CQ's State Fact Finder

CQ's State Fact Finder

Rankings Across America

Victoria Van Son

Congressional Quarterly Inc.

Washington, D.C.

Library of Congress Cataloging-in-Publication Data

Van Son, Victoria, 1956-
    CQ's state fact finder: rankings across America /
Victoria Van Son
    p. cm.
    Includes index.
    ISBN 0-87187-916-6 (cloth).—
    ISBN 0-87187-915-8 (paper)
    1. United States—Statistics. 2. State governments—
United States—Statistics. I. Title.
HA214.V36 1993   93-8929
317.3—dc20   CIP

Contents

Detailed Contents of Subject Rankings

Defense

Education

Energy

Transportation

Preface

CQ's State Fact Finder: Rankings Across America is a comprehensive, user-friendly collection of comparative, detailed data on the states and the District of Columbia. With 325 clear and concise tables, the volume presents raw numerical data and state rankings on a diverse range of subject indicators from business and health to population and education. To compensate for the differences in size and population of states, the raw data are usually converted into percentages, rates, or per capita amounts before the states are ranked. Several conventions were followed in compiling this volume:

- In the subject tables, data are presented not only alphabetically by state but also in rank order in the right-hand column.

- Data are ranked in order from the highest (1) to the lowest (51). This ranking is not meant to impart any value judgments on specific indicators. How a reader analyzes the data is more likely to be a matter of ideology than statistics.

- U.S. summary data for each indicator are listed at the bottom of every table when possible. These national totals and averages provide comparative information and include a rank to show where the United States would be positioned if it were ranked among the states and the District of Columbia.

- Most statistical indicators were carried to three decimals in order to break ties, although the figures are rounded off for consistency in the tables.

- The symbol ''—'' indicates that the indicator is not applicable to the state or District of Columbia; ''NA'' indicates that no data are currently available for the state or District.

- On two tables—Immunization of Two-Year-Olds and Child Abuse Cases Reported—varying methodologies used across the nation prohibit ranking the states.

Care must be taken in interpreting the data from all tables. For example, since the District of Columbia is a highly dense urban area, it usually ranks high on indicators where population density is an important factor (for instance, in the crime tables). The District of Columbia is perhaps best compared against other urban areas, but it is included in this volume, where possible, to complete the view of U.S. population.

The data in this volume have been gathered from the most up-to-date sources available—U.S. Census Bureau, federal agencies, state governments, and nonprofit and private organizations. Those readers interested in more detailed information and limitations of the data should refer to the original source listed at the bottom of each table.

In addition to the tabular presentation of the subject data, there is a handy state profile section that summarizes the rankings on all indicators for each state and the District of Columbia. Thus readers can find a complete portrait of a particular state quickly and easily.

I would like to thank the staff at Congressional Quarterly for recognizing the need for this book. Specifically, I am grateful to Dave Tarr, Nancy Lammers, Jeanne Ferris, Jon Preimesberger, and Jackie Davey for all their efforts. A special thanks goes to Michael Koempel for starting the process and to all the librarians and statisticians who gave so generously of their time. As always, I greatly appreciate the patience, assistance, and kindness of my friends, family, and colleagues who supported me through this arduous process.

Subject Rankings

Agriculture

FARM ACREAGE, 1992

State	Farms	Acres of farmland	Average acreage per farm	Rank by acres of farmland
Alabama	46,000	9,800,000	213	31
Alaska	540	960,000	1,778	44
Arizona	8,000	36,000,000	4,500	8
Arkansas	46,000	15,500,000	337	21
California	81,000	29,800,000	368	14
Colorado	25,500	32,800,000	1,286	12
Connecticut	3,900	410,000	105	49
Delaware	2,700	560,000	207	47
District of Columbia	—	—	—	—
Florida	39,000	10,500,000	269	30
Georgia	46,000	12,100,000	263	27
Hawaii	4,500	1,710,000	380	41
Idaho	21,000	13,500,000	643	24
Illinois	81,000	28,500,000	352	16
Indiana	65,000	16,000,000	246	19
Iowa	102,000	33,400,000	327	11
Kansas	67,000	47,800,000	713	3
Kentucky	91,000	14,100,000	155	23
Louisiana	30,000	8,700,000	290	34
Maine	7,100	1,420,000	200	43
Maryland	15,600	2,200,000	141	40
Massachusetts	6,900	680,000	99	46
Michigan	54,000	10,800,000	200	29
Minnesota	88,000	29,800,000	339	14
Mississippi	38,000	12,800,000	337	25
Missouri	107,000	30,300,000	283	13
Montana	24,600	60,000,000	2,439	2
Nebraska	56,000	47,100,000	841	4
Nevada	2,500	8,900,000	3,560	33
New Hampshire	2,900	470,000	162	48
New Jersey	8,500	880,000	104	45
New Mexico	13,500	44,200,000	3,274	5
New York	38,000	8,200,000	216	36
North Carolina	60,000	9,500,000	158	32
North Dakota	33,000	40,400,000	1,224	7
Ohio	78,000	15,400,000	197	22
Oklahoma	71,000	34,000,000	479	10
Oregon	37,500	17,500,000	467	17
Pennsylvania	52,000	8,000,000	154	37
Rhode Island	700	63,000	90	50
South Carolina	24,500	5,200,000	212	38
South Dakota	35,000	44,200,000	1,263	5
Tennessee	88,000	12,600,000	143	26
Texas	183,000	130,000,000	710	1
Utah	13,200	11,300,000	856	28
Vermont	6,900	1,510,000	219	42
Virginia	44,000	8,700,000	198	34
Washington	38,000	16,000,000	421	19
West Virginia	20,000	3,700,000	185	39
Wisconsin	79,000	17,300,000	219	18
Wyoming	9,200	34,800,000	3,783	9
United States	**2,095,740**	**980,063,000**	**468**	—

Rank in order

By acres of farmland

1. Texas
2. Montana
3. Kansas
4. Nebraska
5. New Mexico
   South Dakota
7. North Dakota
8. Arizona
9. Wyoming
10. Oklahoma
11. Iowa
12. Colorado
13. Missouri
14. California
    Minnesota
16. Illinois
17. Oregon
18. Wisconsin
19. Indiana
    Washington
21. Arkansas
22. Ohio
23. Kentucky
24. Idaho
25. Mississippi
26. Tennessee
27. Georgia
28. Utah
29. Michigan
30. Florida
31. Alabama
32. North Carolina
33. Nevada
34. Louisiana
35. Virginia
36. New York
37. Pennsylvania
38. South Carolina
39. West Virginia
40. Maryland
41. Hawaii
42. Vermont
43. Maine
44. Alaska
45. New Jersey
46. Massachusetts
47. Delaware
48. New Hampshire
49. Connecticut
50. Rhode Island
— District of Columbia

— not applicable.

Source: National Agricultural Statistics Service, *Farm Numbers: Land in Farms* (Washington, D.C.: Department of Agriculture, 1992).

State	Total land area of state (acres)	Acres of farmland	% of state as farmland	Rank by %	By %
Alabama	32,678,000	9,800,000	30.0	32	1. Nebraska
Alaska	365,482,000	960,000	0.3	50	2. Iowa
Arizona	72,688,000	36,000,000	49.5	17	3. Kansas
Arkansas	33,599,000	15,500,000	46.1	21	4. North Dakota
California	100,207,000	29,800,000	29.7	33	5. South Dakota
Colorado	66,486,000	32,800,000	49.3	19	6. Illinois
Connecticut	3,135,000	410,000	13.1	45	7. Texas
Delaware	1,266,000	560,000	44.2	22	8. Oklahoma
District of Columbia	39,000	0	0.0	51	9. Indiana
Florida	34,721,000	10,500,000	30.2	30	10. Missouri
Georgia	37,295,000	12,100,000	32.4	28	11. Montana
Hawaii	4,106,000	1,710,000	41.6	24	12. Ohio
Idaho	52,933,000	13,500,000	25.5	39	13. Minnesota
Illinois	35,795,000	28,500,000	79.6	6	14. New Mexico
Indiana	23,158,000	16,000,000	69.1	9	15. Wyoming
Iowa	35,860,000	33,400,000	93.1	2	16. Kentucky
Kansas	52,511,000	47,800,000	91.0	3	17. Arizona
Kentucky	25,512,000	14,100,000	55.3	16	18. Wisconsin
Louisiana	28,868,000	8,700,000	30.1	31	19. Colorado
Maine	19,848,000	1,420,000	7.2	49	20. Tennessee
Maryland	6,319,000	2,200,000	34.8	26	21. Arkansas
Massachusetts	5,035,000	680,000	13.5	44	22. Delaware
Michigan	36,492,000	10,800,000	29.6	34	23. Mississippi
Minnesota	51,206,000	29,800,000	58.2	13	24. Hawaii
Mississippi	30,223,000	12,800,000	42.4	23	25. Washington
Missouri	44,248,000	30,300,000	68.5	10	26. Maryland
Montana	93,271,000	60,000,000	64.3	11	27. Virginia
Nebraska	49,032,000	47,100,000	96.1	1	28. Georgia
Nevada	70,264,000	8,900,000	12.7	46	29. North Carolina
New Hampshire	5,769,000	470,000	8.1	48	30. Florida
New Jersey	4,814,000	880,000	18.3	43	31. Louisiana
New Mexico	77,766,000	44,200,000	56.8	14	32. Alabama
New York	30,681,000	8,200,000	26.7	38	33. California
North Carolina	31,403,000	9,500,000	30.3	29	34. Michigan
North Dakota	44,453,000	40,400,000	90.9	4	35. Oregon
Ohio	26,222,000	15,400,000	58.7	12	36. Pennsylvania
Oklahoma	44,088,000	34,000,000	77.1	8	37. South Carolina
Oregon	61,599,000	17,500,000	28.4	35	38. New York
Pennsylvania	28,804,000	8,000,000	27.8	36	39. Idaho
Rhode Island	677,000	63,000	9.3	47	40. Vermont
South Carolina	19,374,000	5,200,000	26.8	37	41. West Virginia
South Dakota	48,882,000	44,200,000	90.4	5	42. Utah
Tennessee	26,728,000	12,600,000	47.1	20	43. New Jersey
Texas	168,218,000	130,000,000	77.3	7	44. Massachusetts
Utah	52,697,000	11,300,000	21.4	42	45. Connecticut
Vermont	5,937,000	1,510,000	25.4	40	46. Nevada
Virginia	25,496,000	8,700,000	34.1	27	47. Rhode Island
Washington	42,694,000	16,000,000	37.5	25	48. New Hampshire
West Virginia	15,411,000	3,700,000	24.0	41	49. Maine
Wisconsin	35,011,000	17,300,000	49.4	18	50. Alaska
Wyoming	62,343,000	34,800,000	55.8	15	51. District of Columbia
United States	**2,271,343,000**	**980,063,000**	43.1	23	

Sources: National Agricultural Statistics Service, *Farm Numbers: Land in Farms* (Washington, D.C.: Department of Agriculture, 1992); U.S. Department of Commerce, Bureau of the Census, *Statistical Abstract of the United States, 1992* (Washington, D.C.: Government Printing Office, 1992).

| NET FARM INCOME, 1991 | | | | Rank in order |
State	Net farm income	Per capita	Rank by per capita	By per capita
Alabama	$1,153,300,000	$282.05	16	1. South Dakota
Alaska	3,600,000	6.32	50	2. Nebraska
Arizona	518,600,000	138.29	28	3. North Dakota
Arkansas	1,425,100,000	600.80	7	4. Iowa
California	5,605,100,000	184.50	24	5. Idaho
Colorado	712,300,000	210.93	22	6. Montana
Connecticut	193,900,000	58.92	42	7. Arkansas
Delaware	174,900,000	257.21	18	8. Wyoming
District of Columbia	—	—	—	9. Minnesota
Florida	2,720,700,000	204.92	23	10. Kansas
Georgia	1,471,000,000	222.10	21	11. North Carolina
Hawaii	75,700,000	66.70	39	12. Oklahoma
Idaho	741,000,000	713.19	5	13. Kentucky
Illinois	1,149,500,000	99.58	32	14. Oregon
Indiana	465,100,000	82.91	34	15. Mississippi
Iowa	2,291,100,000	819.71	4	16. Alabama
Kansas	917,200,000	367.62	10	17. Washington
Kentucky	1,071,700,000	288.63	13	18. Delaware
Louisiana	560,700,000	131.87	29	19. Wisconsin
Maine	109,000,000	88.26	33	20. New Mexico
Maryland	387,900,000	79.81	36	21. Georgia
Massachusetts	191,000,000	31.85	48	22. Colorado
Michigan	764,100,000	81.56	35	23. Florida
Minnesota	1,879,900,000	424.17	9	24. California
Mississippi	735,400,000	283.72	15	25. Texas
Missouri	809,700,000	156.98	27	26. Vermont
Montana	515,400,000	637.87	6	27. Missouri
Nebraska	1,954,900,000	1,227.18	2	28. Arizona
Nevada	69,600,000	54.21	43	29. Louisiana
New Hampshire	42,800,000	38.73	45	30. South Carolina
New Jersey	231,400,000	29.82	49	31. Utah
New Mexico	352,800,000	227.91	20	32. Illinois
New York	650,200,000	36.01	47	33. Maine
North Carolina	2,140,500,000	317.72	11	34. Indiana
North Dakota	660,100,000	1,039.53	3	35. Michigan
Ohio	663,200,000	60.63	41	36. Maryland
Oklahoma	940,400,000	296.19	12	37. Virginia
Oregon	830,500,000	284.22	14	38. Tennessee
Pennsylvania	733,200,000	61.30	40	39. Hawaii
Rhode Island	36,800,000	36.65	46	40. Pennsylvania
South Carolina	386,300,000	108.51	30	41. Ohio
South Dakota	1,222,800,000	1,739.40	1	42. Connecticut
Tennessee	372,300,000	75.17	38	43. Nevada
Texas	3,060,800,000	176.43	25	44. West Virginia
Utah	191,100,000	107.97	31	45. New Hampshire
Vermont	91,300,000	161.02	26	46. Rhode Island
Virginia	491,100,000	78.13	37	47. New York
Washington	1,378,100,000	274.63	17	48. Massachusetts
West Virginia	78,300,000	43.48	44	49. New Jersey
Wisconsin	1,186,700,000	239.50	19	50. Alaska
Wyoming	200,400,000	435.65	8	— District of Columbia
United States	$44,608,200,000	$176.89	25	

— not applicable.

Source: Economic Research Service, *Economic Indicators of the Farm Sector: State Financial Summary 1991* (Washington, D.C.: Department of Agriculture, 1993).

State	Government payments	Per capita	Rank by per capita
Alabama	$66,400,000	$16.24	25
Alaska	1,300,000	2.28	44
Arizona	40,500,000	10.80	31
Arkansas	352,800,000	148.74	7
California	260,800,000	8.58	32
Colorado	217,100,000	64.29	13
Connecticut	1,400,000	0.43	48
Delaware	2,700,000	3.97	38
District of Columbia	—	—	—
Florida	40,800,000	3.07	40
Georgia	97,700,000	14.75	26
Hawaii	900,000	0.79	46
Idaho	141,300,000	136.00	8
Illinois	441,400,000	38.24	18
Indiana	210,100,000	37.45	20
Iowa	645,000,000	230.77	6
Kansas	697,900,000	279.72	5
Kentucky	73,400,000	19.77	23
Louisiana	174,600,000	41.06	17
Maine	6,100,000	4.94	35
Maryland	15,300,000	3.15	39
Massachusetts	1,500,000	0.25	49
Michigan	123,700,000	13.20	30
Minnesota	435,800,000	98.33	9
Mississippi	176,300,000	68.02	12
Missouri	268,600,000	52.07	14
Montana	320,100,000	396.16	3
Nebraska	490,700,000	308.04	4
Nevada	5,700,000	4.44	36
New Hampshire	1,500,000	1.36	45
New Jersey	4,100,000	0.53	47
New Mexico	58,400,000	37.73	19
New York	41,200,000	2.28	43
North Carolina	52,800,000	7.84	33
North Dakota	533,900,000	840.79	1
Ohio	156,700,000	14.32	27
Oklahoma	290,900,000	91.62	10
Oregon	89,100,000	30.49	21
Pennsylvania	34,400,000	2.88	42
Rhode Island	100,000	0.10	50
South Carolina	49,400,000	13.88	29
South Dakota	286,200,000	407.11	2
Tennessee	70,300,000	14.19	28
Texas	777,900,000	44.84	15
Utah	33,200,000	18.76	24
Vermont	3,300,000	5.82	34
Virginia	26,600,000	4.23	37
Washington	206,100,000	41.07	16
West Virginia	5,400,000	3.00	41
Wisconsin	150,000,000	30.27	22
Wyoming	33,200,000	72.17	11
United States	**$8,214,400,000**	**$32.57**	**21**

By per capita

1. North Dakota
2. South Dakota
3. Montana
4. Nebraska
5. Kansas
6. Iowa
7. Arkansas
8. Idaho
9. Minnesota
10. Oklahoma
11. Wyoming
12. Mississippi
13. Colorado
14. Missouri
15. Texas
16. Washington
17. Louisiana
18. Illinois
19. New Mexico
20. Indiana
21. Oregon
22. Wisconsin
23. Kentucky
24. Utah
25. Alabama
26. Georgia
27. Ohio
28. Tennessee
29. South Carolina
30. Michigan
31. Arizona
32. California
33. North Carolina
34. Vermont
35. Maine
36. Nevada
37. Virginia
38. Delaware
39. Maryland
40. Florida
41. West Virginia
42. Pennsylvania
43. New York
44. Alaska
45. New Hampshire
46. Hawaii
47. New Jersey
48. Connecticut
49. Massachusetts
50. Rhode Island
— District of Columbia

— not applicable.

Source: Economic Research Service, *Economic Indicators of the Farm Sector: State Financial Summary 1991* (Washington, D.C.: Department of Agriculture, 1993).

Note: Government payments are federal cash payments and payments-in-kind.

FEDERAL COMMODITY LOANS/PRICE SUPPORTS. FISCAL 1991

State	Expenditures	Per capita	Rank by per capita	By per capita
Alabama	$17,224,000	$4.21	31	1. North Dakota
Alaska	0	0.00	49	2. Iowa
Arizona	2,480,000	0.66	40	3. Nebraska
Arkansas	477,290,000	201.22	5	4. South Dakota
California	520,585,000	17.14	22	5. Arkansas
Colorado	220,869,000	65.40	10	6. Minnesota
Connecticut	59,000	0.02	47	7. Mississippi
Delaware	1,040,000	1.53	36	8. Utah
District of Columbia	0	0.00	49	9. Montana
Florida	268,722,000	20.24	19	10. Colorado
Georgia	174,908,000	26.41	17	11. Idaho
Hawaii	685,000	0.60	41	12. Louisiana
Idaho	42,515,000	40.92	11	13. Texas
Illinois	391,314,000	33.90	15	14. Indiana
Indiana	191,071,000	34.06	14	15. Illinois
Iowa	643,852,000	230.36	2	16. Kansas
Kansas	83,333,000	33.40	16	17. Georgia
Kentucky	34,296,000	9.24	26	18. North Carolina
Louisiana	164,979,000	38.80	12	19. Florida
Maine	153,000	0.12	44	20. Missouri
Maryland	8,102,000	1.67	34	21. Michigan
Massachusetts	130,000	0.02	46	22. California
Michigan	187,150,000	19.98	21	23. Wisconsin
Minnesota	675,738,000	152.47	6	24. Ohio
Mississippi	373,028,000	143.92	7	25. Washington
Missouri	103,399,000	20.05	20	26. Kentucky
Montana	64,488,000	79.81	9	27. Wyoming
Nebraska	329,561,000	206.88	3	28. Tennessee
Nevada	71,000	0.06	45	29. Oklahoma
New Hampshire	11,000	0.01	48	30. Oregon
New Jersey	2,546,000	0.33	42	31. Alabama
New Mexico	3,244,000	2.10	33	32. Virginia
New York	22,214,000	1.23	37	33. New Mexico
North Carolina	155,556,000	23.09	18	34. Maryland
North Dakota	265,665,000	418.37	1	35. South Carolina
Ohio	114,375,000	10.46	24	36. Delaware
Oklahoma	13,701,000	4.32	29	37. New York
Oregon	12,425,000	4.25	30	38. Pennsylvania
Pennsylvania	11,400,000	0.95	38	39. West Virginia
Rhode Island	0	0.00	49	40. Arizona
South Carolina	5,916,000	1.66	35	41. Hawaii
South Dakota	142,741,000	203.05	4	42. New Jersey
Tennessee	29,744,000	6.01	28	Vermont
Texas	614,258,000	35.41	13	44. Maine
Utah	170,846,000	96.52	8	45. Nevada
Vermont	186,000	0.33	42	46. Massachusetts
Virginia	19,047,000	3.03	32	47. Connecticut
Washington	52,149,000	10.39	25	48. New Hampshire
West Virginia	1,491,000	0.83	39	49. Alaska
Wisconsin	68,971,000	13.92	23	District of Columbia
Wyoming	2,850,000	6.20	27	Rhode Island
United States	**$6,686,376,000**	**$26.51**	**17**	

Source: U.S. Department of Commerce, Bureau of the Census, *Federal Expenditures by State for Fiscal Year 1991* (Washington, D.C.: Government Printing Office, 1992).

FEDERAL SPENDING ON RURAL DEVELOPMENT. FISCAL 1991

State	Federal expenditures	Per capita	Rank by per capita
Alabama	$108,000	$0.03	39
Alaska	124,000	0.22	12
Arizona	269,000	0.07	28
Arkansas	376,000	0.16	14
California	674,000	0.02	41
Colorado	189,000	0.06	31
Connecticut	0	0.00	48
Delaware	181,000	0.27	8
District of Columbia	0	0.00	48
Florida	196,000	0.02	44
Georgia	403,000	0.06	29
Hawaii	48,000	0.04	36
Idaho	447,000	0.43	4
Illinois	430,000	0.04	37
Indiana	176,000	0.03	38
Iowa	536,000	0.19	13
Kansas	114,000	0.05	35
Kentucky	944,000	0.25	9
Louisiana	2,246,000	0.53	3
Maine	307,000	0.25	10
Maryland	480,000	0.10	23
Massachusetts	11,000	*	47
Michigan	936,000	0.10	22
Minnesota	695,000	0.16	15
Mississippi	380,000	0.15	16
Missouri	243,000	0.05	34
Montana	223,000	0.28	6
Nebraska	150,000	0.09	24
Nevada	172,000	0.13	20
New Hampshire	20,000	0.02	43
New Jersey	171,000	0.02	41
New Mexico	0	0.00	48
New York	943,000	0.05	32
North Carolina	529,000	0.08	26
North Dakota	31,000	0.05	33
Ohio	976,000	0.09	25
Oklahoma	4,343,000	1.37	1
Oregon	430,000	0.15	16
Pennsylvania	889,000	0.07	27
Rhode Island	5,000	0.01	46
South Carolina	963,000	0.27	7
South Dakota	501,000	0.71	2
Tennessee	1,205,000	0.24	11
Texas	1,013,000	0.06	30
Utah	257,000	0.15	18
Vermont	82,000	0.15	18
Virginia	816,000	0.13	21
Washington	113,000	0.02	40
West Virginia	547,000	0.30	5
Wisconsin	46,000	0.01	45
Wyoming	0	0.00	48
United States	**$26,163,000**	**$0.10**	**22**

Rank in order

By per capita

1. Oklahoma
2. South Dakota
3. Louisiana
4. Idaho
5. West Virginia
6. Montana
7. South Carolina
8. Delaware
9. Kentucky
10. Maine
11. Tennessee
12. Alaska
13. Iowa
14. Arkansas
15. Minnesota
16. Mississippi
    Oregon
18. Utah
    Vermont
20. Nevada
21. Virginia
22. Michigan
23. Maryland
24. Nebraska
25. Ohio
26. North Carolina
27. Pennsylvania
28. Arizona
29. Georgia
30. Texas
31. Colorado
32. New York
33. North Dakota
34. Missouri
35. Kansas
36. Hawaii
37. Illinois
38. Indiana
39. Alabama
40. Washington
41. California
    New Jersey
43. New Hampshire
44. Florida
45. Wisconsin
46. Rhode Island
47. Massachusetts
48. Connecticut
    District of Columbia
    New Mexico
    Wyoming

* rounds to less than 0.01.

Source: U.S. Department of Commerce, Bureau of the Census, *Federal Expenditures by State for Fiscal Year 1991* (Washington, D.C.: Government Printing Office, 1992).

Note: Rural development programs are funded under the Department of Agriculture's Farmers Home Administration.

State	Federal expenditures	Per capita	Rank by per capita	By per capita
Alabama	$65,329,000	$15.98	6	1. Virginia
Alaska	5,528,000	9.70	9	2. South Dakota
Arizona	9,756,000	2.60	27	3. Arkansas
Arkansas	71,849,000	30.29	3	4. Iowa
California	0	0.00	40	5. Georgia
Colorado	22,432,000	6.64	16	6. Alabama
Connecticut	0	0.00	40	7. Louisiana
Delaware	0	0.00	40	8. Tennessee
District of Columbia	0	0.00	40	9. Alaska
Florida	64,820,000	4.88	19	10. North Dakota
Georgia	141,899,000	21.43	5	11. Kentucky
Hawaii	0	0.00	40	12. Missouri
Idaho	4,236,000	4.08	21	13. Mississippi
Illinois	0	0.00	40	14. New Mexico
Indiana	13,856,000	2.47	29	15. North Carolina
Iowa	65,708,000	23.51	4	16. Colorado
Kansas	5,057,000	2.03	33	17. Minnesota
Kentucky	33,195,000	8.94	11	18. Maryland
Louisiana	57,618,000	13.55	7	19. Florida
Maine	3,020,000	2.45	32	20. Vermont
Maryland	30,255,000	6.23	18	21. Idaho
Massachusetts	0	0.00	40	22. Oklahoma
Michigan	23,407,000	2.50	28	23. South Carolina
Minnesota	28,480,000	6.43	17	24. Texas
Mississippi	23,061,000	8.90	13	25. Wisconsin
Missouri	46,060,000	8.93	12	26. Montana
Montana	2,178,000	2.70	26	27. Arizona
Nebraska	3,917,000	2.46	31	28. Michigan
Nevada	0	0.00	40	29. Indiana
New Hampshire	631,000	0.57	37	30. Ohio
New Jersey	0	0.00	40	31. Nebraska
New Mexico	12,506,000	8.08	14	32. Maine
New York	8,193,000	0.45	38	33. Kansas
North Carolina	53,448,000	7.93	15	34. Oregon
North Dakota	5,894,000	9.28	10	35. Utah
Ohio	26,976,000	2.47	30	36. Pennsylvania
Oklahoma	12,094,000	3.81	22	37. New Hampshire
Oregon	4,864,000	1.67	34	38. New York
Pennsylvania	11,654,000	0.97	36	39. Washington
Rhode Island	0	0.00	40	40. California
South Carolina	13,453,000	3.78	23	Connecticut
South Dakota	32,769,000	46.61	2	Delaware
Tennessee	52,451,000	10.59	8	District of Columbia
Texas	61,325,000	3.54	24	Hawaii
Utah	2,384,000	1.35	35	Illinois
Vermont	2,500,000	4.41	20	Massachusetts
Virginia	670,467,000	106.66	1	Nevada
Washington	2,268,000	0.45	39	New Jersey
West Virginia	0	0.00	40	Rhode Island
Wisconsin	16,454,000	3.32	25	West Virginia
Wyoming	0	0.00	40	Wyoming
United States	$1,785,338,000	$7.08	16	

Rank in order

Source: U.S. Department of Commerce, Bureau of the Census, *Federal Expenditures by State for Fiscal Year 1991* (Washington, D.C.: Government Printing Office, 1992).

| FOREIGN-OWNED AGRICULTURAL LAND, 1991 | | | | | Rank in order | |
State	Total agricultural acres	Foreign-owned acres	% foreign -owned	Rank by %	By %
Alabama	29,591,000	409,759	1.4	14	1. Maine
Alaska	NA	NA	NA	NA	2. Hawaii
Arizona	40,878,000	326,700	0.8	21	3. New Hampshire
Arkansas	28,672,000	188,329	0.7	27	4. Louisiana
California	49,033,000	915,882	1.9	9	5. Oregon
Colorado	40,945,000	584,455	1.4	13	6. Vermont
Connecticut	2,362,000	1,074	0.0	48	7. Florida
Delaware	1,048,000	5,870	0.6	30	8. Mississippi
District of Columbia	—	—	—	—	9. California
Florida	27,059,000	562,039	2.1	7	10. New Mexico
Georgia	32,289,000	573,040	1.8	12	11. Nevada
Hawaii	3,500,000	175,517	5.0	2	12. Georgia
Idaho	19,152,000	22,944	0.1	42	13. Colorado
Illinois	32,000,000	185,062	0.6	29	14. Alabama
Indiana	20,522,000	79,713	0.4	36	15. Washington
Iowa	33,699,000	32,012	0.1	44	16. South Carolina
Kansas	49,592,000	73,574	0.1	40	17. Maryland
Kentucky	22,799,000	93,226	0.4	35	18. New York
Louisiana	25,016,000	688,373	2.8	4	19. North Carolina
Maine	19,009,000	2,828,483	14.9	1	20. Montana
Maryland	5,111,000	52,186	1.0	17	21. Arizona
Massachusetts	3,786,000	1,934	0.1	47	22. Ohio
Michigan	30,130,000	203,588	0.7	26	23. Tennessee
Minnesota	44,941,000	220,775	0.5	33	24. West Virginia
Mississippi	26,884,000	502,458	1.9	8	25. Texas
Missouri	39,491,000	82,195	0.2	38	26. Michigan
Montana	64,882,000	555,651	0.9	20	27. Arkansas
Nebraska	46,967,000	76,251	0.2	39	28. New Jersey
Nevada	9,916,000	179,912	1.8	11	29. Illinois
New Hampshire	4,599,000	220,199	4.8	3	30. Delaware
New Jersey	3,239,000	19,343	0.6	28	31. Virginia
New Mexico	50,445,000	926,014	1.8	10	32. Wyoming
New York	27,297,000	263,895	1.0	18	33. Minnesota
North Carolina	26,135,000	229,659	0.9	19	34. Utah
North Dakota	41,013,000	30,851	0.1	46	35. Kentucky
Ohio	22,762,000	174,717	0.8	22	36. Indiana
Oklahoma	40,715,000	53,795	0.1	41	37. Pennsylvania
Oregon	27,977,000	746,285	2.7	5	38. Missouri
Pennsylvania	25,027,000	56,824	0.2	37	39. Nebraska
Rhode Island	500,000	0	0.0	49	40. Kansas
South Carolina	16,363,000	190,692	1.2	16	41. Oklahoma
South Dakota	44,403,000	42,882	0.1	43	42. Idaho
Tennessee	23,090,000	174,298	0.8	23	43. South Dakota
Texas	156,768,000	1,078,999	0.7	25	44. Iowa
Utah	15,975,000	68,107	0.4	34	45. Wisconsin
Vermont	5,348,000	120,374	2.3	6	46. North Dakota
Virginia	21,150,000	117,063	0.6	31	47. Massachusetts
Washington	28,383,000	375,841	1.3	15	48. Connecticut
West Virginia	13,695,000	102,459	0.7	24	49. Rhode Island
Wisconsin	30,820,000	23,467	0.1	45	— District of Columbia
Wyoming	32,075,000	170,896	0.5	32	NA Alaska
United States	**1,406,851,000**	**14,808,501**	**1.1**	**17**	

— not applicable. NA not available.

Sources: U.S. Department of Agriculture, Economic Research Service, *Foreign Ownership of U.S. Agricultural Land Through December 31, 1991* (Washington, D.C.: Government Printing Office, 1992); U.S. Department of Commerce, Bureau of the Census, *Statistical Abstract of the United States, 1992* (Washington, D.C.: Government Printing Office, 1992).

Note: Agricultural land includes cropland, pasture land, range land, and forest land.

Business and Economy

State	Gross state product	Per capita	Rank by per capita
Alabama	$67,886,000,000	$16,485.19	43
Alaska	19,582,000,000	37,157.50	2
Arizona	65,306,000,000	18,365.02	36
Arkansas	37,169,000,000	15,448.46	49
California	697,3?1,000,000	23,995.49	8
Colorado	66,180,000,000	19,951.76	21
Connecticut	88,863,000,000	27,435.32	3
Delaware	15,418,000,000	22,909.36	11
District of Columbia	39,363,000,000	65,170.53	1
Florida	226,964,000,000	17,912.08	38
Georgia	129,776,000,000	20,164.08	19
Hawaii	25,755,000,000	23,160.97	10
Idaho	16,339,000,000	16,113.41	47
Illinois	256,478,000,000	22,000.17	14
Indiana	105,314,000,000	18,829.61	32
Iowa	52,574,000,000	18,511.97	34
Kansas	48,829,000,000	19,430.56	24
Kentucky	65,858,000,000	17,670.51	39
Louisiana	79,138,000,000	18,059.79	37
Maine	23,474,000,000	19,209.49	29
Maryland	99,074,000,000	21,106.52	16
Massachusetts	144,791,000,000	24,486.89	7
Michigan	181,827,000,000	19,608.22	23
Minnesota	93,559,000,000	21,492.99	15
Mississippi	38,135,000,000	14,549.79	51
Missouri	100,081,000,000	19,399.30	25
Montana	13,104,000,000	16,258.07	45
Nebraska	31,115,000,000	19,314.09	27
Nevada	27,960,000,000	25,166.52	5
New Hampshire	24,504,000,000	22,135.50	13
New Jersey	203,375,000,000	26,289.43	4
New Mexico	25,414,000,000	16,632.20	42
New York	441,068,000,000	24,572.03	6
North Carolina	130,085,000,000	19,796.84	22
North Dakota	11,231,000,000	17,016.67	41
Ohio	211,545,000,000	19,395.34	26
Oklahoma	52,342,000,000	16,235.11	46
Oregon	52,118,000,000	18,481.56	35
Pennsylvania	227,898,000,000	18,928.41	30
Rhode Island	18,807,000,000	18,844.69	31
South Carolina	60,150,000,000	17,126.99	40
South Dakota	11,135,000,000	15,573.43	48
Tennessee	92,267,000,000	18,677.53	33
Texas	340,057,000,000	20,013.95	20
Utah	28,135,000,000	16,482.13	44
Vermont	11,502,000,000	20,285.71	17
Virginia	136,497,000,000	22,383.90	12
Washington	96,233,000,000	20,212.77	18
West Virginia	27,922,000,000	15,036.08	50
Wisconsin	93,978,000,000	19,309.23	28
Wyoming	11,115,000,000	23,400.00	9
United States	**$5,164,671,000,000**	**$20,805.24**	17

Rank in order

By per capita

1. District of Columbia
2. Alaska
3. Connecticut
4. New Jersey
5. Nevada
6. New York
7. Massachusetts
8. California
9. Wyoming
10. Hawaii
11. Delaware
12. Virginia
13. New Hampshire
14. Illinois
15. Minnesota
16. Maryland
17. Vermont
18. Washington
19. Georgia
20. Texas
21. Colorado
22. North Carolina
23. Michigan
24. Kansas
25. Missouri
26. Ohio
27. Nebraska
28. Wisconsin
29. Maine
30. Pennsylvania
31. Rhode Island
32. Indiana
33. Tennessee
34. Iowa
35. Oregon
36. Arizona
37. Louisiana
38. Florida
39. Kentucky
40. South Carolina
41. North Dakota
42. New Mexico
43. Alabama
44. Utah
45. Montana
46. Oklahoma
47. Idaho
48. South Dakota
49. Arkansas
50. West Virginia
51. Mississippi

Source: Edward A. Trott, Jr., Ann E. Dunbar, and Howard L. Friedenberg, "Gross State Product by Industry, 1977-89," *Survey of Current Business*, December 1991.

Note: Gross state product is measured in current (1989) dollars.

State	Retail sales	Household average	Rank by household average
Alabama	$26,373,000,000	$17,435	40
Alaska	4,669,000,000	24,533	3
Arizona	26,137,000,000	18,703	27
Arkansas ·	15,386,000,000	17,205	43
California	225,066,000,000	21,245	9
Colorado	24,383,000,000	18,864	26
Connecticut	27,729,000,000	22,435	7
Delaware	6,041,000,000	24,145	4
District of Columbia	3,815,000,000	15,360	49
Florida	105,304,000,000	20,056	14
Georgia	46,748,000,000	19,417	22
Hawaii	11,204,000,000	31,121	1
Idaho	6,004,000,000	16,591	47
Illinois	83,479,000,000	19,840	17
Indiana	37,574,000,000	18,153	33
Iowa	18,818,000,000	17,724	37
Kansas	16,656,000,000	17,540	38
Kentucky	23,861,000,000	17,283	42
Louisiana	28,778,000,000	19,260	25
Maine	10,399,000,000	22,149	8
Maryland	36,837,000,000	20,790	11
Massachusetts	50,757,000,000	22,488	6
Michigan	67,785,000,000	19,675	19
Minnesota	33,315,000,000	20,050	15
Mississippi	13,803,000,000	15,131	50
Missouri	36,032,000,000	18,281	32
Montana	5,333,000,000	17,478	39
Nebraska	10,313,000,000	17,113	44
Nevada	9,630,000,000	19,938	16
New Hampshire	11,860,000,000	28,373	2
New Jersey	63,431,000,000	22,579	5
New Mexico	9,378,000,000	17,044	45
New York	124,479,000,000	18,667	29
North Carolina	45,756,000,000	17,995	34
North Dakota	4,467,000,000	18,630	30
Ohio	73,206,000,000	17,880	36
Oklahoma	20,218,000,000	16,780	46
Oregon	22,417,000,000	20,159	13
Pennsylvania	82,990,000,000	18,413	31
Rhode Island	7,325,000,000	19,276	24
South Carolina	23,754,000,000	18,685	28
South Dakota	4,649,000,000	17,921	35
Tennessee	32,422,000,000	17,384	41
Texas	120,459,000,000	19,631	20
Utah	10,581,000,000	19,501	21
Vermont	4,512,000,000	21,223	10
Virginia	47,472,000,000	20,459	12
Washington	36,732,000,000	19,370	23
West Virginia	10,060,000,000	14,718	51
Wisconsin	36,031,000,000	19,691	18
Wyoming	2,726,000,000	16,314	48
United States	**$1,807,183,000,000**	**$19,488**	**22**

By household average

1. Hawaii
2. New Hampshire
3. Alaska
4. Delaware
5. New Jersey
6. Massachusetts
7. Connecticut
8. Maine
9. California
10. Vermont
11. Maryland
12. Virginia
13. Oregon
14. Florida
15. Minnesota
16. Nevada
17. Illinois
18. Wisconsin
19. Michigan
20. Texas
21. Utah
22. Georgia
23. Washington
24. Rhode Island
25. Louisiana
26. Colorado
27. Arizona
28. South Carolina
29. New York
30. North Dakota
31. Pennsylvania
32. Missouri
33. Indiana
34. North Carolina
35. South Dakota
36. Ohio
37. Iowa
38. Kansas
39. Montana
40. Alabama
41. Tennessee
42. Kentucky
43. Arkansas
44. Nebraska
45. New Mexico
46. Oklahoma
47. Idaho
48. Wyoming
49. District of Columbia
50. Mississippi
51. West Virginia

Source: U.S. Department of Commerce, Bureau of the Census, *Statistical Abstract of the United States, 1992* (Washington, D.C.: Government Printing Office, 1992).

SUPERMARKET SALES, 1990				Rank in order

State	Supermarket sales	Per capita	Rank by per capita	By per capita
Alabama	$4,727,000,000	$1,169.76	46	1. New Hampshire
Alaska	1,161,000,000	2,110.91	2	2. Alaska
Arizona	5,728,000,000	1,562.89	10	3. Maine
Arkansas	3,293,000,000	1,400.68	23	4. Hawaii
California	40,044,000,000	1,345.56	26	5. Vermont
Colorado	4,817,000,000	1,462.36	17	6. Louisiana
Connecticut	5,110,000,000	1,554.61	11	7. Nevada
Delaware	1,009,000,000	1,515.02	14	8. New Jersey
District of Columbia	573,000,000	943.99	51	9. Washington
Florida	18,490,000,000	1,429.12	18	10. Arizona
Georgia	8,700,000,000	1,343.01	28	11. Connecticut
Hawaii	1,964,000,000	1,772.56	4	12. Virginia
Idaho	1,335,000,000	1,325.72	30	13. Texas
Illinois	13,491,000,000	1,180.21	44	14. Delaware
Indiana	6,202,000,000	1,118.69	49	15. Massachusetts
Iowa	3,926,000,000	1,413.76	21	16. Montana
Kansas	3,361,000,000	1,356.34	25	17. Colorado
Kentucky	4,593,000,000	1,246.40	39	18. Florida
Louisiana	7,173,000,000	1,699.76	6	19. Oklahoma
Maine	2,284,000,000	1,859.93	3	20. South Carolina
Maryland	6,616,000,000	1,383.81	24	21. Iowa
Massachusetts	9,112,000,000	1,514.63	15	22. Oregon
Michigan	10,443,000,000	1,123.51	47	23. Arkansas
Minnesota	5,723,000,000	1,308.11	34	24. Maryland
Mississippi	2,880,000,000	1,119.32	48	25. Kansas
Missouri	6,670,000,000	1,303.50	35	26. California
Montana	1,198,000,000	1,499.37	16	27. North Carolina
Nebraska	1,861,000,000	1,179.34	45	28. Georgia
Nevada	1,926,000,000	1,602.33	7	29. Pennsylvania
New Hampshire	2,413,000,000	2,175.83	1	30. Idaho
New Jersey	12,182,000,000	1,575.94	8	31. Utah
New Mexico	1,854,000,000	1,223.76	43	32. Rhode Island
New York	23,612,000,000	1,312.51	33	33. New York
North Carolina	8,919,000,000	1,345.45	27	34. Minnesota
North Dakota	788,000,000	1,233.18	42	35. Missouri
Ohio	13,453,000,000	1,240.25	40	36. South Dakota
Oklahoma	4,478,000,000	1,423.39	19	37. West Virginia
Oregon	4,015,000,000	1,412.74	22	38. Wisconsin
Pennsylvania	15,933,000,000	1,340.94	29	39. Kentucky
Rhode Island	1,319,000,000	1,315.05	32	40. Ohio
South Carolina	4,953,000,000	1,420.42	20	41. Wyoming
South Dakota	894,000,000	1,284.48	36	42. North Dakota
Tennessee	5,421,000,000	1,111.54	50	43. New Mexico
Texas	25,989,000,000	1,529.93	13	44. Illinois
Utah	2,270,000,000	1,317.47	31	45. Nebraska
Vermont	978,000,000	1,737.12	5	46. Alabama
Virginia	9,517,000,000	1,538.23	12	47. Michigan
Washington	7,669,000,000	1,575.71	9	48. Mississippi
West Virginia	2,262,000,000	1,261.57	37	49. Indiana
Wisconsin	6,114,000,000	1,249.80	38	50. Tennessee
Wyoming	562,000,000	1,237.89	41	51. District of Columbia
United States	$340,455,000,000	$1,368.88	25	

Source: U.S. Department of Commerce, Bureau of the Census, *Statistical Abstract of the United States, 1992* (Washington, D.C.: Government Printing Office, 1992).

COMMERCIAL BANK ASSETS, 1990

State	Banks	Assets	Per capita	Rank by per capita	By per capita
Alabama	221	$38,900,000,000	$9,626.33	35	1. Delaware
Alaska	8	4,500,000,000	8,181.82	44	2. New York
Arizona	38	32,600,000,000	8,894.95	39	3. District of Columbia
Arkansas	256	21,500,000,000	9,145.04	36	4. South Dakota
California	482	345,300,000,000	11,602.82	20	5. Hawaii
Colorado	446	26,900,000,000	8,166.36	45	6. Illinois
Connecticut	68	36,100,000,000	10,982.66	23	7. Massachusetts
Delaware	47	74,300,000,000	111,561.56	1	8. Rhode Island
District of Columbia	26	18,100,000,000	29,818.78	3	9. Pennsylvania
Florida	430	137,200,000,000	10,604.42	26	10. Nebraska
Georgia	409	70,300,000,000	10,852.11	24	11. Minnesota
Hawaii	21	19,400,000,000	17,509.03	5	12. Missouri
Idaho	22	8,600,000,000	8,540.22	42	13. Iowa
Illinois	1,087	196,900,000,000	17,225.09	6	14. New Jersey
Indiana	301	58,300,000,000	10,515.87	27	15. North Carolina
Iowa	562	34,600,000,000	12,459.49	13	16. Nevada
Kansas	555	29,500,000,000	11,904.76	18	17. Maryland
Kentucky	332	41,400,000,000	11,234.74	22	18. Kansas
Louisiana	231	37,400,000,000	8,862.56	40	19. North Dakota
Maine	21	8,200,000,000	6,677.52	51	20. California
Maryland	103	57,000,000,000	11,922.19	17	21. Virginia
Massachusetts	85	97,900,000,000	16,273.27	7	22. Kentucky
Michigan	235	93,800,000,000	10,091.45	30	23. Connecticut
Minnesota	626	55,500,000,000	12,685.71	11	24. Georgia
Mississippi	123	21,400,000,000	8,317.14	43	25. Vermont
Missouri	544	64,700,000,000	12,644.13	12	26. Florida
Montana	156	7,300,000,000	9,136.42	37	27. Indiana
Nebraska	392	20,200,000,000	12,801.01	10	28. Ohio
Nevada	19	14,400,000,000	11,980.03	16	29. Wyoming
New Hampshire	45	10,000,000,000	9,017.13	38	30. Michigan
New Jersey	131	94,200,000,000	12,186.29	14	31. Texas
New Mexico	91	11,100,000,000	7,326.73	49	32. Tennessee
New York	193	682,200,000,000	37,921.07	2	33. Wisconsin
North Carolina	78	80,200,000,000	12,098.36	15	34. West Virginia
North Dakota	150	7,600,000,000	11,893.58	19	35. Alabama
Ohio	288	113,100,000,000	10,426.85	28	36. Arkansas
Oklahoma	419	26,900,000,000	8,550.54	41	37. Montana
Oregon	50	22,900,000,000	8,057.71	47	38. New Hampshire
Pennsylvania	300	172,400,000,000	14,509.34	9	39. Arizona
Rhode Island	11	14,700,000,000	14,656.03	8	40. Louisiana
South Carolina	85	25,200,000,000	7,226.84	50	41. Oklahoma
South Dakota	125	19,200,000,000	27,586.21	4	42. Idaho
Tennessee	253	47,400,000,000	9,719.09	32	43. Mississippi
Texas	1,184	170,800,000,000	10,054.75	31	44. Alaska
Utah	55	13,800,000,000	8,009.29	48	45. Colorado
Vermont	27	6,100,000,000	10,834.81	25	46. Washington
Virginia	178	69,600,000,000	11,249.39	21	47. Oregon
Washington	94	39,700,000,000	8,156.98	46	48. Utah
West Virginia	180	17,400,000,000	9,704.41	34	49. New Mexico
Wisconsin	473	47,500,000,000	9,709.73	33	50. South Carolina
Wyoming	71	4,600,000,000	10,132.16	29	51. Maine
United States	12,327	$3,369,100,000,000	$13,546.30	10	

Source: U.S. Department of Commerce, Bureau of the Census, *Statistical Abstract of the United States, 1992* (Washington, D.C.: Government Printing Office, 1992).

State	Banks	Insured deposits	Deposits per capita	Rank by per capita
Alabama	221	$31,900,000,000	$7,894.09	35
Alaska	8	3,500,000,000	6,363.64	46
Arizona	38	28,400,000,000	7,748.98	37
Arkansas	256	19,100,000,000	8,124.20	34
California	482	279,700,000,000	9,398.52	20
Colorado	446	22,700,000,000	6,891.32	43
Connecticut	68	31,700,000,000	9,644.05	17
Delaware	47	34,300,000,000	51,501.50	1
District of Columbia	26	15,400,000,000	25,370.68	3
Florida	430	117,000,000,000	9,043.13	22
Georgia	409	53,200,000,000	8,212.41	31
Hawaii	21	16,300,000,000	14,711.19	5
Idaho	22	6,900,000,000	6,852.04	44
Illinois	1,087	154,700,000,000	13,533.37	6
Indiana	301	47,600,000,000	8,585.86	26
Iowa	562	29,200,000,000	10,514.94	12
Kansas	555	26,000,000,000	10,492.33	13
Kentucky	332	33,500,000,000	9,090.91	21
Louisiana	231	32,600,000,000	7,725.12	38
Maine	21	6,900,000,000	5,618.89	50
Maryland	103	45,000,000,000	9,412.26	19
Massachusetts	85	76,600,000,000	12,732.71	7
Michigan	235	76,900,000,000	8,273.27	28
Minnesota	626	45,400,000,000	10,377.14	15
Mississippi	123	18,500,000,000	7,190.05	42
Missouri	544	54,300,000,000	10,611.69	11
Montana	156	6,300,000,000	7,884.86	36
Nebraska	392	17,600,000,000	11,153.36	9
Nevada	19	8,900,000,000	7,404.33	41
New Hampshire	45	8,300,000,000	7,484.22	40
New Jersey	131	78,300,000,000	10,129.37	16
New Mexico	91	9,600,000,000	6,336.63	47
New York	193	476,000,000,000	26,459.14	2
North Carolina	78	58,400,000,000	8,809.78	25
North Dakota	150	6,700,000,000	10,485.13	14
Ohio	288	89,700,000,000	8,269.57	29
Oklahoma	419	23,700,000,000	7,533.38	39
Oregon	50	18,000,000,000	6,333.57	48
Pennsylvania	300	136,300,000,000	11,471.13	8
Rhode Island	11	11,000,000,000	10,967.10	10
South Carolina	85	18,500,000,000	5,305.42	51
South Dakota	125	10,900,000,000	15,660.92	4
Tennessee	253	39,900,000,000	8,181.26	32
Texas	1,184	145,600,000,000	8,571.26	27
Utah	55	10,600,000,000	6,152.06	49
Vermont	27	5,300,000,000	9,413.85	18
Virginia	178	54,700,000,000	8,841.12	24
Washington	94	32,800,000,000	6,739.26	45
West Virginia	180	14,800,000,000	8,254.32	30
Wisconsin	473	39,800,000,000	8,135.73	33
Wyoming	71	4,100,000,000	9,030.84	23
United States	12,327	$2,632,900,000,000	$10,586.22	12

Rank in order

By per capita

1. Delaware
2. New York
3. District of Columbia
4. South Dakota
5. Hawaii
6. Illinois
7. Massachusetts
8. Pennsylvania
9. Nebraska
10. Rhode Island
11. Missouri
12. Iowa
13. Kansas
14. North Dakota
15. Minnesota
16. New Jersey
17. Connecticut
18. Vermont
19. Maryland
20. California
21. Kentucky
22. Florida
23. Wyoming
24. Virginia
25. North Carolina
26. Indiana
27. Texas
28. Michigan
29. Ohio
30. West Virginia
31. Georgia
32. Tennessee
33. Wisconsin
34. Arkansas
35. Alabama
36. Montana
37. Arizona
38. Louisiana
39. Oklahoma
40. New Hampshire
41. Nevada
42. Mississippi
43. Colorado
44. Idaho
45. Washington
46. Alaska
47. New Mexico
48. Oregon
49. Utah
50. Maine
51. South Carolina

Source: U.S. Department of Commerce, Bureau of the Census, *Statistical Abstract of the United States, 1992* (Washington, D.C.: Government Printing Office, 1992).

State	Companies	Rank	Per 100,000 population	
			Rate	Rank
Alabama	5	20	0.12	28
Alaska	0	42	0.00	42
Arizona	2	32	0.05	39
Arkansas	4	22	0.17	21
California	44	3	0.15	23
Colorado	6	19	0.18	20
Connecticut	27	7	0.82	1
Delaware	2	32	0.29	8
District of Columbia	3	31	0.50	2
Florida	7	18	0.05	39
Georgia	11	16	0.17	22
Hawaii	0	42	0.00	42
Idaho	1	37	0.10	32
Illinois	47	2	0.41	3
Indiana	12	15	0.21	16
Iowa	4	22	0.14	24
Kansas	2	32	0.08	35
Kentucky	2	32	0.05	38
Louisiana	4	22	0.09	33
Maine	0	42	0.00	42
Maryland	4	22	0.08	34
Massachusetts	15	11	0.25	13
Michigan	21	9	0.22	15
Minnesota	18	10	0.41	4
Mississippi	0	42	0.00	42
Missouri	15	11	0.29	10
Montana	0	42	0.00	42
Nebraska	4	22	0.25	12
Nevada	0	42	0.00	42
New Hampshire	2	32	0.18	19
New Jersey	25	8	0.32	7
New Mexico	0	42	0.00	42
New York	53	1	0.29	9
North Carolina	8	17	0.12	29
North Dakota	0	42	0.00	42
Ohio	36	4	0.33	6
Oklahoma	4	22	0.13	27
Oregon	4	22	0.14	26
Pennsylvania	29	6	0.24	14
Rhode Island	4	22	0.40	5
South Carolina	4	22	0.11	30
South Dakota	1	37	0.14	25
Tennessee	1	37	0.02	41
Texas	36	4	0.21	17
Utah	1	37	0.06	36
Vermont	0	42	0.00	42
Virginia	13	13	0.21	18
Washington	5	20	0.10	31
West Virginia	1	37	0.06	36
Wisconsin	13	13	0.26	11
Wyoming	0	42	0.00	42
United States	**500**	—	**0.20**	**19**

— not applicable.

Source: "The Fortune 500 Ranked by State," Fortune, April 19, 1993. Copyright © 1993 Time Inc. All rights reserved.
Note: The Fortune 500 companies are the headquarters of the 500 largest U.S. industrial corporations as ranked by Fortune.

Rank in order

By rate per 100,000 population

1. Connecticut
2. District of Columbia
3. Illinois
4. Minnesota
5. Rhode Island
6. Ohio
7. New Jersey
8. Delaware
9. New York
10. Missouri
11. Wisconsin
12. Nebraska
13. Massachusetts
14. Pennsylvania
15. Michigan
16. Indiana
17. Texas
18. Virginia
19. New Hampshire
20. Colorado
21. Arkansas
22. Georgia
23. California
24. Iowa
25. South Dakota
26. Oregon
27. Oklahoma
28. Alabama
29. North Carolina
30. South Carolina
31. Washington
32. Idaho
33. Louisiana
34. Maryland
35. Kansas
36. Utah
   West Virginia
38. Kentucky
39. Arizona
   Florida
41. Tennessee
42. Alaska
   Hawaii
   Maine
   Mississippi
   Montana
   Nevada
   New Mexico
   North Dakota
   Vermont
   Wyoming

| State | Companies | Rank | Per 100,000 population | | Rank in order |
			Rate	Rank	By rate per 100,000 population
Alabama	4	32	0.10	40	1. Idaho
Alaska	0	51	0.00	47	2. Virginia
Arizona	15	9	0.40	5	3. Colorado
Arkansas	0	50	0.00	47	4. Utah
California	78	1	0.26	12	5. Arizona
Colorado	16	8	0.47	3	6. Vermont
Connecticut	8	23	0.24	15	7. Massachusetts
Delaware	2	40	0.29	9	8. New Mexico
District of Columbia	1	46	0.17	26	9. Delaware
Florida	30	4	0.23	17	10. Georgia
Georgia	19	7	0.29	10	11. New Hampshire
Hawaii	0	49	0.00	47	12. California
Idaho	5	28	0.48	1	13. Nebraska
Illinois	13	13	0.11	35	14. Maryland
Indiana	12	15	0.21	22	15. Connecticut
Iowa	2	39	0.07	44	16. Texas
Kansas	4	31	0.16	28	17. Florida
Kentucky	4	30	0.11	37	18. Wisconsin
Louisiana	3	34	0.07	45	19. Oklahoma
Maine	1	45	0.08	41	20. Washington
Maryland	12	14	0.25	14	21. Wyoming
Massachusetts	21	6	0.35	7	22. Indiana
Michigan	11	18	0.12	33	23. Oregon
Minnesota	9	19	0.20	24	24. Minnesota
Mississippi	2	38	0.08	43	25. New Jersey
Missouri	8	22	0.16	29	26. District of Columbia
Montana	0	48	0.00	47	27. Tennessee
Nebraska	4	29	0.25	13	28. Kansas
Nevada	1	44	0.08	42	29. Missouri
New Hampshire	3	33	0.27	11	30. New York
New Jersey	14	11	0.18	25	31. South Dakota
New Mexico	5	27	0.32	8	32. Ohio
New York	26	5	0.14	30	33. Michigan
North Carolina	7	25	0.10	38	Pennsylvania
North Dakota	0	47	0.00	47	35. Illinois
Ohio	13	12	0.12	32	36. West Virginia
Oklahoma	7	24	0.22	19	37. Kentucky
Oregon	6	26	0.21	23	38. North Carolina
Pennsylvania	14	10	0.12	33	39. Rhode Island
Rhode Island	1	43	0.10	39	40. Alabama
South Carolina	2	37	0.06	46	41. Maine
South Dakota	1	42	0.14	31	42. Nevada
Tennessee	8	21	0.16	27	43. Mississippi
Texas	41	2	0.24	16	44. Iowa
Utah	8	20	0.45	4	45. Louisiana
Vermont	2	36	0.35	6	46. South Carolina
Virginia	30	3	0.48	2	47. Alaska
Washington	11	17	0.22	20	Arkansas
West Virginia	2	35	0.11	36	Hawaii
Wisconsin	11	16	0.22	18	Montana
Wyoming	1	41	0.22	21	North Dakota
United States	498	—	0.20	25	

— not applicable.

Source: "The *Inc.* 500: America's Fastest Growing Private Companies," *Inc.*, October 1992. Reprinted with permission, *Inc.* magazine. Copyright 1992 by Goldhirsh Group, Inc., 38 Commercial Wharf, Boston, MA 02110.

Note: The *Inc.* 500 are the 500 fastest-growing private U.S. companies as ranked by *Inc.* Two companies are in Puerto Rico.

State	New business incorporations	Per 1,000 population	
		Rate	Rank
Alabama	6,116	1.50	44
Alaska	1,250	2.19	23
Arizona	9,832	2.62	15
Arkansas	5,326	2.25	21
California	36,561	1.20	51
Colorado	13,583	4.02	4
Connecticut	8,501	2.58	17
Delaware	29,887	43.95	1
District of Columbia	2,256	3.77	5
Florida	81,083	6.11	3
Georgia	18,098	2.73	13
Hawaii	3,792	3.34	9
Idaho	1,944	1.87	33
Illinois	29,068	2.52	18
Indiana	10,205	1.82	36
Iowa	4,531	1.62	41
Kansas	3,930	1.58	43
Kentucky	6,782	1.83	35
Louisiana	8,973	2.11	27
Maine	2,326	1.88	32
Maryland	16,463	3.39	8
Massachusetts	11,706	1.95	29
Michigan	20,099	2.15	26
Minnesota	9,564	2.16	25
Mississippi	3,602	1.39	48
Missouri	9,521	1.85	34
Montana	1,572	1.95	30
Nebraska	3,093	1.94	31
Nevada	11,030	8.59	2
New Hampshire	2,387	2.16	24
New Jersey	27,994	3.61	6
New Mexico	2,713	1.75	38
New York	63,808	3.53	7
North Carolina	11,944	1.77	37
North Dakota	820	1.29	49
Ohio	17,895	1.64	40
Oklahoma	7,073	2.23	22
Oregon	8,375	2.87	11
Pennsylvania	17,340	1.45	46
Rhode Island	2,458	2.45	19
South Carolina	5,700	1.60	42
South Dakota	1,040	1.48	45
Tennessee	8,306	1.68	39
Texas	34,571	1.99	28
Utah	4,973	2.81	12
Vermont	1,486	2.62	16
Virginia	16,883	2.69	14
Washington	11,521	2.30	20
West Virginia	2,219	1.23	50
Wisconsin	6,994	1.41	47
Wyoming	1,386	3.01	10
United States	**628,580**	**2.49**	**19**

Rank in order

By rate per 1,000 population

1. Delaware
2. Nevada
3. Florida
4. Colorado
5. District of Columbia
6. New Jersey
7. New York
8. Maryland
9. Hawaii
10. Wyoming
11. Oregon
12. Utah
13. Georgia
14. Virginia
15. Arizona
16. Vermont
17. Connecticut
18. Illinois
19. Rhode Island
20. Washington
21. Arkansas
22. Oklahoma
23. Alaska
24. New Hampshire
25. Minnesota
26. Michigan
27. Louisiana
28. Texas
29. Massachusetts
30. Montana
31. Nebraska
32. Maine
33. Idaho
34. Missouri
35. Kentucky
36. Indiana
37. North Carolina
38. New Mexico
39. Tennessee
40. Ohio
41. Iowa
42. South Carolina
43. Kansas
44. Alabama
45. South Dakota
46. Pennsylvania
47. Wisconsin
48. Mississippi
49. North Dakota
50. West Virginia
51. California

Source: Dun & Bradstreet Corporation, *New Business Incorporations* (New York: Dun & Bradstreet Corporation, monthly).

BUSINESS FAILURES, 1992				Rank in order
State	**Business failures**	**Per 1,000 population**		**By rate per 1,000 population**
		Rate	**Rank**	
Alabama	1,027	0.25	38	1. Rhode Island
Alaska	144	0.25	36	2. New Hampshire
Arizona	2,230	0.60	3	3. Arizona
Arkansas	480	0.20	43	4. Oklahoma
California	14,685	0.48	7	5. Colorado
Colorado	1,959	0.58	5	6. Georgia
Connecticut	459	0.14	49	7. California
Delaware	160	0.24	40	8. Massachusetts
District of Columbia	198	0.33	24	9. Oregon
Florida	5,229	0.39	15	South Dakota
Georgia	3,390	0.51	6	11. Texas
Hawaii	74	0.07	51	12. Tennessee
Idaho	397	0.38	16	13. Nevada
Illinois	3,068	0.27	33	14. Kansas
Indiana	1,736	0.31	29	15. Florida
Iowa	295	0.11	50	16. Idaho
Kansas	989	0.40	14	17. Virginia
Kentucky	1,234	0.33	22	18. Minnesota
Louisiana	1,103	0.26	34	19. New Jersey
Maine	396	0.32	25	20. Wyoming
Maryland	1,331	0.27	32	21. Nebraska
Massachusetts	2,839	0.47	8	22. Kentucky
Michigan	2,295	0.25	39	Vermont
Minnesota	1,583	0.36	18	24. District of Columbia
Mississippi	523	0.20	43	25. Maine
Missouri	1,609	0.31	27	26. Utah
Montana	160	0.20	46	27. Missouri
Nebraska	536	0.34	21	28. New York
Nevada	515	0.40	13	29. Indiana
New Hampshire	861	0.78	2	30. Pennsylvania
New Jersey	2,758	0.36	19	31. Washington
New Mexico	390	0.25	37	32. Maryland
New York	5,612	0.31	28	33. Illinois
North Carolina	1,351	0.20	45	34. Louisiana
North Dakota	140	0.22	42	35. Ohio
Ohio	2,776	0.25	35	36. Alaska
Oklahoma	1,845	0.58	4	37. New Mexico
Oregon	1,309	0.45	9	38. Alabama
Pennsylvania	3,658	0.31	30	39. Michigan
Rhode Island	911	0.91	1	40. Delaware
South Carolina	603	0.17	48	41. West Virginia
South Dakota	315	0.45	9	42. North Dakota
Tennessee	1,995	0.40	12	43. Arkansas
Texas	7,036	0.41	11	Mississippi
Utah	556	0.31	26	45. North Carolina
Vermont	188	0.33	22	46. Montana
Virginia	2,297	0.37	17	47. Wisconsin
Washington	1,424	0.28	31	48. South Carolina
West Virginia	399	0.22	41	49. Connecticut
Wisconsin	910	0.18	47	50. Iowa
Wyoming	162	0.35	20	51. Hawaii
United States	**88,140**	**0.35**	**21**	

Source: Richard H. Gearhart and Dina M. Silva-Decker, "Business Failures Up 10 Percent in 1992 to a New High of 96,836, According to Dun & Bradstreet," press release, February 10, 1993.

FINANCIAL AID TO MINORITY BUSINESSES, FISCAL 1991

State	Financial aid	Per capita	Rank by per capita
Alabama	$5,168,634	$1.28	14
Alaska	1,447,725	2.63	7
Arizona	9,324,648	2.54	8
Arkansas	1,228,229	0.52	31
California	63,182,352	2.12	10
Colorado	8,995,571	2.73	6
Connecticut	2,382,947	0.73	25
Delaware	0	0.00	41
District of Columbia	12,476,601	20.56	1
Florida	19,834,581	1.53	13
Georgia	20,490,531	3.16	5
Hawaii	7,991,229	7.21	3
Idaho	0	0.00	41
Illinois	8,260,794	0.72	26
Indiana	2,767,502	0.50	33
Iowa	0	0.00	41
Kansas	250,000	0.10	39
Kentucky	158,303	0.04	40
Louisiana	3,693,739	0.88	23
Maine	0	0.00	41
Maryland	2,492,000	0.52	32
Massachusetts	1,445,200	0.24	36
Michigan	2,950,000	0.32	35
Minnesota	4,187,647	0.96	18
Mississippi	5,140,065	2.00	11
Missouri	1,221,900	0.24	37
Montana	0	0.00	41
Nebraska	0	0.00	41
Nevada	1,175,143	0.98	17
New Hampshire	0	0.00	41
New Jersey	7,119,175	0.92	22
New Mexico	22,957,253	15.15	2
New York	16,857,936	0.94	21
North Carolina	7,830,289	1.18	15
North Dakota	1,529,350	2.39	9
Ohio	10,230,773	0.94	20
Oklahoma	4,852,519	1.54	12
Oregon	2,691,860	0.95	19
Pennsylvania	6,499,720	0.55	29
Rhode Island	0	0.00	41
South Carolina	1,584,545	0.45	34
South Dakota	73,000	0.11	38
Tennessee	3,742,815	0.77	24
Texas	60,165,091	3.54	4
Utah	1,146,231	0.67	27
Vermont	0	0.00	41
Virginia	3,348,000	0.54	30
Washington	5,000,013	1.03	16
West Virginia	0	0.00	41
Wisconsin	2,752,291	0.56	28
Wyoming	0	0.00	41
United States	**$344,646,202**	**$1.39**	**14**

Rank in order

By per capita

1. District of Columbia
2. New Mexico
3. Hawaii
4. Texas
5. Georgia
6. Colorado
7. Alaska
8. Arizona
9. North Dakota
10. California
11. Mississippi
12. Oklahoma
13. Florida
14. Alabama
15. North Carolina
16. Washington
17. Nevada
18. Minnesota
19. Oregon
20. Ohio
21. New York
22. New Jersey
23. Louisiana
24. Tennessee
25. Connecticut
26. Illinois
27. Utah
28. Wisconsin
29. Pennsylvania
30. Virginia
31. Arkansas
32. Maryland
33. Indiana
34. South Carolina
35. Michigan
36. Massachusetts
37. Missouri
38. South Dakota
39. Kansas
40. Kentucky
41. Delaware
    Idaho
    Iowa
    Maine
    Montana
    Nebraska
    New Hampshire
    Rhode Island
    Vermont
    West Virginia
    Wyoming

Source: Minority Business Development Agency, *Annual Business Assistance Report, Fiscal Year 1991* (Washington, D.C.: Department of Commerce, 1992)

Note: Financial aid include loans, trade credits, bonds, and equity investments offered through business development centers. Sources of assistance include commercial lenders, Small Business Administration, and state and local government.

WOMEN-OWNED BUSINESSES, 1987				Rank in order

State	Women-owned businesses	% of U.S. businesses	Rank by %	By % of U.S. businesses
Alabama	48,018	27.0	48	1. District of Columbia
Alaska	13,976	28.6	35	2. Hawaii
Arizona	60,567	31.6	7	3. Colorado
Arkansas	35,469	26.3	50	4. Maryland
California	559,821	30.9	18	5. Oregon
Colorado	89,411	34.0	3	6. Virginia
Connecticut	60,924	31.0	17	7. Arizona
Delaware	9,727	31.4	12	8. Kansas
District of Columbia	10,987	37.6	1	9. Washington
Florida	221,361	30.1	25	10. Nevada
Georgia	88,050	28.8	34	11. Minnesota
Hawaii	21,696	35.6	2	12. Delaware
Idaho	18,973	27.9	42	Nebraska
Illinois	177,057	30.8	20	14. Michigan
Indiana	89,949	30.5	23	15. Wyoming
Iowa	53,592	30.8	21	16. Massachusetts
Kansas	53,505	31.5	8	17. Connecticut
Kentucky	53,454	27.6	44	18. California
Louisiana	55,852	27.3	46	19. New Mexico
Maine	23,922	27.1	47	20. Illinois
Maryland	81,891	33.6	4	21. Iowa
Massachusetts	111,376	31.2	16	22. New York
Michigan	133,958	31.4	14	23. Indiana
Minnesota	88,137	31.5	11	24. Vermont
Mississippi	28,976	25.8	51	25. Florida
Missouri	87,658	29.9	26	26. Missouri
Montana	17,747	27.9	43	27. Utah
Nebraska	32,285	31.4	12	28. North Dakota
Nevada	18,831	31.5	10	29. Ohio
New Hampshire	22,713	28.5	38	30. Texas
New Jersey	117,373	28.9	33	31. Wisconsin
New Mexico	25,397	30.9	19	32. West Virginia
New York	284,912	30.6	22	33. New Jersey
North Carolina	93,532	28.4	39	34. Georgia
North Dakota	12,689	29.7	28	35. Alaska
Ohio	154,084	29.6	29	36. South Carolina
Oklahoma	63,690	28.5	37	37. Oklahoma
Oregon	58,941	31.8	5	38. New Hampshire
Pennsylvania	167,362	28.1	40	39. North Carolina
Rhode Island	14,517	27.5	45	40. Pennsylvania
South Carolina	42,604	28.6	36	41. South Dakota
South Dakota	13,374	28.0	41	42. Idaho
Tennessee	67,448	26.8	49	43. Montana
Texas	298,138	29.1	30	44. Kentucky
Utah	29,810	29.8	27	45. Rhode Island
Vermont	13,802	30.5	24	46. Louisiana
Virginia	94,416	31.7	6	47. Maine
Washington	90,285	31.5	9	48. Alabama
West Virginia	22,549	28.9	32	49. Tennessee
Wisconsin	69,185	28.9	31	50. Arkansas
Wyoming	10,796	31.2	15	51. Mississippi
United States	4,114,787	30.0	26	

Source: U.S. Department of Commerce, Bureau of the Census, *1987 Economic Census Characteristics of Business Owners* (Washington, D.C.: Government Printing Office, 1992).

State	Sales & receipts of Women-owned businesses	% of U.S. sales & receipts	Rank by %
Alabama	$3,624,000,000	13.7	37
Alaska	829,000,000	16.6	5
Arizona	2,911,000,000	12.8	41
Arkansas	2,008,000,000	14.6	21
California	31,027,000,000	12.6	42
Colorado	4,261,000,000	15.8	12
Connecticut	5,320,000,000	15.2	17
Delaware	753,000,000	16.2	7
District of Columbia	774,000,000	11.9	49
Florida	16,828,000,000	16.9	3
Georgia	5,874,000,000	12.0	48
Hawaii	857,000,000	13.1	40
Idaho	813,000,000	12.5	43
Illinois	13,884,000,000	14.0	33
Indiana	8,913,000,000	17.6	2
Iowa	2,905,000,000	16.0	9
Kansas	2,661,000,000	15.6	15
Kentucky	3,265,000,000	14.4	26
Louisiana	2,962,000,000	13.8	35
Maine	1,635,000,000	15.7	14
Maryland	5,509,000,000	13.3	39
Massachusetts	11,140,000,000	16.8	4
Michigan	7,889,000,000	12.3	45
Minnesota	4,991,000,000	14.3	27
Mississippi	2,062,000,000	15.7	13
Missouri	5,349,000,000	14.1	31
Montana	930,000,000	16.5	6
Nebraska	1,649,000,000	13.7	36
Nevada	1,414,000,000	14.2	28
New Hampshire	1,858,000,000	14.2	29
New Jersey	13,554,000,000	14.4	24
New Mexico	1,166,000,000	16.0	8
New York	29,970,000,000	14.4	25
North Carolina	6,813,000,000	15.0	19
North Dakota	572,000,000	13.9	34
Ohio	8,872,000,000	12.3	46
Oklahoma	2,948,000,000	15.0	18
Oregon	4,279,000,000	19.4	1
Pennsylvania	13,339,000,000	11.5	51
Rhode Island	1,340,000,000	13.3	38
South Carolina	2,950,000,000	15.9	10
South Dakota	726,000,000	14.1	30
Tennessee	4,226,000,000	12.5	44
Texas	13,385,000,000	11.6	50
Utah	1,392,000,000	14.1	32
Vermont	766,000,000	14.8	20
Virginia	5,952,000,000	14.4	23
Washington	4,689,000,000	12.1	47
West Virginia	1,114,000,000	15.8	11
Wisconsin	4,667,000,000	14.6	22
Wyoming	524,000,000	15.3	16
United States	**$278,138,000,000**	14.0	35

By % of U.S. sales & receipts
1. Oregon
2. Indiana
3. Florida
4. Massachusetts
5. Alaska
6. Montana
7. Delaware
8. New Mexico
9. Iowa
10. South Carolina
11. West Virginia
12. Colorado
13. Mississippi
14. Maine
15. Kansas
16. Wyoming
17. Connecticut
18. Oklahoma
19. North Carolina
20. Vermont
21. Arkansas
22. Wisconsin
23. Virginia
24. New Jersey
25. New York
26. Kentucky
27. Minnesota
28. Nevada
29. New Hampshire
30. South Dakota
31. Missouri
32. Utah
33. Illinois
34. North Dakota
35. Louisiana
36. Nebraska
37. Alabama
38. Rhode Island
39. Maryland
40. Hawaii
41. Arizona
42. California
43. Idaho
44. Tennessee
45. Michigan
46. Ohio
47. Washington
48. Georgia
49. District of Columbia
50. Texas
51. Pennsylvania

Source: U.S. Department of Commerce, Bureau of the Census, *1987 Economic Census Characteristics of Business Owners* (Washington, D.C.: Government Printing Office, 1992).

AFRICAN AMERICAN-OWNED BUSINESSES, 1987				Rank in order
State	**African American-owned businesses**	**% of U.S. businesses**	**Rank by %**	**By % of U.S. businesses**
Alabama	10,085	5.7	9	1. District of Columbia
Alaska	507	1.0	31	2. Maryland
Arizona	1,811	0.9	33	3. Mississippi
Arkansas	4,392	3.3	17	4. South Carolina
California	47,728	2.6	21	5. Louisiana
Colorado	2,871	1.1	30	6. Georgia
Connecticut	4,061	2.1	22	7. Virginia
Delaware	1,399	4.5	10	8. North Carolina
District of Columbia	8,275	28.3	1	9. Alabama
Florida	25,527	3.5	15	10. Delaware
Georgia	21,283	7.0	6	11. Tennessee
Hawaii	399	0.7	39	12. New York
Idaho	94	0.1	48	13. New Jersey
Illinois	19,011	3.3	16	14. Texas
Indiana	5,867	2.0	23	15. Florida
Iowa	703	0.4	42	16. Illinois
Kansas	2,323	1.4	28	17. Arkansas
Kentucky	3,738	1.9	25	18. Michigan
Louisiana	15,331	7.5	5	19. Ohio
Maine	131	0.1	47	20. Missouri
Maryland	21,678	8.9	2	21. California
Massachusetts	4,761	1.3	29	22. Connecticut
Michigan	13,708	3.2	18	23. Indiana
Minnesota	1,448	0.5	40	24. Pennsylvania
Mississippi	9,667	8.6	3	25. Kentucky
Missouri	7,832	2.7	20	26. Nevada
Montana	77	0.1	51	27. Oklahoma
Nebraska	863	0.8	37	28. Kansas
Nevada	1,002	1.7	26	29. Massachusetts
New Hampshire	229	0.3	43	30. Colorado
New Jersey	14,556	3.6	13	31. Alaska
New Mexico	587	0.7	38	32. Wisconsin
New York	36,289	3.9	12	33. Arizona
North Carolina	19,487	5.9	8	34. West Virginia
North Dakota	57	0.1	49	35. Rhode Island
Ohio	15,983	3.1	19	36. Washington
Oklahoma	3,461	1.5	27	37. Nebraska
Oregon	848	0.5	41	38. New Mexico
Pennsylvania	11,728	2.0	24	39. Hawaii
Rhode Island	489	0.9	35	40. Minnesota
South Carolina	12,815	8.6	4	41. Oregon
South Dakota	63	0.1	50	42. Iowa
Tennessee	10,423	4.1	11	43. New Hampshire
Texas	35,725	3.5	14	44. Wyoming
Utah	202	0.2	46	45. Vermont
Vermont	98	0.2	45	46. Utah
Virginia	18,781	6.3	7	47. Maine
Washington	2,583	0.9	36	48. Idaho
West Virginia	727	0.9	34	49. North Dakota
Wisconsin	2,381	1.0	32	50. South Dakota
Wyoming	81	0.2	44	51. Montana
United States	**424,165**	**3.1**	**8**	

Source: U.S. Department of Commerce, Bureau of the Census, *1987 Economic Census Characteristics of Business Owners* (Washington, D.C.: Government Printing Office, 1992).

State	Sales & receipts of African American-owned businesses	% of U.S. sales & receipts	Rank by %
Alabama	$440,000,000	1.7	9
Alaska	14,000,000	0.3	37
Arizona	91,000,000	0.4	31
Arkansas	215,000,000	1.6	11
California	2,364,000,000	1.0	17
Colorado	106,000,000	0.4	33
Connecticut	226,000,000	0.6	24
Delaware	78,000,000	1.7	8
District of Columbia	412,000,000	6.3	1
Florida	1,212,000,000	1.2	12
Georgia	1,180,000,000	2.4	4
Hawaii	12,000,000	0.2	41
Idaho	5,000,000	0.1	49
Illinois	1,100,000,000	1.1	14
Indiana	350,000,000	0.7	23
Iowa	45,000,000	0.2	39
Kansas	154,000,000	0.9	20
Kentucky	120,000,000	0.5	28
Louisiana	532,000,000	2.5	3
Maine	5,000,000	*	50
Maryland	720,000,000	1.7	7
Massachusetts	252,000,000	0.4	34
Michigan	701,000,000	1.1	15
Minnesota	125,000,000	0.4	36
Mississippi	532,000,000	4.1	2
Missouri	336,000,000	0.9	21
Montana	7,000,000	0.1	45
Nebraska	31,000,000	0.3	38
Nevada	39,000,000	0.4	32
New Hampshire	31,000,000	0.2	40
New Jersey	996,000,000	1.1	16
New Mexico	27,000,000	0.4	35
New York	1,886,000,000	0.9	19
North Carolina	746,000,000	1.6	10
North Dakota	1,000,000	*	51
Ohio	626,000,000	0.9	22
Oklahoma	94,000,000	0.5	29
Oregon	34,000,000	0.2	43
Pennsylvania	747,000,000	0.6	25
Rhode Island	18,000,000	0.2	42
South Carolina	444,000,000	2.4	5
South Dakota	5,000,000	0.1	47
Tennessee	386,000,000	1.1	13
Texas	1,084,000,000	0.9	18
Utah	9,000,000	0.1	48
Vermont	7,000,000	0.1	44
Virginia	811,000,000	2.0	6
Washington	176,000,000	0.5	30
West Virginia	39,000,000	0.6	27
Wisconsin	191,000,000	0.6	26
Wyoming	4,000,000	0.1	46
United States	**$19,763,000,000**	1.0	8

SALES & RECEIPTS OF AFRICAN AMERICAN-OWNED BUSINESSES, 1987

Rank in order

% of U.S. sales & receipts

1. District of Columbia
2. Mississippi
3. Louisiana
4. Georgia
5. South Carolina
6. Virginia
7. Maryland
8. Delaware
9. Alabama
10. North Carolina
11. Arkansas
12. Florida
13. Tennessee
14. Illinois
15. Michigan
16. New Jersey
17. California
18. Texas
19. New York
20. Kansas
21. Missouri
22. Ohio
23. Indiana
24. Connecticut
25. Pennsylvania
26. Wisconsin
27. West Virginia
28. Kentucky
29. Oklahoma
30. Washington
31. Arizona
32. Nevada
33. Colorado
34. Massachusetts
35. New Mexico
36. Minnesota
37. Alaska
38. Nebraska
39. Iowa
40. New Hampshire
41. Hawaii
42. Rhode Island
43. Oregon
44. Vermont
45. Montana
46. Wyoming
47. South Dakota
48. Utah
49. Idaho
50. Maine
51. North Dakota

* percent of total rounds to less than 0.1.

Source: U.S. Department of Commerce, Bureau of the Census, *1987 Economic Census Characteristics of Business Owners* (Washington, D.C.: Government Printing Office, 1992).

State	Hispanic-owned businesses	% of U.S. businesses	Rank by %
Alabama	397	0.2	47
Alaska	502	1.0	19
Arizona	9,845	5.1	5
Arkansas	324	0.2	44
California	132,212	7.3	4
Colorado	9,516	3.6	6
Connecticut	2,235	1.1	18
Delaware	184	0.6	30
District of Columbia	762	2.6	10
Florida	64,413	8.8	3
Georgia	1,931	0.6	27
Hawaii	1,226	2.0	11
Idaho	974	1.4	14
Illinois	9,636	1.7	13
Indiana	1,427	0.5	31
Iowa	475	0.3	40
Kansas	1,541	0.9	22
Kentucky	359	0.2	50
Louisiana	2,697	1.3	15
Maine	139	0.2	51
Maryland	2,931	1.2	17
Massachusetts	2,636	0.7	25
Michigan	2,654	0.6	28
Minnesota	751	0.3	41
Mississippi	308	0.3	39
Missouri	1,247	0.4	34
Montana	304	0.5	32
Nebraska	619	0.6	29
Nevada	1,767	3.0	9
New Hampshire	244	0.3	37
New Jersey	12,094	3.0	8
New Mexico	14,299	17.4	1
New York	28,254	3.0	7
North Carolina	918	0.3	38
North Dakota	88	0.2	49
Ohio	1,989	0.4	35
Oklahoma	1,516	0.7	26
Oregon	1,598	0.9	23
Pennsylvania	2,650	0.4	33
Rhode Island	426	0.8	24
South Carolina	393	0.3	42
South Dakota	109	0.2	45
Tennessee	554	0.2	48
Texas	94,754	9.2	2
Utah	1,300	1.3	16
Vermont	118	0.3	43
Virginia	2,716	0.9	21
Washington	2,686	0.9	20
West Virginia	177	0.2	46
Wisconsin	894	0.4	36
Wyoming	584	1.7	12
United States	**422,373**	**3.1**	**7**

By % of U.S. businesses

1. New Mexico
2. Texas
3. Florida
4. California
5. Arizona
6. Colorado
7. New York
8. New Jersey
9. Nevada
10. District of Columbia
11. Hawaii
12. Wyoming
13. Illinois
14. Idaho
15. Louisiana
16. Utah
17. Maryland
18. Connecticut
19. Alaska
20. Washington
21. Virginia
22. Kansas
23. Oregon
24. Rhode Island
25. Massachusetts
26. Oklahoma
27. Georgia
28. Michigan
29. Nebraska
30. Delaware
31. Indiana
32. Montana
33. Pennsylvania
34. Missouri
35. Ohio
36. Wisconsin
37. New Hampshire
38. North Carolina
39. Mississippi
40. Iowa
41. Minnesota
42. South Carolina
43. Vermont
44. Arkansas
45. South Dakota
46. West Virginia
47. Alabama
48. Tennessee
49. North Dakota
50. Kentucky
51. Maine

Source: U.S. Department of Commerce, Bureau of the Census, *1987 Economic Census Characteristics of Business Owners* (Washington, D.C.: Government Printing Office, 1992).

SALES & RECEIPTS OF HISPANIC-OWNED BUSINESSES, 1987

State	Sales & receipts of Hispanic-owned businesses	% of U.S. sales & receipts	Rank by %
Alabama	$30,000,000	0.1	40
Alaska	27,000,000	0.5	15
Arizona	513,000,000	2.3	5
Arkansas	14,000,000	0.1	43
California	8,120,000,000	3.3	4
Colorado	394,000,000	1.5	6
Connecticut	176,000,000	0.5	16
Delaware	6,000,000	0.1	38
District of Columbia	64,000,000	1.0	8
Florida	4,949,000,000	5.0	2
Georgia	145,000,000	0.3	25
Hawaii	58,000,000	0.9	10
Idaho	31,000,000	0.5	18
Illinois	589,000,000	0.6	14
Indiana	106,000,000	0.2	31
Iowa	20,000,000	0.1	41
Kansas	62,000,000	0.4	22
Kentucky	17,000,000	0.1	50
Louisiana	136,000,000	0.6	13
Maine	12,000,000	0.1	39
Maryland	185,000,000	0.4	20
Massachusetts	174,000,000	0.3	27
Michigan	126,000,000	0.2	34
Minnesota	29,000,000	0.1	48
Mississippi	12,000,000	0.1	46
Missouri	50,000,000	0.1	37
Montana	10,000,000	0.2	35
Nebraska	19,000,000	0.2	36
Nevada	142,000,000	1.4	7
New Hampshire	13,000,000	0.1	44
New Jersey	902,000,000	1.0	9
New Mexico	702,000,000	9.6	1
New York	1,556,000,000	0.7	11
North Carolina	93,000,000	0.2	32
North Dakota	2,000,000	*	51
Ohio	192,000,000	0.3	26
Oklahoma	50,000,000	0.3	28
Oregon	110,000,000	0.5	17
Pennsylvania	247,000,000	0.2	30
Rhode Island	40,000,000	0.4	21
South Carolina	16,000,000	0.1	47
South Dakota	4,000,000	0.1	49
Tennessee	35,000,000	0.1	42
Texas	4,108,000,000	3.6	3
Utah	47,000,000	0.5	18
Vermont	5,000,000	0.1	45
Virginia	141,000,000	0.3	24
Washington	141,000,000	0.4	22
West Virginia	14,000,000	0.2	33
Wisconsin	74,000,000	0.2	29
Wyoming	22,000,000	0.6	12
United States	**$24,732,000,000**	1.2	8

By % of U.S. businesses

1. New Mexico
2. Florida
3. Texas
4. California
5. Arizona
6. Colorado
7. Nevada
8. District of Columbia
9. New Jersey
10. Hawaii
11. New York
12. Wyoming
13. Louisiana
14. Illinois
15. Alaska
16. Connecticut
17. Oregon
18. Idaho
     Utah
20. Maryland
21. Rhode Island
22. Kansas
     Washington
24. Virginia
25. Georgia
26. Ohio
27. Massachusetts
28. Oklahoma
29. Wisconsin
30. Pennsylvania
31. Indiana
32. North Carolina
33. West Virginia
34. Michigan
35. Montana
36. Nebraska
37. Missouri
38. Delaware
39. Maine
40. Alabama
41. Iowa
42. Tennessee
43. Arkansas
44. New Hampshire
45. Vermont
46. Mississippi
47. South Carolina
48. Minnesota
49. South Dakota
50. Kentucky
51. North Dakota

* percent of total rounds to less than 0.1.

Source: U.S. Department of Commerce, Bureau of the Census, *1987 Economic Census Characteristics of Business Owners* (Washington, D.C.: Government Printing Office, 1992).

EMPLOYEES IN MANUFACTURING, 1990				Rank in order
State	Manufacturing employees	% of U.S. manufacturing	Rank by %	By % of U.S. manufacturing
Alabama	367,800	2.0	19	1. California
Alaska	13,600	0.1	49	2. New York
Arizona	180,900	1.0	30	3. Ohio
Arkansas	219,000	1.2	26	4. Pennsylvania
California	2,105,900	11.2	1	5. Illinois
Colorado	179,900	1.0	31	6. Texas
Connecticut	345,100	1.8	22	7. Michigan
Delaware	65,800	0.4	40	8. North Carolina
District of Columbia	14,100	0.1	49	9. New Jersey
Florida	497,900	2.6	15	10. Indiana
Georgia	564,500	3.0	11	11. Georgia
Hawaii	20,700	0.1	47	12. Wisconsin
Idaho	60,900	0.3	41	13. Massachusetts
Illinois	1,007,700	5.4	5	14. Tennessee
Indiana	615,500	3.3	10	15. Florida
Iowa	230,400	1.2	25	16. Missouri
Kansas	190,900	1.0	29	Virginia
Kentucky	278,800	1.5	23	18. Minnesota
Louisiana	171,200	0.9	32	19. Alabama
Maine	103,000	0.6	34	South Carolina
Maryland	212,100	1.1	28	Washington
Massachusetts	529,300	2.8	13	22. Connecticut
Michigan	913,100	4.9	7	23. Kentucky
Minnesota	394,500	2.1	18	24. Mississippi
Mississippi	233,400	1.2	24	25. Iowa
Missouri	422,700	2.2	16	26. Arkansas
Montana	20,000	0.1	46	27. Oregon
Nebraska	99,300	0.5	37	28. Maryland
Nevada	25,600	0.1	45	29. Kansas
New Hampshire	92,300	0.5	38	30. Arizona
New Jersey	627,200	3.3	9	31. Colorado
New Mexico	39,900	0.2	43	32. Louisiana
New York	1,150,200	6.1	2	33. Oklahoma
North Carolina	831,800	4.4	8	34. Maine
North Dakota	16,300	0.1	48	35. Rhode Island
Ohio	1,085,100	5.8	3	Utah
Oklahoma	167,500	0.9	33	37. Nebraska
Oregon	216,100	1.2	27	38. New Hampshire
Pennsylvania	1,010,000	5.4	4	39. West Virginia
Rhode Island	101,000	0.5	35	40. Delaware
South Carolina	367,000	2.0	19	41. Idaho
South Dakota	29,700	0.2	44	42. Vermont
Tennessee	503,700	2.7	14	43. New Mexico
Texas	942,700	5.0	6	44. South Dakota
Utah	101,500	0.5	35	45. Nevada
Vermont	44,000	0.2	42	46. Montana
Virginia	422,900	2.2	16	47. Hawaii
Washington	367,300	2.0	19	48. North Dakota
West Virginia	82,200	0.4	39	49. Alaska
Wisconsin	548,000	2.9	12	District of Columbia
Wyoming	10,200	0.1	51	51. Wyoming
United States	18,840,300	100.0	—	

— not applicable.

Source: U.S. Department of Commerce, Bureau of the Census, *1990 Annual Survey of Manufactures, Geographic Area Statistics* (Washington, D.C.: Government Printing Office, 1992).

State	Value of manufacturing shipments	Per capita	Rank by per capita
Alabama	$48,748,000,000	$12,063.35	22
Alaska	3,676,100,000	6,683.82	40
Arizona	22,885,900,000	6,244.45	43
Arkansas	30,493,300,000	12,970.35	17
California	293,190,000,000	9,851.81	31
Colorado	27,701,300,000	8,409.62	37
Connecticut	39,898,100,000	12,138.15	21
Delaware	12,901,000,000	19,370.87	1
District of Columbia	2,152,300,000	3,545.80	50
Florida	60,749,500,000	4,695.43	47
Georgia	84,230,700,000	13,002.58	16
Hawaii	4,202,900,000	3,793.23	48
Idaho	9,183,800,000	9,119.96	33
Illinois	156,674,800,000	13,706.13	13
Indiana	98,618,800,000	17,788.38	2
Iowa	45,926,500,000	16,538.17	5
Kansas	36,349,200,000	14,668.77	9
Kentucky	53,776,500,000	14,593.35	10
Louisiana	65,806,600,000	15,593.98	8
Maine	12,477,200,000	10,160.59	28
Maryland	30,679,400,000	6,416.94	42
Massachusetts	63,796,200,000	10,604.42	27
Michigan	153,386,000,000	16,501.99	6
Minnesota	55,244,100,000	12,627.22	19
Mississippi	30,312,600,000	11,781.03	23
Missouri	67,355,100,000	13,163.01	15
Montana	4,039,900,000	5,056.20	45
Nebraska	20,370,000,000	12,908.75	18
Nevada	2,924,800,000	2,433.28	51
New Hampshire	9,727,200,000	8,771.15	35
New Jersey	87,498,000,000	11,319.28	25
New Mexico	5,547,600,000	3,661.78	49
New York	154,713,900,000	8,599.99	36
North Carolina	116,245,300,000	17,535.87	3
North Dakota	3,012,700,000	4,714.71	46
Ohio	177,786,500,000	16,390.38	7
Oklahoma	28,009,900,000	8,903.34	34
Oregon	31,072,600,000	10,933.36	26
Pennsylvania	136,526,000,000	11,490.15	24
Rhode Island	9,760,900,000	9,731.70	32
South Carolina	46,500,800,000	13,335.47	14
South Dakota	4,532,600,000	6,512.36	41
Tennessee	67,403,600,000	13,820.71	12
Texas	210,584,400,000	12,396.80	20
Utah	13,949,500,000	8,096.05	38
Vermont	5,592,100,000	9,932.68	29
Virginia	61,042,200,000	9,866.20	30
Washington	67,538,000,000	13,876.72	11
West Virginia	12,937,500,000	7,215.56	39
Wisconsin	83,013,400,000	16,969.22	4
Wyoming	2,756,400,000	6,071.37	44
United States	**$2,873,501,600,000**	**$11,553.62**	**24**

Rank in order

By per capita

1. Delaware
2. Indiana
3. North Carolina
4. Wisconsin
5. Iowa
6. Michigan
7. Ohio
8. Louisiana
9. Kansas
10. Kentucky
11. Washington
12. Tennessee
13. Illinois
14. South Carolina
15. Missouri
16. Georgia
17. Arkansas
18. Nebraska
19. Minnesota
20. Texas
21. Connecticut
22. Alabama
23. Mississippi
24. Pennsylvania
25. New Jersey
26. Oregon
27. Massachusetts
28. Maine
29. Vermont
30. Virginia
31. California
32. Rhode Island
33. Idaho
34. Oklahoma
35. New Hampshire
36. New York
37. Colorado
38. Utah
39. West Virginia
40. Alaska
41. South Dakota
42. Maryland
43. Arizona
44. Wyoming
45. Montana
46. North Dakota
47. Florida
48. Hawaii
49. New Mexico
50. District of Columbia
51. Nevada

Source: U.S. Department of Commerce, Bureau of the Census, *1990 Annual Survey of Manufactures, Geographic Area Statistics* (Washington, D.C.: Government Printing Office, 1992).

JAPANESE-OWNED U.S. MANUFACTURING PLANTS, 1989

State	Manufacturing plants	Rank
Alabama	17	20
Alaska	26	15
Arizona	10	28
Arkansas	13	25
California	235	1
Colorado	10	28
Connecticut	9	30
Delaware	2	42
District of Columbia	0	48
Florida	14	23
Georgia	65	4
Hawaii	14	23
Idaho	1	45
Illinois	86	3
Indiana	53	6
Iowa	6	36
Kansas	6	36
Kentucky	49	7
Louisana	4	39
Maine	9	30
Maryland	12	26
Massachusetts	24	16
Michigan	61	5
Minnesota	5	38
Mississippi	7	34
Missouri	15	22
Montana	0	48
Nebraska	9	30
Nevada	9	30
New Hampshire	20	19
New Jersey	47	9
New Mexico	2	42
New York	35	14
North Carolina	43	10
North Dakota	0	48
Ohio	100	2
Oklahoma	11	27
Oregon	22	18
Pennsylvania	36	13
Rhode Island	1	45
South Carolina	23	17
South Dakota	1	45
Tennessee	41	11
Texas	48	8
Utah	4	39
Vermont	4	39
Virginia	17	20
Washington	40	12
West Virginia	2	42
Wisconsin	7	34
Wyoming	0	48
United States	**1,275**	**—**

— not applicable.

Source: Phyllis A. Genther and Donald H. Dalton, *Japanese Direct Investment in U.S. Manufacturing* (Washington, D.C.: Department of Commerce, 1990).

Rank in order

By number of plants

1. California
2. Ohio
3. Illinois
4. Georgia
5. Michigan
6. Indiana
7. Kentucky
8. Texas
9. New Jersey
10. North Carolina
11. Tennessee
12. Washington
13. Pennsylvania
14. New York
15. Alaska
16. Massachusetts
17. South Carolina
18. Oregon
19. New Hampshire
20. Alabama
    Virginia
22. Missouri
23. Florida
    Hawaii
25. Arkansas
26. Maryland
27. Oklahoma
28. Arizona
    Colorado
30. Connecticut
    Maine
    Nebraska
    Nevada
34. Mississippi
    Wisconsin
36. Iowa
    Kansas
38. Minnesota
39. Louisana
    Utah
    Vermont
42. Delaware
    New Mexico
    West Virginia
45. Idaho
    Rhode Island
    South Dakota
48. District of Columbia
    Montana
    North Dakota
    Wyoming

State	Value of exports	Per capita	Rank by per capita	% of state's foreign exports	Rank by %
Alabama	$152,628,000	$37.33	29	4.0	22
Alaska	6,045,000	10.61	45	0.2	51
Arizona	990,787,000	264.21	2	18.1	2
Arkansas	95,929,000	40.44	24	7.3	6
California	5,526,877,000	181.92	4	8.8	4
Colorado	90,148,000	26.69	33	3.1	31
Connecticut	259,395,000	78.82	9	4.6	16
Delaware	127,383,000	187.33	3	7.2	7
District of Columbia	4,103,000	6.86	49	0.7	50
Florida	578,730,000	43.59	23	3.3	27
Georgia	376,741,000	56.88	14	4.7	15
Hawaii	6,535,000	5.76	50	2.7	35
Idaho	32,925,000	31.69	31	3.1	31
Illinois	1,087,100,000	94.18	8	6.6	9
Indiana	259,377,000	46.23	21	4.0	22
Iowa	108,261,000	38.73	27	4.2	18
Kansas	258,266,000	103.51	7	10.9	3
Kentucky	163,489,000	44.03	22	4.6	16
Louisiana	618,114,000	145.37	6	3.7	24
Maine	14,398,000	11.66	44	1.4	43
Maryland	50,728,000	10.44	46	1.3	44
Massachusetts	229,829,000	38.33	28	1.9	39
Michigan	1,628,409,000	173.83	5	7.0	8
Minnesota	216,964,000	48.95	20	3.4	25
Mississippi	100,639,000	38.83	26	5.1	14
Missouri	288,245,000	55.88	15	7.7	5
Montana	9,716,000	12.02	42	3.2	30
Nebraska	64,401,000	40.43	25	5.8	12
Nevada	11,304,000	8.80	47	2.3	37
New Hampshire	37,834,000	34.24	30	3.3	27
New Jersey	452,365,000	58.29	11	4.1	19
New Mexico	18,219,000	11.77	43	5.3	13
New York	886,835,000	49.11	18	2.9	34
North Carolina	330,540,000	49.06	19	3.3	27
North Dakota	3,570,000	5.62	51	0.9	48
Ohio	581,783,000	53.18	16	3.4	25
Oklahoma	80,354,000	25.31	35	4.1	19
Oregon	55,401,000	18.96	39	1.1	46
Pennsylvania	693,727,000	58.00	12	6.1	10
Rhode Island	24,096,000	24.00	36	3.1	31
South Carolina	94,191,000	26.46	34	2.2	38
South Dakota	6,105,000	8.68	48	2.6	36
Tennessee	290,875,000	58.73	10	5.9	11
Texas	15,485,379,000	892.58	1	32.9	1
Utah	39,340,000	22.23	38	1.9	39
Vermont	17,968,000	31.69	31	0.8	49
Virginia	146,028,000	23.23	37	1.3	44
Washington	290,573,000	57.91	13	1.0	47
West Virginia	32,504,000	18.05	40	1.8	41
Wisconsin	249,911,000	50.44	17	4.1	19
Wyoming	6,224,000	13.53	41	1.8	41
United States	**$33,181,288,000**	**$131.58**	7	7.9	5

By % of state's foreign exports
1. Texas
2. Arizona
3. Kansas
4. California
5. Missouri
6. Arkansas
7. Delaware
8. Michigan
9. Illinois
10. Pennsylvania
11. Tennessee
12. Nebraska
13. New Mexico
14. Mississippi
15. Georgia
16. Connecticut
    Kentucky
18. Iowa
19. New Jersey
    Oklahoma
    Wisconsin
22. Alabama
    Indiana
24. Louisiana
25. Minnesota
    Ohio
27. Florida
    New Hampshire
    North Carolina
30. Montana
31. Colorado
    Idaho
    Rhode Island
34. New York
35. Hawaii
36. South Dakota
37. Nevada
38. South Carolina
39. Massachusetts
    Utah
41. West Virginia
    Wyoming
43. Maine
44. Maryland
    Virginia
46. Oregon
47. Washington
48. North Dakota
49. Vermont
50. District of Columbia
51. Alaska

Source: International Trade Administration, *U.S. Exports to Mexico: A State-by-State Overview, 1987-1991* (Washington, D.C.: Department of Commerce, 1992).

CHANGE IN EXPORTS TO MEXICO, 1987-1991						Rank in order
State	Dollar change in exports	Per capita	Rank by per capita	% change in exports	Rank by %	By % change in exports
Alabama	$72,077,000	$17.63	28	89.5	33	1. Hawaii
Alaska	752,000	1.32	45	14.2	45	2. Montana
Arizona	346,109,000	92.30	4	53.7	40	3. Vermont
Arkansas	58,219,000	24.54	23	154.4	22	4. Maine
California	3,269,615,000	107.62	3	144.8	23	5. Delaware
Colorado	20,858,000	6.18	42	30.1	44	6. Nevada
Connecticut	144,017,000	43.76	9	124.8	29	7. Illinois
Delaware	99,350,000	146.10	2	354.4	5	8. New Hampshire
District of Columbia	−829,000	−1.39	48	−16.8	49	9. Pennsylvania
Florida	359,732,000	27.09	21	164.3	21	10. Kentucky
Georgia	268,644,000	40.56	12	248.5	13	11. Virginia
Hawaii	6,475,000	5.70	44	10699.1	1	12. North Carolina
Idaho	21,687,000	20.87	25	193.0	17	13. Georgia
Illinois	808,727,000	70.06	5	290.5	7	Washington
Indiana	−11,552,000	−2.06	49	−4.3	48	15. Wisconsin
Iowa	42,177,000	15.09	32	63.8	38	16. Maryland
Kansas	133,287,000	53.42	8	106.6	30	17. Idaho
Kentucky	120,244,000	32.38	17	277.9	10	18. South Carolina
Louisiana	240,688,000	56.61	7	63.8	38	19. Tennessee
Maine	11,713,000	9.48	37	436.3	4	20. Oregon
Maryland	33,684,000	6.93	39	197.6	16	21. Florida
Massachusetts	129,712,000	21.63	24	129.6	28	22. Arkansas
Michigan	550,539,000	58.77	6	51.1	41	23. California
Minnesota	126,989,000	28.65	19	141.1	24	24. Minnesota
Mississippi	48,129,000	18.57	27	91.7	32	25. Texas
Missouri	89,533,000	17.36	30	45.1	42	26. New Jersey
Montana	8,497,000	10.52	36	697.1	2	27. Ohio
Nebraska	19,854,000	12.46	33	44.6	43	28. Massachusetts
Nevada	8,598,000	6.70	40	317.8	6	29. Connecticut
New Hampshire	28,044,000	25.38	22	286.4	8	30. Kansas
New Jersey	263,157,000	33.91	16	139.1	26	31. New Mexico
New Mexico	9,162,000	5.92	43	101.1	31	32. Mississippi
New York	374,467,000	20.74	26	73.1	36	33. Alabama
North Carolina	235,870,000	35.01	14	249.1	12	34. Wyoming
North Dakota	−36,316,000	−57.19	51	−91.0	51	35. Oklahoma
Ohio	336,550,000	30.77	18	137.2	27	36. New York
Oklahoma	36,107,000	11.37	35	81.6	35	37. Rhode Island
Oregon	35,923,000	12.29	34	184.4	20	38. Iowa
Pennsylvania	512,601,000	42.86	10	283.0	9	Louisiana
Rhode Island	9,432,000	9.39	38	64.3	37	40. Arizona
South Carolina	61,841,000	17.37	29	191.2	18	41. Michigan
South Dakota	746,000	1.06	47	13.9	46	42. Missouri
Tennessee	189,938,000	38.35	13	188.2	19	43. Nebraska
Texas	9,020,256,000	519.93	1	139.5	25	44. Colorado
Utah	2,252,000	1.27	46	6.1	47	45. Alaska
Vermont	15,398,000	27.16	20	599.2	3	46. South Dakota
Virginia	104,971,000	16.70	31	255.7	11	47. Utah
Washington	207,191,000	41.29	11	248.5	13	48. Indiana
West Virginia	−11,485,000	−6.38	50	−26.1	50	49. District of Columbia
Wisconsin	172,588,000	34.83	15	223.2	15	50. West Virginia
Wyoming	2,850,000	6.20	41	84.4	34	51. North Dakota
United States	$18,693,541,000	$74.13	5	128.2	29	

Source: International Trade Administration, *U.S. Exports to Mexico: A State-by-State Overview, 1987-1991* (Washington, D.C.: Department of Commerce, 1992).

EXISTING HOME SALES, 1991

State	Homes sold	Per 100,000 population Rate	Per 100,000 population Rank
Alabama	64,000	1,565.17	22
Alaska	NA	NA	NA
Arizona	79,700	2,125.33	2
Arkansas	43,400	1,829.68	8
California	424,100	1,395.98	34
Colorado	59,600	1,764.88	12
Connecticut	37,600	1,142.51	42
Delaware	10,400	1,529.41	25
District of Columbia	12,500	2,090.30	3
Florida	176,000	1,325.60	40
Georgia	70,700	1,067.49	45
Hawaii	12,200	1,074.89	44
Idaho	19,000	1,828.68	9
Illinois	168,100	1,456.29	31
Indiana	76,000	1,354.72	39
Iowa	54,100	1,935.60	6
Kansas	37,100	1,486.97	29
Kentucky	67,800	1,826.02	10
Louisiana	47,100	1,107.71	43
Maine	NA	NA	NA
Maryland	66,800	1,374.49	36
Massachusetts	49,600	827.22	47
Michigan	145,000	1,547.82	23
Minnesota	66,300	1,495.94	28
Mississippi	35,200	1,358.02	38
Missouri	82,700	1,603.33	20
Montana	13,900	1,720.30	14
Nebraska	19,900	1,249.22	41
Nevada	25,600	1,993.77	5
New Hampshire	9,300	841.63	46
New Jersey	118,800	1,530.93	24
New Mexico	24,400	1,576.23	21
New York	127,200	704.40	49
North Carolina	139,900	2,076.59	4
North Dakota	10,300	1,622.05	17
Ohio	149,800	1,369.41	37
Oklahoma	52,500	1,653.54	15
Oregon	48,100	1,646.13	16
Pennsylvania	179,200	1,498.20	27
Rhode Island	7,800	776.89	48
South Carolina	53,900	1,514.04	26
South Dakota	11,300	1,607.40	19
Tennessee	92,000	1,857.46	7
Texas	242,000	1,394.89	35
Utah	26,300	1,485.88	30
Vermont	8,100	1,428.57	33
Virginia	90,300	1,436.53	32
Washington	86,900	1,731.77	13
West Virginia	43,300	2,404.22	1
Wisconsin	80,000	1,614.53	18
Wyoming	8,200	1,782.61	11
United States	3,220,000	1,276.88	41

NA not available.

Source: National Association of Realtors, *Home Sales* (Washington, D.C.: National Association of Realtors, monthly).

Rank in order

By rate per 100,000 population

1. West Virginia
2. Arizona
3. District of Columbia
4. North Carolina
5. Nevada
6. Iowa
7. Tennessee
8. Arkansas
9. Idaho
10. Kentucky
11. Wyoming
12. Colorado
13. Washington
14. Montana
15. Oklahoma
16. Oregon
17. North Dakota
18. Wisconsin
19. South Dakota
20. Missouri
21. New Mexico
22. Alabama
23. Michigan
24. New Jersey
25. Delaware
26. South Carolina
27. Pennsylvania
28. Minnesota
29. Kansas
30. Utah
31. Illinois
32. Virginia
33. Vermont
34. California
35. Texas
36. Maryland
37. Ohio
38. Mississippi
39. Indiana
40. Florida
41. Nebraska
42. Connecticut
43. Louisiana
44. Hawaii
45. Georgia
46. New Hampshire
47. Massachusetts
48. Rhode Island
49. New York
NA Alaska
NA Maine

State	Single family units	Total housing units	Per 100,000 population Rate	Per 100,000 population Rank
Alabama	13,700	16,500	403.52	24
Alaska	1,300	1,600	280.70	41
Arizona	23,000	25,400	677.33	7
Arkansas	8,200	9,100	383.64	27
California	82,700	109,100	359.12	31
Colorado	12,500	15,400	456.03	20
Connecticut	7,500	8,100	246.13	45
Delaware	4,800	5,500	808.82	3
District of Columbia	200	200	33.45	51
Florida	80,700	98,100	738.87	4
Georgia	35,500	40,800	616.04	9
Hawaii	5,500	8,300	731.28	5
Idaho	7,800	8,500	818.09	2
Illinois	29,700	35,500	307.55	38
Indiana	24,300	27,500	490.20	16
Iowa	7,600	9,500	339.89	35
Kansas	7,900	9,400	376.75	28
Kentucky	11,800	13,800	371.67	30
Louisiana	6,900	8,400	197.55	48
Maine	3,600	3,900	315.79	37
Maryland	17,200	22,700	467.08	18
Massachusetts	12,000	12,800	213.48	46
Michigan	25,600	32,700	349.06	34
Minnesota	20,100	21,900	494.13	15
Mississippi	5,400	6,500	250.77	44
Missouri	15,200	18,100	350.91	33
Montana	2,600	3,300	408.42	23
Nebraska	5,600	7,100	445.70	21
Nevada	10,500	17,500	1,362.93	1
New Hampshire	3,300	3,600	325.79	36
New Jersey	14,400	16,200	208.76	47
New Mexico	4,200	4,600	297.16	40
New York	22,300	27,600	152.84	49
North Carolina	37,700	42,000	623.42	8
North Dakota	1,500	2,900	456.69	19
Ohio	33,500	41,100	375.72	29
Oklahoma	7,600	8,200	258.27	43
Oregon	10,500	15,300	523.61	12
Pennsylvania	31,600	35,800	299.31	39
Rhode Island	2,500	2,800	278.88	42
South Carolina	18,000	19,800	556.18	10
South Dakota	2,200	2,700	384.07	26
Tennessee	21,300	24,000	484.56	17
Texas	54,900	62,000	357.37	32
Utah	8,400	8,900	502.83	14
Vermont	2,000	2,200	388.01	25
Virginia	28,300	34,300	545.66	11
Washington	26,100	34,200	681.55	6
West Virginia	2,000	2,200	122.15	50
Wisconsin	18,900	25,500	514.63	13
Wyoming	1,900	2,000	434.78	22
United States	842,000	1,015,000	402.50	25

HOUSING STARTS, 1991

By rate per 100,000 population

1. Nevada
2. Idaho
3. Delaware
4. Florida
5. Hawaii
6. Washington
7. Arizona
8. North Carolina
9. Georgia
10. South Carolina
11. Virginia
12. Oregon
13. Wisconsin
14. Utah
15. Minnesota
16. Indiana
17. Tennessee
18. Maryland
19. North Dakota
20. Colorado
21. Nebraska
22. Wyoming
23. Montana
24. Alabama
25. Vermont
26. South Dakota
27. Arkansas
28. Kansas
29. Ohio
30. Kentucky
31. California
32. Texas
33. Missouri
34. Michigan
35. Iowa
36. New Hampshire
37. Maine
38. Illinois
39. Pennsylvania
40. New Mexico
41. Alaska
42. Rhode Island
43. Oklahoma
44. Mississippi
45. Connecticut
46. Massachusetts
47. New Jersey
48. Louisiana
49. New York
50. West Virginia
51. District of Columbia

Source: U.S. Department of Commerce, Bureau of the Census, *Statistical Abstract of the United States, 1992* (Washington, D.C.: Government Printing Office, 1992).

Note: Housing starts include only new, privately owned housing units.

State	Average annual pay	Rank	% increase 1990-1991	
			Rate	Rank
Alabama	$21,287	34	4.0	25
Alaska	30,830	2	2.9	50
Arizona	22,207	27	3.6	39
Arkansas	19,008	47	4.4	17
California	27,499	7	5.0	5
Colorado	23,981	14	4.7	11
Connecticut	30,689	3	5.8	1
Delaware	25,647	11	5.0	5
District of Columbia	35,570	1	5.5	3
Florida	21,991	28	4.6	14
Georgia	23,164	21	4.7	11
Hawaii	24,104	13	4.0	25
Idaho	19,688	45	3.7	38
Illinois	26,310	8	3.9	30
Indiana	22,522	25	3.8	36
Iowa	19,810	44	3.0	48
Kansas	21,002	36	3.8	36
Kentucky	20,730	40	3.9	30
Louisiana	21,501	31	4.1	23
Maine	20,870	39	3.6	39
Maryland	25,960	10	5.0	5
Massachusetts	28,041	6	5.0	5
Michigan	26,125	9	3.0	48
Minnesota	23,961	15	3.6	39
Mississippi	18,411	49	3.9	30
Missouri	22,567	24	3.9	30
Montana	18,648	48	4.2	22
Nebraska	19,372	46	4.3	19
Nevada	23,083	22	3.2	45
New Hampshire	23,600	20	4.4	17
New Jersey	29,992	5	5.4	4
New Mexico	20,275	43	4.8	9
New York	30,011	4	3.9	30
North Carolina	21,087	35	4.3	19
North Dakota	18,132	50	2.9	50
Ohio	23,603	19	3.3	43
Oklahoma	20,968	37	3.3	43
Oregon	22,348	26	4.8	9
Pennsylvania	24,393	12	4.0	25
Rhode Island	23,082	23	3.1	46
South Carolina	20,439	42	3.9	30
South Dakota	17,131	51	4.3	19
Tennessee	21,541	30	4.5	16
Texas	23,760	18	4.7	11
Utah	20,874	38	4.0	25
Vermont	21,355	33	4.0	25
Virginia	23,804	17	4.6	14
Washington	23,942	16	5.7	2
West Virginia	21,356	32	3.1	46
Wisconsin	21,838	29	3.5	42
Wyoming	20,591	41	4.1	23
United States	$24,575	12	4.1	23

By average annual pay

1. District of Columbia
2. Alaska
3. Connecticut
4. New York
5. New Jersey
6. Massachusetts
7. California
8. Illinois
9. Michigan
10. Maryland
11. Delaware
12. Pennsylvania
13. Hawaii
14. Colorado
15. Minnesota
16. Washington
17. Virginia
18. Texas
19. Ohio
20. New Hampshire
21. Georgia
22. Nevada
23. Rhode Island
24. Missouri
25. Indiana
26. Oregon
27. Arizona
28. Florida
29. Wisconsin
30. Tennessee
31. Louisiana
32. West Virginia
33. Vermont
34. Alabama
35. North Carolina
36. Kansas
37. Oklahoma
38. Utah
39. Maine
40. Kentucky
41. Wyoming
42. South Carolina
43. New Mexico
44. Iowa
45. Idaho
46. Nebraska
47. Arkansas
48. Montana
49. Mississippi
50. North Dakota
51. South Dakota

Source: U.S. Department of Labor, *"Average Annual Pay by State and Industry, 1991,"* press release USDL 92-631, October 7, 1992.

State	Disposable personal income	Rank	% average annual growth, 1990-1991	
			Rate	Rank
Alabama	$13,843	41	5.89	10
Alaska	18,492	8	5.11	17
Arizona	14,619	37	4.64	23
Arkansas	13,088	47	5.72	12
California	18,000	10	3.52	38
Colorado	16,755	19	5.88	11
Connecticut	22,139	2	2.08	51
Delaware	17,679	12	3.68	36
District of Columbia	19,874	3	3.92	31
Florida	16,820	17	4.44	26
Georgia	15,260	30	5.00	20
Hawaii	17,873	11	4.88	21
Idaho	13,883	40	4.62	24
Illinois	18,046	9	3.46	39
Indiana	15,029	34	3.87	32
Iowa	15,134	31	3.31	42
Kansas	15,930	22	4.09	27
Kentucky	13,757	43	5.58	13
Louisiana	13,489	46	6.99	4
Maine	15,512	28	2.80	47
Maryland	18,901	7	3.76	35
Massachusetts	19,766	4	2.30	50
Michigan	16,301	21	3.12	43
Minnesota	16,394	20	4.06	29
Mississippi	12,259	51	6.15	8
Missouri	15,843	23	5.11	17
Montana	13,729	44	9.06	1
Nebraska	15,644	25	3.81	33
Nevada	17,198	14	5.91	9
New Hampshire	19,738	5	3.81	33
New Jersey	22,323	1	2.57	49
New Mexico	13,047	48	6.35	6
New York	18,996	6	3.10	44
North Carolina	14,833	36	4.60	25
North Dakota	14,065	39	2.82	45
Ohio	15,515	27	3.37	41
Oklahoma	13,671	45	3.64	37
Oregon	15,056	33	5.20	16
Pennsylvania	16,821	16	4.09	27
Rhode Island	16,799	18	2.78	48
South Carolina	13,771	42	5.11	17
South Dakota	14,618	38	5.21	15
Tennessee	14,983	35	6.23	7
Texas	15,289	29	6.37	5
Utah	12,711	50	7.06	2
Vermont	15,840	24	2.82	45
Virginia	17,458	13	3.38	40
Washington	17,136	15	7.01	3
West Virginia	12,779	49	5.23	14
Wisconsin	15,565	26	3.95	30
Wyoming	15,087	32	4.72	22
United States	**$16,644**	20	4.15	27

By disposable personal income

1. New Jersey
2. Connecticut
3. District of Columbia
4. Massachusetts
5. New Hampshire
6. New York
7. Maryland
8. Alaska
9. Illinois
10. California
11. Hawaii
12. Delaware
13. Virginia
14. Nevada
15. Washington
16. Pennsylvania
17. Florida
18. Rhode Island
19. Colorado
20. Minnesota
21. Michigan
22. Kansas
23. Missouri
24. Vermont
25. Nebraska
26. Wisconsin
27. Ohio
28. Maine
29. Texas
30. Georgia
31. Iowa
32. Wyoming
33. Oregon
34. Indiana
35. Tennessee
36. North Carolina
37. Arizona
38. South Dakota
39. North Dakota
40. Idaho
41. Alabama
42. South Carolina
43. Kentucky
44. Montana
45. Oklahoma
46. Louisiana
47. Arkansas
48. New Mexico
49. West Virginia
50. Utah
51. Mississippi

Source: "The Comprehensive Revision of State Personal Income," *Survey of Current Business,* August 1992.
Note: Disposable personal income is measured in current dollars.

MEDIAN INCOME OF FAMILIES WITH CHILDREN, 1986-1990

State	Median income	Rank
Alabama	$26,398	47
Alaska	41,246	6
Arizona	32,397	33
Arkansas	25,717	49
California	36,874	15
Colorado	34,531	25
Connecticut	47,748	1
Delaware	37,106	13
District of Columbia	28,331	46
Florida	30,949	39
Georgia	33,637	30
Hawaii	40,695	7
Idaho	29,591	41
Illinois	36,730	16
Indiana	31,811	35
Iowa	32,931	32
Kansas	35,430	21
Kentucky	28,739	45
Louisiana	29,553	42
Maine	34,119	27
Maryland	42,323	5
Massachusetts	43,463	4
Michigan	37,089	14
Minnesota	38,377	11
Mississippi	24,773	51
Missouri	33,943	28
Montana	28,946	44
Nebraska	33,242	31
Nevada	34,464	26
New Hampshire	44,937	3
New Jersey	47,252	2
New Mexico	25,740	48
New York	35,528	20
North Carolina	31,490	36
North Dakota	33,722	29
Ohio	36,102	19
Oklahoma	29,956	40
Oregon	34,616	24
Pennsylvania	34,955	23
Rhode Island	38,957	9
South Carolina	31,042	37
South Dakota	30,983	38
Tennessee	29,055	43
Texas	32,053	34
Utah	35,101	22
Vermont	36,640	17
Virginia	39,653	8
Washington	37,513	12
West Virginia	25,488	50
Wisconsin	38,636	10
Wyoming	36,620	18
United States	**$34,705**	**24**

Rank in order

By median income

1. Connecticut
2. New Jersey
3. New Hampshire
4. Massachusetts
5. Maryland
6. Alaska
7. Hawaii
8. Virginia
9. Rhode Island
10. Wisconsin
11. Minnesota
12. Washington
13. Delaware
14. Michigan
15. California
16. Illinois
17. Vermont
18. Wyoming
19. Ohio
20. New York
21. Kansas
22. Utah
23. Pennsylvania
24. Oregon
25. Colorado
26. Nevada
27. Maine
28. Missouri
29. North Dakota
30. Georgia
31. Nebraska
32. Iowa
33. Arizona
34. Texas
35. Indiana
36. North Carolina
37. South Carolina
38. South Dakota
39. Florida
40. Oklahoma
41. Idaho
42. Louisiana
43. Tennessee
44. Montana
45. Kentucky
46. District of Columbia
47. Alabama
48. New Mexico
49. Arkansas
50. West Virginia
51. Mississippi

Source: Center for the Study of Social Policy, *Kids Count Data Book: State Profiles of Child Well-Being* (Washington, D.C.: Center for Study of Social Policy, 1992).

Note: Median income is measured in 1990 dollars and represents five-year averages for median annual income for families with related children under age eighteen.

FEDERAL SPENDING ON UNEMPLOYMENT INSURANCE/EMPLOYMENT SERVICES, 1991

State	Expenditures	Per capita	Rank by per capita	By per capita
Alabama	$37,582,000	$9.19	35	1. Alaska
Alaska	23,083,000	40.50	1	2. District of Columbia
Arizona	33,730,000	8.99	39	3. Wyoming
Arkansas	23,769,000	10.02	29	4. North Dakota
California	390,876,000	12.87	16	5. Idaho
Colorado	34,090,000	10.09	28	6. Rhode Island
Connecticut	51,418,000	15.62	8	7. Utah
Delaware	8,455,000	12.43	17	8. Connecticut
District of Columbia	15,156,000	25.34	2	9. Vermont
Florida	88,924,000	6.70	51	10. Nevada
Georgia	55,493,000	8.38	45	11. Montana
Hawaii	12,008,000	10.58	24	12. Maine
Idaho	19,217,000	18.50	5	13. Massachusetts
Illinois	133,668,000	11.58	22	14. New Jersey
Indiana	40,354,000	7.19	50	15. Michigan
Iowa	25,288,000	9.05	38	16. California
Kansas	22,368,000	8.97	40	17. Delaware
Kentucky	32,322,000	8.71	43	18. South Dakota
Louisiana	38,534,000	9.06	37	19. Washington
Maine	17,104,000	13.85	12	20. Oregon
Maryland	44,524,000	9.16	36	21. New Hampshire
Massachusetts	83,021,000	13.85	13	22. Illinois
Michigan	122,212,000	13.05	15	23. New York
Minnesota	41,820,000	9.44	34	24. Hawaii
Mississippi	23,210,000	8.95	41	25. Pennsylvania
Missouri	49,661,000	9.63	32	26. Wisconsin
Montana	11,263,000	13.94	11	27. Nebraska
Nebraska	16,209,000	10.18	27	28. Colorado
Nevada	19,208,000	14.96	10	29. Arkansas
New Hampshire	12,823,000	11.60	21	30. West Virginia
New Jersey	102,564,000	13.22	14	31. New Mexico
New Mexico	15,148,000	9.79	31	32. Missouri
New York	204,525,000	11.33	23	33. Oklahoma
North Carolina	52,900,000	7.85	46	34. Minnesota
North Dakota	12,062,000	19.00	4	35. Alabama
Ohio	96,089,000	8.78	42	36. Maryland
Oklahoma	30,173,000	9.50	33	37. Louisiana
Oregon	34,580,000	11.83	20	38. Iowa
Pennsylvania	125,143,000	10.46	25	39. Arizona
Rhode Island	16,726,000	16.66	6	40. Kansas
South Carolina	30,005,000	8.43	44	41. Mississippi
South Dakota	8,627,000	12.27	18	42. Ohio
Tennessee	36,968,000	7.46	48	43. Kentucky
Texas	135,475,000	7.81	47	44. South Carolina
Utah	29,104,000	16.44	7	45. Georgia
Vermont	8,733,000	15.40	9	46. North Carolina
Virginia	46,339,000	7.37	49	47. Texas
Washington	60,606,000	12.08	19	48. Tennessee
West Virginia	19,006,000	10.00	30	49. Virginia
Wisconsin	50,603,000	10.21	26	50. Indiana
Wyoming	9,066,000	19.71	3	51. Florida
United States	**$2,783,430,000**	**$11.04**	**24**	

Rank in order

Source: U.S. Department of Commerce, Bureau of the Census, *Federal Expenditures by State for Fiscal Year 1991* (Washington, D.C.: Government Printing Office, 1992).

TEEN UNEMPLOYMENT, 1991

State	Unemployed teenagers	Unemployment Rate %	Unemployment Rate Rank
Alabama	23,000	20.0	13
Alaska	3,000	21.1	9
Arizona	19,000	20.6	11
Arkansas	17,000	22.2	4
California	153,000	20.1	12
Colorado	12,000	13.3	43
Connecticut	13,000	13.5	40
Delaware	3,000	16.9	32
District of Columbia	11,000	7.6	50
Florida	69,000	22.1	6
Georgia	28,000	18.9	20
Hawaii	2,000	10.9	47
Idaho	5,000	15.5	36
Illinois	65,000	18.8	23
Indiana	33,000	19.1	18
Iowa	12,000	11.5	46
Kansas	10,000	12.2	45
Kentucky	22,000	21.0	10
Louisiana	23,000	19.0	19
Maine	7,000	15.5	36
Maryland	27,000	22.8	3
Massachusetts	32,000	19.2	17
Michigan	68,000	22.2	4
Minnesota	17,000	10.4	48
Mississippi	17,000	26.4	2
Missouri	32,000	18.2	29
Montana	4,000	17.1	31
Nebraska	4,000	6.7	51
Nevada	5,000	16.3	35
New Hampshire	8,000	22.0	7
New Jersey	32,000	18.3	28
New Mexico	8,000	19.7	16
New York	66,000	18.6	24
North Carolina	34,000	18.9	20
North Dakota	3,000	12.8	44
Ohio	58,000	18.1	30
Oklahoma	15,000	15.5	36
Oregon	15,000	16.7	33
Pennsylvania	63,000	18.5	26
Rhode Island	5,000	18.6	24
South Carolina	18,000	18.9	20
South Dakota	2,000	9.3	49
Tennessee	28,000	18.4	27
Texas	93,000	19.9	15
Utah	10,000	13.4	42
Vermont	3,000	13.5	40
Virginia	35,000	22.0	7
Washington	28,000	20.0	13
West Virginia	13,000	28.4	1
Wisconsin	24,000	14.1	39
Wyoming	3,000	16.5	34
United States	**1,290,000**	**18.6**	**24**

Rank in order

By unemployment rate

1. West Virginia
2. Mississippi
3. Maryland
4. Arkansas
   Michigan
6. Florida
7. New Hampshire
   Virginia
9. Alaska
10. Kentucky
11. Arizona
12. California
13. Alabama
    Washington
15. Texas
16. New Mexico
17. Massachusetts
18. Indiana
19. Louisiana
20. Georgia
    North Carolina
    South Carolina
23. Illinois
24. New York
    Rhode Island
26. Pennsylvania
27. Tennessee
28. New Jersey
29. Missouri
30. Ohio
31. Montana
32. Delaware
33. Oregon
34. Wyoming
35. Nevada
36. Idaho
    Maine
    Oklahoma
39. Wisconsin
40. Connecticut
    Vermont
42. Utah
43. Colorado
44. North Dakota
45. Kansas
46. Iowa
47. Hawaii
48. Minnesota
49. South Dakota
50. District of Columbia
51. Nebraska

Source: U.S. Department of Labor, Bureau of Labor Statistics, *Geographic Profile of Employment and Unemployment, 1991* (Washington, D.C.: Government Printing Office, 1992).

Note: The data are based on the average annual numbers of unemployed teenagers age sixteen to nineteen.

State	Bankruptcy petitions filed	Per 100,000 population		By rate per 100,000 population
		Rate	Rank	
Alabama	27,800	679.87	3	1. Tennessee
Alaska	1,100	192.98	45	2. Georgia
Arizona	19,300	514.67	5	3. Alabama
Arkansas	7,700	324.62	24	4. Nevada
California	124,200	408.82	13	5. Arizona
Colorado	17,000	503.41	7	6. Oklahoma
Connecticut	6,900	209.66	41	7. Colorado
Delaware	1,300	191.18	46	8. Indiana
District of Columbia	1,200	200.67	43	9. Mississippi
Florida	43,400	326.88	22	10. Oregon
Georgia	49,000	739.85	2	11. Utah
Hawaii	1,000	88.11	51	12. Kentucky
Idaho	4,200	404.23	14	13. California
Illinois	40,500	350.86	19	14. Idaho
Indiana	26,800	477.72	8	15. Virginia
Iowa	5,800	207.51	42	16. Ohio
Kansas	9,600	384.77	17	17. Kansas
Kentucky	15,600	420.15	12	18. Minnesota
Louisiana	13,300	312.79	25	19. Illinois
Maine	2,200	178.14	48	20. Washington
Maryland	12,800	263.37	31	21. Missouri
Massachusetts	12,900	215.14	40	22. Florida
Michigan	23,300	248.72	34	23. Wyoming
Minnesota	16,700	376.81	18	24. Arkansas
Mississippi	12,300	474.54	9	25. Louisiana
Missouri	17,300	335.40	21	26. Rhode Island
Montana	2,100	259.90	32	27. New Hampshire
Nebraska	4,500	282.49	29	28. New Mexico
Nevada	6,900	537.38	4	29. Nebraska
New Hampshire	3,400	307.69	27	30. Texas
New Jersey	19,400	250.00	33	31. Maryland
New Mexico	4,500	290.70	28	32. Montana
New York	40,300	223.17	38	33. New Jersey
North Carolina	15,500	230.07	36	34. Michigan
North Dakota	1,200	188.98	47	35. Wisconsin
Ohio	42,800	391.26	16	36. North Carolina
Oklahoma	16,200	510.24	6	37. South Dakota
Oregon	13,500	462.01	10	38. New York
Pennsylvania	20,800	173.90	49	39. West Virginia
Rhode Island	3,100	308.76	26	40. Massachusetts
South Carolina	6,900	193.82	44	41. Connecticut
South Dakota	1,600	227.60	37	42. Iowa
Tennessee	40,600	819.71	1	43. District of Columbia
Texas	46,600	268.60	30	44. South Carolina
Utah	8,000	451.98	11	45. Alaska
Vermont	800	141.09	50	46. Delaware
Virginia	25,300	402.48	15	47. North Dakota
Washington	17,200	342.77	20	48. Maine
West Virginia	4,000	222.10	39	49. Pennsylvania
Wisconsin	12,100	244.20	35	50. Vermont
Wyoming	1,500	326.09	23	51. Hawaii
United States	880,400	349.12	20	

Source: U.S. Department of Commerce, Bureau of the Census, *Statistical Abstract of the United States, 1992* (Washington, D.C.: Government Printing Office, 1992).

State	Patents	Per 1,000 population		Rank in order By rate per 1,000 population
		Rate	Rank	
Alabama	324	0.08	46	1. Delaware
Alaska	54	0.10	44	2. Connecticut
Arizona	921	0.25	17	3. New Jersey
Arkansas	170	0.07	49	4. Massachusetts
California	9,284	0.31	8	5. Minnesota
Colorado	954	0.28	10	6. Michigan
Connecticut	1,642	0.50	2	7. New Hampshire
Delaware	553	0.81	1	8. California
District of Columbia	67	0.11	39	9. Illinois
Florida	2,114	0.16	29	10. Colorado
Georgia	793	0.12	37	11. Ohio
Hawaii	85	0.08	48	12. New York
Idaho	261	0.25	16	13. Wisconsin
Illinois	3,355	0.29	9	14. Pennsylvania
Indiana	1,123	0.20	25	Utah
Iowa	417	0.15	30	16. Idaho
Kansas	329	0.13	35	17. Arizona
Kentucky	329	0.09	45	18. Rhode Island
Louisiana	537	0.13	36	19. Oregon
Maine	130	0.11	40	20. Maryland
Maryland	1,070	0.22	20	21. Vermont
Massachusetts	2,445	0.41	4	Washington
Michigan	3,153	0.34	6	23. Texas
Minnesota	1,631	0.37	5	24. Oklahoma
Mississippi	144	0.06	50	25. Indiana
Missouri	832	0.16	27	26. New Mexico
Montana	109	0.14	32	27. Missouri
Nebraska	162	0.10	41	Virginia
Nevada	172	0.13	33	29. Florida
New Hampshire	361	0.33	7	30. Iowa
New Jersey	3,189	0.41	3	31. North Carolina
New Mexico	261	0.17	26	32. Montana
New York	5,047	0.28	12	33. Nevada
North Carolina	933	0.14	31	South Carolina
North Dakota	63	0.10	42	35. Kansas
Ohio	3,073	0.28	11	36. Louisiana
Oklahoma	672	0.21	24	37. Georgia
Oregon	686	0.24	19	Tennessee
Pennsylvania	3,027	0.25	14	39. District of Columbia
Rhode Island	237	0.24	18	40. Maine
South Carolina	476	0.13	33	41. Nebraska
South Dakota	35	0.05	51	42. North Dakota
Tennessee	594	0.12	37	43. West Virginia
Texas	3,704	0.21	23	44. Alaska
Utah	448	0.25	14	45. Kentucky
Vermont	122	0.22	21	46. Alabama
Virginia	1,013	0.16	27	47. Wyoming
Washington	1,077	0.22	21	48. Hawaii
West Virginia	174	0.10	43	49. Arkansas
Wisconsin	1,342	0.27	13	50. Mississippi
Wyoming	36	0.08	47	51. South Dakota
United States	59,730	0.24	18	

Source: U.S. Department of Commerce, *Commerce News, PTO Issues Record Number of Patents in FY '92*, press release, February 5, 1993.

FEDERAL SPENDING ON COMMUNITY DEVELOPMENT, FISCAL 1991

State	Expenditures	Per capita	Rank by per capita
Alabama	$48,802,000	$11.93	12
Alaska	4,775,000	8.38	39
Arizona	33,831,000	9.02	33
Arkansas	23,797,000	10.03	28
California	254,382,000	8.37	40
Colorado	25,229,000	7.47	47
Connecticut	36,691,000	11.15	19
Delaware	6,626,000	9.74	31
District of Columbia	45,330,000	75.80	1
Florida	108,977,000	8.21	42
Georgia	59,589,000	9.00	34
Hawaii	12,109,000	10.67	24
Idaho	6,750,000	6.50	50
Illinois	169,569,000	14.69	4
Indiana	48,306,000	8.61	37
Iowa	34,072,000	12.19	10
Kansas	22,188,000	8.89	35
Kentucky	39,957,000	10.76	23
Louisiana	59,869,000	14.08	7
Maine	14,883,000	12.05	11
Maryland	41,386,000	8.52	38
Massachusetts	88,010,000	14.68	5
Michigan	105,448,000	11.26	17
Minnesota	41,996,000	9.48	32
Mississippi	25,757,000	9.94	29
Missouri	58,297,000	11.30	16
Montana	9,507,000	11.77	14
Nebraska	17,317,000	10.87	22
Nevada	10,067,000	7.84	45
New Hampshire	10,949,000	9.91	30
New Jersey	100,080,000	12.90	9
New Mexico	15,749,000	10.17	27
New York	330,269,000	18.29	2
North Carolina	54,529,000	8.09	44
North Dakota	6,742,000	10.62	25
Ohio	146,241,000	13.37	8
Oklahoma	26,092,000	8.22	41
Oregon	18,689,000	6.40	51
Pennsylvania	209,220,000	17.49	3
Rhode Island	14,480,000	14.42	6
South Carolina	31,365,000	8.81	36
South Dakota	8,281,000	11.78	13
Tennessee	57,188,000	11.55	15
Texas	191,298,000	11.03	20
Utah	12,616,000	7.13	48
Vermont	5,984,000	10.55	26
Virginia	51,172,000	8.14	43
Washington	37,904,000	7.55	46
West Virginia	20,194,000	11.21	18
Wisconsin	53,929,000	10.88	21
Wyoming	3,171,000	6.89	49
United States	$2,975,794,000	$11.80	13

Rank in order

By per capita

1. District of Columbia
2. New York
3. Pennsylvania
4. Illinois
5. Massachusetts
6. Rhode Island
7. Louisiana
8. Ohio
9. New Jersey
10. Iowa
11. Maine
12. Alabama
13. South Dakota
14. Montana
15. Tennessee
16. Missouri
17. Michigan
18. West Virginia
19. Connecticut
20. Texas
21. Wisconsin
22. Nebraska
23. Kentucky
24. Hawaii
25. North Dakota
26. Vermont
27. New Mexico
28. Arkansas
29. Mississippi
30. New Hampshire
31. Delaware
32. Minnesota
33. Arizona
34. Georgia
35. Kansas
36. South Carolina
37. Indiana
38. Maryland
39. Alaska
40. California
41. Oklahoma
42. Florida
43. Virginia
44. North Carolina
45. Nevada
46. Washington
47. Colorado
48. Utah
49. Wyoming
50. Idaho
51. Oregon

Source: U.S. Department of Commerce, Bureau of the Census, *Federal Expenditures by State for Fiscal Year 1991* (Washington, D.C.: Government Printing Office, 1992).

Note: Community development expenditures are administered by the Department of Housing and Urban Development and provides grants to local jurisdictions for a variety of programs that benefit low- to moderate-income neighborhoods.

State	Expenditures	Per capita	Rank by per capita	By per capita
Alabama	$3,833,000	$0.94	17	1. Alaska
Alaska	3,188,000	5.59	1	2. West Virginia
Arizona	1,286,000	0.34	41	3. North Dakota
Arkansas	3,484,000	1.47	10	4. Vermont
California	6,057,000	0.20	47	5. South Carolina
Colorado	1,585,000	0.47	34	6. Montana
Connecticut	897,000	0.27	45	7. Idaho
Delaware	0	0.00	51	8. Nevada
District of Columbia	643,000	1.08	14	9. Maine
Florida	1,487,000	0.11	49	10. Arkansas
Georgia	6,782,000	1.02	15	11. Mississippi
Hawaii	599,000	0.53	30	12. South Dakota
Idaho	1,682,000	1.62	7	13. Oklahoma
Illinois	4,176,000	0.36	40	14. District of Columbia
Indiana	2,161,000	0.39	39	15. Georgia
Iowa	2,179,000	0.78	22	16. Kentucky
Kansas	2,146,000	0.86	20	17. Alabama
Kentucky	3,595,000	0.97	16	18. New Mexico
Louisiana	1,970,000	0.46	35	19. Oregon
Maine	1,846,000	1.50	9	20. Kansas
Maryland	2,468,000	0.51	32	21. Wyoming
Massachusetts	1,473,000	0.25	46	22. Iowa
Michigan	2,890,000	0.31	44	23. Washington
Minnesota	1,827,000	0.41	37	24. Tennessee
Mississippi	3,475,000	1.34	11	25. Texas
Missouri	3,281,000	0.64	28	26. Ohio
Montana	1,379,000	1.71	6	27. Virginia
Nebraska	791,000	0.50	33	28. Missouri
Nevada	2,060,000	1.60	8	29. Wisconsin
New Hampshire	142,000	0.13	48	30. Hawaii
New Jersey	2,521,000	0.33	43	31. Utah
New Mexico	1,336,000	0.86	18	32. Maryland
New York	6,133,000	0.34	42	33. Nebraska
North Carolina	2,674,000	0.40	38	34. Colorado
North Dakota	1,661,000	2.62	3	35. Louisiana
Ohio	7,085,000	0.65	26	36. Pennsylvania
Oklahoma	3,601,000	1.13	13	37. Minnesota
Oregon	2,518,000	0.86	19	38. North Carolina
Pennsylvania	5,518,000	0.46	36	39. Indiana
Rhode Island	59,000	0.06	50	40. Illinois
South Carolina	6,561,000	1.84	5	41. Arizona
South Dakota	837,000	1.19	12	42. New York
Tennessee	3,328,000	0.67	24	43. New Jersey
Texas	11,449,000	0.66	25	44. Michigan
Utah	908,000	0.51	31	45. Connecticut
Vermont	1,297,000	2.29	4	46. Massachusetts
Virginia	4,032,000	0.64	27	47. California
Washington	3,618,000	0.72	23	48. New Hampshire
West Virginia	4,956,000	2.75	2	49. Florida
Wisconsin	3,039,000	0.61	29	50. Rhode Island
Wyoming	360,000	0.78	21	51. Delaware
United States	$148,882,000	$0.59	30	

Source: U.S. Department of Commerce, Bureau of the Census, *Federal Expenditures by State for Fiscal Year 1991* (Washington, D.C.: Government Printing Office, 1992).

FEDERAL SPENDING ON URBAN DEVELOPMENT ACTION GRANTS, FISCAL 1991

State	Expenditures	Per capita	Rank by per capita	By per capita
Alabama	$728,000	$0.18	15	1. District of Columbia
Alaska	0	0.00	33	2. Ohio
Arizona	0	0.00	33	3. Massachusetts
Arkansas	0	0.00	33	4. New York
California	4,402,000	0.15	19	5. Pennsylvania
Colorado	0	0.00	33	6. Georgia
Connecticut	1,951,000	0.59	9	7. Missouri
Delaware	0	0.00	33	8. Michigan
District of Columbia	1,891,000	3.16	1	9. Connecticut
Florida	1,969,000	0.15	18	10. Kentucky
Georgia	6,384,000	0.96	6	11. New Jersey
Hawaii	0	0.00	33	12. Maryland
Idaho	0	0.00	33	13. Minnesota
Illinois	171,000	0.02	30	14. Tennessee
Indiana	0	0.00	33	15. Alabama
Iowa	110,000	0.04	28	16. West Virginia
Kansas	228,000	0.09	22	17. Wisconsin
Kentucky	1,470,000	0.40	10	18. Florida
Louisiana	102,000	0.02	29	19. California
Maine	0	0.00	33	20. Washington
Maryland	1,612,000	0.33	12	21. Utah
Massachusetts	9,695,000	1.62	3	22. Kansas
Michigan	6,959,000	0.74	8	23. Oklahoma
Minnesota	1,424,000	0.32	13	24. Nebraska
Mississippi	0	0.00	33	South Dakota
Missouri	4,162,000	0.81	7	26. New Mexico
Montana	0	0.00	33	27. Virginia
Nebraska	111,000	0.07	24	28. Iowa
Nevada	0	0.00	33	29. Louisiana
New Hampshire	0	0.00	33	30. Illinois
New Jersey	2,893,000	0.37	11	31. Texas
New Mexico	72,000	0.05	26	32. North Carolina
New York	25,111,000	1.39	4	33. Alaska
North Carolina	36,000	0.01	32	Arizona
North Dakota	0	0.00	33	Arkansas
Ohio	28,739,000	2.63	2	Colorado
Oklahoma	237,000	0.08	23	Delaware
Oregon	0	0.00	33	Hawaii
Pennsylvania	13,823,000	1.16	5	Idaho
Rhode Island	0	0.00	33	Indiana
South Carolina	0	0.00	33	Maine
South Dakota	49,000	0.07	24	Mississippi
Tennessee	956,000	0.19	14	Montana
Texas	209,000	0.01	31	Nevada
Utah	209,000	0.12	21	New Hampshire
Vermont	0	0.00	33	North Dakota
Virginia	285,000	0.05	27	Oregon
Washington	689,000	0.14	20	Rhode Island
West Virginia	285,000	0.16	16	South Carolina
Wisconsin	765,000	0.15	17	Vermont
Wyoming	0	0.00	33	Wyoming
United States	**$128,267,000**	**$0.51**	**10**	

Source: U.S. Department of Commerce, Bureau of the Census, *Federal Expenditures by State for Fiscal Year 1991* (Washington, D.C.: Government Printing Office, 1992).

Crime and Criminal Justice

State	Total crimes	Per 100,000 population		% increase 1990-1991	
		Rate	Rank	Rate	Rank
Alabama	219,400	5,365.6	28	9.2	3
Alaska	32,499	5,701.6	21	10.7	1
Arizona	277,711	7,405.6	4	−6.1	49
Arkansas	122,749	5,174.9	31	6.3	9
California	2,057,513	6,772.6	5	2.6	21
Colorado	205,122	6,074.1	16	0.3	33
Connecticut	176,531	5,364.1	29	−0.4	38
Delaware	39,912	5,869.4	19	9.5	2
District of Columbia	64,393	10,768.1	1	−0.1	34
Florida	1,134,813	8,547.2	2	−3.0	44
Georgia	430,059	6,493.4	7	−4.0	45
Hawaii	67,764	5,970.4	17	−2.2	43
Idaho	43,594	4,195.8	41	3.4	17
Illinois	707,823	6,132.1	15	3.3	18
Indiana	270,279	4,817.8	34	2.9	20
Iowa	115,546	4,134.0	42	0.8	31
Kansas	138,081	5,534.3	24	6.6	6
Kentucky	124,692	3,358.3	48	1.8	27
Louisiana	273,170	6,424.5	8	−1.0	41
Maine	46,531	3,767.1	44	1.9	25
Maryland	301,768	6,209.2	12	6.5	7
Massachusetts	319,128	5,322.3	30	0.5	32
Michigan	575,013	6,138.1	14	2.4	22
Minnesota	199,274	4,496.3	36	−0.9	39
Mississippi	109,402	4,220.8	40	9.1	4
Missouri	279,340	5,415.7	26	5.8	11
Montana	29,477	3,648.1	45	−19.0	51
Nebraska	69,361	4,354.1	39	3.3	18
Nevada	80,876	6,298.8	10	3.9	14
New Hampshire	38,098	3,447.8	47	−5.4	47
New Jersey	421,469	5,431.3	25	−0.3	37
New Mexico	103,396	6,679.3	6	−0.1	34
New York	1,127,651	6,244.6	11	−1.9	42
North Carolina	396,723	5,888.7	18	7.3	5
North Dakota	17,741	2,793.9	50	−4.4	46
Ohio	550,560	5,033.0	33	3.9	14
Oklahoma	179,982	5,668.7	22	1.3	29
Oregon	168,165	5,755.1	20	1.9	25
Pennsylvania	425,638	3,558.5	46	2.4	22
Rhode Island	50,595	5,039.3	32	−5.9	48
South Carolina	219,980	6,179.2	13	2.2	24
South Dakota	21,647	3,079.2	49	5.8	11
Tennessee	265,811	5,366.7	27	6.3	9
Texas	1,356,527	7,819.1	3	−0.1	34
Utah	99,255	5,607.6	23	−0.9	39
Vermont	22,426	3,955.2	43	−8.9	50
Virginia	289,619	4,607.4	35	3.8	16
Washington	316,339	6,304.1	9	1.3	29
West Virginia	47,968	2,663.4	51	6.4	8
Wisconsin	221,283	4,465.9	37	1.6	28
Wyoming	20,189	4,388.9	38	4.2	13
United States	14,872,883	5,897.8	18	1.3	29

TOTAL CRIMES, 1991

Rank in order

By rate per 100,000 population

1. District of Columbia
2. Florida
3. Texas
4. Arizona
5. California
6. New Mexico
7. Georgia
8. Louisiana
9. Washington
10. Nevada
11. New York
12. Maryland
13. South Carolina
14. Michigan
15. Illinois
16. Colorado
17. Hawaii
18. North Carolina
19. Delaware
20. Oregon
21. Alaska
22. Oklahoma
23. Utah
24. Kansas
25. New Jersey
26. Missouri
27. Tennessee
28. Alabama
29. Connecticut
30. Massachusetts
31. Arkansas
32. Rhode Island
33. Ohio
34. Indiana
35. Virginia
36. Minnesota
37. Wisconsin
38. Wyoming
39. Nebraska
40. Mississippi
41. Idaho
42. Iowa
43. Vermont
44. Maine
45. Montana
46. Pennsylvania
47. New Hampshire
48. Kentucky
49. South Dakota
50. North Dakota
51. West Virginia

Source: U.S. Department of Justice, Federal Bureau of Investigation, *Uniform Crime Reports for the United States, 1991* (Washington, D.C.: Government Printing Office, 1992).

VIOLENT CRIMES, 1991						Rank in order
State	Violent crimes	Per 100,000 population		% increase 1990-1991		By rate per 100,000 population
		Rate	Rank	Rate	Rank	
Alabama	34,518	844.2	9	19.1	1	1. District of Columbia
Alaska	3,499	613.9	22	17.0	2	2. Florida
Arizona	25,172	670.7	19	2.8	32	3. New York
Arkansas	14,072	593.3	24	11.5	9	4. California
California	331,122	1,089.9	4	4.3	27	5. Illinois
Colorado	18,887	599.3	23	6.3	21	6. South Carolina
Connecticut	17,761	539.7	27	−2.5	44	7. Maryland
Delaware	4,857	714.3	17	9.0	12	8. Louisiana
District of Columbia	14,671	2,453.3	1	−0.2	39	9. Alabama
Florida	157,243	1,184.3	2	−4.8	45	10. Texas
Georgia	48,894	738.2	14	−2.4	43	11. New Mexico
Hawaii	2,744	241.8	44	−13.9	51	12. Michigan
Idaho	3,016	290.3	41	5.3	24	13. Missouri
Illinois	119,955	1,039.2	5	7.4	14	14. Georgia
Indiana	28,349	505.3	30	6.6	18	15. Massachusetts
Iowa	8,477	303.3	40	1.2	35	16. Tennessee
Kansas	12,465	499.6	31	11.6	8	17. Delaware
Kentucky	16,262	438.8	34	12.2	6	18. Nevada
Louisiana	40,438	951.0	8	5.9	22	19. Arizona
Maine	1,631	132.1	48	−7.8	46	20. North Carolina
Maryland	46,469	956.2	7	4.0	29	21. New Jersey
Massachusetts	44,138	736.1	15	0.0	37	22. Alaska
Michigan	75,232	803.1	12	1.6	33	23. Colorado
Minnesota	14,006	316.0	38	3.2	30	24. Arkansas
Mississippi	10,085	389.1	35	14.3	3	25. Oklahoma
Missouri	39,358	763.0	13	6.7	17	26. Ohio
Montana	1,130	139.9	47	−12.2	50	27. Connecticut
Nebraska	5,330	334.6	37	1.4	34	28. Washington
Nevada	8,693	677.0	18	12.7	5	29. Oregon
New Hampshire	1,318	119.3	49	−9.3	48	30. Indiana
New Jersey	49,257	634.8	21	−2.0	42	31. Kansas
New Mexico	12,922	834.8	11	7.0	15	32. Rhode Island
New York	210,184	1,163.9	3	−1.4	41	33. Pennsylvania
North Carolina	44,355	658.4	20	5.6	23	34. Kentucky
North Dakota	415	65.4	51	−11.5	49	35. Mississippi
Ohio	61,460	561.8	26	11.0	10	36. Virginia
Oklahoma	18,533	583.7	25	6.6	18	37. Nebraska
Oregon	14,795	506.3	29	−0.1	38	38. Minnesota
Pennsylvania	53,824	450.0	33	4.4	26	39. Wyoming
Rhode Island	4,638	462.0	32	7.0	15	40. Iowa
South Carolina	34,621	972.5	6	−0.4	40	41. Idaho
South Dakota	1,281	182.2	46	11.9	7	42. Utah
Tennessee	35,955	725.9	16	8.3	13	43. Wisconsin
Texas	145,743	840.1	10	10.3	11	44. Hawaii
Utah	5,077	286.8	42	1.0	36	45. West Virginia
Vermont	662	116.8	50	−8.2	47	46. South Dakota
Virginia	23,459	373.2	36	6.4	20	47. Montana
Washington	26,224	522.6	28	4.2	28	48. Maine
West Virginia	3,440	191.0	45	12.8	4	49. New Hampshire
Wisconsin	13,723	277.0	43	4.6	25	50. Vermont
Wyoming	1,427	310.2	39	2.9	31	51. North Dakota
United States	1,911,767	758.1	14	3.6	30	

Source: U.S. Department of Justice, Federal Bureau of Investigation, *Uniform Crime Reports for the United States, 1991* (Washington, D.C.: Government Printing Office, 1992).

State	Murders	Per 100,000 population		% increase 1990-1991		By rate per 100,000 population
		Rate	Rank	Rate	Rank	
Alabama	469	11.5	10	−0.9	34	1. District of Columbia
Alaska	42	7.4	23	−1.3	35	2. Louisiana
Arizona	291	7.8	21	1.3	31	3. Texas
Arkansas	264	11.1	14	7.8	19	4. New York
California	3,859	12.7	7	6.7	20	5. Georgia
Colorado	199	5.9	30	40.5	3	Mississippi
Connecticut	187	5.7	31	11.8	12	7. California
Delaware	37	5.4	32	8.0	18	8. Nevada
District of Columbia	482	80.6	1	3.6	29	9. Maryland
Florida	1,248	9.4	19	−12.1	44	10. Alabama
Georgia	849	12.8	5	8.5	16	11. North Carolina
Hawaii	45	4.0	38	0.0	33	12. Illinois
Idaho	19	1.8	48	−33.3	49	South Carolina
Illinois	1,300	11.3	12	9.7	14	14. Arkansas
Indiana	423	7.5	22	21.0	8	15. Tennessee
Iowa	57	2.0	47	5.3	23	16. Michigan
Kansas	153	6.1	29	52.5	2	17. Missouri
Kentucky	253	6.8	26	−5.6	39	New Mexico
Louisiana	720	16.9	2	−1.7	36	19. Florida
Maine	15	1.2	50	−50.0	51	20. Virginia
Maryland	569	11.7	9	1.7	30	21. Arizona
Massachusetts	249	4.2	36	5.0	24	22. Indiana
Michigan	1,009	10.8	16	3.8	28	23. Alaska
Minnesota	131	3.0	43	11.1	13	24. Ohio
Mississippi	332	12.8	5	4.9	25	Oklahoma
Missouri	543	10.5	17	19.3	9	26. Kentucky
Montana	21	2.6	45	−46.9	50	27. Pennsylvania
Nebraska	52	3.3	41	22.2	5	28. West Virginia
Nevada	152	11.8	8	21.6	6	29. Kansas
New Hampshire	40	3.6	40	89.5	1	30. Colorado
New Jersey	406	5.2	33	−7.1	41	31. Connecticut
New Mexico	163	10.5	17	14.1	11	32. Delaware
New York	2,571	14.2	4	−2.1	37	33. New Jersey
North Carolina	769	11.4	11	6.5	21	34. Wisconsin
North Dakota	7	1.1	51	37.5	4	35. Oregon
Ohio	783	7.2	24	18.0	10	36. Massachusetts
Oklahoma	230	7.2	24	−10.0	43	Washington
Oregon	133	4.6	35	21.1	7	38. Hawaii
Pennsylvania	758	6.3	27	−6.0	40	39. Rhode Island
Rhode Island	37	3.7	39	−22.9	47	40. New Hampshire
South Carolina	402	11.3	12	0.9	32	41. Nebraska
South Dakota	12	1.7	49	−15.0	46	Wyoming
Tennessee	547	11.0	15	4.8	26	43. Minnesota
Texas	2,652	15.3	3	8.5	16	44. Utah
Utah	52	2.9	44	−3.3	38	45. Montana
Vermont	12	2.1	46	−8.7	42	46. Vermont
Virginia	583	9.3	20	5.7	22	47. Iowa
Washington	211	4.2	36	−14.3	45	48. Idaho
West Virginia	111	6.2	28	8.8	15	49. South Dakota
Wisconsin	239	4.8	34	4.3	27	50. Maine
Wyoming	15	3.3	41	−32.7	48	51. North Dakota
United States	24,703	9.8	19	4.3	27	

Source: U.S. Department of Justice, Federal Bureau of Investigation, *Uniform Crime Reports for the United States, 1991* (Washington, D.C.: Government Printing Office, 1992).
Note: Murder includes nonnegligent manslaughter.

RAPES, 1991

State	Rapes	Per 100,000 population		% increase 1990-1991	
		Rate	Rank	Rate	Rank
Alabama	1,455	35.6	29	9.2	17
Alaska	523	91.8	1	25.9	1
Arizona	1,590	42.4	20	3.7	26
Arkansas	1,058	44.6	19	3.0	28
California	12,896	42.4	20	−0.5	36
Colorado	1,588	47.0	13	1.7	30
Connecticut	960	29.2	39	4.7	24
Delaware	588	86.5	2	−1.8	38
District of Columbia	214	35.8	28	−28.3	51
Florida	6,865	51.7	11	−1.3	37
Georgia	2,800	42.3	22	−21.1	50
Hawaii	375	33.0	33	1.5	31
Idaho	300	28.9	41	5.9	21
Illinois	4,615	40.0	25	1.5	31
Indiana	2,318	41.3	23	9.0	18
Iowa	583	20.9	49	13.6	10
Kansas	1,118	44.8	18	10.9	14
Kentucky	1,315	35.4	30	22.1	4
Louisiana	1,738	40.9	24	−3.1	41
Maine	270	21.9	48	11.2	12
Maryland	2,229	45.9	16	0.4	35
Massachusetts	1,926	32.1	34	−4.7	43
Michigan	7,372	78.7	3	1.4	33
Minnesota	1,762	39.8	26	17.1	7
Mississippi	1,199	46.3	15	5.0	23
Missouri	1,756	34.0	32	4.6	25
Montana	160	19.8	50	−18.9	49
Nebraska	447	28.1	44	−6.3	45
Nevada	848	66.0	5	6.1	20
New Hampshire	330	29.9	37	−14.1	48
New Jersey	2,259	29.1	40	−2.3	39
New Mexico	811	52.4	10	5.4	22
New York	5,085	28.2	43	−5.4	44
North Carolina	2,331	34.6	31	0.9	34
North Dakota	116	18.3	51	2.8	29
Ohio	5,748	52.5	9	12.2	11
Oklahoma	1,615	50.9	12	8.3	19
Oregon	1,561	53.4	7	13.9	9
Pennsylvania	3,435	28.7	42	11.2	12
Rhode Island	310	30.9	35	25.1	2
South Carolina	2,098	58.9	6	9.7	16
South Dakota	279	39.7	27	15.7	8
Tennessee	2,299	46.4	14	−6.3	45
Texas	9,266	53.4	7	3.7	26
Utah	808	45.6	17	20.6	5
Vermont	173	30.5	36	17.8	6
Virginia	1,879	29.9	37	−3.5	42
Washington	3,529	70.3	4	9.8	15
West Virginia	415	23.0	47	−2.5	40
Wisconsin	1,259	25.4	46	22.7	3
Wyoming	119	25.9	45	−12.2	47
United States	106,593	42.3	22	2.7	30

Rank in order

By rate per 100,000 population

1. Alaska
2. Delaware
3. Michigan
4. Washington
5. Nevada
6. South Carolina
7. Oregon
   Texas
9. Ohio
10. New Mexico
11. Florida
12. Oklahoma
13. Colorado
14. Tennessee
15. Mississippi
16. Maryland
17. Utah
18. Kansas
19. Arkansas
20. Arizona
    California
22. Georgia
23. Indiana
24. Louisiana
25. Illinois
26. Minnesota
27. South Dakota
28. District of Columbia
29. Alabama
30. Kentucky
31. North Carolina
32. Missouri
33. Hawaii
34. Massachusetts
35. Rhode Island
36. Vermont
37. New Hampshire
    Virginia
39. Connecticut
40. New Jersey
41. Idaho
42. Pennsylvania
43. New York
44. Nebraska
45. Wyoming
46. Wisconsin
47. West Virginia
48. Maine
49. Iowa
50. Montana
51. North Dakota

Source: U.S. Department of Justice, Federal Bureau of Investigation, *Uniform Crime Reports for the United States, 1991* (Washington, D.C.: Government Printing Office, 1992).

State	Aggravated assaults	Per 100,000 population		% increase 1990-1991		Rank in order: By rate per 100,000 population
		Rate	Rank	Rate	Rank	
Alabama	26,348	644.4	5	23.8	1	1. District of Columbia
Alaska	2,289	401.6	21	9.3	6	2. South Carolina
Arizona	17,056	454.8	16	2.7	22	3. Florida
Arkansas	9,533	401.9	20	10.0	4	4. New Mexico
California	189,428	623.5	6	1.6	26	5. Alabama
Colorado	13,472	398.9	22	3.6	20	6. California
Connecticut	9,230	280.5	33	−1.9	39	7. Louisiana
Delaware	2,772	407.6	19	2.6	23	8. Illinois
District of Columbia	6,706	1,121.4	1	0.4	30	9. Massachusetts
Florida	96,047	723.4	3	−5.4	45	10. New York
Georgia	27,483	415.0	18	−2.9	42	11. Maryland
Hawaii	1,338	117.9	46	−22.9	51	12. Texas
Idaho	2,482	238.9	36	3.6	20	13. Michigan
Illinois	61,387	531.8	8	1.6	26	14. Missouri
Indiana	19,102	340.5	24	3.7	19	15. Tennessee
Iowa	6,580	235.4	37	−2.0	40	16. Arizona
Kansas	7,741	310.3	26	8.6	8	17. North Carolina
Kentucky	11,610	312.7	25	9.6	5	18. Georgia
Louisiana	26,120	614.3	7	7.9	11	19. Delaware
Maine	1,066	86.3	48	−10.1	47	20. Arkansas
Maryland	23,888	491.5	11	−1.3	36	21. Alaska
Massachusetts	30,294	505.2	9	4.9	17	22. Colorado
Michigan	44,061	470.3	13	0.4	30	23. Oklahoma
Minnesota	7,768	175.3	42	−0.8	34	24. Indiana
Mississippi	5,539	213.7	39	7.9	11	25. Kentucky
Missouri	24,107	467.4	14	2.1	24	26. Kansas
Montana	799	98.9	47	−8.9	46	27. New Jersey
Nebraska	3,970	249.2	35	1.2	28	28. Rhode Island
Nevada	3,681	286.7	32	−1.4	37	29. Washington
New Hampshire	583	52.8	50	−21.9	50	30. Oregon
New Jersey	23,848	307.3	27	−1.2	35	31. Ohio
New Mexico	10,086	651.6	4	7.5	13	32. Nevada
New York	90,186	499.4	10	−2.5	41	33. Connecticut
North Carolina	29,265	434.4	17	1.9	25	34. Wyoming
North Dakota	241	38.0	51	−19.8	49	35. Nebraska
Ohio	31,393	287.0	31	8.4	10	36. Idaho
Oklahoma	12,594	396.7	23	7.1	14	37. Iowa
Oregon	8,714	298.2	30	−4.4	44	38. Pennsylvania
Pennsylvania	26,440	221.1	38	−0.5	33	39. Mississippi
Rhode Island	3,057	304.5	28	8.6	8	40. Virginia
South Carolina	26,029	731.2	2	−3.7	43	41. Utah
South Dakota	858	122.0	44	6.9	15	42. Minnesota
Tennessee	22,566	455.6	15	8.7	7	43. Wisconsin
Texas	84,125	484.9	12	11.4	3	44. South Dakota
Utah	3,241	183.1	41	−1.7	38	45. West Virginia
Vermont	410	72.3	49	−17.1	48	46. Hawaii
Virginia	12,346	196.4	40	4.7	18	47. Montana
Washington	15,181	302.5	29	−0.1	32	48. Maine
West Virginia	2,135	118.5	45	16.1	2	49. Vermont
Wisconsin	6,330	127.7	43	0.8	29	50. New Hampshire
Wyoming	1,214	263.9	34	5.1	16	51. North Dakota
United States	1,092,739	433.3	18	2.2	24	

Source: U.S. Department of Justice, Federal Bureau of Investigation, *Uniform Crime Reports for the United States, 1991* (Washington, D.C.: Government Printing Office, 1992).

State	Property crimes	Per 100,000 population		% increase 1990-1991	
		Rate	Rank	Rate	Rank
Alabama	184,882	4,521.4	32	7.5	5
Alaska	29,000	5,087.7	21	9.9	1
Arizona	252,559	6,734.9	4	−6.9	48
Arkansas	108,677	4,581.7	30	5.7	10
California	1,726,391	5,682.7	9	2.2	24
Colorado	186,235	5,514.8	11	−0.2	35
Connecticut	158,770	4,824.4	25	−0.2	35
Delaware	35,055	5,155.1	19	9.6	2
District of Columbia	49,722	8,314.7	1	0.0	33
Florida	977,570	7,362.9	2	−2.7	44
Georgia	381,165	5,755.2	7	−4.2	45
Hawaii	65,020	5,728.6	8	−1.7	41
Idaho	40,578	3,905.5	40	3.3	16
Illinois	587,868	5,092.9	20	2.5	20
Indiana	241,930	4,312.5	34	2.4	22
Iowa	107,069	3,830.7	43	0.8	29
Kansas	125,616	5,034.7	24	6.1	7
Kentucky	108,430	2,920.3	48	0.4	32
Louisiana	232,732	5,473.5	12	−2.1	43
Maine	44,900	3,635.6	44	2.3	23
Maryland	255,299	5,253.1	15	7.0	6
Massachusetts	274,990	4,586.2	29	0.5	31
Michigan	499,781	5,335.0	13	2.5	20
Minnesota	185,268	4,180.2	37	−1.2	39
Mississippi	99,317	3,831.7	42	8.6	3
Missouri	239,982	4,652.6	27	5.6	11
Montana	28,347	3,508.3	45	−19.2	51
Nebraska	64,031	4,019.5	39	3.5	14
Nevada	72,183	5,621.7	10	2.9	18
New Hampshire	36,780	3,328.5	46	−5.3	47
New Jersey	372,212	4,796.5	26	−0.1	34
New Mexico	90,474	5,844.6	5	−1.0	37
New York	917,467	5,080.7	23	−2.0	42
North Carolina	352,368	5,230.3	17	7.6	4
North Dakota	17,326	2,728.5	50	−4.2	45
Ohio	489,100	4,471.2	33	3.1	17
Oklahoma	161,449	5,085.0	22	0.7	30
Oregon	153,370	5,248.8	16	2.1	25
Pennsylvania	371,814	3,108.6	47	2.1	25
Rhode Island	45,957	4,577.4	31	−7.0	49
South Carolina	185,359	5,206.7	18	2.7	19
South Dakota	20,366	2,897.0	49	5.5	12
Tennessee	229,856	4,640.7	28	5.9	8
Texas	1,210,784	6,979.0	3	−1.2	39
Utah	94,178	5,320.8	14	−1.0	37
Vermont	21,764	3,838.4	41	−8.9	50
Virginia	266,160	4,234.2	35	3.5	14
Washington	290,115	5,781.5	6	1.1	28
West Virginia	44,528	2,472.4	51	5.9	8
Wisconsin	207,560	4,188.9	36	1.4	27
Wyoming	18,762	4,078.7	38	4.3	13
United States	12,961,116	5,139.7	20	1.0	29

Rank in order

By rate per 100,000 population

1. District of Columbia
2. Florida
3. Texas
4. Arizona
5. New Mexico
6. Washington
7. Georgia
8. Hawaii
9. California
10. Nevada
11. Colorado
12. Louisiana
13. Michigan
14. Utah
15. Maryland
16. Oregon
17. North Carolina
18. South Carolina
19. Delaware
20. Illinois
21. Alaska
22. Oklahoma
23. New York
24. Kansas
25. Connecticut
26. New Jersey
27. Missouri
28. Tennessee
29. Massachusetts
30. Arkansas
31. Rhode Island
32. Alabama
33. Ohio
34. Indiana
35. Virginia
36. Wisconsin
37. Minnesota
38. Wyoming
39. Nebraska
40. Idaho
41. Vermont
42. Mississippi
43. Iowa
44. Maine
45. Montana
46. New Hampshire
47. Pennsylvania
48. Kentucky
49. South Dakota
50. North Dakota
51. West Virginia

Source: U.S. Department of Justice, Federal Bureau of Investigation, *Uniform Crime Reports for the United States, 1991* (Washington, D.C.: Government Printing Office, 1992).

| State | Robberies | Per 100,000 population | | % increase 1990-1991 | | Rank in order |
		Rate	Rank	Rate	Rank	By rate per 100,000 population
Alabama	6,246	152.8	23	6.3	28	1. District of Columbia
Alaska	645	113.2	35	47.6	2	2. New York
Arizona	6,215	165.7	22	3.0	37	3. Illinois
Arkansas	3,217	135.6	28	19.8	9	4. California
California	124,939	411.3	4	9.1	26	5. Maryland
Colorado	3,628	107.4	36	18.5	10	6. Florida
Connecticut	7,384	224.4	14	−4.4	47	7. Nevada
Delaware	1,460	214.7	16	30.3	6	8. New Jersey
District of Columbia	7,269	1,215.6	1	0.2	42	9. Texas
Florida	53,083	399.8	6	−4.1	46	10. Louisiana
Georgia	17,762	268.2	11	1.8	39	11. Georgia
Hawaii	986	86.9	38	−4.9	48	12. Missouri
Idaho	215	20.7	46	38.0	3	13. Michigan
Illinois	52,653	456.1	3	15.8	14	14. Connecticut
Indiana	6,506	116.0	34	14.5	16	15. Ohio
Iowa	1,257	45.0	42	14.8	15	16. Delaware
Kansas	3,453	138.4	26	17.7	11	17. Tennessee
Kentucky	3,084	83.1	39	20.3	8	18. Massachusetts
Louisiana	11,860	278.9	10	3.4	36	19. Pennsylvania
Maine	280	22.7	45	−9.6	49	20. North Carolina
Maryland	19,783	407.1	5	11.9	20	21. South Carolina
Massachusetts	11,669	194.6	18	−10.4	50	22. Arizona
Michigan	22,790	243.3	13	4.0	34	23. Alabama
Minnesota	4,345	98.0	37	5.7	29	24. Oregon
Mississippi	3,015	116.3	33	34.9	4	25. Washington
Missouri	12,952	251.1	12	16.0	13	26. Kansas
Montana	150	18.6	48	−14.3	51	27. Virginia
Nebraska	861	54.0	41	5.7	29	28. Arkansas
Nevada	4,012	312.5	7	31.1	5	29. Oklahoma
New Hampshire	365	33.0	44	21.3	7	30. Rhode Island
New Jersey	22,744	293.1	8	−2.6	44	31. New Mexico
New Mexico	1,862	120.3	31	4.5	33	32. Wisconsin
New York	112,342	622.1	2	−0.4	43	33. Mississippi
North Carolina	11,990	178.0	20	17.0	12	34. Indiana
North Dakota	51	8.0	51	2.6	38	35. Alaska
Ohio	23,536	215.2	15	14.2	17	36. Colorado
Oklahoma	4,094	128.9	29	5.7	29	37. Minnesota
Oregon	4,387	150.1	24	4.0	34	38. Hawaii
Pennsylvania	23,191	193.9	19	10.0	24	39. Kentucky
Rhode Island	1,234	122.9	30	0.7	41	40. Utah
South Carolina	6,092	171.1	21	12.3	19	41. Nebraska
South Dakota	132	18.8	47	51.6	1	42. Iowa
Tennessee	10,543	212.9	17	11.3	23	43. West Virginia
Texas	49,700	286.5	9	9.9	25	44. New Hampshire
Utah	976	55.1	40	−3.2	45	45. Maine
Vermont	67	11.8	50	0.9	40	46. Idaho
Virginia	8,651	137.6	27	11.6	22	47. South Dakota
Washington	7,303	145.5	25	11.9	20	48. Montana
West Virginia	779	43.3	43	14.2	17	49. Wyoming
Wisconsin	5,895	119.0	32	5.6	32	50. Vermont
Wyoming	79	17.2	49	8.2	27	51. North Dakota
United States	687,732	272.7	11	6.1	29	

Source: U.S. Department of Justice, Federal Bureau of Investigation, *Uniform Crime Reports for the United States, 1991* (Washington, D.C.: Government Printing Office, 1992).

State	Burglaries	Per 100,000 population		% increase 1990-1991		Rank in order
		Rate	Rank	Rate	Rank	By rate per 100,000 population
Alabama	51,873	1,268.6	16	15.0	3	1. District of Columbia
Alaska	5,582	979.3	34	9.5	9	2. Florida
Arizona	60,281	1,607.5	6	−3.7	42	3. Texas
Arkansas	29,093	1,226.5	20	1.3	29	4. New Mexico
California	424,656	1,397.8	12	3.9	18	5. North Carolina
Colorado	39,117	1,158.3	25	−4.2	43	6. Arizona
Connecticut	39,198	1,191.1	21	−3.0	41	7. Georgia
Delaware	7,668	1,127.6	28	16.2	2	8. Oklahoma
District of Columbia	12,405	2,074.4	1	4.6	17	9. South Carolina
Florida	266,313	2,005.8	2	−7.6	48	10. Louisiana
Georgia	100,317	1,514.7	7	−6.5	47	11. Nevada
Hawaii	14,011	1,234.4	19	0.5	30	12. California
Idaho	8,582	826.0	40	1.6	27	13. Tennessee
Illinois	129,284	1,120.0	30	5.4	14	14. Mississippi
Indiana	54,814	977.1	35	3.6	21	15. Kansas
Iowa	23,267	832.5	39	3.0	24	16. Alabama
Kansas	32,601	1,306.7	15	12.0	4	17. Missouri
Kentucky	29,576	796.6	41	3.9	18	18. Washington
Louisiana	60,017	1,411.5	10	−1.8	37	19. Hawaii
Maine	11,146	902.5	36	9.7	7	20. Arkansas
Maryland	56,258	1,157.6	26	3.4	23	21. Connecticut
Massachusetts	69,977	1,167.1	24	4.9	16	22. Michigan
Michigan	111,126	1,186.2	22	3.8	20	23. Oregon
Minnesota	37,832	853.6	37	−5.9	45	24. Massachusetts
Mississippi	34,524	1,331.9	14	6.4	13	25. Colorado
Missouri	64,643	1,253.3	17	17.6	1	26. Maryland
Montana	4,231	523.6	50	−26.2	51	27. New York
Nebraska	11,574	726.6	45	0.4	31	28. Delaware
Nevada	18,026	1,403.9	11	2.7	25	29. Rhode Island
New Hampshire	8,126	735.4	44	0.0	32	30. Illinois
New Jersey	78,821	1,015.7	33	−0.1	34	31. Ohio
New Mexico	26,672	1,723.0	4	−0.9	35	32. Vermont
New York	204,499	1,132.5	27	−2.4	39	33. New Jersey
North Carolina	114,009	1,692.3	5	10.6	6	34. Alaska
North Dakota	2,367	372.8	51	−12.6	50	35. Indiana
Ohio	115,423	1,055.2	31	7.4	11	36. Maine
Oklahoma	46,934	1,478.2	8	2.1	26	37. Minnesota
Oregon	34,363	1,176.0	23	3.6	21	38. Utah
Pennsylvania	86,074	719.6	46	−1.3	36	39. Iowa
Rhode Island	11,320	1,127.5	29	−11.3	49	40. Idaho
South Carolina	51,793	1,454.9	9	5.4	14	41. Kentucky
South Dakota	4,146	589.8	49	11.8	5	42. Virginia
Tennessee	67,608	1,365.0	13	8.0	10	43. Wisconsin
Texas	312,693	1,802.4	3	−2.7	40	44. New Hampshire
Utah	14,872	840.2	38	−4.6	44	45. Nebraska
Vermont	5,784	1,020.1	32	−6.2	46	46. Pennsylvania
Virginia	49,224	783.1	42	7.1	12	47. Wyoming
Washington	61,996	1,235.5	18	−2.2	38	48. West Virginia
West Virginia	12,009	666.8	48	1.5	28	49. South Dakota
Wisconsin	37,241	751.6	43	0.0	32	50. Montana
Wyoming	3,184	692.2	47	9.7	7	51. North Dakota
United States	3,157,150	1,252.0	18	1.3	29	

Source: U.S. Department of Justice, Federal Bureau of Investigation, *Uniform Crime Reports for the United States, 1991* (Washington, D.C.: Government Printing Office, 1992).

State	Larcenies and thefts	Per 100,000 population		% increase 1990-1991		Rank in order By rate per 100,000 population
		Rate	Rank	Rate	Rank	
Alabama	118,151	2,889.5	33	4.9	9	1. District of Columbia
Alaska	20,375	3,574.6	13	12.8	1	2. Florida
Arizona	159,987	4,266.3	3	−9.3	50	3. Arizona
Arkansas	71,487	3,013.8	27	6.3	6	4. Utah
California	986,120	3,246.0	21	1.5	24	5. Texas
Colorado	132,717	3,930.0	8	1.0	29	6. Hawaii
Connecticut	93,384	2,837.6	37	−1.3	38	7. Washington
Delaware	24,836	3,652.4	10	11.0	2	8. Colorado
District of Columbia	29,182	4,879.9	1	−2.3	45	9. New Mexico
Florida	607,222	4,573.5	2	0.1	33	10. Delaware
Georgia	240,359	3,629.2	11	−2.3	45	11. Georgia
Hawaii	47,195	4,158.1	6	−1.4	39	12. Oregon
Idaho	30,143	2,901.2	32	3.5	14	13. Alaska
Illinois	382,942	3,317.5	20	1.7	22	14. Nevada
Indiana	161,039	2,870.6	34	1.5	24	15. Louisiana
Iowa	79,030	2,827.5	38	0.2	32	16. Michigan
Kansas	84,258	3,377.1	17	4.1	11	17. Kansas
Kentucky	70,855	1,909.1	49	−1.7	42	18. Maryland
Louisiana	148,334	3,488.6	15	−1.7	42	South Carolina
Maine	31,737	2,569.8	43	0.6	30	20. Illinois
Maryland	163,524	3,364.7	18	9.1	3	21. California
Massachusetts	149,930	2,500.5	44	−1.0	36	22. North Carolina
Michigan	324,985	3,469.1	16	3.6	13	23. Wyoming
Minnesota	131,330	2,963.2	29	0.1	33	24. Virginia
Mississippi	57,373	2,213.5	47	6.9	5	25. Nebraska
Missouri	146,533	2,840.9	36	1.5	24	26. Oklahoma
Montana	22,449	2,778.3	39	−18.1	51	27. Arkansas
Nebraska	49,071	3,080.4	25	3.3	15	28. Wisconsin
Nevada	45,781	3,565.5	14	1.8	20	29. Minnesota
New Hampshire	26,220	2,372.9	45	−6.4	48	30. New York
New Jersey	221,544	2,854.9	35	0.4	31	31. Ohio
New Mexico	58,441	3,775.3	9	−1.4	39	32. Idaho
New York	531,681	2,944.3	30	−1.0	36	33. Alabama
North Carolina	218,192	3,238.7	22	6.2	7	34. Indiana
North Dakota	14,154	2,229.0	46	−2.6	47	35. New Jersey
Ohio	318,933	2,915.6	31	1.8	20	36. Missouri
Oklahoma	96,842	3,050.1	26	1.6	23	37. Connecticut
Oregon	105,145	3,598.4	12	1.5	24	38. Iowa
Pennsylvania	228,142	1,907.4	50	5.4	8	39. Montana
Rhode Island	26,664	2,655.8	42	−1.5	41	40. Vermont
South Carolina	119,784	3,364.7	18	1.9	19	41. Tennessee
South Dakota	15,412	2,192.3	48	4.0	12	42. Rhode Island
Tennessee	131,855	2,662.1	41	4.6	10	43. Maine
Texas	734,261	4,232.3	5	−1.7	42	44. Massachusetts
Utah	75,041	4,239.6	4	−0.4	35	45. New Hampshire
Vermont	15,161	2,673.9	40	−8.4	49	46. North Dakota
Virginia	195,652	3,112.5	24	2.7	17	47. Mississippi
Washington	205,814	4,101.5	7	2.2	18	48. South Dakota
West Virginia	29,369	1,630.7	51	7.1	4	49. Kentucky
Wisconsin	148,695	3,000.9	28	1.3	28	50. Pennsylvania
Wyoming	14,867	3,232.0	23	3.3	15	51. West Virginia
United States	8,142,228	3,228.8	24	1.1	29	

Source: U.S. Department of Justice, Federal Bureau of Investigation, *Uniform Crime Reports for the United States, 1991* (Washington, D.C.: Government Printing Office, 1992).

State	Motor vehicle thefts	Per 100,000 population		% increase 1990-1991	
		Rate	Rank	Rate	Rank
Alabama	14,858	363.4	30	4.5	14
Alaska	3,043	533.9	20	−5.6	42
Arizona	32,291	861.1	7	−0.3	30
Arkansas	8,097	341.4	34	18.0	3
California	315,615	1,038.9	2	2.3	23
Colorado	14,401	426.4	27	−0.5	31
Connecticut	26,188	795.7	8	8.9	6
Delaware	2,551	375.1	29	−15.5	49
District of Columbia	8,135	1,360.4	1	1.8	26
Florida	104,035	783.6	10	−5.2	41
Georgia	40,489	611.3	16	−9.2	45
Hawaii	3,814	336.0	36	−11.7	47
Idaho	1,853	178.3	44	7.7	7
Illinois	75,642	655.3	13	1.9	25
Indiana	26,077	464.8	24	5.9	10
Iowa	4,772	170.7	46	0.5	28
Kansas	8,757	351.0	32	4.7	13
Kentucky	7,969	214.6	41	7.6	8
Louisiana	24,381	573.4	17	−4.7	37
Maine	2,017	163.3	47	−7.5	43
Maryland	35,517	730.8	11	3.1	21
Massachusetts	55,083	918.7	6	−0.5	31
Michigan	63,670	679.7	12	−4.8	40
Minnesota	16,106	363.4	30	−0.6	33
Mississippi	7,420	286.3	38	37.9	1
Missouri	28,806	558.5	18	3.5	18
Montana	1,667	206.3	43	−14.9	48
Nebraska	3,386	212.6	42	19.3	2
Nevada	8,376	652.3	14	10.1	5
New Hampshire	2,434	220.3	40	−9.7	46
New Jersey	71,847	925.9	5	−1.4	35
New Mexico	5,361	346.3	33	2.9	22
New York	181,287	1,003.9	3	−3.7	36
North Carolina	20,167	299.3	37	5.5	11
North Dakota	805	126.8	50	−4.7	37
Ohio	54,744	500.4	21	2.0	24
Oklahoma	17,673	556.6	19	−7.5	43
Oregon	13,862	474.4	23	3.4	19
Pennsylvania	57,598	481.5	22	−4.7	37
Rhode Island	7,973	794.1	9	−16.8	50
South Carolina	13,782	387.1	28	0.3	29
South Dakota	808	114.9	51	4.3	15
Tennessee	30,393	613.6	15	7.4	9
Texas	163,830	944.3	4	3.9	16
Utah	4,265	241.0	39	1.4	27
Vermont	819	144.4	49	−30.5	51
Virginia	21,284	338.6	35	3.4	19
Washington	22,305	444.5	25	−0.6	33
West Virginia	3,150	174.9	45	13.6	4
Wisconsin	21,624	436.4	26	4.8	12
Wyoming	711	154.6	48	3.8	17
United States	1,661,718	659.0	13	0.2	30

Rank in order

By rate per 100,000 population

1. District of Columbia
2. California
3. New York
4. Texas
5. New Jersey
6. Massachusetts
7. Arizona
8. Connecticut
9. Rhode Island
10. Florida
11. Maryland
12. Michigan
13. Illinois
14. Nevada
15. Tennessee
16. Georgia
17. Louisiana
18. Missouri
19. Oklahoma
20. Alaska
21. Ohio
22. Pennsylvania
23. Oregon
24. Indiana
25. Washington
26. Wisconsin
27. Colorado
28. South Carolina
29. Delaware
30. Alabama
    Minnesota
32. Kansas
33. New Mexico
34. Arkansas
35. Virginia
36. Hawaii
37. North Carolina
38. Mississippi
39. Utah
40. New Hampshire
41. Kentucky
42. Nebraska
43. Montana
44. Idaho
45. West Virginia
46. Iowa
47. Maine
48. Wyoming
49. Vermont
50. North Dakota
51. South Dakota

Source: U.S. Department of Justice, Federal Bureau of Investigation, *Uniform Crime Reports for the United States, 1991* (Washington, D.C.: Government Printing Office, 1992).

State	Prisoners	Per 100,000 population		By rate per 100,000 population
		Rate	Rank	
Alabama	16,400	392	7	1. District of Columbia
Alaska	1,841	344	11	2. Nevada
Arizona	14,843	398	6	3. South Carolina
Arkansas	7,667	314	18	4. Louisiana
California	98,515	320	16	5. Oklahoma
Colorado	8,347	247	26	6. Arizona
Connecticut	8,585	262	24	7. Alabama
Delaware	2,406	342	12	8. Michigan
District of Columbia	6,893	1,168	1	9. Maryland
Florida	46,531	346	10	10. Florida
Georgia	22,859	342	12	11. Alaska
Hawaii	1,979	172	39	12. Delaware
Idaho	2,211	212	33	Georgia
Illinois	29,115	246	27	14. Mississippi
Indiana	12,876	226	31	15. Ohio
Iowa	4,145	144	45	16. California
Kansas	5,903	230	28	17. New York
Kentucky	9,799	261	25	18. Arkansas
Louisiana	20,307	466	4	19. New Jersey
Maine	1,600	127	47	20. Texas
Maryland	17,824	366	9	Virginia
Massachusetts	8,998	150	42	22. Missouri
Michigan	36,423	387	8	23. North Carolina
Minnesota	3,472	78	50	24. Connecticut
Mississippi	8,848	335	14	25. Kentucky
Missouri	15,411	294	22	26. Colorado
Montana	1,478	182	38	27. Illinois
Nebraska	2,389	146	44	28. Kansas
Nevada	5,879	477	2	29. Oregon
New Hampshire	1,533	132	46	30. Tennessee
New Jersey	23,483	300	19	31. Indiana
New Mexico	3,016	191	35	32. Wyoming
New York	57,862	319	17	33. Idaho
North Carolina	18,288	270	23	34. Pennsylvania
North Dakota	441	68	51	35. New Mexico
Ohio	35,750	323	15	36. South Dakota
Oklahoma	13,376	414	5	37. Washington
Oregon	6,760	229	29	38. Montana
Pennsylvania	23,386	192	34	39. Hawaii
Rhode Island	1,749	172	39	Rhode Island
South Carolina	17,173	473	3	41. Wisconsin
South Dakota	1,374	190	36	42. Massachusetts
Tennessee	11,502	227	30	43. Utah
Texas	51,677	297	20	44. Nebraska
Utah	2,605	149	43	45. Iowa
Vermont	738	125	48	46. New Hampshire
Virginia	18,755	297	20	47. Maine
Washington	9,156	183	37	48. Vermont
West Virginia	1,502	82	49	49. West Virginia
Wisconsin	7,841	158	41	50. Minnesota
Wyoming	1,054	225	32	51. North Dakota
United States	789,261	310	19	

Source: Tracy L. Snell and Danielle C. Morton, "Prisoners in 1991," *Bureau of Justice Statistics Bulletin* (Washington, D.C.: Department of Justice, 1992).

| State | Executions, 1977-1991 | | Prisoners under sentence of death, 12/31/91 | | Rank in order |
	Number	Rank	Number	Rank	By number of executions
Alabama	8	6	119	7	1. Texas
Alaska	—	—	—	—	2. Florida
Arizona	0	17	97	10	3. Louisiana
Arkansas	2	13	34	20	4. Georgia
California	0	17	301	3	5. Virginia
Colorado	0	17	3	32	6. Alabama
Connecticut	0	17	4	30	7. Missouri
Delaware	0	17	7	28	8. Nevada
District of Columbia	—	—	—	—	9. Mississippi
Florida	27	2	311	2	North Carolina
Georgia	15	4	101	9	South Carolina
Hawaii	—	—	—	—	12. Utah
Idaho	0	17	21	22	13. Arkansas
Illinois	1	15	132	5	Indiana
Indiana	2	13	49	16	15. Illinois
Iowa	—	—	—	—	Oklahoma
Kansas	—	—	—	—	17. Arizona
Kentucky	0	17	30	21	California
Louisiana	20	3	37	19	Colorado
Maine	—	—	—	—	Connecticut
Maryland	0	17	16	23	Delaware
Massachusetts	—	—	—	—	Idaho
Michigan	—	—	—	—	Kentucky
Minnesota	—	—	—	—	Maryland
Mississippi	4	9	51	15	Montana
Missouri	6	7	77	12	Nebraska
Montana	0	17	6	29	New Hampshire
Nebraska	0	17	12	24	New Jersey
Nevada	5	8	60	14	New Mexico
New Hampshire	0	17	0	34	Ohio
New Jersey	0	17	4	30	Oregon
New Mexico	0	17	1	33	Pennsylvania
New York	—	—	—	—	South Dakota
North Carolina	4	9	74	13	Tennessee
North Dakota	—	—	—	—	Washington
Ohio	0	17	111	8	Wyoming
Oklahoma	1	15	125	6	— Alaska
Oregon	0	17	9	27	— District of Columbia
Pennsylvania	0	17	137	4	— Hawaii
Rhode Island	—	—	—	—	— Iowa
South Carolina	4	9	45	18	— Kansas
South Dakota	0	17	0	34	— Maine
Tennessee	0	17	97	10	— Massachusetts
Texas	42	1	340	1	— Michigan
Utah	3	12	12	24	— Minnesota
Vermont	—	—	—	—	— New York
Virginia	13	5	47	17	— North Dakota
Washington	0	17	10	26	— Rhode Island
West Virginia	—	—	—	—	— Vermont
Wisconsin	—	—	—	—	— West Virginia
Wyoming	0	17	1	33	— Wisconsin
United States	157	—	2,482	—	

— not applicable (state without death penalty).

Source: Lawrence A. Greenfield, "Capital Punishment 1991," *Bureau of Justice Statistics Bulletin* (Washington, D.C.: Department of Justice, 1992).

State	Expenditures	Per capita	Rank by per capita	Per $1,000 personal income Amount	Per $1,000 personal income Rank
Alabama	$176,812,000	$43.24	41	$2.91	40
Alaska	129,827,000	227.77	1	10.86	1
Arizona	347,329,000	96.62	9	5.89	4
Arkansas	99,568,000	41.98	42	2.98	39
California	2,982,713,000	98.18	7	4.82	15
Colorado	256,967,000	76.09	22	4.12	22
Connecticut	459,799,000	139.71	2	5.48	8
Delaware	82,709,000	121.63	4	6.17	2
District of Columbia	—	—	—	—	—
Florida	924,210,000	69.61	23	3.82	24
Georgia	628,057,000	94.83	10	5.66	6
Hawaii	91,877,000	80.95	18	4.05	23
Idaho	52,688,000	50.71	38	3.42	30
Illinois	661,982,000	57.35	30	2.83	41
Indiana	295,942,000	52.75	36	3.16	35
Iowa	150,815,000	53.96	34	3.15	36
Kansas	208,646,000	83.63	15	4.63	19
Kentucky	208,584,000	56.18	32	3.77	26
Louisiana	258,672,000	60.84	28	4.22	20
Maine	68,009,000	55.07	33	3.22	34
Maryland	506,282,000	104.17	6	4.84	14
Massachusetts	708,076,000	118.09	5	5.21	10
Michigan	815,372,000	87.04	14	4.77	17
Minnesota	167,194,000	37.72	47	2.03	47
Mississippi	91,211,000	35.19	48	2.76	42
Missouri	197,081,000	38.21	46	2.20	46
Montana	45,601,000	56.44	31	3.74	27
Nebraska	66,098,000	41.26	43	2.38	45
Nevada	125,696,000	97.89	8	5.40	9
New Hampshire	43,257,000	39.15	45	1.87	48
New Jersey	633,398,000	81.62	16	3.28	33
New Mexico	123,341,000	79.68	19	5.69	5
New York	2,203,720,000	122.04	3	5.54	7
North Carolina	526,724,000	78.18	21	4.86	13
North Dakota	15,181,000	23.91	49	1.57	50
Ohio	642,984,000	58.78	29	3.37	31
Oklahoma	201,807,000	63.56	24	4.15	21
Oregon	237,256,000	81.20	17	4.82	15
Pennsylvania	541,069,000	45.24	40	2.44	44
Rhode Island	92,086,000	91.72	11	4.87	12
South Carolina	314,469,000	88.33	13	5.93	3
South Dakota	28,258,000	40.20	44	2.57	43
Tennessee	393,752,000	79.50	20	5.08	11
Texas	1,064,135,000	61.34	27	3.73	28
Utah	91,610,000	51.76	37	3.79	25
Vermont	30,319,000	53.47	35	3.07	38
Virginia	567,343,000	90.26	12	4.64	18
Washington	309,694,000	61.72	26	3.36	32
West Virginia	40,470,000	22.47	50	1.64	49
Wisconsin	307,794,000	62.12	25	3.57	29
Wyoming	23,248,000	50.54	39	3.15	36
United States	$19,239,732,000	$76.48	22	$4.14	22

Rank in order

By amount per $1,000 personal income

1. Alaska
2. Delaware
3. South Carolina
4. Arizona
5. New Mexico
6. Georgia
7. New York
8. Connecticut
9. Nevada
10. Massachusetts
11. Tennessee
12. Rhode Island
13. North Carolina
14. Maryland
15. California
    Oregon
17. Michigan
18. Virginia
19. Kansas
20. Louisiana
21. Oklahoma
22. Colorado
23. Hawaii
24. Florida
25. Utah
26. Kentucky
27. Montana
28. Texas
29. Wisconsin
30. Idaho
31. Ohio
32. Washington
33. New Jersey
34. Maine
35. Indiana
36. Iowa
    Wyoming
38. Vermont
39. Arkansas
40. Alabama
41. Illinois
42. Mississippi
43. South Dakota
44. Pennsylvania
45. Nebraska
46. Missouri
47. Minnesota
48. New Hampshire
49. West Virginia
50. North Dakota
— District of Columbia

— not applicable.

Source: U.S. Department of Commerce, Bureau of the Census, *State Government Finances: 1991* (Washington, D.C.: Government Printing Office, 1992).

State	Expenditures	Per capita	Rank by per capita	Per $1,000 personal income Amount	Per $1,000 personal income Rank
Alabama	$76,653,000	$18.75	32	$1.26	22
Alaska	43,067,000	75.56	1	3.60	1
Arizona	114,981,000	30.66	9	1.95	8
Arkansas	37,021,000	15.61	39	1.11	28
California	832,254,000	27.39	13	1.34	18
Colorado	40,136,000	11.89	47	0.64	48
Connecticut	99,256,000	30.16	11	1.18	26
Delaware	36,500,000	53.68	3	2.72	2
District of Columbia	—	—	—	—	—
Florida	251,709,000	18.96	30	1.04	32
Georgia	110,779,000	16.73	36	1.00	36
Hawaii	8,086,000	7.12	50	0.36	50
Idaho	25,025,000	24.09	19	1.62	13
Illinois	234,794,000	20.34	26	1.01	35
Indiana	89,725,000	15.99	38	0.96	39
Iowa	46,324,000	16.57	37	0.97	38
Kansas	30,147,000	12.08	45	0.67	47
Kentucky	105,093,000	28.30	12	1.90	9
Louisiana	114,214,000	26.86	15	1.87	10
Maine	29,951,000	24.25	18	1.42	16
Maryland	272,558,000	56.08	2	2.61	3
Massachusetts	121,887,000	20.33	27	0.90	40
Michigan	191,369,000	20.43	25	1.12	27
Minnesota	88,390,000	19.94	28	1.08	30
Mississippi	32,496,000	12.54	44	0.98	37
Missouri	97,133,000	18.83	31	1.08	29
Montana	21,146,000	26.17	16	1.73	12
Nebraska	33,610,000	20.98	24	1.21	25
Nevada	23,751,000	18.50	33	1.02	33
New Hampshire	24,179,000	21.88	21	1.05	31
New Jersey	239,138,000	30.82	8	1.24	23
New Mexico	47,139,000	30.45	10	2.18	7
New York	319,577,000	17.70	34	0.80	42
North Carolina	142,297,000	21.12	23	1.31	19
North Dakota	6,908,000	10.88	48	0.71	46
Ohio	145,855,000	13.33	41	0.77	44
Oklahoma	41,969,000	13.22	42	0.86	41
Oregon	63,280,000	21.66	22	1.29	20
Pennsylvania	298,807,000	24.98	17	1.35	17
Rhode Island	27,030,000	26.92	14	1.43	15
South Carolina	83,763,000	23.53	20	1.58	14
South Dakota	13,903,000	19.78	29	1.26	21
Tennessee	62,139,000	12.55	43	0.80	43
Texas	206,626,000	11.91	46	0.73	45
Utah	30,003,000	16.95	35	1.24	23
Vermont	23,164,000	40.85	5	2.34	4
Virginia	274,623,000	43.69	4	2.25	5
Washington	164,297,000	32.74	7	1.78	11
West Virginia	25,095,000	13.93	40	1.02	33
Wisconsin	42,131,000	8.50	49	0.49	49
Wyoming	16,379,000	35.61	6	2.22	6
United States	$5,506,357,000	$21.89	21	$1.18	26

— not applicable.

Source: U.S. Department of Commerce, Bureau of the Census, *State Government Finances: 1991* (Washington, D.C.: Government Printing Office, 1992).

Rank in order

By amount per $1,000 personal income

1. Alaska
2. Delaware
3. Maryland
4. Vermont
5. Virginia
6. Wyoming
7. New Mexico
8. Arizona
9. Kentucky
10. Louisiana
11. Washington
12. Montana
13. Idaho
14. South Carolina
15. Rhode Island
16. Maine
17. Pennsylvania
18. California
19. North Carolina
20. Oregon
21. South Dakota
22. Alabama
23. New Jersey
    Utah
25. Nebraska
26. Connecticut
27. Michigan
28. Arkansas
29. Missouri
30. Minnesota
31. New Hampshire
32. Florida
33. Nevada
    West Virginia
35. Illinois
36. Georgia
37. Mississippi
38. Iowa
39. Indiana
40. Massachusetts
41. Oklahoma
42. New York
43. Tennessee
44. Ohio
45. Texas
46. North Dakota
47. Kansas
48. Colorado
49. Wisconsin
50. Hawaii
— District of Columbia

State	Local jails	Inmates	Per 100,000 population Inmate rate	Per 100,000 population Rank
Alabama	110	4,819	117	19
Alaska	5	27	—	—
Arizona	33	6,006	172	9
Arkansas	87	1,994	83	31
California	149	64,216	227	5
Colorado	61	4,882	148	12
Connecticut	—	—	—	—
Delaware	—	—	—	—
District of Columbia	1	1,693	274	2
Florida	102	28,236	229	4
Georgia	196	17,482	276	1
Hawaii	—	—	—	—
Idaho	37	810	81	32
Illinois	95	9,891	85	28
Indiana	90	5,235	94	26
Iowa	90	1,036	37	45
Kansas	94	1,906	76	36
Kentucky	95	4,695	126	18
Louisiana	90	11,222	255	3
Maine	15	669	56	43
Maryland	35	7,486	162	10
Massachusetts	19	5,454	93	27
Michigan	85	9,404	102	21
Minnesota	71	3,227	75	37
Mississippi	96	3,501	134	16
Missouri	123	4,154	81	32
Montana	46	616	77	35
Nebraska	66	1,156	72	42
Nevada	19	2,343	222	6
New Hampshire	11	789	73	40
New Jersey	28	11,124	144	15
New Mexico	34	2,188	145	13
New York	75	25,928	145	13
North Carolina	102	5,469	84	29
North Dakota	26	288	43	44
Ohio	122	9,160	84	29
Oklahoma	100	2,595	80	34
Oregon	39	2,819	102	21
Pennsylvania	75	13,649	114	20
Rhode Island	—	—	—	—
South Carolina	55	3,497	101	23
South Dakota	29	522	73	40
Tennessee	108	10,858	222	6
Texas	275	29,439	175	8
Utah	25	1,261	75	37
Vermont	—	—	—	—
Virginia	95	9,372	156	11
Washington	60	5,934	128	17
West Virginia	52	1,393	74	39
Wisconsin	73	4,667	96	24
Wyoming	22	457	95	25
United States	3,316	343,569	140	16

Rank in order

By rate per 100,000 population

1. Georgia
2. District of Columbia
3. Louisiana
4. Florida
5. California
6. Nevada
   Tennessee
8. Texas
9. Arizona
10. Maryland
11. Virginia
12. Colorado
13. New Mexico
    New York
15. New Jersey
16. Mississippi
17. Washington
18. Kentucky
19. Alabama
20. Pennsylvania
21. Michigan
    Oregon
23. South Carolina
24. Wisconsin
25. Wyoming
26. Indiana
27. Massachusetts
28. Illinois
29. North Carolina
    Ohio
31. Arkansas
32. Idaho
    Missouri
34. Oklahoma
35. Montana
36. Kansas
37. Minnesota
    Utah
39. West Virginia
40. New Hampshire
    South Dakota
42. Nebraska
43. Maine
44. North Dakota
45. Iowa
— Alaska
— Connecticut
— Delaware
— Hawaii
— Rhode Island
— Vermont

— not applicable (state did not operate local jails).

Source: Bureau of Justice Statistics, *Census of Local Jails* (Washington, D.C.: Department of Justice, 1991).

Note: Local jails are correctional facilities not under state or federal jurisdiction. Alaska had primarily an integrated jail-prison system; data from five locally operated jails were included in census.

SPENDING ON LOCAL JAILS, 1988

State	Operating expenditures	Capital expenditures	Total expenditures	Per capita	Rank by per capita
Alabama	$33,835,000	$13,545,000	$47,380,000	$11.77	28
Alaska	1,227,000	3,030,000	4,257,000	—	—
Arizona	48,086,000	147,000	48,233,000	13.64	24
Arkansas	17,311,000	8,373,000	25,684,000	10.96	30
California	523,498,000	136,220,000	659,718,000	23.17	7
Colorado	71,863,000	25,351,000	97,214,000	29.79	4
Connecticut	—	—	—	—	—
Delaware	—	—	—	—	—
District of Columbia	13,563,000	550,000	14,113,000	22.37	9
Florida	316,730,000	44,037,000	360,767,000	29.31	5
Georgia	97,237,000	47,639,000	144,876,000	22.93	8
Hawaii	—	—	—	—	—
Idaho	6,831,000	492,000	7,323,000	7.43	41
Illinois	100,471,000	6,092,000	106,562,000	9.35	36
Indiana	34,514,000	25,808,000	60,322,000	10.98	29
Iowa	16,778,000	12,436,000	29,214,000	10.55	32
Kansas	19,092,000	4,683,000	23,775,000	9.66	34
Kentucky	37,899,000	8,580,000	46,479,000	12.63	27
Louisiana	65,242,000	19,243,000	84,485,000	19.70	12
Maine	9,415,000	6,918,000	16,334,000	13.57	25
Maryland	88,031,000	9,811,000	97,842,000	21.00	11
Massachusetts	75,564,000	13,011,000	88,576,000	14.81	20
Michigan	116,605,000	11,706,000	128,311,000	13.92	23
Minnesota	44,349,000	18,052,000	62,401,000	14.52	21
Mississippi	17,342,000	3,806,000	21,148,000	8.19	38
Missouri	39,010,000	2,150,000	41,160,000	8.10	39
Montana	7,428,000	269,000	7,696,000	9.62	35
Nebraska	14,184,000	1,410,000	15,594,000	9.92	33
Nevada	35,135,000	1,909,000	37,044,000	34.46	3
New Hampshire	11,852,000	4,202,000	16,054,000	14.82	19
New Jersey	127,876,000	9,743,000	137,619,000	17.84	15
New Mexico	25,121,000	353,000	25,474,000	17.09	17
New York	578,439,000	293,851,000	872,290,000	48.61	1
North Carolina	41,956,000	9,800,000	51,756,000	7.98	40
North Dakota	4,788,000	2,331,000	7,119,000	10.87	31
Ohio	104,199,000	36,007,000	140,206,000	12.98	26
Oklahoma	19,427,000	1,812,000	21,239,000	6.70	44
Oregon	38,906,000	26,460,000	65,366,000	23.84	6
Pennsylvania	204,067,000	12,060,000	216,127,000	18.24	14
Rhode Island	—	—	—	—	—
South Carolina	23,340,000	736,000	24,076,000	7.05	43
South Dakota	4,423,000	639,000	5,061,000	7.25	42
Tennessee	71,707,000	34,760,000	106,467,000	22.07	10
Texas	215,108,000	65,273,000	280,381,000	16.82	18
Utah	13,908,000	241,000	14,149,000	8.37	37
Vermont	—	—	—	—	—
Virginia	103,561,000	10,906,000	114,467,000	18.96	13
Washington	64,901,000	766,000	65,667,000	14.15	22
West Virginia	11,793,000	417,000	12,211,000	6.67	45
Wisconsin	50,889,000	33,436,000	84,325,000	17.48	16
Wyoming	7,440,000	11,648,000	19,088,000	41.05	2
United States	**$3,574,941,000**	**$980,709,000**	**$4,555,650,000**	**$19.14**	**13**

Rank in order

By per capita

1. New York
2. Wyoming
3. Nevada
4. Colorado
5. Florida
6. Oregon
7. California
8. Georgia
9. District of Columbia
10. Tennessee
11. Maryland
12. Louisiana
13. Virginia
14. Pennsylvania
15. New Jersey
16. Wisconsin
17. New Mexico
18. Texas
19. New Hampshire
20. Massachusetts
21. Minnesota
22. Washington
23. Michigan
24. Arizona
25. Maine
26. Ohio
27. Kentucky
28. Alabama
29. Indiana
30. Arkansas
31. North Dakota
32. Iowa
33. Nebraska
34. Kansas
35. Montana
36. Illinois
37. Utah
38. Mississippi
39. Missouri
40. North Carolina
41. Idaho
42. South Dakota
43. South Carolina
44. Oklahoma
45. West Virginia
— Alaska
— Connecticut
— Delaware
— Hawaii
— Rhode Island
— Vermont

— not applicable (state did not operate local jails).
Source: Bureau of Justice Statistics, *Census of Local Jails* (Washington, D.C.: Department of Justice, 1991).
Note: Local jails are correctional facilities not under state or federal jurisdiction. Alaska had primarily an integrated jail-prison system; data from five locally operated jails were included in census.

SPENDING PER INMATE FOR LOCAL JAILS, 1988

State	Total expenditures	Expenditure per inmate Amount	Expenditure per inmate Rank
Alabama	$47,380,000	$9,831.92	32
Alaska	4,257,000	—	—
Arizona	48,233,000	8,030.80	42
Arkansas	25,684,000	12,880.64	18
California	659,718,000	10,273.42	29
Colorado	97,214,000	19,912.74	8
Connecticut	—	—	—
Delaware	—	—	—
District of Columbia	14,113,000	8,336.09	39
Florida	360,767,000	12,776.85	19
Georgia	144,876,000	8,287.15	40
Hawaii	—	—	—
Idaho	7,323,000	9,040.74	37
Illinois	106,562,000	10,773.63	28
Indiana	60,322,000	11,522.83	25
Iowa	29,214,000	28,198.84	3
Kansas	23,775,000	12,473.77	21
Kentucky	46,479,000	9,899.68	31
Louisiana	84,485,000	7,528.52	43
Maine	16,334,000	24,415.55	5
Maryland	97,842,000	13,070.00	17
Massachusetts	88,576,000	16,240.56	11
Michigan	128,311,000	13,644.30	15
Minnesota	62,401,000	19,337.16	9
Mississippi	21,148,000	6,040.56	45
Missouri	41,160,000	9,908.52	30
Montana	7,696,000	12,493.51	20
Nebraska	15,594,000	13,489.62	16
Nevada	37,044,000	15,810.50	13
New Hampshire	16,054,000	20,347.28	7
New Jersey	137,619,000	12,371.36	22
New Mexico	25,474,000	11,642.60	24
New York	872,290,000	33,642.78	2
North Carolina	51,756,000	9,463.52	36
North Dakota	7,119,000	24,718.75	4
Ohio	140,206,000	15,306.33	14
Oklahoma	21,239,000	8,184.59	41
Oregon	65,366,000	23,187.66	6
Pennsylvania	216,127,000	15,834.64	12
Rhode Island	—	—	—
South Carolina	24,076,000	6,884.76	44
South Dakota	5,061,000	9,695.40	34
Tennessee	106,467,000	9,805.40	33
Texas	280,381,000	9,524.13	35
Utah	14,149,000	11,220.46	26
Vermont	—	—	—
Virginia	114,467,000	12,213.72	23
Washington	65,667,000	11,066.23	27
West Virginia	12,211,000	8,765.97	38
Wisconsin	84,325,000	18,068.35	10
Wyoming	19,088,000	41,768.05	1
United States	**$4,555,650,000**	**$13,259.78**	**18**

Rank in order

By expenditure per inmate

1. Wyoming
2. New York
3. Iowa
4. North Dakota
5. Maine
6. Oregon
7. New Hampshire
8. Colorado
9. Minnesota
10. Wisconsin
11. Massachusetts
12. Pennsylvania
13. Nevada
14. Ohio
15. Michigan
16. Nebraska
17. Maryland
18. Arkansas
19. Florida
20. Montana
21. Kansas
22. New Jersey
23. Virginia
24. New Mexico
25. Indiana
26. Utah
27. Washington
28. Illinois
29. California
30. Missouri
31. Kentucky
32. Alabama
33. Tennessee
34. South Dakota
35. Texas
36. North Carolina
37. Idaho
38. West Virginia
39. District of Columbia
40. Georgia
41. Oklahoma
42. Arizona
43. Louisiana
44. South Carolina
45. Mississippi
— Alaska
— Connecticut
— Delaware
— Hawaii
— Rhode Island
— Vermont

— not applicable (state did not operate local jails).

Source: Bureau of Justice Statistics, *Census of Local Jails* (Washington, D.C.: Department of Justice, 1991).

Note: Local jails are correctional facilities not under state or federal jurisdiction. Alaska had primarily an integrated jail-prison system; data from five locally operated jails were included in census.

EMPLOYEES AT LOCAL JAILS, 1988

State	Inmates	Employees	Inmate-employee ratio Ratio	Inmate-employee ratio Rank
Alabama	4,819	1,282	3.76	10
Alaska	27	36	—	—
Arizona	6,006	1,506	3.99	7
Arkansas	1,994	922	2.16	38
California	64,216	9,883	6.50	1
Colorado	4,882	1,891	2.58	32
Connecticut	—	—	—	—
Delaware	—	—	—	—
District of Columbia	1,693	600	2.82	25
Florida	28,236	8,045	3.51	15
Georgia	17,482	3,610	4.84	3
Hawaii	—	—	—	—
Idaho	810	310	2.61	30
Illinois	9,891	2,911	3.40	17
Indiana	5,235	1,413	3.71	12
Iowa	1,036	764	1.36	44
Kansas	1,906	923	2.07	39
Kentucky	4,695	1,440	3.26	18
Louisiana	11,222	2,568	4.37	5
Maine	669	400	1.67	43
Maryland	7,486	2,128	3.52	14
Massachusetts	5,454	2,104	2.59	31
Michigan	9,404	2,428	3.87	9
Minnesota	3,227	1,291	2.50	33
Mississippi	3,501	728	4.81	4
Missouri	4,154	1,757	2.36	35
Montana	616	333	1.85	41
Nebraska	1,156	667	1.73	42
Nevada	2,343	777	3.02	23
New Hampshire	789	316	2.50	34
New Jersey	11,124	3,511	3.17	20
New Mexico	2,188	836	2.62	29
New York	25,928	11,901	2.18	37
North Carolina	5,469	1,377	3.97	8
North Dakota	288	224	1.29	45
Ohio	9,160	3,029	3.02	21
Oklahoma	2,595	858	3.02	21
Oregon	2,819	1,063	2.65	27
Pennsylvania	13,649	4,703	2.90	24
Rhode Island	—	—	—	—
South Carolina	3,497	951	3.68	13
South Dakota	522	236	2.21	36
Tennessee	10,858	1,992	5.45	2
Texas	29,439	7,085	4.16	6
Utah	1,261	451	2.80	26
Vermont	—	—	—	—
Virginia	9,372	2,892	3.24	19
Washington	5,934	1,706	3.48	16
West Virginia	1,393	526	2.65	28
Wisconsin	4,667	1,254	3.72	11
Wyoming	457	232	1.97	40
United States	343,569	95,860	3.58	19

Rank in order

By ratio

1. California
2. Tennessee
3. Georgia
4. Mississippi
5. Louisiana
6. Texas
7. Arizona
8. North Carolina
9. Michigan
10. Alabama
11. Wisconsin
12. Indiana
13. South Carolina
14. Maryland
15. Florida
16. Washington
17. Illinois
18. Kentucky
19. Virginia
20. New Jersey
21. Ohio
    Oklahoma
23. Nevada
24. Pennsylvania
25. District of Columbia
26. Utah
27. Oregon
28. West Virginia
29. New Mexico
30. Idaho
31. Massachusetts
32. Colorado
33. Minnesota
34. New Hampshire
35. Missouri
36. South Dakota
37. New York
38. Arkansas
39. Kansas
40. Wyoming
41. Montana
42. Nebraska
43. Maine
44. Iowa
45. North Dakota
— Alaska
— Connecticut
— Delaware
— Hawaii
— Rhode Island
— Vermont

— not applicable (state did not operate local jails).

Source: Bureau of Justice Statistics, *Census of Local Jails* (Washington, D.C.: Department of Justice, 1991).

Note: Local jails are correctional facilities not under state or federal jurisdiction. Alaska had primarily an integrated jail-prison system; data from five locally operated jails were included in census.

JUVENILE CUSTODY RATE, 1989				Rank in order
	Per 100,000 youths			
State	**Rate**		**Rank**	**By rate per 100,000 youths**
Alabama	125		31	1. District of Columbia
Alaska	261		6	2. Nevada
Arizona	188		14	3. Wyoming
Arkansas	97		38	4. South Dakota
California	227		8	5. Iowa
Colorado	157		23	6. Alaska
Connecticut	164		18	7. Kansas
Delaware	123		32	8. California
District of Columbia	467		1	9. Nebraska
Florida	146		26	10. Ohio
Georgia	159		21	11. Indiana
Hawaii	33		51	12. Pennsylvania
Idaho	92		39	13. Michigan
Illinois	84		46	14. Arizona
Indiana	204		11	Oregon
Iowa	281		5	16. Minnesota
Kansas	240		7	17. New York
Kentucky	87		45	18. Connecticut
Louisiana	122		33	North Dakota
Maine	90		42	20. Missouri
Maryland	128		30	21. Georgia
Massachusetts	88		43	22. North Carolina
Michigan	189		13	23. Colorado
Minnesota	179		16	Virginia
Mississippi	92		39	25. Wisconsin
Missouri	162		20	26. Florida
Montana	139		28	South Carolina
Nebraska	213		9	28. Montana
Nevada	348		2	New Mexico
New Hampshire	100		37	30. Maryland
New Jersey	92		39	31. Alabama
New Mexico	139		28	32. Delaware
New York	168		17	33. Louisiana
North Carolina	158		22	34. Rhode Island
North Dakota	164		18	35. Washington
Ohio	205		10	36. Texas
Oklahoma	88		43	37. New Hampshire
Oregon	188		14	38. Arkansas
Pennsylvania	197		12	39. Idaho
Rhode Island	120		34	Mississippi
South Carolina	146		26	New Jersey
South Dakota	322		4	42. Maine
Tennessee	78		48	43. Massachusetts
Texas	103		36	Oklahoma
Utah	80		47	45. Kentucky
Vermont	63		50	46. Illinois
Virginia	157		23	47. Utah
Washington	114		35	48. Tennessee
West Virginia	75		49	49. West Virginia
Wisconsin	156		25	50. Vermont
Wyoming	326		3	51. Hawaii
United States	**156**		**25**	

Source: Center for the Study of Social Policy, *Kids Count Data Book: State Profiles of Child Well-Being* (Washington, D.C.: Center for the Study of Social Policy, 1992).

Note: Juvenile data covers ages ten to fifteen.

FEDERAL SPENDING ON OFFICE OF JUSTICE ASSISTANCE PROGRAMS, FISCAL 1991

State	Expenditures	Per capita	Rank by per capita
Alabama	$8,329,000	$2.04	33
Alaska	2,058,000	3.61	5
Arizona	13,980,000	3.73	3
Arkansas	6,407,000	2.70	14
California	63,205,000	2.08	32
Colorado	8,063,000	2.39	22
Connecticut	6,001,000	1.82	35
Delaware	3,420,000	5.03	1
District of Columbia	2,029,000	3.39	7
Florida	23,891,000	1.80	37
Georgia	11,311,000	1.71	42
Hawaii	3,054,000	2.69	15
Idaho	3,379,000	3.25	8
Illinois	16,508,000	1.43	48
Indiana	9,875,000	1.76	39
Iowa	6,944,000	2.48	18
Kansas	5,201,000	2.09	31
Kentucky	5,604,000	1.51	46
Louisiana	7,379,000	1.74	40
Maine	3,670,000	2.97	11
Maryland	11,578,000	2.38	23
Massachusetts	13,857,000	2.31	25
Michigan	16,097,000	1.72	41
Minnesota	6,566,000	1.48	47
Mississippi	4,196,000	1.62	44
Missouri	12,386,000	2.40	21
Montana	2,932,000	3.63	4
Nebraska	4,062,000	2.55	17
Nevada	3,155,000	2.46	19
New Hampshire	2,990,000	2.71	13
New Jersey	13,932,000	1.80	38
New Mexico	3,501,000	2.26	27
New York	29,631,000	1.64	43
North Carolina	8,844,000	1.31	49
North Dakota	2,055,000	3.24	9
Ohio	19,771,000	1.81	36
Oklahoma	269,000	0.09	51
Oregon	6,544,000	2.24	28
Pennsylvania	13,925,000	1.16	50
Rhode Island	3,890,000	3.88	2
South Carolina	7,723,000	2.17	30
South Dakota	2,211,000	3.15	10
Tennessee	12,737,000	2.57	16
Texas	35,299,000	2.04	34
Utah	4,299,000	2.43	20
Vermont	1,297,000	2.29	26
Virginia	14,574,000	2.32	24
Washington	11,114,000	2.22	29
West Virginia	5,164,000	2.87	12
Wisconsin	7,496,000	1.51	45
Wyoming	1,568,000	3.41	6
United States	**$501,874,000**	**$1.99**	**35**

Rank in order

By per capita

1. Delaware
2. Rhode Island
3. Arizona
4. Montana
5. Alaska
6. Wyoming
7. District of Columbia
8. Idaho
9. North Dakota
10. South Dakota
11. Maine
12. West Virginia
13. New Hampshire
14. Arkansas
15. Hawaii
16. Tennessee
17. Nebraska
18. Iowa
19. Nevada
20. Utah
21. Missouri
22. Colorado
23. Maryland
24. Virginia
25. Massachusetts
26. Vermont
27. New Mexico
28. Oregon
29. Washington
30. South Carolina
31. Kansas
32. California
33. Alabama
34. Texas
35. Connecticut
36. Ohio
37. Florida
38. New Jersey
39. Indiana
40. Louisiana
41. Michigan
42. Georgia
43. New York
44. Mississippi
45. Wisconsin
46. Kentucky
47. Minnesota
48. Illinois
49. North Carolina
50. Pennsylvania
51. Oklahoma

Source: U.S. Department of Commerce, Bureau of the Census, *Federal Expenditures by State for Fiscal Year 1991* (Washington, D.C.: Government Printing Office, 1992).

Defense

DEFENSE GRANTS TO STATE AND LOCAL GOVERNMENTS, FISCAL 1991				Rank in order

State	Federal expenditures	Per capita	Rank by per capita	By per capita
Alabama	$2,296,000	$0.56	13	1. Alaska
Alaska	19,417,000	34.07	1	2. North Dakota
Arizona	1,281,000	0.34	20	3. Idaho
Arkansas	944,000	0.40	17	4. District of Columbia
California	1,419,000	0.05	40	5. New Mexico
Colorado	2,000	*	49	6. Mississippi
Connecticut	142,000	0.04	42	7. Virginia
Delaware	98,000	0.14	34	8. West Virginia
District of Columbia	2,014,000	3.37	4	9. Minnesota
Florida	1,212,000	0.09	38	10. Oregon
Georgia	959,000	0.15	33	11. Montana
Hawaii	255,000	0.23	27	12. Iowa
Idaho	4,112,000	3.96	3	13. Alabama
Illinois	1,739,000	0.15	32	Michigan
Indiana	1,009,000	0.18	28	15. Oklahoma
Iowa	1,706,000	0.61	12	16. Ohio
Kansas	884,000	0.35	18	17. Arkansas
Kentucky	637,000	0.17	30	18. Kansas
Louisiana	185,000	0.04	41	19. Missouri
Maine	34,000	0.03	45	20. Arizona
Maryland	352,000	0.07	39	21. Utah
Massachusetts	129,000	0.02	46	22. New Jersey
Michigan	5,261,000	0.56	13	23. Texas
Minnesota	4,484,000	1.01	9	24. South Dakota
Mississippi	5,062,000	1.95	6	25. Tennessee
Missouri	1,774,000	0.34	19	26. Wyoming
Montana	499,000	0.62	11	27. Hawaii
Nebraska	171,000	0.11	37	28. Indiana
Nevada	175,000	0.14	36	29. South Carolina
New Hampshire	1,000	*	49	30. Kentucky
New Jersey	2,379,000	0.31	22	31. Wisconsin
New Mexico	3,954,000	2.55	5	32. Illinois
New York	760,000	0.04	43	33. Georgia
North Carolina	248,000	0.04	44	34. Delaware
North Dakota	6,140,000	9.67	2	35. Pennsylvania
Ohio	4,553,000	0.42	16	36. Nevada
Oklahoma	1,329,000	0.42	15	37. Nebraska
Oregon	2,133,000	0.73	10	38. Florida
Pennsylvania	1,697,000	0.14	35	39. Maryland
Rhode Island	0	0.00	—	40. California
South Carolina	633,000	0.18	29	41. Louisiana
South Dakota	190,000	0.27	24	42. Connecticut
Tennessee	1,321,000	0.27	25	43. New York
Texas	5,275,000	0.30	23	44. North Carolina
Utah	598,000	0.34	21	45. Maine
Vermont	8,000	0.01	48	46. Massachusetts
Virginia	11,579,000	1.84	7	47. Washington
Washington	86,000	0.02	47	48. Vermont
West Virginia	2,737,000	1.52	8	49. Colorado
Wisconsin	844,000	0.17	31	New Hampshire
Wyoming	113,000	0.25	26	— Rhode Island
United States	**$111,454,000**	**$0.44**	**15**	

— not applicable.   * per capita amount rounds to less than 0.005.

Source: U.S. Department of Commerce, Bureau of the Census, *Federal Expenditure by State for Fiscal Year 1991* (Washington, D.C.: Government Printing Office, 1992).

Note: Funding includes construction of National Guard Centers and activities of U.S. Army Corps of Engineers.

TOTAL DEFENSE PAYROLL, FISCAL 1991

State	Personnel	Payroll	Per capita	Rank by per capita
Alabama	92,972	$2,093,128,000	$511.89	16
Alaska	35,909	902,723,000	1,583.72	4
Arizona	57,725	1,658,485,000	442.26	22
Arkansas	37,640	718,068,000	302.73	31
California	452,213	13,952,250,000	459.26	20
Colorado	75,463	2,172,327,000	643.27	8
Connecticut	28,113	658,537,000	200.10	37
Delaware	14,772	262,125,000	385.48	28
District of Columbia	46,161	1,190,080,000	1,990.10	1
Florida	177,398	6,002,604,000	452.11	21
Georgia	146,160	3,792,894,000	572.69	12
Hawaii	75,245	2,245,154,000	1,978.11	2
Idaho	15,077	281,866,000	271.29	34
Illinois	114,350	1,836,647,000	159.11	43
Indiana	62,766	1,042,936,000	185.91	41
Iowa	24,905	205,409,000	73.49	51
Kansas	55,160	1,250,416,000	501.17	17
Kentucky	78,934	1,806,737,000	486.60	18
Louisiana	73,686	1,413,697,000	332.48	30
Maine	25,148	667,310,000	540.33	14
Maryland	112,959	3,270,639,000	672.97	6
Massachusetts	59,549	1,016,037,000	169.45	42
Michigan	68,323	926,978,000	98.95	48
Minnesota	39,095	363,223,000	81.95	50
Mississippi	51,053	1,062,286,000	409.83	26
Missouri	75,406	1,556,214,000	301.71	32
Montana	14,349	231,879,000	286.98	33
Nebraska	30,496	685,293,000	430.19	23
Nevada	18,931	593,940,000	462.57	19
New Hampshire	9,558	218,559,000	197.79	38
New Jersey	73,132	1,633,871,000	210.55	36
New Mexico	36,865	998,822,000	645.23	7
New York	130,227	1,867,152,000	103.40	47
North Carolina	158,791	3,774,218,000	560.22	13
North Dakota	19,861	331,911,000	522.69	15
Ohio	112,374	2,124,507,000	194.21	39
Oklahoma	76,072	1,893,052,000	596.24	10
Oregon	25,785	430,698,000	147.40	44
Pennsylvania	136,835	2,688,733,000	224.79	35
Rhode Island	16,656	422,392,000	420.71	24
South Carolina	93,450	2,621,924,000	736.50	5
South Dakota	15,925	272,302,000	387.34	27
Tennessee	57,934	943,865,000	190.56	40
Texas	272,412	7,257,502,000	418.32	25
Utah	43,783	1,025,681,000	579.48	11
Vermont	7,191	80,865,000	142.62	45
Virginia	251,569	10,507,498,000	1,671.57	3
Washington	106,553	3,209,286,000	639.55	9
West Virginia	17,180	206,007,000	114.38	46
Wisconsin	40,533	427,480,000	86.27	49
Wyoming	9,029	173,355,000	376.86	29
United States	**3,871,686**	**$96,969,562,000**	**$384.53**	**29**

By per capita

1. District of Columbia
2. Hawaii
3. Virginia
4. Alaska
5. South Carolina
6. Maryland
7. New Mexico
8. Colorado
9. Washington
10. Oklahoma
11. Utah
12. Georgia
13. North Carolina
14. Maine
15. North Dakota
16. Alabama
17. Kansas
18. Kentucky
19. Nevada
20. California
21. Florida
22. Arizona
23. Nebraska
24. Rhode Island
25. Texas
26. Mississippi
27. South Dakota
28. Delaware
29. Wyoming
30. Louisiana
31. Arkansas
32. Missouri
33. Montana
34. Idaho
35. Pennsylvania
36. New Jersey
37. Connecticut
38. New Hampshire
39. Ohio
40. Tennessee
41. Indiana
42. Massachusetts
43. Illinois
44. Oregon
45. Vermont
46. West Virginia
47. New York
48. Michigan
49. Wisconsin
50. Minnesota
51. Iowa

Source: U.S. Department of Defense, Directorate for Information Operations and Reports, *Atlas/Data Abstract for the United States and Selected Areas, Fiscal Year 1991* (Washington, D.C.: Government Printing Office, 1992).

State	Personnel	Payroll	Per capita	Rank by per capita	By per capita
Alabama	72,724	$1,471,123,000	$359.78	7	1. Alaska
Alaska	17,731	397,936,000	698.13	1	2. Hawaii
Arizona	24,431	640,895,000	170.91	20	3. District of Columbia
Arkansas	23,487	278,837,000	117.55	22	4. Virginia
California	109,837	1,950,045,000	64.19	30	5. Kentucky
Colorado	38,243	989,546,000	293.03	10	6. Kansas
Connecticut	11,964	87,697,000	26.65	50	7. Alabama
Delaware	4,392	38,080,000	56.00	40	8. Georgia
District of Columbia	17,363	404,164,000	675.86	3	9. North Carolina
Florida	42,681	824,399,000	62.09	32	10. Colorado
Georgia	94,177	2,326,260,000	351.24	8	11. Maryland
Hawaii	32,486	782,782,000	689.68	2	12. Oklahoma
Idaho	6,823	60,098,000	57.84	37	13. Washington
Illinois	53,642	602,508,000	52.20	42	14. New Mexico
Indiana	36,059	420,946,000	75.03	26	15. Texas
Iowa	17,847	103,983,000	37.20	49	16. South Carolina
Kansas	40,927	948,351,000	380.10	6	17. Missouri
Kentucky	68,653	1,553,823,000	418.48	5	18. Utah
Louisiana	44,808	727,128,000	171.01	19	19. Louisiana
Maine	7,246	62,965,000	50.98	44	20. Arizona
Maryland	52,958	1,349,060,000	277.58	11	21. New Jersey
Massachusetts	34,122	452,877,000	75.53	25	22. Arkansas
Michigan	39,197	409,260,000	43.69	46	23. Mississippi
Minnesota	26,845	171,165,000	38.62	48	24. Pennsylvania
Mississippi	25,167	286,575,000	110.56	23	25. Massachusetts
Missouri	48,204	960,034,000	186.13	17	26. Indiana
Montana	6,482	46,938,000	58.09	36	27. Vermont
Nebraska	11,428	112,320,000	70.51	28	28. Nebraska
Nevada	4,081	63,560,000	49.50	45	29. Tennessee
New Hampshire	5,785	68,216,000	61.73	33	30. California
New Jersey	44,385	935,620,000	120.57	21	31. South Dakota
New Mexico	14,142	299,144,000	193.25	14	32. Florida
New York	82,531	1,024,876,000	56.75	38	33. New Hampshire
North Carolina	80,064	1,979,414,000	293.81	9	34. Oregon
North Dakota	6,297	35,617,000	56.09	39	35. West Virginia
Ohio	42,602	277,739,000	25.39	51	36. Montana
Oklahoma	39,729	827,040,000	260.49	12	37. Idaho
Oregon	15,970	174,991,000	59.89	34	38. New York
Pennsylvania	68,551	973,144,000	81.36	24	39. North Dakota
Rhode Island	5,491	43,374,000	43.20	47	40. Delaware
South Carolina	37,695	663,075,000	186.26	16	41. Wisconsin
South Dakota	6,396	43,726,000	62.20	31	42. Illinois
Tennessee	30,668	338,632,000	68.37	29	43. Wyoming
Texas	145,525	3,277,063,000	188.89	15	44. Maine
Utah	17,472	314,325,000	177.58	18	45. Nevada
Vermont	5,084	40,377,000	71.21	27	46. Michigan
Virginia	88,865	2,821,506,000	448.86	4	47. Rhode Island
Washington	48,440	1,024,103,000	204.09	13	48. Minnesota
West Virginia	11,834	107,538,000	59.71	35	49. Iowa
Wisconsin	28,623	264,499,000	53.38	41	50. Connecticut
Wyoming	2,922	23,799,000	51.74	43	51. Ohio
United States	1,843,076	$34,081,173,000	$135.15	21	

Rank in order

Source: U.S. Department of Defense, Directorate for Information Operations and Reports, *Atlas/Data Abstract for the United States and Selected Areas, Fiscal Year 1991* (Washington, D.C.: Government Printing Office, 1992).

State	Personnel	Payroll	Per capita	Rank by per capita
Alabama	6,266	$127,828,000	$31.26	30
Alaska	2,649	61,420,000	107.75	14
Arizona	10,188	214,154,000	57.11	21
Arkansas	2,381	71,687,000	30.22	31
California	235,118	8,361,578,000	275.23	8
Colorado	5,908	100,938,000	29.89	32
Connecticut	12,681	480,739,000	146.08	12
Delaware	988	13,746,000	20.21	40
District of Columbia	22,948	545,816,000	912.74	3
Florida	79,604	2,979,642,000	224.42	10
Georgia	18,540	484,671,000	73.18	17
Hawaii	31,830	1,143,164,000	1,007.19	1
Idaho	2,474	63,147,000	60.78	20
Illinois	35,328	578,271,000	50.10	23
Indiana	13,603	349,380,000	62.28	19
Iowa	3,326	34,816,000	12.46	47
Kansas	5,759	66,995,000	26.85	34
Kentucky	5,960	136,585,000	36.79	28
Louisiana	11,593	204,949,000	48.20	24
Maine	11,805	448,508,000	363.16	5
Maryland	37,813	1,212,335,000	249.45	9
Massachusetts	9,792	154,386,000	25.75	35
Michigan	11,524	102,624,000	10.95	50
Minnesota	5,593	66,906,000	15.10	44
Mississippi	8,560	314,455,000	121.32	13
Missouri	11,516	148,168,000	28.73	33
Montana	1,137	19,757,000	24.45	36
Nebraska	2,444	34,601,000	21.72	39
Nevada	2,801	100,648,000	78.39	16
New Hampshire	1,602	55,714,000	50.42	22
New Jersey	13,260	371,221,000	47.84	25
New Mexico	2,455	66,522,000	42.97	26
New York	21,492	245,189,000	13.58	46
North Carolina	62,270	1,279,469,000	189.92	11
North Dakota	601	5,753,000	9.06	51
Ohio	12,800	149,596,000	13.68	45
Oklahoma	3,466	73,549,000	23.17	37
Oregon	4,878	116,614,000	39.91	27
Pennsylvania	42,838	1,179,490,000	98.61	15
Rhode Island	8,960	348,522,000	347.13	6
South Carolina	33,790	1,318,604,000	370.39	4
South Dakota	656	8,150,000	11.59	49
Tennessee	17,476	354,237,000	71.52	18
Texas	30,515	601,315,000	34.66	29
Utah	2,277	30,937,000	17.48	42
Vermont	491	9,948,000	17.54	41
Virginia	122,358	5,870,149,000	933.84	2
Washington	39,181	1,559,602,000	310.80	7
West Virginia	2,050	39,883,000	22.14	38
Wisconsin	5,878	60,602,000	12.23	48
Wyoming	459	7,986,000	17.36	43
United States	**1,039,895**	**$32,374,966,000**	**$128.38**	**13**

Rank in order

By per capita

1. Hawaii
2. Virginia
3. District of Columbia
4. South Carolina
5. Maine
6. Rhode Island
7. Washington
8. California
9. Maryland
10. Florida
11. North Carolina
12. Connecticut
13. Mississippi
14. Alaska
15. Pennsylvania
16. Nevada
17. Georgia
18. Tennessee
19. Indiana
20. Idaho
21. Arizona
22. New Hampshire
23. Illinois
24. Louisiana
25. New Jersey
26. New Mexico
27. Oregon
28. Kentucky
29. Texas
30. Alabama
31. Arkansas
32. Colorado
33. Missouri
34. Kansas
35. Massachusetts
36. Montana
37. Oklahoma
38. West Virginia
39. Nebraska
40. Delaware
41. Vermont
42. Utah
43. Wyoming
44. Minnesota
45. Ohio
46. New York
47. Iowa
48. Wisconsin
49. South Dakota
50. Michigan
51. North Dakota

Source: U.S. Department of Defense, Directorate for Information Operations and Reports, *Atlas/Data Abstract for the United States and Selected Areas, Fiscal Year 1991* (Washington, D.C.: Government Printing Office, 1992).

TOTAL AIR FORCE PAYROLL, FISCAL 1991

State	Personnel	Payroll	Per capita	Rank by per capita
Alabama	13,193	$471,444,000	$115.30	27
Alaska	15,478	442,129,000	775.66	1
Arizona	22,396	777,641,000	207.37	14
Arkansas	11,706	365,438,000	154.06	21
California	96,090	3,328,771,000	109.57	29
Colorado	28,484	1,009,716,000	299.00	12
Connecticut	2,294	47,373,000	14.39	51
Delaware	9,367	209,520,000	308.12	10
District of Columbia	5,436	218,682,000	365.69	4
Florida	53,608	2,145,700,000	161.61	20
Georgia	31,827	943,531,000	142.46	23
Hawaii	10,721	312,765,000	275.56	13
Idaho	5,767	158,199,000	152.26	22
Illinois	24,044	609,012,000	52.76	36
Indiana	10,068	196,292,000	34.99	42
Iowa	3,600	62,139,000	22.23	47
Kansas	8,153	224,053,000	89.80	31
Kentucky	2,615	75,881,000	20.44	48
Louisiana	16,949	471,599,000	110.91	28
Maine	6,024	153,613,000	124.38	24
Maryland	16,963	512,731,000	105.50	30
Massachusetts	13,657	344,001,000	57.37	34
Michigan	15,708	352,891,000	37.67	40
Minnesota	6,130	106,342,000	23.99	46
Mississippi	17,130	454,363,000	175.29	19
Missouri	10,850	281,637,000	54.60	35
Montana	6,710	164,666,000	203.79	15
Nebraska	16,589	536,968,000	337.08	6
Nevada	12,004	428,122,000	333.43	7
New Hampshire	1,998	88,138,000	79.76	32
New Jersey	14,192	280,380,000	36.13	41
New Mexico	19,728	617,522,000	398.92	3
New York	23,846	514,588,000	28.50	44
North Carolina	15,048	478,113,000	70.97	33
North Dakota	12,930	289,707,000	456.23	2
Ohio	43,454	1,347,730,000	123.20	25
Oklahoma	32,679	986,793,000	310.80	9
Oregon	4,894	137,510,000	47.06	38
Pennsylvania	12,410	240,885,000	20.14	49
Rhode Island	2,126	27,733,000	27.62	45
South Carolina	21,439	626,784,000	176.06	18
South Dakota	8,856	219,923,000	312.83	8
Tennessee	6,895	210,457,000	42.49	39
Texas	94,423	3,313,489,000	190.99	17
Utah	21,974	630,114,000	356.00	5
Vermont	1,557	28,421,000	50.13	37
Virginia	25,152	1,203,373,000	191.44	16
Washington	18,341	605,210,000	120.61	26
West Virginia	3,267	57,790,000	32.09	43
Wisconsin	5,897	98,091,000	19.80	50
Wyoming	5,572	138,925,000	302.01	11
United States	**890,239**	**$27,546,895,000**	**$109.24**	**30**

Rank in order

By per capita

1. Alaska
2. North Dakota
3. New Mexico
4. District of Columbia
5. Utah
6. Nebraska
7. Nevada
8. South Dakota
9. Oklahoma
10. Delaware
11. Wyoming
12. Colorado
13. Hawaii
14. Arizona
15. Montana
16. Virginia
17. Texas
18. South Carolina
19. Mississippi
20. Florida
21. Arkansas
22. Idaho
23. Georgia
24. Maine
25. Ohio
26. Washington
27. Alabama
28. Louisiana
29. California
30. Maryland
31. Kansas
32. New Hampshire
33. North Carolina
34. Massachusetts
35. Missouri
36. Illinois
37. Vermont
38. Oregon
39. Tennessee
40. Michigan
41. New Jersey
42. Indiana
43. West Virginia
44. New York
45. Rhode Island
46. Minnesota
47. Iowa
48. Kentucky
49. Pennsylvania
50. Wisconsin
51. Connecticut

Source: U.S. Department of Defense, Directorate for Information Operations and Reports, *Atlas/Data Abstract for the United States and Selected Areas, Fiscal Year 1991* (Washington, D.C.: Government Printing Office, 1992).

State	Personnel	Payroll	Per capita	Rank by per capita
Alabama	18,562	$570,964,000	$139.63	29
Alaska	23,302	599,946,000	1,052.54	2
Arizona	23,802	596,828,000	159.15	26
Arkansas	8,748	231,111,000	97.43	33
California	188,702	6,259,825,000	206.05	18
Colorado	38,662	1,019,315,000	301.84	8
Connecticut	7,031	302,245,000	91.84	34
Delaware	4,509	108,299,000	159.26	25
District of Columbia	13,904	454,263,000	759.64	3
Florida	75,029	2,474,259,000	186.36	20
Georgia	60,018	1,657,422,000	250.25	13
Hawaii	42,869	1,341,581,000	1,182.01	1
Idaho	4,373	110,151,000	106.02	31
Illinois	31,817	759,965,000	65.84	36
Indiana	5,575	179,757,000	32.04	42
Iowa	421	15,565,000	5.57	51
Kansas	24,421	719,649,000	288.44	10
Kentucky	38,671	1,079,178,000	290.65	9
Louisiana	26,417	725,758,000	170.69	23
Maine	5,338	195,684,000	158.45	27
Maryland	32,692	888,821,000	182.88	21
Massachusetts	8,481	257,144,000	42.89	38
Michigan	8,275	200,448,000	21.40	44
Minnesota	1,019	33,664,000	7.60	49
Mississippi	12,837	379,854,000	146.55	28
Missouri	14,126	406,643,000	78.84	35
Montana	4,447	99,753,000	123.46	30
Nebraska	12,574	379,118,000	237.99	14
Nevada	9,642	267,673,000	208.47	17
New Hampshire	320	23,453,000	21.22	45
New Jersey	11,343	356,671,000	45.96	37
New Mexico	15,263	390,367,000	252.18	12
New York	24,947	734,432,000	40.67	40
North Carolina	98,044	2,415,029,000	358.47	6
North Dakota	10,016	224,599,000	353.70	7
Ohio	11,657	392,714,000	35.90	41
Oklahoma	26,177	737,820,000	232.38	16
Oregon	1,112	36,140,000	12.37	46
Pennsylvania	5,936	305,898,000	25.57	43
Rhode Island	3,642	165,577,000	164.92	24
South Carolina	38,279	1,314,030,000	369.11	5
South Dakota	6,745	163,723,000	232.89	15
Tennessee	9,261	211,628,000	42.73	39
Texas	112,490	3,082,821,000	177.69	22
Utah	6,145	174,440,000	98.55	32
Vermont	148	5,332,000	9.40	48
Virginia	94,018	4,626,840,000	736.05	4
Washington	36,391	1,306,215,000	260.31	11
West Virginia	640	21,269,000	11.81	47
Wisconsin	974	28,025,000	5.66	50
Wyoming	3,630	86,490,000	188.02	19
United States	1,263,455	$39,118,396,000	$155.12	28

By per capita

1. Hawaii
2. Alaska
3. District of Columbia
4. Virginia
5. South Carolina
6. North Carolina
7. North Dakota
8. Colorado
9. Kentucky
10. Kansas
11. Washington
12. New Mexico
13. Georgia
14. Nebraska
15. South Dakota
16. Oklahoma
17. Nevada
18. California
19. Wyoming
20. Florida
21. Maryland
22. Texas
23. Louisiana
24. Rhode Island
25. Delaware
26. Arizona
27. Maine
28. Mississippi
29. Alabama
30. Montana
31. Idaho
32. Utah
33. Arkansas
34. Connecticut
35. Missouri
36. Illinois
37. New Jersey
38. Massachusetts
39. Tennessee
40. New York
41. Ohio
42. Indiana
43. Pennsylvania
44. Michigan
45. New Hampshire
46. Oregon
47. West Virginia
48. Vermont
49. Minnesota
50. Wisconsin
51. Iowa

Source: U.S. Department of Defense, Directorate for Information Operations and Reports, *Atlas/Data Abstract for the United States and Selected Areas, Fiscal Year 1991* (Washington, D.C.: Government Printing Office, 1992).

ARMY ACTIVE-DUTY PAYROLL, FISCAL 1991

State	Personnel	Payroll	Per capita	Rank by per capita
Alabama	12,985	$379,895,000	$92.91	14
Alaska	9,849	251,349,000	440.96	2
Arizona	6,331	177,933,000	47.45	18
Arkansas	1,235	37,476,000	15.80	26
California	26,909	742,199,000	24.43	19
Colorado	19,988	579,350,000	171.56	8
Connecticut	64	2,492,000	0.76	49
Delaware	53	2,397,000	3.53	34
District of Columbia	5,353	160,318,000	268.09	4
Florida	2,434	107,736,000	8.11	27
Georgia	47,154	1,273,715,000	192.32	7
Hawaii	18,876	531,098,000	467.93	1
Idaho	42	898,000	0.86	47
Illinois	2,068	71,798,000	6.22	28
Indiana	2,365	99,183,000	17.68	25
Iowa	196	8,434,000	3.02	36
Kansas	20,414	611,183,000	244.96	5
Kentucky	37,959	1,060,108,000	285.51	3
Louisiana	15,740	429,246,000	100.95	12
Maine	226	6,835,000	5.53	30
Maryland	10,609	310,554,000	63.90	16
Massachusetts	4,664	135,843,000	22.66	22
Michigan	680	20,352,000	2.17	41
Minnesota	384	13,605,000	3.07	35
Mississippi	282	10,353,000	3.99	33
Missouri	9,640	290,626,000	56.34	17
Montana	9	302,000	0.37	51
Nebraska	81	3,900,000	2.45	38
Nevada	23	931,000	0.73	50
New Hampshire	18	858,000	0.78	48
New Jersey	5,354	156,456,000	20.16	24
New Mexico	1,144	37,026,000	23.92	21
New York	14,075	436,455,000	24.17	20
North Carolina	42,271	1,395,387,000	207.12	6
North Dakota	23	939,000	1.48	45
Ohio	937	26,464,000	2.42	39
Oklahoma	14,114	418,614,000	131.85	10
Oregon	297	5,085,000	1.74	43
Pennsylvania	1,865	67,823,000	5.67	29
Rhode Island	88	2,850,000	2.84	37
South Carolina	9,708	279,933,000	78.63	15
South Dakota	30	1,184,000	1.68	44
Tennessee	576	22,125,000	4.47	32
Texas	57,790	1,644,168,000	94.77	13
Utah	813	40,098,000	22.65	23
Vermont	28	1,189,000	2.10	42
Virginia	28,675	1,068,235,000	169.94	9
Washington	18,878	513,119,000	102.26	11
West Virginia	250	9,685,000	5.38	31
Wisconsin	337	11,316,000	2.28	40
Wyoming	12	541,000	1.18	46
United States	**453,896**	**$13,459,659,000**	**$53.37**	**18**

Rank in order

By per capita

1. Hawaii
2. Alaska
3. Kentucky
4. District of Columbia
5. Kansas
6. North Carolina
7. Georgia
8. Colorado
9. Virginia
10. Oklahoma
11. Washington
12. Louisiana
13. Texas
14. Alabama
15. South Carolina
16. Maryland
17. Missouri
18. Arizona
19. California
20. New York
21. New Mexico
22. Massachusetts
23. Utah
24. New Jersey
25. Indiana
26. Arkansas
27. Florida
28. Illinois
29. Pennsylvania
30. Maine
31. West Virginia
32. Tennessee
33. Mississippi
34. Delaware
35. Minnesota
36. Iowa
37. Rhode Island
38. Nebraska
39. Ohio
40. Wisconsin
41. Michigan
42. Vermont
43. Oregon
44. South Dakota
45. North Dakota
46. Wyoming
47. Idaho
48. New Hampshire
49. Connecticut
50. Nevada
51. Montana

Source: U.S. Department of Defense, Directorate for Information Operations and Reports, *Atlas/Data Abstract for the United States and Selected Areas, Fiscal Year 1991* (Washington, D.C.: Government Printing Office, 1992).

NAVY/MARINE CORPS ACTIVE-DUTY PAYROLL. FISCAL 1991

State	Personnel	Payroll	Per capita	Rank by per capita
Alabama	829	$29,895,000	$7.31	28
Alaska	1,932	44,925,000	78.82	12
Arizona	5,380	86,524,000	23.07	19
Arkansas	250	5,991,000	2.53	40
California	116,918	4,256,510,000	140.11	6
Colorado	921	25,149,000	7.45	27
Connecticut	6,859	295,319,000	89.74	11
Delaware	31	855,000	1.26	45
District of Columbia	4,786	146,383,000	244.79	3
Florida	39,279	1,504,908,000	113.35	8
Georgia	5,188	177,703,000	26.83	18
Hawaii	18,498	642,644,000	566.21	1
Idaho	1,193	28,998,000	27.91	17
Illinois	19,758	400,851,000	34.73	16
Indiana	552	14,916,000	2.66	37
Iowa	83	2,227,000	0.80	47
Kansas	324	11,198,000	4.49	34
Kentucky	386	9,748,000	2.63	38
Louisiana	1,843	62,776,000	14.76	22
Maine	1,850	111,320,000	90.14	10
Maryland	15,453	362,929,000	74.68	13
Massachusetts	1,106	33,733,000	5.63	31
Michigan	717	18,198,000	1.94	43
Minnesota	400	11,402,000	2.57	39
Mississippi	3,270	139,693,000	53.89	14
Missouri	834	27,960,000	5.42	32
Montana	15	466,000	0.58	49
Nebraska	359	10,415,000	6.54	29
Nevada	960	22,968,000	17.89	21
New Hampshire	148	9,724,000	8.80	26
New Jersey	1,375	82,427,000	10.62	24
New Mexico	518	13,816,000	8.93	25
New York	3,250	91,419,000	5.06	33
North Carolina	46,581	789,024,000	117.12	7
North Dakota	9	391,000	0.62	48
Ohio	956	26,158,000	2.39	41
Oklahoma	462	10,943,000	3.45	36
Oregon	426	18,038,000	6.17	30
Pennsylvania	3,515	217,402,000	18.18	20
Rhode Island	3,409	157,068,000	156.44	5
South Carolina	15,515	704,690,000	197.95	4
South Dakota	7	231,000	0.33	50
Tennessee	8,182	172,451,000	34.82	15
Texas	6,563	190,415,000	10.98	23
Utah	135	3,819,000	2.16	42
Vermont	16	640,000	1.13	46
Virginia	50,341	2,990,878,000	475.80	2
Washington	8,881	566,506,000	112.89	9
West Virginia	246	7,201,000	4.00	35
Wisconsin	354	7,678,000	1.55	44
Wyoming	2	77,000	0.17	51
United States	400,878	$14,547,600,000	$57.69	14

Rank in order

By per capita

1. Hawaii
2. Virginia
3. District of Columbia
4. South Carolina
5. Rhode Island
6. California
7. North Carolina
8. Florida
9. Washington
10. Maine
11. Connecticut
12. Alaska
13. Maryland
14. Mississippi
15. Tennessee
16. Illinois
17. Idaho
18. Georgia
19. Arizona
20. Pennsylvania
21. Nevada
22. Louisiana
23. Texas
24. New Jersey
25. New Mexico
26. New Hampshire
27. Colorado
28. Alabama
29. Nebraska
30. Oregon
31. Massachusetts
32. Missouri
33. New York
34. Kansas
35. West Virginia
36. Oklahoma
37. Indiana
38. Kentucky
39. Minnesota
40. Arkansas
41. Ohio
42. Utah
43. Michigan
44. Wisconsin
45. Delaware
46. Vermont
47. Iowa
48. North Dakota
49. Montana
50. South Dakota
51. Wyoming

Source: U.S. Department of Defense, Directorate for Information Operations and Reports, *Atlas/Data Abstract for the United States and Selected Areas, Fiscal Year 1991* (Washington, D.C.: Government Printing Office, 1992).

	AIR FORCE ACTIVE-DUTY PAYROLL, FISCAL 1991				Rank in order

State	Personnel	Payroll	Per capita	Rank by per capita	By per capita
Alabama	4,748	$161,174,000	$39.42	28	1. Alaska
Alaska	11,521	303,672,000	532.76	1	2. North Dakota
Arizona	12,091	332,371,000	88.63	17	3. District of Columbia
Arkansas	7,263	187,644,000	79.11	18	4. South Dakota
California	44,875	1,261,116,000	41.51	27	5. Nebraska
Colorado	17,753	414,816,000	122.84	11	6. New Mexico
Connecticut	108	4,434,000	1.35	51	7. Nevada
Delaware	4,425	105,047,000	154.48	9	8. Wyoming
District of Columbia	3,765	147,562,000	246.76	3	9. Delaware
Florida	33,316	861,615,000	64.90	22	10. Hawaii
Georgia	7,676	206,004,000	31.10	31	11. Colorado
Hawaii	5,495	167,839,000	147.88	10	12. Montana
Idaho	3,138	80,255,000	77.24	19	13. Oklahoma
Illinois	9,991	287,316,000	24.89	33	14. South Carolina
Indiana	2,658	65,658,000	11.70	38	15. Virginia
Iowa	142	4,904,000	1.75	49	16. Mississippi
Kansas	3,683	97,268,000	38.99	29	17. Arizona
Kentucky	326	9,322,000	2.51	45	18. Arkansas
Louisiana	8,834	233,736,000	54.97	24	19. Idaho
Maine	3,262	77,529,000	62.78	23	20. Utah
Maryland	6,630	215,338,000	44.31	26	21. Texas
Massachusetts	2,711	87,568,000	14.60	37	22. Florida
Michigan	6,878	161,898,000	17.28	34	23. Maine
Minnesota	235	8,657,000	1.95	47	24. Louisiana
Mississippi	9,285	229,808,000	88.66	16	25. Washington
Missouri	3,652	88,057,000	17.07	35	26. Maryland
Montana	4,423	98,985,000	122.51	12	27. California
Nebraska	12,134	364,803,000	229.00	5	28. Alabama
Nevada	8,659	243,774,000	189.86	7	29. Kansas
New Hampshire	154	12,871,000	11.65	39	30. North Carolina
New Jersey	4,614	117,788,000	15.18	36	31. Georgia
New Mexico	13,601	339,525,000	219.33	6	32. Ohio
New York	7,622	206,558,000	11.44	40	33. Illinois
North Carolina	9,192	230,618,000	34.23	30	34. Michigan
North Dakota	9,984	223,269,000	351.60	2	35. Missouri
Ohio	9,764	340,092,000	31.09	32	36. New Jersey
Oklahoma	11,601	308,263,000	97.09	13	37. Massachusetts
Oregon	389	13,017,000	4.45	43	38. Indiana
Pennsylvania	556	20,673,000	1.73	50	39. New Hampshire
Rhode Island	145	5,659,000	5.64	42	40. New York
South Carolina	13,056	329,407,000	92.53	14	41. Vermont
South Dakota	6,708	162,308,000	230.88	4	42. Rhode Island
Tennessee	503	17,052,000	3.44	44	43. Oregon
Texas	48,137	1,248,238,000	71.95	21	44. Tennessee
Utah	5,197	130,523,000	73.74	20	45. Kentucky
Vermont	104	3,503,000	6.18	41	46. West Virginia
Virginia	15,002	567,727,000	90.32	15	47. Minnesota
Washington	8,632	226,590,000	45.16	25	48. Wisconsin
West Virginia	144	4,383,000	2.43	46	49. Iowa
Wisconsin	283	9,031,000	1.82	48	50. Pennsylvania
Wyoming	3,616	85,872,000	186.68	8	51. Connecticut
United States	408,681	$11,111,137,000	$44.06	27	

Source: U.S. Department of Defense, Directorate for Information Operations and Reports, *Atlas/Data Abstract for the United States and Selected Areas, Fiscal Year 1991* (Washington, D.C.: Government Printing Office, 1992).

State	Personnel	Payroll	Per capita	Rank by per capita
Alabama	26,003	$782,396,000	$191.34	10
Alaska	4,914	199,657,000	350.28	5
Arizona	9,884	400,335,000	106.76	22
Arkansas	4,896	138,004,000	58.18	35
California	121,289	4,170,352,000	137.27	15
Colorado	13,641	397,983,000	117.85	19
Connecticut	5,009	178,118,000	54.12	37
Delaware	1,780	48,282,000	71.00	31
District of Columbia	17,093	632,731,000	1,058.08	1
Florida	32,396	1,030,361,000	77.60	29
Georgia	37,270	1,078,027,000	162.77	13
Hawaii	18,978	665,950,000	586.74	3
Idaho	1,443	36,732,000	35.35	44
Illinois	19,895	577,050,000	49.99	38
Indiana	15,284	496,984,000	88.59	25
Iowa	1,454	44,988,000	16.10	51
Kansas	6,827	196,057,000	78.58	28
Kentucky	14,195	404,310,000	108.89	21
Louisiana	9,247	258,664,000	60.83	34
Maine	9,333	314,721,000	254.83	7
Maryland	41,860	1,650,173,000	339.54	6
Massachusetts	11,715	374,627,000	62.48	33
Michigan	11,735	387,701,000	41.39	42
Minnesota	2,957	90,210,000	20.35	49
Mississippi	11,279	340,408,000	131.33	17
Missouri	18,655	627,312,000	121.62	18
Montana	1,243	37,840,000	46.83	39
Nebraska	4,031	126,325,000	79.30	27
Nevada	1,924	56,182,000	43.76	41
New Hampshire	1,376	50,907,000	46.07	40
New Jersey	25,753	847,050,000	109.16	20
New Mexico	9,681	311,488,000	201.22	9
New York	17,758	567,595,000	31.43	47
North Carolina	17,527	492,649,000	73.13	30
North Dakota	1,891	52,860,000	83.24	26
Ohio	35,378	1,167,190,000	106.70	23
Oklahoma	22,030	672,802,000	211.91	8
Oregon	2,943	99,657,000	34.11	45
Pennsylvania	50,502	1,584,999,000	132.51	16
Rhode Island	4,284	151,361,000	150.76	14
South Carolina	19,133	580,977,000	163.20	12
South Dakota	1,369	39,370,000	56.00	36
Tennessee	7,894	180,858,000	36.51	43
Texas	56,710	1,616,661,000	93.18	24
Utah	19,747	631,533,000	356.80	4
Vermont	645	18,457,000	32.55	46
Virginia	105,167	3,962,697,000	630.40	2
Washington	28,757	948,560,000	189.03	11
West Virginia	1,747	50,302,000	27.93	48
Wisconsin	3,553	97,862,000	19.75	50
Wyoming	1,100	32,443,000	70.53	32
United States	911,175	$29,900,758,000	$118.57	19

By per capita

1. District of Columbia
2. Virginia
3. Hawaii
4. Utah
5. Alaska
6. Maryland
7. Maine
8. Oklahoma
9. New Mexico
10. Alabama
11. Washington
12. South Carolina
13. Georgia
14. Rhode Island
15. California
16. Pennsylvania
17. Mississippi
18. Missouri
19. Colorado
20. New Jersey
21. Kentucky
22. Arizona
23. Ohio
24. Texas
25. Indiana
26. North Dakota
27. Nebraska
28. Kansas
29. Florida
30. North Carolina
31. Delaware
32. Wyoming
33. Massachusetts
34. Louisiana
35. Arkansas
36. South Dakota
37. Connecticut
38. Illinois
39. Montana
40. New Hampshire
41. Nevada
42. Michigan
43. Tennessee
44. Idaho
45. Oregon
46. Vermont
47. New York
48. West Virginia
49. Minnesota
50. Wisconsin
51. Iowa

Source: U.S. Department of Defense, Directorate for Information Operations and Reports, *Atlas/Data Abstract for the United States and Selected Areas, Fiscal Year 1991* (Washington, D.C.: Government Printing Office, 1992).

State	Personnel	Payroll	Per capita	Rank by per capita		Rank in order By per capita
Alabama	22,072	$666,205,000	$162.93	4		1. District of Columbia
Alaska	2,614	100,127,000	175.66	2		2. Alaska
Arizona	4,696	245,282,000	65.41	12		3. Virginia
Arkansas	3,533	100,846,000	42.52	18		4. Alabama
California	14,230	447,727,000	14.74	37		5. Maryland
Colorado	4,970	150,282,000	44.50	17		6. Hawaii
Connecticut	632	17,325,000	5.26	48		7. New Mexico
Delaware	245	6,713,000	9.87	43		8. Utah
District of Columbia	6,540	189,459,000	316.82	1		9. Missouri
Florida	1,985	54,007,000	4.07	51		10. Kentucky
Georgia	15,300	424,110,000	64.04	13		11. New Jersey
Hawaii	5,148	148,885,000	131.18	6		12. Arizona
Idaho	559	14,289,000	13.75	42		13. Georgia
Illinois	11,441	320,487,000	27.76	24		14. Kansas
Indiana	3,212	105,921,000	18.88	32		15. Mississippi
Iowa	796	24,961,000	8.93	45		16. Oklahoma
Kansas	5,147	145,925,000	58.49	14		17. Colorado
Kentucky	9,632	272,732,000	73.45	10		18. Arkansas
Louisiana	4,711	133,868,000	31.48	23		19. Pennsylvania
Maine	340	8,364,000	6.77	47		20. Nebraska
Maryland	17,050	712,190,000	146.54	5		21. Texas
Massachusetts	5,069	143,762,000	23.98	28		22. Washington
Michigan	7,513	239,861,000	25.60	26		23. Louisiana
Minnesota	1,565	43,694,000	9.86	44		24. Illinois
Mississippi	5,051	149,617,000	57.72	15		25. North Carolina
Missouri	11,980	401,569,000	77.85	9		26. Michigan
Montana	391	11,618,000	14.38	38		27. Oregon
Nebraska	1,879	60,533,000	38.00	20		28. Massachusetts
Nevada	220	6,334,000	4.93	50		29. South Carolina
New Hampshire	561	18,419,000	16.67	34		30. West Virginia
New Jersey	15,973	537,798,000	69.30	11		31. South Dakota
New Mexico	4,920	166,246,000	107.39	7		32. Indiana
New York	9,926	317,107,000	17.56	33		33. New York
North Carolina	6,990	184,500,000	27.39	25		34. New Hampshire
North Dakota	383	10,187,000	16.04	35		35. North Dakota
Ohio	1,981	55,755,000	5.10	49		36. Tennessee
Oklahoma	5,806	163,626,000	51.54	16		37. California
Oregon	2,167	73,578,000	25.18	27		38. Montana
Pennsylvania	13,694	472,445,000	39.50	19		39. Vermont
Rhode Island	314	7,938,000	7.91	46		40. Wyoming
South Carolina	3,176	76,193,000	21.40	29		41. Wisconsin
South Dakota	532	14,889,000	21.18	31		42. Idaho
Tennessee	2,840	79,398,000	16.03	36		43. Delaware
Texas	23,833	629,782,000	36.30	21		44. Minnesota
Utah	5,143	165,436,000	93.47	8		45. Iowa
Vermont	313	7,939,000	14.00	39		46. Rhode Island
Virginia	28,667	1,044,460,000	166.16	3		47. Maine
Washington	6,012	163,586,000	32.60	22		48. Connecticut
West Virginia	1,288	38,344,000	21.29	30		49. Ohio
Wisconsin	2,541	68,332,000	13.79	41		50. Nevada
Wyoming	238	6,393,000	13.90	40		51. Florida
United States	**305,819**	**$9,649,044,000**	**$38.26**	**20**		

Source: U.S. Department of Defense, Directorate for Information Operations and Reports, *Atlas/Data Abstract for the United States and Selected Areas, Fiscal Year 1991* (Washington, D.C.: Government Printing Office, 1992).

State	Personnel	Payroll	Per capita	Rank by per capita
Alabama	72	$1,816,000	$0.44	39
Alaska	221	9,050,000	15.88	19
Arizona	442	13,299,000	3.55	27
Arkansas	10	279,000	0.12	45
California	70,846	2,530,443,000	83.29	9
Colorado	24	891,000	0.26	40
Connecticut	2,941	109,993,000	33.42	15
Delaware	10	334,000	0.49	38
District of Columbia	8,905	369,185,000	617.37	1
Florida	19,152	623,606,000	46.97	12
Georgia	5,001	140,680,000	21.24	18
Hawaii	11,423	428,351,000	377.40	2
Idaho	62	2,028,000	1.95	30
Illinois	2,139	58,383,000	5.06	24
Indiana	7,689	275,970,000	49.19	11
Iowa	6	149,000	0.05	48
Kansas	144	4,078,000	1.63	31
Kentucky	2,640	84,232,000	22.69	17
Louisiana	1,986	55,529,000	13.06	20
Maine	8,097	280,803,000	227.37	4
Maryland	16,462	632,207,000	130.08	7
Massachusetts	702	24,359,000	4.06	26
Michigan	91	2,437,000	0.26	40
Minnesota	38	1,084,000	0.24	42
Mississippi	3,061	103,682,000	40.00	13
Missouri	472	17,839,000	3.46	28
Montana	2	66,000	0.08	46
Nebraska	15	372,000	0.23	43
Nevada	337	9,310,000	7.25	22
New Hampshire	315	13,707,000	12.40	21
New Jersey	6,467	205,117,000	26.43	16
New Mexico	222	7,752,000	5.01	25
New York	722	23,559,000	1.30	33
North Carolina	7,818	236,077,000	35.04	14
North Dakota	1	52,000	0.08	46
Ohio	224	15,972,000	1.46	32
Oklahoma	111	3,228,000	1.02	35
Oregon	20	573,000	0.20	44
Pennsylvania	22,210	771,435,000	64.50	10
Rhode Island	3,633	134,862,000	134.32	6
South Carolina	12,922	426,389,000	119.77	8
South Dakota	0	0	0.00	50
Tennessee	1,118	31,284,000	6.32	23
Texas	1,959	57,675,000	3.32	29
Utah	44	1,835,000	1.04	34
Vermont	1	18,000	0.03	49
Virginia	57,012	2,059,173,000	327.58	3
Washington	19,867	698,012,000	139.10	5
West Virginia	43	1,297,000	0.72	36
Wisconsin	79	2,701,000	0.55	37
Wyoming	0	0	0.00	50
United States	297,778	$10,471,173,000	$41.52	13

By per capita

1. District of Columbia
2. Hawaii
3. Virginia
4. Maine
5. Washington
6. Rhode Island
7. Maryland
8. South Carolina
9. California
10. Pennsylvania
11. Indiana
12. Florida
13. Mississippi
14. North Carolina
15. Connecticut
16. New Jersey
17. Kentucky
18. Georgia
19. Alaska
20. Louisiana
21. New Hampshire
22. Nevada
23. Tennessee
24. Illinois
25. New Mexico
26. Massachusetts
27. Arizona
28. Missouri
29. Texas
30. Idaho
31. Kansas
32. Ohio
33. New York
34. Utah
35. Oklahoma
36. West Virginia
37. Wisconsin
38. Delaware
39. Alabama
40. Colorado
    Michigan
42. Minnesota
43. Nebraska
44. Oregon
45. Arkansas
46. Montana
    North Dakota
48. Iowa
49. Vermont
50. South Dakota
    Wyoming

Source: U.S. Department of Defense, Directorate for Information Operations and Reports, *Atlas/Data Abstract for the United States and Selected Areas, Fiscal Year 1991* (Washington, D.C.: Government Printing Office, 1992).

| AIR FORCE CIVILIAN PAYROLL, FISCAL 1991 | | | | | Rank in order |
State	Personnel	Payroll	Per capita	Rank by per capita	By per capita
Alabama	3,070	$91,642,000	$22.41	25	1. Utah
Alaska	2,028	89,242,000	156.56	3	2. Oklahoma
Arizona	4,036	115,959,000	30.92	19	3. Alaska
Arkansas	1,287	34,773,000	14.66	30	4. District of Columbia
California	25,045	880,326,000	28.98	21	5. New Mexico
Colorado	5,819	174,683,000	51.73	11	6. Hawaii
Connecticut	262	8,072,000	2.45	50	7. Georgia
Delaware	1,500	40,456,000	59.49	10	8. Ohio
District of Columbia	1,234	52,669,000	88.08	4	9. North Dakota
Florida	9,754	299,885,000	22.59	23	10. Delaware
Georgia	15,353	474,805,000	71.69	7	11. Colorado
Hawaii	2,199	82,271,000	72.49	6	12. Wyoming
Idaho	809	19,993,000	19.24	26	13. Texas
Illinois	4,979	151,324,000	13.11	34	14. Nebraska
Indiana	1,347	38,775,000	6.91	41	15. Virginia
Iowa	520	15,407,000	5.51	45	16. South Dakota
Kansas	1,215	35,037,000	14.04	31	17. Montana
Kentucky	217	6,898,000	1.86	51	18. Mississippi
Louisiana	2,214	59,246,000	13.93	32	19. Arizona
Maine	823	23,330,000	18.89	27	20. Nevada
Maryland	3,123	109,263,000	22.48	24	21. California
Massachusetts	3,966	141,733,000	23.64	22	22. Massachusetts
Michigan	2,237	83,200,000	8.88	36	23. Florida
Minnesota	827	26,622,000	6.01	42	24. Maryland
Mississippi	2,971	80,216,000	30.95	18	25. Alabama
Missouri	1,367	41,529,000	8.05	38	26. Idaho
Montana	830	25,638,000	31.73	17	27. Maine
Nebraska	2,102	64,016,000	40.19	14	28. South Carolina
Nevada	1,322	38,928,000	30.32	20	29. Vermont
New Hampshire	327	12,290,000	11.12	35	30. Arkansas
New Jersey	2,018	57,485,000	7.41	40	31. Kansas
New Mexico	3,999	121,856,000	78.72	5	32. Louisiana
New York	4,752	144,430,000	8.00	39	33. Washington
North Carolina	1,310	34,850,000	5.17	47	34. Illinois
North Dakota	1,474	41,787,000	65.81	9	35. New Hampshire
Ohio	19,655	746,021,000	68.20	8	36. Michigan
Oklahoma	15,915	500,278,000	157.57	2	37. Oregon
Oregon	713	23,923,000	8.19	37	38. Missouri
Pennsylvania	1,562	45,905,000	3.84	49	39. New York
Rhode Island	258	5,798,000	5.77	44	40. New Jersey
South Carolina	2,509	64,934,000	18.24	28	41. Indiana
South Dakota	820	23,978,000	34.11	16	42. Minnesota
Tennessee	1,041	29,637,000	5.98	43	43. Tennessee
Texas	28,969	863,569,000	49.78	13	44. Rhode Island
Utah	12,500	413,957,000	233.87	1	45. Iowa
Vermont	272	8,381,000	14.78	29	46. West Virginia
Virginia	4,294	246,594,000	39.23	15	47. North Carolina
Washington	2,287	66,591,000	13.27	33	48. Wisconsin
West Virginia	387	9,865,000	5.48	46	49. Pennsylvania
Wisconsin	798	22,541,000	4.55	48	50. Connecticut
Wyoming	786	23,405,000	50.88	12	51. Kentucky
United States	209,102	$6,814,013,000	$27.02	22	

Source: U.S. Department of Defense, Directorate for Information Operations and Reports, *Atlas/Data Abstract for the United States and Selected Areas, Fiscal Year 1991* (Washington, D.C.: Government Printing Office, 1992).

TOTAL RESERVE AND NATIONAL GUARD PAYROLL, FISCAL 1991

State	Personnel	Payroll	Per capita	Rank by per capita
Alabama	48,407	$191,170,000	$46.75	7
Alaska	7,693	31,340,000	54.98	2
Arizona	24,039	72,190,000	19.25	38
Arkansas	23,996	67,102,000	28.29	22
California	142,222	372,214,000	12.25	47
Colorado	23,160	161,594,000	47.85	6
Connecticut	16,073	38,985,000	11.85	48
Delaware	8,483	35,644,000	52.42	4
District of Columbia	15,164	54,152,000	90.56	1
Florida	69,973	141,317,000	10.64	51
Georgia	48,872	244,140,000	36.86	12
Hawaii	13,398	44,736,000	39.41	10
Idaho	9,261	29,204,000	28.11	23
Illinois	62,638	157,065,000	13.61	44
Indiana	41,907	160,480,000	28.61	21
Iowa	23,030	54,632,000	19.55	37
Kansas	23,912	123,862,000	49.64	5
Kentucky	26,068	93,128,000	25.08	27
Louisiana	38,022	98,307,000	23.12	30
Maine	10,477	27,595,000	22.34	33
Maryland	38,407	140,937,000	29.00	20
Massachusetts	39,353	136,003,000	22.68	31
Michigan	48,313	102,880,000	10.98	50
Minnesota	35,119	96,801,000	21.84	34
Mississippi	26,937	81,991,000	31.63	17
Missouri	42,625	167,232,000	32.42	14
Montana	8,659	25,770,000	31.89	16
Nebraska	13,891	35,597,000	22.35	32
Nevada	7,365	17,399,000	13.55	45
New Hampshire	7,862	20,200,000	18.28	41
New Jersey	36,036	143,175,000	18.45	40
New Mexico	11,921	36,459,000	23.55	29
New York	87,522	203,181,000	11.25	49
North Carolina	43,220	112,700,000	16.73	43
North Dakota	7,954	24,670,000	38.85	11
Ohio	65,339	147,286,000	13.46	46
Oklahoma	27,865	113,840,000	35.86	13
Oregon	21,730	54,532,000	18.66	39
Pennsylvania	80,397	298,845,000	24.98	28
Rhode Island	8,730	26,829,000	26.72	24
South Carolina	36,038	140,399,000	39.44	9
South Dakota	7,811	21,608,000	30.74	18
Tennessee	40,779	104,462,000	21.09	35
Texas	103,212	299,381,000	17.26	42
Utah	17,891	94,182,000	53.21	3
Vermont	6,398	22,383,000	39.48	8
Virginia	52,384	160,245,000	25.49	26
Washington	41,405	128,895,000	25.69	25
West Virginia	14,793	36,398,000	20.21	36
Wisconsin	36,006	159,648,000	32.22	15
Wyoming	4,299	13,657,000	29.69	19
United States	**1,697,056**	**$536,644,200**	**$21.28**	**35**

Rank in order

By per capita

1. District of Columbia
2. Alaska
3. Utah
4. Delaware
5. Kansas
6. Colorado
7. Alabama
8. Vermont
9. South Carolina
10. Hawaii
11. North Dakota
12. Georgia
13. Oklahoma
14. Missouri
15. Wisconsin
16. Montana
17. Mississippi
18. South Dakota
19. Wyoming
20. Maryland
21. Indiana
22. Arkansas
23. Idaho
24. Rhode Island
25. Washington
26. Virginia
27. Kentucky
28. Pennsylvania
29. New Mexico
30. Louisiana
31. Massachusetts
32. Nebraska
33. Maine
34. Minnesota
35. Tennessee
36. West Virginia
37. Iowa
38. Arizona
39. Oregon
40. New Jersey
41. New Hampshire
42. Texas
43. North Carolina
44. Illinois
45. Nevada
46. Ohio
47. California
48. Connecticut
49. New York
50. Michigan
51. Florida

Source: U.S. Department of Defense, Directorate for Information Operations and Reports, *Atlas/Data Abstract for the United States and Selected Areas, Fiscal Year 1991* (Washington, D.C.: Government Printing Office, 1992).

State	Personnel	Payroll	Per capita	Rank by per capita
Alabama	37,667	$158,056,000	$38.65	4
Alaska	5,268	22,820,000	40.04	3
Arizona	13,404	43,784,000	11.68	40
Arkansas	18,719	51,440,000	21.69	19
California	68,698	183,634,000	6.04	50
Colorado	13,285	54,010,000	15.99	28
Connecticut	11,268	30,090,000	9.14	44
Delaware	4,094	13,224,000	19.45	21
District of Columbia	5,470	35,761,000	59.80	1
Florida	38,262	68,064,000	5.13	51
Georgia	31,723	193,403,000	29.20	6
Hawaii	8,462	31,586,000	27.83	10
Idaho	6,222	21,129,000	20.34	20
Illinois	40,133	99,918,000	8.66	45
Indiana	30,482	128,151,000	22.84	14
Iowa	16,855	38,103,000	13.63	34
Kansas	15,366	95,957,000	38.46	5
Kentucky	21,062	82,370,000	22.18	16
Louisiana	24,357	57,462,000	13.51	35
Maine	6,680	17,028,000	13.79	33
Maryland	25,299	87,592,000	18.02	24
Massachusetts	24,389	87,307,000	14.56	31
Michigan	31,004	63,866,000	6.82	49
Minnesota	24,896	64,014,000	14.44	32
Mississippi	19,834	56,312,000	21.73	17
Missouri	26,584	129,074,000	25.02	13
Montana	6,082	17,543,000	21.71	18
Nebraska	9,468	24,835,000	15.59	29
Nevada	3,838	9,153,000	7.13	46
New Hampshire	5,206	13,148,000	11.90	39
New Jersey	23,058	100,922,000	13.01	36
New Mexico	8,078	27,533,000	17.79	25
New York	58,530	126,250,000	6.99	48
North Carolina	30,803	83,190,000	12.35	38
North Dakota	5,891	17,215,000	27.11	11
Ohio	39,684	77,862,000	7.12	47
Oklahoma	19,809	88,630,000	27.91	9
Oregon	13,506	31,864,000	10.90	43
Pennsylvania	52,992	223,444,000	18.68	23
Rhode Island	5,089	16,686,000	16.62	27
South Carolina	24,811	102,769,000	28.87	7
South Dakota	5,834	15,724,000	22.37	15
Tennessee	27,252	61,748,000	12.47	37
Texas	63,902	192,508,000	11.10	42
Utah	11,516	71,575,000	40.44	2
Vermont	4,743	16,339,000	28.82	8
Virginia	31,523	119,266,000	18.97	22
Washington	23,550	76,346,000	15.21	30
West Virginia	10,296	20,544,000	11.41	41
Wisconsin	25,745	130,348,000	26.31	12
Wyoming	2,672	7,840,000	17.04	26
United States	1,083,361	$3,587,437,000	$14.23	33

ARMY RESERVE AND NATIONAL GUARD PAYROLL, FISCAL 1991

Rank in order

By per capita

1. District of Columbia
2. Utah
3. Alaska
4. Alabama
5. Kansas
6. Georgia
7. South Carolina
8. Vermont
9. Oklahoma
10. Hawaii
11. North Dakota
12. Wisconsin
13. Missouri
14. Indiana
15. South Dakota
16. Kentucky
17. Mississippi
18. Montana
19. Arkansas
20. Idaho
21. Delaware
22. Virginia
23. Pennsylvania
24. Maryland
25. New Mexico
26. Wyoming
27. Rhode Island
28. Colorado
29. Nebraska
30. Washington
31. Massachusetts
32. Minnesota
33. Maine
34. Iowa
35. Louisiana
36. New Jersey
37. Tennessee
38. North Carolina
39. New Hampshire
40. Arizona
41. West Virginia
42. Texas
43. Oregon
44. Connecticut
45. Illinois
46. Nevada
47. Ohio
48. New York
49. Michigan
50. California
51. Florida

Source: U.S. Department of Defense, Directorate for Information Operations and Reports, *Atlas/Data Abstract for the United States and Selected Areas, Fiscal Year 1991* (Washington, D.C.: Government Printing Office, 1992).

State	Personnel	Payroll	Per capita	Rank by per capita
Alabama	5,365	$11,718,000	$2.87	17
Alaska	496	716,000	1.26	46
Arizona	4,366	7,047,000	1.88	37
Arkansas	2,121	3,976,000	1.68	40
California	47,354	91,954,000	3.03	14
Colorado	4,963	9,507,000	2.82	18
Connecticut	2,881	3,166,000	0.96	49
Delaware	947	2,081,000	3.06	12
District of Columbia	9,257	17,910,000	29.95	1
Florida	21,173	42,304,000	3.19	10
Georgia	8,351	20,865,000	3.15	11
Hawaii	1,909	2,169,000	1.91	36
Idaho	1,219	2,088,000	2.01	33
Illinois	13,431	27,544,000	2.39	25
Indiana	5,362	9,749,000	1.74	39
Iowa	3,237	6,001,000	2.15	30
Kansas	5,291	15,924,000	6.38	2
Kentucky	2,934	4,407,000	1.19	48
Louisiana	7,764	17,928,000	4.22	6
Maine	1,858	2,827,000	2.29	26
Maryland	5,898	25,346,000	5.22	4
Massachusetts	7,984	18,132,000	3.02	15
Michigan	10,716	20,326,000	2.17	29
Minnesota	5,155	12,347,000	2.79	19
Mississippi	2,229	3,274,000	1.26	46
Missouri	10,210	15,716,000	3.05	13
Montana	1,120	2,229,000	2.76	20
Nebraska	2,070	4,230,000	2.66	23
Nevada	1,504	2,272,000	1.77	38
New Hampshire	1,139	929,000	0.84	50
New Jersey	5,418	6,043,000	0.78	51
New Mexico	1,715	3,051,000	1.97	34
New York	17,520	34,756,000	1.92	35
North Carolina	7,871	14,734,000	2.19	28
North Dakota	591	1,428,000	2.25	27
Ohio	11,620	22,760,000	2.08	31
Oklahoma	2,893	5,324,000	1.68	40
Oregon	4,432	8,627,000	2.95	16
Pennsylvania	17,113	38,774,000	3.24	9
Rhode Island	1,918	3,662,000	3.65	8
South Carolina	5,353	9,757,000	2.74	22
South Dakota	649	1,088,000	1.55	42
Tennessee	8,176	19,364,000	3.91	7
Texas	21,993	47,948,000	2.76	20
Utah	2,098	4,395,000	2.48	24
Vermont	474	857,000	1.51	43
Virginia	15,005	33,629,000	5.35	3
Washington	10,433	23,846,000	4.75	5
West Virginia	1,761	2,481,000	1.38	44
Wisconsin	5,445	10,305,000	2.08	31
Wyoming	457	603,000	1.31	45
United States	**341,239**	**$698,114,000**	**$2.77**	**20**

By per capita

1. District of Columbia
2. Kansas
3. Virginia
4. Maryland
5. Washington
6. Louisiana
7. Tennessee
8. Rhode Island
9. Pennsylvania
10. Florida
11. Georgia
12. Delaware
13. Missouri
14. California
15. Massachusetts
16. Oregon
17. Alabama
18. Colorado
19. Minnesota
20. Montana
   Texas
22. South Carolina
23. Nebraska
24. Utah
25. Illinois
26. Maine
27. North Dakota
28. North Carolina
29. Michigan
30. Iowa
31. Ohio
   Wisconsin
33. Idaho
34. New Mexico
35. New York
36. Hawaii
37. Arizona
38. Nevada
39. Indiana
40. Arkansas
   Oklahoma
42. South Dakota
43. Vermont
44. West Virginia
45. Wyoming
46. Alaska
   Mississippi
48. Kentucky
49. Connecticut
50. New Hampshire
51. New Jersey

Source: U.S. Department of Defense, Directorate for Information Operations and Reports, *Atlas/Data Abstract for the United States and Selected Areas, Fiscal Year 1991* (Washington, D.C.: Government Printing Office, 1992).

State	Personnel	Payroll	Per capita	Rank by per capita	By per capita
Alabama	5,375	$21,396,000	$5.23	23	1. Delaware
Alaska	1,929	7,804,000	13.69	3	2. Colorado
Arizona	6,269	21,359,000	5.70	20	3. Alaska
Arkansas	3,156	11,686,000	4.93	25	4. Wyoming
California	26,170	96,626,000	3.18	41	5. Utah
Colorado	4,912	98,077,000	29.04	2	6. Hawaii
Connecticut	1,924	5,729,000	1.74	48	7. North Dakota
Delaware	3,442	20,339,000	29.91	1	8. Vermont
District of Columbia	437	481,000	0.80	51	9. Mississippi
Florida	10,538	30,949,000	2.33	45	10. South Carolina
Georgia	8,798	29,872,000	4.51	32	11. West Virginia
Hawaii	3,027	10,981,000	9.67	6	12. Montana
Idaho	1,820	5,987,000	5.76	17	13. South Dakota
Illinois	9,074	29,603,000	2.56	43	14. Rhode Island
Indiana	6,063	22,580,000	4.02	36	15. Maine
Iowa	2,938	10,528,000	3.77	39	16. Oklahoma
Kansas	3,255	11,981,000	4.80	27	17. Idaho
Kentucky	2,072	6,351,000	1.71	49	Maryland
Louisiana	5,901	22,917,000	5.39	22	19. Washington
Maine	1,939	7,740,000	6.27	15	20. Arizona
Maryland	7,210	27,999,000	5.76	17	21. New Hampshire
Massachusetts	6,980	30,564,000	5.10	24	22. Louisiana
Michigan	6,593	18,688,000	1.99	47	23. Alabama
Minnesota	5,068	20,440,000	4.61	31	24. Massachusetts
Mississippi	4,874	22,405,000	8.64	9	25. Arkansas
Missouri	5,831	22,442,000	4.35	33	26. Oregon
Montana	1,457	5,998,000	7.42	12	27. Kansas
Nebraska	2,353	6,532,000	4.10	35	28. Tennessee
Nevada	2,023	5,974,000	4.65	30	29. New Jersey
New Hampshire	1,517	6,123,000	5.54	21	30. Nevada
New Jersey	7,560	36,210,000	4.67	29	31. Minnesota
New Mexico	2,128	5,875,000	3.80	38	32. Georgia
New York	11,472	42,175,000	2.34	44	33. Missouri
North Carolina	4,546	14,776,000	2.19	46	34. Ohio
North Dakota	1,472	6,027,000	9.49	7	35. Nebraska
Ohio	14,035	46,664,000	4.27	34	36. Indiana
Oklahoma	5,163	19,886,000	6.26	16	37. Wisconsin
Oregon	3,792	14,041,000	4.81	26	38. New Mexico
Pennsylvania	10,292	36,627,000	3.06	42	39. Iowa
Rhode Island	1,723	6,481,000	6.46	14	40. Texas
South Carolina	5,874	27,873,000	7.83	10	41. California
South Dakota	1,328	4,796,000	6.82	13	42. Pennsylvania
Tennessee	5,351	23,350,000	4.71	28	43. Illinois
Texas	17,317	58,925,000	3.40	40	44. New York
Utah	4,277	18,212,000	10.29	5	45. Florida
Vermont	1,181	5,187,000	9.15	8	46. North Carolina
Virginia	5,856	7,350,000	1.17	50	47. Michigan
Washington	7,422	28,703,000	5.72	19	48. Connecticut
West Virginia	2,736	13,373,000	7.43	11	49. Kentucky
Wisconsin	4,816	18,995,000	3.83	37	50. Virginia
Wyoming	1,170	5,214,000	11.33	4	51. District of Columbia
United States	**272,456**	**$1,080,891,000**	**$4.29**	**34**	

Source: U.S. Department of Defense, Directorate for Information Operations and Reports, *Atlas/Data Abstract for the United States and Selected Areas, Fiscal Year 1991* (Washington, D.C.: Government Printing Office, 1992).

TOTAL RETIRED MILITARY PAYROLL, FISCAL 1991				Rank in order

State	Payroll	Per capita	Rank by per capita	By per capita
Alabama	$548,598,000	$134.16	10	1. Virginia
Alaska	71,780,000	125.93	12	2. Nevada
Arizona	589,132,000	157.10	9	3. Florida
Arkansas	281,851,000	118.82	15	4. Colorado
California	3,149,859,000	103.68	20	5. Hawaii
Colorado	593,435,000	175.73	4	6. New Mexico
Connecticut	139,189,000	42.29	40	7. South Carolina
Delaware	69,900,000	102.79	21	8. Washington
District of Columbia	48,934,000	81.83	30	9. Arizona
Florida	2,356,667,000	177.50	3	10. Alabama
Georgia	813,305,000	122.80	13	11. Texas
Hawaii	192,887,000	169.94	5	12. Alaska
Idaho	105,779,000	101.81	22	13. Georgia
Illinois	342,567,000	29.68	48	14. Maryland
Indiana	205,715,000	36.67	45	15. Arkansas
Iowa	90,224,000	32.28	46	16. Oklahoma
Kansas	210,848,000	84.51	28	17. New Hampshire
Kentucky	230,121,000	61.98	36	18. North Carolina
Louisiana	330,968,000	77.84	32	19. Maine
Maine	129,310,000	104.70	19	20. California
Maryland	590,708,000	121.54	14	21. Delaware
Massachusetts	248,263,000	41.40	42	22. Idaho
Michigan	235,949,000	25.19	50	23. Mississippi
Minnesota	142,548,000	32.16	47	24. Nebraska
Mississippi	260,033,000	100.32	23	25. Tennessee
Missouri	355,027,000	68.83	34	26. Wyoming
Montana	68,516,000	84.80	27	27. Montana
Nebraska	144,253,000	90.55	24	28. Kansas
Nevada	252,686,000	196.80	2	29. Oregon
New Hampshire	123,999,000	112.22	17	30. District of Columbia
New Jersey	286,975,000	36.98	44	31. Rhode Island
New Mexico	260,508,000	168.29	6	32. Louisiana
New York	361,944,000	20.04	51	33. Utah
North Carolina	753,840,000	111.90	18	34. Missouri
North Dakota	29,782,000	46.90	39	35. South Dakota
Ohio	417,317,000	38.15	43	36. Kentucky
Oklahoma	368,590,000	116.09	16	37. Vermont
Oregon	240,369,000	82.26	29	38. West Virginia
Pennsylvania	498,991,000	41.72	41	39. North Dakota
Rhode Island	78,625,000	78.31	31	40. Connecticut
South Carolina	586,518,000	164.75	7	41. Pennsylvania
South Dakota	47,601,000	67.71	35	42. Massachusetts
Tennessee	446,917,000	90.23	25	43. Ohio
Texas	2,258,639,000	130.19	11	44. New Jersey
Utah	125,526,000	70.92	33	45. Indiana
Vermont	34,693,000	61.19	37	46. Iowa
Virginia	1,757,716,000	279.62	1	47. Minnesota
Washington	825,616,000	164.53	8	48. Illinois
West Virginia	98,038,000	54.44	38	49. Wisconsin
Wisconsin	141,945,000	28.65	49	50. Michigan
Wyoming	40,765,000	88.62	26	51. New York
United States	$22,583,966,000	$89.56	26	

Source: U.S. Department of Defense, Directorate for Information Operations and Reports, *Atlas/Data Abstract for the United States and Selected Areas, Fiscal Year 1991* (Washington, D.C.: Government Printing Office, 1992).

State	Payroll	Per capita	Rank by per capita
Alabama	$266,967,000	$65.29	3
Alaska	23,640,000	41.47	15
Arizona	173,896,000	46.37	12
Arkansas	89,075,000	37.55	17
California	576,485,000	18.98	35
Colorado	205,904,000	60.97	5
Connecticut	37,790,000	11.48	44
Delaware	15,746,000	23.16	28
District of Columbia	18,626,000	31.15	22
Florida	594,592,000	44.78	13
Georgia	435,032,000	65.69	2
Hawaii	71,213,000	62.74	4
Idaho	23,782,000	22.89	29
Illinois	110,305,000	9.56	49
Indiana	87,691,000	15.63	40
Iowa	32,485,000	11.62	43
Kansas	95,286,000	38.19	16
Kentucky	138,613,000	37.33	18
Louisiana	106,552,000	25.06	26
Maine	30,738,000	24.89	27
Maryland	238,724,000	49.12	9
Massachusetts	85,965,000	14.34	42
Michigan	85,181,000	9.09	50
Minnesota	49,852,000	11.25	46
Mississippi	70,293,000	27.12	23
Missouri	138,765,000	26.90	24
Montana	17,475,000	21.63	32
Nebraska	23,052,000	14.47	41
Nevada	47,142,000	36.71	19
New Hampshire	35,791,000	32.39	21
New Jersey	140,444,000	18.10	36
New Mexico	68,339,000	44.15	14
New York	145,064,000	8.03	51
North Carolina	316,337,000	46.96	10
North Dakota	7,276,000	11.46	45
Ohio	117,658,000	10.76	48
Oklahoma	156,170,000	49.19	8
Oregon	64,464,000	22.06	30
Pennsylvania	209,432,000	17.51	37
Rhode Island	15,900,000	15.84	39
South Carolina	204,180,000	57.35	6
South Dakota	11,929,000	16.97	38
Tennessee	175,361,000	35.41	20
Texas	810,605,000	46.72	11
Utah	37,216,000	21.03	33
Vermont	14,910,000	26.30	25
Virginia	589,545,000	93.79	1
Washington	271,052,000	54.02	7
West Virginia	38,965,000	21.64	31
Wisconsin	54,503,000	11.00	47
Wyoming	9,025,000	19.62	34
United States	$7,385,033,000	$29.29	23

ARMY RETIRED MILITARY PAYROLL, FISCAL 1991

Rank in order

By per capita

1. Virginia
2. Georgia
3. Alabama
4. Hawaii
5. Colorado
6. South Carolina
7. Washington
8. Oklahoma
9. Maryland
10. North Carolina
11. Texas
12. Arizona
13. Florida
14. New Mexico
15. Alaska
16. Kansas
17. Arkansas
18. Kentucky
19. Nevada
20. Tennessee
21. New Hampshire
22. District of Columbia
23. Mississippi
24. Missouri
25. Vermont
26. Louisiana
27. Maine
28. Delaware
29. Idaho
30. Oregon
31. West Virginia
32. Montana
33. Utah
34. Wyoming
35. California
36. New Jersey
37. Pennsylvania
38. South Dakota
39. Rhode Island
40. Indiana
41. Nebraska
42. Massachusetts
43. Iowa
44. Connecticut
45. North Dakota
46. Minnesota
47. Wisconsin
48. Ohio
49. Illinois
50. Michigan
51. New York

Source: U.S. Department of Defense, Directorate for Information Operations and Reports, *Atlas/Data Abstract for the United States and Selected Areas, Fiscal Year 1991* (Washington, D.C.: Government Printing Office, 1992).

State	Payroll	Per capita	Rank by per capita
Alabama	$84,399,000	$20.64	23
Alaska	6,729,000	11.81	38
Arizona	107,284,000	28.61	14
Arkansas	61,441,000	25.90	19
California	1,482,671,000	48.80	8
Colorado	65,391,000	19.36	25
Connecticut	72,261,000	21.96	20
Delaware	10,476,000	15.41	32
District of Columbia	12,338,000	20.63	24
Florida	808,824,000	60.92	3
Georgia	145,423,000	21.96	20
Hawaii	70,000,000	61.67	2
Idaho	30,033,000	28.91	13
Illinois	91,493,000	7.93	47
Indiana	48,745,000	8.69	45
Iowa	26,439,000	9.46	44
Kansas	35,795,000	14.35	34
Kentucky	38,198,000	10.29	40
Louisiana	68,716,000	16.16	29
Maine	53,558,000	43.37	9
Maryland	191,853,000	39.48	10
Massachusetts	78,162,000	13.04	35
Michigan	61,663,000	6.58	49
Minnesota	42,073,000	9.49	43
Mississippi	67,806,000	26.16	18
Missouri	86,653,000	16.80	28
Montana	16,996,000	21.03	22
Nebraska	19,584,000	12.29	37
Nevada	66,098,000	51.48	6
New Hampshire	31,354,000	28.37	15
New Jersey	77,634,000	10.00	41
New Mexico	41,903,000	27.07	16
New York	95,455,000	5.29	51
North Carolina	239,634,000	35.57	11
North Dakota	3,882,000	6.11	50
Ohio	84,706,000	7.74	48
Oklahoma	54,054,000	17.02	27
Oregon	89,376,000	30.59	12
Pennsylvania	151,879,000	12.70	36
Rhode Island	52,930,000	52.72	5
South Carolina	177,768,000	49.93	7
South Dakota	6,831,000	9.72	42
Tennessee	131,138,000	26.48	17
Texas	305,277,000	17.60	26
Utah	20,888,000	11.80	39
Vermont	8,433,000	14.37	33
Virginia	786,469,000	125.11	1
Washington	271,238,000	54.05	4
West Virginia	28,904,000	16.05	30
Wisconsin	39,918,000	8.06	46
Wyoming	7,306,000	15.88	31
United States	**$6,658,079,000**	**$26.40**	18

Rank in order

By per capita

1. Virginia
2. Hawaii
3. Florida
4. Washington
5. Rhode Island
6. Nevada
7. South Carolina
8. California
9. Maine
10. Maryland
11. North Carolina
12. Oregon
13. Idaho
14. Arizona
15. New Hampshire
16. New Mexico
17. Tennessee
18. Mississippi
19. Arkansas
20. Connecticut
    Georgia
22. Montana
23. Alabama
24. District of Columbia
25. Colorado
26. Texas
27. Oklahoma
28. Missouri
29. Louisiana
30. West Virginia
31. Wyoming
32. Delaware
33. Vermont
34. Kansas
35. Massachusetts
36. Pennsylvania
37. Nebraska
38. Alaska
39. Utah
40. Kentucky
41. New Jersey
42. South Dakota
43. Minnesota
44. Iowa
45. Indiana
46. Wisconsin
47. Illinois
48. Ohio
49. Michigan
50. North Dakota
51. New York

Source: U.S. Department of Defense, Directorate for Information Operations and Reports, *Atlas/Data Abstract for the United States and Selected Areas, Fiscal Year 1991* (Washington, D.C.: Government Printing Office, 1992).

AIR FORCE RETIRED MILITARY PAYROLL, FISCAL 1991				Rank in order
State	**Payroll**	**Per capita**	**Rank by per capita**	**By per capita**
Alabama	$197,232,000	$48.23	18	1. Nevada
Alaska	41,411,000	72.65	5	2. New Mexico
Arizona	307,952,000	82.12	4	3. Colorado
Arkansas	131,335,000	55.37	13	4. Arizona
California	1,090,703,000	35.90	26	5. Alaska
Colorado	322,140,000	95.39	3	6. Florida
Connecticut	29,138,000	8.85	50	7. Texas
Delaware	43,678,000	64.23	8	8. Delaware
District of Columbia	17,970,000	30.05	30	9. Nebraska
Florida	953,251,000	71.80	6	10. Virginia
Georgia	232,850,000	35.16	27	11. South Carolina
Hawaii	51,674,000	45.53	20	12. Washington
Idaho	51,964,000	50.01	16	13. Arkansas
Illinois	140,769,000	12.20	42	14. Wyoming
Indiana	69,279,000	12.35	41	15. New Hampshire
Iowa	31,300,000	11.20	45	16. Idaho
Kansas	79,767,000	31.97	29	17. Oklahoma
Kentucky	53,310,000	14.36	39	18. Alabama
Louisiana	155,700,000	36.62	24	19. Mississippi
Maine	45,014,000	36.45	25	20. Hawaii
Maryland	160,131,000	32.95	28	21. Montana
Massachusetts	84,136,000	14.03	40	22. South Dakota
Michigan	89,105,000	9.51	48	23. Utah
Minnesota	50,623,000	11.42	44	24. Louisiana
Mississippi	121,934,000	47.04	19	25. Maine
Missouri	129,609,000	25.13	35	26. California
Montana	34,045,000	42.13	21	27. Georgia
Nebraska	101,617,000	63.79	9	28. Maryland
Nevada	139,446,000	108.60	1	29. Kansas
New Hampshire	56,854,000	51.45	15	30. District of Columbia
New Jersey	68,897,000	8.88	49	31. Oregon
New Mexico	150,266,000	97.07	2	32. North Carolina
New York	121,425,000	6.72	51	33. North Dakota
North Carolina	197,869,000	29.37	32	34. Tennessee
North Dakota	18,624,000	29.33	33	35. Missouri
Ohio	214,953,000	19.65	37	36. Vermont
Oklahoma	158,366,000	49.88	17	37. Ohio
Oregon	86,529,000	29.61	31	38. West Virginia
Pennsylvania	137,680,000	11.51	43	39. Kentucky
Rhode Island	9,795,000	9.76	46	40. Massachusetts
South Carolina	204,570,000	57.46	11	41. Indiana
South Dakota	28,841,000	41.03	22	42. Illinois
Tennessee	140,418,000	28.35	34	43. Pennsylvania
Texas	1,142,757,000	65.87	7	44. Minnesota
Utah	67,422,000	38.09	23	45. Iowa
Vermont	11,350,000	20.02	36	46. Rhode Island
Virginia	381,702,000	60.72	10	47. Wisconsin
Washington	283,326,000	56.46	12	48. Michigan
West Virginia	30,169,000	16.75	38	49. New Jersey
Wisconsin	47,524,000	9.59	47	50. Connecticut
Wyoming	24,434,000	53.12	14	51. New York
United States	**$8,540,854,000**	**$33.87**	**28**	

Source: U.S. Department of Defense, Directorate for Information Operations and Reports, *Atlas/Data Abstract for the United States and Selected Areas, Fiscal Year 1991* (Washington, D.C.: Government Printing Office, 1992).

State	Amount	Per capita	Rank by per capita
Alabama	$1,833,621,000	$448.43	17
Alaska	560,073,000	982.58	6
Arizona	2,510,578,000	669.49	12
Arkansas	306,363,000	129.16	46
California	24,265,041,000	798.72	9
Colorado	2,663,798,000	788.81	10
Connecticut	4,978,594,000	1,512.79	2
Delaware	132,729,000	195.19	37
District of Columbia	1,516,385,000	2,535.76	1
Florida	5,166,419,000	389.13	24
Georgia	1,983,797,000	299.53	29
Hawaii	697,127,000	614.21	13
Idaho	77,974,000	75.05	51
Illinois	1,790,834,000	155.14	43
Indiana	2,189,522,000	390.29	23
Iowa	458,455,000	164.03	40
Kansas	852,466,000	341.67	28
Kentucky	590,634,000	159.07	41
Louisiana	1,246,478,000	293.15	30
Maine	1,065,372,000	862.65	7
Maryland	4,128,541,000	849.49	8
Massachusetts	6,933,473,000	1,156.35	4
Michigan	1,336,716,000	142.69	44
Minnesota	1,779,751,000	401.57	22
Mississippi	1,792,342,000	691.49	11
Missouri	6,298,111,000	1,221.04	3
Montana	82,340,000	101.91	49
Nebraska	253,020,000	158.83	42
Nevada	249,598,000	194.39	38
New Hampshire	427,057,000	386.48	25
New Jersey	3,492,863,000	450.11	16
New Mexico	681,643,000	440.34	18
New York	6,860,402,000	379.91	26
North Carolina	1,560,584,000	231.64	35
North Dakota	148,658,000	234.11	34
Ohio	4,760,046,000	435.14	19
Oklahoma	778,981,000	245.35	33
Oregon	316,759,000	108.40	48
Pennsylvania	2,948,522,000	246.51	32
Rhode Island	413,225,000	411.58	21
South Carolina	984,748,000	276.61	31
South Dakota	124,947,000	177.73	39
Tennessee	2,058,601,000	415.63	20
Texas	10,225,414,000	589.40	14
Utah	801,672,000	452.92	15
Vermont	71,362,000	125.86	47
Virginia	6,780,702,000	1,078.70	5
Washington	1,759,657,000	350.67	27
West Virginia	152,433,000	84.64	50
Wisconsin	967,548,000	195.27	36
Wyoming	63,322,000	137.66	45
United States	**$124,119,298,000**	**$492.19**	**15**

TOTAL DEFENSE PRIME CONTRACTS, FISCAL 1991

Rank in order

By per capita

1. District of Columbia
2. Connecticut
3. Missouri
4. Massachusetts
5. Virginia
6. Alaska
7. Maine
8. Maryland
9. California
10. Colorado
11. Mississippi
12. Arizona
13. Hawaii
14. Texas
15. Utah
16. New Jersey
17. Alabama
18. New Mexico
19. Ohio
20. Tennessee
21. Rhode Island
22. Minnesota
23. Indiana
24. Florida
25. New Hampshire
26. New York
27. Washington
28. Kansas
29. Georgia
30. Louisiana
31. South Carolina
32. Pennsylvania
33. Oklahoma
34. North Dakota
35. North Carolina
36. Wisconsin
37. Delaware
38. Nevada
39. South Dakota
40. Iowa
41. Kentucky
42. Nebraska
43. Illinois
44. Michigan
45. Wyoming
46. Arkansas
47. Vermont
48. Oregon
49. Montana
50. West Virginia
51. Idaho

Source: U.S. Department of Defense, Directorate for Information Operations and Reports, *Atlas/Data Abstract for the United States and Selected Areas, Fiscal Year 1991* (Washington, D.C.: Government Printing Office, 1992).
Note: Prime contracts include contracts over $25,000.

	ARMY PRIME CONTRACTS, FISCAL 1991			Rank in order

State	Amount	Per capita	Rank by per capita	By per capita
Alabama	$1,185,326,000	$289.88	4	1. Massachusetts
Alaska	141,362,000	248.00	7	2. Arizona
Arizona	1,337,898,000	356.77	2	3. Connecticut
Arkansas	144,986,000	61.12	38	4. Alabama
California	4,098,936,000	134.92	17	5. District of Columbia
Colorado	277,113,000	82.06	29	6. Virginia
Connecticut	1,026,598,000	311.94	3	7. Alaska
Delaware	40,839,000	60.06	39	8. Indiana
District of Columbia	152,008,000	254.19	5	9. New Mexico
Florida	1,491,392,000	112.33	21	10. Minnesota
Georgia	700,664,000	105.79	23	11. Hawaii
Hawaii	218,607,000	192.61	11	12. Ohio
Idaho	33,672,000	32.41	46	13. Maryland
Illinois	449,380,000	38.93	45	14. Missouri
Indiana	1,108,259,000	197.55	8	15. Texas
Iowa	207,266,000	74.16	32	16. Wisconsin
Kansas	318,189,000	127.53	19	17. California
Kentucky	400,826,000	107.95	22	18. North Dakota
Louisiana	365,045,000	85.85	27	19. Kansas
Maine	67,357,000	54.54	41	20. Utah
Maryland	753,129,000	154.96	13	21. Florida
Massachusetts	2,687,372,000	448.19	1	22. Kentucky
Michigan	846,832,000	90.40	26	23. Georgia
Minnesota	855,607,000	193.05	10	24. Mississippi
Mississippi	247,054,000	95.31	24	25. Pennsylvania
Missouri	758,164,000	146.99	14	26. Michigan
Montana	38,276,000	47.37	44	27. Louisiana
Nebraska	29,826,000	18.72	48	28. New Hampshire
Nevada	100,131,000	77.98	30	29. Colorado
New Hampshire	91,048,000	82.40	28	30. Nevada
New Jersey	140,444,000	18.10	49	31. North Carolina
New Mexico	299,728,000	193.62	9	32. Iowa
New York	538,249,000	29.81	47	33. Oklahoma
North Carolina	525,299,000	77.97	31	34. West Virginia
North Dakota	85,536,000	134.70	18	35. South Dakota
Ohio	1,878,734,000	171.75	12	36. Tennessee
Oklahoma	232,138,000	73.11	33	37. Washington
Oregon	145,651,000	49.85	43	38. Arkansas
Pennsylvania	1,119,353,000	93.58	25	39. Delaware
Rhode Island	58,929,000	58.69	40	40. Rhode Island
South Carolina	178,605,000	50.17	42	41. Maine
South Dakota	50,379,000	71.66	35	42. South Carolina
Tennessee	348,734,000	70.41	36	43. Oregon
Texas	2,400,595,000	138.37	15	44. Montana
Utah	206,120,000	116.45	20	45. Illinois
Vermont	8,686,000	15.32	50	46. Idaho
Virginia	1,592,831,000	253.39	6	47. New York
Washington	311,730,000	62.12	37	48. Nebraska
West Virginia	129,669,000	72.00	34	49. New Jersey
Wisconsin	668,818,000	134.98	16	50. Vermont
Wyoming	3,661,000	7.96	51	51. Wyoming
United States	$31,686,758,000	$125.65	20	

Source: U.S. Department of Defense, Directorate for Information Operations and Reports, *Atlas/Data Abstract for the United States and Selected Areas, Fiscal Year 1991* (Washington, D.C.: Government Printing Office, 1992).

Note: Prime contracts include contracts over $25,000.

State	Amount	Per capita	Rank by per capita
Alabama	$97,343,000	$23.81	30
Alaska	63,079,000	110.66	17
Arizona	138,864,000	37.03	28
Arkansas	12,365,000	5.21	45
California	7,289,024,000	239.93	10
Colorado	61,342,000	18.16	35
Connecticut	3,037,046,000	922.83	2
Delaware	9,184,000	13.51	40
District of Columbia	958,344,000	1,602.58	1
Florida	1,201,943,000	90.53	21
Georgia	330,956,000	49.97	27
Hawaii	250,164,000	220.41	11
Idaho	2,800,000	2.69	47
Illinois	246,551,000	21.36	31
Indiana	322,044,000	57.41	26
Iowa	41,850,000	14.97	39
Kansas	46,947,000	18.82	34
Kentucky	48,251,000	13.00	41
Louisiana	589,135,000	138.55	14
Maine	959,649,000	777.04	3
Maryland	1,801,705,000	370.72	7
Massachusetts	1,939,277,000	323.43	9
Michigan	140,504,000	15.00	38
Minnesota	567,261,000	127.99	15
Mississippi	1,304,972,000	503.46	6
Missouri	3,688,878,000	715.18	4
Montana	1,325,000	1.64	49
Nebraska	3,390,000	2.13	48
Nevada	37,477,000	29.19	29
New Hampshire	206,355,000	186.75	13
New Jersey	77,634,000	10.00	44
New Mexico	32,925,000	21.27	32
New York	3,613,706,000	200.12	12
North Carolina	609,530,000	90.47	22
North Dakota	3,259,000	5.13	46
Ohio	640,170,000	58.52	24
Oklahoma	38,922,000	12.26	42
Oregon	35,768,000	12.24	43
Pennsylvania	1,115,975,000	93.30	20
Rhode Island	325,855,000	324.56	8
South Carolina	393,788,000	110.61	18
South Dakota	114,000	0.16	50
Tennessee	98,643,000	19.92	33
Texas	1,758,415,000	101.36	19
Utah	140,246,000	79.24	23
Vermont	32,950,000	58.11	25
Virginia	3,290,856,000	523.52	5
Washington	582,940,000	116.17	16
West Virginia	28,640,000	15.90	37
Wisconsin	80,596,000	16.27	36
Wyoming	47,000	0.10	51
United States	**$39,916,551,000**	**$158.29**	**14**

Rank in order

By per capita

1. District of Columbia
2. Connecticut
3. Maine
4. Missouri
5. Virginia
6. Mississippi
7. Maryland
8. Rhode Island
9. Massachusetts
10. California
11. Hawaii
12. New York
13. New Hampshire
14. Louisiana
15. Minnesota
16. Washington
17. Alaska
18. South Carolina
19. Texas
20. Pennsylvania
21. Florida
22. North Carolina
23. Utah
24. Ohio
25. Vermont
26. Indiana
27. Georgia
28. Arizona
29. Nevada
30. Alabama
31. Illinois
32. New Mexico
33. Tennessee
34. Kansas
35. Colorado
36. Wisconsin
37. West Virginia
38. Michigan
39. Iowa
40. Delaware
41. Kentucky
42. Oklahoma
43. Oregon
44. New Jersey
45. Arkansas
46. North Dakota
47. Idaho
48. Nebraska
49. Montana
50. South Dakota
51. Wyoming

Source: U.S. Department of Defense, Directorate for Information Operations and Reports, *Atlas/Data Abstract for the United States and Selected Areas, Fiscal Year 1991* (Washington, D.C.: Government Printing Office, 1992).
Note: Prime contracts include contracts over $25,000.

State	Amount	Per capita	Rank by per capita	By per capita
Alabama	$335,296,000	$82.00	25	1. Colorado
Alaska	171,927,000	301.63	5	2. California
Arizona	982,291,000	261.94	8	3. Missouri
Arkansas	77,393,000	32.63	37	4. Massachusetts
California	10,954,901,000	360.60	2	5. Alaska
Colorado	2,050,859,000	607.30	1	6. Tennessee
Connecticut	800,958,000	243.38	9	7. Texas
Delaware	53,067,000	78.04	27	8. Arizona
District of Columbia	114,960,000	192.24	11	9. Connecticut
Florida	2,385,053,000	179.64	12	10. Maryland
Georgia	820,210,000	123.84	19	11. District of Columbia
Hawaii	158,866,000	139.97	18	12. Florida
Idaho	16,069,000	15.47	43	13. Kansas
Illinois	652,396,000	56.52	30	14. New Mexico
Indiana	545,879,000	97.30	24	15. Ohio
Iowa	148,501,000	53.13	31	16. Utah
Kansas	427,837,000	171.48	13	17. Virginia
Kentucky	15,032,000	4.05	50	18. Hawaii
Louisiana	60,106,000	14.14	45	19. Georgia
Maine	15,259,000	12.36	47	20. New York
Maryland	1,162,852,000	239.27	10	21. Oklahoma
Massachusetts	2,035,133,000	339.42	4	22. New Hampshire
Michigan	224,544,000	23.97	40	23. Nebraska
Minnesota	166,106,000	37.48	36	24. Indiana
Mississippi	108,981,000	42.05	35	25. Alabama
Missouri	1,759,280,000	341.08	3	26. North Dakota
Montana	25,352,000	31.38	39	27. Delaware
Nebraska	167,724,000	105.29	23	28. Nevada
Nevada	97,918,000	76.26	28	29. Washington
New Hampshire	116,382,000	105.32	22	30. Illinois
New Jersey	68,897,000	8.88	48	31. Iowa
New Mexico	265,388,000	171.44	14	32. Wyoming
New York	2,187,678,000	121.15	20	33. South Dakota
North Carolina	219,149,000	32.53	38	34. Vermont
North Dakota	49,878,000	78.55	26	35. Mississippi
Ohio	1,826,166,000	166.94	15	36. Minnesota
Oklahoma	336,476,000	105.98	21	37. Arkansas
Oregon	36,347,000	12.44	46	38. North Carolina
Pennsylvania	268,042,000	22.41	41	39. Montana
Rhode Island	14,212,000	14.16	44	40. Michigan
South Carolina	74,891,000	21.04	42	41. Pennsylvania
South Dakota	31,115,000	44.26	33	42. South Carolina
Tennessee	1,340,025,000	270.55	6	43. Idaho
Texas	4,592,133,000	264.69	7	44. Rhode Island
Utah	285,709,000	161.42	16	45. Louisiana
Vermont	24,711,000	43.58	34	46. Oregon
Virginia	927,414,000	147.54	17	47. Maine
Washington	345,044,000	68.76	29	48. New Jersey
West Virginia	2,036,000	1.13	51	49. Wisconsin
Wisconsin	38,421,000	7.75	49	50. Kentucky
Wyoming	21,515,000	46.77	32	51. West Virginia
United States	$40,086,667,000	$158.96	17	

Source: U.S. Department of Defense, Directorate for Information Operations and Reports, *Atlas/Data Abstract for the United States and Selected Areas, Fiscal Year 1991* (Washington, D.C.: Government Printing Office, 1992).
Note: Prime contracts include contracts over $25,000.

U.S. MILITARY INSTALLATIONS, 1991

State	Army	Navy	Air Force	Marine Corps	Total	Rank by total
Alabama	4	1	5	0	10	17
Alaska	3	1	7	0	11	10
Arizona	2	0	6	1	9	18
Arkansas	2	0	3	0	5	29
California	10	34	16	7	67	1
Colorado	3	0	6	0	9	18
Connecticut	0	1	2	0	3	38
Delaware	0	0	2	0	2	41
District of Columbia	2	4	1	1	8	23
Florida	0	14	10	0	24	4
Georgia	6	3	5	1	15	8
Hawaii	4	6	2	2	14	9
Idaho	0	0	2	0	2	41
Illinois	4	2	5	0	11	10
Indiana	3	2	3	0	8	23
Iowa	0	0	2	0	2	41
Kansas	2	0	2	0	4	34
Kentucky	3	1	1	0	5	29
Louisiana	1	1	3	0	5	29
Maine	0	2	3	0	5	29
Maryland	7	8	2	0	17	5
Massachusetts	3	1	7	0	11	10
Michigan	2	0	4	0	6	27
Minnesota	0	0	2	0	2	41
Mississippi	0	4	5	0	9	18
Missouri	2	0	6	1	9	18
Montana	0	0	2	0	2	41
Nebraska	0	0	2	0	2	41
Nevada	0	1	3	0	4	34
New Hampshire	0	1	2	0	3	38
New Jersey	4	3	2	0	9	18
New Mexico	1	0	3	0	4	34
New York	6	1	8	1	16	7
North Carolina	2	2	4	3	11	10
North Dakota	0	0	4	0	4	34
Ohio	1	1	9	0	11	10
Oklahoma	2	0	5	0	7	25
Oregon	0	0	2	0	2	41
Pennsylvania	7	7	3	0	17	5
Rhode Island	0	2	3	0	5	29
South Carolina	1	4	4	2	11	10
South Dakota	0	0	2	0	2	41
Tennessee	1	2	4	0	7	25
Texas	6	5	15	0	26	3
Utah	4	0	2	0	6	27
Vermont	0	0	1	0	1	51
Virginia	12	12	2	3	29	2
Washington	1	6	4	0	11	10
West Virginia	0	0	2	0	2	41
Wisconsin	1	0	2	0	3	38
Wyoming	0	0	2	0	2	41
United States	**112**	**132**	**204**	**22**	**470**	**—**

Rank in order

By total

1. California
2. Virginia
3. Texas
4. Florida
5. Maryland
   Pennsylvania
7. New York
8. Georgia
9. Hawaii
10. Alaska
    Illinois
    Massachusetts
    North Carolina
    Ohio
    South Carolina
    Washington
17. Alabama
18. Arizona
    Colorado
    Mississippi
    Missouri
    New Jersey
23. District of Columbia
    Indiana
25. Oklahoma
    Tennessee
27. Michigan
    Utah
29. Arkansas
    Kentucky
    Louisiana
    Maine
    Rhode Island
34. Kansas
    Nevada
    New Mexico
    North Dakota
38. Connecticut
    New Hampshire
    Wisconsin
41. Delaware
    Idaho
    Iowa
    Minnesota
    Montana
    Nebraska
    Oregon
    South Dakota
    West Virginia
    Wyoming
51. Vermont

— not applicable.

Source: U.S. Department of Defense, Military Installations and Properties, September 1991, unpublished data.

State	Federal expenditures	Per capita	Rank by per capita		Rank in order By per capita
Alabama	$2,262,000	$0.55	13		1. Alaska
Alaska	19,416,000	34.06	1		2. North Dakota
Arizona	1,281,000	0.34	16		3. Idaho
Arkansas	338,000	0.14	30		4. District of Columbia
California	1,134,000	0.04	41		5. New Mexico
Colorado	0	0.00	49		6. Virginia
Connecticut	134,000	0.04	40		7. Mississippi
Delaware	95,000	0.14	31		8. West Virginia
District of Columbia	2,014,000	3.37	4		9. Minnesota
Florida	1,208,000	0.09	35		10. Oregon
Georgia	319,000	0.05	37		11. Montana
Hawaii	255,000	0.23	23		12. Michigan
Idaho	4,108,000	3.95	3		13. Alabama
Illinois	1,459,000	0.13	34		14. Iowa
Indiana	1,009,000	0.18	26		15. Ohio
Iowa	1,408,000	0.50	14		16. Arizona
Kansas	654,000	0.26	20		17. Utah
Kentucky	112,000	0.03	43		18. New Jersey
Louisiana	128,000	0.03	43		19. Missouri
Maine	34,000	0.03	45		20. Kansas
Maryland	350,000	0.07	36		21. Wyoming
Massachusetts	93,000	0.02	46		22. Texas
Michigan	5,253,000	0.56	12		23. Hawaii
Minnesota	4,467,000	1.01	9		24. Oklahoma
Mississippi	4,592,000	1.77	7		25. Tennessee
Missouri	1,419,000	0.28	19		26. Indiana
Montana	494,000	0.61	11		27. South Carolina
Nebraska	69,000	0.04	38		28. Wisconsin
Nevada	175,000	0.14	32		29. South Dakota
New Hampshire	0	0.00	49		30. Arkansas
New Jersey	2,379,000	0.31	18		31. Delaware
New Mexico	3,954,000	2.55	5		32. Nevada
New York	755,000	0.04	39		33. Pennsylvania
North Carolina	247,000	0.04	41		34. Illinois
North Dakota	6,017,000	9.48	2		35. Florida
Ohio	4,464,000	0.41	15		36. Maryland
Oklahoma	671,000	0.21	24		37. Georgia
Oregon	2,124,000	0.73	10		38. Nebraska
Pennsylvania	1,576,000	0.13	33		39. New York
Rhode Island	0	0.00	49		40. Connecticut
South Carolina	597,000	0.17	27		41. California
South Dakota	111,000	0.16	29		North Carolina
Tennessee	1,008,000	0.20	25		43. Kentucky
Texas	3,962,000	0.23	22		Louisiana
Utah	598,000	0.34	17		45. Maine
Vermont	7,000	0.01	48		46. Massachusetts
Virginia	11,462,000	1.82	6		47. Washington
Washington	66,000	0.01	47		48. Vermont
West Virginia	2,629,000	1.46	8		49. Colorado
Wisconsin	799,000	0.16	28		New Hampshire
Wyoming	113,000	0.25	21		Rhode Island
United States	**$104,444,000**	**$15.00**	**15**		

Source: U.S. Department of Commerce, Bureau of the Census, *Federal Expenditures by State for Fiscal 1991* (Washington, D.C.: Government Printing Office, 1992).

Education

State	State population	School age population	% of state population	Rank by %
Alabama	4,089,000	776,000	19.0	19
Alaska	570,000	123,000	21.6	4
Arizona	3,750,000	700,000	18.7	25
Arkansas	2,372,000	456,000	19.2	15
California	30,380,000	5,512,000	18.1	34
Colorado	3,377,000	625,000	18.5	28
Connecticut	3,291,000	527,000	16.0	47
Delaware	680,000	117,000	17.2	39
District of Columbia	598,000	78,000	13.0	51
Florida	13,277,000	2,083,000	15.7	50
Georgia	6,623,000	1,252,000	18.9	21
Hawaii	1,135,000	199,000	17.5	38
Idaho	1,039,000	236,000	22.7	2
Illinois	11,543,000	2,111,000	18.3	32
Indiana	5,610,000	1,059,000	18.9	22
Iowa	2,795,000	532,000	19.0	18
Kansas	2,495,000	482,000	19.3	14
Kentucky	3,713,000	703,000	18.9	20
Louisiana	4,252,000	894,000	21.0	7
Maine	1,235,000	224,000	18.1	35
Maryland	4,860,000	824,000	17.0	43
Massachusetts	5,996,000	943,000	15.7	49
Michigan	9,368,000	1,767,000	18.9	23
Minnesota	4,432,000	851,000	19.2	16
Mississippi	2,592,000	549,000	21.2	6
Missouri	5,158,000	962,000	18.7	26
Montana	808,000	165,000	20.4	9
Nebraska	1,593,000	315,000	19.8	12
Nevada	1,284,000	220,000	17.1	42
New Hampshire	1,105,000	195,000	17.7	37
New Jersey	7,760,000	1,277,000	16.5	46
New Mexico	1,548,000	328,000	21.2	5
New York	18,058,000	3,026,000	16.8	45
North Carolina	6,737,000	1,158,000	17.2	40
North Dakota	635,000	127,000	20.0	11
Ohio	10,939,000	2,023,000	18.5	29
Oklahoma	3,175,000	615,000	19.4	13
Oregon	2,922,000	539,000	18.5	30
Pennsylvania	11,961,000	2,014,000	16.8	44
Rhode Island	1,004,000	160,000	15.9	48
South Carolina	3,560,000	668,000	18.8	24
South Dakota	703,000	146,000	20.8	8
Tennessee	4,953,000	884,000	17.9	36
Texas	17,349,000	3,512,000	20.2	10
Utah	1,770,000	468,000	26.4	1
Vermont	567,000	103,000	18.2	33
Virginia	6,286,000	1,078,000	17.2	41
Washington	5,018,000	932,000	18.6	27
West Virginia	1,801,000	331,000	18.4	31
Wisconsin	4,955,000	949,000	19.2	17
Wyoming	460,000	102,000	22.2	3
United States	**252,177,000**	**45,923,000**	**18.2**	**33**

Rank in order

By %

1. Utah
2. Idaho
3. Wyoming
4. Alaska
5. New Mexico
6. Mississippi
7. Louisiana
8. South Dakota
9. Montana
10. Texas
11. North Dakota
12. Nebraska
13. Oklahoma
14. Kansas
15. Arkansas
16. Minnesota
17. Wisconsin
18. Iowa
19. Alabama
20. Kentucky
21. Georgia
22. Indiana
23. Michigan
24. South Carolina
25. Arizona
26. Missouri
27. Washington
28. Colorado
29. Ohio
30. Oregon
31. West Virginia
32. Illinois
33. Vermont
34. California
35. Maine
36. Tennessee
37. New Hampshire
38. Hawaii
39. Delaware
40. North Carolina
41. Virginia
42. Nevada
43. Maryland
44. Pennsylvania
45. New York
46. New Jersey
47. Connecticut
48. Rhode Island
49. Massachusetts
50. Florida
51. District of Columbia

Source: U.S. Department of Commerce, Bureau of the Census, *Statistical Abstract of the United States, 1992* (Washington, D.C.: Government Printing Office, 1992).

Note: "School age" covers ages five to seventeen.

State	Total enrollment		Kindergarten to grade 8		Grades 9 to 12	
	students	Rank	Students	Rank	Students	Rank
Alabama	721,806	21	527,097	21	194,709	21
Alaska	113,874	47	85,297	46	28,577	47
Arizona	639,853	23	479,050	23	160,803	25
Arkansas	436,286	34	313,512	34	122,774	31
California	4,950,474	1	3,614,798	1	1,335,676	1
Colorado	574,213	27	419,929	27	154,284	26
Connecticut	469,123	31	347,396	30	121,727	32
Delaware	99,658	48	72,606	48	27,052	49
District of Columbia	80,694	51	61,274	51	19,420	51
Florida	1,861,592	4	1,369,934	4	491,658	7
Georgia	1,151,687	9	849,082	9	302,605	11
Hawaii	171,708	42	122,840	42	48,868	41
Idaho	220,840	38	160,097	38	60,743	38
Illinois	1,821,407	5	1,309,640	5	511,767	5
Indiana	954,581	13	675,887	13	278,694	12
Iowa	483,652	30	344,874	31	138,778	28
Kansas	437,034	33	319,697	33	117,337	34
Kentucky	636,401	24	459,216	24	177,185	23
Louisiana	784,757	19	586,183	17	198,574	20
Maine	215,149	39	155,218	39	59,931	39
Maryland	715,176	22	526,859	22	188,317	22
Massachusetts	834,314	15	604,234	15	230,080	15
Michigan	1,581,925	8	1,145,558	8	436,367	8
Minnesota	756,374	20	545,556	20	210,818	19
Mississippi	502,417	28	371,674	28	130,743	30
Missouri	812,234	17	584,953	18	227,281	16
Montana	152,974	43	111,172	43	41,802	43
Nebraska	274,081	37	198,080	37	76,001	37
Nevada	201,316	40	149,882	40	51,434	40
New Hampshire	172,785	41	126,309	41	46,476	42
New Jersey	1,089,646	10	783,558	10	306,088	9
New Mexico	301,881	36	208,087	36	93,794	36
New York	2,598,337	3	1,827,936	3	770,401	3
North Carolina	1,086,871	11	783,132	11	303,739	10
North Dakota	117,825	46	84,943	47	32,882	46
Ohio	1,771,516	6	1,257,689	6	513,827	4
Oklahoma	579,087	26	424,901	26	154,186	27
Oregon	484,652	29	350,748	29	133,904	29
Pennsylvania	1,667,834	7	1,172,164	7	495,670	6
Rhode Island	138,813	44	101,797	44	37,016	44
South Carolina	622,112	25	452,033	25	170,079	24
South Dakota	129,164	45	95,169	45	33,995	45
Tennessee	824,595	16	598,111	16	226,484	18
Texas	3,382,887	2	2,510,955	2	871,932	2
Utah	447,891	32	326,266	32	121,625	33
Vermont	95,762	50	70,860	50	24,902	50
Virginia	998,601	12	728,282	12	270,319	13
Washington	839,709	14	612,597	14	227,112	17
West Virginia	322,389	35	224,057	35	98,332	35
Wisconsin	797,621	18	565,520	19	232,101	14
Wyoming	98,226	49	70,941	49	27,285	48
United States	**41,223,804**	—	**28,887,650**	—	**11,336,154**	—

— not applicable.

Source: U.S Department of Education, National Center for Education Statistics, *Digest of Education Statistics, 1992* (Washington, D.C.: Government Printing Office, 1992).

Rank in order

By total enrollment

1. California
2. Texas
3. New York
4. Florida
5. Illinois
6. Ohio
7. Pennsylvania
8. Michigan
9. Georgia
10. New Jersey
11. North Carolina
12. Virginia
13. Indiana
14. Washington
15. Massachusetts
16. Tennessee
17. Missouri
18. Wisconsin
19. Louisiana
20. Minnesota
21. Alabama
22. Maryland
23. Arizona
24. Kentucky
25. South Carolina
26. Oklahoma
27. Colorado
28. Mississippi
29. Oregon
30. Iowa
31. Connecticut
32. Utah
33. Kansas
34. Arkansas
35. West Virginia
36. New Mexico
37. Nebraska
38. Idaho
39. Maine
40. Nevada
41. New Hampshire
42. Hawaii
43. Montana
44. Rhode Island
45. South Dakota
46. North Dakota
47. Alaska
48. Delaware
49. Wyoming
50. Vermont
51. District of Columbia

AVERAGE DAILY ATTENDANCE, 1989-1990					Rank in order
State	Average daily membership (ADM)	Average daily attendance (ADA)	ADA as % of ADM	Rank by %	By %
Alabama	NA	683,833	NA	NA	1. New Mexico
Alaska	105,662	98,213	93.0	33	2. Virginia
Arizona	617,519	557,252	90.2	40	3. Nevada
Arkansas	427,889	403,025	94.2	22	4. Indiana
California	NA	4,893,341	NA	NA	5. Kansas
Colorado	NA	519,419	NA	NA	6. Louisiana
Connecticut	466,195	439,524	94.3	20	7. Wisconsin
Delaware	96,358	89,838	93.2	30	8. South Carolina
District of Columbia	79,430	71,468	90.0	41	9. Nebraska
Florida	1,785,223	1,646,583	92.2	37	South Dakota
Georgia	1,123,527	1,054,097	93.8	24	11. Iowa
Hawaii	169,032	157,360	93.1	31	12. Minnesota
Idaho	NA	203,987	NA	NA	13. Mississippi
Illinois	1,709,939	1,587,733	92.9	34	14. Vermont
Indiana	914,750	884,568	96.7	4	15. Kentucky
Iowa	471,145	450,224	95.6	11	16. Wyoming
Kansas	403,245	388,986	96.5	5	17. Oklahoma
Kentucky	600,226	569,795	94.9	15	18. Utah
Louisiana	755,289	727,125	96.3	6	19. North Carolina
Maine	207,034	195,089	94.2	21	20. Connecticut
Maryland	696,993	620,617	89.0	43	21. Maine
Massachusetts	822,376	763,231	92.8	35	22. Arkansas
Michigan	NA	1,446,996	NA	NA	23. North Dakota
Minnesota	733,010	699,001	95.4	12	24. Georgia
Mississippi	499,660	476,048	95.3	13	25. Tennessee
Missouri	NA	729,693	NA	NA	26. Pennsylvania
Montana	149,539	135,406	90.5	38	27. Washington
Nebraska	266,404	254,754	95.6	9	28. New Jersey
Nevada	177,886	173,149	97.3	3	29. Ohio
New Hampshire	166,640	154,915	93.0	32	30. Delaware
New Jersey	1,067,397	997,561	93.5	28	31. Hawaii
New Mexico	278,790	290,245	104.1	1	32. New Hampshire
New York	2,482,500	2,244,110	90.4	39	33. Alaska
North Carolina	1,065,399	1,004,901	94.3	19	34. Illinois
North Dakota	116,743	109,659	93.9	23	35. Massachusetts
Ohio	1,681,711	1,571,325	93.4	29	36. Rhode Island
Oklahoma	573,200	543,170	94.8	17	37. Florida
Oregon	467,300	419,771	89.8	42	38. Montana
Pennsylvania	1,629,000	1,524,839	93.6	26	39. New York
Rhode Island	135,738	125,934	92.8	36	40. Arizona
South Carolina	593,328	569,028	95.9	8	41. District of Columbia
South Dakota	125,303	119,823	95.6	9	42. Oregon
Tennessee	812,020	761,766	93.8	25	43. Maryland
Texas	NA	3,075,333	NA	NA	NA Alabama
Utah	432,168	408,917	94.6	18	NA California
Vermont	92,282	87,832	95.2	14	NA Colorado
Virginia	976,992	989,197	101.2	2	NA Idaho
Washington	807,655	755,141	93.5	27	NA Michigan
West Virginia	NA	301,947	NA	NA	NA Missouri
Wisconsin	740,308	711,466	96.1	7	NA Texas
Wyoming	96,263	91,277	94.8	16	NA West Virginia
United States	NA	37,778,512	NA		

NA not available.

Source: U.S Department of Education, National Center for Education Statistics, *Digest of Education Statistics, 1992* (Washington, D.C.: Government Printing Office, 1992).

Note: Average daily membership is the average of those students who are enrolled when schools are actually in session.

STUDENT-TEACHER RATIO, FALL 1990

State	Students	Teachers	Student-teacher ratio	Rank by ratio
Alabama	721,806	36,266	19.9	4
Alaska	113,874	6,710	17.0	21
Arizona	639,853	32,987	19.4	8
Arkansas	436,286	25,984	16.8	25
California	4,950,474	217,228	22.8	2
Colorado	574,213	32,342	17.8	15
Connecticut	469,123	34,549	13.6	48
Delaware	99,658	5,961	16.7	27
District of Columbia	80,694	5,950	13.6	49
Florida	1,861,592	108,088	17.2	20
Georgia	1,151,687	63,058	18.3	12
Hawaii	171,708	9,083	18.9	10
Idaho	220,840	11,254	19.6	6
Illinois	1,821,407	108,775	16.7	26
Indiana	954,581	54,509	17.5	16
Iowa	483,652	31,045	15.6	33
Kansas	437,034	29,140	15.0	41
Kentucky	636,401	36,777	17.3	17
Louisiana	784,757	NA	NA	NA
Maine	215,149	15,513	13.9	46
Maryland	715,176	42,562	16.8	24
Massachusetts	834,314	54,003	15.4	37
Michigan	1,581,925	80,008	19.8	5
Minnesota	756,374	43,753	17.3	18
Mississippi	502,417	28,062	17.9	14
Missouri	812,234	52,304	15.5	35
Montana	152,974	9,613	15.9	31
Nebraska	274,081	18,764	14.6	43
Nevada	201,316	10,373	19.4	7
New Hampshire	172,785	10,637	16.2	29
New Jersey	1,089,646	79,886	13.6	47
New Mexico	301,881	16,703	18.1	13
New York	2,598,337	176,390	14.7	42
North Carolina	1,086,871	64,283	16.9	22
North Dakota	117,825	7,591	15.5	36
Ohio	1,771,516	102,714	17.2	19
Oklahoma	579,087	37,221	15.6	34
Oregon	484,652	26,163	18.5	11
Pennsylvania	1,667,834	100,275	16.6	28
Rhode Island	138,813	9,522	14.6	44
South Carolina	622,112	36,963	16.8	23
South Dakota	129,164	8,511	15.2	39
Tennessee	824,595	43,051	19.2	9
Texas	3,382,887	219,298	15.4	38
Utah	447,891	17,884	25.0	1
Vermont	95,762	7,257	13.2	50
Virginia	998,601	63,638	15.7	32
Washington	839,709	41,764	20.1	3
West Virginia	322,389	21,476	15.0	40
Wisconsin	797,621	49,302	16.2	30
Wyoming	98,226	6,784	14.5	45
United States	**41,223,804**	**2,397,351**	**17.2**	**21**

Rank in order

By ratio

1. Utah
2. California
3. Washington
4. Alabama
5. Michigan
6. Idaho
7. Nevada
8. Arizona
9. Tennessee
10. Hawaii
11. Oregon
12. Georgia
13. New Mexico
14. Mississippi
15. Colorado
16. Indiana
17. Kentucky
18. Minnesota
19. Ohio
20. Florida
21. Alaska
22. North Carolina
23. South Carolina
24. Maryland
25. Arkansas
26. Illinois
27. Delaware
28. Pennsylvania
29. New Hampshire
30. Wisconsin
31. Montana
32. Virginia
33. Iowa
34. Oklahoma
35. Missouri
36. North Dakota
37. Massachusetts
38. Texas
39. South Dakota
40. West Virginia
41. Kansas
42. New York
43. Nebraska
44. Rhode Island
45. Wyoming
46. Maine
47. New Jersey
48. Connecticut
49. District of Columbia
50. Vermont
NA Louisiana

NA not available.

Source: U.S Department of Education, National Center for Education Statistics, *Digest of Education Statistics, 1992* (Washington, D.C.: Government Printing Office, 1992).

State	Average annual salary	Rank	% of national average	Rank by %
Alabama	$26,862	39	81.5	39
Alaska	43,435	2	131.7	2
Arizona	30,773	26	93.3	26
Arkansas	23,611	49	71.6	49
California	39,598	4	120.1	4
Colorado	31,819	23	96.5	23
Connecticut	43,808	1	132.8	1
Delaware	35,246	11	106.9	11
District of Columbia	39,497	5	119.8	5
Florida	30,555	27	92.7	27
Georgia	29,172	30	88.5	30
Hawaii	32,541	18	98.7	18
Idaho	25,485	46	77.3	46
Illinois	34,605	13	104.9	13
Indiana	32,434	19	98.4	19
Iowa	27,977	37	84.8	37
Kansas	29,767	28	90.3	28
Kentucky	29,115	31	88.3	31
Louisiana	26,240	42	79.6	42
Maine	28,531	33	86.5	33
Maryland	38,382	7	116.4	7
Massachusetts	36,090	9	109.4	9
Michigan	38,326	8	116.2	8
Minnesota	33,126	15	100.5	15
Mississippi	24,366	48	73.9	48
Missouri	28,290	35	85.8	35
Montana	26,774	40	81.2	40
Nebraska	26,592	41	80.6	41
Nevada	32,209	22	97.7	22
New Hampshire	31,273	24	94.8	24
New Jersey	38,411	6	116.5	6
New Mexico	25,754	44	78.1	44
New York	42,080	3	127.6	3
North Carolina	29,276	29	88.8	29
North Dakota	23,574	50	71.5	50
Ohio	32,615	17	98.9	17
Oklahoma	24,457	47	74.2	47
Oregon	32,300	20	97.9	20
Pennsylvania	36,057	10	109.3	10
Rhode Island	34,997	12	106.1	12
South Carolina	28,301	34	85.8	34
South Dakota	22,376	51	67.9	51
Tennessee	28,248	36	85.7	36
Texas	27,658	38	83.9	38
Utah	25,578	45	77.6	45
Vermont	30,986	25	94.0	25
Virginia	32,239	21	97.8	21
Washington	33,079	16	100.3	16
West Virginia	25,967	43	78.7	43
Wisconsin	33,209	14	100.7	14
Wyoming	28,988	32	87.9	32
United States	**$32,977**	**17**	**100.0**	**17**

SALARIES OF PUBLIC SCHOOL TEACHERS, 1990

Rank in order

By average annual salary

1. Connecticut
2. Alaska
3. New York
4. California
5. District of Columbia
6. New Jersey
7. Maryland
8. Michigan
9. Massachusetts
10. Pennsylvania
11. Delaware
12. Rhode Island
13. Illinois
14. Wisconsin
15. Minnesota
16. Washington
17. Ohio
18. Hawaii
19. Indiana
20. Oregon
21. Virginia
22. Nevada
23. Colorado
24. New Hampshire
25. Vermont
26. Arizona
27. Florida
28. Kansas
29. North Carolina
30. Georgia
31. Kentucky
32. Wyoming
33. Maine
34. South Carolina
35. Missouri
36. Tennessee
37. Iowa
38. Texas
39. Alabama
40. Montana
41. Nebraska
42. Louisiana
43. West Virginia
44. New Mexico
45. Utah
46. Idaho
47. Oklahoma
48. Mississippi
49. Arkansas
50. North Dakota
51. South Dakota

Source: National Education Association, *Rankings of the States, 1992* (Washington, D.C.: National Education Association, 1992); U.S Department of Education, National Center for Education Statistics, *Digest of Education Statistics, 1992* (Washington, D.C.: Government Printing Office, 1992).

PUBLIC SCHOOL TEACHERS WHO ARE MALE, 1991-1992

State	Teachers	% of teachers who are male	Rank by %
Alabama	41,072	20.5	45
Alaska	7,205	32.2	9
Arizona	33,505	28.8	25
Arkansas	25,901	22.0	39
California	221,000	30.3	16
Colorado	33,093	30.1	17
Connecticut	34,770	29.7	22
Delaware	6,096	26.7	33
District of Columbia	6,220	21.6	42
Florida	109,939	23.1	38
Georgia	70,294	16.9	51
Hawaii	10,009	21.5	43
Idaho	11,617	30.8	15
Illinois	109,862	30.0	18
Indiana	55,092	30.0	18
Iowa	31,474	32.2	9
Kansas	29,316	29.8	21
Kentucky	37,350	21.2	44
Louisiana	44,015	18.9	47
Maine	14,815	31.4	12
Maryland	43,314	23.8	36
Massachusetts	55,962	37.9	1
Michigan	80,214	24.3	35
Minnesota	44,903	36.8	2
Mississippi	27,867	18.4	49
Missouri	52,306	23.7	37
Montana	9,883	35.4	5
Nebraska	18,869	29.4	23
Nevada	11,409	27.1	31
New Hampshire	11,464	27.7	29
New Jersey	80,515	28.0	28
New Mexico	17,058	27.2	30
New York	180,300	31.0	14
North Carolina	64,838	19.0	46
North Dakota	7,758	31.6	11
Ohio	103,220	29.3	24
Oklahoma	37,670	25.2	34
Oregon	26,691	36.2	4
Pennsylvania	100,476	36.4	3
Rhode Island	9,586	28.4	26
South Carolina	36,344	17.0	50
South Dakota	8,570	28.4	26
Tennessee	43,075	22.0	39
Texas	212,578	21.7	41
Utah	18,326	31.4	12
Vermont	7,031	32.5	8
Virginia	64,742	18.9	47
Washington	42,925	34.6	7
West Virginia	20,997	26.8	32
Wisconsin	52,028	29.9	20
Wyoming	6,403	35.3	6
United States	**2,429,967**	**27.1**	**31**

Rank in order

By %

1. Massachusetts
2. Minnesota
3. Pennsylvania
4. Oregon
5. Montana
6. Wyoming
7. Washington
8. Vermont
9. Alaska
   Iowa
11. North Dakota
12. Maine
    Utah
14. New York
15. Idaho
16. California
17. Colorado
18. Illinois
    Indiana
20. Wisconsin
21. Kansas
22. Connecticut
23. Nebraska
24. Ohio
25. Arizona
26. Rhode Island
    South Dakota
28. New Jersey
29. New Hampshire
30. New Mexico
31. Nevada
32. West Virginia
33. Delaware
34. Oklahoma
35. Michigan
36. Maryland
37. Missouri
38. Florida
39. Arkansas
    Tennessee
41. Texas
42. District of Columbia
43. Hawaii
44. Kentucky
45. Alabama
46. North Carolina
47. Louisiana
    Virginia
49. Mississippi
50. South Carolina
51. Georgia

Source: National Education Association, *Rankings of the States, 1992* (Washington, D.C.: National Education Association, 1992).

EIGHTH GRADE MATH TEST RESULTS, 1990

State	Average proficiency	Rank	% of students at or above		
			Level 200	Level 250	Level 300
Alabama	252	34	96	52	7
Alaska	—	—	—	—	—
Arizona	259	25	98	61	10
Arkansas	256	28	97	57	7
California	256	28	95	56	11
Colorado	267	13	99	72	14
Connecticut	270	11	98	72	19
Delaware	261	20	97	60	13
District of Columbia	231	38	86	23	2
Florida	255	33	96	54	10
Georgia	258	26	96	59	12
Hawaii	251	35	93	49	10
Idaho	272	8	100	79	15
Illinois	260	22	96	64	12
Indiana	267	13	99	71	14
Iowa	278	3	100	84	21
Kansas	—	—	—	—	—
Kentucky	256	28	98	57	8
Louisiana	246	37	94	43	4
Maine	—	—	—	—	—
Maryland	260	22	96	61	14
Massachusetts	—	—	—	—	—
Michigan	264	16	98	67	13
Minnesota	276	4	99	82	20
Mississippi	—	—	—	—	—
Missouri	—	—	—	—	—
Montana	280	2	100	88	23
Nebraska	276	4	99	81	21
Nevada	—	—	—	—	—
New Hampshire	273	7	100	79	17
New Jersey	269	12	99	72	19
New Mexico	256	28	98	56	8
New York	261	20	96	62	13
North Carolina	250	36	94	49	7
North Dakota	281	1	100	88	24
Ohio	264	16	98	67	12
Oklahoma	263	19	99	67	10
Oregon	271	10	99	76	18
Pennsylvania	266	15	98	69	15
Rhode Island	260	22	96	61	12
South Carolina	—	—	—	—	—
South Dakota	—	—	—	—	—
Tennessee	—	—	—	—	—
Texas	258	26	97	58	10
Utah	—	—	—	—	—
Vermont	—	—	—	—	—
Virginia	264	16	98	64	15
Washington	—	—	—	—	—
West Virginia	256	28	98	56	7
Wisconsin	274	6	99	80	20
Wyoming	272	8	100	80	15
United States	261	20	97	64	12

Rank in order

By average proficiency

1. North Dakota
2. Montana
3. Iowa
4. Minnesota
   Nebraska
6. Wisconsin
7. New Hampshire
8. Idaho
   Wyoming
10. Oregon
11. Connecticut
12. New Jersey
13. Colorado
    Indiana
15. Pennsylvania
16. Michigan
    Ohio
    Virginia
19. Oklahoma
20. Delaware
    New York
22. Illinois
    Maryland
    Rhode Island
25. Arizona
26. Georgia
    Texas
28. Arkansas
    California
    Kentucky
    New Mexico
    West Virginia
33. Florida
34. Alabama
35. Hawaii
36. North Carolina
37. Louisiana
38. District of Columbia
— Alaska
— Kansas
— Maine
— Massachusetts
— Mississippi
— Missouri
— Nevada
— South Carolina
— South Dakota
— Tennessee
— Utah
— Vermont
— Washington

— not applicable.

Source: U.S Department of Education, National Center for Education Statistics, *Digest of Education Statistics, 1992.*

Note: Level 200 indicates ability to perform simple additive reasoning and problem solving. Level 250 indicates ability to perform simple multiplicative reasoning and two-step problem solving. Level 300 indicates ability to perform reasoning and problem solving involving fractions, decimals, percents, elementary geometry, and simple algebra.

State	Total students grades 9 to 12	% of students enrolled in			
		Math	Rank	Science	Rank
Alabama	197,613	73	33	69	25
Alaska	27,582	NA	NA	NA	NA
Arizona	155,919	NA	NA	NA	NA
Arkansas	122,798	90	7	76	12
California	1,269,871	79	27	59	34
Colorado	153,098	NA	NA	NA	NA
Connecticut	123,168	88	9	81	5
Delaware	27,109	86	14	78	8
District of Columbia	18,949	75	30	63	32
Florida	468,910	93	4	87	1
Georgia	298,109	NA	NA	NA	NA
Hawaii	42,828	87	13	71	21
Idaho	57,651	81	22	60	33
Illinois	484,138	70	36	55	35
Indiana	275,914	80	25	71	21
Iowa	132,797	86	14	71	21
Kansas	114,515	80	25	78	8
Kentucky	175,035	88	9	73	17
Louisiana	201,564	85	16	80	6
Maine	60,656	NA	NA	NA	NA
Maryland	185,535	96	2	78	8
Massachusetts	235,350	NA	NA	NA	NA
Michigan	431,833	NA	NA	NA	NA
Minnesota	211,046	74	31	74	16
Mississippi	126,948	83	20	76	12
Missouri	229,868	81	22	78	8
Montana	40,736	88	9	72	18
Nebraska	76,693	78	28	70	25
Nevada	49,357	73	33	49	36
New Hampshire	46,964	NA	NA	NA	NA
New Jersey	293,273	NA	NA	NA	NA
New Mexico	76,062	96	2	67	30
New York	708,794	90	7	83	3
North Carolina	310,919	88	9	71	21
North Dakota	32,896	84	19	82	4
Ohio	524,832	85	16	72	18
Oklahoma	156,971	78	28	65	31
Oregon	131,291	NA	NA	NA	NA
Pennsylvania	480,491	83	20	85	2
Rhode Island	36,882	NA	NA	NA	NA
South Carolina	172,465	97	1	72	18
South Dakota	33,366	NA	NA	NA	NA
Tennessee	229,539	74	31	69	25
Texas	885,269	91	5	69	25
Utah	111,437	NA	NA	NA	NA
Vermont	23,656	NA	NA	NA	NA
Virginia	272,940	91	5	76	12
Washington	224,414	NA	NA	NA	NA
West Virginia	96,398	81	22	75	15
Wisconsin	230,394	85	16	79	7
Wyoming	26,927	73	33	69	25
United States	—	84	19	72	18

HIGH SCHOOL MATH AND SCIENCE ENROLLMENT, 1990

Rank in order

By math enrollment

1. South Carolina
2. Maryland
   New Mexico
4. Florida
5. Texas
   Virginia
7. Arkansas
   New York
9. Connecticut
   Kentucky
   Montana
   North Carolina
13. Hawaii
14. Delaware
   Iowa
16. Louisiana
   Ohio
   Wisconsin
19. North Dakota
20. Mississippi
   Pennsylvania
22. Idaho
   Missouri
   West Virginia
25. Indiana
   Kansas
27. California
28. Nebraska
   Oklahoma
30. District of Columbia
31. Minnesota
   Tennessee
33. Alabama
   Nevada
   Wyoming
36. Illinois
NA Alaska
NA Arizona
NA Colorado
NA Georgia
NA Maine
NA Massachusetts
NA Michigan
NA New Hampshire
NA New Jersey
NA Oregon
NA Rhode Island
NA South Dakota
NA Utah
NA Vermont
NA Washington

— not applicable. NA not available.

Source: Rolf K. Blank and Melanie Dalkilic, *State Indicators of Science and Mathematics Education, 1990* (Washington, D.C.: Council of Chief State School Officers, 1990).

PUBLIC HIGH SCHOOL GRADUATION RATE, 1989-1990

State	9th grade enrollment (fall 1986)	Graduates 1989-1990	Graduation rate %	Graduation rate Rank	Rank in order By graduation rate
Alabama	62,612	40,485	64.7	44	1. Minnesota
Alaska	7,872	5,386	68.4	38	2. North Dakota
Arizona	44,263	32,103	72.5	31	3. Iowa
Arkansas	34,501	26,475	76.7	22	4. Hawaii
California	348,672	236,291	67.8	42	5. South Dakota
Colorado	44,478	32,967	74.1	26	6. Nebraska
Connecticut	37,191	27,842	74.9	25	7. Wisconsin
Delaware	8,103	5,550	68.5	37	8. Montana
District of Columbia	5,884	3,626	61.6	48	9. Utah
Florida	145,470	88,934	61.1	49	10. Vermont
Georgia	90,274	56,605	62.7	47	11. Kansas
Hawaii	11,896	10,325	86.8	4	12. New Jersey
Idaho	15,080	11,971	79.4	13	13. Idaho
Illinois	141,211	108,119	76.6	23	14. Pennsylvania
Indiana	79,787	59,868	75.0	24	15. Wyoming
Iowa	36,316	31,796	87.6	3	16. Maine
Kansas	30,940	25,367	82.0	11	17. Oklahoma
Kentucky	55,038	38,005	69.1	36	18. West Virginia
Louisiana	63,616	36,053	56.7	51	19. Nevada
Maine	17,829	13,839	77.6	16	20. Washington
Maryland	57,118	41,566	72.8	30	21. Massachusetts
Massachusetts	70,205	54,065	77.0	21	22. Arkansas
Michigan	133,796	93,737	70.1	34	23. Illinois
Minnesota	54,693	49,087	89.8	1	24. Indiana
Mississippi	39,196	25,182	64.2	45	25. Connecticut
Missouri	67,105	48,457	72.2	32	26. Colorado
Montana	11,249	9,370	83.3	8	27. Ohio
Nebraska	20,650	17,664	85.5	6	28. New Hampshire
Nevada	12,273	9,477	77.2	19	29. Virginia
New Hampshire	14,547	10,766	74.0	28	30. Maryland
New Jersey	87,477	69,824	79.8	12	31. Arizona
New Mexico	21,820	14,884	68.2	39	32. Missouri
New York	220,033	143,318	65.1	43	33. Oregon
North Carolina	95,311	64,782	68.0	40	34. Michigan
North Dakota	8,733	7,690	88.1	2	35. Rhode Island
Ohio	154,659	114,513	74.0	27	36. Kentucky
Oklahoma	45,930	35,606	77.5	17	37. Delaware
Oregon	35,552	25,473	71.7	33	38. Alaska
Pennsylvania	139,761	110,527	79.1	14	39. New Mexico
Rhode Island	11,238	7,825	69.6	35	40. North Carolina
South Carolina	55,488	32,483	58.5	50	41. Tennessee
South Dakota	8,929	7,650	85.7	5	42. California
Tennessee	67,900	46,094	67.9	41	43. New York
Texas	269,256	172,480	64.1	46	44. Alabama
Utah	26,935	22,373	83.1	9	45. Mississippi
Vermont	6,685	5,500	82.3	10	46. Texas
Virginia	82,294	60,605	73.6	29	47. Georgia
Washington	59,514	45,941	77.2	20	48. District of Columbia
West Virginia	28,278	21,854	77.3	18	49. Florida
Wisconsin	61,791	52,038	84.2	7	50. South Carolina
Wyoming	7,411	5,823	78.6	15	51. Louisiana
United States	**3,256,860**	**2,318,888**	**71.2**	**34**	

Source: U.S. Department of Education, National Center for Education Statistics, unpublished data, 1992.

State	Average age of persons tested	Persons tested	GED credentials issued	Passage rate %	Rank by %
Alabama	25.5	13,095	8,022	61.3	30
Alaska	23.7	2,637	1,623	61.5	29
Arizona	24.4	14,157	9,978	70.5	15
Arkansas	26.7	10,221	7,891	77.2	5
California	25.0	58,625	39,226	66.9	20
Colorado	24.8	10,385	6,818	65.7	22
Connecticut	26.0	7,557	5,306	70.2	16
Delaware	24.8	1,935	821	42.4	47
District of Columbia	24.4	1,525	734	48.1	43
Florida	25.5	50,215	35,673	71.0	13
Georgia	25.8	23,528	15,527	66.0	21
Hawaii	23.1	2,271	1,361	59.9	32
Idaho	25.6	3,682	983	26.7	50
Illinois	26.9	30,481	12,607	41.4	48
Indiana	28.1	15,730	12,520	79.6	2
Iowa	25.5	8,373	5,305	63.4	25
Kansas	25.1	8,185	5,328	65.1	23
Kentucky	28.0	22,491	12,613	56.1	37
Louisiana	23.5	8,874	7,305	82.3	1
Maine	27.0	4,840	3,423	70.7	14
Maryland	25.8	11,692	6,211	53.1	39
Massachusetts	26.1	14,795	10,849	73.3	8
Michigan	25.1	30,660	14,111	46.0	46
Minnesota	25.5	9,906	6,151	62.1	28
Mississippi	24.8	9,594	6,053	63.1	26
Missouri	25.5	11,728	8,543	72.8	9
Montana	24.7	2,726	1,740	63.8	24
Nebraska	25.0	4,494	2,517	56.0	38
Nevada	25.0	3,443	2,734	79.4	3
New Hampshire	26.6	2,963	2,276	76.8	6
New Jersey	25.8	17,524	8,430	48.1	44
New Mexico	25.0	7,172	4,161	58.0	36
New York	25.8	64,360	32,668	50.8	41
North Carolina	26.1	19,220	13,331	69.4	17
North Dakota	27.5	1,469	858	58.4	35
Ohio	28.1	25,388	19,969	78.7	4
Oklahoma	27.7	9,194	6,293	68.4	19
Oregon	25.1	12,623	8,723	69.1	18
Pennsylvania	25.4	26,693	20,378	76.3	7
Rhode Island	25.0	5,576	2,654	47.6	45
South Carolina	25.8	8,506	6,060	71.2	12
South Dakota	25.4	2,216	1,113	50.2	42
Tennessee	27.3	18,792	11,759	62.6	27
Texas	25.2	76,221	39,944	52.4	40
Utah	23.5	5,063	801	15.8	51
Vermont	24.8	1,757	1,264	71.9	11
Virginia	25.9	17,500	10,264	58.7	34
Washington	24.8	16,094	9,523	59.2	33
West Virginia	26.5	6,785	4,155	61.2	31
Wisconsin	25.4	9,971	3,948	39.6	49
Wyoming	27.1	1,810	1,304	72.0	10
United States	25.8	755,033	461,849	61.2	32

Rank in order

By %

1. Louisiana
2. Indiana
3. Nevada
4. Ohio
5. Arkansas
6. New Hampshire
7. Pennsylvania
8. Massachusetts
9. Missouri
10. Wyoming
11. Vermont
12. South Carolina
13. Florida
14. Maine
15. Arizona
16. Connecticut
17. North Carolina
18. Oregon
19. Oklahoma
20. California
21. Georgia
22. Colorado
23. Kansas
24. Montana
25. Iowa
26. Mississippi
27. Tennessee
28. Minnesota
29. Alaska
30. Alabama
31. West Virginia
32. Hawaii
33. Washington
34. Virginia
35. North Dakota
36. New Mexico
37. Kentucky
38. Nebraska
39. Maryland
40. Texas
41. New York
42. South Dakota
43. District of Columbia
44. New Jersey
45. Rhode Island
46. Michigan
47. Delaware
48. Illinois
49. Wisconsin
50. Idaho
51. Utah

Source: American Council on Education, General Educational Development Testing Service, *1991 GED Statistical Report* (Washington, D.C.: American Council on Education, 1991).

Note: Each state has its own minimum score for issuing high school equivalency credentials. The U.S. total for persons tested includes 291 tested in Veterans Administration hospitals.

ADULT ILLITERACY, 1985

State	% of illiteracy among adults	Rank
Alabama	13	19
Alaska	7	48
Arizona	12	21
Arkansas	15	5
California	14	12
Colorado	8	43
Connecticut	12	21
Delaware	11	27
District of Columbia	NA	NA
Florida	15	5
Georgia	14	12
Hawaii	15	5
Idaho	8	43
Illinois	14	12
Indiana	11	27
Iowa	10	35
Kansas	9	38
Kentucky	15	5
Louisiana	16	1
Maine	11	27
Maryland	12	21
Massachusetts	11	27
Michigan	11	27
Minnesota	9	38
Mississippi	16	1
Missouri	12	21
Montana	8	43
Nebraska	9	38
Nevada	9	38
New Hampshire	9	38
New Jersey	14	12
New Mexico	14	12
New York	16	1
North Carolina	14	12
North Dakota	12	21
Ohio	11	27
Oklahoma	11	27
Oregon	8	43
Pennsylvania	12	21
Rhode Island	15	5
South Carolina	15	5
South Dakota	11	27
Tennessee	15	5
Texas	16	1
Utah	6	50
Vermont	10	35
Virginia	13	19
Washington	8	43
West Virginia	14	12
Wisconsin	10	35
Wyoming	7	48
United States	13	19

Rank in order

By %

1. Louisiana
   Mississippi
   New York
   Texas
5. Arkansas
   Florida
   Hawaii
   Kentucky
   Rhode Island
   South Carolina
   Tennessee
12. California
    Georgia
    Illinois
    New Jersey
    New Mexico
    North Carolina
    West Virginia
19. Alabama
    Virginia
21. Arizona
    Connecticut
    Maryland
    Missouri
    North Dakota
    Pennsylvania
27. Delaware
    Indiana
    Maine
    Massachusetts
    Michigan
    Ohio
    Oklahoma
    South Dakota
35. Iowa
    Vermont
    Wisconsin
38. Kansas
    Minnesota
    Nebraska
    Nevada
    New Hampshire
43. Colorado
    Idaho
    Montana
    Oregon
    Washington
48. Alaska
    Wyoming
50. Utah
NA District of Columbia

NA not available.

Source: U.S. Department of Education, *English Language Proficiency Survey* (Washington, D.C.: Department of Education, 1985).

Note: The data is based on a survey taken in 1985. It is the only state-by-state measurement of illiteracy at present.

FEDERAL REVENUE FOR PUBLIC SCHOOLS, 1989-1990

State	Total revenue	Federal revenue	% of total revenue	Rank by %
Alabama	$2,557,836,000	$286,598,000	11.2	5
Alaska	909,380,000	116,277,000	12.8	2
Arizona	2,742,625,000	216,488,000	7.9	16
Arkansas	1,594,428,000	153,637,000	9.6	11
California	24,320,281,000	1,605,281,000	6.6	20
Colorado	2,767,107,000	132,246,000	4.8	42
Connecticut	3,554,800,000	161,933,000	4.6	45
Delaware	542,448,000	39,616,000	7.3	18
District of Columbia	557,089,000	54,591,000	9.8	9
Florida	9,589,961,000	595,711,000	6.2	24
Georgia	5,194,517,000	329,253,000	6.3	23
Hawaii	755,987,000	76,099,000	10.1	7
Idaho	710,841,000	56,891,000	8.0	15
Illinois	9,001,253,000	531,923,000	5.9	26
Indiana	4,349,969,000	211,441,000	4.9	41
Iowa	2,149,710,000	105,270,000	4.9	40
Kansas	2,085,315,000	103,598,000	5.0	38
Kentucky	2,247,379,000	220,813,000	9.8	8
Louisiana	3,058,293,000	309,117,000	10.1	6
Maine	1,154,667,000	62,805,000	5.4	32
Maryland	4,267,441,000	196,285,000	4.6	44
Massachusetts	5,117,504,000	240,192,000	4.7	43
Michigan	8,394,959,000	482,031,000	5.7	29
Minnesota	3,988,317,000	165,059,000	4.1	48
Mississippi	1,573,464,000	243,774,000	15.5	1
Missouri	3,699,939,000	205,179,000	5.5	31
Montana	707,594,000	63,726,000	9.0	12
Nebraska	1,359,712,000	79,742,000	5.9	27
Nevada	860,464,000	36,018,000	4.2	47
New Hampshire	900,843,000	24,944,000	2.8	51
New Jersey	8,763,058,000	336,351,000	3.8	50
New Mexico	1,255,429,000	150,229,000	12.0	3
New York	19,744,546,000	1,014,296,000	5.1	36
North Carolina	4,683,693,000	300,405,000	6.4	22
North Dakota	487,049,000	47,517,000	9.8	10
Ohio	8,617,848,000	462,810,000	5.4	33
Oklahoma	2,172,547,000	121,530,000	5.6	30
Oregon	2,539,734,000	155,250,000	6.1	25
Pennsylvania	10,336,060,000	534,118,000	5.2	35
Rhode Island	844,009,000	41,524,000	4.9	39
South Carolina	2,678,790,000	215,088,000	8.0	14
South Dakota	503,949,000	57,774,000	11.5	4
Tennessee	2,907,714,000	261,676,000	9.0	13
Texas	13,948,117,000	1,012,383,000	7.3	19
Utah	1,326,479,000	86,986,000	6.6	21
Vermont	562,543,000	24,464,000	4.3	46
Virginia	5,101,281,000	268,730,000	5.3	34
Washington	4,192,291,000	243,402,000	5.8	28
West Virginia	1,413,165,000	106,072,000	7.5	17
Wisconsin	4,240,432,000	174,249,000	4.1	49
Wyoming	581,050,000	29,140,000	5.0	37
United States	**$207,583,910,000**	**$12,750,530,000**	**6.1**	**25**

Rank in order

By %

1. Mississippi
2. Alaska
3. New Mexico
4. South Dakota
5. Alabama
6. Louisiana
7. Hawaii
8. Kentucky
9. District of Columbia
10. North Dakota
11. Arkansas
12. Montana
13. Tennessee
14. South Carolina
15. Idaho
16. Arizona
17. West Virginia
18. Delaware
19. Texas
20. California
21. Utah
22. North Carolina
23. Georgia
24. Florida
25. Oregon
26. Illinois
27. Nebraska
28. Washington
29. Michigan
30. Oklahoma
31. Missouri
32. Maine
33. Ohio
34. Virginia
35. Pennsylvania
36. New York
37. Wyoming
38. Kansas
39. Rhode Island
40. Iowa
41. Indiana
42. Colorado
43. Massachusetts
44. Maryland
45. Connecticut
46. Vermont
47. Nevada
48. Minnesota
49. Wisconsin
50. New Jersey
51. New Hampshire

Source: U.S Department of Education, National Center for Education Statistics, *Digest of Education Statistics, 1992* (Washington, D.C.: Government Printing Office, 1992).

Note: Public school data include elementary and secondary schools.

STATE REVENUE FOR PUBLIC SCHOOLS, 1989-1990					Rank in order
State	**Total revenue**	**State revenue**	**% of total revenue**	**Rank by %**	**By %**
Alabama	$2,557,836,000	$1,534,021,000	60.0	11	1. Hawaii
Alaska	909,380,000	567,900,000	62.4	9	2. Washington
Arizona	2,742,625,000	1,194,354,000	43.5	31	3. New Mexico
Arkansas	1,594,428,000	905,487,000	56.8	14	4. Kentucky
California	24,320,281,000	16,260,203,000	66.9	5	5. California
Colorado	2,767,107,000	1,055,366,000	38.1	39	6. North Carolina
Connecticut	3,554,800,000	1,533,343,000	43.1	32	7. Delaware
Delaware	542,448,000	362,161,000	66.8	7	8. West Virginia
District of Columbia	557,089,000	—	—	—	9. Alaska
Florida	9,589,961,000	4,914,474,000	51.2	21	10. Idaho
Georgia	5,194,517,000	2,759,335,000	53.1	19	11. Alabama
Hawaii	755,987,000	660,341,000	87.3	1	12. Indiana
Idaho	710,841,000	427,757,000	60.2	10	13. Oklahoma
Illinois	9,001,253,000	2,952,592,000	32.8	44	14. Arkansas
Indiana	4,349,969,000	2,510,251,000	57.7	12	15. Utah
Iowa	2,149,710,000	1,056,130,000	49.1	24	16. Mississippi
Kansas	2,085,315,000	920,867,000	44.2	28	17. Louisiana
Kentucky	2,247,379,000	1,540,138,000	68.5	4	18. Maine
Louisiana	3,058,293,000	1,696,645,000	55.5	17	19. Georgia
Maine	1,154,667,000	613,447,000	53.1	18	20. Minnesota
Maryland	4,267,441,000	1,609,649,000	37.7	41	21. Florida
Massachusetts	5,117,504,000	1,765,255,000	34.5	42	22. Wyoming
Michigan	8,394,959,000	2,251,071,000	26.8	46	23. South Carolina
Minnesota	3,988,317,000	2,088,236,000	52.4	20	24. Iowa
Mississippi	1,573,464,000	884,024,000	56.2	16	25. Montana
Missouri	3,699,939,000	1,480,193,000	40.0	37	26. Tennessee
Montana	707,594,000	324,888,000	45.9	25	27. North Dakota
Nebraska	1,359,712,000	314,371,000	23.1	49	28. Kansas
Nevada	860,464,000	326,773,000	38.0	40	29. Pennsylvania
New Hampshire	900,843,000	75,684,000	8.4	50	30. Ohio
New Jersey	8,763,058,000	3,486,521,000	39.8	38	31. Arizona
New Mexico	1,255,429,000	893,539,000	71.2	3	32. Connecticut
New York	19,744,546,000	8,044,917,000	40.7	35	33. Rhode Island
North Carolina	4,683,693,000	3,127,946,000	66.8	6	34. Texas
North Dakota	487,049,000	218,041,000	44.8	27	35. New York
Ohio	8,617,848,000	3,754,896,000	43.6	30	36. Wisconsin
Oklahoma	2,172,547,000	1,237,503,000	57.0	13	37. Missouri
Oregon	2,539,734,000	637,971,000	25.1	48	38. New Jersey
Pennsylvania	10,336,060,000	4,511,630,000	43.6	29	39. Colorado
Rhode Island	844,009,000	363,539,000	43.1	33	40. Nevada
South Carolina	2,678,790,000	1,340,255,000	50.0	23	41. Maryland
South Dakota	503,949,000	130,552,000	25.9	47	42. Massachusetts
Tennessee	2,907,714,000	1,330,928,000	45.8	26	43. Virginia
Texas	13,948,117,000	5,847,048,000	41.9	34	44. Illinois
Utah	1,326,479,000	751,040,000	56.6	15	45. Vermont
Vermont	562,543,000	181,330,000	32.2	45	46. Michigan
Virginia	5,101,281,000	1,687,176,000	33.1	43	47. South Dakota
Washington	4,192,291,000	3,000,965,000	71.6	2	48. Oregon
West Virginia	1,413,165,000	928,128,000	65.7	8	49. Nebraska
Wisconsin	4,240,432,000	1,703,555,000	40.2	36	50. New Hampshire
Wyoming	581,050,000	297,225,000	51.2	22	— District of Columbia
United States	**$207,583,910,000**	**$98,059,659,000**	**47.2**	**25**	

— not applicable.

Source: U.S Department of Education, National Center for Education Statistics, *Digest of Education Statistics, 1992* (Washington, D.C.: Government Printing Office, 1992).

Note: Public school data includes elementary and secondary schools.

LOCAL GOVERNMENT REVENUE FOR PUBLIC SCHOOLS, 1989-1990

State	Total revenue	Local revenue	% of total revenue	Rank by %
Alabama	$2,557,836,000	$737,217,000	28.8	41
Alaska	909,380,000	225,203,000	24.8	47
Arizona	2,742,625,000	1,331,784,000	48.6	24
Arkansas	1,594,428,000	535,304,000	33.6	39
California	24,320,281,000	6,454,798,000	26.5	45
Colorado	2,767,107,000	1,579,494,000	57.1	13
Connecticut	3,554,800,000	1,859,524,000	52.3	18
Delaware	542,448,000	140,672,000	25.9	46
District of Columbia	557,089,000	502,498,000	90.2	1
Florida	9,589,961,000	4,079,776,000	42.5	31
Georgia	5,194,517,000	2,105,928,000	40.5	34
Hawaii	755,987,000	19,546,000	2.6	51
Idaho	710,841,000	226,193,000	31.8	40
Illinois	9,001,253,000	5,516,737,000	61.3	9
Indiana	4,349,969,000	1,628,277,000	37.4	36
Iowa	2,149,710,000	988,310,000	46.0	25
Kansas	2,085,315,000	1,060,850,000	50.9	22
Kentucky	2,247,379,000	486,428,000	21.6	49
Louisiana	3,058,293,000	1,052,531,000	34.4	38
Maine	1,154,667,000	478,416,000	41.4	33
Maryland	4,267,441,000	2,461,507,000	57.7	12
Massachusetts	5,117,504,000	3,112,058,000	60.8	10
Michigan	8,394,959,000	5,661,857,000	67.4	5
Minnesota	3,988,317,000	1,735,023,000	43.5	30
Mississippi	1,573,464,000	445,666,000	28.3	42
Missouri	3,699,939,000	2,014,567,000	54.4	16
Montana	707,594,000	318,980,000	45.1	28
Nebraska	1,359,712,000	965,600,000	71.0	3
Nevada	860,464,000	497,673,000	57.8	11
New Hampshire	900,843,000	800,215,000	88.8	2
New Jersey	8,763,058,000	4,940,187,000	56.4	14
New Mexico	1,255,429,000	181,661,000	14.5	50
New York	19,744,546,000	10,685,333,000	54.1	17
North Carolina	4,683,693,000	1,255,342,000	26.8	44
North Dakota	487,049,000	221,490,000	45.5	26
Ohio	8,617,848,000	4,400,142,000	51.1	21
Oklahoma	2,172,547,000	813,514,000	37.4	35
Oregon	2,539,734,000	1,746,513,000	68.8	4
Pennsylvania	10,336,060,000	5,290,312,000	51.2	20
Rhode Island	844,009,000	438,946,000	52.0	19
South Carolina	2,678,790,000	1,123,447,000	41.9	32
South Dakota	503,949,000	315,623,000	62.6	7
Tennessee	2,907,714,000	1,315,110,000	45.2	27
Texas	13,948,117,000	7,088,686,000	50.8	23
Utah	1,326,479,000	488,454,000	36.8	37
Vermont	562,543,000	356,749,000	63.4	6
Virginia	5,101,281,000	3,145,376,000	61.7	8
Washington	4,192,291,000	947,925,000	22.6	48
West Virginia	1,413,165,000	378,965,000	26.8	43
Wisconsin	4,240,432,000	2,362,628,000	55.7	15
Wyoming	581,050,000	254,684,000	43.8	29
United States	**$207,583,910,000**	**$96,773,720,000**	**46.6**	**25**

By %

1. District of Columbia
2. New Hampshire
3. Nebraska
4. Oregon
5. Michigan
6. Vermont
7. South Dakota
8. Virginia
9. Illinois
10. Massachusetts
11. Nevada
12. Maryland
13. Colorado
14. New Jersey
15. Wisconsin
16. Missouri
17. New York
18. Connecticut
19. Rhode Island
20. Pennsylvania
21. Ohio
22. Kansas
23. Texas
24. Arizona
25. Iowa
26. North Dakota
27. Tennessee
28. Montana
29. Wyoming
30. Minnesota
31. Florida
32. South Carolina
33. Maine
34. Georgia
35. Oklahoma
36. Indiana
37. Utah
38. Louisiana
39. Arkansas
40. Idaho
41. Alabama
42. Mississippi
43. West Virginia
44. North Carolina
45. California
46. Delaware
47. Alaska
48. Washington
49. Kentucky
50. New Mexico
51. Hawaii

Source: U.S Department of Education, National Center for Education Statistics, *Digest of Education Statistics, 1992* (Washington, D.C.: Government Printing Office, 1992).

Note: Public school data includes elementary and secondary schools.

		Expenditures per enrollee				By expenditure per enrollee
State	**Total expenditures**	**Amount**	**Rank**	**Per capita expenditure**	**Rank by per capita**	

TOTAL PUBLIC SCHOOL SPENDING, 1989-1990 — Rank in order

State	Total expenditures	Amount	Rank	Per capita expenditure	Rank by per capita	By expenditure per enrollee
Alabama	$2,275,233,000	$3,152.14	48	$552.51	51	1. District of Columbia
Alaska	822,472,000	7,222.65	3	1,560.67	1	2. New Jersey
Arizona	2,260,980,000	3,533.59	41	635.82	42	3. Alaska
Arkansas	1,404,545,000	3,219.32	47	583.77	47	4. Connecticut
California	21,485,782,000	4,340.15	24	739.28	25	5. New York
Colorado	2,451,885,000	4,269.99	25	739.19	26	6. Vermont
Connecticut	3,342,033,000	7,124.00	4	1,031.81	4	7. Massachusetts
Delaware	511,718,000	5,134.74	12	760.35	19	8. Rhode Island
District of Columbia	636,383,000	7,886.37	1	1,053.61	3	9. Pennsylvania
Florida	8,228,531,000	4,420.16	23	649.40	38	10. Maryland
Georgia	4,414,016,000	3,832.65	36	685.83	33	11. Wyoming
Hawaii	699,977,000	4,076.55	32	629.48	43	12. Delaware
Idaho	627,794,000	2,842.75	50	619.13	45	13. Michigan
Illinois	8,125,493,000	4,461.11	22	696.99	31	14. Wisconsin
Indiana	4,024,098,000	4,215.56	27	719.49	28	15. Maine
Iowa	2,004,742,000	4,145.01	30	705.90	30	16. Oregon
Kansas	1,848,302,000	4,229.19	26	735.50	27	17. New Hampshire
Kentucky	2,094,231,000	3,290.74	46	561.91	50	18. Minnesota
Louisiana	2,802,793,000	3,571.54	39	639.62	40	19. Virginia
Maine	1,048,195,000	4,871.95	15	857.77	9	20. Ohio
Maryland	3,845,123,000	5,376.47	10	819.16	11	21. Nebraska
Massachusetts	4,760,390,000	5,705.75	7	805.07	13	22. Illinois
Michigan	8,025,621,000	5,073.33	13	865.48	8	23. Florida
Minnesota	3,474,398,000	4,593.49	18	798.16	14	24. California
Mississippi	1,473,807,000	2,933.43	49	562.31	49	25. Colorado
Missouri	3,288,738,000	4,049.00	33	637.48	41	26. Kansas
Montana	641,345,000	4,192.51	29	795.71	15	27. Indiana
Nebraska	1,233,431,000	4,500.24	21	765.63	18	28. Washington
Nevada	712,898,000	3,541.19	40	641.67	39	29. Montana
New Hampshire	821,671,000	4,755.45	17	742.25	23	30. Iowa
New Jersey	7,971,100,000	7,315.31	2	1,030.39	5	31. West Virginia
New Mexico	1,021,082,000	3,382.40	44	668.25	34	32. Hawaii
New York	18,090,978,000	6,962.52	5	1,007.85	6	33. Missouri
North Carolina	4,288,474,000	3,945.71	34	652.64	37	34. North Carolina
North Dakota	459,391,000	3,898.93	35	696.05	32	35. North Dakota
Ohio	8,070,267,000	4,555.57	20	739.92	24	36. Georgia
Oklahoma	1,907,379,000	3,293.77	45	591.62	46	37. Texas
Oregon	2,317,652,000	4,782.10	16	821.86	10	38. South Carolina
Pennsylvania	9,241,300,000	5,540.90	9	767.55	17	39. Louisiana
Rhode Island	786,969,000	5,669.27	8	788.55	16	40. Nevada
South Carolina	2,326,105,000	3,739.05	38	662.33	35	41. Arizona
South Dakota	447,177,000	3,462.09	42	625.42	44	42. South Dakota
Tennessee	2,790,808,000	3,384.46	43	564.94	48	43. Tennessee
Texas	12,763,954,000	3,773.09	37	751.22	20	44. New Mexico
Utah	1,116,251,000	2,492.24	51	653.93	36	45. Oklahoma
Vermont	546,901,000	5,711.04	6	964.55	7	46. Kentucky
Virginia	4,561,874,000	4,568.27	19	748.09	21	47. Arkansas
Washington	3,534,584,000	4,209.30	28	742.40	22	48. Alabama
West Virginia	1,316,173,000	4,082.56	31	708.76	29	49. Mississippi
Wisconsin	3,929,920,000	4,927.05	14	807.46	12	50. Idaho
Wyoming	509,084,000	5,182.78	11	1,071.76	2	51. Utah
United States	**$187,384,049,000**	**$4,545.53**	**21**	**$754.85**	**20**	

Source: U.S Department of Education, National Center for Education Statistics, *Digest of Education Statistics, 1992* (Washington, D.C.: Government Printing Office, 1992).

Note: Public school data include elementary and secondary schools.

PUBLIC SCHOOL SPENDING ON INSTRUCTION, 1989-1990

State	Expenditures	% of total expenditures	Rank by %
Alabama	$1,409,244,000	61.9	11
Alaska	439,628,000	53.5	44
Arizona	1,318,751,000	58.3	29
Arkansas	735,721,000	52.4	47
California	12,160,178,000	56.6	38
Colorado	1,475,510,000	60.2	18
Connecticut	1,833,643,000	54.9	43
Delaware	346,639,000	67.7	1
District of Columbia	288,184,000	45.3	51
Florida	4,759,763,000	57.8	33
Georgia	2,729,736,000	61.8	12
Hawaii	420,364,000	60.1	20
Idaho	366,630,000	58.4	28
Illinois	4,580,000,000	56.4	40
Indiana	2,332,145,000	58.0	31
Iowa	1,203,193,000	60.0	21
Kansas	1,061,382,000	57.4	34
Kentucky	1,081,298,000	51.6	49
Louisiana	1,639,505,000	58.5	27
Maine	600,373,000	57.3	36
Maryland	2,019,963,000	52.5	46
Massachusetts	2,642,765,000	55.5	41
Michigan	4,157,270,000	51.8	48
Minnesota	2,200,134,000	63.3	4
Mississippi	919,413,000	62.4	7
Missouri	1,989,034,000	60.5	16
Montana	398,079,000	62.1	9
Nebraska	750,669,000	60.9	14
Nevada	431,571,000	60.5	15
New Hampshire	511,957,000	62.3	8
New Jersey	4,233,091,000	53.1	45
New Mexico	594,571,000	58.2	30
New York	11,932,397,000	66.0	2
North Carolina	2,661,413,000	62.1	10
North Dakota	277,047,000	60.3	17
Ohio	4,564,730,000	56.6	39
Oklahoma	1,087,703,000	57.0	37
Oregon	1,358,166,000	58.6	26
Pennsylvania	5,304,025,000	57.4	35
Rhode Island	496,857,000	63.1	5
South Carolina	1,346,483,000	57.9	32
South Dakota	275,338,000	61.6	13
Tennessee	1,658,388,000	59.4	23
Texas	7,084,501,000	55.5	42
Utah	725,087,000	65.0	3
Vermont	327,678,000	59.9	22
Virginia	2,743,571,000	60.1	19
Washington	2,076,608,000	58.8	25
West Virginia	658,555,000	50.0	50
Wisconsin	2,454,141,000	62.4	6
Wyoming	301,001,000	59.1	24
United States	**$108,964,095,000**	**58.2**	**31**

Rank in order

By %

1. Delaware
2. New York
3. Utah
4. Minnesota
5. Rhode Island
6. Wisconsin
7. Mississippi
8. New Hampshire
9. Montana
10. North Carolina
11. Alabama
12. Georgia
13. South Dakota
14. Nebraska
15. Nevada
16. Missouri
17. North Dakota
18. Colorado
19. Virginia
20. Hawaii
21. Iowa
22. Vermont
23. Tennessee
24. Wyoming
25. Washington
26. Oregon
27. Louisiana
28. Idaho
29. Arizona
30. New Mexico
31. Indiana
32. South Carolina
33. Florida
34. Kansas
35. Pennsylvania
36. Maine
37. Oklahoma
38. California
39. Ohio
40. Illinois
41. Massachusetts
42. Texas
43. Connecticut
44. Alaska
45. New Jersey
46. Maryland
47. Arkansas
48. Michigan
49. Kentucky
50. West Virginia
51. District of Columbia

Source: U.S Department of Education, National Center for Education Statistics, *Digest of Education Statistics, 1992* (Washington, D.C.: Government Printing Office, 1992).

Note: Public school data include elementary and secondary schools.

PUBLIC SCHOOL SPENDING ON NONINSTRUCTION. 1989-1990				Rank in order
State	Expenditures	% of total expenditures	Rank by %	By %
Alabama	$198,070,000	8.7	3	1. Nebraska
Alaska	37,562,000	4.6	25	2. South Carolina
Arizona	107,654,000	4.8	23	3. Alabama
Arkansas	118,107,000	8.4	4	4. Arkansas
California	815,429,000	3.8	33	5. Louisiana
Colorado	73,060,000	3.0	45	6. Mississippi
Connecticut	32,321,000	1.0	51	7. North Dakota
Delaware	9,568,000	1.9	49	8. Hawaii
District of Columbia	26,533,000	4.2	30	9. Tennessee
Florida	412,617,000	5.0	18	10. North Carolina
Georgia	266,376,000	6.0	15	11. Utah
Hawaii	49,285,000	7.0	8	12. Texas
Idaho	31,110,000	5.0	19	13. West Virginia
Illinois	297,532,000	3.7	35	14. South Dakota
Indiana	189,244,000	4.7	24	15. Georgia
Iowa	87,734,000	4.4	29	16. Oklahoma
Kansas	88,152,000	4.8	22	17. Ohio
Kentucky	95,566,000	4.6	26	18. Florida
Louisiana	234,410,000	8.4	5	19. Idaho
Maine	29,610,000	2.8	47	20. Washington
Maryland	133,691,000	3.5	38	21. New Mexico
Massachusetts	147,269,000	3.1	43	22. Kansas
Michigan	242,502,000	3.0	44	23. Arizona
Minnesota	143,338,000	4.1	31	24. Indiana
Mississippi	119,758,000	8.1	6	25. Alaska
Missouri	146,684,000	4.5	27	26. Kentucky
Montana	28,213,000	4.4	28	27. Missouri
Nebraska	119,096,000	9.7	1	28. Montana
Nevada	24,508,000	3.4	39	29. Iowa
New Hampshire	29,037,000	3.5	36	30. District of Columbia
New Jersey	203,888,000	2.6	48	31. Minnesota
New Mexico	49,447,000	4.8	21	32. Virginia
New York	566,332,000	3.1	42	33. California
North Carolina	284,685,000	6.6	10	34. Pennsylvania
North Dakota	36,084,000	7.9	7	35. Illinois
Ohio	420,929,000	5.2	17	36. New Hampshire
Oklahoma	108,410,000	5.7	16	37. Wyoming
Oregon	78,768,000	3.4	40	38. Maryland
Pennsylvania	346,623,000	3.8	34	39. Nevada
Rhode Island	14,413,000	1.8	50	40. Oregon
South Carolina	214,535,000	9.2	2	41. Wisconsin
South Dakota	27,169,000	6.1	14	42. New York
Tennessee	194,458,000	7.0	9	43. Massachusetts
Texas	809,828,000	6.3	12	44. Michigan
Utah	70,841,000	6.3	11	45. Colorado
Vermont	16,053,000	2.9	46	46. Vermont
Virginia	179,548,000	3.9	32	47. Maine
Washington	171,992,000	4.9	20	48. New Jersey
West Virginia	80,307,000	6.1	13	49. Delaware
Wisconsin	126,865,000	3.2	41	50. Rhode Island
Wyoming	17,866,000	3.5	37	51. Connecticut
United States	$8,353,075,000	4.5	28	

Source: U.S Department of Education, National Center for Education Statistics, *Digest of Education Statistics, 1992* (Washington, D.C.: Government Printing Office, 1992).

Note: Public school data include elementary and secondary schools.

State	Expenditures	% of total expenditures	Rank by %
Alabama	$667,918,000	29.4	45
Alaska	345,283,000	42.0	1
Arizona	829,807,000	36.7	10
Arkansas	417,505,000	29.7	43
California	8,027,550,000	37.4	5
Colorado	903,315,000	36.8	9
Connecticut	1,021,465,000	30.6	41
Delaware	155,512,000	30.4	42
District of Columbia	235,366,000	37.0	7
Florida	3,054,700,000	37.1	6
Georgia	1,372,772,000	31.1	34
Hawaii	230,328,000	32.9	25
Idaho	194,776,000	31.0	35
Illinois	2,878,965,000	35.4	18
Indiana	1,279,281,000	31.8	32
Iowa	713,815,000	35.6	16
Kansas	655,898,000	35.5	17
Kentucky	647,624,000	30.9	36
Louisiana	900,099,000	32.1	30
Maine	301,413,000	28.8	48
Maryland	1,244,653,000	32.4	27
Massachusetts	1,697,188,000	35.7	15
Michigan	2,931,610,000	36.5	11
Minnesota	1,120,685,000	32.3	29
Mississippi	416,601,000	28.3	50
Missouri	1,153,019,000	35.1	19
Montana	215,053,000	33.5	24
Nebraska	360,461,000	29.2	47
Nevada	256,820,000	36.0	13
New Hampshire	280,676,000	34.2	22
New Jersey	2,730,868,000	34.3	21
New Mexico	377,064,000	36.9	8
New York	5,592,249,000	30.9	37
North Carolina	1,315,344,000	30.7	40
North Dakota	146,259,000	31.8	31
Ohio	3,084,608,000	38.2	2
Oklahoma	557,683,000	29.2	46
Oregon	880,717,000	38.0	3
Pennsylvania	2,993,178,000	32.4	26
Rhode Island	242,391,000	30.8	38
South Carolina	714,302,000	30.7	39
South Dakota	144,670,000	32.4	28
Tennessee	744,797,000	26.7	51
Texas	3,983,101,000	31.2	33
Utah	320,323,000	28.7	49
Vermont	183,609,000	33.6	23
Virginia	1,638,755,000	35.9	14
Washington	1,285,984,000	36.4	12
West Virginia	390,742,000	29.7	44
Wisconsin	1,348,914,000	34.3	20
Wyoming	190,217,000	37.4	4
United States	$63,375,931,000	33.8	23

Rank in order

By %

1. Alaska
2. Ohio
3. Oregon
4. Wyoming
5. California
6. Florida
7. District of Columbia
8. New Mexico
9. Colorado
10. Arizona
11. Michigan
12. Washington
13. Nevada
14. Virginia
15. Massachusetts
16. Iowa
17. Kansas
18. Illinois
19. Missouri
20. Wisconsin
21. New Jersey
22. New Hampshire
23. Vermont
24. Montana
25. Hawaii
26. Pennsylvania
27. Maryland
28. South Dakota
29. Minnesota
30. Louisiana
31. North Dakota
32. Indiana
33. Texas
34. Georgia
35. Idaho
36. Kentucky
37. New York
38. Rhode Island
39. South Carolina
40. North Carolina
41. Connecticut
42. Delaware
43. Arkansas
44. West Virginia
45. Alabama
46. Oklahoma
47. Nebraska
48. Maine
49. Utah
50. Mississippi
51. Tennessee

Source: U.S Department of Education, National Center for Education Statistics, *Digest of Education Statistics, 1992* (Washington, D.C.: Government Printing Office, 1992).

Note: Public school data include elementary and secondary schools.

State	Total expenditures	Expenditures on public schools	% of total expenditures	Rank by %	By %
STATE AND LOCAL GOVERNMENT SPENDING ON PUBLIC SCHOOLS, 1989-1990					**Rank in order**
Alabama	$10,868,400,000	$2,337,600,000	21.5	44	1. Texas
Alaska	5,303,900,000	913,400,000	17.2	49	2. Missouri
Arizona	13,040,000,000	2,824,800,000	21.7	43	3. New Hampshire
Arkansas	5,351,600,000	1,395,400,000	26.1	14	4. Pennsylvania
California	110,724,000,000	24,160,500,000	21.8	42	5. Montana
Colorado	10,705,200,000	2,681,100,000	25.0	25	6. Indiana
Connecticut	13,421,300,000	3,232,800,000	24.1	31	7. Vermont
Delaware	2,574,400,000	549,900,000	21.4	45	8. Maine
District of Columbia	4,019,800,000	573,200,000	14.3	51	9. Virginia
Florida	40,883,800,000	10,024,200,000	24.5	28	10. Nebraska
Georgia	19,648,300,000	5,096,800,000	25.9	16	11. Oregon
Hawaii	4,403,400,000	684,700,000	15.5	50	12. South Carolina
Idaho	2,649,900,000	647,100,000	24.4	29	13. North Carolina
Illinois	34,537,500,000	8,217,400,000	23.8	33	14. Arkansas
Indiana	15,286,000,000	4,121,200,000	27.0	6	15. Ohio
Iowa	8,825,500,000	2,082,000,000	23.6	34	16. Georgia
Kansas	7,492,900,000	1,915,400,000	25.6	23	17. West Virginia
Kentucky	9,605,500,000	1,998,600,000	20.8	47	18. New Jersey
Louisiana	12,926,400,000	2,895,100,000	22.4	38	19. Washington
Maine	4,009,800,000	1,071,600,000	26.7	8	20. Wisconsin
Maryland	16,632,800,000	3,960,700,000	23.8	32	21. South Dakota
Massachusetts	23,133,200,000	4,678,300,000	20.2	48	22. Michigan
Michigan	31,132,200,000	7,987,500,000	25.7	22	23. Kansas
Minnesota	17,121,800,000	4,016,000,000	23.5	35	24. Wyoming
Mississippi	6,592,800,000	1,589,100,000	24.1	30	25. Colorado
Missouri	12,489,400,000	3,658,100,000	29.3	2	26. Utah
Montana	2,512,400,000	698,400,000	27.8	5	27. Oklahoma
Nebraska	4,814,000,000	1,277,800,000	26.5	10	28. Florida
Nevada	4,120,700,000	922,800,000	22.4	39	29. Idaho
New Hampshire	3,286,300,000	931,900,000	28.4	3	30. Mississippi
New Jersey	29,872,300,000	7,726,200,000	25.9	18	31. Connecticut
New Mexico	4,963,100,000	1,134,300,000	22.9	37	32. Maryland
New York	89,937,900,000	19,732,600,000	21.9	41	33. Illinois
North Carolina	18,715,200,000	4,923,800,000	26.3	13	34. Iowa
North Dakota	2,169,700,000	503,800,000	23.2	36	35. Minnesota
Ohio	32,045,500,000	8,324,800,000	26.0	15	36. North Dakota
Oklahoma	8,428,200,000	2,105,200,000	25.0	27	37. New Mexico
Oregon	9,654,700,000	2,554,000,000	26.5	11	38. Louisiana
Pennsylvania	35,617,400,000	10,050,300,000	28.2	4	39. Nevada
Rhode Island	3,673,700,000	809,200,000	22.0	40	40. Rhode Island
South Carolina	9,970,300,000	2,624,100,000	26.3	12	41. New York
South Dakota	1,947,800,000	500,200,000	25.7	21	42. California
Tennessee	12,703,600,000	2,663,600,000	21.0	46	43. Arizona
Texas	47,230,100,000	13,938,900,000	29.5	1	44. Alabama
Utah	4,959,700,000	1,239,100,000	25.0	26	45. Delaware
Vermont	2,026,700,000	543,100,000	26.8	7	46. Tennessee
Virginia	19,493,900,000	5,186,700,000	26.6	9	47. Kentucky
Washington	16,594,200,000	4,279,700,000	25.8	19	48. Massachusetts
West Virginia	4,644,400,000	1,203,100,000	25.9	17	49. Alaska
Wisconsin	16,620,500,000	4,281,200,000	25.8	20	50. Hawaii
Wyoming	2,158,200,000	541,800,000	25.1	24	51. District of Columbia
United States	**$831,540,200,000**	**$202,009,400,000**	24.3	30	

Source: U.S. Department of Commerce, Bureau of the Census, *Government Finances 1989-90* (Washington, D.C.: Government Printing Office, 1991).

Note: Public school data include elementary and secondary schools.

FEDERAL SPENDING ON SCHOOL IMPROVEMENT PROGRAMS, FISCAL 1991

State	Expenditures	Per capita	Rank by per capita
Alabama	$21,858,000	$5.35	18
Alaska	6,042,000	10.60	3
Arizona	16,529,000	4.41	43
Arkansas	12,623,000	5.32	19
California	131,051,000	4.31	44
Colorado	15,124,000	4.48	41
Connecticut	13,815,000	4.20	48
Delaware	6,050,000	8.90	6
District of Columbia	6,024,000	10.07	4
Florida	50,545,000	3.81	51
Georgia	33,385,000	5.04	23
Hawaii	6,130,000	5.40	15
Idaho	6,156,000	5.93	12
Illinois	55,825,000	4.84	28
Indiana	26,879,000	4.79	29
Iowa	13,203,000	4.72	34
Kansas	11,508,000	4.61	37
Kentucky	19,273,000	5.19	20
Louisiana	24,628,000	5.79	13
Maine	6,153,000	4.98	25
Maryland	20,705,000	4.26	46
Massachusetts	24,736,000	4.13	50
Michigan	46,196,000	4.93	26
Minnesota	19,903,000	4.49	40
Mississippi	16,023,000	6.18	10
Missouri	23,903,000	4.63	36
Montana	6,089,000	7.54	8
Nebraska	7,592,000	4.77	31
Nevada	6,118,000	4.77	32
New Hampshire	6,127,000	5.55	14
New Jersey	34,587,000	4.46	42
New Mexico	8,350,000	5.39	16
New York	86,290,000	4.78	30
North Carolina	30,590,000	4.54	38
North Dakota	6,062,000	9.55	5
Ohio	51,773,000	4.73	33
Oklahoma	15,890,000	5.01	24
Oregon	12,486,000	4.27	45
Pennsylvania	54,092,000	4.52	39
Rhode Island	6,094,000	6.07	11
South Carolina	17,999,000	5.06	22
South Dakota	6,071,000	8.64	7
Tennessee	24,060,000	4.86	27
Texas	89,301,000	5.15	21
Utah	10,999,000	6.21	9
Vermont	6,034,000	10.64	2
Virginia	26,640,000	4.24	47
Washington	20,947,000	4.17	49
West Virginia	9,702,000	5.39	17
Wisconsin	23,008,000	4.64	35
Wyoming	6,034,000	13.12	1
United States	**$1,242,803,000**	**$4.93**	**27**

Rank in order

By per capita

1. Wyoming
2. Vermont
3. Alaska
4. District of Columbia
5. North Dakota
6. Delaware
7. South Dakota
8. Montana
9. Utah
10. Mississippi
11. Rhode Island
12. Idaho
13. Louisiana
14. New Hampshire
15. Hawaii
16. New Mexico
17. West Virginia
18. Alabama
19. Arkansas
20. Kentucky
21. Texas
22. South Carolina
23. Georgia
24. Oklahoma
25. Maine
26. Michigan
27. Tennessee
28. Illinois
29. Indiana
30. New York
31. Nebraska
32. Nevada
33. Ohio
34. Iowa
35. Wisconsin
36. Missouri
37. Kansas
38. North Carolina
39. Pennsylvania
40. Minnesota
41. Colorado
42. New Jersey
43. Arizona
44. California
45. Oregon
46. Maryland
47. Virginia
48. Connecticut
49. Washington
50. Massachusetts
51. Florida

Source: U.S. Department of Commerce, Bureau of the Census, *Federal Expenditures by State for Fiscal Year 1991* (Washington, D.C.: Government Printing Office, 1992).

GIFTED AND TALENTED STUDENTS, 1989-1990				Rank in order
State	**Students**	**% of enrollment**	**Rank by %**	**By %**
Alabama	17,827	2.5	32	1. Michigan
Alaska	4,577	4.2	22	2. New Jersey
Arizona	NA	NA	NA	3. Virginia
Arkansas	31,519	7.2	9	4. Nebraska
California	223,712	4.7	18	5. Maryland
Colorado	NA	NA	NA	6. Illinois
Connecticut	NA	NA	NA	7. South Carolina
Delaware	5,025	5.1	15	8. Oklahoma
District of Columbia	NA	NA	50	9. Arkansas
Florida	61,458	3.4	29	10. North Carolina
Georgia	49,384	4.4	21	Texas
Hawaii	8,863	5.2	14	12. New York
Idaho	NA	NA	NA	13. Minnesota
Illinois	141,537	7.9	6	14. Hawaii
Indiana	45,000	4.7	18	15. Delaware
Iowa	18,970	4.0	24	16. Kentucky
Kansas	13,096	3.0	31	17. Pennsylvania
Kentucky	31,825	5.0	16	18. California
Louisiana	19,000	2.4	33	Indiana
Maine	15,785	NA	NA	20. Missouri
Maryland	60,000	8.6	5	21. Georgia
Massachusetts	NA	NA	NA	22. Alaska
Michigan	182,414	11.6	1	Rhode Island
Minnesota	39,725	5.4	13	24. Iowa
Mississippi	18,279	3.6	28	25. South Dakota
Missouri	36,200	4.5	20	26. Ohio
Montana	NA	NA	NA	West Virginia
Nebraska	25,000	9.2	4	28. Mississippi
Nevada	6,389	3.4	29	29. Florida
New Hampshire	NA	NA	NA	Nevada
New Jersey	122,626	11.4	2	31. Kansas
New Mexico	NA	NA	NA	32. Alabama
New York	150,000	5.8	12	33. Louisiana
North Carolina	67,119	6.2	10	34. Tennessee
North Dakota	1,151	1.0	35	35. North Dakota
Ohio	65,486	3.7	26	NA Arizona
Oklahoma	43,297	7.5	8	NA Colorado
Oregon	NA	NA	NA	NA Connecticut
Pennsylvania	80,386	4.9	17	NA District of Columbia
Rhode Island	5,674	4.2	22	NA Idaho
South Carolina	46,961	7.6	7	NA Maine
South Dakota	4,825	3.8	25	NA Massachusetts
Tennessee	15,600	1.9	34	NA Montana
Texas	206,583	6.2	10	NA New Hampshire
Utah	NA	NA	NA	NA New Mexico
Vermont	NA	NA	NA	NA Oregon
Virginia	101,579	10.3	3	NA Utah
Washington	NA	NA	NA	NA Vermont
West Virginia	11,989	3.7	26	NA Washington
Wisconsin	NA	NA	NA	NA Wisconsin
Wyoming	NA	NA	NA	NA Wyoming
United States	**NA**	**NA**	**NA**	

NA not available.

Source: U.S Department of Education, National Center for Education Statistics, *Digest of Education Statistics, 1992* (Washington, D.C.: Government Printing Office, 1992).

FEDERAL SPENDING ON EDUCATION OF STUDENTS WITH DISABILITIES, FISCAL 1991

State	Expenditures	Per capita	Rank by per capita
Alabama	$41,873,000	$10.24	3
Alaska	6,940,000	12.18	1
Arizona	23,840,000	6.36	45
Arkansas	20,074,000	8.46	22
California	187,841,000	6.18	48
Colorado	24,262,000	7.18	38
Connecticut	28,548,000	8.68	18
Delaware	6,666,000	9.80	6
District of Columbia	1,257,000	2.10	51
Florida	93,943,000	7.08	39
Georgia	41,368,000	6.25	47
Hawaii	5,689,000	5.01	50
Idaho	9,140,000	8.80	16
Illinois	114,746,000	9.94	5
Indiana	48,274,000	8.61	19
Iowa	24,734,000	8.85	15
Kansas	18,732,000	7.51	35
Kentucky	33,108,000	8.92	14
Louisiana	30,018,000	7.06	40
Maine	12,063,000	9.77	8
Maryland	37,282,000	7.67	32
Massachusetts	69,613,000	11.61	2
Michigan	71,830,000	7.67	33
Minnesota	33,495,000	7.56	34
Mississippi	25,064,000	9.67	10
Missouri	42,398,000	8.22	26
Montana	7,051,000	8.73	17
Nebraska	13,140,000	8.25	25
Nevada	7,188,000	5.60	49
New Hampshire	8,482,000	7.68	31
New Jersey	76,043,000	9.80	7
New Mexico	13,889,000	8.97	12
New York	133,265,000	7.38	37
North Carolina	50,107,000	7.44	36
North Dakota	5,463,000	8.60	20
Ohio	85,193,000	7.79	29
Oklahoma	26,951,000	8.49	21
Oregon	18,935,000	6.48	44
Pennsylvania	81,135,000	6.78	42
Rhode Island	8,112,000	8.08	28
South Carolina	31,822,000	8.94	13
South Dakota	5,926,000	8.43	23
Tennessee	41,688,000	8.42	24
Texas	133,989,000	7.72	30
Utah	17,626,000	9.96	4
Vermont	4,597,000	8.11	27
Virginia	43,758,000	6.96	41
Washington	31,769,000	6.33	46
West Virginia	17,534,000	9.74	9
Wisconsin	33,234,000	6.71	43
Wyoming	4,382,000	9.53	11
United States	**$2,006,151,000**	**$7.96**	**29**

Rank in order

By per capita

1. Alaska
2. Massachusetts
3. Alabama
4. Utah
5. Illinois
6. Delaware
7. New Jersey
8. Maine
9. West Virginia
10. Mississippi
11. Wyoming
12. New Mexico
13. South Carolina
14. Kentucky
15. Iowa
16. Idaho
17. Montana
18. Connecticut
19. Indiana
20. North Dakota
21. Oklahoma
22. Arkansas
23. South Dakota
24. Tennessee
25. Nebraska
26. Missouri
27. Vermont
28. Rhode Island
29. Ohio
30. Texas
31. New Hampshire
32. Maryland
33. Michigan
34. Minnesota
35. Kansas
36. North Carolina
37. New York
38. Colorado
39. Florida
40. Louisiana
41. Virginia
42. Pennsylvania
43. Wisconsin
44. Oregon
45. Arizona
46. Washington
47. Georgia
48. California
49. Nevada
50. Hawaii
51. District of Columbia

Source: U.S. Department of Commerce, Bureau of the Census, *Federal Expenditures by State for Fiscal Year 1991* (Washington, D.C.: Government Printing Office, 1992).

STUDENT-TEACHER RATIO IN CATHOLIC ELEMENTARY SCHOOLS. 1991-1992

State	Schools	Students	Teachers	Student-teacher ratio Ratio	Student-teacher ratio Rank	Rank in order By ratio
Alabama	44	10,528	688	15.3	39	1. Nevada
Alaska	4	791	55	14.4	46	2. California
Arizona	44	11,672	577	20.2	5	3. Hawaii
Arkansas	32	6,209	462	13.4	49	4. Illinois
California	602	178,007	8,314	21.4	2	5. Arizona
Colorado	46	12,414	750	16.6	28	6. Utah
Connecticut	138	30,573	1,862	16.4	29	7. Louisiana
Delaware	29	10,465	716	14.6	44	8. Pennsylvania
District of Columbia	85	20,854	1,123	18.6	11	9. Michigan
Florida	164	53,638	3,094	17.3	18	10. Ohio
Georgia	28	9,499	569	16.7	24	11. District of Columbia
Hawaii	35	9,112	433	21.0	3	12. New Jersey
Idaho	11	2,042	114	17.9	13	13. Idaho
Illinois	569	170,876	8,211	20.8	4	14. New York
Indiana	186	43,454	2,529	17.2	19	15. Kentucky
Iowa	124	31,297	1,888	16.6	27	16. Virginia
Kansas	95	21,775	1,256	17.3	17	17. Kansas
Kentucky	134	32,328	1,818	17.8	15	18. Florida
Louisiana	183	73,206	3,780	19.4	7	19. Indiana
Maine	21	3,997	269	14.9	42	20. Massachusetts
Maryland	78	22,499	1,346	16.7	22	21. Mississippi
Massachusetts	213	58,512	3,410	17.2	20	22. Maryland
Michigan	306	76,474	4,064	18.8	9	23. Nebraska
Minnesota	206	45,211	3,136	14.4	45	24. Georgia
Mississippi	35	7,994	475	16.8	21	25. North Carolina
Missouri	263	64,257	3,916	16.4	30	26. Washington
Montana	14	2,986	197	15.2	40	27. Iowa
Nebraska	91	21,728	1,301	16.7	23	28. Colorado
Nevada	14	3,432	154	22.3	1	29. Connecticut
New Hampshire	39	6,166	451	13.7	48	30. Missouri
New Jersey	392	108,642	5,992	18.1	12	31. North Dakota
New Mexico	33	6,558	411	16.0	33	32. Oregon
New York	768	224,825	12,593	17.9	14	33. New Mexico
North Carolina	35	8,416	505	16.7	25	34. Texas
North Dakota	30	4,860	299	16.3	31	35. West Virginia
Ohio	472	147,263	7,876	18.7	10	36. Tennessee
Oklahoma	29	6,770	454	14.9	41	37. Wisconsin
Oregon	46	9,052	563	16.1	32	38. Rhode Island
Pennsylvania	666	195,595	10,212	19.2	8	39. Alabama
Rhode Island	55	12,303	784	15.7	38	40. Montana
South Carolina	27	5,863	420	14.0	47	41. Oklahoma
South Dakota	26	4,835	330	14.7	43	42. Maine
Tennessee	38	10,614	673	15.8	36	43. South Dakota
Texas	228	57,611	3,615	15.9	34	44. Delaware
Utah	10	2,658	134	19.8	6	45. Minnesota
Vermont	11	2,222	179	12.4	51	46. Alaska
Virginia	52	16,631	947	17.6	16	47. South Carolina
Washington	77	19,037	1,148	16.6	26	48. New Hampshire
West Virginia	30	5,864	369	15.9	35	49. Arkansas
Wisconsin	374	71,502	4,538	15.8	37	50. Wyoming
Wyoming	7	1,124	84	13.4	50	51. Vermont
United States	7,239	1,964,241	109,084	18.0	13	

Source: National Catholic Educational Association, *Catholic Elementary and Secondary Schools 1991-92: Annual Statistical Report on Schools, Enrollment, and Staffing* (Washington, D.C.: National Catholic Educational Association, 1992).

STUDENT-TEACHER RATIO IN CATHOLIC SECONDARY SCHOOLS, 1991-1992

State	Schools	Students	Teachers	Student-teacher ratio Ratio	Rank	By ratio
Alabama	6	2,424	206	11.8	25	1. Arizona
Alaska	1	148	16	9.3	47	2. Washington
Arizona	9	4,705	266	17.7	1	3. Idaho
Arkansas	5	1,616	145	11.1	32	4. Illinois
California	115	66,255	4,410	15.0	7	5. Pennsylvania
Colorado	7	2,081	184	11.3	29	6. Indiana
Connecticut	25	11,098	961	11.5	27	7. California
Delaware	7	4,301	369	11.7	26	8. Florida
District of Columbia	18	7,609	547	13.9	12	9. Nevada
Florida	30	17,291	1,154	15.0	8	10. Wisconsin
Georgia	7	3,561	296	12.0	23	11. New Jersey
Hawaii	7	2,760	269	10.3	38	12. District of Columbia
Idaho	1	513	32	16.0	3	13. Ohio
Illinois	84	52,105	3,266	16.0	4	14. Michigan
Indiana	23	10,534	683	15.4	6	15. Utah
Iowa	25	7,823	695	11.3	31	16. New York
Kansas	16	5,029	527	9.5	46	17. Kentucky
Kentucky	26	9,488	732	13.0	17	18. New Hampshire
Louisiana	54	22,654	2,035	11.1	33	19. Oklahoma
Maine	3	695	69	10.1	41	20. North Carolina
Maryland	23	8,696	894	9.7	42	21. Massachusetts
Massachusetts	58	23,659	1,919	12.3	21	22. Oregon
Michigan	56	20,329	1,511	13.5	14	23. Georgia
Minnesota	21	7,579	691	11.0	35	24. Virginia
Mississippi	9	1,863	192	9.7	43	25. Alabama
Missouri	43	18,271	1,583	11.5	28	26. Delaware
Montana	4	865	98	8.8	49	27. Connecticut
Nebraska	27	6,220	691	9.0	48	28. Missouri
Nevada	2	1,187	80	14.8	9	29. Colorado
New Hampshire	5	1,830	142	12.9	18	30. Tennessee
New Jersey	80	37,627	2,650	14.2	11	31. Iowa
New Mexico	6	1,412	135	10.5	37	32. Arkansas
New York	131	74,484	5,626	13.2	16	33. Louisiana
North Carolina	3	1,117	90	12.4	20	34. Vermont
North Dakota	5	1,160	115	10.1	40	35. Minnesota
Ohio	78	42,059	3,067	13.7	13	36. Texas
Oklahoma	4	2,060	163	12.6	19	37. New Mexico
Oregon	8	3,068	254	12.1	22	38. Hawaii
Pennsylvania	97	52,282	3,387	15.4	5	39. South Carolina
Rhode Island	10	3,846	401	9.6	44	40. North Dakota
South Carolina	3	1,131	112	10.1	39	41. Maine
South Dakota	5	1,241	130	9.5	45	42. Maryland
Tennessee	11	3,755	333	11.3	30	43. Mississippi
Texas	45	13,330	1,274	10.5	36	44. Rhode Island
Utah	2	1,124	84	13.4	15	45. South Dakota
Vermont	2	599	54	11.1	34	46. Kansas
Virginia	14	4,589	387	11.9	24	47. Alaska
Washington	11	5,781	348	16.6	2	48. Nebraska
West Virginia	8	1,351	175	7.7	50	49. Montana
Wisconsin	27	11,388	788	14.5	10	50. West Virginia
Wyoming	2	29	14	2.1	51	51. Wyoming
United States	**1,269**	**586,622**	**44,250**	**13.3**	**16**	

Source: National Catholic Educational Association, *Catholic Elementary and Secondary Schools 1991-92: Annual Statistical Report on Schools, Enrollment, and Staffing* (Washington, D.C.: National Catholic Educational Association, 1992).

State	Expenditures	Per capita	Rank by per capita	Per $1,000 personal income Amount	Rank
Alabama	$3,508,818,000	$858.11	17	$57.73	10
Alaska	1,098,062,000	1,926.42	1	91.84	1
Arizona	2,807,281,000	748.61	33	47.63	23
Arkansas	1,840,883,000	776.09	30	55.13	18
California	27,217,855,000	895.91	15	43.94	28
Colorado	2,653,866,000	785.86	24	42.55	32
Connecticut	2,334,659,000	709.41	40	27.85	48
Delaware	758,217,000	1,115.03	6	56.60	14
District of Columbia	—	—	—	—	—
Florida	9,096,937,000	685.17	42	37.64	41
Georgia	5,199,458,000	785.06	26	46.89	25
Hawaii	1,268,863,000	1,117.94	5	55.99	16
Idaho	862,416,000	830.04	19	55.92	17
Illinois	7,206,280,000	624.30	45	30.84	46
Indiana	4,404,473,000	785.11	25	46.95	24
Iowa	2,581,131,000	923.48	14	53.92	21
Kansas	1,945,407,000	779.72	27	43.18	29
Kentucky	3,309,670,000	891.37	16	59.79	9
Louisiana	3,464,812,000	814.87	21	56.58	15
Maine	960,894,000	778.05	28	45.44	27
Maryland	3,353,612,000	690.04	41	32.05	44
Massachusetts	3,299,520,000	550.29	49	24.29	49
Michigan	6,948,119,000	741.69	34	40.63	35
Minnesota	4,501,100,000	1,015.59	8	54.74	19
Mississippi	1,902,486,000	733.98	35	57.64	12
Missouri	3,454,018,000	669.64	43	38.56	38
Montana	752,810,000	931.70	12	61.68	8
Nebraska	1,161,219,000	724.86	37	41.87	34
Nevada	997,787,000	777.09	29	42.83	31
New Hampshire	404,343,000	365.92	50	17.47	50
New Jersey	5,830,322,000	751.33	32	30.23	47
New Mexico	1,777,914,000	1,148.52	3	82.02	2
New York	14,580,528,000	807.43	22	36.67	43
North Carolina	6,258,105,000	928.92	13	57.73	10
North Dakota	622,666,000	980.58	9	64.29	6
Ohio	8,008,509,000	732.11	36	41.99	33
Oklahoma	2,597,006,000	817.95	20	53.41	22
Oregon	1,891,945,000	647.48	44	38.46	39
Pennsylvania	6,892,290,000	576.23	48	31.01	45
Rhode Island	724,989,000	722.10	38	38.37	40
South Carolina	3,021,894,000	848.85	18	57.01	13
South Dakota	409,004,000	581.80	47	37.19	42
Tennessee	3,074,195,000	620.67	46	39.65	37
Texas	12,310,342,000	709.57	39	43.18	30
Utah	1,804,567,000	1,019.53	7	74.57	3
Vermont	540,115,000	952.58	11	54.62	20
Virginia	4,868,391,000	774.48	31	39.84	36
Washington	5,748,501,000	1,145.58	4	62.37	7
West Virginia	1,721,050,000	955.61	10	69.90	5
Wisconsin	3,948,375,000	796.85	23	45.83	26
Wyoming	535,714,000	1,164.60	2	72.61	4
United States	$196,461,418,000	$780.91	27	$42.26	33

Rank in order

By per capita

1. Alaska
2. Wyoming
3. New Mexico
4. Washington
5. Hawaii
6. Delaware
7. Utah
8. Minnesota
9. North Dakota
10. West Virginia
11. Vermont
12. Montana
13. North Carolina
14. Iowa
15. California
16. Kentucky
17. Alabama
18. South Carolina
19. Idaho
20. Oklahoma
21. Louisiana
22. New York
23. Wisconsin
24. Colorado
25. Indiana
26. Georgia
27. Kansas
28. Maine
29. Nevada
30. Arkansas
31. Virginia
32. New Jersey
33. Arizona
34. Michigan
35. Mississippi
36. Ohio
37. Nebraska
38. Rhode Island
39. Texas
40. Connecticut
41. Maryland
42. Florida
43. Missouri
44. Oregon
45. Illinois
46. Tennessee
47. South Dakota
48. Pennsylvania
49. Massachusetts
50. New Hampshire
— District of Columbia

— not applicable.

Source: U.S. Department of Commerce, Bureau of the Census, *State Government Finances: 1991* (Washington, D.C.: Government Printing Office, 1992).

STATE AND LOCAL GOVERNMENT SPENDING ON EDUCATION, 1989-1990

State	Total expenditures	Education expenditures	% of total expenditures	Rank by %	Rank in order By %
Alabama	$10,868,400,000	$4,138,000,000	38.1	17	1. Vermont
Alaska	5,303,900,000	1,245,600,000	23.5	50	2. Utah
Arizona	13,040,000,000	4,457,300,000	34.2	36	3. Texas
Arkansas	5,351,600,000	2,166,100,000	40.5	6	4. Indiana
California	110,724,000,000	35,374,600,000	31.9	44	5. Nebraska
Colorado	10,705,200,000	4,019,000,000	37.5	24	6. Arkansas
Connecticut	13,421,300,000	4,070,800,000	30.3	45	7. North Carolina
Delaware	2,574,400,000	954,800,000	37.1	27	8. Missouri
District of Columbia	4,019,800,000	673,900,000	16.8	51	9. South Carolina
Florida	40,883,800,000	13,395,400,000	32.8	41	10. Kansas
Georgia	19,648,300,000	6,993,600,000	35.6	32	11. North Dakota
Hawaii	4,403,400,000	1,113,500,000	25.3	49	12. Iowa
Idaho	2,649,900,000	997,100,000	37.6	21	13. Virginia
Illinois	34,537,500,000	11,837,100,000	34.3	35	14. Wisconsin
Indiana	15,286,000,000	6,266,800,000	41.0	4	15. Oregon
Iowa	8,825,500,000	3,433,000,000	38.9	12	16. Mississippi
Kansas	7,492,900,000	2,950,400,000	39.4	10	17. Alabama
Kentucky	9,605,500,000	3,380,600,000	35.2	34	18. Michigan
Louisiana	12,926,400,000	4,132,100,000	32.0	43	19. Oklahoma
Maine	4,009,800,000	1,462,600,000	36.5	30	20. West Virginia
Maryland	16,632,800,000	5,670,400,000	34.1	37	21. Idaho
Massachusetts	23,133,200,000	6,144,200,000	26.6	48	22. New Mexico
Michigan	31,132,200,000	11,838,300,000	38.0	18	23. Montana
Minnesota	17,121,800,000	5,768,600,000	33.7	39	24. Colorado
Mississippi	6,592,800,000	2,518,700,000	38.2	16	25. Washington
Missouri	12,489,400,000	4,957,700,000	39.7	8	26. New Hampshire
Montana	2,512,400,000	944,700,000	37.6	23	27. Delaware
Nebraska	4,814,000,000	1,961,200,000	40.7	5	28. Ohio
Nevada	4,120,700,000	1,223,800,000	29.7	46	29. Pennsylvania
New Hampshire	3,286,300,000	1,219,100,000	37.1	26	30. Maine
New Jersey	29,872,300,000	10,022,500,000	33.6	40	31. Wyoming
New Mexico	4,963,100,000	1,867,300,000	37.6	22	32. Georgia
New York	89,937,900,000	25,411,200,000	28.3	47	33. South Dakota
North Carolina	18,715,200,000	7,535,700,000	40.3	7	34. Kentucky
North Dakota	2,169,700,000	849,500,000	39.2	11	35. Illinois
Ohio	32,045,500,000	11,876,900,000	37.1	28	36. Arizona
Oklahoma	8,428,200,000	3,192,200,000	37.9	19	37. Maryland
Oregon	9,654,700,000	3,688,600,000	38.2	15	38. Tennessee
Pennsylvania	35,617,400,000	13,198,200,000	37.1	29	39. Minnesota
Rhode Island	3,673,700,000	1,195,200,000	32.5	42	40. New Jersey
South Carolina	9,970,300,000	3,952,400,000	39.6	9	41. Florida
South Dakota	1,947,800,000	692,900,000	35.6	33	42. Rhode Island
Tennessee	12,703,600,000	4,311,200,000	33.9	38	43. Louisiana
Texas	47,230,100,000	19,393,400,000	41.1	3	44. California
Utah	4,959,700,000	2,051,900,000	41.4	2	45. Connecticut
Vermont	2,026,700,000	850,800,000	42.0	1	46. Nevada
Virginia	19,493,900,000	7,558,900,000	38.8	13	47. New York
Washington	16,594,200,000	6,207,700,000	37.4	25	48. Massachusetts
West Virginia	4,644,400,000	1,756,800,000	37.8	20	49. Hawaii
Wisconsin	16,620,500,000	6,442,100,000	38.8	14	50. Alaska
Wyoming	2,158,200,000	783,600,000	36.3	31	51. District of Columbia
United States	**$831,540,200,000**	**$288,148,100,000**	**34.7**	**35**	

Source: U.S. Department of Commerce, Bureau of the Census, *Government Finances, 1989-90* (Washington, D.C.: Government Printing Office, 1991).

Note: Total expenditures are all expenditures other than the specifically enumerated kinds of expenditures classified as utility expenditure, liquor store expenditure, employee-retirement, and other insurance trust expenditure.

HIGHER EDUCATION TUITION AND FEES, 1989-1990

State	Tuition and fees	Per student (FTE)	Rank	By tuition and fees per student
Alabama	$356,067,199	$2,048	38	1. District of Columbia
Alaska	27,977,546	1,514	48	2. Vermont
Arizona	313,814,819	2,030	39	3. Massachusetts
Arkansas	143,531,638	2,030	39	4. New Hampshire
California	2,647,637,169	2,301	33	5. Rhode Island
Colorado	475,018,039	3,405	18	6. Pennsylvania
Connecticut	603,306,134	5,388	7	7. Connecticut
Delaware	143,558,534	4,396	9	8. New York
District of Columbia	580,504,738	9,686	1	9. Delaware
Florida	949,255,057	2,496	31	10. Ohio
Georgia	531,996,567	2,848	26	11. Maine
Hawaii	67,750,814	1,678	46	12. Indiana
Idaho	66,100,575	1,737	45	13. Iowa
Illinois	1,725,314,205	3,641	16	14. New Jersey
Indiana	837,356,825	3,968	12	15. Maryland
Iowa	527,926,999	3,786	13	16. Illinois
Kansas	238,430,392	2,099	37	17. Missouri
Kentucky	280,590,661	2,271	34	18. Colorado
Louisiana	450,647,869	3,008	24	19. Minnesota
Maine	165,576,389	4,111	11	20. Michigan
Maryland	586,474,693	3,654	15	21. South Carolina
Massachusetts	2,361,533,588	7,144	3	22. Virginia
Michigan	1,296,240,813	3,337	20	23. Tennessee
Minnesota	639,105,816	3,398	19	24. Louisiana
Mississippi	193,139,045	1,961	41	25. Wisconsin
Missouri	719,657,546	3,570	17	26. Georgia
Montana	51,198,949	1,656	47	27. Washington
Nebraska	197,591,880	2,506	30	28. Oregon
Nevada	39,570,480	1,273	50	29. South Dakota
New Hampshire	279,193,329	6,495	4	30. Nebraska
New Jersey	796,383,403	3,770	14	31. Florida
New Mexico	81,417,017	1,421	49	32. North Carolina
New York	4,001,451,935	5,296	8	33. California
North Carolina	636,729,272	2,312	32	34. Kentucky
North Dakota	74,387,421	2,108	36	35. West Virginia
Ohio	1,635,813,215	4,146	10	36. North Dakota
Oklahoma	247,323,188	1,871	42	37. Kansas
Oregon	318,401,597	2,773	28	38. Alabama
Pennsylvania	2,642,272,049	6,014	6	39. Arizona
Rhode Island	363,176,717	6,153	5	Arkansas
South Carolina	385,143,679	3,287	21	41. Mississippi
South Dakota	69,731,492	2,697	29	42. Oklahoma
Tennessee	512,979,546	3,029	23	43. Texas
Texas	1,185,310,317	1,857	43	44. Utah
Utah	112,662,100	1,774	44	45. Idaho
Vermont	244,116,891	8,330	2	46. Hawaii
Virginia	756,618,641	3,111	22	47. Montana
Washington	504,147,966	2,846	27	48. Alaska
West Virginia	137,446,824	2,111	35	49. New Mexico
Wisconsin	679,775,400	3,000	25	50. Nevada
Wyoming	21,154,296	1,020	51	51. Wyoming
United States	**$32,902,511,274**	**$3,424**	18	

FTE full-time equivalent.

Source: National Center for Education Statistics, *State Higher Education Profiles* (Washington, D.C.: Department of Education, 1993).

Note: Tuition and fees are educational charges paid by students.

HIGHER EDUCATION REVENUE, 1989-1990

State	Revenues	Per student (FTE)	Rank
Alabama	$1,532,396,358	$8,815	43
Alaska	270,175,615	14,617	6
Arizona	1,334,281,682	8,631	45
Arkansas	682,913,481	9,657	38
California	12,934,690,047	11,268	15
Colorado	1,373,664,678	9,846	32
Connecticut	1,685,504,884	15,052	3
Delaware	350,251,216	10,726	25
District of Columbia	1,254,183,586	20,926	1
Florida	3,471,589,211	9,129	40
Georgia	2,162,265,750	11,574	12
Hawaii	428,266,654	10,606	27
Idaho	341,061,978	8,964	42
Illinois	5,041,211,183	10,638	26
Indiana	2,348,998,065	11,130	18
Iowa	1,523,734,490	10,927	22
Kansas	1,035,411,990	9,116	41
Kentucky	1,211,780,915	9,806	33
Louisiana	1,380,258,467	9,213	39
Maine	448,290,177	11,130	18
Maryland	2,366,819,463	14,746	5
Massachusetts	5,145,123,875	15,564	2
Michigan	3,799,998,661	9,783	35
Minnesota	2,117,030,234	11,255	16
Mississippi	821,115,622	8,339	47
Missouri	2,249,448,274	11,160	17
Montana	213,889,386	6,908	51
Nebraska	766,470,229	9,722	36
Nevada	267,188,043	8,599	46
New Hampshire	537,126,894	12,496	9
New Jersey	2,597,181,153	12,295	10
New Mexico	652,486,546	11,388	14
New York	10,521,143,647	13,925	7
North Carolina	3,214,719,389	11,674	11
North Dakota	307,552,161	8,714	44
Ohio	4,088,455,702	10,363	28
Oklahoma	973,393,296	7,364	50
Oregon	1,172,092,768	10,209	30
Pennsylvania	5,597,118,402	12,740	8
Rhode Island	679,128,508	11,506	13
South Carolina	1,263,852,219	10,788	23
South Dakota	206,078,627	7,969	48
Tennessee	1,858,949,501	10,977	21
Texas	6,303,317,841	9,876	31
Utah	702,248,339	11,055	20
Vermont	435,074,239	14,847	4
Virginia	2,358,577,899	9,699	37
Washington	1,900,187,450	10,727	24
West Virginia	501,747,085	7,707	49
Wisconsin	2,338,388,315	10,319	29
Wyoming	202,985,243	9,789	34
United States	**$106,969,819,438**	**$11,132**	**18**

Rank in order

By revenue per student

1. District of Columbia
2. Massachusetts
3. Connecticut
4. Vermont
5. Maryland
6. Alaska
7. New York
8. Pennsylvania
9. New Hampshire
10. New Jersey
11. North Carolina
12. Georgia
13. Rhode Island
14. New Mexico
15. California
16. Minnesota
17. Missouri
18. Indiana
    Maine
20. Utah
21. Tennessee
22. Iowa
23. South Carolina
24. Washington
25. Delaware
26. Illinois
27. Hawaii
28. Ohio
29. Wisconsin
30. Oregon
31. Texas
32. Colorado
33. Kentucky
34. Wyoming
35. Michigan
36. Nebraska
37. Virginia
38. Arkansas
39. Louisiana
40. Florida
41. Kansas
42. Idaho
43. Alabama
44. North Dakota
45. Arizona
46. Nevada
47. Mississippi
48. South Dakota
49. West Virginia
50. Oklahoma
51. Montana

FTE full-time equivalent.

Source: National Center for Education Statistics, *State Higher Education Profiles* (Washington, D.C.: Department of Education, 1993).

FEDERAL SPENDING ON HIGHER EDUCATION. FISCAL 1990

State	Expenditures	Per student (FTE)	Rank
Alabama	$20,209,404	$116	15
Alaska	949,679	51	35
Arizona	10,362,739	67	28
Arkansas	12,421,601	176	6
California	31,143,788	27	45
Colorado	8,143,747	58	33
Connecticut	7,028,107	63	31
Delaware	2,772,113	85	23
District of Columbia	237,870,076	3,969	1
Florida	8,158,758	21	46
Georgia	16,593,389	89	22
Hawaii	2,698,515	67	28
Idaho	4,022,381	106	16
Illinois	17,893,069	38	41
Indiana	33,888,207	161	7
Iowa	19,310,322	138	11
Kansas	15,981,403	141	9
Kentucky	18,915,311	153	8
Louisiana	14,417,762	96	19
Maine	4,073,701	101	17
Maryland	5,289,694	33	42
Massachusetts	6,196,929	19	47
Michigan	1,432,574	4	48
Minnesota	17,919,220	95	20
Mississippi	21,301,135	216	3
Missouri	15,908,152	79	26
Montana	1,640,480	53	34
Nebraska	6,607,883	84	24
Nevada	50,084	2	49
New Hampshire	92,115	2	49
New Jersey	6,162,407	29	43
New Mexico	8,087,915	141	9
New York	22,279,845	29	43
North Carolina	25,229,713	92	21
North Dakota	7,289,205	207	4
Ohio	20,153,092	51	35
Oklahoma	12,935,980	98	18
Oregon	7,987,949	70	27
Pennsylvania	17,604,997	40	40
Rhode Island	0	0	51
South Carolina	14,271,380	122	14
South Dakota	5,176,910	200	5
Tennessee	13,662,322	81	25
Texas	26,020,255	41	39
Utah	3,902,624	61	32
Vermont	3,796,336	130	13
Virginia	10,895,193	45	37
Washington	7,880,585	44	38
West Virginia	8,810,356	135	12
Wisconsin	15,183,224	67	28
Wyoming	16,462,266	794	2
United States	**$817,084,892**	**$85**	**24**

Rank in order

By expenditures per student

1. District of Columbia
2. Wyoming
3. Mississippi
4. North Dakota
5. South Dakota
6. Arkansas
7. Indiana
8. Kentucky
9. Kansas
   New Mexico
11. Iowa
12. West Virginia
13. Vermont
14. South Carolina
15. Alabama
16. Idaho
17. Maine
18. Oklahoma
19. Louisiana
20. Minnesota
21. North Carolina
22. Georgia
23. Delaware
24. Nebraska
25. Tennessee
26. Missouri
27. Oregon
28. Arizona
    Hawaii
28. Wisconsin
31. Connecticut
32. Utah
33. Colorado
34. Montana
35. Alaska
    Ohio
37. Virginia
38. Washington
39. Texas
40. Pennsylvania
41. Illinois
42. Maryland
43. New Jersey
43. New York
45. California
46. Florida
47. Massachusetts
48. Michigan
49. Nevada
    New Hampshire
51. Rhode Island

FTE full-time equivalent.

Source: National Center for Education Statistics, *State Higher Education Profiles* (Washington, D.C.: Department of Education, 1992).

State	Expenditures	Per capita	Rank by per capita	Per $1,000 personal income Amount	Per $1,000 personal income Rank
Alabama	$1,435,808,000	$351.14	13	$23.62	6
Alaska	281,192,000	493.32	3	23.52	7
Arizona	1,135,005,000	326.35	21	20.76	16
Arkansas	667,107,000	281.24	32	19.98	21
California	7,234,453,000	330.45	18	16.21	34
Colorado	1,295,084,000	387.85	9	21.00	12
Connecticut	697,710,000	212.01	45	8.32	50
Delaware	364,566,000	536.13	1	27.21	4
District of Columbia	—	—	—	—	—
Florida	2,031,172,000	203.27	49	11.17	43
Georgia	1,541,624,000	232.77	40	13.90	39
Hawaii	466,664,000	411.16	7	20.59	17
Idaho	310,213,000	311.59	24	20.99	13
Illinois	2,321,800,000	222.38	43	10.99	44
Indiana	1,960,004,000	349.38	15	20.89	14
Iowa	961,584,000	376.39	11	21.98	9
Kansas	736,409,000	312.78	23	17.32	30
Kentucky	1,127,846,000	303.77	26	20.38	18
Louisiana	1,165,085,000	274.01	35	19.03	25
Maine	331,659,000	270.42	36	15.79	36
Maryland	1,320,719,000	288.35	28	13.39	41
Massachusetts	1,226,672,000	204.62	48	9.03	48
Michigan	3,078,435,000	349.46	14	19.14	24
Minnesota	1,579,937,000	357.30	12	19.26	23
Mississippi	583,376,000	252.24	37	19.81	22
Missouri	1,000,371,000	207.03	46	11.92	42
Montana	199,912,000	251.35	38	16.64	33
Nebraska	526,411,000	348.94	16	20.16	19
Nevada	321,813,000	205.63	47	13.81	40
New Hampshire	239,556,000	216.79	44	10.35	45
New Jersey	1,631,828,000	228.16	41	9.18	47
New Mexico	614,417,000	407.89	8	29.13	3
New York	3,707,149,000	222.97	42	10.13	46
North Carolina	1,904,436,000	346.46	17	21.53	10
North Dakota	323,061,000	510.99	2	33.50	1
Ohio	2,961,165,000	276.60	34	15.86	35
Oklahoma	910,571,000	286.79	30	18.73	26
Oregon	806,404,000	306.66	25	18.21	29
Pennsylvania	1,758,206,000	157.15	50	8.46	49
Rhode Island	278,235,000	277.13	33	14.73	38
South Carolina	1,172,838,000	329.45	19	22.13	8
South Dakota	171,286,000	243.65	39	15.58	37
Tennessee	1,445,858,000	291.92	27	18.65	27
Texas	4,332,859,000	282.06	31	17.16	31
Utah	804,345,000	454.43	4	33.24	2
Vermont	251,439,000	443.46	5	25.43	5
Virginia	2,062,667,000	328.14	20	16.88	32
Washington	1,918,580,000	382.34	10	20.81	15
West Virginia	518,461,000	287.87	29	21.06	11
Wisconsin	1,579,812,000	318.83	22	18.34	28
Wyoming	148,210,000	411.39	6	20.01	20
United States	$65,444,214,000	$284.81	31	$15.41	38

STATE SPENDING ON HIGHER EDUCATION, FISCAL 1991

Rank in order

By per capita

1. Delaware
2. North Dakota
3. Alaska
4. Utah
5. Vermont
6. Wyoming
7. Hawaii
8. New Mexico
9. Colorado
10. Washington
11. Iowa
12. Minnesota
13. Alabama
14. Michigan
15. Indiana
16. Nebraska
17. North Carolina
18. California
19. South Carolina
20. Virginia
21. Arizona
22. Wisconsin
23. Kansas
24. Idaho
25. Oregon
26. Kentucky
27. Tennessee
28. Maryland
29. West Virginia
30. Oklahoma
31. Texas
32. Arkansas
33. Rhode Island
34. Ohio
35. Louisiana
36. Maine
37. Mississippi
38. Montana
39. South Dakota
40. Georgia
41. New Jersey
42. New York
43. Illinois
44. New Hampshire
45. Connecticut
46. Missouri
47. Nevada
48. Massachusetts
49. Florida
50. Pennsylvania
— District of Columbia

— not applicable.

Source: U.S. Department of Commerce, Bureau of the Census, *State Government Finances: 1991* (Washington, D.C.: Government Printing Office, 1992).

STATE AND LOCAL GOVERNMENT SPENDING ON HIGHER EDUCATION, 1989-1990

State	Expenditures	% of total expenditures	Rank by %	Per capita	Rank by per capita
Alabama	$1,344,400,000	12.4	10	$332.69	22
Alaska	245,500,000	4.6	50	446.43	5
Arizona	1,502,400,000	11.5	16	409.94	9
Arkansas	589,400,000	11.0	20	250.71	38
California	10,036,400,000	9.1	32	337.25	20
Colorado	1,257,300,000	11.7	13	381.70	13
Connecticut	652,500,000	4.9	49	198.52	48
Delaware	332,600,000	12.9	5	499.45	1
District of Columbia	100,700,000	2.5	51	165.96	51
Florida	2,661,200,000	6.5	45	205.69	47
Georgia	1,498,500,000	7.6	39	213.33	46
Hawaii	409,700,000	9.3	30	369.75	15
Idaho	309,100,000	11.7	14	306.99	26
Illinois	2,940,500,000	8.5	35	257.24	37
Indiana	1,797,900,000	11.8	12	324.30	23
Iowa	1,204,000,000	13.6	3	433.55	7
Kansas	941,800,000	12.6	9	380.06	14
Kentucky	1,069,400,000	11.1	19	290.19	30
Louisiana	1,011,600,000	7.8	38	239.72	40
Maine	331,300,000	8.3	37	269.75	33
Maryland	1,458,900,000	8.8	34	305.15	28
Massachusetts	1,172,800,000	5.1	47	194.94	49
Michigan	3,550,400,000	11.4	18	381.97	12
Minnesota	1,507,200,000	8.8	33	344.49	19
Mississippi	791,700,000	12.0	11	307.69	25
Missouri	1,142,800,000	9.2	31	223.34	44
Montana	183,200,000	7.3	42	229.27	42
Nebraska	612,700,000	12.7	6	388.31	11
Nevada	272,500,000	6.6	44	226.68	43
New Hampshire	239,900,000	7.3	41	216.30	45
New Jersey	2,027,000,000	6.8	43	262.22	35
New Mexico	666,400,000	13.4	4	439.86	6
New York	4,454,700,000	5.0	48	247.62	39
North Carolina	2,379,300,000	12.7	7	358.92	17
North Dakota	310,000,000	14.3	2	485.08	3
Ohio	3,038,100,000	9.5	29	280.09	32
Oklahoma	962,300,000	11.4	17	305.88	27
Oregon	1,027,800,000	10.6	24	361.63	16
Pennsylvania	2,067,200,000	5.8	46	173.98	50
Rhode Island	270,400,000	7.4	40	269.59	34
South Carolina	1,096,600,000	11.0	21	314.47	24
South Dakota	162,700,000	8.4	36	233.79	41
Tennessee	1,371,500,000	10.8	22	281.21	31
Texas	5,041,800,000	10.7	23	296.81	29
Utah	738,500,000	14.9	1	428.61	8
Vermont	254,800,000	12.6	8	452.50	4
Virginia	2,064,300,000	10.6	25	333.65	21
Washington	1,705,600,000	10.3	27	350.44	18
West Virginia	467,100,000	10.1	28	260.49	36
Wisconsin	1,920,500,000	11.6	15	392.59	10
Wyoming	223,500,000	10.4	26	492.22	2
United States	**$73,418,300,000**	**8.8**	**33**	**$295.20**	**30**

Rank in order

By %

1. Utah
2. North Dakota
3. Iowa
4. New Mexico
5. Delaware
6. Nebraska
7. North Carolina
8. Vermont
9. Kansas
10. Alabama
11. Mississippi
12. Indiana
13. Colorado
14. Idaho
15. Wisconsin
16. Arizona
17. Oklahoma
18. Michigan
19. Kentucky
20. Arkansas
21. South Carolina
22. Tennessee
23. Texas
24. Oregon
25. Virginia
26. Wyoming
27. Washington
28. West Virginia
29. Ohio
30. Hawaii
31. Missouri
32. California
33. Minnesota
34. Maryland
35. Illinois
36. South Dakota
37. Maine
38. Louisiana
39. Georgia
40. Rhode Island
41. New Hampshire
42. Montana
43. New Jersey
44. Nevada
45. Florida
46. Pennsylvania
47. Massachusetts
48. New York
49. Connecticut
50. Alaska
51. District of Columbia

Source: U.S. Department of Commerce, Bureau of the Census, *Government Finances 1989-90* (Washington, D.C.: Government Printing Office, 1991).

STATE AND LOCAL APPROPRIATIONS FOR HIGHER EDUCATION. FISCAL 1990				Rank in order
State	Appropriations	Per student (FTE)	Rank	By appropriations per student
Alabama	$684,251,666	$3,936	28	1. Alaska
Alaska	159,181,245	8,612	1	2. Hawaii
Arizona	689,587,658	4,461	14	3. Wyoming
Arkansas	307,965,812	4,355	17	4. New Mexico
California	5,875,250,913	5,122	5	5. California
Colorado	416,669,348	2,987	44	6. Maryland
Connecticut	359,150,830	3,207	42	7. South Carolina
Delaware	114,488,092	3,506	36	8. New Jersey
District of Columbia	74,958,000	1,251	51	9. North Carolina
Florida	1,638,602,063	4,309	18	10. Nevada
Georgia	862,341,196	4,616	11	11. Georgia
Hawaii	257,625,683	6,380	2	12. Kansas
Idaho	158,952,184	4,177	21	13. Kentucky
Illinois	1,546,752,291	3,264	41	14. Arizona
Indiana	831,712,400	3,941	27	15. Texas
Iowa	514,246,408	3,688	34	16. Utah
Kansas	521,534,777	4,592	12	17. Arkansas
Kentucky	564,322,832	4,567	13	18. Florida
Louisiana	502,246,112	3,352	39	19. Wisconsin
Maine	164,771,277	4,091	23	20. Washington
Maryland	820,259,964	5,110	6	21. Idaho
Massachusetts	568,792,411	1,721	48	22. Oregon
Michigan	1,451,257,908	3,736	33	23. Maine
Minnesota	704,066,878	3,743	32	24. Nebraska
Mississippi	395,225,792	4,014	25	25. Mississippi
Missouri	600,077,088	2,977	45	26. Tennessee
Montana	104,378,082	3,397	38	27. Indiana
Nebraska	319,476,978	4,052	24	28. Alabama
Nevada	145,039,657	4,668	10	29. New York
New Hampshire	65,099,232	1,514	49	30. Virginia
New Jersey	1,049,239,764	4,967	8	31. West Virginia
New Mexico	306,157,407	5,344	4	32. Minnesota
New York	2,882,424,308	3,815	29	33. Michigan
North Carolina	1,363,257,203	4,951	9	34. Iowa
North Dakota	127,747,237	3,620	35	35. North Dakota
Ohio	1,361,201,623	3,450	37	36. Delaware
Oklahoma	439,406,751	3,324	40	37. Ohio
Oregon	472,889,628	4,119	22	38. Montana
Pennsylvania	1,073,012,972	2,442	46	39. Louisiana
Rhode Island	127,965,907	2,168	47	40. Oklahoma
South Carolina	584,510,404	4,989	7	41. Illinois
South Dakota	77,663,408	3,003	43	42. Connecticut
Tennessee	667,592,228	3,942	26	43. South Dakota
Texas	2,830,133,870	4,434	15	44. Colorado
Utah	281,247,670	4,427	16	45. Missouri
Vermont	41,271,115	1,408	50	46. Pennsylvania
Virginia	926,560,433	3,810	30	47. Rhode Island
Washington	750,765,611	4,238	20	48. Massachusetts
West Virginia	247,794,929	3,806	31	49. New Hampshire
Wisconsin	972,301,256	4,290	19	50. Vermont
Wyoming	126,456,393	6,098	3	51. District of Columbia
United States	$38,127,884,894	$3,968	26	

FTE full-time equivalent.

Source: National Center for Education Statistics, *State Higher Education Profiles* (Washington, D.C.: Department of Education, 1993).

FEDERAL SPENDING ON HIGHER EDUCATION ACT INSURED LOANS, FISCAL 1991				Rank in order

State	Expenditures	Per capita	Rank by per capita	By per capita
Alabama	$81,979,000	$20.05	43	1. Indiana
Alaska	0	0.00	50	2. Nebraska
Arizona	267,650,000	71.37	10	3. Minnesota
Arkansas	86,553,000	36.49	27	4. Wisconsin
California	1,099,235,000	36.18	28	5. Pennsylvania
Colorado	257,096,000	76.13	9	6. Massachusetts
Connecticut	137,050,000	41.64	23	7. Vermont
Delaware	14,817,000	21.79	42	8. Iowa
District of Columbia	20,298,000	33.94	32	9. Colorado
Florida	250,784,000	18.89	44	10. Arizona
Georgia	150,329,000	22.70	40	11. Montana
Hawaii	20,686,000	18.23	46	12. North Dakota
Idaho	39,510,000	38.03	25	13. Utah
Illinois	486,085,000	42.11	22	14. New York
Indiana	2,482,114,000	442.44	1	15. Rhode Island
Iowa	221,330,000	79.19	8	16. Oklahoma
Kansas	27,503,000	11.02	48	17. New Hampshire
Kentucky	101,260,000	27.27	38	18. South Dakota
Louisiana	96,225,000	22.63	41	19. Maine
Maine	53,385,000	43.23	19	20. Virginia
Maryland	153,147,000	31.51	35	21. Mississippi
Massachusetts	594,182,000	99.10	6	22. Illinois
Michigan	297,113,000	31.72	34	23. Connecticut
Minnesota	514,419,000	116.07	3	24. Texas
Mississippi	110,312,000	42.56	21	25. Idaho
Missouri	180,735,000	35.04	30	26. Oregon
Montana	55,701,000	68.94	11	27. Arkansas
Nebraska	194,556,000	122.13	2	28. California
Nevada	0	0.00	50	29. Washington
New Hampshire	50,895,000	46.06	17	30. Missouri
New Jersey	236,164,000	30.43	36	31. Tennessee
New Mexico	50,833,000	32.84	33	32. District of Columbia
New York	1,009,924,000	55.93	14	33. New Mexico
North Carolina	109,931,000	16.32	47	34. Michigan
North Dakota	43,569,000	68.61	12	35. Maryland
Ohio	318,373,000	29.10	37	36. New Jersey
Oklahoma	147,102,000	46.33	16	37. Ohio
Oregon	108,013,000	36.97	26	38. Kentucky
Pennsylvania	1,188,707,000	99.38	5	39. South Carolina
Rhode Island	50,302,000	50.10	15	40. Georgia
South Carolina	92,373,000	25.95	39	41. Louisiana
South Dakota	31,760,000	45.18	18	42. Delaware
Tennessee	171,564,000	34.64	31	43. Alabama
Texas	706,461,000	40.72	24	44. Florida
Utah	103,314,000	58.37	13	45. Wyoming
Vermont	52,635,000	92.83	7	46. Hawaii
Virginia	270,781,000	43.08	20	47. North Carolina
Washington	177,126,000	35.30	29	48. Kansas
West Virginia	17,599,000	9.77	49	49. West Virginia
Wisconsin	549,218,000	110.84	4	50. Alaska
Wyoming	8,638,000	18.78	45	Nevada
United States	$13,514,368,000	$53.59	15	

Source: U.S. Department of Commerce, Bureau of the Census, *Federal Expenditures by State for Fiscal Year 1991* (Washington, D.C.: Government Printing Office, 1992).

State	Expenditures	Per capita	Rank by per capita
Alabama	$13,016,000	$3.18	43
Alaska	351,000	0.62	51
Arizona	33,704,000	8.99	12
Arkansas	7,098,000	2.99	45
California	115,533,000	3.80	36
Colorado	25,007,000	7.41	17
Connecticut	12,336,000	3.75	37
Delaware	1,852,000	2.72	46
District of Columbia	6,260,000	10.47	9
Florida	53,572,000	4.04	34
Georgia	11,755,000	1.78	50
Hawaii	4,124,000	3.63	38
Idaho	6,512,000	6.27	23
Illinois	76,753,000	6.65	19
Indiana	50,558,000	9.01	11
Iowa	35,457,000	12.69	6
Kansas	15,674,000	6.28	22
Kentucky	15,249,000	4.11	33
Louisiana	22,911,000	5.39	26
Maine	9,148,000	7.41	16
Maryland	13,080,000	2.69	47
Massachusetts	75,455,000	12.58	7
Michigan	37,159,000	3.97	35
Minnesota	31,362,000	7.08	18
Mississippi	11,812,000	4.56	30
Missouri	30,109,000	5.84	24
Montana	6,839,000	8.46	13
Nebraska	41,299,000	25.93	2
Nevada	2,504,000	1.95	49
New Hampshire	3,322,000	3.01	44
New Jersey	32,763,000	4.22	32
New Mexico	8,215,000	5.31	27
New York	238,925,000	13.23	4
North Carolina	23,351,000	3.47	41
North Dakota	8,163,000	12.86	5
Ohio	69,799,000	6.38	20
Oklahoma	11,295,000	3.56	39
Oregon	6,915,000	2.37	48
Pennsylvania	168,733,000	14.11	3
Rhode Island	7,442,000	7.41	15
South Carolina	11,550,000	3.24	42
South Dakota	32,812,000	46.67	1
Tennessee	17,200,000	3.47	40
Texas	79,106,000	4.56	29
Utah	14,138,000	7.99	14
Vermont	5,860,000	10.34	10
Virginia	36,621,000	5.83	25
Washington	26,475,000	5.28	28
West Virginia	7,803,000	4.33	31
Wisconsin	53,293,000	10.76	8
Wyoming	2,892,000	6.29	21
United States	**$2,207,574,000**	**$8.75**	**13**

By per capita

1. South Dakota
2. Nebraska
3. Pennsylvania
4. New York
5. North Dakota
6. Iowa
7. Massachusetts
8. Wisconsin
9. District of Columbia
10. Vermont
11. Indiana
12. Arizona
13. Montana
14. Utah
15. Rhode Island
16. Maine
17. Colorado
18. Minnesota
19. Illinois
20. Ohio
21. Wyoming
22. Kansas
23. Idaho
24. Missouri
25. Virginia
26. Louisiana
27. New Mexico
28. Washington
29. Texas
30. Mississippi
31. West Virginia
32. New Jersey
33. Kentucky
34. Florida
35. Michigan
36. California
37. Connecticut
38. Hawaii
39. Oklahoma
40. Tennessee
41. North Carolina
42. South Carolina
43. Alabama
44. New Hampshire
45. Arkansas
46. Delaware
47. Maryland
48. Oregon
49. Nevada
50. Georgia
51. Alaska

Source: U.S. Department of Commerce, Bureau of the Census, *Federal Expenditures by State for Fiscal Year 1991* (Washington, D.C.: Government Printing Office, 1992).

Note: Federal expenditures consist entirely of interest subsidies paid to lending institutions.

FEDERAL SPENDING ON PELL GRANTS, FISCAL 1991				Rank in order

State	Expenditures	Per capita	Rank by per capita	By per capita
Alabama	$99,690,000	$24.38	17	1. North Dakota
Alaska	4,962,000	8.71	48	2. Utah
Arizona	94,309,000	25.15	14	3. South Dakota
Arkansas	56,282,000	23.73	19	4. Montana
California	442,932,000	14.58	37	5. Mississippi
Colorado	78,802,000	23.33	20	6. Louisiana
Connecticut	36,322,000	11.04	45	7. Wyoming
Delaware	4,242,000	6.24	50	8. Oklahoma
District of Columbia	−2,593,000	−4.34	51	9. New York
Florida	212,494,000	16.00	34	10. Iowa
Georgia	90,618,000	13.68	42	11. New Mexico
Hawaii	8,393,000	7.39	49	12. Minnesota
Idaho	25,430,000	24.48	15	13. Nebraska
Illinois	188,081,000	16.29	33	14. Arizona
Indiana	110,476,000	19.69	25	15. Idaho
Iowa	73,933,000	26.45	10	16. Kansas
Kansas	60,984,000	24.44	16	17. Alabama
Kentucky	89,897,000	24.21	18	18. Kentucky
Louisiana	126,398,000	29.73	6	19. Arkansas
Maine	17,050,000	13.81	40	20. Colorado
Maryland	53,284,000	10.96	46	21. Ohio
Massachusetts	84,398,000	14.08	39	22. West Virginia
Michigan	196,277,000	20.95	23	23. Michigan
Minnesota	111,843,000	25.24	12	24. Missouri
Mississippi	80,074,000	30.89	5	25. Indiana
Missouri	107,647,000	20.87	24	26. Wisconsin
Montana	25,609,000	31.69	4	27. Rhode Island
Nebraska	40,134,000	25.19	13	28. Oregon
Nevada	17,492,000	13.62	43	29. Tennessee
New Hampshire	10,039,000	9.09	47	30. Texas
New Jersey	86,745,000	11.18	44	31. Pennsylvania
New Mexico	39,766,000	25.69	11	32. South Carolina
New York	492,505,000	27.27	9	33. Illinois
North Carolina	92,877,000	13.79	41	34. Florida
North Dakota	23,539,000	37.07	1	35. Vermont
Ohio	251,888,000	23.03	21	36. Washington
Oklahoma	88,667,000	27.93	8	37. California
Oregon	55,556,000	19.01	28	38. Virginia
Pennsylvania	221,591,000	18.53	31	39. Massachusetts
Rhode Island	19,430,000	19.35	27	40. Maine
South Carolina	58,305,000	16.38	32	41. North Carolina
South Dakota	24,124,000	34.32	3	42. Georgia
Tennessee	93,963,000	18.97	29	43. Nevada
Texas	325,602,000	18.77	30	44. New Jersey
Utah	62,267,000	35.18	2	45. Connecticut
Vermont	8,954,000	15.79	35	46. Maryland
Virginia	89,252,000	14.20	38	47. New Hampshire
Washington	75,742,000	15.09	36	48. Alaska
West Virginia	40,292,000	22.37	22	49. Hawaii
Wisconsin	97,301,000	19.64	26	50. Delaware
Wyoming	12,862,000	27.96	7	51. District of Columbia
United States	$5,110,082,000	$20.26	25	

Source: U.S. Department of Commerce, Bureau of the Census, *State Government Finances: 1991* (Washington, D.C.: Government Printing Office, 1992).

DEFAULT RATE IN PERKINS STUDENT LOAN PROGRAM, 1991					Rank in order
State	**Loans in default**	**Value of loans in default**	**Default rate %**	**Rank by %**	**By %**
Alabama	14,446	$14,203,838	8.4	5	1. Mississippi
Alaska	314	470,244	11.4	2	2. Alaska
Arizona	8,089	9,023,557	6.3	18	3. Louisiana
Arkansas	7,991	7,874,812	7.5	12	4. West Virginia
California	45,405	60,996,182	5.2	33	5. Alabama
Colorado	9,332	11,309,997	5.2	31	6. Texas
Connecticut	6,894	8,396,122	5.0	36	7. North Carolina
Delaware	1,163	1,244,684	4.7	39	8. New Jersey
District of Columbia	3,882	6,096,531	6.1	20	9. Georgia
Florida	17,684	22,557,711	7.3	14	10. Tennessee
Georgia	15,110	15,730,290	7.7	9	11. New York
Hawaii	1,166	1,656,668	5.1	34	12. Arkansas
Idaho	2,234	2,883,097	5.4	28	13. South Carolina
Illinois	22,714	30,008,521	5.3	30	14. Florida
Indiana	9,038	13,015,102	3.7	50	15. Oklahoma
Iowa	9,239	11,467,107	4.4	45	16. Maryland
Kansas	6,994	8,791,192	4.4	43	17. Nevada
Kentucky	10,535	10,826,504	6.1	21	18. Arizona
Louisiana	21,403	20,016,846	10.5	3	19. Virginia
Maine	4,102	5,487,560	5.6	26	20. District of Columbia
Maryland	9,921	11,176,340	6.9	16	21. Kentucky
Massachusetts	19,960	25,547,859	4.6	41	22. Ohio
Michigan	22,780	24,470,085	5.1	35	23. Vermont
Minnesota	9,290	13,361,920	4.1	46	24. Missouri
Mississippi	23,060	16,190,382	12.0	1	25. Oregon
Missouri	13,259	17,806,188	5.7	24	26. Maine
Montana	2,189	2,636,367	4.9	38	27. New Mexico
Nebraska	3,518	4,607,836	4.0	48	28. Idaho
Nevada	902	1,179,265	6.4	17	29. Wyoming
New Hampshire	2,781	4,107,032	4.6	42	30. Illinois
New Jersey	18,020	18,624,066	7.9	8	31. Colorado
New Mexico	3,359	4,347,397	5.5	27	32. Rhode Island
New York	66,433	84,393,349	7.6	11	33. California
North Carolina	20,516	23,902,912	8.0	7	34. Hawaii
North Dakota	2,402	3,137,000	4.0	47	35. Michigan
Ohio	26,875	34,161,648	5.9	22	36. Connecticut
Oklahoma	12,687	14,068,664	7.1	15	37. South Dakota
Oregon	10,379	13,500,451	5.7	25	38. Montana
Pennsylvania	27,237	31,440,573	4.7	40	39. Delaware
Rhode Island	3,923	4,603,632	5.2	32	40. Pennsylvania
South Carolina	10,875	8,533,069	7.5	13	41. Massachusetts
South Dakota	3,197	4,135,554	5.0	37	42. New Hampshire
Tennessee	17,143	18,085,177	7.7	10	43. Kansas
Texas	28,800	35,598,033	8.4	6	44. Washington
Utah	1,835	2,998,695	3.3	51	45. Iowa
Vermont	3,034	3,814,540	5.8	23	46. Minnesota
Virginia	10,513	13,042,995	6.1	19	47. North Dakota
Washington	8,754	12,581,461	4.4	44	48. Nebraska
West Virginia	8,073	.10,217,959	9.0	4	49. Wisconsin
Wisconsin	8,069	12,917,351	3.9	49	50. Indiana
Wyoming	1,215	1,426,970	5.4	29	51. Utah
United States	**628,888**	**$744,730,462**	**6.0**	**22**	

Source: U.S. Department of Education, *Perkins Loan Program Status of Default as of June 30, 1991* (Washington, D.C.: Department of Education, 1992).

STATE SPENDING ON LIBRARIES. FISCAL 1991

State	Expenditures	Per capita	Rank by per capita	Per $1,000 personal income Amount	Per $1,000 personal income Rank
Alabama	$9,453,000	$2.31	31	$0.16	26
Alaska	6,502,000	11.41	2	0.54	2
Arizona	5,747,000	1.53	43	0.10	41
Arkansas	5,547,000	2.34	29	0.17	22
California	53,642,000	1.77	41	0.09	43
Colorado	6,617,000	1.96	39	0.11	39
Connecticut	13,183,000	4.01	10	0.16	25
Delaware	1,826,000	2.69	21	0.14	31
District of Columbia	—	—	—	—	—
Florida	26,311,000	1.98	38	0.11	38
Georgia	20,104,000	3.04	17	0.18	18
Hawaii	35,103,000	30.93	1	1.55	1
Idaho	2,635,000	2.54	23	0.17	20
Illinois	56,930,000	4.93	8	0.24	8
Indiana	6,900,000	1.23	45	0.07	45
Iowa	6,640,000	2.38	27	0.14	30
Kansas	4,359,000	1.75	42	0.10	41
Kentucky	13,103,000	3.53	13	0.24	9
Louisiana	3,010,000	0.71	50	0.05	50
Maine	3,709,000	3.00	18	0.18	19
Maryland	29,029,000	5.97	3	0.28	5
Massachusetts	30,089,000	5.02	7	0.22	11
Michigan	31,521,000	3.37	14	0.18	15
Minnesota	6,348,000	1.43	44	0.08	44
Mississippi	6,072,000	2.34	28	0.18	15
Missouri	5,983,000	1.16	47	0.07	47
Montana	2,249,000	2.78	20	0.18	15
Nebraska	3,666,000	2.30	32	0.13	33
Nevada	6,120,000	4.77	9	0.26	6
New Hampshire	2,688,000	2.43	26	0.12	36
New Jersey	19,672,000	2.54	24	0.10	40
New Mexico	3,374,000	2.18	34	0.16	26
New York	92,400,000	5.12	6	0.23	10
North Carolina	17,958,000	2.67	22	0.17	22
North Dakota	1,880,000	2.96	19	0.19	14
Ohio	12,575,000	1.15	48	0.07	48
Oklahoma	6,150,000	1.94	40	0.13	34
Oregon	3,461,000	1.18	46	0.07	46
Pennsylvania	29,731,000	2.49	25	0.13	32
Rhode Island	5,822,000	5.80	4	0.31	4
South Carolina	7,649,000	2.15	35	0.14	29
South Dakota	2,720,000	3.87	11	0.25	7
Tennessee	11,513,000	2.32	30	0.15	28
Texas	18,655,000	1.08	49	0.07	49
Utah	4,053,000	2.29	33	0.17	21
Vermont	2,169,000	3.83	12	0.22	12
Virginia	19,605,000	3.12	16	0.16	24
Washington	10,448,000	2.08	36	0.11	37
West Virginia	9,242,000	5.13	5	0.38	3
Wisconsin	10,203,000	2.06	37	0.12	35
Wyoming	1,491,000	3.24	15	0.20	13
United States	**$695,857,000**	**$2.77**	**21**	**$0.15**	**28**

Rank in order

By per capita

1. Hawaii
2. Alaska
3. Maryland
4. Rhode Island
5. West Virginia
6. New York
7. Massachusetts
8. Illinois
9. Nevada
10. Connecticut
11. South Dakota
12. Vermont
13. Kentucky
14. Michigan
15. Wyoming
16. Virginia
17. Georgia
18. Maine
19. North Dakota
20. Montana
21. Delaware
22. North Carolina
23. Idaho
24. New Jersey
25. Pennsylvania
26. New Hampshire
27. Iowa
28. Mississippi
29. Arkansas
30. Tennessee
31. Alabama
32. Nebraska
33. Utah
34. New Mexico
35. South Carolina
36. Washington
37. Wisconsin
38. Florida
39. Colorado
40. Oklahoma
41. California
42. Kansas
43. Arizona
44. Minnesota
45. Indiana
46. Oregon
47. Missouri
48. Ohio
49. Texas
50. Louisiana
— District of Columbia

— not applicable.

Source: U.S. Department of Commerce, Bureau of the Census, *State Government Finances: 1991* (Washington, D.C.: Government Printing Office, 1992).

Energy

	TOTAL SPENDING ON ENERGY, 1990						By per capita

| | Per million Btu | | | | Rank by | | |
State	Price	Rank	Expenditures	Per capita	per capita		By per capita
Alabama	$7.92	36	$8,388,000,000	$2,075.72	12		1. Alaska
Alaska	7.03	45	2,128,000,000	3,869.09	1		2. Wyoming
Arizona	11.37	3	6,544,000,000	1,785.54	38		3. Louisiana
Arkansas	8.81	23	4,735,000,000	2,014.04	15		4. Texas
California	9.08	17	48,635,000,000	1,634.24	46		5. North Dakota
Colorado	8.14	35	5,245,000,000	1,592.29	49		6. Indiana
Connecticut	11.62	2	6,131,000,000	1,865.23	31		7. West Virginia
Delaware	9.14	16	1,424,000,000	2,138.14	9		8. Kansas
District of Columbia	11.31	4	1,084,000,000	1,785.83	37		9. Delaware
Florida	10.58	8	20,961,000,000	1,620.11	47		10. Montana
Georgia	8.88	22	12,892,000,000	1,990.12	18		11. Maine
Hawaii	9.76	11	2,186,000,000	1,972.92	22		12. Alabama
Idaho	7.81	39	1,823,000,000	1,810.33	35		13. New Jersey
Illinois	8.74	24	22,442,000,000	1,963.26	24		14. Nevada
Indiana	6.77	46	12,218,000,000	2,203.82	6		15. Arkansas
Iowa	7.71	40	5,164,000,000	1,859.56	32		16. Tennessee
Kansas	7.59	41	5,318,000,000	2,146.09	8		17. Oklahoma
Kentucky	7.91	37	7,323,000,000	1,987.25	19		18. Georgia
Louisiana	6.05	51	13,653,000,000	3,235.31	3		19. Kentucky
Maine	9.54	12	2,549,000,000	2,075.73	11		20. Nebraska
Maryland	9.40	13	7,909,000,000	1,654.26	45		21. South Carolina
Massachusetts	10.57	9	10,557,000,000	1,754.82	42		22. Hawaii
Michigan	8.17	33	16,785,000,000	1,805.81	36		23. New Mexico
Minnesota	8.17	33	7,514,000,000	1,717.49	43		24. Illinois
Mississippi	8.31	31	4,960,000,000	1,927.71	27		25. Ohio
Missouri	8.91	20	9,468,000,000	1,850.30	33		26. South Dakota
Montana	7.87	38	1,686,000,000	2,110.14	10		27. Mississippi
Nebraska	8.43	28	3,126,000,000	1,980.99	20		28. North Carolina
Nevada	9.01	18	2,424,000,000	2,016.64	14		29. Vermont
New Hampshire	11.30	5	1,970,000,000	1,776.38	39		30. Pennsylvania
New Jersey	9.32	14	16,008,000,000	2,070.89	13		31. Connecticut
New Mexico	9.22	15	2,979,000,000	1,966.34	23		32. Iowa
New York	10.68	7	27,550,000,000	1,531.41	51		33. Missouri
North Carolina	10.06	10	12,585,000,000	1,898.48	28		34. Virginia
North Dakota	6.64	48	1,581,000,000	2,474.18	5		35. Idaho
Ohio	8.32	30	21,097,000,000	1,944.96	25		36. Michigan
Oklahoma	7.46	42	6,265,000,000	1,991.42	17		37. District of Columbia
Oregon	8.39	29	5,016,000,000	1,764.95	40		38. Arizona
Pennsylvania	8.63	26	22,238,000,000	1,871.57	30		39. New Hampshire
Rhode Island	10.80	6	1,586,000,000	1,581.26	50		40. Oregon
South Carolina	8.93	19	6,895,000,000	1,977.34	21		41. Washington
South Dakota	8.65	25	1,349,000,000	1,938.22	26		42. Massachusetts
Tennessee	8.61	27	9,719,000,000	1,992.82	16		43. Minnesota
Texas	6.48	49	43,305,000,000	2,549.30	4		44. Wisconsin
Utah	7.16	44	2,755,000,000	1,598.96	48		45. Maryland
Vermont	11.64	1	1,056,000,000	1,875.67	29		46. California
Virginia	8.89	21	11,302,000,000	1,826.73	34		47. Florida
Washington	7.39	43	8,563,000,000	1,759.40	41		48. Utah
West Virginia	6.77	46	3,918,000,000	2,185.16	7		49. Colorado
Wisconsin	8.27	32	8,093,000,000	1,654.33	44		50. Rhode Island
Wyoming	6.46	50	1,531,000,000	3,372.25	2		51. New York
United States	$8.43	29	$472,657,000,000	$1,900.43	28		

Source: U.S. Department of Energy, Energy Information Administration, *State Energy Price and Expenditure Report 1990* (Washington, D.C.: Government Printing Office, 1992).

Note: Expenditures is the money spent by all consumers to purchase energy.

NET GENERATION OF ELECTRICITY, 1990				Rank in order
State	**Net generation (kilowatt hours)**	**Per capita (kilowatt hours)**	**Rank by per capita**	**By per capita**
Alabama	76,200,000,000	18,856.72	8	1. Wyoming
Alaska	4,500,000,000	8,181.82	41	2. West Virginia
Arizona	62,300,000,000	16,998.64	13	3. North Dakota
Arkansas	37,100,000,000	15,780.52	15	4. Montana
California	114,600,000,000	3,850.81	49	5. Washington
Colorado	31,300,000,000	9,502.13	34	6. Kentucky
Connecticut	32,200,000,000	9,796.17	30	7. South Carolina
Delaware	7,100,000,000	10,660.66	28	8. Alabama
District of Columbia	400,000,000	658.98	50	9. New Mexico
Florida	123,500,000,000	9,545.53	33	10. Utah
Georgia	97,600,000,000	15,066.38	17	11. Indiana
Hawaii	8,000,000,000	7,220.22	44	12. Oregon
Idaho	8,600,000,000	8,540.22	40	13. Arizona
Illinois	127,000,000,000	11,110.14	27	14. Nevada
Indiana	97,700,000,000	17,622.66	11	15. Arkansas
Iowa	29,000,000,000	10,442.92	29	16. Tennessee
Kansas	33,900,000,000	13,680.39	22	17. Georgia
Kentucky	73,800,000,000	20,027.14	6	18. Oklahoma
Louisiana	57,400,000,000	13,601.90	23	19. Pennsylvania
Maine	9,100,000,000	7,410.42	43	20. Texas
Maryland	31,500,000,000	6,588.58	46	21. Nebraska
Massachusetts	36,500,000,000	6,067.15	47	22. Kansas
Michigan	89,000,000,000	9,575.04	32	23. Louisiana
Minnesota	39,500,000,000	9,028.57	37	24. North Carolina
Mississippi	23,000,000,000	8,938.98	38	25. Ohio
Missouri	59,000,000,000	11,530.19	26	26. Missouri
Montana	25,700,000,000	32,165.21	4	27. Illinois
Nebraska	21,600,000,000	13,688.21	21	28. Delaware
Nevada	19,300,000,000	16,056.57	14	29. Iowa
New Hampshire	10,800,000,000	9,738.50	31	30. Connecticut
New Jersey	36,500,000,000	4,721.86	48	31. New Hampshire
New Mexico	28,500,000,000	18,811.88	9	32. Michigan
New York	128,700,000,000	7,153.97	45	33. Florida
North Carolina	79,800,000,000	12,038.02	24	34. Colorado
North Dakota	26,800,000,000	41,940.53	3	35. Wisconsin
Ohio	126,500,000,000	11,662.21	25	36. South Dakota
Oklahoma	45,100,000,000	14,335.66	18	37. Minnesota
Oregon	49,000,000,000	17,241.38	12	38. Mississippi
Pennsylvania	165,700,000,000	13,945.46	19	39. Vermont
Rhode Island	600,000,000	598.21	51	40. Idaho
South Carolina	69,300,000,000	19,873.82	7	41. Alaska
South Dakota	6,400,000,000	9,195.40	36	42. Virginia
Tennessee	73,900,000,000	15,152.76	16	43. Maine
Texas	234,500,000,000	13,804.67	20	44. Hawaii
Utah	32,300,000,000	18,746.37	10	45. New York
Vermont	5,000,000,000	8,881.00	39	46. Maryland
Virginia	47,200,000,000	7,628.90	42	47. Massachusetts
Washington	100,500,000,000	20,649.27	5	48. New Jersey
West Virginia	77,400,000,000	43,167.88	2	49. California
Wisconsin	45,600,000,000	9,321.34	35	50. District of Columbia
Wyoming	39,400,000,000	86,784.14	1	51. Rhode Island
United States	2,805,300,000,000	11,279.40	27	

Source: U.S. Department of Commerce, Bureau of the Census, *Statistical Abstract of the United States, 1992* (Washington, D.C.: Government Printing Office, 1992).

State	Average cost		Average annual use		Average annual cost		Rank in order
	Cents	Rank	Kilowatt hours	Rank	Amount	Rank	By average cost
Alabama	5.60	38	31,582	12	$1,767.36	16	1. Rhode Island
Alaska	8.83	9	18,194	44	1,606.46	24	2. New York
Arizona	7.82	13	25,527	24	1,995.36	5	3. Connecticut
Arkansas	6.62	19	23,952	28	1,585.21	27	4. Massachusetts
California	9.27	6	17,245	47	1,597.72	25	5. New Jersey
Colorado	5.93	31	19,180	42	1,136.72	51	6. California
Connecticut	9.61	3	18,818	43	1,809.18	11	7. Hawaii
Delaware	6.62	19	26,652	21	1,765.16	18	8. New Hampshire
District of Columbia	6.25	25	46,348	2	2,898.23	1	9. Alaska
Florida	7.20	16	21,712	37	1,562.89	28	10. Maine
Georgia	6.47	23	26,814	20	1,735.45	20	11. Vermont
Hawaii	9.25	7	22,524	34	2,082.98	2	12. Pennsylvania
Idaho	3.80	50	37,008	5	1,407.34	37	13. Arizona
Illinois	7.63	14	24,003	27	1,832.26	10	14. Illinois
Indiana	5.54	39	28,821	14	1,597.59	26	15. New Mexico
Iowa	5.89	32	23,330	29	1,374.88	40	16. Florida
Kansas	6.56	21	23,165	30	1,520.23	30	17. Michigan
Kentucky	4.81	46	37,025	4	1,780.48	13	18. Maryland
Louisiana	5.88	33	34,930	6	2,053.79	4	19. Arkansas
Maine	8.42	10	17,823	46	1,500.59	31	Delaware
Maryland	6.84	18	26,194	22	1,790.85	12	21. Kansas
Massachusetts	9.54	4	17,053	48	1,627.37	23	22. Missouri
Michigan	7.01	17	20,446	38	1,434.16	36	23. Georgia
Minnesota	5.37	43	24,320	26	1,306.35	47	North Carolina
Mississippi	6.09	28	27,920	16	1,699.36	22	25. District of Columbia
Missouri	6.52	22	22,564	33	1,470.16	33	26. Virginia
Montana	4.22	49	31,719	11	1,339.30	43	27. Ohio
Nebraska	5.39	42	22,918	31	1,236.26	48	28. Mississippi
Nevada	5.61	37	27,812	17	1,561.34	29	South Dakota
New Hampshire	9.13	8	15,387	50	1,404.35	38	30. Texas
New Jersey	9.43	5	19,592	41	1,846.60	9	31. Colorado
New Mexico	7.29	15	20,224	39	1,473.79	32	32. Iowa
New York	9.79	2	18,055	45	1,766.81	17	33. Louisiana
North Carolina	6.47	23	27,492	18	1,779.68	14	34. Oklahoma
North Dakota	5.75	35	22,832	32	1,312.02	46	35. North Dakota
Ohio	6.11	27	30,531	13	1,865.82	8	36. South Carolina
Oklahoma	5.87	34	24,571	25	1,443.11	35	37. Nevada
Oregon	4.24	48	31,902	9	1,351.94	42	38. Alabama
Pennsylvania	8.00	12	22,154	36	1,771.98	15	39. Indiana
Rhode Island	9.99	1	14,638	51	1,462.85	34	40. Utah
South Carolina	5.64	36	33,619	7	1,894.78	7	41. Wisconsin
South Dakota	6.09	28	20,018	40	1,218.66	49	42. Nebraska
Tennessee	5.24	44	33,073	8	1,733.72	21	43. Minnesota
Texas	6.05	30	31,836	10	1,926.19	6	44. Tennessee
Utah	5.46	40	25,610	23	1,399.25	39	45. West Virginia
Vermont	8.05	11	16,478	49	1,326.72	44	46. Kentucky
Virginia	6.12	26	28,505	15	1,745.61	19	47. Wyoming
Washington	3.48	51	38,920	3	1,353.86	41	48. Oregon
West Virginia	4.84	45	27,327	19	1,322.72	45	49. Montana
Wisconsin	5.45	41	22,290	35	1,215.13	50	50. Idaho
Wyoming	4.27	47	48,274	1	2,062.21	3	51. Washington
United States	6.76	19	24,589	25	$1,663.21	23	

Source: Edison Electric Institute, *1991 Statistical Yearbook of the Electric Utility Industry* (Washington, D.C.: Edison Electric Institute), advance release of data, May 1992.

Note: Average cost is cents per kilowatt hours sold. Average annual cost is revenue per customer.

State	Per million Btu Price	Per million Btu Rank	Expenditures	Per capita	Rank by per capita
Alabama	$16.46	35	$3,237,000,000	$801.04	10
Alaska	27.80	1	401,000,000	729.09	23
Arizona	22.82	11	3,181,000,000	867.94	5
Arkansas	19.78	18	1,790,000,000	761.38	14
California	25.98	8	18,418,000,000	618.88	44
Colorado	17.31	32	1,800,000,000	546.45	49
Connecticut	26.83	4	2,489,000,000	757.23	15
Delaware	19.00	21	534,000,000	801.80	9
District of Columbia	17.38	29	584,000,000	962.11	2
Florida	20.62	17	10,098,000,000	780.49	12
Georgia	19.25	20	5,255,000,000	811.21	8
Hawaii	26.53	7	732,000,000	660.65	34
Idaho	11.15	50	685,000,000	680.24	31
Illinois	22.02	14	8,307,000,000	726.71	24
Indiana	15.75	42	3,927,000,000	708.33	27
Iowa	17.37	30	1,745,000,000	628.38	40
Kansas	19.31	19	1,775,000,000	716.30	26
Kentucky	13.17	46	2,707,000,000	734.60	21
Louisiana	17.77	27	3,739,000,000	886.02	4
Maine	22.42	13	882,000,000	718.24	25
Maryland	18.47	24	3,122,000,000	653.00	35
Massachusetts	25.93	9	4,021,000,000	668.38	33
Michigan	20.85	16	5,797,000,000	623.67	42
Minnesota	15.68	43	2,491,000,000	569.37	47
Mississippi	18.05	25	1,915,000,000	744.27	16
Missouri	18.94	22	3,485,000,000	681.06	30
Montana	11.67	49	510,000,000	638.30	36
Nebraska	16.34	37	996,000,000	631.18	39
Nevada	15.77	40	880,000,000	732.11	22
New Hampshire	26.67	5	817,000,000	736.70	17
New Jersey	26.63	6	5,689,000,000	735.96	19
New Mexico	20.99	15	964,000,000	636.30	37
New York	27.51	2	12,088,000,000	671.93	32
North Carolina	18.74	23	5,715,000,000	862.12	6
North Dakota	16.86	34	401,000,000	627.54	41
Ohio	17.33	31	8,322,000,000	767.22	13
Oklahoma	16.08	39	2,316,000,000	736.17	18
Oregon	12.25	48	1,797,000,000	632.30	38
Pennsylvania	22.46	12	8,737,000,000	735.31	20
Rhode Island	26.85	3	588,000,000	586.24	46
South Carolina	16.39	36	3,113,000,000	892.74	3
South Dakota	17.95	26	388,000,000	557.47	48
Tennessee	15.59	44	4,055,000,000	831.45	7
Texas	17.09	33	13,431,000,000	790.66	11
Utah	16.09	38	831,000,000	482.30	51
Vermont	24.24	10	390,000,000	692.72	29
Virginia	17.70	28	4,374,000,000	706.97	28
Washington	10.03	51	3,034,000,000	623.38	43
West Virginia	13.90	45	1,089,000,000	607.36	45
Wisconsin	15.77	40	2,620,000,000	535.57	50
Wyoming	12.37	47	482,000,000	1,061.67	1
United States	**$19.33**	**19**	**$176,742,000,000**	**$710.63**	**27**

SPENDING ON ELECTRICITY, 1990

Rank in order

By per capita

1. Wyoming
2. District of Columbia
3. South Carolina
4. Louisiana
5. Arizona
6. North Carolina
7. Tennessee
8. Georgia
9. Delaware
10. Alabama
11. Texas
12. Florida
13. Ohio
14. Arkansas
15. Connecticut
16. Mississippi
17. New Hampshire
18. Oklahoma
19. New Jersey
20. Pennsylvania
21. Kentucky
22. Nevada
23. Alaska
24. Illinois
25. Maine
26. Kansas
27. Indiana
28. Virginia
29. Vermont
30. Missouri
31. Idaho
32. New York
33. Massachusetts
34. Hawaii
35. Maryland
36. Montana
37. New Mexico
38. Oregon
39. Nebraska
40. Iowa
41. North Dakota
42. Michigan
43. Washington
44. California
45. West Virginia
46. Rhode Island
47. Minnesota
48. South Dakota
49. Colorado
50. Wisconsin
51. Utah

Source: U.S. Department of Energy, Energy Information Administration, *State Energy Price and Expenditure Report 1990* (Washington, D.C.: Government Printing Office, 1992).

Note: Expenditures is the money spent by all consumers to purchase electricity.

	Per million Btu						Rank in order
State	**Price**	**Rank**	**Expenditures**	**Per capita**	**Rank by per capita**		**By per capita**
Alabama	$4.07	31	$842,000,000	$208.36	30		1. Louisiana
Alaska	1.96	51	224,000,000	407.27	4		2. Texas
Arizona	4.48	19	451,000,000	123.06	44		3. Oklahoma
Arkansas	3.27	45	665,000,000	282.86	13		4. Alaska
California	4.31	23	7,830,000,000	263.10	17		5. Illinois
Colorado	3.92	35	821,000,000	249.24	21		6. Michigan
Connecticut	6.40	2	642,000,000	195.31	33		7. Wyoming
Delaware	3.82	38	151,000,000	226.73	26		8. Kansas
District of Columbia	6.40	2	185,000,000	304.78	11		9. Indiana
Florida	3.21	46	1,081,000,000	83.55	47		10. Ohio
Georgia	4.80	12	1,467,000,000	226.46	27		11. District of Columbia
Hawaii	12.24	1	37,000,000	33.39	50		12. Iowa
Idaho	3.43	43	142,000,000	141.01	42		13. Arkansas
Illinois	4.57	16	4,269,000,000	373.46	5		14. New Jersey
Indiana	4.27	25	1,878,000,000	338.74	9		15. Wisconsin
Iowa	3.81	39	803,000,000	289.16	12		16. Pennsylvania
Kansas	3.30	44	871,000,000	351.49	8		17. California
Kentucky	4.10	30	656,000,000	178.02	36		18. Nebraska
Louisiana	2.11	50	2,467,000,000	584.60	1		19. West Virginia
Maine	6.05	5	26,000,000	21.17	51		20. New York
Maryland	5.07	10	884,000,000	184.90	35		21. Colorado
Massachusetts	5.55	7	1,480,000,000	246.01	22		22. Massachusetts
Michigan	4.36	22	3,470,000,000	373.32	6		23. Minnesota
Minnesota	3.87	36	1,066,000,000	243.66	23		24. Utah
Mississippi	2.75	48	558,000,000	216.87	28		25. New Mexico
Missouri	4.69	13	1,108,000,000	216.53	29		26. Delaware
Montana	4.16	28	163,000,000	204.01	31		27. Georgia
Nebraska	3.93	34	415,000,000	262.99	18		28. Mississippi
Nevada	3.68	40	243,000,000	202.16	32		29. Missouri
New Hampshire	6.38	4	92,000,000	82.96	48		30. Alabama
New Jersey	5.05	11	2,185,000,000	282.66	14		31. Montana
New Mexico	3.84	37	349,000,000	230.36	25		32. Nevada
New York	5.25	8	4,614,000,000	256.48	20		33. Connecticut
North Carolina	4.19	26	657,000,000	99.11	46		34. Rhode Island
North Dakota	4.12	29	99,000,000	154.93	39		35. Maryland
Ohio	4.54	18	3,402,000,000	313.64	10		36. Kentucky
Oklahoma	2.80	47	1,307,000,000	415.45	3		37. Tennessee
Oregon	4.28	24	438,000,000	154.12	40		38. South Dakota
Pennsylvania	5.24	9	3,297,000,000	277.48	16		39. North Dakota
Rhode Island	5.80	6	187,000,000	186.44	34		40. Oregon
South Carolina	4.01	32	526,000,000	150.85	41		41. South Carolina
South Dakota	4.41	20	111,000,000	159.48	38		42. Idaho
Tennessee	3.98	33	804,000,000	164.86	37		43. Virginia
Texas	2.47	49	7,319,000,000	430.86	2		44. Arizona
Utah	4.17	27	419,000,000	243.18	24		45. Washington
Vermont	4.65	15	31,000,000	55.06	49		46. North Carolina
Virginia	4.67	14	831,000,000	134.31	43		47. Florida
Washington	3.60	41	554,000,000	113.83	45		48. New Hampshire
West Virginia	4.40	21	471,000,000	262.69	19		49. Vermont
Wisconsin	4.56	17	1,371,000,000	280.25	15		50. Hawaii
Wyoming	3.57	42	163,000,000	359.03	7		51. Maine
United States	**$3.85**	**37**	**$64,121,000,000**	**$257.81**	**20**		

SPENDING ON NATURAL GAS, 1990

Source: U.S. Department of Energy, Energy Information Administration, *State Energy Price and Expenditure Report 1990* (Washington, D.C.: Government Printing Office, 1992).

Note: Expenditures is the money spent by all consumers to purchase natural gas.

SPENDING ON GASOLINE, 1990						Rank in order

State	Per million Btu Price	Per million Btu Rank	Expenditures	Per capita	Rank by per capita	By per capita
Alabama	$8.96	40	$2,303,000,000	$569.91	18	1. Wyoming
Alaska	10.03	5	307,000,000	558.18	23	2. North Dakota
Arizona	9.22	32	1,893,000,000	516.51	34	3. Montana
Arkansas	8.86	42	1,342,000,000	570.82	15	4. Delaware
California	8.57	50	13,700,000,000	460.35	47	5. South Dakota
Colorado	9.29	29	1,726,000,000	523.98	32	6. Vermont
Connecticut	10.06	4	1,636,000,000	497.72	39	7. New Mexico
Delaware	10.26	3	429,000,000	644.14	4	8. Nevada
District of Columbia	10.66	2	225,000,000	370.68	50	9. Oklahoma
Florida	8.85	43	6,581,000,000	508.66	38	10. Maine
Georgia	8.24	51	3,580,000,000	552.64	24	11. Tennessee
Hawaii	11.71	1	530,000,000	478.34	43	12. Nebraska
Idaho	9.15	35	547,000,000	543.20	28	13. Texas
Illinois	9.35	26	5,913,000,000	517.28	33	14. North Carolina
Indiana	8.74	47	2,827,000,000	509.92	37	15. Arkansas
Iowa	9.38	24	1,552,000,000	558.88	22	16. South Carolina
Kansas	8.90	41	1,331,000,000	537.13	30	17. West Virginia
Kentucky	9.25	30	2,080,000,000	564.45	19	18. Alabama
Louisiana	9.47	17	2,174,000,000	515.17	35	19. Kentucky
Maine	9.74	10	719,000,000	585.50	10	20. Missouri
Maryland	9.88	8	2,447,000,000	511.82	36	21. Virginia
Massachusetts	9.53	15	2,789,000,000	463.60	45	22. Iowa
Michigan	8.78	46	4,582,000,000	492.95	41	23. Alaska
Minnesota	9.56	13	2,386,000,000	545.37	26	24. Georgia
Mississippi	9.21	33	1,399,000,000	543.72	27	25. Oregon
Missouri	8.61	49	2,879,000,000	562.63	20	26. Minnesota
Montana	9.56	13	515,000,000	644.56	3	27. Mississippi
Nebraska	9.49	16	915,000,000	579.85	12	28. Idaho
Nevada	9.10	36	710,000,000	590.68	8	29. Washington
New Hampshire	9.66	11	594,000,000	535.62	31	30. Kansas
New Jersey	9.03	38	3,694,000,000	477.88	44	31. New Hampshire
New Mexico	9.23	31	899,000,000	593.40	7	32. Colorado
New York	8.83	44	6,419,000,000	356.81	51	33. Illinois
North Carolina	9.44	21	3,824,000,000	576.86	14	34. Arizona
North Dakota	9.87	9	420,000,000	657.28	2	35. Louisiana
Ohio	9.35	26	5,394,000,000	497.28	40	36. Maryland
Oklahoma	9.00	39	1,851,000,000	588.37	9	37. Indiana
Oregon	9.45	19	1,566,000,000	551.02	25	38. Florida
Pennsylvania	9.35	26	5,247,000,000	441.59	49	39. Connecticut
Rhode Island	10.03	5	459,000,000	457.63	48	40. Ohio
South Carolina	8.80	45	1,988,000,000	570.12	16	41. Michigan
South Dakota	9.40	22	441,000,000	633.62	5	42. Wisconsin
Tennessee	9.40	22	2,846,000,000	583.56	11	43. Hawaii
Texas	9.16	34	9,831,000,000	578.74	13	44. New Jersey
Utah	9.09	37	794,000,000	460.82	46	45. Massachusetts
Vermont	9.66	11	338,000,000	600.36	6	46. Utah
Virginia	9.46	18	3,475,000,000	561.66	21	47. California
Washington	9.45	19	2,639,000,000	542.22	29	48. Rhode Island
West Virginia	9.96	7	1,022,000,000	569.99	17	49. Pennsylvania
Wisconsin	9.38	24	2,391,000,000	488.76	42	50. District of Columbia
Wyoming	8.66	48	321,000,000	707.05	1	51. New York
United States	$9.12	36	$126,472,000,000	$508.51	39	

Source: U.S. Department of Energy, Energy Information Administration, *State Energy Price and Expenditure Report 1990* (Washington, D.C.: Government Printing Office, 1992).
Note: Expenditures is the money spent by all consumrs to purchase gasoline.

State	Per million Btu Price	Per million Btu Rank	Expenditures	Per capita	Rank by per capita		By per capita
Alabama	$7.91	29	$4,066,000,000	$1,006.19	23		1. Alaska
Alaska	7.62	35	1,560,000,000	2,836.36	1		2. Louisiana
Arizona	8.47	8	2,951,000,000	805.18	46		3. Wyoming
Arkansas	8.57	5	2,323,000,000	988.09	26		4. Hawaii
California	7.28	41	23,886,000,000	802.62	47		5. Texas
Colorado	8.17	15	2,616,000,000	794.17	48		6. Maine
Connecticut	7.67	34	3,280,000,000	997.87	25		7. North Dakota
Delaware	6.98	48	806,000,000	1,210.21	11		8. Montana
District of Columbia	8.86	2	329,000,000	542.01	51		9. West Virginia
Florida	7.00	47	10,994,000,000	849.74	38		10. South Dakota
Georgia	7.41	37	6,084,000,000	939.18	32		11. Delaware
Hawaii	6.42	50	1,788,000,000	1,613.72	4		12. New Mexico
Idaho	8.13	18	978,000,000	971.20	28		13. Vermont
Illinois	8.65	3	9,694,000,000	848.04	39		14. Nevada
Indiana	7.52	36	5,834,000,000	1,052.31	18		15. Kansas
Iowa	8.38	11	2,549,000,000	917.90	35		16. Nebraska
Kansas	7.37	38	2,719,000,000	1,097.26	15		17. New Jersey
Kentucky	8.07	21	3,800,000,000	1,031.21	19		18. Indiana
Louisiana	6.89	49	7,894,000,000	1,870.62	2		19. Kentucky
Maine	7.04	46	1,685,000,000	1,372.15	6		20. Washington
Maryland	7.99	25	3,998,000,000	836.23	40		21. Mississippi
Massachusetts	7.19	43	5,624,000,000	934.84	33		22. New Hampshire
Michigan	8.42	10	7,334,000,000	789.03	49		23. Alabama
Minnesota	8.36	12	3,916,000,000	895.09	37		24. Oklahoma
Mississippi	7.32	40	2,615,000,000	1,016.32	21		25. Connecticut
Missouri	7.92	28	4,839,000,000	945.67	31		26. Arkansas
Montana	7.93	27	1,007,000,000	1,260.33	8		27. Oregon
Nebraska	8.43	9	1,716,000,000	1,087.45	16		28. Idaho
Nevada	7.91	29	1,356,000,000	1,128.12	14		29. Tennessee
New Hampshire	7.27	42	1,116,000,000	1,006.31	22		30. Virginia
New Jersey	7.33	39	8,313,000,000	1,075.42	17		31. Missouri
New Mexico	8.09	19	1,717,000,000	1,133.33	12		32. Georgia
New York	7.16	44	12,492,000,000	694.39	50		33. Massachusetts
North Carolina	8.51	7	6,091,000,000	918.84	34		34. North Carolina
North Dakota	8.16	17	836,000,000	1,308.29	7		35. Iowa
Ohio	8.54	6	8,958,000,000	825.85	42		36. South Carolina
Oklahoma	8.02	23	3,159,000,000	1,004.13	24		37. Minnesota
Oregon	7.88	32	2,801,000,000	985.57	27		38. Florida
Pennsylvania	8.09	19	9,663,000,000	813.25	45		39. Illinois
Rhode Island	8.27	14	831,000,000	828.51	41		40. Maryland
South Carolina	7.91	29	3,171,000,000	909.38	36		41. Rhode Island
South Dakota	8.00	24	844,000,000	1,212.64	10		42. Ohio
Tennessee	8.34	13	4,725,000,000	968.83	29		43. Utah
Texas	6.30	51	24,706,000,000	1,454.41	5		44. Wisconsin
Utah	7.94	26	1,420,000,000	824.14	43		45. Pennsylvania
Vermont	9.29	1	637,000,000	1,131.44	13		46. Arizona
Virginia	8.03	22	5,954,000,000	962.34	30		47. California
Washington	7.12	45	4,959,000,000	1,018.90	20		48. Colorado
West Virginia	8.17	15	2,180,000,000	1,215.84	9		49. Michigan
Wisconsin	8.63	4	4,027,000,000	823.18	44		50. New York
Wyoming	7.68	33	840,000,000	1,850.22	3		51. District of Columbia
United States	**$7.54**	36	**$237,681,000,000**	**$955.66**	31		

Source: U.S. Department of Energy, Energy Information Administration, *State Energy Price and Expenditure Report 1990* (Washington, D.C.: Government Printing Office, 1992).

Note: Expenditures is the money spent by all consumers to purshase petroleum.

State	Per million Btu		Expenditures	Per capita	Rank by per capita
	Price	Rank			
Alabama	$1.83	9	$1,238,000,000	$306.36	5
Alaska	3.67	2	45,000,000	81.82	34
Arizona	1.45	33	499,000,000	136.15	23
Arkansas	1.62	25	345,000,000	146.75	15
California	2.01	6	131,000,000	4.40	48
Colorado	1.07	48	353,000,000	107.16	28
Connecticut	2.15	5	55,000,000	16.73	44
Delaware	1.76	16	105,000,000	157.66	14
District of Columbia	1.96	7	3,000,000	4.94	47
Florida	1.85	8	1,156,000,000	89.35	31
Georgia	1.79	12	1,282,000,000	197.90	11
Hawaii	1.82	10	1,000,000	0.90	50
Idaho	1.76	16	18,000,000	17.87	43
Illinois	1.72	19	1,283,000,000	112.24	27
Indiana	1.46	32	1,983,000,000	357.68	4
Iowa	1.16	47	386,000,000	139.00	20
Kansas	1.24	42	338,000,000	136.40	22
Kentucky	1.27	41	1,019,000,000	276.53	6
Louisiana	1.68	20	351,000,000	83.18	33
Maine	2.72	4	18,000,000	14.66	45
Maryland	1.62	25	464,000,000	97.05	30
Massachusetts	1.77	15	200,000,000	33.24	39
Michigan	1.63	24	1,283,000,000	138.03	21
Minnesota	1.32	39	429,000,000	98.06	29
Mississippi	1.66	21	172,000,000	66.85	36
Missouri	1.35	37	728,000,000	142.27	19
Montana	0.70	51	116,000,000	145.18	16
Nebraska	0.78	50	110,000,000	69.71	35
Nevada	1.49	30	247,000,000	205.49	9
New Hampshire	1.82	10	57,000,000	51.40	38
New Jersey	1.79	12	144,000,000	18.63	42
New Mexico	1.32	39	363,000,000	239.60	8
New York	1.66	21	575,000,000	31.96	40
North Carolina	1.79	12	946,000,000	142.71	18
North Dakota	1.18	46	444,000,000	694.84	3
Ohio	1.54	29	2,194,000,000	202.27	10
Oklahoma	1.40	36	388,000,000	123.33	24
Oregon	1.22	44	19,000,000	6.69	46
Pennsylvania	1.57	28	2,245,000,000	188.94	12
Rhode Island	3.58	3	0	0.00	51
South Carolina	1.73	18	499,000,000	143.10	17
South Dakota	1.22	44	40,000,000	57.47	37
Tennessee	1.35	37	813,000,000	166.70	13
Texas	1.44	34	1,919,000,000	112.97	26
Utah	1.24	42	455,000,000	264.07	7
Vermont	3.73	1	1,000,000	1.78	49
Virginia	1.60	27	533,000,000	86.15	32
Washington	1.65	23	141,000,000	28.97	41
West Virginia	1.47	31	1,286,000,000	717.23	2
Wisconsin	1.41	35	560,000,000	114.47	25
Wyoming	0.86	49	396,000,000	872.25	1
United States	$1.49	30	$28,380,000,000	$114.11	26

Rank in order

By per capita

1. Wyoming
2. West Virginia
3. North Dakota
4. Indiana
5. Alabama
6. Kentucky
7. Utah
8. New Mexico
9. Nevada
10. Ohio
11. Georgia
12. Pennsylvania
13. Tennessee
14. Delaware
15. Arkansas
16. Montana
17. South Carolina
18. North Carolina
19. Missouri
20. Iowa
21. Michigan
22. Kansas
23. Arizona
24. Oklahoma
25. Wisconsin
26. Texas
27. Illinois
28. Colorado
29. Minnesota
30. Maryland
31. Florida
32. Virginia
33. Louisiana
34. Alaska
35. Nebraska
36. Mississippi
37. South Dakota
38. New Hampshire
39. Massachusetts
40. New York
41. Washington
42. New Jersey
43. Idaho
44. Connecticut
45. Maine
46. Oregon
47. District of Columbia
48. California
49. Vermont
50. Hawaii
51. Rhode Island

Source: U.S. Department of Energy, Energy Information Administration, *State Energy Price and Expenditure Report 1990* (Washington, D.C.: Government Printing Office, 1992).
Note: Expenditures is the money spent by all consumers to purchase coal.

| State | TOTAL ENERGY CONSUMPTION. 1990 | | | Rank in order |
	Total consumption (trillion Btu)	Per capita (million Btu)	Rank by per capita	By per capita
Alabama	1,571.9	388.9	14	1. Alaska
Alaska	581.6	1,057.5	1	2. Wyoming
Arizona	916.3	250.0	43	3. Louisiana
Arkansas	781.7	332.5	21	4. Texas
California	7,307.0	245.5	44	5. North Dakota
Colorado	913.2	277.2	40	6. West Virginia
Connecticut	732.1	222.7	48	7. Indiana
Delaware	235.5	353.5	18	8. Oklahoma
District of Columbia	169.6	279.3	38	9. Montana
Florida	3,059.3	236.4	45	10. Kansas
Georgia	2,073.8	320.1	26	11. Washington
Hawaii	299.0	269.9	41	12. Kentucky
Idaho	372.7	370.1	15	13. New Mexico
Illinois	3,534.9	309.2	28	14. Alabama
Indiana	2,441.1	440.3	7	15. Idaho
Iowa	899.2	323.8	24	16. Mississippi
Kansas	1,030.2	415.7	10	17. Tennessee
Kentucky	1,454.1	394.6	12	18. Delaware
Louisiana	3,493.7	827.9	3	19. South Carolina
Maine	363.2	295.8	32	20. Ohio
Maryland	1,214.2	253.9	42	21. Arkansas
Massachusetts	1,341.2	222.9	47	22. Oregon
Michigan	2,733.5	294.0	33	23. Nevada
Minnesota	1,317.6	301.1	29	24. Iowa
Mississippi	936.3	363.8	16	25. Nebraska
Missouri	1,475.8	288.4	37	26. Georgia
Montana	338.1	423.1	9	27. Utah
Nebraska	507.9	321.8	25	28. Illinois
Nevada	391.6	325.7	23	29. Minnesota
New Hampshire	242.9	219.0	49	30. Pennsylvania
New Jersey	2,260.1	292.3	36	31. Virginia
New Mexico	597.0	394.0	13	32. Maine
New York	3,583.9	199.2	50	33. Michigan
North Carolina	1,948.0	293.8	34	34. North Carolina
North Dakota	306.8	480.1	5	35. South Dakota
Ohio	3,698.1	340.9	20	36. New Jersey
Oklahoma	1,352.3	429.8	8	37. Missouri
Oregon	927.8	326.4	22	38. District of Columbia
Pennsylvania	3,570.5	300.5	30	39. Wisconsin
Rhode Island	194.7	194.1	51	40. Colorado
South Carolina	1,193.7	342.3	19	41. Hawaii
South Dakota	203.7	292.6	35	42. Maryland
Tennessee	1,752.9	359.4	17	43. Arizona
Texas	9,796.9	576.7	4	44. California
Utah	542.9	315.1	27	45. Florida
Vermont	126.6	224.9	46	46. Vermont
Virginia	1,837.2	296.9	31	47. Massachusetts
Washington	1,953.1	401.3	11	48. Connecticut
West Virginia	806.3	449.7	6	49. New Hampshire
Wisconsin	1,365.5	279.1	39	50. New York
Wyoming	398.3	877.4	2	51. Rhode Island
United States	81,150.8	326.2	23	

Source: U.S. Department of Energy, Energy Information Administration, *State Energy Report: Consumption Estimates 1960-1990* (Washington, D.C.: Government Printing Office, 1992).

State	Total consumption (trillion Btu)	Per capita (million Btu)	Rank by per capita
Alabama	204.4	50.6	11
Alaska	14.5	26.4	46
Arizona	141.4	38.6	25
Arkansas	93.3	39.7	23
California	720.2	24.2	50
Colorado	105.0	31.9	37
Connecticut	92.7	28.2	43
Delaware	28.2	42.3	21
District of Columbia	33.6	55.4	6
Florida	489.7	37.8	26
Georgia	274.4	42.4	20
Hawaii	28.3	25.5	48
Idaho	61.4	61.0	3
Illinois	380.7	33.3	34
Indiana	252.4	45.5	16
Iowa	100.4	36.2	30
Kansas	92.6	37.4	28
Kentucky	208.4	56.6	4
Louisiana	217.7	51.6	9
Maine	39.3	32.0	36
Maryland	169.0	35.3	32
Massachusetts	155.0	25.8	47
Michigan	281.0	30.2	41
Minnesota	160.9	36.8	29
Mississippi	109.6	42.6	19
Missouri	183.9	35.9	31
Montana	44.7	55.9	5
Nebraska	60.9	38.6	24
Nevada	55.7	46.3	13
New Hampshire	30.6	27.6	45
New Jersey	214.4	27.7	44
New Mexico	47.1	31.1	38
New York	441.2	24.5	49
North Carolina	306.8	46.3	14
North Dakota	23.9	37.4	27
Ohio	486.0	44.8	17
Oklahoma	145.0	46.1	15
Oregon	146.6	51.6	10
Pennsylvania	391.5	32.9	35
Rhode Island	21.9	21.8	51
South Carolina	189.8	54.4	7
South Dakota	21.6	31.0	39
Tennessee	263.2	54.0	8
Texas	810.0	47.7	12
Utah	52.5	30.5	40
Vermont	16.0	28.4	42
Virginia	248.0	40.1	22
Washington	310.6	63.8	2
West Virginia	78.9	44.0	18
Wisconsin	167.8	34.3	33
Wyoming	40.1	88.3	1
United States	**9,255.2**	**182.2**	**29**

Rank in order

By per capita

1. Wyoming
2. Washington
3. Idaho
4. Kentucky
5. Montana
6. District of Columbia
7. South Carolina
8. Tennessee
9. Louisiana
10. Oregon
11. Alabama
12. Texas
13. Nevada
14. North Carolina
15. Oklahoma
16. Indiana
17. Ohio
18. West Virginia
19. Mississippi
20. Georgia
21. Delaware
22. Virginia
23. Arkansas
24. Nebraska
25. Arizona
26. Florida
27. North Dakota
28. Kansas
29. Minnesota
30. Iowa
31. Missouri
32. Maryland
33. Wisconsin
34. Illinois
35. Pennsylvania
36. Maine
37. Colorado
38. New Mexico
39. South Dakota
40. Utah
41. Michigan
42. Vermont
43. Connecticut
44. New Jersey
45. New Hampshire
46. Alaska
47. Massachusetts
48. Hawaii
49. New York
50. California
51. Rhode Island

Source: U.S. Department of Energy, Energy Information Administration, *State Energy Report: Consumption Estimates 1960-1990* (Washington, D.C.: Government Printing Office, 1992).

NATURAL GAS CONSUMPTION. 1990				Rank in order
State	Total consumption (trillion Btu)	Per capita (million Btu)	Rank by per capita	By per capita
Alabama	251.0	62.1	22	1. Alaska
Alaska	326.8	594.2	1	2. Louisiana
Arizona	128.7	35.1	41	3. Wyoming
Arkansas	234.4	99.7	9	4. Texas
California	1,923.7	64.6	20	5. Oklahoma
Colorado	240.3	73.0	15	6. New Mexico
Connecticut	100.8	30.7	44	7. Kansas
Delaware	40.1	60.2	23	8. Mississippi
District of Columbia	29.0	47.8	32	9. Arkansas
Florida	341.9	26.4	46	10. Michigan
Georgia	319.4	49.3	31	11. Illinois
Hawaii	2.9	2.6	51	12. Indiana
Idaho	46.7	46.4	35	13. Iowa
Illinois	960.0	84.0	11	14. Utah
Indiana	459.0	82.8	12	15. Colorado
Iowa	219.7	79.1	13	16. West Virginia
Kansas	352.6	142.3	7	17. Ohio
Kentucky	192.2	52.2	29	18. Nebraska
Louisiana	1,636.9	387.9	2	19. Minnesota
Maine	4.3	3.5	50	20. California
Maryland	177.0	37.0	39	21. Wisconsin
Massachusetts	268.0	44.5	36	22. Alabama
Michigan	834.3	89.8	10	23. Delaware
Minnesota	291.7	66.7	19	24. Pennsylvania
Mississippi	262.1	101.9	8	25. New Jersey
Missouri	241.3	47.2	33	26. Nevada
Montana	44.3	55.4	27	27. Montana
Nebraska	109.1	69.1	18	28. North Dakota
Nevada	66.8	55.6	26	29. Kentucky
New Hampshire	14.4	13.0	48	30. New York
New Jersey	439.0	56.8	25	31. Georgia
New Mexico	251.4	165.9	6	32. District of Columbia
New York	888.9	49.4	30	33. Missouri
North Carolina	166.3	25.1	47	34. Tennessee
North Dakota	33.5	52.4	28	35. Idaho
Ohio	777.3	71.7	17	36. Massachusetts
Oklahoma	620.7	197.3	5	37. Oregon
Oregon	111.7	39.3	37	38. South Carolina
Pennsylvania	680.5	57.3	24	39. Maryland
Rhode Island	32.3	32.2	43	40. South Dakota
South Carolina	134.1	38.5	38	41. Arizona
South Dakota	25.4	36.5	40	42. Washington
Tennessee	227.5	46.6	34	43. Rhode Island
Texas	3,747.2	220.6	4	44. Connecticut
Utah	126.9	73.7	14	45. Virginia
Vermont	6.6	11.7	49	46. Florida
Virginia	188.7	30.5	45	47. North Carolina
Washington	167.6	34.4	42	48. New Hampshire
West Virginia	129.0	71.9	16	49. Vermont
Wisconsin	310.9	63.6	21	50. Maine
Wyoming	101.3	223.1	3	51. Hawaii
United States	19,288.4	77.6	14	

Source: U.S. Department of Energy, Energy Information Administration, *State Energy Report: Consumption Estimates 1960-1990* (Washington, D.C.: Government Printing Office, 1992).

PETROLEUM CONSUMPTION, 1990				Rank in order
State	**Total consumption (trillion Btu)**	**Per capita (million Btu)**	**Rank by per capita**	**By per capita**
Alabama	528.6	130.8	22	1. Alaska
Alaska	232.3	422.4	1	2. Louisiana
Arizona	349.8	95.4	50	3. Wyoming
Arkansas	277.6	118.1	35	4. Hawaii
California	3,541.8	119.0	34	5. Texas
Colorado	327.3	99.4	46	6. Delaware
Connecticut	429.0	130.5	23	7. Maine
Delaware	132.4	198.8	6	8. Montana
District of Columbia	37.1	61.1	51	9. North Dakota
Florida	1,573.2	121.6	30	10. Kansas
Georgia	8.0	127.7	25	11. West Virginia
Hawaii	294.3	265.6	4	12. Washington
Idaho	120.2	119.4	33	13. New Jersey
Illinois	1,227.8	107.4	42	14. Mississippi
Indiana	837.9	151.1	16	15. South Dakota
Iowa	304.7	109.7	40	16. Indiana
Kansas	406.6	164.1	10	17. New Mexico
Kentucky	508.7	138.0	20	18. Nevada
Louisiana	1,429.5	338.7	2	19. New Hampshire
Maine	239.2	194.8	7	20. Kentucky
Maryland	501.2	104.8	43	21. Oklahoma
Massachusetts	764.1	127.0	26	22. Alabama
Michigan	892.7	96.0	49	23. Connecticut
Minnesota	495.0	113.1	38	24. Nebraska
Mississippi	393.9	153.1	14	25. Georgia
Missouri	616.7	120.5	31	26. Massachusetts
Montana	146.8	183.7	8	27. Oregon
Nebraska	203.7	129.1	24	28. Virginia
Nevada	171.4	142.6	18	29. Vermont
New Hampshire	153.5	138.4	19	30. Florida
New Jersey	1,201.3	155.4	13	31. Missouri
New Mexico	221.1	145.9	17	32. Tennessee
New York	1,772.6	98.5	47	33. Idaho
North Carolina	730.7	110.2	39	34. California
North Dakota	109.1	170.7	9	35. Arkansas
Ohio	1,113.5	102.7	44	36. South Carolina
Oklahoma	434.1	138.0	21	37. Utah
Oregon	355.2	125.0	27	38. Minnesota
Pennsylvania	1,277.5	107.5	41	39. North Carolina
Rhode Island	100.4	100.1	45	40. Iowa
South Carolina	404.1	115.9	36	41. Pennsylvania
South Dakota	105.5	151.6	15	42. Illinois
Tennessee	586.9	120.3	32	43. Maryland
Texas	4,456.5	262.3	5	44. Ohio
Utah	195.2	113.3	37	45. Rhode Island
Vermont	68.5	121.7	29	46. Colorado
Virginia	753.0	121.7	28	47. New York
Washington	788.6	162.0	12	48. Wisconsin
West Virginia	292.4	163.1	11	49. Michigan
Wisconsin	472.9	96.7	48	50. Arizona
Wyoming	126.0	277.5	3	51. District of Columbia
United States	**33,551.5**	**134.9**	**22**	

Source: U.S. Department of Energy, Energy Information Administration, *State Energy Report: Consumption Estimates 1960-1990* (Washington, D.C.: Government Printing Office, 1992).

State	COAL CONSUMPTION. 1990 Total consumption (trillion Btu)	Per capita (million Btu)	Rank by per capita
Alabama	678.2	167.8	9
Alaska	12.3	22.4	38
Arizona	343.6	93.8	19
Arkansas	212.7	90.5	20
California	65.3	2.2	48
Colorado	328.9	99.8	18
Connecticut	25.6	7.8	44
Delaware	59.5	89.3	22
District of Columbia	1.7	2.8	47
Florida	624.3	48.3	34
Georgia	718.2	110.9	15
Hawaii	0.6	0.5	49
Idaho	10.0	9.9	43
Illinois	747.9	65.4	30
Indiana	1,361.7	245.6	4
Iowa	331.6	119.4	14
Kansas	272.5	110.0	16
Kentucky	804.2	218.2	5
Louisiana	208.4	49.4	33
Maine	6.6	5.4	46
Maryland	286.3	59.9	31
Massachusetts	113.1	18.8	40
Michigan	786.3	84.6	24
Minnesota	324.3	74.1	29
Mississippi	103.8	40.3	36
Missouri	540.6	105.6	17
Montana	166.1	207.9	7
Nebraska	142.0	90.0	21
Nevada	165.7	137.9	10
New Hampshire	31.5	28.4	37
New Jersey	80.8	10.5	42
New Mexico	275.6	181.9	8
New York	346.1	19.2	39
North Carolina	530.1	80.0	27
North Dakota	374.6	586.2	2
Ohio	1,424.7	131.3	11
Oklahoma	277.1	88.1	23
Oregon	15.6	5.5	45
Pennsylvania	1,427.2	120.1	13
Rhode Island	0.1	0.1	51
South Carolina	289.2	82.9	25
South Dakota	32.5	46.7	35
Tennessee	600.2	123.1	12
Texas	1,333.9	78.5	28
Utah	366.3	212.6	6
Vermont	0.2	0.4	50
Virginia	333.0	53.8	32
Washington	85.5	17.6	41
West Virginia	872.6	486.7	3
Wisconsin	397.1	81.2	26
Wyoming	458.3	1,009.5	1
United States	18,996.5	76.4	29

Rank in order

By per capita

1. Wyoming
2. North Dakota
3. West Virginia
4. Indiana
5. Kentucky
6. Utah
7. Montana
8. New Mexico
9. Alabama
10. Nevada
11. Ohio
12. Tennessee
13. Pennsylvania
14. Iowa
15. Georgia
16. Kansas
17. Missouri
18. Colorado
19. Arizona
20. Arkansas
21. Nebraska
22. Delaware
23. Oklahoma
24. Michigan
25. South Carolina
26. Wisconsin
27. North Carolina
28. Texas
29. Minnesota
30. Illinois
31. Maryland
32. Virginia
33. Louisiana
34. Florida
35. South Dakota
36. Mississippi
37. New Hampshire
38. Alaska
39. New York
40. Massachusetts
41. Washington
42. New Jersey
43. Idaho
44. Connecticut
45. Oregon
46. Maine
47. District of Columbia
48. California
49. Hawaii
50. Vermont
51. Rhode Island

Source: U.S. Department of Energy, Energy Information Administration, *State Energy Report: Consumption Estimates 1960-1990* (Washington, D.C.: Government Printing Office, 1992).

		Per 100,000 population	
POWER PLANTS, 1991			
State	**Power plants**	**Rate**	**Rank**
Alabama	35	0.86	36
Alaska	118	20.70	1
Arizona	31	0.83	37
Arkansas	32	1.35	24
California	292	0.96	32
Colorado	65	1.92	16
Connecticut	34	1.03	29
Delaware	10	1.47	22
District of Columbia	2	0.33	51
Florida	69	0.52	48
Georgia	50	0.76	41
Hawaii	17	1.49	21
Idaho	44	4.23	6
Illinois	70	0.61	43
Indiana	44	0.78	38
Iowa	116	4.14	7
Kansas	97	3.88	8
Kentucky	34	0.92	33
Louisiana	37	0.87	35
Maine	58	4.68	5
Maryland	23	0.47	49
Massachusetts	59	0.98	31
Michigan	141	1.50	20
Minnesota	106	2.39	14
Mississippi	20	0.77	40
Missouri	84	1.63	18
Montana	29	3.58	10
Nebraska	80	5.03	3
Nevada	21	1.64	17
New Hampshire	18	1.62	19
New Jersey	31	0.40	50
New Mexico	18	1.16	28
New York	183	1.01	30
North Carolina	61	0.91	34
North Dakota	19	2.97	12
Ohio	58	0.53	46
Oklahoma	38	1.19	26
Oregon	58	1.99	15
Pennsylvania	63	0.53	47
Rhode Island	6	0.60	45
South Carolina	51	1.43	23
South Dakota	24	3.43	11
Tennessee	37	0.75	42
Texas	134	0.77	39
Utah	66	3.73	9
Vermont	64	11.23	2
Virginia	38	0.60	44
Washington	65	1.29	25
West Virginia	21	1.17	27
Wisconsin	121	2.44	13
Wyoming	22	4.78	4
United States	**3,014**	**1.20**	**26**

Rank in order

By rate per 100,000 population

1. Alaska
2. Vermont
3. Nebraska
4. Wyoming
5. Maine
6. Idaho
7. Iowa
8. Kansas
9. Utah
10. Montana
11. South Dakota
12. North Dakota
13. Wisconsin
14. Minnesota
15. Oregon
16. Colorado
17. Nevada
18. Missouri
19. New Hampshire
20. Michigan
21. Hawaii
22. Delaware
23. South Carolina
24. Arkansas
25. Washington
26. Oklahoma
27. West Virginia
28. New Mexico
29. Connecticut
30. New York
31. Massachusetts
32. California
33. Kentucky
34. North Carolina
35. Louisiana
36. Alabama
37. Arizona
38. Indiana
39. Texas
40. Mississippi
41. Georgia
42. Tennessee
43. Illinois
44. Virginia
45. Rhode Island
46. Ohio
47. Pennsylvania
48. Florida
49. Maryland
50. New Jersey
51. District of Columbia

Source: U.S. Department of Energy, Energy Information Administration, *Inventory of Power Plants in the United States, 1991* (Washington, D.C.: Government Printing Office, 1992).

Note: Power plants are all facilities (fossil, steam, nuclear, hydroelectric, etc.) that convert mechanical, chemical, and/or nuclear energy into electric energy.

| State | Nuclear plants | Per 100,000 population | | |
		Rate	Rank	By rate per 100,000 population
Alabama	2	0.05	8	1. Vermont
Alaska	0	0.00	34	2. Nebraska
Arizona	1	0.03	25	3. South Carolina
Arkansas	1	0.04	13	4. New Hampshire
California	2	0.01	33	5. Maine
Colorado	0	0.00	34	6. Connecticut
Connecticut	2	0.06	6	Illinois
Delaware	0	0.00	34	8. Alabama
District of Columbia	0	0.00	34	9. Louisiana
Florida	3	0.02	26	10. Minnesota
Georgia	2	0.03	23	North Carolina
Hawaii	0	0.00	34	12. Michigan
Idaho	0	0.00	34	13. Arkansas
Illinois	7	0.06	6	Pennsylvania
Indiana	0	0.00	34	15. Kansas
Iowa	1	0.04	19	Wisconsin
Kansas	1	0.04	15	17. Mississippi
Kentucky	0	0.00	34	New Jersey
Louisiana	2	0.05	9	19. Iowa
Maine	1	0.08	5	20. Oregon
Maryland	1	0.02	27	21. Massachusetts
Massachusetts	2	0.03	21	22. Virginia
Michigan	4	0.04	12	23. Georgia
Minnesota	2	0.05	10	24. New York
Mississippi	1	0.04	17	25. Arizona
Missouri	1	0.02	30	26. Florida
Montana	0	0.00	34	27. Maryland
Nebraska	2	0.13	2	28. Tennessee
Nevada	0	0.00	34	Washington
New Hampshire	1	0.09	4	30. Missouri
New Jersey	3	0.04	17	31. Ohio
New Mexico	0	0.00	34	32. Texas
New York	5	0.03	24	33. California
North Carolina	3	0.05	10	34. Alaska
North Dakota	0	0.00	34	Colorado
Ohio	2	0.02	31	Delaware
Oklahoma	0	0.00	34	District of Columbia
Oregon	1	0.03	20	Hawaii
Pennsylvania	5	0.04	13	Idaho
Rhode Island	0	0.00	34	Indiana
South Carolina	4	0.11	3	Kentucky
South Dakota	0	0.00	34	Montana
Tennessee	1	0.02	28	Nevada
Texas	2	0.01	32	New Mexico
Utah	0	0.00	34	North Dakota
Vermont	1	0.18	1	Oklahoma
Virginia	2	0.03	22	Rhode Island
Washington	1	0.02	28	South Dakota
West Virginia	0	0.00	34	Utah
Wisconsin	2	0.04	15	West Virginia
Wyoming	0	0.00	34	Wyoming
United States	**71**	**0.03**	**20**	

Source: U.S. Department of Energy, Energy Information Administration, *Inventory of Power Plants in the United States, 1991* (Washington, D.C.: Government Printing Office, 1992).

HYDROELECTRIC POWER PLANTS, 1991				Rank in order
		Per 100,000 population		By rate per
State	Power plants	Rate	Rank	100,000 population
Alabama	21	0.51	22	1. Vermont
Alaska	22	3.86	3	2. Idaho
Arizona	12	0.32	30	3. Alaska
Arkansas	13	0.55	21	4. Maine
California	229	0.75	14	5. Utah
Colorado	31	0.92	12	6. Wyoming
Connecticut	15	0.46	26	7. Montana
Delaware	0	0.00	47	8. Oregon
District of Columbia	0	0.00	47	9. Wisconsin
Florida	3	0.02	45	10. New Hampshire
Georgia	31	0.47	24	11. Washington
Hawaii	2	0.18	35	12. Colorado
Idaho	42	4.04	2	13. South Carolina
Illinois	4	0.03	44	14. California
Indiana	6	0.11	39	15. South Dakota
Iowa	6	0.21	32	16. Nebraska
Kansas	0	0.00	47	17. Michigan
Kentucky	7	0.19	34	18. New York
Louisiana	0	0.00	47	19. North Carolina
Maine	42	3.39	4	20. Tennessee
Maryland	2	0.04	42	21. Arkansas
Massachusetts	23	0.38	28	22. Alabama
Michigan	64	0.68	17	23. Minnesota
Minnesota	22	0.50	23	24. Georgia
Mississippi	0	0.00	47	25. Nevada
Missouri	8	0.16	37	26. Connecticut
Montana	21	2.59	7	27. West Virginia
Nebraska	11	0.69	16	28. Massachusetts
Nevada	6	0.47	25	29. Virginia
New Hampshire	12	1.08	10	30. Arizona
New Jersey	1	0.01	46	31. Oklahoma
New Mexico	3	0.19	33	32. Iowa
New York	123	0.68	18	33. New Mexico
North Carolina	41	0.61	19	34. Kentucky
North Dakota	1	0.16	36	35. Hawaii
Ohio	4	0.04	43	36. North Dakota
Oklahoma	10	0.31	31	37. Missouri
Oregon	52	1.78	8	38. Texas
Pennsylvania	8	0.07	41	39. Indiana
Rhode Island	1	0.10	40	40. Rhode Island
South Carolina	28	0.79	13	41. Pennsylvania
South Dakota	5	0.71	15	42. Maryland
Tennessee	28	0.57	20	43. Ohio
Texas	25	0.14	38	44. Illinois
Utah	50	2.82	5	45. Florida
Vermont	52	9.12	1	46. New Jersey
Virginia	21	0.33	29	47. Delaware
Washington	53	1.06	11	District of Columbia
West Virginia	8	0.44	27	Kansas
Wisconsin	75	1.51	9	Louisiana
Wyoming	12	2.61	6	Mississippi
United States	1,256	0.50	23	

Source: U.S. Department of Energy, Energy Information Administration, *Inventory of Power Plants in the United States, 1991* (Washington, D.C.: Government Printing Office, 1992).

Environment

FEDERALLY OWNED LAND, 1989

State	Total land area (acres)	Federal land (acres)	% of state	Rank
Alabama	32,678,000	550,000	1.7	41
Alaska	365,482,000	247,802,000	67.8	2
Arizona	72,688,000	31,491,000	43.3	8
Arkansas	33,599,000	3,421,000	10.2	18
California	100,207,000	61,043,000	60.9	5
Colorado	66,486,000	22,648,000	34.1	9
Connecticut	3,135,000	14,000	0.4	50
Delaware	1,266,000	30,000	2.4	35
District of Columbia	39,000	11,000	28.2	12
Florida	34,721,000	3,356,000	9.7	20
Georgia	37,295,000	2,292,000	6.1	22
Hawaii	4,106,000	677,000	16.5	15
Idaho	52,933,000	33,122,000	62.6	4
Illinois	35,795,000	494,000	1.4	44
Indiana	23,158,000	470,000	2.0	38
Iowa	35,860,000	159,000	0.4	51
Kansas	52,511,000	690,000	1.3	45
Kentucky	25,512,000	1,391,000	5.5	26
Louisiana	28,868,000	6,538,000	22.6	14
Maine	19,848,000	153,000	0.8	47
Maryland	6,319,000	197,000	3.1	33
Massachusetts	5,035,000	83,000	1.6	42
Michigan	36,492,000	3,565,000	9.8	19
Minnesota	51,206,000	2,387,000	4.7	29
Mississippi	30,223,000	1,671,000	5.5	25
Missouri	44,248,000	2,031,000	4.6	30
Montana	93,271,000	25,863,000	27.7	13
Nebraska	49,032,000	719,000	1.5	43
Nevada	70,264,000	57,803,000	82.3	1
New Hampshire	5,769,000	754,000	13.1	17
New Jersey	4,814,000	136,000	2.8	34
New Mexico	77,766,000	25,747,000	33.1	10
New York	30,681,000	223,000	0.7	49
North Carolina	31,403,000	1,141,000	3.6	32
North Dakota	44,453,000	1,965,000	4.4	31
Ohio	26,222,000	322,000	1.2	46
Oklahoma	44,088,000	874,000	2.0	39
Oregon	61,599,000	29,669,000	48.2	7
Pennsylvania	28,804,000	641,000	2.2	37
Rhode Island	677,000	5,000	0.7	48
South Carolina	19,374,000	434,000	2.2	36
South Dakota	48,882,000	2,744,000	5.6	24
Tennessee	26,728,000	1,322,000	4.9	28
Texas	168,218,000	2,845,000	1.7	40
Utah	52,697,000	33,611,000	63.8	3
Vermont	5,937,000	355,000	6.0	23
Virginia	25,496,000	1,918,000	7.5	21
Washington	42,694,000	12,373,000	29.0	11
West Virginia	15,411,000	2,099,000	13.6	16
Wisconsin	35,011,000	1,906,000	5.4	27
Wyoming	62,343,000	30,407,000	48.8	6
United States	**2,271,343,000**	**662,158,000**	**29.2**	**11**

Rank in order
By % of state

1. Nevada
2. Alaska
3. Utah
4. Idaho
5. California
6. Wyoming
7. Oregon
8. Arizona
9. Colorado
10. New Mexico
11. Washington
12. District of Columbia
13. Montana
14. Louisiana
15. Hawaii
16. West Virginia
17. New Hampshire
18. Arkansas
19. Michigan
20. Florida
21. Virginia
22. Georgia
23. Vermont
24. South Dakota
25. Mississippi
26. Kentucky
27. Wisconsin
28. Tennessee
29. Minnesota
30. Missouri
31. North Dakota
32. North Carolina
33. Maryland
34. New Jersey
35. Delaware
36. South Carolina
37. Pennsylvania
38. Indiana
39. Oklahoma
40. Texas
41. Alabama
42. Massachusetts
43. Nebraska
44. Illinois
45. Kansas
46. Ohio
47. Maine
48. Rhode Island
49. New York
50. Connecticut
51. Iowa

Source: U.S. Department of Commerce, Bureau of the Census, *Statistical Abstract of the United States, 1992* (Washington, D.C.: Government Printing Office, 1992).

State	Total surface area (acres)	Wetlands (acres) 1780s	Wetlands (acres) 1980s	Wetlands lost %	Wetlands lost Rank
Alabama	33,030,000	7,570,000	3,780,000	50.1	21
Alaska	375,300,000	170,200,000	170,000,000	0.1	50
Arizona	72,900,000	930,000	600,000	35.5	34
Arkansas	33,990,000	9,850,000	2,760,000	72.0	10
California	101,560,000	5,000,000	450,000	91.0	1
Colorado	66,720,000	2,000,000	1,000,000	50.0	22
Connecticut	3,210,000	670,000	180,000	73.1	9
Delaware	1,320,000	480,000	220,000	54.2	17
District of Columbia	—	—	—	—	—
Florida	37,480,000	20,330,000	11,040,000	45.7	27
Georgia	37,680,000	6,840,000	5,300,000	22.5	46
Hawaii	4,120,000	60,000	50,000	16.7	48
Idaho	53,470,000	880,000	390,000	55.7	16
Illinois	36,100,000	8,210,000	1,250,000	84.8	6
Indiana	23,230,000	5,600,000	750,000	86.6	5
Iowa	36,030,000	4,000,000	420,000	89.5	3
Kansas	52,650,000	840,000	440,000	47.6	25
Kentucky	25,850,000	1,570,000	300,000	80.9	7
Louisiana	31,050,000	16,190,000	8,780,000	45.8	26
Maine	21,260,000	6,460,000	5,200,000	19.5	47
Maryland	6,770,000	1,650,000	440,000	73.3	8
Massachusetts	5,280,000	820,000	590,000	28.0	42
Michigan	37,260,000	11,200,000	5,580,000	50.2	20
Minnesota	53,800,000	15,070,000	8,700,000	42.3	29
Mississippi	30,540,000	9,870,000	4,070,000	58.8	14
Missouri	44,600,000	4,840,000	640,000	86.8	4
Montana	94,170,000	1,150,000	840,000	27.0	44
Nebraska	49,430,000	2,910,000	1,910,000	34.4	37
Nevada	70,750,000	490,000	240,000	51.0	19
New Hampshire	5,950,000	220,000	200,000	9.1	49
New Jersey	5,020,000	1,500,000	920,000	38.7	31
New Mexico	77,870,000	720,000	480,000	33.3	38
New York	31,730,000	2,560,000	1,030,000	59.8	12
North Carolina	33,660,000	11,090,000	5,690,000	48.7	24
North Dakota	45,230,000	4,930,000	2,490,000	49.5	23
Ohio	26,830,000	5,000,000	480,000	90.4	2
Oklahoma	44,750,000	2,840,000	950,000	66.5	11
Oregon	62,070,000	2,260,000	1,390,000	38.5	32
Pennsylvania	29,010,000	1,130,000	500,000	55.8	15
Rhode Island	780,000	100,000	70,000	30.0	41
South Carolina	19,880,000	6,410,000	4,660,000	27.3	43
South Dakota	49,310,000	2,740,000	1,780,000	35.0	36
Tennessee	27,040,000	1,940,000	790,000	59.3	13
Texas	171,100,000	16,000,000	7,610,000	52.4	18
Utah	54,350,000	800,000	560,000	30.0	40
Vermont	6,150,000	340,000	220,000	35.3	35
Virginia	26,120,000	1,850,000	1,070,000	42.2	30
Washington	43,640,000	1,350,000	940,000	30.4	39
West Virginia	15,480,000	130,000	100,000	23.1	45
Wisconsin	35,940,000	9,800,000	5,330,000	45.6	28
Wyoming	62,660,000	2,000,000	1,250,000	37.5	33
United States	2,314,120,000	391,390,000	274,430,000	29.9	42

LOSS OF WETLANDS, 1780s–1980s

Rank in order

By % of wetlands lost

1. California
2. Ohio
3. Iowa
4. Missouri
5. Indiana
6. Illinois
7. Kentucky
8. Maryland
9. Connecticut
10. Arkansas
11. Oklahoma
12. New York
13. Tennessee
14. Mississippi
15. Pennsylvania
16. Idaho
17. Delaware
18. Texas
19. Nevada
20. Michigan
21. Alabama
22. Colorado
23. North Dakota
24. North Carolina
25. Kansas
26. Louisiana
27. Florida
28. Wisconsin
29. Minnesota
30. Virginia
31. New Jersey
32. Oregon
33. Wyoming
34. Arizona
35. Vermont
36. South Dakota
37. Nebraska
38. New Mexico
39. Washington
40. Utah
41. Rhode Island
42. Massachusetts
43. South Carolina
44. Montana
45. West Virginia
46. Georgia
47. Maine
48. Hawaii
49. New Hampshire
50. Alaska
— District of Columbia

— not applicable.

Source: T. E. Dahl, *Wetland Losses in the United States 1780's to 1980's, Report to Congress* (Washington, D.C.: Department of the Interior, 1991).

ENVIRONMENTAL PROTECTION AGENCY SPENDING, FISCAL 1991				Rank in order
State	**Expenditures**	**Per capita**	**Rank by per capita**	**By per capita**
Alabama	$21,083,000	$5.16	49	1. District of Columbia
Alaska	19,090,000	33.49	2	2. Alaska
Arizona	14,171,000	3.78	51	3. Delaware
Arkansas	16,020,000	6.75	43	4. North Dakota
California	190,657,000	6.28	46	5. New York
Colorado	31,880,000	9.44	28	6. Hawaii
Connecticut	50,628,000	15.38	18	7. West Virginia
Delaware	17,233,000	25.34	3	8. South Dakota
District of Columbia	35,105,000	58.70	1	9. Maine
Florida	105,323,000	7.93	33	10. Maryland
Georgia	52,454,000	7.92	34	11. New Jersey
Hawaii	26,309,000	23.18	6	12. Wyoming
Idaho	13,173,000	12.68	22	13. Vermont
Illinois	146,427,000	12.69	21	14. Wisconsin
Indiana	50,199,000	8.95	31	15. New Hampshire
Iowa	34,747,000	12.43	24	16. Montana
Kansas	22,514,000	9.02	30	17. Michigan
Kentucky	16,680,000	4.49	50	18. Connecticut
Louisiana	30,496,000	7.17	40	19. Minnesota
Maine	25,213,000	20.42	9	20. Rhode Island
Maryland	93,919,000	19.32	10	21. Illinois
Massachusetts	75,438,000	12.58	23	22. Idaho
Michigan	147,050,000	15.70	17	23. Massachusetts
Minnesota	66,827,000	15.08	19	24. Iowa
Mississippi	27,295,000	10.53	27	25. Missouri
Missouri	56,838,000	11.02	25	26. Ohio
Montana	13,304,000	16.47	16	27. Mississippi
Nebraska	11,781,000	7.40	37	28. Colorado
Nevada	7,890,000	6.14	47	29. Oregon
New Hampshire	18,523,000	16.76	15	30. Kansas
New Jersey	148,780,000	19.17	11	31. Indiana
New Mexico	12,221,000	7.89	35	32. Washington
New York	447,865,000	24.80	5	33. Florida
North Carolina	49,623,000	7.37	38	34. Georgia
North Dakota	16,035,000	25.25	4	35. New Mexico
Ohio	117,302,000	10.72	26	36. Virginia
Oklahoma	22,097,000	6.96	42	37. Nebraska
Oregon	26,788,000	9.17	29	38. North Carolina
Pennsylvania	85,873,000	7.18	39	39. Pennsylvania
Rhode Island	14,347,000	14.29	20	40. Louisiana
South Carolina	24,851,000	6.98	41	41. South Carolina
South Dakota	14,594,000	20.76	8	42. Oklahoma
Tennessee	33,080,000	6.68	44	43. Arkansas
Texas	110,974,000	6.40	45	44. Tennessee
Utah	9,761,000	5.51	48	45. Texas
Vermont	10,471,000	18.47	13	46. California
Virginia	47,526,000	7.56	36	47. Nevada
Washington	44,461,000	8.86	32	48. Utah
West Virginia	38,639,000	21.45	7	49. Alabama
Wisconsin	90,626,000	18.29	14	50. Kentucky
Wyoming	8,574,000	18.64	12	51. Arizona
United States	**$2,835,837,000**	**$11.25**	**25**	

Source: U.S. Department of Commerce, Bureau of the Census, *Federal Expenditures by State for Fiscal Year 1991* (Washington, D.C.: Government Printing Office, 1992).

State	Expenditures	Per capita	Rank by per capita		By per capita
	EPA ABATEMENT, CONTROL, AND COMPLIANCE, FISCAL 1991				**Rank in order**
Alabama	$1,819,000	$0.45	47		1. District of Columbia
Alaska	1,753,000	3.08	3		2. Vermont
Arizona	3,247,000	0.87	28		3. Alaska
Arkansas	1,837,000	0.77	37		4. Montana
California	11,115,000	0.37	48		5. Delaware
Colorado	3,843,000	1.14	22		6. Wyoming
Connecticut	2,576,000	0.78	35		7. Idaho
Delaware	1,947,000	2.86	5		8. Rhode Island
District of Columbia	17,621,000	29.47	1		9. North Dakota
Florida	4,205,000	0.32	50		10. South Dakota
Georgia	2,986,000	0.45	46		11. Maryland
Hawaii	1,492,000	1.32	18		12. West Virginia
Idaho	2,643,000	2.54	7		13. Illinois
Illinois	18,548,000	1.61	13		14. New Mexico
Indiana	4,046,000	0.72	40		15. Washington
Iowa	2,404,000	0.86	29		16. New Hampshire
Kansas	3,013,000	1.21	19		17. Nevada
Kentucky	2,429,000	0.65	41		18. Hawaii
Louisiana	3,651,000	0.86	30		19. Kansas
Maine	1,472,000	1.19	20		20. Maine
Maryland	8,267,000	1.70	11		21. Minnesota
Massachusetts	4,480,000	0.75	38		22. Colorado
Michigan	−4,207,000	−0.45	51		23. New Jersey
Minnesota	5,246,000	1.18	21		24. Oregon
Mississippi	2,558,000	0.99	25		25. Mississippi
Missouri	2,429,000	0.47	45		26. Utah
Montana	2,417,000	2.99	4		27. Virginia
Nebraska	1,337,000	0.84	31		28. Arizona
Nevada	1,739,000	1.35	17		29. Iowa
New Hampshire	1,566,000	1.42	16		30. Louisiana
New Jersey	8,069,000	1.04	23		31. Nebraska
New Mexico	2,348,000	1.52	14		32. North Carolina
New York	14,331,000	0.79	33		33. New York
North Carolina	5,433,000	0.81	32		34. Pennsylvania
North Dakota	1,232,000	1.94	9		35. Connecticut
Ohio	7,130,000	0.65	42		36. Wisconsin
Oklahoma	2,343,000	0.74	39		37. Arkansas
Oregon	3,012,000	1.03	24		38. Massachusetts
Pennsylvania	9,384,000	0.79	34		39. Oklahoma
Rhode Island	2,115,000	2.11	8		40. Indiana
South Carolina	1,753,000	0.49	43		41. Kentucky
South Dakota	1,201,000	1.71	10		42. Ohio
Tennessee	2,356,000	0.48	44		43. South Carolina
Texas	6,157,000	0.36	49		44. Tennessee
Utah	1,743,000	0.99	26		45. Missouri
Vermont	2,051,000	3.62	2		46. Georgia
Virginia	5,995,000	0.95	27		47. Alabama
Washington	7,360,000	1.47	15		48. California
West Virginia	3,056,000	1.70	12		49. Texas
Wisconsin	3,871,000	0.78	36		50. Florida
Wyoming	1,290,000	2.80	6		51. Michigan
United States	**$212,394,000**	**$0.84**	**31**		

Source: U.S. Department of Commerce, Bureau of the Census, *Federal Expenditures by State for Fiscal Year 1991* (Washington, D.C.: Government Printing Office, 1992).

Note: Credit amounts (−) reflect refunds of advances from previous years.

STATE SPENDING ON ENVIRONMENTAL PROGRAMS, FISCAL 1988

State	Expenditures	Per capita	Rank by per capita
Alabama	$64,906,954	$15.82	42
Alaska	131,684,237	251.31	2
Arizona	46,612,900	13.36	45
Arkansas	44,188,570	18.45	39
California	1,486,124,000	52.49	8
Colorado	76,150,000	23.07	34
Connecticut	61,996,000	19.18	37
Delaware	33,170,000	50.26	9
District of Columbia	—	—	—
Florida	465,591,276	37.75	13
Georgia	93,344,466	14.72	44
Hawaii	27,832,208	25.35	29
Idaho	61,442,400	61.26	6
Illinois	392,844,000	33.83	18
Indiana	52,766,177	9.50	49
Iowa	88,065,353	31.07	22
Kansas	47,817,000	19.17	38
Kentucky	120,289,400	32.28	21
Louisiana	193,835,955	43.97	11
Maine	39,332,000	32.64	19
Maryland	150,091,393	32.47	20
Massachusetts	237,936,245	40.40	12
Michigan	221,424,840	23.96	32
Minnesota	126,236,105	29.31	28
Mississippi	54,153,592	20.67	35
Missouri	119,907,403	23.32	33
Montana	69,559,793	86.41	3
Nebraska	27,988,000	17.47	40
Nevada	36,487,054	34.62	16
New Hampshire	33,588,000	30.96	23
New Jersey	523,874,000	67.85	4
New Mexico	44,782,182	29.72	27
New York	236,484,000	13.20	46
North Carolina	96,942,764	14.94	43
North Dakota	32,524,000	48.76	10
Ohio	125,669,234	11.58	48
Oklahoma	40,868,619	12.61	47
Oregon	186,438,200	67.38	5
Pennsylvania	288,766,000	24.06	31
Rhode Island	35,878,756	36.13	15
South Carolina	71,124,250	20.50	36
South Dakota	21,264,000	29.82	26
Tennessee	81,180,056	16.58	41
Texas	113,796,559	6.76	50
Utah	51,419,000	30.43	24
Vermont	20,222,111	36.31	14
Virginia	152,149,051	25.29	30
Washington	246,873,000	53.11	7
West Virginia	56,189,209	29.95	25
Wisconsin	167,779,368	34.56	17
Wyoming	128,050,724	267.33	1
United States	**$7,327,640,404**	**$29.89**	**26**

Rank in order

By per capita

1. Wyoming
2. Alaska
3. Montana
4. New Jersey
5. Oregon
6. Idaho
7. Washington
8. California
9. Delaware
10. North Dakota
11. Louisiana
12. Massachusetts
13. Florida
14. Vermont
15. Rhode Island
16. Nevada
17. Wisconsin
18. Illinois
19. Maine
20. Maryland
21. Kentucky
22. Iowa
23. New Hampshire
24. Utah
25. West Virginia
26. South Dakota
27. New Mexico
28. Minnesota
29. Hawaii
30. Virginia
31. Pennsylvania
32. Michigan
33. Missouri
34. Colorado
35. Mississippi
36. South Carolina
37. Connecticut
38. Kansas
39. Arkansas
40. Nebraska
41. Tennessee
42. Alabama
43. North Carolina
44. Georgia
45. Arizona
46. New York
47. Oklahoma
48. Ohio
49. Indiana
50. Texas
— District of Columbia

— not applicable.

Source: R. Steven Brown, John M. Johnson, and Karen Marshall, *Resource Guide to State Environmental Management*, 2d ed. (Lexington, Ky.: Council of State Governments, 1990).

Note: State programs include developing and protecting natural resources.

ENVIRONMENTAL PROGRAMS AS PART OF STATE BUDGET, FISCAL 1988					Rank in order	
State	Total state expenditures	Environmental expenditures	% of state budget	Rank by %	By %	
Alabama	$6,392,000,000	$64,906,954	1.02	41	1.	Wyoming
Alaska	3,179,000,000	131,684,237	4.00	4	2.	Montana
Arizona	4,836,000,000	46,612,900	0.96	43	3.	Idaho
Arkansas	3,849,000,000	44,188,570	1.15	39	4.	Alaska
California	57,084,000,000	1,486,124,000	2.60	9	5.	New Jersey
Colorado	4,612,000,000	76,150,000	1.65	24	6.	Oregon
Connecticut	8,028,000,000	61,996,000	0.77	46	7.	Louisiana
Delaware	1,840,000,000	33,170,000	1.80	19	8.	Washington
District of Columbia	—	—	—	—	9.	California
Florida	18,522,000,000	465,591,276	2.51	11	10.	Nevada
Georgia	8,711,000,000	93,344,466	1.07	40	11.	Florida
Hawaii	3,279,000,000	27,832,208	0.85	44	12.	New Hampshire
Idaho	1,455,000,000	61,442,400	4.22	3	13.	North Dakota
Illinois	17,355,000,000	392,844,000	2.26	14	14.	Illinois
Indiana	7,706,000,000	52,766,177	0.68	47	15.	Vermont
Iowa	6,120,000,000	88,065,353	1.44	32	16.	Maine
Kansas	3,875,000,000	47,817,000	1.23	37	17.	Rhode Island
Kentucky	7,321,000,000	120,289,400	1.64	25	18.	South Dakota
Louisiana	7,354,000,000	193,835,955	2.64	7	19.	Delaware
Maine	2,097,000,000	39,332,000	1.88	16		Utah
Maryland	9,375,000,000	150,091,393	1.60	26	21.	Missouri
Massachusetts	15,225,000,000	237,936,245	1.56	27	22.	Wisconsin
Michigan	15,562,000,000	221,424,840	1.42	33	23.	West Virginia
Minnesota	8,664,000,000	126,236,105	1.46	31	24.	Colorado
Mississippi	3,872,000,000	54,153,592	1.40	34	25.	Kentucky
Missouri	6,948,000,000	119,907,403	1.73	21	26.	Maryland
Montana	1,621,000,000	69,559,793	4.29	2	27.	Massachusetts
Nebraska	2,171,000,000	27,988,000	1.29	36	28.	Pennsylvania
Nevada	1,417,000,000	36,487,054	2.57	10	29.	New Mexico
New Hampshire	1,393,000,000	33,588,000	2.41	12	30.	Virginia
New Jersey	14,504,000,000	523,874,000	3.61	5	31.	Minnesota
New Mexico	3,029,000,000	44,782,182	1.48	29	32.	Iowa
New York	39,895,000,000	236,484,000	0.59	50	33.	Michigan
North Carolina	9,724,000,000	96,942,764	1.00	42	34.	Mississippi
North Dakota	1,400,000,000	32,524,000	2.32	13	35.	Tennessee
Ohio	19,233,000,000	125,669,234	0.65	48	36.	Nebraska
Oklahoma	5,172,000,000	40,868,619	0.79	45	37.	Kansas
Oregon	6,147,000,000	186,438,200	3.03	6	38.	South Carolina
Pennsylvania	19,361,000,000	288,766,000	1.49	28	39.	Arkansas
Rhode Island	1,925,000,000	35,878,756	1.86	17	40.	Georgia
South Carolina	5,891,000,000	71,124,250	1.21	38	41.	Alabama
South Dakota	1,152,000,000	21,264,000	1.85	18	42.	North Carolina
Tennessee	6,041,000,000	81,180,056	1.34	35	43.	Arizona
Texas	18,882,000,000	113,796,559	0.60	49	44.	Hawaii
Utah	2,863,000,000	51,419,000	1.80	19	45.	Oklahoma
Vermont	1,044,000,000	20,222,111	1.94	15	46.	Connecticut
Virginia	10,378,000,000	152,149,051	1.47	30	47.	Indiana
Washington	9,388,000,000	246,873,000	2.63	8	48.	Ohio
West Virginia	3,337,000,000	56,189,209	1.68	23	49.	Texas
Wisconsin	9,860,000,000	167,779,368	1.70	22	50.	New York
Wyoming	1,656,000,000	128,050,724	7.73	1	—	District of Columbia
United States	$430,745,000,000	$7,327,640,404	1.70	23		

— not applicable.

Source: R. Steven Brown, John M. Johnson, and Karen Marshall, *Resource Guide to State Environmental Management,* 2d ed. (Lexington, Ky.: Council of State Governments, 1990).

Note: State programs include developing and protecting natural resources.

STATE SPENDING ON FOREST PROGRAMS, FISCAL 1988				Rank in order
State	Expenditures	Per capita	Rank by per capita	By per capita
Alabama	$21,747,318	$5.30	11	1. Alaska
Alaska	23,190,100	44.26	1	2. Oregon
Arizona	787,000	0.23	48	3. Montana
Arkansas	11,028,491	4.61	14	4. California
California	328,478,000	11.60	4	5. Idaho
Colorado	4,380,000	1.33	37	6. Minnesota
Connecticut	4,336,000	1.34	36	7. Washington
Delaware	1,326,000	2.01	30	8. Mississippi
District of Columbia	—	—	—	9. Georgia
Florida	47,033,632	3.81	18	10. Vermont
Georgia	40,549,000	6.39	9	11. Alabama
Hawaii	3,967,000	3.61	19	12. South Carolina
Idaho	9,939,000	9.91	5	13. Wisconsin
Illinois	3,739,000	0.32	47	14. Arkansas
Indiana	6,308,779	1.14	40	15. North Carolina
Iowa	2,189,000	0.77	42	16. South Dakota
Kansas	NA	NA	NA	17. Nevada
Kentucky	9,090,400	2.44	24	18. Florida
Louisiana	9,889,655	2.24	25	19. Hawaii
Maine	595,000	0.49	45	20. Missouri
Maryland	9,021,290	1.95	31	21. Virginia
Massachusetts	7,985,000	1.36	34	22. Tennessee
Michigan	22,749,363	2.46	23	23. Michigan
Minnesota	42,621,000	9.90	6	24. Kentucky
Mississippi	21,209,774	8.10	8	25. Louisiana
Missouri	17,914,465	3.49	20	26. Wyoming
Montana	10,145,982	12.60	3	27. West Virginia
Nebraska	669,334	0.42	46	28. Pennsylvania
Nevada	4,668,359	4.43	17	29. New York
New Hampshire	1,573,000	1.45	33	30. Delaware
New Jersey	5,239,000	0.68	43	31. Maryland
New Mexico	1,944,000	1.29	38	32. Oklahoma
New York	37,469,000	2.09	29	33. New Hampshire
North Carolina	29,670,288	4.57	15	34. Massachusetts
North Dakota	840,000	1.26	39	35. Rhode Island
Ohio	9,030,240	0.83	41	36. Connecticut
Oklahoma	6,321,868	1.95	32	37. Colorado
Oregon	60,851,197	21.99	2	38. New Mexico
Pennsylvania	25,591,000	2.13	28	39. North Dakota
Rhode Island	1,333,377	1.34	35	40. Indiana
South Carolina	17,031,000	4.91	12	41. Ohio
South Dakota	3,165,000	4.44	16	42. Iowa
Tennessee	14,820,000	3.03	22	43. New Jersey
Texas	8,796,000	0.52	44	44. Texas
Utah	NA	NA	NA	45. Maine
Vermont	3,062,144	5.50	10	46. Nebraska
Virginia	19,728,403	3.28	21	47. Illinois
Washington	41,074,000	8.84	7	48. Arizona
West Virginia	4,000,000	2.13	27	— District of Columbia
Wisconsin	23,346,091	4.81	13	NA Kansas
Wyoming	1,061,827	2.22	26	NA Utah
United States	$981,505,377	$4.00	18	

— not applicable. NA not avaialable.

Source: R. Steven Brown, John M. Johnson, and Karen Marshall, *Resource Guide to State Environmental Management*, 2d ed. (Lexington, Ky.: Council of State Governments, 1990).

Note: Forest expenditures for Utah are included in their land management function.

TOTAL TREE PLANTING, FISCAL 1990

State	Total acres seeded and plated	% of total land area	Rank by %
Alabama	259,657	0.795	4
Alaska	2,211	0.001	48
Arizona	2,371	0.003	43
Arkansas	128,427	0.382	11
California	90,915	0.091	15
Colorado	6,956	0.010	37
Connecticut	693	0.022	29
Delaware	403	0.032	26
District of Columbia	—	—	—
Florida	239,162	0.689	5
Georgia	343,374	0.921	2
Hawaii	215	0.005	39
Idaho	36,274	0.069	18
Illinois	9,836	0.027	28
Indiana	8,841	0.038	24
Iowa	7,874	0.022	29
Kansas	2,864	0.005	39
Kentucky	11,607	0.045	22
Louisiana	163,624	0.567	6
Maine	9,239	0.047	21
Maryland	8,036	0.127	12
Massachusetts	101	0.002	46
Michigan	19,759	0.054	20
Minnesota	39,535	0.077	17
Mississippi	298,932	0.989	1
Missouri	8,052	0.018	33
Montana	38,010	0.041	23
Nebraska	7,036	0.014	36
Nevada	240	*	50
New Hampshire	295	0.005	39
New Jersey	429	0.009	38
New Mexico	2,683	0.003	43
New York	5,970	0.019	32
North Carolina	124,616	0.397	9
North Dakota	6,611	0.015	34
Ohio	5,137	0.020	31
Oklahoma	15,535	0.035	25
Oregon	238,721	0.388	10
Pennsylvania	1,539	0.005	39
Rhode Island	453	0.067	19
South Carolina	174,106	0.899	3
South Dakota	7,276	0.015	34
Tennessee	25,656	0.096	14
Texas	133,394	0.079	16
Utah	827	0.002	46
Vermont	80	0.001	48
Virginia	109,548	0.430	8
Washington	220,666	0.517	7
West Virginia	4,840	0.031	27
Wisconsin	36,812	0.105	13
Wyoming	2,139	0.003	43
United States	**2,861,577**	**0.126**	**13**

Rank in order

By %

1. Mississippi
2. Georgia
3. South Carolina
4. Alabama
5. Florida
6. Louisiana
7. Washington
8. Virginia
9. North Carolina
10. Oregon
11. Arkansas
12. Maryland
13. Wisconsin
14. Tennessee
15. California
16. Texas
17. Minnesota
18. Idaho
19. Rhode Island
20. Michigan
21. Maine
22. Kentucky
23. Montana
24. Indiana
25. Oklahoma
26. Delaware
27. West Virginia
28. Illinois
29. Connecticut
    Iowa
31. Ohio
32. New York
33. Missouri
34. North Dakota
    South Dakota
36. Nebraska
37. Colorado
38. New Jersey
39. Hawaii
    Kansas
    New Hampshire
    Pennsylvania
43. Arizona
    New Mexico
    Wyoming
46. Massachusetts
    Utah
48. Alaska
    Vermont
50. Nevada
— District of Columbia

— not applicable.   * data rounds to less than 0.0005.

Sources: U.S. Department of Agriculture, *Agricultural Statistics, 1991* (Washington, D.C.: Government Printing Office, 1992); U.S. Department of Commerce, Bureau of the Census, *Statistical Abstract of the United States, 1992* (Washington, D.C.: Government Printing Office, 1992).

State	Federal acres seeded and planted	% of total land area	Rank by %
Alabama	6,157	0.019	11
Alaska	1,221	*	32
Arizona	2,096	0.003	22
Arkansas	13,433	0.040	8
California	59,755	0.060	3
Colorado	1,295	0.002	25
Connecticut	0	0.000	47
Delaware	0	0.000	47
District of Columbia	—	—	—
Florida	20,244	0.058	4
Georgia	4,886	0.013	12
Hawaii	0	0.000	47
Idaho	24,897	0.047	5
Illinois	49	*	32
Indiana	93	*	32
Iowa	127	*	32
Kansas	70	*	32
Kentucky	1,087	0.004	20
Louisiana	6,742	0.023	10
Maine	20	*	32
Maryland	21	*	32
Massachusetts	1	*	32
Michigan	2,452	0.007	16
Minnesota	2,922	0.006	17
Mississippi	13,340	0.044	7
Missouri	2,137	0.005	19
Montana	23,772	0.025	9
Nebraska	174	*	32
Nevada	35	*	32
New Hampshire	41	0.001	29
New Jersey	14	*	32
New Mexico	2,453	0.003	22
New York	5	*	32
North Carolina	3,181	0.010	13
North Dakota	128	*	32
Ohio	439	0.002	25
Oklahoma	1,504	0.003	22
Oregon	131,320	0.213	1
Pennsylvania	114	*	32
Rhode Island	0	0.000	47
South Carolina	8,769	0.045	6
South Dakota	752	0.002	25
Tennessee	2,049	0.008	14
Texas	6,094	0.004	20
Utah	774	0.001	29
Vermont	80	0.001	29
Virginia	2,023	0.008	14
Washington	38,046	0.089	2
West Virginia	61	*	32
Wisconsin	1,980	0.006	17
Wyoming	1,201	0.002	25
United States	**388,054**	**0.017**	**12**

FEDERAL TREE PLANTING, FISCAL 1990

Rank in order

Rany by %

1. Oregon
2. Washington
3. California
4. Florida
5. Idaho
6. South Carolina
7. Mississippi
8. Arkansas
9. Montana
10. Louisiana
11. Alabama
12. Georgia
13. North Carolina
14. Tennessee
    Virginia
16. Michigan
17. Minnesota
    Wisconsin
19. Missouri
20. Kentucky
    Texas
22. Arizona
    New Mexico
    Oklahoma
25. Colorado
    Ohio
    South Dakota
    Wyoming
29. New Hampshire
    Utah
    Vermont
32. Alaska
    Illinois
    Indiana
    Iowa
    Kansas
    Maine
    Maryland
    Massachusetts
    Nebraska
    Nevada
    New Jersey
    New York
    North Dakota
    Pennsylvania
    West Virginia
47. Delaware
    Connecticut
    Hawaii
    Rhode Island
— District of Columbia

— not applicable.   * data rounds to less than 0.0005.

Sources: U.S. Department of Agriculture, *Agricultural Statistics, 1991* (Washington, D.C.: Government Printing Office, 1992); U.S. Department of Commerce, Bureau of the Census, *Statistical Abstract of the United States, 1992* (Washington, D.C.: Government Printing Office, 1992).

State	Private acres seeded and planted	% of total land area	Rank by %
Alabama	250,947	0.768	4
Alaska	210	*	45
Arizona	248	*	45
Arkansas	113,524	0.338	10
California	30,740	0.031	24
Colorado	5,531	0.008	37
Connecticut	636	0.020	27
Delaware	403	0.032	22
District of Columbia	—	—	—
Florida	215,423	0.620	5
Georgia	338,163	0.907	2
Hawaii	111	0.003	41
Idaho	9,161	0.017	31
Illinois	9,587	0.027	26
Indiana	8,666	0.037	18
Iowa	7,174	0.020	27
Kansas	2,377	0.005	38
Kentucky	10,520	0.041	17
Louisiana	156,232	0.541	6
Maine	9,092	0.046	16
Maryland	7,725	0.122	12
Massachusetts	100	0.002	43
Michigan	12,854	0.035	21
Minnesota	18,835	0.037	18
Mississippi	275,349	0.911	1
Missouri	5,290	0.012	36
Montana	12,881	0.014	32
Nebraska	6,807	0.014	32
Nevada	130	*	45
New Hampshire	254	0.004	40
New Jersey	155	0.003	41
New Mexico	230	*	45
New York	5,560	0.018	29
North Carolina	120,561	0.384	8
North Dakota	6,254	0.014	32
Ohio	4,698	0.018	29
Oklahoma	14,031	0.032	22
Oregon	98,476	0.160	11
Pennsylvania	1,425	0.005	38
Rhode Island	245	0.036	20
South Carolina	164,489	0.849	3
South Dakota	6,424	0.013	35
Tennessee	23,060	0.086	13
Texas	127,300	0.076	15
Utah	53	*	45
Vermont	0	0.000	50
Virginia	106,733	0.419	7
Washington	163,381	0.383	9
West Virginia	4,586	0.030	25
Wisconsin	30,264	0.086	13
Wyoming	908	0.001	44
United States	**2,387,803**	**0.105**	**13**

— not applicable.   * data rounds to less than 0.0005.

Sources: U.S. Department of Agriculture, *Agricultural Statistics, 1991* (Washington, D.C.: Government Printing Office, 1992); U.S. Department of Commerce, Bureau of the Census, *Statistical Abstract of the United States, 1992* (Washington, D.C.: Government Printing Office, 1992).

State	Expenditures	Per capita	Rank by per capita	By per capita
STATE SPENDING ON AIR QUALITY, FISCAL 1988				**Rank in order**
Alabama	$1,995,038	$0.49	45	1. Hawaii
Alaska	1,556,951	2.97	3	2. Oregon
Arizona	2,822,000	0.81	32	3. Alaska
Arkansas	940,129	0.39	47	4. Connecticut
California	63,736,000	2.25	6	5. Illinois
Colorado	6,434,000	1.95	8	6. California
Connecticut	8,553,000	2.65	4	7. Delaware
Delaware	1,388,000	2.10	7	8. Colorado
District of Columbia	—	—	—	9. Wyoming
Florida	7,186,648	0.58	38	10. New Jersey
Georgia	3,492,789	0.55	40	11. North Dakota
Hawaii	6,729,000	6.13	1	12. Vermont
Idaho	776,600	0.77	35	13. Montana
Illinois	27,457,000	2.36	5	14. Utah
Indiana	4,748,609	0.86	28	15. Washington
Iowa	1,063,000	0.38	48	16. Louisiana
Kansas	2,484,000	1.00	20	17. Kentucky
Kentucky	4,307,400	1.16	17	18. South Dakota
Louisiana	5,116,144	1.16	16	19. Ohio
Maine	659,000	0.55	41	20. Kansas
Maryland	4,587,000	0.99	22	21. New Mexico
Massachusetts	4,900,000	0.83	31	22. Maryland
Michigan	7,850,700	0.85	30	23. Wisconsin
Minnesota	3,350,000	0.78	34	24. Pennsylvania
Mississippi	1,314,532	0.50	43	25. Virginia
Missouri	2,423,469	0.47	46	26. New York
Montana	1,193,128	1.48	13	27. New Hampshire
Nebraska	539,925	0.34	49	28. Indiana
Nevada	549,157	0.52	42	29. West Virginia
New Hampshire	961,000	0.89	27	30. Michigan
New Jersey	12,987,000	1.68	10	31. Massachusetts
New Mexico	1,498,000	0.99	21	32. Arizona
New York	16,148,000	0.90	26	33. Rhode Island
North Carolina	3,240,845	0.50	44	34. Minnesota
North Dakota	1,100,000	1.65	11	35. Idaho
Ohio	11,046,433	1.02	19	36. Texas
Oklahoma	1,971,000	0.61	37	37. Oklahoma
Oregon	10,616,253	3.84	2	38. Florida
Pennsylvania	11,420,000	0.95	24	39. Tennessee
Rhode Island	776,884	0.78	33	40. Georgia
South Carolina	919,000	0.27	50	41. Maine
South Dakota	765,000	1.07	18	42. Nevada
Tennessee	2,840,000	0.58	39	43. Mississippi
Texas	11,486,000	0.68	36	44. North Carolina
Utah	2,097,100	1.24	14	45. Alabama
Vermont	890,214	1.60	12	46. Missouri
Virginia	5,583,249	0.93	25	47. Arkansas
Washington	5,618,000	1.21	15	48. Iowa
West Virginia	1,600,000	0.85	29	49. Nebraska
Wisconsin	4,671,142	0.96	23	50. South Carolina
Wyoming	890,170	1.86	9	— District of Columbia
United States	**$287,278,509**	**$1.17**	**16**	

— not applicable.

Source: R. Steven Brown, John M. Johnson, and Karen Marshall, *Resource Guide to State Environmental Management*, 2d. ed. (Lexington, Ky.: Council of State Governments, 1990).

Note: Hawaii includes some expenditures for water quality in air quality expenditures. South Dakota includes expenditures for hazardous and solid wastes in air quality expenditures.

STATE SPENDING ON WATER QUALITY, FISCAL 1988					Rank in order
State	Expenditures	Per capita	Rank by per capita		By per capita
Alabama	$13,380,396	$3.26	42		1. Wyoming
Alaska	7,352,013	14.03	18		2. New Jersey
Arizona	17,232,000	4.94	35		3. Massachusetts
Arkansas	9,147,405	3.82	38		4. Montana
California	717,886,000	25.35	5		5. California
Colorado	16,478,000	4.99	34		6. Idaho
Connecticut	16,285,000	5.04	33		7. Louisiana
Delaware	9,538,000	14.45	17		8. Illinois
District of Columbia	—	—	—		9. Florida
Florida	251,052,664	20.35	9		10. Wisconsin
Georgia	10,287,558	1.62	48		11. Nevada
Hawaii	8,797,000	8.01	24		12. Rhode Island
Idaho	22,082,300	22.02	6		13. North Dakota
Illinois	243,292,000	20.95	8		14. Iowa
Indiana	18,492,594	3.33	41		15. New Hampshire
Iowa	46,411,367	16.38	14		16. Washington
Kansas	23,487,000	9.41	20		17. Delaware
Kentucky	25,034,000	6.72	26		18. Alaska
Louisiana	96,737,853	21.95	7		19. Michigan
Maine	4,553,000	3.78	39		20. Kansas
Maryland	39,803,000	8.61	22		21. Utah
Massachusetts	168,480,245	28.61	3		22. Maryland
Michigan	102,403,665	11.08	19		23. Missouri
Minnesota	19,622,000	4.56	36		24. Hawaii
Mississippi	5,156,065	1.97	46		25. New Mexico
Missouri	42,861,370	8.34	23		26. Kentucky
Montana	21,483,925	26.69	4		27. South Dakota
Nebraska	6,867,691	4.29	37		28. Oregon
Nevada	19,805,865	18.79	11		29. Tennessee
New Hampshire	17,396,000	16.03	15		30. Pennsylvania
New Jersey	450,008,000	58.28	2		31. Virginia
New Mexico	10,452,300	6.94	25		32. New York
New York	91,372,000	5.10	32		33. Connecticut
North Carolina	12,470,585	1.92	47		34. Colorado
North Dakota	11,870,000	17.80	13		35. Arizona
Ohio	27,121,344	2.50	45		36. Minnesota
Oklahoma	5,162,085	1.59	49		37. Nebraska
Oregon	17,271,195	6.24	28		38. Arkansas
Pennsylvania	66,645,000	5.55	30		39. Maine
Rhode Island	17,950,301	18.08	12		40. Vermont
South Carolina	8,808,000	2.54	44		41. Indiana
South Dakota	4,542,000	6.37	27		42. Alabama
Tennessee	27,576,000	5.63	29		43. West Virginia
Texas	17,658,599	1.05	50		44. South Carolina
Utah	15,236,900	9.02	21		45. Ohio
Vermont	2,069,532	3.72	40		46. Mississippi
Virginia	31,736,804	5.28	31		47. North Carolina
Washington	68,049,000	14.64	16		48. Georgia
West Virginia	5,853,000	3.12	43		49. Oklahoma
Wisconsin	96,084,182	19.79	10		50. Texas
Wyoming	68,346,137	142.69	1		— District of Columbia
United States	$3,057,748,940	$12.47	19		

— not applicable.

Source: R. Steven Brown, John M. Johnson, and Karen Marshall, *Resource Guide to State Environmental Management*, 2d ed. (Lexington, Ky.: Council of State Governments, 1990).

Note: Water quality includes programs for drinking water, water quality, and drinking water. The data for Arkansas includes spending for land management and soil conservation. Data for Hawaii includes spending for drinking water and water resources (water quality is included in air quality.)

FEDERAL GRANTS FOR RURAL WATER AND WASTE DISPOSAL. FISCAL 1991				Rank in order

State	Expenditures	Per capita	Rank by per capita	By per capita
Alabama	$2,974,000	$0.73	27	1. Maine
Alaska	300,000	0.53	31	2. South Dakota
Arizona	365,000	0.10	48	3. Arkansas
Arkansas	6,833,000	2.88	3	4. Idaho
California	1,733,000	0.06	49	5. Oklahoma
Colorado	1,730,000	0.51	32	6. West Virginia
Connecticut	533,000	0.16	44	7. New Hampshire
Delaware	752,000	1.11	14	8. Kentucky
District of Columbia	0	0.00	50	9. Mississippi
Florida	4,581,000	0.35	36	10. Vermont
Georgia	2,725,000	0.41	33	11. Wyoming
Hawaii	0	0.00	50	12. Iowa
Idaho	2,516,000	2.42	4	13. Nebraska
Illinois	4,666,000	0.40	34	14. Delaware
Indiana	1,129,000	0.20	42	15. North Dakota
Iowa	3,494,000	1.25	12	16. Oregon
Kansas	414,000	0.17	43	17. Rhode Island
Kentucky	5,884,000	1.59	8	18. Minnesota
Louisiana	2,968,000	0.70	28	19. Missouri
Maine	4,362,000	3.53	1	Wisconsin
Maryland	1,033,000	0.21	41	21. Nevada
Massachusetts	4,802,000	0.80	25	22. North Carolina
Michigan	2,422,000	0.26	38	23. Virginia
Minnesota	4,383,000	0.99	18	24. South Carolina
Mississippi	3,627,000	1.40	9	25. Massachusetts
Missouri	5,053,000	0.98	19	26. Montana
Montana	621,000	0.77	26	27. Alabama
Nebraska	1,958,000	1.23	13	28. Louisiana
Nevada	1,180,000	0.92	21	29. Ohio
New Hampshire	1,870,000	1.69	7	30. Pennsylvania
New Jersey	1,691,000	0.22	40	31. Alaska
New Mexico	182,000	0.12	47	32. Colorado
New York	4,432,000	0.25	39	33. Georgia
North Carolina	5,906,000	0.88	22	34. Illinois
North Dakota	694,000	1.09	15	35. Tennessee
Ohio	6,580,000	0.60	29	36. Florida
Oklahoma	7,323,000	2.31	5	37. Texas
Oregon	3,162,000	1.08	16	38. Michigan
Pennsylvania	6,402,000	0.54	30	39. New York
Rhode Island	1,076,000	1.07	17	40. New Jersey
South Carolina	2,987,000	0.84	24	41. Maryland
South Dakota	2,092,000	2.98	2	42. Indiana
Tennessee	1,934,000	0.39	35	43. Kansas
Texas	5,885,000	0.34	37	44. Connecticut
Utah	213,000	0.12	46	45. Washington
Vermont	737,000	1.30	10	46. Utah
Virginia	5,334,000	0.85	23	47. New Mexico
Washington	679,000	0.14	45	48. Arizona
West Virginia	3,418,000	1.90	6	49. California
Wisconsin	4,856,000	0.98	19	50. District of Columbia
Wyoming	596,000	1.30	11	Hawaii
United States	$150,675,000	$0.60	29	

Source: U.S. Department of Commerce, Bureau of the Census, *Federal Expenditures by State for Fiscal Year 1991* (Washington, D.C.: Government Printing Office, 1992).
Note: The recipients of the federal grants include state and local governments.

FEDERAL SPENDING ON WASTEWATER TREATMENT WORKS. FISCAL 1991

State	Expenditures	Per capita	Rank by per capita	Rank in order — By per capita
Alabama	$17,283,000	$4.23	46	1. Alaska
Alaska	16,489,000	28.93	1	2. New York
Arizona	8,357,000	2.23	51	3. Hawaii
Arkansas	13,431,000	5.66	41	4. Delaware
California	159,693,000	5.26	44	5. District of Columbia
Colorado	25,231,000	7.47	30	6. West Virginia
Connecticut	46,870,000	14.24	14	7. South Dakota
Delaware	13,800,000	20.29	4	8. Maine
District of Columbia	11,909,000	19.91	5	9. North Dakota
Florida	94,528,000	7.12	32	10. Maryland
Georgia	49,182,000	7.43	31	11. Wisconsin
Hawaii	24,218,000	21.34	3	12. Wyoming
Idaho	8,458,000	8.14	27	13. New Jersey
Illinois	113,562,000	9.84	23	14. Connecticut
Indiana	43,222,000	7.70	28	15. Michigan
Iowa	30,719,000	10.99	19	16. Vermont
Kansas	16,355,000	6.56	34	17. Minnesota
Kentucky	12,897,000	3.47	49	18. New Hampshire
Louisiana	23,103,000	5.43	43	19. Iowa
Maine	22,513,000	18.23	8	20. Massachusetts
Maryland	82,548,000	16.99	10	21. Rhode Island
Massachusetts	65,130,000	10.86	20	22. Missouri
Michigan	122,738,000	13.10	15	23. Illinois
Minnesota	52,576,000	11.86	17	24. Montana
Mississippi	23,147,000	8.93	26	25. Ohio
Missouri	52,481,000	10.17	22	26. Mississippi
Montana	7,907,000	9.79	24	27. Idaho
Nebraska	9,441,000	5.93	37	28. Indiana
Nevada	4,419,000	3.44	50	29. Oregon
New Hampshire	12,724,000	11.51	18	30. Colorado
New Jersey	120,693,000	15.55	13	31. Georgia
New Mexico	6,991,000	4.52	45	32. Florida
New York	424,813,000	23.52	2	33. Washington
North Carolina	38,222,000	5.67	40	34. Kansas
North Dakota	11,176,000	17.60	9	35. Pennsylvania
Ohio	104,905,000	9.59	25	36. Virginia
Oklahoma	17,473,000	5.50	42	37. Nebraska
Oregon	22,029,000	7.54	29	38. South Carolina
Pennsylvania	73,227,000	6.12	35	39. Tennessee
Rhode Island	10,617,000	10.57	21	40. North Carolina
South Carolina	21,096,000	5.93	38	41. Arkansas
South Dakota	13,022,000	18.52	7	42. Oklahoma
Tennessee	28,778,000	5.81	39	43. Louisiana
Texas	69,485,000	4.01	47	44. California
Utah	6,521,000	3.68	48	45. New Mexico
Vermont	7,279,000	12.84	16	46. Alabama
Virginia	38,099,000	6.06	36	47. Texas
Washington	34,056,000	6.79	33	48. Utah
West Virginia	34,540,000	19.18	6	49. Kentucky
Wisconsin	82,492,000	16.65	11	50. Nevada
Wyoming	7,191,000	15.63	12	51. Arizona
United States	$2,378,384,000	$9.43	26	

Source: U.S. Department of Commerce, Bureau of the Census, *Federal Expenditures by State for Fiscal Year 1991* (Washington, D.C.: Government Printing Office, 1992).

HAZARDOUS WASTE SITES ON NATIONAL PRIORITY LIST, 1991				Rank in order
State	Sites	% of U.S. sites	Rank by %	By %
Alabama	12	1.0	27	1. New Jersey
Alaska	6	0.5	43	2. Pennsylvania
Arizona	10	0.8	32	3. California
Arkansas	10	0.8	32	4. New York
California	91	7.6	3	5. Michigan
Colorado	16	1.3	23	6. Florida
Connecticut	15	1.2	24	7. Washington
Delaware	20	1.7	18	8. Minnesota
District of Columbia	0	0.0	51	9. Wisconsin
Florida	52	4.3	6	10. Illinois
Georgia	13	1.1	26	11. Indiana
Hawaii	2	0.2	47	Ohio
Idaho	9	0.7	37	13. Texas
Illinois	37	3.1	10	14. Massachusetts
Indiana	33	2.7	11	15. South Carolina
Iowa	20	1.7	18	16. Missouri
Kansas	11	0.9	30	North Carolina
Kentucky	19	1.6	21	18. Delaware
Louisiana	11	0.9	30	Iowa
Maine	9	0.7	37	Virginia
Maryland	10	0.8	32	21. Kentucky
Massachusetts	25	2.1	14	22. New Hampshire
Michigan	77	6.4	5	23. Colorado
Minnesota	42	3.5	8	24. Connecticut
Mississippi	2	0.2	47	25. Tennessee
Missouri	22	1.8	16	26. Georgia
Montana	8	0.7	39	27. Alabama
Nebraska	8	0.7	39	Rhode Island
Nevada	1	0.1	50	Utah
New Hampshire	17	1.4	22	30. Kansas
New Jersey	109	9.1	1	Louisiana
New Mexico	10	0.8	32	32. Arizona
New York	84	7.0	4	Arkansas
North Carolina	22	1.8	16	Maryland
North Dakota	2	0.2	47	New Mexico
Ohio	33	2.7	11	Oklahoma
Oklahoma	10	0.8	32	37. Idaho
Oregon	8	0.7	39	Maine
Pennsylvania	97	8.1	2	39. Montana
Rhode Island	12	1.0	27	Nebraska
South Carolina	23	1.9	15	Oregon
South Dakota	4	0.3	45	Vermont
Tennessee	14	1.2	25	43. Alaska
Texas	29	2.4	13	44. West Virginia
Utah	12	1.0	27	45. South Dakota
Vermont	8	0.7	39	46. Wyoming
Virginia	20	1.7	18	47. Hawaii
Washington	49	4.1	7	Mississippi
West Virginia	5	0.4	44	North Dakota
Wisconsin	39	3.2	9	50. Nevada
Wyoming	3	0.3	46	51. District of Columbia
United States	1,201	—	—	

— not applicable.

Source: U.S. Department of Commerce, Bureau of the Census, *Statistical Abstract of the United States, 1992* (Washington, D.C.: Government Printing Office, 1992).

State	Expenditures	Per capita	Rank by per capita
Alabama	$1,981,000	$0.48	41
Alaska	848,000	1.49	14
Arizona	2,567,000	0.69	26
Arkansas	752,000	0.32	48
California	19,849,000	0.65	27
Colorado	2,806,000	0.83	24
Connecticut	1,182,000	0.36	47
Delaware	1,486,000	2.19	7
District of Columbia	5,575,000	9.32	1
Florida	6,590,000	0.50	40
Georgia	286,000	0.04	51
Hawaii	599,000	0.53	37
Idaho	2,072,000	1.99	11
Illinois	14,317,000	1.24	17
Indiana	2,931,000	0.52	39
Iowa	1,624,000	0.58	33
Kansas	3,146,000	1.26	16
Kentucky	1,354,000	0.37	46
Louisiana	3,742,000	0.88	21
Maine	1,228,000	0.99	18
Maryland	3,104,000	0.64	28
Massachusetts	5,828,000	0.97	19
Michigan	28,519,000	3.04	5
Minnesota	9,005,000	2.03	9
Mississippi	1,590,000	0.61	30
Missouri	1,928,000	0.37	45
Montana	2,980,000	3.69	4
Nebraska	1,003,000	0.63	29
Nevada	1,732,000	1.35	15
New Hampshire	4,233,000	3.83	3
New Jersey	20,018,000	2.58	6
New Mexico	2,882,000	1.86	12
New York	8,721,000	0.48	42
North Carolina	5,968,000	0.89	20
North Dakota	3,627,000	5.71	2
Ohio	5,267,000	0.48	43
Oklahoma	2,281,000	0.72	25
Oregon	1,747,000	0.60	32
Pennsylvania	3,262,000	0.27	49
Rhode Island	1,615,000	1.61	13
South Carolina	2,002,000	0.56	35
South Dakota	371,000	0.53	37
Tennessee	1,946,000	0.39	44
Texas	35,332,000	2.04	8
Utah	1,497,000	0.85	23
Vermont	1,141,000	2.01	10
Virginia	3,432,000	0.55	36
Washington	3,045,000	0.61	31
West Virginia	1,043,000	0.58	34
Wisconsin	4,263,000	0.86	22
Wyoming	93,000	0.20	50
United States	$245,059,000	$0.97	19

FEDERAL GRANTS FOR HAZARDOUS SUBSTANCE RESPONSE, FISCAL 1991

Rank in order

By per capita

1. District of Columbia
2. North Dakota
3. New Hampshire
4. Montana
5. Michigan
6. New Jersey
7. Delaware
8. Texas
9. Minnesota
10. Vermont
11. Idaho
12. New Mexico
13. Rhode Island
14. Alaska
15. Nevada
16. Kansas
17. Illinois
18. Maine
19. Massachusetts
20. North Carolina
21. Louisiana
22. Wisconsin
23. Utah
24. Colorado
25. Oklahoma
26. Arizona
27. California
28. Maryland
29. Nebraska
30. Mississippi
31. Washington
32. Oregon
33. Iowa
34. West Virginia
35. South Carolina
36. Virginia
37. Hawaii
    South Dakota
39. Indiana
40. Florida
41. Alabama
42. New York
43. Ohio
44. Tennessee
45. Missouri
46. Kentucky
47. Connecticut
48. Arkansas
49. Pennsylvania
50. Wyoming
51. Georgia

Source: U.S. Department of Commerce, Bureau of the Census, *Federal Expenditures by State for Fiscal Year 1991* (Washington, D.C.: Government Printing Office, 1992).

Note: Recipients of federal grants include state and local governments.

STATE SPENDING ON HAZARDOUS WASTE, FISCAL 1988

State	Expenditures	Per capita	Rank by per capita
Alabama	$2,158,257	$0.53	45
Alaska	2,680,727	5.12	9
Arizona	4,691,000	1.35	28
Arkansas	1,777,295	0.74	39
California	176,295,000	6.23	4
Colorado	3,875,000	1.17	32
Connecticut	14,311,000	4.43	13
Delaware	5,004,000	7.58	2
District of Columbia	—	—	—
Florida	53,381,084	4.33	14
Georgia	3,544,180	0.56	43
Hawaii	1,396,000	1.27	30
Idaho	1,828,400	1.82	23
Illinois	52,852,000	4.55	12
Indiana	6,486,164	1.17	33
Iowa	926,000	0.33	49
Kansas	2,750,000	1.10	34
Kentucky	4,013,400	1.08	35
Louisiana	5,215,476	1.18	31
Maine	9,559,000	7.93	1
Maryland	11,038,000	2.39	21
Massachusetts	30,262,000	5.14	8
Michigan	12,630,267	1.37	27
Minnesota	20,503,000	4.76	10
Mississippi	1,096,961	0.42	48
Missouri	2,988,778	0.58	42
Montana	6,085,918	7.56	3
Nebraska	1,008,676	0.63	41
Nevada	499,606	0.47	46
New Hampshire	6,107,000	5.63	6
New Jersey	29,204,000	3.78	15
New Mexico	5,632,800	3.74	16
New York	54,740,000	3.06	17
North Carolina	4,359,331	0.67	40
North Dakota	500,000	0.75	38
Ohio	22,884,648	2.11	22
Oklahoma	1,435,000	0.44	47
Oregon	12,768,753	4.62	11
Pennsylvania	34,681,000	2.89	19
Rhode Island	5,231,623	5.27	7
South Carolina	2,639,000	0.76	36
South Dakota	NA	NA	NA
Tennessee	6,965,000	1.42	26
Texas	9,168,849	0.54	44
Utah	2,194,400	1.30	29
Vermont	1,446,707	2.60	20
Virginia	9,936,747	1.65	24
Washington	27,558,000	5.93	5
West Virginia	5,700,000	3.04	18
Wisconsin	7,090,268	1.46	25
Wyoming	360,425	0.75	37
United States	**$689,460,740**	**$2.81**	**20**

Rank in order

By per capita

1. Maine
2. Delaware
3. Montana
4. California
5. Washington
6. New Hampshire
7. Rhode Island
8. Massachusetts
9. Alaska
10. Minnesota
11. Oregon
12. Illinois
13. Connecticut
14. Florida
15. New Jersey
16. New Mexico
17. New York
18. West Virginia
19. Pennsylvania
20. Vermont
21. Maryland
22. Ohio
23. Idaho
24. Virginia
25. Wisconsin
26. Tennessee
27. Michigan
28. Arizona
29. Utah
30. Hawaii
31. Louisiana
32. Colorado
33. Indiana
34. Kansas
35. Kentucky
36. South Carolina
37. Wyoming
38. North Dakota
39. Arkansas
40. North Carolina
41. Nebraska
42. Missouri
43. Georgia
44. Texas
45. Alabama
46. Nevada
47. Oklahoma
48. Mississippi
49. Iowa
— District of Columbia
NA South Dakota

— not applicable.   NA not available.

Source: R. Steven Brown, John M. Johnson, and Karen Marshall, *Resource Guide to State Environmental Management*, 2d ed. (Lexington, Ky.: Council of State Governments, 1990).

Note: Data includes spending on hazardous and solid waste programs. South Dakota reports this data in air quality expenditures. Hawaii reports hazardous waste, but not solid waste expenditures, in air quality.

Health

| State | 1991 overall ranking | | 1992 overall ranking | | Rank in order |
	Rank	Score	Rank	Score	By 1992 ranking
Alabama	42	−9	41	−10	1. Minnesota
Alaska	49	−15	46	−15	2. Hawaii
Arizona	40	−7	33	−3	3. New Hampshire
Arkansas	40	−7	44	−11	Wisconsin
California	22	5	22	3	5. Nebraska
Colorado	10	13	7	15	Utah
Connecticut	7	15	7	15	7. Colorado
Delaware	28	1	26	0	Connecticut
District of Columbia	—	—	—	—	Iowa
Florida	42	−9	41	−10	Kansas
Georgia	36	−4	36	−4	Vermont
Hawaii	1	24	2	23	12. Massachusetts
Idaho	35	−3	33	−3	13. Virginia
Illinois	32	−2	32	−2	14. Maine
Indiana	18	7	19	7	New Jersey
Iowa	8	14	7	15	Rhode Island
Kansas	8	14	7	15	17. North Dakota
Kentucky	36	−4	40	−7	Ohio
Louisiana	46	−12	46	−15	19. Indiana
Maine	11	12	14	9	20. Pennsylvania
Maryland	23	4	22	3	Washington
Massachusetts	11	12	12	13	22. California
Michigan	28	1	24	1	Maryland
Minnesota	2	21	1	24	24. Michigan
Mississippi	47	−13	49	−18	Oklahoma
Missouri	32	−2	31	−1	26. Delaware
Montana	19	6	26	0	Montana
Nebraska	5	17	5	17	South Dakota
Nevada	44	−10	41	−10	Texas
New Hampshire	3	18	3	18	Wyoming
New Jersey	15	10	14	9	31. Missouri
New Mexico	47	−13	46	−15	32. Illinois
New York	32	−2	36	−4	33. Arizona
North Carolina	30	0	33	−3	Idaho
North Dakota	17	9	17	8	North Carolina
Ohio	19	6	17	8	36. Georgia
Oklahoma	27	2	24	1	New York
Oregon	39	−6	38	−5	38. Oregon
Pennsylvania	19	6	20	6	39. Tennessee
Rhode Island	15	10	14	9	40. Kentucky
South Carolina	44	−10	45	−13	41. Alabama
South Dakota	25	3	26	0	Florida
Tennessee	36	−4	39	−6	Nevada
Texas	30	0	26	0	44. Arkansas
Utah	3	18	5	17	45. South Carolina
Vermont	14	11	7	15	46. Alaska
Virginia	11	12	13	11	Louisiana
Washington	23	4	20	6	New Mexico
West Virginia	50	−16	50	−20	49. Mississippi
Wisconsin	5	17	3	18	50. West Virginia
Wyoming	25	3	26	0	— District of Columbia
United States	**NA**	**NA**	**NA**	**NA**	

— not applicable.   NA not available.

Source: Northwestern National Life, The NWNL State Health Rankings (Minneapolis, Minn.: Northwestern National Life, 1992).

Note: These health rankings are based on Northwestern National Life's analysis of seventeen different indicators, including lifestyle choices, access to health care, disabilities, disease, and mortality. The score columns indicate the percentage a state is above or below the national average on the overall health ranking.

State	Expenditures	Per capita	Rank by per capita	Per $1,000 personal income Amount	Per $1,000 personal income Rank	Rank in order By per capita
Alabama	$342,850,000	$83.85	19	$5.64	12	1. Alaska
Alaska	142,270,000	249.60	1	11.90	1	2. Hawaii
Arizona	282,181,000	75.25	24	4.79	22	3. Delaware
Arkansas	128,557,000	54.20	44	3.85	35	4. Wyoming
California	3,427,654,000	112.83	9	5.53	14	5. Rhode Island
Colorado	197,509,000	58.49	39	3.17	44	6. Michigan
Connecticut	341,777,000	103.85	15	4.08	31	7. Massachusetts
Delaware	103,227,000	151.80	3	7.71	5	8. South Carolina
District of Columbia	—	—	—	—	—	9. California
Florida	1,457,379,000	109.77	12	6.03	10	10. Maryland
Georgia	484,224,000	73.11	26	4.37	25	11. Washington
Hawaii	198,137,000	174.57	2	8.74	3	12. Florida
Idaho	56,787,000	54.66	43	3.68	38	13. New York
Illinois	877,710,000	76.04	23	3.76	36	14. New Mexico
Indiana	301,396,000	53.73	45	3.21	43	15. Connecticut
Iowa	118,513,000	42.40	50	2.48	49	16. Montana
Kansas	137,029,000	54.92	42	3.04	46	17. New Hampshire
Kentucky	195,324,000	52.61	46	3.53	40	18. Maine
Louisiana	300,405,000	70.65	30	4.91	18	19. Alabama
Maine	104,482,000	84.60	18	4.94	17	20. Oregon
Maryland	544,860,000	112.11	10	5.21	15	21. Minnesota
Massachusetts	762,023,000	127.09	7	5.61	13	22. South Dakota
Michigan	1,284,400,000	137.11	6	7.51	6	23. Illinois
Minnesota	356,518,000	80.44	21	4.34	27	24. Arizona
Mississippi	146,126,000	56.38	40	4.43	24	25. Wisconsin
Missouri	306,142,000	59.35	38	3.42	42	26. Georgia
Montana	74,086,000	91.69	16	6.07	9	27. Vermont
Nebraska	112,979,000	70.92	29	4.07	33	28. Oklahoma
Nevada	56,461,000	43.97	49	2.42	50	29. Nebraska
New Hampshire	98,808,000	89.42	17	4.27	28	30. Louisiana
New Jersey	500,009,000	64.43	35	2.59	48	31. North Carolina
New Mexico	161,635,000	104.42	14	7.46	8	32. Pennsylvania
New York	1,920,611,000	106.36	13	4.83	20	33. Virginia
North Carolina	471,143,000	69.93	31	4.35	26	34. Utah
North Dakota	29,671,000	46.73	47	3.06	45	35. New Jersey
Ohio	678,654,000	62.04	37	3.56	39	36. Tennessee
Oklahoma	229,586,000	72.31	28	4.72	23	37. Ohio
Oregon	240,548,000	82.32	20	4.89	19	38. Missouri
Pennsylvania	828,192,000	69.24	32	3.73	37	39. Colorado
Rhode Island	141,678,000	141.11	5	7.50	7	40. Mississippi
South Carolina	429,404,000	120.62	8	8.10	4	41. West Virginia
South Dakota	55,827,000	79.41	22	5.08	16	42. Kansas
Tennessee	312,102,000	63.01	36	4.03	32	43. Idaho
Texas	802,863,000	46.28	48	2.82	47	44. Arkansas
Utah	116,754,000	65.96	34	4.82	21	45. Indiana
Vermont	41,453,000	73.11	27	4.19	30	46. Kentucky
Virginia	430,685,000	68.52	33	3.52	41	47. North Dakota
Washington	550,856,000	109.78	11	5.98	11	48. Texas
West Virginia	100,270,000	55.68	41	4.07	33	49. Nevada
Wisconsin	364,954,000	73.65	25	4.24	29	50. Iowa
Wyoming	65,113,000	141.55	4	8.83	2	— District of Columbia
United States	$21,411,822,000	$85.11	18	$4.61	24	

— not applicable.

Source: U.S. Department of Commerce, Bureau of the Census, *State Government Finances: 1991* (Washington, D.C.: Government Printing Office, 1992).

SUPPORT FOR PUBLIC HEALTH, 1992

State	Support for public health	Score	Rank
Alabama	0.67	−17	35
Alaska	0.46	−42	50
Arizona	0.53	−35	47
Arkansas	0.60	−26	41
California	1.08	34	5
Colorado	0.77	−4	26
Connecticut	1.32	53	1
Delaware	0.53	−34	45
District of Columbia	—	—	—
Florida	0.66	−17	35
Georgia	1.07	34	5
Hawaii	0.91	13	14
Idaho	0.75	−6	29
Illinois	0.90	12	15
Indiana	0.85	6	19
Iowa	0.80	0	23
Kansas	0.70	−13	34
Kentucky	0.62	−23	38
Louisiana	0.66	−18	37
Maine	0.85	6	19
Maryland	0.92	14	13
Massachusetts	1.42	53	1
Michigan	1.14	42	3
Minnesota	1.02	27	8
Mississippi	0.71	−12	33
Missouri	0.76	−5	28
Montana	0.54	−33	44
Nebraska	0.82	2	22
Nevada	0.61	−24	40
New Hampshire	0.97	21	12
New Jersey	1.03	28	7
New Mexico	0.53	−34	45
New York	1.14	42	4
North Carolina	0.72	−10	31
North Dakota	0.62	−23	38
Ohio	1.02	27	8
Oklahoma	0.75	−7	30
Oregon	0.59	−26	41
Pennsylvania	0.86	7	18
Rhode Island	0.98	23	11
South Carolina	0.80	0	23
South Dakota	0.51	−37	49
Tennessee	0.84	4	21
Texas	0.56	−30	43
Utah	0.77	−4	26
Vermont	0.72	−11	32
Virginia	0.88	9	16
Washington	0.87	8	17
West Virginia	0.52	−36	48
Wisconsin	1.02	27	8
Wyoming	0.79	−1	25
United States	**NA**	**NA**	**NA**

Rank in order

By score

1. Connecticut
   Massachusetts
3. Michigan
4. New York
5. California
   Georgia
7. New Jersey
8. Minnesota
   Ohio
   Wisconsin
11. Rhode Island
12. New Hampshire
13. Maryland
14. Hawaii
15. Illinois
16. Virginia
17. Washington
18. Pennsylvania
19. Indiana
    Maine
21. Tennessee
22. Nebraska
23. Iowa
    South Carolina
25. Wyoming
26. Colorado
    Utah
28. Missouri
29. Idaho
30. Oklahoma
31. North Carolina
32. Vermont
33. Mississippi
34. Kansas
35. Alabama
    Florida
37. Louisiana
38. Kentucky
    North Dakota
40. Nevada
41. Arkansas
    Oregon
43. Texas
44. Montana
45. Delaware
    New Mexico
47. Arizona
48. West Virginia
49. South Dakota
50. Alaska
— District of Columbia

— not applicable. NA not available.

Source: Northwestern National Life, *The NWNL State Health Rankings* (Minneapolis, Minn.: Northwestern National Life, 1992).

Note: The support for public health column is Northwestern National Life's ranking of the percentage of the state budget spent on public health divided by the poor population. The score column indicates the percentage a state is above or below the national average on a particular measurement.

State	Average health payments by family	Rank	Average business health payments per family	Rank	Total health payments per family	Rank
Alabama	$4,064	24	$1,541	44	$5,604	37
Alaska	3,846	34	3,910	1	7,756	4
Arizona	3,439	45	1,882	32	5,321	40
Arkansas	3,480	42	1,301	50	4,781	47
California	4,433	13	2,708	7	7,141	11
Colorado	3,933	28	2,141	25	6,073	25
Connecticut	5,421	2	3,890	2	9,312	1
Delaware	4,393	14	2,181	22	6,573	17
District of Columbia	4,300	17	1,754	37	6,054	26
Florida	3,932	29	1,623	41	5,556	39
Georgia	4,159	22	1,633	40	5,792	33
Hawaii	4,596	7	2,594	12	7,190	10
Idaho	3,005	51	1,594	42	4,599	49
Illinois	4,670	6	2,700	9	7,370	7
Indiana	3,972	26	1,957	30	5,930	28
Iowa	4,026	25	2,122	26	6,148	24
Kansas	4,481	11	2,477	15	6,959	13
Kentucky	3,206	48	1,329	48	4,535	50
Louisiana	3,809	35	1,868	33	5,677	35
Maine	3,946	27	2,322	20	6,268	22
Maryland	4,484	10	1,697	38	6,181	23
Massachusetts	5,321	3	3,164	3	8,484	2
Michigan	4,569	8	2,768	4	7,337	8
Minnesota	4,568	9	2,684	10	7,252	9
Mississippi	3,009	50	1,149	51	4,158	51
Missouri	4,362	15	2,353	18	6,715	15
Montana	3,154	49	1,755	36	4,910	45
Nebraska	4,268	19	2,286	21	6,554	19
Nevada	3,897	31	2,393	17	6,290	21
New Hampshire	3,860	33	2,701	8	6,561	18
New Jersey	4,863	5	2,722	6	7,586	6
New Mexico	3,297	47	1,518	45	4,815	46
New York	5,585	1	2,625	11	8,210	3
North Carolina	3,630	40	1,471	46	5,101	43
North Dakota	4,193	21	2,335	19	6,528	20
Ohio	4,474	12	2,531	13	7,005	12
Oklahoma	3,786	36	1,393	47	5,179	42
Oregon	3,900	30	2,146	24	6,045	27
Pennsylvania	4,300	17	2,524	14	6,825	14
Rhode Island	4,914	4	2,733	5	7,647	5
South Carolina	3,414	46	1,308	49	4,722	48
South Dakota	3,863	32	2,056	28	5,919	29
Tennessee	3,487	41	2,152	23	5,639	36
Texas	4,095	23	1,796	35	5,891	31
Utah	3,682	38	2,017	29	5,699	34
Vermont	3,649	39	1,949	31	5,598	38
Virginia	4,358	16	1,547	43	5,906	30
Washington	3,710	37	2,117	27	5,826	32
West Virginia	3,443	44	1,653	39	5,096	44
Wisconsin	4,245	20	2,406	16	6,651	16
Wyoming	3,474	43	1,810	34	5,284	41
United States	**$4,296**	**19**	**$2,239**	**22**	**$6,535**	**20**

1. New York
2. Connecticut
3. Massachusetts
4. Rhode Island
5. New Jersey
6. Illinois
7. Hawaii
8. Michigan
9. Minnesota
10. Maryland
11. Kansas
12. Ohio
13. California
14. Delaware
15. Missouri
16. Virginia
17. District of Columbia
    Pennsylvania
19. Nebraska
20. Wisconsin
21. North Dakota
22. Georgia
23. Texas
24. Alabama
25. Iowa
26. Indiana
27. Maine
28. Colorado
29. Florida
30. Oregon
31. Nevada
32. South Dakota
33. New Hampshire
34. Alaska
35. Louisiana
36. Oklahoma
37. Washington
38. Utah
39. Vermont
40. North Carolina
41. Tennessee
42. Arkansas
43. Wyoming
44. West Virginia
45. Arizona
46. South Carolina
47. New Mexico
48. Kentucky
49. Montana
50. Mississippi
51. Idaho

Source: Families U.S.A. Foundation, *Health Spending: Growing Threat to the Family Budget* (Washington, D.C.: Families U.S.A. Foundation, 1991).

Note: Families are groups of one or more related persons who reside together. Health payments cover the delivery of health services and supplies and the purchase of medical products, including prescription drugs and vision products in retail outlets. It also includes government public health expenditures, the administrative costs of public programs, and the net cost of private insurance.

State	HMO plans	Enrollment	Per 1,000 population		Rank in order
			Rate	Rank	By rate per 1,000 population
Alabama	8	250,939	62.1	34	1. District of Columbia
Alaska	0	0	0.0	48	2. California
Arizona	15	743,169	202.8	11	3. Minnesota
Arkansas	4	46,658	19.8	44	4. Massachusetts
California	50	9,679,139	325.2	2	5. Oregon
Colorado	14	704,665	213.9	10	6. Hawaii
Connecticut	13	726,523	221.0	8	7. Wisconsin
Delaware	6	126,208	189.5	12	8. Connecticut
District of Columbia	4	493,607	813.2	1	9. Rhode Island
Florida	35	1,493,517	115.4	22	10. Colorado
Georgia	8	340,628	52.6	38	11. Arizona
Hawaii	6	261,408	235.9	6	12. Delaware
Idaho	1	18,105	18.0	45	13. Maryland
Illinois	25	1,446,627	126.6	21	14. Utah
Indiana	12	356,112	64.2	31	15. Michigan
Iowa	7	300,377	108.2	25	16. New York
Kansas	9	204,426	82.5	28	17. Washington
Kentucky	7	229,265	62.2	33	18. Ohio
Louisiana	10	247,802	58.7	36	19. New Mexico
Maine	3	30,825	25.1	42	20. Pennsylvania
Maryland	15	904,425	189.2	13	21. Illinois
Massachusetts	20	1,606,979	267.1	4	22. Florida
Michigan	17	1,496,825	161.0	15	23. New Jersey
Minnesota	11	1,240,202	283.5	3	24. Missouri
Mississippi	0	0	0.0	48	25. Iowa
Missouri	15	555,240	108.5	24	26. New Hampshire
Montana	1	6,300	7.9	47	27. Nevada
Nebraska	5	88,415	56.0	37	28. Kansas
Nevada	3	110,144	91.6	27	29. Texas
New Hampshire	3	105,900	95.5	26	30. Vermont
New Jersey	11	887,597	114.8	23	31. Indiana
New Mexico	5	208,433	137.6	19	32. Virginia
New York	35	2,759,961	153.4	16	33. Kentucky
North Carolina	10	279,326	42.1	39	34. Alabama
North Dakota	2	7,740	12.1	46	35. Oklahoma
Ohio	35	1,529,072	141.0	18	36. Louisiana
Oklahoma	6	190,697	60.6	35	37. Nebraska
Oregon	9	741,434	260.9	5	38. Georgia
Pennsylvania	24	1,520,441	128.0	20	39. North Carolina
Rhode Island	4	220,044	219.4	9	40. Tennessee
South Carolina	4	75,391	21.6	43	41. South Dakota
South Dakota	1	22,100	31.8	41	42. Maine
Tennessee	9	192,731	39.5	40	43. South Carolina
Texas	26	1,371,963	80.8	29	44. Arkansas
Utah	9	300,169	174.2	14	45. Idaho
Vermont	1	40,125	71.3	30	46. North Dakota
Virginia	12	385,371	62.3	32	47. Montana
Washington	9	726,492	149.3	17	48. Alaska
West Virginia	0	0	0.0	48	Mississippi
Wisconsin	28	1,115,079	227.9	7	West Virginia
Wyoming	0	0	0.0	48	Wyoming
United States	569	36,453,596	146.6	18	

Source: Group Health Association of America, *1991 National Directory of HMO's*, (Washington, D.C.: GHAA, 1992).
Note: HMO stands for Health Maintenance Organization.

State	1991 recipients	Recipients as % of state population	Rank by %	% increase 1990-1991 Rate	Rank	By % of state population
Alabama	403,255	9.9	24	14.6	21	1. Mississippi
Alaska	51,288	9.0	31	31.3	3	2. District of Columbia
Arizona	313,142	8.4	35	0.0	51	3. Rhode Island
Arkansas	284,674	12.0	12	7.7	40	4. West Virginia
California	4,019,084	13.2	9	10.9	31	5. Louisiana
Colorado	223,444	6.6	49	17.2	15	6. Kentucky
Connecticut	271,903	8.3	37	8.9	36	7. Tennessee
Delaware	50,680	7.5	44	23.6	8	8. New York
District of Columbia	100,065	16.7	2	7.0	45	9. California
Florida	1,248,883	9.4	28	20.3	9	10. Vermont
Georgia	746,241	11.3	15	14.7	20	11. Maine
Hawaii	91,162	8.0	39	7.3	42	12. Arkansas
Idaho	70,060	6.7	48	28.4	4	13. Ohio
Illinois	1,144,272	9.9	22	7.2	44	14. Michigan
Indiana	415,167	7.4	45	19.3	12	15. Georgia
Iowa	261,419	9.4	29	9.1	35	16. Massachusetts
Kansas	209,329	8.4	34	7.7	41	17. Pennsylvania
Kentucky	525,497	14.2	6	12.4	26	18. South Carolina
Louisiana	640,562	15.1	5	9.5	34	19. New Mexico
Maine	150,623	12.2	11	13.2	24	20. Washington
Maryland	362,520	7.5	43	9.7	33	21. Texas
Massachusetts	651,056	10.9	16	10.2	32	22. Illinois
Michigan	1,112,533	11.9	14	6.2	47	23. North Carolina
Minnesota	421,738	9.5	27	10.9	30	24. Alabama
Mississippi	469,684	18.1	1	8.5	38	25. Missouri
Missouri	503,310	9.8	25	12.3	27	26. Oklahoma
Montana	63,615	7.9	42	4.2	50	27. Minnesota
Nebraska	133,751	8.4	32	12.2	28	28. Florida
Nevada	59,296	4.6	51	26.1	6	29. Iowa
New Hampshire	59,684	5.4	50	33.2	2	30. Oregon
New Jersey	614,073	7.9	41	8.3	39	31. Alaska
New Mexico	161,995	10.5	19	24.7	7	32. Nebraska
New York	2,461,537	13.6	8	5.7	49	33. Wisconsin
North Carolina	667,203	9.9	23	18.4	13	34. Kansas
North Dakota	52,539	8.3	36	7.2	43	35. Arizona
Ohio	1,299,285	11.9	13	6.4	46	36. North Dakota
Oklahoma	304,659	9.6	26	11.5	29	37. Connecticut
Oregon	263,303	9.0	30	15.9	19	38. South Dakota
Pennsylvania	1,277,428	10.7	17	8.5	37	39. Hawaii
Rhode Island	163,704	16.3	3	39.9	1	40. Wyoming
South Carolina	375,233	10.5	18	18.3	14	41. New Jersey
South Dakota	57,145	8.1	38	15.9	18	42. Montana
Tennessee	697,411	14.1	7	13.7	22	43. Maryland
Texas	1,728,629	10.0	21	19.9	10	44. Delaware
Utah	129,274	7.3	46	19.4	11	45. Indiana
Vermont	70,699	12.5	10	17.0	16	46. Utah
Virginia	442,073	7.0	47	16.5	17	47. Virginia
Washington	506,279	10.1	20	13.1	25	48. Idaho
West Virginia	283,708	15.8	4	13.4	23	49. Colorado
Wisconsin	415,942	8.4	33	5.9	48	50. New Hampshire
Wyoming	36,804	8.0	40	27.2	5	51. Nevada
United States	28,279,781	11.2	16	12.0	29	

Source: Health Care Financing Administration, unpublished data, 1993.

MEDICALLY UNDERSERVED POPULATION, 1990

State	% of population medically underserved	Rank by %
Alabama	27.6	4
Alaska	0.0	51
Arizona	17.5	18
Arkansas	27.6	4
California	21.5	9
Colorado	14.9	25
Connecticut	4.4	49
Delaware	13.7	28
District of Columbia	25.4	6
Florida	18.7	16
Georgia	20.2	12
Hawaii	8.3	45
Idaho	17.6	17
Illinois	19.8	13
Indiana	12.1	31
Iowa	10.4	38
Kansas	11.8	32
Kentucky	16.4	20
Louisiana	31.8	2
Maine	8.6	44
Maryland	15.0	24
Massachusetts	12.9	29
Michigan	15.2	23
Minnesota	9.9	42
Mississippi	33.3	1
Missouri	14.2	27
Montana	17.0	19
Nebraska	2.9	50
Nevada	10.0	41
New Hampshire	7.6	46
New Jersey	11.1	37
New Mexico	22.9	8
New York	20.8	11
North Carolina	15.7	22
North Dakota	6.2	47
Ohio	14.4	26
Oklahoma	23.6	7
Oregon	11.2	35
Pennsylvania	11.3	34
Rhode Island	11.2	35
South Carolina	19.3	14
South Dakota	10.3	39
Tennessee	18.9	15
Texas	21.3	10
Utah	11.4	33
Vermont	5.3	48
Virginia	10.2	40
Washington	15.9	21
West Virginia	29.7	3
Wisconsin	12.7	30
Wyoming	8.9	43
United States	**17.2**	**19**

Rank in order

By %

1. Mississippi
2. Louisiana
3. West Virginia
4. Alabama
   Arkansas
6. District of Columbia
7. Oklahoma
8. New Mexico
9. California
10. Texas
11. New York
12. Georgia
13. Illinois
14. South Carolina
15. Tennessee
16. Florida
17. Idaho
18. Arizona
19. Montana
20. Kentucky
21. Washington
22. North Carolina
23. Michigan
24. Maryland
25. Colorado
26. Ohio
27. Missouri
28. Delaware
29. Massachusetts
30. Wisconsin
31. Indiana
32. Kansas
33. Utah
34. Pennsylvania
35. Oregon
    Rhode Island
37. New Jersey
38. Iowa
39. South Dakota
40. Virginia
41. Nevada
42. Minnesota
43. Wyoming
44. Maine
45. Hawaii
46. New Hampshire
47. North Dakota
48. Vermont
49. Connecticut
50. Nebraska
51. Alaska

Source: Joseph Tiang-Yau Liu, Carol Regan, Tracy M. Orloff, and Lourdes A. Rivera, *The Health of America's Children 1992: Maternal and Child Health Data Book,* (Washington, D.C.: Children's Defense Fund, 1992).
Note: Medically underserved is defined as living in a community with shortages of physicians and clinics.

State	LACK OF HEALTH CARE ACCESS, 1991 % of population with lack of health care access	Rank by %
Alabama	8.6	12
Alaska	11.8	8
Arizona	5.1	23
Arkansas	7.8	13
California	4.4	27
Colorado	2.9	41
Connecticut	1.8	46
Delaware	1.8	46
District of Columbia	NA	NA
Florida	5.4	21
Georgia	7.7	14
Hawaii	0.3	50
Idaho	15.7	3
Illinois	6.7	16
Indiana	3.8	34
Iowa	3.9	32
Kansas	1.7	48
Kentucky	5.7	20
Louisiana	11.2	9
Maine	4.5	25
Maryland	2.8	42
Massachusetts	3.1	38
Michigan	4.4	27
Minnesota	2.1	44
Mississippi	13.4	6
Missouri	5.3	22
Montana	9.0	11
Nebraska	3.7	36
Nevada	6.2	17
New Hampshire	2.0	45
New Jersey	0.9	49
New Mexico	17.2	1
New York	3.1	38
North Carolina	6.1	19
North Dakota	16.7	2
Ohio	3.8	34
Oklahoma	4.0	31
Oregon	7.1	15
Pennsylvania	2.2	43
Rhode Island	5.1	23
South Carolina	9.9	10
South Dakota	14.7	4
Tennessee	6.2	17
Texas	4.5	25
Utah	4.2	29
Vermont	3.0	40
Virginia	3.3	37
Washington	3.9	32
West Virginia	13.8	5
Wisconsin	4.1	30
Wyoming	12.5	7
United States	**NA**	**NA**

Rank in order

By %
1. New Mexico
2. North Dakota
3. Idaho
4. South Dakota
5. West Virginia
6. Mississippi
7. Wyoming
8. Alaska
9. Louisiana
10. South Carolina
11. Montana
12. Alabama
13. Arkansas
14. Georgia
15. Oregon
16. Illinois
17. Nevada
    Tennessee
19. North Carolina
20. Kentucky
21. Florida
22. Missouri
23. Arizona
    Rhode Island
25. Maine
    Texas
27. California
    Michigan
29. Utah
30. Wisconsin
31. Oklahoma
32. Iowa
    Washington
34. Indiana
    Ohio
36. Nebraska
37. Virginia
38. Massachusetts
    New York
40. Vermont
41. Colorado
42. Maryland
43. Pennsylvania
44. Minnesota
45. New Hampshire
46. Connecticut
    Delaware
48. Kansas
49. New Jersey
50. Hawaii
NA District of Columbia

NA not available.

Source: Northwestern National Life, *The NWNL State Health Rankings* (Minneapolis, Minn.: Northwestern National Life, 1992).
Note: Population with lack of health care access reside in health professional shortage areas.

State	Physicians	Per 100,000 population		By rate per 100,000 population
		Rate	Rank	
Alabama	6,464	158	41	1. District of Columbia
Alaska	734·	146	47	2. Massachusetts
Arizona	6,961	197	21	3. Maryland
Arkansas	3,595	150	45	4. New York
California	70,062	244	9	5. Connecticut
Colorado	6,894	211	16	6. Rhode Island
Connecticut	9,820	305	5	7. Vermont
Delaware	1,329	199	20	8. New Jersey
District of Columbia	3,674	615	1	9. California
Florida	26,123	208	17	10. Hawaii
Georgia	11,144	175	32	11. Pennsylvania
Hawaii	2,491	236	10	12. Minnesota
Idaho	1,259	125	51	13. Virginia
Illinois	24,680	212	15	Washington
Indiana	8,764	157	43	15. Illinois
Iowa	4,280	151	44	16. Colorado
Kansas	4,360	175	32	17. Florida
Kentucky	6,202	168	37	18. Oregon
Louisiana	8,173	188	27	19. New Hampshire
Maine	2,155	178	31	20. Delaware
Maryland	15,484	334	3	21. Arizona
Massachusetts	19,910	337	2	22. Missouri
Michigan	17,129	185	28	Ohio
Minnesota	9,574	220	12	Tennessee
Mississippi	3,455	133	50	25. North Carolina
Missouri	10,100	196	22	26. Wisconsin
Montana	1,263	158	41	27. Louisiana
Nebraska	2,741	172	35	28. Michigan
Nevada	1,746	159	40	Utah
New Hampshire	2,199	200	19	30. New Mexico
New Jersey	18,971	246	8	31. Maine
New Mexico	2,768	183	30	32. Georgia
New York	56,395	315	4	Kansas
North Carolina	12,262	190	25	Texas
North Dakota	1,102	170	36	35. Nebraska
Ohio	21,379	196	22	36. North Dakota
Oklahoma	4,697	147	46	37. Kentucky
Oregon	5,778	205	18	38. West Virginia
Pennsylvania	28,293	235	11	39. South Carolina
Rhode Island	2,515	254	6	40. Nevada
South Carolina	5,541	161	39	41. Alabama
South Dakota	992	140	48	Montana
Tennessee	9,619	196	22	43. Indiana
Texas	29,451	175	32	44. Iowa
Utah	3,145	185	28	45. Arkansas
Vermont	1,432	253	7	46. Oklahoma
Virginia	12,615	213	13	47. Alaska
Washington	10,006	213	13	48. South Dakota
West Virginia	3,086	166	38	49. Wyoming
Wisconsin	9,172	189	26	50. Mississippi
Wyoming	654	139	49	51. Idaho
United States	**532,638**	**216**	**13**	

Source: American Medical Association, *Physician Characteristics and Distribution in the U.S.* (Chicago: AMA, 1991).

| State | Nurses | Per 100,000 population | | Rank in order By rate per 100,000 population |
		Rate	Rank	
Alabama	22,800	557	40	1. District of Columbia
Alaska	2,700	538	41	2. Massachusetts
Arizona	23,700	671	29	3. Rhode Island
Arkansas	12,000	501	43	4. North Dakota
California	167,900	584	36	5. New Hampshire
Colorado	23,400	715	24	Vermont
Connecticut	28,200	875	8	7. Delaware
Delaware	6,000	898	7	8. Connecticut
District of Columbia	9,500	1,591	1	9. Maine
Florida	84,100	669	30	10. Pennsylvania
Georgia	35,800	562	38	11. South Dakota
Hawaii	5,900	559	39	12. Iowa
Idaho	5,300	525	42	13. New York
Illinois	83,600	719	23	14. Minnesota
Indiana	37,900	678	28	15. Nebraska
Iowa	23,100	814	12	16. Washington
Kansas	18,000	723	21	17. Missouri
Kentucky	18,400	498	45	18. Ohio
Louisiana	18,700	430	51	Oregon
Maine	10,200	841	9	20. Nevada
Maryland	33,500	722	22	21. Kansas
Massachusetts	68,000	1,153	2	22. Maryland
Michigan	62,900	679	27	23. Illinois
Minnesota	34,300	788	14	24. Colorado
Mississippi	12,200	469	49	25. Wisconsin
Missouri	38,900	756	17	26. New Jersey
Montana	5,300	662	31	27. Michigan
Nebraska	12,200	763	15	28. Indiana
Nevada	8,200	746	20	29. Arizona
New Hampshire	10,100	917	5	30. Florida
New Jersey	53,400	692	26	31. Montana
New Mexico	7,300	482	47	32. North Carolina
New York	143,300	800	13	33. West Virginia
North Carolina	40,500	626	32	34. Wyoming
North Dakota	6,000	923	4	35. Tennessee
Ohio	81,600	749	18	36. California
Oklahoma	15,100	473	48	37. Virginia
Oregon	21,100	749	18	38. Georgia
Pennsylvania	100,700	837	10	39. Hawaii
Rhode Island	9,300	938	3	40. Alabama
South Carolina	15,900	461	50	41. Alaska
South Dakota	5,900	833	11	42. Idaho
Tennessee	29,100	591	35	43. Arkansas
Texas	81,600	484	46	44. Utah
Utah	8,500	500	44	45. Kentucky
Vermont	5,200	917	5	46. Texas
Virginia	34,400	580	37	47. New Mexico
Washington	35,800	761	16	48. Oklahoma
West Virginia	11,200	603	33	49. Mississippi
Wisconsin	34,500	709	25	50. South Carolina
Wyoming	2,800	594	34	51. Louisiana
United States	**1,666,200**	**676**	**29**	

Source: U.S. Department of Commerce, Bureau of the Census, *Statistical Abstract of the United States, 1992* (Washington, D.C.: Government Printing Office, 1992).

State	Dentists	Per 100,000 population		Rank in order
		Rate	**Rank**	**By rate per 100,000 population**
Alabama	1,700	42	46	1. District of Columbia
Alaska	340	65	15	2. Connecticut
Arizona	1,790	49	36	Hawaii
Arkansas	970	41	49	4. New York
California	17,680	60	20	5. Massachusetts
Colorado	2,320	71	7	New Jersey
Connecticut	2,640	81	2	7. Colorado
Delaware	290	44	45	8. Oregon
District of Columbia	600	100	1	9. Maryland
Florida	6,230	49	36	Minnesota
Georgia	2,950	46	44	Utah
Hawaii	850	81	2	12. Nebraska
Idaho	550	55	27	Wisconsin
Illinois	7,310	64	17	14. Washington
Indiana	2,710	49	36	15. Alaska
Iowa	1,610	58	22	Montana
Kansas	1,280	52	32	17. Illinois
Kentucky	2,020	55	27	18. Michigan
Louisiana	2,050	49	36	Pennsylvania
Maine	580	48	40	20. California
Maryland	3,170	67	9	21. New Hampshire
Massachusetts	4,470	74	5	22. Iowa
Michigan	5,860	63	18	Wyoming
Minnesota	2,930	67	9	24. Vermont
Mississippi	990	39	51	25. Ohio
Missouri	2,790	55	27	Rhode Island
Montana	520	65	15	27. Idaho
Nebraska	1,030	66	12	Kentucky
Nevada	500	42	46	Missouri
New Hampshire	650	59	21	Tennessee
New Jersey	5,740	74	5	31. Virginia
New Mexico	700	47	42	32. Kansas
New York	14,200	79	4	33. North Dakota
North Carolina	2,730	42	46	Oklahoma
North Dakota	320	51	33	South Dakota
Ohio	6,110	56	25	36. Arizona
Oklahoma	1,580	51	33	Florida
Oregon	1,970	69	8	Indiana
Pennsylvania	7,500	63	18	Louisiana
Rhode Island	560	56	25	40. Maine
South Carolina	1,410	41	49	Texas
South Dakota	350	51	33	42. New Mexico
Tennessee	2,660	55	27	West Virginia
Texas	8,140	48	40	44. Georgia
Utah	1,150	67	9	45. Delaware
Vermont	320	57	24	46. Alabama
Virginia	3,210	53	31	Nevada
Washington	3,140	65	14	North Carolina
West Virginia	850	47	42	49. Arkansas
Wisconsin	3,210	66	12	South Carolina
Wyoming	260	58	22	51. Mississippi
United States	**145,500**	**59**	**21**	

Source: U.S. Department of Commerce, Bureau of the Census, *Statistical Abstract of the United States, 1992* (Washington, D.C.: Government Printing Office, 1992).

AVERAGE COST PER HOSPITAL STAY, 1990			Rank in order
State	**Average cost per stay**	**Rank**	**By average cost per stay**
Alabama	$4,175	38	1. District of Columbia
Alaska	6,249	3	2. New York
Arizona	4,877	16	3. Alaska
Arkansas	3,730	49	4. Connecticut
California	5,709	6	5. Hawaii
Colorado	5,209	12	6. California
Connecticut	6,238	4	Massachusetts
Delaware	5,112	14	8. Nevada
District of Columbia	7,876	1	9. Michigan
Florida	5,312	10	10. Florida
Georgia	4,303	36	11. Illinois
Hawaii	6,048	5	12. Colorado
Idaho	3,701	50	13. Pennsylvania
Illinois	5,253	11	14. Delaware
Indiana	4,390	33	15. Missouri
Iowa	4,135	42	16. Arizona
Kansas	4,161	41	17. Rhode Island
Kentucky	3,762	48	18. Ohio
Louisiana	4,575	24	19. Minnesota
Maine	4,604	23	20. Nebraska
Maryland	4,640	22	21. Texas
Massachusetts	5,709	6	22. Maryland
Michigan	5,358	9	23. Maine
Minnesota	4,782	19	24. Louisiana
Mississippi	3,116	51	25. New Jersey
Missouri	5,022	15	26. New Hampshire
Montana	3,973	45	27. Washington
Nebraska	4,675	20	28. North Dakota
Nevada	5,511	8	29. Oregon
New Hampshire	4,544	26	30. Utah
New Jersey	4,573	25	31. North Carolina
New Mexico	4,172	39	Virginia
New York	6,397	2	33. Indiana
North Carolina	4,408	31	34. Vermont
North Dakota	4,468	28	35. Tennessee
Ohio	4,801	18	36. Georgia
Oklahoma	4,302	37	37. Oklahoma
Oregon	4,432	29	38. Alabama
Pennsylvania	5,120	13	39. New Mexico
Rhode Island	4,839	17	40. South Carolina
South Carolina	4,168	40	41. Kansas
South Dakota	3,905	47	42. Iowa
Tennessee	4,340	35	43. Wisconsin
Texas	4,663	21	44. Wyoming
Utah	4,409	30	45. Montana
Vermont	4,343	34	46. West Virginia
Virginia	4,408	31	47. South Dakota
Washington	4,519	27	48. Kentucky
West Virginia	3,918	46	49. Arkansas
Wisconsin	4,083	43	50. Idaho
Wyoming	3,990	44	51. Mississippi
United States	**$4,726**	**20**	

Source: American Hospital Association, *Hospital Statistics* (Chicago: AHA, 1991).

AVERAGE COST PER DAY FOR HOSPITAL CARE, 1990			Rank in order
State	Average daily cost	Rank	By average daily cost
Alabama	$588	36	1. Alaska
Alaska	1,070	1	2. District of Columbia
Arizona	867	4	3. California
Arkansas	534	43	4. Arizona
California	939	3	5. Nevada
Colorado	725	15	6. Utah
Connecticut	825	7	7. Connecticut
Delaware	771	11	8. Washington
District of Columbia	995	2	9. Oregon
Florida	769	12	10. Massachusetts
Georgia	630	31	11. Delaware
Hawaii	638	27	12. Florida
Idaho	547	41	13. Texas
Illinois	717	17	14. New Mexico
Indiana	667	23	15. Colorado
Iowa	495	45	16. Ohio
Kansas	532	44	17. Illinois
Kentucky	563	39	18. Michigan
Louisiana	701	19	19. Louisiana
Maine	574	37	20. Missouri
Maryland	678	21	21. Maryland
Massachusetts	788	10	22. New Hampshire
Michigan	716	18	23. Indiana
Minnesota	536	42	24. Rhode Island
Mississippi	439	48	25. Pennsylvania
Missouri	679	20	26. New York
Montana	405	50	27. Hawaii
Nebraska	490	46	28. Virginia
Nevada	854	5	29. Tennessee
New Hampshire	671	22	30. Oklahoma
New Jersey	613	32	31. Georgia
New Mexico	734	14	32. New Jersey
New York	641	26	33. Vermont
North Carolina	595	34	34. North Carolina
North Dakota	427	49	35. South Carolina
Ohio	720	16	36. Alabama
Oklahoma	632	30	37. Maine
Oregon	800	9	38. West Virginia
Pennsylvania	662	25	39. Kentucky
Rhode Island	663	24	40. Wisconsin
South Carolina	590	35	41. Idaho
South Dakota	391	51	42. Minnesota
Tennessee	633	29	43. Arkansas
Texas	752	13	44. Kansas
Utah	832	6	45. Iowa
Vermont	598	33	46. Nebraska
Virginia	635	28	47. Wyoming
Washington	817	8	48. Mississippi
West Virginia	565	38	49. North Dakota
Wisconsin	554	40	50. Montana
Wyoming	462	47	51. South Dakota
United States	$661	26	

Source: American Hospital Association, *Hospital Statistics* (Chicago: AHA, 1991).

AVERAGE COST PER DAY FOR HOSPITAL ROOM, 1990			Rank in order
State	**Average room charge**	**Rank**	**By average cost per stay**
Alabama	$210	44	1. Connecticut
Alaska	407	3	2. California
Arizona	300	21	3. Alaska
Arkansas	170	50	4. Delaware
California	453	2	5. Vermont
Colorado	321	17	6. Pennsylvania
Connecticut	456	1	7. Utah
Delaware	385	4	8. Massachusetts
District of Columbia	325	16	9. Hawaii
Florida	271	25	10. Rhode Island
Georgia	191	48	11. New York
Hawaii	348	9	12. Oregon
Idaho	259	28	13. Michigan
Illinois	300	21	14. Maine
Indiana	258	29	15. Washington
Iowa	221	39	16. District of Columbia
Kansas	256	30	17. Colorado
Kentucky	242	33	18. Montana
Louisiana	203	47	19. Ohio
Maine	335	14	20. New Hampshire
Maryland	266	27	21. Arizona
Massachusetts	351	8	Illinois
Michigan	337	13	23. Minnesota
Minnesota	282	23	24. New Jersey
Mississippi	167	51	25. Florida
Missouri	268	26	26. Missouri
Montana	318	18	27. Maryland
Nebraska	209	45	28. Idaho
Nevada	251	32	29. Indiana
New Hampshire	304	20	30. Kansas
New Jersey	273	24	31. New Mexico
New Mexico	254	31	32. Nevada
New York	339	11	33. Kentucky
North Carolina	220	40	34. Wyoming
North Dakota	230	35	35. North Dakota
Ohio	308	19	36. Texas
Oklahoma	220	40	West Virginia
Oregon	338	12	38. Wisconsin
Pennsylvania	375	6	39. Iowa
Rhode Island	342	10	40. North Carolina
South Carolina	212	43	Oklahoma
South Dakota	208	46	Virginia
Tennessee	182	49	43. South Carolina
Texas	223	36	44. Alabama
Utah	353	7	45. Nebraska
Vermont	378	5	46. South Dakota
Virginia	220	40	47. Louisiana
Washington	334	15	48. Georgia
West Virginia	223	36	49. Tennessee
Wisconsin	222	38	50. Arkansas
Wyoming	234	34	51. Mississippi
United States	**$285**	**23**	

Source: Health Insurance Association of America, *Survey of Semi-Private Room Charges* (Washington, D.C.: Health Insurance Association of America, 1991).

State	Expenditures	Per capita	Rank by per capita	Per $1,000 personal income Amount	Per $1,000 personal income Rank
Alabama	$705,923,000	$172.64	3	$11.62	1
Alaska	31,609,000	55.45	40	2.64	44
Arizona	75,230,000	20.06	50	1.28	50
Arkansas	165,407,000	69.73	36	4.95	25
California	2,377,993,000	78.27	30	3.84	35
Colorado	187,080,000	55.40	41	3.00	42
Connecticut	687,910,000	209.03	1	8.20	8
Delaware	43,596,000	64.11	37	3.25	41
District of Columbia	—	—	—	—	—
Florida	491,279,000	37.00	48	2.03	47
Georgia	529,250,000	79.91	27	4.77	28
Hawaii	171,610,000	151.20	6	7.57	10
Idaho	30,442,000	29.30	49	1.97	48
Illinois	652,516,000	56.53	39	2.79	43
Indiana	461,749,000	82.31	26	4.92	26
Iowa	457,525,000	163.69	5	9.56	4
Kansas	285,331,000	114.36	15	6.33	18
Kentucky	277,843,000	74.83	33	5.02	24
Louisiana	697,136,000	163.95	4	11.38	2
Maine	73,553,000	59.56	38	3.48	37
Maryland	351,043,000	72.23	35	3.36	38
Massachusetts	841,011,000	140.26	7	6.19	19
Michigan	1,092,771,000	116.65	14	6.39	17
Minnesota	536,654,000	121.09	12	6.53	15
Mississippi	228,720,000	88.24	23	6.93	12
Missouri	409,013,000	79.30	28	4.57	32
Montana	40,536,000	50.17	43	3.32	39
Nebraska	213,008,000	132.96	11	7.68	9
Nevada	48,677,000	37.91	47	2.09	46
New Hampshire	43,854,000	39.69	46	1.89	49
New Jersey	813,156,000	104.79	18	4.22	34
New Mexico	209,973,000	135.64	10	9.69	3
New York	3,431,920,000	190.05	2	8.63	7
North Carolina	613,921,000	91.13	22	5.66	21
North Dakota	63,502,000	100.00	19	6.56	14
Ohio	1,072,703,000	98.06	21	5.62	22
Oklahoma	316,717,000	99.75	20	6.51	16
Oregon	333,374,000	114.09	16	6.78	13
Pennsylvania	1,018,528,000	85.15	25	4.58	31
Rhode Island	112,944,000	112.49	17	5.98	20
South Carolina	487,973,000	137.07	9	9.21	5
South Dakota	36,235,000	51.54	42	3.29	40
Tennessee	391,388,000	79.02	29	5.05	23
Texas	1,312,703,000	75.66	32	4.60	30
Utah	212,173,000	119.87	13	8.77	6
Vermont	22,971,000	40.51	45	2.32	45
Virginia	881,507,000	140.23	8	7.21	11
Washington	437,731,000	87.23	24	4.75	29
West Virginia	87,688,000	48.69	44	3.56	36
Wisconsin	364,506,000	73.56	34	4.23	33
Wyoming	35,625,000	77.45	31	4.83	27
United States	$24,465,507,000	$97.25	22	$5.26	23

Rank in order

By per capita

1. Connecticut
2. New York
3. Alabama
4. Louisiana
5. Iowa
6. Hawaii
7. Massachusetts
8. Virginia
9. South Carolina
10. New Mexico
11. Nebraska
12. Minnesota
13. Utah
14. Michigan
15. Kansas
16. Oregon
17. Rhode Island
18. New Jersey
19. North Dakota
20. Oklahoma
21. Ohio
22. North Carolina
23. Mississippi
24. Washington
25. Pennsylvania
26. Indiana
27. Georgia
28. Missouri
29. Tennessee
30. California
31. Wyoming
32. Texas
33. Kentucky
34. Wisconsin
35. Maryland
36. Arkansas
37. Delaware
38. Maine
39. Illinois
40. Alaska
41. Colorado
42. South Dakota
43. Montana
44. West Virginia
45. Vermont
46. New Hampshire
47. Nevada
48. Florida
49. Idaho
50. Arizona
— District of Columbia

— not applicable.

Source: U.S. Department of Commerce, Bureau of the Census, *State Government Finances: 1991* (Washington, D.C.: Government Printing Office, 1992).

ADEQUACY OF PRENATAL CARE, 1988			Rank in order
State	% of expectant mothers receiving adequate prenatal care	Rank by %	By %
Alabama	67.9	34	1. New Hampshire
Alaska	69.8	26	2. Iowa
Arizona	61.1	47	3. Massachusetts
Arkansas	61.7	45	4. Wisconsin
California	69.0	30	5. Kansas
Colorado	71.1	20	6. Rhode Island
Connecticut	76.3	9	7. Maryland
Delaware	71.1	20	8. Nebraska
District of Columbia	NA	NA	9. Connecticut
Florida	62.8	44	10. Michigan
Georgia	67.1	36	11. Ohio
Hawaii	65.2	38	12. Maine
Idaho	68.6	33	13. Virginia
Illinois	68.7	32	14. Missouri
Indiana	72.3	15	15. Indiana
Iowa	80.4	2	16. North Carolina
Kansas	77.4	5	17. Minnesota
Kentucky	70.8	23	Pennsylvania
Louisiana	66.9	37	19. Utah
Maine	74.2	12	20. Colorado
Maryland	76.9	7	Delaware
Massachusetts	79.4	3	22. Washington
Michigan	76.0	10	23. Kentucky
Minnesota	71.9	17	24. New Jersey
Mississippi	70.0	25	25. Mississippi
Missouri	73.2	14	26. Alaska
Montana	69.1	29	27. Wyoming
Nebraska	76.6	8	28. Oregon
Nevada	64.8	41	29. Montana
New Hampshire	82.1	1	30. California
New Jersey	70.7	24	31. Tennessee
New Mexico	47.3	50	32. Illinois
New York	64.2	42	33. Idaho
North Carolina	72.1	16	34. Alabama
North Dakota	64.9	40	35. South Dakota
Ohio	75.8	11	36. Georgia
Oklahoma	65.2	38	37. Louisiana
Oregon	69.2	28	38. Hawaii
Pennsylvania	71.9	17	Oklahoma
Rhode Island	77.0	6	40. North Dakota
South Carolina	56.4	49	41. Nevada
South Dakota	67.8	35	42. New York
Tennessee	68.9	31	43. West Virginia
Texas	58.5	48	44. Florida
Utah	71.5	19	45. Arkansas
Vermont	61.7	45	Vermont
Virginia	73.4	13	47. Arizona
Washington	71.0	22	48. Texas
West Virginia	63.2	43	49. South Carolina
Wisconsin	78.2	4	50. New Mexico
Wyoming	69.6	27	NA District of Columbia
United States	NA	NA	

NA not available.

Source: Northwestern National Life, *The NWNL State Health Rankings* (Minneapolis, Minn.: Northwestern National Life, 1992).

| | | **Rank in order**

State	% of infants receiving late or no prenatal care	Rank by %	By %
Alabama	6.2	16	1. District of Columbia
Alaska	3.6	41	New Mexico
Arizona	12.0	3	3. Arizona
Arkansas	7.3	10	4. Texas
California	7.2	11	5. Nevada
Colorado	5.7	19	6. South Carolina
Connecticut	3.5	42	7. Florida
Delaware	5.2	24	New York
District of Columbia	13.8	1	9. New Jersey
Florida	8.1	7	10. Arkansas
Georgia	6.8	12	11. California
Hawaii	6.0	17	12. Georgia
Idaho	6.3	14	13. Oklahoma
Illinois	5.2	24	14. Idaho
Indiana	5.0	26	Louisiana
Iowa	2.7	49	16. Alabama
Kansas	4.5	34	17. Hawaii
Kentucky	4.8	30	18. Pennsylvania
Louisiana	6.3	14	19. Colorado
Maine	2.7	49	North Carolina
Maryland	4.2	35	21. Oregon
Massachusetts	3.3	45	Washington
Michigan	4.2	35	23. West Virginia
Minnesota	3.7	39	24. Delaware
Mississippi	4.6	33	Illinois
Missouri	4.8	30	26. Indiana
Montana	4.9	28	South Dakota
Nebraska	3.2	47	28. Montana
Nevada	9.2	5	Tennessee
New Hampshire	3.3	45	30. Kentucky
New Jersey	7.6	9	Missouri
New Mexico	13.8	1	32. Virginia
New York	8.1	7	33. Mississippi
North Carolina	5.7	19	34. Kansas
North Dakota	3.4	44	35. Maryland
Ohio	4.1	37	Michigan
Oklahoma	6.4	13	37. Ohio
Oregon	5.5	21	38. Wyoming
Pennsylvania	5.8	18	39. Minnesota
Rhode Island	3.0	48	Wisconsin
South Carolina	8.9	6	41. Alaska
South Dakota	5.0	26	42. Connecticut
Tennessee	4.9	28	Vermont
Texas	11.3	4	44. North Dakota
Utah	2.7	49	45. Massachusetts
Vermont	3.5	42	New Hampshire
Virginia	4.7	32	47. Nebraska
Washington	5.5	21	48. Rhode Island
West Virginia	5.3	23	49. Iowa
Wisconsin	3.7	39	Maine
Wyoming	3.9	38	Utah
United States	6.4	13	

Source: Joseph Tiang-Yau Liu, Carol Regan, Tracey M. Orloff, and Lourdes A. Rivera, *The Health of America's Children 1992: Maternal and Child Health Data Book,* (Washington, D.C.: Children's Defense Fund, 1992).

INFANTS BORN WITH LOW BIRTH WEIGHT, 1990

State	Infants of low birth weight	% of all births	Rank by %
Alabama	5,334	8.4	6
Alaska	575	4.8	51
Arizona	4,375	6.4	32
Arkansas	2,986	8.2	7
California	35,558	5.8	38
Colorado	4,283	8.0	9
Connecticut	3,309	6.6	29
Delaware	849	7.6	12
District of Columbia	1,785	15.1	1
Florida	14,813	7.4	16
Georgia	9,747	8.7	4
Hawaii	1,445	7.1	21
Idaho	928	5.7	39
Illinois	14,785	7.6	12
Indiana	5,648	6.6	29
Iowa	2,124	5.4	42
Kansas	2,435	6.2	33
Kentucky	3,838	7.1	21
Louisiana	6,650	9.2	3
Maine	892	5.1	46
Maryland	6,229	7.8	11
Massachusetts	5,417	5.9	36
Michigan	11,586	7.6	12
Minnesota	3,437	5.1	46
Mississippi	4,159	9.6	2
Missouri	5,637	7.1	21
Montana	715	6.2	33
Nebraska	1,287	5.3	43
Nevada	1,563	7.2	19
New Hampshire	863	4.9	50
New Jersey	8,489	7.0	27
New Mexico	2,016	7.4	16
New York	22,568	7.6	12
North Carolina	8,344	8.0	9
North Dakota	506	5.5	41
Ohio	11,812	7.1	21
Oklahoma	3,106	6.6	29
Oregon	2,144	5.0	49
Pennsylvania	12,270	7.1	21
Rhode Island	927	6.2	33
South Carolina	5,107	8.7	4
South Dakota	557	5.1	46
Tennessee	6,152	8.2	7
Texas	21,936	6.9	28
Utah	2,074	5.7	39
Vermont	436	5.3	43
Virginia	7,158	7.2	19
Washington	4,177	5.3	43
West Virginia	1,599	7.1	21
Wisconsin	4,273	5.9	36
Wyoming	515	7.4	16
United States	**289,418**	**7.0**	**27**

Rank in order

By %

1. District of Columbia
2. Mississippi
3. Louisiana
4. Georgia
   South Carolina
6. Alabama
7. Arkansas
   Tennessee
9. Colorado
   North Carolina
11. Maryland
12. Delaware
    Illinois
    Michigan
    New York
16. Florida
    New Mexico
    Wyoming
19. Nevada
    Virginia
21. Hawaii
    Kentucky
    Missouri
    Ohio
    Pennsylvania
    West Virginia
27. New Jersey
28. Texas
29. Connecticut
    Indiana
    Oklahoma
32. Arizona
33. Kansas
    Montana
    Rhode Island
36. Massachusetts
    Wisconsin
38. California
39. Idaho
    Utah
41. North Dakota
42. Iowa
43. Nebraska
    Vermont
    Washington
46. Maine
    Minnesota
    South Dakota
49. Oregon
50. New Hampshire
51. Alaska

Source: National Center for Health Statistics, *Monthly Vital Statistics Report* 41, no. 9, supplement (February 25, 1993).
Note: Low birth rate is defined as less than five pounds and eight ounces.

State	Abortions	Per 1,000 women	
		Rate	Rank
Alabama	18,000	18.7	29
Alaska	2,000	18.2	30
Arizona	23,000	28.8	12
Arkansas	6,000	11.6	46
California	312,000	45.9	2
Colorado	19,000	22.4	23
Connecticut	24,000	31.2	9
Delaware	6,000	35.7	6
District of Columbia	26,000	163.3	1
Florida	83,000	31.5	8
Georgia	37,000	23.5	22
Hawaii	11,000	43.0	4
Idaho	2,000	8.2	48
Illinois	73,000	26.4	16
Indiana	16,000	11.9	45
Iowa	9,000	14.6	42
Kansas	11,000	20.1	25
Kentucky	12,000	13.0	43
Louisiana	17,000	16.3	37
Maine	5,000	16.2	38
Maryland	33,000	28.6	13
Massachusetts	44,000	30.2	11
Michigan	63,000	28.5	14
Minnesota	19,000	18.2	30
Mississippi	5,000	8.4	47
Missouri	19,000	16.4	36
Montana	3,000	16.5	35
Nebraska	6,000	17.7	32
Nevada	10,000	40.3	5
New Hampshire	5,000	17.5	33
New Jersey	64,000	35.1	7
New Mexico	7,000	19.1	26
New York	184,000	43.3	3
North Carolina	40,000	25.4	18
North Dakota	2,000	14.9	41
Ohio	53,000	21.0	24
Oklahoma	12,000	16.2	38
Oregon	16,000	23.9	20
Pennsylvania	52,000	18.9	27
Rhode Island	7,000	30.6	10
South Carolina	14,000	16.7	34
South Dakota	1,000	5.7	50
Tennessee	22,000	18.9	27
Texas	101,000	24.8	19
Utah	5,000	12.8	44
Vermont	4,000	25.8	17
Virginia	35,000	23.7	21
Washington	31,000	27.6	15
West Virginia	3,000	7.5	49
Wisconsin	18,000	16.0	40
Wyoming	1,000	5.1	51
United States	**1,591,000**	**27.3**	**16**

ABORTIONS, 1988

Rank in order

By rate per 1,000 women

1. District of Columbia
2. California
3. New York
4. Hawaii
5. Nevada
6. Delaware
7. New Jersey
8. Florida
9. Connecticut
10. Rhode Island
11. Massachusetts
12. Arizona
13. Maryland
14. Michigan
15. Washington
16. Illinois
17. Vermont
18. North Carolina
19. Texas
20. Oregon
21. Virginia
22. Georgia
23. Colorado
24. Ohio
25. Kansas
26. New Mexico
27. Pennsylvania
    Tennessee
29. Alabama
30. Alaska
    Minnesota
32. Nebraska
33. New Hampshire
34. South Carolina
35. Montana
36. Missouri
37. Louisiana
38. Maine
    Oklahoma
40. Wisconsin
41. North Dakota
42. Iowa
43. Kentucky
44. Utah
45. Indiana
46. Arkansas
47. Mississippi
48. Idaho
49. West Virginia
50. South Dakota
51. Wyoming

Source: Reproduced with the permission of The Alan Guttmacher Institute from Stanley K. Henshaw and Jennifer Van Vort, *Abortion Factbook 1992 Edition: Readings, Trends, and State and Local Data to 1988* (New York: The Alan Guttmacher Institute, 1992).

Note: Data for women are based on ages fifteen to forty-four.

IMMUNIZATIONS OF TWO-YEAR OLDS, 1992

State	% of two-year-olds appropriately immunized
Alabama	57
Alaska	58
Arizona	48
Arkansas	57
California	48
Colorado	61
Connecticut	63
Delaware	50
District of Columbia	43
Florida	49
Georgia	51
Hawaii	61
Idaho	48
Illinois	56
Indiana	56
Iowa	54
Kansas	51
Kentucky	60
Louisiana	58
Maine	65
Maryland	57
Massachusetts	65
Michigan	60
Minnesota	61
Mississippi	74
Missouri	43
Montana	53
Nebraska	56
Nevada	42
New Hampshire	66
New Jersey	50
New Mexico	55
New York	59
North Carolina	59
North Dakota	NA
Ohio	38
Oklahoma	44
Oregon	NA
Pennsylvania	56
Rhode Island	69
South Carolina	68
South Dakota	56
Tennessee	71
Texas	30
Utah	41
Vermont	84
Virginia	56
Washington	51
West Virginia	48
Wisconsin	61
Wyoming	54
United States	**NA**

NA not available.

Source: Joseph Tiang-Yau Liu, Carol Regan, Tracey M. Orloff, and Lourdes A. Rivera, *The Health of America's Children: Maternal and Child Health Data Book* (Washington, D.C.: Children's Defense Fund, 1992).

Note: This table is not ranked because state data reflect varying survey methodologies and cannot be compared with each other.

OVERALL RISK FOR HEART DISEASE, 1992

State	Score	Overall ranking on risk factors
Alabama	−2	36
Alaska	0	40
Arizona	−18	6
Arkansas	0	40
California	−15	12
Colorado	−32	1
Connecticut	−8	24
Delaware	−5	30
District of Columbia	—	—
Florida	−3	33
Georgia	−10	19
Hawaii	−15	12
Idaho	−12	17
Illinois	−16	11
Indiana	4	48
Iowa	−3	33
Kansas	0	40
Kentucky	1	45
Louisiana	−11	18
Maine	−3	33
Maryland	−6	28
Massachusetts	−21	2
Michigan	2	46
Minnesota	−13	15
Mississippi	12	50
Missouri	−6	28
Montana	−17	7
Nebraska	−9	22
Nevada	0	39
New Hampshire	−19	4
New Jersey	0	40
New Mexico	−19	4
New York	−7	25
North Carolina	−2	36
North Dakota	−10	19
Ohio	−5	30
Oklahoma	−4	32
Oregon	−15	12
Pennsylvania	−3	22
Rhode Island	−7	25
South Carolina	3	47
South Dakota	−10	19
Tennessee	−1	38
Texas	−13	15
Utah	−20	3
Vermont	−17	7
Virginia	−17	7
Washington	−17	7
West Virginia	7	49
Wisconsin	−7	25
Wyoming	0	40
United States	—	—

Rank in order

By overall ranking on risk factors

1. Colorado
2. Massachusetts
3. Utah
4. New Hampshire
   New Mexico
6. Arizona
7. Montana
   Vermont
   Virginia
   Washington
11. Illinois
12. California
    Hawaii
    Oregon
15. Minnesota
    Texas
17. Idaho
18. Louisiana
19. Georgia
    North Dakota
    South Dakota
22. Nebraska
    Pennsylvania
24. Connecticut
25. New York
    Rhode Island
    Wisconsin
28. Maryland
    Missouri
30. Delaware
    Ohio
32. Oklahoma
33. Florida
    Iowa
    Maine
36. Alabama
    North Carolina
38. Tennessee
39. Nevada
40. Alaska
    Arkansas
    Kansas
    New Jersey
    Wyoming
45. Kentucky
46. Michigan
47. South Carolina
48. Indiana
49. West Virginia
50. Mississippi
— District of Columbia

— not applicable.

Source: Northwestern National Life, *The NWNL State Health Rankings* (Minneapolis, Minn.: Northwestern National Life, 1992).

Note: Northwestern National Life bases its ranking on measurements of hypertension, sedentary lifestyle, and obesity. The score column indicates the percentage a state is above or below the national average.

State	Hypertension %	Hypertension Rank	Sedentary lifestyle %	Sedentary lifestyle Rank	Obesity %	Obesity Rank	By % of population with hypertension
Alabama	18.9	8	60.3	16	23.9	12	1. Mississippi
Alaska	NA	NA	NA	NA	NA	NA	2. West Virginia
Arizona	14.6	38	51.4	36	20.7	34	3. Florida
Arkansas	NA	NA	NA	NA	NA	NA	4. Indiana
California	15.7	30	53.7	30	20.9	32	5. Tennessee
Colorado	12.6	44	44.5	44	16.3	44	6. Pennsylvania
Connecticut	18.9	8	52.0	33	22.6	22	7. Michigan
Delaware	18.7	11	51.4	36	25.5	4	8. Alabama
District of Columbia	—	—	—	—	—	—	Connecticut
Florida	20.1	3	54.8	28	24.1	11	10. Rhode Island
Georgia	16.2	24	62.3	9	20.2	35	11. Delaware
Hawaii	15.6	34	62.4	8	17.6	43	12. Wisconsin
Idaho	14.7	37	58.7	21	21.6	27	13. Maine
Illinois	12.7	43	60.3	16	20.8	33	14. Kentucky
Indiana	20.0	4	61.3	11	25.9	3	15. North Carolina
Iowa	17.3	18	60.6	15	24.6	7	16. New York
Kansas	NA	NA	NA	NA	NA	NA	17. South Carolina
Kentucky	18.1	14	69.1	3	23.4	16	18. Iowa
Louisiana	13.0	42	58.5	22	24.2	9	19. Missouri
Maine	18.2	13	59.8	18	23.7	13	20. Oregon
Maryland	16.3	23	61.6	10	22.8	20	Washington
Massachusetts	15.1	36	49.8	40	18.9	41	22. Nebraska
Michigan	19.2	7	59.3	19	26.4	1	23. Maryland
Minnesota	16.0	27	55.3	26	21.1	31	24. Georgia
Mississippi	23.5	1	66.4	5	26.2	2	Texas
Missouri	16.8	19	61.2	12	22.9	18	Vermont
Montana	15.7	30	52.0	33	20.2	35	27. Minnesota
Nebraska	16.6	22	55.4	25	23.5	14	Oklahoma
Nevada	NA	NA	NA	NA	NA	NA	29. North Dakota
New Hampshire	15.2	35	46.9	43	21.4	30	30. California
New Jersey	NA	NA	NA	NA	NA	NA	Montana
New Mexico	13.1	41	51.0	38	21.6	27	South Dakota
New York	17.8	16	63.2	7	20.0	37	Utah
North Carolina	18.0	15	60.7	14	24.2	9	34. Hawaii
North Dakota	15.9	29	56.4	24	22.7	21	35. New Hampshire
Ohio	14.6	38	69.3	2	22.6	22	36. Massachusetts
Oklahoma	16.0	27	66.3	6	22.9	18	37. Idaho
Oregon	16.7	20	48.9	41	21.5	29	38. Arizona
Pennsylvania	19.3	6	54.9	27	24.5	8	Ohio
Rhode Island	18.8	10	54.7	29	22.3	25	40. Virginia
South Carolina	17.6	17	69.7	1	25.0	5	41. New Mexico
South Dakota	15.7	30	56.9	23	22.6	22	42. Louisiana
Tennessee	19.4	5	61.0	13	23.5	14	43. Illinois
Texas	16.2	24	53.5	32	22.0	26	44. Colorado
Utah	15.7	30	48.8	42	19.5	39	— District of Columbia
Vermont	16.2	24	51.0	38	19.9	38	NA Alaska
Virginia	13.3	40	59.1	20	19.5	39	NA Arkansas
Washington	16.7	20	51.9	35	18.8	42	NA Kansas
West Virginia	21.2	2	67.8	4	24.8	6	NA Nevada
Wisconsin	18.3	12	53.6	31	23.3	17	NA New Jersey
Wyoming	NA	NA	NA	NA	NA	NA	NA Wyoming
United States	—	—	—	—	—	—	

— not applicable.   NA not available.

Source: Northwestern National Life, *The NWNL State Health Rankings* (Minneapolis, Minn.: Northwestern National Life, 1992).
Note: The % columns reflect the percentage of population suffering from condition.

DEATHS DUE TO HEART DISEASE, 1990				Rank in order
		Per 100,000 population		**By rate per 100,000 population**
State	**Deaths**	**Rate**	**Rank**	
Alabama	12,894	319.08	15	1. West Virginia
Alaska	444	80.73	51	2. Pennsylvania
Arizona	8,807	240.30	40	3. Mississippi
Arkansas	7,991	339.90	10	4. Florida
California	67,560	227.02	44	5. New York
Colorado	6,144	186.52	49	6. Missouri
Connecticut	9,596	291.94	28	7. Oklahoma
Delaware	1,894	284.38	29	8. Iowa
District of Columbia	1,887	310.87	17	9. Rhode Island
Florida	45,842	354.32	4	10. Arkansas
Georgia	16,339	252.22	34	11. South Dakota
Hawaii	2,068	186.64	48	12. Kentucky
Idaho	2,212	219.66	45	13. Ohio
Illinois	35,300	308.81	19	14. Nebraska
Indiana	16,968	306.06	21	15. Alabama
Iowa	9,585	345.16	8	16. Tennessee
Kansas	7,667	309.40	18	17. District of Columbia
Kentucky	11,882	322.44	12	18. Kansas
Louisiana	12,422	294.36	27	19. Illinois
Maine	3,697	301.06	23	20. New Jersey
Maryland	11,902	248.94	36	21. Indiana
Massachusetts	17,754	295.11	26	22. North Dakota
Michigan	27,626	297.21	25	23. Maine
Minnesota	10,777	246.33	39	24. Wisconsin
Mississippi	9,220	358.34	3	25. Michigan
Missouri	17,824	348.33	6	26. Massachusetts
Montana	1,979	247.69	38	27. Louisiana
Nebraska	5,039	319.33	14	28. Connecticut
Nevada	2,864	238.27	41	29. Delaware
New Hampshire	2,792	251.76	35	30. North Carolina
New Jersey	23,659	306.07	20	31. South Carolina
New Mexico	3,003	198.22	47	32. Oregon
New York	63,629	353.69	5	33. Vermont
North Carolina	18,564	280.04	30	34. Georgia
North Dakota	1,949	305.01	22	35. New Hampshire
Ohio	34,665	319.58	13	36. Maryland
Oklahoma	10,882	345.90	7	37. Virginia
Oregon	7,599	267.38	32	38. Montana
Pennsylvania	43,494	366.05	2	39. Minnesota
Rhode Island	3,437	342.67	9	40. Arizona
South Carolina	9,333	267.65	31	41. Nevada
South Dakota	2,330	334.77	11	42. Texas
Tennessee	15,498	317.78	16	43. Washington
Texas	39,555	232.86	42	44. California
Utah	2,739	158.97	50	45. Idaho
Vermont	1,426	253.29	33	46. Wyoming
Virginia	15,399	248.89	37	47. New Mexico
Washington	11,238	230.90	43	48. Hawaii
West Virginia	7,099	395.93	1	49. Colorado
Wisconsin	14,612	298.69	24	50. Utah
Wyoming	972	214.10	46	51. Alaska
United States	**720,058**	**289.52**	**29**	

Source: National Center for Health Statistics, *Monthly Vital Statistics Report* 41, no. 7, supplement (January 7, 1993).

| NEW CANCER CASES, 1993 | | | | Rank in order |
| State | Estimated cases | Per 100,000 population | | By rate per 100,000 population |
		Rate	Rank	
Alabama	20,800	508.68	12	1. District of Columbia
Alaska	1,200	210.53	51	2. Florida
Arizona	16,500	440.00	35	3. West Virginia
Arkansas	13,200	556.49	5	4. Pennsylvania
California	120,000	395.00	44	5. Arkansas
Colorado	11,300	334.62	49	6. Rhode Island
Connecticut	16,200	492.25	17	7. Maine
Delaware	3,500	514.71	10	8. New Jersey
District of Columbia	4,000	668.90	1	9. Kentucky
Florida	78,000	587.48	2	10. Delaware
Georgia	27,500	415.22	42	11. Missouri
Hawaii	3,900	343.61	48	12. Alabama
Idaho	4,000	384.99	45	13. Massachusetts
Illinois	55,000	476.48	24	14. Mississippi
Indiana	26,800	477.72	23	15. Iowa
Iowa	13,900	497.32	15	16. Tennessee
Kansas	11,600	464.93	31	17. Connecticut
Kentucky	19,300	519.80	9	18. North Dakota
Louisiana	19,900	468.02	30	19. New York
Maine	6,700	542.51	7	20. Ohio
Maryland	22,500	462.96	33	21. Oregon
Massachusetts	30,500	508.67	13	22. Oklahoma
Michigan	42,000	448.34	34	23. Indiana
Minnesota	19,000	428.70	39	24. Illinois
Mississippi	12,900	497.69	14	25. North Carolina
Missouri	26,500	513.77	11	26. Nebraska
Montana	3,800	470.30	28	27. New Hampshire
Nebraska	7,500	470.81	26	28. Montana
Nevada	5,600	436.14	36	29. South Dakota
New Hampshire	5,200	470.59	27	30. Louisiana
New Jersey	41,000	528.35	8	31. Kansas
New Mexico	5,600	361.76	47	32. Wisconsin
New York	88,000	487.32	19	33. Maryland
North Carolina	32,000	474.99	25	34. Michigan
North Dakota	3,100	488.19	18	35. Arizona
Ohio	53,000	484.51	20	36. Nevada
Oklahoma	15,300	481.89	22	37. South Carolina
Oregon	14,100	482.55	21	38. Virginia
Pennsylvania	67,000	560.15	4	39. Minnesota
Rhode Island	5,500	547.81	6	40. Vermont
South Carolina	15,500	435.39	37	41. Washington
South Dakota	3,300	469.42	29	42. Georgia
Tennessee	24,600	496.67	16	43. Wyoming
Texas	63,000	363.13	46	44. California
Utah	4,500	254.24	50	45. Idaho
Vermont	2,400	423.28	40	46. Texas
Virginia	27,000	429.53	38	47. New Mexico
Washington	21,000	418.49	41	48. Hawaii
West Virginia	10,400	577.46	3	49. Colorado
Wisconsin	23,000	464.18	32	50. Utah
Wyoming	1,900	413.04	43	51. Alaska
United States	1,170,000	463.96	33	

Source: American Cancer Society, *Cancer Facts & Figures—1993* (Atlanta, Ga.: American Cancer Society, Inc., 1993).

Note: Cancer incidence is estimated based on best available data by the American Cancer Society.

DEATHS DUE TO CANCER, 1990				Rank in order
		Per 100,000 population		
State	Deaths	Rate	Rank	By rate per 100,000 population
Alabama	8,657	211.71	18	1. District of Columbia
Alaska	470	82.46	52	2. Florida
Arizona	6,837	182.32	40	3. Pennsylvania
Arkansas	5,702	240.39	6	4. West Virginia
California	48,986	161.24	46	5. Rhode Island
Colorado	4,935	146.14	49	6. Arkansas
Connecticut	6,819	207.20	23	7. New Jersey
Delaware	1,501	220.74	12	8. Kentucky
District of Columbia	1,547	258.70	1	9. Maine
Florida	33,864	255.06	2	10. Missouri
Georgia	11,035	166.62	44	11. Massachusetts
Hawaii	1,655	145.82	50	12. Delaware
Idaho	1,738	167.28	43	13. Ohio
Illinois	24,439	211.72	17	14. Iowa
Indiana	11,662	207.88	21	15. New York
Iowa	6,076	217.39	14	16. Tennessee
Kansas	5,036	201.84	29	17. Illinois
Kentucky	8,426	226.93	8	18. Alabama
Louisiana	8,695	204.49	27	19. North Dakota
Maine	2,792	226.07	9	20. Oklahoma
Maryland	9,832	202.31	28	21. Indiana
Massachusetts	13,444	224.22	11	22. Wisconsin
Michigan	18,449	196.94	33	23. Connecticut
Minnesota	8,122	183.26	39	24. Nebraska
Mississippi	5,325	205.44	26	25. Oregon
Missouri	11,608	225.05	10	26. Mississippi
Montana	1,621	200.62	30	27. Louisiana
Nebraska	3,299	207.09	24	28. Maryland
Nevada	2,248	175.08	42	29. Kansas
New Hampshire	2,122	192.04	36	30. Montana
New Jersey	17,931	231.07	7	31. Vermont
New Mexico	2,265	146.32	48	32. Michigan
New York	38,415	212.73	15	33. North Carolina
North Carolina	13,229	196.36	34	34. South Dakota
North Dakota	1,339	210.87	19	35. New Hampshire
Ohio	23,973	219.15	13	36. South Carolina
Oklahoma	6,656	209.64	20	37. Virginia
Oregon	6,050	207.05	25	38. Minnesota
Pennsylvania	29,850	249.56	3	39. Arizona
Rhode Island	2,427	241.73	5	40. Washington
South Carolina	6,791	190.76	37	41. Nevada
South Dakota	1,365	194.17	35	42. Idaho
Tennessee	10,493	211.85	16	43. Georgia
Texas	28,633	165.04	45	44. Texas
Utah	1,765	99.72	51	45. California
Vermont	1,136	200.35	32	46. Wyoming
Virginia	11,624	184.92	38	47. New Mexico
Washington	9,004	179.43	41	48. Colorado
West Virginia	4,408	244.75	4	49. Hawaii
Wisconsin	10,295	207.77	22	50. Utah
Wyoming	731	158.91	47	51. Alaska
United States	505,322	200.38	31	

Source: National Center for Health Statistics, Advance Report of Final Mortality Statistics, 1990, *Monthly Vital Statistics Report* 41 no. 7, supplement (Hyattsville, Md.: Public Health Service, 1993).

Note: Caution should be used in comparing death rates by state. Death rates are affected by the population composition of the state.

| PREVALENCE OF SMOKING, 1989 | | | | Rank in order |
State	% of popuulation that smoke	Score	Rank by %	By %
Alabama	29.2	16	7	1. West Virginia
Alaska	28.3	12	11	2. Nevada
Arizona	28.4	13	10	3. Kentucky
Arkansas	25.0	−1	28	4. Tennessee
California	19.8	−21	49	5. Delaware
Colorado	25.9	3	23	Missouri
Connecticut	28.0	11	12	7. Alabama
Delaware	29.9	19	5	Michigan
District of Columbia	—	—	—	9. Oklahoma
Florida	24.9	−1	30	10. Arizona
Georgia	26.7	6	20	11. Alaska
Hawaii	22.3	−11	45	12. Connecticut
Idaho	22.6	−10	44	13. North Carolina
Illinois	26.0	3	22	South Carolina
Indiana	25.0	−1	28	15. Louisiana
Iowa	24.9	−1	30	16. New Hampshire
Kansas	22.8	−9	43	Ohio
Kentucky	31.0	23	3	18. Maine
Louisiana	27.2	8	15	Wyoming
Maine	27.0	7	18	20. Georgia
Maryland	26.7	6	20	Maryland
Massachusetts	24.4	−3	33	22. Illinois
Michigan	29.2	16	7	23. Colorado
Minnesota	22.9	−9	42	24. Pennsylvania
Mississippi	24.4	−3	33	Vermont
Missouri	29.9	19	5	26. New Mexico
Montana	24.1	−4	36	27. Texas
Nebraska	23.3	−7	39	28. Arkansas
Nevada	31.2	24	2	Indiana
New Hampshire	27.1	8	16	30. Florida
New Jersey	24.3	−4	35	Iowa
New Mexico	25.2	0	26	Virginia
New York	23.1	−8	40	33. Massachusetts
North Carolina	27.8	10	13	Mississippi
North Dakota	21.1	−16	48	35. New Jersey
Ohio	27.1	8	16	36. Montana
Oklahoma	28.7	14	9	Rhode Island
Oregon	22.3	−12	45	38. Wisconsin
Pennsylvania	25.7	2	24	39. Nebraska
Rhode Island	24.1	−4	36	40. New York
South Carolina	27.8	10	13	41. Washington
South Dakota	21.7	−14	47	42. Minnesota
Tennessee	30.6	22	4	43. Kansas
Texas	25.1	0	27	44. Idaho
Utah	15.3	−25	50	45. Hawaii
Vermont	25.7	2	24	Oregon
Virginia	24.9	−1	30	47. South Dakota
Washington	23.0	−9	41	48. North Dakota
West Virginia	31.8	25	1	49. California
Wisconsin	23.8	−5	38	50. Utah
Wyoming	27.0	7	18	— District of Columbia
United States	NA	—	—	

— not applicable.   NA not available.

Source: Northwestern National Life, *The NWNL State Health Rankings* (Minneapolis, Minn.: Northwestern National Life, 1992).

Note: The score column indicates the percentage a state is above or below the national average on the prevalence of smoking.

State	Persons with diagnosed diabetes	Per 10,000 population		Rank in order — By rate per 10,000 population
		Rate	Rank	
Alabama	117,271	290.28	5	1. District of Columbia
Alaska	10,191	185.29	51	2. Hawaii
Arizona	92,459	251.93	35	3. Florida
Arkansas	68,041	289.54	6	4. Mississippi
California	728,711	244.86	40	5. Alabama
Colorado	74,408	226.16	48	6. Arkansas
Connecticut	87,499	265.95	20	7. Pennsylvania
Delaware	17,799	265.66	21	8. New York
District of Columbia	23,259	381.30	1	9. New Jersey
Florida	401,011	309.90	3	10. North Carolina
Georgia	167,612	258.66	26	11. South Carolina
Hawaii	39,905	359.51	2	12. West Virginia
Idaho	23,608	233.74	46	13. Louisiana
Illinois	305,283	267.09	18	14. Oklahoma
Indiana	141,522	255.46	31	15. Missouri
Iowa	73,627	264.85	23	16. Tennessee
Kansas	63,617	256.52	30	17. Maryland
Kentucky	94,230	255.37	32	18. Illinois
Louisiana	115,508	273.72	13	19. Rhode Island
Maine	30,507	248.02	39	20. Connecticut
Maryland	129,382	270.67	17	21. Delaware
Massachusetts	154,729	257.03	28	22. Ohio
Michigan	241,614	259.80	25	23. Iowa
Minnesota	104,926	239.56	42	24. Virginia
Mississippi	75,551	293.97	4	25. Michigan
Missouri	139,229	271.93	15	26. Georgia
Montana	20,309	253.86	34	27. South Dakota
Nebraska	40,278	254.92	33	28. Massachusetts
Nevada	29,772	248.10	38	29. Oregon
New Hampshire	25,445	229.23	47	30. Kansas
New Jersey	215,481	278.76	9	31. Indiana
New Mexico	35,884	236.08	43	32. Kentucky
New York	505,780	281.15	8	33. Nebraska
North Carolina	184,581	278.40	10	34. Montana
North Dakota	16,039	250.61	37	35. Arizona
Ohio	288,093	265.52	22	36. Wisconsin
Oklahoma	85,969	272.92	14	37. North Dakota
Oregon	72,858	256.54	29	38. Nevada
Pennsylvania	339,436	285.72	7	39. Maine
Rhode Island	26,642	266.42	19	40. California
South Carolina	97,084	278.18	11	41. Washington
South Dakota	18,076	258.23	27	42. Minnesota
Tennessee	132,644	271.81	16	43. New Mexico
Texas	399,166	234.94	44	44. Texas
Utah	33,806	196.55	50	45. Vermont
Vermont	13,112	234.14	45	46. Idaho
Virginia	161,624	261.11	24	47. New Hampshire
Washington	118,617	243.57	41	48. Colorado
West Virginia	49,180	274.75	12	49. Wyoming
Wisconsin	122,916	251.36	36	50. Utah
Wyoming	10,171	226.02	49	51. Alaska
United States	**6,564,462**	**263.94**	**24**	

Source: Centers for Disease Control, *Diabetes in the United States: A Strategy for Prevention* (Atlanta, Ga.: Department of Health and Human Services, 1993).

DEATHS DUE TO DIABETES, 1989

State	Deaths	Per 10,000 population Rate	Per 10,000 population Rank
Alabama	2,111	5.12	40
Alaska	93	1.76	51
Arizona	1,548	4.35	46
Arkansas	1,448	6.01	33
California	16,587	5.71	37
Colorado	1,389	4.18	48
Connecticut	2,407	7.43	10
Delaware	627	9.36	3
District of Columbia	490	8.17	7
Florida	8,061	6.36	27
Georgia	3,295	5.12	41
Hawaii	634	5.71	36
Idaho	470	4.65	43
Illinois	8,003	6.86	14
Indiana	3,920	7.01	13
Iowa	1,921	6.76	20
Kansas	1,512	6.02	32
Kentucky	2,350	6.30	29
Louisiana	2,947	6.73	21
Maine	903	7.40	11
Maryland	3,188	6.80	17
Massachusetts	4,413	7.47	9
Michigan	6,797	7.33	12
Minnesota	2,561	5.89	35
Mississippi	1,784	6.81	16
Missouri	3,521	6.82	15
Montana	439	5.42	38
Nebraska	1,035	6.43	25
Nevada	481	4.33	47
New Hampshire	718	6.47	23
New Jersey	6,519	8.42	5
New Mexico	682	4.46	45
New York	11,677	6.51	22
North Carolina	4,995	7.60	8
North Dakota	422	6.39	26
Ohio	9,376	8.59	4
Oklahoma	1,926	5.98	34
Oregon	1,744	6.18	30
Pennsylvania	11,540	9.59	2
Rhode Island	839	8.39	6
South Carolina	2,231	6.36	28
South Dakota	463	6.43	24
Tennessee	3,025	6.12	31
Texas	7,786	4.58	44
Utah	687	4.02	49
Vermont	386	6.77	19
Virginia	3,247	5.32	39
Washington	2,359	4.96	42
West Virginia	1,812	9.74	1
Wisconsin	3,309	6.80	18
Wyoming	170	3.54	50
United States	**160,848**	**6.48**	**24**

Rank in order

By rate per 10,000 population

1. West Virginia
2. Pennsylvania
3. Delaware
4. Ohio
5. New Jersey
6. Rhode Island
7. District of Columbia
8. North Carolina
9. Massachusetts
10. Connecticut
11. Maine
12. Michigan
13. Indiana
14. Illinois
15. Missouri
16. Mississippi
17. Maryland
18. Wisconsin
19. Vermont
20. Iowa
21. Louisiana
22. New York
23. New Hampshire
24. South Dakota
25. Nebraska
26. North Dakota
27. Florida
28. South Carolina
29. Kentucky
30. Oregon
31. Tennessee
32. Kansas
33. Arkansas
34. Oklahoma
35. Minnesota
36. Hawaii
37. California
38. Montana
39. Virginia
40. Alabama
41. Georgia
42. Washington
43. Idaho
44. Texas
45. New Mexico
46. Arizona
47. Nevada
48. Colorado
49. Utah
50. Wyoming
51. Alaska

Source: Centers for Disease Control, *Diabetes in the United States: A Strategy for Prevention* (Atlanta, Ga.: Department of Health and Human Services, 1993).

Note: Deaths have diabetes as either an underlying or contributory cause.

COST OF DIABETES, 1990				Rank in order

State	Cost of diabetes	Per capita	Rank by per capita	By per capita
Alabama	$458,000,000	$113.34	5	1. District of Columbia
Alaska	40,000,000	72.73	51	2. Hawaii
Arizona	361,000,000	98.50	36	3. Florida
Arkansas	266,000,000	113.14	6	4. Mississippi
California	2,849,000,000	95.73	40	5. Alabama
Colorado	291,000,00C	88.34	48	6. Arkansas
Connecticut	342,000,000	104.05	20	7. Pennsylvania
Delaware	70,000,000	105.11	18	8. New York
District of Columbia	91,000,000	149.92	1	9. South Carolina
Florida	1,568,000,000	121.19	3	10. New Jersey
Georgia	655,000,000	101.11	27	11. North Carolina
Hawaii	156,000,000	140.79	2	12. Louisiana
Idaho	92,000,000	91.36	45	13. West Virginia
Illinois	1,193,000,000	104.37	19	14. Oklahoma
Indiana	553,000,000	99.75	32	15. Tennessee
Iowa	288,000,000	103.71	22	16. Missouri
Kansas	249,000,000	100.48	29	17. Maryland
Kentucky	368,000,000	99.86	31	18. Delaware
Louisiana	452,000,000	107.11	12	19. Illinois
Maine	119,000,000	96.91	38	20. Connecticut
Maryland	506,000,000	105.84	17	21. Ohio
Massachusetts	605,000,000	100.57	28	22. Iowa
Michigan	945,000,000	101.67	26	23. Rhode Island
Minnesota	410,000,000	93.71	42	24. Virginia
Mississippi	295,000,000	114.65	4	25. South Dakota
Missouri	544,000,000	106.31	16	26. Michigan
Montana	79,000,000	98.87	34	27. Georgia
Nebraska	157,000,000	99.49	33	28. Massachusetts
Nevada	116,000,000	96.51	39	29. Kansas
New Hampshire	99,000,000	89.27	47	30. Oregon
New Jersey	842,000,000	108.93	10	31. Kentucky
New Mexico	140,000,000	92.41	43	32. Indiana
New York	1,977,000,000	109.89	8	33. Nebraska
North Carolina	722,000,000	108.92	11	34. Montana
North Dakota	63,000,000	98.59	35	35. North Dakota
Ohio	1,126,000,000	103.81	21	36. Arizona
Oklahoma	336,000,000	106.80	14	37. Wisconsin
Oregon	285,000,000	100.28	30	38. Maine
Pennsylvania	1,327,000,000	111.68	7	39. Nevada
Rhode Island	104,000,000	103.69	23	40. California
South Carolina	380,000,000	108.98	9	41. Washington
South Dakota	71,000,000	102.01	25	42. Minnesota
Tennessee	519,000,000	106.42	15	43. New Mexico
Texas	1,560,000,000	91.83	44	44. Texas
Utah	132,000,000	76.61	50	45. Idaho
Vermont	51,000,000	90.59	46	46. Vermont
Virginia	632,000,000	102.15	24	47. New Hampshire
Washington	464,000,000	95.34	41	48. Colorado
West Virginia	192,000,000	107.08	13	49. Wyoming
Wisconsin	481,000,000	98.32	37	50. Utah
Wyoming	40,000,000	88.11	49	51. Alaska
United States	$25,661,000,000	$103.18	24	

Source: Centers for Disease Control, *Diabetes in the United States: A Strategy for Prevention* (Atlanta, Ga.: Department of Health and Human Services, 1993).

Note: The cost of diabetes includes the total medical care cost and estimated loss of productivity.

AIDS CASES REPORTED, 1992				Rank in order
State	**Cases reported**	**Per 100,000 population**		**By rate per 100,000 population**
		Rate	**Rank**	
Alabama	486	11.89	20	1. District of Columbia
Alaska	15	2.63	48	2. New York
Arizona	391	10.43	25	3. Florida
Arkansas	295	12.44	18	4. California
California	8,621	28.38	4	5. New Jersey
Colorado	411	12.17	19	6. Maryland
Connecticut	647	19.66	9	7. Delaware
Delaware	141	20.74	7	8. Georgia
District of Columbia	742	124.08	1	9. Connecticut
Florida	5,318	40.05	3	10. Nevada
Georgia	1,331	20.10	8	11. Illinois
Hawaii	147	12.95	16	12. Texas
Idaho	36	3.46	45	13. Louisiana
Illinois	2,072	17.95	11	14. Massachusetts
Indiana	404	7.20	35	15. Missouri
Iowa	112	4.01	42	16. Hawaii
Kansas	192	7.70	32	17. Virginia
Kentucky	214	5.76	37	18. Arkansas
Louisiana	718	16.89	13	19. Colorado
Maine	44	3.56	44	20. Alabama
Maryland	1,300	26.75	6	21. Pennsylvania
Massachusetts	880	14.68	14	22. South Carolina
Michigan	729	7.78	31	23. Washington
Minnesota	233	5.26	38	24. Rhode Island
Mississippi	262	10.11	26	25. Arizona
Missouri	711	13.78	15	26. Mississippi
Montana	24	2.97	47	27. Oregon
Nebraska	62	3.89	43	28. North Carolina
Nevada	249	19.39	10	29. Oklahoma
New Hampshire	53	4.80	40	30. Tennessee
New Jersey	2,138	27.55	5	31. Michigan
New Mexico	115	7.43	34	32. Kansas
New York	8,484	46.98	2	33. Utah
North Carolina	641	9.51	28	34. New Mexico
North Dakota	5	0.79	51	35. Indiana
Ohio	770	7.04	36	36. Ohio
Oklahoma	275	8.66	29	37. Kentucky
Oregon	290	9.92	27	38. Minnesota
Pennsylvania	1,366	11.42	21	39. Wisconsin
Rhode Island	106	10.56	24	40. New Hampshire
South Carolina	394	11.07	22	41. Vermont
South Dakota	8	1.14	49	42. Iowa
Tennessee	424	8.56	30	43. Nebraska
Texas	2,987	17.22	12	44. Maine
Utah	135	7.63	33	45. Idaho
Vermont	26	4.59	41	46. West Virginia
Virginia	791	12.58	17	47. Montana
Washington	553	11.02	23	48. Alaska
West Virginia	56	3.11	46	49. South Dakota
Wisconsin	239	4.82	39	50. Wyoming
Wyoming	5	1.09	50	51. North Dakota
United States	**46,648**	**18.50**	**11**	

Source: Centers for Disease Control, *MMWR Morbidity and Mortality Weekly Report* 41, no. 53 (January 8, 1993).

GONORRHEA CASES REPORTED, 1992

State	Cases reported	Per 100,000 population Rate	Rank	By rate per 100,000 population
Alabama	16,914	413.65	5	1. District of Columbia
Alaska	694	121.75	28	2. Georgia
Arizona	4,235	112.93	30	3. Missouri
Arkansas	7,523	317.16	10	4. Mississippi
California	36,874	121.38	29	5. Alabama
Colorado	4,363	129.20	26	6. North Carolina
Connecticut	5,754	174.84	20	7. Louisiana
Delaware	1,787	262.79	13	8. Maryland
District of Columbia	6,669	1,115.22	1	9. Tennessee
Florida	27,827	209.59	17	10. Arkansas
Georgia	36,927	557.56	2	11. South Carolina
Hawaii	498	43.88	41	12. Illinois
Idaho	115	11.07	47	13. Delaware
Illinois	31,207	270.35	12	14. Ohio
Indiana	9,124	162.64	22	15. Virginia
Iowa	1,560	55.81	39	16. Michigan
Kansas	4,716	189.02	18	17. Florida
Kentucky	4,768	128.41	27	18. Kansas
Louisiana	14,724	346.28	7	19. Oklahoma
Maine	88	7.13	49	20. Connecticut
Maryland	16,662	342.84	8	21. New York
Massachusetts	3,608	60.17	37	22. Indiana
Michigan	21,470	229.18	16	23. Nevada
Minnesota	3,006	67.82	34	24. Texas
Mississippi	11,836	456.64	4	25. Pennsylvania
Missouri	28,708	556.57	3	26. Colorado
Montana	110	13.61	44	27. Kentucky
Nebraska	8	0.50	51	28. Alaska
Nevada	2,034	158.41	23	29. California
New Hampshire	129	11.67	46	30. Arizona
New Jersey	7,521	96.92	31	31. New Jersey
New Mexico	946	61.11	36	32. Washington
New York	29,983	166.04	21	33. Wisconsin
North Carolina	24,604	365.21	6	34. Minnesota
North Dakota	59	9.29	48	35. Rhode Island
Ohio	27,761	253.78	14	36. New Mexico
Oklahoma	5,677	178.80	19	37. Massachusetts
Oregon	1,686	57.70	38	38. Oregon
Pennsylvania	17,763	148.51	25	39. Iowa
Rhode Island	636	63.35	35	40. West Virginia
South Carolina	10,522	295.56	11	41. Hawaii
South Dakota	169	24.04	42	42. South Dakota
Tennessee	15,791	318.82	9	43. Utah
Texas	26,010	149.92	24	44. Montana
Utah	345	19.49	43	45. Wyoming
Vermont	26	4.59	50	46. New Hampshire
Virginia	15,855	252.23	15	47. Idaho
Washington	3,938	78.48	32	48. North Dakota
West Virginia	820	45.53	40	49. Maine
Wisconsin	3,869	78.08	33	50. Vermont
Wyoming	61	13.26	45	51. Nebraska
United States	**497,980**	**197.47**	**18**	

Source: Centers for Disease Control, *MMWR Morbidity and Mortality Weekly Report* 41, no. 53 (January 8, 1993).

			SYPHILIS CASES REPORTED, 1992		Rank in order

SYPHILIS CASES REPORTED, 1992

State	Cases reported	Per 100,000 population		Rank in order — By rate per 100,000 population
		Rate	Rank	
Alabama	1,365	33.38	8	1. District of Columbia
Alaska	6	1.05	42	2. Louisiana
Arizona	166	4.43	31	3. Mississippi
Arkansas	862	36.34	5	4. Missouri
California	1,560	5.13	28	5. Arkansas
Colorado	60	1.78	38	6. North Carolina
Connecticut	245	7.44	24	7. South Carolina
Delaware	209	30.74	9	8. Alabama
District of Columbia	431	72.07	1	9. Delaware
Florida	1,608	12.11	18	10. Georgia
Georgia	1,742	26.30	10	11. Tennessee
Hawaii	9	0.79	44	12. Illinois
Idaho	1	0.10	49	13. New York
Illinois	2,370	20.53	12	14. Oklahoma
Indiana	283	5.04	29	15. Wisconsin
Iowa	58	2.08	36	16. Texas
Kansas	201	8.06	22	17. Maryland
Kentucky	181	4.87	30	18. Florida
Louisiana	2,628	61.81	2	19. Virginia
Maine	5	0.40	46	20. Pennsylvania
Maryland	606	12.47	17	21. Michigan
Massachusetts	327	5.45	27	22. Kansas
Michigan	949	10.13	21	23. Ohio
Minnesota	93	2.10	35	24. Connecticut
Mississippi	1,450	55.94	3	25. New Jersey
Missouri	2,296	44.51	4	26. New Hampshire
Montana	7	0.87	43	27. Massachusetts
Nebraska	1	0.06	50	28. California
Nevada	41	3.19	33	29. Indiana
New Hampshire	78	7.06	26	30. Kentucky
New Jersey	549	7.07	25	31. Arizona
New Mexico	44	2.84	34	32. Rhode Island
New York	2,848	15.77	13	33. Nevada
North Carolina	2,384	35.39	6	34. New Mexico
North Dakota	1	0.16	48	35. Minnesota
Ohio	872	7.97	23	36. Iowa
Oklahoma	460	14.49	14	37. Oregon
Oregon	55	1.88	37	38. Colorado
Pennsylvania	1,235	10.33	20	39. Wyoming
Rhode Island	38	3.78	32	40. Washington
South Carolina	1,207	33.90	7	41. West Virginia
South Dakota	0	0.00	51	42. Alaska
Tennessee	1,224	24.71	11	43. Montana
Texas	2,272	13.10	16	44. Hawaii
Utah	7	0.40	45	45. Utah
Vermont	1	0.18	47	46. Maine
Virginia	718	11.42	19	47. Vermont
Washington	74	1.47	40	48. North Dakota
West Virginia	21	1.17	41	49. Idaho
Wisconsin	691	13.95	15	50. Nebraska
Wyoming	8	1.74	39	51. South Dakota
United States	34,547	13.70	16	

Source: Centers for Disease Control, *MMWR Morbidity and Mortality Weekly Report* 41, no. 53 (January 8, 1993).

State	Cases reported	Per 100,000 population		Rank in order By rate per 100,000 population
		Rate	Rank	
Alabama	415	10.15	12	1. New York
Alaska	54	9.47	15	2. Hawaii
Arizona	252	6.72	20	3. District of Columbia
Arkansas	236	9.95	13	4. California
California	4,568	15.04	4	5. Georgia
Colorado	52	1.54	48	6. Texas
Connecticut	145	4.41	35	7. New Jersey
Delaware	53	7.79	19	8. South Carolina
District of Columbia	122	20.40	3	9. Florida
Florida	1,403	10.57	9	10. Illinois
Georgia	879	13.27	5	11. Kentucky
Hawaii	269	23.70	2	12. Alabama
Idaho	26	2.50	40	13. Arkansas
Illinois	1,214	10.52	10	14. Mississippi
Indiana	220	3.92	36	15. Alaska
Iowa	47	1.68	44	16. North Carolina
Kansas	57	2.28	41	17. Tennessee
Kentucky	390	10.50	11	18. Maryland
Louisiana	217	5.10	29	19. Delaware
Maine	21	1.70	43	20. Arizona
Maryland	418	8.60	18	21. Massachusetts
Massachusetts	387	6.45	21	22. Washington
Michigan	486	5.19	27	23. Nevada
Minnesota	149	3.36	38	24. New Mexico
Mississippi	246	9.49	14	25. Virginia
Missouri	233	4.52	34	26. Pennsylvania
Montana	13	1.61	47	27. Michigan
Nebraska	26	1.63	45	28. West Virginia
Nevada	74	5.76	23	29. Louisiana
New Hampshire	18	1.63	46	30. Oklahoma
New Jersey	905	11.66	7	31. Oregon
New Mexico	89	5.75	24	32. Rhode Island
New York	4,459	24.69	1	33. South Dakota
North Carolina	588	8.73	16	34. Missouri
North Dakota	8	1.26	49	35. Connecticut
Ohio	346	3.16	39	36. Indiana
Oklahoma	158	4.98	30	37. Utah
Oregon	137	4.69	31	38. Minnesota
Pennsylvania	658	5.50	26	39. Ohio
Rhode Island	46	4.58	32	40. Idaho
South Carolina	390	10.96	8	41. Kansas
South Dakota	32	4.55	33	42. Wisconsin
Tennessee	431	8.70	17	43. Maine
Texas	2,213	12.76	6	44. Iowa
Utah	68	3.84	37	45. Nebraska
Vermont	7	1.23	50	46. New Hampshire
Virginia	347	5.52	25	47. Montana
Washington	304	6.06	22	48. Colorado
West Virginia	92	5.11	28	49. North Dakota
Wisconsin	105	2.12	42	50. Vermont
Wyoming	0	0.00	51	51. Wyoming
United States	24,073	9.55	14	

Source: Centers for Disease Control, *MMWR Morbidity and Mortality Weekly Report* 41, no. 53 (January 8, 1993).

HEPATITIS CASES REPORTED, 1992

State	Cases reported	Per 100,000 population		Rank in order — By rate per 100,000 population
		Rate	Rank	
Alabama	210	5.14	46	1. Delaware
Alaska	163	28.60	13	2. District of Columbia
Arizona	1,294	34.51	7	3. Tennessee
Arkansas	255	10.75	35	4. Missouri
California	8,876	29.22	12	5. New Mexico
Colorado	1,124	33.28	8	6. Hawaii
Connecticut	85	2.58	49	7. Arizona
Delaware	471	69.26	1	8. Colorado
District of Columbia	380	63.55	2	9. Utah
Florida	1,572	11.84	31	10. South Dakota
Georgia	676	10.21	36	11. Oregon
Hawaii	406	35.77	6	12. California
Idaho	217	20.89	17	13. Alaska
Illinois	1,104	9.56	37	14. Washington
Indiana	1,002	17.86	23	15. Wisconsin
Iowa	98	3.51	48	16. North Dakota
Kansas	215	8.62	39	17. Idaho
Kentucky	249	6.71	44	18. Nebraska
Louisiana	512	12.04	30	19. Wyoming
Maine	62	5.02	47	20. Minnesota
Maryland	680	13.99	27	21. Montana
Massachusetts	786	13.11	29	22. Texas
Michigan	1,233	13.16	28	23. Indiana
Minnesota	867	19.56	20	24. Rhode Island
Mississippi	46	1.77	51	25. Nevada
Missouri	2,141	41.51	4	26. Oklahoma
Montana	153	18.94	21	27. Maryland
Nebraska	322	20.21	18	28. Michigan
Nevada	212	16.51	25	29. Massachusetts
New Hampshire	128	11.58	33	30. Louisiana
New Jersey	840	10.82	34	31. Florida
New Mexico	580	37.47	5	32. New York
New York	2,129	11.79	32	33. New Hampshire
North Carolina	612	9.08	38	34. New Jersey
North Dakota	137	21.57	16	35. Arkansas
Ohio	787	7.19	41	36. Georgia
Oklahoma	462	14.55	26	37. Illinois
Oregon	897	30.70	11	38. North Carolina
Pennsylvania	858	7.17	42	39. Kansas
Rhode Island	177	17.63	24	40. Vermont
South Carolina	77	2.16	50	41. Ohio
South Dakota	220	31.29	10	42. Pennsylvania
Tennessee	2,508	50.64	3	43. Virginia
Texas	3,132	18.05	22	44. Kentucky
Utah	587	33.16	9	45. West Virginia
Vermont	43	7.58	40	46. Alabama
Virginia	435	6.92	43	47. Maine
Washington	1,368	27.26	14	48. Iowa
West Virginia	96	5.33	45	49. Connecticut
Wisconsin	1,270	25.63	15	50. South Carolina
Wyoming	91	19.78	19	51. Mississippi
United States	**42,845**	**16.99**	**25**	

Source: Centers for Disease Control, *MMWR Morbidity and Mortality Weekly Report* 41, no. 53 (January 8, 1993).
Note: Cases include all forms of hepatitis.

RABIES CASES REPORTED, 1992		Per 100,000 population		Rank in order
State	Cases reported	Rate	Rank	By rate per 100,000 population
Alabama	92	2.25	22	1. Delaware
Alaska	15	2.63	21	2. Connecticut
Arizona	70	1.87	25	3. North Dakota
Arkansas	46	1.94	24	4. Wyoming
California	314	1.03	29	5. South Dakota
Colorado	26	0.77	34	6. Kansas
Connecticut	837	25.43	2	7. Maryland
Delaware	213	31.32	1	8. New Jersey
District of Columbia	17	2.84	20	9. Oklahoma
Florida	43	0.32	42	10. New York
Georgia	370	5.59	13	11. Iowa
Hawaii	0	0.00	48	12. Virginia
Idaho	7	0.67	35	13. Georgia
Illinois	39	0.34	41	14. South Carolina
Indiana	19	0.34	39	15. Vermont
Iowa	175	6.26	11	16. Minnesota
Kansas	368	14.75	6	17. Montana
Kentucky	61	1.64	26	18. Pennsylvania
Louisiana	8	0.19	43	19. West Virginia
Maine	0	0.00	48	20. District of Columbia
Maryland	539	11.09	7	21. Alaska
Massachusetts	57	0.95	31	22. Alabama
Michigan	15	0.16	44	23. Texas
Minnesota	168	3.79	16	24. Arkansas
Mississippi	1	0.04	47	25. Arizona
Missouri	34	0.66	37	26. Kentucky
Montana	24	2.97	17	27. Wisconsin
Nebraska	13	0.82	32	28. Nevada
Nevada	17	1.32	28	29. California
New Hampshire	9	0.81	33	30. Tennessee
New Jersey	710	9.15	8	31. Massachusetts
New Mexico	9	0.58	38	32. Nebraska
New York	1,400	7.75	10	33. New Hampshire
North Carolina	45	0.67	36	34. Colorado
North Dakota	150	23.62	3	35. Idaho
Ohio	14	0.13	45	36. North Carolina
Oklahoma	288	9.07	9	37. Missouri
Oregon	2	0.07	46	38. New Mexico
Pennsylvania	355	2.97	18	39. Indiana
Rhode Island	0	0.00	48	Utah
South Carolina	161	4.52	14	41. Illinois
South Dakota	126	17.92	5	42. Florida
Tennessee	48	0.97	30	43. Louisiana
Texas	343	1.98	23	44. Michigan
Utah	6	0.34	39	45. Ohio
Vermont	23	4.06	15	46. Oregon
Virginia	362	5.76	12	47. Mississippi
Washington	0	0.00	48	48. Hawaii
West Virginia	53	2.94	19	Maine
Wisconsin	69	1.39	27	Rhode Island
Wyoming	83	18.04	4	Washington
United States	7,844	3.11	17	

Source: Centers for Disease Control, *MMWR Morbidity and Mortality Weekly Report* 41, no. 53 (January 8, 1993).

LYME DISEASE CASES REPORTED. 1992		Per 100,000 population		Rank in order

State	Cases reported	Rate	Rank	By rate per 100,000 population
Alabama	10	0.24	35	1. Delaware
Alaska	0	0.00	45	2. Connecticut
Arizona	0	0.00	45	3. Rhode Island
Arkansas	21	0.89	18	4. New York
California	194	0.64	24	5. Pennsylvania
Colorado	0	0.00	45	6. New Jersey
Connecticut	1,051	31.94	2	7. New Hampshire
Delaware	218	32.06	1	8. Minnesota
District of Columbia	3	0.50	26	9. Massachusetts
Florida	36	0.27	34	10. Maryland
Georgia	24	0.36	30	11. Missouri
Hawaii	2	0.18	38	12. Virginia
Idaho	2	0.19	37	13. Vermont
Illinois	27	0.23	36	14. Iowa
Indiana	21	0.37	29	15. Wyoming
Iowa	33	1.18	14	16. North Carolina
Kansas	18	0.72	22	17. Nebraska
Kentucky	27	0.73	21	18. Arkansas
Louisiana	6	0.14	41	19. Oklahoma
Maine	5	0.40	28	20. West Virginia
Maryland	177	3.64	10	21. Kentucky
Massachusetts	229	3.82	9	22. Kansas
Michigan	27	0.29	32	23. Tennessee
Minnesota	177	3.99	8	24. California
Mississippi	0	0.00	45	25. Ohio
Missouri	112	2.17	11	26. District of Columbia
Montana	0	0.00	45	27. Texas
Nebraska	15	0.94	17	28. Maine
Nevada	1	0.08	43	29. Indiana
New Hampshire	46	4.16	7	30. Georgia
New Jersey	681	8.78	6	31. Utah
New Mexico	2	0.13	42	32. Michigan
New York	2,955	16.36	4	33. Washington
North Carolina	73	1.08	16	34. Florida
North Dakota	1	0.16	39	35. Alabama
Ohio	57	0.52	25	36. Illinois
Oklahoma	26	0.82	19	37. Idaho
Oregon	0	0.00	45	38. Hawaii
Pennsylvania	1,119	9.36	5	39. North Dakota
Rhode Island	276	27.49	3	40. South Dakota
South Carolina	2	0.06	44	41. Louisiana
South Dakota	1	0.14	40	42. New Mexico
Tennessee	33	0.67	23	43. Nevada
Texas	73	0.42	27	44. South Carolina
Utah	6	0.34	31	45. Alaska
Vermont	8	1.41	13	Arizona
Virginia	113	1.80	12	Colorado
Washington	14	0.28	33	Mississippi
West Virginia	14	0.78	20	Montana
Wisconsin	0	0.00	45	Oregon
Wyoming	5	1.09	15	Wisconsin
United States	7,941	3.15	11	

Source: Centers for Disease Control, *MMWR Morbidity and Mortality Weekly Report* 41, no. 53 (January 8, 1993).

BEER CONSUMPTION, 1990				Rank in order
State	**Beer consumption (gallons)**	**Per capita (gallons per adult)**	**Rank by per capita**	**By per capita**
Alabama	81,022,000	29.18	43	1. Nevada
Alaska	14,607,000	41.17	8	2. New Hampshire
Arizona	104,899,000	41.76	5	3. Wisconsin
Arkansas	46,863,000	28.93	46	4. Texas
California	709,701,000	34.45	26	5. Arizona
Colorado	79,728,000	34.89	23	6. Hawaii
Connecticut	65,238,000	27.27	50	7. New Mexico
Delaware	17,215,000	36.69	18	8. Alaska
District of Columbia	16,225,000	35.70	20	9. Montana
Florida	381,507,000	39.95	11	10. Louisiana
Georgia	144,718,000	32.70	34	11. Florida
Hawaii	32,470,000	41.65	6	12. North Dakota
Idaho	23,048,000	35.39	22	13. Wyoming
Illinois	294,096,000	36.98	16	14. Vermont
Indiana	124,264,000	32.63	35	15. South Carolina
Iowa	65,535,000	34.02	29	16. Illinois
Kansas	48,827,000	28.68	47	17. Nebraska
Kentucky	74,030,000	29.04	44	18. Delaware
Louisiana	111,375,000	40.02	10	19. Pennsylvania
Maine	27,123,000	31.44	38	20. District of Columbia
Maryland	104,108,000	30.52	41	21. Mississippi
Massachusetts	138,445,000	31.74	37	22. Idaho
Michigan	218,292,000	34.18	28	23. Colorado
Minnesota	101,354,000	33.61	31	South Dakota
Mississippi	59,871,000	35.54	21	25. Missouri
Missouri	124,252,000	34.83	25	26. California
Montana	22,230,000	40.85	9	27. Ohio
Nebraska	39,670,000	36.77	17	28. Michigan
Nevada	48,292,000	56.35	1	29. Iowa
New Hampshire	36,470,000	46.87	2	30. Virginia
New Jersey	162,454,000	28.99	45	31. Minnesota
New Mexico	41,250,000	41.24	7	32. Rhode Island
New York	367,567,000	28.51	49	33. Oregon
North Carolina	138,677,000	29.67	42	34. Georgia
North Dakota	17,021,000	39.34	12	35. Indiana
Ohio	258,980,000	34.37	27	36. Washington
Oklahoma	61,817,000	28.61	48	37. Massachusetts
Oregon	66,615,000	33.33	33	38. Maine
Pennsylvania	306,230,000	35.88	19	39. Tennessee
Rhode Island	24,113,000	33.36	32	40. West Virginia
South Carolina	89,170,000	37.46	15	41. Maryland
South Dakota	16,275,000	34.89	23	42. North Carolina
Tennessee	106,589,000	31.15	39	43. Alabama
Texas	483,477,000	42.73	4	44. Kentucky
Utah	21,850,000	21.75	51	45. New Jersey
Vermont	14,687,000	37.66	14	46. Arkansas
Virginia	148,351,000	33.91	30	47. Kansas
Washington	109,067,000	32.13	36	48. Oklahoma
West Virginia	38,857,000	30.77	40	49. New York
Wisconsin	149,312,000	44.21	3	50. Connecticut
Wyoming	11,384,000	38.13	13	51. Utah
United States	**5,989,215,000**	**34.64**	**26**	

Source: Distilled Spirits Council of U.S., Inc., *1990 Statistical Information for the U.S. Liquor Industry* (Washington, D.C.: Distilled Spirits Council of U.S., Inc., 1991).

Note: Adult is defined as age 21 and over.

State	Wine consumption (gallons)	Per capita (gallons per adult)	Rank by per capita	By per capita
Alabama	4,566,000	1.64	40	1. District of Columbia
Alaska	1,466,000	4.13	8	2. Nevada
Arizona	8,668,000	3.45	15	3. California
Arkansas	1,875,000	1.16	47	4. Washington
California	106,397,000	5.12	3	5. Vermont
Colorado	6,263,000	2.74	22	6. New Hampshire
Connecticut	9,197,000	3.84	12	7. New Jersey
Delaware	1,552,000	3.31	17	8. Alaska
District of Columbia	3,050,000	6.71	1	9. Oregon
Florida	32,145,000	3.37	16	10. Massachusetts
Georgia	11,618,000	2.63	25	11. Rhode Island
Hawaii	2,753,000	3.53	14	12. Connecticut
Idaho	1,939,000	2.96	20	13. New York
Illinois	25,954,000	3.26	18	14. Hawaii
Indiana	6,829,000	1.79	37	15. Arizona
Iowa	3,107,000	1.61	41	16. Florida
Kansas	2,003,000	1.18	46	17. Delaware
Kentucky	2,676,000	1.05	49	18. Illinois
Louisiana	5,897,000	2.12	33	19. Maine
Maine	2,586,000	3.00	19	20. Idaho
Maryland	10,079,000	2.96	20	Maryland
Massachusetts	17,298,000	3.97	10	22. Colorado
Michigan	16,128,000	2.53	27	23. Wisconsin
Minnesota	7,202,000	2.39	30	24. Virginia
Mississippi	1,420,000	0.84	51	25. Georgia
Missouri	7,080,000	1.98	35	26. Montana
Montana	1,416,000	2.60	26	27. Michigan
Nebraska	1,927,000	1.79	37	28. New Mexico
Nevada	5,179,000	6.04	2	29. North Carolina
New Hampshire	3,556,000	4.31	6	30. Minnesota
New Jersey	23,712,000	4.23	7	Texas
New Mexico	2,508,000	2.51	28	32. South Carolina
New York	46,719,000	3.62	13	33. Louisiana
North Carolina	11,407,000	2.44	29	34. Wyoming
North Dakota	658,000	1.52	43	35. Missouri
Ohio	14,476,000	1.92	36	36. Ohio
Oklahoma	2,603,000	1.20	45	37. Indiana
Oregon	8,200,000	4.10	9	Nebraska
Pennsylvania	14,085,000	1.65	39	39. Pennsylvania
Rhode Island	2,802,000	3.88	11	40. Alabama
South Carolina	5,493,000	2.31	32	41. Iowa
South Dakota	739,000	1.58	42	42. South Dakota
Tennessee	4,418,000	1.29	44	43. North Dakota
Texas	27,045,000	2.39	30	44. Tennessee
Utah	1,171,000	1.16	47	45. Oklahoma
Vermont	1,687,000	4.33	5	46. Kansas
Virginia	11,718,000	2.68	24	47. Arkansas
Washington	15,124,000	4.48	4	Utah
West Virginia	1,185,000	0.94	50	49. Kentucky
Wisconsin	9,148,000	2.71	23	50. West Virginia
Wyoming	598,000	2.01	34	51. Mississippi
United States	516,116,000	2.96	20	

Source: Distilled Spirits Council of U.S., Inc., *1990 Statistical Information for the U.S. Liquor Industry* (Washington, D.C.: Distilled Spirits Council of U.S., Inc., 1991).

Note: Adult is defined as age 21 and over.

State	Liquor consumption (gallons)	Per capita (gallons per adult)	Rank by per capita
Alabama	4,830,000	1.74	37
Alaska	1,234,000	3.48	4
Arizona	5,859,000	2.33	20
Arkansas	2,774,000	1.71	40
California	49,880,000	2.42	17
Colorado	4,738,000	2.07	30
Connecticut	6,318,000	2.64	10
Delaware	1,505,000	3.21	5
District of Columbia	2,458,000	5.40	2
Florida	26,849,000	2.81	6
Georgia	11,077,000	2.50	15
Hawaii	1,716,000	2.20	26
Idaho	1,085,000	1.67	42
Illinois	18,878,000	2.37	19
Indiana	6,842,000	1.80	35
Iowa	2,682,000	1.39	49
Kansas	2,546,000	1.50	47
Kentucky	4,194,000	1.65	43
Louisiana	6,188,000	2.22	25
Maine	1,999,000	2.32	21
Maryland	8,968,000	2.63	11
Massachusetts	11,623,000	2.67	7
Michigan	14,411,000	2.26	23
Minnesota	8,032,000	2.66	8
Mississippi	3,183,000	1.89	33
Missouri	6,219,000	1.74	37
Montana	1,173,000	2.16	27
Nebraska	1,937,000	1.80	35
Nevada	4,530,000	5.29	3
New Hampshire	4,265,000	5.48	1
New Jersey	14,582,000	2.60	13
New Mexico	1,917,000	1.92	32
New York	27,134,000	2.10	28
North Carolina	8,537,000	1.83	34
North Dakota	1,089,000	2.52	14
Ohio	11,13,0000	1.48	48
Oklahoma	3,358,000	1.55	45
Oregon	4,010,000	2.01	31
Pennsylvania	13,055,000	1.53	46
Rhode Island	1,649,000	2.28	22
South Carolina	6,177,000	2.50	15
South Dakota	1,048,000	2.25	24
Tennessee	5,798,000	1.69	41
Texas	18,675,000	1.65	43
Utah	1,381,000	1.38	50
Vermont	936,000	2.40	18
Virginia	7,812,000	1.74	37
Washington	7,114,000	2.10	28
West Virginia	1,483,000	1.17	51
Wisconsin	8,949,000	2.65	9
Wyoming	781,000	2.62	12
United States	374,409,000	2.16	27

LIQUOR CONSUMPTION. 1990

Rank in order

By per capita

1. New Hampshire
2. District of Columbia
3. Nevada
4. Alaska
5. Delaware
6. Florida
7. Massachusetts
8. Minnesota
9. Wisconsin
10. Connecticut
11. Maryland
12. Wyoming
13. New Jersey
14. North Dakota
15. Georgia
    South Carolina
17. California
18. Vermont
19. Illinois
20. Arizona
21. Maine
22. Rhode Island
23. Michigan
24. South Dakota
25. Louisiana
26. Hawaii
27. Montana
28. New York
    Washington
30. Colorado
31. Oregon
32. New Mexico
33. Mississippi
34. North Carolina
35. Indiana
    Nebraska
37. Alabama
    Missouri
    Virginia
40. Arkansas
41. Tennessee
42. Idaho
43. Kentucky
    Texas
45. Oklahoma
46. Pennsylvania
47. Kansas
48. Ohio
49. Iowa
50. Utah
51. West Virginia

Source: Distilled Spirits Council of U.S., Inc., *1990 Statistical Information for the U.S. Liquor Industry* (Washington, D.C.: Distilled Spirits Council of U.S., Inc., 1991).

Note: Adult is defined as age 21 and over.

ALCOHOL AND DRUG TREATMENT ADMISSIONS, FISCAL 1990

State	Admissions	Per 1,000 population		Rank in order By rate per 1,000 population
		Rate	Rank	
Alabama	14,311	3.54	45	1. Wisconsin
Alaska	11,448	20.81	2	2. Alaska
Arizona	35,951	9.81	15	3. District of Columbia
Arkansas	10,146	4.32	41	4. Colorado
California	212,802	7.15	30	5. Nebraska
Colorado	60,729	18.44	4	6. Massachusetts
Connecticut	32,210	9.80	16	7. South Dakota
Delaware	6,254	9.39	19	8. Rhode Island
District of Columbia	11,786	19.42	3	9. New York
Florida	94,312	7.29	28	10. Minnesota
Georgia	48,072	7.42	25	11. Montana
Hawaii	4,051	3.66	44	12. Nevada
Idaho	6,568	6.52	31	13. Virginia
Illinois	81,867	7.16	29	14. Vermont
Indiana	20,365	3.67	43	15. Arizona
Iowa	22,655	8.16	21	16. Connecticut
Kansas	15,288	6.17	33	17. Maine
Kentucky	19,165	5.20	38	18. South Carolina
Louisiana	14,638	3.47	46	19. Delaware
Maine	11,939	9.72	17	20. Utah
Maryland	38,827	8.12	22	21. Iowa
Massachusetts	91,946	15.28	6	22. Maryland
Michigan	68,697	7.39	26	23. New Mexico
Minnesota	58,536	13.38	10	24. Missouri
Mississippi	12,528	4.87	40	25. Georgia
Missouri	38,795	7.58	24	26. Michigan
Montana	9,789	12.25	11	27. West Virginia
Nebraska	25,512	16.17	5	28. Florida
Nevada	14,264	11.87	12	29. Illinois
New Hampshire	6,452	5.82	35	30. California
New Jersey	46,749	6.05	34	31. Idaho
New Mexico	11,549	7.62	23	32. North Carolina
New York	250,085	13.90	9	33. Kansas
North Carolina	41,395	6.24	32	34. New Jersey
North Dakota	3,149	4.93	39	35. New Hampshire
Ohio	42,677	3.93	42	36. Pennsylvania
Oklahoma	17,237	5.48	37	37. Oklahoma
Oregon	NA	NA	NA	38. Kentucky
Pennsylvania	67,007	5.64	36	39. North Dakota
Rhode Island	14,519	14.48	8	40. Mississippi
South Carolina	33,200	9.52	18	41. Arkansas
South Dakota	10,299	14.80	7	42. Ohio
Tennessee	7,998	1.64	48	43. Indiana
Texas	34,289	2.02	47	44. Hawaii
Utah	15,993	9.28	20	45. Alabama
Vermont	5,526	9.82	14	46. Louisiana
Virginia	64,605	10.44	13	47. Texas
Washington	NA	NA	NA	48. Tennessee
West Virginia	13,103	7.31	27	NA Oregon
Wisconsin	106,096	21.69	1	NA Washington
Wyoming	NA	NA	NA	NA Wyoming
United States	**1,909,409**	**7.68**	**23**	

NA not available.

Source: National Association of State Alcohol and Drug Abuse Directors, *State Resources and Services Related to Alcohol and Other Drug Abuse Problems, FY90,* (Washington, D.C.: National Association of State Alcohol and Drug Abuse Directors, 1991.)

State	Expenditures	Per capita	Rank by per capita
Alabama	$18,732,000	$4.58	24
Alaska	2,734,000	4.80	19
Arizona	18,002,000	4.80	18
Arkansas	8,417,000	3.55	42
California	151,409,000	4.98	16
Colorado	17,518,000	5.19	10
Connecticut	16,576,000	5.04	15
Delaware	3,213,000	4.73	22
District of Columbia	4,896,000	8.19	1
Florida	63,093,000	4.75	21
Georgia	24,845,000	3.75	38
Hawaii	6,078,000	5.36	8
Idaho	2,775,000	2.67	51
Illinois	62,486,000	5.41	7
Indiana	28,563,000	5.09	14
Iowa	8,633,000	3.09	49
Kansas	8,085,000	3.24	46
Kentucky	12,666,000	3.41	43
Louisiana	18,622,000	4.38	27
Maine	4,654,000	3.77	37
Maryland	23,275,000	4.79	20
Massachusetts	36,009,000	6.01	5
Michigan	46,271,000	4.94	17
Minnesota	16,590,000	3.74	39
Mississippi	8,326,000	3.21	47
Missouri	22,790,000	4.42	25
Montana	2,964,000	3.67	41
Nebraska	5,854,000	3.67	40
Nevada	5,656,000	4.40	26
New Hampshire	4,627,000	4.19	32
New Jersey	47,170,000	6.08	4
New Mexico	6,673,000	4.31	28
New York	103,643,000	5.74	6
North Carolina	22,084,000	3.28	45
North Dakota	1,992,000	3.14	48
Ohio	56,647,000	5.18	11
Oklahoma	13,620,000	4.29	30
Oregon	12,584,000	4.31	29
Pennsylvania	61,799,000	5.17	12
Rhode Island	7,336,000	7.31	2
South Carolina	13,635,000	3.83	36
South Dakota	3,759,000	5.35	9
Tennessee	19,986,000	4.04	34
Texas	73,454,000	4.23	31
Utah	9,083,000	5.13	13
Vermont	3,918,000	6.91	3
Virginia	25,551,000	4.06	33
Washington	23,309,000	4.65	23
West Virginia	6,084,000	3.38	44
Wisconsin	19,186,000	3.87	35
Wyoming	1,285,000	2.79	50
United States	$1,268,670,000	$5.03	16

Rank in order

By per capita

1. District of Columbia
2. Rhode Island
3. Vermont
4. New Jersey
5. Massachusetts
6. New York
7. Illinois
8. Hawaii
9. South Dakota
10. Colorado
11. Ohio
12. Pennsylvania
13. Utah
14. Indiana
15. Connecticut
16. California
17. Michigan
18. Arizona
19. Alaska
20. Maryland
21. Florida
22. Delaware
23. Washington
24. Alabama
25. Missouri
26. Nevada
27. Louisiana
28. New Mexico
29. Oregon
30. Oklahoma
31. Texas
32. New Hampshire
33. Virginia
34. Tennessee
35. Wisconsin
36. South Carolina
37. Maine
38. Georgia
39. Minnesota
40. Nebraska
41. Montana
42. Arkansas
43. Kentucky
44. West Virginia
45. North Carolina
46. Kansas
47. Mississippi
48. North Dakota
49. Iowa
50. Wyoming
51. Idaho

Source: U.S. Department of Commerce, Bureau of the Census, *Federal Expenditures by State for Fiscal Year 1991* (Washington, D.C.: Government Printing Office, 1992).

Note: Expenditures are only those made by the Alcohol, Drug Abuse and Mental Health Administration.

State	Expenditures	Per capita	Rank by per capita
Alabama	$24,887,081	$6.16	36
Alaska	26,266,122	47.76	2
Arizona	28,015,935	7.64	31
Arkansas	9,125,802	3.88	47
California	331,247,420	11.13	12
Colorado	34,178,728	10.38	17
Connecticut	75,858,279	23.08	4
Delaware	6,173,445	9.27	22
District of Columbia	41,860,699	68.96	1
Florida	122,303,088	9.45	20
Georgia	49,939,070	7.71	29
Hawaii	9,311,151	8.40	27
Idaho	4,665,403	4.63	45
Illinois	120,813,696	10.57	16
Indiana	34,114,040	6.15	37
Iowa	20,661,283	7.44	32
Kansas	34,147,169	13.78	10
Kentucky	14,805,725	4.02	46
Louisiana	26,496,138	6.28	35
Maine	10,218,607	8.32	28
Maryland	74,320,297	15.55	8
Massachusetts	65,500,598	10.89	13
Michigan	98,992,122	10.65	15
Minnesota	61,472,932	14.05	9
Mississippi	9,579,320	3.72	48
Missouri	27,641,531	5.40	42
Montana	14,373,375	17.99	6
Nebraska	9,544,585	6.05	39
Nevada	6,728,784	5.60	41
New Hampshire	5,187,506	4.68	44
New Jersey	70,088,000	9.07	24
New Mexico	14,662,826	9.68	19
New York	764,569,310	42.50	3
North Carolina	51,086,448	7.71	30
North Dakota	5,867,562	9.18	23
Ohio	61,903,178	5.71	40
Oklahoma	19,280,431	6.13	38
Oregon	NA	NA	NA
Pennsylvania	103,282,332	8.69	26
Rhode Island	17,621,393	17.57	7
South Carolina	35,676,719	10.23	18
South Dakota	4,613,011	6.63	33
Tennessee	31,049,727	6.37	34
Texas	58,634,223	3.45	49
Utah	16,258,766	9.44	21
Vermont	5,999,730	10.66	14
Virginia	54,543,441	8.82	25
Washington	57,244,000	11.76	11
West Virginia	9,182,104	5.12	43
Wisconsin	96,700,029	19.77	5
Wyoming	NA	NA	NA
United States	$2,910,504,536	$11.70	12

Rank in order

By per capita

1. District of Columbia
2. Alaska
3. New York
4. Connecticut
5. Wisconsin
6. Montana
7. Rhode Island
8. Maryland
9. Minnesota
10. Kansas
11. Washington
12. California
13. Massachusetts
14. Vermont
15. Michigan
16. Illinois
17. Colorado
18. South Carolina
19. New Mexico
20. Florida
21. Utah
22. Delaware
23. North Dakota
24. New Jersey
25. Virginia
26. Pennsylvania
27. Hawaii
28. Maine
29. Georgia
30. North Carolina
31. Arizona
32. Iowa
33. South Dakota
34. Tennessee
35. Louisiana
36. Alabama
37. Indiana
38. Oklahoma
39. Nebraska
40. Ohio
41. Nevada
42. Missouri
43. West Virginia
44. New Hampshire
45. Idaho
46. Kentucky
47. Arkansas
48. Mississippi
49. Texas
NA Oregon
NA Wyoming

NA not available.

Source: National Association of State Alcohol and Drug Abuse Directors, *State Resources and Services Related to Alcohol and Other Drug Abuse Problems, FY1990* (Washington, D.C.: National Association of State Alcohol and Drug Abuse Directors, 1991).

Note: Total expenditures include local, state, and federal funding.

STATE SPENDING ON ALCOHOL/DRUG ABUSE SERVICES, FISCAL 1990				Rank in order

State	Expenditures	Per capita	Rank by per capita	By per capita
Alabama	$2,169,352	$0.54	47	1. Alaska
Alaska	11,819,556	21.49	1	2. New York
Arizona	12,920,139	3.53	20	3. Rhode Island
Arkansas	1,344,553	0.57	45	4. Connecticut
California	88,193,000	2.96	27	5. Minnesota
Colorado	11,879,504	3.61	19	6. Massachusetts
Connecticut	42,930,754	13.06	4	7. Washington
Delaware	4,247,746	6.38	10	8. Maryland
District of Columbia	115,437	0.19	49	9. Illinois
Florida	43,195,548	3.34	22	10. Delaware
Georgia	28,329,913	4.37	16	11. Wisconsin
Hawaii	3,138,183	2.83	29	12. Vermont
Idaho	1,651,464	1.64	40	13. Maine
Illinois	78,169,455	6.84	9	14. North Carolina
Indiana	3,051,944	0.55	46	15. North Dakota
Iowa	8,502,098	3.06	26	16. Georgia
Kansas	7,056,975	2.85	28	17. Virginia
Kentucky	6,861,891	1.86	38	18. New Jersey
Louisiana	1,254,000	0.30	48	19. Colorado
Maine	5,856,140	4.77	13	20. Arizona
Maryland	33,078,977	6.92	8	21. Utah
Massachusetts	45,715,763	7.60	6	22. Florida
Michigan	29,968,468	3.22	25	Pennsylvania
Minnesota	33,485,000	7.65	5	24. Nebraska
Mississippi	2,188,124	0.85	43	25. Michigan
Missouri	11,405,097	2.23	32	26. Iowa
Montana	539,893	0.68	44	27. California
Nebraska	5,104,074	3.24	24	28. Kansas
Nevada	2,361,970	1.97	36	29. Hawaii
New Hampshire	2,522,273	2.27	31	30. West Virginia
New Jersey	29,691,000	3.84	18	31. New Hampshire
New Mexico	3,235,328	2.14	34	32. Missouri
New York	268,679,993	14.94	2	33. South Carolina
North Carolina	30,713,724	4.63	14	34. New Mexico
North Dakota	2,945,916	4.61	15	35. Tennessee
Ohio	18,419,003	1.70	39	36. Nevada
Oklahoma	6,047,036	1.92	37	37. Oklahoma
Oregon	NA	NA	NA	38. Kentucky
Pennsylvania	39,678,527	3.34	22	39. Ohio
Rhode Island	13,629,770	13.59	3	40. Idaho
South Carolina	7,525,347	2.16	33	41. South Dakota
South Dakota	610,293	0.88	41	42. Texas
Tennessee	10,022,625	2.06	35	43. Mississippi
Texas	14,482,591	0.85	42	44. Montana
Utah	5,829,227	3.38	21	45. Arkansas
Vermont	3,304,522	5.87	12	46. Indiana
Virginia	24,369,394	3.94	17	47. Alabama
Washington	34,996,000	7.19	7	48. Louisiana
West Virginia	4,457,806	2.49	30	49. District of Columbia
Wisconsin	30,864,728	6.31	11	NA Oregon
Wyoming	NA	NA	NA	NA Wyoming
United States	$1,099,253,225	$4.42	16	

NA not available.

Source: National Association of State Alcohol and Drug Abuse Directors, *State Resources and Services Related to Alcohol and Other Drug Abuse Problems, Fiscal Year 1990* (Washington, D.C.: National Association of State Alcohol and Drug Abuse Directors, 1991).

Note: Expenditures are those made by the state alcohol/drug abuse agency.

State	Cocaine users	Per 1,000 population	
		Rate	Rank
Alabama	29,000	7.2	22
Alaska	3,500	6.6	26
Arizona	46,000	13.7	5
Arkansas	10,000	4.4	38
California	337,000	12.2	6
Colorado	34,000	10.5	9
Connecticut	18,000	5.7	31
Delaware	3,200	4.9	33
District of Columbia	25,000	40.5	1
Florida	98,000	8.2	16
Georgia	54,000	8.7	14
Hawaii	11,000	10.5	9
Idaho	3,700	3.7	40
Illinois	160,000	13.8	4
Indiana	18,000	3.3	41
Iowa	9,000	3.1	43
Kansas	12,000	4.8	35
Kentucky	24,000	6.6	26
Louisiana	34,000	7.6	19
Maine	3,400	2.9	45
Maryland	29,000	6.4	29
Massachusetts	29,000	4.9	33
Michigan	67,000	7.3	21
Minnesota	29,000	6.9	25
Mississippi	6,900	2.6	46
Missouri	59,000	11.5	7
Montana	1,500	1.8	50
Nebraska	14,000	8.6	15
Nevada	25,000	24.9	2
New Hampshire	3,400	3.3	41
New Jersey	72,000	5.4	32
New Mexico	15,000	10.2	12
New York	436,000	24.5	3
North Carolina	45,000	7.0	24
North Dakota	1,300	2.0	49
Ohio	69,000	6.4	29
Oklahoma	25,000	7.7	17
Oregon	18,000	6.5	28
Pennsylvania	86,000	7.2	22
Rhode Island	4,600	4.7	36
South Carolina	14,000	4.0	39
South Dakota	1,300	1.8	50
Tennessee	36,000	7.4	20
Texas	173,000	10.3	11
Utah	13,000	7.7	17
Vermont	1,100	2.1	48
Virginia	55,000	9.4	13
Washington	21,000	4.5	37
West Virginia	4,200	2.2	47
Wisconsin	52,000	10.8	8
Wyoming	1,500	3.1	43
United States	**2,400,000**	**10.0**	**13**

HARD-CORE COCAINE USERS, 1990

Rank in order

By rate per 1,000 population

1. District of Columbia
2. Nevada
3. New York
4. Illinois
5. Arizona
6. California
7. Missouri
8. Wisconsin
9. Colorado
   Hawaii
11. Texas
12. New Mexico
13. Virginia
14. Georgia
15. Nebraska
16. Florida
17. Oklahoma
    Utah
19. Louisiana
20. Tennessee
21. Michigan
22. Alabama
    Pennsylvania
24. North Carolina
25. Minnesota
26. Alaska
    Kentucky
28. Oregon
29. Maryland
    Ohio
31. Connecticut
32. New Jersey
33. Delaware
    Massachusetts
35. Kansas
36. Rhode Island
37. Washington
38. Arkansas
39. South Carolina
40. Idaho
41. Indiana
    New Hampshire
43. Iowa
    Wyoming
45. Maine
46. Mississippi
47. West Virginia
48. Vermont
49. North Dakota
50. Montana
    South Dakota

Source: *U.S. Senate, Committee on Judiciary,* (Washington, D.C.: Government Printing Office, 1990).
Note: Hard core cocaine users are defined as those using cocaine more than once a week.

FEDERAL DRUG GRANTS TO STATES, FISCAL 1991

State	Expenditures	Per capita	Rank by per capita		By per capita
Alabama	$22,100,000	$5.41	27		1. District of Columbia
Alaska	5,400,000	9.47	3		2. Wyoming
Arizona	19,600,000	5.23	35		3. Alaska
Arkansas	12,000,000	5.06	42		4. Vermont
California	160,500,000	5.28	33		5. Delaware
Colorado	18,800,000	5.57	21		6. North Dakota
Connecticut	18,100,000	5.50	23		7. South Dakota
Delaware	6,100,000	8.97	5		8. Rhode Island
District of Columbia	6,700,000	11.20	1		9. Montana
Florida	63,500,000	4.78	50		10. Hawaii
Georgia	32,600,000	4.92	47		11. Utah
Hawaii	7,400,000	6.52	10		12. Louisiana
Idaho	6,100,000	5.87	14		13. New York
Illinois	64,300,000	5.57	20		14. Idaho
Indiana	26,900,000	4.80	49		15. Michigan
Iowa	14,600,000	5.22	36		16. New Jersey
Kansas	12,200,000	4.89	48		17. Maryland
Kentucky	19,800,000	5.33	29		18. New Mexico
Louisiana	26,200,000	6.16	12		19. Nevada
Maine	6,700,000	5.43	26		20. Illinois
Maryland	27,400,000	5.64	17		21. Colorado
Massachusetts	32,600,000	5.44	25		22. New Hampshire
Michigan	53,300,000	5.69	15		23. Connecticut
Minnesota	22,700,000	5.12	40		24. Nebraska
Mississippi	13,800,000	5.32	30		25. Massachusetts
Missouri	26,400,000	5.12	41		26. Maine
Montana	5,700,000	7.05	9		27. Alabama
Nebraska	8,700,000	5.46	24		28. Wisconsin
Nevada	7,200,000	5.61	19		29. Kentucky
New Hampshire	6,100,000	5.52	22		30. Mississippi
New Jersey	43,900,000	5.66	16		31. Pennsylvania
New Mexico	8,700,000	5.62	18		32. Texas
New York	109,600,000	6.07	13		33. California
North Carolina	30,700,000	4.56	51		34. West Virginia
North Dakota	5,300,000	8.35	6		35. Arizona
Ohio	56,400,000	5.16	38		36. Iowa
Oklahoma	16,000,000	5.04	44		37. Oregon
Oregon	15,100,000	5.17	37		38. Ohio
Pennsylvania	63,600,000	5.32	31		39. South Carolina
Rhode Island	7,400,000	7.37	8		40. Minnesota
South Carolina	18,300,000	5.14	39		41. Missouri
South Dakota	5,500,000	7.82	7		42. Arkansas
Tennessee	25,000,000	5.05	43		43. Tennessee
Texas	92,200,000	5.31	32		44. Oklahoma
Utah	11,300,000	6.38	11		45. Washington
Vermont	5,300,000	9.35	4		46. Virginia
Virginia	31,200,000	4.96	46		47. Georgia
Washington	25,100,000	5.00	45		48. Kansas
West Virginia	9,500,000	5.28	34		49. Indiana
Wisconsin	26,500,000	5.35	28		50. Florida
Wyoming	4,700,000	10.22	2		51. North Carolina
United States	**$1,427,700,000**	**$5.66**	**16**		

Source: Office of National Drug Control Policy, *Federal Drug Grants to States* (Washington, D.C.: Executive Office of the President, 1990).

Population

State	1980 population	1990 population	% change 1980-1990	Rank by 1990 population
Alabama	3,894,000	4,041,000	3.8	22
Alaska	402,000	550,000	36.8	50
Arizona	2,718,000	3,665,000	34.8	24
Arkansas	2,286,000	2,351,000	2.8	33
California	23,668,000	29,760,000	25.7	1
Colorado	2,890,000	3,294,000	14.0	26
Connecticut	3,108,000	3,287,000	5.8	27
Delaware	594,000	666,000	12.1	46
District of Columbia	638,000	607,000	−4.9	48
Florida	9,746,000	12,938,000	32.8	4
Georgia	5,463,000	6,478,000	18.6	11
Hawaii	965,000	1,108,000	14.8	41
Idaho	944,000	1,007,000	6.7	42
Illinois	11,427,000	11,431,000	*	6
Indiana	5,490,000	5,544,000	1.0	14
Iowa	2,914,000	2,777,000	−4.7	30
Kansas	2,364,000	2,478,000	4.8	32
Kentucky	3,661,000	3,685,000	0.7	23
Louisiana	4,206,000	4,220,000	0.3	21
Maine	1,125,000	1,228,000	9.2	38
Maryland	4,217,000	4,781,000	13.4	19
Massachusetts	5,737,000	6,016,000	4.9	13
Michigan	9,262,000	9,295,000	0.4	8
Minnesota	4,076,000	4,375,000	7.3	20
Mississippi	2,521,000	2,573,000	2.1	31
Missouri	4,917,000	5,117,000	4.1	15
Montana	787,000	799,000	1.5	44
Nebraska	1,570,000	1,578,000	0.5	36
Nevada	800,000	1,202,000	50.3	39
New Hampshire	921,000	1,109,000	20.4	40
New Jersey	7,365,000	7,730,000	5.0	9
New Mexico	1,303,000	1,515,000	16.3	37
New York	17,558,000	17,990,000	2.5	2
North Carolina	5,882,000	6,629,000	12.7	10
North Dakota	653,000	639,000	−2.1	47
Ohio	10,798,000	10,847,000	0.5	7
Oklahoma	3,025,000	3,146,000	4.0	28
Oregon	2,633,000	2,842,000	7.9	29
Pennsylvania	11,864,000	11,882,000	0.2	5
Rhode Island	947,000	1,003,000	5.9	43
South Carolina	3,122,000	3,487,000	11.7	25
South Dakota	691,000	696,000	0.7	45
Tennessee	4,591,000	4,877,000	6.2	17
Texas	14,229,000	16,987,000	19.4	3
Utah	1,461,000	1,723,000	17.9	35
Vermont	511,000	563,000	10.2	49
Virginia	5,347,000	6,187,000	15.7	12
Washington	4,132,000	4,867,000	17.8	18
West Virginia	1,950,000	1,793,000	−8.1	34
Wisconsin	4,706,000	4,892,000	4.0	16
Wyoming	470,000	454,000	−3.4	51
United States	226,546,000	248,710,000	9.8	20

Rank in order
By 1990 population
1. California
2. New York
3. Texas
4. Florida
5. Pennsylvania
6. Illinois
7. Ohio
8. Michigan
9. New Jersey
10. North Carolina
11. Georgia
12. Virginia
13. Massachusetts
14. Indiana
15. Missouri
16. Wisconsin
17. Tennessee
18. Washington
19. Maryland
20. Minnesota
21. Louisiana
22. Alabama
23. Kentucky
24. Arizona
25. South Carolina
26. Colorado
27. Connecticut
28. Oklahoma
29. Oregon
30. Iowa
31. Mississippi
32. Kansas
33. Arkansas
34. West Virginia
35. Utah
36. Nebraska
37. New Mexico
38. Maine
39. Nevada
40. New Hampshire
41. Hawaii
42. Idaho
43. Rhode Island
44. Montana
45. South Dakota
46. Delaware
47. North Dakota
48. District of Columbia
49. Vermont
50. Alaska
51. Wyoming

* rounds to less than 0.05.

Source: U.S. Department of Commerce, Bureau of the Census, *Statistical Abstract of the United States, 1992* (Washington, D.C.: Government Printing Office, 1992).

POPULATION DENSITY, 1991

State	Population per square mile	Rank
Alabama	80.6	26
Alaska	1.0	51
Arizona	33.0	38
Arkansas	45.5	36
California	194.8	13
Colorado	32.6	39
Connecticut	679.2	5
Delaware	347.9	8
District of Columbia	9,742.9	1
Florida	245.9	11
Georgia	114.3	22
Hawaii	176.7	14
Idaho	12.6	45
Illinois	207.6	12
Indiana	156.4	17
Iowa	50.0	34
Kansas	30.5	40
Kentucky	93.5	24
Louisiana	97.6	23
Maine	40.0	37
Maryland	497.2	6
Massachusetts	765.0	4
Michigan	164.9	15
Minnesota	55.7	32
Mississippi	55.3	33
Missouri	74.9	28
Montana	5.6	49
Nebraska	20.7	43
Nevada	11.7	46
New Hampshire	123.2	19
New Jersey	1,046.0	2
New Mexico	12.8	44
New York	382.4	7
North Carolina	138.3	18
North Dakota	9.2	48
Ohio	267.1	9
Oklahoma	46.2	35
Oregon	30.4	41
Pennsylvania	266.9	10
Rhode Island	961.1	3
South Carolina	118.2	21
South Dakota	9.3	47
Tennessee	120.2	20
Texas	66.2	30
Utah	21.5	42
Vermont	61.3	31
Virginia	158.7	16
Washington	75.4	27
West Virginia	74.8	29
Wisconsin	91.2	25
Wyoming	4.7	50
United States	**71.3**	**30**

Rank in order

By population per square mile

1. District of Columbia
2. New Jersey
3. Rhode Island
4. Massachusetts
5. Connecticut
6. Maryland
7. New York
8. Delaware
9. Ohio
10. Pennsylvania
11. Florida
12. Illinois
13. California
14. Hawaii
15. Michigan
16. Virginia
17. Indiana
18. North Carolina
19. New Hampshire
20. Tennessee
21. South Carolina
22. Georgia
23. Louisiana
24. Kentucky
25. Wisconsin
26. Alabama
27. Washington
28. Missouri
29. West Virginia
30. Texas
31. Vermont
32. Minnesota
33. Mississippi
34. Iowa
35. Oklahoma
36. Arkansas
37. Maine
38. Arizona
39. Colorado
40. Kansas
41. Oregon
42. Utah
43. Nebraska
44. New Mexico
45. Idaho
46. Nevada
47. South Dakota
48. North Dakota
49. Montana
50. Wyoming
51. Alaska

Source: U.S. Department of Commerce, Bureau of the Census, *Statistical Abstract of the United States, 1992* (Washington, D.C.: Government Printing Office, 1992).

POPULATION IN METROPOLITAN AREAS. 1990

State	Metropolitan population	% of state population	Rank by %
Alabama	2,723,000	67.4	28
Alaska	226,000	41.1	41
Arizona	2,896,000	79.0	17
Arkansas	943,000	40.1	43
California	28,493,000	95.7	3
Colorado	2,686,000	81.5	15
Connecticut	3,038,000	92.4	6
Delaware	442,000	66.4	29
District of Columbia	607,000	100.0	1
Florida	11,754,000	90.8	8
Georgia	4,212,000	65.0	31
Hawaii	836,000	75.5	20
Idaho	206,000	20.5	51
Illinois	9,450,000	82.7	12
Indiana	3,796,000	68.5	24
Iowa	1,223,000	44.0	40
Kansas	1,333,000	53.8	36
Kentucky	1,714,000	46.5	39
Louisiana	2,935,000	69.6	22
Maine	441,000	35.9	45
Maryland	4,439,000	92.8	4
Massachusetts	5,438,000	90.4	9
Michigan	7,446,000	80.1	16
Minnesota	2,960,000	67.7	26
Mississippi	776,000	30.2	46
Missouri	3,387,000	66.2	30
Montana	191,000	23.9	49
Nebraska	766,000	48.5	37
Nevada	996,000	82.9	11
New Hampshire	622,000	56.1	35
New Jersey	7,730,000	100.0	1
New Mexico	733,000	48.4	38
New York	16,386,000	91.1	7
North Carolina	3,758,000	56.7	34
North Dakota	257,000	40.2	42
Ohio	8,567,000	79.0	18
Oklahoma	1,870,000	59.4	33
Oregon	1,947,000	68.5	23
Pennsylvania	10,077,000	84.8	10
Rhode Island	928,000	92.5	5
South Carolina	2,113,000	60.6	32
South Dakota	205,000	29.5	48
Tennessee	3,300,000	67.7	25
Texas	13,867,000	81.6	14
Utah	1,336,000	77.5	19
Vermont	131,000	23.3	50
Virginia	4,483,000	72.5	21
Washington	3,976,000	81.7	13
West Virginia	553,000	36.4	44
Wisconsin	3,298,000	67.4	27
Wyoming	134,000	29.5	47
United States	**192,726,000**	**77.5**	**20**

Rank in order

By %

1. District of Columbia
   New Jersey
3. California
4. Maryland
5. Rhode Island
6. Connecticut
7. New York
8. Florida
9. Massachusetts
10. Pennsylvania
11. Nevada
12. Illinois
13. Washington
14. Texas
15. Colorado
16. Michigan
17. Arizona
18. Ohio
19. Utah
20. Hawaii
21. Virginia
22. Louisiana
23. Oregon
24. Indiana
25. Tennessee
26. Minnesota
27. Wisconsin
28. Alabama
29. Delaware
30. Missouri
31. Georgia
32. South Carolina
33. Oklahoma
34. North Carolina
35. New Hampshire
36. Kansas
37. Nebraska
38. New Mexico
39. Kentucky
40. Iowa
41. Alaska
42. North Dakota
43. Arkansas
44. West Virginia
45. Maine
46. Mississippi
47. Wyoming
48. South Dakota
49. Montana
50. Vermont
51. Idaho

Source: U.S. Department of Commerce, Bureau of the Census, *Statistical Abstract of the United States, 1992* (Washington, D.C.: Government Printing Office, 1992).

POPULATION UNDER 18 YEARS OLD, 1990				Rank in order
State	Population under age 18	% of state population	Rank by %	By %
Alabama	1,058,788	26.2	23	1. Utah
Alaska	172,344	31.3	2	2. Alaska
Arizona	981,119	26.8	13	3. Idaho
Arkansas	621,131	26.4	19	4. Wyoming
California	7,750,725	26.0	25	5. New Mexico
Colorado	861,266	26.1	24	6. Louisiana
Connecticut	749,581	22.8	47	7. Mississippi
Delaware	163,341	24.5	40	8. South Dakota
District of Columbia	117,092	19.3	51	9. Texas
Florida	2,866,237	22.2	50	10. Montana
Georgia	1,727,303	26.7	16	11. North Dakota
Hawaii	280,126	25.3	34	12. Nebraska
Idaho	308,405	30.6	3	13. Arizona
Illinois	2,946,366	25.8	30	14. Kansas
Indiana	1,455,964	26.3	22	15. Minnesota
Iowa	718,880	25.9	28	16. Georgia
Kansas	661,614	26.7	14	17. Oklahoma
Kentucky	954,094	25.9	27	18. Michigan
Louisiana	1,227,269	29.1	6	19. Arkansas
Maine	309,002	25.2	35	20. South Carolina
Maryland	1,162,241	24.3	42	21. Wisconsin
Massachusetts	1,353,075	22.5	49	22. Indiana
Michigan	2,458,765	26.5	18	23. Alabama
Minnesota	1,166,783	26.7	15	24. Colorado
Mississippi	746,761	29.0	7	25. California
Missouri	1,314,826	25.7	31	26. Washington
Montana	222,104	27.8	10	27. Kentucky
Nebraska	429,012	27.2	12	28. Iowa
Nevada	296,948	24.7	39	29. Ohio
New Hampshire	278,755	25.1	36	30. Illinois
New Jersey	1,799,462	23.3	46	31. Missouri
New Mexico	446,741	29.5	5	32. Oregon
New York	4,259,549	23.7	44	33. Vermont
North Carolina	1,606,149	24.2	43	34. Hawaii
North Dakota	175,385	27.4	11	35. Maine
Ohio	2,799,744	25.8	29	36. New Hampshire
Oklahoma	837,007	26.6	17	37. Tennessee
Oregon	724,130	25.5	32	38. West Virginia
Pennsylvania	2,794,810	23.5	45	39. Nevada
Rhode Island	225,690	22.5	48	40. Delaware
South Carolina	920,207	26.4	20	41. Virginia
South Dakota	198,462	28.5	8	42. Maryland
Tennessee	1,216,604	24.9	37	43. North Carolina
Texas	4,835,839	28.5	9	44. New York
Utah	627,444	36.4	1	45. Pennsylvania
Vermont	143,083	25.4	33	46. New Jersey
Virginia	1,504,738	24.3	41	47. Connecticut
Washington	1,261,387	25.9	26	48. Rhode Island
West Virginia	443,577	24.7	38	49. Massachusetts
Wisconsin	1,288,982	26.3	21	50. Florida
Wyoming	135,525	29.9	4	51. District of Columbia
United States	63,604,432	25.6	32	

Source: U.S. Department of Commerce, Bureau of the Census, *Statistical Abstract of the United States, 1992* (Washington, D.C.: Government Printing Office, 1992)

State	Population over age 65	% of state population	Rank by %
Alabama	529,000	12.9	24
Alaska	23,000	4.0	51
Arizona	497,000	13.3	20
Arkansas	353,000	14.9	6
California	3,188,000	10.5	45
Colorado	340,000	10.1	49
Connecticut	451,000	13.7	14
Delaware	83,000	12.2	32
District of Columbia	78,000	13.0	23
Florida	2,433,000	18.3	1
Georgia	668,000	10.1	48
Hawaii	130,000	11.5	38
Idaho	125,000	12.0	34
Illinois	1,449,000	12.6	28
Indiana	708,000	12.6	27
Iowa	431,000	15.4	3
Kansas	346,000	13.9	11
Kentucky	471,000	12.7	26
Louisiana	475,000	11.2	40
Maine	167,000	13.5	15
Maryland	530,000	10.9	42
Massachusetts	824,000	13.7	12
Michigan	1,129,000	12.1	33
Minnesota	555,000	12.5	29
Mississippi	323,000	12.5	30
Missouri	725,000	14.1	10
Montana	108,000	13.4	18
Nebraska	225,000	14.1	9
Nevada	139,000	10.8	44
New Hampshire	128,000	11.6	37
New Jersey	1,041,000	13.4	17
New Mexico	169,000	10.9	41
New York	2,356,000	13.0	22
North Carolina	826,000	12.3	31
North Dakota	91,000	14.3	8
Ohio	1,432,000	13.1	21
Oklahoma	429,000	13.5	16
Oregon	401,000	13.7	13
Pennsylvania	1,858,000	15.5	2
Rhode Island	152,000	15.1	4
South Carolina	407,000	11.4	39
South Dakota	104,000	14.8	7
Tennessee	630,000	12.7	25
Texas	1,756,000	10.1	47
Utah	155,000	8.8	50
Vermont	67,000	11.8	35
Virginia	682,000	10.9	43
Washington	589,000	11.7	36
West Virginia	271,000	15.0	5
Wisconsin	661,000	13.3	19
Wyoming	48,000	10.4	46
United States	**31,754,000**	**12.6**	**28**

Rank in order

By %

1. Florida
2. Pennsylvania
3. Iowa
4. Rhode Island
5. West Virginia
6. Arkansas
7. South Dakota
8. North Dakota
9. Nebraska
10. Missouri
11. Kansas
12. Massachusetts
13. Oregon
14. Connecticut
15. Maine
16. Oklahoma
17. New Jersey
18. Montana
19. Wisconsin
20. Arizona
21. Ohio
22. New York
23. District of Columbia
24. Alabama
25. Tennessee
26. Kentucky
27. Indiana
28. Illinois
29. Minnesota
30. Mississippi
31. North Carolina
32. Delaware
33. Michigan
34. Idaho
35. Vermont
36. Washington
37. New Hampshire
38. Hawaii
39. South Carolina
40. Louisiana
41. New Mexico
42. Maryland
43. Virginia
44. Nevada
45. California
46. Wyoming
47. Texas
48. Georgia
49. Colorado
50. Utah
51. Alaska

Source: U.S. Department of Commerce, Bureau of the Census *Statistical Abstract of the United States, 1992* (Washington, D.C.: Government Printing Office, 1992).

| WHITE POPULATION, 1990 | | | | Rank in order | |
State	White population	% of state population	Rank by %	By %	
Alabama	2,976,000	73.6	43	1. Vermont	
Alaska	415,000	75.5	40	2. Maine	
Arizona	2,963,000	80.8	33	3. New Hampshire	
Arkansas	1,945,000	82.7	31	4. Iowa	
California	20,524,000	69.0	47	5. West Virginia	
Colorado	2,905,000	88.2	23	6. North Dakota	
Connecticut	2,859,000	87.0	26	7. Minnesota	
Delaware	535,000	80.3	34	8. Idaho	
District of Columbia	180,000	29.7	51	9. Wyoming	
Florida	10,749,000	83.1	29	10. Nebraska	
Georgia	4,600,000	71.0	44	11. Utah	
Hawaii	370,000	33.4	50	12. Oregon	
Idaho	950,000	94.3	8	13. Montana	
Illinois	8,953,000	78.3	36	14. Wisconsin	
Indiana	5,021,000	90.6	18	15. Kentucky	
Iowa	2,683,000	96.6	4	16. South Dakota	
Kansas	2,232,000	90.1	19	17. Rhode Island	
Kentucky	3,392,000	92.0	15	18. Indiana	
Louisiana	2,839,000	67.3	48	19. Kansas	
Maine	1,208,000	98.4	2	20. Massachusetts	
Maryland	3,394,000	71.0	45	21. Pennsylvania	
Massachusetts	5,405,000	89.8	20	22. Washington	
Michigan	7,756,000	83.4	28	23. Colorado	
Minnesota	4,130,000	94.4	7	24. Ohio	
Mississippi	1,633,000	63.5	49	25. Missouri	
Missouri	4,486,000	87.7	25	26. Connecticut	
Montana	741,000	92.7	13	27. Nevada	
Nebraska	1,481,000	93.9	10	28. Michigan	
Nevada	1,013,000	84.3	27	29. Florida	
New Hampshire	1,087,000	98.0	3	30. Tennessee	
New Jersey	6,130,000	79.3	35	31. Arkansas	
New Mexico	1,146,000	75.6	38	32. Oklahoma	
New York	13,385,000	74.4	42	33. Arizona	
North Carolina	5,008,000	75.5	39	34. Delaware	
North Dakota	604,000	94.5	6	35. New Jersey	
Ohio	9,522,000	87.8	24	36. Illinois	
Oklahoma	2,584,000	82.1	32	37. Virginia	
Oregon	2,637,000	92.8	12	38. New Mexico	
Pennsylvania	10,520,000	88.5	21	39. North Carolina	
Rhode Island	917,000	91.4	17	40. Alaska	
South Carolina	2,407,000	69.0	46	41. Texas	
South Dakota	638,000	91.7	16	42. New York	
Tennessee	4,048,000	83.0	30	43. Alabama	
Texas	12,775,000	75.2	41	44. Georgia	
Utah	1,616,000	93.8	11	45. Maryland	
Vermont	555,000	98.6	1	46. South Carolina	
Virginia	4,792,000	77.5	37	47. California	
Washington	4,309,000	88.5	22	48. Louisiana	
West Virginia	1,726,000	96.3	5	49. Mississippi	
Wisconsin	4,513,000	92.3	14	50. Hawaii	
Wyoming	427,000	94.1	9	51. District of Columbia	
United States	199,686,000	80.3	35		

Source: U.S. Department of Commerce, Bureau of the Census, *Statistical Abstract of the United States, 1992* (Washington, D.C.: Government Printing Office, 1992).

State	African American population	% of state population	Rank by %	By %
Alabama	1,021,000	25.3	6	1. District of Columbia
Alaska	22,000	4.0	32	2. Mississippi
Arizona	111,000	3.0	37	3. Louisiana
Arkansas	374,000	15.9	12	4. South Carolina
California	2,209,000	7.4	25	5. Georgia
Colorado	133,000	4.0	31	6. Alabama
Connecticut	274,000	8.3	22	7. Maryland
Delaware	112,000	16.8	10	8. North Carolina
District of Columbia	400,000	65.9	1	9. Virginia
Florida	1,760,000	13.6	16	10. Delaware
Georgia	1,747,000	27.0	5	11. Tennessee
Hawaii	27,000	2.4	38	12. Arkansas
Idaho	3,000	0.3	50	13. New York
Illinois	1,694,000	14.8	14	14. Illinois
Indiana	432,000	7.8	23	15. Michigan
Iowa	48,000	1.7	41	16. Florida
Kansas	143,000	5.8	28	17. New Jersey
Kentucky	263,000	7.1	26	18. Texas
Louisiana	1,299,000	30.8	3	19. Missouri
Maine	5,000	0.4	48	20. Ohio
Maryland	1,190,000	24.9	7	21. Pennsylvania
Massachusetts	300,000	5.0	30	22. Connecticut
Michigan	1,292,000	13.9	15	23. Indiana
Minnesota	95,000	2.2	39	24. Oklahoma
Mississippi	915,000	35.6	2	25. California
Missouri	548,000	10.7	19	26. Kentucky
Montana	2,000	0.3	51	27. Nevada
Nebraska	57,000	3.6	34	28. Kansas
Nevada	79,000	6.6	27	29. Wisconsin
New Hampshire	7,000	0.6	45	30. Massachusetts
New Jersey	1,037,000	13.4	17	31. Colorado
New Mexico	30,000	2.0	40	32. Alaska
New York	2,859,000	15.9	13	33. Rhode Island
North Carolina	1,456,000	22.0	8	34. Nebraska
North Dakota	4,000	0.6	46	35. West Virginia
Ohio	1,155,000	10.6	20	36. Washington
Oklahoma	234,000	7.4	24	37. Arizona
Oregon	46,000	1.6	42	38. Hawaii
Pennsylvania	1,090,000	9.2	21	39. Minnesota
Rhode Island	39,000	3.9	33	40. New Mexico
South Carolina	1,040,000	29.8	4	41. Iowa
South Dakota	3,000	0.4	47	42. Oregon
Tennessee	778,000	16.0	11	43. Wyoming
Texas	2,022,000	11.9	18	44. Utah
Utah	12,000	0.7	44	45. New Hampshire
Vermont	2,000	0.4	49	46. North Dakota
Virginia	1,163,000	18.8	9	47. South Dakota
Washington	150,000	3.1	36	48. Maine
West Virginia	56,000	3.1	35	49. Vermont
Wisconsin	245,000	5.0	29	50. Idaho
Wyoming	4,000	0.9	43	51. Montana
United States	29,986,000	12.1	18	

Source: U.S. Department of Commerce, Bureau of the Census, *Statistical Abstract of the United States, 1992* (Washington, D.C.: Government Printing Office, 1992).

HISPANIC POPULATION, 1990				Rank in order
State	**Hispanic population**	**% of state population**	**Rank by %**	**By %**
Alabama	25,000	0.6	48	1. New Mexico
Alaska	18,000	3.3	22	2. California
Arizona	688,000	18.8	4	3. Texas
Arkansas	20,000	0.9	42	4. Arizona
California	7,688,000	25.8	2	5. Colorado
Colorado	424,000	12.9	5	6. New York
Connecticut	213,000	6.5	12	7. Florida
Delaware	16,000	2.4	26	8. Nevada
District of Columbia	33,000	5.4	14	9. New Jersey
Florida	1,574,000	12.2	7	10. Illinois
Georgia	109,000	1.7	33	11. Hawaii
Hawaii	81,000	7.3	11	12. Connecticut
Idaho	53,000	5.3	15	13. Wyoming
Illinois	904,000	7.9	10	14. District of Columbia
Indiana	99,000	1.8	32	15. Idaho
Iowa	33,000	1.2	38	16. Utah
Kansas	94,000	3.8	21	17. Massachusetts
Kentucky	22,000	0.6	49	18. Rhode Island
Louisiana	93,000	2.2	28	19. Washington
Maine	7,000	0.6	50	20. Oregon
Maryland	125,000	2.6	24	21. Kansas
Massachusetts	288,000	4.8	17	22. Alaska
Michigan	202,000	2.2	29	23. Oklahoma
Minnesota	54,000	1.2	36	24. Maryland
Mississippi	16,000	0.6	47	25. Virginia
Missouri	62,000	1.2	37	26. Delaware
Montana	12,000	1.5	34	27. Nebraska
Nebraska	37,000	2.3	27	28. Louisiana
Nevada	124,000	10.3	8	29. Michigan
New Hampshire	11,000	1.0	40	30. Pennsylvania
New Jersey	740,000	9.6	9	31. Wisconsin
New Mexico	579,000	38.2	1	32. Indiana
New York	2,214,000	12.3	6	33. Georgia
North Carolina	77,000	1.2	39	34. Montana
North Dakota	5,000	0.8	43	35. Ohio
Ohio	140,000	1.3	35	36. Minnesota
Oklahoma	86,000	2.7	23	37. Missouri
Oregon	113,000	4.0	20	38. Iowa
Pennsylvania	232,000	2.0	30	39. North Carolina
Rhode Island	46,000	4.6	18	40. New Hampshire
South Carolina	31,000	0.9	41	41. South Carolina
South Dakota	5,000	0.7	44	42. Arkansas
Tennessee	33,000	0.7	46	43. North Dakota
Texas	4,340,000	25.5	3	44. South Dakota
Utah	85,000	4.9	16	45. Vermont
Vermont	4,000	0.7	45	46. Tennessee
Virginia	160,000	2.6	25	47. Mississippi
Washington	215,000	4.4	19	48. Alabama
West Virginia	8,000	0.4	51	49. Kentucky
Wisconsin	93,000	1.9	31	50. Maine
Wyoming	26,000	5.7	13	51. West Virginia
United States	**22,354,000**	**9.0**	**10**	

Source: U.S. Department of Commerce, Bureau of the Census, *Statistical Abstract of the United States, 1992* (Washington, D.C.: Government Printing Office, 1992).

Note: Persons of Hispanic origin may be of any race.

| ASIAN AMERICAN POPULATION, 1990 | | | | Rank in order |
State	Asian American population	% of state population	Rank by %	By %
Alabama	22,000	0.5	44	1. Hawaii
Alaska	20,000	3.6	5	2. California
Arizona	55,000	1.5	20	3. Washington
Arkansas	13,000	0.6	43	4. New York
California	2,846,000	9.6	2	5. Alaska
Colorado	60,000	1.8	15	6. New Jersey
Connecticut	51,000	1.6	19	7. Nevada
Delaware	9,000	1.4	21	8. Maryland
District of Columbia	11,000	1.8	16	9. Virginia
Florida	154,000	1.2	23	10. Illinois
Georgia	76,000	1.2	24	11. Oregon
Hawaii	685,000	61.8	1	12. Massachusetts
Idaho	9,000	0.9	32	13. Utah
Illinois	285,000	2.5	10	14. Texas
Indiana	38,000	0.7	38	15. Colorado
Iowa	25,000	0.9	31	16. District of Columbia
Kansas	32,000	1.3	22	17. Rhode Island
Kentucky	18,000	0.5	48	18. Minnesota
Louisiana	41,000	1.0	29	19. Connecticut
Maine	7,000	0.6	42	20. Arizona
Maryland	140,000	2.9	8	21. Delaware
Massachusetts	143,000	2.4	12	22. Kansas
Michigan	105,000	1.1	26	23. Florida
Minnesota	78,000	1.8	18	24. Georgia
Mississippi	13,000	0.5	46	25. Pennsylvania
Missouri	41,000	0.8	35	26. Michigan
Montana	4,000	0.5	47	27. Wisconsin
Nebraska	12,000	0.8	37	28. Oklahoma
Nevada	38,000	3.2	7	29. Louisiana
New Hampshire	9,000	0.8	34	30. New Mexico
New Jersey	273,000	3.5	6	31. Iowa
New Mexico	14,000	0.9	30	32. Idaho
New York	694,000	3.9	4	33. Ohio
North Carolina	52,000	0.8	36	34. New Hampshire
North Dakota	3,000	0.5	49	35. Missouri
Ohio	91,000	0.8	33	36. North Carolina
Oklahoma	34,000	1.1	28	37. Nebraska
Oregon	69,000	2.4	11	38. Indiana
Pennsylvania	137,000	1.2	25	39. Wyoming
Rhode Island	18,000	1.8	17	40. Tennessee
South Carolina	22,000	0.6	41	41. South Carolina
South Dakota	3,000	0.4	50	42. Maine
Tennessee	32,000	0.7	40	43. Arkansas
Texas	319,000	1.9	14	44. Alabama
Utah	33,000	1.9	13	45. Vermont
Vermont	3,000	0.5	45	46. Mississippi
Virginia	159,000	2.6	9	47. Montana
Washington	211,000	4.3	3	48. Kentucky
West Virginia	7,000	0.4	51	49. North Dakota
Wisconsin	54,000	1.1	27	50. South Dakota
Wyoming	3,000	0.7	39	51. West Virginia
United States	7,274,000	2.9	9	

Source: U.S. Department of Commerce, Bureau of the Census, *Statistical Abstract of the United States, 1992* (Washington, D.C.: Government Printing Office, 1992).

Note: Asian Americans include Pacific Islanders.

NATIVE AMERICAN POPULATION, 1990				Rank in order
State	Native American population	% of state population	Rank by %	By %
Alabama	17,000	0.4	26	1. Alaska
Alaska	86,000	15.6	1	2. New Mexico
Arizona	204,000	5.6	6	3. Oklahoma
Arkansas	13,000	0.6	22	4. South Dakota
California	242,000	0.8	18	5. Montana
Colorado	28,000	0.9	17	6. Arizona
Connecticut	7,000	0.2	40	7. North Dakota
Delaware	2,000	0.3	33	8. Wyoming
District of Columbia	1,000	0.2	48	9. Nevada
Florida	36,000	0.3	34	Washington
Georgia	13,000	0.2	42	11. Utah
Hawaii	5,000	0.5	24	12. Idaho
Idaho	14,000	1.4	12	13. Oregon
Illinois	22,000	0.2	45	14. North Carolina
Indiana	13,000	0.2	38	15. Minnesota
Iowa	7,000	0.3	36	16. Kansas
Kansas	22,000	0.9	16	17. Colorado
Kentucky	6,000	0.2	49	18. California
Louisiana	19,000	0.5	25	19. Wisconsin
Maine	6,000	0.5	23	20. Nebraska
Maryland	13,000	0.3	35	21. Michigan
Massachusetts	12,000	0.2	43	22. Arkansas
Michigan	56,000	0.6	21	23. Maine
Minnesota	50,000	1.1	15	24. Hawaii
Mississippi	9,000	0.4	31	25. Louisiana
Missouri	20,000	0.4	28	26. Alabama
Montana	48,000	6.0	5	27. Rhode Island
Nebraska	12,000	0.8	20	28. Missouri
Nevada	20,000	1.7	9	29. Texas
New Hampshire	2,000	0.2	47	30. Vermont
New Jersey	15,000	0.2	44	31. Mississippi
New Mexico	134,000	8.8	2	New York
New York	63,000	0.4	31	33. Delaware
North Carolina	80,000	1.2	14	34. Florida
North Dakota	26,000	4.1	7	35. Maryland
Ohio	20,000	0.2	46	36. Iowa
Oklahoma	252,000	8.0	3	37. Virginia
Oregon	38,000	1.3	13	38. Indiana
Pennsylvania	15,000	0.1	50	39. South Carolina
Rhode Island	4,000	0.4	27	40. Connecticut
South Carolina	8,000	0.2	39	41. Tennessee
South Dakota	51,000	7.3	4	42. Georgia
Tennessee	10,000	0.2	41	43. Massachusetts
Texas	66,000	0.4	29	44. New Jersey
Utah	24,000	1.4	11	45. Illinois
Vermont	2,000	0.4	30	46. Ohio
Virginia	15,000	0.2	37	47. New Hampshire
Washington	81,000	1.7	9	48. District of Columbia
West Virginia	2,000	0.1	51	49. Kentucky
Wisconsin	39,000	0.8	19	50. Pennsylvania
Wyoming	9,000	2.0	8	51. West Virginia
United States	1,959,000	0.8	20	

Source: U.S. Department of Commerce, Bureau of the Census, *Statistical Abstract of the United States, 1992* (Washington, D.C.: Government Printing Office, 1992).

State	Catholic population	% of state population	Rank by %	Rank in order By %
Alabama	124,725	3.1	48	1. District of Columbia
Alaska	44,612	7.8	39	2. Rhode Island
Arizona	667,947	17.8	26	3. Massachusetts
Arkansas	73,568	3.1	47	4. New Jersey
California	7,299,032	24.0	17	5. Connecticut
Colorado	482,264	14.3	30	6. New York
Connecticut	1,342,213	40.8	5	7. Louisiana
Delaware	139,341	20.5	23	8. Wisconsin
District of Columbia	400,000	66.9	1	9. Illinois
Florida	1,660,298	12.5	32	10. Pennsylvania
Georgia	235,707	3.6	46	11. New Mexico
Hawaii	232,780	20.5	22	12. New Hampshire
Idaho	72,051	6.9	40	13. North Dakota
Illinois	3,584,619	31.1	9	14. Minnesota
Indiana	692,938	12.4	33	15. Vermont
Iowa	526,972	18.9	25	16. Michigan
Kansas	373,380	15.0	29	17. California
Kentucky	356,841	9.6	36	18. South Dakota
Louisiana	1,377,768	32.4	7	19. Nebraska
Maine	256,113	20.7	20	20. Maine
Maryland	451,576	9.3	38	21. Texas
Massachusetts	2,923,331	48.8	3	22. Hawaii
Michigan	2,267,122	24.2	16	23. Delaware
Minnesota	1,123,865	25.4	14	24. Ohio
Mississippi	102,471	4.0	44	25. Iowa
Missouri	814,840	15.8	27	26. Arizona
Montana	126,814	15.7	28	27. Missouri
Nebraska	334,530	21.0	19	28. Montana
Nevada	152,000	11.8	34	29. Kansas
New Hampshire	304,541	27.6	12	30. Colorado
New Jersey	3,211,540	41.4	4	31. Wyoming
New Mexico	455,991	29.5	11	32. Florida
New York	7,275,427	40.3	6	33. Indiana
North Carolina	151,170	2.2	51	34. Nevada
North Dakota	173,335	27.3	13	35. Oregon
Ohio	2,203,781	20.2	24	36. Kentucky
Oklahoma	138,284	4.4	43	37. Washington
Oregon	286,461	9.8	35	38. Maryland
Pennsylvania	3,630,959	30.4	10	39. Alaska
Rhode Island	632,931	63.0	2	40. Idaho
South Carolina	80,206	2.3	50	41. Virginia
South Dakota	152,143	21.6	18	42. West Virginia
Tennessee	136,427	2.8	49	43. Oklahoma
Texas	3,582,859	20.7	21	44. Mississippi
Utah	67,120	3.8	45	45. Utah
Vermont	142,208	25.1	15	46. Georgia
Virginia	403,852	6.4	41	47. Arkansas
Washington	470,838	9.4	37	48. Alabama
West Virginia	105,862	5.9	42	49. Tennessee
Wisconsin	1,574,080	31.8	8	50. South Carolina
Wyoming	63,737	13.9	31	51. North Carolina
United States	**53,483,470**	**21.2**	**19**	

Source: P. J. Kenedy & Sons, *The Official Catholic Directory 1991*, (New Providence, N.J.: P. J. Kenedy & Sons, 1991).

State	Estimated Jewish population	% of state population	Rank by %	By %
Alabama	9,000	0.2	40	1. New York
Alaska	2,400	0.4	32	2. New Jersey
Arizona	72,000	2.0	11	3. Florida
Arkansas	1,800	0.1	47	4. Massachusetts
California	923,000	3.1	8	5. Maryland
Colorado	51,000	1.5	14	6. District of Columbia
Connecticut	106,000	3.2	7	7. Connecticut
Delaware	9,500	1.4	15	8. California
District of Columbia	25,500	4.2	6	9. Pennsylvania
Florida	593,000	4.6	3	10. Illinois
Georgia	74,000	1.1	19	11. Arizona
Hawaii	7,000	0.6	27	12. Nevada
Idaho	500	0.1	50	13. Rhode Island
Illinois	257,000	2.2	10	14. Colorado
Indiana	18,000	0.3	36	15. Delaware
Iowa	6,000	0.2	41	16. Ohio
Kansas	14,000	0.6	29	17. Missouri
Kentucky	11,500	0.3	37	18. Michigan
Louisiana	15,500	0.4	34	19. Georgia
Maine	8,500	0.7	24	20. Virginia
Maryland	211,000	4.4	5	21. Vermont
Massachusetts	275,000	4.6	4	22. Wisconsin
Michigan	107,000	1.2	18	23. Minnesota
Minnesota	30,500	0.7	23	24. Maine
Mississippi	1,700	0.1	48	25. Washington
Missouri	61,500	1.2	17	26. Texas
Montana	500	0.1	49	27. Hawaii
Nebraska	7,500	0.5	31	28. New Hampshire
Nevada	20,500	1.7	12	29. Kansas
New Hampshire	7,000	0.6	28	30. Oregon
New Jersey	426,000	5.5	2	31. Nebraska
New Mexico	6,000	0.4	33	32. Alaska
New York	1,644,000	9.1	1	33. New Mexico
North Carolina	16,500	0.2	38	34. Louisiana
North Dakota	700	0.1	45	35. Tennessee
Ohio	131,000	1.2	16	36. Indiana
Oklahoma	5,500	0.2	42	37. Kentucky
Oregon	15,500	0.5	30	38. North Carolina
Pennsylvania	330,000	2.8	9	39. South Carolina
Rhode Island	16,000	1.6	13	40. Alabama
South Carolina	8,000	0.2	39	41. Iowa
South Dakota	350	0.1	50	42. Oklahoma
Tennessee	17,500	0.4	35	43. Utah
Texas	109,000	0.6	26	44. West Virginia
Utah	3,000	0.2	43	45. North Dakota
Vermont	4,500	0.8	21	Wyoming
Virginia	67,500	1.1	20	47. Arkansas
Washington	33,000	0.7	25	48. Mississippi
West Virginia	2,500	0.1	44	49. Montana
Wisconsin	34,500	0.7	22	50. Idaho
Wyoming	500	0.1	45	South Dakota
United States	**5,798,000**	**2.3**	**10**	

Source: Jewish population estimates from *American Jewish Year Book 1992* (New York and Philadelphia: American Jewish Committee and Jewish Publication Society, 1992). Copyright © 1992.

State	Marriages	Per 1,000 population		Rank in order
		Rate	Rank	By rate per 1,000 population
Alabama	43,263	10.5	15	1. Nevada
Alaska	5,730	10.8	11	2. Hawaii
Arizona	37,007	10.2	18	3. South Carolina
Arkansas	35,703	14.8	4	4. Arkansas
California	236,693	7.9	43	5. Idaho
Colorado	31,512	9.4	25	6. Kentucky
Connecticut	27,806	8.6	35	7. Tennessee
Delaware	5,628	8.2	39	8. Virginia
District of Columbia	4,716	7.9	43	9. Utah
Florida	142,292	10.9	10	10. Florida
Georgia	64,359	9.8	20	11. Alaska
Hawaii	18,144	16.1	2	South Dakota
Idaho	14,977	14.6	5	13. Texas
Illinois	97,082	8.3	38	Vermont
Indiana	54,295	9.6	22	15. Alabama
Iowa	24,813	8.7	32	16. Oklahoma
Kansas	23,385	9.2	30	Wyoming
Kentucky	51,291	13.8	6	18. Arizona
Louisiana	41,161	9.4	25	19. Washington
Maine	11,773	9.5	23	20. Georgia
Maryland	46,081	9.7	21	21. Maryland
Massachusetts	47,822	8.1	41	22. Indiana
Michigan	76,137	8.2	39	23. Maine
Minnesota	33,695	7.7	46	Missouri
Mississippi	24,322	9.3	29	25. Colorado
Missouri	49,251	9.5	23	Louisiana
Montana	7,025	8.7	32	New Hampshire
Nebraska	12,484	7.7	46	New York
Nevada	123,356	105.6	1	29. Mississippi
New Hampshire	10,582	9.4	25	30. Kansas
New Jersey	58,012	7.5	48	31. Oregon
New Mexico	13,175	8.5	36	32. Iowa
New York	169,264	9.4	25	Montana
North Carolina	52,070	7.8	45	Ohio
North Dakota	4,779	7.3	49	35. Connecticut
Ohio	95,827	8.7	32	36. New Mexico
Oklahoma	33,162	10.3	16	37. Wisconsin
Oregon	25,211	8.8	31	38. Illinois
Pennsylvania	86,794	7.2	50	39. Delaware
Rhode Island	8,113	8.1	41	Michigan
South Carolina	55,837	15.7	3	41. Massachusetts
South Dakota	7,727	10.8	11	Rhode Island
Tennessee	66,597	13.4	7	43. California
Texas	182,831	10.7	13	District of Columbia
Utah	19,012	11.0	9	45. North Carolina
Vermont	6,144	10.7	13	46. Minnesota
Virginia	71,257	11.5	8	Nebraska
Washington	48,642	10.0	19	48. New Jersey
West Virginia	13,166	7.2	50	49. North Dakota
Wisconsin	41,160	8.4	37	50. Pennsylvania
Wyoming	4,843	10.3	16	West Virginia
United States	2,466,008	9.4	25	

Source: National Center for Health Statistics, *Monthly Vital Statistics Report* 40, no. 13 (September 30, 1992).

DIVORCES, 1990		Per 1,000 population		Rank in order

State	Divorces	Rate	Rank	By rate per 1,000 population
Alabama	25,280	6.1	9	1. Nevada
Alaska	2,921	5.5	12	2. Oklahoma
Arizona	25,096	6.9	3	3. Arizona
Arkansas	16,765	6.9	3	Arkansas
California	127,967	4.3	33	5. Wyoming
Colorado	18,385	5.5	12	6. Idaho
Connecticut	10,301	3.2	46	Tennessee
Delaware	2,985	4.4	31	8. Florida
District of Columbia	2,686	4.5	28	9. Alabama
Florida	81,655	6.3	8	10. Washington
Georgia	35,672	5.5	12	11. Kentucky
Hawaii	5,168	4.6	27	12. Alaska
Idaho	6,634	6.5	6	Colorado
Illinois	44,259	3.8	38	Georgia
Indiana	NA	NA	NA	Mississippi
Iowa	11,060	3.9	37	Oregon
Kansas	12,623	5.0	23	Texas
Kentucky	21,790	5.8	11	18. West Virginia
Louisiana	NA	NA	NA	19. Missouri
Maine	5,275	4.3	33	Montana
Maryland	16,055	3.4	44	North Carolina
Massachusetts	16,781	2.8	49	Utah
Michigan	40,219	4.3	33	23. Kansas
Minnesota	15,421	3.5	43	24. New Mexico
Mississippi	14,444	5.5	12	25. New Hampshire
Missouri	26,351	5.1	19	Ohio
Montana	4,093	5.1	19	27. Hawaii
Nebraska	6,488	4.0	36	28. District of Columbia
Nevada	13,290	11.4	1	South Carolina
New Hampshire	5,279	4.7	25	Vermont
New Jersey	23,612	3.0	48	31. Delaware
New Mexico	7,652	4.9	24	Virginia
New York	57,863	3.2	46	33. California
North Carolina	34,017	5.1	19	Maine
North Dakota	2,326	3.6	41	Michigan
Ohio	50,989	4.7	25	36. Nebraska
Oklahoma	24,919	7.7	2	37. Iowa
Oregon	15,884	5.5	12	38. Illinois
Pennsylvania	40,123	3.3	45	39. Rhode Island
Rhode Island	3,754	3.7	39	South Dakota
South Carolina	16,080	4.5	28	41. North Dakota
South Dakota	2,648	3.7	39	Wisconsin
Tennessee	32,295	6.5	6	43. Minnesota
Texas	94,044	5.5	12	44. Maryland
Utah	8,786	5.1	19	45. Pennsylvania
Vermont	2,616	4.5	28	46. Connecticut
Virginia	27,266	4.4	31	New York
Washington	28,773	5.9	10	48. New Jersey
West Virginia	9,658	5.3	18	49. Massachusetts
Wisconsin	17,832	3.6	41	NA Indiana
Wyoming	3,095	6.6	5	NA Louisiana
United States	**1,119,175**	**4.7**	**25**	

NA not available.

Source: National Center for Health Statistics, *Monthly Vital Statistics Report* 40, no. 13 (September 30, 1992).

State	Births	Per 1,000 population	
		Rate	Rank
Alabama	60,513	14.6	33
Alaska	11,245	21.1	1
Arizona	67,656	18.3	6
Arkansas	34,588	14.2	44
California	605,694	19.8	3
Colorado	53,968	16.1	18
Connecticut	48,282	14.8	29
Delaware	11,175	16.0	19
District of Columbia	9,971	17.0	11
Florida	194,457	14.6	33
Georgia	110,024	16.6	12
Hawaii	20,014	17.5	8
Idaho	17,233	16.6	12
Illinois	193,987	16.5	15
Indiana	84,707	14.9	28
Iowa	36,011	12.6	50
Kansas	37,300	14.6	33
Kentucky	54,913	14.7	30
Louisiana	74,562	17.2	10
Maine	16,581	13.2	48
Maryland	84,452	17.5	8
Massachusetts	86,321	14.5	38
Michigan	153,359	16.4	16
Minnesota	67,020	15.1	25
Mississippi	43,522	16.6	12
Missouri	77,991	15.0	27
Montana	11,544	14.3	43
Nebraska	23,933	14.7	30
Nevada	22,973	18.8	4
New Hampshire	16,060	13.9	46
New Jersey	117,789	15.1	25
New Mexico	28,160	18.0	7
New York	292,400	16.2	17
North Carolina	102,442	15.2	23
North Dakota	9,071	14.0	45
Ohio	158,638	14.4	42
Oklahoma	47,312	14.7	30
Oregon	42,807	14.6	33
Pennsylvania	168,584	13.9	46
Rhode Island	14,591	14.5	38
South Carolina	57,742	16.0	19
South Dakota	11,042	15.4	21
Tennessee	73,104	14.5	38
Texas	325,562	18.8	4
Utah	35,070	20.1	2
Vermont	7,712	13.2	48
Virginia	96,610	15.4	21
Washington	75,734	15.2	23
West Virginia	22,195	12.2	51
Wisconsin	71,736	14.5	38
Wyoming	6,801	14.6	33
United States	**4,095,158**	**16.2**	**17**

By rate per 1,000 population

1. Alaska
2. Utah
3. California
4. Nevada
   Texas
6. Arizona
7. New Mexico
8. Hawaii
   Maryland
10. Louisiana
11. District of Columbia
12. Georgia
    Idaho
    Mississippi
15. Illinois
16. Michigan
17. New York
18. Colorado
19. Delaware
    South Carolina
21. South Dakota
    Virginia
23. North Carolina
    Washington
25. Minnesota
    New Jersey
27. Missouri
28. Indiana
29. Connecticut
30. Kentucky
    Nebraska
    Oklahoma
33. Alabama
    Florida
    Kansas
    Oregon
    Wyoming
38. Massachusetts
    Rhode Island
    Tennessee
    Wisconsin
42. Ohio
43. Montana
44. Arkansas
45. North Dakota
46. New Hampshire
    Pennsylvania
48. Maine
    Vermont
50. Iowa
51. West Virginia

Source: National Center for Health Statistics, *Monthly Vital Statistics Report* 40, no. 13 (September 30, 1992).

BIRTHS TO SINGLE MOTHERS, 1990				Rank in order
State	**Births to single mothers**	**Per 1,000 live births**		**By rate per 1,000 live births**
		Rate	**Rank**	
Alabama	19,131	301.3	13	1. District of Columbia
Alaska	3,113	261.6	25	2. Mississippi
Arizona	22,532	326.6	8	3. Louisiana
Arkansas	10,713	293.9	15	4. New Mexico
California	193,559	315.9	11	5. New York
Colorado	11,374	212.5	41	6. Georgia
Connecticut	13,330	265.9	21	7. South Carolina
Delaware	3,222	289.9	17	8. Arizona
District of Columbia	7,692	649.1	1	9. Illinois
Florida	63,169	316.9	10	10. Florida
Georgia	36,979	328.2	6	11. California
Hawaii	5,088	248.3	31	12. Tennessee
Idaho	2,738	166.6	50	13. Alabama
Illinois	62,148	317.4	9	14. Maryland
Indiana	22,562	261.7	24	15. Arkansas
Iowa	8,282	210.2	42	North Carolina
Kansas	8,397	215.2	40	17. Delaware
Kentucky	12,829	236.0	37	18. Ohio
Louisiana	26,601	368.5	3	19. Pennsylvania
Maine	3,931	226.5	39	20. Missouri
Maryland	23,789	296.5	14	21. Connecticut
Massachusetts	22,886	247.0	32	22. Rhode Island
Michigan	40,289	262.1	23	23. Michigan
Minnesota	14,192	208.7	43	24. Indiana
Mississippi	17,627	404.6	2	25. Alaska
Missouri	22,643	285.7	20	26. Virginia
Montana	2,757	237.4	35	27. Oregon
Nebraska	5,056	207.4	44	28. West Virginia
Nevada	5,480	253.7	29	29. Nevada
New Hampshire	2,967	168.9	49	30. Oklahoma
New Jersey	29,756	243.3	33	31. Hawaii
New Mexico	9,704	354.1	4	32. Massachusetts
New York	98,110	329.7	5	33. New Jersey
North Carolina	30,718	293.9	15	34. Wisconsin
North Dakota	1,699	183.7	47	35. Montana
Ohio	48,289	289.3	18	36. Washington
Oklahoma	11,998	251.8	30	37. Kentucky
Oregon	11,041	257.4	27	38. South Dakota
Pennsylvania	49,258	286.4	19	39. Maine
Rhode Island	3,997	263.0	22	40. Kansas
South Carolina	19,148	326.7	7	41. Colorado
South Dakota	2,515	228.7	38	42. Iowa
Tennessee	22,662	302.3	12	43. Minnesota
Texas	55,435	175.2	48	44. Nebraska
Utah	4,910	135.3	51	45. Vermont
Vermont	1,666	201.4	45	46. Wyoming
Virginia	25,874	260.4	26	47. North Dakota
Washington	18,746	236.5	36	48. Texas
West Virginia	5,743	254.3	28	49. New Hampshire
Wisconsin	17,656	242.2	34	50. Idaho
Wyoming	1,383	198.0	46	51. Utah
United States	**1,165,384**	**280.3**	**21**	

Source: National Center for Health Statistics, *Monthly Vital Statistics Report* 41, no. 9 (February 25, 1993).

State	Births to single teenagers as % of all births	Rank by %	Rank in order By %
Alabama	11.7	5	1. District of Columbia
Alaska	6.3	45	2. Mississippi
Arizona	9.5	15	3 Louisiana
Arkansas	11.1	7	4. South Carolina
California	7.5	28	5. Alabama
Colorado	7.4	31	6. Georgia
Connecticut	6.7	42	7. Arkansas
Delaware	9.8	13	8. New Mexico
District of Columbia	17.2	1	9. North Carolina
Florida	9.6	14	10. Illinois
Georgia	11.4	6	11. Tennessee
Hawaii	7.1	36	12. Ohio
Idaho	5.8	47	13. Delaware
Illinois	10.6	10	14. Florida
Indiana	9.1	18	15. Arizona
Iowa	7.2	35	Missouri
Kansas	7.1	36	17. West Virginia
Kentucky	8.7	21	18. Indiana
Louisiana	12.4	3	19. Oklahoma
Maine	7.5	28	Pennsylvania
Maryland	8.6	22	21. Kentucky
Massachusetts	6.8	41	22. Maryland
Michigan	8.6	22	Michigan
Minnesota	5.9	46	24. Wisconsin
Mississippi	15.8	2	25. Oregon
Missouri	9.5	15	Rhode Island
Montana	6.7	42	Virginia
Nebraska	6.6	44	28. California
Nevada	7.1	36	Maine
New Hampshire	5.2	50	South Dakota
New Jersey	7.1	36	31. Colorado
New Mexico	11.0	8	New York
New York	7.4	31	Texas
North Carolina	10.8	9	34. Washington
North Dakota	5.3	49	35. Iowa
Ohio	10.1	12	36. Hawaii
Oklahoma	8.9	19	Kansas
Oregon	7.9	25	Nevada
Pennsylvania	8.9	19	New Jersey
Rhode Island	7.9	25	40. Wyoming
South Carolina	12.0	4	41. Massachusetts
South Dakota	7.5	28	42. Connecticut
Tennessee	10.3	11	Montana
Texas	7.4	31	44. Nebraska
Utah	4.7	51	45. Alaska
Vermont	5.7	48	46. Minnesota
Virginia	7.9	25	47. Idaho
Washington	7.3	34	48. Vermont
West Virginia	9.3	17	49. North Dakota
Wisconsin	8.0	24	50. New Hampshire
Wyoming	7.0	40	51. Utah
United States	**8.6**	**22**	

Source: Center for the Study of Social Policy, *Kids Count Data Book: State Profiles of Child Well-Being* (Washington, D.C.: Center for the Study of Social Policy, 1992).

ADOPTIONS. 1986				Rank in order
		Per 1,000 population		**By rate per 1,000 population**
State	**Total adoptions**	**Rate**	**Rank**	
Alabama	2,480	0.61	16	1. Alaska
Alaska	662	1.25	1	2. Montana
Arizona	1,303	0.40	40	3. Utah
Arkansas	1,541	0.65	12	4. Maine
California	5,069	0.19	50	5. North Dakota
Colorado	2,036	0.62	14	6. Oklahoma
Connecticut	975	0.31	45	7. Indiana
Delaware	186	0.29	46	8. South Dakota
District of Columbia	326	0.52	22	9. New Mexico
Florida	7,683	0.66	10	10. Florida
Georgia	2,732	0.45	31	11. West Virginia
Hawaii	276	0.26	48	12. Arkansas
Idaho	330	0.33	43	13. Nebraska
Illinois	5,430	0.47	27	14. Colorado
Indiana	3,791	0.69	7	15. Vermont
Iowa	1,504	0.53	20	16. Alabama
Kansas	990	0.40	38	17. Mississippi
Kentucky	1,040	0.28	47	North Carolina
Louisiana	1,683	0.37	41	19. Texas
Maine	873	0.75	4	20. Iowa
Maryland	1,400	0.31	44	21. Missouri
Massachusetts	2,334	0.40	39	22. District of Columbia
Michigan	4,115	0.45	30	23. Rhode Island
Minnesota	2,100	0.50	25	24. New Hampshire
Mississippi	1,468	0.56	17	25. Minnesota
Missouri	2,660	0.53	21	26. Washington
Montana	652	0.80	2	27. Illinois
Nebraska	1,009	0.63	13	28. South Carolina
Nevada	427	0.43	33	29. Wyoming
New Hampshire	512	0.50	24	30. Michigan
New Jersey	1,631	0.21	49	31. Georgia
New Mexico	979	0.66	9	32. Oregon
New York	7,213	0.41	36	33. Nevada
North Carolina	3,535	0.56	17	Tennessee
North Dakota	484	0.71	5	35. Wisconsin
Ohio	1,898	0.18	51	36. New York
Oklahoma	2,350	0.71	6	Virginia
Oregon	1,161	0.43	32	38. Kansas
Pennsylvania	4,105	0.35	42	39. Massachusetts
Rhode Island	493	0.51	23	40. Arizona
South Carolina	1,569	0.46	28	41. Louisiana
South Dakota	482	0.68	8	42. Pennsylvania
Tennessee	2,058	0.43	33	43. Idaho
Texas	8,998	0.54	19	44. Maryland
Utah	1,261	0.76	3	45. Connecticut
Vermont	333	0.62	15	46. Delaware
Virginia	2,348	0.41	36	47. Kentucky
Washington	2,133	0.48	26	48. Hawaii
West Virginia	1,254	0.65	11	49. New Jersey
Wisconsin	1,984	0.42	35	50. California
Wyoming	232	0.46	29	51. Ohio
United States	**104,088**	**0.43**	**32**	

Source: National Committee for Adoption, *Adoption Factbook: U.S. Data, Issues, Regulations and Resources* (Washington, D.C.: National Committee for Adoption, 1989).

ADOPTION OPTION INDEX, 1989			Rank in order
State	**Adoption option index**	**Rank**	**By adoption option index**
Alabama	8.2	37	1. Utah
Alaska	27.1	5	2. Idaho
Arizona	8.3	36	3. South Dakota
Arkansas	27.1	6	4. Oregon
California	4.8	46	5. Alaska
Colorado	9.5	31	6. Arkansas
Connecticut	10.1	27	7. Montana
Delaware	3.5	48	8. Oklahoma
District of Columbia	2.6	49	9. Wyoming
Florida	15.2	16	10. Illinois
Georgia	9.9	30	11. South Carolina
Hawaii	5.0	45	12. Vermont
Idaho	35.4	2	13. Mississippi
Illinois	22.7	10	14. Nebraska
Indiana	8.4	35	15. Wisconsin
Iowa	9.4	33	16. Florida
Kansas	14.2	18	17. West Virginia
Kentucky	13.8	21	18. Kansas
Louisiana	4.1	47	19. Texas
Maine	6.9	41	20. Washington
Maryland	7.2	39	21. Kentucky
Massachusetts	10.0	29	22. Missouri
Michigan	10.9	25	23. North Dakota
Minnesota	9.4	32	24. Rhode Island
Mississippi	17.5	13	25. Michigan
Missouri	11.8	22	26. Pennsylvania
Montana	26.1	7	27. Connecticut
Nebraska	15.7	14	28. Tennessee
Nevada	6.4	42	29. Massachusetts
New Hampshire	5.3	44	30. Georgia
New Jersey	1.4	51	31. Colorado
New Mexico	7.1	40	32. Minnesota
New York	6.4	43	33. Iowa
North Carolina	8.9	34	34. North Carolina
North Dakota	11.5	23	35. Indiana
Ohio	8.1	38	36. Arizona
Oklahoma	25.3	8	37. Alabama
Oregon	30.0	4	38. Ohio
Pennsylvania	10.2	26	39. Maryland
Rhode Island	11.0	24	40. New Mexico
South Carolina	20.9	11	41. Maine
South Dakota	30.9	3	42. Nevada
Tennessee	10.0	28	43. New York
Texas	14.0	19	44. New Hampshire
Utah	51.9	1	45. Hawaii
Vermont	20.3	12	46. California
Virginia	2.2	50	47. Louisiana
Washington	13.9	20	48. Delaware
West Virginia	14.8	17	49. District of Columbia
Wisconsin	15.4	15	50. Virginia
Wyoming	24.6	9	51. New Jersey
United States	**10.0**	**28**	

Source: National Committee for Adoption, *Adoption Factbook: U.S. Data, Issues, Regulations and Resources* (Washington, D.C.: National Committee for Adoption, 1989).

Note: The ''adoption option index'' is a standardized ratio calculated by dividing the number of domestic infant adoptions by the sum of abortions and births to unmarried women, multiplied by 1,000.

| State | Infant deaths | Per 1,000 population | | Rank in order |
		Rate	Rank	By rate per 1,000 population
Alabama	675	11.2	5	1. District of Columbia
Alaska	101	9.0	21	2. Delaware
Arizona	588	8.7	26	3. Georgia
Arkansas	361	10.4	8	4. Mississippi
California	4,748	7.8	34	5. Alabama
Colorado	446	8.3	30	6. North Carolina
Connecticut	355	7.4	40	7. South Carolina
Delaware	142	12.7	2	8. Arkansas
District of Columbia	199	20.0	1	9. Illinois
Florida	1,722	8.9	25	10. Missouri
Georgia	1,364	12.4	3	11. Michigan
Hawaii	131	6.5	47	Oklahoma
Idaho	150	8.7	26	13. Tennessee
Illinois	2,006	10.3	9	Virginia
Indiana	794	9.4	17	15. Louisiana
Iowa	279	7.7	36	16. Ohio
Kansas	352	9.4	17	17. Indiana
Kentucky	452	8.2	31	Kansas
Louisiana	716	9.6	15	New York
Maine	105	6.3	49	Pennsylvania
Maryland	684	8.1	32	21. Alaska
Massachusetts	591	6.8	46	North Dakota
Michigan	1,521	9.9	11	South Dakota
Minnesota	491	7.3	43	West Virginia
Mississippi	490	11.3	4	25. Florida
Missouri	799	10.2	10	26. Arizona
Montana	88	7.6	38	Idaho
Nebraska	177	7.4	40	28. New Jersey
Nevada	162	7.1	45	29. New Mexico
New Hampshire	105	6.5	47	30. Colorado
New Jersey	1,013	8.6	28	31. Kentucky
New Mexico	239	8.5	29	32. Maryland
New York	2,734	9.4	17	Wisconsin
North Carolina	1,123	11.0	6	34. California
North Dakota	82	9.0	21	Rhode Island
Ohio	1,500	9.5	16	36. Iowa
Oklahoma	467	9.9	11	Texas
Oregon	326	7.6	38	38. Montana
Pennsylvania	1,587	9.4	17	Oregon
Rhode Island	114	7.8	34	40. Connecticut
South Carolina	617	10.7	7	Nebraska
South Dakota	99	9.0	21	Washington
Tennessee	709	9.7	13	43. Minnesota
Texas	2,510	7.7	36	44. Wyoming
Utah	210	6.0	51	45. Nevada
Vermont	47	6.1	50	46. Massachusetts
Virginia	938	9.7	13	47. Hawaii
Washington	564	7.4	40	New Hampshire
West Virginia	199	9.0	21	49. Maine
Wisconsin	584	8.1	32	50. Vermont
Wyoming	49	7.2	44	51. Utah
United States	36,505	8.9	25	

Source: National Center for Health Statistics, *Monthly Vital Statistics Report* 40, no. 13 (September 30, 1992).

State	Child deaths	Per 100,000 children		Child suicides	As % of all child deaths	Rank by %	Rank in order — By death rate per 100,000 children
		Rate	Rank				
Alabama	301	35.2	17	8	2.7	10	1. Mississippi
Alaska	61	45.9	2	2	3.3	5	2. Alaska
Arizona	301	39.1	6	3	1.0	39	3. Arkansas
Arkansas	227	45.0	3	2	0.9	41	4. District of Columbia
California	1,857	30.5	37	26	1.4	27	5. South Carolina
Colorado	193	28.3	45	5	2.6	11	6. Arizona
Connecticut	141	24.1	50	2	1.4	26	7. Louisiana
Delaware	46	34.8	19	2	4.3	3	8. North Carolina
District of Columbia	45	40.9	4	0	0.0	49	Wyoming
Florida	842	37.8	11	14	1.7	21	10. Idaho
Georgia	499	35.9	16	5	1.0	38	11. Florida
Hawaii	67	29.5	41	1	1.5	25	12. Nevada
Idaho	92	38.2	10	5	5.4	2	South Dakota
Illinois	792	34.1	22	4	0.5	46	14. New Mexico
Indiana	377	33.4	23	2	0.5	45	15. Montana
Iowa	172	30.9	34	2	1.2	34	16. Georgia
Kansas	163	31.2	32	4	2.5	13	17. Alabama
Kentucky	243	32.5	25	3	1.2	33	Oklahoma
Louisiana	392	39.0	7	10	2.6	12	19. Delaware
Maine	76	32.3	28	1	1.3	30	20. Texas
Maryland	284	31.5	30	3	1.1	37	21. Missouri
Massachusetts	230	22.3	51	1	0.4	47	22. Illinois
Michigan	591	31.3	31	9	1.5	24	23. Indiana
Minnesota	254	28.5	44	6	2.4	17	24. West Virginia
Mississippi	283	47.3	1	8	2.8	8	25. Kentucky
Missouri	348	34.2	21	10	2.9	7	Utah
Montana	63	36.4	15	1	1.6	23	27. North Dakota
Nebraska	103	30.8	36	1	1.0	40	28. Maine
Nevada	82	37.4	12	2	2.4	14	29. Vermont
New Hampshire	64	29.5	41	0	0.0	49	30. Maryland
New Jersey	375	26.6	48	2	0.5	44	31. Michigan
New Mexico	131	36.5	14	1	0.8	42	32. Kansas
New York	1,014	30.1	38	4	0.4	48	Virginia
North Carolina	484	38.5	8	11	2.3	18	34. Iowa
North Dakota	46	32.4	27	1	2.2	20	Oregon
Ohio	645	29.5	41	8	1.2	32	36. Nebraska
Oklahoma	236	35.2	17	3	1.3	31	37. California
Oregon	169	30.9	34	4	2.4	16	38. New York
Pennsylvania	617	28.1	46	7	1.1	35	39. Tennessee
Rhode Island	45	25.3	49	1	2.2	19	40. Wisconsin
South Carolina	297	40.3	5	4	1.3	29	41. Hawaii
South Dakota	58	37.4	12	0	0.0	49	New Hampshire
Tennessee	289	29.9	39	4	1.4	28	Ohio
Texas	1,335	34.3	20	22	1.6	22	44. Minnesota
Utah	166	32.5	25	5	3.0	6	45. Colorado
Vermont	35	31.8	29	2	5.7	1	46. Pennsylvania
Virginia	357	31.2	32	4	1.1	36	47. Washington
Washington	264	27.6	47	2	0.8	43	48. New Jersey
West Virginia	118	33.2	24	4	3.4	4	49. Rhode Island
Wisconsin	294	29.8	40	8	2.7	9	50. Connecticut
Wyoming	42	38.5	8	1	2.4	15	51. Massachusetts
United States	16,206	32.4	27	240	1.5	26	

Source: National Center for Health Statistics, *Vital Statistics of the United States, 1989,* vol. II, *Mortality, Part B* (Hyattsville, Md.: Public Health Service, 1992.)

Note: Data for children are based on ages five to fourteen.

TEEN VIOLENT DEATH RATE, 1989			Rank in order
	Violent deaths per 100,000 teens		**By rate per 100,000 teens**
State	**Rate**	**Rank**	
Alabama	75.5	19	1. District of Columbia
Alaska	153.8	2	2. Alaska
Arizona	86.6	9	3. Nevada
Arkansas	94.7	5	4. New Mexico
California	79.4	14	5. Arkansas
Colorado	66.8	30	6. West Virginia
Connecticut	59.4	39	7. Wyoming
Delaware	42.6	50	8. Oklahoma
District of Columbia	237.1	1	9. Arizona
Florida	74.4	23	10. Louisiana
Georgia	80.6	13	11. Missouri
Hawaii	45.5	46	12. Montana
Idaho	79.0	15	13. Georgia
Illinois	65.6	32	14. California
Indiana	57.3	41	15. Idaho
Iowa	72.5	25	16. South Dakota
Kansas	66.7	31	17. Texas
Kentucky	73.2	24	18. Tennessee
Louisiana	86.4	10	19. Alabama
Maine	50.5	44	20. Michigan
Maryland	69.8	27	21. Oregon
Massachusetts	44.4	49	22. Mississippi
Michigan	75.0	20	23. Florida
Minnesota	61.9	34	24. Kentucky
Mississippi	74.5	22	25. Iowa
Missouri	83.2	11	26. South Carolina
Montana	80.7	12	27. Maryland
Nebraska	57.8	40	28. North Carolina
Nevada	101.4	3	29. Washington
New Hampshire	65.4	33	30. Colorado
New Jersey	41.5	51	31. Kansas
New Mexico	100.9	4	32. Illinois
New York	53.5	42	33. New Hampshire
North Carolina	69.2	28	34. Minnesota
North Dakota	44.7	48	35. Utah
Ohio	53.5	42	36. Virginia
Oklahoma	87.9	8	37. Wisconsin
Oregon	74.9	21	38. Pennsylvania
Pennsylvania	59.6	38	39. Connecticut
Rhode Island	47.1	45	40. Nebraska
South Carolina	70.0	26	41. Indiana
South Dakota	78.4	16	42. New York
Tennessee	75.8	18	Ohio
Texas	78.1	17	44. Maine
Utah	60.7	35	45. Rhode Island
Vermont	45.2	47	46. Hawaii
Virginia	60.5	36	47. Vermont
Washington	67.0	29	48. North Dakota
West Virginia	89.0	6	49. Massachusetts
Wisconsin	60.2	37	50. Delaware
Wyoming	88.2	7	51. New Jersey
United States	**69.3**	**28**	

Source: Center for the Study of Social Policy, *Kids Count Data Book: State Profiles of Child Well-Being* (Washington, D.C.: Center for the Study of Social Policy, 1992).

Note: Data for teens are based on ages fifteen to nineteen.

State	Deaths	Per 1,000 population	
		Rate	Rank
Alabama	38,027	9.2	10
Alaska	2,145	4.0	51
Arizona	29,329	7.9	34
Arkansas	24,230	10.0	6
California	218,735	7.2	45
Colorado	22,334	6.7	48
Connecticut	27,745	8.5	31
Delaware	5,880	8.4	32
District of Columbia	6,961	11.9	1
Florida	135,280	10.1	5
Georgia	52,708	7.9	34
Hawaii	6,715	5.9	49
Idaho	7,789	7.5	41
Illinois	104,389	8.9	20
Indiana	51,780	9.1	14
Iowa	25,906	9.1	14
Kansas	22,511	8.8	22
Kentucky	35,281	9.5	8
Louisiana	38,290	8.8	22
Maine	10,952	8.7	25
Maryland	37,982	7.9	34
Massachusetts	51,366	8.6	28
Michigan	79,972	8.6	28
Minnesota	35,270	7.9	34
Mississippi	25,625	9.8	7
Missouri	53,461	10.3	3
Montana	7,071	8.8	22
Nebraska	14,665	9.0	16
Nevada	9,243	7.5	41
New Hampshire	8,513	7.4	43
New Jersey	69,983	9.0	16
New Mexico	11,116	7.1	46
New York	166,795	9.2	10
North Carolina	58,909	8.7	25
North Dakota	5,648	8.7	25
Ohio	99,104	9.0	16
Oklahoma	30,349	9.5	8
Oregon	25,205	8.6	28
Pennsylvania	123,536	10.2	4
Rhode Island	9,294	9.2	10
South Carolina	29,983	8.3	33
South Dakota	6,594	9.2	10
Tennessee	45,351	9.0	16
Texas	128,926	7.4	43
Utah	9,199	5.3	50
Vermont	4,541	7.7	39
Virginia	49,151	7.8	38
Washington	37,682	7.6	40
West Virginia	19,801	10.9	2
Wisconsin	43,749	8.9	20
Wyoming	3,167	6.8	47
United States	**2,168,238**	**8.5**	**31**

Rank in order

By rate per 1,000 population

1. District of Columbia
2. West Virginia
3. Missouri
4. Pennsylvania
5. Florida
6. Arkansas
7. Mississippi
8. Kentucky
   Oklahoma
10. Alabama
    New York
    Rhode Island
    South Dakota
14. Indiana
    Iowa
16. Nebraska
    New Jersey
    Ohio
    Tennessee
20. Illinois
    Wisconsin
22. Kansas
    Louisiana
    Montana
25. Maine
    North Carolina
    North Dakota
28. Massachusetts
    Michigan
    Oregon
31. Connecticut
32. Delaware
33. South Carolina
34. Arizona
    Georgia
    Maryland
    Minnesota
38. Virginia
39. Vermont
40. Washington
41. Idaho
    Nevada
43. New Hampshire
    Texas
45. California
46. New Mexico
47. Wyoming
48. Colorado
49. Hawaii
50. Utah
51. Alaska

Source: National Center for Health Statistics, *Monthly Vital Statistics Report* 40, no. 13 (September 30, 1992).

Recreation

STATE PARKS AND RECREATION AREAS, 1990					Rank in order
State	Acres	Acreage per capita	Rank by per capita		By per capita
Alabama	50,000	0.01	42		1. Alaska
Alaska	3,169,000	5.76	1		2. Vermont
Arizona	39,000	0.01	43		3. Wyoming
Arkansas	48,000	0.02	37		4. South Dakota
California	1,299,000	0.04	19		5. Kansas
Colorado	233,000	0.07	10		6. Nevada
Connecticut	171,000	0.05	14		7. West Virginia
Delaware	12,000	0.02	40		8. Nebraska
District of Columbia	—	—	—		9. New Mexico
Florida	426,000	0.03	22		10. Colorado
Georgia	57,000	0.01	47		11. Utah
Hawaii	25,000	0.02	32		12. Montana
Idaho	42,000	0.04	20		13. Maine
Illinois	333,000	0.03	26		14. Connecticut
Indiana	57,000	0.01	46		15. Washington
Iowa	63,000	0.02	32		16. Maryland
Kansas	296,000	0.12	5		17. Minnesota
Kentucky	42,000	0.01	43		18. Massachusetts
Louisiana	38,000	0.01	47		19. California
Maine	74,000	0.06	13		20. Idaho
Maryland	226,000	0.05	16		21. New Jersey
Massachusetts	271,000	0.05	18		22. Florida
Michigan	263,000	0.03	27		23. Oregon
Minnesota	200,000	0.05	17		24. New Hampshire
Mississippi	23,000	0.01	47		Oklahoma
Missouri	110,000	0.02	36		26. Illinois
Montana	52,000	0.07	12		27. Michigan
Nebraska	149,000	0.09	8		28. North Dakota
Nevada	142,000	0.12	6		Tennessee
New Hampshire	33,000	0.03	24		30. Texas
New Jersey	302,000	0.04	21		Wisconsin
New Mexico	123,000	0.08	9		32. Hawaii
New York	259,000	0.01	41		Iowa
North Carolina	129,000	0.02	38		Pennsylvania
North Dakota	17,000	0.03	28		South Carolina
Ohio	208,000	0.02	38		36. Missouri
Oklahoma	94,000	0.03	24		37. Arkansas
Oregon	88,000	0.03	23		38. North Carolina
Pennsylvania	277,000	0.02	32		Ohio
Rhode Island	9,000	0.01	47		40. Delaware
South Carolina	79,000	0.02	32		41. New York
South Dakota	92,000	0.13	4		42. Alabama
Tennessee	133,000	0.03	28		43. Arizona
Texas	433,000	0.03	30		Kentucky
Utah	116,000	0.07	11		Virginia
Vermont	171,000	0.30	2		46. Indiana
Virginia	67,000	0.01	43		47. Georgia
Washington	236,000	0.05	15		Louisiana
West Virginia	201,000	0.11	7		Mississippi
Wisconsin	121,000	0.03	30		Rhode Island
Wyoming	120,000	0.26	3		— District of Columbia
United States	11,218,000	0.05	18		

— not applicable.

Source: National Association of State Park Directors, *1991 Annual Information Exchange* (Austin, Tex.: National Association of State Park Directors, 1991).

State	Day visitors	Total visitors	Total visitors per capita	Rank by per capita	By per capita
Alabama	4,721,000	5,800,000	1.44	42	1. Alaska
Alaska	18,727,000	19,813,000	36.02	1	2. Hawaii
Arizona	1,756,000	2,122,000	0.58	49	3. Oregon
Arkansas	6,178,000	6,765,000	2.88	21	4. South Dakota
California	71,429,000	77,811,000	2.62	23	5. Washington
Colorado	7,736,000	8,179,000	2.48	25	6. Rhode Island
Connecticut	6,943,000	7,331,000	2.23	31	7. Kentucky
Delaware	2,454,000	2,748,000	4.13	14	8. Ohio
District of Columbia	—	—	—	—	9. Nebraska
Florida	13,097,000	14,124,000	1.09	46	10. Tennessee
Georgia	11,224,000	14,924,000	2.30	29	11. Oklahoma
Hawaii	18,727,000	19,813,000	17.88	2	12. West Virginia
Idaho	2,197,000	2,463,000	2.45	26	13. Iowa
Illinois	35,978,000	38,457,000	3.36	16	14. Delaware
Indiana	7,800,000	9,450,000	1.71	36	15. Wyoming
Iowa	11,274,000	11,784,000	4.24	13	16. Illinois
Kansas	2,596,000	3,994,000	1.61	38	17. New York
Kentucky	25,693,000	26,704,000	7.25	7	18. Pennsylvania
Louisiana	784,000	1,090,000	0.26	50	19. Utah
Maine	1,979,000	2,188,000	1.78	34	20. New Mexico
Maryland	7,006,000	7,495,000	1.57	39	21. Arkansas
Massachusetts	11,941,000	12,695,000	2.11	32	22. Missouri
Michigan	17,334,000	22,556,000	2.43	27	23. California
Minnesota	6,932,000	7,753,000	1.77	35	24. New Hampshire
Mississippi	3,079,000	3,703,000	1.44	41	25. Colorado
Missouri	13,375,000	14,464,000	2.83	22	26. Idaho
Montana	539,000	697,000	0.87	47	27. Michigan
Nebraska	7,670,000	9,004,000	5.71	9	28. Wisconsin
Nevada	2,524,000	2,721,000	2.26	30	29. Georgia
New Hampshire	2,567,000	2,759,000	2.49	24	30. Nevada
New Jersey	10,061,000	10,503,000	1.36	43	31. Connecticut
New Mexico	1,784,000	4,410,000	2.91	20	32. Massachusetts
New York	55,864,000	58,884,000	3.27	17	33. South Carolina
North Carolina	8,264,000	8,549,000	1.29	44	34. Maine
North Dakota	837,000	982,000	1.54	40	35. Minnesota
Ohio	61,369,000	63,740,000	5.88	8	36. Indiana
Oklahoma	14,351,000	16,613,000	5.28	11	37. Vermont
Oregon	38,034,000	40,201,000	14.15	3	38. Kansas
Pennsylvania	36,773,000	38,388,000	3.23	18	39. Maryland
Rhode Island	6,943,000	7,331,000	7.31	6	40. North Dakota
South Carolina	6,236,000	7,238,000	2.08	33	41. Mississippi
South Dakota	5,365,000	5,739,000	8.25	4	42. Alabama
Tennessee	24,919,000	26,063,000	5.34	10	43. New Jersey
Texas	18,773,000	21,112,000	1.24	45	44. North Carolina
Utah	4,540,000	5,062,000	2.94	19	45. Texas
Vermont	546,000	918,000	1.63	37	46. Florida
Virginia	3,235,000	3,688,000	0.60	48	47. Montana
Washington	37,852,000	40,118,000	8.24	5	48. Virginia
West Virginia	7,829,000	8,470,000	4.72	12	49. Arizona
Wisconsin	10,154,000	11,495,000	2.35	28	50. Louisiana
Wyoming	1,294,000	1,732,000	3.82	15	— District of Columbia
United States	679,283,000	740,643,000	2.98	19	

— not applicable.

Source: National Association of State Park Directors, *1991 Annual Information Exchange* (Austin, Tex.: National Association of State Park Directors, 1991).

State	Revenues	Per capita	Rank by per capita	Revenue as % of operating budget	Rank by %	By per capita
Alabama	$22,303,000	$5.52	6	83.1	5	1. Kentucky
Alaska	1,292,000	2.35	16	17.7	43	2. Vermont
Arizona	2,146,000	0.59	43	32.0	28	3. New Hampshire
Arkansas	10,494,000	4.46	9	55.3	14	4. West Virginia
California	43,170,000	1.45	28	26.8	32	5. New Mexico
Colorado	8,046,000	2.44	15	85.0	4	6. Alabama
Connecticut	2,096,000	0.64	42	25.2	36	7. Delaware
Delaware	3,477,000	5.22	7	45.2	20	8. South Dakota
District of Columbia	—	—	—	—	—	9. Arkansas
Florida	16,878,000	1.31	29	40.0	23	10. Oklahoma
Georgia	11,546,000	1.78	21	45.7	18	11. Tennessee
Hawaii	1,292,000	1.17	33	17.7	43	12. Nebraska
Idaho	1,480,000	1.47	27	41.3	22	13. South Carolina
Illinois	2,491,000	0.22	49	7.8	50	14. Oregon
Indiana	8,281,000	1.49	24	65.8	7	15. Colorado
Iowa	1,245,000	0.45	46	14.6	48	16. Alaska
Kansas	2,350,000	0.95	37	33.3	27	17. Rhode Island
Kentucky	35,642,000	9.67	1	64.2	8	18. Utah
Louisiana	1,756,000	0.42	47	30.9	30	19. Michigan
Maine	1,504,000	1.23	31	36.8	25	20. Mississippi
Maryland	5,108,000	1.07	34	24.2	38	21. Georgia
Massachusetts	9,314,000	1.55	22	50.4	16	22. Massachusetts
Michigan	19,105,000	2.06	19	76.4	6	23. New York
Minnesota	6,448,000	1.47	26	37.6	24	24. Indiana
Mississippi	4,817,000	1.87	20	45.0	21	25. Wisconsin
Missouri	2,787,000	0.55	45	15.8	45	26. Minnesota
Montana	852,000	1.07	35	25.4	33	27. Idaho
Nebraska	4,548,000	2.88	12	58.2	12	28. California
Nevada	811,000	0.68	41	19.0	42	29. Florida
New Hampshire	7,554,000	6.81	3	92.5	3	30. Washington
New Jersey	5,459,000	0.71	40	22.0	41	31. Maine
New Mexico	8,728,000	5.76	5	106.8	1	32. North Dakota
New York	27,752,000	1.54	23	25.4	33	33. Hawaii
North Carolina	1,377,000	0.21	50	15.0	46	34. Maryland
North Dakota	759,000	1.19	32	45.7	18	35. Montana
Ohio	11,255,000	1.04	36	25.4	33	36. Ohio
Oklahoma	12,399,000	3.94	10	59.5	11	37. Kansas
Oregon	7,714,000	2.71	14	31.0	29	38. Wyoming
Pennsylvania	6,675,000	0.56	44	15.0	46	39. Texas
Rhode Island	2,096,000	2.09	17	25.2	36	40. New Jersey
South Carolina	9,698,000	2.78	13	57.9	13	41. Nevada
South Dakota	3,488,000	5.01	8	61.5	10	42. Connecticut
Tennessee	18,275,000	3.75	11	50.5	15	43. Arizona
Texas	12,003,000	0.71	39	34.2	26	44. Pennsylvania
Utah	3,544,000	2.06	18	27.5	31	45. Missouri
Vermont	4,129,000	7.33	2	94.0	2	46. Iowa
Virginia	2,164,000	0.35	48	23.2	39	47. Louisiana
Washington	6,022,000	1.24	30	22.9	40	48. Virginia
West Virginia	11,968,000	6.68	4	49.6	17	49. Illinois
Wisconsin	7,265,000	1.49	25	62.1	9	50. North Carolina
Wyoming	351,000	0.77	38	12.9	49	— District of Columbia
United States	$401,954,000	$1.62	22	—	—	

— not applicable.

Source: National Association of State Park Directors, *1991 Annual Information Exchange* (Austin, Tex.: National Association of State Park Directors, 1991).

Note: Operating budget is the state's budget for parks and recreation areas.

State	Expenditures	Per capita	Rank by per capita
Alabama	$1,579,000	$0.39	47
Alaska	1,432,000	2.51	4
Arizona	2,068,000	0.55	35
Arkansas	973,000	0.41	46
California	16,958,000	0.56	34
Colorado	1,536,000	0.46	42
Connecticut	2,197,000	0.67	28
Delaware	1,313,000	1.93	7
District of Columbia	3,200,000	5.35	2
Florida	23,386,000	1.76	8
Georgia	3,338,000	0.50	37
Hawaii	12,065,000	10.63	1
Idaho	665,000	0.64	30
Illinois	10,348,000	0.90	20
Indiana	2,812,000	0.50	38
Iowa	1,249,000	0.45	43
Kansas	1,072,000	0.43	45
Kentucky	3,302,000	0.89	21
Louisiana	936,000	0.22	49
Maine	755,000	0.61	32
Maryland	7,442,000	1.53	9
Massachusetts	12,624,000	2.11	6
Michigan	9,152,000	0.98	17
Minnesota	4,213,000	0.95	19
Mississippi	514,000	0.20	50
Missouri	4,480,000	0.87	22
Montana	780,000	0.97	18
Nebraska	1,048,000	0.66	29
Nevada	359,000	0.28	48
New Hampshire	519,000	0.47	41
New Jersey	11,703,000	1.51	10
New Mexico	1,119,000	0.72	27
New York	50,981,000	2.82	3
North Carolina	5,428,000	0.81	25
North Dakota	274,000	0.43	44
Ohio	12,130,000	1.11	12
Oklahoma	3,195,000	1.01	14
Oregon	1,537,000	0.53	36
Pennsylvania	11,704,000	0.98	16
Rhode Island	1,010,000	1.01	14
South Carolina	3,633,000	1.02	13
South Dakota	405,000	0.58	33
Tennessee	4,299,000	0.87	23
Texas	3,386,000	0.20	51
Utah	4,284,000	2.42	5
Vermont	479,000	0.85	24
Virginia	4,016,000	0.64	31
Washington	2,396,000	0.48	40
West Virginia	2,384,000	1.32	11
Wisconsin	2,422,000	0.49	39
Wyoming	351,000	0.76	26
United States	**$259,451,000**	**$1.03**	**13**

Rank in order

By per capita

1. Hawaii
2. District of Columbia
3. New York
4. Alaska
5. Utah
6. Massachusetts
7. Delaware
8. Florida
9. Maryland
10. New Jersey
11. West Virginia
12. Ohio
13. South Carolina
14. Oklahoma
    Rhode Island
16. Pennsylvania
17. Michigan
18. Montana
19. Minnesota
20. Illinois
21. Kentucky
22. Missouri
23. Tennessee
24. Vermont
25. North Carolina
26. Wyoming
27. New Mexico
28. Connecticut
29. Nebraska
30. Idaho
31. Virginia
32. Maine
33. South Dakota
34. California
35. Arizona
36. Oregon
37. Georgia
38. Indiana
39. Wisconsin
40. Washington
41. New Hampshire
42. Colorado
43. Iowa
44. North Dakota
45. Kansas
46. Arkansas
47. Alabama
48. Nevada
49. Louisiana
50. Mississippi
51. Texas

Source: U.S. Department of Commerce, Bureau of the Census, *Statistical Abstract of the United States, 1992* (Washington, D.C.: Government Printing Office, 1992).

State	Expenditures	Share of U.S. total	Rank by U.S. share	Per capita	Rank by per capita
Alabama	$3,150,000,000	1.2	27	$764.93	42
Alaska	1,000,000,000	0.4	45	1,897.53	6
Arizona	4,370,000,000	1.6	20	1,228.91	14
Arkansas	2,065,000,000	0.8	36	858.27	38
California	38,241,000,000	14.1	1	1,315.80	10
Colorado	4,844,000,000	1.8	18	1,460.36	9
Connecticut	3,022,000,000	1.1	29	933.00	33
Delaware	748,000,000	0.3	48	1,111.44	20
District of Columbia	2,714,000,000	1.0	31	4,493.38	3
Florida	24,437,000,000	9.0	2	1,928.58	5
Georgia	7,054,000,000	2.6	11	1,096.02	22
Hawaii	5,492,000,000	2.0	16	4,938.85	2
Idaho	1,179,000,000	0.4	41	1,162.72	15
Illinois	10,865,000,000	4.0	5	931.98	34
Indiana	3,493,000,000	1.3	26	624.53	50
Iowa	2,341,000,000	0.9	33	824.30	39
Kansas	2,176,000,000	0.8	34	865.90	37
Kentucky	2,901,000,000	1.1	30	778.37	41
Louisiana	4,161,000,000	1.5	22	949.57	30
Maine	1,357,000,000	0.5	40	1,110.47	21
Maryland	4,273,000,000	1.6	21	910.31	36
Massachusetts	6,252,000,000	2.3	14	1,057.33	24
Michigan	6,427,000,000	2.4	12	693.09	47
Minnesota	3,587,000,000	1.3	25	824.03	40
Mississippi	1,821,000,000	0.7	38	694.77	46
Missouri	5,393,000,000	2.0	17	1,045.36	25
Montana	1,179,000,000	0.4	41	1,462.78	8
Nebraska	1,509,000,000	0.6	39	936.69	31
Nevada	9,753,000,000	3.6	6	8,778.58	1
New Hampshire	1,120,000,000	0.4	44	1,011.74	27
New Jersey	8,974,000,000	3.3	7	1,160.03	16
New Mexico	2,007,000,000	0.7	37	1,313.48	11
New York	18,301,000,000	6.7	3	1,019.55	26
North Carolina	6,306,000,000	2.3	13	959.67	28
North Dakota	702,000,000	0.3	49	1,063.64	23
Ohio	7,253,000,000	2.7	10	664.99	48
Oklahoma	2,362,000,000	0.9	32	732.63	44
Oregon	3,141,000,000	1.2	28	1,113.83	19
Pennsylvania	8,664,000,000	3.2	8	719.60	45
Rhode Island	621,000,000	0.2	51	622.24	51
South Carolina	3,937,000,000	1.4	23	1,121.01	17
South Dakota	679,000,000	0.3	50	949.65	29
Tennessee	5,530,000,000	2.0	15	1,119.43	18
Texas	15,543,000,000	5.7	4	914.78	35
Utah	2,117,000,000	0.8	35	1,240.19	13
Vermont	889,000,000	0.3	47	1,567.90	7
Virginia	7,827,000,000	2.9	9	1,283.54	12
Washington	4,451,000,000	1.6	19	934.89	32
West Virginia	1,161,000,000	0.4	43	625.20	49
Wisconsin	3,647,000,000	1.3	24	749.33	43
Wyoming	990,000,000	0.4	46	2,084.21	4
United States	$272,027,000,000	—	0	$1,095.83	23

Rank in order

By per capita

1. Nevada
2. Hawaii
3. District of Columbia
4. Wyoming
5. Florida
6. Alaska
7. Vermont
8. Montana
9. Colorado
10. California
11. New Mexico
12. Virginia
13. Utah
14. Arizona
15. Idaho
16. New Jersey
17. South Carolina
18. Tennessee
19. Oregon
20. Delaware
21. Maine
22. Georgia
23. North Dakota
24. Massachusetts
25. Missouri
26. New York
27. New Hampshire
28. North Carolina
29. South Dakota
30. Louisiana
31. Nebraska
32. Washington
33. Connecticut
34. Illinois
35. Texas
36. Maryland
37. Kansas
38. Arkansas
39. Iowa
40. Minnesota
41. Kentucky
42. Alabama
43. Wisconsin
44. Oklahoma
45. Pennsylvania
46. Mississippi
47. Michigan
48. Ohio
49. West Virginia
50. Indiana
51. Rhode Island

— not applicable.

Source: U.S. Travel Data Center, *Impact of Travel on State Economies, 1989* (Washington, D.C.: U.S. Travel Data Center, 1991).

Note: Expendiitures for domestic travel are based on total overnight/day trips that are 100 miles or more away from home.

STATE TRAVEL OFFICE BUDGETS, FISCAL 1990				Rank in order

State	Travel office budget	Per capita	Rank by per capita	By per capita
Alabama	$5,417,121	$1.34	28	1. Hawaii
Alaska	12,446,900	22.63	2	2. Alaska
Arizona	5,269,700	1.44	26	3. Wyoming
Arkansas	7,724,944	3.29	8	4. Montana
California	7,500,000	0.25	50	5. South Dakota
Colorado	8,618,300	2.62	12	6. Vermont
Connecticut	1,830,069	0.56	48	7. Nevada
Delaware	939,000	1.41	27	8. Arkansas
District of Columbia	—	—	—	9. Idaho
Florida	10,663,933	0.82	44	10. New Mexico
Georgia	7,949,638	1.23	33	11. Rhode Island
Hawaii	27,939,664	25.22	1	12. Colorado
Idaho	2,786,089	2.77	9	13. South Carolina
Illinois	24,200,000	2.12	19	14. Utah
Indiana	3,500,000	0.63	46	15. New Hampshire
Iowa	4,181,270	1.51	25	16. North Dakota
Kansas	2,136,420	0.86	42	17. Louisiana
Kentucky	6,602,500	1.79	22	18. Tennessee
Louisiana	9,350,542	2.22	17	19. Illinois
Maine	1,607,408	1.31	30	20. Minnesota
Maryland	6,314,348	1.32	29	21. West Virginia
Massachusetts	5,325,900	0.89	41	22. Kentucky
Michigan	8,775,102	0.94	38	23. Oklahoma
Minnesota	8,383,031	1.92	20	24. Wisconsin
Mississippi	2,305,709	0.90	40	25. Iowa
Missouri	6,490,716	1.27	31	26. Arizona
Montana	5,125,859	6.42	4	27. Delaware
Nebraska	1,515,092	0.96	37	28. Alabama
Nevada	5,080,588	4.23	7	29. Maryland
New Hampshire	2,826,000	2.55	15	30. Maine
New Jersey	6,978,000	0.90	39	31. Missouri
New Mexico	4,014,317	2.65	10	32. Virginia
New York	13,197,500	0.73	45	33. Georgia
North Carolina	6,674,313	1.01	36	34. Texas
North Dakota	1,500,000	2.35	16	35. Pennsylvania
Ohio	5,366,055	0.50	49	36. North Carolina
Oklahoma	5,621,394	1.79	23	37. Nebraska
Oregon	2,437,519	0.86	43	38. Michigan
Pennsylvania	14,005,000	1.18	35	39. New Jersey
Rhode Island	2,630,000	2.62	11	40. Mississippi
South Carolina	9,079,000	2.60	13	41. Massachusetts
South Dakota	3,499,949	5.03	5	42. Kansas
Tennessee	10,740,900	2.20	18	43. Oregon
Texas	20,483,460	1.21	34	44. Florida
Utah	4,450,400	2.58	14	45. New York
Vermont	2,456,000	4.36	6	46. Indiana
Virginia	7,731,775	1.25	32	47. Washington
Washington	2,864,936	0.59	47	48. Connecticut
West Virginia	3,352,586	1.87	21	49. Ohio
Wisconsin	8,573,400	1.75	24	50. California
Wyoming	4,125,796	9.09	3	— District of Columbia
United States	**$342,588,143**	**$1.38**	**28**	

— not applicable.

Source: U.S. Travel Data Center, *Survey of State Travel Offices, 1991-1992* (Washington, D.C.: U.S. Travel Data Center, 1992).

Note: State travel offices promote tourism.

Rank in order

State	Lodging facilities	Rooms	Rooms per 100,000 population		By rooms per 100,000 population
			Rate	Rank	
Alabama	375	38,690	957	38	1. Nevada
Alaska	142	10,385	1,888	8	2. Hawaii
Arizona	544	63,499	1,733	10	3. District of Columbia
Arkansas	335	27,257	1,159	24	4. Wyoming
California	3,316	348,443	1,171	23	5. Vermont
Colorado	673	63,380	1,924	7	6. Florida
Connecticut	239	23,201	706	49	7. Colorado
Delaware	104	7,279	1,093	30	8. Alaska
District of Columbia	102	24,515	4,039	3	9. Montana
Florida	2,170	290,129	2,242	6	10. Arizona
Georgia	731	97,254	1,501	17	11. New Mexico
Hawaii	315	67,173	6,063	2	12. South Dakota
Idaho	150	11,149	1,107	28	13. South Carolina
Illinois	859	105,300	921	39	14. Tennessee
Indiana	385	44,758	807	44	15. Virginia
Iowa	383	27,811	1,001	33	16. Utah
Kansas	335	24,637	994	34	17. Georgia
Kentucky	369	37,755	1,025	31	18. North Dakota
Louisiana	311	48,598	1,152	25	19. North Carolina
Maine	281	15,630	1,273	22	20. Nebraska
Maryland	424	45,932	961	37	21. Oregon
Massachusetts	514	54,801	911	40	22. Maine
Michigan	832	74,856	805	45	23. California
Minnesota	495	42,601	974	36	24. Arkansas
Mississippi	221	23,350	908	41	25. Louisiana
Missouri	487	56,498	1,104	29	26. Texas
Montana	243	14,971	1,874	9	27. New Hampshire
Nebraska	439	20,864	1,322	20	28. Idaho
Nevada	410	93,940	7,815	1	29. Missouri
New Hampshire	205	12,713	1,146	27	30. Delaware
New Jersey	443	59,507	770	46	31. Kentucky
New Mexico	291	24,977	1,649	11	32. Oklahoma
New York	1,137	137,623	765	47	33. Iowa
North Carolina	1,179	98,105	1,480	19	34. Kansas
North Dakota	124	9,476	1,483	18	35. Wisconsin
Ohio	722	81,645	753	48	36. Minnesota
Oklahoma	292	31,700	1,008	32	37. Maryland
Oregon	587	37,391	1,316	21	38. Alabama
Pennsylvania	795	81,678	687	50	39. Illinois
Rhode Island	48	4,944	493	51	40. Massachusetts
South Carolina	453	54,614	1,566	13	41. Mississippi
South Dakota	187	10,957	1,574	12	42. Washington
Tennessee	718	76,049	1,559	14	43. West Virginia
Texas	1,419	194,772	1,147	26	44. Indiana
Utah	378	26,473	1,536	16	45. Michigan
Vermont	241	13,834	2,457	5	46. New Jersey
Virginia	853	95,709	1,547	15	47. New York
Washington	482	43,393	892	42	48. Ohio
West Virginia	161	14,764	823	43	49. Connecticut
Wisconsin	792	47,910	979	35	50. Pennsylvania
Wyoming	237	16,253	3,580	4	51. Rhode Island
United States	**27,928**	**2,979,143**	**1,198**	**23**	

Source: "Lodging Industry Census," *Lodging Hospitality*, December 1990.

PARTICIPATION IN EXERCISE WALKING, 1990				Rank in order
State	Participants	% of state population	Rank by %	By %
Alabama	1,391,000	34.4	16	1. Maine
Alaska	NA	NA	NA	2. Montana
Arizona	917,000	25.0	37	3. South Carolina
Arkansas	673,000	28.6	22	4. Iowa
California	7,879,000	26.5	31	5. Idaho
Colorado	949,000	28.8	21	6. West Virginia
Connecticut	574,000	17.5	48	7. Wyoming
Delaware	161,000	24.2	40	8. Rhode Island
District of Columbia	87,000	14.3	49	9. Wisconsin
Florida	3,349,000	25.9	36	10. Tennessee
Georgia	1,949,000	30.1	19	11. North Dakota
Hawaii	NA	NA	NA	12. Oregon
Idaho	386,000	38.3	5	13. Kentucky
Illinois	3,056,000	26.7	28	14. Minnesota
Indiana	1,280,000	23.1	42	15. Louisiana
Iowa	1,068,000	38.5	4	16. Alabama
Kansas	645,000	26.0	34	17. Utah
Kentucky	1,275,000	34.6	13	18. New Mexico
Louisiana	1,454,000	34.5	15	19. Georgia
Maine	569,000	46.3	1	20. Nebraska
Maryland	1,159,000	24.2	39	21. Colorado
Massachusetts	1,589,000	26.4	32	22. Arkansas
Michigan	2,630,000	28.3	23	23. Michigan
Minnesota	1,512,000	34.6	14	24. Texas
Mississippi	627,000	24.4	38	25. South Dakota
Missouri	1,336,000	26.1	33	26. Pennsylvania
Montana	340,000	42.6	2	27. New Jersey
Nebraska	459,000	29.1	20	28. Illinois
Nevada	236,000	19.6	47	29. Washington
New Hampshire	225,000	20.3	46	30. New York
New Jersey	2,078,000	26.9	27	31. California
New Mexico	457,000	30.2	18	32. Massachusetts
New York	4,785,000	26.6	30	33. Missouri
North Carolina	1,717,000	25.9	35	34. Kansas
North Dakota	227,000	35.5	11	35. North Carolina
Ohio	2,615,000	24.1	41	36. Florida
Oklahoma	714,000	22.7	44	37. Arizona
Oregon	994,000	35.0	12	38. Mississippi
Pennsylvania	3,202,000	26.9	26	39. Maryland
Rhode Island	370,000	36.9	8	40. Delaware
South Carolina	1,379,000	39.5	3	41. Ohio
South Dakota	188,000	27.0	25	42. Indiana
Tennessee	1,739,000	35.7	10	43. Virginia
Texas	4,730,000	27.8	24	44. Oklahoma
Utah	564,000	32.7	17	45. Vermont
Vermont	125,000	22.2	45	46. New Hampshire
Virginia	1,426,000	23.0	43	47. Nevada
Washington	1,299,000	26.7	29	48. Connecticut
West Virginia	687,000	38.3	6	49. District of Columbia
Wisconsin	1,774,000	36.3	9	NA Alaska
Wyoming	169,000	37.2	7	NA Hawaii
United States	68,995,000	27.7	25	

NA not available.

Source: National Sporting Goods Association, *Sports Participation in 1990* (Prospect, Ill.: National Sporting Goods Association, 1992).

Note: Participant is defined as someone seven years or older who participates six or more times during the year.

State	Participants	% of state population	Rank by %
Alabama	1,188,000	29.4	19
Alaska	NA	NA	NA
Arizona	1,438,000	39.2	3
Arkansas	569,000	24.2	41
California	7,414,000	24.9	39
Colorado	717,000	21.8	45
Connecticut	899,000	27.4	29
Delaware	191,000	28.7	21
District of Columbia	150,000	24.7	40
Florida	3,932,000	30.4	15
Georgia	1,721,000	26.6	32
Hawaii	NA	NA	NA
Idaho	363,000	36.0	5
Illinois	2,911,000	25.5	36
Indiana	1,546,000	27.9	28
Iowa	875,000	31.5	12
Kansas	525,000	21.2	46
Kentucky	1,127,000	30.6	14
Louisiana	1,358,000	32.2	10
Maine	503,000	41.0	2
Maryland	1,238,000	25.9	35
Massachusetts	1,784,000	29.7	17
Michigan	2,753,000	29.6	18
Minnesota	1,358,000	31.0	13
Mississippi	680,000	26.4	33
Missouri	1,430,000	27.9	27
Montana	380,000	47.6	1
Nebraska	361,000	22.9	43
Nevada	343,000	28.5	24
New Hampshire	317,000	28.6	23
New Jersey	2,504,000	32.4	9
New Mexico	511,000	33.7	8
New York	5,409,000	30.1	16
North Carolina	1,795,000	27.1	31
North Dakota	179,000	28.0	26
Ohio	2,941,000	27.1	30
Oklahoma	551,000	17.5	48
Oregon	751,000	26.4	34
Pennsylvania	3,493,000	29.4	20
Rhode Island	321,000	32.0	11
South Carolina	998,000	28.6	22
South Dakota	102,000	14.7	49
Tennessee	1,378,000	28.3	25
Texas	4,282,000	25.2	37
Utah	603,000	35.0	6
Vermont	141,000	25.0	38
Virginia	1,423,000	23.0	42
Washington	1,095,000	22.5	44
West Virginia	647,000	36.1	4
Wisconsin	1,680,000	34.3	7
Wyoming	84,000	18.5	47
United States	**68,979,000**	**27.7**	**29**

By %

1. Montana
2. Maine
3. Arizona
4. West Virginia
5. Idaho
6. Utah
7. Wisconsin
8. New Mexico
9. New Jersey
10. Louisiana
11. Rhode Island
12. Iowa
13. Minnesota
14. Kentucky
15. Florida
16. New York
17. Massachusetts
18. Michigan
19. Alabama
20. Pennsylvania
21. Delaware
22. South Carolina
23. New Hampshire
24. Nevada
25. Tennessee
26. North Dakota
27. Missouri
28. Indiana
29. Connecticut
30. Ohio
31. North Carolina
32. Georgia
33. Mississippi
34. Oregon
35. Maryland
36. Illinois
37. Texas
38. Vermont
39. California
40. District of Columbia
41. Arkansas
42. Virginia
43. Nebraska
44. Washington
45. Colorado
46. Kansas
47. Wyoming
48. Oklahoma
49. South Dakota
NA Alaska
NA Hawaii

NA not available.

Source: National Sporting Goods Association, *Sports Participation in 1990* (Prospect, Ill.: National Sporting Goods Association, 1992).

Note: Participant is defined as someone seven years or older who participates six or more times during the year.

State	Participants	% of state population	Rank by %
Alabama	445,000	11.0	43
Alaska	NA	NA	NA
Arizona	1,026,000	28.0	9
Arkansas	453,000	19.3	23
California	6,184,000	20.8	20
Colorado	892,000	27.1	12
Connecticut	363,000	11.0	42
Delaware	56,000	8.4	48
District of Columbia	49,000	8.1	49
Florida	1,377,000	10.6	46
Georgia	989,000	15.3	34
Hawaii	NA	NA	NA
Idaho	556,000	55.2	2
Illinois	1,798,000	15.7	33
Indiana	721,000	13.0	40
Iowa	757,000	27.3	11
Kansas	334,000	13.5	37
Kentucky	926,000	25.1	15
Louisiana	755,000	17.9	25
Maine	496,000	40.4	3
Maryland	636,000	13.3	38
Massachusetts	815,000	13.5	36
Michigan	2,431,000	26.2	13
Minnesota	1,307,000	29.9	7
Mississippi	278,000	10.8	44
Missouri	1,171,000	22.9	16
Montana	577,000	72.2	1
Nebraska	313,000	19.8	21
Nevada	329,000	27.4	10
New Hampshire	177,000	16.0	31
New Jersey	824,000	10.7	45
New Mexico	446,000	29.4	8
New York	3,036,000	16.9	27
North Carolina	1,134,000	17.1	26
North Dakota	139,000	21.8	18
Ohio	1,813,000	16.7	28
Oklahoma	506,000	16.1	30
Oregon	1,064,000	37.4	5
Pennsylvania	2,166,000	18.2	24
Rhode Island	160,000	16.0	32
South Carolina	316,000	9.1	47
South Dakota	97,000	13.9	35
Tennessee	636,000	13.0	39
Texas	3,279,000	19.3	22
Utah	678,000	39.4	4
Vermont	94,000	16.7	29
Virginia	770,000	12.4	41
Washington	1,089,000	22.4	17
West Virginia	536,000	29.9	6
Wisconsin	1,272,000	26.0	14
Wyoming	97,000	21.4	19
United States	**46,345,000**	**18.6**	**24**

PARTICIPATION IN CAMPING. 1990

Rank in order

By %

1. Montana
2. Idaho
3. Maine
4. Utah
5. Oregon
6. West Virginia
7. Minnesota
8. New Mexico
9. Arizona
10. Nevada
11. Iowa
12. Colorado
13. Michigan
14. Wisconsin
15. Kentucky
16. Missouri
17. Washington
18. North Dakota
19. Wyoming
20. California
21. Nebraska
22. Texas
23. Arkansas
24. Pennsylvania
25. Louisiana
26. North Carolina
27. New York
28. Ohio
29. Vermont
30. Oklahoma
31. New Hampshire
32. Rhode Island
33. Illinois
34. Georgia
35. South Dakota
36. Massachusetts
37. Kansas
38. Maryland
39. Tennessee
40. Indiana
41. Virginia
42. Connecticut
43. Alabama
44. Mississippi
45. New Jersey
46. Florida
47. South Carolina
48. Delaware
49. District of Columbia
NA Alaska
NA Hawaii

NA not available.

Source: National Sporting Goods Association, *Sports Participation in 1990* (Prospect, Ill.: National Sporting Goods Association, 1992).

Note: Participant is defined as someone seven years or older who participates more than once a year.

State	Participants	% of state population	Rank by %
Alabama	517,000	12.8	39
Alaska	NA	NA	NA
Arizona	663,000	18.1	19
Arkansas	338,000	14.4	31
California	4,149,000	13.9	32
Colorado	582,000	17.7	20
Connecticut	289,000	8.8	46
Delaware	150,000	22.5	7
District of Columbia	103,000	17.0	24
Florida	1,796,000	13.9	33
Georgia	897,000	13.8	34
Hawaii	NA	NA	NA
Idaho	148,000	14.7	29
Illinois	2,416,000	21.1	11
Indiana	1,008,000	18.2	18
Iowa	645,000	23.2	5
Kansas	302,000	12.2	40
Kentucky	779,000	21.1	10
Louisiana	644,000	15.3	27
Maine	282,000	23.0	6
Maryland	799,000	16.7	25
Massachusetts	1,110,000	18.5	17
Michigan	2,203,000	23.7	4
Minnesota	943,000	21.6	9
Mississippi	247,000	9.6	43
Missouri	989,000	19.3	15
Montana	320,000	40.1	1
Nebraska	314,000	19.9	13
Nevada	207,000	17.2	22
New Hampshire	55,000	5.0	49
New Jersey	998,000	12.9	38
New Mexico	365,000	24.1	3
New York	3,535,000	19.7	14
North Carolina	539,000	8.1	47
North Dakota	76,000	11.9	41
Ohio	1,851,000	17.1	23
Oklahoma	283,000	9.0	45
Oregon	526,000	18.5	16
Pennsylvania	2,071,000	17.4	21
Rhode Island	201,000	20.0	12
South Carolina	533,000	15.3	26
South Dakota	63,000	9.1	44
Tennessee	653,000	13.4	36
Texas	2,300,000	13.5	35
Utah	262,000	15.2	28
Vermont	36,000	6.4	48
Virginia	907,000	14.7	30
Washington	648,000	13.3	37
West Virginia	398,000	22.2	8
Wisconsin	1,268,000	25.9	2
Wyoming	53,000	11.7	42
United States	40,463,000	16.3	26

Rank in order

By %

1. Montana
2. Wisconsin
3. New Mexico
4. Michigan
5. Iowa
6. Maine
7. Delaware
8. West Virginia
9. Minnesota
10. Kentucky
11. Illinois
12. Rhode Island
13. Nebraska
14. New York
15. Missouri
16. Oregon
17. Massachusetts
18. Indiana
19. Arizona
20. Colorado
21. Pennsylvania
22. Nevada
23. Ohio
24. District of Columbia
25. Maryland
26. South Carolina
27. Louisiana
28. Utah
29. Idaho
30. Virginia
31. Arkansas
32. California
33. Florida
34. Georgia
35. Texas
36. Tennessee
37. Washington
38. New Jersey
39. Alabama
40. Kansas
41. North Dakota
42. Wyoming
43. Mississippi
44. South Dakota
45. Oklahoma
46. Connecticut
47. North Carolina
48. Vermont
49. New Hampshire
NA Alaska
NA Hawaii

NA not available.

Source: National Sporting Goods Association, *Sports Participation in 1990* (Prospect, Ill.: National Sporting Goods Association, 1992).

Note: Participant is defined as someone seven years or older who participates more than once a year.

State	Bowling leagues	Membership	Per 1,000 population Rate	Per 1,000 population Rank
Alabama	803	15,989	3.9	49
Alaska	320	8,292	14.5	16
Arizona	1,713	40,131	10.7	27
Arkansas	600	13,920	5.9	41
California	11,359	215,927	7.1	37
Colorado	1,990	49,338	14.6	15
Connecticut	1,031	32,033	9.7	29
Delaware	553	13,370	19.7	10
District of Columbia	1,167	35,749	59.8	1
Florida	4,911	114,773	8.6	32
Georgia	1,717	34,967	5.3	45
Hawaii	466	13,448	11.8	24
Idaho	560	14,113	13.6	21
Illinois	5,165	159,487	13.8	19
Indiana	3,392	101,708	18.1	13
Iowa	2,073	57,988	20.7	7
Kansas	1,512	36,937	14.8	14
Kentucky	1,239	31,353	8.4	34
Louisiana	1,069	21,804	5.1	46
Maine	187	5,166	4.2	48
Maryland	1,203	27,674	5.7	44
Massachusetts	790	20,390	3.4	50
Michigan	7,749	250,955	26.8	3
Minnesota	2,964	89,965	20.3	8
Mississippi	316	6,413	2.5	51
Missouri	2,839	70,717	13.7	20
Montana	564	15,985	19.8	9
Nebraska	1,402	39,343	24.7	5
Nevada	798	18,403	14.3	17
New Hampshire	251	5,413	4.9	47
New Jersey	3,032	86,402	11.1	26
New Mexico	577	13,676	8.8	31
New York	8,502	237,272	13.1	22
North Carolina	2,089	42,016	6.2	39
North Dakota	554	16,235	25.6	4
Ohio	7,162	211,205	19.3	11
Oklahoma	1,298	25,564	8.1	35
Oregon	1,386	29,484	10.1	28
Pennsylvania	5,510	143,775	12.0	23
Rhode Island	263	5,755	5.7	43
South Carolina	1,316	23,742	6.7	38
South Dakota	568	16,694	23.7	6
Tennessee	1,349	28,472	5.7	42
Texas	5,321	107,927	6.2	40
Utah	603	16,741	9.5	30
Vermont	243	8,049	14.2	18
Virginia	1,805	45,092	7.2	36
Washington	2,414	55,931	11.1	25
West Virginia	621	15,460	8.6	33
Wisconsin	5,196	142,406	28.7	2
Wyoming	351	8,681	18.9	12
United States	**110,863**	**2,842,330**	**11.4**	**26**

Rank in order

By rate per 1,000 population

1. District of Columbia
2. Wisconsin
3. Michigan
4. North Dakota
5. Nebraska
6. South Dakota
7. Iowa
8. Minnesota
9. Montana
10. Delaware
11. Ohio
12. Wyoming
13. Indiana
14. Kansas
15. Colorado
16. Alaska
17. Nevada
18. Vermont
19. Illinois
20. Missouri
21. Idaho
22. New York
23. Pennsylvania
24. Hawaii
25. Washington
26. New Jersey
27. Arizona
28. Oregon
29. Connecticut
30. Utah
31. New Mexico
32. Florida
33. West Virginia
34. Kentucky
35. Oklahoma
36. Virginia
37. California
38. South Carolina
39. North Carolina
40. Texas
41. Arkansas
42. Tennessee
43. Rhode Island
44. Maryland
45. Georgia
46. Louisiana
47. New Hampshire
48. Maine
49. Alabama
50. Massachusetts
51. Mississippi

Source: American Bowling Congress, *American Bowling Congress Annual Report, 1990-1991* (Greendale, Wis.: American Bowling Congress, 1992).

State	Participants	% of state population	Rank by %	Rank in order By %
Alabama	479,000	11.9	11	1. Montana
Alaska	NA	NA	NA	2. Wyoming
Arizona	409,000	11.2	15	3. South Carolina
Arkansas	147,000	6.3	45	4. Oregon
California	3,214,000	10.8	18	5. Louisiana
Colorado	308,000	9.4	26	6. Utah
Connecticut	185,000	5.6	46	7. Iowa
Delaware	33,000	5.0	47	8. District of Columbia
District of Columbia	76,000	12.5	8	9. Maine
Florida	1,092,000	8.4	34	10. Idaho
Georgia	698,000	10.8	19	11. Alabama
Hawaii	NA	NA	NA	12. North Carolina
Idaho	120,000	11.9	10	13. Texas
Illinois	1,128,000	9.9	24	14. West Virginia
Indiana	480,000	8.7	33	15. Arizona
Iowa	373,000	13.4	7	16. Virginia
Kansas	261,000	10.5	21	17. Wisconsin
Kentucky	351,000	9.5	25	18. California
Louisiana	612,000	14.5	5	19. Georgia
Maine	152,000	12.4	9	20. Nebraska
Maryland	417,000	8.7	32	21. Kansas
Massachusetts	547,000	9.1	29	22. Tennessee
Michigan	756,000	8.1	37	23. Rhode Island
Minnesota	366,000	8.4	35	24. Illinois
Mississippi	161,000	6.3	44	25. Kentucky
Missouri	400,000	7.8	40	26. Colorado
Montana	181,000	22.7	1	27. Washington
Nebraska	168,000	10.6	20	28. New Jersey
Nevada	96,000	8.0	38	29. Massachusetts
New Hampshire	50,000	4.5	48	30. New Mexico
New Jersey	706,000	9.1	28	31. New York
New Mexico	137,000	9.0	30	32. Maryland
New York	1,606,000	8.9	31	33. Indiana
North Carolina	781,000	11.8	12	34. Florida
North Dakota	52,000	8.1	36	35. Minnesota
Ohio	860,000	7.9	39	36. North Dakota
Oklahoma	228,000	7.2	42	37. Michigan
Oregon	463,000	16.3	4	38. Nevada
Pennsylvania	816,000	6.9	43	39. Ohio
Rhode Island	103,000	10.3	23	40. Missouri
South Carolina	580,000	16.6	3	41. South Dakota
South Dakota	54,000	7.8	41	42. Oklahoma
Tennessee	512,000	10.5	22	43. Pennsylvania
Texas	1,955,000	11.5	13	44. Mississippi
Utah	249,000	14.5	6	45. Arkansas
Vermont	16,000	2.8	49	46. Connecticut
Virginia	685,000	11.1	16	47. Delaware
Washington	452,000	9.3	27	48. New Hampshire
West Virginia	201,000	11.2	14	49. Vermont
Wisconsin	530,000	10.8	17	NA Alaska
Wyoming	88,000	19.4	2	NA Hawaii
United States	24,310,000	9.8	8	

NA not available.

Source: National Sporting Goods Association, *Sports Participation in 1990* (Prospect, Ill.: National Sporting Goods Association, 1992).

Note: Participant is defined as someone seven years or older who participates six or more times during the year.

State	Participants	% of state population	Rank by %
Alabama	379,000	9.4	30
Alaska	NA	NA	NA
Arizona	419,000	11.4	10
Arkansas	244,000	10.4	22
California	3,381,000	11.4	11
Colorado	256,000	7.8	42
Connecticut	237,000	7.2	45
Delaware	35,000	5.3	49
District of Columbia	70,000	11.5	9
Florida	1,060,000	8.2	38
Georgia	554,000	8.6	35
Hawaii	NA	NA	NA
Idaho	139,000	13.8	3
Illinois	1,078,000	9.4	27
Indiana	487,000	8.8	34
Iowa	309,000	11.1	13
Kansas	228,000	9.2	31
Kentucky	282,000	7.7	43
Louisiana	499,000	11.8	7
Maine	154,000	12.5	4
Maryland	437,000	9.1	33
Massachusetts	586,000	9.7	25
Michigan	875,000	9.4	29
Minnesota	412,000	9.4	28
Mississippi	169,000	6.6	47
Missouri	550,000	10.7	17
Montana	154,000	19.3	1
Nebraska	156,000	9.9	24
Nevada	134,000	11.1	12
New Hampshire	90,000	8.1	41
New Jersey	835,000	10.8	16
New Mexico	168,000	11.1	14
New York	1,880,000	10.5	21
North Carolina	548,000	8.3	37
North Dakota	45,000	7.0	46
Ohio	881,000	8.1	40
Oklahoma	195,000	6.2	48
Oregon	355,000	12.5	5
Pennsylvania	1,007,000	8.5	36
Rhode Island	106,000	10.6	19
South Carolina	408,000	11.7	8
South Dakota	64,000	9.2	32
Tennessee	370,000	7.6	44
Texas	1,780,000	10.5	20
Utah	258,000	15.0	2
Vermont	46,000	8.2	39
Virginia	631,000	10.2	23
Washington	516,000	10.6	18
West Virginia	198,000	11.0	15
Wisconsin	465,000	9.5	26
Wyoming	54,000	11.9	6
United States	**24,180,000**	**9.7**	**26**

Rank in order

By %

1. Montana
2. Utah
3. Idaho
4. Maine
5. Oregon
6. Wyoming
7. Louisiana
8. South Carolina
9. District of Columbia
10. Arizona
11. California
12. Nevada
13. Iowa
14. New Mexico
15. West Virginia
16. New Jersey
17. Missouri
18. Washington
19. Rhode Island
20. Texas
21. New York
22. Arkansas
23. Virginia
24. Nebraska
25. Massachusetts
26. Wisconsin
27. Illinois
28. Minnesota
29. Michigan
30. Alabama
31. Kansas
32. South Dakota
33. Maryland
34. Indiana
35. Georgia
36. Pennsylvania
37. North Carolina
38. Florida
39. Vermont
40. Ohio
41. New Hampshire
42. Colorado
43. Kentucky
44. Tennessee
45. Connecticut
46. North Dakota
47. Mississippi
48. Oklahoma
49. Delaware
NA Alaska
NA Hawaii

NA not available.

Source: National Sporting Goods Association, *Sports Participation in 1990* (Prospect, Ill.: National Sporting Goods Association, 1992).

Note: Participant is defined as someone seven years or older who participates six or more times during the year.

PARTICIPATION IN GOLF, 1990				Rank in order
State	Participants	% of state population	Rank by %	By %
Alabama	319,000	7.9	30	1. Montana
Alaska	NA	NA	NA	2. Iowa
Arizona	265,000	7.2	39	3. Wisconsin
Arkansas	75,000	3.2	49	4. Nebraska
California	2,283,000	7.7	35	5. West Virginia
Colorado	317,000	9.6	20	6. Wyoming
Connecticut	315,000	9.6	21	7. New Mexico
Delaware	60,000	9.0	25	8. Rhode Island
District of Columbia	20,000	3.3	48	9. Michigan
Florida	1,101,000	8.5	28	10. Minnesota
Georgia	496,000	7.7	36	11. Oregon
Hawaii	NA	NA	NA	12. Washington
Idaho	93,000	9.2	23	13. Ohio
Illinois	1,283,000	11.2	15	14. Indiana
Indiana	645,000	11.6	14	15. Illinois
Iowa	470,000	16.9	2	16. Maine
Kansas	145,000	5.9	45	17. Kentucky
Kentucky	382,000	10.4	17	18. Nevada
Louisiana	278,000	6.6	41	19. South Carolina
Maine	128,000	10.4	16	20. Colorado
Maryland	300,000	6.3	42	21. Connecticut
Massachusetts	457,000	7.6	37	22. North Dakota
Michigan	1,276,000	13.7	9	23. Idaho
Minnesota	584,000	13.3	10	24. New York
Mississippi	117,000	4.5	47	25. Delaware
Missouri	396,000	7.7	33	26. Texas
Montana	176,000	22.0	1	27. Pennsylvania
Nebraska	235,000	14.9	4	28. Florida
Nevada	118,000	9.8	18	29. Virginia
New Hampshire	67,000	6.0	43	30. Alabama
New Jersey	604,000	7.8	31	31. New Jersey
New Mexico	210,000	13.9	7	North Carolina
New York	1,626,000	9.0	24	33. Missouri
North Carolina	518,000	7.8	31	34. Tennessee
North Dakota	60,000	9.4	22	35. California
Ohio	1,270,000	11.7	13	36. Georgia
Oklahoma	223,000	7.1	40	37. Massachusetts
Oregon	355,000	12.5	11	38. South Dakota
Pennsylvania	1,036,000	8.7	27	39. Arizona
Rhode Island	139,000	13.9	8	40. Oklahoma
South Carolina	337,000	9.7	19	41. Louisiana
South Dakota	51,000	7.3	38	42. Maryland
Tennessee	375,000	7.7	34	43. New Hampshire
Texas	1,529,000	9.0	26	44. Vermont
Utah	97,000	5.6	46	45. Kansas
Vermont	34,000	6.0	44	46. Utah
Virginia	501,000	8.1	29	47. Mississippi
Washington	600,000	12.3	12	48. District of Columbia
West Virginia	265,000	14.8	5	49. Arkansas
Wisconsin	762,000	15.6	3	NA Alaska
Wyoming	66,000	14.5	6	NA Hawaii
United States	23,058,000	9.3	23	

NA not available.

Source: National Sporting Goods Association, *Sports Participation in 1990* (Prospect, Ill.: National Sporting Goods Association, 1992).

Note: Participant is defined as someone seven years or older who participates more than once a year.

PARTICIPATION IN SOFTBALL, 1990				Rank in order

State	Participants	% of state population	Rank by %	By %
Alabama	328,000	8.1	28	1. Idaho
Alaska	NA	NA	NA	2. Montana
Arizona	472,000	12.9	5	3. Rhode Island
Arkansas	182,000	7.7	33	4. Iowa
California	2,397,000	8.1	30	5. Arizona
Colorado	258,000	7.8	31	6. Wisconsin
Connecticut	233,000	7.1	36	7. Minnesota
Delaware	45,000	6.8	39	8. District of Columbia
District of Columbia	73,000	12.0	8	9. Louisiana
Florida	768,000	5.9	45	10. Missouri
Georgia	617,000	9.5	16	11. Kentucky
Hawaii	NA	NA	NA	12. Illinois
Idaho	206,000	20.5	1	13. Nebraska
Illinois	1,195,000	10.5	12	14. Massachusetts
Indiana	448,000	8.1	29	15. Utah
Iowa	425,000	15.3	4	16. Georgia
Kansas	166,000	6.7	40	17. North Dakota
Kentucky	387,000	10.5	11	18. New Mexico
Louisiana	471,000	11.2	9	18. Oregon
Maine	84,000	6.8	38	20. Ohio
Maryland	355,000	7.4	35	21. New Jersey
Massachusetts	611,000	10.2	14	22. New York
Michigan	774,000	8.3	25	23. New Hampshire
Minnesota	534,000	12.2	7	24. Wyoming
Mississippi	91,000	3.5	48	25. Michigan
Missouri	571,000	11.2	10	26. West Virginia
Montana	163,000	20.4	2	27. Tennessee
Nebraska	164,000	10.4	13	28. Alabama
Nevada	20,000	1.7	49	29. Indiana
New Hampshire	96,000	8.7	23	30. California
New Jersey	678,000	8.8	21	31. Colorado
New Mexico	137,000	9.0	18	32. Pennsylvania
New York	1,563,000	8.7	22	33. Arkansas
North Carolina	498,000	7.5	34	34. North Carolina
North Dakota	60,000	9.4	17	35. Maryland
Ohio	968,000	8.9	20	36. Connecticut
Oklahoma	155,000	4.9	46	37. Texas
Oregon	257,000	9.0	18	38. Maine
Pennsylvania	920,000	7.7	32	39. Delaware
Rhode Island	164,000	16.4	3	40. Kansas
South Carolina	216,000	6.2	42	41. Washington
South Dakota	29,000	4.2	47	42. South Carolina
Tennessee	401,000	8.2	27	43. Virginia
Texas	1,201,000	7.1	37	44. Vermont
Utah	167,000	9.7	15	45. Florida
Vermont	34,000	6.0	44	46. Oklahoma
Virginia	376,000	6.1	43	47. South Dakota
Washington	315,000	6.5	41	48. Mississippi
West Virginia	149,000	8.3	26	49. Nevada
Wisconsin	620,000	12.7	6	NA Alaska
Wyoming	38,000	8.4	24	NA Hawaii
United States	**21,084,000**	**8.5**	**24**	

NA not available.

Source: National Sporting Goods Association, *Sports Participation in 1990* (Prospect, Ill.: National Sporting Goods Association, 1992).

Note: Participant is defined as someone seven years or older who participates more than once a year.

PARTICIPATION IN HEALTH CLUBS, 1990				Rank in order
State	**Participants**	**% of state population**	**Rank by %**	**By %**
Alabama	216,000	5.3	44	1. Delaware
Alaska	NA	NA	NA	2. Wyoming
Arizona	452,000	12.3	3	3. Arizona
Arkansas	136,000	5.8	43	4. Connecticut
California	3,279,000	11.0	7	5. Colorado
Colorado	366,000	11.1	5	6. District of Columbia
Connecticut	369,000	11.2	4	7. California
Delaware	122,000	18.3	1	8. Massachusetts
District of Columbia	67,000	11.0	6	9. Washington
Florida	977,000	7.6	25	10. Montana
Georgia	591,000	9.1	15	11. Minnesota
Hawaii	NA	NA	NA	12. Rhode Island
Idaho	88,000	8.7	18	13. New Jersey
Illinois	1,038,000	9.1	16	14. Oregon
Indiana	332,000	6.0	42	15. Georgia
Iowa	242,000	8.7	19	16. Illinois
Kansas	94,000	3.8	46	17. New York
Kentucky	225,000	6.1	40	18. Idaho
Louisiana	288,000	6.8	33	19. Iowa
Maine	97,000	7.9	23	20. Oklahoma
Maryland	327,000	6.8	32	21. North Dakota
Massachusetts	644,000	10.7	8	22. New Hampshire
Michigan	732,000	7.9	24	23. Maine
Minnesota	442,000	10.1	11	24. Michigan
Mississippi	54,000	2.1	49	25. Florida
Missouri	333,000	6.5	35	26. North Carolina
Montana	84,000	10.5	10	27. Virginia
Nebraska	101,000	6.4	37	28. Pennsylvania
Nevada	80,000	6.7	34	29. Texas
New Hampshire	88,000	7.9	22	30. Wisconsin
New Jersey	768,000	9.9	13	31. South Dakota
New Mexico	52,000	3.4	47	32. Maryland
New York	1,604,000	8.9	17	33. Louisiana
North Carolina	486,000	7.3	26	34. Nevada
North Dakota	51,000	8.0	21	35. Missouri
Ohio	678,000	6.3	39	36. Tennessee
Oklahoma	255,000	8.1	20	37. Nebraska
Oregon	277,000	9.7	14	38. South Carolina
Pennsylvania	832,000	7.0	28	39. Ohio
Rhode Island	100,000	10.0	12	40. Kentucky
South Carolina	220,000	6.3	38	41. West Virginia
South Dakota	48,000	6.9	31	42. Indiana
Tennessee	315,000	6.5	36	43. Arkansas
Texas	1,185,000	7.0	29	44. Alabama
Utah	85,000	4.9	45	45. Utah
Vermont	15,000	2.7	48	46. Kansas
Virginia	438,000	7.1	27	47. New Mexico
Washington	517,000	10.6	9	48. Vermont
West Virginia	108,000	6.0	41	49. Mississippi
Wisconsin	340,000	7.0	30	NA Alaska
Wyoming	63,000	13.9	2	NA Hawaii
United States	**20,299,000**	**8.2**	**20**	

NA not available.

Source: National Sporting Goods Association, *Sports Participation in 1990* (Prospect, Ill.: National Sporting Goods Association, 1992).

Note: Participant is defined as someone seven years or older who participates more than once a year.

PARTICIPATION IN TENNIS, 1990				Rank in order
State	Participants	% of state population	Rank by %	By %
Alabama	338,000	8.4	12	1. Rhode Island
Alaska	NA	NA	NA	2. New Mexico
Arizona	218,000	5.9	38	3. District of Columbia
Arkansas	113,000	4.8	41	4. West Virginia
California	2,358,000	7.9	17	5. Georgia
Colorado	253,000	7.7	21	6. Connecticut
Connecticut	378,000	11.5	6	7. Oregon
Delaware	35,000	5.3	40	8. Iowa
District of Columbia	94,000	15.5	3	9. Utah
Florida	954,000	7.4	24	10. South Carolina
Georgia	782,000	12.1	5	11. Virginia
Hawaii	NA	NA	NA	12. Alabama
Idaho	68,000	6.8	32	13. Maine
Illinois	823,000	7.2	28	14. North Carolina
Indiana	375,000	6.8	31	15. New Jersey
Iowa	274,000	9.9	8	16. Mississippi
Kansas	136,000	5.5	39	17. California
Kentucky	275,000	7.5	23	18. Michigan
Louisiana	329,000	7.8	19	19. Louisiana
Maine	102,000	8.3	13	20. Wisconsin
Maryland	332,000	6.9	29	21. Colorado
Massachusetts	363,000	6.0	35	22. Montana
Michigan	733,000	7.9	18	23. Kentucky
Minnesota	284,000	6.5	33	24. Florida
Mississippi	206,000	8.0	16	25. New York
Missouri	317,000	6.2	34	26. Pennsylvania
Montana	61,000	7.6	22	27. Texas
Nebraska	107,000	6.8	30	28. Illinois
Nevada	20,000	1.7	47	29. Maryland
New Hampshire	53,000	4.8	42	30. Nebraska
New Jersey	624,000	8.1	15	31. Indiana
New Mexico	235,000	15.5	2	32. Idaho
New York	1,305,000	7.3	25	33. Minnesota
North Carolina	549,000	8.3	14	34. Missouri
North Dakota	9,000	1.4	48	35. Massachusetts
Ohio	649,000	6.0	36	36. Ohio
Oklahoma	138,000	4.4	44	37. Tennessee
Oregon	296,000	10.4	7	38. Arizona
Pennsylvania	861,000	7.2	26	39. Kansas
Rhode Island	200,000	19.9	1	40. Delaware
South Carolina	302,000	8.7	10	41. Arkansas
South Dakota	26,000	3.7	45	42. New Hampshire
Tennessee	291,000	6.0	37	43. Washington
Texas	1,229,000	7.2	27	44. Oklahoma
Utah	163,000	9.5	9	45. South Dakota
Vermont	NA	NA	NA	46. Wyoming
Virginia	528,000	8.5	11	47. Nevada
Washington	223,000	4.6	43	48. North Dakota
West Virginia	226,000	12.6	4	NA Alaska
Wisconsin	379,000	7.7	20	NA Hawaii
Wyoming	9,000	2.0	46	NA Vermont
United States	18,622,000	7.5	23	

NA not available.

Source: National Sporting Goods Association, *Sports Participation in 1990* (Prospect, Ill.: National Sporting Goods Association, 1992).

Note: Participant is defined as someone seven years or older who participates more than once a year.

State	Participants	% of state population	Rank by %
Alabama	267,000	6.6	31
Alaska	NA	NA	NA
Arizona	207,000	5.6	34
Arkansas	303,000	12.9	12
California	857,000	2.9	43
Colorado	359,000	10.9	18
Connecticut	102,000	3.1	42
Delaware	29,000	4.4	38
District of Columbia	NA	NA	NA
Florida	421,000	3.3	41
Georgia	561,000	8.7	23
Hawaii	NA	NA	NA
Idaho	233,000	23.1	2
Illinois	521,000	4.6	36
Indiana	223,000	4.0	40
Iowa	365,000	13.1	11
Kansas	251,000	10.1	20
Kentucky	511,000	13.9	8
Louisiana	580,000	13.7	9
Maine	210,000	17.1	4
Maryland	211,000	4.4	37
Massachusetts	162,000	2.7	44
Michigan	789,000	8.5	25
Minnesota	637,000	14.6	7
Mississippi	344,000	13.4	10
Missouri	796,000	15.6	5
Montana	255,000	31.9	1
Nebraska	196,000	12.4	16
Nevada	93,000	7.7	28
New Hampshire	25,000	2.3	46
New Jersey	195,000	2.5	45
New Mexico	22,000	1.5	48
New York	1,063,000	5.9	32
North Carolina	484,000	7.3	29
North Dakota	82,000	12.8	13
Ohio	561,000	5.2	35
Oklahoma	208,000	6.6	30
Oregon	358,000	12.6	14
Pennsylvania	1,491,000	12.5	15
Rhode Island	18,000	1.8	47
South Carolina	296,000	8.5	24
South Dakota	71,000	10.2	19
Tennessee	378,000	7.8	27
Texas	1,376,000	8.1	26
Utah	201,000	11.7	17
Vermont	49,000	8.7	22
Virginia	357,000	5.8	33
Washington	208,000	4.3	39
West Virginia	383,000	21.4	3
Wisconsin	759,000	15.5	6
Wyoming	44,000	9.7	21
United States	18,114,000	7.3	30

Rank in order

By %

1. Montana
2. Idaho
3. West Virginia
4. Maine
5. Missouri
6. Wisconsin
7. Minnesota
8. Kentucky
9. Louisiana
10. Mississippi
11. Iowa
12. Arkansas
13. North Dakota
14. Oregon
15. Pennsylvania
16. Nebraska
17. Utah
18. Colorado
19. South Dakota
20. Kansas
21. Wyoming
22. Vermont
23. Georgia
24. South Carolina
25. Michigan
26. Texas
27. Tennessee
28. Nevada
29. North Carolina
30. Oklahoma
31. Alabama
32. New York
33. Virginia
34. Arizona
35. Ohio
36. Illinois
37. Maryland
38. Delaware
39. Washington
40. Indiana
41. Florida
42. Connecticut
43. California
44. Massachusetts
45. New Jersey
46. New Hampshire
47. Rhode Island
48. New Mexico
NA Alaska
NA District of Columbia
NA Hawaii

NA not available.

Source: National Sporting Goods Association, *Sports Participation in 1990* (Prospect, Ill.: National Sporting Goods Association, 1992).

Note: Participant is defined as someone seven years or older who participates more than once a year.

| PARTICIPATION IN BASEBALL, 1990 | | | | Rank in order |
State	Participants	% of state population	Rank by %	By %
Alabama	281,000	7.0	19	1. Rhode Island
Alaska	NA	NA	NA	2. Montana
Arizona	247,000	6.7	20	3. Nevada
Arkansas	56,000	2.4	47	4. Iowa
California	1,750,000	5.9	26	5. Idaho
Colorado	181,000	5.5	32	6. West Virginia
Connecticut	115,000	3.5	43	7. Louisiana
Delaware	55,000	8.3	8	8. Delaware
District of Columbia	9,000	1.5	48	9. Illinois
Florida	459,000	3.5	42	10. Missouri
Georgia	292,000	4.5	38	11. New Mexico
Hawaii	NA	NA	NA	12. New York
Idaho	98,000	9.7	5	13. Tennessee
Illinois	922,000	8.1	9	14. Ohio
Indiana	348,000	6.3	22	15. Pennsylvania
Iowa	278,000	10.0	4	16. South Carolina
Kansas	113,000	4.6	37	17. Michigan
Kentucky	197,000	5.3	33	18. New Jersey
Louisiana	367,000	8.7	7	19. Alabama
Maine	69,000	5.6	30	20. Arizona
Maryland	295,000	6.2	24	21. North Dakota
Massachusetts	309,000	5.1	34	22. Indiana
Michigan	667,000	7.2	17	23. Oregon
Minnesota	256,000	5.9	27	24. Maryland
Mississippi	96,000	3.7	41	25. Texas
Missouri	411,000	8.0	10	26. California
Montana	100,000	12.5	2	27. Minnesota
Nebraska	90,000	5.7	28	28. Nebraska
Nevada	121,000	10.1	3	29. Utah
New Hampshire	53,000	4.8	36	30. Maine
New Jersey	543,000	7.0	18	31. South Dakota
New Mexico	119,000	7.9	11	32. Colorado
New York	1,386,000	7.7	12	33. Kentucky
North Carolina	297,000	4.5	39	34. Massachusetts
North Dakota	41,000	6.4	21	35. Wisconsin
Ohio	817,000	7.5	14	36. New Hampshire
Oklahoma	92,000	2.9	44	37. Kansas
Oregon	176,000	6.2	23	38. Georgia
Pennsylvania	876,000	7.4	15	39. North Carolina
Rhode Island	168,000	16.8	1	40. Virginia
South Carolina	255,000	7.3	16	41. Mississippi
South Dakota	39,000	5.6	31	42. Florida
Tennessee	375,000	7.7	13	43. Connecticut
Texas	1,040,000	6.1	25	44. Oklahoma
Utah	97,000	5.6	29	45. Wyoming
Vermont	NA	NA	NA	46. Washington
Virginia	246,000	4.0	40	47. Arkansas
Washington	125,000	2.6	46	48. District of Columbia
West Virginia	164,000	9.1	6	NA Alaska
Wisconsin	248,000	5.1	35	NA Hawaii
Wyoming	13,000	2.9	45	NA Vermont
United States	15,491,000	6.2	23	

NA not available.

Source: National Sporting Goods Association, *Sports Participation in 1990* (Prospect, Ill.: National Sporting Goods Association, 1992).

Note: Participant is defined as someone seven years or older who participates more than once a year.

PARTICIPATION IN BICYCLE RIDING, 1990				Rank in order
State	Participants	% of state population	Rank by %	By %
Alabama	65,200	1.6	43	1. Montana
Alaska	NA	NA	NA	2. Idaho
Arizona	91,900	2.5	18	3. Wyoming
Arkansas	29,900	1.3	48	4. Iowa
California	678,300	2.3	25	5. Minnesota
Colorado	79,800	2.4	21	6. Rhode Island
Connecticut	50,600	1.5	44	7. Utah
Delaware	7,100	1.1	49	8. North Dakota
District of Columbia	9,000	1.5	45	9. West Virginia
Florida	327,300	2.5	17	10. Wisconsin
Georgia	127,500	2.0	33	11. Maine
Hawaii	NA	NA	NA	12. Nevada
Idaho	45,100	4.5	2	13. Michigan
Illinois	278,600	2.4	19	14. Oregon
Indiana	134,500	2.4	20	15. Louisiana
Iowa	102,600	3.7	4	16. New Mexico
Kansas	42,700	1.7	40	17. Florida
Kentucky	81,600	2.2	28	18. Arizona
Louisiana	112,900	2.7	15	19. Illinois
Maine	37,200	3.0	11	20. Indiana
Maryland	90,200	1.9	35	21. Colorado
Massachusetts	135,800	2.3	27	22. South Carolina
Michigan	261,600	2.8	13	23. Missouri
Minnesota	153,800	3.5	5	24. New York
Mississippi	36,500	1.4	47	25. California
Missouri	120,600	2.4	23	26. Ohio
Montana	41,700	5.2	1	27. Massachusetts
Nebraska	34,900	2.2	29	28. Kentucky
Nevada	35,000	2.9	12	29. Nebraska
New Hampshire	18,400	1.7	42	30. South Dakota
New Jersey	156,900	2.0	31	31. New Jersey
New Mexico	39,900	2.6	16	32. North Carolina
New York	417,000	2.3	24	33. Georgia
North Carolina	131,000	2.0	32	34. Vermont
North Dakota	20,700	3.2	8	35. Maryland
Ohio	244,900	2.3	26	36. Washington
Oklahoma	45,000	1.4	46	37. Pennsylvania
Oregon	77,500	2.7	14	38. Tennessee
Pennsylvania	222,000	1.9	37	39. Texas
Rhode Island	35,200	3.5	6	40. Kansas
South Carolina	82,700	2.4	22	41. Virginia
South Dakota	14,900	2.1	30	42. New Hampshire
Tennessee	90,800	1.9	38	43. Alabama
Texas	311,300	1.8	39	44. Connecticut
Utah	56,300	3.3	7	45. District of Columbia
Vermont	11,000	2.0	34	46. Oklahoma
Virginia	104,100	1.7	41	47. Mississippi
Washington	91,600	1.9	36	48. Arkansas
West Virginia	57,700	3.2	9	49. Delaware
Wisconsin	151,300	3.1	10	NA Alaska
Wyoming	17,300	3.8	3	NA Hawaii
United States	5,609,300	2.3	28	

NA not available.

Source: National Sporting Goods Association, *Sports Participation in 1990* (Prospect, Ill.: National Sporting Goods Association, 1992).

Note: Participant is defined as someone seven years or older who participates six or more times during the year.

NUMBER OF BOATS, 1991		Per 1,000 population		Rank in order
State	Boats	Rate	Rank	By rate per 1,000 population
Alabama	233,738	57.2	17	1. Minnesota
Alaska	31,822	55.8	18	2. Wisconsin
Arizona	144,123	38.4	29	3. South Carolina
Arkansas	140,672	59.3	16	4. Michigan
California	815,730	26.9	42	5. Maine
Colorado	81,000	24.0	47	6. New Hampshire
Connecticut	100,800	30.6	41	7. Vermont
Delaware	47,910	70.5	9	8. Mississippi
District of Columbia	6,200	10.4	51	9. Delaware
Florida	685,389	51.6	21	10. Louisiana
Georgia	276,362	41.7	27	11. Idaho
Hawaii	13,592	12.0	50	12. North Dakota
Idaho	67,018	64.5	11	13. Iowa
Illinois	360,894	31.3	39	14. Oregon
Indiana	269,883	48.1	25	15. Oklahoma
Iowa	172,495	61.7	13	16. Arkansas
Kansas	94,413	37.8	30	17. Alabama
Kentucky	138,128	37.2	31	18. Alaska
Louisiana	290,812	68.4	10	19. Missouri
Maine	111,308	90.1	5	20. Montana
Maryland	180,508	37.1	32	21. Florida
Massachusetts	145,789	24.3	44	22. South Dakota
Michigan	863,888	92.2	4	23. Wyoming
Minnesota	723,071	163.1	1	24. Tennessee
Mississippi	185,909	71.7	8	25. Indiana
Missouri	277,473	53.8	19	26. Washington
Montana	43,397	53.7	20	27. Georgia
Nebraska	58,112	36.5	33	28. North Carolina
Nevada	43,163	33.6	37	29. Arizona
New Hampshire	82,100	74.3	6	30. Kansas
New Jersey	155,290	20.0	49	31. Kentucky
New Mexico	36,253	23.4	48	32. Maryland
New York	437,579	24.2	45	33. Nebraska
North Carolina	280,251	41.6	28	34. Ohio
North Dakota	39,480	62.2	12	35. Texas
Ohio	383,136	35.0	34	36. Utah
Oklahoma	190,600	60.0	15	37. Nevada
Oregon	177,043	60.6	14	38. Virginia
Pennsylvania	301,804	25.2	43	39. Illinois
Rhode Island	31,216	31.1	40	40. Rhode Island
South Carolina	333,467	93.7	3	41. Connecticut
South Dakota	35,685	50.8	22	42. California
Tennessee	247,661	50.0	24	43. Pennsylvania
Texas	600,329	34.6	35	44. Massachusetts
Utah	60,243	34.0	36	45. New York
Vermont	41,951	74.0	7	46. West Virginia
Virginia	202,616	32.2	38	47. Colorado
Washington	220,463	43.9	26	48. New Mexico
West Virginia	43,423	24.1	46	49. New Jersey
Wisconsin	500,917	101.1	2	50. Hawaii
Wyoming	23,284	50.6	23	51. District of Columbia
United States	**11,028,390**	**43.7**	**27**	

Source: U.S. Coast Guard, *Boating Statistics, 1991* (Washington, D.C.: Department of Transportation, 1992).

ATTENDANCE AT PARIMUTUEL RACING, 1989

State	Average daily attendance	Per 1,000 population		Rank in order — By attendance per 1,000 population
		Rate	Rank	
Alabama	2,558	0.62	21	1. Arkansas
Alaska	—	—	—	2. Delaware
Arizona	2,686	0.76	19	3. New Hampshire
Arkansas	15,792	6.56	1	4. Nebraska
California	9,076	0.31	28	5. Wyoming
Colorado	1,046	0.32	25	6. Minnesota
Connecticut	—	—	—	7. South Dakota
Delaware	2,597	3.86	2	8. Idaho
District of Columbia	—	—	—	9. Oklahoma
Florida	5,282	0.42	23	10. New Mexico
Georgia	—	—	—	11. North Dakota
Hawaii	—	—	—	12. West Virginia
Idaho	1,647	1.62	8	13. Kentucky
Illinois	4,248	0.36	24	14. Maryland
Indiana	—	—	—	15. Washington
Iowa	2,666	0.94	17	16. Louisiana
Kansas	1,297	0.52	22	17. Iowa
Kentucky	4,631	1.24	13	18. New Jersey
Louisiana	4,183	0.96	16	19. Arizona
Maine	—	—	—	20. Massachusetts
Maryland	5,460	1.16	14	21. Alabama
Massachusetts	3,917	0.66	20	22. Kansas
Michigan	2,922	0.32	25	23. Florida
Minnesota	7,239	1.66	6	24. Illinois
Mississippi	—	—	—	25. Colorado
Missouri	—	—	—	Michigan
Montana	—	—	—	Ohio
Nebraska	4,360	2.71	4	28. California
Nevada	—	—	—	29. Pennsylvania
New Hampshire	4,073	3.68	3	30. New York
New Jersey	6,580	0.85	18	31. Texas
New Mexico	2,396	1.57	10	— Alaska
New York	4,244	0.24	30	— Connecticut
North Carolina	—	—	—	— District of Columbia
North Dakota	925	1.40	11	— Georgia
Ohio	3,431	0.32	25	— Hawaii
Oklahoma	5,129	1.59	9	— Indiana
Oregon	—	—	—	— Maine
Pennsylvania	3,173	0.26	29	— Mississippi
Rhode Island	—	—	—	— Missouri
South Carolina	—	—	—	— Montana
South Dakota	1,188	1.66	7	— Nevada
Tennessee	—	—	—	— North Carolina
Texas	2,195	0.13	31	— Oregon
Utah	—	—	—	— Rhode Island
Vermont	—	—	—	— South Carolina
Virginia	—	—	—	— Tennessee
Washington	4,984	1.05	15	— Utah
West Virginia	2,512	1.35	12	— Vermont
Wisconsin	—	—	—	— Virginia
Wyoming	1,047	2.20	5	— Wisconsin
United States	4,398	0.02	32	

— not applicable.

Source: Association of Racing Commissioners International Inc., *Parimutuel Racing 1989* (Lexington, Ky.: Association of Racing Commissioners International Inc., 1990).

| REVENUE FROM PARIMUTUEL BETTING, 1989 | | Per 1,000 population | | Rank in order |
State	Revenue	Rate	Rank	By rate per 1,000 population
Alabama	$1,105,809	$268.53	28	1. New York
Alaska	—	—	—	2. Connecticut
Arizona	1,112,433	312.83	27	3. California
Arkansas	4,030,694	1,675.27	12	4. Louisiana
California	163,894,648	5,639.29	3	5. Kentucky
Colorado	125,761	37.91	34	6. Illinois
Connecticut	20,452,667	6,314.50	2	7. New Hampshire
Delaware	340,180	505.47	23	8. Oklahoma
District of Columbia	—	—	—	9. Michigan
Florida	13,853,258	1,093.30	15	10. Washington
Georgia	—	—	—	11. Ohio
Hawaii	—	—	—	12. Arkansas
Idaho	323,810	319.34	26	13. New Mexico
Illinois	48,133,884	4,128.83	6	14. West Virginia
Indiana	—	—	—	15. Florida
Iowa	591,958	208.44	29	16. New Jersey
Kansas	243,735	96.99	31	17. Maryland
Kentucky	17,620,401	4,727.77	5	18. Pennsylvania
Louisiana	23,425,248	5,345.79	4	19. Maine
Maine	712,288	582.89	19	20. Minnesota
Maryland	4,478,622	954.12	17	21. Wyoming
Massachusetts	3,046,762	515.27	22	22. Massachusetts
Michigan	22,004,866	2,373.00	9	23. Delaware
Minnesota	2,447,186	562.18	20	24. Nebraska
Mississippi	—	—	—	25. Oregon
Missouri	—	—	—	26. Idaho
Montana	138,856	172.28	30	27. Arizona
Nebraska	648,827	402.75	24	28. Alabama
Nevada	14,222	12.80	37	29. Iowa
New Hampshire	3,191,731	2,883.23	7	30. Montana
New Jersey	8,089,099	1,045.64	16	31. Kansas
New Mexico	2,292,299	1,500.20	13	32. Vermont
New York	189,174,272	10,538.90	1	33. Texas
North Carolina	—	—	—	34. Colorado
North Dakota	15,486	23.46	36	35. South Dakota
Ohio	20,782,460	1,905.42	11	36. North Dakota
Oklahoma	8,886,266	2,756.29	8	37. Nevada
Oregon	1,074,580	381.06	25	— Alaska
Pennsylvania	9,472,650	786.76	18	— District of Columbia
Rhode Island	—	—	—	— Georgia
South Carolina	—	—	—	— Hawaii
South Dakota	26,388	36.91	35	— Indiana
Tennessee	—	—	—	— Mississippi
Texas	713,167	41.97	33	— Missouri
Utah	—	—	—	— North Carolina
Vermont	43,955	77.52	32	— Rhode Island
Virginia	—	—	—	— South Carolina
Washington	9,941,078	2,088.02	10	— Tennessee
West Virginia	2,177,101	1,172.38	14	— Utah
Wisconsin	—	—	—	— Virginia
Wyoming	261,556	550.64	21	— Wisconsin
United States	$584,888,183	$2,356.15	10	

— not applicable.

Source: Association of Racing Commissioners International Inc., *Parimutuel Racing 1989* (Lexington, Ky.: Association of Racing Commissioners International Inc., 1990).

Social Services

FEDERAL GRANTS FOR SOCIAL SERVICES, FISCAL 1991				Rank in order
State	Expenditures	Per capita	Rank by per capita	By per capita
Alabama	$46,459,000	$11.36	19	1. North Dakota
Alaska	6,001,000	10.53	44	2. Wyoming
Arizona	42,404,000	11.31	21	3. Louisiana
Arkansas	28,765,000	12.13	9	4. Indiana
California	331,236,000	10.90	33	5. Oklahoma
Colorado	37,391,000	11.07	27	6. New Hampshire
Connecticut	38,890,000	11.82	11	7. South Dakota
Delaware	6,937,000	10.20	47	8. Pennsylvania
District of Columbia	4,771,000	7.98	51	9. Arkansas
Florida	139,721,000	10.52	45	10. Mississippi
Georgia	76,187,000	11.50	16	11. Connecticut
Hawaii	12,557,000	11.06	28	12. Ohio
Idaho	11,361,000	10.94	32	13. Iowa
Illinois	125,344,000	10.86	34	14. Nebraska
Indiana	72,346,000	12.90	4	15. Tennessee
Iowa	32,420,000	11.60	13	16. Georgia
Kansas	27,709,000	11.11	25	17. Montana
Kentucky	39,125,000	10.54	43	18. Texas
Louisiana	59,307,000	13.95	3	19. Alabama
Maine	13,210,000	10.70	40	20. North Carolina
Maryland	52,337,000	10.77	37	21. Arizona
Massachusetts	60,372,000	10.07	48	22. New Jersey
Michigan	100,811,000	10.76	38	23. New York
Minnesota	48,702,000	10.99	31	24. Vermont
Mississippi	30,815,000	11.89	10	25. Kansas
Missouri	55,121,000	10.69	41	26. Wisconsin
Montana	9,293,000	11.50	17	27. Colorado
Nebraska	18,382,000	11.54	14	28. Hawaii
Nevada	12,126,000	9.44	50	29. Rhode Island
New Hampshire	13,751,000	12.44	6	30. New Mexico
New Jersey	87,457,000	11.27	22	31. Minnesota
New Mexico	17,070,000	11.03	30	32. Idaho
New York	201,565,000	11.16	23	33. California
North Carolina	76,480,000	11.35	20	34. Illinois
North Dakota	10,305,000	16.23	1	35. Virginia
Ohio	127,477,000	11.65	12	36. South Carolina
Oklahoma	39,783,000	12.53	5	37. Maryland
Oregon	31,342,000	10.73	39	38. Michigan
Pennsylvania	148,318,000	12.40	8	39. Oregon
Rhode Island	11,104,000	11.06	29	40. Maine
South Carolina	38,344,000	10.77	36	41. Missouri
South Dakota	8,727,000	12.41	7	42. Utah
Tennessee	56,997,000	11.51	15	43. Kentucky
Texas	197,815,000	11.40	18	44. Alaska
Utah	18,794,000	10.62	42	45. Florida
Vermont	6,309,000	11.13	24	46. Washington
Virginia	68,133,000	10.84	35	47. Delaware
Washington	52,649,000	10.49	46	48. Massachusetts
West Virginia	17,313,000	9.61	49	49. West Virginia
Wisconsin	54,994,000	11.10	26	50. Nevada
Wyoming	6,913,000	15.03	2	51. District of Columbia
United States	$2,847,150,000	$11.29	22	

Source: U.S. Department of Commerce, Bureau of the Census, *Federal Expenditures by State for Fiscal Year 1991* (Washington, D.C.: Government Printing Office, 1992).

STATE SPENDING ON PUBLIC WELFARE, FISCAL 1991

State	Expenditures	Per capita	Rank by per capita	Per $1,000 personal income Amount	Rank	By per capita
Alabama	$1,356,970,000	$331.86	41	$22.33	30	1. Massachusetts
Alaska	434,961,000	763.09	3	36.38	4	2. New York
Arizona	1,034,440,000	275.85	48	17.55	47	3. Alaska
Arkansas	953,593,000	402.02	27	28.56	16	4. Maine
California	18,990,798,000	625.11	7	30.66	8	5. Rhode Island
Colorado	1,131,940,000	335.19	39	18.15	46	6. Connecticut
Connecticut	2,068,735,000	628.60	6	24.67	25	7. California
Delaware	256,892,000	377.78	32	19.18	41	8. Vermont
District of Columbia	—	—	—	—	—	9. Michigan
Florida	4,556,120,000	343.16	38	18.85	43	10. New Jersey
Georgia	2,672,806,000	403.56	25	24.10	28	11. Minnesota
Hawaii	478,011,000	421.16	20	21.09	35	12. Ohio
Idaho	285,200,000	274.49	49	18.49	44	13. Kentucky
Illinois	4,860,235,000	421.05	21	20.80	36	14. Pennsylvania
Indiana	2,271,725,000	404.94	24	24.22	27	15. Wisconsin
Iowa	1,171,292,000	419.07	22	24.47	26	16. Washington
Kansas	825,194,000	330.74	42	18.32	45	17. Maryland
Kentucky	1,936,684,000	521.60	13	34.99	5	18. South Carolina
Louisiana	1,831,817,000	430.81	19	29.91	11	19. Louisiana
Maine	877,679,000	710.67	4	41.51	3	20. Hawaii
Maryland	2,107,771,000	433.70	17	20.14	38	21. Illinois
Massachusetts	5,784,674,000	964.76	1	42.58	2	22. Iowa
Michigan	5,125,229,000	547.10	9	29.97	9	23. Montana
Minnesota	2,375,445,000	535.98	11	28.89	13	24. Indiana
Mississippi	868,399,000	335.03	40	26.31	21	25. Georgia
Missouri	1,771,716,000	343.49	37	19.78	39	26. North Dakota
Montana	331,119,000	409.80	23	27.13	18	27. Arkansas
Nebraska	594,398,000	371.03	33	21.43	34	28. Tennessee
Nevada	262,459,000	204.41	50	11.27	50	29. Oklahoma
New Hampshire	398,299,000	360.45	34	17.21	48	30. West Virginia
New Jersey	4,185,677,000	539.39	10	21.70	33	31. Oregon
New Mexico	537,590,000	347.28	36	24.80	24	32. Delaware
New York	17,015,247,000	942.26	2	42.79	1	33. Nebraska
North Carolina	2,361,902,000	350.59	35	21.79	32	34. New Hampshire
North Dakota	255,754,000	402.76	26	26.40	20	35. North Carolina
Ohio	5,712,108,000	522.18	12	29.95	10	36. New Mexico
Oklahoma	1,263,277,000	397.88	29	25.98	22	37. Missouri
Oregon	1,144,097,000	391.55	31	23.25	29	38. Florida
Pennsylvania	6,115,065,000	511.25	14	27.52	17	39. Colorado
Rhode Island	651,329,000	648.73	5	34.47	7	40. Mississippi
South Carolina	1,538,128,000	432.06	18	29.02	12	41. Alabama
South Dakota	212,120,000	301.74	45	19.29	40	42. Kansas
Tennessee	1,977,532,000	399.26	28	25.50	23	43. Wyoming
Texas	5,393,405,000	310.88	44	18.92	42	44. Texas
Utah	533,666,000	301.51	46	22.05	31	45. South Dakota
Vermont	345,516,000	609.38	8	34.94	6	46. Utah
Virginia	1,814,379,000	288.64	47	14.85	49	47. Virginia
Washington	2,451,817,000	488.60	16	26.60	19	48. Arizona
West Virginia	708,271,000	393.27	30	28.77	15	49. Idaho
Wisconsin	2,480,359,000	500.58	15	28.79	14	50. Nevada
Wyoming	152,107,000	330.67	43	20.62	37	— District of Columbia
United States	$124,463,947,000	$494.73	16	$26.77	19	

— not applicable.

Source: U.S. Department of Commerce, Bureau of the Census, *State Government Finances: 1991* (Washington, D.C.: Government Printing Office, 1992).

State	% of population in poverty	Rank by %
Alabama	18.8	4
Alaska	11.8	34
Arizona	14.8	19
Arkansas	17.3	9
California	15.7	13
Colorado	10.4	38
Connecticut	8.6	48
Delaware	7.5	50
District of Columbia	18.6	6
Florida	15.4	16
Georgia	17.2	10
Hawaii	7.7	49
Idaho	13.9	26
Illinois	13.5	27
Indiana	15.7	13
Iowa	9.6	44
Kansas	12.3	33
Kentucky	18.8	4
Louisiana	19.0	3
Maine	14.1	23
Maryland	9.1	47
Massachusetts	11.0	36
Michigan	14.1	23
Minnesota	12.9	30
Mississippi	23.7	1
Missouri	14.8	19
Montana	15.4	16
Nebraska	9.5	45
Nevada	11.4	35
New Hampshire	7.3	51
New Jersey	9.7	43
New Mexico	22.4	2
New York	15.3	18
North Carolina	14.5	21
North Dakota	14.5	21
Ohio	13.4	29
Oklahoma	17.0	11
Oregon	13.5	27
Pennsylvania	11.0	36
Rhode Island	10.4	38
South Carolina	16.4	12
South Dakota	14.0	25
Tennessee	15.5	15
Texas	17.5	8
Utah	12.9	30
Vermont	12.6	32
Virginia	9.9	40
Washington	9.5	45
West Virginia	17.9	7
Wisconsin	9.9	40
Wyoming	9.9	40
United States	NA	NA

Rank in order

By %

1. Mississippi
2. New Mexico
3. Louisiana
4. Alabama
   Kentucky
6. District of Columbia
7. West Virginia
8. Texas
9. Arkansas
10. Georgia
11. Oklahoma
12. South Carolina
13. California
    Indiana
15. Tennessee
16. Florida
    Montana
18. New York
19. Arizona
    Missouri
21. North Carolina
    North Dakota
23. Maine
    Michigan
25. South Dakota
26. Idaho
27. Illinois
    Oregon
29. Ohio
30. Minnesota
    Utah
32. Vermont
33. Kansas
34. Alaska
35. Nevada
36. Massachusetts
    Pennsylvania
38. Colorado
    Rhode Island
40. Virginia
    Wisconsin
    Wyoming
43. New Jersey
44. Iowa
45. Nebraska
    Washington
47. Maryland
48. Connecticut
49. Hawaii
50. Delaware
51. New Hampshire

Source: Bureau of the Census, *Poverty in the United States, 1991* (Washington, D.C.: Department of Commerce, 1992).

State	% of state population	Rank by %
Alabama	6.5	15
Alaska	4.6	36
Arizona	4.7	33
Arkansas	6.3	18
California	9.4	4
Colorado	4.3	39
Connecticut	4.7	33
Delaware	4.4	38
District of Columbia	10.9	2
Florida	4.6	36
Georgia	7.1	11
Hawaii	5.2	29
Idaho	2.7	50
Illinois	7.1	11
Indiana	3.9	43
Iowa	4.7	33
Kansas	4.1	42
Kentucky	7.9	7
Louisiana	9.8	3
Maine	6.6	13
Maryland	5.1	30
Massachusetts	6.4	16
Michigan	8.6	6
Minnesota	4.9	31
Mississippi	11.4	1
Missouri	5.8	21
Montana	4.9	31
Nebraska	3.7	46
Nevada	2.9	49
New Hampshire	2.2	51
New Jersey	5.3	28
New Mexico	5.8	21
New York	7.7	8
North Carolina	5.7	24
North Dakota	3.6	47
Ohio	7.3	9
Oklahoma	5.6	26
Oregon	4.3	39
Pennsylvania	6.0	19
Rhode Island	6.4	16
South Carolina	5.8	21
South Dakota	4.2	41
Tennessee	7.2	10
Texas	5.4	27
Utah	3.3	48
Vermont	5.7	24
Virginia	3.9	43
Washington	6.0	19
West Virginia	8.8	5
Wisconsin	6.6	13
Wyoming	3.8	45
United States	**6.5**	**15**

By %

1. Mississippi
2. District of Columbia
3. Louisiana
4. California
5. West Virginia
6. Michigan
7. Kentucky
8. New York
9. Ohio
10. Tennessee
11. Georgia
    Illinois
13. Maine
    Wisconsin
15. Alabama
16. Massachusetts
    Rhode Island
18. Arkansas
19. Pennsylvania
    Washington
21. Missouri
    New Mexico
    South Carolina
24. North Carolina
    Vermont
26. Oklahoma
27. Texas
28. New Jersey
29. Hawaii
30. Maryland
31. Minnesota
    Montana
33. Arizona
    Connecticut
    Iowa
36. Alaska
    Florida
38. Delaware
39. Colorado
    Oregon
41. South Dakota
42. Kansas
43. Indiana
    Virginia
45. Wyoming
46. Nebraska
47. North Dakota
48. Utah
49. Nevada
50. Idaho
51. New Hampshire

Source: U.S. Department of Commerce, Bureau of the Census, *Statistical Abstract of the United States, 1992* (Washington, D.C.: Government Printing Office, 1992).

PARTICIPANTS IN FOOD STAMP PROGRAM, 1990					Rank in order
State	Participants	Cost of program	Per capita	Rank by per capita	By per capita
Alabama	460,000	$330,000,000	$81.66	6	1. Mississippi
Alaska	26,000	25,000,000	45.45	29	2. Louisiana
Arizona	348,000	239,000,000	65.21	16	3. West Virginia
Arkansas	231,000	155,000,000	65.93	15	4. Kentucky
California	1,975,000	1,009,000,000	33.90	49	5. Texas
Colorado	226,000	156,000,000	47.36	26	6. Alabama
Connecticut	146,000	72,000,000	21.90	50	7. Ohio
Delaware	35,000	25,000,000	37.54	43	8. New Mexico
District of Columbia	64,000	43,000,000	70.84	13	9. Tennessee
Florida	826,000	609,000,000	47.07	27	10. Hawaii
Georgia	561,000	382,000,000	58.97	21	11. Illinois
Hawaii	76,000	81,000,000	73.10	10	12. Michigan
Idaho	57,000	40,000,000	39.72	36	13. District of Columbia
Illinois	1,041,000	835,000,000	73.05	11	14. South Carolina
Indiana	320,000	226,000,000	40.76	34	15. Arkansas
Iowa	170,000	109,000,000	39.25	37	16. Arizona
Kansas	145,000	96,000,000	38.74	41	17. Missouri
Kentucky	449,000	334,000,000	90.64	4	18. New York
Louisiana	721,000	549,000,000	130.09	2	19. Oklahoma
Maine	98,000	63,000,000	51.30	24	20. Oregon
Maryland	275,000	208,000,000	43.51	30	21. Georgia
Massachusetts	348,000	207,000,000	34.41	47	22. Pennsylvania
Michigan	940,000	663,000,000	71.33	12	23. Montana
Minnesota	268,000	165,000,000	37.71	42	24. Maine
Mississippi	500,000	352,000,000	136.81	1	25. South Dakota
Missouri	441,000	312,000,000	60.97	17	26. Colorado
Montana	56,000	41,000,000	51.31	23	27. Florida
Nebraska	94,000	59,000,000	37.39	44	28. Wyoming
Nevada	53,000	41,000,000	34.11	48	29. Alaska
New Hampshire	35,000	20,000,000	18.03	51	30. Maryland
New Jersey	396,000	289,000,000	37.39	45	31. North Carolina
New Mexico	158,000	117,000,000	77.23	8	32. Rhode Island
New York	1,594,000	1,086,000,000	60.37	18	33. Utah
North Carolina	438,000	282,000,000	42.54	31	34. Indiana
North Dakota	37,000	25,000,000	39.12	38	35. Virginia
Ohio	1,114,000	861,000,000	79.38	7	36. Idaho
Oklahoma	270,000	186,000,000	59.12	19	37. Iowa
Oregon	209,000	168,000,000	59.11	20	38. North Dakota
Pennsylvania	992,000	670,000,000	56.39	22	39. Vermont
Rhode Island	70,000	42,000,000	41.87	32	40. Washington
South Carolina	270,000	240,000,000	68.83	14	41. Kansas
South Dakota	50,000	35,000,000	50.29	25	42. Minnesota
Tennessee	542,000	372,000,000	76.28	9	43. Delaware
Texas	1,946,000	1,429,000,000	84.12	5	44. Nebraska
Utah	101,000	71,000,000	41.21	33	45. New Jersey
Vermont	39,000	22,000,000	39.08	39	46. Wisconsin
Virginia	356,000	247,000,000	39.92	35	47. Massachusetts
Washington	341,000	190,000,000	39.04	40	48. Nevada
West Virginia	259,000	192,000,000	107.08	3	49. California
Wisconsin	281,000	180,000,000	36.79	46	50. Connecticut
Wyoming	27,000	21,000,000	46.26	28	51. New Hampshire
United States	20,472,000	$14,172,000,000	$56.98	22	

Source: U.S. Department of Commerce, Bureau of the Census, *Statistical Abstract of the United States, 1992* (Washington, D.C.: Government Printing Office, 1992).

HOUSEHOLDS IN FOOD STAMP PROGRAM, 1990

State	Households	% of all households	Rank by %
Alabama	169,000	11.2	8
Alaska	9,000	4.8	49
Arizona	120,000	8.8	19
Arkansas	85,000	9.5	14
California	707,000	6.8	29
Colorado	89,000	6.9	28
Connecticut	58,000	4.7	50
Delaware	13,000	5.3	46
District of Columbia	28,000	11.2	8
Florida	315,000	6.1	38
Georgia	210,000	8.9	17
Hawaii	31,000	8.7	20
Idaho	20,000	5.5	44
Illinois	432,000	10.3	12
Indiana	112,000	5.4	45
Iowa	68,000	6.4	37
Kansas	55,000	5.8	41
Kentucky	163,000	11.8	4
Louisiana	252,000	16.8	2
Maine	43,000	9.2	16
Maryland	117,000	6.7	31
Massachusetts	158,000	7.0	27
Michigan	393,000	11.5	6
Minnesota	111,000	6.7	31
Mississippi	178,000	19.5	1
Missouri	171,000	8.7	20
Montana	20,000	6.5	35
Nebraska	37,000	6.1	38
Nevada	23,000	4.9	48
New Hampshire	15,000	3.6	51
New Jersey	157,000	5.6	43
New Mexico	54,000	10.0	13
New York	720,000	10.8	11
North Carolina	171,000	6.8	29
North Dakota	14,000	5.8	41
Ohio	473,000	11.6	5
Oklahoma	107,000	8.9	17
Oregon	90,000	8.2	23
Pennsylvania	427,000	9.5	14
Rhode Island	30,000	7.9	24
South Carolina	96,000	7.6	26
South Dakota	17,000	6.6	34
Tennessee	212,000	11.4	7
Texas	681,000	11.2	8
Utah	36,000	6.7	31
Vermont	18,000	8.5	22
Virginia	148,000	6.5	35
Washington	144,000	7.7	25
West Virginia	97,000	14.1	3
Wisconsin	95,000	5.2	47
Wyoming	10,000	5.9	40
United States	**8,005,000**	**8.7**	**20**

Rank in order

By %

1. Mississippi
2. Louisiana
3. West Virginia
4. Kentucky
5. Ohio
6. Michigan
7. Tennessee
8. Alabama
   District of Columbia
   Texas
11. New York
12. Illinois
13. New Mexico
14. Arkansas
    Pennsylvania
16. Maine
17. Georgia
    Oklahoma
19. Arizona
20. Hawaii
    Missouri
22. Vermont
23. Oregon
24. Rhode Island
25. Washington
26. South Carolina
27. Massachusetts
28. Colorado
29. California
    North Carolina
31. Maryland
    Minnesota
    Utah
34. South Dakota
35. Montana
    Virginia
37. Iowa
38. Florida
    Nebraska
40. Wyoming
41. Kansas
    North Dakota
43. New Jersey
44. Idaho
45. Indiana
46. Delaware
47. Wisconsin
48. Nevada
49. Alaska
50. Connecticut
51. New Hampshire

Source: U.S. Department of Commerce, Bureau of the Census, *Statistical Abstract of the United States, 1992* (Washington, D.C.: Government Printing Office, 1992).

PERCENTAGE OF POOR USING AFDC AND FOOD STAMPS, 1991			Rank in order
State	% of poor	Rank by %	By %
Alabama	45.5	50	1. Alaska
Alaska	99.2	1	2. Hawaii
Arizona	65.0	33	3. California
Arkansas	53.8	46	4. Connecticut
California	91.5	3	5. New York
Colorado	66.9	27	6. Vermont
Connecticut	89.6	4	7. Washington
Delaware	65.3	32	8. Rhode Island
District of Columbia	71.0	20	9. Massachusetts
Florida	61.4	38	10. Minnesota
Georgia	60.4	41	11. Wisconsin
Hawaii	98.7	2	12. Oregon
Idaho	62.2	37	13. New Hampshire
Illinois	66.2	29	14. Maine
Indiana	61.4	38	15. Michigan
Iowa	70.9	21	16. Maryland
Kansas	72.2	17	17. Kansas
Kentucky	57.2	44	18. Pennsylvania
Louisiana	52.6	47	19. New Jersey
Maine	75.4	14	20. District of Columbia
Maryland	72.3	16	21. Iowa
Massachusetts	79.2	9	22. North Dakota
Michigan	72.6	15	23. Utah
Minnesota	78.8	10	24. Montana
Mississippi	44.6	51	25. South Dakota
Missouri	61.3	40	26. Nebraska
Montana	69.2	24	27. Colorado
Nebraska	67.1	26	28. Oklahoma
Nevada	64.2	34	29. Illinois
New Hampshire	75.9	13	30. Ohio
New Jersey	71.1	19	31. Virginia
New Mexico	64.1	36	32. Delaware
New York	89.1	5	33. Arizona
North Carolina	58.3	43	34. Nevada
North Dakota	70.6	22	Wyoming
Ohio	66.1	30	36. New Mexico
Oklahoma	66.3	28	37. Idaho
Oregon	78.4	12	38. Florida
Pennsylvania	72.0	18	Indiana
Rhode Island	79.9	8	40. Missouri
South Carolina	54.3	45	41. Georgia
South Dakota	68.0	25	42. West Virginia
Tennessee	51.9	48	43. North Carolina
Texas	51.5	49	44. Kentucky
Utah	69.3	23	45. South Carolina
Vermont	87.2	6	46. Arkansas
Virginia	65.5	31	47. Louisiana
Washington	80.7	7	48. Tennessee
West Virginia	59.4	42	49. Texas
Wisconsin	78.5	11	50. Alabama
Wyoming	64.2	34	51. Mississippi
United States	67.1	26	

Source: Center for the Study of Social Policy, *Kids Count Data Book: State Profiles of Child Well-Being* (Washington, D.C.: Center for the Study of Social Policy, 1992).

Note: AFDC is Aid to Families with Dependent Children. Percent of poor is percentage of impoverished one-parent families, as defined by the previous year's U.S. poverty threshold, who are using AFDC and food stamps. In 1990, the threshold was $13,360.

FEDERAL SPENDING ON CHILDREN AND FAMILY SERVICES, FISCAL 1991				Rank in order

State	Expenditures	Per capita	Rank by per capita	By per capita
Alabama	$50,981,000	$12.47	21	1. District of Columbia
Alaska	14,485,000	25.41	3	2. Mississippi
Arizona	55,091,000	14.69	14	3. Alaska
Arkansas	34,018,000	14.34	16	4. South Dakota
California	447,717,000	14.74	13	5. North Dakota
Colorado	36,949,000	10.94	29	6. Montana
Connecticut	31,566,000	9.59	43	7. New Mexico
Delaware	8,590,000	12.63	20	8. Wyoming
District of Columbia	35,252,000	58.95	1	9. Hawaii
Florida	105,415,000	7.94	49	10. Vermont
Georgia	59,319,000	8.96	46	11. West Virginia
Hawaii	19,326,000	17.03	9	12. Idaho
Idaho	15,709,000	15.12	12	13. California
Illinois	139,157,000	12.06	23	14. Arizona
Indiana	42,506,000	7.58	50	15. Oklahoma
Iowa	30,220,000	10.81	34	16. Arkansas
Kansas	27,297,000	10.94	29	17. Kentucky
Kentucky	49,125,000	13.23	17	18. South Carolina
Louisiana	52,278,000	12.30	22	19. Washington
Maine	13,420,000	10.87	31	20. Delaware
Maryland	41,886,000	8.62	48	21. Alabama
Massachusetts	70,632,000	11.78	26	22. Louisiana
Michigan	88,991,000	9.50	45	23. Illinois
Minnesota	45,667,000	10.30	38	24. Rhode Island
Mississippi	79,240,000	30.57	2	25. Oregon
Missouri	53,002,000	10.28	39	26. Massachusetts
Montana	15,469,000	19.15	6	27. Nevada
Nebraska	15,670,000	9.84	42	28. Tennessee
Nevada	14,925,000	11.62	27	29. Colorado
New Hampshire	7,920,000	7.17	51	Kansas
New Jersey	77,227,000	9.95	40	31. Maine
New Mexico	28,975,000	18.72	7	32. Virginia
New York	195,986,000	10.85	33	33. New York
North Carolina	71,976,000	10.68	35	34. Iowa
North Dakota	12,376,000	19.49	5	35. North Carolina
Ohio	97,567,000	8.92	47	36. Pennsylvania
Oklahoma	46,557,000	14.66	15	37. Utah
Oregon	34,479,000	11.80	25	38. Minnesota
Pennsylvania	126,602,000	10.59	36	39. Missouri
Rhode Island	11,863,000	11.82	24	40. New Jersey
South Carolina	45,609,000	12.81	18	41. Wisconsin
South Dakota	17,787,000	25.30	4	42. Nebraska
Tennessee	54,736,000	11.05	28	43. Connecticut
Texas	165,567,000	9.54	44	44. Texas
Utah	18,538,000	10.47	37	45. Michigan
Vermont	9,357,000	16.50	10	46. Georgia
Virginia	68,229,000	10.85	32	47. Ohio
Washington	63,641,000	12.68	19	48. Maryland
West Virginia	28,255,000	15.69	11	49. Florida
Wisconsin	49,306,000	9.95	41	50. Indiana
Wyoming	8,236,000	17.90	8	51. New Hampshire
United States	$3,030,367,000	$12.02	24	

Source: U.S. Department of Commerce, Bureau of the Census, *Federal Expenditures by State for Fiscal Year 1991* (Washington, D.C.: Government Printing Office, 1992).

State	Expenditures	Per capita	Rank by per capita
Alabama	$50,507,000	$12.35	10
Alaska	6,428,000	11.28	14
Arizona	41,979,000	11.19	15
Arkansas	29,526,000	12.45	9
California	213,610,000	7.03	44
Colorado	21,807,000	6.46	45
Connecticut	30,726,000	9.34	22
Delaware	5,299,000	7.79	37
District of Columbia	5,776,000	9.66	21
Florida	82,951,000	6.25	48
Georgia	76,204,000	11.51	13
Hawaii	9,907,000	8.73	28
Idaho	13,169,000	12.68	7
Illinois	94,015,000	8.15	33
Indiana	49,402,000	8.81	27
Iowa	22,823,000	8.17	32
Kansas	19,056,000	7.64	39
Kentucky	44,825,000	12.07	12
Louisiana	60,671,000	14.27	4
Maine	15,612,000	12.64	8
Maryland	28,485,000	5.86	50
Massachusetts	34,401,000	5.74	51
Michigan	79,093,000	8.44	30
Minnesota	33,046,000	7.46	41
Mississippi	44,790,000	17.28	1
Missouri	40,858,000	7.92	36
Montana	8,487,000	10.50	20
Nebraska	12,823,000	8.05	35
Nevada	8,062,000	6.28	47
New Hampshire	8,074,000	7.31	42
New Jersey	45,730,000	5.89	49
New Mexico	20,553,000	13.28	6
New York	160,741,000	8.90	26
North Carolina	61,333,000	9.10	23
North Dakota	7,796,000	12.28	11
Ohio	88,153,000	8.06	34
Oklahoma	27,104,000	8.54	29
Oregon	21,829,000	7.47	40
Pennsylvania	97,852,000	8.18	31
Rhode Island	8,956,000	8.92	25
South Carolina	48,170,000	13.53	5
South Dakota	10,317,000	14.68	3
Tennessee	54,356,000	10.97	18
Texas	156,440,000	9.02	24
Utah	19,789,000	11.18	17
Vermont	8,636,000	15.23	2
Virginia	48,077,000	7.65	38
Washington	31,615,000	6.30	46
West Virginia	19,519,000	10.84	19
Wisconsin	35,160,000	7.10	43
Wyoming	5,144,000	11.18	16
United States	$2,275,419,000	$9.02	24

Rank in order

By per capita

1. Mississippi
2. Vermont
3. South Dakota
4. Louisiana
5. South Carolina
6. New Mexico
7. Idaho
8. Maine
9. Arkansas
10. Alabama
11. North Dakota
12. Kentucky
13. Georgia
14. Alaska
15. Arizona
16. Wyoming
17. Utah
18. Tennessee
19. West Virginia
20. Montana
21. District of Columbia
22. Connecticut
23. North Carolina
24. Texas
25. Rhode Island
26. New York
27. Indiana
28. Hawaii
29. Oklahoma
30. Michigan
31. Pennsylvania
32. Iowa
33. Illinois
34. Ohio
35. Nebraska
36. Missouri
37. Delaware
38. Virginia
39. Kansas
40. Oregon
41. Minnesota
42. New Hampshire
43. Wisconsin
44. California
45. Colorado
46. Washington
47. Nevada
48. Florida
49. New Jersey
50. Maryland
51. Massachusetts

Source: U.S. Department of Commerce, Bureau of the Census, *Federal Expenditures by State for Fiscal Year 1991* (Washington, D.C.: Government Printing Office, 1992).

CHILD WELFARE SERVICES, 1989					Rank in order
State	Child welfare workers	Child population	Children per welfare worker	Rank by ratio	By ratio
Alabama	865.00	1,108,000	1,280.9	13	1. Nevada
Alaska	240.50	165,000	686.1	33	2. Indiana
Arizona	817.00	982,000	1,202.0	17	3. New Mexico
Arkansas	621.00	650,000	1,046.7	20	4. Utah
California	4,719.60	7,714,000	1,634.5	5	5. California
Colorado	1,092.00	864,000	791.2	26	6. Mississippi
Connecticut	617.00	759,000	1,230.2	16	7. Virginia
Delaware	233.00	168,000	721.0	32	8. Michigan
District of Columbia	178.00	139,000	780.9	27	9. Texas
Florida	6,252.50	2,872,000	459.3	44	10. Nebraska
Georgia	1,196.00	1,797,000	1,502.5	11	11. Georgia
Hawaii	386.00	288,000	746.1	30	12. Idaho
Idaho	218.00	304,000	1,394.5	12	13. Alabama
Illinois	2,735.00	2,980,000	1,089.6	19	14. Louisiana
Indiana	430.00	1,460,000	3,395.4	2	15. New Hampshire
Iowa	705.00	708,000	1,004.3	21	16. Connecticut
Kansas	1,107.25	659,000	595.2	39	17. Arizona
Kentucky	1,300.50	966,000	742.8	31	18. Oklahoma
Louisiana	1,018.00	1,273,000	1,250.5	14	19. Illinois
Maine	396.50	305,000	769.2	28	20. Arkansas
Maryland	1,709.50	1,161,000	679.2	34	21. Iowa
Massachusetts	2,190.50	1,337,000	610.4	37	22. Washington
Michigan	1,587.00	2,445,000	1,540.6	8	23. Pennsylvania
Minnesota	NA	1,129,000	NA	NA	24. South Carolina
Mississippi	476.00	769,000	1,615.6	6	25. South Dakota
Missouri	2,544.00	1,306,000	513.4	43	26. Colorado
Montana	328.20	217,000	661.2	35	27. District of Columbia
Nebraska	282.00	424,000	1,503.6	10	28. Maine
Nevada	76.50	277,000	3,620.9	1	29. New York
New Hampshire	226.00	279,000	1,234.5	15	30. Hawaii
New Jersey	3,487.00	1,833,000	525.7	42	31. Kentucky
New Mexico	230.00	454,000	1,973.9	3	32. Delaware
New York	5,675.00	4,350,000	766.5	29	33. Alaska
North Carolina	NA	1,642,000	NA	NA	34. Maryland
North Dakota	NA	179,000	NA	NA	35. Montana
Ohio	NA	2,818,000	NA	NA	36. Vermont
Oklahoma	782.00	853,000	1,090.8	18	37. Massachusetts
Oregon	NA	697,000	NA	NA	38. Tennessee
Pennsylvania	3,010.00	2,840,000	943.5	23	39. Kansas
Rhode Island	398.00	231,000	580.4	40	40. Rhode Island
South Carolina	1,015.00	955,000	940.9	24	41. Wisconsin
South Dakota	219.00	196,000	895.0	25	42. New Jersey
Tennessee	2,094.00	1,255,000	599.3	38	43. Missouri
Texas	3,241.00	4,952,000	1,527.9	9	44. Florida
Utah	334.00	631,000	1,889.2	4	45. Wyoming
Vermont	223.00	141,000	632.3	36	NA Minnesota
Virginia	926.00	1,482,000	1,600.4	7	NA North Carolina
Washington	1,227.70	1,216,000	990.5	22	NA North Dakota
West Virginia	NA	463,000	NA	NA	NA Ohio
Wisconsin	2,372.00	1,255,000	529.1	41	NA Oregon
Wyoming	354.00	136,000	384.2	45	NA West Virginia
United States	60,135.25	64,082,000	1,065.6	20	

NA not available.

Source: American Public Welfare Association, *Factbook on Public Child Welfare Services* (Washington, D.C.: American Public Welfare Association, 1990).

Note: The number of child welfare workers is calculated by the full-time equivalents.

CHILD ABUSE CASES REPORTED. 1990

State	Reported cases	Per 100,000 children
Alabama	40,794	385.3
Alaska	7,716	447.8
Arizona	39,207	399.6
Arkansas	23,739	382.2
California	553,782	714.5
Colorado	61,096	709.4
Connecticut	19,831	264.6
Delaware	7,395	452.9
District of Columbia	8,501	726.0
Florida	182,527	636.8
Georgia	86,594	501.3
Hawaii	3,421	122.1
Idaho	13,748	445.8
Illinois	104,449	354.5
Indiana	50,812	349.0
Iowa	35,298	491.0
Kansas	NA	NA
Kentucky	48,645	509.9
Louisiana	43,997	358.5
Maine	9,273	300.1
Maryland	47,146	405.7
Massachusetts	57,983	428.5
Michigan	116,151	472.4
Minnesota	13,620	116.7
Mississippi	16,279	218.0
Missouri	73,399	558.3
Montana	11,029	496.6
Nebraska	15,609	363.9
Nevada	23,220	782.1
New Hampshire	9,509	341.1
New Jersey	54,366	302.1
New Mexico	15,023	336.3
New York	212,767	499.5
North Carolina	74,222	462.1
North Dakota	6,054	345.2
Ohio	107,271	383.2
Oklahoma	47,386	566.1
Oregon	41,685	575.7
Pennsylvania	24,357	87.2
Rhode Island	12,989	575.5
South Carolina	28,615	311.0
South Dakota	11,267	567.6
Tennessee	33,382	274.4
Texas	134,295	277.7
Utah	24,224	386.1
Vermont	2,697	188.5
Virginia	51,548	342.6
Washington	27,092	214.8
West Virginia	24,865	560.5
Wisconsin	38,842	301.3
Wyoming	4,815	355.4
United States	**2,712,917**	**427.2**

NA not available.

Source: Administration for Children and Families, *National Child Abuse and Neglect Data System: Working Paper 1. 1990 Summary Data Component* (Washington, D.C.: Department of Health and Human Services, 1992).

Note: State data on child abuse reflect varying methodologies and cannot be compared with each other. Therefore, this table is not ranked. Kansas did not report data for 1990.

State	Related children	Children below poverty level	%	Rank by %
Alabama	1,044,374	250,485	24.0	9
Alaska	167,172	18,219	10.9	49
Arizona	956,550	207,188	21.7	10
Arkansas	610,863	152,891	25.0	5
California	7,509,141	1,335,512	17.8	20
Colorado	843,242	126,181	15.0	29
Connecticut	735,909	76,572	10.4	50
Delaware	159,941	18,697	11.7	44
District of Columbia	111,308	27,849	25.0	6
Florida	2,792,950	511,595	18.3	18
Georgia	1,696,466	336,020	19.8	16
Hawaii	273,746	30,440	11.1	46
Idaho	302,057	47,585	15.8	26
Illinois	2,895,494	485,706	16.8	25
Indiana	1,428,895	198,545	13.9	35
Iowa	705,446	98,463	14.0	33
Kansas	649,711	90,624	13.9	34
Kentucky	938,325	229,530	24.5	7
Louisiana	1,208,296	377,143	31.2	2
Maine	301,565	39,934	13.2	38
Maryland	1,136,669	124,149	10.9	48
Massachusetts	1,327,013	171,179	12.9	40
Michigan	2,412,856	440,082	18.2	19
Minnesota	1,147,812	142,202	12.4	42
Mississippi	736,090	246,224	33.5	1
Missouri	1,289,705	224,532	17.4	22
Montana	216,898	43,237	19.9	15
Nebraska	422,646	57,026	13.5	37
Nevada	285,255	36,455	12.8	41
New Hampshire	273,284	19,200	7.0	51
New Jersey	1,768,451	195,325	11.0	47
New Mexico	437,572	120,139	27.5	3
New York	4,160,128	782,530	18.8	17
North Carolina	1,578,852	266,933	16.9	23
North Dakota	172,964	29,214	16.9	24
Ohio	2,756,163	484,526	17.6	21
Oklahoma	821,045	175,340	21.4	11
Oregon	702,785	106,549	15.2	28
Pennsylvania	2,742,646	421,750	15.4	27
Rhode Island	222,328	30,022	13.5	36
South Carolina	906,202	188,110	20.8	12
South Dakota	195,221	39,240	20.1	14
Tennessee	1,193,453	247,366	20.7	13
Texas	4,749,480	1,140,367	24.0	8
Utah	618,936	75,504	12.2	43
Vermont	140,289	16,145	11.5	45
Virginia	1,473,533	191,983	13.0	39
Washington	1,223,467	171,257	14.0	32
West Virginia	436,708	112,942	25.9	4
Wisconsin	1,266,105	184,427	14.6	30
Wyoming	132,648	18,702	14.1	31
United States	62,278,655	11,161,836	17.9	20

CHILDREN IN POVERTY, 1989

Rank in order

By %

1. Mississippi
2. Louisiana
3. New Mexico
4. West Virginia
5. Arkansas
6. District of Columbia
7. Kentucky
8. Texas
9. Alabama
10. Arizona
11. Oklahoma
12. South Carolina
13. Tennessee
14. South Dakota
15. Montana
16. Georgia
17. New York
18. Florida
19. Michigan
20. California
21. Ohio
22. Missouri
23. North Carolina
24. North Dakota
25. Illinois
26. Idaho
27. Pennsylvania
28. Oregon
29. Colorado
30. Wisconsin
31. Wyoming
32. Washington
33. Iowa
34. Kansas
35. Indiana
36. Rhode Island
37. Nebraska
38. Maine
39. Virginia
40. Massachusetts
41. Nevada
42. Minnesota
43. Utah
44. Delaware
45. Vermont
46. Hawaii
47. New Jersey
48. Maryland
49. Alaska
50. Connecticut
51. New Hampshire

Source: Children's Defense Fund, *Child Poverty Data* (Washington, D.C.: Children's Defense Fund, 1992).
Note: "Related children" excludes persons under age eighteen who are not related to the head of the household (such as foster children), or who live alone or are teen parents. The Census Bureau's definition of poverty varies by family size. In 1989, a family of four was poor if its income was less than $12,675.

CHILDREN WITHOUT HEALTH INSURANCE, 1987-1991			Rank in order

State	% of children without health insurance	Rank by %	By %
Alabama	27.0	6	1. Texas
Alaska	20.6	18	2. New Mexico
Arizona	27.4	5	3. Arkansas
Arkansas	28.7	3	4. Mississippi
California	22.9	11	5. Arizona
Colorado	18.0	25	6. Alabama
Connecticut	11.7	46	7. Oklahoma
Delaware	18.4	24	8. Florida
District of Columbia	26.0	10	9. Louisiana
Florida	26.8	8	10. District of Columbia
Georgia	19.9	21	11. California
Hawaii	14.4	35	Kentucky
Idaho	21.1	16	13. North Carolina
Illinois	14.3	36	14. Nevada
Indiana	17.8	27	15. South Carolina
Iowa	10.2	50	16. Idaho
Kansas	13.7	39	17. Montana
Kentucky	22.9	11	18. Alaska
Louisiana	26.4	9	19. Oregon
Maine	13.8	38	20. Tennessee
Maryland	17.6	28	21. Georgia
Massachusetts	12.6	44	22. West Virginia
Michigan	11.7	46	23. South Dakota
Minnesota	9.9	51	24. Delaware
Mississippi	28.6	4	25. Colorado
Missouri	16.9	29	Virginia
Montana	20.7	17	27. Indiana
Nebraska	15.9	32	28. Maryland
Nevada	22.1	14	29. Missouri
New Hampshire	16.3	30	30. New Hampshire
New Jersey	13.4	41	31. New York
New Mexico	30.2	2	32. Nebraska
New York	16.0	31	33. Wyoming
North Carolina	22.5	13	34. Washington
North Dakota	11.2	48	35. Hawaii
Ohio	14.1	37	36. Illinois
Oklahoma	26.9	7	37. Ohio
Oregon	20.4	19	38. Maine
Pennsylvania	13.1	42	39. Kansas
Rhode Island	11.8	45	40. Vermont
South Carolina	21.5	15	41. New Jersey
South Dakota	19.1	23	42. Pennsylvania
Tennessee	20.3	20	43. Utah
Texas	30.4	1	44. Massachusetts
Utah	12.8	43	45. Rhode Island
Vermont	13.5	40	46. Connecticut
Virginia	18.0	25	Michigan
Washington	14.5	34	48. North Dakota
West Virginia	19.3	22	49. Wisconsin
Wisconsin	10.9	49	50. Iowa
Wyoming	15.1	33	51. Minnesota
United States	19.3	22	

Source: Center for the Study of Social Policy, *Kids Count Data Book: State Profiles of Child Well-Being* (Washington, D.C.: Center for the Study of Social Policy, 1992).

Note: Data is based on the five-year average of the percent of related children under age eighteen who are not covered by any kind of public or private health insurance, including Medicaid.

| CHILDREN WHO ARE HUNGRY OR AT RISK, 1991 | | | | | Rank in order |
State	% of children who are hungry	Rank by %	% of children who are at risk	Rank by %	By % of children hungry
Alabama	17.0	6	18.0	6	1. Mississippi
Alaska	8.3	48	9.4	48	2. Arkansas
Arizona	12.1	30	13.7	29	3. West Virginia
Arkansas	18.4	2	20.1	2	4. New Mexico
California	13.1	22	14.7	21	5. District of Columbia
Colorado	9.9	44	11.1	43	6. Alabama
Connecticut	7.8	50	8.4	50	7. Louisiana
Delaware	10.6	39	11.2	42	8. Idaho
District of Columbia	17.1	5	16.6	9	9. South Carolina
Florida	13.2	20	14.3	22	10. Iowa
Georgia	13.1	22	14.0	27	Montana
Hawaii	10.8	37	12.9	35	Tennessee
Idaho	15.6	8	18.8	5	13. New York
Illinois	13.9	15	14.1	26	14. Kentucky
Indiana	12.0	31	13.3	31	15. Illinois
Iowa	14.7	10	17.0	7	16. Texas
Kansas	10.5	40	12.3	39	17. Oklahoma
Kentucky	14.3	14	15.5	13	18. South Dakota
Louisiana	15.9	7	16.2	11	19. Michigan
Maine	11.2	36	13.1	34	20. Florida
Maryland	7.9	49	8.5	49	Nebraska
Massachusetts	9.3	47	10.0	47	22. California
Michigan	13.3	19	14.3	22	Georgia
Minnesota	9.8	45	11.4	41	24. Nevada
Mississippi	18.9	1	19.8	3	25. North Dakota
Missouri	12.7	26	14.2	24	26. Missouri
Montana	14.7	10	16.8	8	27. North Carolina
Nebraska	13.2	20	15.4	14	28. Pennsylvania
Nevada	12.9	24	15.0	19	29. Rhode Island
New Hampshire	5.8	51	6.8	51	30. Arizona
New Jersey	10.0	42	10.3	46	31. Indiana
New Mexico	17.2	4	18.9	4	32. Ohio
New York	14.6	13	15.1	17	33. Wisconsin
North Carolina	12.4	27	13.9	28	34. Oregon
North Dakota	12.8	25	15.1	17	Utah
Ohio	11.7	32	12.6	37	36. Maine
Oklahoma	13.5	17	15.2	15	37. Hawaii
Oregon	11.3	34	12.8	36	38. Washington
Pennsylvania	12.3	28	13.3	31	39. Delaware
Rhode Island	12.2	29	13.4	30	40. Kansas
South Carolina	15.0	9	16.3	10	41. Wyoming
South Dakota	13.4	18	15.2	15	42. New Jersey
Tennessee	14.7	10	16.0	12	Vermont
Texas	13.6	16	15.0	19	44. Colorado
Utah	11.3	34	14.2	24	45. Minnesota
Vermont	10.0	42	10.5	45	46. Virginia
Virginia	9.7	46	10.8	44	47. Massachusetts
Washington	10.7	38	12.0	40	48. Alaska
West Virginia	18.3	3	20.3	1	49. Maryland
Wisconsin	11.4	33	13.3	31	50. Connecticut
Wyoming	10.2	41	12.4	38	51. New Hampshire
United States	12.8	25	14.0	27	

Source: Spencer Rich, ''Hunger Said to Afflict 1 in 8 American Children,'' *Washington Post*, March 27, 1991.
Note: Percentage at risk represents children living in households that experienced aspects of hunger. Data are based on children up to age twelve.

| FEDERAL SPENDING ON CHILD NUTRITION PROGRAMS. FISCAL 1991 | | | | Rank in order |
State	Expenditures	Per capita	Rank by per capita	By per capita
Alabama	$122,589,000	$29.98	4	1. Mississippi
Alaska	15,716,000	27.57	9	2. Louisiana
Arizona	86,103,000	22.96	19	3. New Mexico
Arkansas	68,386,000	28.83	7	4. Alabama
California	665,374,000	21.90	24	5. North Dakota
Colorado	58,334,000	17.27	35	6. South Dakota
Connecticut	41,578,000	12.63	49	7. Arkansas
Delaware	13,051,000	19.19	28	8. Texas
District of Columbia	15,411,000	25.77	12	9. Alaska
Florida	273,873,000	20.63	26	10. Kentucky
Georgia	167,006,000	25.22	16	11. South Carolina
Hawaii	21,652,000	19.08	29	12. District of Columbia
Idaho	20,600,000	19.83	27	13. Utah
Illinois	204,122,000	17.68	33	14. Kansas
Indiana	87,224,000	15.55	39	15. West Virginia
Iowa	51,675,000	18.49	30	16. Georgia
Kansas	63,576,000	25.48	14	17. Oklahoma
Kentucky	101,006,000	27.20	10	18. Tennessee
Louisiana	163,481,000	38.45	2	19. Arizona
Maine	22,598,000	18.30	31	20. Montana
Maryland	66,470,000	13.68	44	21. North Carolina
Massachusetts	88,703,000	14.79	42	22. Nebraska
Michigan	141,310,000	15.08	41	23. Minnesota
Minnesota	99,731,000	22.50	23	24. California
Mississippi	123,980,000	47.83	1	25. Wyoming
Missouri	93,738,000	18.17	32	26. Florida
Montana	18,457,000	22.84	20	27. Idaho
Nebraska	36,020,000	22.61	22	28. Delaware
Nevada	13,664,000	10.64	50	29. Hawaii
New Hampshire	10,660,000	9.65	51	30. Iowa
New Jersey	100,005,000	12.89	47	31. Maine
New Mexico	57,324,000	37.03	3	32. Missouri
New York	312,340,000	17.30	34	33. Illinois
North Carolina	153,437,000	22.78	21	34. New York
North Dakota	18,468,000	29.08	5	35. Colorado
Ohio	174,952,000	15.99	37	36. Washington
Oklahoma	77,320,000	24.35	17	37. Ohio
Oregon	46,579,000	15.94	38	38. Oregon
Pennsylvania	160,651,000	13.43	45	39. Indiana
Rhode Island	13,136,000	13.08	46	40. Vermont
South Carolina	94,575,000	26.57	11	41. Michigan
South Dakota	20,395,000	29.01	6	42. Massachusetts
Tennessee	115,159,000	23.25	18	43. Wisconsin
Texas	491,159,000	28.31	8	44. Maryland
Utah	45,519,000	25.72	13	45. Pennsylvania
Vermont	8,814,000	15.55	40	46. Rhode Island
Virginia	80,363,000	12.78	48	47. New Jersey
Washington	83,674,000	16.68	36	48. Virginia
West Virginia	45,610,000	25.33	15	49. Connecticut
Wisconsin	72,724,000	14.68	43	50. Nevada
Wyoming	9,911,000	21.55	25	51. New Hampshire
United States	$5,298,560,000	$21.01	26	

Source: U.S. Department of Commerce, Bureau of the Census, *Federal Expenditures by State for Fiscal Year 1991* (Washington, D.C.: Government Printing Office, 1992).

State	Expenditures	Per capita	Rank by per capita		By per capita
Alabama	$41,000	$0.01	43		1. Wisconsin
Alaska	6,000	0.01	42		2. Vermont
Arizona	167,000	0.05	29		3. Illinois
Arkansas	29,000	0.01	41		4. Minnesota
California	1,005,000	0.03	34		5. Connecticut
Colorado	112,000	0.03	33		6. New Hampshire
Connecticut	669,000	0.20	5		7. Nebraska
Delaware	1,000	*	49		8. Idaho
District of Columbia	19,000	0.03	35		9. Michigan
Florida	119,000	0.01	44		10. Rhode Island
Georgia	25,000	*	48		11. Kansas
Hawaii	8,000	0.01	45		12. New Jersey
Idaho	164,000	0.16	8		13. Ohio
Illinois	3,245,000	0.28	3		14. Maine
Indiana	608,000	0.11	16		15. North Dakota
Iowa	264,000	0.09	20		16. Indiana
Kansas	332,000	0.13	11		17. Missouri
Kentucky	284,000	0.08	25		18. Massachusetts
Louisiana	77,000	0.02	38		19. New York
Maine	145,000	0.12	14		20. Iowa
Maryland	389,000	0.08	23		21. Oregon
Massachusetts	576,000	0.10	18		22. Montana
Michigan	1,376,000	0.15	9		23. Maryland
Minnesota	989,000	0.22	4		24. South Dakota
Mississippi	16,000	0.01	47		25. Kentucky
Missouri	536,000	0.10	17		26. Pennsylvania
Montana	66,000	0.08	22		27. Washington
Nebraska	255,000	0.16	7		28. Nevada
Nevada	68,000	0.05	28		29. Arizona
New Hampshire	218,000	0.20	6		30. Oklahoma
New Jersey	1,025,000	0.13	12		31. Utah
New Mexico	22,000	0.01	40		32. Wyoming
New York	1,705,000	0.09	19		33. Colorado
North Carolina	135,000	0.02	37		34. California
North Dakota	73,000	0.12	15		35. District of Columbia
Ohio	1,307,000	0.12	13		36. West Virginia
Oklahoma	138,000	0.04	30		37. North Carolina
Oregon	249,000	0.09	21		38. Louisiana
Pennsylvania	809,000	0.07	26		39. Virginia
Rhode Island	144,000	0.14	10		40. New Mexico
South Carolina	—	—	—		41. Arkansas
South Dakota	54,000	0.08	24		42. Alaska
Tennessee	—	—	—		43. Alabama
Texas	96,000	0.01	46		44. Florida
Utah	75,000	0.04	31		45. Hawaii
Vermont	166,000	0.29	2		46. Texas
Virginia	100,000	0.02	39		47. Mississippi
Washington	312,000	0.06	27		48. Georgia
West Virginia	39,000	0.02	36		49. Delaware
Wisconsin	2,047,000	0.41	1		— South Carolina
Wyoming	16,000	0.04	32		— Tennessee
United States	**$20,325,000**	**$0.08**	**22**		

— not applicable.   * rounds to less than 0.005.

Source: U.S. Department of Commerce, Bureau of the Census, *Federal Expenditures by State for Fiscal Year 1991* (Washington, D.C.: Government Printing Office, 1992).

NATIONAL SCHOOL LUNCH PROGRAM PARTICIPANTS, 1990

State	Participants	Cost of program	Per capita	Rank by per capita
Alabama	570,000	$77,000,000	$19.05	4
Alaska	39,000	8,000,000	14.55	14
Arizona	331,000	47,000,000	12.82	21
Arkansas	292,000	41,000,000	17.44	6
California	2,147,000	396,000,000	13.31	19
Colorado	282,000	31,000,000	9.41	36
Connecticut	231,000	23,000,000	7.00	48
Delaware	59,000	6,000,000	9.01	39
District of Columbia	47,000	10,000,000	16.47	10
Florida	1,110,000	158,000,000	12.21	25
Georgia	908,000	106,000,000	16.36	11
Hawaii	145,000	14,000,000	12.64	22
Idaho	131,000	14,000,000	13.90	17
Illinois	932,000	131,000,000	11.46	27
Indiana	635,000	54,000,000	9.74	33
Iowa	392,000	31,000,000	11.16	30
Kansas	302,000	29,000,000	11.70	26
Kentucky	498,000	61,000,000	16.55	9
Louisiana	694,000	104,000,000	24.64	2
Maine	108,000	11,000,000	8.96	40
Maryland	347,000	40,000,000	8.37	44
Massachusetts	454,000	44,000,000	7.31	46
Michigan	733,000	82,000,000	8.82	42
Minnesota	489,000	42,000,000	9.60	35
Mississippi	428,000	76,000,000	29.54	1
Missouri	547,000	58,000,000	11.33	29
Montana	84,000	10,000,000	12.52	23
Nebraska	191,000	18,000,000	11.41	28
Nevada	67,000	8,000,000	6.66	50
New Hampshire	91,000	6,000,000	5.41	51
New Jersey	507,000	60,000,000	7.76	45
New Mexico	179,000	30,000,000	19.80	3
New York	1,546,000	232,000,000	12.90	20
North Carolina	749,000	91,000,000	13.73	18
North Dakota	94,000	8,000,000	12.52	23
Ohio	919,000	109,000,000	10.05	32
Oklahoma	362,000	46,000,000	14.62	13
Oregon	234,000	26,000,000	9.15	38
Pennsylvania	990,000	102,000,000	8.58	43
Rhode Island	60,000	7,000,000	6.98	49
South Carolina	451,000	60,000,000	17.21	8
South Dakota	102,000	12,000,000	17.24	7
Tennessee	590,000	68,000,000	13.94	15
Texas	2,003,000	304,000,000	17.90	5
Utah	233,000	24,000,000	13.93	16
Vermont	47,000	4,000,000	7.10	47
Virginia	586,000	60,000,000	9.70	34
Washington	361,000	43,000,000	8.84	41
West Virginia	198,000	29,000,000	16.17	12
Wisconsin	468,000	45,000,000	9.20	37
Wyoming	57,000	5,000,000	11.01	31
United States	**24,019,000**	**$3,098,000,000**	**$12.46**	**25**

Rank in order

By per capita

1. Mississippi
2. Louisiana
3. New Mexico
4. Alabama
5. Texas
6. Arkansas
7. South Dakota
8. South Carolina
9. Kentucky
10. District of Columbia
11. Georgia
12. West Virginia
13. Oklahoma
14. Alaska
15. Tennessee
16. Utah
17. Idaho
18. North Carolina
19. California
20. New York
21. Arizona
22. Hawaii
23. Montana
    North Dakota
25. Florida
26. Kansas
27. Illinois
28. Nebraska
29. Missouri
30. Iowa
31. Wyoming
32. Ohio
33. Indiana
34. Virginia
35. Minnesota
36. Colorado
37. Wisconsin
38. Oregon
39. Delaware
40. Maine
41. Washington
42. Michigan
43. Pennsylvania
44. Maryland
45. New Jersey
46. Massachusetts
47. Vermont
48. Connecticut
49. Rhode Island
50. Nevada
51. New Hampshire

Source: U.S. Department of Commerce, Bureau of the Census, *Statistical Abstract of the United States, 1992* (Washington, D.C.: Government Printing Office, 1992).

State	Enrollment	% of children enrolled	Rank by %	By %
Alabama	13,052	14.9	14	1. Mississippi
Alaska	1,067	12.6	32	2. District of Columbia
Arizona	6,179	7.3	50	3. Maine
Arkansas	8,213	14.8	16	4. Rhode Island
California	52,658	10.0	45	5. Delaware
Colorado	6,696	12.7	31	6. Vermont
Connecticut	5,311	16.9	7	7. Connecticut
Delaware	1,333	17.6	5	8. Hawaii
District of Columbia	2,639	23.6	2	9. New Jersey
Florida	20,575	10.2	44	10. Illinois
Georgia	16,004	12.5	35	11. Maryland
Hawaii	1,974	16.1	8	12. Kentucky
Idaho	1,658	8.9	46	13. Ohio
Illinois	28,802	15.2	10	14. Alabama
Indiana	10,213	13.0	28	15. Wyoming
Iowa	5,266	13.3	25	16. Arkansas
Kansas	4,705	12.5	34	17. West Virginia
Kentucky	12,467	15.1	12	18. Michigan
Louisiana	15,804	11.8	38	19. Massachusetts
Maine	3,132	19.4	3	20. North Carolina
Maryland	7,594	15.2	11	21. Pennsylvania
Massachusetts	10,159	14.4	19	22. Missouri
Michigan	26,174	14.5	18	23. Oklahoma
Minnesota	7,136	12.0	36	24. Tennessee
Mississippi	22,343	26.8	1	25. Iowa
Missouri	11,972	13.6	22	26. South Carolina
Montana	1,961	11.6	39	27. Nebraska
Nebraska	3,154	13.0	27	28. Indiana
Nevada	1,073	6.7	51	29. North Dakota
New Hampshire	1,016	12.0	37	30. Wisconsin
New Jersey	11,688	15.9	9	31. Colorado
New Mexico	4,958	10.9	42	32. Alaska
New York	34,688	11.4	40	33. Virginia
North Carolina	14,083	13.7	20	34. Kansas
North Dakota	1,436	12.8	29	35. Georgia
Ohio	29,132	15.0	13	36. Minnesota
Oklahoma	8,977	13.4	23	37. New Hampshire
Oregon	3,885	8.5	49	38. Louisiana
Pennsylvania	22,414	13.7	21	39. Montana
Rhode Island	2,293	17.8	4	40. New York
South Carolina	9,025	13.2	26	41. South Dakota
South Dakota	1,691	11.0	41	42. New Mexico
Tennessee	12,481	13.4	24	42. Utah
Texas	36,354	8.7	48	44. Florida
Utah	3,455	10.9	42	45. California
Vermont	1,129	17.1	6	46. Idaho
Virginia	9,455	12.6	33	47. Washington
Washington	6,361	8.7	47	48. Texas
West Virginia	5,842	14.6	17	49. Oregon
Wisconsin	9,665	12.8	30	50. Arizona
Wyoming	1,128	14.8	15	51. Nevada
United States	540,470	12.5	35	

Source: Administration for Children and Families, *Project Head Start Statistical Fact Sheet* (Washington, D.C.: Department of Health and Human Services, 1993).

State	Expenditures	Expenditures per enrollee		Rank in order — By expenditure per enrollee
		Amount	Rank	
Alabama	$40,021,964	$3,066.35	37	1. New Jersey
Alaska	4,434,434	4,155.98	7	2. Oregon
Arizona	20,728,619	3,354.69	20	3. New York
Arkansas	22,296,739	2,714.81	50	4. Washington
California	219,422,451	4,166.93	6	5. Massachusetts
Colorado	19,356,537	2,890.76	48	6. California
Connecticut	18,694,171	3,519.90	16	7. Alaska
Delaware	4,454,355	3,341.60	21	8. Idaho
District of Columbia	9,672,828	3,665.34	14	9. Vermont
Florida	67,552,007	3,283.21	22	10. New Hampshire
Georgia	52,222,062	3,263.06	24	11. Hawaii
Hawaii	7,546,855	3,823.13	11	12. Nevada
Idaho	6,745,361	4,068.37	8	13. Pennsylvania
Illinois	99,851,528	3,466.83	18	14. District of Columbia
Indiana	31,054,260	3,040.66	40	15. Maryland
Iowa	16,484,267	3,130.32	33	16. Connecticut
Kansas	14,175,330	3,012.82	43	17. Virginia
Kentucky	38,053,187	3,052.31	38	18. Illinois
Louisiana	48,205,452	3,050.21	39	19. Minnesota
Maine	9,476,482	3,025.70	42	20. Arizona
Maryland	27,042,577	3,561.05	15	21. Delaware
Massachusetts	42,347,733	4,168.49	5	22. Florida
Michigan	82,320,697	3,145.13	31	23. Montana
Minnesota	24,372,925	3,415.49	19	24. Georgia
Mississippi	71,861,269	3,216.28	27	25. Nebraska
Missouri	35,640,966	2,977.03	46	26. West Virginia
Montana	6,436,060	3,282.03	23	27. Mississippi
Nebraska	10,284,366	3,260.74	25	28. Wisconsin
Nevada	4,000,259	3,728.11	12	29. South Dakota
New Hampshire	4,080,060	4,015.81	10	30. Tennessee
New Jersey	54,531,674	4,665.61	1	31. Michigan
New Mexico	13,655,086	2,754.15	49	32. North Carolina
New York	153,857,818	4,435.48	3	33. Iowa
North Carolina	44,259,257	3,142.74	32	34. Texas
North Dakota	4,282,718	2,982.39	45	35. Utah
Ohio	84,964,226	2,916.53	47	36. South Carolina
Oklahoma	24,077,589	2,682.14	51	37. Alabama
Oregon	17,759,794	4,571.38	2	38. Kentucky
Pennsylvania	82,449,145	3,678.47	13	39. Louisiana
Rhode Island	6,964,235	3,037.17	41	40. Indiana
South Carolina	27,716,471	3,071.08	36	41. Rhode Island
South Dakota	5,421,032	3,205.81	29	42. Maine
Tennessee	39,270,659	3,146.44	30	43. Kansas
Texas	113,610,274	3,125.11	34	44. Wyoming
Utah	10,670,343	3,088.38	35	45. North Dakota
Vermont	4,556,350	4,035.74	9	46. Missouri
Virginia	33,134,274	3,504.42	17	47. Ohio
Washington	27,533,139	4,328.43	4	48. Colorado
West Virginia	18,959,220	3,245.33	26	49. New Mexico
Wisconsin	31,052,313	3,212.86	28	50. Arkansas
Wyoming	3,370,989	2,988.47	44	51. Oklahoma
United States	$1,860,932,407	$3,443.17	19	

Source: Administration for Children and Families, *Project Head Start Statistical Fact Sheet* (Washington, D.C.: Department of Health and Human Services, 1993).

State	Expenditures	Per capita	Rank by per capita
Alabama	$40,503,000	$9.91	8
Alaska	5,870,000	10.30	6
Arizona	22,920,000	6.11	39
Arkansas	23,868,000	10.06	7
California	143,583,000	4.73	49
Colorado	20,329,000	6.02	40
Connecticut	14,347,000	4.36	51
Delaware	5,902,000	8.68	17
District of Columbia	10,305,000	17.23	1
Florida	76,664,000	5.77	43
Georgia	48,581,000	7.34	29
Hawaii	6,487,000	5.72	46
Idaho	8,691,000	8.37	20
Illinois	68,754,000	5.96	41
Indiana	43,990,000	7.84	23
Iowa	21,324,000	7.63	25
Kansas	16,988,000	6.81	34
Kentucky	36,161,000	9.74	9
Louisiana	40,789,000	9.59	10
Maine	10,741,000	8.70	16
Maryland	25,687,000	5.29	47
Massachusetts	35,587,000	5.94	42
Michigan	61,367,000	6.55	36
Minnesota	29,860,000	6.74	35
Mississippi	29,801,000	11.50	3
Missouri	40,003,000	7.76	24
Montana	6,939,000	8.59	19
Nebraska	11,328,000	7.11	30
Nevada	5,943,000	4.63	50
New Hampshire	6,916,000	6.26	38
New Jersey	37,496,000	4.83	48
New Mexico	13,609,000	8.79	14
New York	104,163,000	5.77	44
North Carolina	56,322,000	8.36	21
North Dakota	5,838,000	9.19	12
Ohio	83,275,000	7.61	26
Oklahoma	27,528,000	8.67	18
Oregon	20,083,000	6.87	32
Pennsylvania	89,400,000	7.47	27
Rhode Island	6,850,000	6.82	33
South Carolina	32,326,000	9.08	13
South Dakota	6,485,000	9.23	11
Tennessee	43,489,000	8.78	15
Texas	119,530,000	6.89	31
Utah	14,767,000	8.34	22
Vermont	5,912,000	10.43	5
Virginia	39,516,000	6.29	37
Washington	28,779,000	5.74	45
West Virginia	19,022,000	10.56	4
Wisconsin	36,679,000	7.40	28
Wyoming	5,528,000	12.02	2
United States	**$1,751,319,000**	**$6.94**	**31**

Rank in order

By per capita

1. District of Columbia
2. Wyoming
3. Mississippi
4. West Virginia
5. Vermont
6. Alaska
7. Arkansas
8. Alabama
9. Kentucky
10. Louisiana
11. South Dakota
12. North Dakota
13. South Carolina
14. New Mexico
15. Tennessee
16. Maine
17. Delaware
18. Oklahoma
19. Montana
20. Idaho
21. North Carolina
22. Utah
23. Indiana
24. Missouri
25. Iowa
26. Ohio
27. Pennsylvania
28. Wisconsin
29. Georgia
30. Nebraska
31. Texas
32. Oregon
33. Rhode Island
34. Kansas
35. Minnesota
36. Michigan
37. Virginia
38. New Hampshire
39. Arizona
40. Colorado
41. Illinois
42. Massachusetts
43. Florida
44. New York
45. Washington
46. Hawaii
47. Maryland
48. New Jersey
49. California
50. Nevada
51. Connecticut

Source: U.S. Department of Commerce, Bureau of the Census, *Federal Expenditures by State for Fiscal Year 1991* (Washington, D.C.: Government Printing Office, 1992).

State Government

FINANCIAL WORLD'S STATE RANKINGS. 1992			Rank in order
State	**1991 rank**	**1992 rank**	**By 1992 rank**
Alabama	32	22	1. Utah
Alaska	47	33	2. Missouri
Arizona	25	29	3. Maryland
Arkansas	26	34	4. Virginia
California	46	41	5. South Carolina
Colorado	31	25	6. Tennessee
Connecticut	30	46	7. Washington
Delaware	15	16	8. North Carolina
District of Columbia	—	—	9. Minnesota
Florida	10	14	10. Wisconsin
Georgia	20	18	11. Indiana
Hawaii	13	15	12. Iowa
Idaho	35	38	13. Nevada
Illinois	42	36	14. Florida
Indiana	19	11	15. Hawaii
Iowa	23	12	16. Delaware
Kansas	29	40	17. Oregon
Kentucky	24	37	18. Georgia
Louisiana	37	24	19. New Hampshire
Maine	48	48	20. New Jersey
Maryland	4	3	21. Pennsylvania
Massachusetts	49	50	22. Alabama
Michigan	34	26	23. Mississippi
Minnesota	9	9	24. Louisiana
Mississippi	36	23	25. Colorado
Missouri	3	2	26. Michigan
Montana	41	30	27. Texas
Nebraska	21	31	28. Ohio
Nevada	14	13	29. Arizona
New Hampshire	28	19	30. Montana
New Jersey	17	20	31. Nebraska
New Mexico	45	45	32. South Dakota
New York	40	43	33. Alaska
North Carolina	16	8	34. Arkansas
North Dakota	22	42	35. Wyoming
Ohio	33	28	36. Illinois
Oklahoma	39	39	37. Kentucky
Oregon	6	17	38. Idaho
Pennsylvania	27	21	39. Oklahoma
Rhode Island	38	44	40. Kansas
South Carolina	7	5	41. California
South Dakota	18	32	42. North Dakota
Tennessee	5	6	43. New York
Texas	11	27	44. Rhode Island
Utah	2	1	45. New Mexico
Vermont	43	49	46. Connecticut
Virginia	1	4	47. West Virginia
Washington	12	7	48. Maine
West Virginia	44	47	49. Vermont
Wisconsin	8	10	50. Massachusetts
Wyoming	50	35	— District of Columbia
United States	—	—	

— not applicable.

Source: Katherine Barrett and Richard Greene, "The State of the States," *Financial World*, May 12, 1992.

Note: *Financial World* analyzes states using broad measurements of state government budgeting and program evaluation and performance.

State	Governor Salary	Governor Rank	Lt. Governor Salary	Lt. Governor Rank	Secretary of State Salary	Secretary of State Rank	Attorney General Salary	Attorney General Rank
Alabama	$81,151	24	$45,360	32	$57,204	29	$90,475	8
Alaska	81,648	23	76,188	8	—	—	61,008	38
Arizona	75,000	33	—	—	54,600	31	76,400	20
Arkansas	35,000	50	14,000	41	22,500	47	26,500	50
California	114,286	4	85,714	5	85,716	6	102,000	3
Colorado	70,000	41	48,500	30	48,500	39	60,000	39
Connecticut	78,000	30	55,000	22	50,000	38	60,000	39
Delaware	80,000	26	36,500	36	73,700	10	84,700	15
District of Columbia	—	—	—	—	—	—	—	—
Florida	103,909	10	94,040	3	94,040	3	94,040	6
Georgia	91,080	17	70,698	10	72,966	12	74,645	23
Hawaii	94,780	15	90,041	4	—	—	85,302	12
Idaho	75,000	33	20,000	39	62,500	20	67,500	29
Illinois	97,370	13	68,732	12	85,915	5	85,915	11
Indiana	74,100	37	51,199	28	40,889	45	59,202	41
Iowa	76,700	31	60,000	16	60,000	24	73,600	25
Kansas	74,235	36	70,346	11	57,668	27	66,324	32
Kentucky	79,255	29	67,378	13	67,378	17	67,378	30
Louisiana	73,440	38	63,367	15	60,169	22	66,566	31
Maine	70,000	41	—	—	48,152	40	58,240	43
Maryland	120,000	3	100,000	2	70,000	16	100,000	5
Massachusetts	75,000	33	60,000	16	60,000	24	65,000	34
Michigan	106,690	7	80,300	7	109,000	1	109,000	2
Minnesota	109,053	6	59,981	18	59,981	26	85,194	13
Mississippi	75,600	32	40,500	34	54,000	32	61,200	36
Missouri	88,541	19	54,343	24	72,327	13	78,322	18
Montana	54,254	49	54,305	25	36,556	46	49,573	49
Nebraska	65,000	47	47,000	31	52,000	34	64,500	35
Nevada	82,391	22	18,309	40	57,216	28	77,814	19
New Hampshire	79,541	28	—	—	63,430	19	71,007	28
New Jersey	85,000	20	—	—	100,225	2	100,225	4
New Mexico	90,692	18	65,500	14	65,500	18	73,060	26
New York	130,000	1	110,000	1	87,338	4	110,000	1
North Carolina	123,000	2	75,252	9	75,252	8	75,252	22
North Dakota	67,800	46	55,632	21	51,272	36	57,936	44
Ohio	99,986	11	51,709	27	73,861	9	73,861	24
Oklahoma	70,000	41	40,000	35	42,500	43	55,000	45
Oregon	80,000	26	—	—	61,500	21	66,000	33
Pennsylvania	105,000	9	83,000	6	72,000	14	84,000	16
Rhode Island	69,900	45	52,000	26	52,000	34	55,000	45
South Carolina	98,000	12	43,000	33	85,000	7	85,000	14
South Dakota	60,890	48	56,067	20	41,371	44	51,715	47
Tennessee	85,000	20	—	—	73,148	11	89,775	9
Texas	95,301	14	7,140	42	70,476	15	76,192	21
Utah	72,800	39	54,600	23	—	—	58,300	42
Vermont	80,730	25	33,655	37	50,800	37	61,025	37
Virginia	105,882	8	29,550	38	56,603	30	93,100	7
Washington	112,000	5	58,600	19	60,100	23	86,400	10
West Virginia	72,000	40	—	—	43,000	42	50,400	48
Wisconsin	92,283	16	49,673	29	45,088	41	82,706	17
Wyoming	70,000	41	—	—	52,500	33	71,298	27
United States	$84,946	22	$57,076	20	$62,467	21	$73,553	26

Rank in order

By governor's salary

1. New York
2. North Carolina
3. Maryland
4. California
5. Washington
6. Minnesota
7. Michigan
8. Virginia
9. Pennsylvania
10. Florida
11. Ohio
12. South Carolina
13. Illinois
14. Texas
15. Hawaii
16. Wisconsin
17. Georgia
18. New Mexico
19. Missouri
20. New Jersey
    Tennessee
22. Nevada
23. Alaska
24. Alabama
25. Vermont
26. Delaware
    Oregon
28. New Hampshire
29. Kentucky
30. Connecticut
31. Iowa
32. Mississippi
33. Arizona
    Idaho
    Massachusetts
36. Kansas
37. Indiana
38. Louisiana
39. Utah
40. West Virginia
41. Colorado
    Maine
    Oklahoma
    Wyoming
45. Rhode Island
46. North Dakota
47. Nebraska
48. South Dakota
49. Montana
50. Arkansas
— District of Columbia

— not applicable.

Source: Council of State Governments, *The Book of the States: 1992-1993* (Lexington, Ky.: Council of State Governments, 1992).
Note: The governor of New York accepts $100,000. The governor and lieutenant governor of California have taken a voluntary 5 percent cut in statutory salary.

SALARIES OF STATE LEGISLATORS. 1991

State	Salaries	Rank	Per diem
Alabama	—	—	$10
Alaska	$24,012	15	—
Arizona	15,000	25	—
Arkansas	7,500	35	—
California	52,500	2	—
Colorado	17,500	21	—
Connecticut	16,760	23	—
Delaware	24,213	14	—
District of Columbia	—	—	—
Florida	22,560	18	—
Georgia	10,510	31	—
Hawaii	27,000	12	—
Idaho	12,000	27	—
Illinois	37,230	6	—
Indiana	11,600	30	—
Iowa	18,100	19	—
Kansas	—	—	60
Kentucky	—	—	100
Louisiana	16,800	22	—
Maine	7,125	37	—
Maryland	27,000	12	—
Massachusetts	30,000	10	—
Michigan	45,450	4	—
Minnesota	27,979	11	—
Mississippi	10,000	33	—
Missouri	22,870	17	—
Montana	—	—	56
Nebraska	12,000	27	—
Nevada	—	—	130
New Hampshire	100	40	—
New Jersey	35,000	7	—
New Mexico	—	—	75
New York	57,500	1	—
North Carolina	12,504	26	—
North Dakota	—	—	90
Ohio	42,427	5	—
Oklahoma	32,000	9	—
Oregon	11,868	29	—
Pennsylvania	47,000	3	—
Rhode Island	—	—	5
South Carolina	10,400	32	—
South Dakota	4,267	39	—
Tennessee	16,500	24	—
Texas	7,200	36	—
Utah	—	—	65
Vermont	8,160	34	—
Virginia	18,000	20	—
Washington	23,200	16	—
West Virginia	6,500	38	—
Wisconsin	33,622	8	—
Wyoming	—	—	75
United States	**$21,549**	**19**	—

Rank in order
By legislator's salary

1. New York
2. California
3. Pennsylvania
4. Michigan
5. Ohio
6. Illinois
7. New Jersey
8. Wisconsin
9. Oklahoma
10. Massachusetts
11. Minnesota
12. Hawaii
    Maryland
14. Delaware
15. Alaska
16. Washington
17. Missouri
18. Florida
19. Iowa
20. Virginia
21. Colorado
22. Louisiana
23. Connecticut
24. Tennessee
25. Arizona
26. North Carolina
27. Idaho
    Nebraska
29. Oregon
30. Indiana
31. Georgia
32. South Carolina
33. Mississippi
34. Vermont
35. Arkansas
36. Texas
37. Maine
38. West Virginia
39. South Dakota
40. New Hampshire
— Alabama
— District of Columbia
— Kansas
— Kentucky
— Montana
— Nevada
— New Mexico
— North Dakota
— Rhode Island
— Utah
— Wyoming

— not applicable.

Source: Council of State Governments, *The Book of the States: 1992-1993* (Lexington, Ky.: Council of State Governments, 1992).

Note: In several states, legislators receive a per diem amount (with an limit of the number of days) instead of an annual salary. The per diem amounts are listed here but the states are not included in the overall ranking.

State	Women legislators			% of legislature	Rank by %
	Senate	House	Total		
Alabama	1	7	8	5.7	49
Alaska	4	9	13	21.7	21
Arizona	9	23	32	35.6	2
Arkansas	1	12	13	9.6	46
California	6	22	28	23.3	18
Colorado	8	26	34	34.0	3
Connecticut	8	39	47	25.1	13
Delaware	3	6	9	14.5	38
District of Columbia	—	—	—	—	—
Florida	6	22	28	17.5	31
Georgia	6	35	41	17.4	32
Hawaii	6	12	18	23.7	16
Idaho	9	23	32	30.5	7
Illinois	11	30	41	23.2	19
Indiana	13	16	29	19.3	27
Iowa	6	16	22	14.7	37
Kansas	14	33	47	28.5	8
Kentucky	1	5	6	4.3	50
Louisiana	1	9	10	6.9	48
Maine	11	47	58	31.2	6
Maryland	10	34	44	23.4	17
Massachusetts	9	37	46	23.0	20
Michigan	3	26	29	19.6	26
Minnesota	20	35	55	27.4	9
Mississippi	4	15	19	10.9	44
Missouri	1	37	38	19.3	29
Montana	8	21	29	19.3	27
Nebraska	10	—	10	20.4	23
Nevada	5	12	17	27.0	11
New Hampshire	9	133	142	33.5	5
New Jersey	2	13	15	12.5	41
New Mexico	8	14	22	19.6	25
New York	7	27	34	16.1	35
North Carolina	7	24	31	18.2	30
North Dakota	8	16	24	16.3	34
Ohio	5	23	28	21.2	22
Oklahoma	6	8	14	9.4	47
Oregon	7	17	24	26.7	12
Pennsylvania	4	21	25	9.9	45
Rhode Island	11	26	37	24.7	14
South Carolina	3	19	22	12.9	40
South Dakota	7	14	21	20.0	24
Tennessee	3	13	16	12.1	42
Texas	4	25	29	16.0	36
Utah	2	12	14	13.5	39
Vermont	11	50	61	33.9	4
Virginia	4	12	16	11.4	43
Washington	17	41	58	39.5	1
West Virginia	5	17	22	16.4	33
Wisconsin	7	29	36	27.3	10
Wyoming	5	17	22	24.4	15
United States	**336**	**1,180**	**1,516**	**20.4**	**23**

WOMEN IN STATE LEGISLATURES, 1993

Rank in order

By %

1. Washington
2. Arizona
3. Colorado
4. Vermont
5. New Hampshire
6. Maine
7. Idaho
8. Kansas
9. Minnesota
10. Wisconsin
11. Nevada
12. Oregon
13. Connecticut
14. Rhode Island
15. Wyoming
16. Hawaii
17. Maryland
18. California
19. Illinois
20. Massachusetts
21. Alaska
22. Ohio
23. Nebraska
24. South Dakota
25. New Mexico
26. Michigan
27. Indiana
    Montana
29. Missouri
30. North Carolina
31. Florida
32. Georgia
33. West Virginia
34. North Dakota
35. New York
36. Texas
37. Iowa
38. Delaware
39. Utah
40. South Carolina
41. New Jersey
42. Tennessee
43. Virginia
44. Mississippi
45. Pennsylvania
46. Arkansas
47. Oklahoma
48. Louisiana
49. Alabama
50. Kentucky
— District of Columbia

— not applicable.

Source: Data provided by the National Conference of State Legislatures, January 1993.
Note: Nebraska has a nonpartisan, unicameral legislature.

AFRICAN AMERICANS IN STATE LEGISLATURES. 1993

State	African American legislators			% of legislature	Rank by %
	Senate	House	Total		
Alabama	5	19	24	17.1	4
Alaska	0	1	1	1.7	34
Arizona	1	2	3	3.3	29
Arkansas	3	9	12	8.9	15
California	2	7	9	7.5	19
Colorado	1	3	4	4.0	26
Connecticut	1	5	6	3.2	31
Delaware	1	2	3	4.8	24
District of Columbia	0	0	0	0.0	51
Florida	5	14	19	11.9	10
Georgia	8	30	38	16.1	5
Hawaii	0	0	0	0.0	43
Idaho	0	0	0	0.0	43
Illinois	8	14	22	12.4	9
Indiana	2	7	9	6.0	22
Iowa	0	1	1	0.7	40
Kansas	2	3	5	3.0	32
Kentucky	1	1	2	1.4	36
Louisiana	8	25	33	22.9	2
Maine	0	0	0	0.0	43
Maryland	7	30	37	19.7	3
Massachusetts	1	7	8	4.0	26
Michigan	3	11	14	9.5	14
Minnesota	0	1	1	0.5	41
Mississippi	10	32	42	24.1	1
Missouri	3	12	15	7.6	18
Montana	0	0	0	0.0	43
Nebraska	1	0	1	2.0	33
Nevada	1	2	3	4.8	25
New Hampshire	0	2	2	0.5	42
New Jersey	2	10	12	10.0	13
New Mexico	0	0	0	0.0	43
New York	8	21	29	13.7	8
North Carolina	7	17	24	14.1	7
North Dakota	0	0	0	0.0	43
Ohio	3	12	15	11.4	11
Oklahoma	2	3	5	3.4	28
Oregon	1	2	3	3.3	29
Pennsylvania	3	15	18	7.1	20
Rhode Island	1	8	9	6.0	22
South Carolina	7	19	26	15.3	6
South Dakota	1	0	1	1.0	38
Tennessee	3	12	15	11.4	11
Texas	2	14	16	8.8	16
Utah	0	0	0	0.0	43
Vermont	1	2	3	1.7	34
Virginia	5	7	12	8.6	17
Washington	0	2	2	1.4	37
West Virginia	0	1	1	0.7	39
Wisconsin	2	7	9	6.8	21
Wyoming	0	0	0	0.0	43
United States	122	392	514	6.9	21

By %

1. Mississippi
2. Louisiana
3. Maryland
4. Alabama
5. Georgia
6. South Carolina
7. North Carolina
8. New York
9. Illinois
10. Florida
11. Ohio
    Tennessee
13. New Jersey
14. Michigan
15. Arkansas
16. Texas
17. Virginia
18. Missouri
19. California
20. Pennsylvania
21. Wisconsin
22. Indiana
    Rhode Island
24. Delaware
25. Nevada
26. Colorado
    Massachusetts
28. Oklahoma
29. Arizona
    Oregon
31. Connecticut
32. Kansas
33. Nebraska
34. Alaska
    Vermont
36. Kentucky
37. Washington
38. South Dakota
39. West Virginia
40. Iowa
41. Minnesota
42. New Hampshire
43. Hawaii
    Idaho
    Maine
    Montana
    New Mexico
    North Dakota
    Utah
    Wyoming
— District of Columbia

— not applicable.

Source: Data provided by the National Conference of State Legislatures, January 1993.
Note: Nebraska has a nonpartisan, unicameral legislature.

HISPANICS IN STATE LEGISLATURES, 1993

State	Hispanic legislators Senate	House	Total	% of legislature	Rank by %
Alabama	0	0	0	0.0	21
Alaska	0	0	0	0.0	21
Arizona	3	5	8	8.9	3
Arkansas	0	0	0	0.0	21
California	3	7	10	8.3	4
Colorado	3	5	8	8.0	5
Connecticut	0	5	5	2.7	9
Delaware	0	0	0	0.0	21
District of Columbia	—	—	—	—	—
Florida	3	9	12	7.5	6
Georgia	0	0	0	0.0	21
Hawaii	0	0	0	0.0	21
Idaho	0	1	1	1.0	16
Illinois	2	4	6	3.4	8
Indiana	0	1	1	0.7	18
Iowa	0	0	0	0.0	21
Kansas	1	1	2	1.2	12
Kentucky	0	0	0	0.0	21
Louisiana	0	0	0	0.0	21
Maine	0	0	0	0.0	21
Maryland	0	0	0	0.0	21
Massachusetts	0	1	1	0.5	19
Michigan	0	0	0	0.0	21
Minnesota	0	2	2	1.0	14
Mississippi	0	0	0	0.0	21
Missouri	0	0	0	0.0	21
Montana	0	0	0	0.0	21
Nebraska	0	0	0	0.0	21
Nevada	1	0	1	1.6	10
New Hampshire	0	0	0	0.0	21
New Jersey	0	1	1	0.8	17
New Mexico	16	25	41	36.6	1
New York	4	7	11	5.2	7
North Carolina	0	0	0	0.0	21
North Dakota	0	0	0	0.0	21
Ohio	0	0	0	0.0	21
Oklahoma	0	0	0	0.0	21
Oregon	0	0	0	0.0	21
Pennsylvania	0	1	1	0.4	20
Rhode Island	0	0	0	0.0	21
South Carolina	0	0	0	0.0	21
South Dakota	0	0	0	0.0	21
Tennessee	0	0	0	0.0	21
Texas	11	26	37	20.4	2
Utah	0	1	1	1.0	15
Vermont	0	0	0	0.0	21
Virginia	0	0	0	0.0	21
Washington	2	0	2	1.4	11
West Virginia	0	0	0	0.0	21
Wisconsin	0	0	0	0.0	21
Wyoming	1	0	1	1.1	13
United States	**50**	**102**	**152**	**2.0**	**10**

— not applicable.

Source: Data provided by the National Conference of State Legislatures, January 1993.

Note: Nebraska has a nonpartisan, unicameral legislature.

Rank in order

By %

1. New Mexico
2. Texas
3. Arizona
4. California
5. Colorado
6. Florida
7. New York
8. Illinois
9. Connecticut
10. Nevada
11. Washington
12. Kansas
13. Wyoming
14. Minnesota
15. Utah
16. Idaho
17. New Jersey
18. Indiana
19. Massachusetts
20. Pennsylvania
21. Alabama
    Alaska
    Arkansas
    Delaware
    Georgia
    Hawaii
    Iowa
    Kentucky
    Louisiana
    Maine
    Maryland
    Michigan
    Mississippi
    Missouri
    Montana
    Nebraska
    New Hampshire
    North Carolina
    North Dakota
    Ohio
    Oklahoma
    Oregon
    Rhode Island
    South Carolina
    South Dakota
    Tennessee
    Vermont
    Virginia
    West Virginia
    Wisconsin
— District of Columbia

State	Asian American legislators			% of legislature	Rank by %	Rank in order By %
	Senate	House	Total			
Alabama	0	0	0	0.0	6	1. Hawaii
Alaska	0	0	0	0.0	6	2. Oregon
Arizona	0	0	0	0.0	6	3. Washington
Arkansas	0	0	0	0.0	6	4. California
California	0	1	1	0.8	4	5. Florida
Colorado	0	0	0	0.0	6	6. Alabama
Connecticut	0	0	0	0.0	6	Alaska
Delaware	0	0	0	0.0	6	Arizona
District of Columbia	—	—	—	—	—	Arkansas
Florida	0	1	1	0.6	5	Colorado
Georgia	0	0	0	0.0	6	Connecticut
Hawaii	16	31	47	61.8	1	Delaware
Idaho	0	0	0	0.0	6	Georgia
Illinois	0	0	0	0.0	6	Idaho
Indiana	0	0	0	0.0	6	Illinois
Iowa	0	0	0	0.0	6	Indiana
Kansas	0	0	0	0.0	6	Iowa
Kentucky	0	0	0	0.0	6	Kansas
Louisiana	0	0	0	0.0	6	Kentucky
Maine	0	0	0	0.0	6	Louisiana
Maryland	0	0	0	0.0	6	Maine
Massachusetts	0	0	0	0.0	6	Maryland
Michigan	0	0	0	0.0	6	Massachusetts
Minnesota	0	0	0	0.0	6	Michigan
Mississippi	0	0	0	0.0	6	Minnesota
Missouri	0	0	0	0.0	6	Mississippi
Montana	0	0	0	0.0	6	Missouri
Nebraska	0	0	0	0.0	6	Montana
Nevada	0	0	0	0.0	6	Nebraska
New Hampshire	0	0	0	0.0	6	Nevada
New Jersey	0	0	0	0.0	6	New Hampshire
New Mexico	0	0	0	0.0	6	New Jersey
New York	0	0	0	0.0	6	New Mexico
North Carolina	0	0	0	0.0	6	New York
North Dakota	0	0	0	0.0	6	North Carolina
Ohio	0	0	0	0.0	6	North Dakota
Oklahoma	0	0	0	0.0	6	Ohio
Oregon	2	0	2	2.2	2	Oklahoma
Pennsylvania	0	0	0	0.0	6	Pennsylvania
Rhode Island	0	0	0	0.0	6	Rhode Island
South Carolina	0	0	0	0.0	6	South Carolina
South Dakota	0	0	0	0.0	6	South Dakota
Tennessee	0	0	0	0.0	6	Tennessee
Texas	0	0	0	0.0	6	Texas
Utah	0	0	0	0.0	6	Utah
Vermont	0	0	0	0.0	6	Vermont
Virginia	0	0	0	0.0	6	Virginia
Washington	0	3	3	2.0	3	West Virginia
West Virginia	0	0	0	0.0	6	Wisconsin
Wisconsin	0	0	0	0.0	6	Wyoming
Wyoming	0	0	0	0.0	6	— District of Columbia
United States	18	36	54	0.7	5	

— not applicable.

Source: Data provided by the National Conference of State Legislatures, January 1993.

Note: Nebraska has a nonpartisan, unicameral legislature. Asian Americans include Pacific Islanders.

State	Native American legislators			% of legislature	Rank by %
	Senate	House	Total		
Alabama	0	0	0	0.0	12
Alaska	4	6	10	16.7	1
Arizona	1	2	3	3.3	4
Arkansas	0	0	0	0.0	12
California	0	0	0	0.0	12
Colorado	0	0	0	0.0	12
Connecticut	0	0	0	0.0	12
Delaware	0	0	0	0.0	12
District of Columbia	—	—	—	—	—
Florida	0	0	0	0.0	12
Georgia	0	0	0	0.0	12
Hawaii	3	6	9	11.8	2
Idaho	0	0	0	0.0	12
Illinois	0	0	0	0.0	12
Indiana	0	0	0	0.0	12
Iowa	0	0	0	0.0	12
Kansas	0	0	0	0.0	12
Kentucky	0	0	0	0.0	12
Louisiana	0	0	0	0.0	12
Maine	0	0	0	0.0	12
Maryland	0	0	0	0.0	12
Massachusetts	0	0	0	0.0	12
Michigan	0	0	0	0.0	12
Minnesota	1	0	1	0.5	11
Mississippi	0	0	0	0.0	12
Missouri	0	0	0	0.0	12
Montana	1	2	3	2.0	6
Nebraska	0	0	0	0.0	12
Nevada	0	0	0	0.0	12
New Hampshire	0	0	0	0.0	12
New Jersey	0	0	0	0.0	12
New Mexico	2	5	7	6.3	3
New York	0	0	0	0.0	12
North Carolina	0	1	1	0.6	10
North Dakota	1	0	1	0.7	8
Ohio	0	0	0	0.0	12
Oklahoma	1	0	1	0.7	9
Oregon	0	0	0	0.0	12
Pennsylvania	0	0	0	0.0	12
Rhode Island	0	0	0	0.0	12
South Carolina	0	0	0	0.0	12
South Dakota	2	1	3	2.9	5
Tennessee	0	0	0	0.0	12
Texas	0	0	0	0.0	12
Utah	0	0	0	0.0	12
Vermont	0	0	0	0.0	12
Virginia	0	0	0	0.0	12
Washington	0	0	0	0.0	12
West Virginia	0	1	1	0.7	7
Wisconsin	0	0	0	0.0	12
Wyoming	0	0	0	0.0	12
United States	**16**	**24**	**40**	**0.5**	**11**

NATIVE AMERICANS IN STATE LEGISLATURES. 1993

Rank in order

By %

1. Alaska
2. Hawaii
3. New Mexico
4. Arizona
5. South Dakota
6. Montana
7. West Virginia
8. North Dakota
9. Oklahoma
10. North Carolina
11. Minnesota
12. Alabama
    Arkansas
    California
    Colorado
    Connecticut
    Delaware
    Florida
    Georgia
    Idaho
    Illinois
    Indiana
    Iowa
    Kansas
    Kentucky
    Louisiana
    Maine
    Maryland
    Massachusetts
    Michigan
    Mississippi
    Missouri
    Nebraska
    Nevada
    New Hampshire
    New Jersey
    New York
    Ohio
    Oregon
    Pennsylvania
    Rhode Island
    South Carolina
    Tennessee
    Texas
    Utah
    Vermont
    Virginia
    Washington
    Wisconsin
    Wyoming
— District of Columbia

— not applicable.
Source: Data provided by the National Conference of State Legislatures, January 1993.
Note: Nebraska has a nonpartisan, unicameral legislature.

TURNOVER IN STATE LEGISLATURES, 1990-1991					Rank in order
State	Total legislators	Turnovers	% of total	Rank by %	By %
Alabama	140	38	27.1	11	1. Nevada
Alaska	60	21	35.0	4	2. West Virginia
Arizona	90	25	27.8	10	3. North Dakota
Arkansas	135	24	17.8	37	4. Alaska
California	120	23	19.2	31	5. New Hampshire
Colorado	100	20	20.0	28	6. Montana
Connecticut	187	37	19.8	29	7. Idaho
Delaware	62	5	8.1	48	8. South Dakota
District of Columbia	—	—	—	—	9. Massachusetts
Florida	160	30	18.8	35	10. Arizona
Georgia	236	60	25.4	14	11. Alabama
Hawaii	76	11	14.5	41	12. Vermont
Idaho	126	39	31.0	7	13. Maryland
Illinois	177	24	13.6	44	14. Georgia
Indiana	150	23	15.3	38	15. Utah
Iowa	150	29	19.3	30	16. Texas
Kansas	165	38	23.0	19	17. Oklahoma
Kentucky	138	26	18.8	34	18. Maine
Louisiana	144	6	4.2	49	19. Kansas
Maine	186	46	24.7	18	20. Michigan
Maryland	188	48	25.5	13	21. Tennessee
Massachusetts	200	56	28.0	9	22. Washington
Michigan	148	33	22.3	20	23. Rhode Island
Minnesota	201	42	20.9	25	24. North Carolina
Mississippi	174	6	3.4	50	25. Minnesota
Missouri	197	40	20.3	27	26. New Jersey
Montana	150	48	32.0	6	27. Missouri
Nebraska	49	9	18.4	36	28. Colorado
Nevada	63	27	42.9	1	29. Connecticut
New Hampshire	424	142	33.5	5	30. Iowa
New Jersey	120	25	20.8	26	31. California
New Mexico	112	15	13.4	45	32. Wyoming
New York	211	28	13.3	46	33. Wisconsin
North Carolina	170	36	21.2	24	34. Kentucky
North Dakota	159	58	36.5	3	35. Florida
Ohio	132	19	14.4	43	36. Nebraska
Oklahoma	149	37	24.8	17	37. Arkansas
Oregon	90	13	14.4	42	38. Indiana
Pennsylvania	253	37	14.6	40	39. South Carolina
Rhode Island	150	32	21.3	23	40. Pennsylvania
South Carolina	170	26	15.3	39	41. Hawaii
South Dakota	105	30	28.6	8	42. Oregon
Tennessee	132	29	22.0	21	43. Ohio
Texas	181	45	24.9	16	44. Illinois
Utah	104	26	25.0	15	45. New Mexico
Vermont	180	47	26.1	12	46. New York
Virginia	140	16	11.4	47	47. Virginia
Washington	147	32	21.8	22	48. Delaware
West Virginia	134	55	41.0	2	49. Louisiana
Wisconsin	132	25	18.9	33	50. Mississippi
Wyoming	94	18	19.1	32	— District of Columbia
United States	7,461	1,625	21.8	22	

— not applicable.

Source: Council of State Governments, *The Book of the States: 1992-1993* (Lexington, Ky.: Council of State Governments, 1992).

LENGTH OF STATE LEGISLATIVE SESSIONS, 1991

State	Regular session Days	Regular session Rank	Special session Days	Special session Rank
Alabama	105	14	7	18
Alaska	122	9	0	31
Arizona	160	4	26	8
Arkansas	73	24	0	31
California	138	8	0	31
Colorado	120	10	35	5
Connecticut	148	5	140	1
Delaware	54	35	1	27
District of Columbia	—	—	—	—
Florida	59	33	6	19
Georgia	40	38	11	15
Hawaii	64	30	5	22
Idaho	82	21	0	31
Illinois	108	13	86	2
Indiana	61	31	17	12
Iowa	119	11	0	31
Kansas	103	16	0	31
Kentucky	0	42	33	6
Louisiana	85	20	23	10
Maine	72	25	12	14
Maryland	90	17	29	7
Massachusetts	364	1	0	31
Michigan	356	2	0	31
Minnesota	58	34	0	31
Mississippi	81	22	3	25
Missouri	142	6	0	31
Montana	90	17	0	31
Nebraska	90	17	10	16
Nevada	115	12	0	31
New Hampshire	31	41	1	27
New Jersey	65	29	0	31
New Mexico	60	32	10	16
New York	0	42	1	27
North Carolina	0	42	6	19
North Dakota	67	28	5	22
Ohio	0	42	0	31
Oklahoma	70	26	5	22
Oregon	168	3	0	31
Pennsylvania	0	42	0	31
Rhode Island	0	42	0	31
South Carolina	0	42	1	27
South Dakota	40	38	2	26
Tennessee	0	42	0	31
Texas	140	7	37	4
Utah	45	36	6	19
Vermont	74	23	0	31
Virginia	45	36	17	12
Washington	105	14	21	11
West Virginia	68	27	24	9
Wisconsin	0	42	55	3
Wyoming	38	40	0	31
United States	137	9	21	12

Rank in order

By regular session

1. Massachusetts
2. Michigan
3. Oregon
4. Arizona
5. Connecticut
6. Missouri
7. Texas
8. California
9. Alaska
10. Colorado
11. Iowa
12. Nevada
13. Illinois
14. Alabama
    Washington
16. Kansas
17. Maryland
    Montana
    Nebraska
20. Louisiana
21. Idaho
22. Mississippi
23. Vermont
24. Arkansas
25. Maine
26. Oklahoma
27. West Virginia
28. North Dakota
29. New Jersey
30. Hawaii
31. Indiana
32. New Mexico
33. Florida
34. Minnesota
35. Delaware
36. Utah
    Virginia
38. Georgia
    South Dakota
40. Wyoming
41. New Hampshire
42. Kentucky
    New York
    North Carolina
    Ohio
    Pennsylvania
    Rhode Island
    South Carolina
    Tennessee
    Wisconsin
 — District of Columbia

— not applicable.

Source: Council of State Governments, *The Book of the States: 1992-1993* (Lexington, Ky.: Council of State Governments, 1992).

Note: When length of session differed for both chambers of the legislature, the larger of the two sessions was used to calculate this table. The U.S. figure is an average based on the legislatures in session, not fifty state legislatures.

STATE BILLS IN REGULAR SESSION, 1991					Rank in order
State	Bills introduced	Bills enacted	% enacted	Rank by %	By %
Alabama	1,744	732	42.0	10	1. Arkansas
Alaska	669	106	15.8	33	2. Colorado
Arizona	979	322	32.9	19	3. South Dakota
Arkansas	1,865	1,246	66.8	1	4. North Dakota
California	3,521	1,217	34.6	17	5. Virginia
Colorado	524	338	64.5	2	6. Montana
Connecticut	3,353	454	13.5	37	7. Idaho
Delaware	643	190	29.5	23	8. Nevada
District of Columbia	—	—	—	—	9. Utah
Florida	2,338	414	17.7	32	10. Alabama
Georgia	1,556	608	39.1	12	11. New Hampshire
Hawaii	4,379	335	7.7	46	12. Georgia
Idaho	687	348	50.7	7	13. Wyoming
Illinois	4,183	828	19.8	30	14. North Carolina
Indiana	1,722	239	13.9	36	15. Maine
Iowa	1,380	272	19.7	31	16. Maryland
Kansas	1,114	298	26.8	24	17. California
Kentucky	—	—	—	—	18. Louisiana
Louisiana	3,138	1,073	34.2	18	19. Arizona
Maine	1,975	734	37.2	15	20. Oregon
Maryland	2,179	776	35.6	16	21. Nebraska
Massachusetts	6,484	558	8.6	44	22. New Jersey
Michigan	2,094	201	9.6	43	23. Delaware
Minnesota	3,319	356	10.7	42	24. Kansas
Mississippi	2,921	610	20.9	27	25. Oklahoma
Missouri	1,287	153	11.9	39	26. New Mexico
Montana	1,486	824	55.5	6	27. Mississippi
Nebraska	857	276	32.2	21	28. Texas
Nevada	1,493	729	48.8	8	29. Tennessee
New Hampshire	939	389	41.4	11	30. Illinois
New Jersey	1,671	528	31.6	22	31. Iowa
New Mexico	1,579	341	21.6	26	32. Florida
New York	15,506	750	4.8	47	33. Alaska
North Carolina	2,003	761	38.0	14	34. Vermont
North Dakota	1,210	721	59.6	4	35. Washington
Ohio	875	107	12.2	38	36. Indiana
Oklahoma	1,342	344	25.6	25	37. Connecticut
Oregon	2,959	967	32.7	20	38. Ohio
Pennsylvania	3,791	53	1.4	48	39. Missouri
Rhode Island	3,646	429	NA	NA	40. South Carolina
South Carolina	2,099	244	11.6	40	41. West Virginia
South Dakota	685	417	60.9	3	42. Minnesota
Tennessee	3,286	661	20.1	29	43. Michigan
Texas	4,684	971	20.7	28	44. Massachusetts
Utah	691	295	42.7	9	45. Wisconsin
Vermont	856	128	15.0	34	46. Hawaii
Virginia	1,300	742	57.1	5	47. New York
Washington	984	146	14.8	35	48. Pennsylvania
West Virginia	1,624	179	11.0	41	— District of Columbia
Wisconsin	1,247	107	8.6	45	— Kentucky
Wyoming	696	265	38.1	13	NA Rhode Island
United States	2,277	485	21.3	27	

— not applicable. NA not available.

Source: The Council of State Governments, *The Book of the States: 1992-1993* (Lexington, Kentucky: The Council of State Governments, 1992).

Note: Rhode Island is not included in the rankings because bill and resolution introductions are reported as a total. There was no regular session of the Kentucky legislature in 1991.

STATE RESOLUTIONS IN REGULAR SESSION, 1991					Rank in order
State	Resolutions introduced	Resolutions enacted	% enacted	Rank by %	By %
Alabama	636	568	89.3	7	1. Massachusetts
Alaska	163	57	35.0	30	2. New York
Arizona	51	25	49.0	26	3. Maine
Arkansas	263	187	71.1	20	4. Illinois
California	215	100	46.5	27	5. Florida
Colorado	104	79	76.0	18	6. Texas
Connecticut	258	207	80.2	13	7. Alabama
Delaware	285	18	6.3	42	8. Tennessee
District of Columbia	—	—	—	—	9. Georgia
Florida	177	163	92.1	5	10. Virginia
Georgia	979	842	86.0	9	11. North Dakota
Hawaii	1,255	455	36.3	29	12. Louisiana
Idaho	85	46	54.1	25	13. Connecticut
Illinois	2,360	2,245	95.1	4	14. South Carolina
Indiana	17	0	0.0	45	15. Vermont
Iowa	19	3	15.8	38	16. Nevada
Kansas	58	16	27.6	33	17. Utah
Kentucky	—	—	—	—	18. Colorado
Louisiana	641	527	82.2	12	19. Montana
Maine	38	37	97.4	3	20. Arkansas
Maryland	44	5	11.4	40	21. New Hampshire
Massachusetts	4	4	100.0	1	22. Washington
Michigan	37	0	0.0	45	23. Pennsylvania
Minnesota	0	0	0.0	45	24. Mississippi
Mississippi	471	271	57.5	24	25. Idaho
Missouri	40	6	15.0	39	26. Arizona
Montana	108	82	75.9	19	27. California
Nebraska	17	1	5.9	43	28. Wisconsin
Nevada	267	204	76.4	16	29. Hawaii
New Hampshire	78	53	67.9	21	30. Alaska
New Jersey	238	69	29.0	32	31. West Virginia
New Mexico	34	1	2.9	44	32. New Jersey
New York	3,656	3,561	97.4	2	33. Kansas
North Carolina	277	30	10.8	41	34. Oregon
North Dakota	151	127	84.1	11	35. Wyoming
Ohio	102	20	19.6	36	36. Ohio
Oklahoma	76	14	18.4	37	37. Oklahoma
Oregon	111	24	21.6	34	38. Iowa
Pennsylvania	360	231	64.2	23	39. Missouri
Rhode Island	NA	488	NA	NA	40. Maryland
South Carolina	444	352	79.3	14	41. North Carolina
South Dakota	4	0	0.0	45	42. Delaware
Tennessee	971	858	88.4	8	43. Nebraska
Texas	2,424	2,201	90.8	6	44. New Mexico
Utah	117	89	76.1	17	45. Indiana
Vermont	119	91	76.5	15	Michigan
Virginia	472	403	85.4	10	Minnesota
Washington	125	82	65.6	22	South Dakota
West Virginia	198	67	33.8	31	— District of Columbia
Wisconsin	190	77	40.5	28	— Kentucky
Wyoming	49	10	20.4	35	NA Rhode Island
United States	383	306	79.9	14	

— not applicable.   NA not available.

Source: Council of State Governments, *The Book of the States: 1992-1993* (Lexington, Ky.: Council of State Governments, 1992).

Note: Rhode Island is not included in the rankings because bill and resolution introductions are reported as a total. There was no regular session of Kentucky legislature in 1991.

State	Bills introduced	Bills enacted	% enacted	Rank by %
STATE BILLS IN SPECIAL SESSION, 1991				
Alabama	146	29	19.9	22
Alaska	—	—	—	—
Arizona	61	15	24.6	21
Arkansas	—	—	—	—
California	37	7	19.4	NA
Colorado	75	29	38.7	17
Connecticut	55	28	50.9	12
Delaware	1	1	100.0	1
District of Columbia	—	—	—	—
Florida	61	22	36.1	18
Georgia	47	31	66.0	9
Hawaii	1	1	100.0	1
Idaho	—	—	—	—
Illinois	8	0	0.0	29
Indiana	14	1	7.1	27
Iowa	—	—	—	—
Kansas	—	—	—	—
Kentucky	41	17	41.5	16
Louisiana	58	19	32.8	20
Maine	43	40	93.0	5
Maryland	66	6	9.1	25
Massachusetts	—	—	—	—
Michigan	—	—	—	—
Minnesota	—	—	—	—
Mississippi	38	21	55.3	11
Missouri	—	—	—	—
Montana	—	—	—	—
Nebraska	6	1	16.7	23
Nevada	—	—	—	—
New Hampshire	1	1	100.0	1
New Jersey	—	—	—	—
New Mexico	46	6	13.0	24
New York	4	0	0.0	29
North Carolina	23	8	34.8	19
North Dakota	8	7	87.5	6
Ohio	—	—	—	—
Oklahoma	2	2	100.0	1
Oregon	—	—	—	—
Pennsylvania	—	—	—	—
Rhode Island	—	—	—	—
South Carolina	13	10	76.9	7
South Dakota	8	4	50.0	13
Tennessee	—	—	—	—
Texas	596	35	5.9	28
Utah	23	15	65.2	10
Vermont	—	—	—	—
Virginia	35	26	74.3	8
Washington	25	11	44.0	15
West Virginia	58	27	46.6	14
Wisconsin	22	2	9.1	25
Wyoming	—	—	—	—
United States	**53**	**14**	**26.4**	**21**

Rank in order

By %

1. Delaware
   Hawaii
   New Hampshire
   Oklahoma
5. Maine
6. North Dakota
7. South Carolina
8. Virginia
9. Georgia
10. Utah
11. Mississippi
12. Connecticut
13. South Dakota
14. West Virginia
15. Washington
16. Kentucky
17. Colorado
18. Florida
19. North Carolina
20. Louisiana
21. Arizona
22. Alabama
23. Nebraska
24. New Mexico
25. Maryland
    Wisconsin
27. Indiana
28. Texas
29. Illinois
    New York
— Alaska
— Arkansas
— District of Columbia
— Idaho
— Iowa
— Kansas
— Massachusetts
— Michigan
— Minnesota
— Missouri
— Montana
— Nevada
— New Jersey
— Ohio
— Oregon
— Pennsylvania
— Rhode Island
— Tennessee
— Vermont
— Wyoming
NA California

— not applicable.   NA not available.

Source: Council of State Governments, *The Book of the States: 1992-1993* (Lexington, Ky.: Council of State Governments, 1992).
Note: Nineteen legislatures did not hold special sessions in 1991. California's special session was still active as of December 31, 1991, so the state is not included in the rankings.

STATE RESOLUTIONS IN SPECIAL SESSION, 1991					Rank in order
State	**Resolutions introduced**	**Resolutions enacted**	**% enacted**	**Rank by %**	**By %**
Alabama	119	104	87.4	13	1. Connecticut
Alaska	—	—	—	—	Florida
Arizona	17	1	5.9	18	Georgia
Arkansas	—	—	—	—	Mississippi
California	4	2	50.0	NA	North Dakota
Colorado	17	15	88.2	11	Wisconsin
Connecticut	28	28	100.0	1	7. Virginia
Delaware	0	0	0.0	19	8. Texas
District of Columbia	—	—	—	—	9. Washington
Florida	12	12	100.0	1	10. Illinois
Georgia	125	125	100.0	1	11. Colorado
Hawaii	0	0	0.0	19	12. West Virginia
Idaho	—	—	—	—	13. Alabama
Illinois	23	21	91.3	10	14. Kentucky
Indiana	0	0	0.0	19	15. Louisiana
Iowa	—	—	—	—	16. North Carolina
Kansas	—	—	—	—	Utah
Kentucky	261	220	84.3	14	18. Arizona
Louisiana	80	63	78.8	15	19. Delaware
Maine	0	0	0.0	19	Hawaii
Maryland	1	0	0.0	19	Indiana
Massachusetts	—	—	—	—	Maine
Michigan	—	—	—	—	Maryland
Minnesota	—	—	—	—	Nebraska
Mississippi	9	9	100.0	1	New Hampshire
Missouri	—	—	—	—	New Mexico
Montana	—	—	—	—	New York
Nebraska	9	0	0.0	19	Oklahoma
Nevada	—	—	—	—	South Carolina
New Hampshire	0	0	0.0	19	South Dakota
New Jersey	—	—	—	—	— Alaska
New Mexico	0	0	0.0	19	— Arkansas
New York	0	0	0.0	19	— District of Columbia
North Carolina	4	3	75.0	16	— Idaho
North Dakota	2	2	100.0	1	— Iowa
Ohio	—	—	—	—	— Kansas
Oklahoma	0	0	0.0	19	— Massachusetts
Oregon	—	—	—	—	— Michigan
Pennsylvania	—	—	—	—	— Minnesota
Rhode Island	—	—	—	—	— Missouri
South Carolina	0	0	0.0	19	— Montana
South Dakota	0	0	0.0	19	— Nevada
Tennessee	—	—	—	—	— New Jersey
Texas	867	805	92.8	8	— Ohio
Utah	4	3	75.0	16	— Oregon
Vermont	—	—	—	—	— Pennsylvania
Virginia	78	77	98.7	7	— Rhode Island
Washington	12	11	91.7	9	— Tennessee
West Virginia	32	28	87.5	12	— Vermont
Wisconsin	2	2	100.0	1	— Wyoming
Wyoming	0	0	0.0	50	NA California
United States	**57**	**51**	**89.5**	**11**	

— not applicable.   NA not available.

Source: Council of State Governments, *The Book of the States: 1992-1993* (Lexington, Ky.: Council of State Governments, 1992).

Note: Nineteen legislatures did not hold special sessions in 1991. California's special session was still active as of December 31, 1991, and the state is not included in the rankings.

| | | | | Rank in order

State	Total cabinet positions	Women appointed	% of cabinet	Rank by %	By %
Alabama	21	2	9.5	32	1. Maryland
Alaska	15	1	6.7	34	2. Washington
Arizona	NA	NA	NA	NA	3. Minnesota
Arkansas	16	3	18.8	19	4. Louisiana
California	10	2	20.0	17	Massachusetts
Colorado	18	3	16.7	22	6. Maine
Connecticut	24	6	25.0	9	Michigan
Delaware	18	2	11.1	28	8. Pennsylvania
District of Columbia	—	—	—	—	9. Connecticut
Florida	—	—	—	—	New Mexico
Georgia	—	—	—	—	New York
Hawaii	16	3	18.8	19	Virginia
Idaho	18	2	11.1	28	13. Rhode Island
Illinois	NA	NA	NA	NA	14. North Carolina
Indiana	—	—	—	—	Wisconsin
Iowa	NA	NA	NA	NA	16. Montana
Kansas	10	2	20.0	17	17. California
Kentucky	13	1	7.7	33	Kansas
Louisiana	10	3	30.0	4	19. Arkansas
Maine	14	4	28.6	6	Hawaii
Maryland	17	7	41.2	1	21. South Dakota
Massachusetts	10	3	30.0	4	22. Colorado
Michigan	14	4	28.6	6	West Virginia
Minnesota	22	7	31.9	3	24. Ohio
Mississippi	—	—	—	—	25. New Jersey
Missouri	10	1	10.0	31	26. Utah
Montana	19	4	21.1	16	27. Tennessee
Nebraska	NA	NA	NA	NA	28. Delaware
Nevada	19	1	5.3	36	Idaho
New Hampshire	—	—	—	—	Vermont
New Jersey	19	3	15.8	25	31. Missouri
New Mexico	16	4	25.0	9	32. Alabama
New York	20	5	25.0	9	33. Kentucky
North Carolina	9	2	22.2	14	34. Alaska
North Dakota	15	1	6.7	34	North Dakota
Ohio	25	4	16.0	24	36. Nevada
Oklahoma	NA	NA	NA	NA	— District of Columbia
Oregon	NA	NA	NA	NA	— Florida
Pennsylvania	18	5	27.8	8	— Georgia
Rhode Island	21	5	23.8	13	— Indiana
South Carolina	—	—	—	—	— Mississippi
South Dakota	22	4	18.2	21	— New Hampshire
Tennessee	22	3	13.6	27	— South Carolina
Texas	—	—	—	—	— Texas
Utah	14	2	14.3	26	— Wyoming
Vermont	9	1	11.1	28	NA Arizona
Virginia	8	2	25.0	9	NA Illinois
Washington	24	8	33.3	2	NA Iowa
West Virginia	6	1	16.7	22	NA Nebraska
Wisconsin	9	2	22.2	14	NA Oklahoma
Wyoming	—	—	—	—	NA Oregon
United States	—	—	—	—	

— not applicable.   NA not available.

Source: National Women's Political Caucus, *The Appointment of Women: A Survey of Governors' Cabinets, 1989-1991* (Washington, D.C.: National Women's Political Caucus, 1991).

Note: Florida, Georgia, Indiana, Mississippi, New Hampshire, South Carolina, Texas, and Wyoming have elected or noncabinet governmental structures.

State	Expenditures	Per capita	Rank by per capita	By per capita
TOTAL FEDERAL FUNDING TO STATE GOVERNMENTS, FISCAL 1991				**Rank in order**
Alabama	$18,464,000,000	$4,515.53	15	1. District of Columbia
Alaska	3,655,000,000	6,412.28	2	2. Alaska
Arizona	15,491,000,000	4,130.93	28	3. Virginia
Arkansas	9,053,000,000	3,816.61	36	4. Maryland
California	127,684,000,000	4,202.90	24	5. New Mexico
Colorado	16,474,000,000	4,878.29	11	6. Hawaii
Connecticut	16,460,000,000	5,001.52	10	7. Massachusetts
Delaware	2,435,000,000	3,580.88	43	8. North Dakota
District of Columbia	19,105,000,000	31,948.16	1	9. Missouri
Florida	56,276,000,000	4,238.61	21	10. Connecticut
Georgia	23,739,000,000	3,584.33	42	11. Colorado
Hawaii	6,162,000,000	5,429.08	6	12. Montana
Idaho	4,287,000,000	4,126.08	29	13. Rhode Island
Illinois	40,767,000,000	3,531.75	45	14. Maine
Indiana	18,806,000,000	3,352.23	50	15. Alabama
Iowa	10,306,000,000	3,687.30	41	16. South Dakota
Kansas	10,519,000,000	4,216.03	23	17. Mississippi
Kentucky	15,231,000,000	4,102.07	30	18. Washington
Louisiana	16,270,000,000	3,826.44	35	19. New York
Maine	5,601,000,000	4,535.22	14	20. Wyoming
Maryland	29,507,000,000	6,071.40	4	21. Florida
Massachusetts	31,449,000,000	5,245.00	7	22. Tennessee
Michigan	31,565,000,000	3,369.45	49	23. Kansas
Minnesota	16,366,000,000	3,692.69	40	24. California
Mississippi	11,240,000,000	4,336.42	17	25. South Carolina
Missouri	26,410,000,000	5,120.20	9	26. West Virginia
Montana	3,743,000,000	4,632.43	12	27. Pennsylvania
Nebraska	6,419,000,000	4,029.50	32	28. Arizona
Nevada	4,922,000,000	3,833.33	34	29. Idaho
New Hampshire	3,874,000,000	3,505.88	46	30. Kentucky
New Jersey	30,862,000,000	3,977.06	33	31. Oklahoma
New Mexico	9,338,000,000	6,032.30	5	32. Nebraska
New York	76,790,000,000	4,252.41	19	33. New Jersey
North Carolina	23,243,000,000	3,450.05	47	34. Nevada
North Dakota	3,253,000,000	5,122.84	8	35. Louisiana
Ohio	41,414,000,000	3,785.90	37	36. Arkansas
Oklahoma	12,973,000,000	4,085.98	31	37. Ohio
Oregon	10,457,000,000	3,578.71	44	38. Utah
Pennsylvania	49,463,000,000	4,135.36	27	39. Texas
Rhode Island	4,604,000,000	4,585.66	13	40. Minnesota
South Carolina	14,907,000,000	4,187.36	25	41. Iowa
South Dakota	3,106,000,000	4,418.21	16	42. Georgia
Tennessee	20,890,000,000	4,217.65	22	43. Delaware
Texas	64,472,000,000	3,716.18	39	44. Oregon
Utah	6,694,000,000	3,781.92	38	45. Illinois
Vermont	1,930,000,000	3,403.88	48	46. New Hampshire
Virginia	38,674,000,000	6,152.40	3	47. North Carolina
Washington	21,529,000,000	4,290.36	18	48. Vermont
West Virginia	7,465,000,000	4,144.92	26	49. Michigan
Wisconsin	16,246,000,000	3,278.71	51	50. Indiana
Wyoming	1,951,000,000	4,241.30	20	51. Wisconsin
United States	**$1,096,493,000,000**	**$4,348.11**	**17**	

Source: U.S. Department of Commerce, Bureau of the Census, *Federal Expenditures by State for Fiscal Year 1991* (Washington, D.C.: Government Printing Office, 1992).

State	Expenditures	Per capita	Rank by per capita	Per $1,000 personal income		By amount per $1,000 personal income
				Amount	Rank	
Alabama	$8,855,260,000	$2,165.63	34	$145.70	26	1. Alaska
Alaska	4,941,025,000	8,668.46	1	413.27	1	2. Wyoming
Arizona	7,872,052,000	2,099.21	37	133.55	33	3. New Mexico
Arkansas	4,649,190,000	1,960.03	45	139.24	30	4. Hawaii
California	85,639,976,000	2,818.96	17	138.27	32	5. Montana
Colorado	6,992,288,000	2,070.56	38	112.10	44	6. West Virginia
Connecticut	11,114,721,000	3,377.31	8	132.57	34	7. North Dakota
Delaware	2,318,072,000	3,408.93	6	173.03	10	8. Rhode Island
District of Columbia	—	—	—	—	—	9. Vermont
Florida	25,167,779,000	1,895.59	47	104.12	47	10. Delaware
Georgia	13,286,331,000	2,006.09	43	119.82	40	11. Louisiana
Hawaii	4,510,034,000	3,973.60	2	199.00	4	12. Washington
Idaho	2,305,140,000	2,218.61	33	149.46	21	13. Utah
Illinois	24,619,161,000	2,132.82	35	105.36	46	14. South Carolina
Indiana	11,547,519,000	2,058.38	39	123.10	36	15. Maine
Iowa	6,819,816,000	2,440.01	27	142.47	28	16. Kentucky
Kansas	5,134,222,000	2,057.80	40	113.97	43	17. New York
Kentucky	9,047,773,000	2,436.78	28	163.46	16	18. Mississippi
Louisiana	10,537,155,000	2,478.16	26	172.07	11	19. Minnesota
Maine	3,514,633,000	2,845.86	15	166.21	15	20. Massachusetts
Maryland	12,576,285,000	2,587.71	20	120.20	38	21. Idaho
Massachusetts	20,348,875,000	3,393.74	7	149.78	20	Oklahoma
Michigan	24,036,582,000	2,565.82	21	140.56	29	23. Nevada
Minnesota	12,730,356,000	2,872.37	14	154.83	19	24. Oregon
Mississippi	5,171,284,000	1,995.09	44	156.66	18	25. Ohio
Missouri	9,254,189,000	1,794.14	49	103.32	49	26. Alabama
Montana	2,384,343,000	2,950.92	12	195.36	5	27. Wisconsin
Nebraska	3,266,203,000	2,038.83	41	117.77	42	28. Iowa
Nevada	3,435,503,000	2,675.63	18	147.46	23	29. Michigan
New Hampshire	2,135,163,000	1,932.27	46	92.24	50	30. Arkansas
New Jersey	23,250,454,000	2,996.19	11	120.54	37	31. North Carolina
New Mexico	4,526,761,000	2,924.26	13	208.83	3	32. California
New York	64,320,860,000	3,561.90	4	161.77	17	33. Arizona
North Carolina	15,036,215,000	2,231.89	32	138.72	31	34. Connecticut
North Dakota	1,792,841,000	2,823.37	16	185.10	7	35. South Dakota
Ohio	27,790,759,000	2,540.52	22	145.71	25	36. Indiana
Oklahoma	7,266,779,000	2,288.75	30	149.46	21	37. New Jersey
Oregon	7,248,922,000	2,480.81	25	147.34	24	38. Maryland
Pennsylvania	26,709,513,000	2,233.05	31	120.19	39	39. Pennsylvania
Rhode Island	3,465,349,000	3,451.54	5	183.41	8	40. Georgia
South Carolina	8,970,344,000	2,519.76	23	169.23	14	41. Tennessee
South Dakota	1,416,513,000	2,014.95	42	128.81	35	42. Nebraska
Tennessee	9,237,787,000	1,865.09	48	119.14	41	43. Kansas
Texas	29,525,988,000	1,701.88	50	103.57	48	44. Colorado
Utah	4,108,339,000	2,321.10	29	169.77	13	45. Virginia
Vermont	1,735,886,000	3,061.53	10	175.54	9	46. Illinois
Virginia	13,351,971,000	2,124.08	36	109.25	45	47. Florida
Washington	15,666,047,000	3,121.97	9	169.96	12	48. Texas
West Virginia	4,740,556,000	2,632.18	19	192.53	6	49. Missouri
Wisconsin	12,448,441,000	2,512.30	24	144.50	27	50. New Hampshire
Wyoming	1,813,108,000	3,941.54	3	245.75	2	— District of Columbia
United States	$628,634,363,000	$2,498.76	25	$135.23	33	

— not applicable.

Source: U.S. Department of Commerce, Bureau of the Census, *State Government Finances: 1991* (Washington, D.C.: Government Printing Office, 1992).

State	Expenditures	Per capita	Rank by per capita	Per $1,000 personal income	
				Amount	Rank
Alabama	$8,050,247,000	$1,968.76	35	$132.46	23
Alaska	4,493,231,000	7,882.86	1	375.81	1
Arizona	7,118,181,000	1,898.18	40	120.76	32
Arkansas	4,315,084,000	1,819.18	43	129.24	25
California	75,033,397,000	2,469.83	17	121.14	31
Colorado	6,089,428,000	1,803.21	45	97.62	46
Connecticut	9,806,921,000	2,979.92	7	116.97	34
Delaware	2,151,640,000	3,164.18	4	160.61	9
District of Columbia	—	—	—	—	—
Florida	23,628,437,000	1,779.65	46	97.75	45
Georgia	12,280,305,000	1,854.19	42	110.75	38
Hawaii	4,174,449,000	3,677.93	2	184.20	4
Idaho	2,055,374,000	1,978.22	32	133.27	22
Illinois	22,167,969,000	1,920.47	38	94.87	47
Indiana	10,966,648,000	1,954.84	36	116.91	35
Iowa	6,383,519,000	2,283.91	19	133.35	21
Kansas	4,706,960,000	1,886.56	41	104.48	40
Kentucky	8,247,566,000	2,221.27	21	149.00	12
Louisiana	9,592,363,000	2,255.96	20	156.64	10
Maine	3,095,441,000	2,506.43	15	146.38	13
Maryland	10,776,479,000	2,217.38	23	103.00	41
Massachusetts	18,265,374,000	3,046.26	5	134.44	20
Michigan	20,748,884,000	2,214.87	24	121.34	30
Minnesota	11,688,084,000	2,637.20	11	142.15	17
Mississippi	4,680,374,000	1,805.70	44	141.79	18
Missouri	8,478,125,000	1,643.68	48	94.65	49
Montana	2,058,039,000	2,547.08	14	168.62	6
Nebraska	3,191,803,000	1,992.39	30	115.09	36
Nevada	2,556,872,000	1,991.33	31	109.75	39
New Hampshire	1,748,813,000	1,582.64	49	75.55	50
New Jersey	19,398,772,000	2,499.84	16	100.57	44
New Mexico	4,203,656,000	2,715.54	10	193.92	3
New York	53,916,492,000	2,985.74	6	135.60	19
North Carolina	13,805,168,000	2,049.16	28	127.36	28
North Dakota	1,653,192,000	2,603.45	13	170.68	5
Ohio	22,324,368,000	2,040.81	29	117.05	33
Oklahoma	6,270,902,000	1,975.09	33	128.98	26
Oregon	6,292,079,000	2,153.35	26	127.89	27
Pennsylvania	22,879,014,000	1,912.80	39	102.95	42
Rhode Island	2,749,576,000	2,738.62	9	145.53	14
South Carolina	7,698,481,000	2,162.49	25	145.24	15
South Dakota	1,356,187,000	1,929.14	37	123.32	29
Tennessee	8,596,037,000	1,735.52	47	110.86	37
Texas	27,025,896,000	1,557.78	50	94.80	48
Utah	3,692,298,000	2,086.04	27	152.58	11
Vermont	1,606,774,000	2,833.82	8	162.48	7
Virginia	12,389,500,000	1,970.97	34	101.37	43
Washington	13,170,331,000	2,624.62	12	142.89	16
West Virginia	3,996,068,000	2,218.81	22	162.30	8
Wisconsin	11,340,393,000	2,288.68	18	131.64	24
Wyoming	1,637,792,000	3,560.42	3	221.98	2
United States	$554,552,983,000	$2,204.29	25	$119.29	33

By amount per $1,000 personal income

1. Alaska
2. Wyoming
3. New Mexico
4. Hawaii
5. North Dakota
6. Montana
7. Vermont
8. West Virginia
9. Delaware
10. Louisiana
11. Utah
12. Kentucky
13. Maine
14. Rhode Island
15. South Carolina
16. Washington
17. Minnesota
18. Mississippi
19. New York
20. Massachusetts
21. Iowa
22. Idaho
23. Alabama
24. Wisconsin
25. Arkansas
26. Oklahoma
27. Oregon
28. North Carolina
29. South Dakota
30. Michigan
31. California
32. Arizona
33. Ohio
34. Connecticut
35. Indiana
36. Nebraska
37. Tennessee
38. Georgia
39. Nevada
40. Kansas
41. Maryland
42. Pennsylvania
43. Virginia
44. New Jersey
45. Florida
46. Colorado
47. Illinois
48. Texas
49. Missouri
50. New Hampshire
— District of Columbia

— not applicable.

Source: U.S. Department of Commerce, Bureau of the Census, *State Government Finances: 1991* (Washington, D.C.: Government Printing Office, 1992).

Note: General expenditures are all government expenditures other than utility, liquor store, and insurance trust expenditures.

STATE DEBT. FISCAL 1991

State	Total long-term debt	Per capita	Rank by per capita
Alabama	$4,213,842,000	$1,030.53	35
Alaska	5,290,972,000	9,282.41	1
Arizona	2,539,685,000	677.25	43
Arkansas	1,764,450,000	743.87	42
California	31,956,108,000	1,051.88	32
Colorado	2,659,408,000	787.51	41
Connecticut	13,006,152,000	3,952.04	4
Delaware	3,215,375,000	4,728.49	2
District of Columbia	—	—	—
Florida	11,083,642,000	834.80	39
Georgia	3,651,646,000	551.36	46
Hawaii	4,201,628,000	3,701.87	6
Idaho	1,122,423,000	1,080.29	29
Illinois	18,238,449,000	1,580.04	18
Indiana	4,623,993,000	824.24	40
Iowa	1,620,256,000	579.70	44
Kansas	336,964,000	135.06	50
Kentucky	6,024,486,000	1,622.54	17
Louisiana	10,728,679,000	2,523.21	10
Maine	2,584,646,000	2,092.83	14
Maryland	7,527,848,000	1,548.94	19
Massachusetts	21,101,790,000	3,519.31	7
Michigan	10,109,004,000	1,079.10	31
Minnesota	3,940,713,000	889.15	38
Mississippi	1,412,925,000	545.11	47
Missouri	5,775,342,000	1,119.69	28
Montana	1,611,458,000	1,994.38	16
Nebraska	1,595,738,000	1,001.72	36
Nevada	1,708,027,000	1,330.24	23
New Hampshire	4,126,744,000	3,734.61	5
New Jersey	19,039,169,000	2,453.50	12
New Mexico	1,751,531,000	1,131.48	27
New York	51,804,160,000	2,868.77	8
North Carolina	3,489,720,000	517.99	48
North Dakota	963,767,000	1,517.74	21
Ohio	11,367,331,000	1,039.16	33
Oklahoma	3,729,656,000	1,174.69	26
Oregon	6,450,578,000	2,207.59	13
Pennsylvania	11,640,349,000	973.19	37
Rhode Island	4,392,975,000	4,375.47	3
South Carolina	4,189,096,000	1,176.71	25
South Dakota	1,753,731,000	2,494.64	11
Tennessee	2,789,937,000	563.28	45
Texas	7,686,504,000	443.05	49
Utah	1,911,495,000	1,079.94	30
Vermont	1,485,874,000	2,620.59	9
Virginia	6,500,254,000	1,034.08	34
Washington	6,519,718,000	1,299.27	24
West Virginia	2,769,644,000	1,537.84	20
Wisconsin	6,624,538,000	1,336.94	22
Wyoming	921,627,000	2,003.54	15
United States	**$345,554,047,000**	**$1,370.28**	**22**

Rank in order

By per capita

1. Alaska
2. Delaware
3. Rhode Island
4. Connecticut
5. New Hampshire
6. Hawaii
7. Massachusetts
8. New York
9. Vermont
10. Louisiana
11. South Dakota
12. New Jersey
13. Oregon
14. Maine
15. Wyoming
16. Montana
17. Kentucky
18. Illinois
19. Maryland
20. West Virginia
21. North Dakota
22. Wisconsin
23. Nevada
24. Washington
25. South Carolina
26. Oklahoma
27. New Mexico
28. Missouri
29. Idaho
30. Utah
31. Michigan
32. California
33. Ohio
34. Virginia
35. Alabama
36. Nebraska
37. Pennsylvania
38. Minnesota
39. Florida
40. Indiana
41. Colorado
42. Arkansas
43. Arizona
44. Iowa
45. Tennessee
46. Georgia
47. Mississippi
48. North Carolina
49. Texas
50. Kansas
— District of Columbia

— not applicable.

Source: U.S. Department of Commerce, Bureau of the Census, *State Government Finances: 1991* (Washington, D.C.: Government Printing Office, 1992).

State	Expenditures	Per capita	Rank by per capita	Per $1,000 personal income Amount	Per $1,000 personal income Rank	By amount per $1,000 personal income
Alabama	$275,353,000	$67.34	35	$4.53	25	1. Alaska
Alaska	483,182,000	847.69	1	40.41	1	2. Delaware
Arizona	187,183,000	49.92	44	3.18	41	3. Rhode Island
Arkansas	130,201,000	54.89	41	3.90	34	4. Louisiana
California	2,195,669,000	72.27	31	3.54	38	5. South Dakota
Colorado	234,943,000	69.57	34	3.77	36	6. Vermont
Connecticut	742,603,000	225.65	5	8.86	11	7. New Hampshire
Delaware	207,242,000	304.77	2	15.47	2	8. Massachusetts
District of Columbia	—	—	—	—	—	9. Hawaii
Florida	694,414,000	52.30	43	2.87	44	10. Oregon
Georgia	234,536,000	35.41	47	2.12	46	11. Connecticut
Hawaii	230,308,000	202.91	7	10.16	9	12. Maine
Idaho	94,574,000	91.02	23	6.13	19	13. North Dakota
Illinois	1,292,228,000	111.95	18	5.53	21	14. New York
Indiana	320,008,000	57.04	40	3.41	40	15. Montana
Iowa	146,895,000	52.56	42	3.07	42	16. New Jersey
Kansas	31,114,000	12.47	50	0.69	50	17. West Virginia
Kentucky	378,733,000	102.00	19	6.84	18	18. Kentucky
Louisiana	830,016,000	195.21	10	13.55	4	19. Idaho
Maine	171,670,000	139.00	15	8.12	12	20. Utah
Maryland	463,139,000	95.30	21	4.43	27	21. Illinois
Massachusetts	1,384,585,000	230.92	4	10.19	8	22. Wisconsin
Michigan	660,449,000	70.50	32	3.86	35	23. New Mexico
Minnesota	284,496,000	64.19	36	3.46	39	24. Nevada
Mississippi	96,407,000	37.19	46	2.92	43	25. Alabama
Missouri	363,602,000	70.49	33	4.06	32	26. Nebraska
Montana	93,512,000	115.73	17	7.66	15	27. Maryland
Nebraska	124,148,000	77.50	27	4.48	26	28. Washington
Nevada	120,761,000	94.05	22	5.18	24	29. Pennsylvania
New Hampshire	243,699,000	220.54	6	10.53	7	30. Ohio
New Jersey	1,403,499,000	180.86	11	7.28	16	31. South Carolina
New Mexico	116,936,000	75.54	29	5.39	23	32. Missouri
New York	3,160,473,000	175.02	12	7.95	14	33. Virginia
North Carolina	224,668,000	33.35	49	2.07	48	34. Arkansas
North Dakota	77,812,000	122.54	16	8.03	13	35. Michigan
Ohio	797,471,000	72.90	30	4.18	30	36. Colorado
Oklahoma	181,693,000	57.23	39	3.74	37	37. Oklahoma
Oregon	465,565,000	159.33	14	9.46	10	38. California
Pennsylvania	943,134,000	78.85	26	4.24	29	39. Minnesota
Rhode Island	289,175,000	288.02	3	15.31	3	40. Indiana
South Carolina	217,178,000	61.01	38	4.10	31	41. Arizona
South Dakota	138,066,000	196.40	8	12.55	5	42. Iowa
Tennessee	198,556,000	40.09	45	2.56	45	43. Mississippi
Texas	598,499,000	34.50	48	2.10	47	44. Florida
Utah	140,594,000	79.43	25	5.81	20	45. Tennessee
Vermont	110,966,000	195.71	9	11.22	6	46. Georgia
Virginia	478,340,000	76.10	28	3.91	33	47. Texas
Washington	407,388,000	81.19	24	4.42	28	48. North Carolina
West Virginia	176,898,000	98.22	20	7.18	17	49. Wyoming
Wisconsin	474,970,000	62.12	37	5.51	22	50. Kansas
Wyoming	75,325,000	163.75	13	1.02	49	— District of Columbia
United States	**$23,392,876,000**	**$92.98**	**23**	**$5.03**	**25**	

— not applicable.

Source: U.S. Department of Commerce, Bureau of the Census, *State Government Finances: 1991* (Washington, D.C.: Government Printing Office, 1992).

	TOTAL STATE TAX REVENUE, FISCAL 1991			Rank in order
State	Expenditures	Per capita	Rank by per capita	By per capita
Alabama	$3,942,565,000	$964.19	44	1. Alaska
Alaska	1,806,131,000	3,168.65	1	2. Hawaii
Arizona	4,710,745,000	1,256.20	19	3. Delaware
Arkansas	2,366,105,000	997.51	42	4. Massachusetts
California	44,874,424,000	1,477.10	10	5. Washington
Colorado	3,213,833,000	951.68	45	6. Minnesota
Connecticut	4,983,328,000	1,514.23	8	7. New York
Delaware	1,165,492,000	1,713.96	3	8. Connecticut
District of Columbia	—	—	—	9. New Jersey
Florida	13,764,055,000	1,036.68	39	10. California
Georgia	7,154,525,000	1,080.25	35	11. Wisconsin
Hawaii	2,639,152,000	2,325.24	2	12. Wyoming
Idaho	1,204,607,000	1,159.39	27	13. Kentucky
Illinois	13,291,517,000	1,151.48	28	14. New Mexico
Indiana	6,182,409,000	1,102.03	32	15. Maryland
Iowa	3,447,460,000	1,233.44	21	16. Nevada
Kansas	2,796,415,000	1,120.81	29	17. West Virginia
Kentucky	5,043,183,000	1,358.25	13	18. Maine
Louisiana	4,309,467,000	1,013.52	40	19. Arizona
Maine	1,558,231,000	1,261.73	18	20. Rhode Island
Maryland	6,401,428,000	1,317.17	15	21. Iowa
Massachusetts	9,683,597,000	1,615.01	4	22. Oklahoma
Michigan	11,103,151,000	1,185.22	25	23. Vermont
Minnesota	7,050,698,000	1,590.86	6	24. North Dakota
Mississippi	2,460,836,000	949.40	46	25. Michigan
Missouri	4,996,388,000	968.67	43	26. North Carolina
Montana	817,679,000	1,011.98	41	27. Idaho
Nebraska	1,767,368,000	1,109.46	30	28. Illinois
Nevada	1,682,602,000	1,310.44	16	29. Kansas
New Hampshire	624,627,000	565.27	50	30. Nebraska
New Jersey	11,644,652,000	1,500.60	9	31. South Carolina
New Mexico	2,085,690,000	1,347.34	14	32. Indiana
New York	28,299,769,000	1,567.16	7	33. Virginia
North Carolina	7,850,043,000	1,165.21	26	34. Pennsylvania
North Dakota	755,054,000	1,189.06	24	35. Georgia
Ohio	11,555,584,000	1,056.37	36	36. Ohio
Oklahoma	3,861,985,000	1,216.37	22	37. Utah
Oregon	3,029,829,000	1,036.90	38	38. Oregon
Pennsylvania	13,021,344,000	1,088.65	34	39. Florida
Rhode Island	1,256,652,000	1,251.65	20	40. Louisiana
South Carolina	3,933,214,000	1,104.84	31	41. Montana
South Dakota	528,248,000	751.42	49	42. Arkansas
Tennessee	4,310,573,000	870.30	48	43. Missouri
Texas	16,016,913,000	923.22	47	44. Alabama
Utah	1,860,817,000	1,051.31	37	45. Colorado
Vermont	684,519,000	1,207.26	23	46. Mississippi
Virginia	6,852,365,000	1,090.10	33	47. Texas
Washington	7,989,522,000	1,592.17	5	48. Tennessee
West Virginia	2,328,132,000	1,292.69	17	49. South Dakota
Wisconsin	7,016,734,000	1,416.09	11	50. New Hampshire
Wyoming	637,452,000	1,385.77	12	— District of Columbia
United States	$310,561,109,000	$1,231.52	22	

— not applicable.

Source: U.S. Department of Commerce, Bureau of the Census, *State Government Finances: 1991* (Washington, D.C.: Government Printing Office, 1992).

State	Tax revenue	Per capita	Rank by per capita	% of total state revenue	Rank by %		By per capita
Alabama	$2,022,653,000	$494.66	39	51.3	20		1. Hawaii
Alaska	96,674,000	169.60	49	5.4	50		2. Washington
Arizona	2,677,036,000	713.88	9	56.8	11		3. Nevada
Arkansas	1,258,163,000	530.42	34	53.2	18		4. Connecticut
California	18,721,452,000	616.24	17	41.7	39		5. New Jersey
Colorado	1,366,667,000	404.70	45	42.5	38		6. Florida
Connecticut	3,407,057,000	1,035.27	4	68.4	7		7. New Mexico
Delaware	170,477,000	250.70	47	14.6	48		8. Texas
District of Columbia	—	—	—	—	—		9. Arizona
Florida	10,884,691,000	819.82	6	79.1	3		10. West Virginia
Georgia	3,497,055,000	528.02	35	48.9	28		11. Minnesota
Hawaii	1,598,490,000	1,408.36	1	60.6	9		12. Rhode Island
Idaho	587,765,000	565.70	25	48.8	29		13. Tennessee
Illinois	6,632,507,000	574.59	23	49.9	26		14. North Dakota
Indiana	3,385,256,000	603.43	18	54.8	13		15. Wisconsin
Iowa	1,506,257,000	538.91	30	43.7	34		16. Mississippi
Kansas	1,348,119,000	540.33	29	48.2	30		17. California
Kentucky	2,150,471,000	579.17	22	42.6	37		18. Indiana
Louisiana	2,125,805,000	499.95	38	49.3	27		19. Maine
Maine	744,774,000	603.06	19	47.8	31		20. Nebraska
Maryland	2,641,718,000	543.56	28	41.3	40		21. South Carolina
Massachusetts	2,946,443,000	491.40	40	30.4	46		22. Kentucky
Michigan	4,513,241,000	481.77	42	40.6	42		23. Illinois
Minnesota	3,037,426,000	685.34	11	43.1	35		24. South Dakota
Mississippi	1,600,978,000	617.66	16	65.1	8		25. Idaho
Missouri	2,503,050,000	485.28	41	50.1	24		26. Vermont
Montana	183,377,000	226.95	48	22.4	47		27. Pennsylvania
Nebraska	959,270,000	602.18	20	54.3	15		28. Maryland
Nevada	1,436,754,000	1,118.97	3	85.4	1		29. Kansas
New Hampshire	312,063,000	282.41	46	50.0	25		30. Iowa
New Jersey	6,363,602,000	820.05	5	54.6	14		31. New York
New Mexico	1,250,442,000	807.78	7	60.0	10		32. Utah
New York	9,686,126,000	536.39	31	34.2	45		33. Ohio
North Carolina	3,126,370,000	464.06	43	39.8	43		34. Arkansas
North Dakota	419,793,000	661.09	14	55.6	12		35. Georgia
Ohio	5,803,212,000	530.51	33	50.2	23		36. Oklahoma
Oklahoma	1,658,748,000	522.44	36	43.0	36		37. Wyoming
Oregon	424,301,000	145.21	50	14.0	49		38. Louisiana
Pennsylvania	6,544,459,000	547.15	27	50.3	22		39. Alabama
Rhode Island	676,966,000	674.27	12	53.9	16		40. Massachusetts
South Carolina	2,093,427,000	588.04	21	53.2	17		41. Missouri
South Dakota	400,595,000	569.84	24	75.8	5		42. Michigan
Tennessee	3,299,700,000	666.20	13	76.5	4		43. North Carolina
Texas	12,877,251,000	742.25	8	80.4	2		44. Virginia
Utah	943,438,000	533.02	32	50.7	21		45. Colorado
Vermont	313,268,000	552.50	26	45.8	32		46. New Hampshire
Virginia	2,791,294,000	444.05	44	40.7	41		47. Delaware
Washington	5,994,394,000	1,194.58	2	75.0	6		48. Montana
West Virginia	1,235,863,000	686.21	10	53.1	19		49. Alaska
Wisconsin	3,084,971,000	622.60	15	44.0	33		50. Oregon
Wyoming	230,812,000	501.77	37	36.2	44		— District of Columbia
United States	**$153,534,721,000**	**$608.84**	**18**	**49.4**	**27**		

STATE REVENUE FROM TAX ON SALES AND GROSS RECEIPTS, FISCAL 1991

Rank in order

— not applicable.

Source: U.S. Department of Commerce, Bureau of the Census, *State Government Tax Collections: 1991* (Washington, D.C.: Government Printing Office, 1992).

STATE REVENUE FROM GENERAL SALES TAX. FISCAL 1991

State	Tax revenue	Per capita	Rank by per capita	% of total state revenue	Rank by %	By per capita
Alabama	$1,049,526,000	$256.67	40	26.6	35	1. Hawaii
Alaska	—	—	—	—	—	2. Washington
Arizona	2,005,801,000	534.88	7	42.6	11	3. Connecticut
Arkansas	876,900,000	369.69	25	37.1	16	4. Nevada
California	14,339,942,000	472.02	11	32.0	25	5. Florida
Colorado	844,572,000	250.10	42	26.3	36	6. New Mexico
Connecticut	2,438,653,000	741.01	3	48.9	6	7. Arizona
Delaware	—	—	—	—	—	8. New Jersey
District of Columbia	—	—	—	—	—	9. Texas
Florida	8,138,690,000	612.99	5	59.1	2	10. Tennessee
Georgia	2,656,792,000	401.15	21	37.1	15	11. California
Hawaii	1,278,737,000	1,126.64	1	48.5	7	12. West Virginia
Idaho	404,164,000	388.99	23	33.6	22	13. Indiana
Illinois	4,163,801,000	360.72	28	31.3	27	14. Rhode Island
Indiana	2,538,335,000	452.47	13	41.1	12	15. Minnesota
Iowa	977,056,000	349.57	32	28.3	33	16. Mississippi
Kansas	918,211,000	368.02	26	32.8	23	17. Utah
Kentucky	1,299,665,000	350.03	31	25.8	37	18. Wisconsin
Louisiana	1,308,090,000	307.64	38	30.4	30	19. South Carolina
Maine	497,069,000	402.49	20	31.9	26	20. Maine
Maryland	1,540,887,000	317.06	37	24.1	39	21. Georgia
Massachusetts	1,909,438,000	318.45	36	19.7	43	22. Nebraska
Michigan	3,190,647,000	340.59	33	28.7	32	23. Idaho
Minnesota	1,963,433,000	443.01	15	27.8	34	24. North Dakota
Mississippi	1,120,155,000	432.16	16	45.5	9	25. Arkansas
Missouri	1,863,374,000	361.26	27	37.3	14	26. Kansas
Montana	—	—	—	—	—	27. Missouri
Nebraska	624,259,000	391.88	22	35.3	19	28. Illinois
Nevada	826,288,000	643.53	4	49.1	5	29. South Dakota
New Hampshire	—	—	—	—	—	30. Pennsylvania
New Jersey	4,042,805,000	520.98	8	34.7	21	31. Kentucky
New Mexico	939,242,000	606.75	6	45.0	10	32. Iowa
New York	5,751,832,000	318.52	35	20.3	42	33. Michigan
North Carolina	1,689,871,000	250.83	41	21.5	41	34. Ohio
North Dakota	235,255,000	370.48	24	31.2	28	35. New York
Ohio	3,574,539,000	326.77	34	30.9	29	36. Massachusetts
Oklahoma	963,548,000	303.48	39	25.0	38	37. Maryland
Oregon	—	—	—	—	—	38. Louisiana
Pennsylvania	4,197,700,000	350.95	30	32.2	24	39. Oklahoma
Rhode Island	448,402,000	446.62	14	35.7	18	40. Alabama
South Carolina	1,437,473,000	403.79	19	36.5	17	41. North Carolina
South Dakota	247,974,000	352.74	29	46.9	8	42. Colorado
Tennessee	2,363,252,000	477.14	10	54.8	3	43. Virginia
Texas	8,294,921,000	478.12	9	51.8	4	44. Vermont
Utah	739,633,000	417.87	17	39.7	13	— Alaska
Vermont	125,611,000	221.54	44	18.4	44	— Delaware
Virginia	1,558,873,000	247.99	43	22.7	40	— District of Columbia
Washington	4,758,204,000	948.23	2	59.6	1	— Montana
West Virginia	817,368,000	453.84	12	35.1	20	— New Hampshire
Wisconsin	2,026,711,000	409.02	18	28.9	31	— Oregon
Wyoming	—	—	—	—	—	— Wyoming
United States	$103,165,478,000	$409.10	18	33.2	23	

— not applicable.

Source: U.S. Department of Commerce, Bureau of the Census, *State Government Tax Collections: 1991* (Washington, D.C.: Government Printing Office, 1992).

State	Tax revenue	Per capita	Rank by per capita	% of total state revenue	Rank by %
Alabama	$382,073,000	$93.44	14	9.7	11
Alaska	82,624,000	144.95	2	4.6	43
Arizona	287,793,000	76.75	24	6.1	31
Arkansas	150,859,000	63.60	42	6.4	25
California	2,130,937,000	70.14	35	4.7	42
Colorado	221,528,000	65.60	40	6.9	21
Connecticut	269,917,000	82.02	22	5.4	37
Delaware	358,510,000	527.22	1	30.8	1
District of Columbia	—	—	—	—	51
Florida	937,132,000	70.58	34	6.8	22
Georgia	194,328,000	29.34	50	2.7	49
Hawaii	34,048,000	30.00	49	1.3	50
Idaho	106,171,000	102.19	11	8.8	15
Illinois	817,275,000	70.80	33	6.1	30
Indiana	215,351,000	38.39	48	3.5	47
Iowa	323,165,000	115.62	9	9.4	12
Kansas	170,841,000	68.47	37	6.1	31
Kentucky	272,440,000	73.38	30	5.4	39
Louisiana	385,408,000	90.64	18	8.9	14
Maine	93,019,000	75.32	28	6.0	33
Maryland	239,729,000	49.33	46	3.7	46
Massachusetts	389,477,000	64.96	41	4.0	45
Michigan	696,207,000	74.32	29	6.3	27
Minnesota	521,215,000	117.60	8	7.4	19
Mississippi	159,276,000	61.45	43	6.5	24
Missouri	371,753,000	72.07	32	7.4	18
Montana	96,568,000	119.52	6	11.8	5
Nebraska	110,526,000	69.38	36	6.3	28
Nevada	174,199,000	135.67	3	10.4	8
New Hampshire	98,759,000	89.38	19	15.8	2
New Jersey	585,154,000	75.41	27	5.0	40
New Mexico	132,651,000	85.69	21	6.4	26
New York	935,643,000	51.81	45	3.3	48
North Carolina	510,649,000	75.80	25	6.5	23
North Dakota	58,151,000	91.58	17	7.7	17
Ohio	824,988,000	75.42	26	7.1	20
Oklahoma	374,600,000	117.98	7	9.7	10
Oregon	376,623,000	128.89	4	12.4	3
Pennsylvania	1,369,409,000	114.49	10	10.5	7
Rhode Island	72,742,000	72.45	31	5.8	35
South Carolina	242,102,000	68.01	38	6.2	29
South Dakota	65,000,000	92.46	15	12.3	4
Tennessee	454,329,000	91.73	16	10.5	6
Texas	1,657,332,000	95.53	13	10.3	9
Utah	75,061,000	42.41	47	4.0	44
Vermont	54,229,000	95.64	12	7.9	16
Virginia	376,559,000	59.90	44	5.5	36
Washington	432,318,000	86.15	20	5.4	38
West Virginia	138,826,000	77.08	23	6.0	34
Wisconsin	333,442,000	67.29	39	4.8	41
Wyoming	57,686,000	125.40	5	9.0	13
United States	**$19,418,622,000**	**$77.00**	**24**	**6.3**	**29**

STATE REVENUE FROM LICENSES, FISCAL 1991

Rank in order

By per capita

1. Delaware
2. Alaska
3. Nevada
4. Oregon
5. Wyoming
6. Montana
7. Oklahoma
8. Minnesota
9. Iowa
10. Pennsylvania
11. Idaho
12. Vermont
13. Texas
14. Alabama
15. South Dakota
16. Tennessee
17. North Dakota
18. Louisiana
19. New Hampshire
20. Washington
21. New Mexico
22. Connecticut
23. West Virginia
24. Arizona
25. North Carolina
26. Ohio
27. New Jersey
28. Maine
29. Michigan
30. Kentucky
31. Rhode Island
32. Missouri
33. Illinois
34. Florida
35. California
36. Nebraska
37. Kansas
38. South Carolina
39. Wisconsin
40. Colorado
41. Massachusetts
42. Arkansas
43. Mississippi
44. Virginia
45. New York
46. Maryland
47. Utah
48. Indiana
49. Hawaii
50. Georgia
— District of Columbia

— not applicable.

Source: U.S. Department of Commerce, Bureau of the Census, *State Government Tax Collections: 1991* (Washington, D.C.: Government Printing Office, 1992).

STATE REVENUE FROM MOTOR VEHICLE LICENSES, FISCAL 1991

State	Tax revenue	Per capita	Rank by per capita	% of total state revenue	Rank by %	By per capita
Alabama	$141,015,000	$34.49	35	3.6	23	1. Oklahoma
Alaska	20,760,000	36.42	33	1.1	48	2. Oregon
Arizona	209,350,000	55.83	9	4.4	15	3. Minnesota
Arkansas	74,193,000	31.28	38	3.1	29	4. Iowa
California	1,239,599,000	40.80	23	2.8	34	5. Wyoming
Colorado	99,353,000	29.42	44	3.1	31	6. New Mexico
Connecticut	165,318,000	50.23	15	3.3	28	7. Vermont
Delaware	20,508,000	30.16	40	1.8	47	8. North Dakota
District of Columbia	—	—	—	—	—	9. Arizona
Florida	533,113,000	40.15	25	3.9	19	10. South Dakota
Georgia	78,734,000	11.89	50	1.1	49	11. Idaho
Hawaii	20,935,000	18.45	48	0.8	50	12. Michigan
Idaho	56,402,000	54.29	11	4.7	11	13. Illinois
Illinois	597,981,000	51.81	13	4.5	14	14. Rhode Island
Indiana	165,706,000	29.54	43	2.7	37	15. Connecticut
Iowa	220,730,000	78.97	4	6.4	5	16. West Virginia
Kansas	106,728,000	42.78	20	3.8	20	17. Montana
Kentucky	141,080,000	38.00	29	2.8	33	18. New Hampshire
Louisiana	78,273,000	18.41	49	1.8	46	19. Nevada
Maine	47,904,000	38.79	27	3.1	32	20. Kansas
Maryland	144,195,000	29.67	42	2.3	42	21. Texas
Massachusetts	243,568,000	40.62	24	2.5	39	22. New Jersey
Michigan	490,222,000	52.33	12	4.4	16	23. California
Minnesota	363,922,000	82.11	3	5.2	8	24. Massachusetts
Mississippi	64,248,000	24.79	45	2.6	38	25. Florida
Missouri	194,014,000	37.61	30	3.9	18	26. Virginia
Montana	37,007,000	45.80	17	4.5	13	27. Maine
Nebraska	55,175,000	34.64	34	3.1	30	28. Washington
Nevada	56,982,000	44.38	19	3.4	27	29. Kentucky
New Hampshire	50,457,000	45.66	18	8.1	1	30. Missouri
New Jersey	316,855,000	40.83	22	2.7	36	31. Pennsylvania
New Mexico	103,468,000	66.84	6	5.0	10	32. Ohio
New York	537,935,000	29.79	41	1.9	44	33. Alaska
North Carolina	214,325,000	31.81	37	2.7	35	34. Nebraska
North Dakota	37,866,000	59.63	8	5.0	9	35. Alabama
Ohio	399,016,000	36.48	32	3.5	25	36. Wisconsin
Oklahoma	279,644,000	88.08	1	7.2	3	37. North Carolina
Oregon	243,259,000	83.25	2	8.0	2	38. Arkansas
Pennsylvania	446,355,000	37.32	31	3.4	26	39. Tennessee
Rhode Island	51,934,000	51.73	14	4.1	17	40. Delaware
South Carolina	72,463,000	20.36	47	1.8	45	41. New York
South Dakota	38,174,000	54.30	10	7.2	4	42. Maryland
Tennessee	152,357,000	30.76	39	3.5	24	43. Indiana
Texas	725,608,000	41.82	21	4.5	12	44. Colorado
Utah	41,497,000	23.45	46	2.2	43	45. Mississippi
Vermont	35,353,000	62.35	7	5.2	7	46. Utah
Virginia	245,912,000	39.12	26	3.6	22	47. South Carolina
Washington	193,546,000	38.57	28	2.4	40	48. Hawaii
West Virginia	83,676,000	46.46	16	3.6	21	49. Louisiana
Wisconsin	158,643,000	32.02	36	2.3	41	50. Georgia
Wyoming	35,994,000	78.25	5	5.6	6	— District of Columbia
United States	**$10,131,352,000**	**$40.18**	25	3.3	29	

— not applicable.

Source: U.S. Department of Commerce, Bureau of the Census, *State Government Tax Collections: 1991* (Washington, D.C.: Government Printing Office, 1992).

STATE REVENUE FROM INDIVIDUAL INCOME TAXES, FISCAL 1991						Rank in order
State	Tax revenue	Per capital	Rank by per capita	% of total state revenue	Rank by %	By per capita
Alabama	$1,174,230,000	$287.17	35	29.8	32	1. Massachusetts
Alaska	—	—	—	—	—	2. New York
Arizona	1,245,645,000	332.17	33	26.4	34	3. Hawaii
Arkansas	793,880,000	334.69	32	33.6	28	4. Delaware
California	16,817,244,000	553.56	9	37.5	15	5. Oregon
Colorado	1,466,285,000	434.20	18	45.6	6	6. Minnesota
Connecticut	474,609,000	144.21	41	9.5	41	7. Wisconsin
Delaware	461,723,000	679.00	4	39.6	11	8. Maryland
District of Columbia	—	—	—	—	—	9. California
Florida	—	—	—	—	—	10. North Carolina
Georgia	2,947,681,000	445.07	16	41.2	10	11. Virginia
Hawaii	872,734,000	768.93	3	33.1	29	12. Iowa
Idaho	446,148,000	429.40	19	37.0	17	13. Maine
Illinois	4,538,545,000	393.19	23	34.1	24	14. Kentucky
Indiana	2,183,972,000	389.30	25	35.3	20	15. Vermont
Iowa	1,343,571,000	480.71	12	39.0	12	16. Georgia
Kansas	880,740,000	353.00	30	31.5	31	17. New Jersey
Kentucky	1,693,339,000	456.06	14	33.6	27	18. Colorado
Louisiana	803,592,000	188.99	38	18.6	38	19. Idaho
Maine	580,748,000	470.24	13	37.3	16	20. Rhode Island
Maryland	2,931,020,000	603.09	8	45.8	5	21. Michigan
Massachusetts	5,343,387,000	891.16	1	55.2	2	22. Utah
Michigan	3,787,197,000	404.27	21	34.1	26	23. Illinois
Minnesota	2,974,554,000	671.15	6	42.2	9	24. South Carolina
Mississippi	479,602,000	185.03	39	19.5	37	25. Indiana
Missouri	1,829,224,000	354.64	29	36.6	18	26. Ohio
Montana	282,960,000	350.20	31	34.6	22	27. Oklahoma
Nebraska	603,112,000	378.60	28	34.1	25	28. Nebraska
Nevada	—	—	—	—	—	29. Missouri
New Hampshire	36,949,000	33.44	42	5.9	42	30. Kansas
New Jersey	3,391,026,000	436.99	17	29.1	33	31. Montana
New Mexico	369,455,000	238.67	37	17.7	39	32. Arkansas
New York	14,482,059,000	801.98	2	51.2	3	33. Arizona
North Carolina	3,534,474,000	524.64	10	45.0	7	34. West Virginia
North Dakota	114,273,000	179.96	40	15.1	40	35. Alabama
Ohio	4,217,200,000	385.52	26	36.5	19	36. Pennsylvania
Oklahoma	1,218,279,000	383.71	27	31.5	30	37. New Mexico
Oregon	1,983,705,000	678.89	5	65.5	1	38. Louisiana
Pennsylvania	3,274,656,000	273.78	36	25.1	35	39. Mississippi
Rhode Island	429,247,000	427.54	20	34.2	23	40. North Dakota
South Carolina	1,386,648,000	389.51	24	35.3	21	41. Connecticut
South Dakota	—	—	—	—	—	42. New Hampshire
Tennessee	97,033,000	19.59	43	2.3	43	43. Tennessee
Texas	—	—	—	—	—	— Alaska
Utah	714,915,000	403.91	22	38.4	13	— District of Columbia
Vermont	257,517,000	454.18	15	37.6	14	— Florida
Virginia	3,236,011,000	514.80	11	47.2	4	— Nevada
Washington	—	—	—	—	—	— South Dakota
West Virginia	576,340,000	320.01	34	24.8	36	— Texas
Wisconsin	3,003,381,000	606.13	7	42.8	8	— Washington
Wyoming	—	—	—	—	—	— Wyoming
United States	$99,278,910,000	$393.69	23	32.0	30	

— not applicable.

Source: U.S. Department of Commerce, Bureau of the Census, *State Government Tax Collections: 1991* (Washington, D.C.: Government Printing Office, 1992).

State	Tax revenue	Per capita	Rank by per capita	% of total state revenue	Rank by %	By per capita
Alabama	$168,253,000	$41.15	44	4.3	36	1. Alaska
Alaska	253,649,000	445.00	1	14.0	3	2. Delaware
Arizona	192,325,000	51.29	34	4.1	39	3. Michigan
Arkansas	122,240,000	51.54	32	5.2	27	4. Connecticut
California	4,440,479,000	146.17	5	9.9	6	5. California
Colorado	114,514,000	33.91	45	3.6	44	6. New Jersey
Connecticut	515,879,000	156.75	4	10.4	5	7. Massachusetts
Delaware	122,457,000	180.08	2	10.5	4	8. New York
District of Columbia	—	—	—	—	—	9. New Hampshire
Florida	582,149,000	43.85	40	4.2	37	10. West Virginia
Georgia	416,558,000	62.90	24	5.8	24	11. Minnesota
Hawaii	116,380,000	102.54	12	4.4	35	12. Hawaii
Idaho	59,712,000	57.47	27	5.0	29	13. Wisconsin
Illinois	940,759,000	81.50	18	7.1	17	14. Montana
Indiana	310,394,000	55.33	28	5.0	28	15. Kentucky
Iowa	201,929,000	72.25	22	5.9	23	16. Kansas
Kansas	212,950,000	85.35	16	7.6	12	17. Pennsylvania
Kentucky	319,351,000	86.01	15	6.3	21	18. Illinois
Louisiana	326,659,000	76.83	20	7.6	13	19. North Dakota
Maine	76,053,000	61.58	25	4.9	31	20. Louisiana
Maryland	255,488,000	52.57	31	4.0	41	21. North Carolina
Massachusetts	719,569,000	120.01	7	7.4	14	22. Iowa
Michigan	1,593,109,000	170.06	3	14.3	2	23. Tennessee
Minnesota	458,271,000	103.40	11	6.5	19	24. Georgia
Mississippi	139,823,000	53.94	30	5.7	25	25. Maine
Missouri	224,759,000	43.58	41	4.5	33	26. Ohio
Montana	70,784,000	87.60	14	8.7	8	27. Idaho
Nebraska	81,948,000	51.44	33	4.6	32	28. Indiana
Nevada	—	—	—	—	—	29. South Dakota
New Hampshire	122,205,000	110.59	9	19.6	1	30. Mississippi
New Jersey	1,030,620,000	132.81	6	8.9	7	31. Maryland
New Mexico	48,989,000	31.65	46	2.3	46	32. Arkansas
New York	2,030,332,000	112.43	8	7.2	16	33. Nebraska
North Carolina	499,958,000	74.21	21	6.4	20	34. Arizona
North Dakota	50,911,000	80.18	19	6.7	18	35. Oregon
Ohio	630,183,000	57.61	26	5.5	26	36. Vermont
Oklahoma	137,582,000	43.33	42	3.6	45	37. Utah
Oregon	149,074,000	51.02	35	4.9	30	38. Rhode Island
Pennsylvania	1,011,966,000	84.61	17	7.8	11	39. Virginia
Rhode Island	45,966,000	45.78	38	3.7	43	40. Florida
South Carolina	151,433,000	42.54	43	3.9	42	41. Missouri
South Dakota	38,578,000	54.88	29	7.3	15	42. Oklahoma
Tennessee	345,542,000	69.76	23	8.0	10	43. South Carolina
Texas	—	—	—	—	—	44. Alabama
Utah	82,463,000	46.59	37	4.4	34	45. Colorado
Vermont	27,387,000	48.30	36	4.0	40	46. New Mexico
Virginia	285,106,000	45.36	39	4.2	38	— District of Columbia
Washington	—	—	—	—	—	— Nevada
West Virginia	191,214,000	106.17	10	8.2	9	— Texas
Wisconsin	440,918,000	88.98	13	6.3	22	— Washington
Wyoming	—	—	—	—	—	— Wyoming
United States	$20,356,868,000	$80.73	19	6.6	19	

— not applicable.

Source: U.S. Department of Commerce, Bureau of the Census, *State Government Tax Collections: 1991* (Washington, D.C.: Government Printing Office, 1992).

STATE REVENUE FROM SEVERANCE TAXES, FISCAL 1991						Rank in order

State	Tax revenue	Per capita	Rank by per capita	% of total state revenue	Rank by %	By per capita
Alabama	$71,731,000	$17.54	16	1.8	15	1. Alaska
Alaska	1,284,746,000	2,253.94	1	71.1	1	2. Wyoming
Arizona	—	—	—	—	—	3. North Dakota
Arkansas	16,744,000	7.06	19	0.7	19	4. New Mexico
California	35,649,000	1.17	24	0.1	25	5. Louisiana
Colorado	10,460,000	3.10	22	0.3	22	6. Oklahoma
Connecticut	—	—	—	—	—	7. Montana
Delaware	—	—	—	—	—	8. West Virginia
District of Columbia	—	—	—	—	—	9. Texas
Florida	71,938,000	5.42	20	0.5	20	10. Kentucky
Georgia	—	—	—	—	—	11. Kansas
Hawaii	—	—	—	—	—	12. Utah
Idaho	652,000	0.63	26	0.1	26	13. Oregon
Illinois	—	—	—	—	—	14. Mississippi
Indiana	803,000	0.14	32	*	33	15. Nevada
Iowa	—	—	—	—	—	16. Alabama
Kansas	99,619,000	39.93	11	3.6	11	17. Washington
Kentucky	212,596,000	57.26	10	4.2	10	18. South Dakota
Louisiana	578,430,000	136.04	5	13.4	4	19. Arkansas
Maine	—	—	—	—	—	20. Florida
Maryland	—	—	—	—	—	21. Michigan
Massachusetts	—	—	—	—	—	22. Colorado
Michigan	48,895,000	5.22	21	0.4	21	23. Nebraska
Minnesota	2,212,000	0.50	27	*	28	24. California
Mississippi	51,182,000	19.75	14	2.1	14	25. Ohio
Missouri	42,000	0.01	34	*	34	26. Idaho
Montana	82,913,000	102.62	7	10.1	7	27. Minnesota
Nebraska	3,201,000	2.01	23	0.2	23	28. Tennessee
Nevada	23,951,000	18.65	15	1.4	17	29. Wisconsin
New Hampshire	127,000	0.12	33	*	31	30. North Carolina
New Jersey	—	—	—	—	—	31. Virginia
New Mexico	256,431,000	165.65	4	12.3	5	32. Indiana
New York	—	—	—	—	—	33. New Hampshire
North Carolina	1,648,000	0.25	30	*	29	34. Missouri
North Dakota	108,015,000	170.10	3	14.3	3	— Arizona
Ohio	9,461,000	0.87	25	0.1	24	— Connecticut
Oklahoma	415,528,000	130.88	6	10.8	6	— Delaware
Oregon	63,079,000	21.59	13	2.1	13	— District of Columbia
Pennsylvania	—	—	—	—	—	— Georgia
Rhode Island	—	—	—	—	—	— Hawaii
South Carolina	—	—	—	—	—	— Illinois
South Dakota	8,070,000	11.48	18	1.5	16	— Iowa
Tennessee	1,447,000	0.29	28	*	27	— Maine
Texas	1,355,104,000	78.11	9	8.5	8	— Maryland
Utah	39,851,000	22.52	12	2.1	12	— Massachusetts
Vermont	—	—	—	—	—	— New Jersey
Virginia	1,461,000	0.23	31	*	29	— New York
Washington	70,050,000	13.96	17	0.9	18	— Pennsylvania
West Virginia	173,001,000	96.06	8	7.4	9	— Rhode Island
Wisconsin	1,334,000	0.27	29	*	32	— South Carolina
Wyoming	266,540,000	579.44	2	41.8	2	— Vermont
United States	**$5,366,911,000**	**$21.28**	**14**	**1.7**	**16**	

— not applicable.   * rounds to less than 0.05.

Source: U.S. Department of Commerce, Bureau of the Census, *State Government Tax Collections: 1991* (Washington, D.C.: Government Printing Office, 1992).

State	Tax revenue	Per capita	Rank by per capita	% of total state revenue	Rank by %
Alabama	$94,215,000	$23.04	13	2.4	12
Alaska	85,007,000	149.14	3	4.7	7
Arizona	278,945,000	74.39	6	5.9	5
Arkansas	8,854,000	3.73	25	0.4	25
California	2,233,393,000	73.52	7	5.0	6
Colorado	7,493,000	2.22	30	0.2	30
Connecticut	12,000	*	42	*	42
Delaware	—	—	—	—	—
District of Columbia	—	—	—	—	—
Florida	430,334,000	32.41	11	3.1	8
Georgia	26,923,000	4.07	24	0.4	24
Hawaii	—	—	—	—	—
Idaho	99,000	0.10	40	*	39
Illinois	228,436,000	19.79	14	1.7	14
Indiana	4,910,000	0.88	36	0.1	35
Iowa	—	—	—	—	—
Kansas	32,961,000	13.21	18	1.2	17
Kentucky	323,373,000	87.09	5	6.4	4
Louisiana	47,394,000	11.15	20	1.1	19
Maine	44,558,000	36.08	9	2.9	10
Maryland	179,901,000	37.02	8	2.8	11
Massachusetts	616,000	0.10	39	*	40
Michigan	327,607,000	34.97	10	3.0	9
Minnesota	7,625,000	1.72	32	0.1	33
Mississippi	22,221,000	8.57	23	0.9	21
Missouri	12,669,000	2.46	29	0.3	28
Montana	77,405,000	95.80	4	9.5	3
Nebraska	2,142,000	1.35	33	0.1	32
Nevada	34,221,000	26.65	12	2.0	13
New Hampshire	335,000	0.30	37	0.1	37
New Jersey	16,722,000	2.16	31	0.1	31
New Mexico	21,118,000	13.64	17	1.0	20
New York	—	—	—	—	—
North Carolina	92,478,000	13.73	16	1.2	18
North Dakota	2,133,000	3.36	27	0.3	27
Ohio	10,501,000	0.96	34	0.1	34
Oklahoma	—	—	—	—	—
Oregon	142,000	0.05	41	*	41
Pennsylvania	157,714,000	13.19	19	1.2	16
Rhode Island	9,835,000	9.80	22	0.8	22
South Carolina	11,954,000	3.36	26	0.3	26
South Dakota	—	—	—	—	—
Tennessee	—	—	—	—	—
Texas	—	—	—	—	—
Utah	278,000	0.16	38	*	38
Vermont	9,785,000	17.26	15	1.4	15
Virginia	17,271,000	2.75	28	0.3	29
Washington	1,235,137,000	246.14	1	15.5	1
West Virginia	1,694,000	0.94	35	0.1	36
Wisconsin	49,225,000	9.93	21	0.7	23
Wyoming	80,115,000	174.16	2	12.6	2
United States	$6,227,751,000	$24.70	13	2.0	14

Rank in order

By per capita

1. Washington
2. Wyoming
3. Alaska
4. Montana
5. Kentucky
6. Arizona
7. California
8. Maryland
9. Maine
10. Michigan
11. Florida
12. Nevada
13. Alabama
14. Illinois
15. Vermont
16. North Carolina
17. New Mexico
18. Kansas
19. Pennsylvania
20. Louisiana
21. Wisconsin
22. Rhode Island
23. Mississippi
24. Georgia
25. Arkansas
26. South Carolina
27. North Dakota
28. Virginia
29. Missouri
30. Colorado
31. New Jersey
32. Minnesota
33. Nebraska
34. Ohio
35. West Virginia
36. Indiana
37. New Hampshire
38. Utah
39. Massachusetts
40. Idaho
41. Oregon
42. Connecticut
— Delaware
— District of Columbia
— Hawaii
— Iowa
— New York
— Oklahoma
— South Dakota
— Tennessee
— Texas

— not applicable. * indicates less than 0.005 in per capita data and less than 0.05 in % of total state revenue.

Source: U.S. Department of Commerce, Bureau of the Census, *State Government Tax Collections: 1991* (Washington, D.C.: Government Printing Office, 1992).

State	Tax revenue	Per capita	Rank by per capita	% of total state revenue	Rank by %
Alabama	$18,265,000	$4.47	42	0.5	38
Alaska	3,266,000	5.73	38	0.2	50
Arizona	29,001,000	7.73	31	0.6	31
Arkansas	8,550,000	3.61	45	0.4	41
California	495,270,000	16.30	14	1.1	17
Colorado	15,306,000	4.53	41	0.5	37
Connecticut	266,868,000	81.09	1	5.4	1
Delaware	19,403,000	28.53	5	1.7	11
District of Columbia	—	—	—	—	—
Florida	294,531,000	22.18	9	2.1	7
Georgia	41,262,000	6.23	34	0.6	34
Hawaii	11,860,000	10.45	23	0.4	39
Idaho	2,364,000	2.28	50	0.2	49
Illinois	111,476,000	9.66	28	0.8	26
Indiana	81,723,000	14.57	17	1.3	14
Iowa	68,977,000	24.68	7	2.0	8
Kansas	51,185,000	20.52	10	1.8	9
Kentucky	68,727,000	18.51	12	1.4	13
Louisiana	42,179,000	9.92	26	1.0	24
Maine	11,713,000	9.48	29	0.8	29
Maryland	73,447,000	15.11	16	1.1	15
Massachusetts	249,516,000	41.61	2	2.6	5
Michigan	119,581,000	12.77	18	1.1	19
Minnesota	26,665,000	6.02	37	0.4	40
Mississippi	7,754,000	2.99	46	0.3	45
Missouri	53,286,000	10.33	24	1.1	21
Montana	9,340,000	11.56	21	1.1	16
Nebraska	4,531,000	2.84	47	0.3	47
Nevada	13,477,000	10.50	22	0.8	27
New Hampshire	22,354,000	20.23	11	3.6	3
New Jersey	212,826,000	27.43	6	1.8	10
New Mexico	6,604,000	4.27	43	0.3	44
New York	709,923,000	39.31	4	2.5	6
North Carolina	84,466,000	12.54	19	1.1	20
North Dakota	1,778,000	2.80	48	0.2	48
Ohio	60,039,000	5.49	39	0.5	35
Oklahoma	39,450,000	12.43	20	1.0	23
Oregon	17,842,000	6.11	35	0.6	33
Pennsylvania	497,565,000	41.60	3	3.8	2
Rhode Island	18,422,000	18.35	13	1.5	12
South Carolina	36,058,000	10.13	25	0.9	25
South Dakota	15,914,000	22.64	8	3.0	4
Tennessee	44,056,000	8.90	30	1.0	22
Texas	127,226,000	7.33	33	0.8	28
Utah	4,811,000	2.72	49	0.3	46
Vermont	3,452,000	6.09	36	0.5	36
Virginia	46,883,000	7.46	32	0.7	30
Washington	48,946,000	9.75	27	0.6	32
West Virginia	7,563,000	4.20	44	0.3	43
Wisconsin	75,657,000	15.27	15	1.1	18
Wyoming	2,299,000	5.00	40	0.4	41
United States	**$4,283,657,000**	**$16.99**	**14**	**1.4**	**13**

STATE REVENUE FROM DEATH AND GIFT TAXES, FISCAL 1991

Rank in order

By per capita

1. Connecticut
2. Massachusetts
3. Pennsylvania
4. New York
5. Delaware
6. New Jersey
7. Iowa
8. South Dakota
9. Florida
10. Kansas
11. New Hampshire
12. Kentucky
13. Rhode Island
14. California
15. Wisconsin
16. Maryland
17. Indiana
18. Michigan
19. North Carolina
20. Oklahoma
21. Montana
22. Nevada
23. Hawaii
24. Missouri
25. South Carolina
26. Louisiana
27. Washington
28. Illinois
29. Maine
30. Tennessee
31. Arizona
32. Virginia
33. Texas
34. Georgia
35. Oregon
36. Vermont
37. Minnesota
38. Alaska
39. Ohio
40. Wyoming
41. Colorado
42. Alabama
43. New Mexico
44. West Virginia
45. Arkansas
46. Mississippi
47. Nebraska
48. North Dakota
49. Utah
50. Idaho
— District of Columbia

— not applicable.

Source: U.S. Department of Commerce, Bureau of the Census, *State Government Tax Collections: 1991* (Washington, D.C.: Government Printing Office, 1992).

State	Tax revenue	Per capita	Rank by per capita	% of total state revenue	Rank by %
Alabama	$11,145,000	$2.73	21	0.3	18
Alaska	—	—	—	—	—
Arizona	—	—	—	—	—
Arkansas	6,110,000	2.58	22	0.3	21
California	—	—	—	—	—
Colorado	—	—	—	—	—
Connecticut	48,986,000	14.89	7	1.0	10
Delaware	31,448,000	46.25	1	2.7	3
District of Columbia	—	—	—	—	—
Florida	563,280,000	42.43	2	4.1	2
Georgia	15,150,000	2.29	23	0.2	23
Hawaii	5,640,000	4.97	17	0.2	22
Idaho	—	—	—	—	—
Illinois	22,519,000	1.95	25	0.2	24
Indiana	—	—	—	—	—
Iowa	3,561,000	1.27	28	0.1	28
Kansas	—	—	—	—	—
Kentucky	2,886,000	0.78	29	0.1	29
Louisiana	—	—	—	—	—
Maine	7,366,000	5.96	12	0.5	13
Maryland	56,855,000	11.70	9	0.9	11
Massachusetts	34,589,000	5.77	13	0.4	15
Michigan	—	—	—	—	—
Minnesota	22,730,000	5.13	16	0.3	16
Mississippi	—	—	—	—	—
Missouri	—	—	—	—	—
Montana	—	—	—	—	—
Nebraska	2,638,000	1.66	26	0.1	26
Nevada	—	—	—	—	—
New Hampshire	31,835,000	28.81	4	5.1	1
New Jersey	44,702,000	5.76	14	0.4	14
New Mexico	—	—	—	—	—
New York	455,686,000	25.24	5	1.6	5
North Carolina	—	—	—	—	—
North Dakota	—	—	—	—	—
Ohio	—	—	—	—	—
Oklahoma	4,256,000	1.34	27	0.1	27
Oregon	15,063,000	5.16	15	0.5	12
Pennsylvania	165,575,000	13.84	8	1.3	7
Rhode Island	3,425,000	3.41	19	0.3	19
South Carolina	11,592,000	3.26	20	0.3	17
South Dakota	91,000	0.13	30	*	30
Tennessee	46,195,000	9.33	11	1.1	8
Texas	—	—	—	—	—
Utah	—	—	—	—	—
Vermont	10,528,000	18.57	6	1.5	6
Virginia	70,986,000	11.29	10	1.0	9
Washington	208,677,000	41.59	3	2.6	4
West Virginia	3,631,000	2.02	24	0.2	25
Wisconsin	18,769,000	3.79	18	0.3	20
Wyoming	—	—	—	—	—
United States	$1,925,644,000	$7.64	12	0.6	12

Rank in order

By per capita

1. Delaware
2. Florida
3. Washington
4. New Hampshire
5. New York
6. Vermont
7. Connecticut
8. Pennsylvania
9. Maryland
10. Virginia
11. Tennessee
12. Maine
13. Massachusetts
14. New Jersey
15. Oregon
16. Minnesota
17. Hawaii
18. Wisconsin
19. Rhode Island
20. South Carolina
21. Alabama
22. Arkansas
23. Georgia
24. West Virginia
25. Illinois
26. Nebraska
27. Oklahoma
28. Iowa
29. Kentucky
30. South Dakota
— Alaska
— Arizona
— California
— Colorado
— District of Columbia
— Idaho
— Indiana
— Kansas
— Louisiana
— Michigan
— Mississippi
— Missouri
— Montana
— Nevada
— New Mexico
— North Carolina
— North Dakota
— Ohio
— Texas
— Utah
— Wyoming

— not applicable. * data rounds to less than 0.05.

Source: U.S. Department of Commerce, Bureau of the Census, *State Government Tax Collections: 1991* (Washington, D.C.: Government Printing Office, 1992).

State	Tax revenue	Per capita	Rank by per capita	% of total state revenue	Rank by %
Alabama	$290,447,000	$71.03	41	7.4	29
Alaska	39,917,000	70.03	43	2.2	48
Arizona	362,018,000	96.54	23	7.7	27
Arkansas	224,929,000	94.83	25	9.5	12
California	2,002,287,000	65.91	45	4.5	46
Colorado	331,515,000	98.17	21	10.3	8
Connecticut	329,815,000	100.22	19	6.6	36
Delaware	66,216,000	97.38	22	5.7	42
District of Columbia	—	—	—	—	—
Florida	821,776,000	61.90	46	6.0	40
Georgia	451,169,000	68.12	44	6.3	39
Hawaii	53,188,000	46.86	49	2.0	49
Idaho	112,305,000	108.09	13	9.3	15
Illinois	1,024,492,000	88.75	32	7.7	26
Indiana	581,740,000	103.70	17	9.4	14
Iowa	330,530,000	118.26	6	9.6	11
Kansas	234,725,000	94.08	28	8.4	23
Kentucky	350,369,000	94.36	27	6.9	34
Louisiana	443,770,000	104.37	15	10.3	9
Maine	130,005,000	105.27	14	8.3	24
Maryland	443,563,000	91.27	31	6.9	35
Massachusetts	464,222,000	77.42	38	4.8	45
Michigan	733,501,000	78.30	37	6.6	37
Minnesota	457,571,000	103.24	18	6.5	38
Mississippi	305,100,000	117.71	7	12.4	6
Missouri	364,998,000	70.76	42	7.3	31
Montana	110,246,000	136.44	2	13.5	4
Nebraska	222,715,000	139.81	1	12.6	5
Nevada	120,487,000	93.84	29	7.2	32
New Hampshire	90,820,000	82.19	35	14.5	3
New Jersey	400,186,000	51.57	48	3.4	47
New Mexico	175,944,000	113.66	10	8.4	22
New York	506,704,000	28.06	50	1.8	50
North Carolina	825,425,000	122.52	4	10.5	7
North Dakota	75,917,000	119.55	5	10.1	10
Ohio	1,035,492,000	94.66	26	9.0	17
Oklahoma	330,819,000	104.20	16	8.6	20
Oregon	258,969,000	88.63	33	8.5	21
Pennsylvania	722,713,000	60.42	47	5.6	44
Rhode Island	74,602,000	74.31	39	5.9	41
South Carolina	340,112,000	95.54	24	8.6	19
South Dakota	78,686,000	111.93	11	14.9	1
Tennessee	635,248,000	128.26	3	14.7	2
Texas	1,509,285,000	87.00	34	9.4	13
Utah	131,057,000	74.04	40	7.0	33
Vermont	52,213,000	92.09	30	7.6	28
Virginia	617,586,000	98.25	20	9.0	16
Washington	584,960,000	116.57	8	7.3	30
West Virginia	205,981,000	114.37	9	8.8	18
Wisconsin	546,508,000	110.29	12	7.8	25
Wyoming	36,116,000	78.51	36	5.7	43
United States	**$20,638,959,000**	**$81.84**	**36**	**6.6**	**36**

STATE REVENUE FROM TAX ON MOTOR FUELS, FISCAL 1991

Rank in order

By per capita

1. Nebraska
2. Montana
3. Tennessee
4. North Carolina
5. North Dakota
6. Iowa
7. Mississippi
8. Washington
9. West Virginia
10. New Mexico
11. South Dakota
12. Wisconsin
13. Idaho
14. Maine
15. Louisiana
16. Oklahoma
17. Indiana
18. Minnesota
19. Connecticut
20. Virginia
21. Colorado
22. Delaware
23. Arizona
24. South Carolina
25. Arkansas
26. Ohio
27. Kentucky
28. Kansas
29. Nevada
30. Vermont
31. Maryland
32. Illinois
33. Oregon
34. Texas
35. New Hampshire
36. Wyoming
37. Michigan
38. Massachusetts
39. Rhode Island
40. Utah
41. Alabama
42. Missouri
43. Alaska
44. Georgia
45. California
46. Florida
47. Pennsylvania
48. New Jersey
49. Hawaii
50. New York
— District of Columbia

— not applicable.

Source: U.S. Department of Commerce, Bureau of the Census, *State Government Tax Collections: 1991* (Washington, D.C.: Government Printing Office, 1992).

STATE REVENUE FROM TAX ON TOBACCO PRODUCTS, FISCAL 1991

State	Tax revenue	Per capita	Rank by per capita	% of total state revenue	Rank by %
Alabama	$68,801,000	$16.83	36	1.7	30
Alaska	16,713,000	29.32	12	0.9	44
Arizona	51,796,000	13.81	41	1.1	41
Arkansas	62,300,000	26.27	18	2.6	8
California	755,531,000	24.87	21	1.7	31
Colorado	61,135,000	18.10	33	1.9	23
Connecticut	114,926,000	34.92	7	2.3	14
Delaware	17,188,000	25.28	20	1.5	36
District of Columbia	—	—	—	—	—
Florida	428,042,000	32.24	10	3.1	3
Georgia	85,207,000	12.87	43	1.2	40
Hawaii	26,263,000	23.14	24	1.0	42
Idaho	15,259,000	14.69	40	1.3	38
Illinois	319,038,000	27.64	17	2.4	11
Indiana	110,115,000	19.63	31	1.8	27
Iowa	86,523,000	30.96	11	2.5	10
Kansas	54,584,000	21.88	26	2.0	22
Kentucky	14,278,000	3.85	48	0.3	48
Louisiana	84,199,000	19.80	28	2.0	21
Maine	43,843,000	35.50	6	2.8	6
Maryland	61,320,000	12.62	44	1.0	43
Massachusetts	144,423,000	24.09	23	1.5	35
Michigan	259,342,000	27.68	16	2.3	13
Minnesota	153,737,000	34.69	8	2.2	17
Mississippi	50,914,000	19.64	30	2.1	19
Missouri	78,062,000	15.13	39	1.6	33
Montana	12,740,000	15.77	38	1.6	34
Nebraska	38,962,000	24.46	22	2.2	15
Nevada	50,296,000	39.17	1	3.0	5
New Hampshire	39,923,000	36.13	4	6.4	1
New Jersey	275,833,000	35.55	5	2.4	12
New Mexico	17,517,000	11.32	46	0.8	46
New York	603,433,000	33.42	9	2.1	18
North Carolina	15,190,000	2.26	50	0.2	50
North Dakota	16,519,000	26.01	19	2.2	16
Ohio	211,836,000	19.37	32	1.8	25
Oklahoma	69,632,000	21.93	25	1.8	26
Oregon	83,230,000	28.48	14	2.7	7
Pennsylvania	213,418,000	17.84	34	1.6	32
Rhode Island	37,792,000	37.64	2	3.0	4
South Carolina	30,335,000	8.52	47	0.8	47
South Dakota	13,899,000	19.77	29	2.6	9
Tennessee	79,309,000	16.01	37	1.8	24
Texas	637,000,000	36.72	3	4.0	2
Utah	23,298,000	13.16	42	1.3	39
Vermont	12,093,000	21.33	27	1.8	28
Virginia	15,458,000	2.46	49	0.2	49
Washington	140,253,000	27.95	15	1.8	29
West Virginia	31,741,000	17.62	35	1.4	37
Wisconsin	141,452,000	28.55	13	2.0	20
Wyoming	5,456,000	11.86	45	0.9	45
United States	**$5,980,154,000**	**$23.71**	**24**	**1.9**	**23**

Rank in order

By per capita

1. Nevada
2. Rhode Island
3. Texas
4. New Hampshire
5. New Jersey
6. Maine
7. Connecticut
8. Minnesota
9. New York
10. Florida
11. Iowa
12. Alaska
13. Wisconsin
14. Oregon
15. Washington
16. Michigan
17. Illinois
18. Arkansas
19. North Dakota
20. Delaware
21. California
22. Nebraska
23. Massachusetts
24. Hawaii
25. Oklahoma
26. Kansas
27. Vermont
28. Louisiana
29. South Dakota
30. Mississippi
31. Indiana
32. Ohio
33. Colorado
34. Pennsylvania
35. West Virginia
36. Alabama
37. Tennessee
38. Montana
39. Missouri
40. Idaho
41. Arizona
42. Utah
43. Georgia
44. Maryland
45. Wyoming
46. New Mexico
47. South Carolina
48. Kentucky
49. Virginia
50. North Carolina
— District of Columbia

— not applicable.

Source: U.S. Department of Commerce, Bureau of the Census, *State Government Tax Collections: 1991* (Washington, D.C.: Government Printing Office, 1992).

EXCISE TAX ON CIGARETTES, FISCAL 1991			Rank in order
State	Tax per package (cents)	**Rank**	**By tax rate**
Alabama	16.5	38	1. Minnesota
Alaska	29.0	16	2. Texas
Arizona	18.0	30	3. Connecticut
Arkansas	21.0	27	New Jersey
California	35.0	8	5. New York
Colorado	20.0	28	6. Rhode Island
Connecticut	40.0	3	7. Iowa
Delaware	24.0	22	8. California
District of Columbia	—	—	Nevada
Florida	33.9	11	10. Washington
Georgia	12.0	44	11. Florida
Hawaii	—	—	12. Maine
Idaho	18.0	30	13. Illinois
Illinois	30.0	13	North Dakota
Indiana	15.5	40	Wisconsin
Iowa	36.0	7	16. Alaska
Kansas	24.0	22	17. Oregon
Kentucky	3.0	47	18. Nebraska
Louisiana	20.0	28	19. Massachusetts
Maine	33.0	12	20. Michigan
Maryland	16.0	39	New Hampshire
Massachusetts	26.0	19	22. Delaware
Michigan	25.0	20	Kansas
Minnesota	43.0	1	24. Oklahoma
Mississippi	18.0	30	South Dakota
Missouri	13.0	42	Utah
Montana	18.0	30	27. Arkansas
Nebraska	27.0	18	28. Colorado
Nevada	35.0	8	Louisiana
New Hampshire	25.0	20	30. Arizona
New Jersey	40.0	3	Idaho
New Mexico	15.0	41	Mississippi
New York	39.0	5	Montana
North Carolina	2.0	49	Ohio
North Dakota	30.0	13	Pennsylvania
Ohio	18.0	30	36. Vermont
Oklahoma	23.0	24	West Virginia
Oregon	28.0	17	38. Alabama
Pennsylvania	18.0	30	39. Maryland
Rhode Island	37.0	6	40. Indiana
South Carolina	7.0	46	41. New Mexico
South Dakota	23.0	24	42. Missouri
Tennessee	13.0	42	Tennessee
Texas	41.0	2	44. Georgia
Utah	23.0	24	Wyoming
Vermont	17.0	36	46. South Carolina
Virginia	2.5	48	47. Kentucky
Washington	34.0	10	48. Virginia
West Virginia	17.0	36	49. North Carolina
Wisconsin	30.0	13	— Hawaii
Wyoming	12.0	44	— District of Columbia
United States	**22.9**	**27**	

— not applicable.

Source: U.S. Department of Commerce, Bureau of the Census, *State Government Tax Collections: 1991* (Washington, D.C.: Government Printing Office, 1992).

Note: Hawaii's excise tax on cigarettes is 40% of the wholesale price.

EXCISE TAX ON GASOLINE, FISCAL 1991			Rank in order
State	**Tax per gallon (cents)**	**Rank**	**By tax rate**
Alabama	11.0	42	1. Nebraska
Alaska	8.0	47	2. Washington
Arizona	18.0	22	3. North Carolina
Arkansas	18.5	20	4. Wisconsin
California	15.0	35	5. Colorado
Colorado	22.0	5	Connecticut
Connecticut	22.0	5	Idaho
Delaware	19.0	17	8. Massachusetts
District of Columbia	—	—	Rhode Island
Florida	4.0	50	10. Iowa
Georgia	7.5	49	Louisiana
Hawaii	11.0	42	Minnesota
Idaho	22.0	5	Montana
Illinois	19.0	17	Ohio
Indiana	15.0	35	Oregon
Iowa	20.0	10	Tennessee
Kansas	16.0	31	17. Delaware
Kentucky	15.0	35	Illinois
Louisiana	20.0	10	Utah
Maine	17.0	26	20. Arkansas
Maryland	18.5	20	Maryland
Massachusetts	21.0	8	22. Arizona
Michigan	15.0	35	Mississippi
Minnesota	20.0	10	South Dakota
Mississippi	18.0	22	25. Virginia
Missouri	11.0	42	26. Maine
Montana	20.0	10	North Dakota
Nebraska	23.9	1	Oklahoma
Nevada	16.3	29	29. Nevada
New Hampshire	16.0	31	30. New Mexico
New Jersey	10.5	45	31. Kansas
New Mexico	16.2	30	New Hampshire
New York	8.0	47	South Carolina
North Carolina	22.3	3	34. West Virginia
North Dakota	17.0	26	35. California
Ohio	20.0	10	Indiana
Oklahoma	17.0	26	Kentucky
Oregon	20.0	10	Michigan
Pennsylvania	12.0	41	Texas
Rhode Island	21.0	8	Vermont
South Carolina	16.0	31	41. Pennsylvania
South Dakota	18.0	22	42. Alabama
Tennessee	20.0	10	Hawaii
Texas	15.0	35	Missouri
Utah	19.0	17	45. New Jersey
Vermont	15.0	35	46. Wyoming
Virginia	17.5	25	47. Alaska
Washington	23.0	2	New York
West Virginia	15.5	34	49. Georgia
Wisconsin	22.2	4	50. Florida
Wyoming	9.0	46	— District of Columbia
United States	**16.7**	**29**	

— not applicable.

Source: U.S. Department of Commerce, Bureau of the Census, *State Government Tax Collections: 1991* (Washington, D.C.: Government Printing Office, 1992).

State	Total revenues	Net lottery revenues	% of total state revenue	Rank by %
Alabama	$9,767,445,000	—	—	—
Alaska	6,355,069,000	—	—	—
Arizona	9,016,008,000	$106,586,000	1.2	16
Arkansas	4,809,850,000	—	—	—
California	90,783,734,000	947,872,000	1.0	20
Colorado	7,863,081,000	78,321,000	1.0	21
Connecticut	9,816,213,000	222,547,000	2.3	8
Delaware	2,442,824,000	27,876,000	1.1	17
District of Columbia	—	—	—	—
Florida	25,754,050,000	982,390,000	3.8	1
Georgia	13,866,289,000	—	—	—
Hawaii	4,915,536,000	—	—	—
Idaho	2,583,740,000	25,648,000	1.0	22
Illinois	25,092,123,000	636,436,000	2.5	4
Indiana	12,288,307,000	179,689,000	1.5	14
Iowa	7,136,778,000	56,281,000	0.8	27
Kansas	5,249,018,000	33,749,000	0.6	31
Kentucky	9,951,015,000	74,689,000	0.8	28
Louisiana	10,764,100,000	—	—	—
Maine	3,222,152,000	44,657,000	1.4	15
Maryland	12,478,513,000	363,722,000	2.9	2
Massachusetts	18,727,292,000	528,012,000	2.8	3
Michigan	24,504,726,000	474,906,000	1.9	12
Minnesota	13,701,385,000	123,759,000	0.9	23
Mississippi	5,794,489,000	—	—	—
Missouri	10,001,999,000	88,347,000	0.9	24
Montana	2,358,921,000	10,925,000	0.5	32
Nebraska	3,435,806,000	—	—	—
Nevada	3,552,707,000	—	—	—
New Hampshire	2,088,359,000	43,552,000	2.1	11
New Jersey	24,743,271,000	567,646,000	2.3	7
New Mexico	4,912,601,000	—	—	—
New York	65,715,331,000	999,602,000	1.5	13
North Carolina	15,266,228,000	—	—	—
North Dakota	1,997,559,000	—	—	—
Ohio	31,271,463,000	726,349,000	2.3	6
Oklahoma	7,819,349,000	—	—	—
Oregon	8,201,014,000	59,449,000	0.7	29
Pennsylvania	27,085,979,000	644,027,000	2.4	5
Rhode Island	3,305,336,000	27,593,000	0.8	25
South Carolina	9,412,827,000	—	—	—
South Dakota	1,597,245,000	33,384,000	2.1	10
Tennessee	9,544,386,000	—	—	—
Texas	33,772,746,000	—	—	—
Utah	4,343,966,000	—	—	—
Vermont	1,703,027,000	18,767,000	1.1	18
Virginia	14,522,813,000	328,069,000	2.3	9
Washington	16,394,269,000	134,521,000	0.8	26
West Virginia	4,895,902,000	35,243,000	0.7	30
Wisconsin	14,137,205,000	149,177,000	1.1	19
Wyoming	1,979,132,000	—	—	—
United States	**$661,393,178,000**	**$8,773,791,000**	**1.3**	**16**

- not applicable.

Source: U.S. Department of Commerce, Bureau of the Census, *State Government Finances: 1991* (Washington, D.C.: Government Printing Office, 1992).

Table header: STATE REVENUE FROM LOTTERIES, FISCAL 1991

Rank in order

By %
1. Florida
2. Maryland
3. Massachusetts
4. Illinois
5. Pennsylvania
6. Ohio
7. New Jersey
8. Connecticut
9. Virginia
10. South Dakota
11. New Hampshire
12. Michigan
13. New York
14. Indiana
15. Maine
16. Arizona
17. Delaware
18. Vermont
19. Wisconsin
20. California
21. Colorado
22. Idaho
23. Minnesota
24. Missouri
25. Rhode Island
26. Washington
27. Iowa
28. Kentucky
29. Oregon
30. West Virginia
31. Kansas
32. Montana
— Alabama
— Alaska
— Arkansas
— District of Columbia
— Georgia
— Hawaii
— Louisiana
— Mississippi
— Nebraska
— Nevada
— New Mexico
— North Carolina
— North Dakota
— Oklahoma
— South Carolina
— Tennessee
— Texas
— Utah
— Wyoming

Transportation

	MOTOR VEHICLE REGISTRATIONS, 1991			Rank in order
		Per 1,000 population		By rate per 1,000
State	Registrations	Rate	Rank	population
Alabama	3,698,602	904.53	8	1. Wyoming
Alaska	470,903	826.15	16	2. Idaho
Arizona	2,848,537	759.61	29	3. South Dakota
Arkansas	1,479,637	623.79	48	4. North Dakota
California	22,252,741	732.48	35	5. Iowa
Colorado	3,045,247	901.76	9	6. Montana
Connecticut	2,588,777	786.62	24	7. Tennessee
Delaware	533,567	784.66	25	8. Alabama
District of Columbia	246,390	412.02	51	9. Colorado
Florida	9,980,076	751.68	31	10. Nebraska
Georgia	5,714,189	862.78	12	11. Washington
Hawaii	785,004	691.63	44	12. Georgia
Idaho	1,055,369	1,015.70	2	13. Oregon
Illinois	8,192,744	709.76	40	14. New Mexico
Indiana	4,413,624	786.74	23	15. Oklahoma
Iowa	2,668,436	954.72	5	16. Alaska
Kansas	1,879,442	753.28	30	17. New Hampshire
Kentucky	2,962,763	797.94	19	18. Virginia
Louisiana	3,045,788	716.32	38	19. Kentucky
Maine	978,849	792.59	21	20. Ohio
Maryland	3,630,236	746.96	32	21. Maine
Massachusetts	3,663,843	611.05	49	22. Vermont
Michigan	7,244,938	773.37	27	23. Indiana
Minnesota	3,273,153	738.53	34	24. Connecticut
Mississippi	1,887,441	728.18	37	25. Delaware
Missouri	3,950,125	765.83	28	26. North Carolina
Montana	765,754	947.72	6	27. Michigan
Nebraska	1,404,444	881.64	10	28. Missouri
Nevada	881,274	686.35	45	29. Arizona
New Hampshire	906,464	820.33	17	30. Kansas
New Jersey	5,518,957	711.21	39	31. Florida
New Mexico	1,320,488	853.03	14	32. Maryland
New York	9,771,437	541.11	50	33. Wisconsin
North Carolina	5,216,177	774.26	26	34. Minnesota
North Dakota	628,672	990.04	4	35. California
Ohio	8,684,599	793.91	20	36. Texas
Oklahoma	2,669,312	840.73	15	37. Mississippi
Oregon	2,506,950	857.96	13	38. Louisiana
Pennsylvania	8,037,808	672.00	46	39. New Jersey
Rhode Island	628,407	625.90	47	40. Illinois
South Carolina	2,471,245	694.17	43	41. West Virginia
South Dakota	701,987	998.56	3	42. Utah
Tennessee	4,541,676	916.96	7	43. South Carolina
Texas	12,696,540	731.83	36	44. Hawaii
Utah	1,229,730	694.76	42	45. Nevada
Vermont	446,819	788.04	22	46. Pennsylvania
Virginia	5,022,222	798.95	18	47. Rhode Island
Washington	4,403,604	877.56	11	48. Arkansas
West Virginia	1,273,444	707.08	41	49. Massachusetts
Wisconsin	3,684,938	743.68	33	50. New York
Wyoming	468,566	1,018.60	1	51. District of Columbia
United States	188,371,935	746.98	32	

Source: Federal Highway Administration, *Selected Highway Statistics and Charts, 1991* (Washington, D.C.: Department of Transportation, 1992).

| AUTOMOBILE REGISTRATIONS, 1991 | | Per 1,000 population | | Rank in order |
State	Registrations	Rate	Rank	By rate per 1,000 population
Alabama	2,711,952	663.23	4	1. Connecticut
Alaska	296,840	520.77	40	2. Tennessee
Arizona	2,023,279	539.54	32	3. Iowa
Arkansas	957,617	403.72	50	4. Alabama
California	17,231,516	567.20	27	5. Colorado
Colorado	2,219,708	657.30	5	6. New Jersey
Connecticut	2,443,651	742.53	1	7. Ohio
Delaware	410,611	603.84	15	8. Oregon
District of Columbia	228,602	382.28	51	9. New Hampshire
Florida	7,910,254	595.79	20	10. Maryland
Georgia	3,991,270	602.64	16	11. Idaho
Hawaii	680,083	599.19	18	12. Washington
Idaho	641,482	617.40	11	13. Maine
Illinois	6,628,157	574.21	26	14. Virginia
Indiana	3,233,272	576.34	25	15. Delaware
Iowa	1,906,608	682.15	3	16. Georgia
Kansas	1,242,751	498.10	44	17. Michigan
Kentucky	1,941,932	523.01	39	18. Hawaii
Louisiana	2,001,937	470.82	45	19. South Dakota
Maine	755,300	611.58	13	20. Florida
Maryland	3,008,571	619.05	10	21. North Dakota
Massachusetts	3,159,888	527.00	37	22. Nebraska
Michigan	5,643,831	602.46	17	23. Minnesota
Minnesota	2,563,511	578.41	23	24. Vermont
Mississippi	1,443,017	556.72	28	25. Indiana
Missouri	2,787,925	540.51	31	26. Illinois
Montana	449,831	556.72	28	27. California
Nebraska	928,817	583.06	22	28. Mississippi
Nevada	602,085	468.91	47	Montana
New Hampshire	709,408	642.00	9	30. North Carolina
New Jersey	5,058,227	651.83	6	31. Missouri
New Mexico	824,490	532.62	35	32. Arizona
New York	8,494,221	470.39	46	33. Oklahoma
North Carolina	3,712,709	551.09	30	34. Pennsylvania
North Dakota	373,544	588.26	21	35. New Mexico
Ohio	7,056,813	645.11	7	36. Wyoming
Oklahoma	1,708,496	538.11	33	37. Massachusetts
Oregon	1,883,875	644.72	8	38. South Carolina
Pennsylvania	6,430,499	537.62	34	39. Kentucky
Rhode Island	520,389	518.32	41	40. Alaska
South Carolina	1,869,500	525.14	38	41. Rhode Island
South Dakota	420,172	597.68	19	42. Texas
Tennessee	3,642,146	735.34	2	43. Wisconsin
Texas	8,666,111	499.52	42	44. Kansas
Utah	799,478	451.68	48	45. Louisiana
Vermont	327,593	577.77	24	46. New York
Virginia	3,825,498	608.57	14	47. Nevada
Washington	3,090,975	615.98	12	48. Utah
West Virginia	778,632	432.33	49	49. West Virginia
Wisconsin	2,474,621	499.42	43	50. Arkansas
Wyoming	243,928	530.28	36	51. District of Columbia
United States	**142,955,623**	**566.89**	**28**	

Source: Federal Highway Administration, *Selected Highway Statistics and Charts, 1991* (Washington, D.C.: Department of Transportation, 1992).

| State | Registrations | Per 1,000 population | |
		Rate	Rank
Alabama	986,650	241.29	20
Alaska	174,063	305.37	7
Arizona	825,258	220.07	25
Arkansas	522,020	220.08	24
California	5,021,225	165.28	38
Colorado	825,539	244.46	17
Connecticut	145,126	44.10	50
Delaware	122,956	180.82	33
District of Columbia	17,788	29.75	51
Florida	2,069,822	155.90	40
Georgia	1,722,919	260.14	14
Hawaii	104,921	92.44	46
Idaho	413,887	398.35	4
Illinois	1,564,587	135.54	42
Indiana	1,180,352	210.40	28
Iowa	761,828	272.57	12
Kansas	636,691	255.19	15
Kentucky	1,020,831	274.93	10
Louisiana	1,043,851	245.50	16
Maine	223,549	181.01	32
Maryland	621,665	127.92	44
Massachusetts	503,955	84.05	47
Michigan	1,601,107	170.91	36
Minnesota	709,642	160.12	39
Mississippi	444,424	171.46	35
Missouri	1,162,200	225.32	22
Montana	315,923	390.99	5
Nebraska	475,627	298.57	9
Nevada	279,189	217.44	26
New Hampshire	197,056	178.33	34
New Jersey	460,730	59.37	49
New Mexico	495,998	320.41	6
New York	1,277,216	70.73	48
North Carolina	1,503,468	223.17	23
North Dakota	255,128	401.78	2
Ohio	1,627,786	148.81	41
Oklahoma	960,816	302.62	8
Oregon	623,075	213.24	27
Pennsylvania	1,607,309	134.38	43
Rhode Island	108,018	107.59	45
South Carolina	601,745	169.03	37
South Dakota	281,815	400.88	3
Tennessee	899,530	181.61	31
Texas	4,030,429	232.32	21
Utah	430,252	243.08	19
Vermont	119,226	210.28	29
Virginia	1,196,724	190.38	30
Washington	1,312,629	261.58	13
West Virginia	494,812	274.74	11
Wisconsin	1,210,317	244.26	18
Wyoming	224,638	488.34	1
United States	**45,416,312**	**180.10**	**34**

Rank in order

By rate per 1,000 population

1. Wyoming
2. North Dakota
3. South Dakota
4. Idaho
5. Montana
6. New Mexico
7. Alaska
8. Oklahoma
9. Nebraska
10. Kentucky
11. West Virginia
12. Iowa
13. Washington
14. Georgia
15. Kansas
16. Louisiana
17. Colorado
18. Wisconsin
19. Utah
20. Alabama
21. Texas
22. Missouri
23. North Carolina
24. Arkansas
25. Arizona
26. Nevada
27. Oregon
28. Indiana
29. Vermont
30. Virginia
31. Tennessee
32. Maine
33. Delaware
34. New Hampshire
35. Mississippi
36. Michigan
37. South Carolina
38. California
39. Minnesota
40. Florida
41. Ohio
42. Illinois
43. Pennsylvania
44. Maryland
45. Rhode Island
46. Hawaii
47. Massachusetts
48. New York
49. New Jersey
50. Connecticut
51. District of Columbia

Source: Federal Highway Administration, *Selected Highway Statistics and Charts, 1991* (Washington, D.C.: Department of Transportation, 1992).

MOTORCYCLE REGISTRATIONS. 1991		Per 1,000 population		Rank in order

State	Registrations	Rate	Rank	By rate per 1,000 population
Alabama	40,645	9.94	42	1. Iowa
Alaska	11,016	19.33	21	2. Wisconsin
Arizona	80,517	21.47	17	3. Wyoming
Arkansas	14,000	5.90	50	4. South Dakota
California	651,370	21.44	18	5. New Hampshire
Colorado	88,868	26.32	10	6. Vermont
Connecticut	50,882	15.46	27	7. Idaho
Delaware	9,232	13.58	33	8. North Dakota
District of Columbia	2,057	3.44	51	9. Maine
Florida	196,031	14.77	30	10. Colorado
Georgia	77,524	11.71	36	11. Montana
Hawaii	20,857	18.38	23	12. Minnesota
Idaho	33,198	31.95	7	13. Kansas
Illinois	184,380	15.97	26	14. Washington
Indiana	96,812	17.26	25	15. Rhode Island
Iowa	165,451	59.20	1	16. Ohio
Kansas	59,224	23.74	13	17. Arizona
Kentucky	34,000	9.16	45	18. California
Louisiana	32,332	7.60	49	19. Oregon
Maine	37,141	30.07	9	20. New Mexico
Maryland	54,906	11.30	37	21. Alaska
Massachusetts	53,649	8.95	46	22. Oklahoma
Michigan	166,125	17.73	24	23. Hawaii
Minnesota	112,367	25.35	12	24. Michigan
Mississippi	26,198	10.11	41	25. Indiana
Missouri	60,783	11.78	35	26. Illinois
Montana	21,185	26.22	11	27. Connecticut
Nebraska	20,667	12.97	34	28. Nevada
Nevada	19,833	15.45	28	29. Tennessee
New Hampshire	36,692	33.21	5	30. Florida
New Jersey	86,096	11.10	38	31. Pennsylvania
New Mexico	32,083	20.73	20	32. Utah
New York	197,851	10.96	39	33. Delaware
North Carolina	58,406	8.67	47	34. Nebraska
North Dakota	19,181	30.21	8	35. Missouri
Ohio	235,975	21.57	16	36. Georgia
Oklahoma	58,990	18.58	22	37. Maryland
Oregon	62,369	21.35	19	38. New Jersey
Pennsylvania	167,326	13.99	31	39. New York
Rhode Island	23,125	23.03	15	40. Texas
South Carolina	29,406	8.26	48	41. Mississippi
South Dakota	24,152	34.36	4	42. Alabama
Tennessee	74,290	15.00	29	43. West Virginia
Texas	185,167	10.67	40	44. Virginia
Utah	24,473	13.83	32	45. Kentucky
Vermont	18,433	32.51	6	46. Massachusetts
Virginia	61,327	9.76	44	47. North Carolina
Washington	115,613	23.04	14	48. South Carolina
West Virginia	17,642	9.80	43	49. Louisiana
Wisconsin	210,378	42.46	2	50. Arkansas
Wyoming	16,812	36.55	3	51. District of Columbia
United States	4,177,037	16.56	26	

Source: Federal Highway Administration, *Selected Highway Statistics and Charts, 1991* (Washington, D.C.: Department of Transportation, 1992).

State	Driver licenses	Per 1,000 population Rate	Per 1,000 population Rank	% increase 1990-1991 Rate	% increase 1990-1991 Rank
Alabama	2,937,981	718.51	14	6.7	3
Alaska	318,000	557.90	51	1.2	21
Arizona	2,400,002	640.00	42	2.4	10
Arkansas	1,720,270	725.24	10	−0.1	41
California	19,930,785	656.05	39	0.4	34
Colorado	2,083,864	617.08	44	2.0	14
Connecticut	2,212,725	672.36	33	−0.1	41
Delaware	495,281	728.35	8	2.2	11
District of Columbia	406,270	679.38	29	−1.5	47
Florida	9,692,974	730.06	6	5.0	5
Georgia	4,610,271	696.10	22	2.9	9
Hawaii	699,664	616.44	45	3.3	8
Idaho	711,662	684.95	27	1.1	24
Illinois	7,359,537	637.58	43	0.9	25
Indiana	3,453,186	615.54	46	−4.1	50
Iowa	1,856,650	664.28	37	−0.8	46
Kansas	1,780,520	713.64	17	3.9	6
Kentucky	2,413,670	650.06	41	0.5	32
Louisiana	2,594,762	610.25	47	0.7	27
Maine	888,963	719.81	12	0.2	35
Maryland	3,213,900	661.30	38	−4.4	51
Massachusetts	4,205,850	701.44	20	−0.6	45
Michigan	6,433,993	686.81	24	−0.1	41
Minnesota	2,545,936	574.44	49	0.7	27
Mississippi	1,924,696	742.55	3	2.1	13
Missouri	3,732,342	723.60	11	1.2	21
Montana	580,313	718.21	15	−3.9	49
Nebraska	1,068,695	670.87	34	−1.8	48
Nevada	908,684	707.70	19	7.4	1
New Hampshire	847,564	767.03	2	0.5	32
New Jersey	5,659,994	729.38	7	1.3	20
New Mexico	1,081,437	698.60	21	0.7	27
New York	10,266,741	568.54	50	0.1	38
North Carolina	4,547,443	675.00	30	−0.1	41
North Dakota	425,935	670.76	35	0.2	35
Ohio	7,470,352	682.91	28	0.6	31
Oklahoma	2,283,068	719.08	13	0.2	35
Oregon	2,373,660	812.34	1	7.3	2
Pennsylvania	7,950,559	664.71	36	0.7	27
Rhode Island	676,228	673.53	32	0.8	26
South Carolina	2,401,642	674.62	31	1.2	21
South Dakota	500,564	712.04	18	1.7	18
Tennessee	3,393,127	685.07	25	1.8	17
Texas	11,293,184	650.94	40	1.4	19
Utah	1,067,030	602.84	48	2.0	14
Vermont	412,369	727.28	9	0.1	38
Virginia	4,651,070	739.91	5	6.0	4
Washington	3,490,585	695.61	23	3.4	7
West Virginia	1,285,627	713.84	16	0.1	38
Wisconsin	3,394,428	685.05	26	2.0	14
Wyoming	341,023	741.35	4	2.2	11
United States	168,995,076	670.15	36	1.2	21

DRIVER LICENSES, 1991

Rank in order

By rate per 1,000 population

1. Oregon
2. New Hampshire
3. Mississippi
4. Wyoming
5. Virginia
6. Florida
7. New Jersey
8. Delaware
9. Vermont
10. Arkansas
11. Missouri
12. Maine
13. Oklahoma
14. Alabama
15. Montana
16. West Virginia
17. Kansas
18. South Dakota
19. Nevada
20. Massachusetts
21. New Mexico
22. Georgia
23. Washington
24. Michigan
25. Tennessee
26. Wisconsin
27. Idaho
28. Ohio
29. District of Columbia
30. North Carolina
31. South Carolina
32. Rhode Island
33. Connecticut
34. Nebraska
35. North Dakota
36. Pennsylvania
37. Iowa
38. Maryland
39. California
40. Texas
41. Kentucky
42. Arizona
43. Illinois
44. Colorado
45. Hawaii
46. Indiana
47. Louisiana
48. Utah
49. Minnesota
50. New York
51. Alaska

Source: Federal Highway Administration, *Selected Highway Statistics and Charts, 1991* (Washington, D.C.: Department of Transportation, 1992).

FEDERAL SPENDING ON HIGHWAY TRUST FUND, FISCAL 1991				Rank in order

State	Expenditures	Per capita	Rank by per capita	By per capita
Alabama	$237,986,000	$58.20	27	1. Alaska
Alaska	165,342,000	290.07	1	2. Wyoming
Arizona	219,435,000	58.52	26	3. Montana
Arkansas	160,704,000	67.75	22	4. Hawaii
California	1,384,449,000	45.57	46	5. District of Columbia
Colorado	275,042,000	81.45	15	6. Connecticut
Connecticut	464,769,000	141.22	6	7. North Dakota
Delaware	68,830,000	101.22	11	8. Rhode Island
District of Columbia	86,240,000	144.21	5	9. South Dakota
Florida	418,103,000	31.49	51	10. Idaho
Georgia	318,104,000	48.03	44	11. Delaware
Hawaii	164,976,000	145.35	4	12. Nevada
Idaho	115,026,000	110.71	10	13. Vermont
Illinois	454,977,000	39.42	48	14. New Mexico
Indiana	320,171,000	57.07	30	15. Colorado
Iowa	193,639,000	69.28	21	16. Washington
Kansas	153,554,000	61.54	24	17. Louisiana
Kentucky	172,050,000	46.34	45	18. West Virginia
Louisiana	302,308,000	71.10	17	19. Nebraska
Maine	68,393,000	55.38	33	20. Maryland
Maryland	340,124,000	69.98	20	21. Iowa
Massachusetts	337,034,000	56.21	32	22. Arkansas
Michigan	358,076,000	38.22	49	23. Oklahoma
Minnesota	235,498,000	53.14	36	24. Kansas
Mississippi	149,505,000	57.68	28	25. Missouri
Missouri	307,738,000	59.66	25	26. Arizona
Montana	137,609,000	170.31	3	27. Alabama
Nebraska	111,700,000	70.12	19	28. Mississippi
Nevada	108,733,000	84.68	12	29. Oregon
New Hampshire	62,183,000	56.27	31	30. Indiana
New Jersey	395,502,000	50.97	39	31. New Hampshire
New Mexico	127,975,000	82.67	14	32. Massachusetts
New York	682,204,000	37.78	50	33. Maine
North Carolina	345,692,000	51.31	37	34. Texas
North Dakota	86,151,000	135.67	7	35. Tennessee
Ohio	559,501,000	51.15	38	36. Minnesota
Oklahoma	211,909,000	66.74	23	37. North Carolina
Oregon	167,393,000	57.29	29	38. Ohio
Pennsylvania	592,054,000	49.50	42	39. New Jersey
Rhode Island	132,138,000	131.61	8	40. South Carolina
South Carolina	180,544,000	50.71	40	41. Virginia
South Dakota	90,656,000	128.96	9	42. Pennsylvania
Tennessee	263,671,000	53.23	35	43. Wisconsin
Texas	952,068,000	54.88	34	44. Georgia
Utah	80,509,000	45.49	47	45. Kentucky
Vermont	47,877,000	84.44	13	46. California
Virginia	313,984,000	49.95	41	47. Utah
Washington	389,206,000	77.56	16	48. Illinois
West Virginia	127,412,000	70.75	18	49. Michigan
Wisconsin	238,246,000	48.08	43	50. New York
Wyoming	117,932,000	256.37	2	51. Florida
United States	$14,081,440,000	$55.84	33	

Source: U.S. Department of Commerce, Bureau of the Census, *Federal Expenditures by State for Fiscal Year 1991* (Washington, D.C.: Government Printing Office, 1992).

FEDERAL SPENDING ON MASS TRANSPORTATION. FISCAL 1991				Rank in order
State	Expenditures	Per capita	Rank by per capita	By per capita
Alabama	$14,567,000	$3.56	34	1. District of Columbia
Alaska	1,754,000	3.08	39	2. New York
Arizona	19,134,000	5.10	24	3. Illinois
Arkansas	8,768,000	3.70	32	4. Connecticut
California	412,844,000	13.59	12	5. New Jersey
Colorado	37,902,000	11.22	15	6. Maryland
Connecticut	94,398,000	28.68	4	7. Missouri
Delaware	2,470,000	3.63	33	8. Massachusetts
District of Columbia	298,556,000	499.26	1	9. Pennsylvania
Florida	101,229,000	7.62	21	10. Georgia
Georgia	109,015,000	16.46	10	11. Rhode Island
Hawaii	10,926,000	9.63	17	12. California
Idaho	1,499,000	1.44	49	13. Washington
Illinois	433,928,000	37.59	3	14. Oregon
Indiana	50,923,000	9.08	19	15. Colorado
Iowa	8,037,000	2.88	41	16. Ohio
Kansas	5,981,000	2.40	45	17. Hawaii
Kentucky	15,090,000	4.06	29	18. Louisiana
Louisiana	38,959,000	9.16	18	19. Indiana
Maine	3,475,000	2.81	43	20. Wisconsin
Maryland	106,803,000	21.98	6	21. Florida
Massachusetts	106,354,000	17.74	8	22. Michigan
Michigan	52,202,000	5.57	22	23. Minnesota
Minnesota	23,893,000	5.39	23	24. Arizona
Mississippi	5,787,000	2.23	48	25. North Carolina
Missouri	92,153,000	17.87	7	26. Utah
Montana	2,383,000	2.95	40	27. Wyoming
Nebraska	6,605,000	4.15	28	28. Nebraska
Nevada	1,171,000	0.91	50	29. Kentucky
New Hampshire	3,160,000	2.86	42	30. Tennessee
New Jersey	193,956,000	24.99	5	31. Virginia
New Mexico	3,705,000	2.39	46	32. Arkansas
New York	814,709,000	45.12	2	33. Delaware
North Carolina	30,574,000	4.54	25	34. Alabama
North Dakota	1,980,000	3.12	38	35. South Carolina
Ohio	115,508,000	10.56	16	36. Oklahoma
Oklahoma	10,869,000	3.42	36	37. South Dakota
Oregon	34,167,000	11.69	14	38. North Dakota
Pennsylvania	199,639,000	16.69	9	39. Alaska
Rhode Island	15,062,000	15.00	11	40. Montana
South Carolina	12,373,000	3.48	35	41. Iowa
South Dakota	2,307,000	3.28	37	42. New Hampshire
Tennessee	19,840,000	4.01	30	43. Maine
Texas	15,047,000	0.87	51	44. West Virginia
Utah	7,753,000	4.38	26	45. Kansas
Vermont	1,355,000	2.39	47	46. New Mexico
Virginia	24,214,000	3.85	31	47. Vermont
Washington	62,051,000	12.37	13	48. Mississippi
West Virginia	4,448,000	2.47	44	49. Idaho
Wisconsin	39,275,000	7.93	20	50. Nevada
Wyoming	1,974,000	4.29	27	51. Texas
United States	$3,825,769,000	$15.17	11	

Source: U.S. Department of Commerce, Bureau of the Census, *Federal Expenditures by State for Fiscal Year 1991* (Washington, D.C.: Government Printing Office, 1992).

State	Expenditures	Per capita	Rank by per capita	Per 1,000 personal income	
				Amount	Rank
Alabama	$679,371,000	$166.15	40	$11.18	31
Alaska	501,887,000	880.50	1	41.98	2
Arizona	1,094,076,000	291.75	9	18.56	8
Arkansas	459,403,000	193.68	30	13.76	20
California	3,888,891,000	128.01	48	6.26	49
Colorado	670,712,000	198.61	27	10.75	33
Connecticut	1,019,058,000	309.65	5	12.15	28
Delaware	257,350,000	378.46	2	19.21	6
District of Columbia	—	—	—	—	—
Florida	1,778,850,000	133.98	47	7.36	46
Georgia	1,019,880,000	153.99	42	9.20	42
Hawaii	276,620,000	243.72	18	12.21	27
Idaho	278,597,000	268.14	14	18.06	10
Illinois	2,375,834,000	205.82	26	10.17	38
Indiana	1,044,286,000	186.15	35	11.13	32
Iowa	866,714,000	310.09	4	18.11	9
Kansas	633,246,000	253.81	15	14.06	18
Kentucky	826,158,000	222.50	22	14.93	17
Louisiana	842,546,000	198.15	28	13.76	20
Maine	286,969,000	232.36	20	13.57	23
Maryland	1,187,070,000	244.25	17	11.35	30
Massachusetts	699,095,000	116.59	49	5.15	50
Michigan	1,436,775,000	153.37	43	8.40	44
Minnesota	1,011,745,000	228.28	21	12.30	26
Mississippi	496,226,000	191.45	32	15.03	16
Missouri	902,654,000	175.00	37	10.08	39
Montana	272,279,000	336.98	3	22.31	3
Nebraska	434,941,000	271.50	11	15.68	15
Nevada	242,575,000	188.92	33	10.41	36
New Hampshire	175,348,000	158.69	41	7.58	45
New Jersey	1,372,131,000	176.82	36	7.11	47
New Mexico	364,475,000	235.45	19	16.81	12
New York	2,569,144,000	142.27	46	6.46	48
North Carolina	1,389,936,000	206.31	25	12.82	24
North Dakota	196,408,000	309.30	6	20.28	5
Ohio	2,046,757,000	187.11	34	10.73	34
Oklahoma	778,673,000	245.25	16	16.02	13
Oregon	783,904,000	268.28	13	15.93	14
Pennsylvania	2,362,726,000	197.54	29	10.63	35
Rhode Island	194,402,000	193.63	31	10.29	37
South Carolina	510,991,000	143.54	45	9.64	40
South Dakota	209,354,000	297.80	8	19.04	7
Tennessee	1,060,615,000	214.14	24	13.68	22
Texas	2,612,497,000	150.58	44	9.16	43
Utah	300,314,000	169.67	38	12.41	25
Vermont	169,872,000	299.60	7	17.18	11
Virginia	1,696,901,000	269.95	12	13.88	19
Washington	1,104,748,000	220.16	23	11.99	29
West Virginia	500,904,000	278.13	10	20.34	4
Wisconsin	829,118,000	8.50	50	9.62	41
Wyoming	324,757,000	167.33	39	44.02	1
United States	$47,037,783,000	$186.97	35	$10.12	39

STATE SPENDING ON HIGHWAYS, FISCAL 1991

Rank in order

By per capita

1. Alaska
2. Delaware
3. Montana
4. Iowa
5. Connecticut
6. North Dakota
7. Vermont
8. South Dakota
9. Arizona
10. West Virginia
11. Nebraska
12. Virginia
13. Oregon
14. Idaho
15. Kansas
16. Oklahoma
17. Maryland
18. Hawaii
19. New Mexico
20. Maine
21. Minnesota
22. Kentucky
23. Washington
24. Tennessee
25. North Carolina
26. Illinois
27. Colorado
28. Louisiana
29. Pennsylvania
30. Arkansas
31. Rhode Island
32. Mississippi
33. Nevada
34. Ohio
35. Indiana
36. New Jersey
37. Missouri
38. Utah
39. Wyoming
40. Alabama
41. New Hampshire
42. Georgia
43. Michigan
44. Texas
45. South Carolina
46. New York
47. Florida
48. California
49. Massachusetts
50. Wisconsin
— District of Columbia

— not applicable.

Source: U.S. Department of Commerce, Bureau of the Census, *State Government Finances: 1991* (Washington, D.C.: Government Printing Office, 1992).

HIGHWAY DEFICIENCY. 1989			Rank in order
State	**% of interstate highways rated in poor condition**	**Rank by %**	**By %**
Alabama	15.5	11	1. Florida
Alaska	15.6	10	2. Idaho
Arizona	23.5	5	3. Rhode Island
Arkansas	13.1	19	4. New Hampshire
California	10.6	28	5. Arizona
Colorado	7.2	35	6. Mississippi
Connecticut	3.6	42	7. West Virginia
Delaware	12.0	22	8. Montana
District of Columbia	—	—	9. Pennsylvania
Florida	56.6	1	10. Alaska
Georgia	11.0	25	11. Alabama
Hawaii	10.4	29	12. Kansas
Idaho	27.7	2	13. Oregon
Illinois	3.3	44	14. Louisiana
Indiana	13.2	18	15. Maine
Iowa	2.9	45	Nebraska
Kansas	14.8	12	17. Tennessee
Kentucky	11.9	23	18. Indiana
Louisiana	13.9	14	19. Arkansas
Maine	13.6	15	20. Nevada
Maryland	5.4	38	21. South Dakota
Massachusetts	10.1	32	22. Delaware
Michigan	10.8	26	23. Kentucky
Minnesota	2.2	49	24. New Jersey
Mississippi	22.9	6	25. Georgia
Missouri	10.7	27	26. Michigan
Montana	17.3	8	27. Missouri
Nebraska	13.6	15	28. California
Nevada	12.7	20	29. Hawaii
New Hampshire	25.2	4	Virginia
New Jersey	11.4	24	31. Wisconsin
New Mexico	7.7	33	32. Massachusetts
New York	2.5	46	33. New Mexico
North Carolina	5.4	38	34. Ohio
North Dakota	1.8	50	35. Colorado
Ohio	7.5	34	36. Vermont
Oklahoma	6.1	37	37. Oklahoma
Oregon	14.2	13	38. Maryland
Pennsylvania	17.2	9	North Carolina
Rhode Island	26.8	3	40. Wyoming
South Carolina	2.5	46	41. Texas
South Dakota	12.1	21	42. Connecticut
Tennessee	13.5	17	Utah
Texas	5.0	41	44. Illinois
Utah	3.6	42	45. Iowa
Vermont	6.2	36	46. New York
Virginia	10.4	29	South Carolina
Washington	2.3	48	48. Washington
West Virginia	19.1	7	49. Minnesota
Wisconsin	10.2	31	50. North Dakota
Wyoming	5.2	40	— District of Columbia
United States	**NA**	**NA**	

— not applicable.   NA not available.

Source: U.S. Congress, House of Representatives, *The Status of the Nation's Highways and Bridges: Conditions and Performance, 1991.*

BRIDGE DEFICIENCY, 1990			Rank in order
State	% of bridges rated as deficient	Rank by %	By %
Alabama	41.5	19	1. New York
Alaska	25.7	43	2. West Virginia
Arizona	12.7	50	3. Massachusetts
Arkansas	25.3	45	4. Rhode Island
California	30.0	37	5. Missouri
Colorado	38.9	24	6. Vermont
Connecticut	48.6	11	7. New Jersey
Delaware	31.2	34	8. Hawaii
District of Columbia	—	—	9. Mississippi
Florida	26.1	41	10. Louisiana
Georgia	30.7	36	11. Connecticut
Hawaii	49.2	8	12. Kentucky
Idaho	27.1	40	13. Oklahoma
Illinois	31.4	33	14. Pennsylvania
Indiana	36.1	27	15. Nebraska
Iowa	34.3	30	16. North Carolina
Kansas	39.7	21	17. North Dakota
Kentucky	48.0	12	18. New Hampshire
Louisiana	48.7	10	19. Alabama
Maine	39.6	23	20. Michigan
Maryland	38.6	25	21. Kansas
Massachusetts	56.9	3	22. Tennessee
Michigan	40.0	20	23. Maine
Minnesota	25.4	44	24. Colorado
Mississippi	48.7	9	25. Maryland
Missouri	53.5	5	26. South Dakota
Montana	25.9	42	27. Indiana
Nebraska	44.5	15	28. Ohio
Nevada	23.5	46	29. Virginia
New Hampshire	42.5	18	30. Iowa
New Jersey	50.8	7	31. Wisconsin
New Mexico	18.4	49	32. Washington
New York	70.5	1	33. Illinois
North Carolina	43.8	16	34. Delaware
North Dakota	43.2	17	35. Texas
Ohio	35.4	28	36. Georgia
Oklahoma	47.7	13	37. California
Oregon	27.3	38	38. Oregon
Pennsylvania	47.5	14	39. Utah
Rhode Island	53.6	4	40. Idaho
South Carolina	22.5	48	41. Florida
South Dakota	37.8	26	42. Montana
Tennessee	39.6	22	43. Alaska
Texas	30.8	35	44. Minnesota
Utah	27.3	39	45. Arkansas
Vermont	51.3	6	46. Nevada
Virginia	35.0	29	47. Wyoming
Washington	31.5	32	48. South Carolina
West Virginia	58.7	2	49. New Mexico
Wisconsin	32.8	31	50. Arizona
Wyoming	23.0	47	— District of Columbia
United States	NA	NA	

— not applicable.   NA not available.

Source: U.S. Congress, House of Representatives, *Highway Bridge Replacement and Rehabilitation Program, 1991* (Washington, D.C.: Government Printing Office, 1991).

TRAFFIC FATALITIES. 1991				Rank in order
State	**Fatalities**	**Per 1,000 population**		**By rate per 100,000 population**
		Rate	**Rank**	
Alabama	1,112	27.20	2	1. New Mexico
Alaska	101	17.72	24	2. Alabama
Arizona	816	21.76	13	3. Mississippi
Arkansas	608	25.63	5	4. Wyoming
California	4,685	15.42	32	5. Arkansas
Colorado	543	16.08	31	6. Idaho
Connecticut	310	9.42	49	7. South Carolina
Delaware	102	15.00	35	8. Montana
District of Columbia	63	10.54	47	9. Nevada
Florida	2,464	18.56	21	10. West Virginia
Georgia	1,389	20.97	14	11. Tennessee
Hawaii	135	11.89	45	12. Kentucky
Idaho	264	25.41	6	13. Arizona
Illinois	1,448	12.54	43	14. Georgia
Indiana	1,022	18.22	22	15. Oklahoma
Iowa	488	17.46	25	16. South Dakota
Kansas	409	16.39	29	17. North Carolina
Kentucky	826	22.25	12	18. Louisiana
Louisiana	856	20.13	18	19. Missouri
Maine	204	16.52	28	20. Vermont
Maryland	694	14.28	39	21. Florida
Massachusetts	552	9.21	50	22. Indiana
Michigan	1,408	15.03	34	23. Texas
Minnesota	531	11.98	44	24. Alaska
Mississippi	699	26.97	3	25. Iowa
Missouri	1,011	19.60	19	26. Nebraska
Montana	200	24.75	8	27. Oregon
Nebraska	275	17.26	26	28. Maine
Nevada	297	23.13	9	29. Kansas
New Hampshire	143	12.94	42	30. Wisconsin
New Jersey	784	10.10	48	31. Colorado
New Mexico	469	30.30	1	32. California
New York	2,009	11.13	46	33. Utah
North Carolina	1,369	20.32	17	34. Michigan
North Dakota	94	14.80	38	35. Delaware
Ohio	1,635	14.95	37	36. Virginia
Oklahoma	651	20.50	15	37. Ohio
Oregon	484	16.56	27	38. North Dakota
Pennsylvania	1,661	13.89	40	39. Maryland
Rhode Island	88	8.77	51	40. Pennsylvania
South Carolina	890	25.00	7	41. Washington
South Dakota	143	20.34	16	42. New Hampshire
Tennessee	1,113	22.47	11	43. Illinois
Texas	3,078	17.74	23	44. Minnesota
Utah	271	15.31	33	45. Hawaii
Vermont	110	19.40	20	46. New York
Virginia	942	14.99	36	47. District of Columbia
Washington	682	13.59	41	48. New Jersey
West Virginia	415	23.04	10	49. Connecticut
Wisconsin	797	16.09	30	50. Massachusetts
Wyoming	122	26.52	4	51. Rhode Island
United States	**41,462**	**16.44**	**29**	

Source: U.S. Department of Transportation, National Highway Traffic Safety Administration, *1991 Traffic Fatality Facts* (Washington, D.C.: U.S. Department of Transportation, 1992).

TRAFFIC FATALITIES PER MILES TRAVELED, 1991						Rank in order
State	Fatalities	Vehicle miles traveled	Per 100 million vehicle miles			By rate per 100 million vehicle miles
			Rate	Rank		
Alabama	1,112	42,729,000,000	2.60	6		1. Nevada
Alaska	101	4,045,000,000	2.50	9		2. Arkansas
Arizona	816	36,595,000,000	2.23	14		3. Mississippi
Arkansas	608	21,405,000,000	2.84	2		4. New Mexico
California	4,685	260,656,000,000	1.80	33		5. West Virginia
Colorado	543	27,834,000,000	1.95	22		6. Alabama
Connecticut	310	26,323,000,000	1.18	51		7. South Carolina
Delaware	102	6,589,000,000	1.55	44		8. Idaho
District of Columbia	63	3,223,000,000	1.96	21		9. Alaska
Florida	2,464	110,692,000,000	2.23	15		10. Kentucky
Georgia	1,389	72,784,000,000	1.91	26		11. Tennessee
Hawaii	135	7,939,000,000	1.70	40		12. Montana
Idaho	264	10,189,000,000	2.59	8		13. Louisiana
Illinois	1,448	84,100,000,000	1.72	38		14. Arizona
Indiana	1,022	54,470,000,000	1.88	28		15. Florida
Iowa	488	23,163,000,000	2.11	17		16. North Carolina
Kansas	409	23,020,000,000	1.78	34		17. Iowa
Kentucky	826	33,985,000,000	2.43	10		18. South Dakota
Louisiana	856	38,139,000,000	2.24	13		19. Wyoming
Maine	204	11,757,000,000	1.74	37		20. Missouri
Maryland	694	40,908,000,000	1.70	41		21. District of Columbia
Massachusetts	552	45,461,000,000	1.21	50		22. Colorado
Michigan	1,408	82,239,000,000	1.71	39		23. Nebraska
Minnesota	531	38,832,000,000	1.37	47		24. Oklahoma
Mississippi	699	24,895,000,000	2.81	3		25. Pennsylvania
Missouri	1,011	51,586,000,000	1.96	20		26. Georgia
Montana	200	8,473,000,000	2.36	12		27. Vermont
Nebraska	275	14,173,000,000	1.94	23		28. Indiana
Nevada	297	10,334,000,000	2.87	1		29. Texas
New Hampshire	143	9,790,000,000	1.46	46		30. New York
New Jersey	784	59,797,000,000	1.31	48		31. Ohio
New Mexico	469	17,035,000,000	2.75	4		32. Utah
New York	2,009	107,494,000,000	1.87	30		33. California
North Carolina	1,369	63,460,000,000	2.16	16		34. Kansas
North Dakota	94	5,878,000,000	1.60	42		35. Oregon
Ohio	1,635	88,099,000,000	1.86	31		36. Wisconsin
Oklahoma	651	33,616,000,000	1.94	24		37. Maine
Oregon	484	27,305,000,000	1.77	35		38. Illinois
Pennsylvania	1,661	86,230,000,000	1.93	25		39. Michigan
Rhode Island	88	7,002,000,000	1.26	49		40. Hawaii
South Carolina	890	34,332,000,000	2.59	7		41. Maryland
South Dakota	143	6,825,000,000	2.10	18		42. North Dakota
Tennessee	1,113	46,496,000,000	2.39	11		43. Virginia
Texas	3,078	164,405,000,000	1.87	29		44. Delaware
Utah	271	14,882,000,000	1.82	32		45. Washington
Vermont	110	5,773,000,000	1.91	27		46. New Hampshire
Virginia	942	60,829,000,000	1.55	43		47. Minnesota
Washington	682	46,211,000,000	1.48	45		48. New Jersey
West Virginia	415	15,472,000,000	2.68	5		49. Rhode Island
Wisconsin	797	45,150,000,000	1.77	36		50. Massachusetts
Wyoming	122	5,973,000,000	2.04	19		51. Connecticut
United States	41,462	2,168,591,000,000	1.91	26		

Source: U.S. Department of Transportation, National Highway Traffic Safety Administration, *1991 Traffic Fatality Facts* (Washington, D.C.: U.S. Department of Transportation, 1992).

MOTORCYCLIST FATALITIES, 1991

State	Fatalities	% of total traffic fatalities Rate	% of total traffic fatalities Rank	Per 100,000 population Rate	Per 100,000 population Rank
Alabama	38	3.4	49	0.93	36
Alaska	11	10.9	6	1.93	5
Arizona	60	7.4	22	1.60	7
Arkansas	23	3.8	48	0.97	33
California	515	11.0	5	1.70	6
Colorado	45	8.3	15	1.33	16
Connecticut	29	9.4	13	0.88	41
Delaware	7	6.9	26	1.03	29
District of Columbia	6	9.5	12	1.00	32
Florida	177	7.2	24	1.33	16
Georgia	60	4.3	44	0.91	39
Hawaii	18	13.3	3	1.59	9
Idaho	12	4.5	41	1.16	26
Illinois	111	7.7	20	0.96	34
Indiana	82	8.0	18	1.46	12
Iowa	40	8.2	16	1.43	13
Kansas	49	12.0	4	1.96	4
Kentucky	34	4.1	46	0.92	37
Louisiana	28	3.3	50	0.66	49
Maine	30	14.7	2	2.43	3
Maryland	49	7.1	25	1.01	31
Massachusetts	42	7.6	21	0.70	46
Michigan	85	6.0	32	0.91	38
Minnesota	42	7.9	19	0.95	35
Mississippi	15	2.1	51	0.58	50
Missouri	41	4.1	47	0.80	44
Montana	10	5.0	39	1.24	22
Nebraska	14	5.1	38	0.88	42
Nevada	18	6.1	31	1.40	15
New Hampshire	14	9.8	9	1.27	21
New Jersey	41	5.2	36	0.53	51
New Mexico	38	8.1	17	2.46	2
New York	124	6.2	30	0.69	47
North Carolina	71	5.2	37	1.05	28
North Dakota	9	9.6	11	1.42	14
Ohio	164	10.0	7	1.50	11
Oklahoma	37	5.7	34	1.17	25
Oregon	35	7.2	23	1.20	24
Pennsylvania	107	6.4	27	0.90	40
Rhode Island	16	18.2	1	1.59	8
South Carolina	44	4.9	40	1.24	23
South Dakota	9	6.3	29	1.28	20
Tennessee	50	4.5	42	1.01	30
Texas	131	4.3	45	0.76	45
Utah	23	8.5	14	1.30	19
Vermont	6	5.5	35	1.06	27
Virginia	42	4.5	43	0.67	48
Washington	43	6.3	28	0.86	43
West Virginia	24	5.8	33	1.33	16
Wisconsin	77	9.7	10	1.55	10
Wyoming	12	9.8	8	2.61	1
United States	2,808	6.8	27	1.11	27

Rank in order

By rate per 100,000 population

1. Wyoming
2. New Mexico
3. Maine
4. Kansas
5. Alaska
6. California
7. Arizona
8. Rhode Island
9. Hawaii
10. Wisconsin
11. Ohio
12. Indiana
13. Iowa
14. North Dakota
15. Nevada
16. Colorado
    Florida
    West Virginia
19. Utah
20. South Dakota
21. New Hampshire
22. Montana
23. South Carolina
24. Oregon
25. Oklahoma
26. Idaho
27. Vermont
28. North Carolina
29. Delaware
30. Tennessee
31. Maryland
32. District of Columbia
33. Arkansas
34. Illinois
35. Minnesota
36. Alabama
37. Kentucky
38. Michigan
39. Georgia
40. Pennsylvania
41. Connecticut
42. Nebraska
43. Washington
44. Missouri
45. Texas
46. Massachusetts
47. New York
48. Virginia
49. Louisiana
50. Mississippi
51. New Jersey

Source: U.S. Department of Transportation, National Highway Traffic Safety Administration, *1991 Motorcycle Fatal Crash Facts* (Washington, D.C.: U.S. Department of Transportation, 1991).

State	Fatalities	% of total traffic fatalities		Per 100,000 population	
		Rate	Rank	Rate	Rank
Alabama	13	1.2	34	0.32	19
Alaska	3	3.0	5	0.53	7
Arizona	30	3.7	3	0.80	2
Arkansas	5	0.8	43	0.21	37
California	112	2.4	13	0.37	14
Colorado	14	2.6	12	0.42	9
Connecticut	5	1.6	25	0.15	44
Delaware	3	2.9	6	0.44	8
District of Columbia	1	1.6	26	0.17	40
Florida	118	4.8	1	0.89	1
Georgia	20	1.4	33	0.30	22
Hawaii	2	1.5	30	0.18	39
Idaho	4	1.5	27	0.39	12
Illinois	27	1.9	17	0.23	32
Indiana	19	1.9	19	0.34	16
Iowa	9	1.8	20	0.32	18
Kansas	7	1.7	24	0.28	23
Kentucky	9	1.1	36	0.24	30
Louisiana	23	2.7	9	0.54	5
Maine	1	0.5	49	0.08	49
Maryland	8	1.2	35	0.17	41
Massachusetts	13	2.4	15	0.22	35
Michigan	38	2.7	8	0.41	10
Minnesota	8	1.5	28	0.18	38
Mississippi	7	1.0	40	0.27	26
Missouri	5	0.5	48	0.10	48
Montana	2	1.0	41	0.25	29
Nebraska	4	1.5	32	0.25	28
Nevada	3	1.0	39	0.23	32
New Hampshire	0	0.0	51	0.00	51
New Jersey	21	2.7	10	0.27	25
New Mexico	4	0.9	42	0.26	27
New York	69	3.4	4	0.38	13
North Carolina	36	2.6	11	0.53	6
North Dakota	1	1.1	38	0.16	43
Ohio	30	1.8	21	0.27	24
Oklahoma	4	0.6	47	0.13	46
Oregon	9	1.9	18	0.31	20
Pennsylvania	18	1.1	37	0.15	45
Rhode Island	4	4.5	2	0.40	11
South Carolina	21	2.4	14	0.59	3
South Dakota	4	2.8	7	0.57	4
Tennessee	8	0.7	46	0.16	42
Texas	53	1.7	23	0.31	21
Utah	4	1.5	31	0.23	34
Vermont	2	1.8	22	0.35	15
Virginia	21	2.2	16	0.33	17
Washington	5	0.7	45	0.10	47
West Virginia	1	0.2	50	0.06	50
Wisconsin	12	1.5	29	0.24	30
Wyoming	1	0.8	44	0.22	35
United States	841	2.0	17	0.33	18

PEDALCYCLIST FATALITIES, 1991

Rank in order

By rate per 100,000 population

1. Florida
2. Arizona
3. South Carolina
4. South Dakota
5. Louisiana
6. North Carolina
7. Alaska
8. Delaware
9. Colorado
10. Michigan
11. Rhode Island
12. Idaho
13. New York
14. California
15. Vermont
16. Indiana
17. Virginia
18. Iowa
19. Alabama
20. Oregon
21. Texas
22. Georgia
23. Kansas
24. Ohio
25. New Jersey
26. Mississippi
27. New Mexico
28. Nebraska
29. Montana
30. Kentucky
    Wisconsin
32. Illinois
    Nevada
34. Utah
35. Massachusetts
    Wyoming
37. Arkansas
38. Minnesota
39. Hawaii
40. District of Columbia
41. Maryland
42. Tennessee
43. North Dakota
44. Connecticut
45. Pennsylvania
46. Oklahoma
47. Washington
48. Missouri
49. Maine
50. West Virginia
51. New Hampshire

Source: U.S. Department of Transportation, National Highway Traffic Safety Administration, *1991 Pedalcyclist Fatal Crash Facts* (Washington, D.C.: U.S. Department of Transportation, 1992).

State	Fatalities	% of total traffic fatalities		Per 100,000 population		Rank in order By rate per 100,000 population
		Rate	Rank	Rate	Rank	
Alabama	102	9.2	31	2.49	14	1. New Mexico
Alaska	17	16.8	10	2.98	8	2. District of Columbia
Arizona	117	14.3	16	3.12	6	3. Florida
Arkansas	53	8.7	34	2.23	19	4. South Carolina
California	883	18.8	9	2.91	10	5. Louisiana
Colorado	48	8.8	33	1.42	39	6. Arizona
Connecticut	50	16.1	12	1.52	36	7. Nevada
Delaware	16	15.7	14	2.35	16	8. Alaska
District of Columbia	24	38.1	1	4.01	2	9. Texas
Florida	493	20.0	5	3.71	3	10. California
Georgia	161	11.6	24	2.43	15	11. Maryland
Hawaii	26	19.3	7	2.29	18	12. North Carolina
Idaho	17	6.4	46	1.64	31	13. New York
Illinois	220	15.2	15	1.91	23	14. Alabama
Indiana	88	8.6	35	1.57	34	15. Georgia
Iowa	35	7.2	42	1.25	44	16. Delaware
Kansas	20	4.9	49	0.80	49	17. New Jersey
Kentucky	52	6.3	48	1.40	41	18. Hawaii
Louisiana	138	16.1	13	3.25	5	19. Arkansas
Maine	9	4.4	50	0.73	50	20. Tennessee
Maryland	140	20.2	4	2.88	11	21. Mississippi
Massachusetts	106	19.2	8	1.77	27	22. Pennsylvania
Michigan	177	12.6	22	1.89	24	23. Illinois
Minnesota	60	11.3	25	1.35	42	24. Michigan
Mississippi	51	7.3	40	1.97	21	25. West Virginia
Missouri	73	7.2	41	1.42	40	26. Oregon
Montana	14	7.0	43	1.73	29	27. Massachusetts
Nebraska	18	6.5	45	1.13	47	28. Virginia
Nevada	40	13.5	21	3.12	7	29. Montana
New Hampshire	14	9.8	30	1.27	43	30. Utah
New Jersey	179	22.8	3	2.31	17	31. Idaho
New Mexico	91	19.4	6	5.88	1	32. Vermont
New York	488	24.3	2	2.70	13	33. Oklahoma
North Carolina	189	13.8	19	2.81	12	34. Indiana
North Dakota	6	6.4	47	0.95	48	35. Ohio
Ohio	169	10.3	29	1.55	35	36. Connecticut
Oklahoma	50	7.7	38	1.58	33	37. Washington
Oregon	53	11.0	28	1.81	26	38. South Dakota
Pennsylvania	231	13.9	18	1.93	22	39. Colorado
Rhode Island	12	13.6	20	1.20	46	40. Missouri
South Carolina	125	14.0	17	3.51	4	41. Kentucky
South Dakota	10	7.0	44	1.42	38	42. Minnesota
Tennessee	101	9.1	32	2.04	20	43. New Hampshire
Texas	511	16.6	11	2.95	9	44. Iowa
Utah	30	11.1	26	1.70	30	45. Wisconsin
Vermont	9	8.2	36	1.59	32	46. Rhode Island
Virginia	111	11.8	23	1.77	28	47. Nebraska
Washington	75	11.0	27	1.50	37	48. North Dakota
West Virginia	33	8.0	37	1.83	25	49. Kansas
Wisconsin	60	7.5	39	1.21	45	50. Maine
Wyoming	2	1.6	51	0.44	51	51. Wyoming
United States	5,797	14.0	18	2.30	18	

Source: U.S. Department of Transportation, National Highway Traffic Safety Administration, *1991 Pedestrian Fatal Crash Facts* (Washington, D.C.: U.S. Department of Transportation).

| | REGISTERED AIRCRAFT, 1990 | | | | Rank in order |
| | | | Per 10,000 population | | By rate per 10,000 population |
State	Registered aircraft	Rate	Rank		
Alabama	4,139	10.25	29		1. Alaska
Alaska	8,886	161.56	1		2. Delaware
Arizona	6,307	17.19	13		3. Montana
Arkansas	3,039	12.93	21		4. North Dakota
California	35,240	11.84	25		5. Idaho
Colorado	5,360	16.29	15		6. Wyoming
Connecticut	2,513	7.64	40		7. Nevada
Delaware	2,804	41.85	2		8. Oregon
District of Columbia	550	9.02	33		9. South Dakota
Florida	16,631	12.85	22		10. New Mexico
Georgia	6,092	9.40	31		11. New Hampshire
Hawaii	776	6.99	42		12. Kansas
Idaho	2,535	25.10	5		13. Arizona
Illinois	9,078	7.94	39		14. Washington
Indiana	4,688	8.46	38		15. Colorado
Iowa	3,409	12.26	23		16. Oklahoma
Kansas	4,458	17.98	12		17. Nebraska
Kentucky	2,043	5.54	49		18. Minnesota
Louisiana	3,782	8.96	34		19. Maine
Maine	1,627	13.23	19		20. Vermont
Maryland	3,256	6.81	44		21. Arkansas
Massachusetts	3,906	6.49	47		22. Florida
Michigan	8,778	9.44	30		23. Iowa
Minnesota	6,085	13.89	18		24. Texas
Mississippi	2,293	8.92	35		25. California
Missouri	5,488	10.72	28		26. Utah
Montana	2,666	33.33	3		27. Wisconsin
Nebraska	2,377	15.04	17		28. Missouri
Nevada	2,907	24.23	7		29. Alabama
New Hampshire	2,037	18.35	11		30. Michigan
New Jersey	4,731	6.12	48		31. Georgia
New Mexico	2,852	18.76	10		32. North Carolina
New York	8,513	4.73	50		33. District of Columbia
North Carolina	6,067	9.15	32		34. Louisiana
North Dakota	1,958	30.59	4		35. Mississippi
Ohio	9,201	8.48	37		36. Tennessee
Oklahoma	4,868	15.45	16		37. Ohio
Oregon	6,622	23.32	8		38. Indiana
Pennsylvania	7,809	6.57	46		39. Illinois
Rhode Island	473	4.73	51		40. Connecticut
South Carolina	2,433	6.97	43		41. West Virginia
South Dakota	1,629	23.27	9		42. Hawaii
Tennessee	4,267	8.74	36		43. South Carolina
Texas	20,556	12.10	24		44. Maryland
Utah	1,855	10.79	26		45. Virginia
Vermont	726	12.96	20		46. Pennsylvania
Virginia	4,097	6.62	45		47. Massachusetts
Washington	8,173	16.78	14		48. New Jersey
West Virginia	1,274	7.12	41		49. Kentucky
Wisconsin	5,263	10.76	27		50. New York
Wyoming	1,113	24.73	6		51. Rhode Island
United States	268,230	10.78	28		

Source: Federal Aviation Administration, *Census U.S. Civil Aircraft, Calendar Year 1990* (Washington, D.C.: U.S. Department of Transportation, 1992).

| State | Registered pilots | Per 10,000 population | | Rank in order |
		Rate	Rank	By rate per 10,000 population
Alabama	9,256	22.91	36	1. Alaska
Alaska	9,715	176.64	1	2. North Dakota
Arizona	16,219	44.19	7	3. Colorado
Arkansas	5,990	25.49	31	4. Montana
California	96,656	32.48	19	5. Washington
Colorado	16,484	50.10	3	6. Nevada
Connecticut	8,643	26.27	27	7. Arizona
Delaware	1,737	25.93	28	8. Idaho
District of Columbia	569	9.33	51	9. New Hampshire
Florida	48,500	37.48	13	10. Wyoming
Georgia	18,827	29.05	25	11. Minnesota
Hawaii	3,505	31.58	22	12. Kansas
Idaho	4,367	43.24	8	13. Florida
Illinois	26,271	22.98	35	14. Oregon
Indiana	12,596	22.74	37	15. South Dakota
Iowa	7,334	26.38	26	16. Utah
Kansas	9,426	38.01	12	17. Oklahoma
Kentucky	6,041	16.37	47	18. Vermont
Louisiana	7,969	18.88	43	19. California
Maine	3,877	31.52	23	20. New Mexico
Maryland	10,082	21.09	39	21. Nebraska
Massachusetts	12,407	20.61	40	22. Hawaii
Michigan	19,958	21.46	38	23. Maine
Minnesota	16,966	38.74	11	24. Texas
Mississippi	4,695	18.27	45	25. Georgia
Missouri	13,057	25.50	30	26. Iowa
Montana	3,842	48.03	4	27. Connecticut
Nebraska	5,003	31.67	21	28. Delaware
Nevada	5,437	45.31	6	29. Tennessee
New Hampshire	4,793	43.18	9	30. Missouri
New Jersey	14,375	18.60	44	31. Arkansas
New Mexico	4,897	32.22	20	32. Virginia
New York	24,599	13.67	50	33. Wisconsin
North Carolina	15,574	23.49	34	34. North Carolina
North Dakota	3,277	51.20	2	35. Illinois
Ohio	21,755	20.05	42	36. Alabama
Oklahoma	10,702	33.98	17	37. Indiana
Oregon	10,429	36.72	14	38. Michigan
Pennsylvania	21,413	18.02	46	39. Maryland
Rhode Island	1,585	15.85	48	40. Massachusetts
South Carolina	7,060	20.23	41	41. South Carolina
South Dakota	2,513	35.90	15	42. Ohio
Tennessee	12,593	25.81	29	43. Louisiana
Texas	51,835	30.51	24	44. New Jersey
Utah	6,000	34.88	16	45. Mississippi
Vermont	1,830	32.68	18	46. Pennsylvania
Virginia	15,641	25.27	32	47. Kentucky
Washington	22,548	46.30	5	48. Rhode Island
West Virginia	2,504	13.99	49	49. West Virginia
Wisconsin	12,003	24.55	33	50. New York
Wyoming	1,941	43.13	10	51. District of Columbia
United States	675,296	27.15	26	

Source: Federal Aviation Administration, *Census U.S. Civil Aircraft, Calendar Year 1990* (Washington, D.C.: U.S. Department of Transportation, 1992).

FEDERAL SPENDING ON AIRPORT AND AIRWAY TRUST FUND, FISCAL 1991				Rank in order
State	Expenditures	Per capita	Rank by per capita	By per capita
Alabama	$11,881,000	$2.91	43	1. Alaska
Alaska	38,439,000	67.44	1	2. Hawaii
Arizona	45,426,000	12.11	6	3. Nevada
Arkansas	14,800,000	6.24	22	4. Colorado
California	73,823,000	2.43	47	5. Wyoming
Colorado	121,580,000	36.00	4	6. Arizona
Connecticut	11,084,000	3.37	39	7. Montana
Delaware	49,000	0.07	51	8. Tennessee
District of Columbia	71,000	0.12	50	9. Missouri
Florida	101,497,000	7.64	16	10. Nebraska
Georgia	44,349,000	6.70	20	11. South Dakota
Hawaii	44,687,000	39.37	2	12. Illinois
Idaho	5,365,000	5.16	28	13. Utah
Illinois	93,893,000	8.13	12	14. Indiana
Indiana	44,241,000	7.89	14	15. Maine
Iowa	10,672,000	3.82	38	16. Florida
Kansas	12,509,000	5.01	29	17. Kentucky
Kentucky	27,527,000	7.41	17	18. Washington
Louisiana	30,439,000	7.16	19	19. Louisiana
Maine	9,479,000	7.68	15	20. Georgia
Maryland	13,249,000	2.73	46	21. North Dakota
Massachusetts	16,353,000	2.73	45	22. Arkansas
Michigan	26,623,000	2.84	44	23. Pennsylvania
Minnesota	20,609,000	4.65	32	24. New Mexico
Mississippi	8,200,000	3.16	40	25. Texas
Missouri	44,852,000	8.70	9	26. New Hampshire
Montana	8,717,000	10.79	7	27. Wisconsin
Nebraska	13,665,000	8.58	10	28. Idaho
Nevada	47,940,000	37.34	3	29. Kansas
New Hampshire	5,979,000	5.41	26	30. Ohio
New Jersey	11,357,000	1.46	49	31. New York
New Mexico	8,676,000	5.60	24	32. Minnesota
New York	86,426,000	4.79	31	33. Rhode Island
North Carolina	28,937,000	4.30	35	34. Oklahoma
North Dakota	4,121,000	6.49	21	35. North Carolina
Ohio	53,114,000	4.86	30	36. West Virginia
Oklahoma	13,758,000	4.33	34	37. Oregon
Oregon	11,907,000	4.07	37	38. Iowa
Pennsylvania	73,744,000	6.17	23	39. Connecticut
Rhode Island	4,660,000	4.64	33	40. Mississippi
South Carolina	7,541,000	2.12	48	41. Virginia
South Dakota	5,780,000	8.22	11	42. Vermont
Tennessee	49,036,000	9.90	8	43. Alabama
Texas	96,532,000	5.56	25	44. Michigan
Utah	13,969,000	7.89	13	45. Massachusetts
Vermont	1,682,000	2.97	42	46. Maryland
Virginia	18,757,000	2.98	41	47. California
Washington	36,744,000	7.32	18	48. South Carolina
West Virginia	7,412,000	4.12	36	49. New Jersey
Wisconsin	25,649,000	5.18	27	50. District of Columbia
Wyoming	9,928,000	21.58	5	51. Delaware
United States	$1,540,876,000	$6.11	24	

Source: U.S. Department of Commerce, Bureau of the Census, *Federal Expenditures by State for Fiscal Year 1991* (Washington, D.C.: Government Printing Office, 1992).

AIRCRAFT FATALITIES, 1992					Rank in order

State	Aircraft involved in accidents	Fatalities	Fatalities per 100,000 population		By fatalities rate per 100,000 population
			Rate	Rank	
Alabama	40	25	0.61	14	1. Alaska
Alaska	171	45	7.90	1	2. Hawaii
Arizona	81	40	1.07	9	3. Montana
Arkansas	56	7	0.30	26	4. Wyoming
California	256	154	0.51	16	5. Nevada
Colorado	83	48	1.42	6	6. Colorado
Connecticut	21	6	0.18	36	7. Idaho
Delaware	5	7	1.03	10	8. North Dakota
District of Columbia	0	0	0.00	50	9. Arizona
Florida	116	51	0.38	20	10. Delaware
Georgia	49	15	0.23	29	11. Washington
Hawaii	19	28	2.47	2	West Virginia
Idaho	34	13	1.25	7	13. New Mexico
Illinois	58	26	0.23	30	14. Alabama
Indiana	27	7	0.13	45	15. Nebraska
Iowa	23	2	0.07	47	16. California
Kansas	23	5	0.20	33	17. Oklahoma
Kentucky	22	7	0.19	35	18. Wisconsin
Louisiana	24	7	0.17	41	19. Maine
Maine	20	5	0.41	19	20. Florida
Maryland	23	13	0.27	28	21. Oregon
Massachusetts	30	9	0.15	42	22. North Carolina
Michigan	60	20	0.21	31	23. Mississippi
Minnesota	25	9	0.20	32	24. Utah
Mississippi	20	9	0.35	23	25. Virginia
Missouri	38	9	0.17	39	26. Arkansas
Montana	26	19	2.35	3	27. New Hampshire
Nebraska	18	9	0.57	15	28. Maryland
Nevada	27	21	1.64	5	29. Georgia
New Hampshire	9	3	0.27	27	30. Illinois
New Jersey	27	5	0.06	48	31. Michigan
New Mexico	25	11	0.71	13	32. Minnesota
New York	32	9	0.05	49	33. Kansas
North Carolina	47	25	0.37	22	34. Rhode Island
North Dakota	16	7	1.10	8	35. Kentucky
Ohio	53	15	0.14	44	36. Connecticut
Oklahoma	34	15	0.47	17	Tennessee
Oregon	43	11	0.38	21	38. Texas
Pennsylvania	46	13	0.11	46	39. Missouri
Rhode Island	2	2	0.20	34	40. South Carolina
South Carolina	31	6	0.17	40	41. Louisiana
South Dakota	8	1	0.14	43	42. Massachusetts
Tennessee	24	9	0.18	36	43. South Dakota
Texas	118	31	0.18	38	44. Ohio
Utah	24	6	0.34	24	45. Indiana
Vermont	4	0	0.00	50	46. Pennsylvania
Virginia	31	21	0.33	25	47. Iowa
Washington	79	39	0.78	11	48. New Jersey
West Virginia	16	14	0.78	11	49. New York
Wisconsin	38	22	0.44	18	50. District of Columbia
Wyoming	16	8	1.74	4	Vermont
United States	2,118	889	0.35	23	

Source: National Transportation Safety Board, 1993.

State Rankings

Agriculture
State Ranking

Farm Acreage	31
Farmland as Portion of State	32
Net Farm Income	16
Government Payments to Farms	25
Federal Commodity Loans/Price Supports	31
Federal Spending on Rural Development	39
Rural Electric and Telephone Loan Guarantees	6
Foreign-Owned Agricultural Land	14

Business and Economy
State Ranking

Gross State Product	43
Retail Sales	40
Supermarket Sales	46
Commercial Bank Assets	35
Insured Commercial Bank Deposits	35
Fortune 500 Companies	28
Inc. 500 Companies	40
New Business Incorporations	44
Business Failures	38
Financial Aid to Minority Businesses	14
Women-Owned Businesses	48
Sales & Receipts of Women-Owned Businesses	37
African American-Owned Businesses	9
Sales & Receipts of African American-Owned Businesses	9
Hispanic-Owned Businesses	47
Sales & Receipts of Hispanic-Owned Businesses	40
Employees in Manufacturing	19
Manufacturing Shipments	22
Japanese-Owned U.S. Manufacturing Plants	20
Exports to Mexico	22
Change in Exports to Mexico	33
Existing Home Sales	22
Housing Starts	24
Average Annual Pay	34
Disposable Personal Income	41
Median Income of Families with Children	47
Federal Spending on Unemployment Insurance/Employment Services	35
Teen Unemployment	13
Bankruptcy Petitions Filed	3
Patents Issued to State Residents	46
Federal Spending on Community Development	12
Federal Spending on Economic Development Administration	17
Federal Spending on Urban Development Action Grants	15

Crime and Criminal Justice
State Ranking

Total Crimes	28
Violent Crimes	9
Murders	10
Rapes	29
Aggravated Assaults	5
Property Crimes	32
Robberies	23
Burglaries	16
Larcenies and Thefts	33
Motor Vehicle Thefts	30
State and Federal Prisoners	7
Capital Punishment	6
State Spending on Corrections	40
State Spending on Police	22
Inmates in Local Jails	19
Spending on Local Jails	28
Spending per Inmate for Local Jails	32
Employees at Local Jails	10
Juvenile Custody Rate	31
Federal Spending on Office of Justice Assistance Programs	33

Defense
State Ranking

Defense Grants to State and Local Governments	13
Total Defense Payroll	16
Total Army Payroll	7
Total Navy/Marine Corps Payroll	30
Total Air Force Payroll	27
Total Active-Duty Payroll	29
Army Active-Duty Payroll	14
Navy/Marine Corps Active-Duty Payroll	28
Air Force Active-Duty Payroll	28
Total Civilian Payroll	10
Army Civilian Payroll	4
Navy/Marine Corps Civilian Payroll	39
Air Force Civilian Payroll	25
Total Reserve and National Guard Payroll	7
Army Reserve and National Guard Payroll	4
Navy/Marine Corps Reserve and National Guard Payroll	17
Air Force Reserve and National Guard Payroll	23
Total Retired Military Payroll	10
Army Retired Military Payroll	3
Navy/Marine Corps Retired Military Payroll	23
Air Force Retired Military Payroll	18
Total Defense Prime Contracts	17
Army Prime Contracts	4
Navy/Marine Corps Prime Contracts	30
Air Force Prime Contracts	25
U.S. Military Installations	17
Construction of National Guard Centers	13

Education
State Ranking

School Age Population	19
Public Elementary and Secondary School Enrollment	21
Average Daily Attendance	NA
Student-Teacher Ratio	4
Salaries of Public School Teachers	39
Public School Teachers Who Are Male	45
Eighth Grade Math Test Results	34
High School Math Enrollment	33
Public High School Graduation Rate	44
General Educational Development (GED) Test Results	30
Adult Illiteracy	19
Federal Revenue for Public Schools	5
State Revenue for Public Schools	11
Local Government Revenue for Public Schools	41
Total Public School Spending	48
Public School Spending on Instruction	11
Public School Spending on Noninstruction	3
Public School Spending on Support Staff	45
State and Local Government Spending on Public Schools	44
Federal Spending on School Improvement Programs	18
Gifted and Talented Students	32
Federal Spending on Education of Students with Disabilities	3
Student-Teacher Ratio in Catholic Elementary Schools	39
Student-Teacher Ratio in Catholic Secondary Schools	25
State Spending on Education	17
State and Local Government Spending on Education	17
Higher Education Tuition and Fees	38
Higher Education Revenue	43
Federal Spending on Higher Education	15
State Spending on Higher Education	13
State and Local Government Spending on Higher Education	22
State and Local Appropriations for Higher Education	28
Federal Spending on Higher Education Act Insured Loans	43
Federal Spending on National Guaranteed Student Loans	43
Federal Spending on Pell Grants	17
Default Rate in Perkins Student Loan Program	5
State Spending on Libraries	31

Energy
State Ranking

Total Spending on Energy	12
Net Generation of Electricity	8
Cost of Electricity	38
Spending on Electricity	10
Spending on Natural Gas	30
Spending on Gasoline	18
Spending on Petroleum	23
Spending on Coal	5
Total Energy Consumption	14
Electricity Consumption	11
Natural Gas Consumption	22
Petroleum Consumption	22
Coal Consumption	9
Power Plants	36
Nuclear Power Plants	8
Hydroelectric Power Plants	22

Environment
State Ranking

Federally Owned Land (acreage)	41
Loss of Wetlands	21
Environmental Protection Agency Spending	49
EPA Abatement, Control, and Compliance	47
State Spending on Environmental Programs	42
Environmental Programs as Part of State Budget	41
State Spending on Forest Programs	11
Total Tree Planting	4
Federal Tree Planting	11
Private Tree Planting	4
State Spending on Air Quality	45
State Spending on Water Quality	42
Federal Grants for Rural Water and Waste Disposal	27
Federal Spending on Wastewater Treatment Works	46
Hazardous Waste Sites on National Priority List	27

Federal Grants for Hazardous Substance
Response 41
State Spending on Hazardous Waste 45

Health

State Ranking

State Health Rankings 41
State Spending on Health 19
Support for Public Health 35
Family and Business Spending on Health
Care 24
HMO Enrollment 34
Medicaid Recipients 24
Medically Underserved Population 4
Lack of Health Care Access 12
Active Nonfederal Physicians 41
Active Nonfederal Nurses 40
Active Nonfederal Dentists 46
Average Cost per Hospital Stay 38
Average Cost per Day for Hospital Care 36
Average Cost per Day for Hospital
Room 44
State Spending on Hospitals 3
Adequacy of Prenatal Care 34
Infants Born Receiving Late or No
Prenatal Care 16
Infants Born with Low Birth Weight 6
Abortions 29
Immunizations of Two-Year-Olds —
Overall Risk for Heart Disease 36
Risk Factor for Heart Disease
(hypertension) 8
Deaths Due to Heart Disease 15
New Cancer Cases 12
Deaths Due to Cancer 18
Prevalence of Smoking 7
Prevalence of Diabetes 5
Deaths Due to Diabetes 40
Cost of Diabetes 5
AIDS Cases Reported 20
Gonorrhea Cases Reported 5
Syphilis Cases Reported 8
Tuberculosis Cases Reported 12
Hepatitis Cases Reported 46
Rabies Cases Reported 22
Lyme Disease Cases Reported 35
Beer Consumption 43
Wine Consumption 40
Liquor Consumption 37
Alcohol and Drug Treatment Admissions 45
Federal Spending on Alcohol, Drug
Abuse, and Mental Health 24
Total Spending on Alcohol/Drug Abuse
Services 36
State Spending on Alcohol/Drug Abuse
Services 47
Hard-Core Cocaine Users 22
Federal Drug Grants to States 27

Population

State Ranking

Population 22
Population Density 26
Population in Metropolitan Areas 28
Population Under 18 Years Old 23
Population Over 65 Years Old 24
White Population 43
African American Population 6
Hispanic Population 48
Asian American Population 44
Native American Population 26
Catholic Population 48

Jewish Population 40
Marriages 15
Divorces 9
Births 33
Births to Single Mothers 13
Births to Single Teenagers 5
Adoptions 16
Adoption Option Index 37
Infant Mortality 5
Child Deaths and Suicides 17
Teen Violent Death Rate 19
Deaths 10

Recreation

State Ranking

State Parks and Recreation Areas 42
Visitors to State Parks and Recreation
Areas 42
Revenues from State Parks and
Recreation Areas 6
Spending on State Arts Agencies 47
Domestic Travel Spending 42
State Travel Office Budgets 28
Lodging Industry (rooms) 38
Participation in Exercise Walking 16
Participation in Swimming 19
Participation in Camping 43
Participation in Bowling 39
Bowling League Membership 49
Participation in Running/Jogging 11
Participation in Aerobics 30
Participation in Golf 30
Participation in Softball 28
Participation in Health Clubs 44
Participation in Tennis 12
Participation in Hunting 31
Participation in Baseball 19
Participation in Bicycle Riding 43
Number of Boats 17
Attendance at Parimutuel Racing 21
Revenue from Parimutuel Betting 28

Social Services

State Ranking

Federal Grants for Social Services 19
State Spending on Public Welfare 41
Persons in Poverty 4
Public Aid Recipients 15
Participants in Food Stamp Program 6
Households in Food Stamp Program 8
Percentage of Poor Using AFDC and
Food Stamps 50
Federal Spending on Children and
Family Services 21
Federal Women, Infants, and Children
Food Program 10
Child Welfare Services 13
Child Abuse Cases Reported —
Children in Poverty 9
Children Without Health Insurance 6
Children Who Are Hungry or at Risk 6
Federal Spending on Child Nutrition
Programs 4
Federal Spending on Special Milk
Program 43
National School Lunch Program
Participants 4
Head Start Enrollment 14
Head Start Spending 37
Federal Spending on Rehabilitation
Services/Handicapped Research 8

State Government

State Ranking

Financial World's State Rankings 22
Salaries of State Officials (governor) 24
Salaries of State Legislators —
Women in State Legislatures 49
African Americans in State Legislatures 4
Hispanics in State Legislatures 21
Asian Americans in State Legislatures 6
Native Americans in State Legislatures 12
Turnover in State Legislatures 11
Length of State Legislative Sessions 14
State Bills in Regular Session 10
State Resolutions in Regular Session 7
State Bills in Special Session 22
State Resolutions in Special Session 13
Women in State Cabinets 32
Total Federal Funding to State
Governments 15
Total State Spending 26
State General Expenditures 23
State Debt 35
State Spending on Interest on the
General Debt 25
Total State Tax Revenue 44
State Revenue from Tax on Sales and
Gross Receipts 39
State Revenue from General Sales Tax 40
State Revenue from Licenses 14
State Revenue from Motor Vehicle
Licenses 35
State Revenue from Individual Income
Taxes 35
State Revenue from Corporation Net
Income Taxes 44
State Revenue from Severance Taxes 16
State Revenue from Property Taxes 13
State Revenue from Death and Gift
Taxes 42
State Revenue from Documentary and
Stock Transfers 21
State Revenue from Tax on Motor Fuels 41
State Revenue from Tax on Tobacco
Products 36
Excise Tax on Cigarettes 38
Excise Tax on Gasoline 42
State Revenue from Lotteries —

Transportation

State Ranking

Motor Vehicle Registrations 8
Automobile Registrations 4
Bus and Truck Registrations 20
Motorcycle Registrations 42
Driver Licenses 14
Federal Spending on Highway Trust
Fund 27
Federal Spending on Mass
Transportation 34
State Spending on Highways 40
Highway Deficiency 11
Bridge Deficiency 19
Traffic Fatalities 2
Traffic Fatalities per Miles Traveled 6
Motorcyclist Fatalities 36
Pedalcyclist Fatalities 19
Pedestrian Fatalities 14
Registered Aircraft 29
Registered Pilots 36
Federal Spending on Airport and
Airway Trust Fund 43
Aircraft Fatalities 14

— *not applicable* NA *not available*

Agriculture
State Ranking

Farm Acreage	44
Farmland as Portion of State	50
Net Farm Income	50
Government Payments to Farms	44
Federal Commodity Loans/Price Supports	49
Federal Spending on Rural Development	12
Rural Electric and Telephone Loan Guarantees	9
Foreign-Owned Agricultural Land	NA

Business and Economy
State Ranking

Gross State Product	2
Retail Sales	3
Supermarket Sales	2
Commercial Bank Assets	44
Insured Commercial Bank Deposits	46
Fortune 500 Companies	42
Inc. 500 Companies	47
New Business Incorporations	23
Business Failures	36
Financial Aid to Minority Businesses	7
Women-Owned Businesses	35
Sales & Receipts of Women-Owned Businesses	5
African American-Owned Businesses	31
Sales & Receipts of African American-Owned Businesses	37
Hispanic-Owned Businesses	19
Sales & Receipts of Hispanic-Owned Businesses	15
Employees in Manufacturing	49
Manufacturing Shipments	40
Japanese-Owned U.S. Manufacturing Plants	15
Exports to Mexico	51
Change in Exports to Mexico	45
Existing Home Sales	NA
Housing Starts	41
Average Annual Pay	2
Disposable Personal Income	8
Median Income of Families with Children	6
Federal Spending on Unemployment Insurance/Employment Services	1
Teen Unemployment	9
Bankruptcy Petitions Filed	45
Patents Issued to State Residents	44
Federal Spending on Community Development	39
Federal Spending on Economic Development Administration	1
Federal Spending on Urban Development Action Grants	33

Crime and Criminal Justice
State Ranking

Total Crimes	21
Violent Crimes	22
Murders	23
Rapes	1
Aggravated Assaults	21
Property Crimes	21
Robberies	35
Burglaries	34
Larcenies and Thefts	13
Motor Vehicle Thefts	20
State and Federal Prisoners	11
Capital Punishment	—
State Spending on Corrections	1
State Spending on Police	1
Inmates in Local Jails	—
Spending on Local Jails	—
Spending per Inmate for Local Jails	—
Employees at Local Jails	—
Juvenile Custody Rate	6
Federal Spending on Office of Justice Assistance Programs	5

Defense
State Ranking

Defense Grants to State and Local Governments	1
Total Defense Payroll	4
Total Army Payroll	1
Total Navy/Marine Corps Payroll	14
Total Air Force Payroll	1
Total Active-Duty Payroll	2
Army Active-Duty Payroll	2
Navy/Marine Corps Active-Duty Payroll	12
Air Force Active-Duty Payroll	1
Total Civilian Payroll	5
Army Civilian Payroll	2
Navy/Marine Corps Civilian Payroll	19
Air Force Civilian Payroll	3
Total Reserve and National Guard Payroll	2
Army Reserve and National Guard Payroll	3
Navy/Marine Corps Reserve and National Guard Payroll	46
Air Force Reserve and National Guard Payroll	3
Total Retired Military Payroll	12
Army Retired Military Payroll	15
Navy/Marine Corps Retired Military Payroll	38
Air Force Retired Military Payroll	5
Total Defense Prime Contracts	6
Army Prime Contracts	7
Navy/Marine Corps Prime Contracts	17
Air Force Prime Contracts	5
U.S. Military Installations	10
Construction of National Guard Centers	1

Education
State Ranking

School Age Population	4
Public Elementary and Secondary School Enrollment	47
Average Daily Attendance	33
Student-Teacher Ratio	21
Salaries of Public School Teachers	2
Public School Teachers Who Are Male	9
Eighth Grade Math Test Results	—
High School Math Enrollment	NA
Public High School Graduation Rate	38
General Educational Development (GED) Test Results	29
Adult Illiteracy	48
Federal Revenue for Public Schools	2
State Revenue for Public Schools	9
Local Government Revenue for Public Schools	47
Total Public School Spending	3
Public School Spending on Instruction	44
Public School Spending on Noninstruction	25
Public School Spending on Support Staff	1
State and Local Government Spending on Public Schools	49
Federal Spending on School Improvement Programs	3
Gifted and Talented Students	22
Federal Spending on Education of Students with Disabilities	1
Student-Teacher Ratio in Catholic Elementary Schools	46
Student-Teacher Ratio in Catholic Secondary Schools	47
State Spending on Education	1
State and Local Government Spending on Education	50
Higher Education Tuition and Fees	48
Higher Education Revenue	6
Federal Spending on Higher Education	35
State Spending on Higher Education	3
State and Local Government Spending on Higher Education	50
State and Local Appropriations for Higher Education	1
Federal Spending on Higher Education Act Insured Loans	50
Federal Spending on National Guaranteed Student Loans	51
Federal Spending on Pell Grants	48
Default Rate in Perkins Student Loan Program	2
State Spending on Libraries	2

Energy
State Ranking

Total Spending on Energy	1
Net Generation of Electricity	41
Cost of Electricity	9
Spending on Electricity	23
Spending on Natural Gas	4
Spending on Gasoline	23
Spending on Petroleum	1
Spending on Coal	34
Total Energy Consumption	1
Electricity Consumption	46
Natural Gas Consumption	1
Petroleum Consumption	1
Coal Consumption	38
Power Plants	1
Nuclear Power Plants	34
Hydroelectric Power Plants	3

Environment
State Ranking

Federally Owned Land (acreage)	2
Loss of Wetlands	50
Environmental Protection Agency Spending	2
EPA Abatement, Control, and Compliance	3
State Spending on Environmental Programs	2
Environmental Programs as Part of State Budget	4
State Spending on Forest Programs	1
Total Tree Planting	48
Federal Tree Planting	32
Private Tree Planting	45
State Spending on Air Quality	3
State Spending on Water Quality	18
Federal Grants for Rural Water and Waste Disposal	31
Federal Spending on Wastewater Treatment Works	1
Hazardous Waste Sites on National Priority List	43

Federal Grants for Hazardous Substance
Response 14
State Spending on Hazardous Waste 9

Health — State Ranking

State Health Rankings 46
State Spending on Health 1
Support for Public Health 50
Family and Business Spending on Health Care 34
HMO Enrollment 48
Medicaid Recipients 31
Medically Underserved Population 51
Lack of Health Care Access 8
Active Nonfederal Physicians 47
Active Nonfederal Nurses 41
Active Nonfederal Dentists 15
Average Cost per Hospital Stay 3
Average Cost per Day for Hospital Care 1
Average Cost per Day for Hospital Room 3
State Spending on Hospitals 40
Adequacy of Prenatal Care 26
Infants Born Receiving Late or No Prenatal Care 41
Infants Born with Low Birth Weight 51
Abortions 30
Immunizations of Two-Year-Olds —
Overall Risk for Heart Disease 40
Risk Factor for Heart Disease (hypertension) NA
Deaths Due to Heart Disease 51
New Cancer Cases 51
Deaths Due to Cancer 51
Prevalence of Smoking 11
Prevalence of Diabetes 51
Deaths Due to Diabetes 51
Cost of Diabetes 51
AIDS Cases Reported 48
Gonorrhea Cases Reported 28
Syphilis Cases Reported 42
Tuberculosis Cases Reported 15
Hepatitis Cases Reported 13
Rabies Cases Reported 21
Lyme Disease Cases Reported 45
Beer Consumption 8
Wine Consumption 8
Liquor Consumption 4
Alcohol and Drug Treatment Admissions 2
Federal Spending on Alcohol, Drug Abuse, and Mental Health 19
Total Spending on Alcohol/Drug Abuse Services 2
State Spending on Alcohol/Drug Abuse Services 1
Hard-Core Cocaine Users 26
Federal Drug Grants to States 3

Population — State Ranking

Population 50
Population Density 51
Population in Metropolitan Areas 41
Population Under 18 Years Old 2
Population Over 65 Years Old 51
White Population 40
African American Population 32
Hispanic Population 22
Asian American Population 5
Native American Population 1
Catholic Population 39

Jewish Population 32
Marriages 11
Divorces 12
Births 1
Births to Single Mothers 25
Births to Single Teenagers 45
Adoptions 1
Adoption Option Index 5
Infant Mortality 21
Child Deaths and Suicides 2
Teen Violent Death Rate 2
Deaths 51

Recreation — State Ranking

State Parks and Recreation Areas 1
Visitors to State Parks and Recreation Areas 1
Revenues from State Parks and Recreation Areas 16
Spending on State Arts Agencies 4
Domestic Travel Spending 6
State Travel Office Budgets 2
Lodging Industry (rooms) 8
Participation in Exercise Walking NA
Participation in Swimming NA
Participation in Camping NA
Participation in Bowling NA
Bowling League Membership 16
Participation in Running/Jogging NA
Participation in Aerobics NA
Participation in Golf NA
Participation in Softball NA
Participation in Health Clubs NA
Participation in Tennis NA
Participation in Hunting NA
Participation in Baseball NA
Participation in Bicycle Riding NA
Number of Boats 18
Attendance at Parimutuel Racing —
Revenue from Parimutuel Betting —

Social Services — State Ranking

Federal Grants for Social Services 44
State Spending on Public Welfare 3
Persons in Poverty 34
Public Aid Recipients 36
Participants in Food Stamp Program 29
Households in Food Stamp Program 49
Percentage of Poor Using AFDC and Food Stamps 1
Federal Spending on Children and Family Services 3
Federal Women, Infants, and Children Food Program 14
Child Welfare Services 33
Child Abuse Cases Reported —
Children in Poverty 49
Children Without Health Insurance 18
Children Who Are Hungry or at Risk 48
Federal Spending on Child Nutrition Programs 9
Federal Spending on Special Milk Program 42
National School Lunch Program Participants 14
Head Start Enrollment 32
Head Start Spending 7
Federal Spending on Rehabilitation Services/Handicapped Research 6

State Government — State Ranking

Financial World's State Rankings 33
Salaries of State Officials (governor) 23
Salaries of State Legislators 15
Women in State Legislatures 21
African Americans in State Legislatures 34
Hispanics in State Legislatures 21
Asian Americans in State Legislatures 6
Native Americans in State Legislatures 1
Turnover in State Legislatures 4
Length of State Legislative Sessions 9
State Bills in Regular Session 33
State Resolutions in Regular Session 30
State Bills in Special Session —
State Resolutions in Special Session —
Women in State Cabinets 34
Total Federal Funding to State Governments 2
Total State Spending 1
State General Expenditures 1
State Debt 1
State Spending on Interest on the General Debt 1
Total State Tax Revenue 1
State Revenue from Tax on Sales and Gross Receipts 49
State Revenue from General Sales Tax —
State Revenue from Licenses 2
State Revenue from Motor Vehicle Licenses 33
State Revenue from Individual Income Taxes —
State Revenue from Corporation Net Income Taxes 1
State Revenue from Severance Taxes 1
State Revenue from Property Taxes 3
State Revenue from Death and Gift Taxes 38
State Revenue from Documentary and Stock Transfers —
State Revenue from Tax on Motor Fuels 43
State Revenue from Tax on Tobacco Products 12
Excise Tax on Cigarettes 16
Excise Tax on Gasoline 47
State Revenue from Lotteries —

Transportation — State Ranking

Motor Vehicle Registrations 16
Automobile Registrations 40
Bus and Truck Registrations 7
Motorcycle Registrations 21
Driver Licenses 51
Federal Spending on Highway Trust Fund 1
Federal Spending on Mass Transportation 39
State Spending on Highways 1
Highway Deficiency 10
Bridge Deficiency 43
Traffic Fatalities 24
Traffic Fatalities per Miles Traveled 9
Motorcyclist Fatalities 5
Pedalcyclist Fatalities 7
Pedestrian Fatalities 8
Registered Aircraft 1
Registered Pilots 1
Federal Spending on Airport and Airway Trust Fund 1
Aircraft Fatalities 1

— not applicable NA not available

Agriculture
State Ranking

Farm Acreage	8
Farmland as Portion of State	17
Net Farm Income	28
Government Payments to Farms	31
Federal Commodity Loans/Price Supports	40
Federal Spending on Rural Development	28
Rural Electric and Telephone Loan Guarantees	27
Foreign-Owned Agricultural Land	21

Business and Economy
State Ranking

Gross State Product	36
Retail Sales	27
Supermarket Sales	10
Commercial Bank Assets	39
Insured Commercial Bank Deposits	37
Fortune 500 Companies	39
Inc. 500 Companies	5
New Business Incorporations	15
Business Failures	3
Financial Aid to Minority Businesses	8
Women-Owned Businesses	7
Sales & Receipts of Women-Owned Businesses	41
African American-Owned Businesses	33
Sales & Receipts of African American-Owned Businesses	31
Hispanic-Owned Businesses	5
Sales & Receipts of Hispanic-Owned Businesses	5
Employees in Manufacturing	30
Manufacturing Shipments	43
Japanese-Owned U.S. Manufacturing Plants	28
Exports to Mexico	2
Change in Exports to Mexico	40
Existing Home Sales	2
Housing Starts	7
Average Annual Pay	27
Disposable Personal Income	37
Median Income of Families with Children	33
Federal Spending on Unemployment Insurance/Employment Services	39
Teen Unemployment	11
Bankruptcy Petitions Filed	5
Patents Issued to State Residents	17
Federal Spending on Community Development	33
Federal Spending on Economic Development Administration	41
Federal Spending on Urban Development Action Grants	33

Crime and Criminal Justice
State Ranking

Total Crimes	4
Violent Crimes	19
Murders	21
Rapes	20
Aggravated Assaults	16
Property Crimes	4
Robberies	22
Burglaries	6
Larcenies and Thefts	3
Motor Vehicle Thefts	7
State and Federal Prisoners	6
Capital Punishment	17

State Spending on Corrections	4
State Spending on Police	8
Inmates in Local Jails	9
Spending on Local Jails	24
Spending per Inmate for Local Jails	42
Employees at Local Jails	7
Juvenile Custody Rate	14
Federal Spending on Office of Justice Assistance Programs	3

Defense
State Ranking

Defense Grants to State and Local Governments	20
Total Defense Payroll	22
Total Army Payroll	20
Total Navy/Marine Corps Payroll	21
Total Air Force Payroll	14
Total Active-Duty Payroll	26
Army Active-Duty Payroll	18
Navy/Marine Corps Active-Duty Payroll	19
Air Force Active-Duty Payroll	17
Total Civilian Payroll	22
Army Civilian Payroll	12
Navy/Marine Corps Civilian Payroll	27
Air Force Civilian Payroll	19
Total Reserve and National Guard Payroll	38
Army Reserve and National Guard Payroll	40
Navy/Marine Corps Reserve and National Guard Payroll	37
Air Force Reserve and National Guard Payroll	20
Total Retired Military Payroll	9
Army Retired Military Payroll	12
Navy/Marine Corps Retired Military Payroll	14
Air Force Retired Military Payroll	4
Total Defense Prime Contracts	12
Army Prime Contracts	2
Navy/Marine Corps Prime Contracts	28
Air Force Prime Contracts	8
U.S. Military Installations	18
Construction of National Guard Centers	16

Education
State Ranking

School Age Population	25
Public Elementary and Secondary School Enrollment	23
Average Daily Attendance	40
Student-Teacher Ratio	8
Salaries of Public School Teachers	26
Public School Teachers Who Are Male	25
Eighth Grade Math Test Results	25
High School Math Enrollment	NA
Public High School Graduation Rate	31
General Educational Development (GED) Test Results	15
Adult Illiteracy	21
Federal Revenue for Public Schools	16
State Revenue for Public Schools	31
Local Government Revenue for Public Schools	24
Total Public School Spending	41
Public School Spending on Instruction	29
Public School Spending on Noninstruction	23
Public School Spending on Support Staff	10
State and Local Government Spending on Public Schools	43

Federal Spending on School Improvement Programs	43
Gifted and Talented Students	NA
Federal Spending on Education of Students with Disabilities	45
Student-Teacher Ratio in Catholic Elementary Schools	5
Student-Teacher Ratio in Catholic Secondary Schools	1
State Spending on Education	33
State and Local Government Spending on Education	36
Higher Education Tuition and Fees	39
Higher Education Revenue	45
Federal Spending on Higher Education	28
State Spending on Higher Education	21
State and Local Government Spending on Higher Education	16
State and Local Appropriations for Higher Education	14
Federal Spending on Higher Education Act Insured Loans	10
Federal Spending on National Guaranteed Student Loans	12
Federal Spending on Pell Grants	14
Default Rate in Perkins Student Loan Program	18
State Spending on Libraries	43

Energy
State Ranking

Total Spending on Energy	38
Net Generation of Electricity	13
Cost of Electricity	13
Spending on Electricity	5
Spending on Natural Gas	44
Spending on Gasoline	34
Spending on Petroleum	46
Spending on Coal	23
Total Energy Consumption	43
Electricity Consumption	25
Natural Gas Consumption	41
Petroleum Consumption	50
Coal Consumption	19
Power Plants	37
Nuclear Power Plants	25
Hydroelectric Power Plants	30

Environment
State Ranking

Federally Owned Land (acreage)	8
Loss of Wetlands	34
Environmental Protection Agency Spending	51
EPA Abatement, Control, and Compliance	28
State Spending on Environmental Programs	45
Environmental Programs as Part of State Budget	43
State Spending on Forest Programs	48
Total Tree Planting	43
Federal Tree Planting	22
Private Tree Planting	45
State Spending on Air Quality	32
State Spending on Water Quality	35
Federal Grants for Rural Water and Waste Disposal	48
Federal Spending on Wastewater Treatment Works	51
Hazardous Waste Sites on National Priority List	32

Federal Grants for Hazardous Substance
  Response 26
State Spending on Hazardous Waste 28

Health   *State Ranking*

State Health Rankings 33
State Spending on Health 24
Support for Public Health 47
Family and Business Spending on Health
  Care 45
HMO Enrollment 11
Medicaid Recipients 35
Medically Underserved Population 18
Lack of Health Care Access 23
Active Nonfederal Physicians 21
Active Nonfederal Nurses 29
Active Nonfederal Dentists 36
Average Cost per Hospital Stay 16
Average Cost per Day for Hospital Care 4
Average Cost per Day for Hospital Room 21
State Spending on Hospitals 50
Adequacy of Prenatal Care 47
Infants Born Receiving Late or No
  Prenatal Care 3
Infants Born with Low Birth Weight 32
Abortions 12
Immunizations of Two-Year-Olds —
Overall Risk for Heart Disease 6
Risk Factor for Heart Disease
  (hypertension) 38
Deaths Due to Heart Disease 40
New Cancer Cases 35
Deaths Due to Cancer 39
Prevalence of Smoking 10
Prevalence of Diabetes 35
Deaths Due to Diabetes 46
Cost of Diabetes 36
AIDS Cases Reported 25
Gonorrhea Cases Reported· 30
Syphilis Cases Reported 31
Tuberculosis Cases Reported 20
Hepatitis Cases Reported 7
Rabies Cases Reported 25
Lyme Disease Cases Reported 45
Beer Consumption 5
Wine Consumption 15
Liquor Consumption 20
Alcohol and Drug Treatment Admissions 15
Federal Spending on Alcohol, Drug
  Abuse, and Mental Health 18
Total Spending on Alcohol/Drug Abuse
  Services 31
State Spending on Alcohol/Drug Abuse
  Services 20
Hard-Core Cocaine Users 5
Federal Drug Grants to States 35

Population   *State Ranking*

Population 24
Population Density 38
Population in Metropolitan Areas 17
Population Under 18 Years Old 13
Population Over 65 Years Old 20
White Population 33
African American Population 37
Hispanic Population 4
Asian American Population 20
Native American Population 6
Catholic Population 26

Jewish Population 11
Marriages 18
Divorces 3
Births 6
Births to Single Mothers 8
Births to Single Teenagers 15
Adoptions 40
Adoption Option Index 36
Infant Mortality 26
Child Deaths and Suicides 6
Teen Violent Death Rate 9
Deaths 34

Recreation   *State Ranking*

State Parks and Recreation Areas 43
Visitors to State Parks and Recreation
  Areas 49
Revenues from State Parks and
  Recreation Areas 43
Spending on State Arts Agencies 35
Domestic Travel Spending 14
State Travel Office Budgets 26
Lodging Industry (rooms) 10
Participation in Exercise Walking 37
Participation in Swimming 3
Participation in Camping 9
Participation in Bowling 19
Bowling League Membership 27
Participation in Running/Jogging 15
Participation in Aerobics 10
Participation in Golf 39
Participation in Softball 5
Participation in Health Clubs 3
Participation in Tennis 38
Participation in Hunting 34
Participation in Baseball 20
Participation in Bicycle Riding 18
Number of Boats 29
Attendance at Parimutuel Racing 19
Revenue from Parimutuel Betting 27

Social Services   *State Ranking*

Federal Grants for Social Services 21
State Spending on Public Welfare 48
Persons in Poverty 19
Public Aid Recipients 33
Participants in Food Stamp Program 16
Households in Food Stamp Program 19
Percentage of Poor Using AFDC and
  Food Stamps 33
Federal Spending on Children and
  Family Services 14
Federal Women, Infants, and Children
  Food Program 15
Child Welfare Services 17
Child Abuse Cases Reported —
Children in Poverty 10
Children Without Health Insurance 5
Children Who Are Hungry or at Risk 30
Federal Spending on Child Nutrition
  Programs 19
Federal Spending on Special Milk
  Program 29
National School Lunch Program
  Participants 21
Head Start Enrollment 50
Head Start Spending 20
Federal Spending on Rehabilitation
  Services/Handicapped Research 39

State Government   *State Ranking*

Financial World's State Rankings 29
Salaries of State Officials (governor) 33
Salaries of State Legislators 25
Women in State Legislatures 2
African Americans in State Legislatures 29
Hispanics in State Legislatures 3
Asian Americans in State Legislatures 6
Native Americans in State Legislatures 4
Turnover in State Legislatures 10
Length of State Legislative Sessions 4
State Bills in Regular Session 19
State Resolutions in Regular Session 26
State Bills in Special Session 21
State Resolutions in Special Session 18
Women in State Cabinets NA
Total Federal Funding to State
  Governments 28
Total State Spending 33
State General Expenditures 32
State Debt 43
State Spending on Interest on the
  General Debt 41
Total State Tax Revenue 19
State Revenue from Tax on Sales and
  Gross Receipts 9
State Revenue from General Sales Tax 7
State Revenue from Licenses 24
State Revenue from Motor Vehicle
  Licenses 9
State Revenue from Individual Income
  Taxes 33
State Revenue from Corporation Net
  Income Taxes 34
State Revenue from Severance Taxes —
State Revenue from Property Taxes 6
State Revenue from Death and Gift
  Taxes 31
State Revenue from Documentary and
  Stock Transfers —
State Revenue from Tax on Motor Fuels 23
State Revenue from Tax on Tobacco
  Products 41
Excise Tax on Cigarettes 30
Excise Tax on Gasoline 22
State Revenue from Lotteries 16

Transportation   *State Ranking*

Motor Vehicle Registrations 29
Automobile Registrations 32
Bus and Truck Registrations 25
Motorcycle Registrations 17
Driver Licenses 42
Federal Spending on Highway Trust
  Fund 26
Federal Spending on Mass
  Transportation 24
State Spending on Highways 9
Highway Deficiency 5
Bridge Deficiency 50
Traffic Fatalities 13
Traffic Fatalities per Miles Traveled 14
Motorcyclist Fatalities 7
Pedalcyclist Fatalities 2
Pedestrian Fatalities 6
Registered Aircraft 13
Registered Pilots 7
Federal Spending on Airport and
  Airway Trust Fund 6
Aircraft Fatalities 9

— *not applicable* NA *not available*

Agriculture
State Ranking

Farm Acreage	21
Farmland as Portion of State	21
Net Farm Income	7
Government Payments to Farms	7
Federal Commodity Loans/Price Supports	5
Federal Spending on Rural Development	14
Rural Electric and Telephone Loan Guarantees	3
Foreign-Owned Agricultural Land	27

Business and Economy
State Ranking

Gross State Product	49
Retail Sales	43
Supermarket Sales	23
Commercial Bank Assets	36
Insured Commercial Bank Deposits	34
Fortune 500 Companies	21
Inc. 500 Companies	47
New Business Incorporations	21
Business Failures	43
Financial Aid to Minority Businesses	31
Women-Owned Businesses	50
Sales & Receipts of Women-Owned Businesses	21
African American-Owned Businesses	17
Sales & Receipts of African American-Owned Businesses	11
Hispanic-Owned Businesses	44
Sales & Receipts of Hispanic-Owned Businesses	43
Employees in Manufacturing	26
Manufacturing Shipments	17
Japanese-Owned U.S. Manufacturing Plants	25
Exports to Mexico	6
Change in Exports to Mexico	22
Existing Home Sales	8
Housing Starts	27
Average Annual Pay	47
Disposable Personal Income	47
Median Income of Families with Children	49
Federal Spending on Unemployment Insurance/Employment Services	29
Teen Unemployment	4
Bankruptcy Petitions Filed	24
Patents Issued to State Residents	49
Federal Spending on Community Development	28
Federal Spending on Economic Development Administration	10
Federal Spending on Urban Development Action Grants	33

Crime and Criminal Justice
State Ranking

Total Crimes	31
Violent Crimes	24
Murders	14
Rapes	19
Aggravated Assaults	20
Property Crimes	30
Robberies	28
Burglaries	20
Larcenies and Thefts	27
Motor Vehicle Thefts	34
State and Federal Prisoners	18
Capital Punishment	13

State Spending on Corrections	39
State Spending on Police	28
Inmates in Local Jails	31
Spending on Local Jails	30
Spending per Inmate for Local Jails	18
Employees at Local Jails	38
Juvenile Custody Rate	38
Federal Spending on Office of Justice Assistance Programs	14

Defense
State Ranking

Defense Grants to State and Local Governments	17
Total Defense Payroll	31
Total Army Payroll	22
Total Navy/Marine Corps Payroll	31
Total Air Force Payroll	21
Total Active-Duty Payroll	33
Army Active-Duty Payroll	26
Navy/Marine Corps Active-Duty Payroll	40
Air Force Active-Duty Payroll	18
Total Civilian Payroll	35
Army Civilian Payroll	18
Navy/Marine Corps Civilian Payroll	45
Air Force Civilian Payroll	30
Total Reserve and National Guard Payroll	22
Army Reserve and National Guard Payroll	19
Navy/Marine Corps Reserve and National Guard Payroll	40
Air Force Reserve and National Guard Payroll	25
Total Retired Military Payroll	15
Army Retired Military Payroll	17
Navy/Marine Corps Retired Military Payroll	19
Air Force Retired Military Payroll	13
Total Defense Prime Contracts	46
Army Prime Contracts	38
Navy/Marine Corps Prime Contracts	45
Air Force Prime Contracts	37
U.S. Military Installations	29
Construction of National Guard Centers	30

Education
State Ranking

School Age Population	15
Public Elementary and Secondary School Enrollment	34
Average Daily Attendance	22
Student-Teacher Ratio	25
Salaries of Public School Teachers	49
Public School Teachers Who Are Male	39
Eighth Grade Math Test Results	28
High School Math Enrollment	7
Public High School Graduation Rate	22
General Educational Development (GED) Test Results	5
Adult Illiteracy	5
Federal Revenue for Public Schools	11
State Revenue for Public Schools	14
Local Government Revenue for Public Schools	39
Total Public School Spending	47
Public School Spending on Instruction	47
Public School Spending on Noninstruction	4
Public School Spending on Support Staff	43
State and Local Government Spending on Public Schools	14

Federal Spending on School Improvement Programs	19
Gifted and Talented Students	9
Federal Spending on Education of Students with Disabilities	22
Student-Teacher Ratio in Catholic Elementary Schools	49
Student-Teacher Ratio in Catholic Secondary Schools	32
State Spending on Education	30
State and Local Government Spending on Education	6
Higher Education Tuition and Fees	39
Higher Education Revenue	38
Federal Spending on Higher Education	6
State Spending on Higher Education	32
State and Local Government Spending on Higher Education	20
State and Local Appropriations for Higher Education	17
Federal Spending on Higher Education Act Insured Loans	27
Federal Spending on National Guaranteed Student Loans	45
Federal Spending on Pell Grants	19
Default Rate in Perkins Student Loan Program	12
State Spending on Libraries	29

Energy
State Ranking

Total Spending on Energy	15
Net Generation of Electricity	15
Cost of Electricity	19
Spending on Electricity	14
Spending on Natural Gas	13
Spending on Gasoline	15
Spending on Petroleum	26
Spending on Coal	15
Total Energy Consumption	21
Electricity Consumption	23
Natural Gas Consumption	9
Petroleum Consumption	35
Coal Consumption	20
Power Plants	24
Nuclear Power Plants	13
Hydroelectric Power Plants	21

Environment
State Ranking

Federally Owned Land (acreage)	18
Loss of Wetlands	10
Environmental Protection Agency Spending	43
EPA Abatement, Control, and Compliance	37
State Spending on Environmental Programs	39
Environmental Programs as Part of State Budget	39
State Spending on Forest Programs	14
Total Tree Planting	11
Federal Tree Planting	8
Private Tree Planting	10
State Spending on Air Quality	47
State Spending on Water Quality	38
Federal Grants for Rural Water and Waste Disposal	3
Federal Spending on Wastewater Treatment Works	41
Hazardous Waste Sites on National Priority List	32

Federal Grants for Hazardous Substance Response	48
State Spending on Hazardous Waste	39

Health — State Ranking

State Health Rankings	44
State Spending on Health	44
Support for Public Health	41
Family and Business Spending on Health Care	42
HMO Enrollment	44
Medicaid Recipients	12
Medically Underserved Population	4
Lack of Health Care Access	13
Active Nonfederal Physicians	45
Active Nonfederal Nurses	43
Active Nonfederal Dentists	49
Average Cost per Hospital Stay	49
Average Cost per Day for Hospital Care	43
Average Cost per Day for Hospital Room	50
State Spending on Hospitals	36
Adequacy of Prenatal Care	45
Infants Born Receiving Late or No Prenatal Care	10
Infants Born with Low Birth Weight	7
Abortions	46
Immunizations of Two-Year-Olds	—
Overall Risk for Heart Disease	40
Risk Factor for Heart Disease (hypertension)	NA
Deaths Due to Heart Disease	10
New Cancer Cases	5
Deaths Due to Cancer	6
Prevalence of Smoking	28
Prevalence of Diabetes	6
Deaths Due to Diabetes	33
Cost of Diabetes	6
AIDS Cases Reported	18
Gonorrhea Cases Reported	10
Syphilis Cases Reported	5
Tuberculosis Cases Reported	13
Hepatitis Cases Reported	35
Rabies Cases Reported	24
Lyme Disease Cases Reported	18
Beer Consumption	46
Wine Consumption	47
Liquor Consumption	40
Alcohol and Drug Treatment Admissions	41
Federal Spending on Alcohol, Drug Abuse, and Mental Health	42
Total Spending on Alcohol/Drug Abuse Services	47
State Spending on Alcohol/Drug Abuse Services	45
Hard-Core Cocaine Users	38
Federal Drug Grants to States	42

Population — State Ranking

Population	33
Population Density	36
Population in Metropolitan Areas	43
Population Under 18 Years Old	19
Population Over 65 Years Old	6
White Population	31
African American Population	12
Hispanic Population	42
Asian American Population	43
Native American Population	22
Catholic Population	47

Jewish Population	47
Marriages	4
Divorces	3
Births	44
Births to Single Mothers	15
Births to Single Teenagers	7
Adoptions	12
Adoption Option Index	6
Infant Mortality	8
Child Deaths and Suicides	3
Teen Violent Death Rate	5
Deaths	6

Recreation — State Ranking

State Parks and Recreation Areas	37
Visitors to State Parks and Recreation Areas	21
Revenues from State Parks and Recreation Areas	9
Spending on State Arts Agencies	46
Domestic Travel Spending	38
State Travel Office Budgets	8
Lodging Industry (rooms)	24
Participation in Exercise Walking	22
Participation in Swimming	41
Participation in Camping	23
Participation in Bowling	31
Bowling League Membership	41
Participation in Running/Jogging	45
Participation in Aerobics	22
Participation in Golf	49
Participation in Softball	33
Participation in Health Clubs	43
Participation in Tennis	41
Participation in Hunting	12
Participation in Baseball	47
Participation in Bicycle Riding	48
Number of Boats	16
Attendance at Parimutuel Racing	1
Revenue from Parimutuel Betting	12

Social Services — State Ranking

Federal Grants for Social Services	9
State Spending on Public Welfare	27
Persons in Poverty	9
Public Aid Recipients	18
Participants in Food Stamp Program	15
Households in Food Stamp Program	14
Percentage of Poor Using AFDC and Food Stamps	46
Federal Spending on Children and Family Services	16
Federal Women, Infants, and Children Food Program	9
Child Welfare Services	20
Child Abuse Cases Reported	—
Children in Poverty	5
Children Without Health Insurance	3
Children Who Are Hungry or at Risk	2
Federal Spending on Child Nutrition Programs	7
Federal Spending on Special Milk Program	41
National School Lunch Program Participants	6
Head Start Enrollment	16
Head Start Spending	50
Federal Spending on Rehabilitation Services/Handicapped Research	7

State Government — State Ranking

Financial World's State Rankings	34
Salaries of State Officials (governor)	50
Salaries of State Legislators	35
Women in State Legislatures	46
African Americans in State Legislatures	15
Hispanics in State Legislatures	21
Asian Americans in State Legislatures	6
Native Americans in State Legislatures	12
Turnover in State Legislatures	37
Length of State Legislative Sessions	24
State Bills in Regular Session	1
State Resolutions in Regular Session	20
State Bills in Special Session	—
State Resolutions in Special Session	—
Women in State Cabinets	19
Total Federal Funding to State Governments	36
Total State Spending	30
State General Expenditures	25
State Debt	42
State Spending on Interest on the General Debt	34
Total State Tax Revenue	42
State Revenue from Tax on Sales and Gross Receipts	34
State Revenue from General Sales Tax	25
State Revenue from Licenses	42
State Revenue from Motor Vehicle Licenses	38
State Revenue from Individual Income Taxes	32
State Revenue from Corporation Net Income Taxes	32
State Revenue from Severance Taxes	19
State Revenue from Property Taxes	25
State Revenue from Death and Gift Taxes	45
State Revenue from Documentary and Stock Transfers	22
State Revenue from Tax on Motor Fuels	25
State Revenue from Tax on Tobacco Products	18
Excise Tax on Cigarettes	27
Excise Tax on Gasoline	20
State Revenue from Lotteries	—

Transportation — State Ranking

Motor Vehicle Registrations	48
Automobile Registrations	50
Bus and Truck Registrations	24
Motorcycle Registrations	50
Driver Licenses	10
Federal Spending on Highway Trust Fund	22
Federal Spending on Mass Transportation	32
State Spending on Highways	30
Highway Deficiency	19
Bridge Deficiency	45
Traffic Fatalities	5
Traffic Fatalities per Miles Traveled	2
Motorcyclist Fatalities	33
Pedalcyclist Fatalities	37
Pedestrian Fatalities	19
Registered Aircraft	21
Registered Pilots	31
Federal Spending on Airport and Airway Trust Fund	22
Aircraft Fatalities	26

— *not applicable*   NA *not available*

Agriculture
State Ranking

Farm Acreage	14
Farmland as Portion of State	33
Net Farm Income	24
Government Payments to Farms	32
Federal Commodity Loans/Price Supports	22
Federal Spending on Rural Development	41
Rural Electric and Telephone Loan Guarantees	40
Foreign-Owned Agricultural Land	9

Business and Economy
State Ranking

Gross State Product	8
Retail Sales	9
Supermarket Sales	26
Commercial Bank Assets	20
Insured Commercial Bank Deposits	20
Fortune 500 Companies	23
Inc. 500 Companies	12
New Business Incorporations	51
Business Failures	7
Financial Aid to Minority Businesses	10
Women-Owned Businesses	18
Sales & Receipts of Women-Owned Businesses	42
African American-Owned Businesses	21
Sales & Receipts of African American-Owned Businesses	17
Hispanic-Owned Businesses	4
Sales & Receipts of Hispanic-Owned Businesses	4
Employees in Manufacturing	1
Manufacturing Shipments	31
Japanese-Owned U.S. Manufacturing Plants	1
Exports to Mexico	4
Change in Exports to Mexico	23
Existing Home Sales	34
Housing Starts	31
Average Annual Pay	7
Disposable Personal Income	10
Median Income of Families with Children	15
Federal Spending on Unemployment Insurance/Employment Services	16
Teen Unemployment	12
Bankruptcy Petitions Filed	13
Patents Issued to State Residents	8
Federal Spending on Community Development	40
Federal Spending on Economic Development Administration	47
Federal Spending on Urban Development Action Grants	19

Crime and Criminal Justice
State Ranking

Total Crimes	5
Violent Crimes	4
Murders	7
Rapes	20
Aggravated Assaults	6
Property Crimes	9
Robberies	4
Burglaries	12
Larcenies and Thefts	21
Motor Vehicle Thefts	2
State and Federal Prisoners	16
Capital Punishment	17

State Spending on Corrections	15
State Spending on Police	18
Inmates in Local Jails	5
Spending on Local Jails	7
Spending per Inmate for Local Jails	29
Employees at Local Jails	1
Juvenile Custody Rate	8
Federal Spending on Office of Justice Assistance Programs	32

Defense
State Ranking

Defense Grants to State and Local Governments	40
Total Defense Payroll	20
Total Army Payroll	30
Total Navy/Marine Corps Payroll	8
Total Air Force Payroll	29
Total Active-Duty Payroll	18
Army Active-Duty Payroll	19
Navy/Marine Corps Active-Duty Payroll	6
Air Force Active-Duty Payroll	27
Total Civilian Payroll	15
Army Civilian Payroll	37
Navy/Marine Corps Civilian Payroll	9
Air Force Civilian Payroll	21
Total Reserve and National Guard Payroll	47
Army Reserve and National Guard Payroll	50
Navy/Marine Corps Reserve and National Guard Payroll	14
Air Force Reserve and National Guard Payroll	41
Total Retired Military Payroll	20
Army Retired Military Payroll	35
Navy/Marine Corps Retired Military Payroll	8
Air Force Retired Military Payroll	26
Total Defense Prime Contracts	9
Army Prime Contracts	17
Navy/Marine Corps Prime Contracts	10
Air Force Prime Contracts	2
U.S. Military Installations	1
Construction of National Guard Centers	41

Education
State Ranking

School Age Population	34
Public Elementary and Secondary School Enrollment	1
Average Daily Attendance	NA
Student-Teacher Ratio	2
Salaries of Public School Teachers	4
Public School Teachers Who Are Male	16
Eighth Grade Math Test Results	28
High School Math Enrollment	27
Public High School Graduation Rate	42
General Educational Development (GED) Test Results	20
Adult Illiteracy	12
Federal Revenue for Public Schools	20
State Revenue for Public Schools	5
Local Government Revenue for Public Schools	45
Total Public School Spending	24
Public School Spending on Instruction	38
Public School Spending on Noninstruction	33
Public School Spending on Support Staff	5
State and Local Government Spending on Public Schools	42

Federal Spending on School Improvement Programs	44
Gifted and Talented Students	18
Federal Spending on Education of Students with Disabilities	48
Student-Teacher Ratio in Catholic Elementary Schools	2
Student-Teacher Ratio in Catholic Secondary Schools	7
State Spending on Education	15
State and Local Government Spending on Education	44
Higher Education Tuition and Fees	33
Higher Education Revenue	15
Federal Spending on Higher Education	45
State Spending on Higher Education	18
State and Local Government Spending on Higher Education	32
State and Local Appropriations for Higher Education	5
Federal Spending on Higher Education Act Insured Loans	28
Federal Spending on National Guaranteed Student Loans	36
Federal Spending on Pell Grants	37
Default Rate in Perkins Student Loan Program	33
State Spending on Libraries	41

Energy
State Ranking

Total Spending on Energy	46
Net Generation of Electricity	49
Cost of Electricity	6
Spending on Electricity	44
Spending on Natural Gas	17
Spending on Gasoline	47
Spending on Petroleum	47
Spending on Coal	48
Total Energy Consumption	44
Electricity Consumption	50
Natural Gas Consumption	20
Petroleum Consumption	34
Coal Consumption	48
Power Plants	32
Nuclear Power Plants	33
Hydroelectric Power Plants	14

Environment
State Ranking

Federally Owned Land (acreage)	5
Loss of Wetlands	1
Environmental Protection Agency Spending	46
EPA Abatement, Control, and Compliance	48
State Spending on Environmental Programs	8
Environmental Programs as Part of State Budget	9
State Spending on Forest Programs	4
Total Tree Planting	15
Federal Tree Planting	3
Private Tree Planting	24
State Spending on Air Quality	6
State Spending on Water Quality	5
Federal Grants for Rural Water and Waste Disposal	49
Federal Spending on Wastewater Treatment Works	44
Hazardous Waste Sites on National Priority List	3

Federal Grants for Hazardous Substance
Response — 27
State Spending on Hazardous Waste — 4

Health — *State Ranking*

State Health Rankings — 22
State Spending on Health — 9
Support for Public Health — 5
Family and Business Spending on Health
Care — 13
HMO Enrollment — 2
Medicaid Recipients — 9
Medically Underserved Population — 9
Lack of Health Care Access — 27
Active Nonfederal Physicians — 9
Active Nonfederal Nurses — 36
Active Nonfederal Dentists — 20
Average Cost per Hospital Stay — 6
Average Cost per Day for Hospital Care — 3
Average Cost per Day for Hospital Room — 2
State Spending on Hospitals — 30
Adequacy of Prenatal Care — 30
Infants Born Receiving Late or No
Prenatal Care — 11
Infants Born with Low Birth Weight — 38
Abortions — 2
Immunizations of Two-Year-Olds — —
Overall Risk for Heart Disease — 12
Risk Factor for Heart Disease
(hypertension) — 30
Deaths Due to Heart Disease — 44
New Cancer Cases — 44
Deaths Due to Cancer — 45
Prevalence of Smoking — 49
Prevalence of Diabetes — 40
Deaths Due to Diabetes — 37
Cost of Diabetes — 40
AIDS Cases Reported — 4
Gonorrhea Cases Reported — 29
Syphilis Cases Reported — 28
Tuberculosis Cases Reported — 4
Hepatitis Cases Reported — 12
Rabies Cases Reported — 29
Lyme Disease Cases Reported — 24
Beer Consumption — 26
Wine Consumption — 3
Liquor Consumption — 17
Alcohol and Drug Treatment Admissions — 30
Federal Spending on Alcohol, Drug
Abuse, and Mental Health — 16
Total Spending on Alcohol/Drug Abuse
Services — 12
State Spending on Alcohol/Drug Abuse
Services — 27
Hard-Core Cocaine Users — 6
Federal Drug Grants to States — 33

Population — *State Ranking*

Population — 1
Population Density — 13
Population in Metropolitan Areas — 3
Population Under 18 Years Old — 25
Population Over 65 Years Old — 45
White Population — 47
African American Population — 25
Hispanic Population — 2
Asian American Population — 2
Native American Population — 18
Catholic Population — 17

Jewish Population — 8
Marriages — 43
Divorces — 33
Births — 3
Births to Single Mothers — 11
Births to Single Teenagers — 28
Adoptions — 50
Adoption Option Index — 46
Infant Mortality — 34
Child Deaths and Suicides — 37
Teen Violent Death Rate — 14
Deaths — 45

Recreation — *State Ranking*

State Parks and Recreation Areas — 19
Visitors to State Parks and Recreation
Areas — 23
Revenues from State Parks and
Recreation Areas — 28
Spending on State Arts Agencies — 34
Domestic Travel Spending — 10
State Travel Office Budgets — 50
Lodging Industry (rooms) — 23
Participation in Exercise Walking — 31
Participation in Swimming — 39
Participation in Camping — 20
Participation in Bowling — 32
Bowling League Membership — 37
Participation in Running/Jogging — 18
Participation in Aerobics — 11
Participation in Golf — 35
Participation in Softball — 30
Participation in Health Clubs — 7
Participation in Tennis — 17
Participation in Hunting — 43
Participation in Baseball — 26
Participation in Bicycle Riding — 25
Number of Boats — 42
Attendance at Parimutuel Racing — 28
Revenue from Parimutuel Betting — 3

Social Services — *State Ranking*

Federal Grants for Social Services — 33
State Spending on Public Welfare — 7
Persons in Poverty — 13
Public Aid Recipients — 4
Participants in Food Stamp Program — 49
Households in Food Stamp Program — 29
Percentage of Poor Using AFDC and
Food Stamps — 3
Federal Spending on Children and
Family Services — 13
Federal Women, Infants, and Children
Food Program — 44
Child Welfare Services — 5
Child Abuse Cases Reported — —
Children in Poverty — 20
Children Without Health Insurance — 11
Children Who Are Hungry or at Risk — 22
Federal Spending on Child Nutrition
Programs — 24
Federal Spending on Special Milk
Program — 34
National School Lunch Program
Participants — 19
Head Start Enrollment — 45
Head Start Spending — 6
Federal Spending on Rehabilitation
Services/Handicapped Research — 49

State Government — *State Ranking*

Financial World's State Rankings — 41
Salaries of State Officials (governor) — 4
Salaries of State Legislators — 2
Women in State Legislatures — 18
African Americans in State Legislatures — 19
Hispanics in State Legislatures — 4
Asian Americans in State Legislatures — 4
Native Americans in State Legislatures — 12
Turnover in State Legislatures — 31
Length of State Legislative Sessions — 8
State Bills in Regular Session — 17
State Resolutions in Regular Session — 27
State Bills in Special Session — NA
State Resolutions in Special Session — NA
Women in State Cabinets — 17
Total Federal Funding to State
Governments — 24
Total State Spending — 32
State General Expenditures — 31
State Debt — 32
State Spending on Interest on the
General Debt — 38
Total State Tax Revenue — 10
State Revenue from Tax on Sales and
Gross Receipts — 17
State Revenue from General Sales Tax — 11
State Revenue from Licenses — 35
State Revenue from Motor Vehicle
Licenses — 23
State Revenue from Individual Income
Taxes — 9
State Revenue from Corporation Net
Income Taxes — 5
State Revenue from Severance Taxes — 24
State Revenue from Property Taxes — 7
State Revenue from Death and Gift
Taxes — 14
State Revenue from Documentary and
Stock Transfers — —
State Revenue from Tax on Motor Fuels — 45
State Revenue from Tax on Tobacco
Products — 21
Excise Tax on Cigarettes — 8
Excise Tax on Gasoline — 35
State Revenue from Lotteries — 20

Transportation — *State Ranking*

Motor Vehicle Registrations — 35
Automobile Registrations — 27
Bus and Truck Registrations — 38
Motorcycle Registrations — 18
Driver Licenses — 39
Federal Spending on Highway Trust
Fund — 46
Federal Spending on Mass
Transportation — 12
State Spending on Highways — 48
Highway Deficiency — 28
Bridge Deficiency — 37
Traffic Fatalities — 32
Traffic Fatalities per Miles Traveled — 33
Motorcyclist Fatalities — 6
Pedalcyclist Fatalities — 14
Pedestrian Fatalities — 10
Registered Aircraft — 25
Registered Pilots — 19
Federal Spending on Airport and
Airway Trust Fund — 47
Aircraft Fatalities — 16

— *not applicable* NA *not available*

Agriculture
State Ranking

Farm Acreage	12
Farmland as Portion of State	19
Net Farm Income	22
Government Payments to Farms	13
Federal Commodity Loans/Price Supports	10
Federal Spending on Rural Development	31
Rural Electric and Telephone Loan Guarantees	16
Foreign-Owned Agricultural Land	13

Business and Economy
State Ranking

Gross State Product	21
Retail Sales	26
Supermarket Sales	17
Commercial Bank Assets	45
Insured Commercial Bank Deposits	43
Fortune 500 Companies	20
Inc. 500 Companies	3
New Business Incorporations	4
Business Failures	5
Financial Aid to Minority Businesses	6
Women-Owned Businesses	3
Sales & Receipts of Women-Owned Businesses	12
African American-Owned Businesses	30
Sales & Receipts of African American-Owned Businesses	33
Hispanic-Owned Businesses	6
Sales & Receipts of Hispanic-Owned Businesses	6
Employees in Manufacturing	31
Manufacturing Shipments	37
Japanese-Owned U.S. Manufacturing Plants	28
Exports to Mexico	31
Change in Exports to Mexico	44
Existing Home Sales	12
Housing Starts	20
Average Annual Pay	14
Disposable Personal Income	19
Median Income of Families with Children	25
Federal Spending on Unemployment Insurance/Employment Services	28
Teen Unemployment	43
Bankruptcy Petitions Filed	7
Patents Issued to State Residents	10
Federal Spending on Community Development	47
Federal Spending on Economic Development Administration	34
Federal Spending on Urban Development Action Grants	33

Crime and Criminal Justice
State Ranking

Total Crimes	16
Violent Crimes	23
Murders	30
Rapes	13
Aggravated Assaults	22
Property Crimes	11
Robberies	36
Burglaries	25
Larcenies and Thefts	8
Motor Vehicle Thefts	27
State and Federal Prisoners	26
Capital Punishment	17

State Spending on Corrections	22
State Spending on Police	48
Inmates in Local Jails	12
Spending on Local Jails	4
Spending per Inmate for Local Jails	8
Employees at Local Jails	32
Juvenile Custody Rate	23
Federal Spending on Office of Justice Assistance Programs	22

Defense
State Ranking

Defense Grants to State and Local Governments	49
Total Defense Payroll	8
Total Army Payroll	10
Total Navy/Marine Corps Payroll	32
Total Air Force Payroll	12
Total Active-Duty Payroll	8
Army Active-Duty Payroll	8
Navy/Marine Corps Active-Duty Payroll	27
Air Force Active-Duty Payroll	11
Total Civilian Payroll	19
Army Civilian Payroll	17
Navy/Marine Corps Civilian Payroll	40
Air Force Civilian Payroll	11
Total Reserve and National Guard Payroll	6
Army Reserve and National Guard Payroll	28
Navy/Marine Corps Reserve and National Guard Payroll	18
Air Force Reserve and National Guard Payroll	2
Total Retired Military Payroll	4
Army Retired Military Payroll	5
Navy/Marine Corps Retired Military Payroll	25
Air Force Retired Military Payroll	3
Total Defense Prime Contracts	10
Army Prime Contracts	29
Navy/Marine Corps Prime Contracts	35
Air Force Prime Contracts	1
U.S. Military Installations	18
Construction of National Guard Centers	49

Education
State Ranking

School Age Population	28
Public Elementary and Secondary School Enrollment	27
Average Daily Attendance	NA
Student-Teacher Ratio	15
Salaries of Public School Teachers	23
Public School Teachers Who Are Male	17
Eighth Grade Math Test Results	13
High School Math Enrollment	NA
Public High School Graduation Rate	26
General Educational Development (GED) Test Results	22
Adult Illiteracy	43
Federal Revenue for Public Schools	42
State Revenue for Public Schools	39
Local Government Revenue for Public Schools	13
Total Public School Spending	25
Public School Spending on Instruction	18
Public School Spending on Noninstruction	45
Public School Spending on Support Staff	9
State and Local Government Spending on Public Schools	25

Federal Spending on School Improvement Programs	41
Gifted and Talented Students	NA
Federal Spending on Education of Students with Disabilities	38
Student-Teacher Ratio in Catholic Elementary Schools	28
Student-Teacher Ratio in Catholic Secondary Schools	29
State Spending on Education	24
State and Local Government Spending on Education	24
Higher Education Tuition and Fees	18
Higher Education Revenue	32
Federal Spending on Higher Education	33
State Spending on Higher Education	9
State and Local Government Spending on Higher Education	13
State and Local Appropriations for Higher Education	44
Federal Spending on Higher Education Act Insured Loans	9
Federal Spending on National Guaranteed Student Loans	17
Federal Spending on Pell Grants	20
Default Rate in Perkins Student Loan Program	31
State Spending on Libraries	39

Energy
State Ranking

Total Spending on Energy	49
Net Generation of Electricity	34
Cost of Electricity	31
Spending on Electricity	49
Spending on Natural Gas	21
Spending on Gasoline	32
Spending on Petroleum	48
Spending on Coal	28
Total Energy Consumption	40
Electricity Consumption	37
Natural Gas Consumption	15
Petroleum Consumption	46
Coal Consumption	18
Power Plants	16
Nuclear Power Plants	34
Hydroelectric Power Plants	12

Environment
State Ranking

Federally Owned Land (acreage)	9
Loss of Wetlands	22
Environmental Protection Agency Spending	28
EPA Abatement, Control, and Compliance	22
State Spending on Environmental Programs	34
Environmental Programs as Part of State Budget	24
State Spending on Forest Programs	37
Total Tree Planting	37
Federal Tree Planting	25
Private Tree Planting	37
State Spending on Air Quality	8
State Spending on Water Quality	34
Federal Grants for Rural Water and Waste Disposal	32
Federal Spending on Wastewater Treatment Works	30
Hazardous Waste Sites on National Priority List	23

— *not applicable*   *NA not available*

Agriculture
State Ranking

Farm Acreage	49
Farmland as Portion of State	45
Net Farm Income	42
Government Payments to Farms	48
Federal Commodity Loans/Price Supports	47
Federal Spending on Rural Development	48
Rural Electric and Telephone Loan Guarantees	40
Foreign-Owned Agricultural Land	48

Business and Economy
State Ranking

Gross State Product	3
Retail Sales	7
Supermarket Sales	11
Commercial Bank Assets	23
Insured Commercial Bank Deposits	17
Fortune 500 Companies	1
Inc. 500 Companies	3
New Business Incorporations	17
Business Failures	49
Financial Aid to Minority Businesses	25
Women-Owned Businesses	17
Sales & Receipts of Women-Owned Businesses	17
African American-Owned Businesses	22
Sales & Receipts of African American-Owned Businesses	24
Hispanic-Owned Businesses	18
Sales & Receipts of Hispanic-Owned Businesses	16
Employees in Manufacturing	22
Manufacturing Shipments	21
Japanese-Owned U.S. Manufacturing Plants	30
Exports to Mexico	16
Change in Exports to Mexico	29
Existing Home Sales	42
Housing Starts	45
Average Annual Pay	3
Disposable Personal Income	2
Median Income of Families with Children	1
Federal Spending on Unemployment Insurance/Employment Services	8
Teen Unemployment	40
Bankruptcy Petitions Filed	41
Patents Issued to State Residents	2
Federal Spending on Community Development	19
Federal Spending on Economic Development Administration	45
Federal Spending on Urban Development Action Grants	9

Crime and Criminal Justice
State Ranking

Total Crimes	29
Violent Crimes	27
Murders	31
Rapes	39
Aggravated Assaults	33
Property Crimes	25
Robberies	14
Burglaries	21
Larcenies and Thefts	37
Motor Vehicle Thefts	8
State and Federal Prisoners	24
Capital Punishment	17

State Spending on Corrections	8
State Spending on Police	26
Inmates in Local Jails	—
Spending on Local Jails	—
Spending per Inmate for Local Jails	—
Employees at Local Jails	—
Juvenile Custody Rate	18
Federal Spending on Office of Justice Assistance Programs	35

Defense
State Ranking

Defense Grants to State and Local Governments	42
Total Defense Payroll	37
Total Army Payroll	50
Total Navy/Marine Corps Payroll	12
Total Air Force Payroll	51
Total Active-Duty Payroll	34
Army Active-Duty Payroll	49
Navy/Marine Corps Active-Duty Payroll	11
Air Force Active-Duty Payroll	51
Total Civilian Payroll	37
Army Civilian Payroll	48
Navy/Marine Corps Civilian Payroll	15
Air Force Civilian Payroll	50
Total Reserve and National Guard Payroll	48
Army Reserve and National Guard Payroll	44
Navy/Marine Corps Reserve and National Guard Payroll	49
Air Force Reserve and National Guard Payroll	48
Total Retired Military Payroll	40
Army Retired Military Payroll	44
Navy/Marine Corps Retired Military Payroll	20
Air Force Retired Military Payroll	50
Total Defense Prime Contracts	2
Army Prime Contracts	3
Navy/Marine Corps Prime Contracts	2
Air Force Prime Contracts	9
U.S. Military Installations	38
Construction of National Guard Centers	40

Education
State Ranking

School Age Population	47
Public Elementary and Secondary School Enrollment	31
Average Daily Attendance	20
Student-Teacher Ratio	48
Salaries of Public School Teachers	1
Public School Teachers Who Are Male	22
Eighth Grade Math Test Results	11
High School Math Enrollment	9
Public High School Graduation Rate	25
General Educational Development (GED) Test Results	16
Adult Illiteracy	21
Federal Revenue for Public Schools	45
State Revenue for Public Schools	32
Local Government Revenue for Public Schools	18
Total Public School Spending	4
Public School Spending on Instruction	43
Public School Spending on Noninstruction	51
Public School Spending on Support Staff	41
State and Local Government Spending on Public Schools	31

Federal Spending on School Improvement Programs	48
Gifted and Talented Students	NA
Federal Spending on Education of Students with Disabilities	18
Student-Teacher Ratio in Catholic Elementary Schools	29
Student-Teacher Ratio in Catholic Secondary Schools	27
State Spending on Education	40
State and Local Government Spending on Education	45
Higher Education Tuition and Fees	7
Higher Education Revenue	3
Federal Spending on Higher Education	31
State Spending on Higher Education	45
State and Local Government Spending on Higher Education	49
State and Local Appropriations for Higher Education	42
Federal Spending on Higher Education Act Insured Loans	23
Federal Spending on National Guaranteed Student Loans	37
Federal Spending on Pell Grants	45
Default Rate in Perkins Student Loan Program	36
State Spending on Libraries	10

Energy
State Ranking

Total Spending on Energy	31
Net Generation of Electricity	30
Cost of Electricity	3
Spending on Electricity	15
Spending on Natural Gas	33
Spending on Gasoline	39
Spending on Petroleum	25
Spending on Coal	44
Total Energy Consumption	48
Electricity Consumption	43
Natural Gas Consumption	44
Petroleum Consumption	23
Coal Consumption	44
Power Plants	29
Nuclear Power Plants	6
Hydroelectric Power Plants	26

Environment
State Ranking

Federally Owned Land (acreage)	50
Loss of Wetlands	9
Environmental Protection Agency Spending	18
EPA Abatement, Control, and Compliance	35
State Spending on Environmental Programs	37
Environmental Programs as Part of State Budget	46
State Spending on Forest Programs	36
Total Tree Planting	29
Federal Tree Planting	47
Private Tree Planting	27
State Spending on Air Quality	4
State Spending on Water Quality	33
Federal Grants for Rural Water and Waste Disposal	44
Federal Spending on Wastewater Treatment Works	14
Hazardous Waste Sites on National Priority List	24

Federal Grants for Hazardous Substance
   Response   47
State Spending on Hazardous Waste   13

Health   *State Ranking*

State Health Rankings   7
State Spending on Health   15
Support for Public Health   1
Family and Business Spending on Health
   Care   2
HMO Enrollment   8
Medicaid Recipients   37
Medically Underserved Population   49
Lack of Health Care Access   46
Active Nonfederal Physicians   5
Active Nonfederal Nurses   8
Active Nonfederal Dentists   2
Average Cost per Hospital Stay   4
Average Cost per Day for Hospital Care   7
Average Cost per Day for Hospital Room   1
State Spending on Hospitals   1
Adequacy of Prenatal Care   9
Infants Born Receiving Late or No
   Prenatal Care   42
Infants Born with Low Birth Weight   29
Abortions   9
Immunizations of Two-Year-Olds   —
Overall Risk for Heart Disease   23
Risk Factor for Heart Disease
   (hypertension)   8
Deaths Due to Heart Disease   28
New Cancer Cases   17
Deaths Due to Cancer   23
Prevalence of Smoking   12
Prevalence of Diabetes   20
Deaths Due to Diabetes   10
Cost of Diabetes   20
AIDS Cases Reported   9
Gonorrhea Cases Reported   20
Syphilis Cases Reported   24
Tuberculosis Cases Reported   35
Hepatitis Cases Reported   49
Rabies Cases Reported   2
Lyme Disease Cases Reported   2
Beer Consumption   50
Wine Consumption   12
Liquor Consumption   10
Alcohol and Drug Treatment Admissions   16
Federal Spending on Alcohol, Drug
   Abuse, and Mental Health   15
Total Spending on Alcohol/Drug Abuse
   Services   4
State Spending on Alcohol/Drug Abuse
   Services   4
Hard-Core Cocaine Users   31
Federal Drug Grants to States   23

Population   *State Ranking*

Population   27
Population Density   5
Population in Metropolitan Areas   6
Population Under 18 Years Old   47
Population Over 65 Years Old   14
White Population   26
African American Population   22
Hispanic Population   12
Asian American Population   19
Native American Population   40
Catholic Population   5

Jewish Population   7
Marriages   35
Divorces   46
Births   29
Births to Single Mothers   21
Births to Single Teenagers   42
Adoptions   45
Adoption Option Index   27
Infant Mortality   40
Child Deaths and Suicides   50
Teen Violent Death Rate   39
Deaths   31

Recreation   *State Ranking*

State Parks and Recreation Areas   14
Visitors to State Parks and Recreation
   Areas   31
Revenues from State Parks and
   Recreation Areas   42
Spending on State Arts Agencies   28
Domestic Travel Spending   33
State Travel Office Budgets   48
Lodging Industry (rooms)   49
Participation in Exercise Walking   48
Participation in Swimming   29
Participation in Camping   42
Participation in Bowling   46
Bowling League Membership   29
Participation in Running/Jogging   46
Participation in Aerobics   45
Participation in Golf   21
Participation in Softball   36
Participation in Health Clubs   4
Participation in Tennis   6
Participation in Hunting   42
Participation in Baseball   43
Participation in Bicycle Riding   44
Number of Boats   41
Attendance at Parimutuel Racing   —
Revenue from Parimutuel Betting   2

Social Services   *State Ranking*

Federal Grants for Social Services   11
State Spending on Public Welfare   6
Persons in Poverty   48
Public Aid Recipients   33
Participants in Food Stamp Program   50
Households in Food Stamp Program   50
Percentage of Poor Using AFDC and
   Food Stamps   4
Federal Spending on Children and
   Family Services   43
Federal Women, Infants, and Children
   Food Program   22
Child Welfare Services   16
Child Abuse Cases Reported   —
Children in Poverty   50
Children Without Health Insurance   46
Children Who Are Hungry or at Risk   50
Federal Spending on Child Nutrition
   Programs   49
Federal Spending on Special Milk
   Program   5
National School Lunch Program
   Participants   48
Head Start Enrollment   7
Head Start Spending   16
Federal Spending on Rehabilitation
   Services/Handicapped Research   51

State Government   *State Ranking*

Financial World's State Rankings   46
Salaries of State Officials (governor)   30
Salaries of State Legislators   23
Women in State Legislatures   13
African Americans in State Legislatures   31
Hispanics in State Legislatures   9
Asian Americans in State Legislatures   6
Native Americans in State Legislatures   12
Turnover in State Legislatures   29
Length of State Legislative Sessions   5
State Bills in Regular Session   37
State Resolutions in Regular Session   13
State Bills in Special Session   12
State Resolutions in Special Session   1
Women in State Cabinets   9
Total Federal Funding to State
   Governments   10
Total State Spending   34
State General Expenditures   34
State Debt   4
State Spending on Interest on the
   General Debt   11
Total State Tax Revenue   8
State Revenue from Tax on Sales and
   Gross Receipts   4
State Revenue from General Sales Tax   3
State Revenue from Licenses   22
State Revenue from Motor Vehicle
   Licenses   15
State Revenue from Individual Income
   Taxes   41
State Revenue from Corporation Net
   Income Taxes   4
State Revenue from Severance Taxes   —
State Revenue from Property Taxes   42
State Revenue from Death and Gift
   Taxes   1
State Revenue from Documentary and
   Stock Transfers   7
State Revenue from Tax on Motor Fuels   19
State Revenue from Tax on Tobacco
   Products   7
Excise Tax on Cigarettes   3
Excise Tax on Gasoline   5
State Revenue from Lotteries   8

Transportation   *State Ranking*

Motor Vehicle Registrations   24
Automobile Registrations   1
Bus and Truck Registrations   50
Motorcycle Registrations   27
Driver Licenses   33
Federal Spending on Highway Trust
   Fund   6
Federal Spending on Mass
   Transportation   4
State Spending on Highways   5
Highway Deficiency   42
Bridge Deficiency   11
Traffic Fatalities   49
Traffic Fatalities per Miles Traveled   51
Motorcyclist Fatalities   41
Pedalcyclist Fatalities   44
Pedestrian Fatalities   36
Registered Aircraft   40
Registered Pilots   27
Federal Spending on Airport and
   Airway Trust Fund   39
Aircraft Fatalities   36

— *not applicable*   *NA not available*

Agriculture
State Ranking

Farm Acreage	47
Farmland as Portion of State	22
Net Farm Income	18
Government Payments to Farms	38
Federal Commodity Loans/Price Supports	36
Federal Spending on Rural Development	8
Rural Electric and Telephone Loan Guarantees	40
Foreign-Owned Agricultural Land	30

Business and Economy
State Ranking

Gross State Product	11
Retail Sales	4
Supermarket Sales	14
Commercial Bank Assets	1
Insured Commercial Bank Deposits	1
Fortune 500 Companies	8
Inc. 500 Companies	9
New Business Incorporations	1
Business Failures	40
Financial Aid to Minority Businesses	41
Women-Owned Businesses	12
Sales & Receipts of Women-Owned Businesses	7
African American-Owned Businesses	10
Sales & Receipts of African American-Owned Businesses	8
Hispanic-Owned Businesses	30
Sales & Receipts of Hispanic-Owned Businesses	38
Employees in Manufacturing	40
Manufacturing Shipments	1
Japanese-Owned U.S. Manufacturing Plants	42
Exports to Mexico	7
Change in Exports to Mexico	5
Existing Home Sales	25
Housing Starts	3
Average Annual Pay	11
Disposable Personal Income	12
Median Income of Families with Children	13
Federal Spending on Unemployment Insurance/Employment Services	17
Teen Unemployment	32
Bankruptcy Petitions Filed	46
Patents Issued to State Residents	1
Federal Spending on Community Development	31
Federal Spending on Economic Development Administration	51
Federal Spending on Urban Development Action Grants	33

Crime and Criminal Justice
State Ranking

Total Crimes	19
Violent Crimes	17
Murders	32
Rapes	2
Aggravated Assaults	19
Property Crimes	19
Robberies	16
Burglaries	28
Larcenies and Thefts	10
Motor Vehicle Thefts	29
State and Federal Prisoners	12
Capital Punishment	17

State Spending on Corrections	2
State Spending on Police	2
Inmates in Local Jails	—
Spending on Local Jails	—
Spending per Inmate for Local Jails	—
Employees at Local Jails	—
Juvenile Custody Rate	32
Federal Spending on Office of Justice Assistance Programs	1

Defense
State Ranking

Defense Grants to State and Local Governments	34
Total Defense Payroll	28
Total Army Payroll	40
Total Navy/Marine Corps Payroll	40
Total Air Force Payroll	10
Total Active-Duty Payroll	25
Army Active-Duty Payroll	34
Navy/Marine Corps Active-Duty Payroll	45
Air Force Active-Duty Payroll	9
Total Civilian Payroll	31
Army Civilian Payroll	43
Navy/Marine Corps Civilian Payroll	38
Air Force Civilian Payroll	10
Total Reserve and National Guard Payroll	4
Army Reserve and National Guard Payroll	21
Navy/Marine Corps Reserve and National Guard Payroll	12
Air Force Reserve and National Guard Payroll	1
Total Retired Military Payroll	21
Army Retired Military Payroll	28
Navy/Marine Corps Retired Military Payroll	32
Air Force Retired Military Payroll	8
Total Defense Prime Contracts	37
Army Prime Contracts	39
Navy/Marine Corps Prime Contracts	40
Air Force Prime Contracts	27
U.S. Military Installations	41
Construction of National Guard Centers	31

Education
State Ranking

School Age Population	39
Public Elementary and Secondary School Enrollment	48
Average Daily Attendance	30
Student-Teacher Ratio	27
Salaries of Public School Teachers	11
Public School Teachers Who Are Male	33
Eighth Grade Math Test Results	20
High School Math Enrollment	14
Public High School Graduation Rate	37
General Educational Development (GED) Test Results	47
Adult Illiteracy	27
Federal Revenue for Public Schools	18
State Revenue for Public Schools	7
Local Government Revenue for Public Schools	46
Total Public School Spending	12
Public School Spending on Instruction	1
Public School Spending on Noninstruction	49
Public School Spending on Support Staff	42
State and Local Government Spending on Public Schools	45

Federal Spending on School Improvement Programs	6
Gifted and Talented Students	15
Federal Spending on Education of Students with Disabilities	6
Student-Teacher Ratio in Catholic Elementary Schools	44
Student-Teacher Ratio in Catholic Secondary Schools	26
State Spending on Education	6
State and Local Government Spending on Education	27
Higher Education Tuition and Fees	9
Higher Education Revenue	25
Federal Spending on Higher Education	23
State Spending on Higher Education	1
State and Local Government Spending on Higher Education	5
State and Local Appropriations for Higher Education	36
Federal Spending on Higher Education Act Insured Loans	42
Federal Spending on National Guaranteed Student Loans	46
Federal Spending on Pell Grants	50
Default Rate in Perkins Student Loan Program	39
State Spending on Libraries	21

Energy
State Ranking

Total Spending on Energy	9
Net Generation of Electricity	28
Cost of Electricity	19
Spending on Electricity	9
Spending on Natural Gas	26
Spending on Gasoline	4
Spending on Petroleum	11
Spending on Coal	14
Total Energy Consumption	18
Electricity Consumption	21
Natural Gas Consumption	23
Petroleum Consumption	6
Coal Consumption	22
Power Plants	22
Nuclear Power Plants	34
Hydroelectric Power Plants	47

Environment
State Ranking

Federally Owned Land (acreage)	35
Loss of Wetlands	17
Environmental Protection Agency Spending	3
EPA Abatement, Control, and Compliance	5
State Spending on Environmental Programs	9
Environmental Programs as Part of State Budget	19
State Spending on Forest Programs	30
Total Tree Planting	26
Federal Tree Planting	47
Private Tree Planting	22
State Spending on Air Quality	7
State Spending on Water Quality	17
Federal Grants for Rural Water and Waste Disposal	14
Federal Spending on Wastewater Treatment Works	4
Hazardous Waste Sites on National Priority List	18

Federal Grants for Hazardous Substance
   Response   7
State Spending on Hazardous Waste   2

Health   *State Ranking*

State Health Rankings   26
State Spending on Health   3
Support for Public Health   45
Family and Business Spending on Health
   Care   14
HMO Enrollment   12
Medicaid Recipients   44
Medically Underserved Population   28
Lack of Health Care Access   46
Active Nonfederal Physicians   20
Active Nonfederal Nurses   7
Active Nonfederal Dentists   45
Average Cost per Hospital Stay   14
Average Cost per Day for Hospital Care   11
Average Cost per Day for Hospital Room   4
State Spending on Hospitals   37
Adequacy of Prenatal Care   20
Infants Born Receiving Late or No
   Prenatal Care   24
Infants Born with Low Birth Weight   12
Abortions   6
Immunizations of Two-Year-Olds   —
Overall Risk for Heart Disease   29
Risk Factor for Heart Disease
   (hypertension)   11
Deaths Due to Heart Disease   29
New Cancer Cases   10
Deaths Due to Cancer   12
Prevalence of Smoking   5
Prevalence of Diabetes   21
Deaths Due to Diabetes   3
Cost of Diabetes   18
AIDS Cases Reported   7
Gonorrhea Cases Reported   13
Syphilis Cases Reported   9
Tuberculosis Cases Reported   19
Hepatitis Cases Reported   1
Rabies Cases Reported   1
Lyme Disease Cases Reported   1
Beer Consumption   18
Wine Consumption   17
Liquor Consumption   5
Alcohol and Drug Treatment Admissions   19
Federal Spending on Alcohol, Drug
   Abuse, and Mental Health   22
Total Spending on Alcohol/Drug Abuse
   Services   22
State Spending on Alcohol/Drug Abuse
   Services   10
Hard-Core Cocaine Users   33
Federal Drug Grants to States   5

Population   *State Ranking*

Population   46
Population Density   8
Population in Metropolitan Areas   29
Population Under 18 Years Old   40
Population Over 65 Years Old   32
White Population   34
African American Population   10
Hispanic Population   26
Asian American Population   21
Native American Population   33
Catholic Population   23

Jewish Population   15
Marriages   39
Divorces   31
Births   19
Births to Single Mothers   17
Births to Single Teenagers   13
Adoptions   46
Adoption Option Index   48
Infant Mortality   2
Child Deaths and Suicides   19
Teen Violent Death Rate   50
Deaths   32

Recreation   *State Ranking*

State Parks and Recreation Areas   40
Visitors to State Parks and Recreation
   Areas   14
Revenues from State Parks and
   Recreation Areas   7
Spending on State Arts Agencies   7
Domestic Travel Spending   20
State Travel Office Budgets   27
Lodging Industry (rooms)   30
Participation in Exercise Walking   40
Participation in Swimming   21
Participation in Camping   48
Participation in Bowling   7
Bowling League Membership   10
Participation in Running/Jogging   47
Participation in Aerobics   49
Participation in Golf   25
Participation in Softball   39
Participation in Health Clubs   1
Participation in Tennis   40
Participation in Hunting   38
Participation in Baseball   8
Participation in Bicycle Riding   49
Number of Boats   9
Attendance at Parimutuel Racing   2
Revenue from Parimutuel Betting   23

Social Services   *State Ranking*

Federal Grants for Social Services   47
State Spending on Public Welfare   32
Persons in Poverty   50
Public Aid Recipients   38
Participants in Food Stamp Program   43
Households in Food Stamp Program   46
Percentage of Poor Using AFDC and
   Food Stamps   32
Federal Spending on Children and
   Family Services   20
Federal Women, Infants, and Children
   Food Program   37
Child Welfare Services   32
Child Abuse Cases Reported   —
Children in Poverty   44
Children Without Health Insurance   24
Children Who Are Hungry or at Risk   39
Federal Spending on Child Nutrition
   Programs   28
Federal Spending on Special Milk
   Program   49
National School Lunch Program
   Participants   39
Head Start Enrollment   5
Head Start Spending   21
Federal Spending on Rehabilitation
   Services/Handicapped Research   17

State Government   *State Ranking*

Financial World's State Rankings   16
Salaries of State Officials (governor)   26
Salaries of State Legislators   14
Women in State Legislatures   38
African Americans in State Legislatures   24
Hispanics in State Legislatures   21
Asian Americans in State Legislatures   6
Native Americans in State Legislatures   13
Turnover in State Legislatures   48
Length of State Legislative Sessions   35
State Bills in Regular Session   23
State Resolutions in Regular Session   42
State Bills in Special Session   1
State Resolutions in Special Session   19
Women in State Cabinets   28
Total Federal Funding to State
   Governments   43
Total State Spending   10
State General Expenditures   9
State Debt   2
State Spending on Interest on the
   General Debt   2
Total State Tax Revenue   3
State Revenue from Tax on Sales and
   Gross Receipts   47
State Revenue from General Sales Tax   —
State Revenue from Licenses   1
State Revenue from Motor Vehicle
   Licenses   40
State Revenue from Individual Income
   Taxes   4
State Revenue from Corporation Net
   Income Taxes   2
State Revenue from Severance Taxes   —
State Revenue from Property Taxes   —
State Revenue from Death and Gift
   Taxes   5
State Revenue from Documentary and
   Stock Transfers   1
State Revenue from Tax on Motor Fuels   22
State Revenue from Tax on Tobacco
   Products   20
Excise Tax on Cigarettes   22
Excise Tax on Gasoline   17
State Revenue from Lotteries   17

Transportation   *State Ranking*

Motor Vehicle Registrations   25
Automobile Registrations   15
Bus and Truck Registrations   33
Motorcycle Registrations   33
Driver Licenses   8
Federal Spending on Highway Trust
   Fund   11
Federal Spending on Mass
   Transportation   33
State Spending on Highways   2
Highway Deficiency   22
Bridge Deficiency   34
Traffic Fatalities   35
Traffic Fatalities per Miles Traveled   44
Motorcyclist Fatalities   29
Pedalcyclist Fatalities   8
Pedestrian Fatalities   16
Registered Aircraft   2
Registered Pilots   28
Federal Spending on Airport and
   Airway Trust Fund   51
Aircraft Fatalities   10

— *not applicable*   NA *not available*

Agriculture
State Ranking

Farm Acreage	—
Farmland as Portion of State	51
Net Farm Income	—
Government Payments to Farms	—
Federal Commodity Loans/Price Supports	49
Federal Spending on Rural Development	48
Rural Electric and Telephone Loan Guarantees	40
Foreign-Owned Agricultural Land	—

Business and Economy
State Ranking

Gross State Product	1
Retail Sales	49
Supermarket Sales	51
Commercial Bank Assets	3
Insured Commercial Bank Deposits	3
Fortune 500 Companies	2
Inc. 500 Companies	26
New Business Incorporations	5
Business Failures	24
Financial Aid to Minority Businesses	1
Women-Owned Businesses	1
Sales & Receipts of Women-Owned Businesses	49
African American-Owned Businesses	1
Sales & Receipts of African American-Owned Businesses	1
Hispanic-Owned Businesses	10
Sales & Receipts of Hispanic-Owned Businesses	8
Employees in Manufacturing	49
Manufacturing Shipments	50
Japanese-Owned U.S. Manufacturing Plants	48
Exports to Mexico	50
Change in Exports to Mexico	49
Existing Home Sales	3
Housing Starts	51
Average Annual Pay	1
Disposable Personal Income	3
Median Income of Families with Children	46
Federal Spending on Unemployment Insurance/Employment Services	2
Teen Unemployment	50
Bankruptcy Petitions Filed	43
Patents Issued to State Residents	39
Federal Spending on Community Development	1
Federal Spending on Economic Development Administration	14
Federal Spending on Urban Development Action Grants	1

Crime and Criminal Justice
State Ranking

Total Crimes	1
Violent Crimes	1
Murders	1
Rapes	28
Aggravated Assaults	1
Property Crimes	1
Robberies	1
Burglaries	1
Larcenies and Thefts	1
Motor Vehicle Thefts	1
State and Federal Prisoners	1
Capital Punishment	—
State Spending on Corrections	—
State Spending on Police	—
Inmates in Local Jails	2
Spending on Local Jails	9
Spending per Inmate for Local Jails	39
Employees at Local Jails	25
Juvenile Custody Rate	1
Federal Spending on Office of Justice Assistance Programs	7

Defense
State Ranking

Defense Grants to State and Local Governments	4
Total Defense Payroll	1
Total Army Payroll	3
Total Navy/Marine Corps Payroll	3
Total Air Force Payroll	4
Total Active-Duty Payroll	3
Army Active-Duty Payroll	4
Navy/Marine Corps Active-Duty Payroll	3
Air Force Active-Duty Payroll	3
Total Civilian Payroll	1
Army Civilian Payroll	1
Navy/Marine Corps Civilian Payroll	1
Air Force Civilian Payroll	4
Total Reserve and National Guard Payroll	1
Army Reserve and National Guard Payroll	1
Navy/Marine Corps Reserve and National Guard Payroll	1
Air Force Reserve and National Guard Payroll	51
Total Retired Military Payroll	30
Army Retired Military Payroll	22
Navy/Marine Corps Retired Military Payroll	24
Air Force Retired Military Payroll	30
Total Defense Prime Contracts	1
Army Prime Contracts	5
Navy/Marine Corps Prime Contracts	1
Air Force Prime Contracts	11
U.S. Military Installations	23
Construction of National Guard Centers	4

Education
State Ranking

School Age Population	51
Public Elementary and Secondary School Enrollment	51
Average Daily Attendance	41
Student-Teacher Ratio	49
Salaries of Public School Teachers	5
Public School Teachers Who Are Male	42
Eighth Grade Math Test Results	38
High School Math Enrollment	30
Public High School Graduation Rate	48
General Educational Development (GED) Test Results	43
Adult Illiteracy	NA
Federal Revenue for Public Schools	9
State Revenue for Public Schools	—
Local Government Revenue for Public Schools	1
Total Public School Spending	1
Public School Spending on Instruction	51
Public School Spending on Noninstruction	30
Public School Spending on Support Staff	7
State and Local Government Spending on Public Schools	51
Federal Spending on School Improvement Programs	4
Gifted and Talented Students	NA
Federal Spending on Education of Students with Disabilities	51
Student-Teacher Ratio in Catholic Elementary Schools	11
Student-Teacher Ratio in Catholic Secondary Schools	12
State Spending on Education	—
State and Local Government Spending on Education	51
Higher Education Tuition and Fees	1
Higher Education Revenue	1
Federal Spending on Higher Education	1
State Spending on Higher Education	—
State and Local Government Spending on Higher Education	51
State and Local Appropriations for Higher Education	51
Federal Spending on Higher Education Act Insured Loans	32
Federal Spending on National Guaranteed Student Loans	9
Federal Spending on Pell Grants	51
Default Rate in Perkins Student Loan Program	20
State Spending on Libraries	—

Energy
State Ranking

Total Spending on Energy	37
Net Generation of Electricity	50
Cost of Electricity	25
Spending on Electricity	2
Spending on Natural Gas	11
Spending on Gasoline	50
Spending on Petroleum	51
Spending on Coal	47
Total Energy Consumption	38
Electricity Consumption	6
Natural Gas Consumption	32
Petroleum Consumption	51
Coal Consumption	47
Power Plants	51
Nuclear Power Plants	34
Hydroelectric Power Plants	47

Environment
State Ranking

Federally Owned Land (acreage)	12
Loss of Wetlands	—
Environmental Protection Agency Spending	1
EPA Abatement, Control, and Compliance	1
State Spending on Environmental Programs	—
Environmental Programs as Part of State Budget	—
State Spending on Forest Programs	—
Total Tree Planting	—
Federal Tree Planting	—
Private Tree Planting	—
State Spending on Air Quality	—
State Spending on Water Quality	—
Federal Grants for Rural Water and Waste Disposal	50
Federal Spending on Wastewater Treatment Works	5
Hazardous Waste Sites on National Priority List	51

Federal Grants for Hazardous Substance
   Response   1
State Spending on Hazardous Waste   —

Health   *State Ranking*

State Health Rankings   —
State Spending on Health   —
Support for Public Health   —
Family and Business Spending on Health
   Care   17
HMO Enrollment   1
Medicaid Recipients   2
Medically Underserved Population   6
Lack of Health Care Access   NA
Active Nonfederal Physicians   1
Active Nonfederal Nurses   1
Active Nonfederal Dentists   1
Average Cost per Hospital Stay   1
Average Cost per Day for Hospital Care   2
Average Cost per Day for Hospital Room   16
State Spending on Hospitals   —
Adequacy of Prenatal Care   NA
Infants Born Receiving Late or No
   Prenatal Care   1
Infants Born with Low Birth Weight   1
Abortions   1
Immunizations of Two-Year-Olds   —
Overall Risk for Heart Disease   —
Risk Factor for Heart Disease
   (hypertension)   —
Deaths Due to Heart Disease   17
New Cancer Cases   1
Deaths Due to Cancer   1
Prevalence of Smoking   —
Prevalence of Diabetes   1
Deaths Due to Diabetes   7
Cost of Diabetes   1
AIDS Cases Reported   1
Gonorrhea Cases Reported   1
Syphilis Cases Reported   1
Tuberculosis Cases Reported   3
Hepatitis Cases Reported   2
Rabies Cases Reported   20
Lyme Disease Cases Reported   26
Beer Consumption   20
Wine Consumption   1
Liquor Consumption   2
Alcohol and Drug Treatment Admissions   3
Federal Spending on Alcohol, Drug
   Abuse, and Mental Health   1
Total Spending on Alcohol/Drug Abuse
   Services   1
State Spending on Alcohol/Drug Abuse
   Services   49
Hard-Core Cocaine Users   1
Federal Drug Grants to States   1

Population   *State Ranking*

Population   48
Population Density   1
Population in Metropolitan Areas   1
Population Under 18 Years Old   51
Population Over 65 Years Old   23
White Population   51
African American Population   1
Hispanic Population   14
Asian American Population   16
Native American Population   48
Catholic Population   1

Jewish Population   6
Marriages   43
Divorces   28
Births   11
Births to Single Mothers   1
Births to Single Teenagers   1
Adoptions   22
Adoption Option Index   49
Infant Mortality   1
Child Deaths and Suicides   4
Teen Violent Death Rate   1
Deaths   1

Recreation   *State Ranking*

State Parks and Recreation Areas   —
Visitors to State Parks and Recreation
   Areas   —
Revenues from State Parks and
   Recreation Areas   —
Spending on State Arts Agencies   2
Domestic Travel Spending   3
State Travel Office Budgets   —
Lodging Industry (rooms)   3
Participation in Exercise Walking   49
Participation in Swimming   40
Participation in Camping   49
Participation in Bowling   24
Bowling League Membership   1
Participation in Running/Jogging   8
Participation in Aerobics   9
Participation in Golf   48
Participation in Softball   8
Participation in Health Clubs   6
Participation in Tennis   3
Participation in Hunting   NA
Participation in Baseball   48
Participation in Bicycle Riding   45
Number of Boats   51
Attendance at Parimutuel Racing   —
Revenue from Parimutuel Betting   —

Social Services   *State Ranking*

Federal Grants for Social Services   51
State Spending on Public Welfare   —
Persons in Poverty   6
Public Aid Recipients   2
Participants in Food Stamp Program   13
Households in Food Stamp Program   8
Percentage of Poor Using AFDC and
   Food Stamps   20
Federal Spending on Children and
   Family Services   1
Federal Women, Infants, and Children
   Food Program   21
Child Welfare Services   27
Child Abuse Cases Reported   —
Children in Poverty   6
Children Without Health Insurance   10
Children Who Are Hungry or at Risk   5
Federal Spending on Child Nutrition
   Programs   12
Federal Spending on Special Milk
   Program   35
National School Lunch Program
   Participants   10
Head Start Enrollment   2
Head Start Spending   14
Federal Spending on Rehabilitation
   Services and Handicapped Research   1

State Government   *State Ranking*

Financial World's State Rankings   —
Salaries of State Officials (governor)   —
Salaries of State Legislators   —
Women in State Legislatures   —
African Americans in State Legislatures   —
Hispanics in State Legislatures   —
Asian Americans in State Legislatures   —
Native Americans in State Legislatures   —
Turnover in State Legislatures   —
Length of State Legislative Sessions   —
State Bills in Regular Session   —
State Resolutions in Regular Session   —
State Bills in Special Session   —
State Resolutions in Special Session   —
Women in State Cabinets   —
Total Federal Funding to State (District)
   Governments   1
Total State Spending   —
State General Expenditures   —
State Debt   —
State Spending on Interest on the
   General Debt   —
Total State Tax Revenue   —
State Revenue from Tax on Sales and
   Gross Receipts   —
State Revenue from General Sales Tax   —
State Revenue from Licenses   —
State Revenue from Motor Vehicle
   Licenses   —
State Revenue from Individual Income
   Taxes   —
State Revenue from Corporation Net
   Income Taxes   —
State Revenue from Severance Taxes   —
State Revenue from Property Taxes   —
State Revenue from Death and Gift
   Taxes   —
State Revenue from Documentary and
   Stock Transfers   —
State Revenue from Tax on Motor Fuels   —
State Revenue from Tax on Tobacco
   Products   —
Excise Tax on Cigarettes   —
Excise Tax on Gasoline   —
State Revenue from Lotteries   —

Transportation   *State Ranking*

Motor Vehicle Registrations   51
Automobile Registrations   51
Bus and Truck Registrations   51
Motorcycle Registrations   51
Driver Licenses   29
Federal Spending on Highway Trust
   Fund   5
Federal Spending on Mass
   Transportation   1
State Spending on Highways   —
Highway Deficiency   —
Bridge Deficiency   —
Traffic Fatalities   47
Traffic Fatalities per Miles Traveled   21
Motorcyclist Fatalities   32
Pedalcyclist Fatalities   40
Pedestrian Fatalities   2
Registered Aircraft   33
Registered Pilots   51
Federal Spending on Airport and
   Airway Trust Fund   50
Aircraft Fatalities   50

— *not applicable*   NA *not available*

Agriculture
State Ranking

Farm Acreage	30
Farmland as Portion of State	30
Net Farm Income	23
Government Payments to Farms	40
Federal Commodity Loans/Price Supports	19
Federal Spending on Rural Development	44
Rural Electric and Telephone Loan Guarantees	19
Foreign-Owned Agricultural Land	7

Business and Economy
State Ranking

Gross State Product	38
Retail Sales	14
Supermarket Sales	18
Commercial Bank Assets	26
Insured Commercial Bank Deposits	22
Fortune 500 Companies	39
Inc. 500 Companies	17
New Business Incorporations	3
Business Failures	15
Financial Aid to Minority Businesses	13
Women-Owned Businesses	25
Sales & Receipts of Women-Owned Businesses	3
African American-Owned Businesses	15
Sales & Receipts of African American-Owned Businesses	12
Hispanic-Owned Businesses	3
Sales & Receipts of Hispanic-Owned Businesses	2
Employees in Manufacturing	15
Manufacturing Shipments	47
Japanese-Owned U.S. Manufacturing Plants	23
Exports to Mexico	27
Change in Exports to Mexico	21
Existing Home Sales	40
Housing Starts	4
Average Annual Pay	28
Disposable Personal Income	17
Median Income of Families with Children	39
Federal Spending on Unemployment Insurance/Employment Services	51
Teen Unemployment	6
Bankruptcy Petitions Filed	22
Patents Issued to State Residents	29
Federal Spending on Community Development	42
Federal Spending on Economic Development Administration	49
Federal Spending on Urban Development Action Grants	18

Crime and Criminal Justice
State Ranking

Total Crimes	2
Violent Crimes	2
Murders	19
Rapes	11
Aggravated Assaults	3
Property Crimes	2
Robberies	6
Burglaries	2
Larcenies and Thefts	2
Motor Vehicle Thefts	10
State and Federal Prisoners	10
Capital Punishment	2

State Spending on Corrections	24
State Spending on Police	32
Inmates in Local Jails	4
Spending on Local Jails	5
Spending per Inmate for Local Jails	19
Employees at Local Jails	15
Juvenile Custody Rate	26
Federal Spending on Office of Justice Assistance Programs	37

Defense
State Ranking

Defense Grants to State and Local Governments	38
Total Defense Payroll	21
Total Army Payroll	32
Total Navy/Marine Corps Payroll	10
Total Air Force Payroll	20
Total Active-Duty Payroll	20
Army Active-Duty Payroll	27
Navy/Marine Corps Active-Duty Payroll	8
Air Force Active-Duty Payroll	22
Total Civilian Payroll	29
Army Civilian Payroll	51
Navy/Marine Corps Civilian Payroll	12
Air Force Civilian Payroll	23
Total Reserve and National Guard Payroll	51
Army Reserve and National Guard Payroll	51
Navy/Marine Corps Reserve and National Guard Payroll	10
Air Force Reserve and National Guard Payroll	45
Total Retired Military Payroll	3
Army Retired Military Payroll	13
Navy/Marine Corps Retired Military Payroll	3
Air Force Retired Military Payroll	6
Total Defense Prime Contracts	24
Army Prime Contracts	21
Navy/Marine Corps Prime Contracts	21
Air Force Prime Contracts	12
U.S. Military Installations	4
Construction of National Guard Centers	35

Education
State Ranking

School Age Population	50
Public Elementary and Secondary School Enrollment	4
Average Daily Attendance	37
Student-Teacher Ratio	20
Salaries of Public School Teachers	27
Public School Teachers Who Are Male	38
Eighth Grade Math Test Results	33
High School Math Enrollment	4
Public High School Graduation Rate	49
General Educational Development (GED) Test Results	13
Adult Illiteracy	5
Federal Revenue for Public Schools	24
State Revenue for Public Schools	21
Local Government Revenue for Public Schools	31
Total Public School Spending	23
Public School Spending on Instruction	33
Public School Spending on Noninstruction	18
Public School Spending on Support Staff	6
State and Local Government Spending on Public Schools	28

Federal Spending on School Improvement Programs	51
Gifted and Talented Students	29
Federal Spending on Education of Students with Disabilities	39
Student-Teacher Ratio in Catholic Elementary Schools	18
Student-Teacher Ratio in Catholic Secondary Schools	8
State Spending on Education	42
State and Local Government Spending on Education	41
Higher Education Tuition and Fees	31
Higher Education Revenue	40
Federal Spending on Higher Education	46
State Spending on Higher Education	49
State and Local Government Spending on Higher Education	45
State and Local Appropriations for Higher Education	18
Federal Spending on Higher Education Act Insured Loans	44
Federal Spending on National Guaranteed Student Loans	34
Federal Spending on Pell Grants	34
Default Rate in Perkins Student Loan Program	14
State Spending on Libraries	38

Energy
State Ranking

Total Spending on Energy	47
Net Generation of Electricity	33
Cost of Electricity	16
Spending on Electricity	12
Spending on Natural Gas	47
Spending on Gasoline	38
Spending on Petroleum	38
Spending on Coal	31
Total Energy Consumption	45
Electricity Consumption	26
Natural Gas Consumption	46
Petroleum Consumption	30
Coal Consumption	34
Power Plants	48
Nuclear Power Plants	26
Hydroelectric Power Plants	45

Environment
State Ranking

Federally Owned Land (acreage)	20
Loss of Wetlands	27
Environmental Protection Agency Spending	33
EPA Abatement, Control, and Compliance	50
State Spending on Environmental Programs	13
Environmental Programs as Part of State Budget	11
State Spending on Forest Programs	18
Total Tree Planting	5
Federal Tree Planting	4
Private Tree Planting	5
State Spending on Air Quality	38
State Spending on Water Quality	9
Federal Grants for Rural Water and Waste Disposal	36
Federal Spending on Wastewater Treatment Works	32
Hazardous Waste Sites on National Priority List	6

Federal Grants for Hazardous Substance
Response 40
State Spending on Hazardous Waste 14

Health · *State Ranking*

State Health Rankings 41
State Spending on Health 12
Support for Public Health 35
Family and Business Spending on Health
Care 29
HMO Enrollment 22
Medicaid Recipients 28
Medically Underserved Population 16
Lack of Health Care Access 21
Active Nonfederal Physicians 17
Active Nonfederal Nurses 30
Active Nonfederal Dentists 36
Average Cost per Hospital Stay 10
Average Cost per Day for Hospital Care 12
Average Cost per Day for Hospital Room 25
State Spending on Hospitals 48
Adequacy of Prenatal Care 44
Infants Born Receiving Late or No
Prenatal Care 7
Infants Born with Low Birth Weight 16
Abortions 8
Immunizations of Two-Year-Olds —
Overall Risk for Heart Disease 32
Risk Factor for Heart Disease
(hypertension) 3
Deaths Due to Heart Disease 4
New Cancer Cases 2
Deaths Due to Cancer 2
Prevalence of Smoking 30
Prevalence of Diabetes 3
Deaths Due to Diabetes 27
Cost of Diabetes 3
AIDS Cases Reported 3
Gonorrhea Cases Reported 17
Syphilis Cases Reported 18
Tuberculosis Cases Reported 9
Hepatitis Cases Reported 31
Rabies Cases Reported 42
Lyme Disease Cases Reported 34
Beer Consumption 11
Wine Consumption 16
Liquor Consumption 6
Alcohol and Drug Treatment Admissions 28
Federal Spending on Alcohol, Drug
Abuse, and Mental Health 21
Total Spending on Alcohol/Drug Abuse
Services 20
State Spending on Alcohol/Drug Abuse
Services 22
Hard-Core Cocaine Users 16
Federal Drug Grants to States 50

Population · · · · · · · · · · · · · · · · · *State Ranking*

Population 4
Population Density 11
Population in Metropolitan Areas 8
Population Under 18 Years Old 50
Population Over 65 Years Old 1
White Population 29
African American Population 16
Hispanic Population 7
Asian American Population 23
Native American Population 34
Catholic Population 32

Jewish Population 3
Marriages 10
Divorces 8
Births 33
Births to Single Mothers 10
Births to Single Teenagers 14
Adoptions 10
Adoption Option Index 16
Infant Mortality 25
Child Deaths and Suicides 11
Teen Violent Death Rate 23
Deaths 5

Recreation · · · · · · · · · · · · · · · · · *State Ranking*

State Parks and Recreation Areas 22
Visitors to State Parks and Recreation
Areas 46
Revenues from State Parks and
Recreation Areas 29
Spending on State Arts Agencies 8
Domestic Travel Spending 5
State Travel Office Budgets 44
Lodging Industry (rooms) 6
Participation in Exercise Walking 36
Participation in Swimming 15
Participation in Camping 46
Participation in Bowling 33
Bowling League Membership 32
Participation in Running/Jogging 34
Participation in Aerobics 38
Participation in Golf 28
Participation in Softball 45
Participation in Health Clubs 25
Participation in Tennis 24
Participation in Hunting 41
Participation in Baseball 42
Participation in Bicycle Riding 17
Number of Boats 21
Attendance at Parimutuel Racing 23
Revenue from Parimutuel Betting 15

Social Services · · · · · · · · · · · · · · · *State Ranking*

Federal Grants for Social Services 45
State Spending on Public Welfare 38
Persons in Poverty 16
Public Aid Recipients 36
Participants in Food Stamp Program 27
Households in Food Stamp Program 38
Percentage of Poor Using AFDC and
Food Stamps 38
Federal Spending on Children and
Family Services 49
Federal Women, Infants, and Children
Food Program 48
Child Welfare Services 44
Child Abuse Cases Reported —
Children in Poverty 18
Children Without Health Insurance 8
Children Who Are Hungry or at Risk 20
Federal Spending on Child Nutrition
Programs 26
Federal Spending on Special Milk
Program 44
National School Lunch Program
Participants 25
Head Start Enrollment 44
Head Start Spending 22
Federal Spending on Rehabilitation
Services/Handicapped Research 43

State Government · · · · · · · · · · · *State Ranking*

Financial World's State Rankings 14
Salaries of State Officials (governor) 10
Salaries of State Legislators 18
Women in State Legislatures 31
African Americans in State Legislatures 10
Hispanics in State Legislatures 6
Asian Americans in State Legislatures 5
Native Americans in State Legislatures 12
Turnover in State Legislatures 35
Length of State Legislative Sessions 33
State Bills in Regular Session 32
State Resolutions in Regular Session 5
State Bills in Special Session 18
State Resolutions in Special Session 1
Women in State Cabinets —
Total Federal Funding to State
Governments 21
Total State Spending 47
State General Expenditures 45
State Debt 39
State Spending on Interest on the
General Debt 44
Total State Tax Revenue 39
State Revenue from Tax on Sales and
Gross Receipts 6
State Revenue from General Sales Tax 5
State Revenue from Licenses 34
State Revenue from Motor Vehicle
Licenses 25
State Revenue from Individual Income
Taxes —
State Revenue from Corporation Net
Income Taxes 40
State Revenue from Severance Taxes 20
State Revenue from Property Taxes 11
State Revenue from Death and Gift
Taxes 9
State Revenue from Documentary and
Stock Transfers 2
State Revenue from Tax on Motor Fuels 46
State Revenue from Tax on Tobacco
Products 10
Excise Tax on Cigarettes 11
Excise Tax on Gasoline 50
State Revenue from Lotteries 1

Transportation · · · · · · · · · · · · · · *State Ranking*

Motor Vehicle Registrations 31
Automobile Registrations 20
Bus and Truck Registrations 40
Motorcycle Registrations 30
Driver Licenses 6
Federal Spending on Highway Trust
Fund 51
Federal Spending on Mass
Transportation 21
State Spending on Highways 47
Highway Deficiency 1
Bridge Deficiency 41
Traffic Fatalities 21
Traffic Fatalities per Miles Traveled 15
Motorcyclist Fatalities 16
Pedalcyclist Fatalities 1
Pedestrian Fatalities 3
Registered Aircraft 22
Registered Pilots 13
Federal Spending on Airport and
Airway Trust Fund 16
Aircraft Fatalities 20

— *not applicable* NA *not available*

Agriculture
State Ranking

Farm Acreage	27
Farmland as Portion of State	28
Net Farm Income	21
Government Payments to Farms	26
Federal Commodity Loans/Price Supports	17
Federal Spending on Rural Development	29
Rural Electric and Telephone Loan Guarantees	5
Foreign-Owned Agricultural Land	12

Business and Economy
State Ranking

Gross State Product	19
Retail Sales	22
Supermarket Sales	28
Commercial Bank Assets	24
Insured Commercial Bank Deposits	31
Fortune 500 Companies	22
Inc. 500 Companies	10
New Business Incorporations	13
Business Failures	6
Financial Aid to Minority Businesses	5
Women-Owned Businesses	34
Sales & Receipts of Women-Owned Businesses	48
African American-Owned Businesses	6
Sales & Receipts of African American-Owned Businesses	4
Hispanic-Owned Businesses	27
Sales & Receipts of Hispanic-Owned Businesses	25
Employees in Manufacturing	11
Manufacturing Shipments	16
Japanese-Owned U.S. Manufacturing Plants	4
Exports to Mexico	15
Change in Exports to Mexico	13
Existing Home Sales	45
Housing Starts	9
Average Annual Pay	21
Disposable Personal Income	30
Median Income of Families with Children	30
Federal Spending on Unemployment Insurance/Employment Services	45
Teen Unemployment	20
Bankruptcy Petitions Filed	2
Patents Issued to State Residents	37
Federal Spending on Community Development	34
Federal Spending on Economic Development Administration	15
Federal Spending on Urban Development Action Grants	6

Crime and Criminal Justice
State Ranking

Total Crimes	7
Violent Crimes	14
Murders	5
Rapes	22
Aggravated Assaults	18
Property Crimes	7
Robberies	11
Burglaries	7
Larcenies and Thefts	11
Motor Vehicle Thefts	16
State and Federal Prisoners	12
Capital Punishment	4

State Spending on Corrections	6
State Spending on Police	36
Inmates in Local Jails	1
Spending on Local Jails	8
Spending per Inmate for Local Jails	40
Employees at Local Jails	3
Juvenile Custody Rate	21
Federal Spending on Office of Justice Assistance Programs	42

Defense
State Ranking

Defense Grants to State and Local Governments	33
Total Defense Payroll	12
Total Army Payroll	8
Total Navy/Marine Corps Payroll	17
Total Air Force Payroll	23
Total Active-Duty Payroll	13
Army Active-Duty Payroll	7
Navy/Marine Corps Active-Duty Payroll	18
Air Force Active-Duty Payroll	31
Total Civilian Payroll	13
Army Civilian Payroll	13
Navy/Marine Corps Civilian Payroll	18
Air Force Civilian Payroll	7
Total Reserve and National Guard Payroll	12
Army Reserve and National Guard Payroll	6
Navy/Marine Corps Reserve and National Guard Payroll	11
Air Force Reserve and National Guard Payroll	32
Total Retired Military Payroll	13
Army Retired Military Payroll	2
Navy/Marine Corps Retired Military Payroll	20
Air Force Retired Military Payroll	27
Total Defense Prime Contracts	29
Army Prime Contracts	23
Navy/Marine Corps Prime Contracts	27
Air Force Prime Contracts	19
U.S. Military Installations	8
Construction of National Guard Centers	37

Education
State Ranking

School Age Population	21
Public Elementary and Secondary School Enrollment	9
Average Daily Attendance	24
Student-Teacher Ratio	12
Salaries of Public School Teachers	30
Public School Teachers Who Are Male	51
Eighth Grade Math Test Results	26
High School Math Enrollment	NA
Public High School Graduation Rate	47
General Educational Development (GED) Test Results	21
Adult Illiteracy	12
Federal Revenue for Public Schools	23
State Revenue for Public Schools	19
Local Government Revenue for Public Schools	34
Total Public School Spending	36
Public School Spending on Instruction	12
Public School Spending on Noninstruction	15
Public School Spending on Support Staff	34
State and Local Government Spending on Public Schools	16

Federal Spending on School Improvement Programs	23
Gifted and Talented Students	21
Federal Spending on Education of Students with Disabilities	47
Student-Teacher Ratio in Catholic Elementary Schools	24
Student-Teacher Ratio in Catholic Secondary Schools	23
State Spending on Education	26
State and Local Government Spending on Education	32
Higher Education Tuition and Fees	26
Higher Education Revenue	12
Federal Spending on Higher Education	22
State Spending on Higher Education	40
State and Local Government Spending on Higher Education	39
State and Local Appropriations for Higher Education	11
Federal Spending on Higher Education Act Insured Loans	40
Federal Spending on National Guaranteed Student Loans	50
Federal Spending on Pell Grants	42
Default Rate in Perkins Student Loan Program	9
State Spending on Libraries	17

Energy
State Ranking

Total Spending on Energy	18
Net Generation of Electricity	17
Cost of Electricity	23
Spending on Electricity	8
Spending on Natural Gas	27
Spending on Gasoline	24
Spending on Petroleum	32
Spending on Coal	11
Total Energy Consumption	26
Electricity Consumption	20
Natural Gas Consumption	31
Petroleum Consumption	25
Coal Consumption	15
Power Plants	41
Nuclear Power Plants	23
Hydroelectric Power Plants	24

Environment
State Ranking

Federally Owned Land (acreage)	22
Loss of Wetlands	46
Environmental Protection Agency Spending	34
EPA Abatement, Control, and Compliance	46
State Spending on Environmental Programs	44
Environmental Programs as Part of State Budget	40
State Spending on Forest Programs	9
Total Tree Planting	2
Federal Tree Planting	12
Private Tree Planting	2
State Spending on Air Quality	40
State Spending on Water Quality	48
Federal Grants for Rural Water and Waste Disposal	33
Federal Spending on Wastewater Treatment Works	31
Hazardous Waste Sites on National Priority List	26

Federal Grants for Hazardous Substance
   Response   51
State Spending on Hazardous Waste   43

Health   *State Ranking*

State Health Rankings   36
State Spending on Health   26
Support for Public Health   5
Family and Business Spending on Health
   Care   22
HMO Enrollment   38
Medicaid Recipients   15
Medically Underserved Population   12
Lack of Health Care Access   14
Active Nonfederal Physicians   32
Active Nonfederal Nurses   38
Active Nonfederal Dentists   44
Average Cost per Hospital Stay   36
Average Cost per Day for Hospital Care   31
Average Cost per Day for Hospital Room   48
State Spending on Hospitals   27
Adequacy of Prenatal Care   36
Infants Born Receiving Late or No
   Prenatal Care   12
Infants Born with Low Birth Weight   4
Abortions   22
Immunizations of Two-Year-Olds   —
Overall Risk for Heart Disease   19
Risk Factor for Heart Disease
   (hypertension)   24
Deaths Due to Heart Disease   34
New Cancer Cases   42
Deaths Due to Cancer   43
Prevalence of Smoking   20
Prevalence of Diabetes   26
Deaths Due to Diabetes   41
Cost of Diabetes   27
AIDS Cases Reported   8
Gonorrhea Cases Reported   2
Syphilis Cases Reported   10
Tuberculosis Cases Reported   5
Hepatitis Cases Reported   36
Rabies Cases Reported   13
Lyme Disease Cases Reported   30
Beer Consumption   34
Wine Consumption   25
Liquor Consumption   15
Alcohol and Drug Treatment Admissions   25
Federal Spending on Alcohol, Drug
   Abuse, and Mental Health   38
Total Spending on Alcohol/Drug Abuse
   Services   29
State Spending on Alcohol/Drug Abuse
   Services   16
Hard-Core Cocaine Users   14
Federal Drug Grants to States   47

Population   *State Ranking*

Population   11
Population Density   22
Population in Metropolitan Areas   31
Population Under 18 Years Old   16
Population Over 65 Years Old   48
White Population   44
African American Population   5
Hispanic Population   33
Asian American Population   24
Native American Population   42
Catholic Population   46

Jewish Population   19
Marriages   20
Divorces   12
Births   12
Births to Single Mothers   6
Births to Single Teenagers   6
Adoptions   31
Adoption Option Index   30
Infant Mortality   3
Child Deaths and Suicides   16
Teen Violent Death Rate   13
Deaths   34

Recreation   *State Ranking*

State Parks and Recreation Areas   47
Visitors to State Parks and Recreation
   Areas   29
Revenues from State Parks and
   Recreation Areas   21
Spending on State Arts Agencies   37
Domestic Travel Spending   22
State Travel Office Budgets   33
Lodging Industry (rooms)   17
Participation in Exercise Walking   19
Participation in Swimming   32
Participation in Camping   34
Participation in Bowling   34
Bowling League Membership   45
Participation in Running/Jogging   19
Participation in Aerobics   35
Participation in Golf   36
Participation in Softball   16
Participation in Health Clubs   15
Participation in Tennis   5
Participation in Hunting   23
Participation in Baseball   38
Participation in Bicycle Riding   33
Number of Boats   27
Attendance at Parimutuel Racing   —
Revenue from Parimutuel Betting   —

Social Services   *State Ranking*

Federal Grants for Social Services   16
State Spending on Public Welfare   25
Persons in Poverty   10
Public Aid Recipients   11
Participants in Food Stamp Program   21
Households in Food Stamp Program   17
Percentage of Poor Using AFDC and
   Food Stamps   41
Federal Spending on Children and
   Family Services   46
Federal Women, Infants, and Children
   Food Program   13
Child Welfare Services   11
Child Abuse Cases Reported   —
Children in Poverty   16
Children Without Health Insurance   21
Children Who Are Hungry or at Risk   22
Federal Spending on Child Nutrition
   Programs   16
Federal Spending on Special Milk
   Program   48
National School Lunch Program
   Participants   11
Head Start Enrollment   35
Head Start Spending   24
Federal Spending on Rehabilitation
   Services/Handicapped Research   29

State Government   *State Ranking*

Financial World's State Rankings   18
Salaries of State Officials (governor)   17
Salaries of State Legislators   31
Women in State Legislatures   32
African Americans in State Legislatures   5
Hispanics in State Legislatures   21
Asian Americans in State Legislatures   6
Native Americans in State Legislatures   12
Turnover in State Legislatures   14
Length of State Legislative Sessions   38
State Bills in Regular Session   12
State Resolutions in Regular Session   9
State Bills in Special Session   9
State Resolutions in Special Session   1
Women in State Cabinets   —
Total Federal Funding to State
   Governments   42
Total State Spending   40
State General Expenditures   38
State Debt   46
State Spending on Interest on the
   General Debt   46
Total State Tax Revenue   35
State Revenue from Tax on Sales and
   Gross Receipts   35
State Revenue from General Sales Tax   21
State Revenue from Licenses   50
State Revenue from Motor Vehicle
   Licenses   50
State Revenue from Individual Income
   Taxes   16
State Revenue from Corporation Net
   Income Taxes   24
State Revenue from Severance Taxes   —
State Revenue from Property Taxes   24
State Revenue from Death and Gift
   Taxes   34
State Revenue from Documentary and
   Stock Transfers   23
State Revenue from Tax on Motor Fuels   44
State Revenue from Tax on Tobacco
   Products   43
Excise Tax on Cigarettes   44
Excise Tax on Gasoline   49
State Revenue from Lotteries   —

Transportation   *State Ranking*

Motor Vehicle Registrations   12
Automobile Registrations   16
Bus and Truck Registrations   14
Motorcycle Registrations   36
Driver Licenses   22
Federal Spending on Highway Trust
   Fund   44
Federal Spending on Mass
   Transportation   10
State Spending on Highways   42
Highway Deficiency   25
Bridge Deficiency   36
Traffic Fatalities   14
Traffic Fatalities per Miles Traveled   26
Motorcyclist Fatalities   39
Pedalcyclist Fatalities   22
Pedestrian Fatalities   15
Registered Aircraft   31
Registered Pilots   25
Federal Spending on Airport and
   Airway Trust Fund   20
Aircraft Fatalities   29

— not applicable   NA not available

Agriculture · State Ranking

Farm Acreage	41
Farmland as Portion of State	24
Net Farm Income	39
Government Payments to Farms	46
Federal Commodity Loans/Price Supports	41
Federal Spending on Rural Development	36
Rural Electric and Telephone Loan Guarantees	40
Foreign-Owned Agricultural Land	2

Business and Economy · State Ranking

Gross State Product	10
Retail Sales	1
Supermarket Sales	4
Commercial Bank Assets	5
Insured Commercial Bank Deposits	5
Fortune 500 Companies	42
Inc. 500 Companies	47
New Business Incorporations	9
Business Failures	51
Financial Aid to Minority Businesses	3
Women-Owned Businesses	2
Sales & Receipts of Women-Owned Businesses	40
African American-Owned Businesses	39
Sales & Receipts of African American-Owned Businesses	41
Hispanic-Owned Businesses	11
Sales & Receipts of Hispanic-Owned Businesses	10
Employees in Manufacturing	47
Manufacturing Shipments	48
Japanese-Owned U.S. Manufacturing Plants	23
Exports to Mexico	35
Change in Exports to Mexico	1
Existing Home Sales	44
Housing Starts	5
Average Annual Pay	13
Disposable Personal Income	11
Median Income of Families with Children	7
Federal Spending on Unemployment Insurance/Employment Services	24
Teen Unemployment	47
Bankruptcy Petitions Filed	51
Patents Issued to State Residents	48
Federal Spending on Community Development	24
Federal Spending on Economic Development Administration	30
Federal Spending on Urban Development Action Grants	33

Crime and Criminal Justice · State Ranking

Total Crimes	17
Violent Crimes	44
Murders	38
Rapes	33
Aggravated Assaults	46
Property Crimes	8
Robberies	38
Burglaries	19
Larcenies and Thefts	6
Motor Vehicle Thefts	36
State and Federal Prisoners	39
Capital Punishment	—
State Spending on Corrections	23
State Spending on Police	50
Inmates in Local Jails	—
Spending on Local Jails	—
Spending per Inmate for Local Jails	—
Employees at Local Jails	—
Juvenile Custody Rate	51
Federal Spending on Office of Justice Assistance Programs	15

Defense · State Ranking

Defense Grants to State and Local Governments	27
Total Defense Payroll	2
Total Army Payroll	2
Total Navy/Marine Corps Payroll	1
Total Air Force Payroll	13
Total Active-Duty Payroll	1
Army Active-Duty Payroll	1
Navy/Marine Corps Active-Duty Payroll	1
Air Force Active-Duty Payroll	10
Total Civilian Payroll	3
Army Civilian Payroll	6
Navy/Marine Corps Civilian Payroll	2
Air Force Civilian Payroll	6
Total Reserve and National Guard Payroll	10
Army Reserve and National Guard Payroll	10
Navy/Marine Corps Reserve and National Guard Payroll	36
Air Force Reserve and National Guard Payroll	6
Total Retired Military Payroll	5
Army Retired Military Payroll	4
Navy/Marine Corps Retired Military Payroll	2
Air Force Retired Military Payroll	20
Total Defense Prime Contracts	13
Army Prime Contracts	11
Navy/Marine Corps Prime Contracts	11
Air Force Prime Contracts	18
U.S. Military Installations	9
Construction of National Guard Centers	23

Education · State Ranking

School Age Population	38
Public Elementary and Secondary School Enrollment	42
Average Daily Attendance	31
Student-Teacher Ratio	10
Salaries of Public School Teachers	18
Public School Teachers Who Are Male	43
Eighth Grade Math Test Results	35
High School Math Enrollment	13
Public High School Graduation Rate	4
General Educational Development (GED) Test Results	32
Adult Illiteracy	5
Federal Revenue for Public Schools	7
State Revenue for Public Schools	1
Local Government Revenue for Public Schools	51
Total Public School Spending	32
Public School Spending on Instruction	20
Public School Spending on Noninstruction	8
Public School Spending on Support Staff	25
State and Local Government Spending on Public Schools	50
Federal Spending on School Improvement Programs	15
Gifted and Talented Students	14
Federal Spending on Education of Students with Disabilities	50
Student-Teacher Ratio in Catholic Elementary Schools	3
Student-Teacher Ratio in Catholic Secondary Schools	38
State Spending on Education	5
State and Local Government Spending on Education	49
Higher Education Tuition and Fees	46
Higher Education Revenue	27
Federal Spending on Higher Education	28
State Spending on Higher Education	7
State and Local Government Spending on Higher Education	30
State and Local Appropriations for Higher Education	2
Federal Spending on Higher Education Act Insured Loans	46
Federal Spending on National Guaranteed Student Loans	38
Federal Spending on Pell Grants	49
Default Rate in Perkins Student Loan Program	34
State Spending on Libraries	1

Energy · State Ranking

Total Spending on Energy	22
Net Generation of Electricity	44
Cost of Electricity	7
Spending on Electricity	34
Spending on Natural Gas	50
Spending on Gasoline	43
Spending on Petroleum	4
Spending on Coal	50
Total Energy Consumption	41
Electricity Consumption	48
Natural Gas Consumption	51
Petroleum Consumption	4
Coal Consumption	49
Power Plants	21
Nuclear Power Plants	34
Hydroelectric Power Plants	35

Environment · State Ranking

Federally Owned Land (acreage)	15
Loss of Wetlands	48
Environmental Protection Agency Spending	6
EPA Abatement, Control, and Compliance	18
State Spending on Environmental Programs	29
Environmental Programs as Part of State Budget	44
State Spending on Forest Programs	19
Total Tree Planting	39
Federal Tree Planting	47
Private Tree Planting	41
State Spending on Air Quality	1
State Spending on Water Quality	24
Federal Grants for Rural Water and Waste Disposal	50
Federal Spending on Wastewater Treatment Works	3
Hazardous Waste Sites on National Priority List	47

Federal Grants for Hazardous Substance
  Response — 37
State Spending on Hazardous Waste — 30

Health — State Ranking

State Health Rankings — 2
State Spending on Health — 2
Support for Public Health — 14
Family and Business Spending on Health
  Care — 7
HMO Enrollment — 6
Medicaid Recipients — 39
Medically Underserved Population — 45
Lack of Health Care Access — 50
Active Nonfederal Physicians — 10
Active Nonfederal Nurses — 39
Active Nonfederal Dentists — 2
Average Cost per Hospital Stay — 5
Average Cost per Day for Hospital Care — 27
Average Cost per Day for Hospital Room — 9
State Spending on Hospitals — 6
Adequacy of Prenatal Care — 38
Infants Born Receiving Late or No
  Prenatal Care — 17
Infants Born with Low Birth Weight — 21
Abortions — 4
Immunizations of Two-Year-Olds — —
Overall Risk for Heart Disease — 12
Risk Factor for Heart Disease
  (hypertension) — 34
Deaths Due to Heart Disease — 48
New Cancer Cases — 48
Deaths Due to Cancer — 49
Prevalence of Smoking — 45
Prevalence of Diabetes — 2
Deaths Due to Diabetes — 36
Cost of Diabetes — 2
AIDS Cases Reported — 16
Gonorrhea Cases Reported — 41
Syphilis Cases Reported — 44
Tuberculosis Cases Reported — 2
Hepatitis Cases Reported — 6
Rabies Cases Reported — 48
Lyme Disease Cases Reported — 38
Beer Consumption — 6
Wine Consumption — 14
Liquor Consumption — 26
Alcohol and Drug Treatment Admissions — 44
Federal Spending on Alcohol, Drug
  Abuse, and Mental Health — 8
Total Spending on Alcohol/Drug Abuse
  Services — 27
State Spending on Alcohol/Drug Abuse
  Services — 29
Hard-Core Cocaine Users — 9
Federal Drug Grants to States — 10

Population — State Ranking

Population — 41
Population Density — 14
Population in Metropolitan Areas — 20
Population Under 18 Years Old — 34
Population Over 65 Years Old — 38
White Population — 50
African American Population — 38
Hispanic Population — 11
Asian American Population — 1
Native American Population — 24
Catholic Population — 22

Jewish Population — 27
Marriages — 2
Divorces — 27
Births — 8
Births to Single Mothers — 31
Births to Single Teenagers — 36
Adoptions — 48
Adoption Option Index — 45
Infant Mortality — 47
Child Deaths and Suicides — 41
Teen Violent Death Rate — 46
Deaths — 49

Recreation — State Ranking

State Parks and Recreation Areas — 32
Visitors to State Parks and Recreation
  Areas — 2
Revenues from State Parks and
  Recreation Areas — 33
Spending on State Arts Agencies — 1
Domestic Travel Spending — 2
State Travel Office Budgets — 1
Lodging Industry (rooms) — 2
Participation in Exercise Walking — NA
Participation in Swimming — NA
Participation in Camping — NA
Participation in Bowling — NA
Bowling League Membership — 24
Participation in Running/Jogging — NA
Participation in Aerobics — NA
Participation in Golf — NA
Participation in Softball — NA
Participation in Health Clubs — NA
Participation in Tennis — NA
Participation in Hunting — NA
Participation in Baseball — NA
Participation in Bicycle Riding — NA
Number of Boats — 50
Attendance at Parimutuel Racing — —
Revenue from Parimutuel Betting — —

Social Services — State Ranking

Federal Grants for Social Services — 28
State Spending on Public Welfare — 20
Persons in Poverty — 49
Public Aid Recipients — 29
Participants in Food Stamp Program — 10
Households in Food Stamp Program — 20
Percentage of Poor Using AFDC and
  Food Stamps — 2
Federal Spending on Children and
  Family Services — 9
Federal Women, Infants, and Children
  Food Program — 28
Child Welfare Services — 30
Child Abuse Cases Reported — —
Children in Poverty — 46
Children Without Health Insurance — 35
Children Who Are Hungry or at Risk — 37
Federal Spending on Child Nutrition
  Programs — 29
Federal Spending on Special Milk
  Program — 45
National School Lunch Program
  Participants — 22
Head Start Enrollment — 8
Head Start Spending — 11
Federal Spending on Rehabilitation
  Services and Handicapped Research — 46

State Government — State Ranking

Financial World's State Rankings — 15
Salaries of State Officials (governor) — 15
Salaries of State Legislators — 12
Women in State Legislatures — 16
African Americans in State Legislatures — 43
Hispanics in State Legislatures — 21
Asian Americans in State Legislatures — 1
Native Americans in State Legislatures — 2
Turnover in State Legislatures — 41
Length of State Legislative Sessions — 30
State Bills in Regular Session — 46
State Resolutions in Regular Session — 29
State Bills in Special Session — 1
State Resolutions in Special Session — 19
Women in State Cabinets — 19
Total Federal Funding to State
  Governments — 6
Total State Spending — 4
State General Expenditures — 4
State Debt — 6
State Spending on Interest on the
  General Debt — 9
Total State Tax Revenue — 2
State Revenue from Tax on Sales and
  Gross Receipts — 1
State Revenue from General Sales Tax — 1
State Revenue from Licenses — 49
State Revenue from Motor Vehicle
  Licenses — 48
State Revenue from Individual Income
  Taxes — 3
State Revenue from Corporation Net
  Income Taxes — 12
State Revenue from Severance Taxes — —
State Revenue from Property Taxes — —
State Revenue from Death and Gift
  Taxes — 23
State Revenue from Documentary and
  Stock Transfers — 17
State Revenue from Tax on Motor Fuels — 49
State Revenue from Tax on Tobacco
  Products — 24
Excise Tax on Cigarettes — —
Excise Tax on Gasoline — 42
State Revenue from Lotteries — —

Transportation — State Ranking

Motor Vehicle Registrations — 44
Automobile Registrations — 18
Bus and Truck Registrations — 46
Motorcycle Registrations — 23
Driver Licenses — 45
Federal Spending on Highway Trust
  Fund — 4
Federal Spending on Mass
  Transportation — 17
State Spending on Highways — 18
Highway Deficiency — 29
Bridge Deficiency — 8
Traffic Fatalities — 45
Traffic Fatalities per Miles Traveled — 40
Motorcyclist Fatalities — 9
Pedalcyclist Fatalities — 39
Pedestrian Fatalities — 18
Registered Aircraft — 42
Registered Pilots — 22
Federal Spending on Airport and
  Airway Trust Fund — 2
Aircraft Fatalities — 2

— *not applicable*   NA *not available*

Agriculture
State Ranking

Farm Acreage 24
Farmland as Portion of State 39
Net Farm Income 5
Government Payments to Farms 8
Federal Commodity Loans/Price
  Supports 11
Federal Spending on Rural
  Development 4
Rural Electric and Telephone Loan
  Guarantees 21
Foreign-Owned Agricultural Land 42

Business and Economy
State Ranking

Gross State Product 47
Retail Sales 47
Supermarket Sales 30
Commercial Bank Assets 42
Insured Commercial Bank Deposits 44
Fortune 500 Companies 32
Inc. 500 Companies 1
New Business Incorporations 33
Business Failures 16
Financial Aid to Minority Businesses 41
Women-Owned Businesses 42
Sales & Receipts of Women-Owned
  Businesses 43
African American-Owned Businesses 48
Sales & Receipts of African American-
  Owned Businesses 49
Hispanic-Owned Businesses 14
Sales & Receipts of Hispanic-Owned
  Businesses 18
Employees in Manufacturing 41
Manufacturing Shipments 33
Japanese-Owned U.S. Manufacturing
  Plants 45
Exports to Mexico 31
Change in Exports to Mexico 17
Existing Home Sales 9
Housing Starts 2
Average Annual Pay 45
Disposable Personal Income 40
Median Income of Families with
  Children 41
Federal Spending on Unemployment
  Insurance/Employment Services 5
Teen Unemployment 36
Bankruptcy Petitions Filed 14
Patents Issued to State Residents 16
Federal Spending on Community
  Development 50
Federal Spending on Economic
  Development Administration 7
Federal Spending on Urban
  Development Action Grants 33

Crime and Criminal Justice
State Ranking

Total Crimes 41
Violent Crimes 41
Murders 48
Rapes 41
Aggravated Assaults 36
Property Crimes 40
Robberies 46
Burglaries 40
Larcenies and Thefts 32
Motor Vehicle Thefts 44
State and Federal Prisoners 33
Capital Punishment 17

State Spending on Corrections 30
State Spending on Police 13
Inmates in Local Jails 32
Spending on Local Jails 41
Spending per Inmate for Local Jails 37
Employees at Local Jails 30
Juvenile Custody Rate 39
Federal Spending on Office of Justice
  Assistance Programs 8

Defense
State Ranking

Defense Grants to State and Local
  Governments 3
Total Defense Payroll 34
Total Army Payroll 37
Total Navy/Marine Corps Payroll 20
Total Air Force Payroll 22
Total Active-Duty Payroll 31
Army Active-Duty Payroll 47
Navy/Marine Corps Active-Duty Payroll 17
Air Force Active-Duty Payroll 19
Total Civilian Payroll 44
Army Civilian Payroll 42
Navy/Marine Corps Civilian Payroll 30
Air Force Civilian Payroll 26
Total Reserve and National Guard
  Payroll 23
Army Reserve and National Guard
  Payroll 20
Navy/Marine Corps Reserve and
  National Guard Payroll 33
Air Force Reserve and National Guard
  Payroll 17
Total Retired Military Payroll 22
Army Retired Military Payroll 29
Navy/Marine Corps Retired Military
  Payroll 13
Air Force Retired Military Payroll 16
Total Defense Prime Contracts 51
Army Prime Contracts 46
Navy/Marine Corps Prime Contracts 47
Air Force Prime Contracts 43
U.S. Military Installations 41
Construction of National Guard Centers 3

Education
State Ranking

School Age Population 2
Public Elementary and Secondary
  School Enrollment 38
Average Daily Attendance NA
Student-Teacher Ratio 6
Salaries of Public School Teachers 46
Public School Teachers Who Are Male 15
Eighth Grade Math Test Results 8
High School Math Enrollment 22
Public High School Graduation Rate 13
General Educational Development
  (GED) Test Results 50
Adult Illiteracy 43
Federal Revenue for Public Schools 15
State Revenue for Public Schools 10
Local Government Revenue for Public
  Schools 40
Total Public School Spending 50
Public School Spending on Instruction 28
Public School Spending on
  Noninstruction 19
Public School Spending on Support
  Staff 35
State and Local Government Spending
  on Public Schools 29

Federal Spending on School
  Improvement Programs 12
Gifted and Talented Students NA
Federal Spending on Education of
  Students with Disabilities 16
Student-Teacher Ratio in Catholic
  Elementary Schools 13
Student-Teacher Ratio in Catholic
  Secondary Schools 3
State Spending on Education 19
State and Local Government Spending
  on Education 21
Higher Education Tuition and Fees 45
Higher Education Revenue 42
Federal Spending on Higher Education 16
State Spending on Higher Education 24
State and Local Government Spending
  on Higher Education 14
State and Local Appropriations for
  Higher Education 21
Federal Spending on Higher Education
  Act Insured Loans 25
Federal Spending on National
  Guaranteed Student Loans 23
Federal Spending on Pell Grants 15
Default Rate in Perkins Student Loan
  Program 28
State Spending on Libraries 23

Energy
State Ranking

Total Spending on Energy 35
Net Generation of Electricity 40
Cost of Electricity 50
Spending on Electricity 31
Spending on Natural Gas 42
Spending on Gasoline 28
Spending on Petroleum 28
Spending on Coal 43
Total Energy Consumption 15
Electricity Consumption 3
Natural Gas Consumption 35
Petroleum Consumption 33
Coal Consumption 43
Power Plants 6
Nuclear Power Plants 34
Hydroelectric Power Plants 2

Environment
State Ranking

Federally Owned Land (acreage) 4
Loss of Wetlands 16
Environmental Protection Agency
  Spending 22
EPA Abatement, Control, and
  Compliance 7
State Spending on Environmental
  Programs 6
Environmental Programs as Part of State
  Budget 3
State Spending on Forest Programs 5
Total Tree Planting 18
Federal Tree Planting 5
Private Tree Planting 31
State Spending on Air Quality 35
State Spending on Water Quality 6
Federal Grants for Rural Water and
  Waste Disposal 4
Federal Spending on Wastewater
  Treatment Works 27
Hazardous Waste Sites on National
  Priority List 37

Federal Grants for Hazardous Substance
Response | 11
State Spending on Hazardous Waste | 23

Health | State Ranking

State Health Rankings | 33
State Spending on Health | 43
Support for Public Health | 29
Family and Business Spending on Health
Care | 51
HMO Enrollment | 45
Medicaid Recipients | 48
Medically Underserved Population | 17
Lack of Health Care Access | 3
Active Nonfederal Physicians | 51
Active Nonfederal Nurses | 42
Active Nonfederal Dentists | 27
Average Cost per Hospital Stay | 50
Average Cost per Day for Hospital Care | 41
Average Cost per Day for Hospital Room | 28
State Spending on Hospitals | 49
Adequacy of Prenatal Care | 33
Infants Born Receiving Late or No
Prenatal Care | 14
Infants Born with Low Birth Weight | 39
Abortions | 48
Immunizations of Two-Year-Olds | —
Overall Risk for Heart Disease | 17
Risk Factor for Heart Disease
(hypertension) | 37
Deaths Due to Heart Disease | 45
New Cancer Cases | 45
Deaths Due to Cancer | 42
Prevalence of Smoking | 44
Prevalence of Diabetes | 46
Deaths Due to Diabetes | 43
Cost of Diabetes | 45
AIDS Cases Reported | 45
Gonorrhea Cases Reported | 47
Syphilis Cases Reported | 49
Tuberculosis Cases Reported | 40
Hepatitis Cases Reported | 17
Rabies Cases Reported | 35
Lyme Disease Cases Reported | 37
Beer Consumption | 22
Wine Consumption | 20
Liquor Consumption | 42
Alcohol and Drug Treatment Admissions | 31
Federal Spending on Alcohol, Drug
Abuse, and Mental Health | 51
Total Spending on Alcohol/Drug Abuse
Services | 45
State Spending on Alcohol/Drug Abuse
Services | 40
Hard-Core Cocaine Users | 40
Federal Drug Grants to States | 14

Population | State Ranking

Population | 42
Population Density | 45
Population in Metropolitan Areas | 51
Population Under 18 Years Old | 3
Population Over 65 Years Old | 34
White Population | 8
African American Population | 50
Hispanic Population | 15
Asian American Population | 32
Native American Population | 12
Catholic Population | 40

Jewish Population | 50
Marriages | 5
Divorces | 6
Births | 12
Births to Single Mothers | 50
Births to Single Teenagers | 47
Adoptions | 43
Adoption Option Index | 2
Infant Mortality | 26
Child Deaths and Suicides | 10
Teen Violent Death Rate | 15
Deaths | 41

Recreation | State Ranking

State Parks and Recreation Areas | 20
Visitors to State Parks and Recreation
Areas | 26
Revenues from State Parks and
Recreation Areas | 27
Spending on State Arts Agencies | 30
Domestic Travel Spending | 15
State Travel Office Budgets | 9
Lodging Industry (rooms) | 28
Participation in Exercise Walking | 5
Participation in Swimming | 5
Participation in Camping | 2
Participation in Bowling | 29
Bowling League Membership | 21
Participation in Running/Jogging | 10
Participation in Aerobics | 3
Participation in Golf | 23
Participation in Softball | 1
Participation in Health Clubs | 18
Participation in Tennis | 32
Participation in Hunting | 2
Participation in Baseball | 5
Participation in Bicycle Riding | 2
Number of Boats | 11
Attendance at Parimutuel Racing | 8
Revenue from Parimutuel Betting | 26

Social Services | State Ranking

Federal Grants for Social Services | 32
State Spending on Public Welfare | 49
Persons in Poverty | 26
Public Aid Recipients | 50
Participants in Food Stamp Program | 36
Households in Food Stamp Program | 44
Percentage of Poor Using AFDC and
Food Stamps | 37
Federal Spending on Children and
Family Services | 12
Federal Women, Infants, and Children
Food Program | 7
Child Welfare Services | 12
Child Abuse Cases Reported | —
Children in Poverty | 26
Children Without Health Insurance | 16
Children Who Are Hungry or at Risk | 8
Federal Spending on Child Nutrition
Programs | 27
Federal Spending on Special Milk
Program | 8
National School Lunch Program
Participants | 17
Head Start Enrollment | 46
Head Start Spending | 8
Federal Spending on Rehabilitation
Services/Handicapped Research | 20

State Government | State Ranking

Financial World's State Rankings | 38
Salaries of State Officials (governor) | 33
Salaries of State Legislators | 27
Women in State Legislatures | 7
African Americans in State Legislatures | 43
Hispanics in State Legislatures | 16
Asian Americans in State Legislatures | 6
Native Americans in State Legislatures | 12
Turnover in State Legislatures | 7
Length of State Legislative Sessions | 21
State Bills in Regular Session | 7
State Resolutions in Regular Session | 25
State Bills in Special Session | —
State Resolutions in Special Session | —
Women in State Cabinets | 28
Total Federal Funding to State
Governments | 29
Total State Spending | 21
State General Expenditures | 22
State Debt | 29
State Spending on Interest on the
General Debt | 19
Total State Tax Revenue | 27
State Revenue from Tax on Sales and
Gross Receipts | 25
State Revenue from General Sales Tax | 23
State Revenue from Licenses | 11
State Revenue from Motor Vehicle
Licenses | 11
State Revenue from Individual Income
Taxes | 19
State Revenue from Corporation Net
Income Taxes | 27
State Revenue from Severance Taxes | 26
State Revenue from Property Taxes | 40
State Revenue from Death and Gift
Taxes | 50
State Revenue from Documentary and
Stock Transfers | —
State Revenue from Tax on Motor Fuels | 13
State Revenue from Tax on Tobacco
Products | 40
Excise Tax on Cigarettes | 30
Excise Tax on Gasoline | 5
State Revenue from Lotteries | 22

Transportation | State Ranking

Motor Vehicle Registrations | 2
Automobile Registrations | 11
Bus and Truck Registrations | 4
Motorcycle Registrations | 7
Driver Licenses | 27
Federal Spending on Highway Trust
Fund | 10
Federal Spending on Mass
Transportation | 49
State Spending on Highways | 14
Highway Deficiency | 2
Bridge Deficiency | 40
Traffic Fatalities | 6
Traffic Fatalities per Miles Traveled | 8
Motorcyclist Fatalities | 26
Pedalcyclist Fatalities | 12
Pedestrian Fatalities | 31
Registered Aircraft | 5
Registered Pilots | 8
Federal Spending on Airport and
Airway Trust Fund | 28
Aircraft Fatalities | 7

— *not applicable*   NA *not available*

Agriculture
State Ranking

Farm Acreage	16
Farmland as Portion of State	6
Net Farm Income	32
Government Payments to Farms	18
Federal Commodity Loans/Price Supports	15
Federal Spending on Rural Development	37
Rural Electric and Telephone Loan Guarantees	40
Foreign-Owned Agricultural Land	29

Business and Economy
State Ranking

Gross State Product	14
Retail Sales	17
Supermarket Sales	44
Commercial Bank Assets	6
Insured Commercial Bank Deposits	6
Fortune 500 Companies	3
Inc. 500 Companies	35
New Business Incorporations	18
Business Failures	33
Financial Aid to Minority Businesses	26
Women-Owned Businesses	20
Sales & Receipts of Women-Owned Businesses	33
African American-Owned Businesses	16
Sales & Receipts of African American-Owned Businesses	14
Hispanic-Owned Businesses	13
Sales & Receipts of Hispanic-Owned Businesses	14
Employees in Manufacturing	5
Manufacturing Shipments	13
Japanese-Owned U.S. Manufacturing Plants	3
Exports to Mexico	9
Change in Exports to Mexico	7
Existing Home Sales	31
Housing Starts	38
Average Annual Pay	8
Disposable Personal Income	9
Median Income of Families with Children	16
Federal Spending on Unemployment Insurance/Employment Services	22
Teen Unemployment	23
Bankruptcy Petitions Filed	19
Patents Issued to State Residents	9
Federal Spending on Community Development	4
Federal Spending on Economic Development Administration	40
Federal Spending on Urban Development Action Grants	30

Crime and Criminal Justice
State Ranking

Total Crimes	15
Violent Crimes	5
Murders	12
Rapes	25
Aggravated Assaults	8
Property Crimes	20
Robberies	3
Burglaries	30
Larcenies and Thefts	20
Motor Vehicle Thefts	13
State and Federal Prisoners	27
Capital Punishment	15

State Spending on Corrections	41
State Spending on Police	35
Inmates in Local Jails	28
Spending on Local Jails	36
Spending per Inmate for Local Jails	28
Employees at Local Jails	17
Juvenile Custody Rate	46
Federal Spending on Office of Justice Assistance Programs	48

Defense
State Ranking

Defense Grants to State and Local Governments	32
Total Defense Payroll	43
Total Army Payroll	42
Total Navy/Marine Corps Payroll	23
Total Air Force Payroll	36
Total Active-Duty Payroll	36
Army Active-Duty Payroll	28
Navy/Marine Corps Active-Duty Payroll	16
Air Force Active-Duty Payroll	33
Total Civilian Payroll	38
Army Civilian Payroll	24
Navy/Marine Corps Civilian Payroll	24
Air Force Civilian Payroll	34
Total Reserve and National Guard Payroll	44
Army Reserve and National Guard Payroll	45
Navy/Marine Corps Reserve and National Guard Payroll	25
Air Force Reserve and National Guard Payroll	43
Total Retired Military Payroll	48
Army Retired Military Payroll	49
Navy/Marine Corps Retired Military Payroll	47
Air Force Retired Military Payroll	42
Total Defense Prime Contracts	43
Army Prime Contracts	45
Navy/Marine Corps Prime Contracts	31
Air Force Prime Contracts	30
U.S. Military Installations	10
Construction of National Guard Centers	34

Education
State Ranking

School Age Population	32
Public Elementary and Secondary School Enrollment	5
Average Daily Attendance	34
Student-Teacher Ratio	26
Salaries of Public School Teachers	13
Public School Teachers Who Are Male	18
Eighth Grade Math Test Results	22
High School Math Enrollment	36
Public High School Graduation Rate	23
General Educational Development (GED) Test Results	48
Adult Illiteracy	12
Federal Revenue for Public Schools	26
State Revenue for Public Schools	44
Local Government Revenue for Public Schools	9
Total Public School Spending	22
Public School Spending on Instruction	40
Public School Spending on Noninstruction	35
Public School Spending on Support Staff	18
State and Local Government Spending on Public Schools	33

Federal Spending on School Improvement Programs	28
Gifted and Talented Students	6
Federal Spending on Education of Students with Disabilities	5
Student-Teacher Ratio in Catholic Elementary Schools	4
Student-Teacher Ratio in Catholic Secondary Schools	4
State Spending on Education	45
State and Local Government Spending on Education	35
Higher Education Tuition and Fees	16
Higher Education Revenue	26
Federal Spending on Higher Education	41
State Spending on Higher Education	43
State and Local Government Spending on Higher Education	35
State and Local Appropriations for Higher Education	41
Federal Spending on Higher Education Act Insured Loans	22
Federal Spending on National Guaranteed Student Loans	19
Federal Spending on Pell Grants	33
Default Rate in Perkins Student Loan Program	30
State Spending on Libraries	8

Energy
State Ranking

Total Spending on Energy	24
Net Generation of Electricity	27
Cost of Electricity	14
Spending on Electricity	24
Spending on Natural Gas	5
Spending on Gasoline	33
Spending on Petroleum	39
Spending on Coal	27
Total Energy Consumption	28
Electricity Consumption	34
Natural Gas Consumption	11
Petroleum Consumption	42
Coal Consumption	30
Power Plants	43
Nuclear Power Plants	6
Hydroelectric Power Plants	44

Environment
State Ranking

Federally Owned Land (acreage)	44
Loss of Wetlands	6
Environmental Protection Agency Spending	21
EPA Abatement, Control, and Compliance	13
State Spending on Environmental Programs	18
Environmental Programs as Part of State Budget	14
State Spending on Forest Programs	47
Total Tree Planting	28
Federal Tree Planting	32
Private Tree Planting	26
State Spending on Air Quality	5
State Spending on Water Quality	8
Federal Grants for Rural Water and Waste Disposal	34
Federal Spending on Wastewater Treatment Works	23
Hazardous Waste Sites on National Priority List	10

Federal Grants for Hazardous Substance
Response 17
State Spending on Hazardous Waste 12

Health — State Ranking

State Health Rankings 32
State Spending on Health 23
Support for Public Health 15
Family and Business Spending on Health
Care 6
HMO Enrollment 21
Medicaid Recipients 22
Medically Underserved Population 13
Lack of Health Care Access 16
Active Nonfederal Physicians 15
Active Nonfederal Nurses 23
Active Nonfederal Dentists 17
Average Cost per Hospital Stay 11
Average Cost per Day for Hospital Care 17
Average Cost per Day for Hospital Room 21
State Spending on Hospitals 39
Adequacy of Prenatal Care 32
Infants Born Receiving Late or No
Prenatal Care 24
Infants Born with Low Birth Weight 12
Abortions 16
Immunizations of Two-Year-Olds —
Overall Risk for Heart Disease 11
Risk Factor for Heart Disease
(hypertension) 43
Deaths Due to Heart Disease 19
New Cancer Cases 24
Deaths Due to Cancer 17
Prevalence of Smoking 22
Prevalence of Diabetes 18
Deaths Due to Diabetes 14
Cost of Diabetes 19
AIDS Cases Reported 11
Gonorrhea Cases Reported 12
Syphilis Cases Reported 12
Tuberculosis Cases Reported 10
Hepatitis Cases Reported 37
Rabies Cases Reported 41
Lyme Disease Cases Reported 36
Beer Consumption 16
Wine Consumption 18
Liquor Consumption 19
Alcohol and Drug Treatment Admissions 29
Federal Spending on Alcohol, Drug
Abuse, and Mental Health 7
Total Spending on Alcohol/Drug Abuse
Services 16
State Spending on Alcohol/Drug Abuse
Services 9
Hard-Core Cocaine Users 4
Federal Drug Grants to States 20

Population — State Ranking

Population 6
Population Density 12
Population in Metropolitan Areas 12
Population Under 18 Years Old 30
Population Over 65 Years Old 28
White Population 36
African American Population 14
Hispanic Population 10
Asian American Population 10
Native American Population 45
Catholic Population 9

Jewish Population 10
Marriages 38
Divorces 38
Births 15
Births to Single Mothers 9
Births to Single Teenagers 10
Adoptions 27
Adoption Option Index 10
Infant Mortality 9
Child Deaths and Suicides 22
Teen Violent Death Rate 32
Deaths 20

Recreation — State Ranking

State Parks and Recreation Areas 26
Visitors to State Parks and Recreation
Areas 16
Revenues from State Parks and
Recreation Areas 49
Spending on State Arts Agencies 20
Domestic Travel Spending 34
State Travel Office Budgets 19
Lodging Industry (rooms) 39
Participation in Exercise Walking 28
Participation in Swimming 36
Participation in Camping 33
Participation in Bowling 11
Bowling League Membership 19
Participation in Running/Jogging 24
Participation in Aerobics 27
Participation in Golf 15
Participation in Softball 12
Participation in Health Clubs 16
Participation in Tennis 28
Participation in Hunting 36
Participation in Baseball 9
Participation in Bicycle Riding 19
Number of Boats 39
Attendance at Parimutuel Racing 24
Revenue from Parimutuel Betting 6

Social Services — State Ranking

Federal Grants for Social Services 34
State Spending on Public Welfare 21
Persons in Poverty 27
Public Aid Recipients 11
Participants in Food Stamp Program 11
Households in Food Stamp Program 12
Percentage of Poor Using AFDC and
Food Stamps 29
Federal Spending on Children and
Family Services 23
Federal Women, Infants, and Children
Food Program 33
Child Welfare Services 19
Child Abuse Cases Reported —
Children in Poverty 25
Children Without Health Insurance 36
Children Who Are Hungry or at Risk 15
Federal Spending on Child Nutrition
Programs 33
Federal Spending on Special Milk
Program 3
National School Lunch Program
Participants 27
Head Start Enrollment 10
Head Start Spending 18
Federal Spending on Rehabilitation
Services/Handicapped Research 41

State Government — State Ranking

Financial World's State Rankings 36
Salaries of State Officials (governor) 13
Salaries of State Legislators 6
Women in State Legislatures 19
African Americans in State Legislatures 9
Hispanics in State Legislatures 8
Asian Americans in State Legislatures 6
Native Americans in State Legislatures 12
Turnover in State Legislatures 44
Length of State Legislative Sessions 13
State Bills in Regular Session 30
State Resolutions in Regular Session 4
State Bills in Special Session 29
State Resolutions in Special Session 10
Women in State Cabinets NA
Total Federal Funding to State
Governments 45
Total State Spending 46
State General Expenditures 47
State Debt 18
State Spending on Interest on the
General Debt 21
Total State Tax Revenue 28
State Revenue from Tax on Sales and
Gross Receipts 23
State Revenue from General Sales Tax 28
State Revenue from Licenses 33
State Revenue from Motor Vehicle
Licenses 13
State Revenue from Individual Income
Taxes 23
State Revenue from Corporation Net
Income Taxes 18
State Revenue from Severance Taxes —
State Revenue from Property Taxes 14
State Revenue from Death and Gift
Taxes 28
State Revenue from Documentary and
Stock Transfers 25
State Revenue from Tax on Motor Fuels 32
State Revenue from Tax on Tobacco
Products 17
Excise Tax on Cigarettes 13
Excise Tax on Gasoline 17
State Revenue from Lotteries 4

Transportation — State Ranking

Motor Vehicle Registrations 40
Automobile Registrations 26
Bus and Truck Registrations 42
Motorcycle Registrations 26
Driver Licenses 43
Federal Spending on Highway Trust
Fund 48
Federal Spending on Mass
Transportation 3
State Spending on Highways 26
Highway Deficiency 44
Bridge Deficiency 33
Traffic Fatalities 43
Traffic Fatalities per Miles Traveled 38
Motorcyclist Fatalities 34
Pedalcyclist Fatalities 32
Pedestrian Fatalities 23
Registered Aircraft 39
Registered Pilots 35
Federal Spending on Airport and
Airway Trust Fund 12
Aircraft Fatalities 30

— *not applicable* NA *not available*

Agriculture
State Ranking

Farm Acreage	19
Farmland as Portion of State	9
Net Farm Income	34
Government Payments to Farms	20
Federal Commodity Loans/Price Supports	14
Federal Spending on Rural Development	38
Rural Electric and Telephone Loan Guarantees	29
Foreign-Owned Agricultural Land	36

Business and Economy
State Ranking

Gross State Product	32
Retail Sales	33
Supermarket Sales	49
Commercial Bank Assets	27
Insured Commercial Bank Deposits	26
Fortune 500 Companies	16
Inc. 500 Companies	22
New Business Incorporations	36
Business Failures	29
Financial Aid to Minority Businesses	33
Women-Owned Businesses	23
Sales & Receipts of Women-Owned Businesses	2
African American-Owned Businesses	23
Sales & Receipts of African American-Owned Businesses	23
Hispanic-Owned Businesses	31
Sales & Receipts of Hispanic-Owned Businesses	31
Employees in Manufacturing	10
Manufacturing Shipments	2
Japanese-Owned U.S. Manufacturing Plants	6
Exports to Mexico	22
Change in Exports to Mexico	48
Existing Home Sales	39
Housing Starts	16
Average Annual Pay	25
Disposable Personal Income	34
Median Income of Families with Children	35
Federal Spending on Unemployment Insurance/Employment Services	50
Teen Unemployment	18
Bankruptcy Petitions Filed	8
Patents Issued to State Residents	25
Federal Spending on Community Development	37
Federal Spending on Economic Development Administration	39
Federal Spending on Urban Development Action Grants	33

Crime and Criminal Justice
State Ranking

Total Crimes	34
Violent Crimes	30
Murders	22
Rapes	23
Aggravated Assaults	24
Property Crimes	34
Robberies	34
Burglaries	35
Larcenies and Thefts	34
Motor Vehicle Thefts	24
State and Federal Prisoners	31
Capital Punishment	13

State Spending on Corrections	35
State Spending on Police	39
Inmates in Local Jails	26
Spending on Local Jails	29
Spending per Inmate for Local Jails	25
Employees at Local Jails	12
Juvenile Custody Rate	11
Federal Spending on Office of Justice Assistance Programs	39

Defense
State Ranking

Defense Grants to State and Local Governments	28
Total Defense Payroll	41
Total Army Payroll	26
Total Navy/Marine Corps Payroll	19
Total Air Force Payroll	42
Total Active-Duty Payroll	42
Army Active-Duty Payroll	25
Navy/Marine Corps Active-Duty Payroll	37
Air Force Active-Duty Payroll	38
Total Civilian Payroll	25
Army Civilian Payroll	32
Navy/Marine Corps Civilian Payroll	11
Air Force Civilian Payroll	41
Total Reserve and National Guard Payroll	21
Army Reserve and National Guard Payroll	14
Navy/Marine Corps Reserve and National Guard Payroll	39
Air Force Reserve and National Guard Payroll	36
Total Retired Military Payroll	45
Army Retired Military Payroll	40
Navy/Marine Corps Retired Military Payroll	45
Air Force Retired Military Payroll	41
Total Defense Prime Contracts	23
Army Prime Contracts	8
Navy/Marine Corps Prime Contracts	26
Air Force Prime Contracts	24
U.S. Military Installations	23
Construction of National Guard Centers	26

Education
State Ranking

School Age Population	22
Public Elementary and Secondary School Enrollment	13
Average Daily Attendance	4
Student-Teacher Ratio	16
Salaries of Public School Teachers	19
Public School Teachers Who Are Male	18
Eighth Grade Math Test Results	13
High School Math Enrollment	25
Public High School Graduation Rate	24
General Educational Development (GED) Test Results	2
Adult Illiteracy	27
Federal Revenue for Public Schools	41
State Revenue for Public Schools	12
Local Government Revenue for Public Schools	36
Total Public School Spending	27
Public School Spending on Instruction	31
Public School Spending on Noninstruction	24
Public School Spending on Support Staff	32
State and Local Government Spending on Public Schools	6

Federal Spending on School Improvement Programs	29
Gifted and Talented Students	18
Federal Spending on Education of Students with Disabilities	19
Student-Teacher Ratio in Catholic Elementary Schools	19
Student-Teacher Ratio in Catholic Secondary Schools	6
State Spending on Education	25
State and Local Government Spending on Education	4
Higher Education Tuition and Fees	12
Higher Education Revenue	18
Federal Spending on Higher Education	7
State Spending on Higher Education	15
State and Local Government Spending on Higher Education	12
State and Local Appropriations for Higher Education	27
Federal Spending on Higher Education Act Insured Loans	1
Federal Spending on National Guaranteed Student Loans	11
Federal Spending on Pell Grants	25
Default Rate in Perkins Student Loan Program	50
State Spending on Libraries	45

Energy
State Ranking

Total Spending on Energy	6
Net Generation of Electricity	11
Cost of Electricity	39
Spending on Electricity	27
Spending on Natural Gas	9
Spending on Gasoline	37
Spending on Petroleum	18
Spending on Coal	4
Total Energy Consumption	7
Electricity Consumption	16
Natural Gas Consumption	12
Petroleum Consumption	16
Coal Consumption	4
Power Plants	38
Nuclear Power Plants	34
Hydroelectric Power Plants	39

Environment
State Ranking

Federally Owned Land (acreage)	38
Loss of Wetlands	5
Environmental Protection Agency Spending	31
EPA Abatement, Control, and Compliance	40
State Spending on Environmental Programs	49
Environmental Programs as Part of State Budget	47
State Spending on Forest Programs	40
Total Tree Planting	24
Federal Tree Planting	32
Private Tree Planting	18
State Spending on Air Quality	28
State Spending on Water Quality	41
Federal Grants for Rural Water and Waste Disposal	42
Federal Spending on Wastewater Treatment Works	28
Hazardous Waste Sites on National Priority List	11

Federal Grants for Hazardous Substance
Response 39
State Spending on Hazardous Waste 33

Health · State Ranking

State Health Rankings 19
State Spending on Health 45
Support for Public Health 19
Family and Business Spending on Health Care 26
HMO Enrollment 31
Medicaid Recipients 45
Medically Underserved Population 31
Lack of Health Care Access 34
Active Nonfederal Physicians 43
Active Nonfederal Nurses 28
Active Nonfederal Dentists 36
Average Cost per Hospital Stay 33
Average Cost per Day for Hospital Care 23
Average Cost per Day for Hospital Room 29
State Spending on Hospitals 26
Adequacy of Prenatal Care 15
Infants Born Receiving Late or No Prenatal Care 26
Infants Born with Low Birth Weight 29
Abortions 45
Immunizations of Two-Year-Olds —
Overall Risk for Heart Disease 48
Risk Factor for Heart Disease (hypertension) 4
Deaths Due to Heart Disease 21
New Cancer Cases 23
Deaths Due to Cancer 21
Prevalence of Smoking 28
Prevalence of Diabetes 31
Deaths Due to Diabetes 13
Cost of Diabetes 32
AIDS Cases Reported 35
Gonorrhea Cases Reported 22
Syphilis Cases Reported 29
Tuberculosis Cases Reported 36
Hepatitis Cases Reported 23
Rabies Cases Reported 39
Lyme Disease Cases Reported 29
Beer Consumption 35
Wine Consumption 37
Liquor Consumption 35
Alcohol and Drug Treatment Admissions 43
Federal Spending on Alcohol, Drug Abuse, and Mental Health 14
Total Spending on Alcohol/Drug Abuse Services 37
State Spending on Alcohol/Drug Abuse Services 46
Hard-Core Cocaine Users 41
Federal Drug Grants to States 49

Population · State Ranking

Population 14
Population Density 17
Population in Metropolitan Areas 24
Population Under 18 Years Old 22
Population Over 65 Years Old 27
White Population 18
African American Population 23
Hispanic Population 32
Asian American Population 38
Native American Population 38
Catholic Population 33

Jewish Population 36
Marriages 22
Divorces NA
Births 28
Births to Single Mothers 24
Births to Single Teenagers 18
Adoptions 7
Adoption Option Index 35
Infant Mortality 17
Child Deaths and Suicides 23
Teen Violent Death Rate 41
Deaths 14

Recreation · State Ranking

State Parks and Recreation Areas 46
Visitors to State Parks and Recreation Areas 36
Revenues from State Parks and Recreation Areas 24
Spending on State Arts Agencies 38
Domestic Travel Spending 50
State Travel Office Budgets 46
Lodging Industry (rooms) 44
Participation in Exercise Walking 42
Participation in Swimming 28
Participation in Camping 40
Participation in Bowling 18
Bowling League Membership 13
Participation in Running/Jogging 33
Participation in Aerobics 34
Participation in Golf 14
Participation in Softball 29
Participation in Health Clubs 42
Participation in Tennis 31
Participation in Hunting 40
Participation in Baseball 22
Participation in Bicycle Riding 20
Number of Boats 25
Attendance at Parimutuel Racing —
Revenue from Parimutuel Betting —

Social Services · State Ranking

Federal Grants for Social Services 4
State Spending on Public Welfare 24
Persons in Poverty 13
Public Aid Recipients 43
Participants in Food Stamp Program 34
Households in Food Stamp Program 45
Percentage of Poor Using AFDC and Food Stamps 38
Federal Spending on Children and Family Services 50
Federal Women, Infants, and Children Food Program 27
Child Welfare Services 2
Child Abuse Cases Reported —
Children in Poverty 35
Children Without Health Insurance 27
Children Who Are Hungry or at Risk 31
Federal Spending on Child Nutrition Programs 39
Federal Spending on Special Milk Program 16
National School Lunch Program Participants 33
Head Start Enrollment 28
Head Start Spending 40
Federal Spending on Rehabilitation Services/Handicapped Research 23

State Government · State Ranking

Financial World's State Rankings 11
Salaries of State Officials (governor) 37
Salaries of State Legislators 30
Women in State Legislatures 27
African Americans in State Legislatures 22
Hispanics in State Legislatures 18
Asian Americans in State Legislatures 6
Native Americans in State Legislatures 12
Turnover in State Legislatures 38
Length of State Legislative Sessions 31
State Bills in Regular Session 36
State Resolutions in Regular Session 45
State Bills in Special Session 27
State Resolutions in Special Session 19
Women in State Cabinets —
Total Federal Funding to State Governments 50
Total State Spending 36
State General Expenditures 35
State Debt 40
State Spending on Interest on the General Debt 40
Total State Tax Revenue 32
State Revenue from Tax on Sales and Gross Receipts 18
State Revenue from General Sales Tax 13
State Revenue from Licenses 48
State Revenue from Motor Vehicle Licenses 43
State Revenue from Individual Income Taxes 25
State Revenue from Corporation Net Income Taxes 28
State Revenue from Severance Taxes 32
State Revenue from Property Taxes 36
State Revenue from Death and Gift Taxes 17
State Revenue from Documentary and Stock Transfers —
State Revenue from Tax on Motor Fuels 17
State Revenue from Tax on Tobacco Products 31
Excise Tax on Cigarettes 40
Excise Tax on Gasoline 35
State Revenue from Lotteries 14

Transportation · State Ranking

Motor Vehicle Registrations 23
Automobile Registrations 25
Bus and Truck Registrations 28
Motorcycle Registrations 25
Driver Licenses 46
Federal Spending on Highway Trust Fund 30
Federal Spending on Mass Transportation 19
State Spending on Highways 35
Highway Deficiency 18
Bridge Deficiency 27
Traffic Fatalities 22
Traffic Fatalities per Miles Traveled 28
Motorcyclist Fatalities 12
Pedalcyclist Fatalities 16
Pedestrian Fatalities 34
Registered Aircraft 38
Registered Pilots 37
Federal Spending on Airport and Airway Trust Fund 14
Aircraft Fatalities 45

— *not applicable* NA *not available*

Agriculture
State Ranking

Farm Acreage	11
Farmland as Portion of State	2
Net Farm Income	4
Government Payments to Farms	6
Federal Commodity Loans/Price Supports	2
Federal Spending on Rural Development	13
Rural Electric and Telephone Loan Guarantees	4
Foreign-Owned Agricultural Land	44

Business and Economy
State Ranking

Gross State Product	34
Retail Sales	37
Supermarket Sales	21
Commercial Bank Assets	13
Insured Commercial Bank Deposits	12
Fortune 500 Companies	24
Inc. 500 Companies	44
New Business Incorporations	41
Business Failures	50
Financial Aid to Minority Businesses	41
Women-Owned Businesses	21
Sales & Receipts of Women-Owned Businesses	9
African American-Owned Businesses	42
Sales & Receipts of African American-Owned Businesses	39
Hispanic-Owned Businesses	40
Sales & Receipts of Hispanic-Owned Businesses	41
Employees in Manufacturing	25
Manufacturing Shipments	5
Japanese-Owned U.S. Manufacturing Plants	36
Exports to Mexico	18
Change in Exports to Mexico	38
Existing Home Sales	6
Housing Starts	35
Average Annual Pay	44
Disposable Personal Income	31
Median Income of Families with Children	32
Federal Spending on Unemployment Insurance/Employment Services	38
Teen Unemployment	46
Bankruptcy Petitions Filed	42
Patents Issued to State Residents	30
Federal Spending on Community Development	10
Federal Spending on Economic Development Administration	22
Federal Spending on Urban Development Action Grants	28

Crime and Criminal Justice
State Ranking

Total Crimes	42
Violent Crimes	40
Murders	47
Rapes	49
Aggravated Assaults	37
Property Crimes	43
Robberies	42
Burglaries	39
Larcenies and Thefts	38
Motor Vehicle Thefts	46
State and Federal Prisoners	45
Capital Punishment	—

State Spending on Corrections	36
State Spending on Police	38
Inmates in Local Jails	45
Spending on Local Jails	32
Spending per Inmate for Local Jails	3
Employees at Local Jails	44
Juvenile Custody Rate	5
Federal Spending on Office of Justice Assistance Programs	18

Defense
State Ranking

Defense Grants to State and Local Governments	12
Total Defense Payroll	51
Total Army Payroll	49
Total Navy/Marine Corps Payroll	47
Total Air Force Payroll	47
Total Active-Duty Payroll	51
Army Active-Duty Payroll	36
Navy/Marine Corps Active-Duty Payroll	47
Air Force Active-Duty Payroll	49
Total Civilian Payroll	51
Army Civilian Payroll	45
Navy/Marine Corps Civilian Payroll	48
Air Force Civilian Payroll	45
Total Reserve and National Guard Payroll	37
Army Reserve and National Guard Payroll	34
Navy/Marine Corps Reserve and National Guard Payroll	30
Air Force Reserve and National Guard Payroll	39
Total Retired Military Payroll	46
Army Retired Military Payroll	43
Navy/Marine Corps Retired Military Payroll	44
Air Force Retired Military Payroll	45
Total Defense Prime Contracts	40
Army Prime Contracts	32
Navy/Marine Corps Prime Contracts	39
Air Force Prime Contracts	31
U.S. Military Installations	41
Construction of National Guard Centers	14

Education
State Ranking

School Age Population	18
Public Elementary and Secondary School Enrollment	30
Average Daily Attendance	11
Student-Teacher Ratio	33
Salaries of Public School Teachers	37
Public School Teachers Who Are Male	9
Eighth Grade Math Test Results	3
High School Math Enrollment	14
Public High School Graduation Rate	3
General Educational Development (GED) Test Results	25
Adult Illiteracy	35
Federal Revenue for Public Schools	40
State Revenue for Public Schools	24
Local Government Revenue for Public Schools	25
Total Public School Spending	30
Public School Spending on Instruction	21
Public School Spending on Noninstruction	29
Public School Spending on Support Staff	16
State and Local Government Spending on Public Schools	34

Federal Spending on School Improvement Programs	34
Gifted and Talented Students	24
Federal Spending on Education of Students with Disabilities	15
Student-Teacher Ratio in Catholic Elementary Schools	27
Student-Teacher Ratio in Catholic Secondary Schools	31
State Spending on Education	14
State and Local Government Spending on Education	12
Higher Education Tuition and Fees	13
Higher Education Revenue	22
Federal Spending on Higher Education	11
State Spending on Higher Education	11
State and Local Government Spending on Higher Education	3
State and Local Appropriations for Higher Education	34
Federal Spending on Higher Education Act Insured Loans	8
Federal Spending on National Guaranteed Student Loans	6
Federal Spending on Pell Grants	10
Default Rate in Perkins Student Loan Program	45
State Spending on Libraries	27

Energy
State Ranking

Total Spending on Energy	32
Net Generation of Electricity	29
Cost of Electricity	32
Spending on Electricity	40
Spending on Natural Gas	12
Spending on Gasoline	22
Spending on Petroleum	35
Spending on Coal	20
Total Energy Consumption	24
Electricity Consumption	30
Natural Gas Consumption	13
Petroleum Consumption	40
Coal Consumption	14
Power Plants	7
Nuclear Power Plants	19
Hydroelectric Power Plants	32

Environment
State Ranking

Federally Owned Land (acreage)	51
Loss of Wetlands	3
Environmental Protection Agency Spending	24
EPA Abatement, Control, and Compliance	29
State Spending on Environmental Programs	22
Environmental Programs as Part of State Budget	32
State Spending on Forest Programs	42
Total Tree Planting	29
Federal Tree Planting	32
Private Tree Planting	27
State Spending on Air Quality	48
State Spending on Water Quality	14
Federal Grants for Rural Water and Waste Disposal	12
Federal Spending on Wastewater Treatment Works	19
Hazardous Waste Sites on National Priority List	18

Federal Grants for Hazardous Substance Response	33
State Spending on Hazardous Waste	49

Health | State Ranking

State Health Rankings	7
State Spending on Health	50
Support for Public Health	23
Family and Business Spending on Health Care	25
HMO Enrollment	25
Medicaid Recipients	29
Medically Underserved Population	38
Lack of Health Care Access	32
Active Nonfederal Physicians	44
Active Nonfederal Nurses	12
Active Nonfederal Dentists	22
Average Cost per Hospital Stay	42
Average Cost per Day for Hospital Care	45
Average Cost per Day for Hospital Room	39
State Spending on Hospitals	5
Adequacy of Prenatal Care	2
Infants Born Receiving Late or No Prenatal Care	49
Infants Born with Low Birth Weight	42
Abortions	42
Immunizations of Two-Year-Olds	—
Overall Risk for Heart Disease	32
Risk Factor for Heart Disease (hypertension)	18
Deaths Due to Heart Disease	8
New Cancer Cases	15
Deaths Due to Cancer	14
Prevalence of Smoking	30
Prevalence of Diabetes	23
Deaths Due to Diabetes	20
Cost of Diabetes	22
AIDS Cases Reported	42
Gonorrhea Cases Reported	39
Syphilis Cases Reported	36
Tuberculosis Cases Reported	44
Hepatitis Cases Reported	48
Rabies Cases Reported	11
Lyme Disease Cases Reported	14
Beer Consumption	29
Wine Consumption	41
Liquor Consumption	49
Alcohol and Drug Treatment Admissions	21
Federal Spending on Alcohol, Drug Abuse, and Mental Health	49
Total Spending on Alcohol/Drug Abuse Services	32
State Spending on Alcohol/Drug Abuse Services	26
Hard-Core Cocaine Users	43
Federal Drug Grants to States	36

Population | State Ranking

Population	30
Population Density	34
Population in Metropolitan Areas	40
Population Under 18 Years Old	28
Population Over 65 Years Old	3
White Population	4
African American Population	41
Hispanic Population	38
Asian American Population	31
Native American Population	36
Catholic Population	25

Jewish Population	41
Marriages	32
Divorces	37
Births	50
Births to Single Mothers	42
Births to Single Teenagers	35
Adoptions	20
Adoption Option Index	33
Infant Mortality	36
Child Deaths and Suicides	34
Teen Violent Death Rate	25
Deaths	14

Recreation | State Ranking

State Parks and Recreation Areas	32
Visitors to State Parks and Recreation Areas	13
Revenues from State Parks and Recreation Areas	46
Spending on State Arts Agencies	43
Domestic Travel Spending	39
State Travel Office Budgets	25
Lodging Industry (rooms)	33
Participation in Exercise Walking	4
Participation in Swimming	12
Participation in Camping	11
Participation in Bowling	5
Bowling League Membership	7
Participation in Running/Jogging	7
Participation in Aerobics	13
Participation in Golf	2
Participation in Softball	4
Participation in Health Clubs	19
Participation in Tennis	8
Participation in Hunting	11
Participation in Baseball	4
Participation in Bicycle Riding	4
Number of Boats	13
Attendance at Parimutuel Racing	17
Revenue from Parimutuel Betting	29

Social Services | State Ranking

Federal Grants for Social Services	13
State Spending on Public Welfare	22
Persons in Poverty	44
Public Aid Recipients	33
Participants in Food Stamp Program	37
Households in Food Stamp Program	37
Percentage of Poor Using AFDC and Food Stamps	21
Federal Spending on Children and Family Services	34
Federal Women, Infants, and Children Food Program	32
Child Welfare Services	21
Child Abuse Cases Reported	—
Children in Poverty	33
Children Without Health Insurance	50
Children Who Are Hungry or at Risk	10
Federal Spending on Child Nutrition Programs	30
Federal Spending on Special Milk Program	20
National School Lunch Program Participants	30
Head Start Enrollment	25
Head Start Spending	33
Federal Spending on Rehabilitation Services/Handicapped Research	25

State Government | State Ranking

Financial World's State Rankings	12
Salaries of State Officials (governor)	31
Salaries of State Legislators	19
Women in State Legislatures	37
African Americans in State Legislatures	40
Hispanics in State Legislatures	21
Asian Americans in State Legislatures	6
Native Americans in State Legislatures	12
Turnover in State Legislatures	30
Length of State Legislative Sessions	11
State Bills in Regular Session	31
State Resolutions in Regular Session	38
State Bills in Special Session	—
State Resolutions in Special Session	—
Women in State Cabinets	NA
Total Federal Funding to State Governments	41
Total State Spending	28
State General Expenditures	21
State Debt	44
State Spending on Interest on the General Debt	42
Total State Tax Revenue	21
State Revenue from Tax on Sales and Gross Receipts	30
State Revenue from General Sales Tax	32
State Revenue from Licenses	9
State Revenue from Motor Vehicle Licenses	4
State Revenue from Individual Income Taxes	12
State Revenue from Corporation Net Income Taxes	22
State Revenue from Severance Taxes	—
State Revenue from Property Taxes	—
State Revenue from Death and Gift Taxes	7
State Revenue from Documentary and Stock Transfers	28
State Revenue from Tax on Motor Fuels	6
State Revenue from Tax on Tobacco Products	11
Excise Tax on Cigarettes	7
Excise Tax on Gasoline	10
State Revenue from Lotteries	27

Transportation | State Ranking

Motor Vehicle Registrations	5
Automobile Registrations	3
Bus and Truck Registrations	12
Motorcycle Registrations	1
Driver Licenses	37
Federal Spending on Highway Trust Fund	21
Federal Spending on Mass Transportation	41
State Spending on Highways	4
Highway Deficiency	45
Bridge Deficiency	30
Traffic Fatalities	25
Traffic Fatalities per Miles Traveled	17
Motorcyclist Fatalities	13
Pedalcyclist Fatalities	18
Pedestrian Fatalities	44
Registered Aircraft	23
Registered Pilots	26
Federal Spending on Airport and Airway Trust Fund	38
Aircraft Fatalities	47

— not applicable   NA not available

Agriculture
State Ranking

Farm Acreage	3
Farmland as Portion of State	3
Net Farm Income	10
Government Payments to Farms	5
Federal Commodity Loans/Price Supports	16
Federal Spending on Rural Development	35
Rural Electric and Telephone Loan Guarantees	33
Foreign-Owned Agricultural Land	40

Business and Economy
State Ranking

Gross State Product	24
Retail Sales	38
Supermarket Sales	25
Commercial Bank Assets	18
Insured Commercial Bank Deposits	13
Fortune 500 Companies	35
Inc. 500 Companies	28
New Business Incorporations	43
Business Failures	14
Financial Aid to Minority Businesses	39
Women-Owned Businesses	8
Sales & Receipts of Women-Owned Businesses	15
African American-Owned Businesses	28
Sales & Receipts of African American-Owned Businesses	20
Hispanic-Owned Businesses	22
Sales & Receipts of Hispanic-Owned Businesses	22
Employees in Manufacturing	29
Manufacturing Shipments	9
Japanese-Owned U.S. Manufacturing Plants	36
Exports to Mexico	3
Change in Exports to Mexico	30
Existing Home Sales	29
Housing Starts	28
Average Annual Pay	36
Disposable Personal Income	22
Median Income of Families with Children	21
Federal Spending on Unemployment Insurance/Employment Services	40
Teen Unemployment	45
Bankruptcy Petitions Filed	17
Patents Issued to State Residents	35
Federal Spending on Community Development	35
Federal Spending on Economic Development Administration	20
Federal Spending on Urban Development Action Grants	22

Crime and Criminal Justice
State Ranking

Total Crimes	24
Violent Crimes	31
Murders	29
Rapes	18
Aggravated Assaults	26
Property Crimes	24
Robberies	26
Burglaries	15
Larcenies and Thefts	17
Motor Vehicle Thefts	32
State and Federal Prisoners	28
Capital Punishment	—

State Spending on Corrections	19
State Spending on Police	47
Inmates in Local Jails	36
Spending on Local Jails	34
Spending per Inmate for Local Jails	21
Employees at Local Jails	39
Juvenile Custody Rate	7
Federal Spending on Office of Justice Assistance Programs	31

Defense
State Ranking

Defense Grants to State and Local Governments	18
Total Defense Payroll	17
Total Army Payroll	6
Total Navy/Marine Corps Payroll	34
Total Air Force Payroll	31
Total Active-Duty Payroll	10
Army Active-Duty Payroll	5
Navy/Marine Corps Active-Duty Payroll	34
Air Force Active-Duty Payroll	29
Total Civilian Payroll	28
Army Civilian Payroll	14
Navy/Marine Corps Civilian Payroll	31
Air Force Civilian Payroll	31
Total Reserve and National Guard Payroll	5
Army Reserve and National Guard Payroll	5
Navy/Marine Corps Reserve and National Guard Payroll	2
Air Force Reserve and National Guard Payroll	27
Total Retired Military Payroll	28
Army Retired Military Payroll	16
Navy/Marine Corps Retired Military Payroll	34
Air Force Retired Military Payroll	29
Total Defense Prime Contracts	28
Army Prime Contracts	19
Navy/Marine Corps Prime Contracts	34
Air Force Prime Contracts	13
U.S. Military Installations	34
Construction of National Guard Centers	20

Education
State Ranking

School Age Population	14
Public Elementary and Secondary School Enrollment	33
Average Daily Attendance	5
Student-Teacher Ratio	41
Salaries of Public School Teachers	28
Public School Teachers Who Are Male	21
Eighth Grade Math Test Results	—
High School Math Enrollment	25
Public High School Graduation Rate	11
General Educational Development (GED) Test Results	23
Adult Illiteracy	38
Federal Revenue for Public Schools	38
State Revenue for Public Schools	28
Local Government Revenue for Public Schools	22
Total Public School Spending	26
Public School Spending on Instruction	34
Public School Spending on Noninstruction	22
Public School Spending on Support Staff	17
State and Local Government Spending on Public Schools	23

Federal Spending on School Improvement Programs	37
Gifted and Talented Students	31
Federal Spending on Education of Students with Disabilities	35
Student-Teacher Ratio in Catholic Elementary Schools	17
Student-Teacher Ratio in Catholic Secondary Schools	46
State Spending on Education	27
State and Local Government Spending on Education	10
Higher Education Tuition and Fees	37
Higher Education Revenue	41
Federal Spending on Higher Education	9
State Spending on Higher Education	23
State and Local Government Spending on Higher Education	9
State and Local Appropriations for Higher Education	12
Federal Spending on Higher Education Act Insured Loans	48
Federal Spending on National Guaranteed Student Loans	22
Federal Spending on Pell Grants	16
Default Rate in Perkins Student Loan Program	43
State Spending on Libraries	42

Energy
State Ranking

Total Spending on Energy	8
Net Generation of Electricity	22
Cost of Electricity	21
Spending on Electricity	26
Spending on Natural Gas	8
Spending on Gasoline	30
Spending on Petroleum	15
Spending on Coal	22
Total Energy Consumption	10
Electricity Consumption	28
Natural Gas Consumption	7
Petroleum Consumption	10
Coal Consumption	16
Power Plants	8
Nuclear Power Plants	15
Hydroelectric Power Plants	47

Environment
State Ranking

Federally Owned Land (acreage)	45
Loss of Wetlands	25
Environmental Protection Agency Spending	30
EPA Abatement, Control, and Compliance	19
State Spending on Environmental Programs	38
Environmental Programs as Part of State Budget	37
State Spending on Forest Programs	NA
Total Tree Planting	39
Federal Tree Planting	32
Private Tree Planting	38
State Spending on Air Quality	20
State Spending on Water Quality	20
Federal Grants for Rural Water and Waste Disposal	43
Federal Spending on Wastewater Treatment Works	34
Hazardous Waste Sites on National Priority List	30

Federal Grants for Hazardous Substance
Response 16
State Spending on Hazardous Waste 34

Health *State Ranking*

State Health Rankings 7
State Spending on Health 42
Support for Public Health 34
Family and Business Spending on Health
Care 11
HMO Enrollment 28
Medicaid Recipients 34
Medically Underserved Population 32
Lack of Health Care Access 48
Active Nonfederal Physicians 32
Active Nonfederal Nurses 21
Active Nonfederal Dentists 32
Average Cost per Hospital Stay 41
Average Cost per Day for Hospital Care 44
Average Cost per Day for Hospital Room 30
State Spending on Hospitals 15
Adequacy of Prenatal Care 5
Infants Born Receiving Late or No
Prenatal Care 34
Infants Born with Low Birth Weight 33
Abortions 25
Immunizations of Two-Year-Olds —
Overall Risk for Heart Disease 40
Risk Factor for Heart Disease
(hypertension) NA
Deaths Due to Heart Disease 18
New Cancer Cases 31
Deaths Due to Cancer 29
Prevalence of Smoking 43
Prevalence of Diabetes 30
Deaths Due to Diabetes 32
Cost of Diabetes 29
AIDS Cases Reported 32
Gonorrhea Cases Reported 18
Syphilis Cases Reported 22
Tuberculosis Cases Reported 41
Hepatitis Cases Reported 39
Rabies Cases Reported 6
Lyme Disease Cases Reported 22
Beer Consumption 47
Wine Consumption 46
Liquor Consumption 47
Alcohol and Drug Treatment Admissions 33
Federal Spending on Alcohol, Drug
Abuse, and Mental Health 46
Total Spending on Alcohol/Drug Abuse
Services 10
State Spending on Alcohol/Drug Abuse
Services 28
Hard-Core Cocaine Users 35
Federal Drug Grants to States 48

Population *State Ranking*

Population 32
Population Density 40
Population in Metropolitan Areas 36
Population Under 18 Years Old 14
Population Over 65 Years Old 11
White Population 19
African American Population 28
Hispanic Population 21
Asian American Population 22
Native American Population 16
Catholic Population 29

Jewish Population 29
Marriages 30
Divorces 23
Births 33
Births to Single Mothers 40
Births to Single Teenagers 36
Adoptions 38
Adoption Option Index 18
Infant Mortality 17
Child Deaths and Suicides 32
Teen Violent Death Rate 31
Deaths 22

Recreation *State Ranking*

State Parks and Recreation Areas 5
Visitors to State Parks and Recreation
Areas 38
Revenues from State Parks and
Recreation Areas 37
Spending on State Arts Agencies 45
Domestic Travel Spending 37
State Travel Office Budgets 42
Lodging Industry (rooms) 34
Participation in Exercise Walking 34
Participation in Swimming 46
Participation in Camping 37
Participation in Bowling 40
Bowling League Membership 14
Participation in Running/Jogging 21
Participation in Aerobics 31
Participation in Golf 45
Participation in Softball 40
Participation in Health Clubs 46
Participation in Tennis 39
Participation in Hunting 20
Participation in Baseball 37
Participation in Bicycle Riding 40
Number of Boats 30
Attendance at Parimutuel Racing 22
Revenue from Parimutuel Betting 31

Social Services *State Ranking*

Federal Grants for Social Services 25
State Spending on Public Welfare 42
Persons in Poverty 33
Public Aid Recipients 42
Participants in Food Stamp Program 41
Households in Food Stamp Program 41
Percentage of Poor Using AFDC and
Food Stamps 17
Federal Spending on Children and
Family Services 29
Federal Women, Infants, and Children
Food Program 39
Child Welfare Services 39
Child Abuse Cases Reported —
Children in Poverty 34
Children Without Health Insurance 39
Children Who Are Hungry or at Risk 40
Federal Spending on Child Nutrition
Programs 14
Federal Spending on Special Milk
Program 11
National School Lunch Program
Participants 26
Head Start Enrollment 34
Head Start Spending 43
Federal Spending on Rehabilitation
Services/Handicapped Research 34

State Government *State Ranking*

Financial World's State Rankings 40
Salaries of State Officials (governor) 36
Salaries of State Legislators —
Women in State Legislatures 8
African Americans in State Legislatures 32
Hispanics in State Legislatures 12
Asian Americans in State Legislatures 6
Native Americans in State Legislatures 12
Turnover in State Legislatures 19
Length of State Legislative Sessions 16
State Bills in Regular Session 24
State Resolutions in Regular Session 33
State Bills in Special Session —
State Resolutions in Special Session —
Women in State Cabinets 17
Total Federal Funding to State
Governments 23
Total State Spending 43
State General Expenditures 40
State Debt 50
State Spending on Interest on the
General Debt 50
Total State Tax Revenue 29
State Revenue from Tax on Sales and
Gross Receipts 29
State Revenue from General Sales Tax 26
State Revenue from Licenses 37
State Revenue from Motor Vehicle
Licenses 20
State Revenue from Individual Income
Taxes 30
State Revenue from Corporation Net
Income Taxes 16
State Revenue from Severance Taxes 11
State Revenue from Property Taxes 18
State Revenue from Death and Gift
Taxes 10
State Revenue from Documentary and
Stock Transfers —
State Revenue from Tax on Motor Fuels 28
State Revenue from Tax on Tobacco
Products 26
Excise Tax on Cigarettes 22
Excise Tax on Gasoline 31
State Revenue from Lotteries 31

Transportation *State Ranking*

Motor Vehicle Registrations 30
Automobile Registrations 44
Bus and Truck Registrations 15
Motorcycle Registrations 13
Driver Licenses 17
Federal Spending on Highway Trust
Fund 24
Federal Spending on Mass
Transportation 45
State Spending on Highways 15
Highway Deficiency 12
Bridge Deficiency 21
Traffic Fatalities 29
Traffic Fatalities per Miles Traveled 34
Motorcyclist Fatalities 4
Pedalcyclist Fatalities 23
Pedestrian Fatalities 49
Registered Aircraft 12
Registered Pilots 12
Federal Spending on Airport and
Airway Trust Fund 29
Aircraft Fatalities 33

— not applicable   NA not available

Agriculture
State Ranking

Farm Acreage	23
Farmland as Portion of State	16
Net Farm Income	13
Government Payments to Farms	23
Federal Commodity Loans/Price Supports	26
Federal Spending on Rural Development	9
Rural Electric and Telephone Loan Guarantees	11
Foreign-Owned Agricultural Land	35

Business and Economy
State Ranking

Gross State Product	39
Retail Sales	42
Supermarket Sales	39
Commercial Bank Assets	22
Insured Commercial Bank Deposits	21
Fortune 500 Companies	38
Inc. 500 Companies	37
New Business Incorporations	35
Business Failures	22
Financial Aid to Minority Businesses	40
Women-Owned Businesses	44
Sales & Receipts of Women-Owned Businesses	26
African American-Owned Businesses	25
Sales & Receipts of African American-Owned Businesses	28
Hispanic-Owned Businesses	50
Sales & Receipts of Hispanic-Owned Businesses	50
Employees in Manufacturing	23
Manufacturing Shipments	10
Japanese-Owned U.S. Manufacturing Plants	7
Exports to Mexico	16
Change in Exports to Mexico	10
Existing Home Sales	10
Housing Starts	30
Average Annual Pay	40
Disposable Personal Income	43
Median Income of Families with Children	45
Federal Spending on Unemployment Insurance/Employment Services	43
Teen Unemployment	10
Bankruptcy Petitions Filed	12
Patents Issued to State Residents	45
Federal Spending on Community Development	23
Federal Spending on Economic Development Administration	16
Federal Spending on Urban Development Action Grants	10

Crime and Criminal Justice
State Ranking

Total Crimes	48
Violent Crimes	34
Murders	26
Rapes	30
Aggravated Assaults	25
Property Crimes	48
Robberies	39
Burglaries	41
Larcenies and Thefts	49
Motor Vehicle Thefts	41
State and Federal Prisoners	25
Capital Punishment	17

State Spending on Corrections	26
State Spending on Police	9
Inmates in Local Jails	18
Spending on Local Jails	27
Spending per Inmate for Local Jails	31
Employees at Local Jails	18
Juvenile Custody Rate	45
Federal Spending on Office of Justice Assistance Programs	46

Defense
State Ranking

Defense Grants to State and Local Governments	30
Total Defense Payroll	18
Total Army Payroll	5
Total Navy/Marine Corps Payroll	28
Total Air Force Payroll	48
Total Active-Duty Payroll	9
Army Active-Duty Payroll	3
Navy/Marine Corps Active-Duty Payroll	38
Air Force Active-Duty Payroll	45
Total Civilian Payroll	21
Army Civilian Payroll	10
Navy/Marine Corps Civilian Payroll	17
Air Force Civilian Payroll	51
Total Reserve and National Guard Payroll	27
Army Reserve and National Guard Payroll	16
Navy/Marine Corps Reserve and National Guard Payroll	48
Air Force Reserve and National Guard Payroll	49
Total Retired Military Payroll	36
Army Retired Military Payroll	18
Navy/Marine Corps Retired Military Payroll	40
Air Force Retired Military Payroll	39
Total Defense Prime Contracts	41
Army Prime Contracts	22
Navy/Marine Corps Prime Contracts	41
Air Force Prime Contracts	50
U.S. Military Installations	29
Construction of National Guard Centers	43

Education
State Ranking

School Age Population	20
Public Elementary and Secondary School Enrollment	24
Average Daily Attendance	15
Student-Teacher Ratio	17
Salaries of Public School Teachers	31
Public School Teachers Who Are Male	44
Eighth Grade Math Test Results	28
High School Math Enrollment	9
Public High School Graduation Rate	36
General Educational Development (GED) Test Results	37
Adult Illiteracy	5
Federal Revenue for Public Schools	8
State Revenue for Public Schools	4
Local Government Revenue for Public Schools	49
Total Public School Spending	46
Public School Spending on Instruction	49
Public School Spending on Noninstruction	26
Public School Spending on Support Staff	36
State and Local Government Spending on Public Schools	47

Federal Spending on School Improvement Programs	20
Gifted and Talented Students	16
Federal Spending on Education of Students with Disabilities	14
Student-Teacher Ratio in Catholic Elementary Schools	15
Student-Teacher Ratio in Catholic Secondary Schools	17
State Spending on Education	16
State and Local Government Spending on Education	34
Higher Education Tuition and Fees	34
Higher Education Revenue	33
Federal Spending on Higher Education	8
State Spending on Higher Education	26
State and Local Government Spending on Higher Education	19
State and Local Appropriations for Higher Education	13
Federal Spending on Higher Education Act Insured Loans	38
Federal Spending on National Guaranteed Student Loans	33
Federal Spending on Pell Grants	18
Default Rate in Perkins Student Loan Program	21
State Spending on Libraries	13

Energy
State Ranking

Total Spending on Energy	19
Net Generation of Electricity	6
Cost of Electricity	46
Spending on Electricity	21
Spending on Natural Gas	36
Spending on Gasoline	19
Spending on Petroleum	19
Spending on Coal	6
Total Energy Consumption	12
Electricity Consumption	4
Natural Gas Consumption	29
Petroleum Consumption	20
Coal Consumption	5
Power Plants	33
Nuclear Power Plants	34
Hydroelectric Power Plants	34

Environment
State Ranking

Federally Owned Land (acreage)	26
Loss of Wetlands	7
Environmental Protection Agency Spending	50
EPA Abatement, Control, and Compliance	41
State Spending on Environmental Programs	21
Environmental Programs as Part of State Budget	25
State Spending on Forest Programs	24
Total Tree Planting	22
Federal Tree Planting	20
Private Tree Planting	17
State Spending on Air Quality	17
State Spending on Water Quality	26
Federal Grants for Rural Water and Waste Disposal	8
Federal Spending on Wastewater Treatment Works	49
Hazardous Waste Sites on National Priority List	21

Federal Grants for Hazardous Substance
  Response 46
State Spending on Hazardous Waste 35

Health

State Ranking

State Health Rankings 40
State Spending on Health 46
Support for Public Health 38
Family and Business Spending on Health
  Care 48
HMO Enrollment 33
Medicaid Recipients 6
Medically Underserved Population 20
Lack of Health Care Access 20
Active Nonfederal Physicians 37
Active Nonfederal Nurses 45
Active Nonfederal Dentists 27
Average Cost per Hospital Stay 48
Average Cost per Day for Hospital Care 39
Average Cost per Day for Hospital Room 33
State Spending on Hospitals 33
Adequacy of Prenatal Care 23
Infants Born Receiving Late or No
  Prenatal Care 30
Infants Born with Low Birth Weight 21
Abortions 43
Immunizations of Two-Year-Olds —
Overall Risk for Heart Disease 45
Risk Factor for Heart Disease
  (hypertension) 14
Deaths Due to Heart Disease 12
New Cancer Cases 9
Deaths Due to Cancer 8
Prevalence of Smoking 3
Prevalence of Diabetes 32
Deaths Due to Diabetes 29
Cost of Diabetes 31
AIDS Cases Reported 37
Gonorrhea Cases Reported 7
Syphilis Cases Reported 30
Tuberculosis Cases Reported 11
Hepatitis Cases Reported 44
Rabies Cases Reported 26
Lyme Disease Cases Reported 21
Beer Consumption 44
Wine Consumption 49
Liquor Consumption 43
Alcohol and Drug Treatment Admissions 38
Federal Spending on Alcohol, Drug
  Abuse, and Mental Health 43
Total Spending on Alcohol/Drug Abuse
  Services 46
State Spending on Alcohol/Drug Abuse
  Services 38
Hard-Core Cocaine Users 26
Federal Drug Grants to States 29

Population

State Ranking

Population 23
Population Density 24
Population in Metropolitan Areas 39
Population Under 18 Years Old 27
Population Over 65 Years Old 26
White Population 15
African American Population 26
Hispanic Population 49
Asian American Population 48
Native American Population 49
Catholic Population 36

Jewish Population 37
Marriages 6
Divorces 11
Births 30
Births to Single Mothers 37
Births to Single Teenagers 21
Adoptions 47
Adoption Option Index 21
Infant Mortality 31
Child Deaths and Suicides 25
Teen Violent Death Rate 24
Deaths 8

Recreation

State Ranking

State Parks and Recreation Areas 43
Visitors to State Parks and Recreation
  Areas 7
Revenues from State Parks and
  Recreation Areas 1
Spending on State Arts Agencies 21
Domestic Travel Spending 41
State Travel Office Budgets 22
Lodging Industry (rooms) 31
Participation in Exercise Walking 13
Participation in Swimming 14
Participation in Camping 15
Participation in Bowling 10
Bowling League Membership 34
Participation in Running/Jogging 25
Participation in Aerobics 43
Participation in Golf 17
Participation in Softball 11
Participation in Health Clubs 40
Participation in Tennis 23
Participation in Hunting 8
Participation in Baseball 33
Participation in Bicycle Riding 28
Number of Boats 31
Attendance at Parimutuel Racing 13
Revenue from Parimutuel Betting 5

Social Services

State Ranking

Federal Grants for Social Services 43
State Spending on Public Welfare 13
Persons in Poverty 4
Public Aid Recipients 7
Participants in Food Stamp Program 4
Households in Food Stamp Program 4
Percentage of Poor Using AFDC and
  Food Stamps 44
Federal Spending on Children and
  Family Services 17
Federal Women, Infants, and Children
  Food Program 12
Child Welfare Services 31
Child Abuse Cases Reported —
Children in Poverty 7
Children Without Health Insurance 11
Children Who Are Hungry or at Risk 14
Federal Spending on Child Nutrition
  Programs 10
Federal Spending on Special Milk
  Program 25
National School Lunch Program
  Participants 9
Head Start Enrollment 12
Head Start Spending 38
Federal Spending on Rehabilitation
  Services/Handicapped Research 9

State Government

State Ranking

Financial World's State Rankings 37
Salaries of State Officials (governor) 29
Salaries of State Legislators —
Women in State Legislatures 50
African Americans in State Legislatures 36
Hispanics in State Legislatures 21
Asian Americans in State Legislatures 6
Native Americans in State Legislatures 12
Turnover in State Legislatures 34
Length of State Legislative Sessions 42
State Bills in Regular Session —
State Resolutions in Regular Session —
State Bills in Special Session 16
State Resolutions in Special Session 14
Women in State Cabinets 33
Total Federal Funding to State
  Governments 30
Total State Spending 16
State General Expenditures 12
State Debt 17
State Spending on Interest on the
  General Debt 18
Total State Tax Revenue 13
State Revenue from Tax on Sales and
  Gross Receipts 22
State Revenue from General Sales Tax 31
State Revenue from Licenses 30
State Revenue from Motor Vehicle
  Licenses 29
State Revenue from Individual Income
  Taxes 14
State Revenue from Corporation Net
  Income Taxes 15
State Revenue from Severance Taxes 10
State Revenue from Property Taxes 5
State Revenue from Death and Gift
  Taxes 12
State Revenue from Documentary and
  Stock Transfers 29
State Revenue from Tax on Motor Fuels 27
State Revenue from Tax on Tobacco
  Products 48
Excise Tax on Cigarettes 47
Excise Tax on Gasoline 35
State Revenue from Lotteries 28

Transportation

State Ranking

Motor Vehicle Registrations 19
Automobile Registrations 39
Bus and Truck Registrations 10
Motorcycle Registrations 45
Driver Licenses 41
Federal Spending on Highway Trust
  Fund 45
Federal Spending on Mass
  Transportation 29
State Spending on Highways 22
Highway Deficiency 23
Bridge Deficiency 12
Traffic Fatalities 12
Traffic Fatalities per Miles Traveled 10
Motorcyclist Fatalities 37
Pedalcyclist Fatalities 30
Pedestrian Fatalities 41
Registered Aircraft 49
Registered Pilots 47
Federal Spending on Airport and
  Airway Trust Fund 17
Aircraft Fatalities 35

— *not applicable*   NA *not available*

Agriculture
State Ranking

Farm Acreage	34
Farmland as Portion of State	31
Net Farm Income	29
Government Payments to Farms	17
Federal Commodity Loans/Price Supports	12
Federal Spending on Rural Development	3
Rural Electric and Telephone Loan Guarantees	7
Foreign-Owned Agricultural Land	4

Business and Economy
State Ranking

Gross State Product	37
Retail Sales	25
Supermarket Sales	6
Commercial Bank Assets	40
Insured Commercial Bank Deposits	38
Fortune 500 Companies	33
Inc. 500 Companies	45
New Business Incorporations	27
Business Failures	34
Financial Aid to Minority Businesses	23
Women-Owned Businesses	46
Sales & Receipts of Women-Owned Businesses	35
African American-Owned Businesses	5
Sales & Receipts of African American-Owned Businesses	3
Hispanic-Owned Businesses	15
Sales & Receipts of Hispanic-Owned Businesses	13
Employees in Manufacturing	32
Manufacturing Shipments	8
Japanese-Owned U.S. Manufacturing Plants	39
Exports to Mexico	24
Change in Exports to Mexico	38
Existing Home Sales	43
Housing Starts	48
Average Annual Pay	31
Disposable Personal Income	46
Median Income of Families with Children	42
Federal Spending on Unemployment Insurance/Employment Services	37
Teen Unemployment	19
Bankruptcy Petitions Filed	25
Patents Issued to State Residents	36
Federal Spending on Community Development	7
Federal Spending on Economic Development Administration	35
Federal Spending on Urban Development Action Grants	29

Crime and Criminal Justice
State Ranking

Total Crimes	8
Violent Crimes	8
Murders	2
Rapes	24
Aggravated Assaults	7
Property Crimes	12
Robberies	10
Burglaries	10
Larcenies and Thefts	15
Motor Vehicle Thefts	17
State and Federal Prisoners	4
Capital Punishment	3

State Spending on Corrections	20
State Spending on Police	10
Inmates in Local Jails	3
Spending on Local Jails	12
Spending per Inmate for Local Jails	43
Employees at Local Jails	5
Juvenile Custody Rate	33
Federal Spending on Office of Justice Assistance Programs	40

Defense
State Ranking

Defense Grants to State and Local Governments	41
Total Defense Payroll	30
Total Army Payroll	19
Total Navy/Marine Corps Payroll	24
Total Air Force Payroll	28
Total Active-Duty Payroll	23
Army Active-Duty Payroll	12
Navy/Marine Corps Active-Duty Payroll	22
Air Force Active-Duty Payroll	24
Total Civilian Payroll	34
Army Civilian Payroll	23
Navy/Marine Corps Civilian Payroll	20
Air Force Civilian Payroll	32
Total Reserve and National Guard Payroll	30
Army Reserve and National Guard Payroll	35
Navy/Marine Corps Reserve and National Guard Payroll	6
Air Force Reserve and National Guard Payroll	22
Total Retired Military Payroll	32
Army Retired Military Payroll	26
Navy/Marine Corps Retired Military Payroll	29
Air Force Retired Military Payroll	24
Total Defense Prime Contracts	30
Army Prime Contracts	27
Navy/Marine Corps Prime Contracts	14
Air Force Prime Contracts	45
U.S. Military Installations	29
Construction of National Guard Centers	43

Education
State Ranking

School Age Population	7
Public Elementary and Secondary School Enrollment	19
Average Daily Attendance	6
Student-Teacher Ratio	NA
Salaries of Public School Teachers	42
Public School Teachers Who Are Male	47
Eighth Grade Math Test Results	37
High School Math Enrollment	16
Public High School Graduation Rate	51
General Educational Development (GED) Test Results	1
Adult Illiteracy	1
Federal Revenue for Public Schools	6
State Revenue for Public Schools	17
Local Government Revenue for Public Schools	38
Total Public School Spending	39
Public School Spending on Instruction	27
Public School Spending on Noninstruction	5
Public School Spending on Support Staff	30
State and Local Government Spending on Public Schools	38

Federal Spending on School Improvement Programs	13
Gifted and Talented Students	33
Federal Spending on Education of Students with Disabilities	40
Student-Teacher Ratio in Catholic Elementary Schools	7
Student-Teacher Ratio in Catholic Secondary Schools	33
State Spending on Education	21
State and Local Government Spending on Education	43
Higher Education Tuition and Fees	24
Higher Education Revenue	39
Federal Spending on Higher Education	19
State Spending on Higher Education	35
State and Local Government Spending on Higher Education	38
State and Local Appropriations for Higher Education	39
Federal Spending on Higher Education Act Insured Loans	41
Federal Spending on National Guaranteed Student Loans	26
Federal Spending on Pell Grants	6
Default Rate in Perkins Student Loan Program	3
State Spending on Libraries	50

Energy
State Ranking

Total Spending on Energy	3
Net Generation of Electricity	23
Cost of Electricity	33
Spending on Electricity	4
Spending on Natural Gas	1
Spending on Gasoline	35
Spending on Petroleum	2
Spending on Coal	33
Total Energy Consumption	3
Electricity Consumption	9
Natural Gas Consumption	2
Petroleum Consumption	2
Coal Consumption	33
Power Plants	35
Nuclear Power Plants	9
Hydroelectric Power Plants	47

Environment
State Ranking

Federally Owned Land (acreage)	14
Loss of Wetlands	26
Environmental Protection Agency Spending	40
EPA Abatement, Control, and Compliance	30
State Spending on Environmental Programs	11
Environmental Programs as Part of State Budget	7
State Spending on Forest Programs	25
Total Tree Planting	6
Federal Tree Planting	10
Private Tree Planting	6
State Spending on Air Quality	16
State Spending on Water Quality	7
Federal Grants for Rural Water and Waste Disposal	28
Federal Spending on Wastewater Treatment Works	43
Hazardous Waste Sites on National Priority List	30

Federal Grants for Hazardous Substance
Response 21
State Spending on Hazardous Waste 31

Health — State Ranking

State Health Rankings	46
State Spending on Health	30
Support for Public Health	37
Family and Business Spending on Health Care	35
HMO Enrollment	36
Medicaid Recipients	5
Medically Underserved Population	2
Lack of Health Care Access	9
Active Nonfederal Physicians	27
Active Nonfederal Nurses	51
Active Nonfederal Dentists	36
Average Cost per Hospital Stay	24
Average Cost per Day for Hospital Care	19
Average Cost per Day for Hospital Room	47
State Spending on Hospitals	4
Adequacy of Prenatal Care	37
Infants Born Receiving Late or No Prenatal Care	14
Infants Born with Low Birth Weight	3
Abortions	37
Immunizations of Two-Year-Olds	—
Overall Risk for Heart Disease	18
Risk Factor for Heart Disease (hypertension)	42
Deaths Due to Heart Disease	27
New Cancer Cases	30
Deaths Due to Cancer	27
Prevalence of Smoking	15
Prevalence of Diabetes	13
Deaths Due to Diabetes	21
Cost of Diabetes	12
AIDS Cases Reported	13
Gonorrhea Cases Reported	7
Syphilis Cases Reported	2
Tuberculosis Cases Reported	29
Hepatitis Cases Reported	30
Rabies Cases Reported	43
Lyme Disease Cases Reported	41
Beer Consumption	10
Wine Consumption	33
Liquor Consumption	25
Alcohol and Drug Treatment Admissions	46
Federal Spending on Alcohol, Drug Abuse, and Mental Health	27
Total Spending on Alcohol/Drug Abuse Services	35
State Spending on Alcohol/Drug Abuse Services	48
Hard-Core Cocaine Users	19
Federal Drug Grants to States	12

Population — State Ranking

Population	21
Population Density	23
Population in Metropolitan Areas	22
Population Under 18 Years Old	6
Population Over 65 Years Old	40
White Population	48
African American Population	3
Hispanic Population	28
Asian American Population	29
Native American Population	25
Catholic Population	7

— not applicable   NA not available

Jewish Population	34
Marriages	25
Divorces	NA
Births	10
Births to Single Mothers	3
Births to Single Teenagers	3
Adoptions	41
Adoption Option Index	47
Infant Mortality	15
Child Deaths and Suicides	7
Teen Violent Death Rate	10
Deaths	22

Recreation — State Ranking

State Parks and Recreation Areas	47
Visitors to State Parks and Recreation Areas	50
Revenues from State Parks and Recreation Areas	47
Spending on State Arts Agencies	49
Domestic Travel Spending	30
State Travel Office Budgets	17
Lodging Industry (rooms)	25
Participation in Exercise Walking	15
Participation in Swimming	10
Participation in Camping	25
Participation in Bowling	27
Bowling League Membership	46
Participation in Running/Jogging	5
Participation in Aerobics	7
Participation in Golf	41
Participation in Softball	9
Participation in Health Clubs	33
Participation in Tennis	19
Participation in Hunting	9
Participation in Baseball	7
Participation in Bicycle Riding	15
Number of Boats	10
Attendance at Parimutuel Racing	16
Revenue from Parimutuel Betting	4

Social Services — State Ranking

Federal Grants for Social Services	3
State Spending on Public Welfare	19
Persons in Poverty	3
Public Aid Recipients	3
Participants in Food Stamp Program	2
Households in Food Stamp Program	2
Percentage of Poor Using AFDC and Food Stamps	47
Federal Spending on Children and Family Services	22
Federal Women, Infants, and Children Food Program	4
Child Welfare Services	14
Child Abuse Cases Reported	—
Children in Poverty	2
Children Without Health Insurance	9
Children Who Are Hungry or at Risk	7
Federal Spending on Child Nutrition Programs	2
Federal Spending on Special Milk Program	38
National School Lunch Program Participants	2
Head Start Enrollment	38
Head Start Spending	39
Federal Spending on Rehabilitation Services/Handicapped Research	10

State Government — State Ranking

Financial World's State Rankings	24
Salaries of State Officials (governor)	38
Salaries of State Legislators	22
Women in State Legislatures	48
African Americans in State Legislatures	2
Hispanics in State Legislatures	21
Asian Americans in State Legislatures	6
Native Americans in State Legislatures	12
Turnover in State Legislatures	49
Length of State Legislative Sessions	20
State Bills in Regular Session	18
State Resolutions in Regular Session	12
State Bills in Special Session	20
State Resolutions in Special Session	15
Women in State Cabinets	4
Total Federal Funding to State Governments	35
Total State Spending	11
State General Expenditures	10
State Debt	10
State Spending on Interest on the General Debt	4
Total State Tax Revenue	40
State Revenue from Tax on Sales and Gross Receipts	38
State Revenue from General Sales Tax	38
State Revenue from Licenses	18
State Revenue from Motor Vehicle Licenses	49
State Revenue from Individual Income Taxes	38
State Revenue from Corporation Net Income Taxes	20
State Revenue from Severance Taxes	5
State Revenue from Property Taxes	20
State Revenue from Death and Gift Taxes	26
State Revenue from Documentary and Stock Transfers	—
State Revenue from Tax on Motor Fuels	15
State Revenue from Tax on Tobacco Products	28
Excise Tax on Cigarettes	28
Excise Tax on Gasoline	10
State Revenue from Lotteries	—

Transportation — State Ranking

Motor Vehicle Registrations	38
Automobile Registrations	45
Bus and Truck Registrations	16
Motorcycle Registrations	49
Driver Licenses	47
Federal Spending on Highway Trust Fund	17
Federal Spending on Mass Transportation	18
State Spending on Highways	28
Highway Deficiency	14
Bridge Deficiency	10
Traffic Fatalities	18
Traffic Fatalities per Miles Traveled	13
Motorcyclist Fatalities	49
Pedalcyclist Fatalities	5
Pedestrian Fatalities	5
Registered Aircraft	34
Registered Pilots	43
Federal Spending on Airport and Airway Trust Fund	19
Aircraft Fatalities	41

Agriculture
State Ranking

Farm Acreage	43
Farmland as Portion of State	49
Net Farm Income	33
Government Payments to Farms	35
Federal Commodity Loans/Price Supports	44
Federal Spending on Rural Development	10
Rural Electric and Telephone Loan Guarantees	32
Foreign-Owned Agricultural Land	1

Business and Economy
State Ranking

Gross State Product	29
Retail Sales	8
Supermarket Sales	3
Commercial Bank Assets	51
Insured Commercial Bank Deposits	50
Fortune 500 Companies	42
Inc. 500 Companies	41
New Business Incorporations	32
Business Failures	25
Financial Aid to Minority Businesses	41
Women-Owned Businesses	47
Sales & Receipts of Women-Owned Businesses	14
African American-Owned Businesses	47
Sales & Receipts of African American-Owned Businesses	50
Hispanic-Owned Businesses	51
Sales & Receipts of Hispanic-Owned Businesses	39
Employees in Manufacturing	34
Manufacturing Shipments	28
Japanese-Owned U.S. Manufacturing Plants	30
Exports to Mexico	43
Change in Exports to Mexico	4
Existing Home Sales	NA
Housing Starts	37
Average Annual Pay	39
Disposable Personal Income	28
Median Income of Families with Children	27
Federal Spending on Unemployment Insurance/Employment Services	12
Teen Unemployment	36
Bankruptcy Petitions Filed	48
Patents Issued to State Residents	40
Federal Spending on Community Development	11
Federal Spending on Economic Development Administration	9
Federal Spending on Urban Development Action Grants	33

Crime and Criminal Justice
State Ranking

Total Crimes	44
Violent Crimes	48
Murders	50
Rapes	48
Aggravated Assaults	48
Property Crimes	44
Robberies	45
Burglaries	36
Larcenies and Thefts	43
Motor Vehicle Thefts	47
State and Federal Prisoners	47
Capital Punishment	—

State Spending on Corrections	34
State Spending on Police	16
Inmates in Local Jails	43
Spending on Local Jails	25
Spending per Inmate for Local Jails	5
Employees at Local Jails	43
Juvenile Custody Rate	42
Federal Spending on Office of Justice Assistance Programs	11

Defense
State Ranking

Defense Grants to State and Local Governments	45
Total Defense Payroll	14
Total Army Payroll	44
Total Navy/Marine Corps Payroll	5
Total Air Force Payroll	24
Total Active-Duty Payroll	27
Army Active-Duty Payroll	30
Navy/Marine Corps Active-Duty Payroll	10
Air Force Active-Duty Payroll	23
Total Civilian Payroll	7
Army Civilian Payroll	47
Navy/Marine Corps Civilian Payroll	4
Air Force Civilian Payroll	27
Total Reserve and National Guard Payroll	33
Army Reserve and National Guard Payroll	33
Navy/Marine Corps Reserve and National Guard Payroll	26
Air Force Reserve and National Guard Payroll	15
Total Retired Military Payroll	19
Army Retired Military Payroll	27
Navy/Marine Corps Retired Military Payroll	9
Air Force Retired Military Payroll	25
Total Defense Prime Contracts	7
Army Prime Contracts	41
Navy/Marine Corps Prime Contracts	3
Air Force Prime Contracts	47
U.S. Military Installations	29
Construction of National Guard Centers	45

Education
State Ranking

School Age Population	35
Public Elementary and Secondary School Enrollment	39
Average Daily Attendance	21
Student-Teacher Ratio	46
Salaries of Public School Teachers	33
Public School Teachers Who Are Male	12
Eighth Grade Math Test Results	—
High School Math Enrollment	NA
Public High School Graduation Rate	16
General Educational Development (GED) Test Results	14
Adult Illiteracy	27
Federal Revenue for Public Schools	32
State Revenue for Public Schools	18
Local Government Revenue for Public Schools	33
Total Public School Spending	15
Public School Spending on Instruction	36
Public School Spending on Noninstruction	47
Public School Spending on Support Staff	48
State and Local Government Spending on Public Schools	8

Federal Spending on School Improvement Programs	25
Gifted and Talented Students	NA
Federal Spending on Education of Students with Disabilities	8
Student-Teacher Ratio in Catholic Elementary Schools	42
Student-Teacher Ratio in Catholic Secondary Schools	41
State Spending on Education	28
State and Local Government Spending on Education	30
Higher Education Tuition and Fees	11
Higher Education Revenue	18
Federal Spending on Higher Education	17
State Spending on Higher Education	36
State and Local Government Spending on Higher Education	37
State and Local Appropriations for Higher Education	23
Federal Spending on Higher Education Act Insured Loans	19
Federal Spending on National Guaranteed Student Loans	16
Federal Spending on Pell Grants	40
Default Rate in Perkins Student Loan Program	26
State Spending on Libraries	18

Energy
State Ranking

Total Spending on Energy	11
Net Generation of Electricity	43
Cost of Electricity	10
Spending on Electricity	25
Spending on Natural Gas	51
Spending on Gasoline	10
Spending on Petroleum	6
Spending on Coal	45
Total Energy Consumption	32
Electricity Consumption	36
Natural Gas Consumption	50
Petroleum Consumption	7
Coal Consumption	46
Power Plants	5
Nuclear Power Plants	5
Hydroelectric Power Plants	4

Environment
State Ranking

Federally Owned Land (acreage)	47
Loss of Wetlands	47
Environmental Protection Agency Spending	9
EPA Abatement, Control, and Compliance	20
State Spending on Environmental Programs	19
Environmental Programs as Part of State Budget	16
State Spending on Forest Programs	45
Total Tree Planting	21
Federal Tree Planting	32
Private Tree Planting	16
State Spending on Air Quality	41
State Spending on Water Quality	39
Federal Grants for Rural Water and Waste Disposal	1
Federal Spending on Wastewater Treatment Works	8
Hazardous Waste Sites on National Priority List	37

Federal Grants for Hazardous Substance
Response — 18
State Spending on Hazardous Waste — 1

Health   *State Ranking*

State Health Rankings — 14
State Spending on Health — 18
Support for Public Health — 19
Family and Business Spending on Health
Care — 27
HMO Enrollment — 42
Medicaid Recipients — 11
Medically Underserved Population — 44
Lack of Health Care Access — 25
Active Nonfederal Physicians — 31
Active Nonfederal Nurses — 9
Active Nonfederal Dentists — 40
Average Cost per Hospital Stay — 23
Average Cost per Day for Hospital Care — 37
Average Cost per Day for Hospital Room — 14
State Spending on Hospitals — 38
Adequacy of Prenatal Care — 12
Infants Born Receiving Late or No
Prenatal Care — 49
Infants Born with Low Birth Weight — 46
Abortions — 38
Immunizations of Two-Year-Olds — —
Overall Risk for Heart Disease — 32
Risk Factor for Heart Disease
(hypertension) — 13
Deaths Due to Heart Disease — 23
New Cancer Cases — 7
Deaths Due to Cancer — 9
Prevalence of Smoking — 18
Prevalence of Diabetes — 39
Deaths Due to Diabetes — 11
Cost of Diabetes — 38
AIDS Cases Reported — 44
Gonorrhea Cases Reported — 49
Syphilis Cases Reported — 46
Tuberculosis Cases Reported — 43
Hepatitis Cases Reported — 47
Rabies Cases Reported — 48
Lyme Disease Cases Reported — 28
Beer Consumption — 38
Wine Consumption — 19
Liquor Consumption — 21
Alcohol and Drug Treatment Admissions — 17
Federal Spending on Alcohol, Drug
Abuse, and Mental Health — 37
Total Spending on Alcohol/Drug Abuse
Services — 28
State Spending on Alcohol/Drug Abuse
Services — 13
Hard-Core Cocaine Users — 45
Federal Drug Grants to States — 26

Population   *State Ranking*

Population — 38
Population Density — 37
Population in Metropolitan Areas — 45
Population Under 18 Years Old — 35
Population Over 65 Years Old — 15
White Population — 2
African American Population — 48
Hispanic Population — 50
Asian American Population — 42
Native American Population — 23
Catholic Population — 20

Jewish Population — 24
Marriages — 23
Divorces — 33
Births — 48
Births to Single Mothers — 39
Births to Single Teenagers — 28
Adoptions — 4
Adoption Option Index — 41
Infant Mortality — 49
Child Deaths and Suicides — 28
Teen Violent Death Rate — 44
Deaths — 25

Recreation   *State Ranking*

State Parks and Recreation Areas — 13
Visitors to State Parks and Recreation
Areas — 34
Revenues from State Parks and
Recreation Areas — 31
Spending on State Arts Agencies — 32
Domestic Travel Spending — 21
State Travel Office Budgets — 30
Lodging Industry (rooms) — 22
Participation in Exercise Walking — 1
Participation in Swimming — 2
Participation in Camping — 3
Participation in Bowling — 6
Bowling League Membership — 48
Participation in Running/Jogging — 9
Participation in Aerobics — 4
Participation in Golf — 16
Participation in Softball — 38
Participation in Health Clubs — 23
Participation in Tennis — 13
Participation in Hunting — 4
Participation in Baseball — 30
Participation in Bicycle Riding — 11
Number of Boats — 5
Attendance at Parimutuel Racing — —
Revenue from Parimutuel Betting — 19

Social Services   *State Ranking*

Federal Grants for Social Services — 40
State Spending on Public Welfare — 4
Persons in Poverty — 23
Public Aid Recipients — 13
Participants in Food Stamp Program — 24
Households in Food Stamp Program — 16
Percentage of Poor Using AFDC and
Food Stamps — 14
Federal Spending on Children and
Family Services — 31
Federal Women, Infants, and Children
Food Program — 8
Child Welfare Services — 28
Child Abuse Cases Reported — —
Children in Poverty — 38
Children Without Health Insurance — 38
Children Who Are Hungry or at Risk — 36
Federal Spending on Child Nutrition
Programs — 31
Federal Spending on Special Milk
Program — 14
National School Lunch Program
Participants — 40
Head Start Enrollment — 3
Head Start Spending — 42
Federal Spending on Rehabilitation
Services/Handicapped Research — 16

State Government   *State Ranking*

Financial World's State Rankings — 48
Salaries of State Officials (governor) — 41
Salaries of State Legislators — 37
Women in State Legislatures — 6
African Americans in State Legislatures — 43
Hispanics in State Legislatures — 21
Asian Americans in State Legislatures — 6
Native Americans in State Legislatures — 12
Turnover in State Legislatures — 18
Length of State Legislative Sessions — 25
State Bills in Regular Session — 15
State Resolutions in Regular Session — 5
State Bills in Special Session — 3
State Resolutions in Special Session — 19
Women in State Cabinets — 6
Total Federal Funding to State
Governments — 14
Total State Spending — 15
State General Expenditures — 13
State Debt — 14
State Spending on Interest on the
General Debt — 12
Total State Tax Revenue — 18
State Revenue from Tax on Sales and
Gross Receipts — 19
State Revenue from General Sales Tax — 20
State Revenue from Licenses — 28
State Revenue from Motor Vehicle
Licenses — 27
State Revenue from Individual Income
Taxes — 13
State Revenue from Corporation Net
Income Taxes — 25
State Revenue from Severance Taxes — —
State Revenue from Property Taxes — 9
State Revenue from Death and Gift
Taxes — 29
State Revenue from Documentary and
Stock Transfers — 12
State Revenue from Tax on Motor Fuels — 14
State Revenue from Tax on Tobacco
Products — 6
Excise Tax on Cigarettes — 12
Excise Tax on Gasoline — 26
State Revenue from Lotteries — 15

Transportation   *State Ranking*

Motor Vehicle Registrations — 21
Automobile Registrations — 13
Bus and Truck Registrations — 32
Motorcycle Registrations — 9
Driver Licenses — 12
Federal Spending on Highway Trust
Fund — 33
Federal Spending on Mass
Transportation — 43
State Spending on Highways — 20
Highway Deficiency — 15
Bridge Deficiency — 23
Traffic Fatalities — 28
Traffic Fatalities per Miles Traveled — 37
Motorcyclist Fatalities — 3
Pedalcyclist Fatalities — 49
Pedestrian Fatalities — 50
Registered Aircraft — 19
Registered Pilots — 23
Federal Spending on Airport and
Airway Trust Fund — 15
Aircraft Fatalities — 19

— not applicable   NA not available

Agriculture · State Ranking

Farm Acreage	40
Farmland as Portion of State	26
Net Farm Income	36
Government Payments to Farms	39
Federal Commodity Loans/Price Supports	34
Federal Spending on Rural Development	23
Rural Electric and Telephone Loan Guarantees	18
Foreign-Owned Agricultural Land	17

Business and Economy · State Ranking

Gross State Product	16
Retail Sales	11
Supermarket Sales	24
Commercial Bank Assets	17
Insured Commercial Bank Deposits	19
Fortune 500 Companies	34
Inc. 500 Companies	14
New Business Incorporations	8
Business Failures	32
Financial Aid to Minority Businesses	32
Women-Owned Businesses	4
Sales & Receipts of Women-Owned Businesses	39
African American-Owned Businesses	2
Sales & Receipts of African American-Owned Businesses	7
Hispanic-Owned Businesses	17
Sales & Receipts of Hispanic-Owned Businesses	20
Employees in Manufacturing	28
Manufacturing Shipments	42
Japanese-Owned U.S. Manufacturing Plants	26
Exports to Mexico	44
Change in Exports to Mexico	16
Existing Home Sales	36
Housing Starts	18
Average Annual Pay	10
Disposable Personal Income	7
Median Income of Families with Children	5
Federal Spending on Unemployment Insurance/Employment Services	36
Teen Unemployment	3
Bankruptcy Petitions Filed	31
Patents Issued to State Residents	20
Federal Spending on Community Development	38
Federal Spending on Economic Development Administration	32
Federal Spending on Urban Development Action Grants	12

Crime and Criminal Justice · State Ranking

Total Crimes	12
Violent Crimes	7
Murders	9
Rapes	16
Aggravated Assaults	11
Property Crimes	15
Robberies	5
Burglaries	26
Larcenies and Thefts	18
Motor Vehicle Thefts	11
State and Federal Prisoners	9
Capital Punishment	17
State Spending on Corrections	14
State Spending on Police	3
Inmates in Local Jails	10
Spending on Local Jails	11
Spending per Inmate for Local Jails	17
Employees at Local Jails	14
Juvenile Custody Rate	30
Federal Spending on Office of Justice Assistance Programs	23

Defense · State Ranking

Defense Grants to State and Local Governments	39
Total Defense Payroll	6
Total Army Payroll	11
Total Navy/Marine Corps Payroll	9
Total Air Force Payroll	30
Total Active-Duty Payroll	21
Army Active-Duty Payroll	16
Navy/Marine Corps Active-Duty Payroll	13
Air Force Active-Duty Payroll	26
Total Civilian Payroll	6
Army Civilian Payroll	5
Navy/Marine Corps Civilian Payroll	7
Air Force Civilian Payroll	24
Total Reserve and National Guard Payroll	20
Army Reserve and National Guard Payroll	24
Navy/Marine Corps Reserve and National Guard Payroll	4
Air Force Reserve and National Guard Payroll	17
Total Retired Military Payroll	14
Army Retired Military Payroll	9
Navy/Marine Corps Retired Military Payroll	10
Air Force Retired Military Payroll	28
Total Defense Prime Contracts	8
Army Prime Contracts	13
Navy/Marine Corps Prime Contracts	7
Air Force Prime Contracts	10
U.S. Military Installations	5
Construction of National Guard Centers	36

Education · State Ranking

School Age Population	43
Public Elementary and Secondary School Enrollment	22
Average Daily Attendance	43
Student-Teacher Ratio	24
Salaries of Public School Teachers	7
Public School Teachers Who Are Male	36
Eighth Grade Math Test Results	22
High School Math Enrollment	2
Public High School Graduation Rate	30
General Educational Development (GED) Test Results	39
Adult Illiteracy	21
Federal Revenue for Public Schools	44
State Revenue for Public Schools	41
Local Government Revenue for Public Schools	12
Total Public School Spending	10
Public School Spending on Instruction	46
Public School Spending on Noninstruction	38
Public School Spending on Support Staff	27
State and Local Government Spending on Public Schools	32
Federal Spending on School Improvement Programs	46
Gifted and Talented Students	5
Federal Spending on Education of Students with Disabilities	32
Student-Teacher Ratio in Catholic Elementary Schools	22
Student-Teacher Ratio in Catholic Secondary Schools	42
State Spending on Education	41
State and Local Government Spending on Education	37
Higher Education Tuition and Fees	15
Higher Education Revenue	5
Federal Spending on Higher Education	42
State Spending on Higher Education	28
State and Local Government Spending on Higher Education	34
State and Local Appropriations for Higher Education	6
Federal Spending on Higher Education Act Insured Loans	35
Federal Spending on National Guaranteed Student Loans	47
Federal Spending on Pell Grants	46
Default Rate in Perkins Student Loan Program	16
State Spending on Libraries	3

Energy · State Ranking

Total Spending on Energy	45
Net Generation of Electricity	46
Cost of Electricity	18
Spending on Electricity	35
Spending on Natural Gas	35
Spending on Gasoline	36
Spending on Petroleum	40
Spending on Coal	30
Total Energy Consumption	42
Electricity Consumption	32
Natural Gas Consumption	39
Petroleum Consumption	43
Coal Consumption	31
Power Plants	49
Nuclear Power Plants	27
Hydroelectric Power Plants	42

Environment · State Ranking

Federally Owned Land (acreage)	33
Loss of Wetlands	8
Environmental Protection Agency Spending	10
EPA Abatement, Control, and Compliance	11
State Spending on Environmental Programs	20
Environmental Programs as Part of State Budget	26
State Spending on Forest Programs	31
Total Tree Planting	12
Federal Tree Planting	32
Private Tree Planting	12
State Spending on Air Quality	22
State Spending on Water Quality	22
Federal Grants for Rural Water and Waste Disposal	41
Federal Spending on Wastewater Treatment Works	10
Hazardous Waste Sites on National Priority List	32

Federal Grants for Hazardous Substance
Response ... 28
State Spending on Hazardous Waste ... 21

Health
State Ranking

State Health Rankings ... 22
State Spending on Health ... 10
Support for Public Health ... 13
Family and Business Spending on Health
Care ... 10
HMO Enrollment ... 13
Medicaid Recipients ... 43
Medically Underserved Population ... 24
Lack of Health Care Access ... 42
Active Nonfederal Physicians ... 3
Active Nonfederal Nurses ... 22
Active Nonfederal Dentists ... 9
Average Cost per Hospital Stay ... 22
Average Cost per Day for Hospital Care ... 21
Average Cost per Day for Hospital Room ... 27
State Spending on Hospitals ... 35
Adequacy of Prenatal Care ... 7
Infants Born Receiving Late or No
Prenatal Care ... 35
Infants Born with Low Birth Weight ... 11
Abortions ... 13
Immunizations of Two-Year-Olds ... —
Overall Risk for Heart Disease ... 27
Risk Factor for Heart Disease
(hypertension) ... 23
Deaths Due to Heart Disease ... 36
New Cancer Cases ... 33
Deaths Due to Cancer ... 28
Prevalence of Smoking ... 20
Prevalence of Diabetes ... 17
Deaths Due to Diabetes ... 17
Cost of Diabetes ... 17
AIDS Cases Reported ... 6
Gonorrhea Cases Reported ... 8
Syphilis Cases Reported ... 17
Tuberculosis Cases Reported ... 18
Hepatitis Cases Reported ... 27
Rabies Cases Reported ... 7
Lyme Disease Cases Reported ... 10
Beer Consumption ... 41
Wine Consumption ... 20
Liquor Consumption ... 11
Alcohol and Drug Treatment Admissions ... 22
Federal Spending on Alcohol, Drug
Abuse, and Mental Health ... 20
Total Spending on Alcohol/Drug Abuse
Services ... 8
State Spending on Alcohol/Drug Abuse
Services ... 8
Hard-Core Cocaine Users ... 29
Federal Drug Grants to States ... 17

Population
State Ranking

Population ... 19
Population Density ... 6
Population in Metropolitan Areas ... 4
Population Under 18 Years Old ... 42
Population Over 65 Years Old ... 42
White Population ... 45
African American Population ... 7
Hispanic Population ... 24
Asian American Population ... 8
Native American Population ... 35
Catholic Population ... 38

Jewish Population ... 5
Marriages ... 21
Divorces ... 44
Births ... 8
Births to Single Mothers ... 14
Births to Single Teenagers ... 22
Adoptions ... 44
Adoption Option Index ... 39
Infant Mortality ... 32
Child Deaths and Suicides ... 30
Teen Violent Death Rate ... 27
Deaths ... 34

Recreation
State Ranking

State Parks and Recreation Areas ... 16
Visitors to State Parks and Recreation
Areas ... 39
Revenues from State Parks and
Recreation Areas ... 34
Spending on State Arts Agencies ... 9
Domestic Travel Spending ... 36
State Travel Office Budgets ... 29
Lodging Industry (rooms) ... 37
Participation in Exercise Walking ... 39
Participation in Swimming ... 35
Participation in Camping ... 38
Participation in Bowling ... 25
Bowling League Membership ... 44
Participation in Running/Jogging ... 32
Participation in Aerobics ... 33
Participation in Golf ... 42
Participation in Softball ... 35
Participation in Health Clubs ... 32
Participation in Tennis ... 29
Participation in Hunting ... 37
Participation in Baseball ... 24
Participation in Bicycle Riding ... 35
Number of Boats ... 32
Attendance at Parimutuel Racing ... 14
Revenue from Parimutuel Betting ... 17

Social Services
State Ranking

Federal Grants for Social Services ... 37
State Spending on Public Welfare ... 17
Persons in Poverty ... 47
Public Aid Recipients ... 30
Participants in Food Stamp Program ... 30
Households in Food Stamp Program ... 31
Percentage of Poor Using AFDC and
Food Stamps ... 16
Federal Spending on Children and
Family Services ... 48
Federal Women, Infants, and Children
Food Program ... 50
Child Welfare Services ... 34
Child Abuse Cases Reported ... —
Children in Poverty ... 48
Children Without Health Insurance ... 28
Children Who Are Hungry or at Risk ... 49
Federal Spending on Child Nutrition
Programs ... 44
Federal Spending on Special Milk
Program ... 23
National School Lunch Program
Participants ... 44
Head Start Enrollment ... 11
Head Start Spending ... 15
Federal Spending on Rehabilitation
Services/Handicapped Research ... 47

State Government
State Ranking

Financial World's State Rankings ... 3
Salaries of State Officials (governor) ... 3
Salaries of State Legislators ... 12
Women in State Legislatures ... 17
African Americans in State Legislatures ... 3
Hispanics in State Legislatures ... 21
Asian Americans in State Legislatures ... 6
Native Americans in State Legislatures ... 12
Turnover in State Legislatures ... 13
Length of State Legislative Sessions ... 17
State Bills in Regular Session ... 16
State Resolutions in Regular Session ... 40
State Bills in Special Session ... 25
State Resolutions in Special Session ... 19
Women in State Cabinets ... 1
Total Federal Funding to State
Governments ... 4
Total State Spending ... 38
State General Expenditures ... 41
State Debt ... 19
State Spending on Interest on the
General Debt ... 27
Total State Tax Revenue ... 15
State Revenue from Tax on Sales and
Gross Receipts ... 28
State Revenue from General Sales Tax ... 37
State Revenue from Licenses ... 46
State Revenue from Motor Vehicle
Licenses ... 42
State Revenue from Individual Income
Taxes ... 8
State Revenue from Corporation Net
Income Taxes ... 31
State Revenue from Severance Taxes ... —
State Revenue from Property Taxes ... 8
State Revenue from Death and Gift
Taxes ... 16
State Revenue from Documentary and
Stock Transfers ... 9
State Revenue from Tax on Motor Fuels ... 31
State Revenue from Tax on Tobacco
Products ... 44
Excise Tax on Cigarettes ... 39
Excise Tax on Gasoline ... 20
State Revenue from Lotteries ... 2

Transportation
State Ranking

Motor Vehicle Registrations ... 32
Automobile Registrations ... 10
Bus and Truck Registrations ... 44
Motorcycle Registrations ... 37
Driver Licenses ... 38
Federal Spending on Highway Trust
Fund ... 20
Federal Spending on Mass
Transportation ... 6
State Spending on Highways ... 17
Highway Deficiency ... 38
Bridge Deficiency ... 25
Traffic Fatalities ... 39
Traffic Fatalities per Miles Traveled ... 41
Motorcyclist Fatalities ... 31
Pedalcyclist Fatalities ... 41
Pedestrian Fatalities ... 11
Registered Aircraft ... 44
Registered Pilots ... 39
Federal Spending on Airport and
Airway Trust Fund ... 46
Aircraft Fatalities ... 28

— *not applicable*   NA *not available*

Agriculture | *State Ranking*

Farm Acreage	46
Farmland as Portion of State	44
Net Farm Income	48
Government Payments to Farms	49
Federal Commodity Loans/Price Supports	46
Federal Spending on Rural Development	47
Rural Electric and Telephone Loan Guarantees	40
Foreign-Owned Agricultural Land	47

Business and Economy | *State Ranking*

Gross State Product	7
Retail Sales	6
Supermarket Sales	15
Commercial Bank Assets	7
Insured Commercial Bank Deposits	7
Fortune 500 Companies	13
Inc. 500 Companies	7
New Business Incorporations	29
Business Failures	8
Financial Aid to Minority Businesses	36
Women-Owned Businesses	16
Sales & Receipts of Women-Owned Businesses	4
African American-Owned Businesses	29
Sales & Receipts of African American-Owned Businesses	34
Hispanic-Owned Businesses	25
Sales & Receipts of Hispanic-Owned Businesses	27
Employees in Manufacturing	13
Manufacturing Shipments	27
Japanese-Owned U.S. Manufacturing Plants	16
Exports to Mexico	39
Change in Exports to Mexico	28
Existing Home Sales	47
Housing Starts	46
Average Annual Pay	6
Disposable Personal Income	4
Median Income of Families with Children	4
Federal Spending on Unemployment Insurance/Employment Services	13
Teen Unemployment	17
Bankruptcy Petitions Filed	40
Patents Issued to State Residents	4
Federal Spending on Community Development	5
Federal Spending on Economic Development Administration	46
Federal Spending on Urban Development Action Grants	3

Crime and Criminal Justice | *State Ranking*

Total Crimes	30
Violent Crimes	15
Murders	36
Rapes	34
Aggravated Assaults	9
Property Crimes	29
Robberies	18
Burglaries	24
Larcenies and Thefts	44
Motor Vehicle Thefts	6
State and Federal Prisoners	42
Capital Punishment	—

State Spending on Corrections	10
State Spending on Police	40
Inmates in Local Jails	27
Spending on Local Jails	20
Spending per Inmate for Local Jails	11
Employees at Local Jails	31
Juvenile Custody Rate	43
Federal Spending on Office of Justice Assistance Programs	25

Defense | *State Ranking*

Defense Grants to State and Local Governments	46
Total Defense Payroll	42
Total Army Payroll	25
Total Navy/Marine Corps Payroll	35
Total Air Force Payroll	34
Total Active-Duty Payroll	38
Army Active-Duty Payroll	22
Navy/Marine Corps Active-Duty Payroll	31
Air Force Active-Duty Payroll	37
Total Civilian Payroll	33
Army Civilian Payroll	28
Navy/Marine Corps Civilian Payroll	26
Air Force Civilian Payroll	22
Total Reserve and National Guard Payroll	31
Army Reserve and National Guard Payroll	31
Navy/Marine Corps Reserve and National Guard Payroll	15
Air Force Reserve and National Guard Payroll	24
Total Retired Military Payroll	42
Army Retired Military Payroll	42
Navy/Marine Corps Retired Military Payroll	35
Air Force Retired Military Payroll	40
Total Defense Prime Contracts	4
Army Prime Contracts	1
Navy/Marine Corps Prime Contracts	9
Air Force Prime Contracts	4
U.S. Military Installations	10
Construction of National Guard Centers	46

Education | *State Ranking*

School Age Population	49
Public Elementary and Secondary School Enrollment	15
Average Daily Attendance	35
Student-Teacher Ratio	37
Salaries of Public School Teachers	9
Public School Teachers Who Are Male	1
Eighth Grade Math Test Results	—
High School Math Enrollment	NA
Public High School Graduation Rate	21
General Educational Development (GED) Test Results	8
Adult Illiteracy	27
Federal Revenue for Public Schools	43
State Revenue for Public Schools	42
Local Government Revenue for Public Schools	10
Total Public School Spending	7
Public School Spending on Instruction	41
Public School Spending on Noninstruction	43
Public School Spending on Support Staff	15
State and Local Government Spending on Public Schools	48

Federal Spending on School Improvement Programs	50
Gifted and Talented Students	NA
Federal Spending on Education of Students with Disabilities	2
Student-Teacher Ratio in Catholic Elementary Schools	20
Student-Teacher Ratio in Catholic Secondary Schools	21
State Spending on Education	49
State and Local Government Spending on Education	48
Higher Education Tuition and Fees	3
Higher Education Revenue	2
Federal Spending on Higher Education	47
State Spending on Higher Education	48
State and Local Government Spending on Higher Education	47
State and Local Appropriations for Higher Education	48
Federal Spending on Higher Education Act Insured Loans	6
Federal Spending on National Guaranteed Student Loans	7
Federal Spending on Pell Grants	39
Default Rate in Perkins Student Loan Program	41
State Spending on Libraries	7

Energy | *State Ranking*

Total Spending on Energy	42
Net Generation of Electricity	47
Cost of Electricity	4
Spending on Electricity	33
Spending on Natural Gas	22
Spending on Gasoline	45
Spending on Petroleum	33
Spending on Coal	39
Total Energy Consumption	47
Electricity Consumption	47
Natural Gas Consumption	36
Petroleum Consumption	26
Coal Consumption	40
Power Plants	31
Nuclear Power Plants	21
Hydroelectric Power Plants	28

Environment | *State Ranking*

Federally Owned Land (acreage)	42
Loss of Wetlands	42
Environmental Protection Agency Spending	23
EPA Abatement, Control, and Compliance	38
State Spending on Environmental Programs	12
Environmental Programs as Part of State Budget	27
State Spending on Forest Programs	34
Total Tree Planting	46
Federal Tree Planting	32
Private Tree Planting	43
State Spending on Air Quality	31
State Spending on Water Quality	3
Federal Grants for Rural Water and Waste Disposal	25
Federal Spending on Wastewater Treatment Works	20
Hazardous Waste Sites on National Priority List	14

Federal Grants for Hazardous Substance
Response 19
State Spending on Hazardous Waste 8

Health
State Ranking

State Health Rankings	12
State Spending on Health	7
Support for Public Health	1
Family and Business Spending on Health Care	3
HMO Enrollment	4
Medicaid Recipients	16
Medically Underserved Population	29
Lack of Health Care Access	38
Active Nonfederal Physicians	2
Active Nonfederal Nurses	2
Active Nonfederal Dentists	5
Average Cost per Hospital Stay	6
Average Cost per Day for Hospital Care	10
Average Cost per Day for Hospital Room	8
State Spending on Hospitals	7
Adequacy of Prenatal Care	3
Infants Born Receiving Late or No Prenatal Care	45
Infants Born with Low Birth Weight	36
Abortions	11
Immunizations of Two-Year-Olds	—
Overall Risk for Heart Disease	2
Risk Factor for Heart Disease (hypertension)	36
Deaths Due to Heart Disease	26
New Cancer Cases	13
Deaths Due to Cancer	11
Prevalence of Smoking	33
Prevalence of Diabetes	28
Deaths Due to Diabetes	9
Cost of Diabetes	28
AIDS Cases Reported	14
Gonorrhea Cases Reported	37
Syphilis Cases Reported	27
Tuberculosis Cases Reported	21
Hepatitis Cases Reported	29
Rabies Cases Reported	31
Lyme Disease Cases Reported	9
Beer Consumption	37
Wine Consumption	10
Liquor Consumption	7
Alcohol and Drug Treatment Admissions	6
Federal Spending on Alcohol, Drug Abuse, and Mental Health	5
Total Spending on Alcohol/Drug Abuse Services	13
State Spending on Alcohol/Drug Abuse Services	6
Hard-Core Cocaine Users	33
Federal Drug Grants to States	25

Population
State Ranking

Population	13
Population Density	4
Population in Metropolitan Areas	9
Population Under 18 Years Old	49
Population Over 65 Years Old	12
White Population	20
African American Population	30
Hispanic Population	17
Asian American Population	12
Native American Population	43
Catholic Population	3

Jewish Population	4
Marriages	41
Divorces	49
Births	38
Births to Single Mothers	32
Births to Single Teenagers	41
Adoptions	39
Adoption Option Index	29
Infant Mortality	46
Child Deaths and Suicides	51
Teen Violent Death Rate	49
Deaths	28

Recreation
State Ranking

State Parks and Recreation Areas	18
Visitors to State Parks and Recreation Areas	32
Revenues from State Parks and Recreation Areas	22
Spending on State Arts Agencies	6
Domestic Travel Spending	24
State Travel Office Budgets	41
Lodging Industry (rooms)	40
Participation in Exercise Walking	32
Participation in Swimming	17
Participation in Camping	36
Participation in Bowling	17
Bowling League Membership	50
Participation in Running/Jogging	29
Participation in Aerobics	25
Participation in Golf	37
Participation in Softball	14
Participation in Health Clubs	8
Participation in Tennis	35
Participation in Hunting	44
Participation in Baseball	34
Participation in Bicycle Riding	27
Number of Boats	44
Attendance at Parimutuel Racing	20
Revenue from Parimutuel Betting	22

Social Services
State Ranking

Federal Grants for Social Services	48
State Spending on Public Welfare	1
Persons in Poverty	36
Public Aid Recipients	16
Participants in Food Stamp Program	47
Households in Food Stamp Program	27
Percentage of Poor Using AFDC and Food Stamps	9
Federal Spending on Children and Family Services	26
Federal Women, Infants, and Children Food Program	51
Child Welfare Services	37
Child Abuse Cases Reported	—
Children in Poverty	40
Children Without Health Insurance	44
Children Who Are Hungry or at Risk	47
Federal Spending on Child Nutrition Programs	42
Federal Spending on Special Milk Program	18
National School Lunch Program Participants	46
Head Start Enrollment	19
Head Start Spending	5
Federal Spending on Rehabilitation Services/Handicapped Research	42

State Government
State Ranking

Financial World's State Rankings	50
Salaries of State Officials (governor)	33
Salaries of State Legislators	10
Women in State Legislatures	20
African Americans in State Legislatures	26
Hispanics in State Legislatures	19
Asian Americans in State Legislatures	6
Native Americans in State Legislatures	12
Turnover in State Legislatures	9
Length of State Legislative Sessions	1
State Bills in Regular Session	44
State Resolutions in Regular Session	1
State Bills in Special Session	—
State Resolutions in Special Session	—
Women in State Cabinets	4
Total Federal Funding to State Governments	7
Total State Spending	20
State General Expenditures	20
State Debt	7
State Spending on Interest on the General Debt	8
Total State Tax Revenue	4
State Revenue from Tax on Sales and Gross Receipts	40
State Revenue from General Sales Tax	36
State Revenue from Licenses	41
State Revenue from Motor Vehicle Licenses	24
State Revenue from Individual Income Taxes	1
State Revenue from Corporation Net Income Taxes	7
State Revenue from Severance Taxes	—
State Revenue from Property Taxes	39
State Revenue from Death and Gift Taxes	2
State Revenue from Documentary and Stock Transfers	13
State Revenue from Tax on Motor Fuels	38
State Revenue from Tax on Tobacco Products	23
Excise Tax on Cigarettes	19
Excise Tax on Gasoline	8
State Revenue from Lotteries	3

Transportation
State Ranking

Motor Vehicle Registrations	49
Automobile Registrations	37
Bus and Truck Registrations	47
Motorcycle Registrations	46
Driver Licenses	20
Federal Spending on Highway Trust Fund	32
Federal Spending on Mass Transportation	8
State Spending on Highways	49
Highway Deficiency	32
Bridge Deficiency	3
Traffic Fatalities	50
Traffic Fatalities per Miles Traveled	50
Motorcyclist Fatalities	46
Pedalcyclist Fatalities	35
Pedestrian Fatalities	27
Registered Aircraft	47
Registered Pilots	40
Federal Spending on Airport and Airway Trust Fund	45
Aircraft Fatalities	42

— *not applicable*   NA *not available*

Agriculture
State Ranking

Farm Acreage	29
Farmland as Portion of State	34
Net Farm Income	35
Government Payments to Farms	30
Federal Commodity Loans/Price Supports	21
Federal Spending on Rural Development	22
Rural Electric and Telephone Loan Guarantees	28
Foreign-Owned Agricultural Land	26

Business and Economy
State Ranking

Gross State Product	23
Retail Sales	19
Supermarket Sales	47
Commercial Bank Assets	30
Insured Commercial Bank Deposits	28
Fortune 500 Companies	15
Inc. 500 Companies	33
New Business Incorporations	26
Business Failures	39
Financial Aid to Minority Businesses	35
Women-Owned Businesses	14
Sales & Receipts of Women-Owned Businesses	45
African American-Owned Businesses	18
Sales & Receipts of African American-Owned Businesses	15
Hispanic-Owned Businesses	28
Sales & Receipts of Hispanic-Owned Businesses	34
Employees in Manufacturing	7
Manufacturing Shipments	6
Japanese-Owned U.S. Manufacturing Plants	5
Exports to Mexico	8
Change in Exports to Mexico	41
Existing Home Sales	23
Housing Starts	34
Average Annual Pay	9
Disposable Personal Income	21
Median Income of Families with Children	14
Federal Spending on Unemployment Insurance/Employment Services	15
Teen Unemployment	4
Bankruptcy Petitions Filed	34
Patents Issued to State Residents	6
Federal Spending on Community Development	17
Federal Spending on Economic Development Administration	44
Federal Spending on Urban Development Action Grants	8

Crime and Criminal Justice
State Ranking

Total Crimes	14
Violent Crimes	12
Murders	16
Rapes	3
Aggravated Assaults	13
Property Crimes	13
Robberies	13
Burglaries	22
Larcenies and Thefts	16
Motor Vehicle Thefts	12
State and Federal Prisoners	8
Capital Punishment	—
State Spending on Corrections	17
State Spending on Police	27
Inmates in Local Jails	21
Spending on Local Jails	23
Spending per Inmate for Local Jails	15
Employees at Local Jails	9
Juvenile Custody Rate	13
Federal Spending on Office of Justice Assistance Programs	41

Defense
State Ranking

Defense Grants to State and Local Governments	13
Total Defense Payroll	48
Total Army Payroll	46
Total Navy/Marine Corps Payroll	50
Total Air Force Payroll	40
Total Active-Duty Payroll	44
Army Active-Duty Payroll	41
Navy/Marine Corps Active-Duty Payroll	43
Air Force Active-Duty Payroll	34
Total Civilian Payroll	42
Army Civilian Payroll	26
Navy/Marine Corps Civilian Payroll	40
Air Force Civilian Payroll	36
Total Reserve and National Guard Payroll	50
Army Reserve and National Guard Payroll	49
Navy/Marine Corps Reserve and National Guard Payroll	29
Air Force Reserve and National Guard Payroll	47
Total Retired Military Payroll	50
Army Retired Military Payroll	50
Navy/Marine Corps Retired Military Payroll	49
Air Force Retired Military Payroll	48
Total Defense Prime Contracts	44
Army Prime Contracts	26
Navy/Marine Corps Prime Contracts	38
Air Force Prime Contracts	40
U.S. Military Installations	27
Construction of National Guard Centers	12

Education
State Ranking

School Age Population	23
Public Elementary and Secondary School Enrollment	8
Average Daily Attendance	NA
Student-Teacher Ratio	5
Salaries of Public School Teachers	8
Public School Teachers Who Are Male	35
Eighth Grade Math Test Results	16
High School Math Enrollment	NA
Public High School Graduation Rate	34
General Educational Development (GED) Test Results	46
Adult Illiteracy	27
Federal Revenue for Public Schools	29
State Revenue for Public Schools	46
Local Government Revenue for Public Schools	5
Total Public School Spending	13
Public School Spending on Instruction	48
Public School Spending on Noninstruction	44
Public School Spending on Support Staff	11
State and Local Government Spending on Public Schools	22
Federal Spending on School Improvement Programs	26
Gifted and Talented Students	1
Federal Spending on Education of Students with Disabilities	33
Student-Teacher Ratio in Catholic Elementary Schools	9
Student-Teacher Ratio in Catholic Secondary Schools	14
State Spending on Education	34
State and Local Government Spending on Education	18
Higher Education Tuition and Fees	20
Higher Education Revenue	35
Federal Spending on Higher Education	48
State Spending on Higher Education	14
State and Local Government Spending on Higher Education	18
State and Local Appropriations for Higher Education	33
Federal Spending on Higher Education Act Insured Loans	34
Federal Spending on National Guaranteed Student Loans	35
Federal Spending on Pell Grants	23
Default Rate in Perkins Student Loan Program	35
State Spending on Libraries	14

Energy
State Ranking

Total Spending on Energy	36
Net Generation of Electricity	32
Cost of Electricity	17
Spending on Electricity	42
Spending on Natural Gas	6
Spending on Gasoline	41
Spending on Petroleum	49
Spending on Coal	21
Total Energy Consumption	33
Electricity Consumption	41
Natural Gas Consumption	10
Petroleum Consumption	49
Coal Consumption	24
Power Plants	20
Nuclear Power Plants	12
Hydroelectric Power Plants	17

Environment
State Ranking

Federally Owned Land (acreage)	19
Loss of Wetlands	20
Environmental Protection Agency Spending	17
EPA Abatement, Control, and Compliance	51
State Spending on Environmental Programs	32
Environmental Programs as Part of State Budget	33
State Spending on Forest Programs	23
Total Tree Planting	20
Federal Tree Planting	16
Private Tree Planting	21
State Spending on Air Quality	30
State Spending on Water Quality	19
Federal Grants for Rural Water and Waste Disposal	38
Federal Spending on Wastewater Treatment Works	15
Hazardous Waste Sites on National Priority List	5

Federal Grants for Hazardous Substance
Response | 5
State Spending on Hazardous Waste | 27

Health | State Ranking

State Health Rankings | 24
State Spending on Health | 6
Support for Public Health | 3
Family and Business Spending on Health
Care | 8
HMO Enrollment | 15
Medicaid Recipients | 14
Medically Underserved Population | 23
Lack of Health Care Access | 27
Active Nonfederal Physicians | 28
Active Nonfederal Nurses | 27
Active Nonfederal Dentists | 18
Average Cost per Hospital Stay | 9
Average Cost per Day for Hospital Care | 18
Average Cost per Day for Hospital Room | 13
State Spending on Hospitals | 14
Adequacy of Prenatal Care | 10
Infants Born Receiving Late or No
Prenatal Care | 35
Infants Born with Low Birth Weight | 12
Abortions | 14
Immunizations of Two-Year-Olds | —
Overall Risk for Heart Disease | 46
Risk Factor for Heart Disease
(hypertension) | 7
Deaths Due to Heart Disease | 25
New Cancer Cases | 34
Deaths Due to Cancer | 32
Prevalence of Smoking | 7
Prevalence of Diabetes | 25
Deaths Due to Diabetes | 12
Cost of Diabetes | 26
AIDS Cases Reported | 31
Gonorrhea Cases Reported | 16
Syphilis Cases Reported | 21
Tuberculosis Cases Reported | 27
Hepatitis Cases Reported | 28
Rabies Cases Reported | 44
Lyme Disease Cases Reported | 32
Beer Consumption | 28
Wine Consumption | 27
Liquor Consumption | 23
Alcohol and Drug Treatment Admissions | 26
Federal Spending on Alcohol, Drug
Abuse, and Mental Health | 17
Total Spending on Alcohol/Drug Abuse
Services | 15
State Spending on Alcohol/Drug Abuse
Services | 25
Hard-Core Cocaine Users | 21
Federal Drug Grants to States | 15

Population | State Ranking

Population | 8
Population Density | 15
Population in Metropolitan Areas | 16
Population Under 18 Years Old | 18
Population Over 65 Years Old | 33
White Population | 28
African American Population | 15
Hispanic Population | 29
Asian American Population | 26
Native American Population | 21
Catholic Population | 16

Jewish Population | 18
Marriages | 39
Divorces | 33
Births | 16
Births to Single Mothers | 23
Births to Single Teenagers | 22
Adoptions | 30
Adoption Option Index | 25
Infant Mortality | 11
Child Deaths and Suicides | 31
Teen Violent Death Rate | 20
Deaths | 28

Recreation | State Ranking

State Parks and Recreation Areas | 27
Visitors to State Parks and Recreation
Areas | 27
Revenues from State Parks and
Recreation Areas | 19
Spending on State Arts Agencies | 17
Domestic Travel Spending | 47
State Travel Office Budgets | 38
Lodging Industry (rooms) | 45
Participation in Exercise Walking | 23
Participation in Swimming | 18
Participation in Camping | 13
Participation in Bowling | 4
Bowling League Membership | 3
Participation in Running/Jogging | 37
Participation in Aerobics | 29
Participation in Golf | 9
Participation in Softball | 25
Participation in Health Clubs | 24
Participation in Tennis | 18
Participation in Hunting | 25
Participation in Baseball | 17
Participation in Bicycle Riding | 13
Number of Boats | 4
Attendance at Parimutuel Racing | 25
Revenue from Parimutuel Betting | 9

Social Services | State Ranking

Federal Grants for Social Services | 38
State Spending on Public Welfare | 9
Persons in Poverty | 23
Public Aid Recipients | 6
Participants in Food Stamp Program | 12
Households in Food Stamp Program | 6
Percentage of Poor Using AFDC and
Food Stamps | 15
Federal Spending on Children and
Family Services | 45
Federal Women, Infants, and Children
Food Program | 30
Child Welfare Services | 8
Child Abuse Cases Reported | —
Children in Poverty | 19
Children Without Health Insurance | 46
Children Who Are Hungry or at Risk | 19
Federal Spending on Child Nutrition
Programs | 41
Federal Spending on Special Milk
Program | 9
National School Lunch Program
Participants | 42
Head Start Enrollment | 18
Head Start Spending | 31
Federal Spending on Rehabilitation
Services/Handicapped Research | 36

State Government | State Ranking

Financial World's State Rankings | 26
Salaries of State Officials (governor) | 7
Salaries of State Legislators | 4
Women in State Legislatures | 26
African Americans in State Legislatures | 14
Hispanics in State Legislatures | 21
Asian Americans in State Legislatures | 6
Native Americans in State Legislatures | 12
Turnover in State Legislatures | 20
Length of State Legislative Sessions | 2
State Bills in Regular Session | 43
State Resolutions in Regular Session | 45
State Bills in Special Session | —
State Resolutions in Special Session | —
Women in State Cabinets | 6
Total Federal Funding to State
Governments | 49
Total State Spending | 29
State General Expenditures | 30
State Debt | 31
State Spending on Interest on the
General Debt | 35
Total State Tax Revenue | 25
State Revenue from Tax on Sales and
Gross Receipts | 42
State Revenue from General Sales Tax | 33
State Revenue from Licenses | 29
State Revenue from Motor Vehicle
Licenses | 12
State Revenue from Individual Income
Taxes | 21
State Revenue from Corporation Net
Income Taxes | 3
State Revenue from Severance Taxes | 21
State Revenue from Property Taxes | 10
State Revenue from Death and Gift
Taxes | 18
State Revenue from Documentary and
Stock Transfers | —
State Revenue from Tax on Motor Fuels | 37
State Revenue from Tax on Tobacco
Products | 16
Excise Tax on Cigarettes | 20
Excise Tax on Gasoline | 35
State Revenue from Lotteries | 12

Transportation | State Ranking

Motor Vehicle Registrations | 27
Automobile Registrations | 17
Bus and Truck Registrations | 36
Motorcycle Registrations | 24
Driver Licenses | 24
Federal Spending on Highway Trust
Fund | 49
Federal Spending on Mass
Transportation | 22
State Spending on Highways | 43
Highway Deficiency | 26
Bridge Deficiency | 20
Traffic Fatalities | 34
Traffic Fatalities per Miles Traveled | 39
Motorcyclist Fatalities | 38
Pedalcyclist Fatalities | 10
Pedestrian Fatalities | 24
Registered Aircraft | 30
Registered Pilots | 38
Federal Spending on Airport and
Airway Trust Fund | 44
Aircraft Fatalities | 31

— *not applicable*   NA *not available*

Agriculture
State Ranking

Farm Acreage	14
Farmland as Portion of State	13
Net Farm Income	9
Government Payments to Farms	9
Federal Commodity Loans/Price Supports	6
Federal Spending on Rural Development	15
Rural Electric and Telephone Loan Guarantees	17
Foreign-Owned Agricultural Land	33

Business and Economy
State Ranking

Gross State Product	15
Retail Sales	15
Supermarket Sales	34
Commercial Bank Assets	11
Insured Commercial Bank Deposits	15
Fortune 500 Companies	4
Inc. 500 Companies	24
New Business Incorporations	25
Business Failures	18
Financial Aid to Minority Businesses	18
Women-Owned Businesses	11
Sales & Receipts of Women-Owned Businesses	27
African American-Owned Businesses	40
Sales & Receipts of African American-Owned Businesses	36
Hispanic-Owned Businesses	41
Sales & Receipts of Hispanic-Owned Businesses	48
Employees in Manufacturing	18
Manufacturing Shipments	19
Japanese-Owned U.S. Manufacturing Plants	38
Exports to Mexico	25
Change in Exports to Mexico	24
Existing Home Sales	28
Housing Starts	15
Average Annual Pay	15
Disposable Personal Income	20
Median Income of Families with Children	11
Federal Spending on Unemployment Insurance/Employment Services	34
Teen Unemployment	48
Bankruptcy Petitions Filed	18
Patents Issued to State Residents	5
Federal Spending on Community Development	32
Federal Spending on Economic Development Administration	37
Federal Spending on Urban Development Action Grants	13

Crime and Criminal Justice
State Ranking

Total Crimes	36
Violent Crimes	38
Murders	43
Rapes	26
Aggravated Assaults	42
Property Crimes	37
Robberies	37
Burglaries	37
Larcenies and Thefts	29
Motor Vehicle Thefts	30
State and Federal Prisoners	50
Capital Punishment	—

State Spending on Corrections	47
State Spending on Police	30
Inmates in Local Jails	37
Spending on Local Jails	21
Spending per Inmate for Local Jails	9
Employees at Local Jails	33
Juvenile Custody Rate	16
Federal Spending on Office of Justice Assistance Programs	47

Defense
State Ranking

Defense Grants to State and Local Governments	9
Total Defense Payroll	50
Total Army Payroll	48
Total Navy/Marine Corps Payroll	44
Total Air Force Payroll	46
Total Active-Duty Payroll	49
Army Active-Duty Payroll	35
Navy/Marine Corps Active-Duty Payroll	39
Air Force Active-Duty Payroll	47
Total Civilian Payroll	49
Army Civilian Payroll	44
Navy/Marine Corps Civilian Payroll	42
Air Force Civilian Payroll	42
Total Reserve and National Guard Payroll	34
Army Reserve and National Guard Payroll	32
Navy/Marine Corps Reserve and National Guard Payroll	19
Air Force Reserve and National Guard Payroll	31
Total Retired Military Payroll	47
Army Retired Military Payroll	46
Navy/Marine Corps Retired Military Payroll	43
Air Force Retired Military Payroll	44
Total Defense Prime Contracts	22
Army Prime Contracts	10
Navy/Marine Corps Prime Contracts	15
Air Force Prime Contracts	36
U.S. Military Installations	41
Construction of National Guard Centers	9

Education
State Ranking

School Age Population	16
Public Elementary and Secondary School Enrollment	20
Average Daily Attendance	12
Student-Teacher Ratio	18
Salaries of Public School Teachers	15
Public School Teachers Who Are Male	2
Eighth Grade Math Test Results	4
High School Math Enrollment	31
Public High School Graduation Rate	1
General Educational Development (GED) Test Results	28
Adult Illiteracy	38
Federal Revenue for Public Schools	48
State Revenue for Public Schools	20
Local Government Revenue for Public Schools	30
Total Public School Spending	18
Public School Spending on Instruction	4
Public School Spending on Noninstruction	31
Public School Spending on Support Staff	29
State and Local Government Spending on Public Schools	35

Federal Spending on School Improvement Programs	40
Gifted and Talented Students	13
Federal Spending on Education of Students with Disabilities	34
Student-Teacher Ratio in Catholic Elementary Schools	45
Student-Teacher Ratio in Catholic Secondary Schools	35
State Spending on Education	8
State and Local Government Spending on Education	39
Higher Education Tuition and Fees	19
Higher Education Revenue	16
Federal Spending on Higher Education	20
State Spending on Higher Education	12
State and Local Government Spending on Higher Education	33
State and Local Appropriations for Higher Education	32
Federal Spending on Higher Education Act Insured Loans	3
Federal Spending on National Guaranteed Student Loans	18
Federal Spending on Pell Grants	12
Default Rate in Perkins Student Loan Program	46
State Spending on Libraries	44

Energy
State Ranking

Total Spending on Energy	43
Net Generation of Electricity	37
Cost of Electricity	43
Spending on Electricity	47
Spending on Natural Gas	23
Spending on Gasoline	26
Spending on Petroleum	37
Spending on Coal	29
Total Energy Consumption	29
Electricity Consumption	29
Natural Gas Consumption	19
Petroleum Consumption	38
Coal Consumption	29
Power Plants	14
Nuclear Power Plants	10
Hydroelectric Power Plants	23

Environment
State Ranking

Federally Owned Land (acreage)	29
Loss of Wetlands	29
Environmental Protection Agency Spending	19
EPA Abatement, Control, and Compliance	21
State Spending on Environmental Programs	28
Environmental Programs as Part of State Budget	31
State Spending on Forest Programs	6
Total Tree Planting	17
Federal Tree Planting	17
Private Tree Planting	18
State Spending on Air Quality	34
State Spending on Water Quality	36
Federal Grants for Rural Water and Waste Disposal	18
Federal Spending on Wastewater Treatment Works	17
Hazardous Waste Sites on National Priority List	8

Federal Grants for Hazardous Substance
  Response   9
State Spending on Hazardous Waste   10

Health   *State Ranking*

State Health Rankings   1
State Spending on Health   21
Support for Public Health   8
Family and Business Spending on Health
  Care   9
HMO Enrollment   3
Medicaid Recipients   27
Medically Underserved Population   42
Lack of Health Care Access   44
Active Nonfederal Physicians   12
Active Nonfederal Nurses   14
Active Nonfederal Dentists   9
Average Cost per Hospital Stay   19
Average Cost per Day for Hospital Care   42
Average Cost per Day for Hospital Room   23
State Spending on Hospitals   12
Adequacy of Prenatal Care   17
Infants Born Receiving Late or No
  Prenatal Care   39
Infants Born with Low Birth Weight   46
Abortions   30
Immunizations of Two-Year-Olds   —
Overall Risk for Heart Disease   15
Risk Factor for Heart Disease
  (hypertension)   27
Deaths Due to Heart Disease   39
New Cancer Cases   39
Deaths Due to Cancer   39
Prevalence of Smoking   42
Prevalence of Diabetes   42
Deaths Due to Diabetes   35
Cost of Diabetes   42
AIDS Cases Reported   38
Gonorrhea Cases Reported   34
Syphilis Cases Reported   35
Tuberculosis Cases Reported   38
Hepatitis Cases Reported   20
Rabies Cases Reported   16
Lyme Disease Cases Reported   8
Beer Consumption   31
Wine Consumption   30
Liquor Consumption   8
Alcohol and Drug Treatment Admissions   10
Federal Spending on Alcohol, Drug
  Abuse, and Mental Health   39
Total Spending on Alcohol/Drug Abuse
  Services   9
State Spending on Alcohol/Drug Abuse
  Services   5
Hard-Core Cocaine Users   25
Federal Drug Grants to States   40

Population   *State Ranking*

Population   20
Population Density   32
Population in Metropolitan Areas   26
Population Under 18 Years Old   15
Population Over 65 Years Old   29
White Population   7
African American Population   39
Hispanic Population   36
Asian American Population   18
Native American Population   15
Catholic Population   14

Jewish Population   23
Marriages   46
Divorces   43
Births   25
Births to Single Mothers   43
Births to Single Teenagers   46
Adoptions   25
Adoption Option Index   32
Infant Mortality   43
Child Deaths and Suicides   44
Teen Violent Death Rate   34
Deaths   34

Recreation   *State Ranking*

State Parks and Recreation Areas   17
Visitors to State Parks and Recreation
  Areas   35
Revenues from State Parks and
  Recreation Areas   26
Spending on State Arts Agencies   19
Domestic Travel Spending   40
State Travel Office Budgets   20
Lodging Industry (rooms)   36
Participation in Exercise Walking   14
Participation in Swimming   13
Participation in Camping   7
Participation in Bowling   9
Bowling League Membership   8
Participation in Running/Jogging   35
Participation in Aerobics   28
Participation in Golf   10
Participation in Softball   7
Participation in Health Clubs   11
Participation in Tennis   33
Participation in Hunting   7
Participation in Baseball   27
Participation in Bicycle Riding   5
Number of Boats   1
Attendance at Parimutuel Racing   6
Revenue from Parimutuel Betting   20

Social Services   *State Ranking*

Federal Grants for Social Services   31
State Spending on Public Welfare   11
Persons in Poverty   30
Public Aid Recipients   31
Participants in Food Stamp Program   42
Households in Food Stamp Program   31
Percentage of Poor Using AFDC and
  Food Stamps   10
Federal Spending on Children and
  Family Services   38
Federal Women, Infants, and Children
  Food Program   41
Child Welfare Services   NA
Child Abuse Cases Reported   —
Children in Poverty   42
Children Without Health Insurance   51
Children Who Are Hungry or at Risk   45
Federal Spending on Child Nutrition
  Programs   23
Federal Spending on Special Milk
  Program   4
National School Lunch Program
  Participants   35
Head Start Enrollment   36
Head Start Spending   19
Federal Spending on Rehabilitation
  Services/Handicapped Research   35

State Government   *State Ranking*

Financial World's State Rankings   9
Salaries of State Officials (governor)   6
Salaries of State Legislators   11
Women in State Legislatures   9
African Americans in State Legislatures   41
Hispanics in State Legislatures   14
Asian Americans in State Legislatures   6
Native Americans in State Legislatures   11
Turnover in State Legislatures   25
Length of State Legislative Sessions   34
State Bills in Regular Session   42
State Resolutions in Regular Session   45
State Bills in Special Session   —
State Resolutions in Special Session   —
Women in State Cabinets   3
Total Federal Funding to State
  Governments   40
Total State Spending   19
State General Expenditures   17
State Debt   38
State Spending on Interest on the
  General Debt   39
Total State Tax Revenue   6
State Revenue from Tax on Sales and
  Gross Receipts   11
State Revenue from General Sales Tax   15
State Revenue from Licenses   8
State Revenue from Motor Vehicle
  Licenses   3
State Revenue from Individual Income
  Taxes   6
State Revenue from Corporation Net
  Income Taxes   11
State Revenue from Severance Taxes   27
State Revenue from Property Taxes   32
State Revenue from Death and Gift
  Taxes   37
State Revenue from Documentary and
  Stock Transfers   16
State Revenue from Tax on Motor Fuels   18
State Revenue from Tax on Tobacco
  Products   8
Excise Tax on Cigarettes   1
Excise Tax on Gasoline   10
State Revenue from Lotteries   23

Transportation   *State Ranking*

Motor Vehicle Registrations   34
Automobile Registrations   23
Bus and Truck Registrations   39
Motorcycle Registrations   12
Driver Licenses   49
Federal Spending on Highway Trust
  Fund   21
Federal Spending on Mass
  Transportation   36
State Spending on Highways   23
Highway Deficiency   49
Bridge Deficiency   44
Traffic Fatalities   44
Traffic Fatalities per Miles Traveled   47
Motorcyclist Fatalities   35
Pedalcyclist Fatalities   38
Pedestrian Fatalities   42
Registered Aircraft   18
Registered Pilots   11
Federal Spending on Airport and
  Airway Trust Fund   32
Aircraft Fatalities   32

— not applicable   NA not available

Agriculture
State Ranking

Farm Acreage	25
Farmland as Portion of State	23
Net Farm Income	15
Government Payments to Farms	12
Federal Commodity Loans/Price Supports	7
Federal Spending on Rural Development	16
Rural Electric and Telephone Loan Guarantees	13
Foreign-Owned Agricultural Land	8

Business and Economy
State Ranking

Gross State Product	51
Retail Sales	50
Supermarket Sales	48
Commercial Bank Assets	43
Insured Commercial Bank Deposits	42
Fortune 500 Companies	42
Inc. 500 Companies	43
New Business Incorporations	48
Business Failures	43
Financial Aid to Minority Businesses	11
Women-Owned Businesses	51
Sales & Receipts of Women-Owned Businesses	13
African American-Owned Businesses	3
Sales & Receipts of African American-Owned Businesses	2
Hispanic-Owned Businesses	39
Sales & Receipts of Hispanic-Owned Businesses	46
Employees in Manufacturing	24
Manufacturing Shipments	23
Japanese-Owned U.S. Manufacturing Plants	34
Exports to Mexico	14
Change in Exports to Mexico	32
Existing Home Sales	38
Housing Starts	44
Average Annual Pay	49
Disposable Personal Income	51
Median Income of Families with Children	51
Federal Spending on Unemployment Insurance/Employment Services	41
Teen Unemployment	2
Bankruptcy Petitions Filed	9
Patents Issued to State Residents	50
Federal Spending on Community Development	29
Federal Spending on Economic Development Administration	11
Federal Spending on Urban Development Action Grants	33

Crime and Criminal Justice
State Ranking

Total Crimes	40
Violent Crimes	35
Murders	5
Rapes	15
Aggravated Assaults	39
Property Crimes	42
Robberies	33
Burglaries	14
Larcenies and Thefts	47
Motor Vehicle Thefts	38
State and Federal Prisoners	14
Capital Punishment	9

State Spending on Corrections	42
State Spending on Police	37
Inmates in Local Jails	16
Spending on Local Jails	38
Spending per Inmate for Local Jails	45
Employees at Local Jails	4
Juvenile Custody Rate	39
Federal Spending on Office of Justice Assistance Programs	44

Defense
State Ranking

Defense Grants to State and Local Governments	6
Total Defense Payroll	26
Total Army Payroll	23
Total Navy/Marine Corps Payroll	13
Total Air Force Payroll	19
Total Active-Duty Payroll	28
Army Active-Duty Payroll	33
Navy/Marine Corps Active-Duty Payroll	14
Air Force Active-Duty Payroll	16
Total Civilian Payroll	17
Army Civilian Payroll	15
Navy/Marine Corps Civilian Payroll	13
Air Force Civilian Payroll	18
Total Reserve and National Guard Payroll	17
Army Reserve and National Guard Payroll	17
Navy/Marine Corps Reserve and National Guard Payroll	46
Air Force Reserve and National Guard Payroll	9
Total Retired Military Payroll	23
Army Retired Military Payroll	23
Navy/Marine Corps Retired Military Payroll	18
Air Force Retired Military Payroll	19
Total Defense Prime Contracts	11
Army Prime Contracts	24
Navy/Marine Corps Prime Contracts	6
Air Force Prime Contracts	35
U.S. Military Installations	18
Construction of National Guard Centers	7

Education
State Ranking

School Age Population	6
Public Elementary and Secondary School Enrollment	28
Average Daily Attendance	13
Student-Teacher Ratio	14
Salaries of Public School Teachers	48
Public School Teachers Who Are Male	49
Eighth Grade Math Test Results	—
High School Math Enrollment	20
Public High School Graduation Rate	45
General Educational Development (GED) Test Results	26
Adult Illiteracy	1
Federal Revenue for Public Schools	1
State Revenue for Public Schools	16
Local Government Revenue for Public Schools	42
Total Public School Spending	49
Public School Spending on Instruction	7
Public School Spending on Noninstruction	6
Public School Spending on Support Staff	50
State and Local Government Spending on Public Schools	30

Federal Spending on School Improvement Programs	10
Gifted and Talented Students	28
Federal Spending on Education of Students with Disabilities	10
Student-Teacher Ratio in Catholic Elementary Schools	21
Student-Teacher Ratio in Catholic Secondary Schools	43
State Spending on Education	35
State and Local Government Spending on Education	16
Higher Education Tuition and Fees	41
Higher Education Revenue	47
Federal Spending on Higher Education	3
State Spending on Higher Education	37
State and Local Government Spending on Higher Education	11
State and Local Appropriations for Higher Education	25
Federal Spending on Higher Education Act Insured Loans	21
Federal Spending on National Guaranteed Student Loans	30
Federal Spending on Pell Grants	5
Default Rate in Perkins Student Loan Program	1
State Spending on Libraries	28

Energy
State Ranking

Total Spending on Energy	27
Net Generation of Electricity	38
Cost of Electricity	28
Spending on Electricity	16
Spending on Natural Gas	28
Spending on Gasoline	27
Spending on Petroleum	21
Spending on Coal	36
Total Energy Consumption	16
Electricity Consumption	19
Natural Gas Consumption	8
Petroleum Consumption	14
Coal Consumption	36
Power Plants	40
Nuclear Power Plants	17
Hydroelectric Power Plants	47

Environment
State Ranking

Federally Owned Land (acreage)	25
Loss of Wetlands	14
Environmental Protection Agency Spending	27
EPA Abatement, Control, and Compliance	25
State Spending on Environmental Programs	35
Environmental Programs as Part of State Budget	34
State Spending on Forest Programs	8
Total Tree Planting	1
Federal Tree Planting	7
Private Tree Planting	1
State Spending on Air Quality	43
State Spending on Water Quality	46
Federal Grants for Rural Water and Waste Disposal	9
Federal Spending on Wastewater Treatment Works	26
Hazardous Waste Sites on National Priority List	47

Federal Grants for Hazardous Substance Response	30
State Spending on Hazardous Waste	48

Health · State Ranking

State Health Rankings	49
State Spending on Health	40
Support for Public Health	33
Family and Business Spending on Health Care	50
HMO Enrollment	48
Medicaid Recipients	1
Medically Underserved Population	1
Lack of Health Care Access	6
Active Nonfederal Physicians	50
Active Nonfederal Nurses	49
Active Nonfederal Dentists	51
Average Cost per Hospital Stay	51
Average Cost per Day for Hospital Care	48
Average Cost per Day for Hospital Room	51
State Spending on Hospitals	23
Adequacy of Prenatal Care	25
Infants Born Receiving Late or No Prenatal Care	33
Infants Born with Low Birth Weight	2
Abortions	47
Immunizations of Two-Year-Olds	—
Overall Risk for Heart Disease	50
Risk Factor for Heart Disease (hypertension)	1
Deaths Due to Heart Disease	3
New Cancer Cases	14
Deaths Due to Cancer	26
Prevalence of Smoking	33
Prevalence of Diabetes	4
Deaths Due to Diabetes	16
Cost of Diabetes	4
AIDS Cases Reported	26
Gonorrhea Cases Reported	4
Syphilis Cases Reported	3
Tuberculosis Cases Reported	14
Hepatitis Cases Reported	51
Rabies Cases Reported	47
Lyme Disease Cases Reported	45
Beer Consumption	21
Wine Consumption	51
Liquor Consumption	33
Alcohol and Drug Treatment Admissions	40
Federal Spending on Alcohol, Drug Abuse, and Mental Health	47
Total Spending on Alcohol/Drug Abuse Services	48
State Spending on Alcohol/Drug Abuse Services	43
Hard-Core Cocaine Users	46
Federal Drug Grants to States	30

Population · State Ranking

Population	31
Population Density	33
Population in Metropolitan Areas	46
Population Under 18 Years Old	7
Population Over 65 Years Old	30
White Population	49
African American Population	2
Hispanic Population	47
Asian American Population	46
Native American Population	31
Catholic Population	44

Jewish Population	48
Marriages	29
Divorces	12
Births	12
Births to Single Mothers	2
Births to Single Teenagers	2
Adoptions	17
Adoption Option Index	13
Infant Mortality	4
Child Deaths and Suicides	1
Teen Violent Death Rate	22
Deaths	7

Recreation · State Ranking

State Parks and Recreation Areas	47
Visitors to State Parks and Recreation Areas	41
Revenues from State Parks and Recreation Areas	20
Spending on State Arts Agencies	50
Domestic Travel Spending	46
State Travel Office Budgets	40
Lodging Industry (rooms)	41
Participation in Exercise Walking	38
Participation in Swimming	33
Participation in Camping	44
Participation in Bowling	43
Bowling League Membership	51
Participation in Running/Jogging	44
Participation in Aerobics	47
Participation in Golf	47
Participation in Softball	48
Participation in Health Clubs	49
Participation in Tennis	16
Participation in Hunting	10
Participation in Baseball	41
Participation in Bicycle Riding	47
Number of Boats	8
Attendance at Parimutuel Racing	—
Revenue from Parimutuel Betting	—

Social Services · State Ranking

Federal Grants for Social Services	10
State Spending on Public Welfare	40
Persons in Poverty	1
Public Aid Recipients	1
Participants in Food Stamp Program	1
Households in Food Stamp Program	1
Percentage of Poor Using AFDC and Food Stamps	51
Federal Spending on Children and Family Services	2
Federal Women, Infants, and Children Food Program	1
Child Welfare Services	6
Child Abuse Cases Reported	—
Children in Poverty	1
Children Without Health Insurance	4
Children Who Are Hungry or at Risk	1
Federal Spending on Child Nutrition Programs	1
Federal Spending on Special Milk Program	47
National School Lunch Program Participants	1
Head Start Enrollment	1
Head Start Spending	27
Federal Spending on Rehabilitation Services/Handicapped Research	3

State Government · State Ranking

Financial World's State Rankings	23
Salaries of State Officials (governor)	32
Salaries of State Legislators	33
Women in State Legislatures	44
African Americans in State Legislatures	1
Hispanics in State Legislatures	21
Asian Americans in State Legislatures	6
Native Americans in State Legislatures	12
Turnover in State Legislatures	50
Length of State Legislative Sessions	22
State Bills in Regular Session	27
State Resolutions in Regular Session	24
State Bills in Special Session	11
State Resolutions in Special Session	1
Women in State Cabinets	—
Total Federal Funding to State Governments	17
Total State Spending	18
State General Expenditures	18
State Debt	47
State Spending on Interest on the General Debt	43
Total State Tax Revenue	46
State Revenue from Tax on Sales and Gross Receipts	16
State Revenue from General Sales Tax	16
State Revenue from Licenses	43
State Revenue from Motor Vehicle Licenses	45
State Revenue from Individual Income Taxes	39
State Revenue from Corporation Net Income Taxes	30
State Revenue from Severance Taxes	14
State Revenue from Property Taxes	23
State Revenue from Death and Gift Taxes	46
State Revenue from Documentary and Stock Transfers	—
State Revenue from Tax on Motor Fuels	7
State Revenue from Tax on Tobacco Products	30
Excise Tax on Cigarettes	30
Excise Tax on Gasoline	22
State Revenue from Lotteries	—

Transportation · State Ranking

Motor Vehicle Registrations	37
Automobile Registrations	28
Bus and Truck Registrations	35
Motorcycle Registrations	41
Driver Licenses	3
Federal Spending on Highway Trust Fund	28
Federal Spending on Mass Transportation	48
State Spending on Highways	32
Highway Deficiency	6
Bridge Deficiency	9
Traffic Fatalities	3
Traffic Fatalities per Miles Traveled	3
Motorcyclist Fatalities	50
Pedalcyclist Fatalities	26
Pedestrian Fatalities	21
Registered Aircraft	35
Registered Pilots	45
Federal Spending on Airport and Airway Trust Fund	40
Aircraft Fatalities	23

— not applicable   NA not available

Agriculture
State Ranking

Farm Acreage	13
Farmland as Portion of State	10
Net Farm Income	27
Government Payments to Farms	14
Federal Commodity Loans/Price Supports	20
Federal Spending on Rural Development	34
Rural Electric and Telephone Loan Guarantees	12
Foreign-Owned Agricultural Land	38

Business and Economy
State Ranking

Gross State Product	25
Retail Sales	32
Supermarket Sales	35
Commercial Bank Assets	12
Insured Commercial Bank Deposits	11
Fortune 500 Companies	10
Inc. 500 Companies	29
New Business Incorporations	34
Business Failures	27
Financial Aid to Minority Businesses	37
Women-Owned Businesses	26
Sales & Receipts of Women-Owned Businesses	31
African American-Owned Businesses	20
Sales & Receipts of African American-Owned Businesses	21
Hispanic-Owned Businesses	34
Sales & Receipts of Hispanic-Owned Businesses	37
Employees in Manufacturing	16
Manufacturing Shipments	15
Japanese-Owned U.S. Manufacturing Plants	22
Exports to Mexico	5
Change in Exports to Mexico	42
Existing Home Sales	20
Housing Starts	33
Average Annual Pay	24
Disposable Personal Income	23
Median Income of Families with Children	28
Federal Spending on Unemployment Insurance/Employment Services	32
Teen Unemployment	29
Bankruptcy Petitions Filed	21
Patents Issued to State Residents	27
Federal Spending on Community Development	16
Federal Spending on Economic Development Administration	28
Federal Spending on Urban Development Action Grants	7

Crime and Criminal Justice
State Ranking

Total Crimes	26
Violent Crimes	13
Murders	17
Rapes	32
Aggravated Assaults	14
Property Crimes	27
Robberies	12
Burglaries	17
Larcenies and Thefts	36
Motor Vehicle Thefts	18
State and Federal Prisoners	22
Capital Punishment	7

State Spending on Corrections	46
State Spending on Police	29
Inmates in Local Jails	32
Spending on Local Jails	39
Spending per Inmate for Local Jails	30
Employees at Local Jails	35
Juvenile Custody Rate	20
Federal Spending on Office of Justice Assistance Programs	21

Defense
State Ranking

Defense Grants to State and Local Governments	19
Total Defense Payroll	32
Total Army Payroll	17
Total Navy/Marine Corps Payroll	33
Total Air Force Payroll	35
Total Active-Duty Payroll	35
Army Active-Duty Payroll	17
Navy/Marine Corps Active-Duty Payroll	32
Air Force Active-Duty Payroll	35
Total Civilian Payroll	18
Army Civilian Payroll	9
Navy/Marine Corps Civilian Payroll	28
Air Force Civilian Payroll	38
Total Reserve and National Guard Payroll	14
Army Reserve and National Guard Payroll	13
Navy/Marine Corps Reserve and National Guard Payroll	13
Air Force Reserve and National Guard Payroll	33
Total Retired Military Payroll	34
Army Retired Military Payroll	24
Navy/Marine Corps Retired Military Payroll	28
Air Force Retired Military Payroll	35
Total Defense Prime Contracts	3
Army Prime Contracts	14
Navy/Marine Corps Prime Contracts	4
Air Force Prime Contracts	3
U.S. Military Installations	18
Construction of National Guard Centers	19

Education
State Ranking

School Age Population	26
Public Elementary and Secondary School Enrollment	17
Average Daily Attendance	NA
Student-Teacher Ratio	35
Salaries of Public School Teachers	35
Public School Teachers Who Are Male	37
Eighth Grade Math Test Results	—
High School Math Enrollment	22
Public High School Graduation Rate	32
General Educational Development (GED) Test Results	9
Adult Illiteracy	21
Federal Revenue for Public Schools	31
State Revenue for Public Schools	37
Local Government Revenue for Public Schools	16
Total Public School Spending	33
Public School Spending on Instruction	16
Public School Spending on Noninstruction	27
Public School Spending on Support Staff	19
State and Local Government Spending on Public Schools	2

Federal Spending on School Improvement Programs	36
Gifted and Talented Students	20
Federal Spending on Education of Students with Disabilities	26
Student-Teacher Ratio in Catholic Elementary Schools	30
Student-Teacher Ratio in Catholic Secondary Schools	28
State Spending on Education	43
State and Local Government Spending on Education	8
Higher Education Tuition and Fees	17
Higher Education Revenue	17
Federal Spending on Higher Education	26
State Spending on Higher Education	46
State and Local Government Spending on Higher Education	31
State and Local Appropriations for Higher Education	45
Federal Spending on Higher Education Act Insured Loans	30
Federal Spending on National Guaranteed Student Loans	24
Federal Spending on Pell Grants	24
Default Rate in Perkins Student Loan Program	24
State Spending on Libraries	47

Energy
State Ranking

Total Spending on Energy	33
Net Generation of Electricity	26
Cost of Electricity	22
Spending on Electricity	30
Spending on Natural Gas	29
Spending on Gasoline	20
Spending on Petroleum	31
Spending on Coal	19
Total Energy Consumption	37
Electricity Consumption	31
Natural Gas Consumption	33
Petroleum Consumption	31
Coal Consumption	17
Power Plants	18
Nuclear Power Plants	30
Hydroelectric Power Plants	37

Environment
State Ranking

Federally Owned Land (acreage)	30
Loss of Wetlands	4
Environmental Protection Agency Spending	25
EPA Abatement, Control, and Compliance	45
State Spending on Environmental Programs	33
Environmental Programs as Part of State Budget	21
State Spending on Forest Programs	20
Total Tree Planting	33
Federal Tree Planting	19
Private Tree Planting	36
State Spending on Air Quality	46
State Spending on Water Quality	23
Federal Grants for Rural Water and Waste Disposal	19
Federal Spending on Wastewater Treatment Works	22
Hazardous Waste Sites on National Priority List	16

— not applicable   NA not available

Agriculture
State Ranking

Farm Acreage	2
Farmland as Portion of State	11
Net Farm Income	6
Government Payments to Farms	3
Federal Commodity Loans/Price Supports	9
Federal Spending on Rural Development	6
Rural Electric and Telephone Loan Guarantees	26
Foreign-Owned Agricultural Land	20

Business and Economy
State Ranking

Gross State Product	45
Retail Sales	39
Supermarket Sales	16
Commercial Bank Assets	37
Insured Commercial Bank Deposits	36
Fortune 500 Companies	42
Inc. 500 Companies	47
New Business Incorporations	30
Business Failures	46
Financial Aid to Minority Businesses	41
Women-Owned Businesses	43
Sales & Receipts of Women-Owned Businesses	6
African American-Owned Businesses	51
Sales & Receipts of African American-Owned Businesses	45
Hispanic-Owned Businesses	32
Sales & Receipts of Hispanic-Owned Businesses	35
Employees in Manufacturing	46
Manufacturing Shipments	45
Japanese-Owned U.S. Manufacturing Plants	48
Exports to Mexico	30
Change in Exports to Mexico	2
Existing Home Sales	14
Housing Starts	23
Average Annual Pay	48
Disposable Personal Income	44
Median Income of Families with Children	44
Federal Spending on Unemployment Insurance/Employment Services	11
Teen Unemployment	31
Bankruptcy Petitions Filed	32
Patents Issued to State Residents	32
Federal Spending on Community Development	14
Federal Spending on Economic Development Administration	6
Federal Spending on Urban Development Action Grants	33

Crime and Criminal Justice
State Ranking

Total Crimes	45
Violent Crimes	47
Murders	45
Rapes	50
Aggravated Assaults	47
Property Crimes	45
Robberies	48
Burglaries	50
Larcenies and Thefts	39
Motor Vehicle Thefts	43
State and Federal Prisoners	38
Capital Punishment	17

State Spending on Corrections	27
State Spending on Police	
Inmates in Local Jails	12
Spending on Local Jails	35
Spending per Inmate for Local Jails	20
Employees at Local Jails	41
Juvenile Custody Rate	28
Federal Spending on Office of Justice Assistance Programs	4

Defense
State Ranking

Defense Grants to State and Local Governments	11
Total Defense Payroll	33
Total Army Payroll	36
Total Navy/Marine Corps Payroll	36
Total Air Force Payroll	15
Total Active-Duty Payroll	30
Army Active-Duty Payroll	51
Navy/Marine Corps Active-Duty Payroll	49
Air Force Active-Duty Payroll	12
Total Civilian Payroll	39
Army Civilian Payroll	38
Navy/Marine Corps Civilian Payroll	46
Air Force Civilian Payroll	17
Total Reserve and National Guard Payroll	16
Army Reserve and National Guard Payroll	18
Navy/Marine Corps Reserve and National Guard Payroll	20
Air Force Reserve and National Guard Payroll	12
Total Retired Military Payroll	27
Army Retired Military Payroll	32
Navy/Marine Corps Retired Military Payroll	22
Air Force Retired Military Payroll	21
Total Defense Prime Contracts	49
Army Prime Contracts	44
Navy/Marine Corps Prime Contracts	49
Air Force Prime Contracts	39
U.S. Military Installations	41
Construction of National Guard Centers	11

Education
State Ranking

School Age Population	9
Public Elementary and Secondary School Enrollment	43
Average Daily Attendance	38
Student-Teacher Ratio	31
Salaries of Public School Teachers	40
Public School Teachers Who Are Male	5
Eighth Grade Math Test Results	2
High School Math Enrollment	9
Public High School Graduation Rate	8
General Educational Development (GED) Test Results	24
Adult Illiteracy	43
Federal Revenue for Public Schools	12
State Revenue for Public Schools	25
Local Government Revenue for Public Schools	28
Total Public School Spending	29
Public School Spending on Instruction	9
Public School Spending on Noninstruction	28
Public School Spending on Support Staff	24
State and Local Government Spending on Public Schools	5

Federal Spending on School Improvement Programs	8
Gifted and Talented Students	NA
Federal Spending on Education of Students with Disabilities	17
Student-Teacher Ratio in Catholic Elementary Schools	40
Student-Teacher Ratio in Catholic Secondary Schools	49
State Spending on Education	12
State and Local Government Spending on Education	23
Higher Education Tuition and Fees	47
Higher Education Revenue	51
Federal Spending on Higher Education	34
State Spending on Higher Education	38
State and Local Government Spending on Higher Education	42
State and Local Appropriations for Higher Education	38
Federal Spending on Higher Education Act Insured Loans	11
Federal Spending on National Guaranteed Student Loans	13
Federal Spending on Pell Grants	4
Default Rate in Perkins Student Loan Program	38
State Spending on Libraries	20

Energy
State Ranking

Total Spending on Energy	10
Net Generation of Electricity	4
Cost of Electricity	49
Spending on Electricity	36
Spending on Natural Gas	31
Spending on Gasoline	3
Spending on Petroleum	8
Spending on Coal	16
Total Energy Consumption	9
Electricity Consumption	5
Natural Gas Consumption	27
Petroleum Consumption	8
Coal Consumption	7
Power Plants	10
Nuclear Power Plants	34
Hydroelectric Power Plants	7

Environment
State Ranking

Federally Owned Land (acreage)	13
Loss of Wetlands	44
Environmental Protection Agency Spending	16
EPA Abatement, Control, and Compliance	4
State Spending on Environmental Programs	3
Environmental Programs as Part of State Budget	2
State Spending on Forest Programs	3
Total Tree Planting	23
Federal Tree Planting	9
Private Tree Planting	32
State Spending on Air Quality	13
State Spending on Water Quality	4
Federal Grants for Rural Water and Waste Disposal	26
Federal Spending on Wastewater Treatment Works	24
Hazardous Waste Sites on National Priority List	39

Federal Grants for Hazardous Substance
  Response 4
State Spending on Hazardous Waste 3

Health | State Ranking

State Health Rankings 26
State Spending on Health 16
Support for Public Health 44
Family and Business Spending on Health
  Care 49
HMO Enrollment 47
Medicaid Recipients 42
Medically Underserved Population 19
Lack of Health Care Access 11
Active Nonfederal Physicians 41
Active Nonfederal Nurses 31
Active Nonfederal Dentists 15
Average Cost per Hospital Stay 45
Average Cost per Day for Hospital Care 50
Average Cost per Day for Hospital Room 18
State Spending on Hospitals 43
Adequacy of Prenatal Care 29
Infants Born Receiving Late or No
  Prenatal Care 28
Infants Born with Low Birth Weight 33
Abortions 35
Immunizations of Two-Year-Olds —
Overall Risk for Heart Disease 7
Risk Factor for Heart Disease
  (hypertension) 30
Deaths Due to Heart Disease 38
New Cancer Cases 28
Deaths Due to Cancer 30
Prevalence of Smoking 36
Prevalence of Diabetes 34
Deaths Due to Diabetes 38
Cost of Diabetes 34
AIDS Cases Reported 47
Gonorrhea Cases Reported 44
Syphilis Cases Reported 43
Tuberculosis Cases Reported 47
Hepatitis Cases Reported 21
Rabies Cases Reported 17
Lyme Disease Cases Reported 45
Beer Consumption 9
Wine Consumption 26
Liquor Consumption 27
Alcohol and Drug Treatment Admissions 11
Federal Spending on Alcohol, Drug
  Abuse, and Mental Health 41
Total Spending on Alcohol/Drug Abuse
  Services 6
State Spending on Alcohol/Drug Abuse
  Services 44
Hard-Core Cocaine Users 50
Federal Drug Grants to States 9

Population | State Ranking

Population 44
Population Density 49
Population in Metropolitan Areas 49
Population Under 18 Years Old 10
Population Over 65 Years Old 18
White Population 13
African American Population 51
Hispanic Population 34
Asian American Population 47
Native American Population 5
Catholic Population 28

Jewish Population 49
Marriages 32
Divorces 19
Births 43
Births to Single Mothers 35
Births to Single Teenagers 42
Adoptions 2
Adoption Option Index 7
Infant Mortality 38
Child Deaths and Suicides 15
Teen Violent Death Rate 12
Deaths 22

Recreation | State Ranking

State Parks and Recreation Areas 12
Visitors to State Parks and Recreation
  Areas 47
Revenues from State Parks and
  Recreation Areas 35
Spending on State Arts Agencies 18
Domestic Travel Spending 8
State Travel Office Budgets 4
Lodging Industry (rooms) 9
Participation in Exercise Walking 2
Participation in Swimming 1
Participation in Camping 1
Participation in Bowling 1
Bowling League Membership 9
Participation in Running/Jogging 1
Participation in Aerobics 1
Participation in Golf 1
Participation in Softball 2
Participation in Health Clubs 10
Participation in Tennis 22
Participation in Hunting 1
Participation in Baseball 2
Participation in Bicycle Riding 1
Number of Boats 20
Attendance at Parimutuel Racing —
Revenue from Parimutuel Betting 30

Social Services | State Ranking

Federal Grants for Social Services 17
State Spending on Public Welfare 23
Persons in Poverty 16
Public Aid Recipients 31
Participants in Food Stamp Program 23
Households in Food Stamp Program 35
Percentage of Poor Using AFDC and
  Food Stamps 24
Federal Spending on Children and
  Family Services 6
Federal Women, Infants, and Children
  Food Program 20
Child Welfare Services 35
Child Abuse Cases Reported —
Children in Poverty 15
Children Without Health Insurance 17
Children Who Are Hungry or at Risk 10
Federal Spending on Child Nutrition
  Programs 20
Federal Spending on Special Milk
  Program 22
National School Lunch Program
  Participants 23
Head Start Enrollment 39
Head Start Spending 23
Federal Spending on Rehabilitation
  Services/Handicapped Research 19

State Government | State Ranking

Financial World's State Rankings 30
Salaries of State Officials (governor) 49
Salaries of State Legislators —
Women in State Legislatures 27
African Americans in State Legislatures 43
Hispanics in State Legislatures 21
Asian Americans in State Legislatures 6
Native Americans in State Legislatures 6
Turnover in State Legislatures 6
Length of State Legislative Sessions 17
State Bills in Regular Session 6
State Resolutions in Regular Session 19
State Bills in Special Session —
State Resolutions in Special Session —
Women in State Cabinets 16
Total Federal Funding to State
  Governments 12
Total State Spending 5
State General Expenditures 6
State Debt 16
State Spending on Interest on the
  General Debt 15
Total State Tax Revenue 41
State Revenue from Tax on Sales and
  Gross Receipts 48
State Revenue from General Sales Tax —
State Revenue from Licenses 6
State Revenue from Motor Vehicle
  Licenses 17
State Revenue from Individual Income
  Taxes 31
State Revenue from Corporation Net
  Income Taxes 14
State Revenue from Severance Taxes 7
State Revenue from Property Taxes 4
State Revenue from Death and Gift
  Taxes 21
State Revenue from Documentary and
  Stock Transfers —
State Revenue from Tax on Motor Fuels 2
State Revenue from Tax on Tobacco
  Products 38
Excise Tax on Cigarettes 30
Excise Tax on Gasoline 10
State Revenue from Lotteries 32

Transportation | State Ranking

Motor Vehicle Registrations 6
Automobile Registrations 28
Bus and Truck Registrations 5
Motorcycle Registrations 11
Driver Licenses 15
Federal Spending on Highway Trust
  Fund 3
Federal Spending on Mass
  Transportation 40
State Spending on Highways 3
Highway Deficiency 8
Bridge Deficiency 42
Traffic Fatalities 8
Traffic Fatalities per Miles Traveled 12
Motorcyclist Fatalities 22
Pedalcyclist Fatalities 29
Pedestrian Fatalities 29
Registered Aircraft 3
Registered Pilots 4
Federal Spending on Airport and
  Airway Trust Fund 7
Aircraft Fatalities 3

— not applicable   NA not available

Agriculture
State Ranking

Farm Acreage	4
Farmland as Portion of State	1
Net Farm Income	2
Government Payments to Farms	4
Federal Commodity Loans/Price Supports	3
Federal Spending on Rural Development	24
Rural Electric and Telephone Loan Guarantees	31
Foreign-Owned Agricultural Land	39

Business and Economy
State Ranking

Gross State Product	27
Retail Sales	44
Supermarket Sales	45
Commercial Bank Assets	10
Insured Commercial Bank Deposits	9
Fortune 500 Companies	12
Inc. 500 Companies	13
New Business Incorporations	31
Business Failures	21
Financial Aid to Minority Businesses	41
Women-Owned Businesses	12
Sales & Receipts of Women-Owned Businesses	36
African American-Owned Businesses	37
Sales & Receipts of African American-Owned Businesses	38
Hispanic-Owned Businesses	29
Sales & Receipts of Hispanic-Owned Businesses	36
Employees in Manufacturing	37
Manufacturing Shipments	18
Japanese-Owned U.S. Manufacturing Plants	30
Exports to Mexico	12
Change in Exports to Mexico	43
Existing Home Sales	41
Housing Starts	21
Average Annual Pay	46
Disposable Personal Income	25
Median Income of Families with Children	31
Federal Spending on Unemployment Insurance/Employment Services	27
Teen Unemployment	51
Bankruptcy Petitions Filed	29
Patents Issued to State Residents	41
Federal Spending on Community Development	22
Federal Spending on Economic Development Administration	33
Federal Spending on Urban Development Action Grants	24

Crime and Criminal Justice
State Ranking

Total Crimes	39
Violent Crimes	37
Murders	41
Rapes	44
Aggravated Assaults	35
Property Crimes	39
Robberies	41
Burglaries	45
Larcenies and Thefts	25
Motor Vehicle Thefts	42
State and Federal Prisoners	44
Capital Punishment	17

State Spending on Corrections	45
State Spending on Police	25
Inmates in Local Jails	42
Spending on Local Jails	33
Spending per Inmate for Local Jails	16
Employees at Local Jails	42
Juvenile Custody Rate	9
Federal Spending on Office of Justice Assistance Programs	17

Defense
State Ranking

Defense Grants to State and Local Governments	37
Total Defense Payroll	23
Total Army Payroll	28
Total Navy/Marine Corps Payroll	39
Total Air Force Payroll	6
Total Active-Duty Payroll	14
Army Active-Duty Payroll	38
Navy/Marine Corps Active-Duty Payroll	29
Air Force Active-Duty Payroll	5
Total Civilian Payroll	27
Army Civilian Payroll	20
Navy/Marine Corps Civilian Payroll	43
Air Force Civilian Payroll	14
Total Reserve and National Guard Payroll	32
Army Reserve and National Guard Payroll	29
Navy/Marine Corps Reserve and National Guard Payroll	23
Air Force Reserve and National Guard Payroll	35
Total Retired Military Payroll	24
Army Retired Military Payroll	41
Navy/Marine Corps Retired Military Payroll	37
Air Force Retired Military Payroll	9
Total Defense Prime Contracts	42
Army Prime Contracts	48
Navy/Marine Corps Prime Contracts	48
Air Force Prime Contracts	23
U.S. Military Installations	41
Construction of National Guard Centers	38

Education
State Ranking

School Age Population	12
Public Elementary and Secondary School Enrollment	37
Average Daily Attendance	9
Student-Teacher Ratio	43
Salaries of Public School Teachers	41
Public School Teachers Who Are Male	23
Eighth Grade Math Test Results	4
High School Math Enrollment	28
Public High School Graduation Rate	6
General Educational Development (GED) Test Results	38
Adult Illiteracy	38
Federal Revenue for Public Schools	27
State Revenue for Public Schools	49
Local Government Revenue for Public Schools	3
Total Public School Spending	21
Public School Spending on Instruction	14
Public School Spending on Noninstruction	1
Public School Spending on Support Staff	47
State and Local Government Spending on Public Schools	10

Federal Spending on School Improvement Programs	31
Gifted and Talented Students	4
Federal Spending on Education of Students with Disabilities	25
Student-Teacher Ratio in Catholic Elementary Schools	23
Student-Teacher Ratio in Catholic Secondary Schools	48
State Spending on Education	37
State and Local Government Spending on Education	5
Higher Education Tuition and Fees	30
Higher Education Revenue	36
Federal Spending on Higher Education	24
State Spending on Higher Education	16
State and Local Government Spending on Higher Education	6
State and Local Appropriations for Higher Education	24
Federal Spending on Higher Education Act Insured Loans	2
Federal Spending on National Guaranteed Student Loans	2
Federal Spending on Pell Grants	13
Default Rate in Perkins Student Loan Program	48
State Spending on Libraries	32

Energy
State Ranking

Total Spending on Energy	20
Net Generation of Electricity	21
Cost of Electricity	42
Spending on Electricity	39
Spending on Natural Gas	18
Spending on Gasoline	12
Spending on Petroleum	16
Spending on Coal	35
Total Energy Consumption	25
Electricity Consumption	24
Natural Gas Consumption	18
Petroleum Consumption	24
Coal Consumption	21
Power Plants	3
Nuclear Power Plants	2
Hydroelectric Power Plants	16

Environment
State Ranking

Federally Owned Land (acreage)	43
Loss of Wetlands	37
Environmental Protection Agency Spending	37
EPA Abatement, Control, and Compliance	31
State Spending on Environmental Programs	40
Environmental Programs as Part of State Budget	36
State Spending on Forest Programs	46
Total Tree Planting	36
Federal Tree Planting	32
Private Tree Planting	32
State Spending on Air Quality	49
State Spending on Water Quality	37
Federal Grants for Rural Water and Waste Disposal	13
Federal Spending on Wastewater Treatment Works	37
Hazardous Waste Sites on National Priority List	39

Federal Grants for Hazardous Substance
Response 29
State Spending on Hazardous Waste 41

Health — *State Ranking*

State Health Rankings 5
State Spending on Health 29
Support for Public Health 22
Family and Business Spending on Health
Care 19
HMO Enrollment 37
Medicaid Recipients 32
Medically Underserved Population 50
Lack of Health Care Access 36
Active Nonfederal Physicians 35
Active Nonfederal Nurses 15
Active Nonfederal Dentists 12
Average Cost per Hospital Stay 20
Average Cost per Day for Hospital Care 46
Average Cost per Day for Hospital Room 45
State Spending on Hospitals 11
Adequacy of Prenatal Care 8
Infants Born Receiving Late or No
Prenatal Care 47
Infants Born with Low Birth Weight 43
Abortions 32
Immunizations of Two-Year-Olds —
Overall Risk for Heart Disease 22
Risk Factor for Heart Disease
(hypertension) 22
Deaths Due to Heart Disease 14
New Cancer Cases 26
Deaths Due to Cancer 24
Prevalence of Smoking 39
Prevalence of Diabetes 33
Deaths Due to Diabetes 25
Cost of Diabetes 33
AIDS Cases Reported 43
Gonorrhea Cases Reported 51
Syphilis Cases Reported 50
Tuberculosis Cases Reported 45
Hepatitis Cases Reported 18
Rabies Cases Reported 32
Lyme Disease Cases Reported 17
Beer Consumption 17
Wine Consumption 37
Liquor Consumption 35
Alcohol and Drug Treatment Admissions 5
Federal Spending on Alcohol, Drug
Abuse, and Mental Health 40
Total Spending on Alcohol/Drug Abuse
Services 39
State Spending on Alcohol/Drug Abuse
Services 24
Hard-Core Cocaine Users 15
Federal Drug Grants to States 24

Population — *State Ranking*

Population 36
Population Density 43
Population in Metropolitan Areas 37
Population Under 18 Years Old 12
Population Over 65 Years Old 9
White Population 10
African American Population 34
Hispanic Population 27
Asian American Population 37
Native American Population 20
Catholic Population 19

Jewish Population 31
Marriages 46
Divorces 36
Births 30
Births to Single Mothers 44
Births to Single Teenagers 44
Adoptions 13
Adoption Option Index 14
Infant Mortality 40
Child Deaths and Suicides 36
Teen Violent Death Rate 40
Deaths 16

Recreation — *State Ranking*

State Parks and Recreation Areas 8
Visitors to State Parks and Recreation
Areas 9
Revenues from State Parks and
Recreation Areas 12
Spending on State Arts Agencies 29
Domestic Travel Spending 31
State Travel Office Budgets 37
Lodging Industry (rooms) 20
Participation in Exercise Walking 20
Participation in Swimming 43
Participation in Camping 21
Participation in Bowling 13
Bowling League Membership 5
Participation in Running/Jogging 20
Participation in Aerobics 24
Participation in Golf 4
Participation in Softball 13
Participation in Health Clubs 37
Participation in Tennis 30
Participation in Hunting 16
Participation in Baseball 28
Participation in Bicycle Riding 29
Number of Boats 33
Attendance at Parimutuel Racing 4
Revenue from Parimutuel Betting 24

Social Services — *State Ranking*

Federal Grants for Social Services 14
State Spending on Public Welfare 33
Persons in Poverty 45
Public Aid Recipients 46
Participants in Food Stamp Program 44
Households in Food Stamp Program 38
Percentage of Poor Using AFDC and
Food Stamps 26
Federal Spending on Children and
Family Services 42
Federal Women, Infants, and Children
Food Program 35
Child Welfare Services 10
Child Abuse Cases Reported —
Children in Poverty 37
Children Without Health Insurance 32
Children Who Are Hungry or at Risk 20
Federal Spending on Child Nutrition
Programs 22
Federal Spending on Special Milk
Program 7
National School Lunch Program
Participants 28
Head Start Enrollment 27
Head Start Spending 25
Federal Spending on Rehabilitation
Services/Handicapped Research 30

State Government — *State Ranking*

Financial World's State Rankings 31
Salaries of State Officials (governor) 47
Salaries of State Legislators 27
Women in State Legislatures 23
African Americans in State Legislatures 33
Hispanics in State Legislatures 21
Asian Americans in State Legislatures 6
Native Americans in State Legislatures 12
Turnover in State Legislatures 36
Length of State Legislative Sessions 17
State Bills in Regular Session 21
State Resolutions in Regular Session 43
State Bills in Special Session 23
State Resolutions in Special Session 19
Women in State Cabinets NA
Total Federal Funding to State
Governments 32
Total State Spending 42
State General Expenditures 36
State Debt 36
State Spending on Interest on the
General Debt 26
Total State Tax Revenue 30
State Revenue from Tax on Sales and
Gross Receipts 20
State Revenue from General Sales Tax 22
State Revenue from Licenses 36
State Revenue from Motor Vehicle
Licenses 34
State Revenue from Individual Income
Taxes 28
State Revenue from Corporation Net
Income Taxes 33
State Revenue from Severance Taxes 23
State Revenue from Property Taxes 33
State Revenue from Death and Gift
Taxes 47
State Revenue from Documentary and
Stock Transfers 26
State Revenue from Tax on Motor Fuels 1
State Revenue from Tax on Tobacco
Products 22
Excise Tax on Cigarettes 18
Excise Tax on Gasoline 1
State Revenue from Lotteries —

Transportation — *State Ranking*

Motor Vehicle Registrations 10
Automobile Registrations 22
Bus and Truck Registrations 9
Motorcycle Registrations 34
Driver Licenses 34
Federal Spending on Highway Trust
Fund 19
Federal Spending on Mass
Transportation 28
State Spending on Highways 11
Highway Deficiency 15
Bridge Deficiency 15
Traffic Fatalities 26
Traffic Fatalities per Miles Traveled 23
Motorcyclist Fatalities 42
Pedalcyclist Fatalities 28
Pedestrian Fatalities 47
Registered Aircraft 17
Registered Pilots 21
Federal Spending on Airport and
Airway Trust Fund 10
Aircraft Fatalities 15

— *not applicable* NA *not available*

Agriculture
State Ranking

Farm Acreage	33
Farmland as Portion of State	46
Net Farm Income	43
Government Payments to Farms	36
Federal Commodity Loans/Price Supports	45
Federal Spending on Rural Development	20
Rural Electric and Telephone Loan Guarantees	40
Foreign-Owned Agricultural Land	11

Business and Economy
State Ranking

Gross State Product	5
Retail Sales	16
Supermarket Sales	7
Commercial Bank Assets	16
Insured Commercial Bank Deposits	41
Fortune 500 Companies	42
Inc. 500 Companies	42
New Business Incorporations	2
Business Failures	13
Financial Aid to Minority Businesses	17
Women-Owned Businesses	10
Sales & Receipts of Women-Owned Businesses	28
African American-Owned Businesses	26
Sales & Receipts of African American-Owned Businesses	32
Hispanic-Owned Businesses	9
Sales & Receipts of Hispanic-Owned Businesses	7
Employees in Manufacturing	45
Manufacturing Shipments	51
Japanese-Owned U.S. Manufacturing Plants	30
Exports to Mexico	37
Change in Exports to Mexico	6
Existing Home Sales	5
Housing Starts	1
Average Annual Pay	22
Disposable Personal Income	14
Median Income of Families with Children	26
Federal Spending on Unemployment Insurance/Employment Services	10
Teen Unemployment	35
Bankruptcy Petitions Filed	4
Patents Issued to State Residents	33
Federal Spending on Community Development	45
Federal Spending on Economic Development Administration	8
Federal Spending on Urban Development Action Grants	33

Crime and Criminal Justice
State Ranking

Total Crimes	10
Violent Crimes	18
Murders	8
Rapes	5
Aggravated Assaults	32
Property Crimes	10
Robberies	7
Burglaries	11
Larcenies and Thefts	14
Motor Vehicle Thefts	14
State and Federal Prisoners	2
Capital Punishment	8

State Spending on Corrections	9
State Spending on Police	33
Inmates in Local Jails	6
Spending on Local Jails	3
Spending per Inmate for Local Jails	13
Employees at Local Jails	23
Juvenile Custody Rate	2
Federal Spending on Office of Justice Assistance Programs	19

Defense
State Ranking

Defense Grants to State and Local Governments	36
Total Defense Payroll	19
Total Army Payroll	45
Total Navy/Marine Corps Payroll	16
Total Air Force Payroll	7
Total Active-Duty Payroll	17
Army Active-Duty Payroll	50
Navy/Marine Corps Active-Duty Payroll	21
Air Force Active-Duty Payroll	7
Total Civilian Payroll	41
Army Civilian Payroll	50
Navy/Marine Corps Civilian Payroll	22
Air Force Civilian Payroll	20
Total Reserve and National Guard Payroll	45
Army Reserve and National Guard Payroll	46
Navy/Marine Corps Reserve and National Guard Payroll	38
Air Force Reserve and National Guard Payroll	30
Total Retired Military Payroll	2
Army Retired Military Payroll	19
Navy/Marine Corps Retired Military Payroll	6
Air Force Retired Military Payroll	1
Total Defense Prime Contracts	38
Army Prime Contracts	30
Navy/Marine Corps Prime Contracts	29
Air Force Prime Contracts	28
U.S. Military Installations	34
Construction of National Guard Centers	32

Education
State Ranking

School Age Population	42
Public Elementary and Secondary School Enrollment	40
Average Daily Attendance	3
Student-Teacher Ratio	7
Salaries of Public School Teachers	22
Public School Teachers Who Are Male	31
Eighth Grade Math Test Results	—
High School Math Enrollment	33
Public High School Graduation Rate	19
General Educational Development (GED) Test Results	3
Adult Illiteracy	38
Federal Revenue for Public Schools	47
State Revenue for Public Schools	40
Local Government Revenue for Public Schools	11
Total Public School Spending	40
Public School Spending on Instruction	15
Public School Spending on Noninstruction	39
Public School Spending on Support Staff	13
State and Local Government Spending on Public Schools	39

Federal Spending on School Improvement Programs	32
Gifted and Talented Students	29
Federal Spending on Education of Students with Disabilities	49
Student-Teacher Ratio in Catholic Elementary Schools	1
Student-Teacher Ratio in Catholic Secondary Schools	9
State Spending on Education	29
State and Local Government Spending on Education	46
Higher Education Tuition and Fees	50
Higher Education Revenue	46
Federal Spending on Higher Education	49
State Spending on Higher Education	47
State and Local Government Spending on Higher Education	44
State and Local Appropriations for Higher Education	10
Federal Spending on Higher Education Act Insured Loans	50
Federal Spending on National Guaranteed Student Loans	49
Federal Spending on Pell Grants	43
Default Rate in Perkins Student Loan Program	17
State Spending on Libraries	9

Energy
State Ranking

Total Spending on Energy	14
Net Generation of Electricity	14
Cost of Electricity	37
Spending on Electricity	22
Spending on Natural Gas	32
Spending on Gasoline	8
Spending on Petroleum	14
Spending on Coal	9
Total Energy Consumption	23
Electricity Consumption	13
Natural Gas Consumption	26
Petroleum Consumption	18
Coal Consumption	10
Power Plants	17
Nuclear Power Plants	34
Hydroelectric Power Plants	25

Environment
State Ranking

Federally Owned Land (acreage)	1
Loss of Wetlands	19
Environmental Protection Agency Spending	47
EPA Abatement, Control, and Compliance	17
State Spending on Environmental Programs	16
Environmental Programs as Part of State Budget	10
State Spending on Forest Programs	17
Total Tree Planting	50
Federal Tree Planting	32
Private Tree Planting	45
State Spending on Air Quality	42
State Spending on Water Quality	11
Federal Grants for Rural Water and Waste Disposal	21
Federal Spending on Wastewater Treatment Works	50
Hazardous Waste Sites on National Priority List	50

Federal Grants for Hazardous Substance
  Response 15
State Spending on Hazardous Waste ... 46

Health

State Ranking

State Health Rankings 41
State Spending on Health 49
Support for Public Health 40
Family and Business Spending on Health
  Care 31
HMO Enrollment 27
Medicaid Recipients 51
Medically Underserved Population 41
Lack of Health Care Access 17
Active Nonfederal Physicians 40
Active Nonfederal Nurses 20
Active Nonfederal Dentists 46
Average Cost per Hospital Stay 8
Average Cost per Day for Hospital Care . 5
Average Cost per Day for Hospital Room . 32
State Spending on Hospitals 47
Adequacy of Prenatal Care 41
Infants Born Receiving Late or No
  Prenatal Care 5
Infants Born with Low Birth Weight ... 19
Abortions 5
Immunizations of Two-Year-Olds .... —
Overall Risk for Heart Disease 39
Risk Factor for Heart Disease
  (hypertension) .... NA
Deaths Due to Heart Disease 41
New Cancer Cases 36
Deaths Due to Cancer 41
Prevalence of Smoking 2
Prevalence of Diabetes 38
Deaths Due to Diabetes 47
Cost of Diabetes 39
AIDS Cases Reported 10
Gonorrhea Cases Reported 23
Syphilis Cases Reported 33
Tuberculosis Cases Reported 23
Hepatitis Cases Reported 25
Rabies Cases Reported 28
Lyme Disease Cases Reported 43
Beer Consumption 1
Wine Consumption 2
Liquor Consumption 3
Alcohol and Drug Treatment Admissions 12
Federal Spending on Alcohol, Drug
  Abuse, and Mental Health 26
Total Spending on Alcohol/Drug Abuse
  Services 41
State Spending on Alcohol/Drug Abuse
  Services 36
Hard-Core Cocaine Users 2
Federal Drug Grants to States 19

Population

State Ranking

Population 39
Population Density 46
Population in Metropolitan Areas 11
Population Under 18 Years Old 39
Population Over 65 Years Old 44
White Population 27
African American Population 27
Hispanic Population 8
Asian American Population 7
Native American Population 9
Catholic Population 34

Jewish Population 12
Marriages 1
Divorces 1
Births 4
Births to Single Mothers 29
Births to Single Teenagers 36
Adoptions 33
Adoption Option Index 42
Infant Mortality 45
Child Deaths and Suicides 12
Teen Violent Death Rate 3
Deaths 41

Recreation

State Ranking

State Parks and Recreation Areas 6
Visitors to State Parks and Recreation
  Areas 30
Revenues from State Parks and
  Recreation Areas 41
Spending on State Arts Agencies 48
Domestic Travel Spending 1
State Travel Office Budgets 7
Lodging Industry (rooms) 1
Participation in Exercise Walking 47
Participation in Swimming 24
Participation in Camping 10
Participation in Bowling 22
Bowling League Membership 17
Participation in Running/Jogging 38
Participation in Aerobics 12
Participation in Golf 18
Participation in Softball 49
Participation in Health Clubs 34
Participation in Tennis 47
Participation in Hunting 28
Participation in Baseball 3
Participation in Bicycle Riding 12
Number of Boats 37
Attendance at Parimutuel Racing .... —
Revenue from Parimutuel Betting 37

Social Services

State Ranking

Federal Grants for Social Services 50
State Spending on Public Welfare 50
Persons in Poverty 35
Public Aid Recipients 49
Participants in Food Stamp Program ... 48
Households in Food Stamp Program ... 48
Percentage of Poor Using AFDC and
  Food Stamps 34
Federal Spending on Children and
  Family Services 27
Federal Women, Infants, and Children
  Food Program 47
Child Welfare Services 1
Child Abuse Cases Reported .... —
Children in Poverty 41
Children Without Health Insurance 14
Children Who Are Hungry or at Risk ... 24
Federal Spending on Child Nutrition
  Programs 50
Federal Spending on Special Milk
  Program 28
National School Lunch Program
  Participants 50
Head Start Enrollment 51
Head Start Spending 12
Federal Spending on Rehabilitation
  Services/Handicapped Research 50

State Government

State Ranking

Financial World's State Rankings 13
Salaries of State Officials (governor) ... 22
Salaries of State Legislators .... —
Women in State Legislatures 11
African Americans in State Legislatures . 25
Hispanics in State Legislatures 10
Asian Americans in State Legislatures .. 6
Native Americans in State Legislatures . 12
Turnover in State Legislatures 1
Length of State Legislative Sessions ... 12
State Bills in Regular Session 8
State Resolutions in Regular Session ... 16
State Bills in Special Session .... —
State Resolutions in Special Session ... —
Women in State Cabinets 36
Total Federal Funding to State
  Governments 34
Total State Spending 23
State General Expenditures 39
State Debt 23
State Spending on Interest on the
  General Debt 24
Total State Tax Revenue 16
State Revenue from Tax on Sales and
  Gross Receipts 3
State Revenue from General Sales Tax .. 4
State Revenue from Licenses 3
State Revenue from Motor Vehicle
  Licenses 19
State Revenue from Individual Income
  Taxes .... —
State Revenue from Corporation Net
  Income Taxes .... —
State Revenue from Severance Taxes ... 15
State Revenue from Property Taxes 12
State Revenue from Death and Gift
  Taxes 22
State Revenue from Documentary and
  Stock Transfers .... —
State Revenue from Tax on Motor Fuels . 29
State Revenue from Tax on Tobacco
  Products 1
Excise Tax on Cigarettes 8
Excise Tax on Gasoline 29
State Revenue from Lotteries .... —

Transportation

State Ranking

Motor Vehicle Registrations 45
Automobile Registrations 47
Bus and Truck Registrations 26
Motorcycle Registrations 28
Driver Licenses 19
Federal Spending on Highway Trust
  Fund 12
Federal Spending on Mass
  Transportation 50
State Spending on Highways 33
Highway Deficiency 20
Bridge Deficiency 46
Traffic Fatalities 9
Traffic Fatalities per Miles Traveled 1
Motorcyclist Fatalities 15
Pedalcyclist Fatalities 32
Pedestrian Fatalities 7
Registered Aircraft 7
Registered Pilots 6
Federal Spending on Airport and
  Airway Trust Fund 3
Aircraft Fatalities 5

— *not applicable*   NA *not available*

Agriculture
State Ranking

Farm Acreage	48
Farmland as Portion of State	48
Net Farm Income	45
Government Payments to Farms	45
Federal Commodity Loans/Price Supports	48
Federal Spending on Rural Development	43
Rural Electric and Telephone Loan Guarantees	37
Foreign-Owned Agricultural Land	3

Business and Economy
State Ranking

Gross State Product	13
Retail Sales	2
Supermarket Sales	1
Commercial Bank Assets	38
Insured Commercial Bank Deposits	40
Fortune 500 Companies	19
Inc. 500 Companies	11
New Business Incorporations	24
Business Failures	2
Financial Aid to Minority Businesses	41
Women-Owned Businesses	38
Sales & Receipts of Women-Owned Businesses	29
African American-Owned Businesses	43
Sales & Receipts of African American-Owned Businesses	40
Hispanic-Owned Businesses	37
Sales & Receipts of Hispanic-Owned Businesses	44
Employees in Manufacturing	38
Manufacturing Shipments	35
Japanese-Owned U.S. Manufacturing Plants	19
Exports to Mexico	27
Change in Exports to Mexico	8
Existing Home Sales	46
Housing Starts	36
Average Annual Pay	20
Disposable Personal Income	5
Median Income of Families with Children	3
Federal Spending on Unemployment Insurance/Employment Services	21
Teen Unemployment	7
Bankruptcy Petitions Filed	27
Patents Issued to State Residents	7
Federal Spending on Community Development	30
Federal Spending on Economic Development Administration	48
Federal Spending on Urban Development Action Grants	33

Crime and Criminal Justice
State Ranking

Total Crimes	47
Violent Crimes	49
Murders	40
Rapes	37
Aggravated Assaults	50
Property Crimes	46
Robberies	44
Burglaries	44
Larcenies and Thefts	45
Motor Vehicle Thefts	40
State and Federal Prisoners	46
Capital Punishment	17

State Spending on Corrections	48
State Spending on Police	31
Inmates in Local Jails	40
Spending on Local Jails	19
Spending per Inmate for Local Jails	7
Employees at Local Jails	34
Juvenile Custody Rate	37
Federal Spending on Office of Justice Assistance Programs	13

Defense
State Ranking

Defense Grants to State and Local Governments	49
Total Defense Payroll	38
Total Army Payroll	33
Total Navy/Marine Corps Payroll	22
Total Air Force Payroll	32
Total Active-Duty Payroll	45
Army Active-Duty Payroll	48
Navy/Marine Corps Active-Duty Payroll	26
Air Force Active-Duty Payroll	39
Total Civilian Payroll	40
Army Civilian Payroll	34
Navy/Marine Corps Civilian Payroll	21
Air Force Civilian Payroll	35
Total Reserve and National Guard Payroll	41
Army Reserve and National Guard Payroll	39
Navy/Marine Corps Reserve and National Guard Payroll	50
Air Force Reserve and National Guard Payroll	21
Total Retired Military Payroll	17
Army Retired Military Payroll	21
Navy/Marine Corps Retired Military Payroll	15
Air Force Retired Military Payroll	15
Total Defense Prime Contracts	25
Army Prime Contracts	28
Navy/Marine Corps Prime Contracts	13
Air Force Prime Contracts	22
U.S. Military Installations	38
Construction of National Guard Centers	49

Education
State Ranking

School Age Population	37
Public Elementary and Secondary School Enrollment	41
Average Daily Attendance	32
Student-Teacher Ratio	29
Salaries of Public School Teachers	24
Public School Teachers Who Are Male	29
Eighth Grade Math Test Results	7
High School Math Enrollment	NA
Public High School Graduation Rate	28
General Educational Development (GED) Test Results	6
Adult Illiteracy	38
Federal Revenue for Public Schools	51
State Revenue for Public Schools	50
Local Government Revenue for Public Schools	2
Total Public School Spending	17
Public School Spending on Instruction	8
Public School Spending on Noninstruction	36
Public School Spending on Support Staff	22
State and Local Government Spending on Public Schools	3

Federal Spending on School Improvement Programs	14
Gifted and Talented Students	NA
Federal Spending on Education of Students with Disabilities	31
Student-Teacher Ratio in Catholic Elementary Schools	48
Student-Teacher Ratio in Catholic Secondary Schools	18
State Spending on Education	50
State and Local Government Spending on Education	26
Higher Education Tuition and Fees	4
Higher Education Revenue	9
Federal Spending on Higher Education	49
State Spending on Higher Education	44
State and Local Government Spending on Higher Education	41
State and Local Appropriations for Higher Education	49
Federal Spending on Higher Education Act Insured Loans	17
Federal Spending on National Guaranteed Student Loans	44
Federal Spending on Pell Grants	47
Default Rate in Perkins Student Loan Program	42
State Spending on Libraries	26

Energy
State Ranking

Total Spending on Energy	39
Net Generation of Electricity	31
Cost of Electricity	8
Spending on Electricity	17
Spending on Natural Gas	48
Spending on Gasoline	31
Spending on Petroleum	22
Spending on Coal	38
Total Energy Consumption	49
Electricity Consumption	45
Natural Gas Consumption	48
Petroleum Consumption	19
Coal Consumption	37
Power Plants	19
Nuclear Power Plants	4
Hydroelectric Power Plants	10

Environment
State Ranking

Federally Owned Land (acreage)	17
Loss of Wetlands	49
Environmental Protection Agency Spending	15
EPA Abatement, Control, and Compliance	16
State Spending on Environmental Programs	23
Environmental Programs as Part of State Budget	12
State Spending on Forest Programs	33
Total Tree Planting	39
Federal Tree Planting	29
Private Tree Planting	40
State Spending on Air Quality	27
State Spending on Water Quality	15
Federal Grants for Rural Water and Waste Disposal	7
Federal Spending on Wastewater Treatment Works	18
Hazardous Waste Sites on National Priority List	22

Federal Grants for Hazardous Substance
  Response 3
State Spending on Hazardous Waste 6

Health | State Ranking

State Health Rankings 3
State Spending on Health 17
Support for Public Health 12
Family and Business Spending on Health
  Care 33
HMO Enrollment 26
Medicaid Recipients 50
Medically Underserved Population 46
Lack of Health Care Access 45
Active Nonfederal Physicians 19
Active Nonfederal Nurses 5
Active Nonfederal Dentists 21
Average Cost per Hospital Stay 26
Average Cost per Day for Hospital Care 22
Average Cost per Day for Hospital Room 20
State Spending on Hospitals 46
Adequacy of Prenatal Care 1
Infants Born Receiving Late or No
  Prenatal Care 45
Infants Born with Low Birth Weight 50
Abortions 33
Immunizations of Two-Year-Olds —
Overall Risk for Heart Disease 4
Risk Factor for Heart Disease
  (hypertension) 35
Deaths Due to Heart Disease 35
New Cancer Cases 27
Deaths Due to Cancer 35
Prevalence of Smoking 16
Prevalence of Diabetes 47
Deaths Due to Diabetes 23
Cost of Diabetes 47
AIDS Cases Reported 40
Gonorrhea Cases Reported 46
Syphilis Cases Reported 26
Tuberculosis Cases Reported 46
Hepatitis Cases Reported 33
Rabies Cases Reported 33
Lyme Disease Cases Reported 7
Beer Consumption 2
Wine Consumption 6
Liquor Consumption 1
Alcohol and Drug Treatment Admissions 35
Federal Spending on Alcohol, Drug
  Abuse, and Mental Health 32
Total Spending on Alcohol/Drug Abuse
  Services 44
State Spending on Alcohol/Drug Abuse
  Services 31
Hard-Core Cocaine Users 41
Federal Drug Grants to States 22

Population | State Ranking

Population 40
Population Density 19
Population in Metropolitan Areas 35
Population Under 18 Years Old 36
Population Over 65 Years Old 37
White Population 3
African American Population 45
Hispanic Population 40
Asian American Population 34
Native American Population 47
Catholic Population 12

Jewish Population 28
Marriages 25
Divorces 25
Births 46
Births to Single Mothers 49
Births to Single Teenagers 50
Adoptions 24
Adoption Option Index 44
Infant Mortality 47
Child Deaths and Suicides 41
Teen Violent Death Rate 33
Deaths 43

Recreation | State Ranking

State Parks and Recreation Areas 24
Visitors to State Parks and Recreation
  Areas 24
Revenues from State Parks and
  Recreation Areas 3
Spending on State Arts Agencies 41
Domestic Travel Spending 27
State Travel Office Budgets 15
Lodging Industry (rooms) 27
Participation in Exercise Walking 46
Participation in Swimming 23
Participation in Camping 31
Participation in Bowling 49
Bowling League Membership 47
Participation in Running/Jogging 48
Participation in Aerobics 41
Participation in Golf 43
Participation in Softball 23
Participation in Health Clubs 22
Participation in Tennis 42
Participation in Hunting 46
Participation in Baseball 36
Participation in Bicycle Riding 42
Number of Boats 6
Attendance at Parimutuel Racing 3
Revenue from Parimutuel Betting 7

Social Services | State Ranking

Federal Grants for Social Services 6
State Spending on Public Welfare 34
Persons in Poverty 51
Public Aid Recipients 51
Participants in Food Stamp Program 51
Households in Food Stamp Program 51
Percentage of Poor Using AFDC and
  Food Stamps 13
Federal Spending on Children and
  Family Services 51
Federal Women, Infants, and Children
  Food Program 42
Child Welfare Services 15
Child Abuse Cases Reported —
Children in Poverty 51
Children Without Health Insurance 30
Children Who Are Hungry or at Risk 51
Federal Spending on Child Nutrition
  Programs 51
Federal Spending on Special Milk
  Program 6
National School Lunch Program
  Participants 51
Head Start Enrollment 37
Head Start Spending 10
Federal Spending on Rehabilitation
  Services/Handicapped Research 38

State Government | State Ranking

Financial World's State Rankings 19
Salaries of State Officials (governor) 28
Salaries of State Legislators 40
Women in State Legislatures 5
African Americans in State Legislatures 42
Hispanics in State Legislatures 21
Asian Americans in State Legislatures 6
Native Americans in State Legislatures 12
Turnover in State Legislatures 5
Length of State Legislative Sessions 41
State Bills in Regular Session 11
State Resolutions in Regular Session 21
State Bills in Special Session 1
State Resolutions in Special Session 19
Women in State Cabinets —
Total Federal Funding to State
  Governments 46
Total State Spending 50
State General Expenditures 50
State Debt 5
State Spending on Interest on the
  General Debt 7
Total State Tax Revenue 50
State Revenue from Tax on Sales and
  Gross Receipts 46
State Revenue from General Sales Tax —
State Revenue from Licenses 19
State Revenue from Motor Vehicle
  Licenses 18
State Revenue from Individual Income
  Taxes 42
State Revenue from Corporation Net
  Income Taxes 9
State Revenue from Severance Taxes 33
State Revenue from Property Taxes 37
State Revenue from Death and Gift
  Taxes 11
State Revenue from Documentary and
  Stock Transfers 4
State Revenue from Tax on Motor Fuels 35
State Revenue from Tax on Tobacco
  Products 4
Excise Tax on Cigarettes 20
Excise Tax on Gasoline 31
State Revenue from Lotteries 11

Transportation | State Ranking

Motor Vehicle Registrations 17
Automobile Registrations 9
Bus and Truck Registrations 34
Motorcycle Registrations 5
Driver Licenses 2
Federal Spending on Highway Trust
  Fund 31
Federal Spending on Mass
  Transportation 42
State Spending on Highways 41
Highway Deficiency 4
Bridge Deficiency 18
Traffic Fatalities 42
Traffic Fatalities per Miles Traveled 46
Motorcyclist Fatalities 21
Pedalcyclist Fatalities 51
Pedestrian Fatalities 43
Registered Aircraft 11
Registered Pilots 9
Federal Spending on Airport and
  Airway Trust Fund 26
Aircraft Fatalities 27

— *not applicable* NA *not available*

Agriculture
State Ranking

Farm Acreage	45
Farmland as Portion of State	43
Net Farm Income	49
Government Payments to Farms	47
Federal Commodity Loans/Price Supports	42
Federal Spending on Rural Development	41
Rural Electric and Telephone Loan Guarantees	40
Foreign-Owned Agricultural Land	28

Business and Economy
State Ranking

Gross State Product	4
Retail Sales	5
Supermarket Sales	8
Commercial Bank Assets	14
Insured Commercial Bank Deposits	16
Fortune 500 Companies	7
Inc. 500 Companies	25
New Business Incorporations	6
Business Failures	19
Financial Aid to Minority Businesses	22
Women-Owned Businesses	33
Sales & Receipts of Women-Owned Businesses	24
African American-Owned Businesses	13
Sales & Receipts of African American-Owned Businesses	16
Hispanic-Owned Businesses	8
Sales & Receipts of Hispanic-Owned Businesses	9
Employees in Manufacturing	9
Manufacturing Shipments	25
Japanese-Owned U.S. Manufacturing Plants	9
Exports to Mexico	19
Change in Exports to Mexico	26
Existing Home Sales	24
Housing Starts	47
Average Annual Pay	5
Disposable Personal Income	1
Median Income of Families with Children	2
Federal Spending on Unemployment Insurance/Employment Services	14
Teen Unemployment	28
Bankruptcy Petitions Filed	33
Patents Issued to State Residents	3
Federal Spending on Community Development	9
Federal Spending on Economic Development Administration	43
Federal Spending on Urban Development Action Grants	11

Crime and Criminal Justice
State Ranking

Total Crimes	25
Violent Crimes	21
Murders	33
Rapes	40
Aggravated Assaults	27
Property Crimes	26
Robberies	8
Burglaries	33
Larcenies and Thefts	35
Motor Vehicle Thefts	5
State and Federal Prisoners	19
Capital Punishment	17

State Spending on Corrections	33
State Spending on Police	23
Inmates in Local Jails	15
Spending on Local Jails	15
Spending per Inmate for Local Jails	22
Employees at Local Jails	20
Juvenile Custody Rate	39
Federal Spending on Office of Justice Assistance Programs	38

Defense
State Ranking

Defense Grants to State and Local Governments	22
Total Defense Payroll	36
Total Army Payroll	21
Total Navy/Marine Corps Payroll	25
Total Air Force Payroll	41
Total Active-Duty Payroll	37
Army Active-Duty Payroll	24
Navy/Marine Corps Active-Duty Payroll	24
Air Force Active-Duty Payroll	36
Total Civilian Payroll	20
Army Civilian Payroll	11
Navy/Marine Corps Civilian Payroll	16
Air Force Civilian Payroll	40
Total Reserve and National Guard Payroll	40
Army Reserve and National Guard Payroll	36
Navy/Marine Corps Reserve and National Guard Payroll	51
Air Force Reserve and National Guard Payroll	29
Total Retired Military Payroll	44
Army Retired Military Payroll	36
Navy/Marine Corps Retired Military Payroll	41
Air Force Retired Military Payroll	49
Total Defense Prime Contracts	16
Army Prime Contracts	49
Navy/Marine Corps Prime Contracts	44
Air Force Prime Contracts	48
U.S. Military Installations	18
Construction of National Guard Centers	18

Education
State Ranking

School Age Population	46
Public Elementary and Secondary School Enrollment	10
Average Daily Attendance	28
Student-Teacher Ratio	47
Salaries of Public School Teachers	6
Public School Teachers Who Are Male	28
Eighth Grade Math Test Results	12
High School Math Enrollment	NA
Public High School Graduation Rate	12
General Educational Development (GED) Test Results	44
Adult Illiteracy	12
Federal Revenue for Public Schools	50
State Revenue for Public Schools	38
Local Government Revenue for Public Schools	14
Total Public School Spending	2
Public School Spending on Instruction	45
Public School Spending on Noninstruction	48
Public School Spending on Support Staff	21
State and Local Government Spending on Public Schools	18

Federal Spending on School Improvement Programs	42
Gifted and Talented Students	2
Federal Spending on Education of Students with Disabilities	7
Student-Teacher Ratio in Catholic Elementary Schools	12
Student-Teacher Ratio in Catholic Secondary Schools	11
State Spending on Education	32
State and Local Government Spending on Education	40
Higher Education Tuition and Fees	14
Higher Education Revenue	10
Federal Spending on Higher Education	43
State Spending on Higher Education	41
State and Local Government Spending on Higher Education	43
State and Local Appropriations for Higher Education	8
Federal Spending on Higher Education Act Insured Loans	36
Federal Spending on National Guaranteed Student Loans	32
Federal Spending on Pell Grants	44
Default Rate in Perkins Student Loan Program	8
State Spending on Libraries	24

Energy
State Ranking

Total Spending on Energy	13
Net Generation of Electricity	48
Cost of Electricity	5
Spending on Electricity	19
Spending on Natural Gas	14
Spending on Gasoline	44
Spending on Petroleum	17
Spending on Coal	42
Total Energy Consumption	36
Electricity Consumption	44
Natural Gas Consumption	25
Petroleum Consumption	13
Coal Consumption	42
Power Plants	50
Nuclear Power Plants	17
Hydroelectric Power Plants	46

Environment
State Ranking

Federally Owned Land (acreage)	34
Loss of Wetlands	31
Environmental Protection Agency Spending	11
EPA Abatement, Control, and Compliance	23
State Spending on Environmental Programs	4
Environmental Programs as Part of State Budget	5
State Spending on Forest Programs	43
Total Tree Planting	38
Federal Tree Planting	32
Private Tree Planting	41
State Spending on Air Quality	10
State Spending on Water Quality	2
Federal Grants for Rural Water and Waste Disposal	40
Federal Spending on Wastewater Treatment Works	13
Hazardous Waste Sites on National Priority List	1

Federal Grants for Hazardous Substance
  Response 6
State Spending on Hazardous Waste 15

Health   *State Ranking*

State Health Rankings 14
State Spending on Health 35
Support for Public Health 7
Family and Business Spending on Health
  Care 5
HMO Enrollment 23
Medicaid Recipients 41
Medically Underserved Population 37
Lack of Health Care Access 49
Active Nonfederal Physicians 8
Active Nonfederal Nurses 26
Active Nonfederal Dentists 5
Average Cost per Hospital Stay 25
Average Cost per Day for Hospital Care 32
Average Cost per Day for Hospital Room 24
State Spending on Hospitals 18
Adequacy of Prenatal Care 24
Infants Born Receiving Late or No
  Prenatal Care 9
Infants Born with Low Birth Weight 27
Abortions 7
Immunizations of Two-Year-Olds —
Overall Risk for Heart Disease 40
Risk Factor for Heart Disease
  (hypertension) NA
Deaths Due to Heart Disease 20
New Cancer Cases 8
Deaths Due to Cancer 7
Prevalence of Smoking 35
Prevalence of Diabetes 9
Deaths Due to Diabetes 5
Cost of Diabetes 10
AIDS Cases Reported 5
Gonorrhea Cases Reported 31
Syphilis Cases Reported 25
Tuberculosis Cases Reported 7
Hepatitis Cases Reported 34
Rabies Cases Reported 8
Lyme Disease Cases Reported 6
Beer Consumption 45
Wine Consumption 7
Liquor Consumption 13
Alcohol and Drug Treatment Admissions 34
Federal Spending on Alcohol, Drug
  Abuse, and Mental Health 4
Total Spending on Alcohol/Drug Abuse
  Services 24
State Spending on Alcohol/Drug Abuse
  Services 18
Hard-Core Cocaine Users 32
Federal Drug Grants to States 16

Population   *State Ranking*

Population 9
Population Density 2
Population in Metropolitan Areas 1
Population Under 18 Years Old 46
Population Over 65 Years Old 17
White Population 35
African American Population 17
Hispanic Population 9
Asian American Population 6
Native American Population 44
Catholic Population 4

Jewish Population 2
Marriages 48
Divorces 48
Births 25
Births to Single Mothers 33
Births to Single Teenagers 36
Adoptions 49
Adoption Option Index 51
Infant Mortality 28
Child Deaths and Suicides 48
Teen Violent Death Rate 51
Deaths 16

Recreation   *State Ranking*

State Parks and Recreation Areas 21
Visitors to State Parks and Recreation
  Areas 43
Revenues from State Parks and
  Recreation Areas 40
Spending on State Arts Agencies 10
Domestic Travel Spending 16
State Travel Office Budgets 39
Lodging Industry (rooms) 46
Participation in Exercise Walking 27
Participation in Swimming 9
Participation in Camping 45
Participation in Bowling 38
Bowling League Membership 26
Participation in Running/Jogging 28
Participation in Aerobics 16
Participation in Golf 31
Participation in Softball 21
Participation in Health Clubs 13
Participation in Tennis 15
Participation in Hunting 45
Participation in Baseball 18
Participation in Bicycle Riding 31
Number of Boats 49
Attendance at Parimutuel Racing 18
Revenue from Parimutuel Betting 16

Social Services   *State Ranking*

Federal Grants for Social Services 22
State Spending on Public Welfare 10
Persons in Poverty 43
Public Aid Recipients 28
Participants in Food Stamp Program 45
Households in Food Stamp Program 43
Percentage of Poor Using AFDC and
  Food Stamps 19
Federal Spending on Children and
  Family Services 40
Federal Women, Infants, and Children
  Food Program 49
Child Welfare Services 42
Child Abuse Cases Reported —
Children in Poverty 47
Children Without Health Insurance 41
Children Who Are Hungry or at Risk 42
Federal Spending on Child Nutrition
  Programs 47
Federal Spending on Special Milk
  Program 12
National School Lunch Program
  Participants 45
Head Start Enrollment 9
Head Start Spending 1
Federal Spending on Rehabilitation
  Services/Handicapped Research 48

State Government   *State Ranking*

Financial World's State Rankings 20
Salaries of State Officials (governor) 20
Salaries of State Legislators 7
Women in State Legislatures 41
African Americans in State Legislatures 13
Hispanics in State Legislatures 17
Asian Americans in State Legislatures 6
Native Americans in State Legislatures 12
Turnover in State Legislatures 26
Length of State Legislative Sessions 29
State Bills in Regular Session 22
State Resolutions in Regular Session 32
State Bills in Special Session —
State Resolutions in Special Session —
Women in State Cabinets 25
Total Federal Funding to State
  Governments 33
Total State Spending 37
State General Expenditures 44
State Debt 12
State Spending on Interest on the
  General Debt 16
Total State Tax Revenue 9
State Revenue from Tax on Sales and
  Gross Receipts 5
State Revenue from General Sales Tax 8
State Revenue from Licenses 27
State Revenue from Motor Vehicle
  Licenses 22
State Revenue from Individual Income
  Taxes 17
State Revenue from Corporation Net
  Income Taxes 6
State Revenue from Severance Taxes —
State Revenue from Property Taxes 31
State Revenue from Death and Gift
  Taxes 6
State Revenue from Documentary and
  Stock Transfers 14
State Revenue from Tax on Motor Fuels 48
State Revenue from Tax on Tobacco
  Products 5
Excise Tax on Cigarettes 3
Excise Tax on Gasoline 45
State Revenue from Lotteries 7

Transportation   *State Ranking*

Motor Vehicle Registrations 39
Automobile Registrations 6
Bus and Truck Registrations 49
Motorcycle Registrations 38
Driver Licenses 7
Federal Spending on Highway Trust
  Fund 39
Federal Spending on Mass
  Transportation 5
State Spending on Highways 36
Highway Deficiency 24
Bridge Deficiency 7
Traffic Fatalities 48
Traffic Fatalities per Miles Traveled 48
Motorcyclist Fatalities 51
Pedalcyclist Fatalities 25
Pedestrian Fatalities 17
Registered Aircraft 48
Registered Pilots 44
Federal Spending on Airport and
  Airway Trust Fund 49
Aircraft Fatalities 48

— *not applicable* NA *not available*

Agriculture

	State Ranking
Farm Acreage	5
Farmland as Portion of State	14
Net Farm Income	20
Government Payments to Farms	19
Federal Commodity Loans/Price Supports	33
Federal Spending on Rural Development	48
Rural Electric and Telephone Loan Guarantees	14
Foreign-Owned Agricultural Land	10

Business and Economy

	State Ranking
Gross State Product	42
Retail Sales	45
Supermarket Sales	43
Commercial Bank Assets	49
Insured Commercial Bank Deposits	47
Fortune 500 Companies	42
Inc. 500 Companies	8
New Business Incorporations	38
Business Failures	37
Financial Aid to Minority Businesses	2
Women-Owned Businesses	19
Sales & Receipts of Women-Owned Businesses	8
African American-Owned Businesses	38
Sales & Receipts of African American-Owned Businesses	35
Hispanic-Owned Businesses	1
Sales & Receipts of Hispanic-Owned Businesses	1
Employees in Manufacturing	43
Manufacturing Shipments	49
Japanese-Owned U.S. Manufacturing Plants	42
Exports to Mexico	13
Change in Exports to Mexico	31
Existing Home Sales	21
Housing Starts	40
Average Annual Pay	43
Disposable Personal Income	48
Median Income of Families with Children	48
Federal Spending on Unemployment Insurance/Employment Services	31
Teen Unemployment	16
Bankruptcy Petitions Filed	28
Patents Issued to State Residents	26
Federal Spending on Community Development	27
Federal Spending on Economic Development Administration	18
Federal Spending on Urban Development Action Grants	26

Crime and Criminal Justice

	State Ranking
Total Crimes	6
Violent Crimes	11
Murders	17
Rapes	10
Aggravated Assaults	4
Property Crimes	5
Robberies	31
Burglaries	4
Larcenies and Thefts	9
Motor Vehicle Thefts	33
State and Federal Prisoners	35
Capital Punishment	17
State Spending on Corrections	5
State Spending on Police	7
Inmates in Local Jails	13
Spending on Local Jails	17
Spending per Inmate for Local Jails	24
Employees at Local Jails	29
Juvenile Custody Rate	28
Federal Spending on Office of Justice Assistance Programs	27

Defense

	State Ranking
Defense Grants to State and Local Governments	5
Total Defense Payroll	7
Total Army Payroll	14
Total Navy/Marine Corps Payroll	26
Total Air Force Payroll	3
Total Active-Duty Payroll	12
Army Active-Duty Payroll	21
Navy/Marine Corps Active-Duty Payroll	25
Air Force Active-Duty Payroll	6
Total Civilian Payroll	9
Army Civilian Payroll	7
Navy/Marine Corps Civilian Payroll	25
Air Force Civilian Payroll	5
Total Reserve and National Guard Payroll	29
Army Reserve and National Guard Payroll	25
Navy/Marine Corps Reserve and National Guard Payroll	34
Air Force Reserve and National Guard Payroll	38
Total Retired Military Payroll	6
Army Retired Military Payroll	14
Navy/Marine Corps Retired Military Payroll	16
Air Force Retired Military Payroll	2
Total Defense Prime Contracts	18
Army Prime Contracts	9
Navy/Marine Corps Prime Contracts	32
Air Force Prime Contracts	14
U.S. Military Installations	34
Construction of National Guard Centers	5

Education

	State Ranking
School Age Population	5
Public Elementary and Secondary School Enrollment	36
Average Daily Attendance	1
Student-Teacher Ratio	13
Salaries of Public School Teachers	44
Public School Teachers Who Are Male	30
Eighth Grade Math Test Results	28
High School Math Enrollment	2
Public High School Graduation Rate	39
General Educational Development (GED) Test Results	36
Adult Illiteracy	12
Federal Revenue for Public Schools	3
State Revenue for Public Schools	3
Local Government Revenue for Public Schools	50
Total Public School Spending	44
Public School Spending on Instruction	30
Public School Spending on Noninstruction	21
Public School Spending on Support Staff	8
State and Local Government Spending on Public Schools	37
Federal Spending on School Improvement Programs	16
Gifted and Talented Students	NA
Federal Spending on Education of Students with Disabilities	12
Student-Teacher Ratio in Catholic Elementary Schools	33
Student-Teacher Ratio in Catholic Secondary Schools	37
State Spending on Education	3
State and Local Government Spending on Education	22
Higher Education Tuition and Fees	49
Higher Education Revenue	14
Federal Spending on Higher Education	9
State Spending on Higher Education	8
State and Local Government Spending on Higher Education	4
State and Local Appropriations for Higher Education	4
Federal Spending on Higher Education Act Insured Loans	33
Federal Spending on National Guaranteed Student Loans	27
Federal Spending on Pell Grants	11
Default Rate in Perkins Student Loan Program	27
State Spending on Libraries	34

Energy

	State Ranking
Total Spending on Energy	23
Net Generation of Electricity	9
Cost of Electricity	15
Spending on Electricity	37
Spending on Natural Gas	25
Spending on Gasoline	7
Spending on Petroleum	12
Spending on Coal	8
Total Energy Consumption	13
Electricity Consumption	38
Natural Gas Consumption	6
Petroleum Consumption	17
Coal Consumption	8
Power Plants	28
Nuclear Power Plants	34
Hydroelectric Power Plants	33

Environment

	State Ranking
Federally Owned Land (acreage)	10
Loss of Wetlands	38
Environmental Protection Agency Spending	35
EPA Abatement, Control, and Compliance	14
State Spending on Environmental Programs	27
Environmental Programs as Part of State Budget	29
State Spending on Forest Programs	38
Total Tree Planting	43
Federal Tree Planting	22
Private Tree Planting	45
State Spending on Air Quality	21
State Spending on Water Quality	25
Federal Grants for Rural Water and Waste Disposal	47
Federal Spending on Wastewater Treatment Works	45
Hazardous Waste Sites on National Priority List	32

Federal Grants for Hazardous Substance
Response — 12
State Spending on Hazardous Waste — 16

Health
State Ranking

State Health Rankings — 46
State Spending on Health — 14
Support for Public Health — 45
Family and Business Spending on Health
Care — 47
HMO Enrollment — 19
Medicaid Recipients — 19
Medically Underserved Population — 8
Lack of Health Care Access — 1
Active Nonfederal Physicians — 30
Active Nonfederal Nurses — 47
Active Nonfederal Dentists — 42
Average Cost per Hospital Stay — 39
Average Cost per Day for Hospital Care — 14
Average Cost per Day for Hospital Room — 31
State Spending on Hospitals — 10
Adequacy of Prenatal Care — 50
Infants Born Receiving Late or No
Prenatal Care — 1
Infants Born with Low Birth Weight — 16
Abortions — 26
Immunizations of Two-Year-Olds — —
Overall Risk for Heart Disease — 4
Risk Factor for Heart Disease
(hypertension) — 41
Deaths Due to Heart Disease — 47
New Cancer Cases — 47
Deaths Due to Cancer — 47
Prevalence of Smoking — 26
Prevalence of Diabetes — 43
Deaths Due to Diabetes — 45
Cost of Diabetes — 43
AIDS Cases Reported — 34
Gonorrhea Cases Reported — 36
Syphilis Cases Reported — 34
Tuberculosis Cases Reported — 24
Hepatitis Cases Reported — 5
Rabies Cases Reported — 38
Lyme Disease Cases Reported — 42
Beer Consumption — 7
Wine Consumption — 28
Liquor Consumption — 32
Alcohol and Drug Treatment Admissions — 23
Federal Spending on Alcohol, Drug
Abuse, and Mental Health — 28
Total Spending on Alcohol/Drug Abuse
Services — 19
State Spending on Alcohol/Drug Abuse
Services — 34
Hard-Core Cocaine Users — 12
Federal Drug Grants to States — 18

Population
State Ranking

Population — 37
Population Density — 44
Population in Metropolitan Areas — 38
Population Under 18 Years Old — 5
Population Over 65 Years Old — 41
White Population — 38
African American Population — 40
Hispanic Population — 1
Asian American Population — 30
Native American Population — 2
Catholic Population — 11

Jewish Population — 33
Marriages — 36
Divorces — 24
Births — 7
Births to Single Mothers — 4
Births to Single Teenagers — 8
Adoptions — 9
Adoption Option Index — 40
Infant Mortality — 29
Child Deaths and Suicides — 14
Teen Violent Death Rate — 4
Deaths — 46

Recreation
State Ranking

State Parks and Recreation Areas — 9
Visitors to State Parks and Recreation
Areas — 20
Revenues from State Parks and
Recreation Areas — 5
Spending on State Arts Agencies — 27
Domestic Travel Spending — 11
State Travel Office Budgets — 10
Lodging Industry (rooms) — 11
Participation in Exercise Walking — 18
Participation in Swimming — 8
Participation in Camping — 8
Participation in Bowling — 3
Bowling League Membership — 31
Participation in Running/Jogging — 30
Participation in Aerobics — 14
Participation in Golf — 7
Participation in Softball — 18
Participation in Health Clubs — 47
Participation in Tennis — 2
Participation in Hunting — 48
Participation in Baseball — 11
Participation in Bicycle Riding — 16
Number of Boats — 48
Attendance at Parimutuel Racing — 10
Revenue from Parimutuel Betting — 13

Social Services
State Ranking

Federal Grants for Social Services — 30
State Spending on Public Welfare — 36
Persons in Poverty — 2
Public Aid Recipients — 21
Participants in Food Stamp Program — 8
Households in Food Stamp Program — 13
Percentage of Poor Using AFDC and
Food Stamps — 36
Federal Spending on Children and
Family Services — 7
Federal Women, Infants, and Children
Food Program — 6
Child Welfare Services — 3
Child Abuse Cases Reported — —
Children in Poverty — 3
Children Without Health Insurance — 2
Children Who Are Hungry or at Risk — 4
Federal Spending on Child Nutrition
Programs — 3
Federal Spending on Special Milk
Program — 40
National School Lunch Program
Participants — 3
Head Start Enrollment — 42
Head Start Spending — 49
Federal Spending on Rehabilitation
Services/Handicapped Research — 14

State Government
State Ranking

Financial World's State Rankings — 45
Salaries of State Officials (governor) — 18
Salaries of State Legislators — —
Women in State Legislatures — 25
African Americans in State Legislatures — 43
Hispanics in State Legislatures — 1
Asian Americans in State Legislatures — 6
Native Americans in State Legislatures — 3
Turnover in State Legislatures — 45
Length of State Legislative Sessions — 32
State Bills in Regular Session — 26
State Resolutions in Regular Session — 44
State Bills in Special Session — 24
State Resolutions in Special Session — 19
Women in State Cabinets — 9
Total Federal Funding to State
Governments — 5
Total State Spending — 3
State General Expenditures — 3
State Debt — 27
State Spending on Interest on the
General Debt — 23
Total State Tax Revenue — 14
State Revenue from Tax on Sales and
Gross Receipts — 7
State Revenue from General Sales Tax — 6
State Revenue from Licenses — 21
State Revenue from Motor Vehicle
Licenses — 6
State Revenue from Individual Income
Taxes — 37
State Revenue from Corporation Net
Income Taxes — 46
State Revenue from Severance Taxes — 4
State Revenue from Property Taxes — 17
State Revenue from Death and Gift
Taxes — 43
State Revenue from Documentary and
Stock Transfers — —
State Revenue from Tax on Motor Fuels — 10
State Revenue from Tax on Tobacco
Products — 46
Excise Tax on Cigarettes — 41
Excise Tax on Gasoline — 30
State Revenue from Lotteries — —

Transportation
State Ranking

Motor Vehicle Registrations — 14
Automobile Registrations — 35
Bus and Truck Registrations — 6
Motorcycle Registrations — 20
Driver Licenses — 21
Federal Spending on Highway Trust
Fund — 14
Federal Spending on Mass
Transportation — 46
State Spending on Highways — 19
Highway Deficiency — 33
Bridge Deficiency — 49
Traffic Fatalities — 1
Traffic Fatalities per Miles Traveled — 4
Motorcyclist Fatalities — 2
Pedalcyclist Fatalities — 27
Pedestrian Fatalities — 1
Registered Aircraft — 10
Registered Pilots — 20
Federal Spending on Airport and
Airway Trust Fund — 24
Aircraft Fatalities — 13

— *not applicable*   NA *not available*

Agriculture
State Ranking

Farm Acreage	36
Farmland as Portion of State	38
Net Farm Income	47
Government Payments to Farms	43
Federal Commodity Loans/Price Supports	37
Federal Spending on Rural Development	32
Rural Electric and Telephone Loan Guarantees	38
Foreign-Owned Agricultural Land	18

Business and Economy
State Ranking

Gross State Product	6
Retail Sales	29
Supermarket Sales	33
Commercial Bank Assets	2
Insured Commercial Bank Deposits	2
Fortune 500 Companies	9
Inc. 500 Companies	30
New Business Incorporations	7
Business Failures	28
Financial Aid to Minority Businesses	21
Women-Owned Businesses	22
Sales & Receipts of Women-Owned Businesses	25
African American-Owned Businesses	12
Sales & Receipts of African American-Owned Businesses	19
Hispanic-Owned Businesses	7
Sales & Receipts of Hispanic-Owned Businesses	11
Employees in Manufacturing	2
Manufacturing Shipments	36
Japanese-Owned U.S. Manufacturing Plants	14
Exports to Mexico	34
Change in Exports to Mexico	36
Existing Home Sales	49
Housing Starts	49
Average Annual Pay	4
Disposable Personal Income	6
Median Income of Families with Children	20
Federal Spending on Unemployment Insurance/Employment Services	23
Teen Unemployment	24
Bankruptcy Petitions Filed	38
Patents Issued to State Residents	12
Federal Spending on Community Development	2
Federal Spending on Economic Development Administration	42
Federal Spending on Urban Development Action Grants	4

Crime and Criminal Justice
State Ranking

Total Crimes	11
Violent Crimes	3
Murders	4
Rapes	43
Aggravated Assaults	10
Property Crimes	23
Robberies	2
Burglaries	27
Larcenies and Thefts	30
Motor Vehicle Thefts	3
State and Federal Prisoners	17
Capital Punishment	—

State Spending on Corrections	7
State Spending on Police	42
Inmates in Local Jails	13
Spending on Local Jails	1
Spending per Inmate for Local Jails	2
Employees at Local Jails	37
Juvenile Custody Rate	17
Federal Spending on Office of Justice Assistance Programs	43

Defense
State Ranking

Defense Grants to State and Local Governments	43
Total Defense Payroll	47
Total Army Payroll	38
Total Navy/Marine Corps Payroll	46
Total Air Force Payroll	44
Total Active-Duty Payroll	40
Army Active-Duty Payroll	20
Navy/Marine Corps Active-Duty Payroll	33
Air Force Active-Duty Payroll	40
Total Civilian Payroll	47
Army Civilian Payroll	33
Navy/Marine Corps Civilian Payroll	33
Air Force Civilian Payroll	39
Total Reserve and National Guard Payroll	49
Army Reserve and National Guard Payroll	48
Navy/Marine Corps Reserve and National Guard Payroll	35
Air Force Reserve and National Guard Payroll	44
Total Retired Military Payroll	51
Army Retired Military Payroll	51
Navy/Marine Corps Retired Military Payroll	51
Air Force Retired Military Payroll	51
Total Defense Prime Contracts	26
Army Prime Contracts	47
Navy/Marine Corps Prime Contracts	12
Air Force Prime Contracts	20
U.S. Military Installations	7
Construction of National Guard Centers	39

Education
State Ranking

School Age Population	45
Public Elementary and Secondary School Enrollment	3
Average Daily Attendance	39
Student-Teacher Ratio	42
Salaries of Public School Teachers	3
Public School Teachers Who Are Male	14
Eighth Grade Math Test Results	20
High School Math Enrollment	7
Public High School Graduation Rate	43
General Educational Development (GED) Test Results	41
Adult Illiteracy	1
Federal Revenue for Public Schools	36
State Revenue for Public Schools	35
Local Government Revenue for Public Schools	17
Total Public School Spending	5
Public School Spending on Instruction	2
Public School Spending on Noninstruction	42
Public School Spending on Support Staff	37
State and Local Government Spending on Public Schools	41

Federal Spending on School Improvement Programs	30
Gifted and Talented Students	12
Federal Spending on Education of Students with Disabilities	37
Student-Teacher Ratio in Catholic Elementary Schools	14
Student-Teacher Ratio in Catholic Secondary Schools	16
State Spending on Education	22
State and Local Government Spending on Education	47
Higher Education Tuition and Fees	8
Higher Education Revenue	7
Federal Spending on Higher Education	43
State Spending on Higher Education	42
State and Local Government Spending on Higher Education	48
State and Local Appropriations for Higher Education	29
Federal Spending on Higher Education Act Insured Loans	14
Federal Spending on National Guaranteed Student Loans	4
Federal Spending on Pell Grants	9
Default Rate in Perkins Student Loan Program	11
State Spending on Libraries	6

Energy
State Ranking

Total Spending on Energy	51
Net Generation of Electricity	45
Cost of Electricity	2
Spending on Electricity	32
Spending on Natural Gas	20
Spending on Gasoline	51
Spending on Petroleum	50
Spending on Coal	40
Total Energy Consumption	50
Electricity Consumption	49
Natural Gas Consumption	30
Petroleum Consumption	47
Coal Consumption	39
Power Plants	30
Nuclear Power Plants	24
Hydroelectric Power Plants	18

Environment
State Ranking

Federally Owned Land (acreage)	49
Loss of Wetlands	12
Environmental Protection Agency Spending	5
EPA Abatement, Control, and Compliance	33
State Spending on Environmental Programs	46
Environmental Programs as Part of State Budget	50
State Spending on Forest Programs	29
Total Tree Planting	32
Federal Tree Planting	32
Private Tree Planting	29
State Spending on Air Quality	26
State Spending on Water Quality	32
Federal Grants for Rural Water and Waste Disposal	39
Federal Spending on Wastewater Treatment Works	2
Hazardous Waste Sites on National Priority List	4

Federal Grants for Hazardous Substance
Response | 42
State Spending on Hazardous Waste | 17

Health | State Ranking

State Health Rankings | 36
State Spending on Health | 13
Support for Public Health | 4
Family and Business Spending on Health
Care | 1
HMO Enrollment | 16
Medicaid Recipients | 8
Medically Underserved Population | 11
Lack of Health Care Access | 38
Active Nonfederal Physicians | 4
Active Nonfederal Nurses | 13
Active Nonfederal Dentists | 4
Average Cost per Hospital Stay | 2
Average Cost per Day for Hospital Care | 26
Average Cost per Day for Hospital Room | 11
State Spending on Hospitals | 2
Adequacy of Prenatal Care | 42
Infants Born Receiving Late or No
Prenatal Care | 7
Infants Born with Low Birth Weight | 12
Abortions | 3
Immunizations of Two-Year-Olds | —
Overall Risk for Heart Disease | 24
Risk Factor for Heart Disease
(hypertension) | 16
Deaths Due to Heart Disease | 5
New Cancer Cases | 19
Deaths Due to Cancer | 15
Prevalence of Smoking | 40
Prevalence of Diabetes | 8
Deaths Due to Diabetes | 22
Cost of Diabetes | 8
AIDS Cases Reported | 2
Gonorrhea Cases Reported | 21
Syphilis Cases Reported | 13
Tuberculosis Cases Reported | 1
Hepatitis Cases Reported | 32
Rabies Cases Reported | 10
Lyme Disease Cases Reported | 4
Beer Consumption | 49
Wine Consumption | 13
Liquor Consumption | 28
Alcohol and Drug Treatment Admissions | 9
Federal Spending on Alcohol, Drug
Abuse, and Mental Health | 6
Total Spending on Alcohol/Drug Abuse
Services | 3
State Spending on Alcohol/Drug Abuse
Services | 2
Hard-Core Cocaine Users | 3
Federal Drug Grants to States | 13

Population | State Ranking

Population | 2
Population Density | 7
Population in Metropolitan Areas | 7
Population Under 18 Years Old | 44
Population Over 65 Years Old | 22
White Population | 42
African American Population | 13
Hispanic Population | 6
Asian American Population | 4
Native American Population | 31
Catholic Population | 6

Jewish Population | 1
Marriages | 25
Divorces | 46
Births | 17
Births to Single Mothers | 5
Births to Single Teenagers | 31
Adoptions | 36
Adoption Option Index | 43
Infant Mortality | 17
Child Deaths and Suicides | 38
Teen Violent Death Rate | 42
Deaths | 10

Recreation | State Ranking

State Parks and Recreation Areas | 41
Visitors to State Parks and Recreation
Areas | 17
Revenues from State Parks and
Recreation Areas | 23
Spending on State Arts Agencies | 3
Domestic Travel Spending | 26
State Travel Office Budgets | 45
Lodging Industry (rooms) | 47
Participation in Exercise Walking | 30
Participation in Swimming | 16
Participation in Camping | 27
Participation in Bowling | 14
Bowling League Membership | 22
Participation in Running/Jogging | 31
Participation in Aerobics | 21
Participation in Golf | 24
Participation in Softball | 22
Participation in Health Clubs | 17
Participation in Tennis | 25
Participation in Hunting | 32
Participation in Baseball | 12
Participation in Bicycle Riding | 24
Number of Boats | 45
Attendance at Parimutuel Racing | 30
Revenue from Parimutuel Betting | 1

Social Services | State Ranking

Federal Grants for Social Services | 23
State Spending on Public Welfare | 2
Persons in Poverty | 18
Public Aid Recipients | 8
Participants in Food Stamp Program | 18
Households in Food Stamp Program | 11
Percentage of Poor Using AFDC and
Food Stamps | 5
Federal Spending on Children and
Family Services | 33
Federal Women, Infants, and Children
Food Program | 26
Child Welfare Services | 29
Child Abuse Cases Reported | —
Children in Poverty | 17
Children Without Health Insurance | 31
Children Who Are Hungry or at Risk | 13
Federal Spending on Child Nutrition
Programs | 34
Federal Spending on Special Milk
Program | 19
National School Lunch Program
Participants | 20
Head Start Enrollment | 40
Head Start Spending | 3
Federal Spending on Rehabilitation
Services/Handicapped Research | 44

State Government | State Ranking

Financial World's State Rankings | 43
Salaries of State Officials (governor) | 1
Salaries of State Legislators | 1
Women in State Legislatures | 35
African Americans in State Legislatures | 8
Hispanics in State Legislatures | 7
Asian Americans in State Legislatures | 6
Native Americans in State Legislatures | 12
Turnover in State Legislatures | 46
Length of State Legislative Sessions | 42
State Bills in Regular Session | 47
State Resolutions in Regular Session | 2
State Bills in Special Session | 29
State Resolutions in Special Session | 19
Women in State Cabinets | 9
Total Federal Funding to State
Governments | 19
Total State Spending | 17
State General Expenditures | 19
State Debt | 8
State Spending on Interest on the
General Debt | 14
Total State Tax Revenue | 7
State Revenue from Tax on Sales and
Gross Receipts | 31
State Revenue from General Sales Tax | 35
State Revenue from Licenses | 45
State Revenue from Motor Vehicle
Licenses | 41
State Revenue from Individual Income
Taxes | 2
State Revenue from Corporation Net
Income Taxes | 8
State Revenue from Severance Taxes | —
State Revenue from Property Taxes | —
State Revenue from Death and Gift
Taxes | 4
State Revenue from Documentary and
Stock Transfers | 5
State Revenue from Tax on Motor Fuels | 50
State Revenue from Tax on Tobacco
Products | 9
Excise Tax on Cigarettes | 5
Excise Tax on Gasoline | 47
State Revenue from Lotteries | 13

Transportation | State Ranking

Motor Vehicle Registrations | 50
Automobile Registrations | 46
Bus and Truck Registrations | 48
Motorcycle Registrations | 39
Driver Licenses | 50
Federal Spending on Highway Trust
Fund | 50
Federal Spending on Mass
Transportation | 2
State Spending on Highways | 46
Highway Deficiency | 46
Bridge Deficiency | 1
Traffic Fatalities | 46
Traffic Fatalities per Miles Traveled | 30
Motorcyclist Fatalities | 47
Pedalcyclist Fatalities | 13
Pedestrian Fatalities | 13
Registered Aircraft | 50
Registered Pilots | 50
Federal Spending on Airport and
Airway Trust Fund | 31
Aircraft Fatalities | 49

— *not applicable* NA *not available*

Agriculture
State Ranking

Farm Acreage	32
Farmland as Portion of State	29
Net Farm Income	11
Government Payments to Farms	33
Federal Commodity Loans/Price Supports	18
Federal Spending on Rural Development	26
Rural Electric and Telephone Loan Guarantees	15
Foreign-Owned Agricultural Land	19

Business and Economy
State Ranking

Gross State Product	22
Retail Sales	34
Supermarket Sales	27
Commercial Bank Assets	15
Insured Commercial Bank Deposits	25
Fortune 500 Companies	29
Inc. 500 Companies	38
New Business Incorporations	37
Business Failures	45
Financial Aid to Minority Businesses	15
Women-Owned Businesses	39
Sales & Receipts of Women-Owned Businesses	19
African American-Owned Businesses	8
Sales & Receipts of African American-Owned Businesses	10
Hispanic-Owned Businesses	38
Sales & Receipts of Hispanic-Owned Businesses	32
Employees in Manufacturing	8
Manufacturing Shipments	3
Japanese-Owned U.S. Manufacturing Plants	10
Exports to Mexico	27
Change in Exports to Mexico	12
Existing Home Sales	4
Housing Starts	8
Average Annual Pay	35
Disposable Personal Income	36
Median Income of Families with Children	36
Federal Spending on Unemployment Insurance/Employment Services	46
Teen Unemployment	20
Bankruptcy Petitions Filed	36
Patents Issued to State Residents	31
Federal Spending on Community Development	44
Federal Spending on Economic Development Administration	38
Federal Spending on Urban Development Action Grants	32

Crime and Criminal Justice
State Ranking

Total Crimes	18
Violent Crimes	20
Murders	11
Rapes	31
Aggravated Assaults	17
Property Crimes	17
Robberies	20
Burglaries	5
Larcenies and Thefts	22
Motor Vehicle Thefts	37
State and Federal Prisoners	23
Capital Punishment	9

State Spending on Corrections	13
State Spending on Police	19
Inmates in Local Jails	29
Spending on Local Jails	40
Spending per Inmate for Local Jails	36
Employees at Local Jails	8
Juvenile Custody Rate	22
Federal Spending on Office of Justice Assistance Programs	49

Defense
State Ranking

Defense Grants to State and Local Governments	44
Total Defense Payroll	13
Total Army Payroll	9
Total Navy/Marine Corps Payroll	11
Total Air Force Payroll	33
Total Active-Duty Payroll	6
Army Active-Duty Payroll	6
Navy/Marine Corps Active-Duty Payroll	7
Air Force Active-Duty Payroll	30
Total Civilian Payroll	30
Army Civilian Payroll	25
Navy/Marine Corps Civilian Payroll	14
Air Force Civilian Payroll	47
Total Reserve and National Guard Payroll	43
Army Reserve and National Guard Payroll	38
Navy/Marine Corps Reserve and National Guard Payroll	28
Air Force Reserve and National Guard Payroll	46
Total Retired Military Payroll	18
Army Retired Military Payroll	10
Navy/Marine Corps Retired Military Payroll	11
Air Force Retired Military Payroll	32
Total Defense Prime Contracts	35
Army Prime Contracts	31
Navy/Marine Corps Prime Contracts	22
Air Force Prime Contracts	38
U.S. Military Installations	10
Construction of National Guard Centers	41

Education
State Ranking

School Age Population	40
Public Elementary and Secondary School Enrollment	11
Average Daily Attendance	19
Student-Teacher Ratio	22
Salaries of Public School Teachers	29
Public School Teachers Who Are Male	46
Eighth Grade Math Test Results	36
High School Math Enrollment	9
Public High School Graduation Rate	40
General Educational Development (GED) Test Results	17
Adult Illiteracy	12
Federal Revenue for Public Schools	22
State Revenue for Public Schools	6
Local Government Revenue for Public Schools	44
Total Public School Spending	34
Public School Spending on Instruction	10
Public School Spending on Noninstruction	10
Public School Spending on Support Staff	40
State and Local Government Spending on Public Schools	13

Federal Spending on School Improvement Programs	38
Gifted and Talented Students	10
Federal Spending on Education of Students with Disabilities	36
Student-Teacher Ratio in Catholic Elementary Schools	25
Student-Teacher Ratio in Catholic Secondary Schools	20
State Spending on Education	13
State and Local Government Spending on Education	7
Higher Education Tuition and Fees	32
Higher Education Revenue	11
Federal Spending on Higher Education	21
State Spending on Higher Education	17
State and Local Government Spending on Higher Education	7
State and Local Appropriations for Higher Education	9
Federal Spending on Higher Education Act Insured Loans	47
Federal Spending on National Guaranteed Student Loans	41
Federal Spending on Pell Grants	41
Default Rate in Perkins Student Loan Program	7
State Spending on Libraries	22

Energy
State Ranking

Total Spending on Energy	28
Net Generation of Electricity	24
Cost of Electricity	23
Spending on Electricity	6
Spending on Natural Gas	46
Spending on Gasoline	14
Spending on Petroleum	34
Spending on Coal	18
Total Energy Consumption	34
Electricity Consumption	14
Natural Gas Consumption	47
Petroleum Consumption	39
Coal Consumption	27
Power Plants	34
Nuclear Power Plants	10
Hydroelectric Power Plants	19

Environment
State Ranking

Federally Owned Land (acreage)	32
Loss of Wetlands	24
Environmental Protection Agency Spending	38
EPA Abatement, Control, and Compliance	32
State Spending on Environmental Programs	43
Environmental Programs as Part of State Budget	42
State Spending on Forest Programs	15
Total Tree Planting	9
Federal Tree Planting	13
Private Tree Planting	8
State Spending on Air Quality	44
State Spending on Water Quality	47
Federal Grants for Rural Water and Waste Disposal	22
Federal Spending on Wastewater Treatment Works	40
Hazardous Waste Sites on National Priority List	16

Federal Grants for Hazardous Substance
Response — 20
State Spending on Hazardous Waste — 40

Health — *State Ranking*

State Health Rankings — 33
State Spending on Health — 31
Support for Public Health — 31
Family and Business Spending on Health
Care — 40
HMO Enrollment — 39
Medicaid Recipients — 23
Medically Underserved Population — 22
Lack of Health Care Access — 19
Active Nonfederal Physicians — 25
Active Nonfederal Nurses — 32
Active Nonfederal Dentists — 46
Average Cost per Hospital Stay — 31
Average Cost per Day for Hospital Care — 34
Average Cost per Day for Hospital Room — 40
State Spending on Hospitals — 22
Adequacy of Prenatal Care — 16
Infants Born Receiving Late or No
Prenatal Care — 19
Infants Born with Low Birth Weight — 9
Abortions — 18
Immunizations of Two-Year-Olds — —
Overall Risk for Heart Disease — 36
Risk Factor for Heart Disease
(hypertension) — 15
Deaths Due to Heart Disease — 30
New Cancer Cases — 25
Deaths Due to Cancer — 33
Prevalence of Smoking — 13
Prevalence of Diabetes — 10
Deaths Due to Diabetes — 8
Cost of Diabetes — 11
AIDS Cases Reported — 28
Gonorrhea Cases Reported — 6
Syphilis Cases Reported — 6
Tuberculosis Cases Reported — 16
Hepatitis Cases Reported — 38
Rabies Cases Reported — 36
Lyme Disease Cases Reported — 16
Beer Consumption — 42
Wine Consumption — 29
Liquor Consumption — 34
Alcohol and Drug Treatment Admissions — 32
Federal Spending on Alcohol, Drug
Abuse, and Mental Health — 45
Total Spending on Alcohol/Drug Abuse
Services — 30
State Spending on Alcohol/Drug Abuse
Services — 14
Hard-Core Cocaine Users — 24
Federal Drug Grants to States — 51

Population — *State Ranking*

Population — 10
Population Density — 18
Population in Metropolitan Areas — 34
Population Under 18 Years Old — 43
Population Over 65 Years Old — 31
White Population — 39
African American Population — 8
Hispanic Population — 39
Asian American Population — 36
Native American Population — 14
Catholic Population — 51

Jewish Population — 38
Marriages — 45
Divorces — 19
Births — 23
Births to Single Mothers — 15
Births to Single Teenagers — 9
Adoptions — 17
Adoption Option Index — 34
Infant Mortality — 6
Child Deaths and Suicides — .8
Teen Violent Death Rate — 28
Deaths — 25

Recreation — *State Ranking*

State Parks and Recreation Areas — 38
Visitors to State Parks and Recreation
Areas — 44
Revenues from State Parks and
Recreation Areas — 50
Spending on State Arts Agencies — 25
Domestic Travel Spending — 28
State Travel Office Budgets — 36
Lodging Industry (rooms) — 19
Participation in Exercise Walking — 35
Participation in Swimming — 31
Participation in Camping — 26
Participation in Bowling — 47
Bowling League Membership — 39
Participation in Running/Jogging — 12
Participation in Aerobics — 37
Participation in Golf — 31
Participation in Softball — 34
Participation in Health Clubs — 26
Participation in Tennis — 14
Participation in Hunting — 29
Participation in Baseball — 39
Participation in Bicycle Riding — 32
Number of Boats — 28
Attendance at Parimutuel Racing — —
Revenue from Parimutuel Betting — —

Social Services — *State Ranking*

Federal Grants for Social Services — 20
State Spending on Public Welfare — 35
Persons in Poverty — 21
Public Aid Recipients — 24
Participants in Food Stamp Program — 31
Households in Food Stamp Program — 29
Percentage of Poor Using AFDC and
Food Stamps — 43
Federal Spending on Children and
Family Services — 35
Federal Women, Infants, and Children
Food Program — 23
Child Welfare Services — NA
Child Abuse Cases Reported — —
Children in Poverty — 23
Children Without Health Insurance — 13
Children Who Are Hungry or at Risk — 27
Federal Spending on Child Nutrition
Programs — 21
Federal Spending on Special Milk
Program — 37
National School Lunch Program
Participants — 18
Head Start Enrollment — 20
Head Start Spending — 32
Federal Spending on Rehabilitation
Services/Handicapped Research — 21

State Government — *State Ranking*

Financial World's State Rankings — 8
Salaries of State Officials (governor) — 2
Salaries of State Legislators — 26
Women in State Legislatures — 30
African Americans in State Legislatures — 7
Hispanics in State Legislatures — 21
Asian Americans in State Legislatures — 6
Native Americans in State Legislatures — 10
Turnover in State Legislatures — 24
Length of State Legislative Sessions — 42
State Bills in Regular Session — 14
State Resolutions in Regular Session — 41
State Bills in Special Session — 19
State Resolutions in Special Session — 16
Women in State Cabinets — 14
Total Federal Funding to State
Governments — 47
Total State Spending — 31
State General Expenditures — 28
State Debt — 48
State Spending on Interest on the
General Debt — 48
Total State Tax Revenue — 26
State Revenue from Tax on Sales and
Gross Receipts — 43
State Revenue from General Sales Tax — 41
State Revenue from Licenses — 25
State Revenue from Motor Vehicle
Licenses — 37
State Revenue from Individual Income
Taxes — 10
State Revenue from Corporation Net
Income Taxes — 21
State Revenue from Severance Taxes — 30
State Revenue from Property Taxes — 16
State Revenue from Death and Gift
Taxes — 19
State Revenue from Documentary and
Stock Transfers — —
State Revenue from Tax on Motor Fuels — 4
State Revenue from Tax on Tobacco
Products — 50
Excise Tax on Cigarettes — 49
Excise Tax on Gasoline — 3
State Revenue from Lotteries — —

Transportation — *State Ranking*

Motor Vehicle Registrations — 26
Automobile Registrations — 30
Bus and Truck Registrations — 23
Motorcycle Registrations — 47
Driver Licenses — 30
Federal Spending on Highway Trust
Fund — 37
Federal Spending on Mass
Transportation — 25
State Spending on Highways — 25
Highway Deficiency — 38
Bridge Deficiency — 16
Traffic Fatalities — 17
Traffic Fatalities per Miles Traveled — 16
Motorcyclist Fatalities — 28
Pedalcyclist Fatalities — 6
Pedestrian Fatalities — 12
Registered Aircraft — 32
Registered Pilots — 34
Federal Spending on Airport and
Airway Trust Fund — 35
Aircraft Fatalities — 22

— *not applicable*   NA *not available*

Agriculture
State Ranking

Farm Acreage	7
Farmland as Portion of State	4
Net Farm Income	3
Government Payments to Farms	1
Federal Commodity Loans/Price Supports	1
Federal Spending on Rural Development	33
Rural Electric and Telephone Loan Guarantees	10
Foreign-Owned Agricultural Land	46

Business and Economy
State Ranking

Gross State Product	41
Retail Sales	30
Supermarket Sales	42
Commercial Bank Assets	19
Insured Commercial Bank Deposits	14
Fortune 500 Companies	42
Inc. 500 Companies	47
New Business Incorporations	49
Business Failures	42
Financial Aid to Minority Businesses	9
Women-Owned Businesses	28
Sales & Receipts of Women-Owned Businesses	34
African American-Owned Businesses	49
Sales & Receipts of African American-Owned Businesses	51
Hispanic-Owned Businesses	49
Sales & Receipts of Hispanic-Owned Businesses	51
Employees in Manufacturing	48
Manufacturing Shipments	46
Japanese-Owned U.S. Manufacturing Plants	48
Exports to Mexico	48
Change in Exports to Mexico	51
Existing Home Sales	17
Housing Starts	19
Average Annual Pay	50
Disposable Personal Income	39
Median Income of Families with Children	29
Federal Spending on Unemployment Insurance/Employment Services	4
Teen Unemployment	44
Bankruptcy Petitions Filed	47
Patents Issued to State Residents	42
Federal Spending on Community Development	25
Federal Spending on Economic Development Administration	3
Federal Spending on Urban Development Action Grants	33

Crime and Criminal Justice
State Ranking

Total Crimes	50
Violent Crimes	51
Murders	51
Rapes	51
Aggravated Assaults	51
Property Crimes	50
Robberies	51
Burglaries	51
Larcenies and Thefts	46
Motor Vehicle Thefts	50
State and Federal Prisoners	51
Capital Punishment	—

State Spending on Corrections	50
State Spending on Police	46
Inmates in Local Jails	44
Spending on Local Jails	31
Spending per Inmate for Local Jails	4
Employees at Local Jails	45
Juvenile Custody Rate	18
Federal Spending on Office of Justice Assistance Programs	9

Defense
State Ranking

Defense Grants to State and Local Governments	2
Total Defense Payroll	15
Total Army Payroll	39
Total Navy/Marine Corps Payroll	51
Total Air Force Payroll	2
Total Active-Duty Payroll	7
Army Active-Duty Payroll	45
Navy/Marine Corps Active-Duty Payroll	48
Air Force Active-Duty Payroll	2
Total Civilian Payroll	26
Army Civilian Payroll	35
Navy/Marine Corps Civilian Payroll	46
Air Force Civilian Payroll	9
Total Reserve and National Guard Payroll	11
Army Reserve and National Guard Payroll	11
Navy/Marine Corps Reserve and National Guard Payroll	27
Air Force Reserve and National Guard Payroll	7
Total Retired Military Payroll	39
Army Retired Military Payroll	45
Navy/Marine Corps Retired Military Payroll	50
Air Force Retired Military Payroll	33
Total Defense Prime Contracts	34
Army Prime Contracts	18
Navy/Marine Corps Prime Contracts	46
Air Force Prime Contracts	26
U.S. Military Installations	34
Construction of National Guard Centers	2

Education
State Ranking

School Age Population	11
Public Elementary and Secondary School Enrollment	46
Average Daily Attendance	23
Student-Teacher Ratio	36
Salaries of Public School Teachers	50
Public School Teachers Who Are Male	11
Eighth Grade Math Test Results	1
High School Math Enrollment	19
Public High School Graduation Rate	2
General Educational Development (GED) Test Results	35
Adult Illiteracy	21
Federal Revenue for Public Schools	10
State Revenue for Public Schools	27
Local Government Revenue for Public Schools	26
Total Public School Spending	35
Public School Spending on Instruction	17
Public School Spending on Noninstruction	7
Public School Spending on Support Staff	31
State and Local Government Spending on Public Schools	36

Federal Spending on School Improvement Programs	5
Gifted and Talented Students	35
Federal Spending on Education of Students with Disabilities	20
Student-Teacher Ratio in Catholic Elementary Schools	31
Student-Teacher Ratio in Catholic Secondary Schools	40
State Spending on Education	9
State and Local Government Spending on Education	11
Higher Education Tuition and Fees	36
Higher Education Revenue	44
Federal Spending on Higher Education	4
State Spending on Higher Education	2
State and Local Government Spending on Higher Education	2
State and Local Appropriations for Higher Education	35
Federal Spending on Higher Education Act Insured Loans	12
Federal Spending on National Guaranteed Student Loans	5
Federal Spending on Pell Grants	1
Default Rate in Perkins Student Loan Program	47
State Spending on Libraries	19

Energy
State Ranking

Total Spending on Energy	5
Net Generation of Electricity	3
Cost of Electricity	35
Spending on Electricity	41
Spending on Natural Gas	39
Spending on Gasoline	2
Spending on Petroleum	7
Spending on Coal	3
Total Energy Consumption	5
Electricity Consumption	27
Natural Gas Consumption	28
Petroleum Consumption	9
Coal Consumption	2
Power Plants	12
Nuclear Power Plants	34
Hydroelectric Power Plants	36

Environment
State Ranking

Federally Owned Land (acreage)	31
Loss of Wetlands	23
Environmental Protection Agency Spending	4
EPA Abatement, Control, and Compliance	9
State Spending on Environmental Programs	10
Environmental Programs as Part of State Budget	13
State Spending on Forest Programs	39
Total Tree Planting	34
Federal Tree Planting	32
Private Tree Planting	32
State Spending on Air Quality	11
State Spending on Water Quality	13
Federal Grants for Rural Water and Waste Disposal	15
Federal Spending on Wastewater Treatment Works	9
Hazardous Waste Sites on National Priority List	47

Federal Grants for Hazardous Substance
  Response   2
State Spending on Hazardous Waste   38

Health   *State Ranking*

State Health Rankings   17
State Spending on Health   47
Support for Public Health   38
Family and Business Spending on Health
  Care   21
HMO Enrollment   46
Medicaid Recipients   36
Medically Underserved Population   47
Lack of Health Care Access   2
Active Nonfederal Physicians   36
Active Nonfederal Nurses   4
Active Nonfederal Dentists   33
Average Cost per Hospital Stay   28
Average Cost per Day for Hospital Care   49
Average Cost per Day for Hospital Room   35
State Spending on Hospitals   19
Adequacy of Prenatal Care   40
Infants Born Receiving Late or No
  Prenatal Care   44
Infants Born with Low Birth Weight   41
Abortions   41
Immunizations of Two-Year-Olds   —
Overall Risk for Heart Disease   19
Risk Factor for Heart Disease
  (hypertension)   29
Deaths Due to Heart Disease   22
New Cancer Cases   18
Deaths Due to Cancer   19
Prevalence of Smoking   48
Prevalence of Diabetes   37
Deaths Due to Diabetes   26
Cost of Diabetes   35
AIDS Cases Reported   51
Gonorrhea Cases Reported   48
Syphilis Cases Reported   48
Tuberculosis Cases Reported   49
Hepatitis Cases Reported   16
Rabies Cases Reported   3
Lyme Disease Cases Reported   39
Beer Consumption   12
Wine Consumption   43
Liquor Consumption   14
Alcohol and Drug Treatment Admissions 39
Federal Spending on Alcohol, Drug
  Abuse, and Mental Health   48
Total Spending on Alcohol/Drug Abuse
  Services   23
State Spending on Alcohol/Drug Abuse
  Services   15
Hard-Core Cocaine Users   49
Federal Drug Grants to States   6

Population   *State Ranking*

Population   47
Population Density   48
Population in Metropolitan Areas   42
Population Under 18 Years Old   11
Population Over 65 Years Old   8
White Population   6
African American Population   46
Hispanic Population   43
Asian American Population   49
Native American Population   7
Catholic Population   13

Jewish Population   45
Marriages   49
Divorces   41
Births   45
Births to Single Mothers   47
Births to Single Teenagers   49
Adoptions   5
Adoption Option Index   23
Infant Mortality   21
Child Deaths and Suicides   27
Teen Violent Death Rate   48
Deaths   25

Recreation   *State Ranking*

State Parks and Recreation Areas   28
Visitors to State Parks and Recreation
  Areas   40
Revenues from State Parks and
  Recreation Areas   32
Spending on State Arts Agencies   44
Domestic Travel Spending   23
State Travel Office Budgets   16
Lodging Industry (rooms)   18
Participation in Exercise Walking   11
Participation in Swimming   26
Participation in Camping   18
Participation in Bowling   41
Bowling League Membership   4
Participation in Running/Jogging   36
Participation in Aerobics   46
Participation in Golf   22
Participation in Softball   17
Participation in Health Clubs   21
Participation in Tennis   48
Participation in Hunting   13
Participation in Baseball   21
Participation in Bicycle Riding   8
Number of Boats   12
Attendance at Parimutuel Racing   11
Revenue from Parimutuel Betting   36

Social Services   *State Ranking*

Federal Grants for Social Services   1
State Spending on Public Welfare   26
Persons in Poverty   21
Public Aid Recipients   47
Participants in Food Stamp Program   38
Households in Food Stamp Program   41
Percentage of Poor Using AFDC and
  Food Stamps   22
Federal Spending on Children and
  Family Services   5
Federal Women, Infants, and Children
  Food Program   11
Child Welfare Services   NA
Child Abuse Cases Reported   —
Children in Poverty   24
Children Without Health Insurance   48
Children Who Are Hungry or at Risk   25
Federal Spending on Child Nutrition
  Programs   5
Federal Spending on Special Milk
  Program   15
National School Lunch Program
  Participants   23
Head Start Enrollment   29
Head Start Spending   45
Federal Spending on Rehabilitation
  Services/Handicapped Research   12

State Government   *State Ranking*

Financial World's State Rankings   42
Salaries of State Officials (governor)   46
Salaries of State Legislators   —
Women in State Legislatures   34
African Americans in State Legislatures   43
Hispanics in State Legislatures   21
Asian Americans in State Legislatures   6
Native Americans in State Legislatures   8
Turnover in State Legislatures   3
Length of State Legislative Sessions   28
State Bills in Regular Session   4
State Resolutions in Regular Session   11
State Bills in Special Session   6
State Resolutions in Special Session   1
Women in State Cabinets   34
Total Federal Funding to State
  Governments   8
Total State Spending   7
State General Expenditures   5
State Debt   21
State Spending on Interest on the
  General Debt   13
Total State Tax Revenue   24
State Revenue from Tax on Sales and
  Gross Receipts   14
State Revenue from General Sales Tax   24
State Revenue from Licenses   17
State Revenue from Motor Vehicle
  Licenses   8
State Revenue from Individual Income
  Taxes   40
State Revenue from Corporation Net
  Income Taxes   19
State Revenue from Severance Taxes   3
State Revenue from Property Taxes   27
State Revenue from Death and Gift
  Taxes   48
State Revenue from Documentary and
  Stock Transfers   —
State Revenue from Tax on Motor Fuels   5
State Revenue from Tax on Tobacco
  Products   19
Excise Tax on Cigarettes   13
Excise Tax on Gasoline   26
State Revenue from Lotteries   —

Transportation   *State Ranking*

Motor Vehicle Registrations   4
Automobile Registrations   21
Bus and Truck Registrations   2
Motorcycle Registrations   8
Driver Licenses   35
Federal Spending on Highway Trust
  Fund   7
Federal Spending on Mass
  Transportation   38
State Spending on Highways   6
Highway Deficiency   50
Bridge Deficiency   17
Traffic Fatalities   38
Traffic Fatalities per Miles Traveled   42
Motorcyclist Fatalities   14
Pedalcyclist Fatalities   43
Pedestrian Fatalities   48
Registered Aircraft   4
Registered Pilots   2
Federal Spending on Airport and
  Airway Trust Fund   21
Aircraft Fatalities   8

— *not applicable* NA *not available*

Agriculture
State Ranking

Farm Acreage	22
Farmland as Portion of State	12
Net Farm Income	41
Government Payments to Farms	27
Federal Commodity Loans/Price Supports	24
Federal Spending on Rural Development	25
Rural Electric and Telephone Loan Guarantees	30
Foreign-Owned Agricultural Land	22

Business and Economy
State Ranking

Gross State Product	26
Retail Sales	36
Supermarket Sales	40
Commercial Bank Assets	28
Insured Commercial Bank Deposits	29
Fortune 500 Companies	6
Inc. 500 Companies	32
New Business Incorporations	40
Business Failures	35
Financial Aid to Minority Businesses	20
Women-Owned Businesses	29
Sales & Receipts of Women-Owned Businesses	46
African American-Owned Businesses	19
Sales & Receipts of African American-Owned Businesses	22
Hispanic-Owned Businesses	35
Sales & Receipts of Hispanic-Owned Businesses	26
Employees in Manufacturing	3
Manufacturing Shipments	7
Japanese-Owned U.S. Manufacturing Plants	2
Exports to Mexico	25
Change in Exports to Mexico	27
Existing Home Sales	37
Housing Starts	29
Average Annual Pay	19
Disposable Personal Income	27
Median Income of Families with Children	19
Federal Spending on Unemployment Insurance/Employment Services	42
Teen Unemployment	30
Bankruptcy Petitions Filed	16
Patents Issued to State Residents	11
Federal Spending on Community Development	8
Federal Spending on Economic Development Administration	26
Federal Spending on Urban Development Action Grants	2

Crime and Criminal Justice
State Ranking

Total Crimes	33
Violent Crimes	26
Murders	24
Rapes	9
Aggravated Assaults	31
Property Crimes	33
Robberies	15
Burglaries	31
Larcenies and Thefts	31
Motor Vehicle Thefts	21
State and Federal Prisoners	15
Capital Punishment	17

State Spending on Corrections	31
State Spending on Police	44
Inmates in Local Jails	29
Spending on Local Jails	26
Spending per Inmate for Local Jails	14
Employees at Local Jails	21
Juvenile Custody Rate	10
Federal Spending on Office of Justice Assistance Programs	36

Defense
State Ranking

Defense Grants to State and Local Governments	16
Total Defense Payroll	39
Total Army Payroll	51
Total Navy/Marine Corps Payroll	45
Total Air Force Payroll	25
Total Active-Duty Payroll	41
Army Active-Duty Payroll	39
Navy/Marine Corps Active-Duty Payroll	41
Air Force Active-Duty Payroll	32
Total Civilian Payroll	23
Army Civilian Payroll	49
Navy/Marine Corps Civilian Payroll	32
Air Force Civilian Payroll	8
Total Reserve and National Guard Payroll	46
Army Reserve and National Guard Payroll	47
Navy/Marine Corps Reserve and National Guard Payroll	31
Air Force Reserve and National Guard Payroll	34
Total Retired Military Payroll	43
Army Retired Military Payroll	48
Navy/Marine Corps Retired Military Payroll	48
Air Force Retired Military Payroll	37
Total Defense Prime Contracts	19
Army Prime Contracts	12
Navy/Marine Corps Prime Contracts	24
Air Force Prime Contracts	15
U.S. Military Installations	10
Construction of National Guard Centers	15

Education
State Ranking

School Age Population	29
Public Elementary and Secondary School Enrollment	6
Average Daily Attendance	29
Student-Teacher Ratio	19
Salaries of Public School Teachers	17
Public School Teachers Who Are Male	24
Eighth Grade Math Test Results	16
High School Math Enrollment	16
Public High School Graduation Rate	27
General Educational Development (GED) Test Results	4
Adult Illiteracy	27
Federal Revenue for Public Schools	33
State Revenue for Public Schools	30
Local Government Revenue for Public Schools	21
Total Public School Spending	20
Public School Spending on Instruction	39
Public School Spending on Noninstruction	17
Public School Spending on Support Staff	2
State and Local Government Spending on Public Schools	15

Federal Spending on School Improvement Programs	33
Gifted and Talented Students	26
Federal Spending on Education of Students with Disabilities	29
Student-Teacher Ratio in Catholic Elementary Schools	10
Student-Teacher Ratio in Catholic Secondary Schools	13
State Spending on Education	36
State and Local Government Spending on Education	28
Higher Education Tuition and Fees	10
Higher Education Revenue	28
Federal Spending on Higher Education	35
State Spending on Higher Education	34
State and Local Government Spending on Higher Education	29
State and Local Appropriations for Higher Education	37
Federal Spending on Higher Education Act Insured Loans	37
Federal Spending on National Guaranteed Student Loans	20
Federal Spending on Pell Grants	21
Default Rate in Perkins Student Loan Program	22
State Spending on Libraries	48

Energy
State Ranking

Total Spending on Energy	25
Net Generation of Electricity	25
Cost of Electricity	27
Spending on Electricity	13
Spending on Natural Gas	10
Spending on Gasoline	40
Spending on Petroleum	42
Spending on Coal	10
Total Energy Consumption	20
Electricity Consumption	17
Natural Gas Consumption	17
Petroleum Consumption	44
Coal Consumption	11
Power Plants	46
Nuclear Power Plants	31
Hydroelectric Power Plants	43

Environment
State Ranking

Federally Owned Land (acreage)	46
Loss of Wetlands	2
Environmental Protection Agency Spending	26
EPA Abatement, Control, and Compliance	42
State Spending on Environmental Programs	48
Environmental Programs as Part of State Budget	48
State Spending on Forest Programs	41
Total Tree Planting	31
Federal Tree Planting	25
Private Tree Planting	29
State Spending on Air Quality	19
State Spending on Water Quality	45
Federal Grants for Rural Water and Waste Disposal	29
Federal Spending on Wastewater Treatment Works	25
Hazardous Waste Sites on National Priority List	11

Federal Grants for Hazardous Substance
  Response   43
State Spending on Hazardous Waste   22

Health   *State Ranking*

State Health Rankings   17
State Spending on Health   37
Support for Public Health   8
Family and Business Spending on Health
  Care   12
HMO Enrollment   18
Medicaid Recipients   13
Medically Underserved Population   26
Lack of Health Care Access   34
Active Nonfederal Physicians   22
Active Nonfederal Nurses   18
Active Nonfederal Dentists   25
Average Cost per Hospital Stay   18
Average Cost per Day for Hospital Care   16
Average Cost per Day for Hospital Room   19
State Spending on Hospitals   21
Adequacy of Prenatal Care   11
Infants Born Receiving Late or No
  Prenatal Care   37
Infants Born with Low Birth Weight   21
Abortions   24
Immunizations of Two-Year-Olds   —
Overall Risk for Heart Disease   29
Risk Factor for Heart Disease
  (hypertension)   38
Deaths Due to Heart Disease   13
New Cancer Cases   20
Deaths Due to Cancer   13
Prevalence of Smoking   16
Prevalence of Diabetes   22
Deaths Due to Diabetes   4
Cost of Diabetes   21
AIDS Cases Reported   36
Gonorrhea Cases Reported   14
Syphilis Cases Reported   23
Tuberculosis Cases Reported   39
Hepatitis Cases Reported   41
Rabies Cases Reported   45
Lyme Disease Cases Reported   25
Beer Consumption   27
Wine Consumption   36
Liquor Consumption   48
Alcohol and Drug Treatment Admissions   42
Federal Spending on Alcohol, Drug
  Abuse, and Mental Health   11
Total Spending on Alcohol/Drug Abuse
  Services   40
State Spending on Alcohol/Drug Abuse
  Services   39
Hard-Core Cocaine Users   29
Federal Drug Grants to States   38

Population   *State Ranking*

Population   7
Population Density   9
Population in Metropolitan Areas   18
Population Under 18 Years Old   29
Population Over 65 Years Old   21
White Population   24
African American Population   20
Hispanic Population   35
Asian American Population   33
Native American Population   46
Catholic Population   24

Jewish Population   16
Marriages   32
Divorces   25
Births   42
Births to Single Mothers   18
Births to Single Teenagers   12
Adoptions   51
Adoption Option Index   38
Infant Mortality   16
Child Deaths and Suicides   41
Teen Violent Death Rate   42
Deaths   16

Recreation   *State Ranking*

State Parks and Recreation Areas   38
Visitors to State Parks and Recreation
  Areas   8
Revenues from State Parks and
  Recreation Areas   36
Spending on State Arts Agencies   12
Domestic Travel Spending   48
State Travel Office Budgets   49
Lodging Industry (rooms)   48
Participation in Exercise Walking   41
Participation in Swimming   30
Participation in Camping   28
Participation in Bowling   23
Bowling League Membership   11
Participation in Running/Jogging   39
Participation in Aerobics   40
Participation in Golf   13
Participation in Softball   20
Participation in Health Clubs   39
Participation in Tennis   36
Participation in Hunting   35
Participation in Baseball   14
Participation in Bicycle Riding   26
Number of Boats   34
Attendance at Parimutuel Racing   25
Revenue from Parimutuel Betting   11

Social Services   *State Ranking*

Federal Grants for Social Services   12
State Spending on Public Welfare   12
Persons in Poverty   29
Public Aid Recipients   9
Participants in Food Stamp Program   7
Households in Food Stamp Program   5
Percentage of Poor Using AFDC and
  Food Stamps   30
Federal Spending on Children and
  Family Services   47
Federal Women, Infants, and Children
  Food Program   34
Child Welfare Services   NA
Child Abuse Cases Reported   —
Children in Poverty   21
Children Without Health Insurance   37
Children Who Are Hungry or at Risk   32
Federal Spending on Child Nutrition
  Programs   37
Federal Spending on Special Milk
  Program   13
National School Lunch Program
  Participants   32
Head Start Enrollment   13
Head Start Spending   47
Federal Spending on Rehabilitation
  Services/Handicapped Research   26

State Government   *State Ranking*

Financial World's State Rankings   28
Salaries of State Officials (governor)   11
Salaries of State Legislators   5
Women in State Legislatures   22
African Americans in State Legislatures   11
Hispanics in State Legislatures   21
Asian Americans in State Legislatures   6
Native Americans in State Legislatures   12
Turnover in State Legislatures   43
Length of State Legislative Sessions   42
State Bills in Regular Session   38
State Resolutions in Regular Session   36
State Bills in Special Session   —
State Resolutions in Special Session   —
Women in State Cabinets   24
Total Federal Funding to State
  Governments   37
Total State Spending   25
State General Expenditures   33
State Debt   33
State Spending on Interest on the
  General Debt   30
Total State Tax Revenue   36
State Revenue from Tax on Sales and
  Gross Receipts   33
State Revenue from General Sales Tax   34
State Revenue from Licenses   26
State Revenue from Motor Vehicle
  Licenses   32
State Revenue from Individual Income
  Taxes   26
State Revenue from Corporation Net
  Income Taxes   26
State Revenue from Severance Taxes   25
State Revenue from Property Taxes   34
State Revenue from Death and Gift
  Taxes   39
State Revenue from Documentary and
  Stock Transfers   —
State Revenue from Tax on Motor Fuels   26
State Revenue from Tax on Tobacco
  Products   32
Excise Tax on Cigarettes   30
Excise Tax on Gasoline   10
State Revenue from Lotteries   6

Transportation   *State Ranking*

Motor Vehicle Registrations   20
Automobile Registrations   7
Bus and Truck Registrations   41
Motorcycle Registrations   16
Driver Licenses   28
Federal Spending on Highway Trust
  Fund   38
Federal Spending on Mass
  Transportation   16
State Spending on Highways   34
Highway Deficiency   34
Bridge Deficiency   28
Traffic Fatalities   37
Traffic Fatalities per Miles Traveled   31
Motorcyclist Fatalities   11
Pedalcyclist Fatalities   24
Pedestrian Fatalities   35
Registered Aircraft   37
Registered Pilots   42
Federal Spending on Airport and
  Airway Trust Fund   30
Aircraft Fatalities   44

— *not applicable* NA *not available*

Agriculture
State Ranking

Farm Acreage	10
Farmland as Portion of State	8
Net Farm Income	12
Government Payments to Farms	10
Federal Commodity Loans/Price Supports	29
Federal Spending on Rural Development	1
Rural Electric and Telephone Loan Guarantees	22
Foreign-Owned Agricultural Land	41

Business and Economy
State Ranking

Gross State Product	46
Retail Sales	46
Supermarket Sales	19
Commercial Bank Assets	41
Insured Commercial Bank Deposits	39
Fortune 500 Companies	27
Inc. 500 Companies	19
New Business Incorporations	22
Business Failures	4
Financial Aid to Minority Businesses	12
Women-Owned Businesses	37
Sales & Receipts of Women-Owned Businesses	18
African American-Owned Businesses	27
Sales & Receipts of African American-Owned Businesses	29
Hispanic-Owned Businesses	26
Sales & Receipts of Hispanic-Owned Businesses	28
Employees in Manufacturing	33
Manufacturing Shipments	34
Japanese-Owned U.S. Manufacturing Plants	27
Exports to Mexico	19
Change in Exports to Mexico	35
Existing Home Sales	15
Housing Starts	43
Average Annual Pay	37
Disposable Personal Income	45
Median Income of Families with Children	40
Federal Spending on Unemployment Insurance/Employment Services	33
Teen Unemployment	36
Bankruptcy Petitions Filed	6
Patents Issued to State Residents	24
Federal Spending on Community Development	41
Federal Spending on Economic Development Administration	13
Federal Spending on Urban Development Action Grants	23

Crime and Criminal Justice
State Ranking

Total Crimes	22
Violent Crimes	25
Murders	24
Rapes	12
Aggravated Assaults	23
Property Crimes	22
Robberies	29
Burglaries	8
Larcenies and Thefts	26
Motor Vehicle Thefts	19
State and Federal Prisoners	5
Capital Punishment	15
State Spending on Corrections	21
State Spending on Police	41
Inmates in Local Jails	34
Spending on Local Jails	44
Spending per Inmate for Local Jails	41
Employees at Local Jails	21
Juvenile Custody Rate	43
Federal Spending on Office of Justice Assistance Programs	51

Defense
State Ranking

Defense Grants to State and Local Governments	15
Total Defense Payroll	10
Total Army Payroll	12
Total Navy/Marine Corps Payroll	37
Total Air Force Payroll	9
Total Active-Duty Payroll	16
Army Active-Duty Payroll	10
Navy/Marine Corps Active-Duty Payroll	36
Air Force Active-Duty Payroll	13
Total Civilian Payroll	8
Army Civilian Payroll	16
Navy/Marine Corps Civilian Payroll	35
Air Force Civilian Payroll	2
Total Reserve and National Guard Payroll	13
Army Reserve and National Guard Payroll	9
Navy/Marine Corps Reserve and National Guard Payroll	40
Air Force Reserve and National Guard Payroll	16
Total Retired Military Payroll	16
Army Retired Military Payroll	8
Navy/Marine Corps Retired Military Payroll	27
Air Force Retired Military Payroll	17
Total Defense Prime Contracts	33
Army Prime Contracts	33
Navy/Marine Corps Prime Contracts	42
Air Force Prime Contracts	21
U.S. Military Installations	25
Construction of National Guard Centers	24

Education
State Ranking

School Age Population	13
Public Elementary and Secondary School Enrollment	26
Average Daily Attendance	17
Student-Teacher Ratio	34
Salaries of Public School Teachers	47
Public School Teachers Who Are Male	34
Eighth Grade Math Test Results	19
High School Math Enrollment	28
Public High School Graduation Rate	17
General Educational Development (GED) Test Results	19
Adult Illiteracy	27
Federal Revenue for Public Schools	30
State Revenue for Public Schools	13
Local Government Revenue for Public Schools	35
Total Public School Spending	45
Public School Spending on Instruction	37
Public School Spending on Noninstruction	16
Public School Spending on Support Staff	46
State and Local Government Spending on Public Schools	27
Federal Spending on School Improvement Programs	24
Gifted and Talented Students	8
Federal Spending on Education of Students with Disabilities	21
Student-Teacher Ratio in Catholic Elementary Schools	41
Student-Teacher Ratio in Catholic Secondary Schools	19
State Spending on Education	20
State and Local Government Spending on Education	19
Higher Education Tuition and Fees	42
Higher Education Revenue	50
Federal Spending on Higher Education	18
State Spending on Higher Education	30
State and Local Government Spending on Higher Education	17
State and Local Appropriations for Higher Education	40
Federal Spending on Higher Education Act Insured Loans	16
Federal Spending on National Guaranteed Student Loans	39
Federal Spending on Pell Grants	8
Default Rate in Perkins Student Loan Program	15
State Spending on Libraries	40

Energy
State Ranking

Total Spending on Energy	17
Net Generation of Electricity	18
Cost of Electricity	34
Spending on Electricity	18
Spending on Natural Gas	3
Spending on Gasoline	9
Spending on Petroleum	24
Spending on Coal	24
Total Energy Consumption	8
Electricity Consumption	15
Natural Gas Consumption	5
Petroleum Consumption	21
Coal Consumption	23
Power Plants	26
Nuclear Power Plants	34
Hydroelectric Power Plants	31

Environment
State Ranking

Federally Owned Land (acreage)	39
Loss of Wetlands	11
Environmental Protection Agency Spending	42
EPA Abatement, Control, and Compliance	39
State Spending on Environmental Programs	47
Environmental Programs as Part of State Budget	45
State Spending on Forest Programs	32
Total Tree Planting	25
Federal Tree Planting	22
Private Tree Planting	22
State Spending on Air Quality	37
State Spending on Water Quality	49
Federal Grants for Rural Water and Waste Disposal	5
Federal Spending on Wastewater Treatment Works	42
Hazardous Waste Sites on National Priority List	32

Federal Grants for Hazardous Substance
Response — 25
State Spending on Hazardous Waste — 47

Health   State Ranking

State Health Rankings — 24
State Spending on Health — 28
Support for Public Health — 30
Family and Business Spending on Health
Care — 36
HMO Enrollment — 35
Medicaid Recipients — 26
Medically Underserved Population — 7
Lack of Health Care Access — 31
Active Nonfederal Physicians — 46
Active Nonfederal Nurses — 48
Active Nonfederal Dentists — 33
Average Cost per Hospital Stay — 37
Average Cost per Day for Hospital Care — 30
Average Cost per Day for Hospital Room — 40
State Spending on Hospitals — 20
Adequacy of Prenatal Care — 38
Infants Born Receiving Late or No
Prenatal Care — 13
Infants Born with Low Birth Weight — 29
Abortions — 38
Immunizations of Two-Year-Olds — —
Overall Risk for Heart Disease — 31
Risk Factor for Heart Disease
(hypertension) — 27
Deaths Due to Heart Disease — 7
New Cancer Cases — 22
Deaths Due to Cancer — 20
Prevalence of Smoking — 9
Prevalence of Diabetes — 14
Deaths Due to Diabetes — 34
Cost of Diabetes — 14
AIDS Cases Reported — 29
Gonorrhea Cases Reported — 19
Syphilis Cases Reported — 14
Tuberculosis Cases Reported — 30
Hepatitis Cases Reported — 26
Rabies Cases Reported — 9
Lyme Disease Cases Reported — 19
Beer Consumption — 48
Wine Consumption — 45
Liquor Consumption — 45
Alcohol and Drug Treatment Admissions — 37
Federal Spending on Alcohol, Drug
Abuse, and Mental Health — 30
Total Spending on Alcohol/Drug Abuse
Services — 38
State Spending on Alcohol/Drug Abuse
Services — 37
Hard-Core Cocaine Users — 17
Federal Drug Grants to States — 44

Population   State Ranking

Population — 28
Population Density — 35
Population in Metropolitan Areas — 33
Population Under 18 Years Old — 17
Population Over 65 Years Old — 16
White Population — 32
African American Population — 24
Hispanic Population — 23
Asian American Population — 28
Native American Population — 3
Catholic Population — 43

— not applicable   NA not available

Jewish Population — 42
Marriages — 16
Divorces — 2
Births — 30
Births to Single Mothers — 30
Births to Single Teenagers — 19
Adoptions — 6
Adoption Option Index — 8
Infant Mortality — 11
Child Deaths and Suicides — 17
Teen Violent Death Rate — 8
Deaths — 8

Recreation   State Ranking

State Parks and Recreation Areas — 24
Visitors to State Parks and Recreation
Areas — 11
Revenues from State Parks and
Recreation Areas — 10
Spending on State Arts Agencies — 14
Domestic Travel Spending — 44
State Travel Office Budgets — 23
Lodging Industry (rooms) — 32
Participation in Exercise Walking — 44
Participation in Swimming — 48
Participation in Camping — 30
Participation in Bowling — 45
Bowling League Membership — 35
Participation in Running/Jogging — 42
Participation in Aerobics — 48
Participation in Golf — 40
Participation in Softball — 46
Participation in Health Clubs — 20
Participation in Tennis — 44
Participation in Hunting — 30
Participation in Baseball — 44
Participation in Bicycle Riding — 46
Number of Boats — 15
Attendance at Parimutuel Racing — 9
Revenue from Parimutuel Betting — 8

Social Services   State Ranking

Federal Grants for Social Services — 5
State Spending on Public Welfare — 29
Persons in Poverty — 11
Public Aid Recipients — 26
Participants in Food Stamp Program — 19
Households in Food Stamp Program — 17
Percentage of Poor Using AFDC and
Food Stamps — 28
Federal Spending on Children and
Family Services — 15
Federal Women, Infants, and Children
Food Program — 29
Child Welfare Services — 18
Child Abuse Cases Reported — —
Children in Poverty — 11
Children Without Health Insurance — 7
Children Who Are Hungry or at Risk — 17
Federal Spending on Child Nutrition
Programs — 17
Federal Spending on Special Milk
Program — 30
National School Lunch Program
Participants — 13
Head Start Enrollment — 23
Head Start Spending — 51
Federal Spending on Rehabilitation
Services/Handicapped Research — 18

State Government   State Ranking

Financial World's State Rankings — 39
Salaries of State Officials (governor) — 41
Salaries of State Legislators — 9
Women in State Legislatures — 47
African Americans in State Legislatures — 28
Hispanics in State Legislatures — 21
Asian Americans in State Legislatures — 6
Native Americans in State Legislatures — 9
Turnover in State Legislatures — 17
Length of State Legislative Sessions — 26
State Bills in Regular Session — 25
State Resolutions in Regular Session — 37
State Bills in Special Session — 1
State Resolutions in Special Session — 19
Women in State Cabinets — NA
Total Federal Funding to State
Governments — 31
Total State Spending — 21
State General Expenditures — 26
State Debt — 26
State Spending on Interest on the
General Debt — 37
Total State Tax Revenue — 22
State Revenue from Tax on Sales and
Gross Receipts — 36
State Revenue from General Sales Tax — 39
State Revenue from Licenses — 7
State Revenue from Motor Vehicle
Licenses — 1
State Revenue from Individual Income
Taxes — 27
State Revenue from Corporation Net
Income Taxes — 42
State Revenue from Severance Taxes — 6
State Revenue from Property Taxes — —
State Revenue from Death and Gift
Taxes — 20
State Revenue from Documentary and
Stock Transfers — 27
State Revenue from Tax on Motor Fuels — 16
State Revenue from Tax on Tobacco
Products — 25
Excise Tax on Cigarettes — 24
Excise Tax on Gasoline — 26
State Revenue from Lotteries — —

Transportation   State Ranking

Motor Vehicle Registrations — 15
Automobile Registrations — 33
Bus and Truck Registrations — 8
Motorcycle Registrations — 22
Driver Licenses — 13
Federal Spending on Highway Trust
Fund — 23
Federal Spending on Mass
Transportation — 36
State Spending on Highways — 16
Highway Deficiency — 37
Bridge Deficiency — 13
Traffic Fatalities — 15
Traffic Fatalities per Miles Traveled — 24
Motorcyclist Fatalities — 25
Pedalcyclist Fatalities — 46
Pedestrian Fatalities — 33
Registered Aircraft — 16
Registered Pilots — 17
Federal Spending on Airport and
Airway Trust Fund — 34
Aircraft Fatalities — 17

Agriculture   *State Ranking*

Farm Acreage	17
Farmland as Portion of State	35
Net Farm Income	14
Government Payments to Farms	21
Federal Commodity Loans/Price Supports	30
Federal Spending on Rural Development	16
Rural Electric and Telephone Loan Guarantees	34
Foreign-Owned Agricultural Land	5

Business and Economy   *State Ranking*

Gross State Product	35
Retail Sales	13
Supermarket Sales	22
Commercial Bank Assets	47
Insured Commercial Bank Deposits	48
Fortune 500 Companies	26
Inc. 500 Companies	23
New Business Incorporations	11
Business Failures	9
Financial Aid to Minority Businesses	19
Women-Owned Businesses	5
Sales & Receipts of Women-Owned Businesses	1
African American-Owned Businesses	41
Sales & Receipts of African American-Owned Businesses	43
Hispanic-Owned Businesses	23
Sales & Receipts of Hispanic-Owned Businesses	17
Employees in Manufacturing	27
Manufacturing Shipments	26
Japanese-Owned U.S. Manufacturing Plants	18
Exports to Mexico	46
Change in Exports to Mexico	20
Existing Home Sales	16
Housing Starts	12
Average Annual Pay	26
Disposable Personal Income	33
Median Income of Families with Children	24
Federal Spending on Unemployment Insurance/Employment Services	20
Teen Unemployment	33
Bankruptcy Petitions Filed	10
Patents Issued to State Residents	19
Federal Spending on Community Development	51
Federal Spending on Economic Development Administration	19
Federal Spending on Urban Development Action Grants	33

Crime and Criminal Justice   *State Ranking*

Total Crimes	20
Violent Crimes	29
Murders	35
Rapes	7
Aggravated Assaults	30
Property Crimes	16
Robberies	24
Burglaries	23
Larcenies and Thefts	12
Motor Vehicle Thefts	23
State and Federal Prisoners	29
Capital Punishment	17

State Spending on Corrections	15
State Spending on Police	20
Inmates in Local Jails	21
Spending on Local Jails	6
Spending per Inmate for Local Jails	6
Employees at Local Jails	27
Juvenile Custody Rate	14
Federal Spending on Office of Justice Assistance Programs	28

Defense   *State Ranking*

Defense Grants to State and Local Governments	10
Total Defense Payroll	44
Total Army Payroll	34
Total Navy/Marine Corps Payroll	27
Total Air Force Payroll	38
Total Active-Duty Payroll	46
Army Active-Duty Payroll	43
Navy/Marine Corps Active-Duty Payroll	30
Air Force Active-Duty Payroll	43
Total Civilian Payroll	45
Army Civilian Payroll	27
Navy/Marine Corps Civilian Payroll	44
Air Force Civilian Payroll	37
Total Reserve and National Guard Payroll	39
Army Reserve and National Guard Payroll	43
Navy/Marine Corps Reserve and National Guard Payroll	16
Air Force Reserve and National Guard Payroll	26
Total Retired Military Payroll	29
Army Retired Military Payroll	30
Navy/Marine Corps Retired Military Payroll	12
Air Force Retired Military Payroll	31
Total Defense Prime Contracts	48
Army Prime Contracts	43
Navy/Marine Corps Prime Contracts	43
Air Force Prime Contracts	46
U.S. Military Installations	41
Construction of National Guard Centers	10

Education   *State Ranking*

School Age Population	30
Public Elementary and Secondary School Enrollment	29
Average Daily Attendance	42
Student-Teacher Ratio	11
Salaries of Public School Teachers	20
Public School Teachers Who Are Male	4
Eighth Grade Math Test Results	10
High School Math Enrollment	NA
Public High School Graduation Rate	33
General Educational Development (GED) Test Results	18
Adult Illiteracy	43
Federal Revenue for Public Schools	25
State Revenue for Public Schools	48
Local Government Revenue for Public Schools	4
Total Public School Spending	16
Public School Spending on Instruction	26
Public School Spending on Noninstruction	40
Public School Spending on Support Staff	3
State and Local Government Spending on Public Schools	11

Federal Spending on School Improvement Programs	45
Gifted and Talented Students	NA
Federal Spending on Education of Students with Disabilities	44
Student-Teacher Ratio in Catholic Elementary Schools	32
Student-Teacher Ratio in Catholic Secondary Schools	22
State Spending on Education	44
State and Local Government Spending on Education	15
Higher Education Tuition and Fees	28
Higher Education Revenue	30
Federal Spending on Higher Education	27
State Spending on Higher Education	25
State and Local Government Spending on Higher Education	24
State and Local Appropriations for Higher Education	22
Federal Spending on Higher Education Act Insured Loans	26
Federal Spending on National Guaranteed Student Loans	48
Federal Spending on Pell Grants	28
Default Rate in Perkins Student Loan Program	25
State Spending on Libraries	46

Energy   *State Ranking*

Total Spending on Energy	40
Net Generation of Electricity	12
Cost of Electricity	48
Spending on Electricity	38
Spending on Natural Gas	40
Spending on Gasoline	25
Spending on Petroleum	27
Spending on Coal	46
Total Energy Consumption	22
Electricity Consumption	10
Natural Gas Consumption	37
Petroleum Consumption	27
Coal Consumption	45
Power Plants	15
Nuclear Power Plants	20
Hydroelectric Power Plants	8

Environment   *State Ranking*

Federally Owned Land (acreage)	7
Loss of Wetlands	32
Environmental Protection Agency Spending	29
EPA Abatement, Control, and Compliance	24
State Spending on Environmental Programs	5
Environmental Programs as Part of State Budget	6
State Spending on Forest Programs	2
Total Tree Planting	10
Federal Tree Planting	1
Private Tree Planting	11
State Spending on Air Quality	2
State Spending on Water Quality	28
Federal Grants for Rural Water and Waste Disposal	16
Federal Spending on Wastewater Treatment Works	29
Hazardous Waste Sites on National Priority List	39

Federal Grants for Hazardous Substance Response	32
State Spending on Hazardous Waste	11

Health
State Ranking

State Health Rankings	38
State Spending on Health	20
Support for Public Health	41
Family and Business Spending on Health Care	30
HMO Enrollment	5
Medicaid Recipients	30
Medically Underserved Population	35
Lack of Health Care Access	15
Active Nonfederal Physicians	18
Active Nonfederal Nurses	18
Active Nonfederal Dentists	8
Average Cost per Hospital Stay	29
Average Cost per Day for Hospital Care	9
Average Cost per Day for Hospital Room	12
State Spending on Hospitals	16
Adequacy of Prenatal Care	28
Infants Born Receiving Late or No Prenatal Care	21
Infants Born with Low Birth Weight	49
Abortions	20
Immunizations of Two-Year-Olds	—
Overall Risk for Heart Disease	12
Risk Factor for Heart Disease (hypertension)	20
Deaths Due to Heart Disease	32
New Cancer Cases	21
Deaths Due to Cancer	25
Prevalence of Smoking	45
Prevalence of Diabetes	29
Deaths Due to Diabetes	30
Cost of Diabetes	30
AIDS Cases Reported	27
Gonorrhea Cases Reported	38
Syphilis Cases Reported	37
Tuberculosis Cases Reported	31
Hepatitis Cases Reported	11
Rabies Cases Reported	46
Lyme Disease Cases Reported	45
Beer Consumption	33
Wine Consumption	9
Liquor Consumption	31
Alcohol and Drug Treatment Admissions	NA
Federal Spending on Alcohol, Drug Abuse, and Mental Health	29
Total Spending on Alcohol/Drug Abuse Services	NA
State Spending on Alcohol/Drug Abuse Services	NA
Hard-Core Cocaine Users	28
Federal Drug Grants to States	37

Population
State Ranking

Population	29
Population Density	41
Population in Metropolitan Areas	23
Population Under 18 Years Old	32
Population Over 65 Years Old	13
White Population	12
African American Population	42
Hispanic Population	20
Asian American Population	11
Native American Population	13
Catholic Population	35

Jewish Population	30
Marriages	31
Divorces	12
Births	33
Births to Single Mothers	27
Births to Single Teenagers	25
Adoptions	32
Adoption Option Index	4
Infant Mortality	38
Child Deaths and Suicides	34
Teen Violent Death Rate	21
Deaths	28

Recreation
State Ranking

State Parks and Recreation Areas	23
Visitors to State Parks and Recreation Areas	3
Revenues from State Parks and Recreation Areas	14
Spending on State Arts Agencies	36
Domestic Travel Spending	19
State Travel Office Budgets	43
Lodging Industry (rooms)	21
Participation in Exercise Walking	12
Participation in Swimming	34
Participation in Camping	5
Participation in Bowling	16
Bowling League Membership	28
Participation in Running/Jogging	4
Participation in Aerobics	5
Participation in Golf	11
Participation in Softball	18
Participation in Health Clubs	14
Participation in Tennis	7
Participation in Hunting	14
Participation in Baseball	23
Participation in Bicycle Riding	14
Number of Boats	14
Attendance at Parimutuel Racing	—
Revenue from Parimutuel Betting	25

Social Services
State Ranking

Federal Grants for Social Services	39
State Spending on Public Welfare	31
Persons in Poverty	27
Public Aid Recipients	39
Participants in Food Stamp Program	20
Households in Food Stamp Program	23
Percentage of Poor Using AFDC and Food Stamps	12
Federal Spending on Children and Family Services	25
Federal Women, Infants, and Children Food Program	40
Child Welfare Services	NA
Child Abuse Cases Reported	—
Children in Poverty	28
Children Without Health Insurance	19
Children Who Are Hungry or at Risk	34
Federal Spending on Child Nutrition Programs	38
Federal Spending on Special Milk Program	21
National School Lunch Program Participants	38
Head Start Enrollment	49
Head Start Spending	2
Federal Spending on Rehabilitation Services/Handicapped Research	32

State Government
State Ranking

Financial World's State Rankings	17
Salaries of State Officials (governor)	26
Salaries of State Legislators	29
Women in State Legislatures	12
African Americans in State Legislatures	29
Hispanics in State Legislatures	21
Asian Americans in State Legislatures	2
Native Americans in State Legislatures	12
Turnover in State Legislatures	42
Length of State Legislative Sessions	3
State Bills in Regular Session	20
State Resolutions in Regular Session	34
State Bills in Special Session	—
State Resolutions in Special Session	—
Women in State Cabinets	NA
Total Federal Funding to State Governments	44
Total State Spending	24
State General Expenditures	27
State Debt	13
State Spending on Interest on the General Debt	10
Total State Tax Revenue	38
State Revenue from Tax on Sales and Gross Receipts	50
State Revenue from General Sales Tax	—
State Revenue from Licenses	4
State Revenue from Motor Vehicle Licenses	2
State Revenue from Individual Income Taxes	5
State Revenue from Corporation Net Income Taxes	35
State Revenue from Severance Taxes	13
State Revenue from Property Taxes	41
State Revenue from Death and Gift Taxes	35
State Revenue from Documentary and Stock Transfers	15
State Revenue from Tax on Motor Fuels	33
State Revenue from Tax on Tobacco Products	14
Excise Tax on Cigarettes	17
Excise Tax on Gasoline	10
State Revenue from Lotteries	29

Transportation
State Ranking

Motor Vehicle Registrations	13
Automobile Registrations	8
Bus and Truck Registrations	27
Motorcycle Registrations	19
Driver Licenses	1
Federal Spending on Highway Trust Fund	29
Federal Spending on Mass Transportation	14
State Spending on Highways	13
Highway Deficiency	13
Bridge Deficiency	38
Traffic Fatalities	27
Traffic Fatalities per Miles Traveled	35
Motorcyclist Fatalities	24
Pedalcyclist Fatalities	20
Pedestrian Fatalities	26
Registered Aircraft	8
Registered Pilots	14
Federal Spending on Airport and Airway Trust Fund	37
Aircraft Fatalities	21

— not applicable   NA not available

Agriculture
State Ranking

Farm Acreage	37
Farmland as Portion of State	36
Net Farm Income	40
Government Payments to Farms	42
Federal Commodity Loans/Price Supports	38
Federal Spending on Rural Development	27
Rural Electric and Telephone Loan Guarantees	36
Foreign-Owned Agricultural Land	37

Business and Economy
State Ranking

Gross State Product	30
Retail Sales	31
Supermarket Sales	29
Commercial Bank Assets	9
Insured Commercial Bank Deposits	8
Fortune 500 Companies	14
Inc. 500 Companies	33
New Business Incorporations	46
Business Failures	30
Financial Aid to Minority Businesses	29
Women-Owned Businesses	40
Sales & Receipts of Women-Owned Businesses	51
African American-Owned Businesses	24
Sales & Receipts of African American-Owned Businesses	25
Hispanic-Owned Businesses	33
Sales & Receipts of Hispanic-Owned Businesses	30
Employees in Manufacturing	4
Manufacturing Shipments	24
Japanese-Owned U.S. Manufacturing Plants	13
Exports to Mexico	10
Change in Exports to Mexico	9
Existing Home Sales	27
Housing Starts	39
Average Annual Pay	12
Disposable Personal Income	16
Median Income of Families with Children	23
Federal Spending on Unemployment Insurance/Employment Services	25
Teen Unemployment	26
Bankruptcy Petitions Filed	49
Patents Issued to State Residents	14
Federal Spending on Community Development	3
Federal Spending on Economic Development Administration	36
Federal Spending on Urban Development Action Grants	5

Crime and Criminal Justice
State Ranking

Total Crimes	46
Violent Crimes	33
Murders	27
Rapes	42
Aggravated Assaults	38
Property Crimes	47
Robberies	19
Burglaries	46
Larcenies and Thefts	50
Motor Vehicle Thefts	22
State and Federal Prisoners	34
Capital Punishment	17

State Spending on Corrections	44
State Spending on Police	17
Inmates in Local Jails	20
Spending on Local Jails	14
Spending per Inmate for Local Jails	12
Employees at Local Jails	24
Juvenile Custody Rate	12
Federal Spending on Office of Justice Assistance Programs	50

Defense
State Ranking

Defense Grants to State and Local Governments	35
Total Defense Payroll	35
Total Army Payroll	24
Total Navy/Marine Corps Payroll	15
Total Air Force Payroll	49
Total Active-Duty Payroll	43
Army Active-Duty Payroll	29
Navy/Marine Corps Active-Duty Payroll	20
Air Force Active-Duty Payroll	50
Total Civilian Payroll	16
Army Civilian Payroll	19
Navy/Marine Corps Civilian Payroll	10
Air Force Civilian Payroll	49
Total Reserve and National Guard Payroll	28
Army Reserve and National Guard Payroll	23
Navy/Marine Corps Reserve and National Guard Payroll	9
Air Force Reserve and National Guard Payroll	42
Total Retired Military Payroll	41
Army Retired Military Payroll	37
Navy/Marine Corps Retired Military Payroll	36
Air Force Retired Military Payroll	43
Total Defense Prime Contracts	32
Army Prime Contracts	25
Navy/Marine Corps Prime Contracts	20
Air Force Prime Contracts	41
U.S. Military Installations	5
Construction of National Guard Centers	33

Education
State Ranking

School Age Population	44
Public Elementary and Secondary School Enrollment	7
Average Daily Attendance	26
Student-Teacher Ratio	28
Salaries of Public School Teachers	10
Public School Teachers Who Are Male	3
Eighth Grade Math Test Results	15
High School Math Enrollment	20
Public High School Graduation Rate	14
General Educational Development (GED) Test Results	7
Adult Illiteracy	21
Federal Revenue for Public Schools	35
State Revenue for Public Schools	29
Local Government Revenue for Public Schools	20
Total Public School Spending	9
Public School Spending on Instruction	35
Public School Spending on Noninstruction	34
Public School Spending on Support Staff	26
State and Local Government Spending on Public Schools	4

Federal Spending on School Improvement Programs	39
Gifted and Talented Students	17
Federal Spending on Education of Students with Disabilities	42
Student-Teacher Ratio in Catholic Elementary Schools	8
Student-Teacher Ratio in Catholic Secondary Schools	5
State Spending on Education	48
State and Local Government Spending on Education	29
Higher Education Tuition and Fees	6
Higher Education Revenue	8
Federal Spending on Higher Education	40
State Spending on Higher Education	50
State and Local Government Spending on Higher Education	46
State and Local Appropriations for Higher Education	46
Federal Spending on Higher Education Act Insured Loans	5
Federal Spending on National Guaranteed Student Loans	3
Federal Spending on Pell Grants	31
Default Rate in Perkins Student Loan Program	40
State Spending on Libraries	25

Energy
State Ranking

Total Spending on Energy	30
Net Generation of Electricity	19
Cost of Electricity	12
Spending on Electricity	20
Spending on Natural Gas	16
Spending on Gasoline	49
Spending on Petroleum	45
Spending on Coal	12
Total Energy Consumption	30
Electricity Consumption	35
Natural Gas Consumption	24
Petroleum Consumption	41
Coal Consumption	13
Power Plants	47
Nuclear Power Plants	13
Hydroelectric Power Plants	41

Environment
State Ranking

Federally Owned Land (acreage)	37
Loss of Wetlands	15
Environmental Protection Agency Spending	39
EPA Abatement, Control, and Compliance	34
State Spending on Environmental Programs	31
Environmental Programs as Part of State Budget	28
State Spending on Forest Programs	28
Total Tree Planting	39
Federal Tree Planting	32
Private Tree Planting	38
State Spending on Air Quality	24
State Spending on Water Quality	30
Federal Grants for Rural Water and Waste Disposal	30
Federal Spending on Wastewater Treatment Works	35
Hazardous Waste Sites on National Priority List	2

Federal Grants for Hazardous Substance
Response | 49
State Spending on Hazardous Waste | 19

Health | *State Ranking*

State Health Rankings | 20
State Spending on Health | 32
Support for Public Health | 18
Family and Business Spending on Health
Care | 17
HMO Enrollment | 20
Medicaid Recipients | 17
Medically Underserved Population | 34
Lack of Health Care Access | 43
Active Nonfederal Physicians | 11
Active Nonfederal Nurses | 10
Active Nonfederal Dentists | 18
Average Cost per Hospital Stay | 13
Average Cost per Day for Hospital Care | 25
Average Cost per Day for Hospital Room | 6
State Spending on Hospitals | 25
Adequacy of Prenatal Care | 17
Infants Born Receiving Late or No
Prenatal Care | 18
Infants Born with Low Birth Weight | 21
Abortions | 27
Immunizations of Two-Year-Olds | —
Overall Risk for Heart Disease | 22
Risk Factor for Heart Disease
(hypertension) | 6
Deaths Due to Heart Disease | 2
New Cancer Cases | 4
Deaths Due to Cancer | 3
Prevalence of Smoking | 24
Prevalence of Diabetes | 7
Deaths Due to Diabetes | 2
Cost of Diabetes | 7
AIDS Cases Reported | 21
Gonorrhea Cases Reported | 25
Syphilis Cases Reported | 20
Tuberculosis Cases Reported | 26
Hepatitis Cases Reported | 42
Rabies Cases Reported | 18
Lyme Disease Cases Reported | 5
Beer Consumption | 19
Wine Consumption | 39
Liquor Consumption | 46
Alcohol and Drug Treatment Admissions | 36
Federal Spending on Alcohol, Drug
Abuse, and Mental Health | 12
Total Spending on Alcohol/Drug Abuse
Services | 26
State Spending on Alcohol/Drug Abuse
Services | 22
Hard-Core Cocaine Users | 22
Federal Drug Grants to States | 31

Population | *State Ranking*

Population | 5
Population Density | 10
Population in Metropolitan Areas | 10
Population Under 18 Years Old | 45
Population Over 65 Years Old | 2
White Population | 21
African American Population | 21
Hispanic Population | 30
Asian American Population | 25
Native American Population | 50
Catholic Population | 10

Jewish Population | 9
Marriages | 50
Divorces | 45
Births | 46
Births to Single Mothers | 19
Births to Single Teenagers | 19
Adoptions | 42
Adoption Option Index | 26
Infant Mortality | 17
Child Deaths and Suicides | 46
Teen Violent Death Rate | 38
Deaths | 4

Recreation | *State Ranking*

State Parks and Recreation Areas | 32
Visitors to State Parks and Recreation
Areas | 18
Revenues from State Parks and
Recreation Areas | 44
Spending on State Arts Agencies | 16
Domestic Travel Spending | 45
State Travel Office Budgets | 35
Lodging Industry (rooms) | 50
Participation in Exercise Walking | 26
Participation in Swimming | 20
Participation in Camping | 24
Participation in Bowling | 21
Bowling League Membership | 23
Participation in Running/Jogging | 43
Participation in Aerobics | 36
Participation in Golf | 27
Participation in Softball | 32
Participation in Health Clubs | 28
Participation in Tennis | 26
Participation in Hunting | 15
Participation in Baseball | 15
Participation in Bicycle Riding | 37
Number of Boats | 43
Attendance at Parimutuel Racing | 29
Revenue from Parimutuel Betting | 18

Social Services | *State Ranking*

Federal Grants for Social Services | 8
State Spending on Public Welfare | 14
Persons in Poverty | 36
Public Aid Recipients | 19
Participants in Food Stamp Program | 22
Households in Food Stamp Program | 14
Percentage of Poor Using AFDC and
Food Stamps | 18
Federal Spending on Children and
Family Services | 36
Federal Women, Infants, and Children
Food Program | 31
Child Welfare Services | 23
Child Abuse Cases Reported | —
Children in Poverty | 27
Children Without Health Insurance | 42
Children Who Are Hungry or at Risk | 28
Federal Spending on Child Nutrition
Programs | 45
Federal Spending on Special Milk
Program | 26
National School Lunch Program
Participants | 43
Head Start Enrollment | 21
Head Start Spending | 13
Federal Spending on Rehabilitation
Services/Handicapped Research | 27

State Government | *State Ranking*

Financial World's State Rankings | 21
Salaries of State Officials (governor) | 9
Salaries of State Legislators | 3
Women in State Legislatures | 45
African Americans in State Legislatures | 20
Hispanics in State Legislatures | 20
Asian Americans in State Legislatures | 6
Native Americans in State Legislatures | 12
Turnover in State Legislatures | 40
Length of State Legislative Sessions | 42
State Bills in Regular Session | 48
State Resolutions in Regular Session | 23
State Bills in Special Session | —
State Resolutions in Special Session | —
Women in State Cabinets | 8
Total Federal Funding to State
Governments | 27
Total State Spending | 39
State General Expenditures | 42
State Debt | 37
State Spending on Interest on the
General Debt | 29
Total State Tax Revenue | 34
State Revenue from Tax on Sales and
Gross Receipts | 27
State Revenue from General Sales Tax | 30
State Revenue from Licenses | 10
State Revenue from Motor Vehicle
Licenses | 31
State Revenue from Individual Income
Taxes | 36
State Revenue from Corporation Net
Income Taxes | 17
State Revenue from Severance Taxes | —
State Revenue from Property Taxes | 19
State Revenue from Death and Gift
Taxes | 3
State Revenue from Documentary and
Stock Transfers | 8
State Revenue from Tax on Motor Fuels | 47
State Revenue from Tax on Tobacco
Products | 34
Excise Tax on Cigarettes | 30
Excise Tax on Gasoline | 41
State Revenue from Lotteries | 5

Transportation | *State Ranking*

Motor Vehicle Registrations | 46
Automobile Registrations | 34
Bus and Truck Registrations | 43
Motorcycle Registrations | 31
Driver Licenses | 36
Federal Spending on Highway Trust
Fund | 42
Federal Spending on Mass
Transportation | 9
State Spending on Highways | 29
Highway Deficiency | 9
Bridge Deficiency | 14
Traffic Fatalities | 40
Traffic Fatalities per Miles Traveled | 25
Motorcyclist Fatalities | 40
Pedalcyclist Fatalities | 45
Pedestrian Fatalities | 22
Registered Aircraft | 46
Registered Pilots | 46
Federal Spending on Airport and
Airway Trust Fund | 23
Aircraft Fatalities | 46

— *not applicable* NA *not available*

Agriculture

State Ranking

Farm Acreage	50
Farmland as Portion of State	47
Net Farm Income	46
Government Payments to Farms	50
Federal Commodity Loans/Price Supports	49
Federal Spending on Rural Development	46
Rural Electric and Telephone Loan Guarantees	40
Foreign-Owned Agricultural Land	49

Business and Economy

State Ranking

Gross State Product	31
Retail Sales	24
Supermarket Sales	32
Commercial Bank Assets	8
Insured Commercial Bank Deposits	10
Fortune 500 Companies	5
Inc. 500 Companies	39
New Business Incorporations	19
Business Failures	1
Financial Aid to Minority Businesses	41
Women-Owned Businesses	45
Sales & Receipts of Women-Owned Businesses	38
African American-Owned Businesses	35
Sales & Receipts of African American-Owned Businesses	42
Hispanic-Owned Businesses	24
Sales & Receipts of Hispanic-Owned Businesses	21
Employees in Manufacturing	35
Manufacturing Shipments	32
Japanese-Owned U.S. Manufacturing Plants	45
Exports to Mexico	31
Change in Exports to Mexico	37
Existing Home Sales	48
Housing Starts	42
Average Annual Pay	23
Disposable Personal Income	18
Median Income of Families with Children	9
Federal Spending on Unemployment Insurance/Employment Services	6
Teen Unemployment	24
Bankruptcy Petitions Filed	26
Patents Issued to State Residents	18
Federal Spending on Community Development	6
Federal Spending on Economic Development Administration	50
Federal Spending on Urban Development Action Grants	33

Crime and Criminal Justice

State Ranking

Total Crimes	32
Violent Crimes	32
Murders	39
Rapes	35
Aggravated Assaults	28
Property Crimes	31
Robberies	30
Burglaries	29
Larcenies and Thefts	42
Motor Vehicle Thefts	9
State and Federal Prisoners	39
Capital Punishment	—

State Spending on Corrections	12
State Spending on Police	15
Inmates in Local Jails	—
Spending on Local Jails	—
Spending per Inmate for Local Jails	—
Employees at Local Jails	—
Juvenile Custody Rate	34
Federal Spending on Office of Justice Assistance Programs	2

Defense

State Ranking

Defense Grants to State and Local Governments	—
Total Defense Payroll	24
Total Army Payroll	47
Total Navy/Marine Corps Payroll	6
Total Air Force Payroll	45
Total Active-Duty Payroll	24
Army Active-Duty Payroll	37
Navy/Marine Corps Active-Duty Payroll	5
Air Force Active-Duty Payroll	42
Total Civilian Payroll	14
Army Civilian Payroll	46
Navy/Marine Corps Civilian Payroll	6
Air Force Civilian Payroll	44
Total Reserve and National Guard Payroll	24
Army Reserve and National Guard Payroll	27
Navy/Marine Corps Reserve and National Guard Payroll	8
Air Force Reserve and National Guard Payroll	14
Total Retired Military Payroll	31
Army Retired Military Payroll	39
Navy/Marine Corps Retired Military Payroll	5
Air Force Retired Military Payroll	46
Total Defense Prime Contracts	21
Army Prime Contracts	40
Navy/Marine Corps Prime Contracts	8
Air Force Prime Contracts	44
U.S. Military Installations	29
Construction of National Guard Centers	49

Education

State Ranking

School Age Population	48
Public Elementary and Secondary School Enrollment	44
Average Daily Attendance	36
Student-Teacher Ratio	44
Salaries of Public School Teachers	12
Public School Teachers Who Are Male	26
Eighth Grade Math Test Results	22
High School Math Enrollment	NA
Public High School Graduation Rate	35
General Educational Development (GED) Test Results	45
Adult Illiteracy	5
Federal Revenue for Public Schools	39
State Revenue for Public Schools	33
Local Government Revenue for Public Schools	19
Total Public School Spending	8
Public School Spending on Instruction	5
Public School Spending on Noninstruction	50
Public School Spending on Support Staff	38
State and Local Government Spending on Public Schools	40

Federal Spending on School Improvement Programs	11
Gifted and Talented Students	22
Federal Spending on Education of Students with Disabilities	28
Student-Teacher Ratio in Catholic Elementary Schools	38
Student-Teacher Ratio in Catholic Secondary Schools	44
State Spending on Education	38
State and Local Government Spending on Education	42
Higher Education Tuition and Fees	5
Higher Education Revenue	13
Federal Spending on Higher Education	51
State Spending on Higher Education	33
State and Local Government Spending on Higher Education	40
State and Local Appropriations for Higher Education	47
Federal Spending on Higher Education Act Insured Loans	15
Federal Spending on National Guaranteed Student Loans	15
Federal Spending on Pell Grants	27
Default Rate in Perkins Student Loan Program	32
State Spending on Libraries	4

Energy

State Ranking

Total Spending on Energy	50
Net Generation of Electricity	51
Cost of Electricity	1
Spending on Electricity	46
Spending on Natural Gas	34
Spending on Gasoline	48
Spending on Petroleum	41
Spending on Coal	51
Total Energy Consumption	51
Electricity Consumption	51
Natural Gas Consumption	43
Petroleum Consumption	45
Coal Consumption	51
Power Plants	45
Nuclear Power Plants	34
Hydroelectric Power Plants	40

Environment

State Ranking

Federally Owned Land (acreage)	48
Loss of Wetlands	41
Environmental Protection Agency Spending	20
EPA Abatement, Control, and Compliance	8
State Spending on Environmental Programs	15
Environmental Programs as Part of State Budget	17
State Spending on Forest Programs	35
Total Tree Planting	19
Federal Tree Planting	47
Private Tree Planting	20
State Spending on Air Quality	33
State Spending on Water Quality	12
Federal Grants for Rural Water and Waste Disposal	17
Federal Spending on Wastewater Treatment Works	21
Hazardous Waste Sites on National Priority List	27

Federal Grants for Hazardous Substance
    Response   13
State Spending on Hazardous Waste   7

Health   *State Ranking*

State Health Rankings   14
State Spending on Health   5
Support for Public Health   11
Family and Business Spending on Health
    Care   4
HMO Enrollment   9
Medicaid Recipients   3
Medically Underserved Population   35
Lack of Health Care Access   23
Active Nonfederal Physicians   6
Active Nonfederal Nurses   3
Active Nonfederal Dentists   25
Average Cost per Hospital Stay   17
Average Cost per Day for Hospital Care   24
Average Cost per Day for Hospital Room   10
State Spending on Hospitals   17
Adequacy of Prenatal Care   6
Infants Born Receiving Late or No
    Prenatal Care   48
Infants Born with Low Birth Weight   33
Abortions   10
Immunizations of Two-Year-Olds   —
Overall Risk for Heart Disease   24
Risk Factor for Heart Disease
    (hypertension)   10
Deaths Due to Heart Disease   9
New Cancer Cases   6
Deaths Due to Cancer   5
Prevalence of Smoking   36
Prevalence of Diabetes   19
Deaths Due to Diabetes   6
Cost of Diabetes   23
AIDS Cases Reported   24
Gonorrhea Cases Reported   35
Syphilis Cases Reported   32
Tuberculosis Cases Reported   32
Hepatitis Cases Reported   24
Rabies Cases Reported   48
Lyme Disease Cases Reported   3
Beer Consumption   32
Wine Consumption   11
Liquor Consumption   22
Alcohol and Drug Treatment Admissions   8
Federal Spending on Alcohol, Drug
    Abuse, and Mental Health   2
Total Spending on Alcohol/Drug Abuse
    Services   7
State Spending on Alcohol/Drug Abuse
    Services   3
Hard-Core Cocaine Users   36
Federal Drug Grants to States   8

Population   *State Ranking*

Population   43
Population Density   3
Population in Metropolitan Areas   5
Population Under 18 Years Old   48
Population Over 65 Years Old   4
White Population   17
African American Population   33
Hispanic Population   18
Asian American Population   17
Native American Population   27
Catholic Population   2

Jewish Population   13
Marriages   41
Divorces   39
Births   38
Births to Single Mothers   22
Births to Single Teenagers   25
Adoptions   23
Adoption Option Index   24
Infant Mortality   34
Child Deaths and Suicides   49
Teen Violent Death Rate   45
Deaths   10

Recreation   *State Ranking*

State Parks and Recreation Areas   47
Visitors to State Parks and Recreation
    Areas   6
Revenues from State Parks and
    Recreation Areas   17
Spending on State Arts Agencies   14
Domestic Travel Spending   51
State Travel Office Budgets   11
Lodging Industry (rooms)   51
Participation in Exercise Walking   8
Participation in Swimming   11
Participation in Camping   32
Participation in Bowling   12
Bowling League Membership   43
Participation in Running/Jogging   23
Participation in Aerobics   19
Participation in Golf   8
Participation in Softball   3
Participation in Health Clubs   12
Participation in Tennis   1
Participation in Hunting   47
Participation in Baseball   1
Participation in Bicycle Riding   6
Number of Boats   40
Attendance at Parimutuel Racing   —
Revenue from Parimutuel Betting   —

Social Services   *State Ranking*

Federal Grants for Social Services   29
State Spending on Public Welfare   5
Persons in Poverty   38
Public Aid Recipients   16
Participants in Food Stamp Program   32
Households in Food Stamp Program   24
Percentage of Poor Using AFDC and
    Food Stamps   8
Federal Spending on Children and
    Family Services   24
Federal Women, Infants, and Children
    Food Program   25
Child Welfare Services   40
Child Abuse Cases Reported   —
Children in Poverty   36
Children Without Health Insurance   45
Children Who Are Hungry or at Risk   29
Federal Spending on Child Nutrition
    Programs   46
Federal Spending on Special Milk
    Program   10
National School Lunch Program
    Participants   49
Head Start Enrollment   4
Head Start Spending   41
Federal Spending on Rehabilitation
    Services/Handicapped Research   33

State Government   *State Ranking*

Financial World's State Rankings   44
Salaries of State Officials (governor)   45
Salaries of State Legislators   —
Women in State Legislatures   14
African Americans in State Legislatures   22
Hispanics in State Legislatures   21
Asian Americans in State Legislatures   6
Native Americans in State Legislatures   12
Turnover in State Legislatures   23
Length of State Legislative Sessions   42
State Bills in Regular Session   NA
State Resolutions in Regular Session   NA
State Bills in Special Session   —
State Resolutions in Special Session   —
Women in State Cabinets   13
Total Federal Funding to State
    Governments   13
Total State Spending   8
State General Expenditures   14
State Debt   3
State Spending on Interest on the
    General Debt   3
Total State Tax Revenue   20
State Revenue from Tax on Sales and
    Gross Receipts   12
State Revenue from General Sales Tax   14
State Revenue from Licenses   31
State Revenue from Motor Vehicle
    Licenses   14
State Revenue from Individual Income
    Taxes   20
State Revenue from Corporation Net
    Income Taxes   38
State Revenue from Severance Taxes   —
State Revenue from Property Taxes   22
State Revenue from Death and Gift
    Taxes   13
State Revenue from Documentary and
    Stock Transfers   19
State Revenue from Tax on Motor Fuels   39
State Revenue from Tax on Tobacco
    Products   2
Excise Tax on Cigarettes   6
Excise Tax on Gasoline   8
State Revenue from Lotteries   25

Transportation   *State Ranking*

Motor Vehicle Registrations   47
Automobile Registrations   41
Bus and Truck Registrations   45
Motorcycle Registrations   15
Driver Licenses   32
Federal Spending on Highway Trust
    Fund   8
Federal Spending on Mass
    Transportation   11
State Spending on Highways   31
Highway Deficiency   3
Bridge Deficiency   4
Traffic Fatalities   51
Traffic Fatalities per Miles Traveled   49
Motorcyclist Fatalities   8
Pedalcyclist Fatalities   11
Pedestrian Fatalities   46
Registered Aircraft   51
Registered Pilots   48
Federal Spending on Airport and
    Airway Trust Fund   33
Aircraft Fatalities   34

— *not applicable*   NA *not available*

Agriculture   State Ranking

Farm Acreage	38
Farmland as Portion of State	37
Net Farm Income	30
Government Payments to Farms	29
Federal Commodity Loans/Price Supports	35
Federal Spending on Rural Development	7
Rural Electric and Telephone Loan Guarantees	23
Foreign-Owned Agricultural Land	16

Business and Economy   State Ranking

Gross State Product	40
Retail Sales	28
Supermarket Sales	20
Commercial Bank Assets	50
Insured Commercial Bank Deposits	51
Fortune 500 Companies	30
Inc. 500 Companies	46
New Business Incorporations	42
Business Failures	48
Financial Aid to Minority Businesses	34
Women-Owned Businesses	36
Sales & Receipts of Women-Owned Businesses	10
African American-Owned Businesses	4
Sales & Receipts of African American-Owned Businesses	5
Hispanic-Owned Businesses	42
Sales & Receipts of Hispanic-Owned Businesses	47
Employees in Manufacturing	19
Manufacturing Shipments	14
Japanese-Owned U.S. Manufacturing Plants	17
Exports to Mexico	38
Change in Exports to Mexico	18
Existing Home Sales	26
Housing Starts	10
Average Annual Pay	42
Disposable Personal Income	42
Median Income of Families with Children	37
Federal Spending on Unemployment Insurance/Employment Services	44
Teen Unemployment	20
Bankruptcy Petitions Filed	44
Patents Issued to State Residents	33
Federal Spending on Community Development	36
Federal Spending on Economic Development Administration	5
Federal Spending on Urban Development Action Grants	33

Crime and Criminal Justice   State Ranking

Total Crimes	13
Violent Crimes	6
Murders	12
Rapes	6
Aggravated Assaults	2
Property Crimes	18
Robberies	21
Burglaries	9
Larcenies and Thefts	18
Motor Vehicle Thefts	28
State and Federal Prisoners	3
Capital Punishment	9

State Spending on Corrections	3
State Spending on Police	14
Inmates in Local Jails	23
Spending on Local Jails	43
Spending per Inmate for Local Jails	44
Employees at Local Jails	13
Juvenile Custody Rate	26
Federal Spending on Office of Justice Assistance Programs	30

Defense   State Ranking

Defense Grants to State and Local Governments	29
Total Defense Payroll	5
Total Army Payroll	16
Total Navy/Marine Corps Payroll	4
Total Air Force Payroll	18
Total Active-Duty Payroll	5
Army Active-Duty Payroll	15
Navy/Marine Corps Active-Duty Payroll	4
Air Force Active-Duty Payroll	14
Total Civilian Payroll	12
Army Civilian Payroll	29
Navy/Marine Corps Civilian Payroll	8
Air Force Civilian Payroll	28
Total Reserve and National Guard Payroll	9
Army Reserve and National Guard Payroll	7
Navy/Marine Corps Reserve and National Guard Payroll	22
Air Force Reserve and National Guard Payroll	10
Total Retired Military Payroll	7
Army Retired Military Payroll	6
Navy/Marine Corps Retired Military Payroll	7
Air Force Retired Military Payroll	11
Total Defense Prime Contracts	31
Army Prime Contracts	42
Navy/Marine Corps Prime Contracts	18
Air Force Prime Contracts	42
U.S. Military Installations	10
Construction of National Guard Centers	27

Education   State Ranking

School Age Population	24
Public Elementary and Secondary School Enrollment	25
Average Daily Attendance	8
Student-Teacher Ratio	23
Salaries of Public School Teachers	34
Public School Teachers Who Are Male	50
Eighth Grade Math Test Results	—
High School Math Enrollment	1
Public High School Graduation Rate	50
General Educational Development (GED) Test Results	12
Adult Illiteracy	5
Federal Revenue for Public Schools	14
State Revenue for Public Schools	23
Local Government Revenue for Public Schools	32
Total Public School Spending	38
Public School Spending on Instruction	32
Public School Spending on Noninstruction	2
Public School Spending on Support Staff	39
State and Local Government Spending on Public Schools	12

Federal Spending on School Improvement Programs	22
Gifted and Talented Students	7
Federal Spending on Education of Students with Disabilities	13
Student-Teacher Ratio in Catholic Elementary Schools	47
Student-Teacher Ratio in Catholic Secondary Schools	39
State Spending on Education	18
State and Local Government Spending on Education	9
Higher Education Tuition and Fees	21
Higher Education Revenue	23
Federal Spending on Higher Education	14
State Spending on Higher Education	19
State and Local Government Spending on Higher Education	21
State and Local Appropriations for Higher Education	7
Federal Spending on Higher Education Act Insured Loans	39
Federal Spending on National Guaranteed Student Loans	42
Federal Spending on Pell Grants	32
Default Rate in Perkins Student Loan Program	13
State Spending on Libraries	35

Energy   State Ranking

Total Spending on Energy	21
Net Generation of Electricity	7
Cost of Electricity	36
Spending on Electricity	3
Spending on Natural Gas	41
Spending on Gasoline	16
Spending on Petroleum	36
Spending on Coal	17
Total Energy Consumption	19
Electricity Consumption	7
Natural Gas Consumption	38
Petroleum Consumption	36
Coal Consumption	25
Power Plants	23
Nuclear Power Plants	3
Hydroelectric Power Plants	13

Environment   State Ranking

Federally Owned Land (acreage)	36
Loss of Wetlands	43
Environmental Protection Agency Spending	41
EPA Abatement, Control, and Compliance	43
State Spending on Environmental Programs	36
Environmental Programs as Part of State Budget	38
State Spending on Forest Programs	12
Total Tree Planting	3
Federal Tree Planting	6
Private Tree Planting	3
State Spending on Air Quality	50
State Spending on Water Quality	44
Federal Grants for Rural Water and Waste Disposal	24
Federal Spending on Wastewater Treatment Works	38
Hazardous Waste Sites on National Priority List	15

Federal Grants for Hazardous Substance
    Response   35
State Spending on Hazardous Waste   36

Health   *State Ranking*

State Health Rankings   45
State Spending on Health   8
Support for Public Health   23
Family and Business Spending on Health
    Care   46
HMO Enrollment   43
Medicaid Recipients   18
Medically Underserved Population   14
Lack of Health Care Access   10
Active Nonfederal Physicians   39
Active Nonfederal Nurses   50
Active Nonfederal Dentists   49
Average Cost per Hospital Stay   40
Average Cost per Day for Hospital Care   35
Average Cost per Day for Hospital Room   43
State Spending on Hospitals   9
Adequacy of Prenatal Care   49
Infants Born Receiving Late or No
    Prenatal Care   6
Infants Born with Low Birth Weight   4
Abortions   34
Immunizations of Two-Year-Olds   —
Overall Risk for Heart Disease   47
Risk Factor for Heart Disease
    (hypertension)   17
Deaths Due to Heart Disease   31
New Cancer Cases   37
Deaths Due to Cancer   36
Prevalence of Smoking   13
Prevalence of Diabetes   11
Deaths Due to Diabetes   28
Cost of Diabetes   9
AIDS Cases Reported   22
Gonorrhea Cases Reported   11
Syphilis Cases Reported   7
Tuberculosis Cases Reported   8
Hepatitis Cases Reported   50
Rabies Cases Reported   14
Lyme Disease Cases Reported   44
Beer Consumption   15
Wine Consumption   32
Liquor Consumption   15
Alcohol and Drug Treatment Admissions   18
Federal Spending on Alcohol, Drug
    Abuse, and Mental Health   36
Total Spending on Alcohol/Drug Abuse
    Services   18
State Spending on Alcohol/Drug Abuse
    Services   33
Hard-Core Cocaine Users   39
Federal Drug Grants to States   39

Population   *State Ranking*

Population   25
Population Density   21
Population in Metropolitan Areas   32
Population Under 18 Years Old   20
Population Over 65 Years Old   39
White Population   46
African American Population   4
Hispanic Population   41
Asian American Population   41
Native American Population   39
Catholic Population   50

Jewish Population   39
Marriages   3
Divorces   28
Births   19
Births to Single Mothers   7
Births to Single Teenagers   4
Adoptions   28
Adoption Option Index   11
Infant Mortality   7
Child Deaths and Suicides   5
Teen Violent Death Rate   26
Deaths   33

Recreation   *State Ranking*

State Parks and Recreation Areas   32
Visitors to State Parks and Recreation
    Areas   33
Revenues from State Parks and
    Recreation Areas   13
Spending on State Arts Agencies   13
Domestic Travel Spending   17
State Travel Office Budgets   13
Lodging Industry (rooms)   13
Participation in Exercise Walking   3
Participation in Swimming   22
Participation in Camping   47
Participation in Bowling   26
Bowling League Membership   38
Participation in Running/Jogging   3
Participation in Aerobics   8
Participation in Golf   19
Participation in Softball   42
Participation in Health Clubs   38
Participation in Tennis   10
Participation in Hunting   24
Participation in Baseball   16
Participation in Bicycle Riding   22
Number of Boats   3
Attendance at Parimutuel Racing   —
Revenue from Parimutuel Betting   —

Social Services   *State Ranking*

Federal Grants for Social Services   36
State Spending on Public Welfare   18
Persons in Poverty   12
Public Aid Recipients   21
Participants in Food Stamp Program   14
Households in Food Stamp Program   26
Percentage of Poor Using AFDC and
    Food Stamps   45
Federal Spending on Children and
    Family Services   18
Federal Women, Infants, and Children
    Food Program   5
Child Welfare Services   24
Child Abuse Cases Reported   —
Children in Poverty   12
Children Without Health Insurance   15
Children Who Are Hungry or at Risk   9
Federal Spending on Child Nutrition
    Programs   11
Federal Spending on Special Milk
    Program   —
National School Lunch Program
    Participants   8
Head Start Enrollment   26
Head Start Spending   36
Federal Spending on Rehabilitation
    Services/Handicapped Research   13

State Government   *State Ranking*

Financial World's State Rankings   5
Salaries of State Officials (governor)   12
Salaries of State Legislators   32
Women in State Legislatures   40
African Americans in State Legislatures   6
Hispanics in State Legislatures   21
Asian Americans in State Legislatures   6
Native Americans in State Legislatures   12
Turnover in State Legislatures   39
Length of State Legislative Sessions   42
State Bills in Regular Session   40
State Resolutions in Regular Session   14
State Bills in Special Session   7
State Resolutions in Special Session   19
Women in State Cabinets   —
Total Federal Funding to State
    Governments   25
Total State Spending   14
State General Expenditures   15
State Debt   25
State Spending on Interest on the
    General Debt   31
Total State Tax Revenue   31
State Revenue from Tax on Sales and
    Gross Receipts   21
State Revenue from General Sales Tax   19
State Revenue from Licenses   38
State Revenue from Motor Vehicle
    Licenses   47
State Revenue from Individual Income
    Taxes   24
State Revenue from Corporation Net
    Income Taxes   43
State Revenue from Severance Taxes   —
State Revenue from Property Taxes   26
State Revenue from Death and Gift
    Taxes   25
State Revenue from Documentary and
    Stock Transfers   20
State Revenue from Tax on Motor Fuels   24
State Revenue from Tax on Tobacco
    Products   47
Excise Tax on Cigarettes   46
Excise Tax on Gasoline   31
State Revenue from Lotteries   —

Transportation   *State Ranking*

Motor Vehicle Registrations   43
Automobile Registrations   38
Bus and Truck Registrations   37
Motorcycle Registrations   48
Driver Licenses   31
Federal Spending on Highway Trust
    Fund   40
Federal Spending on Mass
    Transportation   35
State Spending on Highways   45
Highway Deficiency   46
Bridge Deficiency   48
Traffic Fatalities   7
Traffic Fatalities per Miles Traveled   7
Motorcyclist Fatalities   23
Pedalcyclist Fatalities   3
Pedestrian Fatalities   4
Registered Aircraft   43
Registered Pilots   41
Federal Spending on Airport and
    Airway Trust Fund   48
Aircraft Fatalities   40

— *not applicable*   NA *not available*

Agriculture
State Ranking

Farm Acreage	5
Farmland as Portion of State	5
Net Farm Income	1
Government Payments to Farms	2
Federal Commodity Loans/Price Supports	4
Federal Spending on Rural Development	2
Rural Electric and Telephone Loan Guarantees	2
Foreign-Owned Agricultural Land	43

Business and Economy
State Ranking

Gross State Product	48
Retail Sales	35
Supermarket Sales	36
Commercial Bank Assets	4
Insured Commercial Bank Deposits	4
Fortune 500 Companies	25
Inc. 500 Companies	31
New Business Incorporations	45
Business Failures	9
Financial Aid to Minority Businesses	38
Women-Owned Businesses	41
Sales & Receipts of Women-Owned Businesses	30
African American-Owned Businesses	50
Sales & Receipts of African American-Owned Businesses	47
Hispanic-Owned Businesses	45
Sales & Receipts of Hispanic-Owned Businesses	49
Employees in Manufacturing	44
Manufacturing Shipments	41
Japanese-Owned U.S. Manufacturing Plants	45
Exports to Mexico	36
Change in Exports to Mexico	46
Existing Home Sales	19
Housing Starts	26
Average Annual Pay	51
Disposable Personal Income	38
Median Income of Families with Children	38
Federal Spending on Unemployment Insurance/Employment Services	18
Teen Unemployment	49
Bankruptcy Petitions Filed	37
Patents Issued to State Residents	51
Federal Spending on Community Development	13
Federal Spending on Economic Development Administration	12
Federal Spending on Urban Development Action Grants	24

Crime and Criminal Justice
State Ranking

Total Crimes	49
Violent Crimes	46
Murders	49
Rapes	27
Aggravated Assaults	44
Property Crimes	49
Robberies	47
Burglaries	49
Larcenies and Thefts	48
Motor Vehicle Thefts	51
State and Federal Prisoners	36
Capital Punishment	17

State Spending on Corrections	43
State Spending on Police	21
Inmates in Local Jails	40
Spending on Local Jails	42
Spending per Inmate for Local Jails	34
Employees at Local Jails	36
Juvenile Custody Rate	4
Federal Spending on Office of Justice Assistance Programs	10

Defense
State Ranking

Defense Grants to State and Local Governments	24
Total Defense Payroll	27
Total Army Payroll	31
Total Navy/Marine Corps Payroll	49
Total Air Force Payroll	8
Total Active-Duty Payroll	15
Army Active-Duty Payroll	44
Navy/Marine Corps Active-Duty Payroll	50
Air Force Active-Duty Payroll	4
Total Civilian Payroll	36
Army Civilian Payroll	31
Navy/Marine Corps Civilian Payroll	50
Air Force Civilian Payroll	16
Total Reserve and National Guard Payroll	18
Army Reserve and National Guard Payroll	15
Navy/Marine Corps Reserve and National Guard Payroll	42
Air Force Reserve and National Guard Payroll	13
Total Retired Military Payroll	35
Army Retired Military Payroll	38
Navy/Marine Corps Retired Military Payroll	42
Air Force Retired Military Payroll	22
Total Defense Prime Contracts	39
Army Prime Contracts	35
Navy/Marine Corps Prime Contracts	50
Air Force Prime Contracts	33
U.S. Military Installations	41
Construction of National Guard Centers	29

Education
State Ranking

School Age Population	8
Public Elementary and Secondary School Enrollment	45
Average Daily Attendance	9
Student-Teacher Ratio	39
Salaries of Public School Teachers	51
Public School Teachers Who Are Male	26
Eighth Grade Math Test Results	—
High School Math Enrollment	NA
Public High School Graduation Rate	5
General Educational Development (GED) Test Results	42
Adult Illiteracy	27
Federal Revenue for Public Schools	4
State Revenue for Public Schools	47
Local Government Revenue for Public Schools	7
Total Public School Spending	42
Public School Spending on Instruction	13
Public School Spending on Noninstruction	14
Public School Spending on Support Staff	28
State and Local Government Spending on Public Schools	21

Federal Spending on School Improvement Programs	7
Gifted and Talented Students	25
Federal Spending on Education of Students with Disabilities	23
Student-Teacher Ratio in Catholic Elementary Schools	43
Student-Teacher Ratio in Catholic Secondary Schools	45
State Spending on Education	47
State and Local Government Spending on Education	33
Higher Education Tuition and Fees	29
Higher Education Revenue	48
Federal Spending on Higher Education	5
State Spending on Higher Education	39
State and Local Government Spending on Higher Education	36
State and Local Appropriations for Higher Education	43
Federal Spending on Higher Education Act Insured Loans	18
Federal Spending on National Guaranteed Student Loans	1
Federal Spending on Pell Grants	3
Default Rate in Perkins Student Loan Program	37
State Spending on Libraries	11

Energy
State Ranking

Total Spending on Energy	26
Net Generation of Electricity	36
Cost of Electricity	28
Spending on Electricity	48
Spending on Natural Gas	38
Spending on Gasoline	5
Spending on Petroleum	10
Spending on Coal	37
Total Energy Consumption	35
Electricity Consumption	39
Natural Gas Consumption	40
Petroleum Consumption	15
Coal Consumption	35
Power Plants	11
Nuclear Power Plants	34
Hydroelectric Power Plants	15

Environment
State Ranking

Federally Owned Land (acreage)	24
Loss of Wetlands	36
Environmental Protection Agency Spending	8
EPA Abatement, Control, and Compliance	10
State Spending on Environmental Programs	26
Environmental Programs as Part of State Budget	18
State Spending on Forest Programs	16
Total Tree Planting	34
Federal Tree Planting	25
Private Tree Planting	35
State Spending on Air Quality	18
State Spending on Water Quality	27
Federal Grants for Rural Water and Waste Disposal	2
Federal Spending on Wastewater Treatment Works	7
Hazardous Waste Sites on National Priority List	45

Federal Grants for Hazardous Substance
Response | 37
State Spending on Hazardous Waste | NA

Health

	State Ranking
State Health Rankings	26
State Spending on Health	22
Support for Public Health	49
Family and Business Spending on Health Care	32
HMO Enrollment	41
Medicaid Recipients	38
Medically Underserved Population	39
Lack of Health Care Access	4
Active Nonfederal Physicians	48
Active Nonfederal Nurses	11
Active Nonfederal Dentists	33
Average Cost per Hospital Stay	47
Average Cost per Day for Hospital Care	51
Average Cost per Day for Hospital Room	46
State Spending on Hospitals	42
Adequacy of Prenatal Care	35
Infants Born Receiving Late or No Prenatal Care	26
Infants Born with Low Birth Weight	46
Abortions	50
Immunizations of Two-Year-Olds	—
Overall Risk for Heart Disease	19
Risk Factor for Heart Disease (hypertension)	30
Deaths Due to Heart Disease	11
New Cancer Cases	29
Deaths Due to Cancer	34
Prevalence of Smoking	47
Prevalence of Diabetes	27
Deaths Due to Diabetes	24
Cost of Diabetes	25
AIDS Cases Reported	49
Gonorrhea Cases Reported	42
Syphilis Cases Reported	51
Tuberculosis Cases Reported	33
Hepatitis Cases Reported	10
Rabies Cases Reported	5
Lyme Disease Cases Reported	40
Beer Consumption	23
Wine Consumption	42
Liquor Consumption	24
Alcohol and Drug Treatment Admissions	7
Federal Spending on Alcohol, Drug Abuse, and Mental Health	9
Total Spending on Alcohol/Drug Abuse Services	33
State Spending on Alcohol/Drug Abuse Services	41
Hard-Core Cocaine Users	50
Federal Drug Grants to States	7

Population

	State Ranking
Population	45
Population Density	47
Population in Metropolitan Areas	48
Population Under 18 Years Old	8
Population Over 65 Years Old	7
White Population	16
African American Population	47
Hispanic Population	44
Asian American Population	50
Native American Population	4
Catholic Population	18

Jewish Population	50
Marriages	11
Divorces	39
Births	21
Births to Single Mothers	38
Births to Single Teenagers	28
Adoptions	8
Adoption Option Index	3
Infant Mortality	21
Child Deaths and Suicides	12
Teen Violent Death Rate	16
Deaths	10

Recreation

	State Ranking
State Parks and Recreation Areas	4
Visitors to State Parks and Recreation Areas	4
Revenues from State Parks and Recreation Areas	8
Spending on State Arts Agencies	33
Domestic Travel Spending	29
State Travel Office Budgets	5
Lodging Industry (rooms)	12
Participation in Exercise Walking	25
Participation in Swimming	49
Participation in Camping	35
Participation in Bowling	44
Bowling League Membership	6
Participation in Running/Jogging	41
Participation in Aerobics	32
Participation in Golf	38
Participation in Softball	47
Participation in Health Clubs	31
Participation in Tennis	45
Participation in Hunting	19
Participation in Baseball	31
Participation in Bicycle Riding	30
Number of Boats	22
Attendance at Parimutuel Racing	7
Revenue from Parimutuel Betting	35

Social Services

	State Ranking
Federal Grants for Social Services	7
State Spending on Public Welfare	45
Persons in Poverty	25
Public Aid Recipients	41
Participants in Food Stamp Program	25
Households in Food Stamp Program	34
Percentage of Poor Using AFDC and Food Stamps	25
Federal Spending on Children and Family Services	4
Federal Women, Infants, and Children Food Program	3
Child Welfare Services	25
Child Abuse Cases Reported	—
Children in Poverty	14
Children Without Health Insurance	23
Children Who Are Hungry or at Risk	18
Federal Spending on Child Nutrition Programs	6
Federal Spending on Special Milk Program	24
National School Lunch Program Participants	7
Head Start Enrollment	41
Head Start Spending	29
Federal Spending on Rehabilitation Services/Handicapped Research	11

State Government

	State Ranking
Financial World's State Rankings	32
Salaries of State Officials (governor)	48
Salaries of State Legislators	39
Women in State Legislatures	24
African Americans in State Legislatures	38
Hispanics in State Legislatures	21
Asian Americans in State Legislatures	6
Native Americans in State Legislatures	5
Turnover in State Legislatures	8
Length of State Legislative Sessions	38
State Bills in Regular Session	3
State Resolutions in Regular Session	45
State Bills in Special Session	13
State Resolutions in Special Session	19
Women in State Cabinets	21
Total Federal Funding to State Governments	16
Total State Spending	35
State General Expenditures	29
State Debt	11
State Spending on Interest on the General Debt	5
Total State Tax Revenue	49
State Revenue from Tax on Sales and Gross Receipts	24
State Revenue from General Sales Tax	29
State Revenue from Licenses	15
State Revenue from Motor Vehicle Licenses	10
State Revenue from Individual Income Taxes	—
State Revenue from Corporation Net Income Taxes	29
State Revenue from Severance Taxes	18
State Revenue from Property Taxes	—
State Revenue from Death and Gift Taxes	8
State Revenue from Documentary and Stock Transfers	20
State Revenue from Tax on Motor Fuels	11
State Revenue from Tax on Tobacco Products	29
Excise Tax on Cigarettes	24
Excise Tax on Gasoline	22
State Revenue from Lotteries	10

Transportation

	State Ranking
Motor Vehicle Registrations	3
Automobile Registrations	19
Bus and Truck Registrations	3
Motorcycle Registrations	4
Driver Licenses	18
Federal Spending on Highway Trust Fund	9
Federal Spending on Mass Transportation	37
State Spending on Highways	8
Highway Deficiency	21
Bridge Deficiency	26
Traffic Fatalities	16
Traffic Fatalities per Miles Traveled	18
Motorcyclist Fatalities	20
Pedalcyclist Fatalities	4
Pedestrian Fatalities	38
Registered Aircraft	9
Registered Pilots	15
Federal Spending on Airport and Airway Trust Fund	11
Aircraft Fatalities	43

— *not applicable* NA *not available*

Agriculture
State Ranking

Farm Acreage	26
Farmland as Portion of State	20
Net Farm Income	38
Government Payments to Farms	28
Federal Commodity Loans/Price Supports	28
Federal Spending on Rural Development	11
Rural Electric and Telephone Loan Guarantees	8
Foreign-Owned Agricultural Land	23

Business and Economy
State Ranking

Gross State Product	33
Retail Sales	41
Supermarket Sales	50
Commercial Bank Assets	32
Insured Commercial Bank Deposits	32
Fortune 500 Companies	41
Inc. 500 Companies	27
New Business Incorporations	39
Business Failures	12
Financial Aid to Minority Businesses	24
Women-Owned Businesses	49
Sales & Receipts of Women-Owned Businesses	44
African American-Owned Businesses	11
Sales & Receipts of African American-Owned Businesses	13
Hispanic-Owned Businesses	48
Sales & Receipts of Hispanic-Owned Businesses	42
Employees in Manufacturing	14
Manufacturing Shipments	12
Japanese-Owned U.S. Manufacturing Plants	11
Exports to Mexico	11
Change in Exports to Mexico	19
Existing Home Sales	7
Housing Starts	17
Average Annual Pay	30
Disposable Personal Income	35
Median Income of Families with Children	43
Federal Spending on Unemployment Insurance/Employment Services	48
Teen Unemployment	27
Bankruptcy Petitions Filed	1
Patents Issued to State Residents	37
Federal Spending on Community Development	15
Federal Spending on Economic Development Administration	24
Federal Spending on Urban Development Action Grants	14

Crime and Criminal Justice
State Ranking

Total Crimes	27
Violent Crimes	16
Murders	15
Rapes	14
Aggravated Assaults	15
Property Crimes	28
Robberies	17
Burglaries	13
Larcenies and Thefts	41
Motor Vehicle Thefts	15
State and Federal Prisoners	30
Capital Punishment	17
State Spending on Corrections	11
State Spending on Police	43
Inmates in Local Jails	6
Spending on Local Jails	10
Spending per Inmate for Local Jails	33
Employees at Local Jails	2
Juvenile Custody Rate	48
Federal Spending on Office of Justice Assistance Programs	16

Defense
State Ranking

Defense Grants to State and Local Governments	25
Total Defense Payroll	40
Total Army Payroll	29
Total Navy/Marine Corps Payroll	18
Total Air Force Payroll	39
Total Active-Duty Payroll	39
Army Active-Duty Payroll	32
Navy/Marine Corps Active-Duty Payroll	15
Air Force Active-Duty Payroll	44
Total Civilian Payroll	43
Army Civilian Payroll	36
Navy/Marine Corps Civilian Payroll	23
Air Force Civilian Payroll	43
Total Reserve and National Guard Payroll	35
Army Reserve and National Guard Payroll	37
Navy/Marine Corps Reserve and National Guard Payroll	7
Air Force Reserve and National Guard Payroll	28
Total Retired Military Payroll	25
Army Retired Military Payroll	20
Navy/Marine Corps Retired Military Payroll	17
Air Force Retired Military Payroll	34
Total Defense Prime Contracts	20
Army Prime Contracts	36
Navy/Marine Corps Prime Contracts	33
Air Force Prime Contracts	6
U.S. Military Installations	25
Construction of National Guard Centers	25

Education
State Ranking

School Age Population	36
Public Elementary and Secondary School Enrollment	16
Average Daily Attendance	25
Student-Teacher Ratio	9
Salaries of Public School Teachers	36
Public School Teachers Who Are Male	39
Eighth Grade Math Test Results	—
High School Math Enrollment	31
Public High School Graduation Rate	41
General Educational Development (GED) Test Results	27
Adult Illiteracy	5
Federal Revenue for Public Schools	13
State Revenue for Public Schools	26
Local Government Revenue for Public Schools	27
Total Public School Spending	43
Public School Spending on Instruction	23
Public School Spending on Noninstruction	9
Public School Spending on Support Staff	51
State and Local Government Spending on Public Schools	46
Federal Spending on School Improvement Programs	27
Gifted and Talented Students	34
Federal Spending on Education of Students with Disabilities	24
Student-Teacher Ratio in Catholic Elementary Schools	36
Student-Teacher Ratio in Catholic Secondary Schools	30
State Spending on Education	46
State and Local Government Spending on Education	38
Higher Education Tuition and Fees	23
Higher Education Revenue	21
Federal Spending on Higher Education	25
State Spending on Higher Education	27
State and Local Government Spending on Higher Education	22
State and Local Appropriations for Higher Education	26
Federal Spending on Higher Education Act Insured Loans	31
Federal Spending on National Guaranteed Student Loans	40
Federal Spending on Pell Grants	29
Default Rate in Perkins Student Loan Program	10
State Spending on Libraries	30

Energy
State Ranking

Total Spending on Energy	16
Net Generation of Electricity	16
Cost of Electricity	44
Spending on Electricity	7
Spending on Natural Gas	37
Spending on Gasoline	11
Spending on Petroleum	29
Spending on Coal	13
Total Energy Consumption	17
Electricity Consumption	8
Natural Gas Consumption	34
Petroleum Consumption	32
Coal Consumption	12
Power Plants	42
Nuclear Power Plants	28
Hydroelectric Power Plants	20

Environment
State Ranking

Federally Owned Land (acreage)	28
Loss of Wetlands	13
Environmental Protection Agency Spending	44
EPA Abatement, Control, and Compliance	44
State Spending on Environmental Programs	41
Environmental Programs as Part of State Budget	35
State Spending on Forest Programs	22
Total Tree Planting	14
Federal Tree Planting	14
Private Tree Planting	13
State Spending on Air Quality	39
State Spending on Water Quality	29
Federal Grants for Rural Water and Waste Disposal	35
Federal Spending on Wastewater Treatment Works	39
Hazardous Waste Sites on National Priority List	25

Federal Grants for Hazardous Substance
Response 44
State Spending on Hazardous Waste 26

Health
State Ranking

State Health Rankings 39
State Spending on Health 36
Support for Public Health 21
Family and Business Spending on Health
Care 41
HMO Enrollment 40
Medicaid Recipients 7
Medically Underserved Population 15
Lack of Health Care Access 17
Active Nonfederal Physicians 22
Active Nonfederal Nurses 35
Active Nonfederal Dentists 27
Average Cost per Hospital Stay 35
Average Cost per Day for Hospital Care 29
Average Cost per Day for Hospital Room 49
State Spending on Hospitals 29
Adequacy of Prenatal Care 31
Infants Born Receiving Late or No
Prenatal Care 28
Infants Born with Low Birth Weight 7
Abortions 27
Immunizations of Two-Year-Olds —
Overall Risk for Heart Disease 38
Risk Factor for Heart Disease
(hypertension) 5
Deaths Due to Heart Disease 16
New Cancer Cases 16
Deaths Due to Cancer 16
Prevalence of Smoking 4
Prevalence of Diabetes 16
Deaths Due to Diabetes 31
Cost of Diabetes 15
AIDS Cases Reported 30
Gonorrhea Cases Reported 9
Syphilis Cases Reported 11
Tuberculosis Cases Reported 17
Hepatitis Cases Reported 3
Rabies Cases Reported 30
Lyme Disease Cases Reported 23
Beer Consumption 39
Wine Consumption 44
Liquor Consumption 41
Alcohol and Drug Treatment Admissions 48
Federal Spending on Alcohol, Drug
Abuse, and Mental Health 34
Total Spending on Alcohol/Drug Abuse
Services 34
State Spending on Alcohol/Drug Abuse
Services 35
Hard-Core Cocaine Users 20
Federal Drug Grants to States 43

Population
State Ranking

Population 17
Population Density 20
Population in Metropolitan Areas 25
Population Under 18 Years Old 37
Population Over 65 Years Old 25
White Population 30
African American Population 11
Hispanic Population 46
Asian American Population 40
Native American Population 41
Catholic Population 49

Jewish Population 35
Marriages 7
Divorces 6
Births 38
Births to Single Mothers 12
Births to Single Teenagers 11
Adoptions 33
Adoption Option Index 28
Infant Mortality 13
Child Deaths and Suicides 39
Teen Violent Death Rate 18
Deaths 16

Recreation
State Ranking

State Parks and Recreation Areas 28
Visitors to State Parks and Recreation
Areas 10
Revenues from State Parks and
Recreation Areas 11
Spending on State Arts Agencies 23
Domestic Travel Spending 18
State Travel Office Budgets 18
Lodging Industry (rooms) 14
Participation in Exercise Walking 10
Participation in Swimming 25
Participation in Camping 39
Participation in Bowling 36
Bowling League Membership 42
Participation in Running/Jogging 22
Participation in Aerobics 44
Participation in Golf 34
Participation in Softball 27
Participation in Health Clubs 36
Participation in Tennis 37
Participation in Hunting 27
Participation in Baseball 13
Participation in Bicycle Riding 38
Number of Boats 24
Attendance at Parimutuel Racing —
Revenue from Parimutuel Betting —

Social Services
State Ranking

Federal Grants for Social Services 15
State Spending on Public Welfare 28
Persons in Poverty 15
Public Aid Recipients 10
Participants in Food Stamp Program 9
Households in Food Stamp Program 7
Percentage of Poor Using AFDC and
Food Stamps 48
Federal Spending on Children and
Family Services 28
Federal Women, Infants, and Children
Food Program 18
Child Welfare Services 38
Child Abuse Cases Reported —
Children in Poverty 13
Children Without Health Insurance 20
Children Who Are Hungry or at Risk 10
Federal Spending on Child Nutrition
Programs 18
Federal Spending on Special Milk
Program —
National School Lunch Program
Participants 15
Head Start Enrollment 24
Head Start Spending 30
Federal Spending on Rehabilitation
Services/Handicapped Research 15

State Government
State Ranking

Financial World's State Rankings 6
Salaries of State Officials (governor) 20
Salaries of State Legislators 24
Women in State Legislatures 42
African Americans in State Legislatures 11
Hispanics in State Legislatures 21
Asian Americans in State Legislatures 6
Native Americans in State Legislatures 12
Turnover in State Legislatures 21
Length of State Legislative Sessions 42
State Bills in Regular Session 29
State Resolutions in Regular Session 8
State Bills in Special Session —
State Resolutions in Special Session —
Women in State Cabinets 27
Total Federal Funding to State
Governments 22
Total State Spending 41
State General Expenditures 37
State Debt 45
State Spending on Interest on the
General Debt 45
Total State Tax Revenue 48
State Revenue from Tax on Sales and
Gross Receipts 13
State Revenue from General Sales Tax 10
State Revenue from Licenses 16
State Revenue from Motor Vehicle
Licenses 39
State Revenue from Individual Income
Taxes 43
State Revenue from Corporation Net
Income Taxes 23
State Revenue from Severance Taxes 28
State Revenue from Property Taxes —
State Revenue from Death and Gift
Taxes 30
State Revenue from Documentary and
Stock Transfers 11
State Revenue from Tax on Motor Fuels 3
State Revenue from Tax on Tobacco
Products 37
Excise Tax on Cigarettes 42
Excise Tax on Gasoline 10
State Revenue from Lotteries —

Transportation
State Ranking

Motor Vehicle Registrations 7
Automobile Registrations 2
Bus and Truck Registrations 31
Motorcycle Registrations 29
Driver Licenses 25
Federal Spending on Highway Trust
Fund 35
Federal Spending on Mass
Transportation 30
State Spending on Highways 24
Highway Deficiency 17
Bridge Deficiency 22
Traffic Fatalities 11
Traffic Fatalities per Miles Traveled 11
Motorcyclist Fatalities 30
Pedalcyclist Fatalities 42
Pedestrian Fatalities 20
Registered Aircraft 36
Registered Pilots 29
Federal Spending on Airport and
Airway Trust Fund 8
Aircraft Fatalities 36

— not applicable NA not available

Agriculture *State Ranking*

Farm Acreage 1
Farmland as Portion of State 7
Net Farm Income 25
Government Payments to Farms 15
Federal Commodity Loans/Price
 Supports 13
Federal Spending on Rural
 Development 30
Rural Electric and Telephone Loan
 Guarantees 24
Foreign-Owned Agricultural Land 25

Business and Economy *State Ranking*

Gross State Product 20
Retail Sales 20
Supermarket Sales 13
Commercial Bank Assets 31
Insured Commercial Bank Deposits 27
Fortune 500 Companies 17
Inc. 500 Companies 16
New Business Incorporations 28
Business Failures 11
Financial Aid to Minority Businesses 4
Women-Owned Businesses 30
Sales & Receipts of Women-Owned
 Businesses 50
African American-Owned Businesses 14
Sales & Receipts of African American-
 Owned Businesses 18
Hispanic-Owned Businesses 2
Sales & Receipts of Hispanic-Owned
 Businesses 3
Employees in Manufacturing 6
Manufacturing Shipments 20
Japanese-Owned U.S. Manufacturing
 Plants 8
Exports to Mexico 1
Change in Exports to Mexico 25
Existing Home Sales 35
Housing Starts 32
Average Annual Pay 18
Disposable Personal Income 29
Median Income of Families with
 Children 34
Federal Spending on Unemployment
 Insurance/Employment Services 47
Teen Unemployment 15
Bankruptcy Petitions Filed 30
Patents Issued to State Residents 23
Federal Spending on Community
 Development 20
Federal Spending on Economic
 Development Administration 25
Federal Spending on Urban
 Development Action Grants 31

Crime and Criminal Justice *State Ranking*

Total Crimes 3
Violent Crimes 10
Murders 3
Rapes 7
Aggravated Assaults 12
Property Crimes 3
Robberies 9
Burglaries 3
Larcenies and Thefts 5
Motor Vehicle Thefts 4
State and Federal Prisoners 20
Capital Punishment 1

State Spending on Corrections 28
State Spending on Police 45
Inmates in Local Jails 8
Spending on Local Jails 18
Spending per Inmate for Local Jails 35
Employees at Local Jails 6
Juvenile Custody Rate 36
Federal Spending on Office of Justice
 Assistance Programs 34

Defense *State Ranking*

Defense Grants to State and Local
 Governments 23
Total Defense Payroll 25
Total Army Payroll 15
Total Navy/Marine Corps Payroll 29
Total Air Force Payroll 17
Total Active-Duty Payroll 22
Army Active-Duty Payroll 13
Navy/Marine Corps Active-Duty Payroll 23
Air Force Active-Duty Payroll 21
Total Civilian Payroll 24
Army Civilian Payroll 21
Navy/Marine Corps Civilian Payroll 29
Air Force Civilian Payroll 13
Total Reserve and National Guard
 Payroll 42
Army Reserve and National Guard
 Payroll 42
Navy/Marine Corps Reserve and
 National Guard Payroll 20
Air Force Reserve and National Guard
 Payroll 40
Total Retired Military Payroll 11
Army Retired Military Payroll 11
Navy/Marine Corps Retired Military
 Payroll 26
Air Force Retired Military Payroll 7
Total Defense Prime Contracts 14
Army Prime Contracts 15
Navy/Marine Corps Prime Contracts 19
Air Force Prime Contracts 7
U.S. Military Installations 3
Construction of National Guard Centers 22

Education *State Ranking*

School Age Population 10
Public Elementary and Secondary
 School Enrollment 2
Average Daily Attendance NA
Student-Teacher Ratio 38
Salaries of Public School Teachers 38
Public School Teachers Who Are Male 41
Eighth Grade Math Test Results 26
High School Math Enrollment 5
Public High School Graduation Rate 46
General Educational Development
 (GED) Test Results 40
Adult Illiteracy 1
Federal Revenue for Public Schools 19
State Revenue for Public Schools 34
Local Government Revenue for Public
 Schools 23
Total Public School Spending 37
Public School Spending on Instruction 42
Public School Spending on
 Noninstruction 12
Public School Spending on Support
 Staff 33
State and Local Government Spending
 on Public Schools 1

Federal Spending on School
 Improvement Programs 21
Gifted and Talented Students 10
Federal Spending on Education of
 Students with Disabilities 30
Student-Teacher Ratio in Catholic
 Elementary Schools 34
Student-Teacher Ratio in Catholic
 Secondary Schools 36
State Spending on Education 39
State and Local Government Spending
 on Education 3
Higher Education Tuition and Fees 43
Higher Education Revenue 31
Federal Spending on Higher Education 39
State Spending on Higher Education 31
State and Local Government Spending
 on Higher Education 23
State and Local Appropriations for
 Higher Education 15
Federal Spending on Higher Education
 Act Insured Loans 24
Federal Spending on National
 Guaranteed Student Loans 29
Federal Spending on Pell Grants 30
Default Rate in Perkins Student Loan
 Program 6
State Spending on Libraries 49

Energy *State Ranking*

Total Spending on Energy 4
Net Generation of Electricity 20
Cost of Electricity 30
Spending on Electricity 11
Spending on Natural Gas 2
Spending on Gasoline 13
Spending on Petroleum 5
Spending on Coal 26
Total Energy Consumption 4
Electricity Consumption 12
Natural Gas Consumption 4
Petroleum Consumption 5
Coal Consumption 28
Power Plants 39
Nuclear Power Plants 32
Hydroelectric Power Plants 38

Environment *State Ranking*

Federally Owned Land (acreage) 40
Loss of Wetlands 18
Environmental Protection Agency
 Spending 45
EPA Abatement, Control, and
 Compliance 49
State Spending on Environmental
 Programs 50
Environmental Programs as Part of State
 Budget 49
State Spending on Forest Programs 44
Total Tree Planting 16
Federal Tree Planting 20
Private Tree Planting 15
State Spending on Air Quality 36
State Spending on Water Quality 50
Federal Grants for Rural Water and
 Waste Disposal 37
Federal Spending on Wastewater
 Treatment Works 47
Hazardous Waste Sites on National
 Priority List 13

Federal Grants for Hazardous Substance
  Response 8
State Spending on Hazardous Waste 44

Health   State Ranking

State Health Rankings 26
State Spending on Health 48
Support for Public Health 43
Family and Business Spending on Health
  Care 23
HMO Enrollment 29
Medicaid Recipients 21
Medically Underserved Population 10
Lack of Health Care Access 25
Active Nonfederal Physicians 32
Active Nonfederal Nurses 46
Active Nonfederal Dentists 40
Average Cost per Hospital Stay 21
Average Cost per Day for Hospital Care 13
Average Cost per Day for Hospital Room 36
State Spending on Hospitals 32
Adequacy of Prenatal Care 48
Infants Born Receiving Late or No
  Prenatal Care 4
Infants Born with Low Birth Weight 28
Abortions 19
Immunizations of Two-Year-Olds —
Overall Risk for Heart Disease 15
Risk Factor for Heart Disease
  (hypertension) 24
Deaths Due to Heart Disease 42
New Cancer Cases 46
Deaths Due to Cancer 44
Prevalence of Smoking 27
Prevalence of Diabetes 44
Deaths Due to Diabetes 44
Cost of Diabetes 44
AIDS Cases Reported 12
Gonorrhea Cases Reported 24
Syphilis Cases Reported 16
Tuberculosis Cases Reported 6
Hepatitis Cases Reported 22
Rabies Cases Reported 23
Lyme Disease Cases Reported 27
Beer Consumption 4
Wine Consumption 30
Liquor Consumption 43
Alcohol and Drug Treatment Admissions 47
Federal Spending on Alcohol, Drug
  Abuse, and Mental Health 31
Total Spending on Alcohol/Drug Abuse
  Services 49
State Spending on Alcohol/Drug Abuse
  Services 42
Hard-Core Cocaine Users 11
Federal Drug Grants to States 32

Population   State Ranking

Population 3
Population Density 30
Population in Metropolitan Areas 14
Population Under 18 Years Old 9
Population Over 65 Years Old 47
White Population 41
African American Population 18
Hispanic Population 3
Asian American Population 14
Native American Population 29
Catholic Population 21

Jewish Population 26
Marriages 13
Divorces 12
Births 4
Births to Single Mothers 48
Births to Single Teenagers 31
Adoptions 19
Adoption Option Index 19
Infant Mortality 36
Child Deaths and Suicides 20
Teen Violent Death Rate 17
Deaths 43

Recreation   State Ranking

State Parks and Recreation Areas 30
Visitors to State Parks and Recreation
  Areas 45
Revenues from State Parks and
  Recreation Areas 39
Spending on State Arts Agencies 51
Domestic Travel Spending 35
State Travel Office Budgets 34
Lodging Industry (rooms) 26
Participation in Exercise Walking 24
Participation in Swimming 37
Participation in Camping 22
Participation in Bowling 35
Bowling League Membership 40
Participation in Running/Jogging 13
Participation in Aerobics 20
Participation in Golf 26
Participation in Softball 37
Participation in Health Clubs 29
Participation in Tennis 27
Participation in Hunting 26
Participation in Baseball 25
Participation in Bicycle Riding 39
Number of Boats 35
Attendance at Parimutuel Racing 31
Revenue from Parimutuel Betting 33

Social Services   State Ranking

Federal Grants for Social Services 18
State Spending on Public Welfare 44
Persons in Poverty 8
Public Aid Recipients 27
Participants in Food Stamp Program 5
Households in Food Stamp Program 8
Percentage of Poor Using AFDC and
  Food Stamps 49
Federal Spending on Children and
  Family Services 44
Federal Women, Infants, and Children
  Food Program 24
Child Welfare Services 9
Child Abuse Cases Reported —
Children in Poverty 8
Children Without Health Insurance 1
Children Who Are Hungry or at Risk 16
Federal Spending on Child Nutrition
  Programs 8
Federal Spending on Special Milk
  Program 46
National School Lunch Program
  Participants 5
Head Start Enrollment 48
Head Start Spending 34
Federal Spending on Rehabilitation
  Services/Handicapped Research 31

State Government   State Ranking

Financial World's State Rankings 27
Salaries of State Officials (governor) 14
Salaries of State Legislators 36
Women in State Legislatures 36
African Americans in State Legislatures 16
Hispanics in State Legislatures 2
Asian Americans in State Legislatures 6
Native Americans in State Legislatures 12
Turnover in State Legislatures 16
Length of State Legislative Sessions 7
State Bills in Regular Session 28
State Resolutions in Regular Session 6
State Bills in Special Session 28
State Resolutions in Special Session 8
Women in State Cabinets —
Total Federal Funding to State
  Governments 39
Total State Spending 48
State General Expenditures 48
State Debt 49
State Spending on Interest on the
  General Debt 47
Total State Tax Revenue 47
State Revenue from Tax on Sales and
  Gross Receipts 8
State Revenue from General Sales Tax 9
State Revenue from Licenses 13
State Revenue from Motor Vehicle
  Licenses 21
State Revenue from Individual Income
  Taxes —
State Revenue from Corporation Net
  Income Taxes —
State Revenue from Severance Taxes 9
State Revenue from Property Taxes —
State Revenue from Death and Gift
  Taxes 33
State Revenue from Documentary and
  Stock Transfers —
State Revenue from Tax on Motor Fuels 34
State Revenue from Tax on Tobacco
  Products 3
Excise Tax on Cigarettes 2
Excise Tax on Gasoline 35
State Revenue from Lotteries —

Transportation   State Ranking

Motor Vehicle Registrations 36
Automobile Registrations 42
Bus and Truck Registrations 21
Motorcycle Registrations 40
Driver Licenses 40
Federal Spending on Highway Trust
  Fund 34
Federal Spending on Mass
  Transportation 51
State Spending on Highways 44
Highway Deficiency 41
Bridge Deficiency 35
Traffic Fatalities 23
Traffic Fatalities per Miles Traveled 29
Motorcyclist Fatalities 45
Pedalcyclist Fatalities 21
Pedestrian Fatalities 9
Registered Aircraft 24
Registered Pilots 24
Federal Spending on Airport and
  Airway Trust Fund 25
Aircraft Fatalities 38

— not applicable   NA not available

Agriculture
State Ranking

Farm Acreage	28
Farmland as Portion of State	42
Net Farm Income	31
Government Payments to Farms	24
Federal Commodity Loans/Price Supports	8
Federal Spending on Rural Development	18
Rural Electric and Telephone Loan Guarantees	35
Foreign-Owned Agricultural Land	34

Business and Economy
State Ranking

Gross State Product	44
Retail Sales	21
Supermarket Sales	31
Commercial Bank Assets	48
Insured Commercial Bank Deposits	49
Fortune 500 Companies	36
Inc. 500 Companies	4
New Business Incorporations	12
Business Failures	26
Financial Aid to Minority Businesses	27
Women-Owned Businesses	27
Sales & Receipts of Women-Owned Businesses	32
African American-Owned Businesses	46
Sales & Receipts of African American-Owned Businesses	48
Hispanic-Owned Businesses	16
Sales & Receipts of Hispanic-Owned Businesses	18
Employees in Manufacturing	35
Manufacturing Shipments	38
Japanese-Owned U.S. Manufacturing Plants	39
Exports to Mexico	39
Change in Exports to Mexico	47
Existing Home Sales	30
Housing Starts	14
Average Annual Pay	38
Disposable Personal Income	50
Median Income of Families with Children	22
Federal Spending on Unemployment Insurance/Employment Services	7
Teen Unemployment	42
Bankruptcy Petitions Filed	11
Patents Issued to State Residents	14
Federal Spending on Community Development	48
Federal Spending on Economic Development Administration	31
Federal Spending on Urban Development Action Grants	21

Crime and Criminal Justice
State Ranking

Total Crimes	23
Violent Crimes	42
Murders	44
Rapes	17
Aggravated Assaults	41
Property Crimes	14
Robberies	40
Burglaries	38
Larcenies and Thefts	4
Motor Vehicle Thefts	39
State and Federal Prisoners	43
Capital Punishment	12

State Spending on Corrections	25
State Spending on Police	23
Inmates in Local Jails	37
Spending on Local Jails	37
Spending per Inmate for Local Jails	26
Employees at Local Jails	26
Juvenile Custody Rate	47
Federal Spending on Office of Justice Assistance Programs	20

Defense
State Ranking

Defense Grants to State and Local Governments	21
Total Defense Payroll	11
Total Army Payroll	18
Total Navy/Marine Corps Payroll	42
Total Air Force Payroll	5
Total Active-Duty Payroll	32
Army Active-Duty Payroll	23
Navy/Marine Corps Active-Duty Payroll	42
Air Force Active-Duty Payroll	20
Total Civilian Payroll	4
Army Civilian Payroll	8
Navy/Marine Corps Civilian Payroll	34
Air Force Civilian Payroll	1
Total Reserve and National Guard Payroll	3
Army Reserve and National Guard Payroll	2
Navy/Marine Corps Reserve and National Guard Payroll	24
Air Force Reserve and National Guard Payroll	5
Total Retired Military Payroll	33
Army Retired Military Payroll	33
Navy/Marine Corps Retired Military Payroll	39
Air Force Retired Military Payroll	23
Total Defense Prime Contracts	15
Army Prime Contracts	20
Navy/Marine Corps Prime Contracts	23
Air Force Prime Contracts	16
U.S. Military Installations	27
Construction of National Guard Centers	17

Education
State Ranking

School Age Population	1
Public Elementary and Secondary School Enrollment	32
Average Daily Attendance	18
Student-Teacher Ratio	1
Salaries of Public School Teachers	45
Public School Teachers Who Are Male	12
Eighth Grade Math Test Results	—
High School Math Enrollment	NA
Public High School Graduation Rate	9
General Educational Development (GED) Test Results	51
Adult Illiteracy	50
Federal Revenue for Public Schools	21
State Revenue for Public Schools	15
Local Government Revenue for Public Schools	37
Total Public School Spending	51
Public School Spending on Instruction	3
Public School Spending on Noninstruction	11
Public School Spending on Support Staff	49
State and Local Government Spending on Public Schools	26

Federal Spending on School Improvement Programs	9
Gifted and Talented Students	NA
Federal Spending on Education of Students with Disabilities	4
Student-Teacher Ratio in Catholic Elementary Schools	6
Student-Teacher Ratio in Catholic Secondary Schools	15
State Spending on Education	7
State and Local Government Spending on Education	2
Higher Education Tuition and Fees	44
Higher Education Revenue	20
Federal Spending on Higher Education	32
State Spending on Higher Education	4
State and Local Government Spending on Higher Education	1
State and Local Appropriations for Higher Education	16
Federal Spending on Higher Education Act Insured Loans	13
Federal Spending on National Guaranteed Student Loans	14
Federal Spending on Pell Grants	2
Default Rate in Perkins Student Loan Program	51
State Spending on Libraries	33

Energy
State Ranking

Total Spending on Energy	48
Net Generation of Electricity	10
Cost of Electricity	40
Spending on Electricity	51
Spending on Natural Gas	24
Spending on Gasoline	46
Spending on Petroleum	43
Spending on Coal	7
Total Energy Consumption	27
Electricity Consumption	40
Natural Gas Consumption	14
Petroleum Consumption	37
Coal Consumption	6
Power Plants	9
Nuclear Power Plants	34
Hydroelectric Power Plants	5

Environment
State Ranking

Federally Owned Land (acreage)	3
Loss of Wetlands	40
Environmental Protection Agency Spending	48
EPA Abatement, Control, and Compliance	26
State Spending on Environmental Programs	24
Environmental Programs as Part of State Budget	19
State Spending on Forest Programs	NA
Total Tree Planting	46
Federal Tree Planting	29
Private Tree Planting	45
State Spending on Air Quality	14
State Spending on Water Quality	21
Federal Grants for Rural Water and Waste Disposal	46
Federal Spending on Wastewater Treatment Works	48
Hazardous Waste Sites on National Priority List	27

Federal Grants for Hazardous Substance
  Response   23
State Spending on Hazardous Waste   29

Health   *State Ranking*

State Health Rankings	5
State Spending on Health	34
Support for Public Health	26
Family and Business Spending on Health Care	38
HMO Enrollment	14
Medicaid Recipients	46
Medically Underserved Population	33
Lack of Health Care Access	29
Active Nonfederal Physicians	28
Active Nonfederal Nurses	44
Active Nonfederal Dentists	9
Average Cost per Hospital Stay	30
Average Cost per Day for Hospital Care	6
Average Cost per Day for Hospital Room	7
State Spending on Hospitals	13
Adequacy of Prenatal Care	19
Infants Born Receiving Late or No Prenatal Care	49
Infants Born with Low Birth Weight	39
Abortions	44
Immunizations of Two-Year-Olds	—
Overall Risk for Heart Disease	3
Risk Factor for Heart Disease (hypertension)	30
Deaths Due to Heart Disease	50
New Cancer Cases	50
Deaths Due to Cancer	50
Prevalence of Smoking	50
Prevalence of Diabetes	50
Deaths Due to Diabetes	49
Cost of Diabetes	50
AIDS Cases Reported	33
Gonorrhea Cases Reported	43
Syphilis Cases Reported	45
Tuberculosis Cases Reported	37
Hepatitis Cases Reported	9
Rabies Cases Reported	39
Lyme Disease Cases Reported	31
Beer Consumption	51
Wine Consumption	47
Liquor Consumption	50
Alcohol and Drug Treatment Admissions	20
Federal Spending on Alcohol, Drug Abuse, and Mental Health	13
Total Spending on Alcohol/Drug Abuse Services	21
State Spending on Alcohol/Drug Abuse Services	21
Hard-Core Cocaine Users	17
Federal Drug Grants to States	11

Population   *State Ranking*

Population	35
Population Density	42
Population in Metropolitan Areas	19
Population Under 18 Years Old	1
Population Over 65 Years Old	50
White Population	11
African American Population	44
Hispanic Population	16
Asian American Population	13
Native American Population	11
Catholic Population	45

Jewish Population	43
Marriages	9
Divorces	19
Births	2
Births to Single Mothers	51
Births to Single Teenagers	51
Adoptions	3
Adoption Option Index	1
Infant Mortality	51
Child Deaths and Suicides	25
Teen Violent Death Rate	35
Deaths	50

Recreation   *State Ranking*

State Parks and Recreation Areas	11
Visitors to State Parks and Recreation Areas	19
Revenues from State Parks and Recreation Areas	18
Spending on State Arts Agencies	5
Domestic Travel Spending	13
State Travel Office Budgets	14
Lodging Industry (rooms)	16
Participation in Exercise Walking	17
Participation in Swimming	6
Participation in Camping	4
Participation in Bowling	28
Bowling League Membership	30
Participation in Running/Jogging	6
Participation in Aerobics	2
Participation in Golf	46
Participation in Softball	15
Participation in Health Clubs	45
Participation in Tennis	9
Participation in Hunting	17
Participation in Baseball	29
Participation in Bicycle Riding	7
Number of Boats	36
Attendance at Parimutuel Racing	—
Revenue from Parimutuel Betting	—

Social Services   *State Ranking*

Federal Grants for Social Services	42
State Spending on Public Welfare	46
Persons in Poverty	30
Public Aid Recipients	48
Participants in Food Stamp Program	33
Households in Food Stamp Program	31
Percentage of Poor Using AFDC and Food Stamps	23
Federal Spending on Children and Family Services	37
Federal Women, Infants, and Children Food Program	17
Child Welfare Services	4
Child Abuse Cases Reported	—
Children in Poverty	43
Children Without Health Insurance	43
Children Who Are Hungry or at Risk	34
Federal Spending on Child Nutrition Programs	13
Federal Spending on Special Milk Program	31
National School Lunch Program Participants	16
Head Start Enrollment	42
Head Start Spending	35
Federal Spending on Rehabilitation Services/Handicapped Research	22

State Government   *State Ranking*

Financial World's State Rankings	1
Salaries of State Officials (governor)	39
Salaries of State Legislators	—
Women in State Legislatures	39
African Americans in State Legislatures	43
Hispanics in State Legislatures	15
Asian Americans in State Legislatures	6
Native Americans in State Legislatures	12
Turnover in State Legislatures	15
Length of State Legislative Sessions	36
State Bills in Regular Session	9
State Resolutions in Regular Session	17
State Bills in Special Session	10
State Resolutions in Special Session	16
Women in State Cabinets	26
Total Federal Funding to State Governments	38
Total State Spending	13
State General Expenditures	11
State Debt	30
State Spending on Interest on the General Debt	20
Total State Tax Revenue	37
State Revenue from Tax on Sales and Gross Receipts	32
State Revenue from General Sales Tax	17
State Revenue from Licenses	47
State Revenue from Motor Vehicle Licenses	46
State Revenue from Individual Income Taxes	22
State Revenue from Corporation Net Income Taxes	37
State Revenue from Severance Taxes	12
State Revenue from Property Taxes	38
State Revenue from Death and Gift Taxes	49
State Revenue from Documentary and Stock Transfers	—
State Revenue from Tax on Motor Fuels	40
State Revenue from Tax on Tobacco Products	42
Excise Tax on Cigarettes	24
Excise Tax on Gasoline	17
State Revenue from Lotteries	—

Transportation   *State Ranking*

Motor Vehicle Registrations	42
Automobile Registrations	48
Bus and Truck Registrations	19
Motorcycle Registrations	32
Driver Licenses	48
Federal Spending on Highway Trust Fund	47
Federal Spending on Mass Transportation	26
State Spending on Highways	38
Highway Deficiency	42
Bridge Deficiency	39
Traffic Fatalities	33
Traffic Fatalities per Miles Traveled	32
Motorcyclist Fatalities	19
Pedalcyclist Fatalities	34
Pedestrian Fatalities	30
Registered Aircraft	26
Registered Pilots	16
Federal Spending on Airport and Airway Trust Fund	13
Aircraft Fatalities	24

— *not applicable*   NA *not available*

Agriculture
State Ranking

Farm Acreage	42
Farmland as Portion of State	40
Net Farm Income	26
Government Payments to Farms	34
Federal Commodity Loans/Price Supports	42
Federal Spending on Rural Development	18
Rural Electric and Telephone Loan Guarantees	20
Foreign-Owned Agricultural Land	6

Business and Economy
State Ranking

Gross State Product	17
Retail Sales	10
Supermarket Sales	5
Commercial Bank Assets	25
Insured Commercial Bank Deposits	18
Fortune 500 Companies	42
Inc. 500 Companies	6
New Business Incorporations	16
Business Failures	22
Financial Aid to Minority Businesses	41
Women-Owned Businesses	24
Sales & Receipts of Women-Owned Businesses	20
African American-Owned Businesses	45
Sales & Receipts of African American-Owned Businesses	44
Hispanic-Owned Businesses	43
Sales & Receipts of Hispanic-Owned Businesses	45
Employees in Manufacturing	42
Manufacturing Shipments	29
Japanese-Owned U.S. Manufacturing Plants	39
Exports to Mexico	49
Change in Exports to Mexico	3
Existing Home Sales	33
Housing Starts	25
Average Annual Pay	33
Disposable Personal Income	24
Median Income of Families with Children	17
Federal Spending on Unemployment Insurance/Employment Services	9
Teen Unemployment	40
Bankruptcy Petitions Filed	50
Patents Issued to State Residents	21
Federal Spending on Community Development	26
Federal Spending on Economic Development Administration	4
Federal Spending on Urban Development Action Grants	33

Crime and Criminal Justice
State Ranking

Total Crimes	43
Violent Crimes	50
Murders	46
Rapes	36
Aggravated Assaults	49
Property Crimes	41
Robberies	50
Burglaries	32
Larcenies and Thefts	40
Motor Vehicle Thefts	49
State and Federal Prisoners	48
Capital Punishment	—

State Spending on Corrections	38
State Spending on Police	4
Inmates in Local Jails	—
Spending on Local Jails	—
Spending per Inmate for Local Jails	—
Employees at Local Jails	—
Juvenile Custody Rate	50
Federal Spending on Office of Justice Assistance Programs	26

Defense
State Ranking

Defense Grants to State and Local Governments	48
Total Defense Payroll	45
Total Army Payroll	27
Total Navy/Marine Corps Payroll	41
Total Air Force Payroll	37
Total Active-Duty Payroll	48
Army Active-Duty Payroll	42
Navy/Marine Corps Active-Duty Payroll	46
Air Force Active-Duty Payroll	41
Total Civilian Payroll	46
Army Civilian Payroll	39
Navy/Marine Corps Civilian Payroll	49
Air Force Civilian Payroll	29
Total Reserve and National Guard Payroll	8
Army Reserve and National Guard Payroll	8
Navy/Marine Corps Reserve and National Guard Payroll	43
Air Force Reserve and National Guard Payroll	8
Total Retired Military Payroll	37
Army Retired Military Payroll	25
Navy/Marine Corps Retired Military Payroll	33
Air Force Retired Military Payroll	36
Total Defense Prime Contracts	47
Army Prime Contracts	50
Navy/Marine Corps Prime Contracts	25
Air Force Prime Contracts	34
U.S. Military Installations	51
Construction of National Guard Centers	48

Education
State Ranking

School Age Population	33
Public Elementary and Secondary School Enrollment	50
Average Daily Attendance	14
Student-Teacher Ratio	50
Salaries of Public School Teachers	25
Public School Teachers Who Are Male	8
Eighth Grade Math Test Results	—
High School Math Enrollment	NA
Public High School Graduation Rate	10
General Educational Development (GED) Test Results	11
Adult Illiteracy	35
Federal Revenue for Public Schools	46
State Revenue for Public Schools	45
Local Government Revenue for Public Schools	6
Total Public School Spending	6
Public School Spending on Instruction	22
Public School Spending on Noninstruction	46
Public School Spending on Support Staff	23
State and Local Government Spending on Public Schools	7

Federal Spending on School Improvement Programs	2
Gifted and Talented Students	NA
Federal Spending on Education of Students with Disabilities	27
Student-Teacher Ratio in Catholic Elementary Schools	51
Student-Teacher Ratio in Catholic Secondary Schools	34
State Spending on Education	11
State and Local Government Spending on Education	1
Higher Education Tuition and Fees	2
Higher Education Revenue	4
Federal Spending on Higher Education	13
State Spending on Higher Education	5
State and Local Government Spending on Higher Education	8
State and Local Appropriations for Higher Education	50
Federal Spending on Higher Education Act Insured Loans	7
Federal Spending on National Guaranteed Student Loans	10
Federal Spending on Pell Grants	35
Default Rate in Perkins Student Loan Program	23
State Spending on Libraries	12

Energy
State Ranking

Total Spending on Energy	29
Net Generation of Electricity	39
Cost of Electricity	11
Spending on Electricity	29
Spending on Natural Gas	49
Spending on Gasoline	6
Spending on Petroleum	13
Spending on Coal	49
Total Energy Consumption	46
Electricity Consumption	42
Natural Gas Consumption	49
Petroleum Consumption	29
Coal Consumption	50
Power Plants	2
Nuclear Power Plants	1
Hydroelectric Power Plants	1

Environment
State Ranking

Federally Owned Land (acreage)	23
Loss of Wetlands	35
Environmental Protection Agency Spending	13
EPA Abatement, Control, and Compliance	2
State Spending on Environmental Programs	14
Environmental Programs as Part of State Budget	15
State Spending on Forest Programs	10
Total Tree Planting	48
Federal Tree Planting	29
Private Tree Planting	50
State Spending on Air Quality	12
State Spending on Water Quality	40
Federal Grants for Rural Water and Waste Disposal	10
Federal Spending on Wastewater Treatment Works	16
Hazardous Waste Sites on National Priority List	39

Federal Grants for Hazardous Substance
Response 10
State Spending on Hazardous Waste 20

Health | State Ranking

State Health Rankings 7
State Spending on Health 27
Support for Public Health 32
Family and Business Spending on Health
Care 39
HMO Enrollment 30
Medicaid Recipients 10
Medically Underserved Population 48
Lack of Health Care Access 40
Active Nonfederal Physicians 7
Active Nonfederal Nurses 5
Active Nonfederal Dentists 24
Average Cost per Hospital Stay 34
Average Cost per Day for Hospital Care 33
Average Cost per Day for Hospital Room 5
State Spending on Hospitals 45
Adequacy of Prenatal Care 45
Infants Born Receiving Late or No
Prenatal Care 42
Infants Born with Low Birth Weight 43
Abortions 17
Immunizations of Two-Year-Olds —
Overall Risk for Heart Disease 7
Risk Factor for Heart Disease
(hypertension) 24
Deaths Due to Heart Disease 33
New Cancer Cases 40
Deaths Due to Cancer 31
Prevalence of Smoking 24
Prevalence of Diabetes 45
Deaths Due to Diabetes 19
Cost of Diabetes 46
AIDS Cases Reported 41
Gonorrhea Cases Reported 50
Syphilis Cases Reported 47
Tuberculosis Cases Reported 50
Hepatitis Cases Reported 40
Rabies Cases Reported 15
Lyme Disease Cases Reported 13
Beer Consumption 14
Wine Consumption 5
Liquor Consumption 18
Alcohol and Drug Treatment Admissions 14
Federal Spending on Alcohol, Drug
Abuse, and Mental Health 3
Total Spending on Alcohol/Drug Abuse
Services 14
State Spending on Alcohol/Drug Abuse
Services 12
Hard-Core Cocaine Users 48
Federal Drug Grants to States 4

Population | State Ranking

Population 49
Population Density 31
Population in Metropolitan Areas 50
Population Under 18 Years Old 33
Population Over 65 Years Old 35
White Population 1
African American Population 49
Hispanic Population 45
Asian American Population 45
Native American Population 30
Catholic Population 15

Jewish Population 21
Marriages 13
Divorces 28
Births 48
Births to Single Mothers 45
Births to Single Teenagers 48
Adoptions 15
Adoption Option Index 12
Infant Mortality 50
Child Deaths and Suicides 29
Teen Violent Death Rate 47
Deaths 39

Recreation | State Ranking

State Parks and Recreation Areas 2
Visitors to State Parks and Recreation
Areas 37
Revenues from State Parks and
Recreation Areas 2
Spending on State Arts Agencies 24
Domestic Travel Spending 7
State Travel Office Budgets 6
Lodging Industry (rooms) 5
Participation in Exercise Walking 45
Participation in Swimming 38
Participation in Camping 29
Participation in Bowling 48
Bowling League Membership 18
Participation in Running/Jogging 49
Participation in Aerobics 39
Participation in Golf 44
Participation in Softball 44
Participation in Health Clubs 48
Participation in Tennis NA
Participation in Hunting 22
Participation in Baseball —
Participation in Bicycle Riding 34
Number of Boats 7
Attendance at Parimutuel Racing NA
Revenue from Parimutuel Betting 32

Social Services | State Ranking

Federal Grants for Social Services 24
State Spending on Public Welfare 8
Persons in Poverty 32
Public Aid Recipients 24
Participants in Food Stamp Program 39
Households in Food Stamp Program 22
Percentage of Poor Using AFDC and
Food Stamps 6
Federal Spending on Children and
Family Services 10
Federal Women, Infants, and Children
Food Program 2
Child Welfare Services 36
Child Abuse Cases Reported —
Children in Poverty 45
Children Without Health Insurance 40
Children Who Are Hungry or at Risk 42
Federal Spending on Child Nutrition
Programs 40
Federal Spending on Special Milk
Program 2
National School Lunch Program
Participants 47
Head Start Enrollment 6
Head Start Spending 9
Federal Spending on Rehabilitation
Services/Handicapped Research 5

State Government | State Ranking

Financial World's State Rankings 49
Salaries of State Officials (governor) 25
Salaries of State Legislators 34
Women in State Legislatures 4
African Americans in State Legislatures 34
Hispanics in State Legislatures 21
Asian Americans in State Legislatures 6
Native Americans in State Legislatures 12
Turnover in State Legislatures 12
Length of State Legislative Sessions 23
State Bills in Regular Session 34
State Resolutions in Regular Session 15
State Bills in Special Session —
State Resolutions in Special Session —
Women in State Cabinets 28
Total Federal Funding to State
Governments 48
Total State Spending 9
State General Expenditures 7
State Debt 9
State Spending on Interest on the
General Debt 6
Total State Tax Revenue 23
State Revenue from Tax on Sales and
Gross Receipts 26
State Revenue from General Sales Tax 44
State Revenue from Licenses 12
State Revenue from Motor Vehicle
Licenses 7
State Revenue from Individual Income
Taxes 15
State Revenue from Corporation Net
Income Taxes 36
State Revenue from Severance Taxes —
State Revenue from Property Taxes 15
State Revenue from Death and Gift
Taxes 36
State Revenue from Documentary and
Stock Transfers 6
State Revenue from Tax on Motor Fuels 30
State Revenue from Tax on Tobacco
Products 27
Excise Tax on Cigarettes 36
Excise Tax on Gasoline 35
State Revenue from Lotteries 18

Transportation | State Ranking

Motor Vehicle Registrations 22
Automobile Registrations 24
Bus and Truck Registrations 29
Motorcycle Registrations 6
Driver Licenses 9
Federal Spending on Highway Trust
Fund 13
Federal Spending on Mass
Transportation 47
State Spending on Highways 7
Highway Deficiency 36
Bridge Deficiency 6
Traffic Fatalities 20
Traffic Fatalities per Miles Traveled 27
Motorcyclist Fatalities 27
Pedalcyclist Fatalities 15
Pedestrian Fatalities 32
Registered Aircraft 20
Registered Pilots 18
Federal Spending on Airport and
Airway Trust Fund 42
Aircraft Fatalities 50

— *not applicable* NA *not available*

Agriculture *State Ranking*

Farm Acreage	35
Farmland as Portion of State	27
Net Farm Income	37
Government Payments to Farms	37
Federal Commodity Loans/Price Supports	32
Federal Spending on Rural Development	21
Rural Electric and Telephone Loan Guarantees	1
Foreign-Owned Agricultural Land	31

Business and Economy *State Ranking*

Gross State Product	12
Retail Sales	12
Supermarket Sales	12
Commercial Bank Assets	21
Insured Commercial Bank Deposits	24
Fortune 500 Companies	18
Inc. 500 Companies	2
New Business Incorporations	14
Business Failures	17
Financial Aid to Minority Businesses	30
Women-Owned Businesses	6
Sales & Receipts of Women-Owned Businesses	23
African American-Owned Businesses	7
Sales & Receipts of African American-Owned Businesses	6
Hispanic-Owned Businesses	21
Sales & Receipts of Hispanic-Owned Businesses	24
Employees in Manufacturing	16
Manufacturing Shipments	30
Japanese-Owned U.S. Manufacturing Plants	20
Exports to Mexico	44
Change in Exports to Mexico	11
Existing Home Sales	32
Housing Starts	11
Average Annual Pay	17
Disposable Personal Income	13
Median Income of Families with Children	8
Federal Spending on Unemployment Insurance/Employment Services	49
Teen Unemployment	7
Bankruptcy Petitions Filed	15
Patents Issued to State Residents	27
Federal Spending on Community Development	43
Federal Spending on Economic Development Administration	27
Federal Spending on Urban Development Action Grants	27

Crime and Criminal Justice *State Ranking*

Total Crimes	35
Violent Crimes	36
Murders	20
Rapes	37
Aggravated Assaults	40
Property Crimes	35
Robberies	27
Burglaries	42
Larcenies and Thefts	24
Motor Vehicle Thefts	35
State and Federal Prisoners	20
Capital Punishment	5
State Spending on Corrections	18
State Spending on Police	5
Inmates in Local Jails	11
Spending on Local Jails	13
Spending per Inmate for Local Jails	23
Employees at Local Jails	19
Juvenile Custody Rate	23
Federal Spending on Office of Justice Assistance Programs	24

Defense *State Ranking*

Defense Grants to State and Local Governments	7
Total Defense Payroll	3
Total Army Payroll	4
Total Navy/Marine Corps Payroll	2
Total Air Force Payroll	16
Total Active-Duty Payroll	4
Army Active-Duty Payroll	9
Navy/Marine Corps Active-Duty Payroll	2
Air Force Active-Duty Payroll	15
Total Civilian Payroll	2
Army Civilian Payroll	3
Navy/Marine Corps Civilian Payroll	3
Air Force Civilian Payroll	15
Total Reserve and National Guard Payroll	26
Army Reserve and National Guard Payroll	22
Navy/Marine Corps Reserve and National Guard Payroll	3
Air Force Reserve and National Guard Payroll	50
Total Retired Military Payroll	1
Army Retired Military Payroll	1
Navy/Marine Corps Retired Military Payroll	1
Air Force Retired Military Payroll	10
Total Defense Prime Contracts	5
Army Prime Contracts	6
Navy/Marine Corps Prime Contracts	5
Air Force Prime Contracts	17
U.S. Military Installations	2
Construction of National Guard Centers	6

Education *State Ranking*

School Age Population	41
Public Elementary and Secondary School Enrollment	12
Average Daily Attendance	2
Student-Teacher Ratio	32
Salaries of Public School Teachers	21
Public School Teachers Who Are Male	47
Eighth Grade Math Test Results	16
High School Math Enrollment	5
Public High School Graduation Rate	29
General Educational Development (GED) Test Results	34
Adult Illiteracy	19
Federal Revenue for Public Schools	34
State Revenue for Public Schools	43
Local Government Revenue for Public Schools	8
Total Public School Spending	19
Public School Spending on Instruction	19
Public School Spending on Noninstruction	32
Public School Spending on Support Staff	14
State and Local Government Spending on Public Schools	9

Federal Spending on School Improvement Programs	47
Gifted and Talented Students	3
Federal Spending on Education of Students with Disabilities	41
Student-Teacher Ratio in Catholic Elementary Schools	16
Student-Teacher Ratio in Catholic Secondary Schools	24
State Spending on Education	31
State and Local Government Spending on Education	13
Higher Education Tuition and Fees	22
Higher Education Revenue	37
Federal Spending on Higher Education	37
State Spending on Higher Education	20
State and Local Government Spending on Higher Education	25
State and Local Appropriations for Higher Education	30
Federal Spending on Higher Education Act Insured Loans	20
Federal Spending on National Guaranteed Student Loans	25
Federal Spending on Pell Grants	38
Default Rate in Perkins Student Loan Program	19
State Spending on Libraries	16

Energy *State Ranking*

Total Spending on Energy	34
Net Generation of Electricity	42
Cost of Electricity	26
Spending on Electricity	28
Spending on Natural Gas	43
Spending on Gasoline	21
Spending on Petroleum	30
Spending on Coal	32
Total Energy Consumption	31
Electricity Consumption	22
Natural Gas Consumption	45
Petroleum Consumption	28
Coal Consumption	32
Power Plants	44
Nuclear Power Plants	22
Hydroelectric Power Plants	29

Environment *State Ranking*

Federally Owned Land (acreage)	21
Loss of Wetlands	30
Environmental Protection Agency Spending	36
EPA Abatement, Control, and Compliance	27
State Spending on Environmental Programs	30
Environmental Programs as Part of State Budget	30
State Spending on Forest Programs	21
Total Tree Planting	8
Federal Tree Planting	14
Private Tree Planting	7
State Spending on Air Quality	25
State Spending on Water Quality	31
Federal Grants for Rural Water and Waste Disposal	23
Federal Spending on Wastewater Treatment Works	36
Hazardous Waste Sites on National Priority List	18

Federal Grants for Hazardous Substance
  Response 36
State Spending on Hazardous Waste 24

Health | State Ranking

State Health Rankings 13
State Spending on Health 33
Support for Public Health 16
Family and Business Spending on Health
  Care 16
HMO Enrollment 32
Medicaid Recipients 47
Medically Underserved Population 40
Lack of Health Care Access 37
Active Nonfederal Physicians 13
Active Nonfederal Nurses 37
Active Nonfederal Dentists 31
Average Cost per Hospital Stay 31
Average Cost per Day for Hospital Care 28
Average Cost per Day for Hospital Room 40
State Spending on Hospitals 8
Adequacy of Prenatal Care 13
Infants Born Receiving Late or No
  Prenatal Care 32
Infants Born with Low Birth Weight 19
Abortions 21
Immunizations of Two-Year-Olds —
Overall Risk for Heart Disease 7
Risk Factor for Heart Disease
  (hypertension) 40
Deaths Due to Heart Disease 37
New Cancer Cases 38
Deaths Due to Cancer 37
Prevalence of Smoking 30
Prevalence of Diabetes 24
Deaths Due to Diabetes 39
Cost of Diabetes 24
AIDS Cases Reported 17
Gonorrhea Cases Reported 15
Syphilis Cases Reported 19
Tuberculosis Cases Reported 25
Hepatitis Cases Reported 43
Rabies Cases Reported 12
Lyme Disease Cases Reported 12
Beer Consumption 30
Wine Consumption 24
Liquor Consumption 37
Alcohol and Drug Treatment Admissions 13
Federal Spending on Alcohol, Drug
  Abuse, and Mental Health 33
Total Spending on Alcohol/Drug Abuse
  Services 25
State Spending on Alcohol/Drug Abuse
  Services 17
Hard-Core Cocaine Users 13
Federal Drug Grants to States 46

Population | State Ranking

Population 12
Population Density 16
Population in Metropolitan Areas 21
Population Under 18 Years Old 41
Population Over 65 Years Old 43
White Population 37
African American Population 9
Hispanic Population 25
Asian American Population 9
Native American Population 37
Catholic Population 41

Jewish Population 20
Marriages 8
Divorces 31
Births 21
Births to Single Mothers 26
Births to Single Teenagers 25
Adoptions 36
Adoption Option Index 50
Infant Mortality 13
Child Deaths and Suicides 32
Teen Violent Death Rate 36
Deaths 38

Recreation | State Ranking

State Parks and Recreation Areas 43
Visitors to State Parks and Recreation
  Areas 48
Revenues from State Parks and
  Recreation Areas 48
Spending on State Arts Agencies 31
Domestic Travel Spending 12
State Travel Office Budgets 32
Lodging Industry (rooms) 15
Participation in Exercise Walking 43
Participation in Swimming 42
Participation in Camping 41
Participation in Bowling 30
Bowling League Membership 36
Participation in Running/Jogging 16
Participation in Aerobics 23
Participation in Golf 29
Participation in Softball 43
Participation in Health Clubs 27
Participation in Tennis 11
Participation in Hunting 33
Participation in Baseball 40
Participation in Bicycle Riding 41
Number of Boats 38
Attendance at Parimutuel Racing —
Revenue from Parimutuel Betting —

Social Services | State Ranking

Federal Grants for Social Services 35
State Spending on Public Welfare 47
Persons in Poverty 40
Public Aid Recipients 43
Participants in Food Stamp Program 35
Households in Food Stamp Program 35
Percentage of Poor Using AFDC and
  Food Stamps 31
Federal Spending on Children and
  Family Services 32
Federal Women, Infants, and Children
  Food Program 38
Child Welfare Services 7
Child Abuse Cases Reported —
Children in Poverty 39
Children Without Health Insurance 25
Children Who Are Hungry or at Risk 46
Federal Spending on Child Nutrition
  Programs 48
Federal Spending on Special Milk
  Program 39
National School Lunch Program
  Participants 34
Head Start Enrollment 33
Head Start Spending 17
Federal Spending on Rehabilitation
  Services/Handicapped Research 37

State Government | State Ranking

Financial World's State Rankings 4
Salaries of State Officials (governor) 8
Salaries of State Legislators 20
Women in State Legislatures 43
African Americans in State Legislatures 17
Hispanics in State Legislatures 21
Asian Americans in State Legislatures 6
Native Americans in State Legislatures 12
Turnover in State Legislatures 47
Length of State Legislative Sessions 36
State Bills in Regular Session 5
State Resolutions in Regular Session 10
State Bills in Special Session 8
State Resolutions in Special Session 7
Women in State Cabinets 9
Total Federal Funding to State
  Governments 3
Total State Spending 45
State General Expenditures 43
State Debt 34
State Spending on Interest on the
  General Debt 33
Total State Tax Revenue 33
State Revenue from Tax on Sales and
  Gross Receipts 44
State Revenue from General Sales Tax 43
State Revenue from Licenses 44
State Revenue from Motor Vehicle
  Licenses 26
State Revenue from Individual Income
  Taxes 11
State Revenue from Corporation Net
  Income Taxes 39
State Revenue from Severance Taxes 31
State Revenue from Property Taxes 28
State Revenue from Death and Gift
  Taxes 32
State Revenue from Documentary and
  Stock Transfers 10
State Revenue from Tax on Motor Fuels 20
State Revenue from Tax on Tobacco
  Products 49
Excise Tax on Cigarettes 48
Excise Tax on Gasoline 25
State Revenue from Lotteries 9

Transportation | State Ranking

Motor Vehicle Registrations 18
Automobile Registrations 14
Bus and Truck Registrations 30
Motorcycle Registrations 44
Driver Licenses 5
Federal Spending on Highway Trust
  Fund 41
Federal Spending on Mass
  Transportation 31
State Spending on Highways 12
Highway Deficiency 29
Bridge Deficiency 29
Traffic Fatalities 36
Traffic Fatalities per Miles Traveled 43
Motorcyclist Fatalities 48
Pedalcyclist Fatalities 17
Pedestrian Fatalities 28
Registered Aircraft 45
Registered Pilots 32
Federal Spending on Airport and
  Airway Trust Fund 41
Aircraft Fatalities 25

— *not applicable*   NA *not available*

Agriculture
State Ranking

Farm Acreage	19
Farmland as Portion of State	25
Net Farm Income	17
Government Payments to Farms	16
Federal Commodity Loans/Price Supports	25
Federal Spending on Rural Development	40
Rural Electric and Telephone Loan Guarantees	39
Foreign-Owned Agricultural Land	15

Business and Economy
State Ranking

Gross State Product	18
Retail Sales	23
Supermarket Sales	9
Commercial Bank Assets	46
Insured Commercial Bank Deposits	45
Fortune 500 Companies	31
Inc. 500 Companies	20
New Business Incorporations	20
Business Failures	31
Financial Aid to Minority Businesses	16
Women-Owned Businesses	9
Sales & Receipts of Women-Owned Businesses	47
African American-Owned Businesses	36
Sales & Receipts of African American-Owned Businesses	30
Hispanic-Owned Businesses	20
Sales & Receipts of Hispanic-Owned Businesses	22
Employees in Manufacturing	19
Manufacturing Shipments	11
Japanese-Owned U.S. Manufacturing Plants	12
Exports to Mexico	47
Change in Exports to Mexico	13
Existing Home Sales	13
Housing Starts	6
Average Annual Pay	16
Disposable Personal Income	15
Median Income of Families with Children	12
Federal Spending on Unemployment Insurance/Employment Services	19
Teen Unemployment	13
Bankruptcy Petitions Filed	20
Patents Issued to State Residents	21
Federal Spending on Community Development	46
Federal Spending on Economic Development Administration	23
Federal Spending on Urban Development Action Grants	20

Crime and Criminal Justice
State Ranking

Total Crimes	9
Violent Crimes	28
Murders	36
Rapes	4
Aggravated Assaults	29
Property Crimes	6
Robberies	25
Burglaries	18
Larcenies and Thefts	7
Motor Vehicle Thefts	25
State and Federal Prisoners	37
Capital Punishment	17

State Spending on Corrections	32
State Spending on Police	11
Inmates in Local Jails	17
Spending on Local Jails	22
Spending per Inmate for Local Jails	27
Employees at Local Jails	16
Juvenile Custody Rate	35
Federal Spending on Office of Justice Assistance Programs	29

Defense
State Ranking

Defense Grants to State and Local Governments	47
Total Defense Payroll	9
Total Army Payroll	13
Total Navy/Marine Corps Payroll	7
Total Air Force Payroll	26
Total Active-Duty Payroll	11
Army Active-Duty Payroll	11
Navy/Marine Corps Active-Duty Payroll	9
Air Force Active-Duty Payroll	25
Total Civilian Payroll	11
Army Civilian Payroll	22
Navy/Marine Corps Civilian Payroll	5
Air Force Civilian Payroll	33
Total Reserve and National Guard Payroll	25
Army Reserve and National Guard Payroll	30
Navy/Marine Corps Reserve and National Guard Payroll	5
Air Force Reserve and National Guard Payroll	19
Total Retired Military Payroll	8
Army Retired Military Payroll	7
Navy/Marine Corps Retired Military Payroll	4
Air Force Retired Military Payroll	12
Total Defense Prime Contracts	27
Army Prime Contracts	37
Navy/Marine Corps Prime Contracts	16
Air Force Prime Contracts	29
U.S. Military Installations	10
Construction of National Guard Centers	47

Education
State Ranking

School Age Population	27
Public Elementary and Secondary School Enrollment	14
Average Daily Attendance	27
Student-Teacher Ratio	3
Salaries of Public School Teachers	16
Public School Teachers Who Are Male	7
Eighth Grade Math Test Results	—
High School Math Enrollment	NA
Public High School Graduation Rate	20
General Educational Development (GED) Test Results	33
Adult Illiteracy	43
Federal Revenue for Public Schools	28
State Revenue for Public Schools	2
Local Government Revenue for Public Schools	48
Total Public School Spending	28
Public School Spending on Instruction	25
Public School Spending on Noninstruction	20
Public School Spending on Support Staff	12
State and Local Government Spending on Public Schools	19

Federal Spending on School Improvement Programs	49
Gifted and Talented Students	NA
Federal Spending on Education of Students with Disabilities	46
Student-Teacher Ratio in Catholic Elementary Schools	26
Student-Teacher Ratio in Catholic Secondary Schools	2
State Spending on Education	4
State and Local Government Spending on Education	25
Higher Education Tuition and Fees	27
Higher Education Revenue	24
Federal Spending on Higher Education	38
State Spending on Higher Education	10
State and Local Government Spending on Higher Education	27
State and Local Appropriations for Higher Education	20
Federal Spending on Higher Education Act Insured Loans	29
Federal Spending on National Guaranteed Student Loans	28
Federal Spending on Pell Grants	36
Default Rate in Perkins Student Loan Program	44
State Spending on Libraries	36

Energy
State Ranking

Total Spending on Energy	41
Net Generation of Electricity	5
Cost of Electricity	51
Spending on Electricity	43
Spending on Natural Gas	45
Spending on Gasoline	29
Spending on Petroleum	20
Spending on Coal	41
Total Energy Consumption	11
Electricity Consumption	2
Natural Gas Consumption	42
Petroleum Consumption	12
Coal Consumption	41
Power Plants	25
Nuclear Power Plants	28
Hydroelectric Power Plants	11

Environment
State Ranking

Federally Owned Land (acreage)	11
Loss of Wetlands	39
Environmental Protection Agency Spending	32
EPA Abatement, Control, and Compliance	15
State Spending on Environmental Programs	7
Environmental Programs as Part of State Budget	8
State Spending on Forest Programs	7
Total Tree Planting	7
Federal Tree Planting	2
Private Tree Planting	9
State Spending on Air Quality	15
State Spending on Water Quality	16
Federal Grants for Rural Water and Waste Disposal	45
Federal Spending on Wastewater Treatment Works	33
Hazardous Waste Sites on National Priority List	7

Federal Grants for Hazardous Substance
  Response 31
State Spending on Hazardous Waste 5

Health State Ranking

State Health Rankings 20
State Spending on Health 11
Support for Public Health 17
Family and Business Spending on Health
  Care 37
HMO Enrollment 17
Medicaid Recipients 20
Medically Underserved Population 21
Lack of Health Care Access 32
Active Nonfederal Physicians 13
Active Nonfederal Nurses 16
Active Nonfederal Dentists 14
Average Cost per Hospital Stay 27
Average Cost per Day for Hospital Care 8
Average Cost per Day for Hospital Room 15
State Spending on Hospitals 24
Adequacy of Prenatal Care 22
Infants Born Receiving Late or No
  Prenatal Care 21
Infants Born with Low Birth Weight 43
Abortions 15
Immunizations of Two-Year-Olds —
Overall Risk for Heart Disease 7
Risk Factor for Heart Disease
  (hypertension) 20
Deaths Due to Heart Disease 43
New Cancer Cases 41
Deaths Due to Cancer 40
Prevalence of Smoking 41
Prevalence of Diabetes 41
Deaths Due to Diabetes 42
Cost of Diabetes 41
AIDS Cases Reported 23
Gonorrhea Cases Reported 32
Syphilis Cases Reported 40
Tuberculosis Cases Reported 22
Hepatitis Cases Reported 14
Rabies Cases Reported 48
Lyme Disease Cases Reported 33
Beer Consumption 36
Wine Consumption 4
Liquor Consumption 28
Alcohol and Drug Treatment
  Admissions NA
Federal Spending on Alcohol, Drug
  Abuse, and Mental Health 23
Total Spending on Alcohol/Drug Abuse
  Services 11
State Spending on Alcohol/Drug Abuse
  Services 7
Hard-Core Cocaine Users 37
Federal Drug Grants to States 45

Population State Ranking

Population 18
Population Density 27
Population in Metropolitan Areas 13
Population Under 18 Years Old 26
Population Over 65 Years Old 36
White Population 22
African American Population 36
Hispanic Population 19
Asian American Population 3
Native American Population 9
Catholic Population 37

Jewish Population 25
Marriages 19
Divorces 10
Births 23
Births to Single Mothers 36
Births to Single Teenagers 34
Adoptions 26
Adoption Option Index 20
Infant Mortality 40
Child Deaths and Suicides 47
Teen Violent Death Rate 29
Deaths 40

Recreation State Ranking

State Parks and Recreation Areas 15
Visitors to State Parks and Recreation
  Areas 5
Revenues from State Parks and
  Recreation Areas 30
Spending on State Arts Agencies 40
Domestic Travel Spending 32
State Travel Office Budgets 47
Lodging Industry (rooms) 42
Participation in Exercise Walking 29
Participation in Swimming 44
Participation in Camping 17
Participation in Bowling 37
Bowling League Membership 25
Participation in Running/Jogging 27
Participation in Aerobics 18
Participation in Golf 12
Participation in Softball 41
Participation in Health Clubs 9
Participation in Tennis 43
Participation in Hunting 39
Participation in Baseball 46
Participation in Bicycle Riding 36
Number of Boats 26
Attendance at Parimutuel Racing 15
Revenue from Parimutuel Betting 10

Social Services State Ranking

Federal Grants for Social Services 46
State Spending on Public Welfare 16
Persons in Poverty 45
Public Aid Recipients 19
Participants in Food Stamp Program 40
Households in Food Stamp Program 25
Percentage of Poor Using AFDC and
  Food Stamps 7
Federal Spending on Children and
  Family Services 19
Federal Women, Infants, and Children
  Food Program 46
Child Welfare Services 22
Child Abuse Cases Reported —
Children in Poverty 32
Children Without Health Insurance 34
Children Who Are Hungry or at Risk 38
Federal Spending on Child Nutrition
  Programs 36
Federal Spending on Special Milk
  Program 27
National School Lunch Program
  Participants 41
Head Start Enrollment 47
Head Start Spending 4
Federal Spending on Rehabilitation
  Services/Handicapped Research 45

State Government State Ranking

Financial World's State Rankings 7
Salaries of State Officials (governor) 5
Salaries of State Legislators 16
Women in State Legislatures 1
African Americans in State Legislatures 37
Hispanics in State Legislatures 11
Asian Americans in State Legislatures 3
Native Americans in State Legislatures 12
Turnover in State Legislatures 22
Length of State Legislative Sessions 14
State Bills in Regular Session 35
State Resolutions in Regular Session 22
State Bills in Special Session 15
State Resolutions in Special Session 9
Women in State Cabinets 2
Total Federal Funding to State
  Governments 18
Total State Spending 12
State General Expenditures 16
State Debt 24
State Spending on Interest on the
  General Debt 28
Total State Tax Revenue 5
State Revenue from Tax on Sales and
  Gross Receipts 2
State Revenue from General Sales Tax 2
State Revenue from Licenses 20
State Revenue from Motor Vehicle
  Licenses 28
State Revenue from Individual Income
  Taxes —
State Revenue from Corporation Net
  Income Taxes —
State Revenue from Severance Taxes 17
State Revenue from Property Taxes 1
State Revenue from Death and Gift
  Taxes 27
State Revenue from Documentary and
  Stock Transfers 3
State Revenue from Tax on Motor Fuels 8
State Revenue from Tax on Tobacco
  Products 15
Excise Tax on Cigarettes 10
Excise Tax on Gasoline 2
State Revenue from Lotteries 26

Transportation State Ranking

Motor Vehicle Registrations 11
Automobile Registrations 12
Bus and Truck Registrations 13
Motorcycle Registrations 14
Driver Licenses 23
Federal Spending on Highway Trust
  Fund 16
Federal Spending on Mass
  Transportation 13
State Spending on Highways 23
Highway Deficiency 48
Bridge Deficiency 32
Traffic Fatalities 41
Traffic Fatalities per Miles Traveled 45
Motorcyclist Fatalities 43
Pedalcyclist Fatalities 47
Pedestrian Fatalities 37
Registered Aircraft 14
Registered Pilots 5
Federal Spending on Airport and
  Airway Trust Fund 18
Aircraft Fatalities 11

— *not applicable* NA *not available*

Agriculture
State Ranking

Farm Acreage	39
Farmland as Portion of State	41
Net Farm Income	44
Government Payments to Farms	41
Federal Commodity Loans/Price Supports	39
Federal Spending on Rural Development	5
Rural Electric and Telephone Loan Guarantees	40
Foreign-Owned Agricultural Land	24

Business and Economy
State Ranking

Gross State Product	50
Retail Sales	51
Supermarket Sales	37
Commercial Bank Assets	34
Insured Commercial Bank Deposits	30
Fortune 500 Companies	36
Inc. 500 Companies	36
New Business Incorporations	50
Business Failures	41
Financial Aid to Minority Businesses	41
Women-Owned Businesses	32
Sales & Receipts of Women-Owned Businesses	11
African American-Owned Businesses	34
Sales & Receipts of African American-Owned Businesses	27
Hispanic-Owned Businesses	46
Sales & Receipts of Hispanic-Owned Businesses	33
Employees in Manufacturing	39
Manufacturing Shipments	39
Japanese-Owned U.S. Manufacturing Plants	42
Exports to Mexico	41
Change in Exports to Mexico	50
Existing Home Sales	1
Housing Starts	50
Average Annual Pay	46
Disposable Personal Income	49
Median Income of Families with Children	50
Federal Spending on Unemployment Insurance/Employment Services	30
Teen Unemployment	1
Bankruptcy Petitions Filed	39
Patents Issued to State Residents	43
Federal Spending on Community Development	18
Federal Spending on Economic Development Administration	2
Federal Spending on Urban Development Action Grants	16

Crime and Criminal Justice
State Ranking

Total Crimes	51
Violent Crimes	45
Murders	28
Rapes	47
Aggravated Assaults	45
Property Crimes	51
Robberies	43
Burglaries	48
Larcenies and Thefts	51
Motor Vehicle Thefts	45
State and Federal Prisoners	49
Capital Punishment	—

State Spending on Corrections	49
State Spending on Police	33
Inmates in Local Jails	39
Spending on Local Jails	45
Spending per Inmate for Local Jails	38
Employees at Local Jails	28
Juvenile Custody Rate	49
Federal Spending on Office of Justice Assistance Programs	12

Defense
State Ranking

Defense Grants to State and Local Governments	8
Total Defense Payroll	46
Total Army Payroll	35
Total Navy/Marine Corps Payroll	38
Total Air Force Payroll	43
Total Active-Duty Payroll	47
Army Active-Duty Payroll	31
Navy/Marine Corps Active-Duty Payroll	35
Air Force Active-Duty Payroll	46
Total Civilian Payroll	48
Army Civilian Payroll	30
Navy/Marine Corps Civilian Payroll	36
Air Force Civilian Payroll	46
Total Reserve and National Guard Payroll	36
Army Reserve and National Guard Payroll	41
Navy/Marine Corps Reserve and National Guard Payroll	44
Air Force Reserve and National Guard Payroll	11
Total Retired Military Payroll	38
Army Retired Military Payroll	31
Navy/Marine Corps Retired Military Payroll	30
Air Force Retired Military Payroll	38
Total Defense Prime Contracts	50
Army Prime Contracts	34
Navy/Marine Corps Prime Contracts	37
Air Force Prime Contracts	51
U.S. Military Installations	41
Construction of National Guard Centers	8

Education
State Ranking

School Age Population	31
Public Elementary and Secondary School Enrollment	35
Average Daily Attendance	NA
Student-Teacher Ratio	40
Salaries of Public School Teachers	43
Public School Teachers Who Are Male	32
Eighth Grade Math Test Results	28
High School Math Enrollment	22
Public High School Graduation Rate	18
General Educational Development (GED) Test Results	31
Adult Illiteracy	12
Federal Revenue for Public Schools	17
State Revenue for Public Schools	8
Local Government Revenue for Public Schools	43
Total Public School Spending	31
Public School Spending on Instruction	50
Public School Spending on Noninstruction	13
Public School Spending on Support Staff	44
State and Local Government Spending on Public Schools	17

Federal Spending on School Improvement Programs	17
Gifted and Talented Students	26
Federal Spending on Education of Students with Disabilities	9
Student-Teacher Ratio in Catholic Elementary Schools	35
Student-Teacher Ratio in Catholic Secondary Schools	50
State Spending on Education	10
State and Local Government Spending on Education	20
Higher Education Tuition and Fees	35
Higher Education Revenue	49
Federal Spending on Higher Education	12
State Spending on Higher Education	29
State and Local Government Spending on Higher Education	28
State and Local Appropriations for Higher Education	31
Federal Spending on Higher Education Act Insured Loans	49
Federal Spending on National Guaranteed Student Loans	31
Federal Spending on Pell Grants	22
Default Rate in Perkins Student Loan Program	4
State Spending on Libraries	5

Energy
State Ranking

Total Spending on Energy	7
Net Generation of Electricity	2
Cost of Electricity	45
Spending on Electricity	45
Spending on Natural Gas	19
Spending on Gasoline	17
Spending on Petroleum	9
Spending on Coal	2
Total Energy Consumption	6
Electricity Consumption	18
Natural Gas Consumption	16
Petroleum Consumption	11
Coal Consumption	3
Power Plants	27
Nuclear Power Plants	34
Hydroelectric Power Plants	27

Environment
State Ranking

Federally Owned Land (acreage)	16
Loss of Wetlands	45
Environmental Protection Agency Spending	7
EPA Abatement, Control, and Compliance	12
State Spending on Environmental Programs	25
Environmental Programs as Part of State Budget	23
State Spending on Forest Programs	27
Total Tree Planting	27
Federal Tree Planting	32
Private Tree Planting	25
State Spending on Air Quality	29
State Spending on Water Quality	43
Federal Grants for Rural Water and Waste Disposal	6
Federal Spending on Wastewater Treatment Works	6
Hazardous Waste Sites on National Priority List	44

Federal Grants for Hazardous Substance
   Response   34
State Spending on Hazardous Waste   18

Health   *State Ranking*

State Health Rankings   50
State Spending on Health   41
Support for Public Health   48
Family and Business Spending on Health
   Care   44
HMO Enrollment   48
Medicaid Recipients   4
Medically Underserved Population   3
Lack of Health Care Access   5
Active Nonfederal Physicians   38
Active Nonfederal Nurses   33
Active Nonfederal Dentists   42
Average Cost per Hospital Stay   46
Average Cost per Day for Hospital Care   38
Average Cost per Day for Hospital Room   36
State Spending on Hospitals   44
Adequacy of Prenatal Care   43
Infants Born Receiving Late or No
   Prenatal Care   23
Infants Born with Low Birth Weight   21
Abortions   49
Immunizations of Two-Year-Olds   —
Overall Risk for Heart Disease   49
Risk Factor for Heart Disease
   (hypertension)   2
Deaths Due to Heart Disease   1
New Cancer Cases   3
Deaths Due to Cancer   4
Prevalence of Smoking   1
Prevalence of Diabetes   12
Deaths Due to Diabetes   1
Cost of Diabetes   13
AIDS Cases Reported   46
Gonorrhea Cases Reported   40
Syphilis Cases Reported   41
Tuberculosis Cases Reported   28
Hepatitis Cases Reported   45
Rabies Cases Reported   19
Lyme Disease Cases Reported   20
Beer Consumption   40
Wine Consumption   50
Liquor Consumption   51
Alcohol and Drug Treatment Admissions 27
Federal Spending on Alcohol, Drug
   Abuse, and Mental Health   44
Total Spending on Alcohol/Drug Abuse
   Services   43
State Spending on Alcohol/Drug Abuse
   Services   30
Hard-Core Cocaine Users   47
Federal Drug Grants to States   34

Population   *State Ranking*

Population   34
Population Density   29
Population in Metropolitan Areas   44
Population Under 18 Years Old   38
Population Over 65 Years Old   5
White Population   5
African American Population   35
Hispanic Population   51
Asian American Population   51
Native American Population   51
Catholic Population   42

Jewish Population   44
Marriages   50
Divorces   18
Births   51
Births to Single Mothers   28
Births to Single Teenagers   17
Adoptions   11
Adoption Option Index   17
Infant Mortality   21
Child Deaths and Suicides   24
Teen Violent Death Rate   6
Deaths   2

Recreation   *State Ranking*

State Parks and Recreation Areas   7
Visitors to State Parks and Recreation
   Areas   12
Revenues from State Parks and
   Recreation Areas   4
Spending on State Arts Agencies   11
Domestic Travel Spending   49
State Travel Office Budgets   21
Lodging Industry (rooms)   43
Participation in Exercise Walking   6
Participation in Swimming   4
Participation in Camping   6
Participation in Bowling   8
Bowling League Membership   33
Participation in Running/Jogging   14
Participation in Aerobics   15
Participation in Golf   5
Participation in Softball   26
Participation in Health Clubs   41
Participation in Tennis   4
Participation in Hunting   3
Participation in Baseball   6
Participation in Bicycle Riding   9
Number of Boats   46
Attendance at Parimutuel Racing   12
Revenue from Parimutuel Betting   14

Social Services   *State Ranking*

Federal Grants for Social Services   49
State Spending on Public Welfare   30
Persons in Poverty   7
Public Aid Recipients   5
Participants in Food Stamp Program   3
Households in Food Stamp Program   3
Percentage of Poor Using AFDC and
   Food Stamps   42
Federal Spending on Children and
   Family Services   11
Federal Women, Infants, and Children
   Food Program   19
Child Welfare Services   NA
Child Abuse Cases Reported   —
Children in Poverty   4
Children Without Health Insurance   22
Children Who Are Hungry or at Risk   3
Federal Spending on Child Nutrition
   Programs   15
Federal Spending on Special Milk
   Program   36
National School Lunch Program
   Participants   12
Head Start Enrollment   17
Head Start Spending   26
Federal Spending on Rehabilitation
   Services/Handicapped Research   4

State Government   *State Ranking*

Financial World's State Rankings   47
Salaries of State Officials (governor)   40
Salaries of State Legislators   38
Women in State Legislatures   33
African Americans in State Legislatures   39
Hispanics in State Legislatures   21
Asian Americans in State Legislatures   6
Native Americans in State Legislatures   7
Turnover in State Legislatures   2
Length of State Legislative Sessions   27
State Bills in Regular Session   41
State Resolutions in Regular Session   31
State Bills in Special Session   14
State Resolutions in Special Session   12
Women in State Cabinets   22
Total Federal Funding to State
   Governments   26
Total State Spending   6
State General Expenditures   8
State Debt   20
State Spending on Interest on the
   General Debt   17
Total State Tax Revenue   17
State Revenue from Tax on Sales and
   Gross Receipts   10
State Revenue from General Sales Tax   12
State Revenue from Licenses   23
State Revenue from Motor Vehicle
   Licenses   16
State Revenue from Individual Income
   Taxes   34
State Revenue from Corporation Net
   Income Taxes   10
State Revenue from Severance Taxes   8
State Revenue from Property Taxes   35
State Revenue from Death and Gift
   Taxes   44
State Revenue from Documentary and
   Stock Transfers   24
State Revenue from Tax on Motor Fuels   9
State Revenue from Tax on Tobacco
   Products   35
Excise Tax on Cigarettes   36
Excise Tax on Gasoline   34
State Revenue from Lotteries   30

Transportation   *State Ranking*

Motor Vehicle Registrations   41
Automobile Registrations   49
Bus and Truck Registrations   11
Motorcycle Registrations   43
Driver Licenses   16
Federal Spending on Highway Trust
   Fund   18
Federal Spending on Mass
   Transportation   44
State Spending on Highways   10
Highway Deficiency   7
Bridge Deficiency   2
Traffic Fatalities   10
Traffic Fatalities per Miles Traveled   5
Motorcyclist Fatalities   16
Pedalcyclist Fatalities   50
Pedestrian Fatalities   25
Registered Aircraft   41
Registered Pilots   49
Federal Spending on Airport and
   Airway Trust Fund   36
Aircraft Fatalities   11

— *not applicable*   NA *not available*

Agriculture
State Ranking

Farm Acreage	18
Farmland as Portion of State	18
Net Farm Income	19
Government Payments to Farms	22
Federal Commodity Loans/Price Supports	23
Federal Spending on Rural Development	45
Rural Electric and Telephone Loan Guarantees	25
Foreign-Owned Agricultural Land	45

Business and Economy
State Ranking

Gross State Product	28
Retail Sales	18
Supermarket Sales	38
Commercial Bank Assets	33
Insured Commercial Bank Deposits	33
Fortune 500 Companies	11
Inc. 500 Companies	18
New Business Incorporations	47
Business Failures	47
Financial Aid to Minority Businesses	28
Women-Owned Businesses	31
Sales & Receipts of Women-Owned Businesses	22
African American-Owned Businesses	32
Sales & Receipts of African American-Owned Businesses	26
Hispanic-Owned Businesses	36
Sales & Receipts of Hispanic-Owned Businesses	29
Employees in Manufacturing	12
Manufacturing Shipments	4
Japanese-Owned U.S. Manufacturing Plants	34
Exports to Mexico	19
Change in Exports to Mexico	15
Existing Home Sales	18
Housing Starts	13
Average Annual Pay	29
Disposable Personal Income	26
Median Income of Families with Children	10
Federal Spending on Unemployment Insurance/Employment Services	26
Teen Unemployment	39
Bankruptcy Petitions Filed	35
Patents Issued to State Residents	13
Federal Spending on Community Development	21
Federal Spending on Economic Development Administration	29
Federal Spending on Urban Development Action Grants	17

Crime and Criminal Justice
State Ranking

Total Crimes	37
Violent Crimes	43
Murders	34
Rapes	46
Aggravated Assaults	43
Property Crimes	36
Robberies	32
Burglaries	43
Larcenies and Thefts	28
Motor Vehicle Thefts	26
State and Federal Prisoners	41
Capital Punishment	—

State Spending on Corrections	29
State Spending on Police	49
Inmates in Local Jails	24
Spending on Local Jails	16
Spending per Inmate for Local Jails	10
Employees at Local Jails	11
Juvenile Custody Rate	25
Federal Spending on Office of Justice Assistance Programs	45

Defense
State Ranking

Defense Grants to State and Local Governments	31
Total Defense Payroll	49
Total Army Payroll	41
Total Navy/Marine Corps Payroll	48
Total Air Force Payroll	50
Total Active-Duty Payroll	50
Army Active-Duty Payroll	40
Navy/Marine Corps Active-Duty Payroll	44
Air Force Active-Duty Payroll	48
Total Civilian Payroll	50
Army Civilian Payroll	41
Navy/Marine Corps Civilian Payroll	37
Air Force Civilian Payroll	48
Total Reserve and National Guard Payroll	15
Army Reserve and National Guard Payroll	12
Navy/Marine Corps Reserve and National Guard Payroll	31
Air Force Reserve and National Guard Payroll	37
Total Retired Military Payroll	49
Army Retired Military Payroll	47
Navy/Marine Corps Retired Military Payroll	46
Air Force Retired Military Payroll	47
Total Defense Prime Contracts	36
Army Prime Contracts	16
Navy/Marine Corps Prime Contracts	36
Air Force Prime Contracts	49
U.S. Military Installations	38
Construction of National Guard Centers	28

Education
State Ranking

School Age Population	17
Public Elementary and Secondary School Enrollment	18
Average Daily Attendance	7
Student-Teacher Ratio	30
Salaries of Public School Teachers	14
Public School Teachers Who Are Male	20
Eighth Grade Math Test Results	6
High School Math Enrollment	16
Public High School Graduation Rate	7
General Educational Development (GED) Test Results	49
Adult Illiteracy	35
Federal Revenue for Public Schools	49
State Revenue for Public Schools	36
Local Government Revenue for Public Schools	15
Total Public School Spending	14
Public School Spending on Instruction	6
Public School Spending on Noninstruction	41
Public School Spending on Support Staff	20
State and Local Government Spending on Public Schools	20

Federal Spending on School Improvement Programs	35
Gifted and Talented Students	NA
Federal Spending on Education of Students with Disabilities	43
Student-Teacher Ratio in Catholic Elementary Schools	37
Student-Teacher Ratio in Catholic Secondary Schools	10
State Spending on Education	23
State and Local Government Spending on Education	14
Higher Education Tuition and Fees	25
Higher Education Revenue	29
Federal Spending on Higher Education	28
State Spending on Higher Education	22
State and Local Government Spending on Higher Education	15
State and Local Appropriations for Higher Education	19
Federal Spending on Higher Education Act Insured Loans	4
Federal Spending on National Guaranteed Student Loans	8
Federal Spending on Pell Grants	26
Default Rate in Perkins Student Loan Program	49
State Spending on Libraries	37

Energy
State Ranking

Total Spending on Energy	44
Net Generation of Electricity	35
Cost of Electricity	41
Spending on Electricity	50
Spending on Natural Gas	15
Spending on Gasoline	42
Spending on Petroleum	44
Spending on Coal	25
Total Energy Consumption	39
Electricity Consumption	33
Natural Gas Consumption	21
Petroleum Consumption	48
Coal Consumption	26
Power Plants	13
Nuclear Power Plants	15
Hydroelectric Power Plants	9

Environment
State Ranking

Federally Owned Land (acreage)	27
Loss of Wetlands	28
Environmental Protection Agency Spending	14
EPA Abatement, Control, and Compliance	36
State Spending on Environmental Programs	17
Environmental Programs as Part of State Budget	22
State Spending on Forest Programs	13
Total Tree Planting	13
Federal Tree Planting	17
Private Tree Planting	13
State Spending on Air Quality	23
State Spending on Water Quality	10
Federal Grants for Rural Water and Waste Disposal	19
Federal Spending on Wastewater Treatment Works	11
Hazardous Waste Sites on National Priority List	9

Federal Grants for Hazardous Substance
  Response 22
State Spending on Hazardous Waste 25

Health   *State Ranking*

State Health Rankings 3
State Spending on Health 25
Support for Public Health 8
Family and Business Spending on Health
  Care 20
HMO Enrollment 7
Medicaid Recipients 33
Medically Underserved Population 30
Lack of Health Care Access 30
Active Nonfederal Physicians 26
Active Nonfederal Nurses 25
Active Nonfederal Dentists 12
Average Cost per Hospital Stay 43
Average Cost per Day for Hospital Care 40
Average Cost per Day for Hospital Room 38
State Spending on Hospitals 34
Adequacy of Prenatal Care 4
Infants Born Receiving Late or No
  Prenatal Care 39
Infants Born with Low Birth Weight 36
Abortions 40
Immunizations of Two-Year-Olds —
Overall Risk for Heart Disease 24
Risk Factor for Heart Disease
  (hypertension) 12
Deaths Due to Heart Disease 24
New Cancer Cases 32
Deaths Due to Cancer 22
Prevalence of Smoking 38
Prevalence of Diabetes 36
Deaths Due to Diabetes 18
Cost of Diabetes 37
AIDS Cases Reported 39
Gonorrhea Cases Reported 33
Syphilis Cases Reported 15
Tuberculosis Cases Reported 42
Hepatitis Cases Reported 15
Rabies Cases Reported 27
Lyme Disease Cases Reported 45
Beer Consumption 3
Wine Consumption 23
Liquor Consumption 9
Alcohol and Drug Treatment Admissions 1
Federal Spending on Alcohol, Drug
  Abuse, and Mental Health 35
Total Spending on Alcohol/Drug Abuse
  Services 5
State Spending on Alcohol/Drug Abuse
  Services 11
Hard-Core Cocaine Users 8
Federal Drug Grants to States 28

Population   *State Ranking*

Population 16
Population Density 25
Population in Metropolitan Areas 27
Population Under 18 Years Old 21
Population Over 65 Years Old 19
White Population 14
African American Population 29
Hispanic Population 31
Asian American Population 27
Native American Population 19
Catholic Population 8

Jewish Population 22
Marriages 37
Divorces 41
Births 38
Births to Single Mothers 34
Births to Single Teenagers 24
Adoptions 35
Adoption Option Index 15
Infant Mortality 32
Child Deaths and Suicides 40
Teen Violent Death Rate 37
Deaths 20

Recreation   *State Ranking*

State Parks and Recreation Areas 30
Visitors to State Parks and Recreation
  Areas 28
Revenues from State Parks and
  Recreation Areas 25
Spending on State Arts Agencies 39
Domestic Travel Spending 43
State Travel Office Budgets 24
Lodging Industry (rooms) 35
Participation in Exercise Walking 9
Participation in Swimming 7
Participation in Camping 14
Participation in Bowling 2
Bowling League Membership 2
Participation in Running/Jogging 17
Participation in Aerobics 26
Participation in Golf 3
Participation in Softball 6
Participation in Health Clubs 30
Participation in Tennis 20
Participation in Hunting 6
Participation in Baseball 35
Participation in Bicycle Riding 10
Number of Boats 2
Attendance at Parimutuel Racing —
Revenue from Parimutuel Betting —

Social Services   *State Ranking*

Federal Grants for Social Services 26
State Spending on Public Welfare 15
Persons in Poverty 40
Public Aid Recipients 13
Participants in Food Stamp Program 46
Households in Food Stamp Program 47
Percentage of Poor Using AFDC and
  Food Stamps 11
Federal Spending on Children and
  Family Services 41
Federal Women, Infants, and Children
  Food Program 43
Child Welfare Services 41
Child Abuse Cases Reported —
Children in Poverty 30
Children Without Health Insurance 49
Children Who Are Hungry or at Risk 33
Federal Spending on Child Nutrition
  Programs 43
Federal Spending on Special Milk
  Program 1
National School Lunch Program
  Participants 37
Head Start Enrollment 30
Head Start Spending 28
Federal Spending on Rehabilitation
  Services/Handicapped Research 28

State Government   *State Ranking*

Financial World's State Rankings 10
Salaries of State Officials (governor) 16
Salaries of State Legislators 8
Women in State Legislatures 10
African Americans in State Legislatures 21
Hispanics in State Legislatures 21
Asian Americans in State Legislatures 6
Native Americans in State Legislatures 12
Turnover in State Legislatures 33
Length of State Legislative Sessions 42
State Bills in Regular Session 45
State Resolutions in Regular Session 28
State Bills in Special Session 25
State Resolutions in Special Session 1
Women in State Cabinets 14
Total Federal Funding to State
  Governments 51
Total State Spending 27
State General Expenditures 24
State Debt 22
State Spending on Interest on the
  General Debt 22
Total State Tax Revenue 11
State Revenue from Tax on Sales and
  Gross Receipts 15
State Revenue from General Sales Tax 18
State Revenue from Licenses 39
State Revenue from Motor Vehicle
  Licenses 36
State Revenue from Individual Income
  Taxes 7
State Revenue from Corporation Net
  Income Taxes 13
State Revenue from Severance Taxes 29
State Revenue from Property Taxes 21
State Revenue from Death and Gift
  Taxes 15
State Revenue from Documentary and
  Stock Transfers 18
State Revenue from Tax on Motor Fuels 12
State Revenue from Tax on Tobacco
  Products 13
Excise Tax on Cigarettes 13
Excise Tax on Gasoline 4
State Revenue from Lotteries 19

Transportation   *State Ranking*

Motor Vehicle Registrations 33
Automobile Registrations 43
Bus and Truck Registrations 18
Motorcycle Registrations 2
Driver Licenses 26
Federal Spending on Highway Trust
  Fund 43
Federal Spending on Mass
  Transportation 20
State Spending on Highways 50
Highway Deficiency 31
Bridge Deficiency 31
Traffic Fatalities 30
Traffic Fatalities per Miles Traveled 36
Motorcyclist Fatalities 10
Pedalcyclist Fatalities 30
Pedestrian Fatalities 45
Registered Aircraft 27
Registered Pilots 33
Federal Spending on Airport and
  Airway Trust Fund 27
Aircraft Fatalities 18

— *not applicable* NA *not available*

Agriculture — *State Ranking*

Farm Acreage	9
Farmland as Portion of State	15
Net Farm Income	8
Government Payments to Farms	11
Federal Commodity Loans/Price Supports	27
Federal Spending on Rural Development	48
Rural Electric and Telephone Loan Guarantees	40
Foreign-Owned Agricultural Land	32

Business and Economy — *State Ranking*

Gross State Product	9
Retail Sales	48
Supermarket Sales	41
Commercial Bank Assets	29
Insured Commercial Bank Deposits	23
Fortune 500 Companies	42
Inc. 500 Companies	21
New Business Incorporations	10
Business Failures	20
Financial Aid to Minority Businesses	41
Women-Owned Businesses	15
Sales & Receipts of Women-Owned Businesses	16
African American-Owned Businesses	44
Sales & Receipts of African American-Owned Businesses	46
Hispanic-Owned Businesses	12
Sales & Receipts of Hispanic-Owned Businesses	12
Employees in Manufacturing	51
Manufacturing Shipments	44
Japanese-Owned U.S. Manufacturing Plants	48
Exports to Mexico	41
Change in Exports to Mexico	34
Existing Home Sales	11
Housing Starts	22
Average Annual Pay	41
Disposable Personal Income	32
Median Income of Families with Children	18
Federal Spending on Unemployment Insurance/Eemployment Services	3
Teen Unemployment	34
Bankruptcy Petitions Filed	23
Patents Issued to State Residents	47
Federal Spending on Community Development	49
Federal Spending on Economic Development Administration	21
Federal Spending on Urban Development Action Grants	33

Crime and Criminal Justice — *State Ranking*

Total Crimes	38
Violent Crimes	39
Murders	41
Rapes	45
Aggravated Assaults	34
Property Crimes	38
Robberies	49
Burglaries	47
Larcenies and Thefts	23
Motor Vehicle Thefts	48
State and Federal Prisoners	32
Capital Punishment	17

State Spending on Corrections	36
State Spending on Police	6
Inmates in Local Jails	25
Spending on Local Jails	2
Spending per Inmate for Local Jails	1
Employees at Local Jails	40
Juvenile Custody Rate	3
Federal Spending on Office of Justice Assistance Programs	6

Defense — *State Ranking*

Defense Grants to State and Local Governments	26
Total Defense Payroll	29
Total Army Payroll	43
Total Navy/Marine Corps Payroll	43
Total Air Force Payroll	11
Total Active-Duty Payroll	19
Army Active-Duty Payroll	46
Navy/Marine Corps Active-Duty Payroll	51
Air Force Active-Duty Payroll	8
Total Civilian Payroll	32
Army Civilian Payroll	40
Navy/Marine Corps Civilian Payroll	50
Air Force Civilian Payroll	12
Total Reserve and National Guard Payroll	19
Army Reserve and National Guard Payroll	26
Navy/Marine Corps Reserve and National Guard Payroll	45
Air Force Reserve and National Guard Payroll	4
Total Retired Military Payroll	26
Army Retired Military Payroll	34
Navy/Marine Corps Retired Military Payroll	31
Air Force Retired Military Payroll	14
Total Defense Prime Contracts	45
Army Prime Contracts	51
Navy/Marine Corps Prime Contracts	51
Air Force Prime Contracts	32
U.S. Military Installations	41
Construction of National Guard Centers	21

Education — *State Ranking*

School Age Population	3
Public Elementary and Secondary School Enrollment	49
Average Daily Attendance	16
Student-Teacher Ratio	45
Salaries of Public School Teachers	32
Public School Teachers Who Are Male	6
Eighth Grade Math Test Results	8
High School Math Enrollment	33
Public High School Graduation Rate	15
General Educational Development (GED) Test Results	10
Adult Illiteracy	48
Federal Revenue for Public Schools	37
State Revenue for Public Schools	22
Local Government Revenue for Public Schools	29
Total Public School Spending	11
Public School Spending on Instruction	24
Public School Spending on Noninstruction	37
Public School Spending on Support Staff	4
State and Local Government Spending on Public Schools	24

Federal Spending on School Improvement Programs	1
Gifted and Talented Students	NA
Federal Spending on Education of Students with Disabilities	11
Student-Teacher Ratio in Catholic Elementary Schools	50
Student-Teacher Ratio in Catholic Secondary Schools	51
State Spending on Education	2
State and Local Government Spending on Education	31
Higher Education Tuition and Fees	51
Higher Education Revenue	34
Federal Spending on Higher Education	2
State Spending on Higher Education	6
State and Local Government Spending on Higher Education	26
State and Local Appropriations for Higher Education	3
Federal Spending on Higher Education Act Insured Loans	45
Federal Spending on National Guaranteed Student Loans	21
Federal Spending on Pell Grants	7
Default Rate in Perkins Student Loan Program	29
State Spending on Libraries	15

Energy — *State Ranking*

Total Spending on Energy	2
Net Generation of Electricity	1
Cost of Electricity	47
Spending on Electricity	1
Spending on Natural Gas	7
Spending on Gasoline	1
Spending on Petroleum	3
Spending on Coal	1
Total Energy Consumption	2
Electricity Consumption	1
Natural Gas Consumption	3
Petroleum Consumption	3
Coal Consumption	1
Power Plants	4
Nuclear Power Plants	34
Hydroelectric Power Plants	6

Environment — *State Ranking*

Federally Owned Land (acreage)	6
Loss of Wetlands	33
Environmental Protection Agency Spending	12
EPA Abatement, Control, and Compliance	6
State Spending on Environmental Programs	1
Environmental Programs as Part of State Budget	1
State Spending on Forest Programs	26
Total Tree Planting	43
Federal Tree Planting	25
Private Tree Planting	44
State Spending on Air Quality	9
State Spending on Water Quality	1
Federal Grants for Rural Water and Waste Disposal	11
Federal Spending on Wastewater Treatment Works	12
Hazardous Waste Sites on National Priority List	46

Federal Grants for Hazardous Substance
   Response 50
State Spending on Hazardous Waste 37

Health   *State Ranking*

State Health Rankings	26
State Spending on Health	4
Support for Public Health	25
Family and Business Spending on Health Care	43
HMO Enrollment	48
Medicaid Recipients	40
Medically Underserved Population	43
Lack of Health Care Access	7
Active Nonfederal Physicians	49
Active Nonfederal Nurses	34
Active Nonfederal Dentists	22
Average Cost per Hospital Stay	44
Average Cost per Day for Hospital Care	47
Average Cost per Day for Hospital Room	34
State Spending on Hospitals	31
Adequacy of Prenatal Care	27
Infants Born Receiving Late or No Prenatal Care	38
Infants Born with Low Birth Weight	16
Abortions	51
Immunizations of Two-Year-Olds	—
Overall Risk for Heart Disease	40
Risk Factor for Heart Disease (hypertension)	NA
Deaths Due to Heart Disease	46
New Cancer Cases	43
Deaths Due to Cancer	46
Prevalence of Smoking	18
Prevalence of Diabetes	49
Deaths Due to Diabetes	50
Cost of Diabetes	49
AIDS Cases Reported	50
Gonorrhea Cases Reported	45
Syphilis Cases Reported	39
Tuberculosis Cases Reported	51
Hepatitis Cases Reported	19
Rabies Cases Reported	4
Lyme Disease Cases Reported	15
Beer Consumption	13
Wine Consumption	34
Liquor Consumption	12
Alcohol and Drug Treatment Admissions	NA
Federal Spending on Alcohol, Drug Abuse, and Mental Health	50
Total Spending on Alcohol/Drug Abuse Services	NA
State Spending on Alcohol/Drug Abuse Services	NA
Hard-Core Cocaine Users	43
Federal Drug Grants to States	2

Population   *State Ranking*

Population	51
Population Density	50
Population in Metropolitan Areas	47
Population Under 18 Years Old	4
Population Over 65 Years Old	46
White Population	9
African American Population	43
Hispanic Population	13
Asian American Population	39
Native American Population	8
Catholic Population	31

Jewish Population	45
Marriages	16
Divorces	5
Births	33
Births to Single Mothers	46
Births to Single Teenagers	40
Adoptions	29
Adoption Option Index	9
Infant Mortality	44
Child Deaths and Suicides	8
Teen Violent Death Rate	7
Deaths	47

Recreation   *State Ranking*

State Parks and Recreation Areas	3
Visitors to State Parks and Recreation Areas	15
Revenues from State Parks and Recreation Areas	38
Spending on State Arts Agencies	26
Domestic Travel Spending	4
State Travel Office Budgets	3
Lodging Industry (rooms)	4
Participation in Exercise Walking	7
Participation in Swimming	47
Participation in Camping	19
Participation in Bowling	42
Bowling League Membership	12
Participation in Running/Jogging	2
Participation in Aerobics	6
Participation in Golf	6
Participation in Softball	24
Participation in Health Clubs	2
Participation in Tennis	46
Participation in Hunting	21
Participation in Baseball	45
Participation in Bicycle Riding	3
Number of Boats	23
Attendance at Parimutuel Racing	5
Revenue from Parimutuel Betting	21

Social Services   *State Ranking*

Federal Grants for Social Services	2
State Spending on Public Welfare	43
Persons in Poverty	40
Public Aid Recipients	45
Participants in Food Stamp Program	28
Households in Food Stamp Program	40
Percentage of Poor Using AFDC and Food Stamps	34
Federal Spending on Children and Family Services	8
Federal Women, Infants, and Children Food Program	16
Child Welfare Services	45
Child Abuse Cases Reported	—
Children in Poverty	31
Children Without Health Insurance	33
Children Who Are Hungry or at Risk	41
Federal Spending on Child Nutrition Programs	25
Federal Spending on Special Milk Program	32
National School Lunch Program Participants	31
Head Start Enrollment	15
Head Start Spending	44
Federal Spending on Rehabilitation Services/Handicapped Research	2

State Government   *State Ranking*

Financial World's State Rankings	35
Salaries of State Officials (governor)	41
Salaries of State Legislators	—
Women in State Legislatures	15
African Americans in State Legislatures	43
Hispanics in State Legislatures	13
Asian Americans in State Legislatures	6
Native Americans in State Legislatures	12
Turnover in State Legislatures	32
Length of State Legislative Sessions	40
State Bills in Regular Session	13
State Resolutions in Regular Session	35
State Bills in Special Session	—
State Resolutions in Special Session	—
Women in State Cabinets	—
Total Federal Funding to State Governments	20
Total State Spending	2
State General Expenditures	2
State Debt	15
State Spending on Interest on the General Debt	49
Total State Tax Revenue	12
State Revenue from Tax on Sales and Gross Receipts	37
State Revenue from General Sales Tax	—
State Revenue from Licenses	5
State Revenue from Motor Vehicle Licenses	5
State Revenue from Individual Income Taxes	—
State Revenue from Corporation Net Income Taxes	—
State Revenue from Severance Taxes	2
State Revenue from Property Taxes	2
State Revenue from Death and Gift Taxes	40
State Revenue from Documentary and Stock Transfers	—
State Revenue from Tax on Motor Fuels	36
State Revenue from Tax on Tobacco Products	45
Excise Tax on Cigarettes	44
Excise Tax on Gasoline	46
State Revenue from Lotteries	—

Transportation   *State Ranking*

Motor Vehicle Registrations	1
Automobile Registrations	36
Bus and Truck Registrations	1
Motorcycle Registrations	3
Driver Licenses	4
Federal Spending on Highway Trust Fund	2
Federal Spending on Mass Transportation	27
State Spending on Highways	39
Highway Deficiency	40
Bridge Deficiency	47
Traffic Fatalities	4
Traffic Fatalities per Miles Traveled	19
Motorcyclist Fatalities	1
Pedalcyclist Fatalities	35
Pedestrian Fatalities	51
Registered Aircraft	6
Registered Pilots	10
Federal Spending on Airport and Airway Trust Fund	5
Aircraft Fatalities	4

— *not applicable*   NA *not available*

Copyrights and Permissions

Index